THE NEW HORIZON
LADDER DICTIONARY
of the English Language

Newly Updated

The Ladder Dictionary has a core vocabulary of the 6,000 most frequently used words in the English language. The clear, easily understandable entries make it particularly suitable for people learning English as a second language, younger readers, and those with reading difficulties. Publication of this updated edition is especially timely due to the increasing numbers of non-native English speakers in schools and businesses. For this edition, besides many changes within the body of the dictionary, the place-name appendix has been fully revised and enlarged to reflect the changes that have occurred throughout the world in recent years.

The New Horizon Ladder Dictionary

of the English Language

REVISED AND ENLARGED EDITION

By
John Robert Shaw
and
Sara Janet Shaw

A SIGNET BOOK

SIGNET
Published by New American Library, a division of
Penguin Group (USA) Inc., 375 Hudson Street,
New York, New York 10014, U.S.A.
Penguin Books Ltd, 80 Strand,
London WC2R 0RL, England
Penguin Books Australia Ltd, 250 Camberwell Road,
Camberwell, Victoria 3124, Australia
Penguin Books Canada Ltd, 10 Alcorn Avenue,
Toronto, Ontario, Canada M4V 3B2
Penguin Books (N.Z.) Ltd, Cnr Rosedale and Airborne Roads,
Albany, Auckland 1310, New Zealand

Penguin Books Ltd, Registered Offices:
80 Strand, London WC2R 0RL, England

First published by Signet, an imprint of New American Library,
a division of Penguin Group (USA) Inc.

First Printing, September 1970
First Printing (Revised Edition), December 1990
First Printing (Revised Appendix IV), August 1996
10 9 8

Contents

v

Acknowledgments

The original research and preparation of the manuscript of the first edition of this dictionary were supported by the United States Information Agency, which wanted a dictionary in simple English for use in its overseas program among foreign readers of English as a second language.

We want to express our deep gratitude for everything that the late Donald E. McNeil did for us. He encouraged us to undertake the original project and gave us invaluable advice and help at its start and continued to do so until his death.

In addition, we want to thank Ann Newton for selecting and writing the phonetics for the first edition of the dictionary. We also wish to thank Richard W. Elliott, who made it easier to prepare our manuscript by providing solutions to a number of computer problems.

Finally, we want to express our appreciation to Hugh Rawson, our editor and the Director of Penguin Reference Books with whom it has been such a pleasure to work, for his helpful advice and suggestions.

Introduction

What this dictionary offers. This edition of *The New Horizon Ladder Dictionary* includes 6,000 main entries based on the most frequently used words in written English—words a person will most often see and need to know in reading general English literature. Five thousand of these main entries constitute a vocabulary developed by the United States Information Agency as a result of reviewing frequency word counts and English-teaching word lists and of consulting a number of English teachers. This vocabulary was used, tested and revised over a period of twelve years in the preparation of books in English at differing levels of reading difficulty for readers of varied ages and interests. In this edition, these 5,000 main entries have been expanded and 1,000 more main entries have been added to reflect the many changes in usage of the English language in the United States in recent years. Also included in the body of the dictionary are many of the most frequently used prefixes and suffixes.

There are also a number of additional main entries that are combined words. Most of these are words or phrases that are constructed from two or more of the 5,000 basic words, prefixes and/or suffixes which are frequently used in English. These combined words are listed separately because in combined form they have a new meaning. The meaning of the word *afternoon* is clear from the two words that combine to make it, *after* and *noon*. The usual meaning of *high school*, however, is not completely clear from the two words *high* and *school*. *High school*, therefore, is included as an entry word. Other examples are *firecracker* and *runner-up*.

Word Levels. For English-teaching purposes, the basic 5,000 main entries are divided into five levels or ladder rungs of approximately 1,000 words each, according to the frequency of their use. After each of those words a number in parentheses (*) appears, showing the level at which the word is located. Words on the first level, shown by (*1*), are among the thousand most frequently used words in written English. Those on the second level, shown by (*2*), are among the second thousand most frequently used words. Those on the third (*3*), fourth (*4*) and fifth (*5*) levels follow the same pattern of frequency.

Arrangement of Words. The words in this dictionary are arranged in order according to the letters of the alphabet: *A, B, C, D, E, F, G, H, I, J, K, L, M, N, O, P, Q, R, S, T, U, V, W, X, Y, Z.* For example, the word **clear** comes after the word **cleanser** because *r* comes after *n* in the alphabet; both come before the word **clench** because *a* comes before *n*.

An example of a dictionary entry explained in detail. When you look at the word **clear** in this dictionary, this is what you will find:

clear (1) [kliːrʹ], *adj.* 1. easily understood; plain. **Ex.** *His explanation was clear.* 2. bright; uncloudy. **Ex.** *The sky is clear today.* 3. free from doubt; certain. **Ex.** *It was a clear case of murder.* 4. free of anything that might block. **Ex.** *The road is clear.* —*v.* 1. remove persons or things; empty. **Ex.** *She is the one who clears the table after meals.* 2. prove or declare innocent. **Ex.** *The lawyer's defense cleared the accused man.* 3. become clear. **Ex.** *The weather will clear in the afternoon.* —**clear'ance,** *n.* the act of clearing; the result of being cleared. **Ex.** *They received clearance to start work.* —**clear'ness,** *n.* the state of being clear. —**clear'ly,** *adv.* —**clear'ing,** *n.* land where there are no trees. —**clear out,** make a cleared place. **Ex.** *He cleared out the room.* —**clear up,** 1. make clear or plain. **Ex.** *He cleared up the mystery.* 2. make neat. **Ex.** *He cleared up the room.*

The word **clear** is printed in dark type so that it is easy to find. It is the main entry word. The word **clear** and all the information about it that follows is called an entry. Following the entry word is the number *(1)*. This shows that **clear** is on the 1,000-word vocabulary level.

Next the pronunciation of the word in the United States is shown in this way [kliːrʹ]. The pronunciation key follows the introduction to the dictionary and, in an abbreviated form for quick reference, is printed at the bottom of every fourth page. This pronunciation key, an adaptation of the Trager-Smith system, is used widely by experts in teaching spoken English.

Following the pronunciation, the part of speech is shown by the letters *adj.*, an abbreviation for the word *adjective.* The abbreviations used in this dictionary for the parts of speech are:

noun—*n.*	article—*art.*	preposition—*prep.*
pronoun—*pron.*	verb—*v.*	conjunction—*conj.*
adjective—*adj.*	adverb—*adv.*	interjection—*interj.*

There is a definition for each of these parts of speech in the main section of the dictionary. See also "A Brief Explanation of English Grammar."

Four meanings are given for the word **clear** used as an adjective. The meaning numbered *1.* is the most frequently occurring meaning. The meanings numbered *2., 3.,* etc., occur in that order of frequency. This rule should not be regarded too strictly, however, since the frequency of meanings may be extremely close in some cases.

In order to help make each meaning of a word easily understood, an example is usually given showing how the word is used in a sentence conveying that meaning. These examples, which are preceded by the letters **Ex.,** also assist readers in adding that meaning to the vocabulary they are readily able to use.

Following the meanings of **clear** as an adjective and the examples of its use as an adjective is the letter *v.* As we have seen above, this is the abbreviation for *verb* and means that the word **clear** is also used as a verb. Three meanings are then given for the word **clear** as a verb and an example is given for each.

Next are the words **clear'ance** and **clear'ness,** each divided into syllables, followed by the letter *n.* for *noun* and a definition. **Clear'ance** also has an example. The next word, **clear'ly,** is followed by the letters *adv.* for *adverb.* Since the most common meanings of **clearly** can be understood from the meanings for the adjective **clear** and the suffix -**ly,** no separate definitions or examples are given. The next word, the noun **clear'ing,** has a different meaning, and therefore has a definition.

Two expressions are included. The first, **clear out,** formed by adding the word **out** to **clear,** is used as a verb; the second, **clear up,** formed by adding the word **up** to **clear,** is also used as a verb. Expressions like these are common uses of the entry word in a phrase or combined form. Definitions and often examples of use are given for such phrases. The reader will find, too, that frequently the extra word does not change the basic meaning but is added to give emphasis or liveliness to the language. **Clear out** means substantially the same thing as **clear.**

Words with the same spelling may actually have several very different, unrelated meanings. When this is the case, there is generally a separate main entry listing for each unrelated meaning. For example, the word *bear* used as a verb has a number of related meanings: support; carry, be equipped, furnished or marked with; bring forth; produce, yield, give birth to; endure, suffer. The word *bear* used as a noun, however, means a kind of animal. Consequently there are two main entries for *bear.* The word *net* used as an adjective means remaining after all necessary expenses are paid. The word *net* used as a verb has a related meaning, earn as a profit. The word *net* used as a noun, however, can mean either a special kind of material or a device of such material used to catch fish, insects, etc. Consequently there are two main entries for *net.*

Not all the possible combinations of an entry word with prefixes, suffixes and other entries are listed in the dictionary. Similarly, not all the various tenses of regular verbs, plurals formed by regular means, the extent or degree of adjectives and adverbs usually formed by adding -*er* or -*est,* are included. If a form of one of the basic 5,600 words of the vocabulary cannot be located in the dictionary, the reader can usually determine its meaning by studying the meanings given for the basic word and the prefixes or suffixes involved, together with "A Brief Explanation of English Grammar," which follows the "Ladder Dictionary Pronunciation Key."

Ladder Dictionary Pronunciation Key

symbol	example	symbol	example
a	far	b	boat
æ	am	d	dark
e	get	f	far
ey	late	g	go
i	in	h	home
iy	see	k	cold
ɔ	all	l	let
ow	go	m	man
u	put	n	net
uw	too	p	part
ə	but, ago	r	red
ər	fur	s	sit
aw	out	t	ten
ay	life	v	very
oy	boy	w	went
		y	yes
		z	zoo

ŋ	ring		
θ	think	:	preceding vowel lengthened
ð	that	'	primary stress on preceding syllable
ž	measure		
š	ship	`	secondary stress on preceding syllable
ǰ	edge		
č	child	( )	sounds enclosed by parentheses are frequently not pronounced

A Brief Explanation of English Grammar

Parts of Speech

The names given to words according to the work each does in a sentence are called the parts of speech. The nine common parts of speech in English are:

noun	*adverb*
pronoun	*preposition*
adjective	*conjunction*
article	*interjection*
verb	

The definition of each of these nine parts of speech is contained in the main part of this dictionary. The abbreviations used in this dictionary for these parts of speech are given in the "Introduction" and "Appendix II."

Noun

A noun is the name of a person, place or thing. A common noun is the name of one kind of a person, place or thing. **Exs.** *girl, teacher, school, city, money, vegetable.* A proper noun is the name of a particular person, place or thing. **Exs.** *Mary, John, Mr. Smith, San Francisco, New York City, North America, The Star Spangled Banner, White House, New Year's Day.* See also **Clauses,** page xviii.

Verb

A verb is a word that shows action or expresses a state or condition of being or existence and usually makes a statement about the subject. There are, however, special forms of verbs that are used differently. A *gerund* is a verb form ending in *ing* that is used as a noun. **Exs.** *Running is his favorite form of exercise. She enjoys reading to her little brother.* A *participle* is a verb form that can be used as an adjective or as a verb when combined with forms of the verb *be* or *have*. The adjective form ending in *ing* is called a present participle. In order to tell whether a verb ending in *ing* is a gerund or a participle, it is necessary to see how it is being used. **Exs.** *They could hear the sound of the running brook. It was time for the reading lesson. She was running to catch up with her friend. He had run all the way to school. What book are you reading? I have not yet read that book.* Other common endings of the adjective forms of a participle are *-ed, -d, -en, -n* and *-t*. Adjective forms with these endings are called past participles. An *infinitive* is a verb form, usually preceded by the word *to*, that can be used as a noun, adjective or verb. **Exs.** *She likes to run every morning before breakfast. I would like to read another book by that same author. I have no time to run today. She didn't bring anything to read. He was too frightened to run. She stood up to read.*

Adjective

An adjective describes or tells something about the noun or pronoun with which it is used. **Exs.** *She is wearing a pretty dress. Who was the last one to leave the room?* See also **Clauses**, page xviii.

Article

An article is used before a noun to identify the word as a noun rather than as another part of speech. There are only three articles: *a* and *an*, which are indefinite, and *the*, which is definite. Sometimes these three words are classified as adjectives. **Ex.** *There were several things on the table: a bowl of fruit, an article cut from the newspaper and the book that I had started to read.*

Adverb

An adverb describes or tells something about a verb, an adjective or another adverb. **Exs.** *He worked rapidly. This is an unusually difficult problem she finished very quickly.* See also **Clauses**, page xviii.

Preposition

A preposition is a word with a meaning of relationship, position, direction, time, etc., which is used to join a noun or pronoun to some other word in the sentence. **Exs.** *The people went into the house. I bought the book from him.*

Conjunction

A conjunction is used to join together sentences, phrases or words. **Exs.** *They were going to leave, but we urged them to stay for dinner. The children have a rest period in the morning and in the afternoon. I have to buy some butter, milk and eggs.*

Interjection

An interjection is a word or words used to show feeling or emotion and having no grammatical relation to the rest of the sentence. **Exs.** *Alas! Oh dear! Oh no! Ouch! Well!*

Pronoun

A pronoun is a word used instead of a noun. Pronouns are given various names according to the kind of person, place or thing they replace, or according to the special work they do in the sentence.

A *personal pronoun* takes the place of a particular person, place or thing.

	Singular	*Plural*
1st person	I, me	we, us
2nd person	you	you

	Singular	*Plural*
3rd person	he, him she, her it	they, them

An *indefinite pronoun* takes the place of any person, place or thing; some of the most common are: each, either, neither, one, everybody, everyone, nobody, no one, anybody, anyone, somebody, someone, several, few, both, many, some, any, none, all and most. **Ex.** *Someone is knocking at the door.*

A *relative pronoun* introduces a clause and relates to another word or idea in the main clause. The most common relative pronouns are: who, whom, whose, which and that. **Ex.** *I would like to speak to the person who helped me yesterday.*

An *interrogative pronoun* asks a question. The interrogative pronouns are who, whom, whose, which and what. **Ex.** *Who is going with you?*

Construction of a Sentence

A sentence expresses a complete thought and can stand alone grammatically. The essential parts of a sentence are the subject and the verb. The subject is the person who or the thing that does something or the person about whom or the thing about which something is said. The verb is the word which shows the action or the state of being.

Ex. *She laughed.*
  She is the subject that does something; *laughed* is the verb that shows the action.

Ex. *Mother was very old.*
  Mother is the subject about whom something is said; *was* is the verb that shows the state of being of the subject.

The word that receives the action of a verb is called the direct object.

Ex. *The birds ate the seed.*
  Seed is the direct object that receives the action of the verb *ate*.

Sometimes a word following a verb is not an object but refers to or describes the subject. The verb joins the two.

Ex. *The house looks new.*
  New describes the subject *house* and is joined to it by the verb *looks*.

Ex. *That boy is my friend.*
  Friend refers to and describes the subject *boy* and is joined to it by the verb *is*.

Modifiers

Modifiers are words or groups of words which describe other words. The most common modifiers are adjectives, which describe nouns or pronouns, and adverbs, which describe verbs, adjectives or other adverbs.

Ex. *The old man walked slowly to the door.*
Old is an adjective that describes the noun *man,* and *slowly* is an adverb that describes the verb *walked.*

Prepositional phrases are groups of words used as modifiers. Such phrases consist of a preposition, a noun or a pronoun and often one or more adjectives which describe the noun or pronoun. These phrases are used in the same ways that adjectives or adverbs are used. The noun or pronoun in the phrase is called the object of the preposition.

Ex. *The girl in the red hat is my sister.*
In the red hat is a prepositional phrase used like an adjective to describe *girl. Hat* is the object of the preposition *in.*

Participial and infinitve phrases, groups of words used as modifiers, consist of a participle or an infinitive and one or more other words. Participial phrases are always used as adjectival modifiers. Infinitive phrases may be used as either adjectival or adverbial modifiers.

Ex. *I waved to the boy riding the bicycle.*
Riding the bicycle is a participial phrase used as an adjective modifying the noun *boy.*

Ex. *He went to buy bread.*
To buy bread is an infinitive phrase used as an adverb modifying the verb *went.*

Clauses

Clauses are groups of words that contain a subject and a verb and usually other words, such as objects and modifiers, but that are written as part of a sentence. If the clause could have been written as a separate sentence, it is called a main clause.

Ex. *We saw a flash of lightning, and then we heard thunder.*
In this sentence there are two main clauses: one, *We saw a flash of lightning,* and two, *then we heard thunder.*

A clause which is not the main clause is called a subordinate clause and may be used as an adjective or adverb. Such a clause is usually introduced by a relative pronoun or by a conjunction.

Ex. *The man whom you saw in the car is my brother.*
Whom you saw in the car is a subordinate clause used as an adjective modifying the noun *man. The man is my brother* is the main clause.

Ex. *When you leave, please lock the door.*
When you leave is a subordinate clause used as an adverb modifying the verb *lock.* *Please lock the door* is the main clause.

Clauses are also used as nouns.

Ex. *That he liked to spend money was well known.*
That he liked to spend money is a noun clause used at the subject of the verb *was.*

Changes of Form—Nouns

A change in the form of a noun is usually used to show whether it is singular or plural, one or more than one. The plural of most nouns is formed by adding *-s.*

Exs. *School, schools; book, books; car, cars.*

The plural of some nouns is formed by adding *-es.*
Exs. *Box, boxes; dress, dresses.*

The plural of some nouns ending in *y* is formed by changing *y* to *i* and adding *-es.*
Exs. *Fly, flies; lady, ladies.*

The plurals of a few nouns are formed by considerable changes in spelling. When the plural of a noun is formed in this manner, the singular and plural forms are usually listed in the dictionary as separate entries.
Exs. *Child, children; tooth, teeth.*

The singular and the plural of a few nouns are the same.
Exs. *Sheep, sheep; deer, deer.*

The possessive of nouns is used to show that something is owned by or is related to someone or something. The possessive is usually formed by adding an apostrophe (') and the letter *-s* to a singular noun and by adding an apostrophe to a plural noun ending in the letter *s* and by adding an apostrophe and the letter *s* to a plural noun not ending in the letter *s.*

Exs. *John's book; the box's cover; the boys' hats; the children's toys.*

Changes of Form—Adjectives, Adverbs

A change in the form of an adjective or an adverb, used to show differing extent or degree, is called a comparison. For most adjectives and adverbs of one syllable, this comparison is made by adding *-er* or *-est.*
Exs. *Old, older, oldest; fast, faster, fastest.*
More or *most* and *less* or *least* are used before some adjectives and adverbs to show comparison.

Exs. *Beautiful, more beautiful, most beautiful; rapidly, less rapidly, least rapidly.*

Some adjectives and adverbs use a different word for each difference of extent or degree.

Exs.			
	good	*better*	*best*
	well	*better*	*best*
	many	*more*	*most*
	bad	*worse*	*worst*

Changes of Form—Verbs

A change in the form of a verb is used to show differing times a particular action or state of being occurs, occurred or will occur. The different time forms are called tenses. Some of the more frequently used tenses are:

Present tense—shows actions or being now.

Past—   " " " "   before now.

Future—   " " " "   not yet begun.

Present Perfect— " " " "   in the past and continuing into the present.

Past Perfect—   " " " "   completed in the past before some other past action.

Future Perfect—   " " " "   that will be completed before some other future action.

The tenses of most verbs are formed in the same way. For example, *-ed* is added to the present tense of the verb to form the past tense. Use of the word *will* forms the future tense. Such verbs are called regular verbs. The tenses of regular verbs are all formed in the same way as the verb *walk*, which is given as an example.

Present		**Present Perfect**	
Singular	**Plural**	**Singular**	**Plural**
I walk	*we walk*	*I have walked*	*we have walked*
you walk	*you walk*	*you have walked*	*you have walked*
he, she walks	*they walk*	*he, she has walked*	*they have walked*

Past

		Past Perfect	
I walked	*we walked*	*I had walked*	*we had walked*
you walked	*you walked*	*you had walked*	*you had walked*
he, she walked	*they walked*	*he, she had walked*	*they had walked*

Future

		Future Perfect	
I will walk	*we will walk*	*I will have walked*	*we will have walked*
you will walk	*you will walk*	*you will have walked*	*you will have walked*
he, she will walk	*they will walk*	*he, she will have walked*	*they will have walked*

Certain verbs are called irregular because the various tenses are not formed in the same way. These verbs, examples of which are *be* and *go*, usually have separate dictionary entries for each of the differing forms. The following are the tenses of the most frequently used verb, *be*.

Present

Singular	**Plural**	**Present Perfect**	
		Singular	**Plural**
I am	*we are*	*I have been*	*we have been*
you are	*you are*	*you have been*	*you have been*
he, she is	*they are*	*he, she has been*	*they have been*

Past

		Past Perfect	
I was	*we were*	*I had been*	*we had been*
you were	*you were*	*you had been been*	*you had been*
he, she was	*they were*	*he, she had*	*they had been*

Future

		Future Perfect	
I will be	*we will be*	*I will have been*	*we will have been*
you will be	*you will be*	*you will have been*	*you will have been*
he, she will be	*they will be*	*he, she will have been*	*they will have been*

A

A, a (1) [ey'], *n.* the first letter of the English alphabet.

a (1) [ey', ə], *adj.* 1. one, one kind of; each; any. **Ex.** *I planted a tree.* 2. used with groups or numbers. **Exs.** *A few; a certain number; a thousand.* *A* is also called an indefinite article and is used before words beginning with most letters except a, e, i, o and u.

a- (1) [ə], *prefix.* on, to, toward, in, into. **Exs.** *Sleep, asleep; live, alive; side, aside.*

abandon (3) [əbæn'dən], *v.* leave completely and finally. **Ex.** *The captain ordered the passengers and crew to abandon ship.* —*n.* careless or wild freedom. **Ex.** *He spent money with abandon.*

abbreviate (5) [əbriy'viyeyt'], *v.* shorten by cutting out part. **Ex.** *His book was abbreviated to appear in a magazine.*

abbreviation (5) [əbriy`viyey'šən], *n.* a shortened form of a word or group of words. **Exs.** *Mr. for mister; Sun. for Sunday; St. for Street and Saint.*

abdomen (5) [æb'dəmən, æbdow'mən], *n.* the middle part of the body, which contains the stomach and other important inner parts. —**ab·dom'i·nal**, *adj.*

abduct [æbdəkt'], *v.* carry away by force and hold, usually for payment of some kind; kidnap. **Ex.** *Two American citizens were abducted by terrorists yesterday.* —**ab·duc'tion**, *n.*

abide (4) [əbayd'], 1. endure; bear. **Ex.** *She cannot abide his smoking.* 2. act in accordance with; obey. **Ex.** *We will abide by your decision.*

ability (2) [əbil'ətiy], *n.* power or skill in mental or physical action. **Ex.** *He no longer has the ability to carry such heavy loads.*

a, far; æ, am; e, get; ey, late; i, in; iy, see; ɔ, all; ow, go; u, put; uw, too; ə, but, ago; ər, fur; aw, out; ay, life; oy, boy; ŋ, ring; θ, think; ð, that; ž, measure; š, ship; j, edge; č, child.

able (1) [ey'bəl], *adj.* 1. having the power or ability to do something. **Ex.** *He was not able to return home.* 2. showing unusual skill or knowledge; clever. **Ex.** *An able teacher helped him in school.* —**a'bly,** *adv.*

-able (1) [əbəl], *suffix.* 1. that can or may be done. **Exs.** *Drink, drinkable; read, readable.* 2. that exists as a condition. **Exs.** *Fashion, fashionable; peace, peaceable.*

abnormal (5) [æbnɔr'məl], *adj.* not usual; odd. **Ex.** *His abnormal behavior shows that something is wrong.* —**ab·nor'mal·ly,** *adv.* **Ex.** *The dry season was abnormally long.* —**ab'nor·mal'i·ty,** *n.*

aboard (4) [əbɔrd'], *adv., prep.* on, in or into a ship, bus, train, etc. **Exs.** *The captain of the ship welcomed the visitors aboard. The passengers aboard the plane were served dinner.*

abolish (3) [əbal'iš], *v.* end completely; destroy. **Ex.** *They are working to abolish racism* —**ab·o·li'tion,** *n.* total ending of. **Ex.** *He hoped for the abolition of all wars.*

abominable (5) [əbam'ənə'bəl], *adj.* hateful; bad and unpleasant. **Ex.** *Murder is an abominable crime.* —**a·bom'i·na·bly,** *adv.*

abort [əbɔrt], *v.* 1. interrupt and bring to an end because of a problem. **Ex.** *The launching of the spacecraft was aborted because of a computer failure.* 2. end a pregnancy ahead of time. **Ex.** *To save the mother's life, the doctor aborted the baby.* —**a·bor'tion,** *n.*

about (1) [əbawt'], *prep.* concerning; of. **Ex.** *A dictionary is a book about words.* —*adv.* 1. almost; nearly. **Ex.** *It is about five o'clock.* 2. in all directions; around. **Ex.** *The man looked about before crossing the street.*

above (1) [əbəv'], *prep.* 1. in or at a higher place than. **Ex.** *His room is above mine.* 2. higher in rank than. **Ex.** *In the army a major ranks above a captain.* —*adv.* in or at a higher place; overhead. **Ex.** *The clouds above were moving fast.*

abreast [əbrest'], *adv., adj.* 1. beside; not in front or behind. **Ex.** *The two runners finished the race abreast of each other.* 2. being informed. **Ex.** *He kept abreast of the situation by phone.*

abridge [əbrij'], *v.* shorten a book, speech, etc.; condense. **Ex.** *The 150 pages of the book were abridged to 100.* —**a·bridged',** *adj.* —**a·bridg'ment,** *n.*

abroad (2) [əbrɔ:d'], *adv.* in a foreign country. **Ex.** *They are traveling abroad.*

abrupt (4) [əbrəpt'], *adj.* 1. unexpected and sudden. **Ex.** *The car came to an abrupt stop.* 2. unpleasantly short. **Ex.** *His abrupt words made me unhappy.* —**a·brupt'ly**, *adv.*

absent (2) [æb'sənt], *adj.* 1. not present; away. **Ex.** *The student was absent from school.* 2. not existing; lacking. **Ex.** *The adventures he read about were absent from his own life.* —**ab'sence**, *n.* the condition of not being present. **Ex.** *His absence was noted.* —**ab`sen·tee'**, *n.* someone not present.

absent-minded [æb'sənt mayn'ded], *adj.* absent mentally; forgetful. **Ex.** *In his absent-minded way, he mailed the letter without a stamp.* —**ab'sent·mind'ed·ly**, *adv.*

absolute (2) [æb'səluwt`], *adj.* 1. perfect; complete. **Ex.** *I have absolute faith in his honesty.* 2. without limit. **Ex.** *The leaders had absolute authority.* —**ab`so·lute'ly**, *adv.*

absolve (5) [əbsalv'], *v.* free from guilt, responsibility or punishment for a sin or crime. **Ex.** *The judge absolved the man of the crime.*

absorb (4) [əbsɔrb'], *v.* 1. hold the full attention. **Ex.** *Absorbed in his work, he did not hear the doorbell ring.* 2. take in; suck up. **Ex.** *We used paper towels to absorb the water.* —**ab·sorb'ent**, *adj.* —**ab·sorp'tion**, *n.*

abstain [æbsteyn'], *v.* by one's own choice keep from doing, eating or drinking certain things. **Ex.** *Our congressman abstained from voting because he thought the proposed legislation was inadequate.* —**ab·sten'tion**, *n.* the act of keeping oneself from doing something, particularly voting. —**ab'sti·nence,** *n.* the act of keeping from doing things which give one pleasure, such as eating and drinking.

abstract (5) [æb'strækt], *adj.* 1. considered apart from the particular matter, substance or case. **Ex.** *The judge was criticized for having only an abstract idea of justice.* 2. expressing a quality apart from any object. **Ex.** *Beauty is an abstract idea.* 3. difficult to understand. **Ex.** *Some authors are not popular because their writings are too abstract.*

absurd (4) [əbsərd'], *adj.* so unreasonable as to be laughable; foolish. **Ex.** *Your story is too absurd to believe.* —**ab·surd'ly**, *adv.* —**ab·surd'i·ty**, *n.* the state or quality of being foolish. **Ex.** *The absurdity of the situation made everyone laugh.*

abundance (4) [əbən'dəns], *n.* a large amount. **Ex.** *We have had an abundance of rain this year.* —**a·bun'dant**, *adj.* —**a·bun'dant·ly**, *adv.*

abuse (4) [əbyuwz'], v. 1. use incorrectly or wrongly. **Ex.** *The judge abused his authority.* 2. treat badly, either physically or in speech. **Ex.** *He abused the man by beating and cursing him.* —n. 1. wrong or bad use. **Ex.** *His abuse of power has turned his friends against him.* 2. cruel treatment. **Ex.** *The man's abuse of the horse made people angry.* —**a·bu'sive**, *adj.* —**a·bu'sive·ly**, *adv.*

academic (3) [æk`ədem'ik], *adj.* 1. concerning a school, college or university, or teaching. **Ex.** *He left the business world to return to academic life.* 2. concerning theoretical and classical matters rather than technical and practical ones. **Ex.** *Philosophy is an academic subject.* —**ac'a·dem'i·cal·ly**, *adv.*

academy (5) [əkæd'əmiy], *n.* 1. an organization of people promoting the arts or sciences. **Ex.** *He is a member of the National Academy of Sciences.* 2. a secondary or preparatory school, often private. **Ex.** *After graduating from the academy, he went to college.* 3. a place of training in a special subject. **Ex.** *His daughter attends an academy of music.*

accelerate [æksel'əreyt], *v.* speed up; go or cause to go or come about more quickly. **Exs.** *The sled accelerated as it went down the icy slope. Can you accelerate the processing of applications?* —**ac·cel`e·ra'tion**, *n.*

accent (3) [æk'sent`], *n.* 1. stronger force or stress given to a word or part of a word in speaking. **Ex.** *The accent in the word* about *is on* bout. 2. a special, national or regional way of speaking. **Ex.** *She speaks English with a foreign accent.* —v. say a word or part of a word with increased force. **Ex.** *Do not accent the a in* about. —**accent mark**'

accept (1) [æksept'], *v.* take a thing that is offered. **Ex.** *He was happy to accept the gift.* 2. receive with favor. **Ex.** *We accept your offer.* 3. believe, agree to. **Ex.** *Do you accept what he is saying?* —**ac·cept'a·ble**, *adj.* —**ac·cept'a·bly**, *adv.* —**ac·cept'ance**, *n.*

access (5) [æk'ses`], *n.* 1. the right to enter, approach, or use. **Ex.** *You have access to a good library.* 2. a way or place of approach. **Ex.** *This street will provide the quickest access to the park.* —**ac·ces'si·bil'i·ty**, *n.* —**ac·ces'si·ble**, *adj.*

accessory (5) [ækses'əriy], *n.* 1. something which adds to comfort, appearance or usefulness but is not needed. **Exs.** *Is air conditioning available as an accessory with this car? Her red hat and gloves were colorful accessories to her gray coat.* 2. an individual who aids another in committing a crime. Ex. *He was an accessory because he provided a car for the robbers.*

accident (2) [æk'sədənt], *n.* 1. a happening that causes damage or hurt. Ex. *He broke his leg in an automobile accident.* 2. an unexpected and unplanned happening. Ex. *It was only by accident that we arrived at the same time.* —**ac`ci·den'tal,** *adj.* —**ac`ci·den'tal·ly,** *adv.*

accommodate (5) [əkam'ədeyt`], *v.* 1. do a favor for; help; aid. Ex. *He accommodated his friend with a loan.* 2. provide with room and sometimes food; have space for. Ex. *The hotel can accommodate fifty guests.* —**ac·com'mo·dat`ing,** *adj.* —**ac·com'mo·da'tions,** *n.* lodging, food and service. Ex. *Where can we find inexpensive accommodations?*

accompany (2) [əkəm'pəniy], *v.* 1. join; go with. Ex. *I will accompany him on the trip.* 2. put with; cause to go with. Ex. *He accompanied his talk with pictures.* 3. play music with a singer or another performer or performers. Ex. *A pianist accompanied the singer.* —**ac·com'pa·nist,** *n.* one who accompanies.

accomplice [əkam'plis], *n.* one who assists in a wrongdoing. Ex. *The robber's accomplice was also caught.*

accomplish (2) [əkam'pliš], *v.* do; perform; finish successfully. Ex. *We accomplished our task.* —**ac·com'plish·ment,** *n.* a completed task; a skill. Ex. *We admire her accomplishments.*

accord (4) [əkɔrd'], *v.* 1. be in agreement. Ex. *Their story did not accord with the facts.* 2. grant; reward. Ex. *He was accorded the honors he deserved.* —*n.* agreement. Ex. *They were in accord.* —**ac·cor'dance,** *n.* —**ac·cord'ing·ly,** *adv.* in a fitting manner. Ex. *Be polite and you will be treated accordingly.* —**ac·cord'ing to.** 1. in agreement with. Ex. *The building of the road was completed according to plan.* 2. said or declared by. Ex. *According to the newspaper, it will rain tomorrow.* 3. in a certain order. Ex. *They stood in line according to height.*

account (2) [əkawnt'], *v.* give a reason for; explain. Ex. *How do you account for your accident?* —*n.* 1. story; explanation. Ex. *Give an account of your trip.* 2. record of money received and paid. Ex. *The bank sends me a monthly statement of my* *account.* —**ac·count'ant,** *n.* one whose work is keeping or examining accounts or business records. —**on account,** as partial payment. **Ex.** *He paid him some on account.* —**on account of,** because of. **Ex.** *We stayed home on account of the rain.*

accumulate (4) [əkyuwm'yəleyt'], *v.* collect or bring together; increase in amount or number. **Ex.** *He wants to accumulate more paintings for his collection.* —**ac·cu'mu·la'tion,** *n.*

accurate (4) [æk'yurət], *adj.* exact; correct; right. **Ex.** *My watch keeps accurate time.* —**ac'cu·ra·cy,** *n.* —**ac'cu·rate·ly,** *adv.*

accuse (2) [əkyuwz'], *v.* charge with a wrongdoing or crime; blame; find fault with. **Ex.** *They accused him of stealing.* —**ac'cu·sa'tion,** *n.* a charge of wrongdoing. —**ac·cused',** *n.* one who is charged with a wrongdoing. —**ac·cus'er,** *n.* one who accuses. —**ac·cus'ing,** *adj.* —**ac·cus'ing·ly,** *adv.*

accustom (2) [əkəs'təm], *v.* become familiar with by use or habit. **Ex.** *She could not accustom herself to a hot climate.* —**accustomed to,** in the habit of. **Ex.** *He is accustomed to sleeping late.*

ache (3) [eyk'], *v.* suffer continued pain. **Ex.** *My tooth aches.* —*n.* pain. **Ex.** *I have a backache.*

achieve (3) [əčiyv'], *v.* 1. accomplish; complete successfully; do. **Ex.** *They were able to achieve their purpose quickly.* 2. get through effort. **Ex.** *The men fought bravely and finally achieved victory.* —**a·chieve'ment,** *n.*

acid (3) [æ'sid], *n.* 1. a chemical substance containing hydrogen that can be replaced by a metal. 2. a sour substance. **Ex.** *Vinegar is an acid.* —*adj.* 1. sharp or biting to the taste. **Ex.** *The lemon is an acid fruit.* 2. sharp or biting in manner. **Ex.** *His acid comments about her work upset her.* —**ac'id·ly,** *adv.* —**a·cid'i·ty,** *n.*

acknowledge (4) [æknal'ij], *v.* 1. admit as true. **Ex.** *She acknowledged her mistake.* 2. answer or express thanks for something. **Ex.** *They acknowledged the gift.* —**ac·knowl'edg·ment,** *n.*

acorn (5) [ey'kɔrn], *n.* nut or fruit, of the oak tree.

ACORN

acquaint (5) [əkweynt'], *v.* 1. make known to; make familiar. **Ex.** *Please acquaint me with the facts.* 2. know personally. **Ex.** *These two women are acquainted with each other.* —**ac·quaint'ance,** *n.*

acquire (3) [əkwayr'], v. get as one's own; become the owner of; gain by some means. **Exs.** *He acquired a fortune. She acquired a Ph.D. after many years of study.* —**ac·qui·si'tion,** n.

acquit [əkwit'], v. declare an accused person innocent of a crime or wrongdoing. **Ex.** *The jury acquitted her of dealing in drugs.* —**ac·quit'tal,** n.

acre (2) [ey'kər], n. piece of land that measures 43,560 square feet or 4,840 square yards.

across (1) [əkrɔːs'], prep. 1. from one side of to the other. **Ex.** *He walked across the bridge.* 2. on the other side of. **Ex.** *He lives across the street.* —**adv.** from one side to another. **Ex.** *We went across by boat.*

act (1) [ækt'], n. 1. thing that is done. **Ex.** *Feeding the hungry child was a kind act.* 2. law; judgment. **Ex.** *The lawmakers passed an act to increase taxes.* v. 1. do something. **Ex.** *Think before you act.* 2. produce an effect. **Ex.** *The medicine acted immediately.* 3. behave. **Ex.** *His dog acts in a strange manner.* 4. perform on the stage. **Ex.** *He acted the part of the king in the play.*

action (1) [æk'šən], n. 1. something done; act. **Ex.** *His action was wise and helpful.* 2. process of doing something. **Ex.** *We need less talk and more action.* — **in action,** moving; doing —**take action,** do something about. **Ex.** *He promised to take action on our problem.*

active (2) [æk'tiv], adj. 1. busy; moving all the time. **Ex.** *She is a very active person.* 2. working; in progress or motion. **Ex.** *He was active in community affairs.* —**ac'tive·ly,** adv. —**ac'tiv·ist,** n. one who is active in social and political causes. —**ac·tiv'i·ty,** n.

actor (3) [æk'tər], n. one who performs in a play or motion picture. **Ex.** *The actor spoke his lines clearly.* —**ac'tress,** n. a female who performs in a play or motion picture.

actual (2) [æk'čuwəl], adj. really existing; real; true. **Ex.** *He is the one who has the actual power.* —**ac'tu·al'i·ty,** n. —**ac'tu·al·ly,** adv.

acute (4) [əkyuwt'], adj. 1. very severe. **Ex.** *The pain was acute.* 2. keen and quick in seeing, hearing, thinking, etc. **Ex.** *A dog has an acute sense of smell.* —**a·cute'ly,** adv.

adapt (5) [ədæpt'], v. change to fit needs or new conditions. **Ex.** *Some people find it difficult to adapt themselves to urban life.* —**a·dapt'a·ble,** adj. —**ad'ap·ta'tion,** n.

add (1) [æd'], *v.* 1. join to increase the number, size or importance. Ex. *His unexpected illness added to the family expenses.* 2. find the sum of two or more numbers. Ex. *When you add 5 and 2, the total is 7.* 3. say or write further. Ex. *She said that she would be late and added that she was sorry.* —**ad·di'tion**, *n.* —**ad·di'tion·al**, *adj.*

addict [æd'ikt], *n.* a person controlled by some habit, usually harmful, such as taking drugs. Ex. *She is afraid that her brother is a drug addict.* —**ad·dict'ed**, *adj.* controlled by; relying on for help or support. Ex. *He is addicted to tobacco.* —**ad·dic'tion**, *n.* —**ad·dic'tive**, *adj.* causing a person to become an addict. Ex. *The doctor warned that the medicine he was prescribing contained an addictive drug.*

address (2) [ədres', æd'res], *n.* 1. number, street and place where one lives. Ex. *To what address shall I deliver this package?* 2. speech or writing directed to a person or group. Ex. *He gave an address to the graduates.* —*v.* speak to; talk to. Ex. *He always addressed us kindly.*

adequate (4) [æd'əkwət], *adj.* as much as required; enough; sufficient. Ex. *They had an adequate amount of money for the trip.* —**ad'e·qua·cy**, *n.* —**ad'e·quate·ly**, *adv.*

adhere (5) [ədhi:r'], *v.* 1. hold tightly to. Ex. *The wet clothing adhered to his body.* 2. be devoted to. Ex. *He no longer adheres to those beliefs.* —**ad·her'ence**, *n.* the act of adhering. Ex. *He was well known for his adherence to the rules.* —**ad·her'ent**, *n.* a person who adheres. Ex. *The candidate was surrounded by his adherents.*

adhesive [ædhiy'siv] *n.* a substance, such as glue, that causes things to stick together. Ex. *She used an adhesive to paste the pictures on the pages of her album.* —*adj.*

adjacent (5) [əjey'sənt], *adj.* near or next to; neighboring. Ex. *There is a school adjacent to my house.*

adjective (5) [æj'əktiv], *n.* a part of speech that describes or tells something about the noun or pronoun with which it is used. Ex. *In the sentence, "The new teacher is very young,"* the words new *and* young *are adjectives.* See **A Brief Explanation of English Grammar.**

adjoin (4) [əjoyn'], *v.* be joined with or to; be next to and touching. Ex. *His land adjoins mine.*

adjourn (4) [əjərn'], *v.* end a meeting or other gathering until a future time. Ex. *The meeting was adjourned until next week.* —**ad·journ'ment**, *n.*

adjust (4) [əjəst'], *v.* 1. change or move into position for use; change to meet new conditions. **Ex.** *You can adjust your chair to make it more comfortable.* 2. fix; arrange the parts to make them work correctly. **Ex.** *Please adjust my watch.* 3. settle; put in order. **Ex.** *Please adjust my account to show the correct purchase price.* —**ad·just'ment,** *n.* —**ad·just'er,** *n.*

administer (5) [ædmin'əstər], *v.* 1. manage; be in charge of. **Ex.** *A new principal is administering the school.* 2. give out. **Ex.** *The chief justice administered the oath of office to the incoming president.* 3. give medicine or treatment. **Ex.** *The nurse administered the medicine.*

administration (3) [ædmin·əstrey'šən], *n.* 1. management of work or of an office. **Ex.** *Who is responsible for the administration of this division?* 2. the operation or functioning of a government. **Ex.** *The mayor was praised for his administration of the city.* 3. group of men who have the powers to operate a government. **Ex.** *The present administration is very capable.* —**ad·min'is·tra'tor,** *n.* —**ad·min'is·trate,** *v.* —**ad·min'is·tra'tive,** *adj.* **Ex.** *He is looking for an administrative position.*

admiral (4) [æd'mərəl], *n.* an officer of the highest rank in the navy; commanding officer of a fleet of ships or a navy.

admire (2) [ædmayr'], *v.* regard with wonder, pleasure and approval. **Ex.** *They all admired her beauty.* —**ad'mi·ra'tion,** *n.* —**ad'mi·ra·ble,** *adj.* deserving high praise; worth great respect. **Ex.** *Her patience is admirable.* —**ad'mi·ra·bly,** *adv.*

admission (3) [ædmiš'ən], *n.* 1. permission to enter. **Ex.** *Admission to the club is open to everyone.* 2. price paid for entering. **Ex.** *Admission to that theater is expensive.* 3. confession of a belief, error or crime; admitting that something is true or false. **Ex.** *His quick admission of his mistake was in his favor.* —**ad·mis'si·ble,** *adj.* allowed; permitted. —**ad·mis'si·bil'i·ty,** *n.*

admit (2) [ædmit'], *v.* 1. tell the truth about; confess. **Ex.** *The criminal admitted his guilt.* 2. allow to enter. **Ex.** *Please admit me to the room.* —**ad·mit'tance,** *n.* permission for physical entry. **Ex.** *We were denied admittance to the building.*

admonish (5) [ædman'iš], *v.* warn of a fault; advise against doing something. **Ex.** *He admonished his friend not to be late for work.* —**ad'mo·ni'tion,** *n.*

ado (5) [əduw'], *n.* trouble; fuss. **Ex.** *There was much ado about the President's visit.*

adolescence (5) [ædəles'əns], *n.* period between being a child and an adult; youth. —**ad'o·les'cent**, *n.* a boy or a girl, generally between the ages of 13 and 19. **Ex.** *As an adolescent, he had many problems.* —*adj.* in the period between being a child and an adult.

adopt (3) [ədapt'], *v.* 1. take and use as one's own. **Ex.** *He adopted their customs without difficulty.* 2. choose and take as a member of one's family by law. **Ex.** *The family adopted the child.* 3. choose or follow. **Ex.** *They decided to adopt the suggestion.* —**a·dop'tion**, *n.*

adore (5) [ədɔːr'], *v.* regard with the greatest love and respect. **Ex.** *He adores his wife.* —**ad'o·ra'tion**, *n.*

adorn (4) [ədɔrn'], *v.* add beauty; decorate; make pleasing to the eye. **Ex.** *Jewels adorned her neck and arms.* —**a·dorn'ment**, *n.*

adult (2) [æd'əlt, ədəlt'], *n.* a person who is fully grown or of responsible age according to law. **Ex.** *An adult went with the children.* —*adj.* 1. fully developed in body and mind. **Ex.** *He is an adult person.* 2. designed for grown people. **Ex.** *The school offers adult education courses.*

advance (1) [ædvæns'], *v.* 1. move or go forward. **Ex.** *The army advanced up the hill.* 2. help to move forward; help to succeed. **Ex.** *They are trying to advance the cause of peace.* —*n.* 1. forward movement. **Ex.** *The army has made an advance.* 2. raise in rank. **Ex.** *His new job is an advance for him.* —*adj.* 1. in front. **Ex.** *Ten soldiers formed the advance guard.* 2. ahead of time. **Ex.** *Please give me two weeks' advance notice.*

advantage (2) [ædvæn'tij], *n.* 1. superior or favored position. **Ex.** *His excellent education gives him an advantage in his new job.* —**ad'van·ta'geous**, *adj.* —**ad'van·ta'geous·ly**, *adv.* —**take advantage of.** 1. make use of. **Ex.** *Take advantage of these low prices to save money.* 2. make unfair use of. **Ex.** *He takes advantage of his employer's absence to do less work.*

adventure (2) [ædven'čər], *n.* 1. an exciting and often dangerous thing to do. **Ex.** *Hunting lions is an adventure.* 2. an unusual and stirring experience. **Ex.** *It was an adventure to ride in an airplane for the first time.* —**ad·ven'tur·ous**, *adj.* —**ad·ven'tur·ous·ly**, *adv.*

adverb (5) [æd'vərb], *n.* a part of speech that describes or tells something about a verb, adjective or another adverb. **Ex.** *In the sentence, "The boy laughed happily," the word* happily *is an adverb.* See **A Brief Explanation of English Grammar.**

adverse (5) [æd'vərs`, ədvərs'], *adj.* 1. acting against. **Ex.** *Adverse winds prevented the boat from entering the harbor.* 2. opposed; opposed to one's interest. **Ex.** *Adverse circumstances caused him to lose all his money.* —**ad·verse·ly,** *adv.* —**ad·ver'si·ty,** *n.* trouble. —**ad'ver·sar·y,** *n.* a person against whom one fights; an opponent.

advertise (3) [æd'vərtayz`], *v.* praise some product publicly, as in a newspaper, on radio or television or by a similar means, to cause people to want to buy it. **Ex.** *This company uses billboards to advertise its products.* —**ad'ver·tis'er,** *n.*

advertisement (3) [ædvərtayz'mənt, ædvər'tizmənt], *n.* a public announcement in a newspaper, on radio or television, etc. praising some product. **Ex.** *He learned that the house was for sale through an advertisement.*

advice (2) [ædvays'], *n.* opinion about what to do or how to do something. **Ex.** *He gave me some good advice about buying a house.*

advise (3) [ædvayz'], *v.* 1. suggest an action; warn. **Exs.** *The doctor advised him to rest. They were advised of the danger.* 2. inform. **Ex.** *He advised us of an increase in taxes.* —**ad·vis'er,** *n.*

advocate (4) [æd'vəkeyt`], *v.* speak or write in favor of. **Ex.** *He advocated a moderate course.*

advocate (4) [æd'vəkit], *n.* one who speaks and writes in support of a cause. **Ex.** *He is an advocate of reforms in the tax laws.*

affair (2) [əfe:r'], *n.* happening; event; business matter. **Exs.** *The wedding was a memorable affair. The sale of the house will be a difficult affair.*

affect (2) [əfekt'], *v.* 1. act on or produce an effect on; change. **Ex.** *Any change in the weather affects the crops.* 2. make an impression on the mind or feelings. **Ex.** *The sad news affected him deeply.*

affection (2) [əfek'šən], *n.* warm liking; friendly feeling or emotion. **Ex.** *The girl had great affection for her little sister.* —**af·fec'tion·ate,** *adj.* —**af·fec'tion·ate·ly,** *adv.*

affirm (4) [əfərm'], *v.* state something with certainty; declare. **Ex.** *He affirmed his innocence.* —**af·firm'a·tive,** *adj.* answering yes; showing agreement. **Ex.** *There were ten affirmative votes.* —**af·firm'a·tive·ly,** *adv.*

afflict (5) [əflikt'], *v.* cause pain or suffering; trouble greatly. **Ex.** *He was afflicted with a lingering illness.* —**af·flic'tion,** *n.*

afford (2) [əfɔrd'], *v.* 1. have the money for. **Ex.** *They can afford to buy a house.* 2. be able to spare or give up for some purpose. **Ex.** *He could not afford the time for a vacation.* 3. do something without damage to health, good name, etc. **Ex.** *A man in his position cannot afford to have his honesty doubted.*

afraid (1) [əfreyd'], *adj.* feeling fear; frightened. **Ex.** *I am afraid of big dogs.*

after (1) [æf'tər], *prep.* 1. following behind. **Ex.** *The soldiers walked in line, one after another.* 2. later in time than. **Ex.** *I will see you after lunch.* 3. as a result of; because of. **Ex.** *After his treatment of me, I never want to see him again.* 4. looking for. **Ex.** *The soldiers were after him.* 5. with the same or similar name as. **Ex.** *She was named after her aunt.* —*adv.* later; behind. **Ex.** *He left an hour after.* —*conj.* following the time that something else happened. **Ex.** *They arrived after the others had left.*

aftermath (3) [æf'tərmæθ'], *n.* result or aftereffect of something, usually bad. **Ex.** *He had to wear eyeglasses as an aftermath of the accident.*

afternoon [æf'ternuwn'], *n.* the period of the day between noon and sunset. **Ex.** *Can you visit us this afternoon?*

afterward (2) [æf'tərwərd], *adv.* later. **Ex.** *First we will go to the theater, then afterward to dinner.*

again (1) [əgen', əgeyn'], *adv.* 1. once more; another time. **Ex.** *I do not understand; tell me again.* 2. as before. **Ex.** *He left home for a while but is back again.* —**again and again.** repeatedly. **Ex.** *I have explained it again and again.*

against (1) [əgenst'], *prep.* 1. not in agreement with; opposed to. **Ex.** *The soldiers fought bravely against the enemy.* 2. in contact with. **Ex.** *The boy leaned against the wall.* 3. in the other direction. **Ex.** *He swam up the river against the current.* 4. in comparison or relation to. **Ex.** *Against the snow, the white rabbit was invisible.*

age (1) [eyj], *n.* 1. length of life; number of years old. **Ex.** *What is your age?* 2. period of life. **Ex.** *He studied painting in* his old age. 3. a time or period. **Ex.** *This is the computer age.* —*v.* grow old. **Ex.** *He is aging quickly.* —**a'ged,** *adj.*

-age (1) [ij], *suffix.* 1. act of; state of. **Exs.** *Marry, marriage; parent, parentage.* 2. cost of; amount of. **Exs.** *post, postage; foot, footage.* 3. place for. **Ex.** *orphan, orphanage.*

agency (3) [ey'jənsiy], *n.* office or business of a person or company. **Ex.** *The employment agency found her a job as a secretary.*

agent (3) [ey'jənt], *n.* 1. a person who represents another. **Ex.** *He is a sales agent for a steel company.* 2. a substance that causes an effect. **Ex.** *A chemical agent is used to make paper white.*

aggregate (5) [æg'rəgit], *adj.* considered as a group or total. **Ex.** *The company's aggregate debts amounted to more than two million dollars.* —*n.* the total; the complete amount. **Ex.** *The aggregate of his debts was less than three hundred dollars.*

aggressive (5) [əgres'iv], *adj.* 1. ready to attack or fight others. **Ex.** *He is so aggressive that others avoid him.* 2. active; energetic. **Ex.** *We need an aggressive leader.* —**ag·gres'sive·ly,** *adv.* —**ag·gres'sion,** *n.* the act of starting an attack, a fight, etc. **Ex.** *We considered the arrest of our citizens an act of aggression.* —**ag·gres'sive·ness,** *n.* quality of being aggressive. **Ex.** *His aggressiveness made us dislike him.* —**ag·gres'sor,** *n.* one who starts a fight or war.

agile (5) [æj'əl], *adj.* moving quickly and easily; active. **Ex.** *The ballet dancer was exceptionally agile.* —**a·gil'i·ty,** *n.* quality of being able to move quickly.

agitate (4) [æj'əteyt`], *v.* 1. move violently; shake. **Ex.** *The wind agitated the trees.* 2. distress; upset. **Ex.** *The girl's unexplained absence agitated her mother.* 3. attempt to excite into action. **Ex.** *The newspapers were agitating for a change in the tax laws.* —**ag'i·ta`tor,** *n.* one who agitates. **Ex.** *Agitators made the crowd angry.* —**ag'i·ta'tion,** *n.* the state of being agitated or of agitating.

ago (1) [əgow'], *adj.* past; gone; before now. **Ex.** *It happened two days ago.* —*adv.* in the past. **Ex.** *I knew him long ago.*

agony (4) [æg'əniy], *n.* great physical or mental pain; suffering. **Ex.** *He was in agony from his illness.* —**ag'o·nize,** *v.*

—**ag'o·niz`ing**, *adj.* causing suffering. **Ex.** *It was an agonizing decision.* —**ag'o·niz`ing·ly**, *adv.*

agree (1) [əgriy'], *v.* 1. think the same. **Ex.** *We both agree that it is a good book.* 2. consent to. **Ex.** *They agreed to the plan.* —**a·gree'a·ble**, *adj.* cooperative; friendly. **Ex.** *He is an agreeable person.* —**a·gree'a·ble·ness**, *n.* —**a·gree'a·bly**, *adv.* —**a·gree'ment**, *n.*

agriculture (3) [æg'rikəl`čər], *n.* art or science of farming; raising crops, cattle, and other farm animals. —**ag'ri·cul'tur·al**, *adj.*

ah [a], *interj.* exclamation of surprise, pleasure, pain or any emotion. **Exs.** *Ah! So he was the guilty one! Ah! How nice to see you!*

ahead (2) [əhed'], *adv.* in front; in advance. **Ex.** *He walked ahead of me in the line.*

aid (2) [eyd'], *n.* help. **Ex.** *A nurse gave the wounded man aid.* —*v.* help; assist. **Ex.** *They gave money to aid the flood victims.*

ail (5) [eyl'], *v.* feel sick. **Ex.** *The old man is ailing and needs a doctor's care.* —**ail'ment**, *n.* sickness; illness. **Ex.** *Fortunately, your ailment is not serious.*

aim (2) [eym'], *n.* 1. purpose. **Ex.** *His aim was to prevent trouble.* 2. act of pointing a gun. **Ex.** *His aim was bad and he did not kill the deer.* —*v.* 1. try; direct one's efforts towards a purpose. **Ex.** *She aimed at perfection.* 2. point or direct something at a person or object. **Ex.** *He aimed his questions at the senator.*

air (1) [e:r'], *n.* 1. the mixture of gases that are on and above the earth and that we breathe. **Ex.** *The birds rose in the air.* 2. general feeling or effect. **Ex.** *He spoke with an air of secrecy.* —*v.* 1. allow air to enter. **Ex.** *We opened the windows to air the room.* 2. give public expression to thoughts. **Ex.** *He aired his opinions to all of his friends.* —**air'i·ly**, *adv.* in a light manner. **Ex.** *He spoke airily about his bad luck.* —**air'y**, *adj.*

air-condition [e:r'kandišan], *v.* lower the temperature and humidity of the air in a building or a room by means of air conditioning equipment. **Ex.** *We have decided to air-condition our house.* —**air' con·di'tion·er**, *n.* machine used to air-condition.

aircraft [e:r'kræft], *n.* All types of flying machines, including helicopters and gliders.

air force [eːr'fɔrs], *n.* a large group of people together with aircraft organized for air war. **Ex.** *He wants to be a pilot in the air force.*

airplane (1) [eːr'pleyn`], *n.* a flying machine used for carrying people and materials through the air.

AIRPLANE

airport (2) [eːr'pɔrt`], *n.* a specially prepared place where airplanes are loaded and fueled, leave the ground, and come down.

aisle (4) [ayl`], *n.* a path for walking between or along the rows of seats, such as in a theater. **Ex.** *The aisle was only wide enough for two people.*

AISLE

-al (3) [əl], *suffix.* 1. the act or process of. **Exs.** *Refuse, refusal; arrive, arrival.* 2. of, like, or with reference to. **Exs.** *Accident, accidental; music, musical.*

alarm (3) [əlarm`], *n.* 1. sudden fear caused by possible danger. **Ex.** *They were filled with alarm when they saw the fire.* 2. any sound or signal warning of danger. **Ex.** *They rang the bell to sound the alarm.* 3. a device for making a warning noise. **Ex.** *They rang the fire alarm.* —*v.* make fearful. **Ex.** *The spreading fire alarmed us.* —**a·larm`ist,** *n.* a person who alarms others, often without cause. **Ex.** *Only the alarmists thought there was danger of war.*

alarm clock [əlarm` klak`], *n.* a clock that can be set to ring or make another sound at a certain time. **Ex.** *Please set the alarm clock for 7:30 a.m.*

album (5) [æl'bəm], *n.* book with blank pages in which to place pictures, stamps, etc. **Ex.** *He had placed all his snapshots in an album.*

alcohol (3) [æl'kəhɔl`], *n.* a strong, colorless fluid usually made from grains. **Ex.** *Drinks such as beer, whiskey and wine contain alcohol.* —**al`co·hol`ic,** *adj.* of or containing alcohol. **Ex.** *At the party they served both alcoholic and nonalcoholic drinks.* —*n.* a person suffering from the effects of drinking too much alcohol. —**al`co·hol·ism,** *n.* the condition of being an alcoholic. **Ex.** *His alcoholism affected his work.*

ale (5) [eyl`], *n.* an alcoholic drink similar to beer. **Ex.** *He liked the bitter taste of the ale.*

alert (4) [ələrt], adj. 1. watchful and ready. Ex. *The policeman on the corner was alert to the possibility of trouble.* 2. quick in thought or action. Ex. *The old man was still alert.* —n. an alarm; a warning. Ex. *During the war people ran for shelter when the alert was sounded.* —v. warn. Ex. *They alerted everyone to the danger.* —**a·lert'ly,** adv. —**a·lert'ness,** n.

alien (4) [ey'liyən], n. a foreign-born person who is not a citizen of the country in which he lives. Ex. *The government keeps a record of all aliens.* —adj. belonging to a different country or people; strange; foreign. Ex. *After ten years his alien speech was still noticeable.* —**al'ien·ate,** v. make unfriendly. Ex. *His bad manners alienated people who did not know him well.* —**al'ien·a'tion,** n. feeling of strangeness or of not belonging. Ex. *He felt a strong sense of alienation because he could not speak English.*

alive [əliv'], adj. 1. living; not dead. Ex. *Although growing weaker, he is still alive.* 2. full of energy; full of life. Ex. *Despite her age, she is more alive than many younger women.*

all (1) [ɔːl'], adj. 1. the whole of. Ex. *All the money has been spent.* 2. each one of. Ex. *I invited all my friends.* 3. any whatever. Ex. *He is guilty beyond all doubt.* —pron. the whole quantity. Ex. *Eat all of your dinner.* —n. everything, everyone. Ex. *All was lost in the fire.* —**after all,** despite everything. Ex. *He succeeded after all.* —**all but,** except for. Ex. *All but three of the students left the room.* —**all over,** 1. ended. Ex. *The party is all over.* 2. everywhere. Ex. *You see those signs all over town.* —**all right,** 1. satisfactory; good; correct. Ex. *Is it all right for me to leave?* 2. unhurt; well. Ex. *Is she all right?* 3. yes. Ex. *All right, I will go with you.* —**at all,** under any condition. Ex. *He would not see her at all.*

allay (5) [əley'], v. quiet; put at rest. Ex. *The doctor's friendly manner helped allay the patient's fears.*

allege (4) [əlej'], v. 1. declare positively but without proof. Ex. *The shopkeeper alleged that the boy stole some fruit.* 2. declare as a reason; give as an excuse for an act. Ex. *He alleged poor vision as a cause of the accident.* —**al·le·ga'tion,** n.

allegiance (4) [əliy'jəns], n. 1. loyalty or faithfulness to a government, ruler, cause, etc. Ex. *His allegiance to the party was never in question.*

alley (4) [æl'iy], n. a narrow street between or behind buildings. Ex. *The truck was too large to pass through the alley.*

alliance [əlay'əns], *n.* the act of uniting; a union of interests between or among states by agreement or treaty, of families by marriage, etc.; the agreement itself. **Ex.** *The alliance between the two nations strengthened each of them economically.*

allocate [æl'əkeyt`], *v.* 1. set apart for a special purpose. **Ex.** *This land has been allocated for the new high school.* 2. divide among many according to a plan; allot. **Ex.** *They are deciding how to allocate the office space.*

allot (5) [əlat'], *v.* give each his share; distribute. **Ex.** *Each soldier was allotted an extra blanket.* —**al·lot'ment,** *n.*

allow (1) [əlaw'], *v.* 1. permit. **Ex.** *Smoking is not allowed here.* 2. provide for. **Ex.** *Allow enough time for breakfast before you leave.* —**al·low'ance,** *n.* an amount of food, money, etc. given for a special purpose. **Ex.** *They gave their son a weekly allowance for lunch.* —**make allowance for,** consider the circumstances. **Ex.** *You must make allowance for the fact that he is a child.*

alloy (5) [æl'oy], *n.* a substance consisting of two or more metals mixed together. **Ex.** *Red gold is an alloy of gold and copper.*

allude (5) [əluwd'], *v.* refer to or mention in a slight or indirect way. **Ex.** *Your letter alludes to a matter that I had forgotten.* —**al·lu'sion,** *n.* a reference to. **Ex.** *In his talk he made several allusions to the American Constitution.*

allure (5) [əluwr'], *n.* charm. **Ex.** *For me, the country has more allure than the city.* —**al·lur'ing,** *adj.* charming. **Ex.** *She is an alluring young woman.*

ally (4) [æ`lay', əlay'], *n.* a country, person, group, etc. joined with another for some special purpose. **Ex.** *They are allies in the war against drugs.* —*v.* join by agreement, treaty, or marriage. **Ex.** *They are allied by their desire for better schools.* —**al·li'ance,** *n.* the act of allying; the agreement.

almanac [ɔl'mænæk`], *n.* a yearly publication which has information about a wide variety of subjects, generally including a calendar, the daily times of sunrise, sunset and the high and low tides, weather conditions, etc. **Ex.** *You can find the population figures of the largest cities in the United States in a world almanac.*

almost (1) [ɔl'mowst], *adv.* nearly; a little less than; not quite. **Ex.** *It is almost ten o'clock.*

alone (1) [əlown'], *adj.* 1. away from others; by oneself or itself. **Ex.** *The man was alone in the car.* 2. not including anyone or anything else. **Ex.** *Man cannot live by bread alone.* —*adv.* by oneself. **Ex.** *Don't bring anyone with you; come alone.*

along (1) [əlɔːŋ'], *prep.* on or beside the length of. **Ex.** *They walked along the road.* —*adv.* 1. forward; onward. **Ex.** *They were late and had to hurry along.* 2. together. **Ex.** *I will go along with you.* —**get along,** manage. **Ex.** *How can you get along on such a small salary?*

aloof (5) [əluwf'], *adj.* distant; disinterested. **Ex.** *He has few friends because of his aloof manner.* —*adv.* at a distance but within view; apart. **Ex.** *He stood aloof from the others.* —**a·loof'ness,** *n.*

aloud [əlawd'], *adv.* 1. in a voice strong enough to be heard; out loud. **Ex.** *Read this announcement to yourselves as I read it aloud.* 2. in a loud voice. **Ex.** *He cried aloud as he fell.*

alphabet (3) [æl'fəbet'], *n.* the letters used in a language, arranged in a certain order. **Ex.** *The first three letters of the English alphabet are A, B, C.* —**al'pha·bet'i·cal,** *adj.* —**al'pha·bet'i·cal·ly,** *adv.* —**al'pha·bet·ize,** *v.* arrange in the order of the alphabet.

already (1) [ɔlred'iy], *adv.* before a certain time. **Ex.** *When I reached the house, he had already gone.*

also (1) [ɔːl'sow'], *adv.* as well; besides; too. **Ex.** *Will he also come?*

altar (4) [ɔl'tər], *n.* a raised structure or table used in religious services. **Ex.** *The marriage ceremony was performed at the altar.*

alter (3) [ɔl'tər], *v.* make different in some way; change. **Ex.** *The tailor will alter the suit to fit you.* —**al'tera'tion,** *n.* a change.

alternate (4) [ɔl'tərneyt'], *v.* say or do by turns, one after the other. **Ex.** *The teacher alternated between written and spoken work.* —*adj.* by turn, one after the other; every other. **Ex.** *She went into the city on alternate Fridays.* —**al'ter·nate·ly,** *adv.*

alternative (5) [ɔltər'nətiv], *n.* choice between two or more things, only one of which can be chosen. **Ex.** *He had the alternative of coming with us or staying at home.* —*adj.* offering a choice between two or more things. **Ex.** *We had alterna-*

tive plans in case it rained on the day of the picnic. —**al·ter'na·tive·ly,** *adv.*

although (1) [ɔlðow'], *conj.* even if; in spite of the fact. **Ex.** *I will go, although I would rather stay home.*

altitude (4) [æl'tətuwd`, æl'tətyuwd`], *n.* 1. height above a certain level, especially above sea level. **Ex.** *At what altitude is the plane flying?* 2. a position that is high. **Ex.** *The altitude made it difficult to breathe.*

altogether (3) [ɔltəgeð'ər], *adv.* completely; entirely. **Ex.** *This noise is altogether unnecessary.* 2. considering everything. **Ex.** *Altogether it was a successful day.*

aluminum [əluw'mənəm], *n.* a silvery gray metal that is light in weight, does not rust, and is widely used in manufacturing. **Ex.** *These pots and pans are made of aluminum.*

always (1) [ɔl'weyz], *adv.* 1. at all times. **Ex.** *He is always happy.* 2. forever. **Ex.** *His bravery will always be remembered.*

am (1) [æm'], *v.* present tense of the verb *be*, used with *I*. **Ex.** *I am a student now.*

amateur (4) [æm'əčər], *n.* 1. one who does something for enjoyment rather than professionally for money. **Ex.** *The actors in the play were very good amateurs.* 2. an unskilled person. **Ex.** *This artist paints like an amateur.* —*adj.* in the manner of a beginner or amateur. **Ex.** *He is an amateur gardener, but his flowers are beautiful.* —**am·a·teur'ish,** *adj.* —**am·a·teur'ish·ly,** *adv.*

amaze (4) [əmeyz'], *v.* surprise; astonish greatly. **Ex.** *I was amazed by his skill at the piano.* —**a·maze'ment,** *n.* —**a·maz'ing,** *adj.* —**a·maz'ing·ly,** *adv.*

ambassador (4) [æmbæs'ədər], *n.* an official of the highest rank sent by one government as its representative to another. **Ex.** *The ambassador was called home for consultation.* —**am·bas'sa·dor'i·al,** *adj.*

ambition (3) [æmbi'šən], *n.* 1. eagerness or great desire for success, wealth, power, etc. **Ex.** *His ambition caused him to work hard.* 2. the object of such desire. **Ex.** *His ambition was to become a scientist.* —**am·bi'tious,** *adj.* determined to succeed. **Ex.** *Because he is ambitious, he works after school.* —**am·bi'tious·ly,** *adv.*

ambulance [æm'byələns], *n.* a vehicle specially designed to carry persons who are sick or injured. **Ex.** *We called an ambulance to take my brother to the hospital.*

amend (3) [əmend'], *v.* 1. make correct; change for the better; improve. **Ex.** *I would like to amend the statement I made yesterday.* 2. alter. **Ex.** *The Constitution of the United States has been amended more than twenty times.* —a·**mend'ment,** *n.*

amiable (5) [ey'miəbəl], *adj.* friendly; good-natured. **Ex.** *He spoke in an amiable manner.* —a·**mi·a·bil'i·ty,** *n.* —a·**mi·a·bly,** *adv.*

amid (5) [əmid'], *prep.* surrounded by; in the middle of. **Ex.** *The teacher stood amid the crowd of students.*

amiss (5) [əmis'], *adv.* improperly; in the wrong way. **Ex.** *From his angry looks, we knew something had gone amiss.* —*adj.* improper; faulty; wrong. **Ex.** *If anything is amiss in the house, we will attend to it.*

ammunition (5) [æm'yəniš'ən], *n.* 1. anything that is hurled or thrown from a weapon or exploded, such as bullets, bombs, etc. **Ex.** *The soldiers still had their guns but were out of ammunition.* 2. any material useful in defense or attack. **Ex.** *His vote for the tax increase was ammunition for his opponent.*

among (1) [əməŋ'], *prep.* 1. in company with; in the midst of. **Ex.** *There are strangers among us.* 2. in the class or group of. **Ex.** *There were disagreements among the members of the family.* 3. with shares to each of three or more. **Ex.** *The estate was divided equally among the six children.*

amount (1) [əmawnt'], *n.* 1. quantity. **Ex.** *She used only a small amount of sugar in the cake.* 2. total of. **Ex.** *The amount of money we needed to pay the whole bill was very little.* —*v.* reach a total of. **Ex.** *The bill amounts to more than I can pay.*

ample (4) [æm'pəl], *adj.* 1. large in size; having enough space. **Ex.** *There is ample room for two people to sit here.* 2. sufficient for the purpose or the needs; more than enough. **Ex.** *Their supply of food was ample for the winter.* —**am'ply,** *adv.*

amplify [æm'pləfay], *v.* 1. enlarge; explain in additional detail. **Ex.** *Please amplify your answer.* 2. make more powerful or louder. **Ex.** *They amplified the music so that it could be heard outdoors.* —**am'pli·fi'·er,** *n.*

amuse (3) [əmyuwz'], *v.* 1. entertain; cause to laugh. **Ex.** *The actors amused us all.* 2. cause time to pass agreeably. **Ex.** *The guests amused themselves by playing a game.* —a·**mus'ing,** *adj.* —a·**mus'ing·ly,** *adv.* —a·**muse'ment,** *n.*

an (1) [æn', ən], *adj.* or *art.* 1. one; one kind of; any. **Ex.** *He told an interesting story.* 2. in or for each. **Ex.** *The car's speed was twenty-five miles an hour. An* is also called an *indefinite article* and is used instead of *a* before words beginning with a vowel sound.

-an (3) [ən], *suffix.* 1. belonging to; relating to. **Exs.** *America, American; Mexico, Mexican.* 2. one who works in or in the field of. **Exs.** *library, librarian; history, historian.*

analysis (4) [ənæl'əsis], *n.* separation of a whole into parts in order to examine each of the parts. **Ex.** *The blood analysis was made at the hospital.*

analyze (5) [æn'əlayz`], *v.* examine something by separating it into parts. **Ex.** *He analyzed the political situation before deciding to run for office.* —**an`a·lyst**, *n.* —**an`a·lyt'ic**, *adj.* —**an`a·lyt'i·cal·ly**, *adv.*

-ance (1) [əns], *suffix.* act of, condition of or quality of. **Exs.** *Assist, assistance; grieve, grievance; avoid, avoidance.*

ancestor (4) [æn'sestər], *n.* a person in one's family who lived many years before. **Ex.** *His ancestors came to this country 200 years ago.* —**an·ces'tral**, *adj.* —**an'ces·try**, *n.* ancestors as a group. **Ex.** *His ancestry is European.*

anchor (3) [æŋ'kər], *n.* something, usually made of metal, lowered by a chain to the bottom of a body of water to hold a ship in a particular place. **Ex.** *The ship dropped anchor just outside the harbor.* —*v.* 1. fasten with an anchor. **Ex.** *The fisherman anchored his boat near the shore.* 2. fasten firmly. **Ex.** *The pupil's desks were anchored to the floor.* —**an'chor·age**, *n.* a place where ships anchor.

ancient (2) [eyn'šənt], *adj.* 1. in the early years of history; belonging to the distant past. **Ex.** *We are reading the history of ancient Rome.* 2. very old. **Ex.** *That ancient ruin was once a temple.*

and (1) [ænd'], *conj.* 1. with **Ex.** *His brother and his sister are going.* 2. also. **Ex.** *The soup is good and hot.* 3. added to. **Ex.** *Four and five are nine.*

anecdote (5) [æn'ikdowt`], *n.* a brief account of an interesting event. **Ex.** *He told many anecdotes about his experiences as a teacher.* —**a'nec·do`tal**, *adj.*

---

a, far; æ, am; e, get; ey, late; i, in; iy, see; ɔ, all; ow, go; u, put; uw, too; ə, but, ago; ər, fur; aw, out; ay, life; oy, boy; ŋ, ring; θ, think; ð, that; ž, measure; š, ship; ǰ, edge; č, child.

angel (3) [eyn'jəl], *n.* 1. a spiritual, heavenly being; a messenger of God, usually pictured with a human body and wings. 2. a person with the good qualities of such a being. **Ex.** *The children were angels while you were gone.* —**an·gel'ic,** *adj.* —**an·gel'i·cal·ly,** *adv.*

anger (1) [æŋ'gər], *n.* strong, unfriendly feeling usually caused by thoughts that one has been wronged. **Ex.** *The unjust tax laws caused great anger.* —*v.* cause this feeling. **Ex.** *The man angered her when he hit the child.*

angle (3) [æŋ'gəl], *n.* 1. figure made by two straight lines going out from a point; the space inside two such lines. 2. a particular way of thinking. **Ex.** *We must consider this problem from all angles.*

ANGLE 1

angry (1) [æŋ'griy], *adj.* feeling or showing anger. **Ex.** *An angry crowd gathered in the street and shouted loudly.* —**an'gri·ly,** *adv.*

anguish (4) [æŋ'gwiš], *n.* great pain, either of body or mind. **Exs.** *In his anguish, the wounded man screamed. Her daughter's behavior caused her great anguish.* —**an'guished,** *adj.* **Ex.** *She gave an anguished cry when she heard the news.*

animal (1) [æn'əməl], *n.* any living being, not a plant, that can feel and move by itself. **Ex.** *Dogs, birds, fish and people are animals.* —*adj.* relating to animals. **Ex.** *Meat contains animal fats.*

ankle (3) [æŋ'kəl], *n.* the joint between the foot and the leg. **Ex.** *She broke her ankle.*

annex (5) [əneks'], *v.* attach, join or add, especially to something larger or more important. **Ex.** *The city annexed a neighboring village.* —*n.* a building near or added to a larger or more important building. **Ex.** *The hospital laboratory is in the annex.* —**an'nex·a'tion,** *n.* the adding or joining of something to something else.

anniversary (5) [æn'əvər'səriy], *n.* 1. yearly date on which some special event occurred in the past. **Ex.** *August twenty-fourth is our wedding anniversary.* 2. the celebration of such a date.

announce (2) [ənawns'], *v.* 1. cause to be known; give first public notice. **Ex.** *They will announce the names of the winners tonight.* 2. state the approach or the presence of. **Ex.** *A man stood at the door to announce the arrival of the guests.*

—**an·nounc'er,** *n.* one who announces. —**an·nounce·ment,** *n.* that which is announced.

annoy (3) [ənoy'], *v.* anger slightly; worry; disturb; bother. **Ex.** *The noise of the passing trucks annoyed him.* —**an·noy'ance,** *n.*

annual (3) [æn'yuwəl], *adj.* once in each year. **Ex.** *New Year's Day is an annual holiday.* —**an·nu·al·ly,** *adv.*

another (1) [ənəð'ər], *adj., pron.* 1. a second; a further. **Ex.** *When you finish your cake, have another piece, if you would like another.* 2. a different; of a different kind. **Ex.** *We're sure that you know another story; tell us another.* —**one another,** each other. **Ex.** *They love one another very much.*

answer (1) [æn'sər], *n.* 1. a reply to a question or argument. **Ex.** *What is your answer to this question?* 2. the solution to a problem. **Ex.** *The teacher said his answer was correct.* —*v.* give a reply in words, action or writing. **Ex.** *He answered my letter quickly.* —**an'swer·able,** *adj.* required to give an accounting; responsible. **Ex.** *He is answerable to the manager of the company for the use of this money.*

ant (3) [ænt'], *n.* a small insect.

-ant (1) [ənt], *suffix.* a person or thing that does something, is acted upon or is used for. **Exs.** *serve, servant; command, commandant.* 2. doing; showing; having. **Exs.** *Extravagance, extravagant; reliance, reliant.*

ANT

antagonist (5) [æntæg'ənist], *n.* one who is opposed to another, especially in battle or in a contest; opponent; rival. **Ex.** *His antagonist was better armed than he.* —**an·tag'o·nism,** *n.* a strong feeling of unfriendliness or hatred between people or groups. **Ex.** *Their antagonism sprang from a boyhood rivalry.* —**an·tag'o·nis'tic,** *adj.* —**an·tag'o·nis'ti·cal·ly,** *adv.*

antelope (5) [ænt'təlowp'], *n.* a fast-running animal similar to a deer.

ANTELOPE

antenna [ænten'ə], *n.* a single metal rod or wire or a number of them used in sending or receiving radio or television broadcasts. **Ex.** *Since we put an antenna on the roof, our television reception is much better.*

anti- [æn'tay, æn'tiy], *prefix.* against; opposed to. **Exs.** *aircraft, antiaircraft; freeze, antifreeze.*

anticipate (4) [æntis'əpəyt`], *v.* 1. expect. **Ex.** *Everyone anticipated the party with pleasure.* 2. think of and deal with something in advance. **Ex.** *We took our umbrellas because we anticipated rain.* —**an·tic`i·pa'tion,** *n.*

antique (5) [æntiyk'], *adj.* of a time long past. **Ex.** *They have some beautiful antique furniture.* —*n.* an object of ancient art. **Ex.** *You can see the antiques of Greece and Rome in museums.* —**an·tiq'ui·ty,** *n.* ancient times.

anxiety (2) [æŋzay'ətiy], *n.* worry caused by uncertainty. **Ex.** *She felt great anxiety about her new job.*

anxious (2) [æŋk'šəs], *adj.* 1. greatly troubled; worried. **Ex.** *He is anxious about his health.* 2. desiring greatly. **Ex.** *These merchants are anxious to please.* —**anx'ious·ly,** *adv.*

any (1) [en'iy], *adj.* 1. of an undetermined amount. **Ex.** *Do you have any money?* 2. of no particular one. **Ex.** *Take any book you like.* 3. some. **Ex.** *Do you want any cream in your coffee?* 4. every. **Ex.** *He can answer any question about this subject.* —*adv.* to some degree; to some extent. **Ex.** *Is the patient any better?* —*pron.* one; some. **Ex.** *He did not buy any.*

anybody [en'iybə`diy, en'iyba`diy], *pron.* any person. **Ex.** *Can anybody tell me the time?*

anyhow (3) [en'iyhaw`], *adv.* in any case; regardless of difficulty or argument. **Ex.** *Though her father did not like the young man, she married him anyhow.*

anyone [en'iywən`], *pron.* any person. **Ex.** *I did not see anyone I knew at the meeting.*

anything [en'iyθiŋ`], *pron.* any thing, act, condition, event or fact. **Exs.** *Did you do anything interesting during your vacation? Did you buy anything to eat?* —*adv.* in any degree. **Ex.** *Their house is not anything like ours.*

anyway [en'iywey`], *adv.* in any case; nevertheless. **Ex.** *He was told not to go, but he went anyway.*

anywhere [en'iyhwe:r`], *adv.* at, in or to any place. **Exs.** *I cannot find the book anywhere. Are you going anywhere this evening?*

apart (2) [əpart'], *adv.* 1. separately, in place or time. **Ex.** *He lived apart from his parents while he attended school.* 2. in two or more parts. **Ex.** *The children took the clock apart to see how it worked.*

apartment (2) [əpart'mənt], *n.* a room or group of connected rooms within a building, arranged for housekeeping. **Ex.** *There are several apartments for rent in that building.* **—a part'-ment house,** *n.* a building that contains a number of apartments. **Ex.** *Our apartment house has 800 units.*

ape (5) [eyp'], *n.* a large monkey with no tail.

apologize (3) [əpal'əjayz'], *v.* express regrets for a mistake made or injury done. **Ex.** *He apologized for his error.* **—a·pol'o·get'ic,** *adj.* **—a·pol'o·get'i·cal·ly,** *adv.*

APE

apology (3) [əpal'əjiy], *n.* expression of regret for; statement that one is sorry. **Ex.** *I owe you an apology for being late.*

appall (5) [əpɔːl'], *v.* fill with horror, shock or fear. **Ex.** *They were appalled by the sight of the bloody shirt.* **—ap·pall'ing,** *adj.* **—ap·pall'ing·ly,** *adv.*

apparatus (4) [æp'ərey'təs, æp'əræt'əs], *n.* tools, equipment, machinery, etc. for a special kind of work. **Ex.** *The town had recently purchased some new fire-fighting apparatus.*

apparel (5) [æpær'əl, əper'əl], *n.* a person's outer clothing, suits, dresses, etc. **Ex.** *A shop selling women's apparel is at the corner.*

apparent (3) [əpær'ənt, əper'ənt], *adj.* 1. evident; capable of being clearly seen or understood. **Ex.** *His fear was apparent to all.* 2. seeming rather than actual. **Ex.** *The apparent spot on the wall was only a shadow.* **—ap·par'ent·ly,** *adv.*

appeal (2) [əpiyl'], *v.* 1. ask for aid. **Ex.** *After their house burned, they appealed for clothing.* 2. offer attraction, interest or enjoyment. **Ex.** *The large house appealed to him.* 3. ask a higher court to review a law case. **—n.** 1. a call for aid, support or mercy; a request. **Ex.** *Their appeal for money was soon answered.* 2. *power to attract.* **Ex.** *His ideas had great appeal for young people.* 3. a request for a review of a law case by a higher court. **—ap·peal'ing,** *adj.* **—ap·peal'ing·ly,** *adv.*

appear (1) [əpi:r'], *v.* 1. seem; look as if. **Ex.** *He appears to be happy.* 2. come into sight. **Ex.** *The ship appeared in the* distance. 3. come or be placed before the public. **Ex.** *She appeared in a new movie.* —**ap·pear'ance,** *n.* 1. act of appearing. **Ex.** *She made a late appearance at the party.* 2. outward look. **Ex.** *From his appearance, we knew he was ill.*

appease (5) [əpiyz'], *v.* 1. satisfy; make quiet; calm. **Ex.** *The food appeased his hunger.* 2. make peace, often by sacrificing a moral principle. **Ex.** *Only complete surrender would appease the enemy.* —**ap·peas'er,** *n.* —**ap·pease'ment,** *n.*

append (5) [əpend'], *v.* add or attach as something extra. **Ex.** *The author appended a list of references at the end of his book.*

appendix (5) [əpen'diks], *n.* 1. material added at the end of a complete book or other written work. **Ex.** *The appendix contains some useful information.* 2. a small tube in the abdomen which has no known use. —**ap·pen·di·ci'tis,** *n.* inflamed, diseased state of the appendix.

appetite (4) [æp'ətayt`], *n.* 1. a desire to eat or drink. **Ex.** *His appetite decreased when he became sick.* 2. any desire. **Ex.** *They have an appetite for travel.* —**ap'pe·tiz'ing,** *adj.* —**ap'pe·tiz'er,** *n.* small pieces of food or drink taken before a meal to improve appetites. **Ex.** *Fruit juice was served as an appetizer.*

applaud (4) [əplɔːd'], *v.* 1. express approval by hitting the hands together. **Ex.** *The audience applauded the actors.* 2. praise; express approval. **Ex.** *We applaud your decision.*

applause (4) [əplɔːz'], *n.* striking the hands together, shouting or other outward expressions of approval. **Ex.** *The applause was loud and long.*

apple (1) [æp'əl], *n.* a red, yellow or green round, firm fruit with small seeds.

appliance (5) [əplay'əns], *n.* a device for a particular use, usually electrically operated. **Ex.** *Our house has many useful electrical appliances.*

APPLE

apply (2) [əplay'], *v.* 1. use. **Ex.** *He applied his knowledge of chemistry to the problem.* 2. place in contact with; put on. **Ex.** *He immediately applied some medicine to the wound.* 3. ask for. **Ex.** *She applied for the job.* —**ap'pli·ca·ble,** *adj.* —**ap'pli·cant,** *n.* one who applies for a job. —**ap'pli·ca'tion,** *n.* a request.

appoint (2) [əpoynt'], *v.* 1. select for a position; place in office. **Ex.** *They appointed him president of the company.* 2. decide upon. **Ex.** *We must appoint a time and place for the meeting.*

appointment (2) [əpoynt'mənt], *n.* 1. selection for position or office. **Ex.** *The committee favored the appointment of a new secretary.* 2. established time; engagement. **Ex.** *I have an appointment with my doctor at four o'clock.*

appreciate (3) [əpriy'šiyeyt'], *v.* 1. recognize or feel the worth of. **Ex.** *He does not appreciate art.* 2. be grateful for. **Ex.** *The boy appreciated the gift.* 3. recognize; understand; sympathize. **Ex.** *He appreciated the difficulties of making the trip.* — **ap·pre'ci·a'tive,** *adj.* —**ap·pre'ci·a·tive·ly,** *adv.* —**ap·pre'ci·a'tion,** *n.*

apprehend (5) [æp'rihend'], *v.* seize; arrest. **Ex.** *The police apprehended the criminal.*

apprehension (4) [æp'rihen'šən], *n.* 1. dread or fear of coming evil. **Ex.** *He had some apprehension about going into the forest alone.* 2. act of seizing or arresting. **Ex.** *The apprehension of the thief was done quickly.* —**ap'pre·hen'sive,** *adj.* —**ap·pre·hen'sive·ly,** *adv.*

apprentice (5) [əpren'tis], *n.* a person helping a skilled worker in a trade in order to learn; a learner; a beginner. **Ex.** *He is an apprentice in the building trade.* —*v.* put under the care of an employer for instruction in an art or trade. **Ex.** *The young man was apprenticed to a shoemaker.* —**ap·pren'tice·ship,** *n.*

approach (2) [əprowč'], *v.* 1. move near to in space, time, quality, etc. **Ex.** *The car approached the city.* 2. go to with a request. **Ex.** *The boy approached his father for permission to go on the trip.* —*n.* 1. act of coming closer. **Ex.** *They were frightened by the man's approach.* 2. means of entrance; road or path. **Ex.** *The approach to the house was lined with trees.* —**ap·proach'able,** *adj.* friendly; willing to talk and listen.

appropriate (4) [əprow'priyət], *adj.* proper or fitting for a particular person, purpose, etc. **Ex.** *He made a speech appropriate to the holiday.* —**ap·pro'pri·ate·ly,** *adv.* —**ap·pro'pri·ate·ness,** *n.*

appropriate (4) [əprow'priyeyt'], *v.* 1. set apart for a special purpose. **Ex.** *The city appropriated money for a new bridge.* 2. take possession of; take for one's self. **Ex.** *After the boy's parents died, an uncle appropriated their property.* —**ap·pro·pri·a'tion,** *n.* 1. act of appropriating. 2. that which is appropriated.

approve (3) [əpruwv'], *v.* 1. speak or think favorably of; consider to be good. **Ex.** *Do you approve of my choice?* 2. give

one's consent to. **Ex.** *The president did not approve the plan.*
—**ap·prov'al**, *n.* —**ap·prov'ing**, *adj.* —**ap·prov'ing·ly**, *adv.*

approximate (3) [əprak'səmət'], *adj.* very similar; not exact but
nearly so. **Ex.** *What is the approximate amount you need?*
—**ap·prox'i·mate·ly**, *adv.*

approximate (3) [əprak'sameyt'], *v.* be or make very similar.
Ex. *This copy approximates the original.* —**ap·prox'i·ma'tion**, *n.*

April (1) [ey'prəl], *n.* fourth month of the
year.

APRON

apron (4) [ey'prən], *n.* article of clothing worn
over the front part of one's clothes to cover
and protect them while working.

apt (4) [æpt'], *adj.* 1. suitable; proper. **Ex.**
*Although not prepared to talk, he made
some apt remarks.* 2. likely. **Ex.** *Please
remind me, for I am apt to forget.* 3. quick
to learn. **Ex.** *The girl is an apt pupil.* —**apt'ly**, *adv.* —**apt'ness**, *n.*

-ar (3) [ər], *suffix.* 1. belonging to; referring to; like; of the
nature of. **Exs.** *Pole, polar; line, linear.* 2. one who. **Exs.**
Beg, beggar; lie, liar.

arbor (5) [ar'bər], *n.* a place covered and shaded by trees or
vines on a frame. **Ex.** *They sat under the grape arbor.*

arc (5) [ark'], *n.* a curved line; a line that is part of a circle.

ARCH

arch (2) [arč'], *n.* 1. a curved part of a building
used to hold up the material above it. 2. any
curve in the form of an arch. —*v.* 1. cover
or provide with an arch. **Ex.** *The bridge arches
over the river.* 2. form or bend into the shape
of an arch. **Ex.** *She arched her eyebrows in
surprise.*

architect (4) [ar'kətekt'], *n.* a person who designs
buildings and checks to see that they are properly built. **Ex.**
We employed an architect to plan our house.

architecture (4) [ar'kətek'čər], *n.* 1. the art or science of designing
buildings. 2. a method or style of building. **Ex.** *Greek architecture and modern architecture are quite different.* —**ar'chi·tec'
tur·al**, *adj.* —**ar'chi·tec'tur·al·ly**, *adv.*

are (1) [a:r'], *v.* present tense of the verb *be* used with *you, we,
they* and plural nouns. **Ex.** *We are friends now.*

area (2) [er'iyə], *n.* 1. a region on the earth's surface. **Ex.** *They traveled through a mountainous area.* 2. an amount of space within boundaries. **Ex.** *The area of their land is two acres.* 3. extent of a subject. **Ex.** *The study of the deep ocean is an important area of research.*

area code [er'iyə kowd], *n.* numbers used before a regular telephone number to reach a particular area when making a long-distance call. **Ex.** *The area code for Washington, D. C. is 202.*

aren't [aːrnt'], *v.* short form or contraction for *are not.* **Ex.** *Aren't you coming with us?*

argue (2) [ar'gyuw], *v.* 1. offer reasons for or against something. **Ex.** *They argued against going home so early.* 2. disagree; quarrel. **Ex.** *The drunken man argued loudly with the taxi driver.* —**ar'gu·ment,** *n.* —**ar'gu·able,** *adj.* —**ar·gu·men'ta·tive,** *adj.* always ready to quarrel.

arise (3) [ərayz'], *v.* 1. move upward; stand up; get out of bed. **Ex.** *I always arise at seven o'clock in the morning.* 2. appear; come into being. **Ex.** *New problems arise every day.*

arisen [ərizən'], *v.* past participle of *arise.* **Ex.** *He had arisen before the alarm clock rang.*

aristocrat (5) [əris'təkræt'], *n.* 1. a person of high rank, birth or title. **Ex.** *For many years only aristocrats were members of the government.* 2. one who has the characteristics of a ruling or upper class of society. **Ex.** *The governor came from a poor family but had the manners of an aristocrat.* —**a·ris'to·crat'ic,** *adj.*

arithmetic (5) [əriθ'mətik'], *n.* the science or study of using numbers. **Ex.** *Arithmetic was his favorite subject in school.* —**ar'ith·met'i·cal,** *adj.* —**ar'ith·met'i·cal·ly,** *adv.*

arm (1) [arm'], *n.* 1. part of the human body from the shoulder to the hand. 2. anything like a human arm. **Ex.** *The coat was hanging over the arm of a chair.* —*v.* 1. give guns or other things with which to fight. **Ex.** *The soldiers were armed with guns.* 2. strengthen; furnish with protection. **Ex.** *He was armed against the cold with warm clothing.* —**armed,** *adj.*

ARM

armament (5) [ar'məmənt], *n.* the weapons, supplies and military force for fighting a war. **Ex.** *A large percentage of the budget was allocated for armaments.*

armchair [arm'če:r], *n.* a chair with supports for the arms. **Ex.** *There was an armchair at each end of the dining room table.*

armistice (5) [ar'məstis], *n.* the stopping of fighting for a brief time, by agreement. **Ex.** *During the armistice, they developed a plan for ending the war.*

armor (3) [ar'mər], *n.* 1. protective covering on a ship, plane, tank, etc. **Ex.** *The rifle fire did not damage the armor of the tank.* 2. protective covering for the body, usually made of metal or leather. **Ex.** *As armor, the President wore a bullet-proof vest.*

arms (1) [armz'], *n.* guns and other things soldiers use to fight in battle; weapons. **Ex.** *The soldiers laid down their arms and surrendered.*

army (1) [ar'miy], *n.* 1. a large group of soldiers organized for land war. **Ex.** *The army prevented the enemy from entering the city.* 2. a great number. **Ex.** *An army of children marched down the street.*

arose (3) [ərowz'], *v.* past tense of *arise.* **Ex.** *He arose early today.*

around (1) [ərawnd'], *adv.* 1. in a circle; on every side. **Ex.** *Come around and listen.* 2. in the opposite direction. **Ex.** *They turned around and ran.* —*prep.* 1. about; encircling. **Ex.** *She wore some beads around her neck.* 2. here and there. **Ex.** *Let us drive around the city for a while.* 3. somewhere in or near. **Ex.** *Stay around the school until I come for you.* 4. near in time or amount. **Ex.** *I will see you around five o'clock.*

arouse (5) [ərawz'], *v.* 1. awaken. **Ex.** *They aroused the boy from a deep sleep.* 2. excite to action or a high degree of emotion. **Ex.** *The speaker aroused the crowd.* —**a·roused'**, *adj.*

arrange (2) [əreynj'], *v.* 1. put in order. **Ex.** *Arrange the papers on the table.* 2. prepare; plan. **Ex.** *We will arrange a meeting for next week.* —**ar·range'ment**, *n.* —**ar·rang'er**, *n.* person who arranges, especially music for different instruments.

array (4) [ərey'], *v.* 1. clothe in fine garments. **Ex.** *The dancers were arrayed in colorful costumes.* 2. place in order; line up or arrange, especially soldiers. **Ex.** *The soldiers were arrayed* *in front of the general.* —*n.* 1. order; battle order. **Ex.** *The troops were in battle array.* 2. an impressive group of things on exhibition. **Ex.** *There was an array of jewels in the shop window.*

arrest (3) [ərest'], *v.* 1. seize a person by legal authority. **Ex.** *The policeman arrested him.* 2. stop. **Ex.** *National and local government agencies are working together to arrest the flow of drugs.* 3. attract. **Ex.** *The story arrested my attention.* —*n.* seizure by legal authority. **Ex.** *They placed the man under arrest.*

arrive (1) [ərayv'], *v.* 1. come to a particular place. **Ex.** *I will arrive on the two o'clock bus.* 2. reach a point or a state by effort. **Ex.** *After much discussion, they arrived at a decision.* —**ar·riv'al,** *n.*

arrow (3) [ær'ow], *n.* 1. a long, thin piece of wood with a sharply pointed tip and feathers at the other end, used as a weapon and shot from a bow. 2. a mark in the form of an arrow which shows direction. **Ex.** *Follow the arrows on the wall.*

art (1) [art'], *n.* 1. the expression or making of something that is beautiful; the thing made or expressed. **Ex.** *These paintings are good examples of modern art.* 2. skilled workmanship. **Ex.** *This ring is a fine example of the jeweler's art.* 3. the general principles of an area of learning. **Ex.** *She is skilled in the art of cooking.* —**art'ist,** *n.* —**ar·tis'tic,** *adj.* —**ar·tis'ti·cal·ly,** *adv.* —**arts,** *n.* certain fields of study outside of science, such as music, dance, language, etc.

artery (5) [ar'təriy], *n.* 1. a blood vessel that carries blood from the heart to other parts of the body. 2. a channel of transportation or communication. **Ex.** *This river was once a main artery of transportation.* —**ar·te'ri·al,** *adj.*

article (1) [ar'təkəl], *n.* 1. a piece of writing on a special subject. **Ex.** *Have you read this newspaper article?* 2. an individual piece or thing. **Ex.** *He lost several articles of clothing.* 3. the indefinite articles *a* and *an* and the definite article *the* used before a noun to identify it as a noun rather than another part of speech.

artificial (4) [ar'təfiš'əl], *adj.* 1. made by humans; not natural. **Ex.** *The artificial flowers were made of silk.* 2. not true; not honest. **Ex.** *Her smile is artificial.* —**ar'ti·fi'cial·ly,** *adv.* —**ar'ti·fi·ci·al'i·ty,** *n.*

artillery (4) [artil'əriy], *n.* 1. large, heavy guns moved on wheeled carriers. **Ex.** *The artillery was the deciding factor in the battle.* 2. the part of the army that uses such guns.

-ary (1) [əriy], *suffix.* relating to; connected with; like. **Ex.** *Honor, honorary; custom, customary; literature, literary.*

as (1) [æz'], *adv.* equally; in the same amount, degree or manner; like. **Ex.** *She is as pretty as her mother.* —*conj.* 1. to the same degree or amount that; in the same manner. *He grew straight as a tree.* **Ex.** 2. while; when. **Ex.** *As I sat there, I thought of many things.* 3. because. **Ex.** *As you are not dressed yet, I will leave without you.* —*pron.* 1. who; which; that. **Ex.** *The store is in the same building as my office.* 2. a fact that. **Ex.** *It is red, as anyone can see.* —*prep.* in the idea, character or condition of. **Ex.** *He was treated as a child.*

ascend (4) [əsend'], *v.* climb or move upward; rise. **Ex.** *He ascended the stairs to the second floor.*

ascent (5) [əsent'], *n.* 1. act of rising; upward movement; rise. **Ex.** *His ascent in the business world was rapid.* 2. way or means of going up; upward slope. **Ex.** *The ascent to the top of the hill was steep.*

ash (3) [æš'], *n.* the powdery material that remains after burning. **Ex.** *The paper burned to ashes.* —**ashen,** *adj.* pale; the color of ashes.

ashamed (3) [əšeymd'], *v.* feeling shame because one has done wrong, failed, etc. **Ex.** *I feel ashamed of the way I acted at your party.*

aside (əsayd'], *adv.* to one side; away. **Ex.** *Why did you turn aside?*

ask (1) [æsk'], *v.* 1. put a question to; seek information. **Ex.** *Ask her when the train leaves.* 2. demand as a price. **Ex.** *You are asking too much for this furniture.* 3. invite. **Ex.** *We asked guests for dinner.*

asleep [əsliyp'], *adj.* sleeping. **Ex.** *I was asleep and did not hear him knock.*

aspect (3) [æs'pekt'], *n.* 1. appearance, look. **Ex.** *To the men in the boat, the rocky shore had a frightening aspect.* 2. a way in which a thing may be viewed or considered. **Ex.** *All aspects of the question must be examined.*

aspire (5) [əspayr'], *v.* desire eagerly, especially something high or great. **Ex.** *He aspired to be a leader.* —**as·pir'ant,** *n.* —**as·pi·ra'tion,** *n.*

assail (4) [əseyl'], *v.* attack violently, either by words or by repeated blows. **Ex.** *He assailed them with bad language.*

—**as·sail'ant,** *n.* attacker. **Ex.** *The assailant has been caught by the police.*

assault (4) [əsɔlt'], *n.* violent attack with weapons or blows or by words and arguments. **Ex.** *We were not prepared for the assault.* —*v.* make an attack.

assemble (3) [əsem'bəl], *v.* 1. collect; gather into one place or group. **Ex.** *The students assembled in the classroom.* 2. put or fit parts together. **Ex.** *The workmen assembled the new machine.* —**as·sem'bly,** *n.* a group of people meeting for a particular purpose. —**As·sem'bly,** *n.* parliament; legislature.

assent (5) [əsent'], *v.* agree; admit the truth of; consent. **Ex.** *He assented to the plan.* —*n.* agreement; act of assenting.

assert (5) [əsərt'], *v.* 1. state as true; declare; state with certainty. **Ex.** *She asserted that she was innocent.* 2. insist on; claim. **Ex.** *He asserted his rights to a share in the profits.* —**as·ser'tion,** *n.*

assess [əses'], *v.* 1. place an estimated value on property for taxation, insurance, etc. **Ex.** *They assessed the damage to the car at three thousand dollars.* 2. establish a rate of taxation, fine, etc. **Ex.** *The city assesses one-family houses at $1.50 for each $100 valuation.* 3. judge the quality of someone's work, performance, etc. **Ex.** *How would you assess his behavior these part few weeks?*

asset (5) [æ'set'], *n.* something of value that is owned; a valuable quality. **Exs.** *Among his assets was a collection of stamps. His honesty is an asset to us.*

assign (3) [əsayn'], *v.* 1. give as a job or work. **Ex.** *The teacher assigned us ten problems for homework.* 2. appoint. **Ex.** *Two new professors were assigned to the science department.* 3. select; fix exactly. **Ex.** *We must assign a day for the meeting.* —**as·sign'ment,** *n.*

assist (3) [əsist'], *v.* aid; help. **Ex.** *I will need two people to assist me in this demonstration.* —**as·sist'ance,** *n.* the act of helping. —**as·sist'ant,** *n.* a helper.

associate (2) [əsow'šiyeyt'], *v.* 1. connect in thought. **Ex.** *He associated spring with romance.* 2. join as a companion or partner. **Ex.** *She likes to associate with people who are her own age.*

a, far; æ, am; e, get; ey, late; i, in; iy, see; ɔ, all; ow, go; u, put; uw, too; ə, but, ago; ər, fur; aw, out; ay, life; oy, boy; ŋ, ring; θ, think; ð, that; ž, measure; š, ship; j, edge; č, child.

associate (2) [əsow'šiyət], *n.* each of two or more partners in an enterprise; companion. **Ex.** *The three men are business associates.*

association (2) [əsow`šiyey'šən], *n.* 1. group of people organized for a common purpose. **Ex.** *He is a member of the lawyers' association.* 2. fellowship; partnership. **Ex.** *The two men formed a business association.* 3. the act of associating; the fact of being associated. **Ex.** *His association with criminals is known to the police.*

assorted (5) [əsɔr'təd], *adj.* of different kinds. **Ex.** *She received a box of assorted cheeses.* **—as·sort'ment,** *n.* variety. **Ex.** *The store had a large assortment of styles.*

assume (2) [əsuwm'], *v.* 1. believe or accept as a fact; suppose. **Ex.** *I assume that you can do the work.* 2. take responsibility for. **Ex.** *She will assume care of the child during the mother's illness.* 3. pretend to be or to have. **Ex.** *Although he was nervous, he assumed an appearance of confidence.* **—as·sump' tion,** *n.*

assure (2) [əšu:r'], *v.* 1. say with certainty; satisfy, as by a promise; give confidence to. **Ex.** *He assured them that he was able to do the work.* 2. make something certain. **Ex.** *The warm weather assured the success of our trip to the seashore.* **—as·sur'ance,** *n.* **—as·sured',** *adj.*

astonish (3) [əstan'iš], *v.* cause to wonder; surprise greatly. **Ex.** *The size of the elephant astonished the little boy.* **—as·ton' ish·ment,** *n.* **—as·ton'ish·ing,** *adj.* **—as·ton'ish·ing·ly,** *adv.*

astronaut (5) [æs'trənɔt], *n.* a person who is trained to operate a spaceship; one who makes a flight into space. **Ex.** *On television we watched the astronauts journey to the moon.*

astronomy (5) [əstran'əmiy], *n.* the science of the stars, moon, planets and other heavenly bodies. **—as·tron'o·mer,** *n.* one who is an expert in astronomy. **—as·tro·nom'i·cal,** *adj.* 1. connected with astronomy. 2. very large, like the numbers used in astronomy. **Ex.** *His salary is astronomical.*

asylum [əsay'ləm], *n.* a place offering shelter and protection; a refuge, often given by a government of one country to people fleeing another for political reasons. **Ex.** *He was given asylum in the embassy.*

at (1) [æt'], *prep.* present on, in or near to. **Ex.** *I met him at the station.* 2. to or toward. **Ex.** *The dog rushed at the stranger.* 3.

occupied with; busy with. **Ex.** *The family was at dinner.* 4. in a situation or condition of. **Ex.** *They seemed at ease with one another.* 5. because of; caused by. **Ex.** *She was frightened at the sight of blood.* 6. showing a point in or period of time. **Ex.** *He often works at night.* 7. in relation to the value or cost of. **Ex.** *Tomatoes are selling at a low price.* —**at last,** finally. **Ex.** *At last she saw him.* —**at once,** now; immediately. **Ex.** *Do the work at once.*

ate (2) [eyt'], *v.* past tense of *eat*. **Ex.** *I ate breakfast this morning.*

-ate (3) [eyt, ət], *suffix.* become or cause to become. **Exs.** *Active, activate; valid, validate.* 2. having the character of. **Exs.** *Affection, affectionate; fortune, fortunate.*

athlete (4) [æθ'liyt'], *n.* a person trained in a sport that requires strength, speed and skill. **Ex.** *The young athlete was much admired for his speed.*

athletic (4) [æθlet'ik], *adj.* 1. concerning athletes or sports. **Ex.** *The game was played on the athletic field.* 2. strong; of a muscular build. **Ex.** *She has a very athletic appearance.* —**ath·let'i·cal·ly,** *adv.* —**ath·let'ics,** *n.* the games and sports of athletes.

atlas [æt'ləs], *n.* a book containing a collection of maps. **Ex.** *We used an atlas in planning our trip.*

atmosphere (3) [æt'məsfi:r'], *n.* 1. the air surrounding the earth; the gases surrounding a planet or star. **Ex.** *Scientists are concerned about unfavorable changes in the earth's atmosphere.* 2. the air in a certain place. **Ex.** *The mountain atmosphere was dry and cool.* 3. the general feeling of a place or thing. **Ex.** *The old house had an atmosphere of neglect.* —**at'mos·pher'ic,** *adj.*

atom (3) [æt'əm], *n.* a bit of matter so small that anything smaller is not the same matter. —**a·tom'ic,** *adj.* of or concerning atoms. **Ex.** *Atomic energy is created when atoms are split.* —**a·tom'ic bomb',** *n.* a very powerful bomb that gets its force from splitting atoms and releasing their energy.

attach (3) [ətæč'], *v.* 1. bind; fasten; tie; connect. **Ex.** *A card was attached to the gift.* 2. bring close together by feelings of fondness, affection or love. **Ex.** *My uncle is very attached to my brother.* 3. assign to, as if connected. **Ex.** *He attaches great importance to the report.* —**at·tach'ment,** *n.*

attack (2) [ətæk'], *v.* 1. start a fight or battle against. **Ex.** *At what hour will our forces attack?* 2. direct unfavorable words

against; blame violently. **Ex.** *The writer attacked the government
in his newspaper articles.* 3. go to work with energy. **Ex.** *They
attacked the work eagerly in order to finish it by noon.* 4. act upon
injuriously; harm. **Ex.** *Disease attacked the roses in our garden.* —*n.* 1. act of attacking. 2. a military action that aims at destroying the enemy. 3. being seized by disease. **Ex.** *He had a
heart attack.*

attain (3) [əteyn'], *v.* 1. accomplish or reach by effort; gain. **Ex.** *She
attained fame as a writer.* 2. arrive at. **Ex.** *My father has attained
the age of sixty-five.* —**at·tain'ment,** *n.*

attempt (1) [ətempt'], *v.* make an effort; try. **Ex.** *The doctor attempted to save the dying man.* —*n.* an effort; a try. **Ex.** *This is
his second attempt to win that prize.*

attend (2) [ətend'], *v.* 1. be present at; go to. **Ex.** *They attend school
five days a week.* 2. care for. **Ex.** *A nurse attends her.* —**at·tend'
ance,** *n.* the act of attending. —**at·tend'ant,** *n.* one who attends.

attention (2) [əten'šən], *n.* 1. the act of keeping one's mind
on a subject. **Ex.** *They listened with great attention.* 2. care;
consideration. **Ex.** *Your request will receive my personal attention.* 3. act of kindness. **Ex.** *She appreciated her nephew's
small attentions.*

attentive (3) [əten'tiv], *adj.* 1. listening closely; observant. **Ex.**
He is a very attentive student. 2. polite; kind; thoughtful. **Ex.**
He is always attentive toward his wife. —**at·ten'tive·ly,** *adv.*
—**at·ten'tive·ness,** *n.*

attic (4) [æt'ik], *n.* a room or space in the part of a house directly
under the roof. **Ex.** *We have some of our suitcases stored in
the attic.*

attire (4) [ətayr'], *v.* dress. **Ex.** *She was attired in a beautiful silk
gown for the dance.* —*n.* clothes, especially rich or splendid
garments. **Ex.** *The bride's attire was particularly lovely.*

attitude (2) [æt'ətuwd', æt'ətyuwd'], *n.* 1. a manner; a way of
behaving, feeling, etc. toward someone or something. **Ex.** *He
took a sympathetic attitude toward my problem.* 2. position of
the body in relation to a person or thing. **Ex.** *The robber
assumed a threatening attitude.*

attorney (4) [ətər'niy], *n.* lawyer; one who has been given the
right to act in legal matters for another. **Ex.** *The court appointed an attorney for the accused man.*

attract (3) [ətrækt'], *v.* cause to come closer; pull toward one's self. **Ex.** *The beautiful girl attracted much attention.* —**at·trac'tion,** *n.* —**at·trac'tive,** *adj.* —**at·trac'tive·ly,** *adv.* in a way that attracts.

attribute (4) [ətrib'yut], *v.* regard something as coming from a particular person or thing. **Ex.** *This poem is attributed to Shakespeare.*

attribute (4) [æt'rəbyuwt'], *n.* a characteristic or quality that is part of the nature of a person or a thing. **Ex.** *One of her attributes is her generosity.* —**at'tri·bu'tion,** *n.*

auction (5) [ɔk'šən], *n.* a public sale of property to the highest bidder. **Ex.** *The farm was sold at auction.* —*v.* sell at auction. **Ex.** *The paintings were auctioned off at high prices.* —**auc·tion·eer',** *n.* one who conducts an auction.

audience (3) [ɔ:'diyəns], *n.* 1. a group of people watching or listening to a speaker or a performer. **Ex.** *The audience was very enthusiastic.* 2. an interview with a high-ranking person. **Ex.** *The ambassador had an audience with the queen.*

audio [ɔ:d'iyow], *adj.* of or having to do with hearing or sound; of or having to do with the broadcasting of sound. **Ex.** *His work involves the audio aspects of television.*

auditorium [ɔ:ditɔr'iyəm], **n.** a large room in a school, theater, church, etc. where people can sit to hear a concert, watch a play, listen to a lecture, etc. **Ex.** *The auditorium opens at two o'clock for this afternoon's performance.*

August (1) [ɔ:'gəst], *n.* the eighth month of the year.

aunt (1) [ænt'] *n.* the sister of one's father or mother; an uncle's wife.

austere (5) [ɔsti:r'], *adj.* 1. severe or stern in appearance or manner. **Ex.** *The judge had an austere look on his face as he spoke to the criminal.* 2. simple in manner of living or acting. **Ex.** *The old man's life was very austere.* 3. plain; without decorations. **Ex.** *The austere room seemed dark and cold.* —**aus·tere'ly,** *adv.* —**aus·ter'i·ty,** *n.*

authentic (5) [ɔθen'tik], *adj.* 1. worthy of acceptance; true. **Ex.** *We need an authentic report of his activities.* 2. of the authorship or origin claimed; real; genuine. **Ex.** *This is an authentic*

a, far; æ, am; e, get; ey, late; i, in; iy, see; ɔ, all; ow, go; u, put; uw, too; ə, but, ago; ər, fur; aw, out; ay, life; oy, boy; ŋ, ring; θ, think; ð, that; ž, measure; š, ship; j, edge; č, child.

tenth-century painting. —**au·then'ti·cate,** *v.* prove to be real. —**au'then·tic'i·ty,** *n.*

author (2) [ɔː'θər], *n.* 1. a person who writes a novel, poem, play, etc. 2. the beginner or creator of anything. **Ex.** *She was the author of the plan to improve the schools.*

authority (2) [əθɔr'ətiy], *n.* 1. the right to control, command or order. **Ex.** *By what authority do you order me to do this?* 2. a person with such rights or powers. **Ex.** *The judge is the authority in this case.* 3. a person or book considered as the correct source of information or advice. **Ex.** *What is your authority for this date?*

authorize (3) [ɔː'θərayz'], *v.* 1. give someone the power or right to do something. **Ex.** *The president of the company authorized the manager to hire ten new workmen.* 2. give official permission to do something. **Ex.** *They authorized the construction of the building.* —**au'thor·i·za'tion,** *n.*

autobiography [ɔ'təbayag'rəfiy], *n.* the story of a person's life written by the person himself. **Ex.** *The explorer's autobiography was an exciting story.*

automatic (4) [ɔ'təmæt'ik], *adj.* 1. having the power of moving by itself, especially machinery or mechanical devices. **Ex.** *An automatic timer turns the street lights on at night and off in the morning.* 2. done without conscious thought or effort. **Ex.** *Her automatic reaction was to refuse the invitation.* —**au'to·mat'i·cal·ly,** *adv.*

automation (4) [ɔ'təmey'šən], *n.* a system or process of producing goods or information in which much or all of the work is done by automatically controlled machines. **Ex.** *The automation of this factory made it necessary for some workers to find new jobs.*

automobile (2) [ɔː'təmowbiyl'], *n.* a motor car especially for passengers. **Ex.** *This automobile seats five passengers.* —**au'to·mo'tive,** *adj.* concerning automobiles.

AUTOMOBILE

autumn (2) [ɔː'təm], *n.* the season between summer and winter; fall.

avail (4) [əveyl'], *n.* use or benefit. **Ex.** *She cried, but her tears were to no avail.* —**avail oneself of,** make use of. **Ex.** *You should avail yourself of the opportunity to travel now.*

available (3) [əveyl'əbəl], *adj.* obtainable; ready for use or service. **Ex.** *Have you tried every available remedy?* —**a·vail'a·bil'i·ty,** *n.*

avenue (2) [æv'ənuw`, æv'ənyuw`], *n.* 1. a wide street. **Ex.** *The avenue was lined with trees.* 2. a way or opening to something. **Ex.** *He could find no avenue of escape from his problem.*

average (2) [æv'(ə)rij], *adj.* normal; ordinary. **Ex.** *She is an average student.* —*n.* 1. the number produced by adding two or more quantities and then dividing by the number of quantities added. **Ex.** *The average of three, four and five is four (3 + 4 + 5 = 12 ÷ 3 = 4).* 2. the ordinary, normal or typical amount. **Ex.** *On the average, how many students are absent each day?* —*v.* find an average of. **Ex.** *Average these numbers for me.*

avert (5) [əvərt'], *v.* 1. turn aside or away. **Ex.** *She averted her glance from the corpse.* 2. prevent. **Ex.** *He averted an automobile accident by stopping quickly.* —**a·ver'sion,** *n.* strong feeling of dislike. **Ex.** *He felt an aversion to the man.*

aviation (5) [ey`viyey'šən], *n.* the art or science of flying airplanes. **Ex.** *He hopes to have a career in aviation.* —**a'vi·a·-tor,** *n.* a man who flies airplanes. —**a'vi·a·trix,** *n.* a woman who flies airplanes.

avocado [æv`əka'dow], *n.* a pear-shaped fruit with a dark green skin and pale green flesh around a large seed. **Ex.** *She served an avocado and grapefruit salad at lunch.*

avoid (2) [əvoyd'], *v.* keep away from. **Ex.** *He avoids me because he owes me money.* —**a·void'a·ble,** *adj.* —**a·void'ance,** *n.*

awake [əweyk'], *adj.* not sleeping. **Ex.** *He was already awake when I went to call him.*

award (4) [əword'], *v.* give after careful consideration. **Ex.** *He was awarded first prize.* —*n.* the thing given; a prize. **Ex.** *He received an award for his fine work.*

aware (3) [əwe:r'], *adj.* informed; conscious; understanding. **Ex.** *He drove carefully, aware of the danger of the icy road.* —**a·ware'ness,** *n.*

away (1) [əwey'], *adv.* 1. aside; out of one's possession. **Ex.** *Either give the clothes away or throw them away.* 2. from this or that place. **Ex.** *We are going away.* 3. out of existence. **Ex.** *The daylight is fading away.* —*adj.* 1. absent. **Ex.** *He will be away for two days.* 2. at a distance. **Ex.** *How far away is the school?*

awe (4) [ɔː'], *n.* respectful fear and wonder inspired by what is grand. **Ex.** *Looking up at the mountain, they were filled with* awe. —*v*. inspire with awe. **Ex.** *They were awed by the sight of the beautiful gardens.*

awful (2) [ɔː'fəl], *adj*. terrible; frightening. **Ex.** *It was an awful experience.* —**aw'ful·ly**, *adv*. 1. very; extremely. **Ex.** *He's awfully busy just now.* 2. badly; terribly. **Ex.** *When she behaves so awfully, I don't know what to do with her.*

awkward (4) [ɔk'wərd], *adj*. 1. lacking in ease, grace or skill. **Ex.** *He had many accidents because he was so awkward.* 2. not convenient; embarrassing. **Ex.** *You have asked me an awkward question.* 3. difficult to use or handle. **Ex.** *The chair was placed in an awkward position.* —**awk'ward·ly**, *adv*. —**awk'ward·ness**, *n*.

awoke [əwowk'], past tense of *awake*. **Ex.** *He awoke at six in the morning.*

ax, axe (2) [æks'], *n*. a tool used for cutting, chopping or splitting wood.

AX

axis (5) [æk'səs], *n*. the real or imaginary straight line about which something turns. **Ex.** *The earth turns on its axis once every twenty-four hours.*

axle (5) [æk'səl], *n*. the rod or bar on which a wheel turns or which turns with the wheel.

AXLE

B

B, b [biy'], *n*. the second letter of the English alphabet.

baby (1) [bey'biy], *n*. 1. very young child; infant. **Ex.** *The baby is only two weeks old.* 2. youngest member of a family. **Ex.** *The baby of the family is already ten years old.* —*adj*. like, of or for a baby. **Ex.** *She prefers to make baby clothes rather than to buy them.* —**ba'by-sit`**, care for a child or children for a short period while the parents are away. **Ex.** *She baby-sits to earn spending money.* —**baby-sitter.**

bachelor (3) [bæč'ələr], *n.* 1. a man who has not married. **Ex.** *As a bachelor, he's often invited to dinner parties.* 2. one who has received the first or lowest degree given by a university. **Ex.** *He is a bachelor of arts.*

back (1) [bæk'], *n.* 1. the rear of the human body. **Ex.** *He lay on his back looking at the sky.* 2. in most animals, the upper part of the body from the neck to the end of the backbone. **Ex.** *He placed the saddle on the horse's back.* 3. the part of anything which is opposite the front. **Ex.** *Are the children playing out back?* 4. something at or on the back for support. **Ex.** *He leaned against the back of the chair.* —*adv.* to or at a former place, time or condition. **Ex.** *We are not going back.* —*adj.* rear; away from the front. **Ex.** *Shut the back door.* —*v.* 1. move backward or to the rear. **Ex.** *Back the truck away from the door.* 2. help and encourage, sometimes with money. **Ex.** *Which candidate are you backing?* —**back and forth,** one way and then the opposite way. **Ex.** *He went back and forth between the houses.* —**in back of,** behind. **Ex.** *She was in back of me in the line.*

background (4) [bæk'grawnd'], *n.* 1. the parts of a scene or picture that are or seem to be behind something else. **Ex.** *It is difficult to see who the people in the background are.* 2. any circumstances that help to explain events that follow. **Ex.** *In order to understand the war better, they are studying its background.* 3. education and experience. **Ex.** *He does not have the background for the job.*

backlog [bæk'lɔːg], *n.* an accumulation of tasks not done or things not attended to. **Ex.** *We have such a large backlog that we cannot take any new applications.*

backward (3) [bæk'wərd], *adv.* 1. away from the front; toward the rear. **Ex.** *Looking backward, he saw a man following him.* 2. other than the usual way; wrongly. **Ex.** *This part of the machine was put in backward.* —*adj.* 1. directed toward the back or past. **Ex.** *She gave a backward glance at her old home.* 2. slow in learning or developing. **Ex.** *These backward children are receiving special lessons to help them to read.*

bacon (4) [bey'kən], *n.* meat from the back or sides of a pig, salted and smoked. **Ex.** *He had bacon and eggs for breakfast.*

bacteria (5) [bæk'tir'iyə], *n. pl.* one-celled living things, too small to be seen without a microscope, which cause rotting, souring, etc. **Ex.** *Bacteria are everywhere; some are helpful, while others cause disease.* **—bac·te'ri·al,** *adj.*

bad (1) [bæd'], *adj.* 1. not good; useless; unpleasant. **Ex.** *He has bad manners.* 2. wicked. **Ex.** *Robbing the bank was only one of the bad things that he did.* 3. faulty; incorrect. **Ex.** *His spelling is bad.* *—n.* that which is not good; that which is wicked; that which is faulty. **Ex.** *You will just have to accept the bad with the good.* **—bad'ly,** *adv.*

badge (5) [bæj'], *n.* a special mark or pin worn to show membership or authority. **Ex.** *The policeman's badge was a silver star.*

baffle (5) [bæf'əl], *v.* puzzle; confuse. **Ex.** *The student's failure baffled the teacher.*

bag (1) [bæg'], *n.* 1. container made of paper, cloth or other soft material. **Ex.** *She carried the food in a large bag.* 2. a woman's purse. **Ex.** *She left her bag on the table.* 3. a suitcase. **Ex.** *Are you going to check your bags?* **—bag'gy,** *adj.* like a bag; loose. **Ex.** *His trousers were baggy at the knees.*

baggage (4) [bæg'ij], *n.* suitcases, boxes, etc. used in traveling. **Ex.** *I need help in carrying my baggage onto the train.*

bail [beyl'], *n.* money deposited with the court to make sure that an arrested person when released will return for trial. **Ex.** *His bail was set at fifty thousand dollars.*

bait (4) [beyt'], *n.* 1. food used as a lure to catch fish or trap animals. **Ex.** *What kind of bait are you using?* 2. anything used to attract a person. **Ex.** *A diamond ring left on the table was used as bait to catch the thief.* *—v.* prepare a hook or a trap with bait. **Ex.** *He baited the fishhook with a worm.*

bake (2) [beyk'], *v.* 1. cook by dry heat, usually in an oven. **Ex.** *My mother bakes bread every week.* 2. dry or harden by heat. **Ex.** *The bricks were baked in the sun after they were shaped.* **—bak'er,** *n.* one who bakes. **—bak'er·y,** *n.* a place where bread, cakes, etc. are made; such a place together with a connected shop where the baked goods are sold and sometimes eaten. **Ex.** *I stopped at the bakery to buy some bread.*

balance (2) [bæl'əns], *n.* 1. equality in amount, weight, importance or value between two things. **Ex.** *The artist tried to keep* *a balance of light and dark in his paintings.* 2. equal distribution of weight which keeps one steady. **Ex.** *You must learn to keep your balance in order to ride a bicycle.* 3. an amount of money in a bank account. **Ex.** *My bank balance is very low.* 4. the amount of money still owed on a bill. **Ex.** *When can you pay the balance? —v.* 1. keep or make steady by equal weight distribution. **Ex.** *She balanced the book on her head.* 2. mentally weigh two things to learn which is of more value, more importance, etc. **Ex.** *He balanced his chances of winning or losing.* 3. find the difference, if any, between what one has or is owed and what one has spent or owes. **Ex.** *He balances his accounts every month.*

balcony (5) [bæl'kəniy], *n.* 1. a platform with a railing, built out from the wall of a building. 2. an upper floor in a theater or hall that extends out over the floor below. **Ex.** *Do you prefer theater seats on the main floor or in the balcony?*

BALCONY 1

bald (5) [bɔːld'], *adj.* lacking hair on the head. **Ex.** *My father was completely bald by the time he was forty.* **—bald'ness,** *n.*

bale (5) [beyl'], *n.* a large bundle of some material, closely pressed together and tied for storage or shipping. **Ex.** *The men loaded the bales of cotton onto the ship. —v.* make into bales. **Ex.** *The farmer was baling hay in the field.*

balk (5) [bɔːk'], *v.* 1. refuse to move or do. **Ex.** *The horse balked when he had a heavy load.* 2. stop from doing something. **Ex.** *He was balked in his efforts to obtain the land.* **—balk'y,** *adj.*

ball (1) [bɔːl'], *n.* 1. a round or egg-shaped object, used in a game. **Ex.** *The children were playing with the ball.* 2. any round shape. **Ex.** *During the thunderstorm he saw a ball of fire come down from the sky.*

BALL 1

ball (1) [bɔːl'], *n.* a large dancing party. **Ex.** *She danced at the President's ball.*

ballad (5) [bæl'əd], *n.* a poem or song that tells a story. **Ex.** *The girl sang an old ballad.*

ballet [bæl-ey'], *n.* a kind of dance using formal, graceful techniques, often telling a story, and usually performed in costume.

Ex. *The company presented a dozen short pieces from classical ballets.*

balloon (4) [bəluwn'], *n.* 1. a bag of strong, light material that rises and floats in the air when filled with a gas lighter than air. 2. a rubber bag that can be filled with air or gas, used as a child's toy. Ex. *The little girl held tightly to the string of her balloon.* —*v.* fill up and swell out like a balloon. Ex. *The sails ballooned out in the wind.*

BALLOON 1

ballot (4) [bæl'ət], *n.* 1. a piece of paper used in voting. Ex. *They counted the ballots to see who had won the election.* 2. a method of secret voting in which printed sheets of paper are used. Ex. *They voted by ballot.*

ballpoint pen [bɔ:l'poynt' pen'], *n.* a pen with a ball at the writing end that rolls ink onto the paper. Ex. *This ballpoint pen writes with a fine line.*

balmy (5) [ba:m'iy], *adj.* soft and gentle; mild. Ex. *A balmy breeze was blowing.*

bamboo (5) [bæm'buw'], *n.* a woody, treelike grass, with hollow jointed stems, used for making furniture, poles, etc. Ex. *The mirror was framed with bamboo.*

ban (5) [bæn'], *v.* not allow; forbid; prohibit. Ex. *The sale of liquor to children is banned.* —*n.* an official prohibition against something. Ex. *There is a ban on smoking in the theater.*

banana (3) [bənæn'ə], *n.* a large plant that grows in hot climates and bears bunches of yellow fruit; also the fruit itself.

BANANA

band (2) [bænd'], *n.* 1. a group of persons united for a common purpose. Ex. *A band of thieves broke into the house.* 2. a group of persons who play music together. Ex. *A band played for the dance.* 3. a thin, flat strip of material for binding or decorating. Ex. *Her hat was trimmed with a velvet band.* —*v.* 1. join together in a group. Ex. *The settlers banded together for protection.* 2. place a band around. Ex. *They banded the pieces of wood together.*

bandage (4) [bæn'dij], *n.* a strip of cloth or other material used for covering and binding a wound. Ex. *The bandage on his leg was to be changed every day.*

bandit (5) [bæn'dət], *n.* a robber; an outlaw. **Ex.** *Bandits robbed the train.*

bang (4) [bæŋ'], *n.* a loud sudden noise, as the shooting of a gun or the violent closing of a door. **Ex.** *The wind blew the door closed with a bang.* —*v.* 1. strike violently or noisily. **Ex.** *He banged on the door.* 2. make a loud noise. **Ex.** *We heard the drums bang in the distance.*

banish (4) [bæn'iš], *v.* 1. officially require a person to leave a country as a punishment. **Ex.** *The king banished the man for his crimes.* 2. dismiss; send away. **Ex.** *The widow attempted to banish her grief.* —**ban'ish·ment**, *n.*

banister [bæn'is-tər], *n.* a railing at the side of a staircase. **Ex.** *He leaned over the banister to see who was downstairs.*

bank (1) [bæŋk'], *n.* 1. a place where money is kept for safety and where other business with money is done. **Ex.** *He went to the bank for money.* 2. a place where supplies are stored for later use. **Ex.** *The Red Cross operates a blood bank.* —*v.* place money in a bank. **Ex.** *He banked part of his money every week.* —**bank'er**, *n.* a person who directs the work of or owns all or part of a bank. —**bank'ing**, *n.* the business done at a bank or by a banker.

bank (1) [bæŋk'], *n.* 1. the high ground on the edges of a river or stream. **Ex.** *He sat on the bank with his feet in the water.* 2. a pile; a mass. **Ex.** *The bank of dark clouds suggests rain.* —*v.* 1. form into a bank. **Ex.** *The snow was banked on each side of the road.* 2. cover a fire with ashes so that it will burn more slowly. **Ex.** *They banked the fire before they left the house.*

bankrupt (5) [bæŋk'rəpt'], *adj.* 1. unable to pay one's debts. **Ex.** *The court has declared him bankrupt.* 2. completely lacking; without. **Ex.** *He is bankrupt of ideas.* —*v.* make poor; make bankrupt; ruin. **Ex.** *His own generosity bankrupted him.*

banner (4) [bæn'ər], *n.* 1. flag of a country, state, or organization. 2. piece of cloth, paper or other material, with writing or symbols on it. **Ex.** *The marchers in the parade carried banners that said "Peace."*

banquet (4) [bæŋ'kwət], *n.* a feast conducted with great ceremony and often followed by speeches. **Ex.** *A banquet was given in honor of the mayor.*

a, far; æ, am; e, get; ey, late; i, in; iy, see; ɔ, all; ow, go; u, put; uw, too; ə, but, ago; ər, fur; aw, out; ay, life; oy, boy; ŋ, ring; θ, think; ð, that; ž, measure; š, ship; ǰ, edge; č, child.

bar (2) [baːr'], *n.* 1. a piece of solid material, greater in length than in width. **Ex.** *Please put a new bar of soap in the bathroom.* 2. a long, narrow piece of wood or metal used to stop, enclose, support, fasten, lift, etc. **Ex.** *The iron bars of the prison windows were two inches apart.* 3. anything that blocks the way and stops action. **Ex.** *Poor eyesight was a bar to his becoming a pilot.* 4. a long, high table or counter at which liquor or food is served; the place in which there is such a table. **Ex.** *Your friends are having drinks at the bar.* 4. the profession of law; lawyers as a group. **Ex.** *He has been admitted to the bar.* —*v.* 1. provide or secure with a bar. **Ex.** *The door was barred.* 2. shut out; prevent; block. **Ex.** *They barred the way to strangers.*

barbarian (5) [barber'iyən], *n.* a rough, uncivilized person; a savage. **Ex.** *People who behave like barbarians are not welcome at this hotel.* —**bar·bar'ic,** *adj.*

barbecue [bar'bi·kyuw], *n.* 1. an outdoor fire, usually with an iron grill framework, over which meat is cooked. **Ex.** *We are going to cook hamburgers on the barbecue tonight.* 2. the meal or gathering at which meat prepared this way is eaten. **Ex.** *We are joining our neighbors for a barbecue tonight.* —*v.* cook meat over an open fire, usually moistening it with a highly flavored sauce. **Ex.** *How long will it take to barbecue this pork roast?*

barber (3) [bar'bər], *n.* one whose work is to cut hair.

bare (2) [beːr'], *adj.* 1. without clothing or covering. **Ex.** *The children walked on the sand with bare feet.* 2. empty. **Ex.** *The room was bare of furnishings.* 3. plain; without additions. **Ex.** *What are the bare facts of the matter?* 4. just sufficient; mere. **Ex.** *The settlers had only the bare necessities of life.* —**bare'ly,** *adv.* —*v.* reveal; uncover. **Ex.** *She bared her shoulders to the sun.*

bargain (3) [bar'gən], *n.* 1. a businesslike agreement between persons. **Ex.** *He made a bargain to lend his neighbor a horse in return for the use of his plow.* 2. something bought or offered for sale at less than the usual cost. **Ex.** *Mother always shops for bargains.* —*v.* try to buy or sell something at a good price. **Ex.** *He bargained with the merchant for an hour before he bought the rug.* —**bargain for,** seek; expect. **Ex.** *He received more letters than he bargained for.*

barge (4) [barj'], *n.* a large, flat-bottomed boat without a motor, used for carrying goods on waterways. **Ex.** *The barge was loaded with coal.*

bark (2) [bark'], *n.* the hard, outside covering of a tree. **Ex.** *The bark of the tree was badly damaged when the car hit it.*

bark (2) [bark'], *n.* the sudden, sharp cry of a dog or other animal. —*v.* 1. make a sudden sharp cry or series of cries, as a dog. **Ex.** *Our dog barks when strangers come to the door.* 2. speak or shout roughly. **Ex.** *The captain barked his orders.*

barley (5) [bar'liy], *n.* 1. a grasslike plant that produces seed or grain. 2. the seeds of this plant which are used to make some liquors, put in soup or feed to animals.

barn (2) [barn'], *n.* a farm building for storing crops, housing farm animals, etc. **Ex.** *The cows are in the barn.*

barometer [bəram'ətər], *n.* an instrument for measuring atmospheric pressure in order to forecast weather and to determine elevation above sea level. **Ex.** *Has the barometer shown falling pressure over the last twenty-four hours?* —**bar`o·met'ric,** *adj.*

barracks (5) [bær'əks], *n.* a building or buildings for housing soldiers. **Ex.** *Two hundred soldiers live in that barracks.*

barrel (3) [bær'əl], *n.* 1. a large container usually made of curved strips of wood that are held together with wooden or metal bands. 2. the tubelike part of a gun from which the shot comes. **Ex.** *He cleaned the barrel of his gun.*

BARREL 1

barren (4) [bær'ən], *adj.* 1. unproductive. **Ex.** *The barren land could produce little food.* 2. unable to produce young. **Ex.** *His wife was barren.*

barricade (5) [bær'əkeyd'], *n.* 1. anything built to bar or serving to bar passage, especially something built roughly and hurriedly, as in a street or entrance. **Ex.** *The cars were stopped at the police barricade.* 2. any barrier to entry. —*v.* shut in or defend with a barricade. **Ex.** *They barricaded the street while it was being repaired.*

barrier (4) [bær'iyər], *n.* 1. anything that prevents approach or attack. **Ex.** *Countries can no longer depend on mountain barriers for protection.* 2. anything that prevents progress or causes difficulty. **Ex.** *High tariffs are a barrier to international trade.*

barter (5) [bar'tər], *v.* Exchange or trade articles or services without using money. **Ex.** *She bartered eggs for wool.* —*n.* the act of bartering.

base (2) [beys'], *n.* 1. the bottom or support on which a thing stands or rests. **Ex.** *The base of the lamp was made of wood.* 2. the main part on which the rest depends or from which the rest began. **Ex.** *The ship returned to its base for supplies.* —*v.* make or form a foundation for; place or establish on a foundation. **Ex.** *He based his request for a raise on his past performance.* —*adj.* at the base of; supporting. **Ex.** *We sent to our base camp for supplies.*

base (2) [beys'], *adj.* 1. morally bad; mean; selfish. **Ex.** *His base character caused his associates to dislike him.* 2. poor in quality; low in value compared to something else. **Ex.** *Brass and iron are base metals.* —**base'ly,** *adv.* —**base'ness,** *n.*

baseball (5) [beys'bɔ:l'], *n.* 1. an American game played with a bat and ball by two teams of nine persons each, on a playing field shaped like a diamond. 2. the ball used in playing this game.

basement (2) [beys'mənt], *n.* the lowest level of a building, partly or completely underground. **Ex.** *In this hot weather the basement is cool and comfortable.*

bashful [bæsh'fəl], *adj.* uncomfortable and shy with others. **Ex.** *He is bashful with girls.*

basic (2) [bey'sik], *adj.* of or forming a base; main. **Ex.** *Here is a list of our basic needs.* —**ba'sically,** *adv.*

basin (3) [bey'sən], *n.* 1. a shallow bowl for holding water or other liquid. **Ex.** *He washed his hands and face in a basin of water.* 2. land drained by a river. **Ex.** *The basin of this river has rich farmland.*

basis (3) [bey'səs], *n.* essential facts or reasons; foundation which supports something. **Ex.** *What is the basis for your opinion?*

basket (1) [bæs'kət], *n.* 1. any container made by passing strips of grasses, thin strips of wood or other material under and over each other. **Ex.** *Please put the basket of fruit on the table.* 2. a metal ring with an open net attached through which a large ball can be passed.

BASKET

basketball [bæs'kət·bɔ:l'], *n.* 1. a game with five players on each of two teams, who try to throw a large ball through the elevated open string basket belonging to the other. **Ex.** *He hopes to play professional basketball when he graduates from college.* 2. the ball used in the game.

bat (4) [bæt'], *n.* a strong, solid stick or club, especially one used for hitting a ball in games. —*v.* strike or hit, as with a bat. **Ex.** *He batted stones with a stick.*

bat (4) [bæt'], *n.* a furry animal that looks like a mouse with wings. **Ex.** *Bats usually fly in the dark.*

bath (2) [bæθ'], *n.* 1. act of washing or cleaning the body with water. **Ex.** *Take a warm bath before going to bed.* 2. water for washing the body. **Ex.** *The bath was too cold.* 3. a room equipped for bathing; the bathroom. **Ex.** *Each room in this hotel has a bath.*

bathe (3) [beyð'], *v.* 1. wash; go swimming. **Ex.** *He liked to bathe in the river.* 2. wet or moisten with liquid. **Ex.** *The doctor told him to bathe the wound with hot water.*

bathroom [bæθ'ruwm'], *n.* a room equipped with a wash basin, bathtub and/or shower for washing the body and a toilet for eliminating body waste. **Ex.** *As soon as the bathroom is free, I would like to take a shower.*

batter (4) [bæt'ər], *v.* 1. break to pieces by pounding. **Ex.** *The police battered the door with their clubs.* 2. damage by rough use. **Ex.** *The boys had battered the furniture.* —*n.* 1. the beaten mixture of flour and liquid used for making bread, cake, etc. **Ex.** *Add a little more milk to the batter.* 2. a person who strikes, or bats, a ball in games.

battery (4) [bæt'(ə)riy], *n.* a small container or connected group of containers that retain electric current and are capable of discharging the current when needed. **Ex.** *The battery could not start the car.*

battle (1) [bæt'əl], *n.* 1. a fight between opposing armed forces. **Ex.** *We won the battle on the second day.* 2. war or armed fighting in general. **Ex.** *He was wounded in battle.* 3. any fight or struggle. **Ex.** *That editor fought many battles for a free press.* —*v.* fight; struggle. **Ex.** *The seamen battled the storm.*

bay (1) [bey'], *n.* a large area of water formed by a deep cut into the shore of a sea or ocean. **Ex.** *Chesapeake Bay is near Washington, D.C.*

be (1) [biy'], *v.* (These are the common forms of *be*. In the present: I *am*; you, we, they *are*; he, she, it *is*. In the past: I,

a, far; æ, am; e, get; ey, late; i, in; iy, see; ɔ, all; ow, go; u, put; uw, too; ə, but, ago; ər, fur; aw, out; ay, life; oy, boy; ŋ, ring; θ, think; ð, that; ž, measure; š, ship; j, edge; č, child.

he, she, it *was*; you, we, they *were*. In the future: I, you, he, she, it, we, they *will be*.) 1. equal in meaning. **Ex.** *That man is my teacher.* 2. have a noted quality or character. **Ex.** *Your sister is kind.* 3. exist; live. **Ex.** *Many years ago a house was on the corner of that street.*

beach (2) [biyč'], *n.* a smooth area of sand and small stones on the shore of an ocean, lake, etc. **Ex.** *Two boys are walking on the beach.*

bead (3) [biyd'], *n.* a small piece of glass, stone, etc., with a hole in it so that it can be put on a string. **Ex.** *She usually wore a string of beads around her neck.*

beak (4) [biyk'], *n.* the long, horny points extending out from a bird's mouth; a bill. **Ex.** *The mother bird held the worm in her beak.*

beam (3) [biym'], *n.* 1. any long, heavy piece of wood or metal cut for use, especially in the structure or supports of a building or ship. **Ex.** *This beam is rotten and will have to be replaced.* 2. a ray of light. **Ex.** *Sunbeams came through the open window.* 3. a continuous radio or other electrical signal. **Ex.** *The airplane followed the radio beam.* —*v.* 1. shine; send forth light. **Ex.** *The sun beamed brightly.* 2. smile broadly. **Ex.** *The teacher beamed at the students.* 3. aim radio signals. **Ex.** *The* Voice of America *programs are beamed around the world.*

bean (1) [biyn'], *n.* 1. the seed of certain plants that grows in a case and is used for food, sometimes with its case. **Ex.** *We are having baked beans for dinner tonight.* 2. a plant that produces beans. 3. a beanlike seed. **Ex.** *The store had large containers of coffee beans.*

BEAN 1

bear (2) [be:r'], *v.* 1. support. **Ex.** *The beams bear the weight of the roof.* 2. carry. **Ex.** *They came bearing gifts.* 3. be equipped, furnished, or marked with. **Ex.** *Soldiers bear arms.* 4. bring forth; produce; yield; give birth to. **Ex.** *These trees bear good apples.* 5. endure; suffer. **Ex.** *I cannot bear his shouting.* —**bear down,** push down or against. **Ex.** *Bear down on the lid and the box will close.* —**bear out,** confirm; prove. **Ex.** *His actions bear out what I said about him.* —**bear up,** continue bravely. **Ex.** *How can she bear up under all her troubles?*

bear (2) [be:r'], *n.* a large, wild animal with a short tail.

beard (3) [bi:rd'], *n.* the hair that grows on a man's chin and face. —**bearded,** *adj.* having a beard. —**beard'less,** *adj.* without a beard. **Ex.** *That man has a long beard, but his son is beardless.*

BEAR

bearing (5) [ber'iŋ], *n.* 1. manner of carrying one's self; behavior. **Ex.** *She was a woman of graceful bearing.* 2. reference or relation to. **Ex.** *Do these facts have any bearing on your problem?* 3. direction or relative position. **Ex.** *He looked at the map to get his bearings.*

beast (2) [biyst'], *n.* 1. any four-footed animal. **Ex.** *The ox and the horse are beasts of burden.* 2. a person who acts cruelly, like an uncontrolled animal. **Ex.** *He behaves like a beast toward his wife.* —**beast'ly,** *adj.* —**beast'li·ness,** *n.*

beat (2) [biyt'], *v.* 1. strike or hit repeatedly. **Ex.** *We heard the rain beating against the window.* 2. move or make a sound in an even, regular manner. **Ex.** *Her heart was beating rapidly.* 3. defeat. **Ex.** *Our team beat the visiting team in a football game.* —*n.* 1. a stroke or blow. **Ex.** *The beat of his heart was not regular.* 2. the sound made by a stroke or blow. **Ex.** *We heard the beat of the drum.* —**beat about** or **around the bush,** approach indirectly. **Ex.** *He should stop beating around the bush and tell us what he wants.* —**beat a retreat,** retreat. **Ex.** *The soldiers beat a retreat to their camp.*

beaten (2) [biyt'ən], *adj.* 1. made smooth by continuous walking on. **Ex.** *A beaten path led to his door.* 2. hammered thin or fine into a required shape. **Ex.** *The temple roof was covered with beaten gold.* 3. hit by many blows; whipped. **Ex.** *Add the sugar to the beaten eggs.* 4. defeated. **Ex.** *The beaten team returned home.*

beaten (2) [biy'tən], *v.* past participle of *beat.* **Ex.** *Our team had beaten the opposing team by five points.*

beauty (1) [byuw'tiy], *n.* 1. the appearance or sound of any object or person that is pleasant; loveliness. **Ex.** *The city was famous for the beauty of its flower gardens.* 2. a person or thing that has beauty. **Ex.** *That girl is a famous beauty.* —**beau'ti·ful,** *adj.* —**beau'ti·fy,** *v.* make beautiful. **Ex.** *He beautified the yard with flowers.* —**beau'ti·cian,** *n.* someone who cuts and styles the hair of females, treats their skin, etc. **Ex.** *She waited in the beauty shop for her favorite beautician.*

beaver (5) [biy'vər], *n.* an animal which has valuable brown fur, a broad flat tail, strong teeth able to cut wood and the ability to swim. **Ex.** *The beavers were building a dam.*

became (1) [bikeym'], *v.* past tense of *become*. **Ex.** *Their son became a doctor.*

because (1) [bikɔ:z', bikəz'], *conj.* for the reason that; since. **Ex.** *We did not go because it rained.* —*adv.* as a result of; on account of. **Ex.** *He was absent because of illness.*

become (1) [bikəm'], *v.* 1. come to be. **Ex.** *The seeds will become flowers in the summer.* 2. be right or suitable; have a pleasing effect. **Ex.** *That dress becomes her.* —**be·com'ing,** *adj.* suitable; having a pleasing effect. **Ex.** *That color is becoming to you.* —**become of,** happen to. **Ex.** *We asked what had become of his sister.*

bed (1) [bed'], *n.* 1. a piece of furniture to sleep or rest in or on. **Ex.** *This room has a double bed.* 2. a piece of ground used for growing plants. **Ex.** *They have many flower beds in their garden.* 3. the ground at the bottom of a body of water. **Ex.** *The bed of the stream was dry.*

BED

bedroom [bed'ruwm], *n.* a room in which to sleep. **Ex.** *We have just redecorated our guest bedroom.*

bedspread [bed'spred'], *n.* a covering for a bed. **Ex.** *She used a beautiful patchwork quilt as a bedspread.*

bee (2) [biy'], *n.* a small insect that often lives in organized groups and stings to protect itself.

beef (3) [biyf'], *n.* meat from a bull, cow or steer. **Ex.** *They ate roast beef for dinner.*

been (1) [bin'], *v.* past participle of *be*. **Ex.** *Where have you been for the past two days?*

BEE

beer (4) [bi:r'], *n.* an alcoholic drink with a slightly bitter taste, made from grain. **Ex.** *He likes to drink cold beer on a hot day.*

beetle (4) [biy'təl], *n.* an insect with four wings, the outer two of which are hard and protect the inner wings when folded.

before (1) [bifɔ:r'], *prep.* 1. earlier than, or ahead of in time, place, worth, etc. **Ex.** *He arrived*

BEETLE

before noon. 2. in the presence or sight of. **Ex.** *He stood before the judge.* —*conj.* 1. earlier than the time that. **Ex.** *Think before you speak.* 2. rather than. **Ex.** *They would go hungry before they would ask for help.* —*adv.* 1. in front; in advance; ahead. **Ex.** *The boy walked along the road, while the dog ran before.* 2. in a past time. **Ex.** *I never saw that book before.* 3. at an earlier time; sooner. **Ex.** *I can meet you at noon but not before.* —**be·fore'hand,** *adv.* ahead of time; earlier. **Ex.** *He had packed his bags beforehand.*

beg (2) [beg'], *v.* 1. ask that something be given without payment. **Ex.** *A little boy stood on the corner begging for food.* 2. ask for humbly and seriously. **Ex.** *The captured soldier begged for mercy.* —**beg'gar,** *n.* one who lives by begging; one who is very poor.

began (1) [bigæn'], *v.* past tense of *begin.* **Ex.** *He began his new job yesterday.*

begin (1) [bigin'], *v.* start; take the first step toward doing. **Ex.** *When does school begin?* —**be·gin'ner,** *n.* one who begins. **Ex.** *He is in a class for beginners.* —**be·gin'ning,** *n.* a start. **Ex.** *Business was rather slow at the beginning of the year.*

begun (2) [bigən'], *v.* past participle of *begin.* **Ex.** *I am already tired, and the day has just begun.*

behalf (4) [bihæf'], *n.* support; part. **Ex.** *My employer spoke in my behalf.*

behave (3) [biheyv'], *v.* 1. conduct oneself or itself; act; do. **Ex.** *That man behaves as if he were ill.* 2. act properly. **Ex.** *We hope the children will behave themselves in public.*

behavior (3) [biheyv'yər], *n.* act or manner of behaving oneself; conduct. **Ex.** *His unkind behavior offended her.*

behind (1) [bihaynd'], *prep.* 1. at the back of; in back of. **Ex.** *There is a garden behind the house.* 2. after; later than. **Ex.** *The train arrived behind time.* 3. less advanced than. **Ex.** *He is behind his class in history.* —*adv.* back in place or time. **Ex.** *He came, but his family stayed behind.* —*adj.* at the back of. **Ex.** *He is in the car behind.*

being (1) [biy'iŋ], *n.* 1. a person, animal, or other living thing. **Ex.** *We do not know if there are beings on other planets.* 2.

existence; life. **Ex.** *The town came into being about two hundred years ago.*

belief (3) [biliyf'], *n.* 1. that which is believed. **Ex.** *I do not like to discuss my religious beliefs.* 2. anything believed or accepted as true; opinion. **Ex.** *It is my belief that we should go ahead with the plan.* 3. faith; trust; confidence. **Ex.** *Nothing can change my belief in his honesty.*

believe (1) [biliyv'], *v.* 1. accept as true. **Ex.** *I believe what you say.* 2. have faith, trust, confidence in. **Ex.** *Many people believe there is a God.* 3. think. **Ex.** *I believe he has returned.*

bell (1) [bel'], *n.* 1. an object or device that rings when struck. **Ex.** *I heard the door bell ring.* 2. anything that looks or sounds like a bell. **Ex.** *Each flower was a tiny white bell.*

bellow (4) [bel'ow], *v.* make a loud cry, like that of a bull; roar. **Ex.** *He bellowed in pain.* —*n.* the act or sound of bellowing. **Ex.** *He answered with a bellow.*

BELL 1

belly (5) [bel'iy], *n.* 1. the lower front part of a person's body; the stomach. **Ex.** *The belly of the starving child was swollen.* 2. the underpart of an animal's body.

belong (1) [bilɔ:ŋ'], *v.* 1. be suited to; have a place or position which is correct for it. **Ex.** *The lamp belongs on this table.* 2. be owned by; be the property of. **Ex.** *This book does not belong to me.* 3. be part of; be connected to. **Ex.** *The garden belongs to this house.* —**be·long'ings,** *n.* possessions; the things one owns. **Ex.** *She packed all her belongings in a box and took them with her.*

beloved (3) [beləvd', bilʌv'əd'], *adj.* greatly loved. **Ex.** *He grieved at the death of his beloved wife.* —*n.* one who is greatly loved. **Ex.** *She is his beloved.*

below (1) [bilow'], *adv.* under; in a lower place. **Ex.** *Read the note written below.* —*prep.* lower than in position, rank, amount, etc. **Ex.** *His office is on the floor below this one.*

belt (2) [belt'], *n.* 1. a band or strip of leather, cloth, etc., worn around the middle of the body. **Ex.** *She wore a belt that matched her dress.* 2. a broad loop placed around two wheels, so that the wheels will turn together.

BELT 2

bench (3) [benč'], *n.* 1. a long metal, wooden or stone seat for two or more

people. **Ex.** *They ate their lunch sitting on a bench in the park.*
2. the seat on which a judge sits in court; the position or office of a judge. **Ex.** *He was appointed to the bench.*

bend (2) [bend'], *v.* 1. force into a different or particular shape, especially a curved shape. **Ex.** *The strong man was able to bend the bar of iron.* 2. stoop; lean over. **Ex.** *You have to bend down to see the marks on the floor.* 3. cause to submit, bow or yield. **Ex.** *The father could not bend the boy to his will.* —*n.* 1. act of bending. 2. something curved. **Ex.** *They turned at the bend in the road.*

beneath (2) [biniyθ'], *prep.* 1. below; under and covered by; in a lower place than. **Ex.** *A wooden floor is beneath the rug.* 2. unworthy of. **Ex.** *It is beneath you to lie.* —*adv.* below something; in a lower place. **Ex.** *He lives on the floor beneath.*

benefit (2) [ben'əfit], *n.* help; act of kindness. **Ex.** *The students had the benefit of a fine library.* —*v.* do good; be of service to; help. **Ex.** *The new hospital will benefit all the people.* —**ben`e·fi'cial,** *adj.*

benevolent (5) [bənev'ələnt], *adj.* desiring or doing good for others; kind. **Ex.** *The free food was given by a benevolent person.* —**be·nev'o·lence,** *n.* —**be·nev'o·lent·ly,** *adv.*

bent (2) [bent'], *v.* past tense and participle of *bend.* **Ex.** *He bent the stick until it broke.*

bent (2) [bent'], *adj.* curved; no longer straight. **Ex.** *You can use a bent pin as a fishhook.*

berry (3) [ber'iy], *n.* any soft, small juicy fruit. **Ex.** *We had berries and cream for dessert.*

beside (1) [bisayd'], *prep.* 1. at or by the side of; near. **Ex.** *We live beside a lake.* 2. compared by putting by the side of. **Ex.** *My fingers are small beside yours.* —**beside oneself,** very troubled or upset; very excited. **Ex.** *She was beside herself when she saw the broken window.*

besides (2) [bisaydz'], *adv.* also; in addition. **Ex.** *We are too tired to go; besides, it is raining.* —*prep.* in addition to; other than. **Ex.** *Besides your teacher, who else was with you?*

besiege (5) [bisiyj'], *v.* 1. surround with armed forces. **Ex.** *The army besieged the town.* 2. surround; make many requests. **Ex.** *The students besieged the teacher with questions.*

best (1) [best'], *adj.* better than any others in quality, results, position, etc. **Ex.** *These are the best books on the subject.*

—*adv.* in a way that is better than any other. **Ex.** *The boy who writes best will win the prize.* —*n.* that which is better than any other person or thing. **Ex.** *My school is the best in the city.* —**get the best of,** beat; defeat. **Ex.** *I got the best of him in that game.* —**make the best of,** do as well as one can under unfavorable circumstances. **Ex.** *He made the best of his illness by studying in bed.*

bestow (4) [bistow'], *v.* give; present to; confer on. **Ex.** *The president of the college bestowed honorary degrees upon a writer and a scientist.* —**be·stow'al,** *n.*

bet (4) [bet'], *n.* 1. an agreement that if someone is proved wrong about something he will pay money or other penalty to the person who is right. **Ex.** *I made a bet with my friend that it would rain before noon today.* 2. the thing which is promised. **Ex.** *Our bet was a good dinner.* —*v.* make such an agreement. **Ex.** *He bet a week's salary on a horse in the third race.* —**bet'tor,** *n.* one who bets.

betray (3) [bitrey'], *v.* 1. assist or support an enemy of one's country or friends. **Ex.** *He betrayed us by telling the enemy where we were.* 2. reveal intentionally or unintentionally. **Ex.** *Her eyes betrayed her real feelings.* —**be·tray'al,** *n.* act of betraying. —**be·tray'er,** *n.* one who betrays.

better (1) [bet'ər], *adj.* 1. more valuable; more desirable; finer in quality; etc. **Ex.** *This is a better house than mine.* 2. improved in health. **Ex.** *She was very ill, but she is better today.* —*adv.* in a more excellent manner or higher degree. **Ex.** *You understand the lesson better than I do.* —*v.* make more desirable or valuable; impróve. **Ex.** *Rest will better the sick child's health.* —*n.* 1. that which is finer. **Ex.** *This painting is the better of the two.* 2. advantage; victory. **Ex.** *The big dog got the better of the little one.* —**better off,** in an improved condition. **Ex.** *He is better off without a car.* —**for the better,** in the direction of improvement. **Ex.** *His health changed for the better.* —**get the better of,** beat; defeat. **Ex.** *He got the better of his enemies.*

between (1) [bitwiyn'], *prep.* 1. in the space or time that separates. **Exs.** *The lunch hour is between twelve and one o'clock. The table is between the door and the window.* 2. connecting. **Ex.** *There is a bus line between the two cities.* 3. involving two. **Ex.** *Why must there be quarrels between us?* —*adv.* being in or doing some action in the space separating two things. **Ex.** *They saw two large buildings with a small house between.*

—**in between,** in the space or time that separates. **Ex.** *I walked in between the buildings.*

beverage (5) [bev'ərij], *n.* a drink of any kind. **Ex.** *What beverage do you want with your dinner?*

beware (4) [biwe:r'], *v.* be on guard against. **Ex.** *Beware of the big dog.*

bewilder (4) [biwil'dər], *v.* puzzle or confuse greatly. **Ex.** *The busy streets bewildered her.* —**be·wil'der·ment,** *n.*

beyond (1) [biyand'], *prep.* 1. on or to the far side of; farther than. **Ex.** *The sea is beyond the mountains.* 2. outside or past the limits, understanding or reach of. **Ex.** *He was beyond the doctor's help and died.* 3. superior to; better than; greater than, etc. **Ex.** *He received a fortune beyond his expectations.*

bias (5) [bay'əs], *n.* 1. a mental attitude, especially one that prevents the fair consideration of a question. **Ex.** *He liked old-fashioned ways and had a bias against change.* 2. a line cut or sewn across the weave of cloth. **Ex.** *You must cut this material on the bias.* —*v.* influence or be influenced strongly, especially unfairly or against. **Ex.** *Why do you think he is biased against you?*

BIAS 2

Bible (3) [bay'bəl], *n.* the sacred book of some world religions.

bicycle (1) [bay'sik`əl], *n.* a machine for riding with two wheels, one behind the other. —**bi'cy·clist,** *n.* one who rides a bicycle.

BICYCLE

bid (4) [bid'], *v.* 1. command. **Ex.** *Do as you are bid.* 2. say, as a greeting. **Ex.** *We always bid our friends good morning.* 3. offer as a price, usually at a public sale. **Ex.** *What am I bid for this painting?* —*n.* 1. an offer or that which is offered. **Ex.** *His bid was higher than any other.* 2. an attempt or effort to win or attract. **Ex.** *With his sad story, he made a bid for our sympathy.* —**bid'der,** *n.*

big (1) [big'], *adj.* 1. large in size or amount. **Ex.** *He is a big man.* 2. important. **Ex.** *The boy's first birthday was a big event in the family.* —**big'ness,** *n.*

a, far; æ, am; e, get; ey, late; i, in; iy, see; ɔ, all; ow, go; u, put; uw, too; ɔ, but, ago; ər, fur; aw, out; ay, life; oy, boy; ŋ, ring; θ, think; ð, that; ž, measure; š, ship; j, edge; č, child.

bigot [big'ət], *n.* a person who does not have a reasonable attitude toward others who hold differing opinions about religion, race, politics, etc. **Ex.** *I did not realize what a bigot he is.* —**big'ot·ed**, *adj.* —**big'ot·ry**, *n.*

bill (2) [bil'], *n.* 1. a paper showing money owed for goods or services supplied; the amount owed. **Ex.** *He gave them a bill for the food they bought in the shop.* 2. in government, a law being considered by the lawmakers. **Ex.** *Congress will vote today on a bill to increase taxes.* 3. a piece of paper money. **Ex.** *He handed me a ten-dollar bill.* —*v.* send a paper showing money owed and requesting payment. **Ex.** *The store will bill me later for the dresses I bought today.*

bill (2) [bil'], *n.* the hard hornlike points extending out from a bird's mouth.

billboard [bil'bord], *n.* a framework supporting a large board on which an advertisement is displayed, frequently along highways. **Ex.** *Looking at the billboards helps to amuse the children on a long ride.*

billion (4) [bil'yən], *n.* and *adj.* a thousand million (1,000,000,000).

billow (5) [bil'ow], *n.* 1. a large wave of water. **Ex.** *The ship was tossed by the ocean billows.* 2. any large rolling mass like a wave, such as of smoke or flame. —*v.* rise and swell in large waves. **Ex.** *The smoke billowed from the burning house.* —**bil'low·y**, *adj.*

bind (2) [baynd'], *v.* 1. tie together or fasten with a band or cord. **Ex.** *Please bind these papers in one package.* 2. place under obligation by a promise or agreement. **Ex.** *This agreement binds you to pay the full amount.* 3. treat a wound by putting a cloth or bandage on it. **Ex.** *The doctor will bind that wound.* —**bind'er**, *n.* a person or thing that binds. —**bind'ing**, *n.* a cover within which the pages of a book are fastened together. —*adj.* having authority; obligatory. **Ex.** *The new law is binding immediately.*

binoculars [bənak'yulərz], *n.* an instrument for making distant objects seem closer and larger by the use of two short telescopes joined together through which the viewer looks with both eyes at the same time. **Ex.** *Through his binoculars he was able to see the distant fishing boats.*

BINOCULARS

biography (5) [bayag'rəfiy], *n.* the story of one person's life written by another. —**bi·og'ra·pher,** *n.* the writer of a biography. —**bi`o·graph'i·cal,** *adj.*

biology (3) [bayal'əjiy], *n.* the science of life or living things in all their shapes and forms. —**bi`o·log'i·cal,** *adj.* concerning the science of biology. —**bi·ol'o·gist,** *n.* a person who studies and works in the field of biology.

birch (4) [bərč'], *n.* 1. a hardwood tree with a smooth white outer bark that peels off in thin layers. 2. the wood itself.

bird (1) [bərd'], *n.* any warm-blooded, egg-laying, feathered animal that has wings and usually flies. **Ex.** *We watched the birds building a nest.*

birth (2) [birθ'], *n.* 1. act of being born. **Ex.** *The birth of their first child was a happy time.* 2. origin; family background. **Ex.** *He returned to the land of his birth.* 3. beginning. **Ex.** *The birth of the United Nations occurred in the city of San Francisco in 1945.* —**birth' con·trol',** *n.* use of various means to limit the number of children conceived or born. **Ex.** *After their fourth child, they practiced birth control.* —**birth' date',** *n.* —**birth'day,** *n.*

biscuit (4) [bis'kit], *n.* a kind of bread baked in small, soft cakes. **Ex.** *She served hot biscuits with the chicken.*

bishop (3) [biš'əp], *n.* a minister or priest in charge of a district of several churches.

bit (2) [bit'], *n.* a small piece or quantity. **Ex.** *She gave him a bit of ice cream.*

bit (2) [bit'], *v.* past tense of *bite.* **Ex.** *The dog bit the postman.*

bite (2) [bayt'], *v.* cut into, usually with the teeth. **Ex.** *My dog will bite strangers.* —*n.* 1. the act of biting. **Ex.** *An animal bite should be treated by a doctor.* 2. a mouthful; a little. **Ex.** *Please have a bite of cake.*

bitten (2) [bit'ən], *v.* past participle of *bite.* **Ex.** *He had been badly bitten by the lion.*

bitter (2) [bit'ər], *adj.* 1. having a sharp, unpleasant taste. **Ex.** *The coffee was so strong that it tasted bitter.* 2. hard to receive or bear. **Ex.** *They learned a bitter lesson from the unpleasant experience.* 3. causing pain; stinging. **Ex.** *Their hands felt frozen in the bitter cold.* 4. showing great dislike. **Ex.** *He felt bitter hatred against his enemy.* —**bit'ter·ly,** *adv.* —**bit'ter·ness,** *n.*

black (1) [blæk'], *adj.* the darkest color. **Ex.** *With no moon shining the night was black.* —**black'ness,** *n.*

blackboard (3) [blæk'bɔrd`], *n.* a dark, smooth surface used for writing on with chalk. **Ex.** *The teacher wrote the questions on the blackboard.*

blackmail [blæk'meyl], *n.* a threat to reveal some wrongdoing or something embarrassing about an individual, organization, etc. unless money is paid. **Ex.** *He was convicted of blackmail and sent to prison.*

blacksmith (3) [blæk'smiθ`], *n.* a person who shapes iron or other metals into various things. **Ex.** *The blacksmith made shoes for the farmer's horses.*

blade (3) [bleyd'], *n.* 1. the sharp, cutting part of an instrument, especially of a knife. 2. narrow leaf of a plant. **Ex.** *He was chewing a blade of grass.* 3. the thin, flat wide section of something, such as the blade of an oar. **Ex.** *The rapidly moving blades of the fan helped to cool the room.*

blame (2) [bleym'], *v.* regard as responsible for a mistake; consider guilty of. **Ex.** *They blamed the driver for the accident.* —*n.* the responsibility for what is wrong. **Ex.** *I will accept the blame.*

blank (2) [blæŋk'], *adj.* 1. not written or printed on. **Ex.** *He handed her a blank sheet of paper.* 2. showing no attention, interest or understanding. **Ex.** *The student gave the teacher a blank look.* —*n.* an empty space to be filled on a written or printed form. **Ex.** *Write your name in the blank on this form.* —**blank'ly,** *adv.* —**blank'ness,** *n.*

blanket (2) [blæŋ'kit], *n.* 1. a large piece of soft material, often wool, used as a covering for warmth. **Ex.** *In the winter, I sleep with two blankets on my bed.* 2. any thin, large covering like a blanket. **Ex.** *A blanket of flowers covered the grave.* —*v.* cover with, or as with, a blanket. **Ex.** *Snow blanketed the earth.*

blast (3) [blæst'], *n.* 1. a sudden blowing or rush of wind. **Ex.** *The blast of wind almost knocked us off our feet.* 2. the sound made by blowing any wind instrument. **Ex.** *The blast of horns was heard over the hill.* 3. the sound made by anything exploding. **Ex.** *We heard a blast from the burning building.* —*v.* tear to pieces or destroy by exploding something. **Ex.** *The engineers are blasting the mountainside in order to build a new road.* —**blast off,** *v.* send up into space. **Ex.** *The space ship blasted off on time.*

blaze (3) [bleyz'], *n.* 1. a brightly burning flame or fire. **Ex.** *We could see the blaze for miles.* 2. a strong, bright light. **Ex.** *We were blinded for a moment by the blaze of the car's lights.* —*v.* burn with a bright flame or light. **Ex.** *The fire blazed out of control.*

bleach (5) [bliyč'], *v.* make white, colorless or stainless. **Ex.** *She bleached the white linen tablecloth.* —*n.* any product, usually a chemical, used to bleach.

bleak (5) [bliyk'], *adj.* 1. bare, cold and usually open to winds. **Ex.** *The climbers reached the bleak mountaintop.* 2. cold and sharp. **Ex.** *A bleak wind was blowing.* 3. cheerless. **Ex.** *The jobless man had a bleak view of life.* —**bleak'ly,** *adv.* —**bleak'ness,** *n.*

bleat (5) [bliyt'], *n.* a thin, high cry, as that of a sheep or goat. —*v.* make such a cry. **Ex.** *The lambs were bleating because they were hungry.*

bled (2) [bled'], *v.* past tense and participle of *bleed.* **Exs.** *His wound bled for more than an hour. It had bled through the bandage.*

bleed (2) [bliyd'], *v.* lose blood. **Ex.** *His wounded leg began to bleed again.*

blend (4) [blend'], *v.* 1. mix completely together so that the things mixed cannot be separated. **Ex.** *Yellow and blue blend to make green.* 2. prepare varieties of wine, tobacco, etc. by mixing several together. **Ex.** *What blend of coffee would you like?* 3. mix pleasantly. **Ex.** *The children's voices blended in song.* —*n.* a mixture of different kinds. **Ex.** *We like this blend of tea.*

blender [blen'dər], *n.* a small electric machine that mixes liquids together or turns solid food into a partially liquid or liquid state. **Ex.** *We put fresh strawberries, a little sugar and some milk in the blender to make a refreshing drink.*

bless (3) [bles'], *v.* 1. make or pronounce holy by prayer. **Ex.** *They asked the minister to bless the food.* 2. make happy or fortunate. **Ex.** *God blessed them with many children.*

blew (3) [bluw'], *v.* past tense of blow. **Ex.** *The wind blew outside the house.*

blight (5) [blayt'], *n.* 1. any widespread disease which destroys plants. **Ex.** *Blight ruined the potato crop.* 2. anything which

a, far; æ, am; e, get; ey, late; i, in; iy, see; ɔ, all; ow, go; u, put; uw, too; ə, but, ago; ər, fur; aw, out; ay, life; oy, boy; ŋ, ring; θ, think; ð, that; ž, measure; š, ship; ǰ, edge; č, child.

destroys or damages. **Ex.** *Slums are a blight on this city.* —*v.* damage; destroy. **Ex.** *Insects blighted the fruit trees.*

blind (2) [blaynd'], *adj.* 1. unable to see. **Ex.** *He helped the blind man across the street.* 2. unable or unwilling to understand or judge. **Ex.** *He was blind to his own faults.* —*v.* cause to be unable to see. **Ex.** *For a moment, the sun blinded him.* —**blind'ly**, *adv.* —**blind'ness**, *n.* —**blind al'ley**, *n.* a narrow street open at only one end; a situation like this. **Ex.** *Her job is just a blind alley.* —**blind'fold'**, *v.* cover the eyes with a band of material so that one cannot see. **Ex.** *They blind-folded the prisoner.* —*n.* that which is used to cover the eyes so that one cannot see.

blind (2) [blaynd'], *n.* a covering for a window made of cloth, thin slats of wood or other material on a roller to keep out light and to provide privacy. **Ex.** *Just pull the blind halfway down.*

blink (4) [bliŋk'], *v.* 1. open and close the eyes often and quickly. **Ex.** *She blinked at the sun.* 2. shine unsteadily. **Ex.** *The light blinked on and off.*

bliss (5) [blis'], *n.* a great gladness or happiness. **Ex.** *Her unhappiness turned to bliss when she heard his voice.* —**bliss'ful**, *adj.*

blister (5) [blis'tər], *n.* a raised place in the skin with fluid underneath, caused by a burn or other injury. —*v.* cause a blister to form. **Ex.** *He blistered his hands in the fire.*

block (2) [blak'], *n.* 1. a solid mass of wood, stone, ice, etc. with some flat surface. **Ex.** *Blocks of ice floated down the river.* 2. a portion of a town or city enclosed by four streets; a square block. **Ex.** *Many people live on this block.* 3. the length or distance of one side of this square. **Ex.** *He lives eight blocks from school.* 4. anything which stops movement or progress. **Ex.** *The police formed a roadblock to catch the criminal.* —*v.* hold back to prevent passage or progress. **Ex.** *The automobile accident blocked traffic.*

blond, blonde (3) [bland'], *adj.* of light yellow; light-colored. **Ex.** *My daughter has blond hair.* —*n.* a person whose hair is blond. **Ex.** *Both she and her sister are blondes.*

blood (1) [bləd'], *n.* 1. the red fluid that flows through the body, carrying oxygen and other needed materials to the parts of the body and taking away wastes. **Ex.** *She was weak from loss of blood.* 2. family line. **Ex.** *He claimed to be of royal blood.* —**blood'y**, *adj.*

bloom (3) [bluwm'], *n.* 1. flower of a plant. **Ex.** *This lily has three blooms.* 2. state of having flowers. **Ex.** *The roses are in bloom.* —*v.* produce or yield blossoms. **Ex.** *With enough sun this plant will bloom.*

blossom (3) [blas'əm], *n.* 1. a flower, especially of a plant that bears fruit. **Ex.** *These orange blossoms have a sweet smell.* 2. the state of having flowers. **Ex.** *The apple trees are in blossom.* —*v.* 1. flower; bloom. **Ex.** *The tree blossomed for the first time this spring.* 2. develop. **Ex.** *The girl's beauty blossomed as she grew.*

blot (4) [blat'], *n.* 1. spot or stain. **Ex.** *The spilled ink left a blot on the paper.* 2. a stain on character or reputation; shame. **Ex.** *The boy's arrest was a blot on the family's good name.* —*v.* 1. make a spot or stain on. 2. dry with a special paper that absorbs moisture. —**blot out,** *eliminate; destroy.* **Ex.** *She tried to blot out the unhappy memory.* —**blot'ter,** a paper that absorbs moisture.

blouse (5) [blaws'], *n.* outer clothing, like a shirt, worn by women and girls.

blow (1) [blow'], *v.* 1. move with force; be in motion. **Ex.** *A strong wind began to blow.* 2. carry or be carried by blowing. **Ex.** *The wind is blowing the papers off my desk.* 3. cause to make a sound by forcing air through. **Ex.** *Blow your horn.* 4. force air out or in to clear. **Ex.** *Use your handkerchief to blow your*

BLOUSE

nose. —**blow up,** 1. fill with air. **Ex.** *He used a small pump to blow up the bicycle tire.* 2. explode or cause to explode. **Ex.** *They used a bomb to blow up the bridge.*

blow (1) [blow'], *n.* 1. a hard hit with the hand or some instrument. **Ex.** *He was knocked to the ground by a blow on the head.* 2. a shock. **Ex.** *His sudden death was a great blow to the family.*

blown [blown'], *v.* past participle of *blow.* **Ex.** *We were blown out of our seats by the explosion.*

blue (1) [bluw'], *n.* a color like that of a clear sky. **Ex.** *Blue is my favorite color.* —*adj.* having the color of a clear sky. **Ex.** *She is wearing a blue dress.*

blueberry [bluw'ber`iy], *n.* a small, round, smooth, dark blue edible berry that grows on a small bush. **Ex.** *Blueberry muffins for breakfast are a real treat.*

blue jay [bluw' jey'], *n.* a blue bird with touches of black and white and a small bunch of standing blue feathers on its head. **Ex.** *The blue jays were scolding the cat.*

blueprint [bluw'print'], *n.* a printed copy, with white lines on a blue background, of a plan drawn by an architect or other professional person for constructing a building, road, dam, etc. **Ex.** *After seeing the blueprint, they issued a license for the construction of the elevator.*

bluff (4) [bləf'], *n.* a high, steep cliff or hill. **Ex.** *The house on the bluff had a fine view of the ocean.* —*adj.* rough and unusual in speech but good natured. **Ex.** *The bluff sailor was well liked by the villagers.* —**bluff'ness.** *n.*

bluff (4) [bləf'], *v.* fool; deceive by pretense. **Ex.** *He bluffed them into thinking he was brave.* —*n.* act of bluffing. **Ex.** *His threat was just a bluff.*

blunder (4) [blən'dər], *n.* a careless or stupid mistake. **Ex.** *His failure to lock the door was a serious blunder.* —*v.* make a careless or stupid mistake. **Ex.** *She blundered and told them our secrets.*

blunt (5) [blənt'], *adj.* 1. having a thick or dull edge or point. **Ex.** *I cannot cut thin slices with that blunt knife.* 2. plain, almost rude, in speech or manner; impolite. **Ex.** *His answer to my request was a blunt "No."* —*v.* make dull. **Ex.** *Constant use had blunted the knife.*

blur (5) [blə:r'], *v.* make less clear or readable. **Ex.** *Water had spilled on the letter and blurred the writing.* —*n.* 1. a stain or spot that makes something unclear. **Ex.** *There is a blur in the first line.* 2. something unclear or confused. **Ex.** *The memory of the evening was just a blur to him.* —**blur'ry,** *adj.*

blush (3) [bləš'], *v.* redden in the face, as from shame, confusion, etc. **Ex.** *She blushed when she saw her mistake.* —*n.* a reddening of the face. **Ex.** *There was a faint blush to her cheeks.*

board (1) [bord'], *n.* 1. a long, wide piece of wood, cut thin. **Ex.** *What kind of boards are you going to use for the floor?* 2. a group of persons chosen to manage a business, group, etc. **Ex.** *The board of directors of the bank meets today.* 3. food, especially meals, served for payment. **Ex.** *The amount he pays for room and board is very reasonable.* —*v.* 1. cover with boards. **Ex.** *They boarded up the windows of their house during the storm.* 2. receive or provide meals for pay. **Ex.** *He* *boards at that house.* —**board'er**, *n.* one who rents a room and pays for meals in the home of another. —**board'ing school'**, *n.* a school at which the students live and receive meals. **Ex.** *The children are home from boarding school for spring vacation.*

board (1) [bord'], *v.* go on, as a ship, plane or train. **Ex.** *You can board the ship at two o'clock.* —**on board,** on a ship, train or plane.

boast (3) [bowst'], *v.* 1. praise oneself, one's family or one's possessions too much. **Ex.** *He boasted about his skills.* 2. possess or display with deserved pride. **Ex.** *The town boasts an excellent new school.* —*n.* a thing boasted about. **Ex.** *It was his boast that he was the best student in the school.* —**boast'ful,** *adj.* —**boast'ful·ly, boast'ing·ly,** *adv.* —**boast'ful ·ness,** *n.*

boat (1) [bowt'], *n.* a small vessel for travel on water.

body (1) [bad'iy], *n.* 1. the whole physical structure of an animal or person. **Ex.** *He exercised every day to keep his body strong.* 2. the physical remains of a dead person or animal. **Ex.** *The body was lowered into the grave.* 3. the main part of an animal or person, not including

BOAT

the head, arms, and legs; the main or central part of anything. **Ex.** *He liked the design of the body of the car.* 4. a group considered as a single thing. **Ex.** *The people went to the meeting in a body.* 5. a separate part of anything. **Ex.** *He saw a body of land across the water.* —**bod'i·ly,** *adv., adj.*

bodyguard [bad'iygard'], *n.* a person or group of persons who watch over and protect an individual who might be in danger. **Ex.** *The police assigned a bodyguard to their chief witness in the murder case.*

boil (2) [boyl'], *v.* 1. heat a liquid until steam and bubbles form. **Ex.** *The water for the tea is boiling.* 2. cook by boiling in water. **Ex.** *Boil the rice for dinner.* —*n.* 1. act or state of boiling. **Ex.** *The water came to a boil.* 2. hard, swelling sore on the body. **Ex.** *The boil on my arm is painful.* —**boil'er,** *n.* a metal tank in which water is boiled.

bold (3) [bowld'], *adj.* 1. ready to face danger; unafraid. **Ex.** *He was young, strong and bold.* 2. rude; not respectful. **Ex.** *They did not like his bold manners.* —**bold'ly**, *adv.*

bolt (3) [bowlt'], *n.* 1. a threaded rod, usually metal, onto which a small metal nut can be screwed. **Ex.** *Parts of many machines are held together by bolts.* 2. a movable bar that slides into an opening to fasten a door, gate, window, etc. 3. a sudden flash of lightning. **Ex.** *A bolt of lightning struck the old tree.* —*v.* 1. fasten with bolts; lock. **Ex.** *Be sure to bolt the door.* 2. leave suddenly.

BOLT AND NUT

Ex. *He bolted from the room when he saw the policeman.*

bomb (3) [bam'], *n.* a metal or plastic container filled with material that explodes with great force. **Ex.** *Bombs were dropped from the planes.* —*v.* attack or destroy with bombs. **Ex.** *The airplanes bombed the city.*

bond (4) [band'], *n.* 1. anything that ties or fastens. **Ex.** *They loosened the prisoner's bonds and set him free.* 2. something that unites people and holds them together. **Ex.** *The bond of friendship between them was very strong.* 3. a printed or written promise to pay back principal and interest, given by a corporation or government, in return for a loan of money. **Ex.** *The government sold bonds to get money for a new school.*

bone (1) [bown'], *n.* the hard material of which the frame, or skeleton, of the body is made; pieces of this material. **Ex.** *He broke a bone in his finger.* —**bon'y**, *adj.* 1. full of bones. **Ex.** *This fish is bony.* 2. having large bones; without much flesh on the bones. **Ex.** *He had a thin, bony face.*

bonus (5) [bow'nəs], *n.* something given or paid in addition to what is usual or due. **Ex.** *Every worker received the equivalent of two weeks' salary as a bonus at Christmas.*

book (1) [buk'], *n.* a fairly long, written or printed work or record. **Ex.** *He is writing a book about the history of this country.* —**note'book,** *n.* a number of sheets of blank paper bound together at one side within a cover, used for writing notes. **Ex.** *I need a notebook for school.*

book [buk'], *v.* have set aside for one's use. **Ex.** *She booked a hotel room for two.*

bookend [buk'end], *n.* a pair of supports to hold up a row of books.

bookkeeper [buk'kiy`pər], *n.* one who keeps the records of money received and spent for a business, store, government office, etc. **Ex.** *The bookkeeper was questioned about irregularities in the company's accounts.*

boom (4) [buwm'], *v.* 1. make a long, deep sound. **Ex.** *The big guns boomed.* 2. grow or develop rapidly. **Ex.** *The town boomed after gold was discovered.* —*n.* 1. a deep hollow sound. **Ex.** *The boom of drums could be heard in the distance.* 2. sudden, rapid growth. **Ex.** *There has been a boom in new office buildings in the downtown area.*

boot (3) [buwt'], *n.* a covering for the foot and leg. —*v.* kick. **Ex.** *He booted the ball.*

booth (4) [buwθ'], *n.* a small, often enclosed space, used for a special purpose. **Ex.** *He went into the telephone booth to call his wife.*

BOOT

border (2) [bɔr'dər], *n.* 1. the line between two countries; the frontier. **Ex.** *The Rio Grande River is part of the border between the United States and Mexico.* 2. the outer part or edge. **Ex.** *There was a border of flowers along the path to the house.* —*v.* touch at the edge or limit. **Ex.** *Both Canada and Mexico border on the United States.*

bore (2) [bɔːr'], *v.* 1. cause to tire by dullness. **Ex.** *People who talk about themselves all the time bore me.* 2. make a hole in, as by drilling. **Ex.** *We need to bore two holes in that board.* —*n.* a person or thing that tires by dullness. **Ex.** *She is a bore.* —**bored,** *adj.*

born (1) [bɔrn'], *v.* past participle of *bear* (give birth). **Ex.** *The baby was born yesterday.* —*adj.* 1. brought into existence. **Ex.** *The newly born child cried loudly.* 2. possessing from birth the quality stated. **Ex.** *He is a born leader.*

borne (4) [bɔrn'], *v.* past participle of *bear* (carry). **Ex.** *He has borne the burden much too long.*

borough (5) [bər'ow], *n.* 1. a certain type of town or village that governs itself. 2. one of the political divisions of New York City.

borrow (1) [bar'ow], *v.* 1. obtain the use of something by promising to return it. **Ex.** *He borrowed enough money to buy a house.* 2. copy; imitate. **Ex.** *All the ideas in his book are borrowed from other writers.*

boss (3) [bɔːs'], *n.* one who directs the work of others; a manager. **Ex.** *He was the boss of fifty men.* —*v.*

both (1) [bowθ'], *adj., pron.* the two together. **Ex.** *Both men are here.* —*conj.* as well as; not only but; equally. **Ex.** *She was both young and pretty.*

bother (3) [baðˈər], *v.* give trouble to; worry; disturb; annoy. **Ex.** *I have some questions to ask, but I do not want to bother you now.* —*n.* trouble; inconvenience. **Ex.** *What a bother it is to go out in this heat!*

bottle (1) [batˈəl], *n.* 1. a container usually made of glass or plastic, with a narrow opening and no handles. 2. the contents of a bottle. **Ex.** *He took a drink from a bottle of water.*

BOTTLE

bottleneck [batˈəl·nek], *n.* the point where a road narrows or has an obstruction and causes a slow-down in traffic; anything that causes a slowdown in activity. **Ex.** *Our letters are not going out promptly because there is a bottleneck in the mailroom.*

bottom (1) [batˈəm], *n.* 1. the lowest part of something. **Ex.** *The water must be raised from the bottom of the well.* 2. the base or underside; the part under and supporting the rest. **Ex.** *There is a mark on the bottom of the dish.* 3. the ground under a body of water. **Ex.** *The bottom of the river is sandy.*

bough (3) [baw'], *n.* branch of a tree, usually a large limb. **Ex.** *The bough bent under the weight of the snow.*

bought (2) [bɔːt'], *v.* past tense and participle of *buy.* **Exs.** *He bought that book yesterday. She found she had not bought enough material.*

boulder (5) [bowlˈdər], *n.* a large, round, smooth rock. **Ex.** *The boulder was too heavy to move.*

bounce (4) [bawns'], *v.* 1. throw an object against something to make it return. **Ex.** *The little girl is bouncing her rubber ball.* 2. spring back; leap suddenly. **Ex.** *She bounced out of the chair.* —*n.* 1. ability to spring back. **Ex.** *This ball does not have enough bounce.* 2. spring or leap. **Ex.** *He jumped to his feet with a bounce.*

bound (2) [bawnd'], *n.* limit; boundary. **Ex.** *Her joy knew no bounds.* —*v.* form the boundary of. **Ex.** *The Atlantic Ocean bounds the United States on the east.*

bound (2) [bawnd'], *v.* past tense and participle of *bind.* **Exs.** *They bound him with a rope. They had the books bound with* *leather.* —*adj.* 1. tied. **Ex.** *They released the bound ankles of the prisoner.* 2. required. **Ex.** *You are bound by law to pay this tax.* 3. sure. **Ex.** *He is bound to succeed.*

bound (2) [bawnd'], *n.* a jump; a leap onward or upward. **Ex.** *He was on the train with one bound.* —*v.* move by sudden leaps; jump. **Ex.** *He bounded from the train.*

bound (2) [bawnd'], *adj.* traveling in the direction of; on the way to. **Ex.** *This airplane is bound for New York.*

boundary (3) [bawn'd(ə)ry], *n.* border; a limiting line. **Ex.** *High mountains form the boundary between the two countries.*

bounty (5) [bawn'tiy], *n.* 1. generosity in giving. **Ex.** *The bounty of nature is seen at harvest time.* 2. whatever is given generously. **Ex.** *The orphans were grateful for the woman's bounty.* 3. a reward given for killing certain dangerous or destructive animals. **Ex.** *A bounty was offered for dead rats.* —**boun'ti·ful,** *adj.*

bouquet (5) [buw'key', bow'key'], *n.* a bunch of flowers. **Ex.** *The bride carried a bouquet of white roses.*

bourgeois (5) [bur'žwa:', bur'žwa:'], *n.* a member of the middle class, such as a property owner or businessman; one neither very rich nor very poor. —*adj.* belonging to or like the middle class. **Ex.** *Those are bourgeois ideas.* —**bour'geois·ie',** *n.* the middle class.

bout (5) [bawt'], *n.* 1. a contest; a conflict. **Ex.** *He won the first bout.* 2. a spell; a difficult or strenuous period of time. **Ex.** *He had a long bout of illness.*

bow (2) [baw'], *v.* 1. bend the body, head, or knee in greeting or to show respect. **Ex.** *They bowed to each other as they passed in the street.* 2. submit. **Ex.** *We must bow to authority.* 3. curve; bend. **Ex.** *The old man was bowed by age.*

bow (2) [bow'], *n.* 1. a weapon, made of a curved strip of wood with a cord connecting the two ends, used to shoot an arrow. 2. a long, thin piece of wood with tightly stretched horsehairs attached at each end, used in playing certain stringed instruments, such as the violin. 3. anything bent or curved. **Ex.** *She saw a rainbow in the sky after the rain.* 3. a type of knot with two or more open loops. **Ex.** *She fastened her hair with a bow.*

BOW AND ARROW

bowl (2) [bowl'], *n.* 1. a deep, round dish. **Ex.** *Help yourself to the fruit in the bowl.* 2. the quantity a bowl contains. **Ex.** *He ate only one bowl of rice.*

bowl [bowl'], *v.* throw or roll a wooden ball in order to knock down a standing object or group of objects. **Ex.** *Would you like to bowl with our team?* —**bow'ling,** *n.* the game in which one bowls.

box (1) [baks'], *n.* a blow with the inside of the hand or with the fist. **Ex.** *She gave the boy a box on the ear.* —*v.* 1. fight with the fists. 2. strike with the hand or fist. —**box'ing,** *n.* the sport of fistfighting, wearing padded gloves.

BOX 1

box (1) [baks'], *n.* 1. a container made of firm material, usually with a removable cover or lid. 2. the quantity contained in a box. **Ex.** *The child ate the whole box of candy.*

box office [baks'ɔːf'is], *n.* a place in a theater, stadium, auditorium, etc. at which tickets are sold. **Ex.** *They are holding our tickets at the box office.*

boy (1) [boy'], *n.* a male child. **Ex.** *There were no boys in the family.* —**boy'ish,** *adj.*

boycott [boy'kat], *v.* keep from doing business or having relations with a country, group, business, etc. in order to force a change. **Ex.** *They boycotted the bus company because of the fare increase.* —*n.*

brace (4) [breys'], *n.* anything that supports something firmly or holds parts together or in place. **Ex.** *She wore a brace to support her knee.* —*v.* 1. provide a support to make stronger. **Ex.** *The carpenter braced the leg of the chair.* 2. prepare oneself for a shock. **Ex.** *Seeing her worried expression, he braced himself for the bad news.*

bracelet (4) [breys'lət], *n.* an attractive band or chain worn about the wrist or arm. **Ex.** *Her bracelet is made of gold.*

bracket (5) [bræk'ət], *n.* 1. an *L*-shaped support fastened to a wall under a shelf to support the shelf. 2. one of two marks [ ] used in writing to enclose certain words or phrases. **Ex.** *[These words are between brackets.]*

brag (5) [bræg'], *v.* praise one's own ability, possessions, or actions too much. **Ex.** *She is always bragging about her children.* —**bragg'art,** *n.*

braid (4) [breyd'], *v.* divide into three or more parts and weave together, as hair, ribbon, etc. **Ex.** *She braids her hair every day.* —*n.* 1. a length of hair woven together. **Ex.** *Her braids come down to her waist.* 2. a narrow, woven band or tape used to decorate. **Ex.** *The army general had a lot of gold braid on his uniform.*

braille [breyl'], *n.* a system of printing for the blind using raised dots in various arrangements to represent letters of the alphabet and numerals, which can be read by touching them.

brain (2) [breyn'], *n.* 1. the soft, gray matter that fills the head of humans and animals and is the center of feeling and thinking. 2. understanding; intelligence. **Ex.** *She had brains as well as beauty.*

brake (4) [breyk'], *n.* a mechanical device for stopping the motion of a wheel or wheels. **Ex.** *The accident occurred when his brakes failed.* —*v.* slow the motion by using a brake. **Ex.** *He braked his car to a full stop.*

bran [bræn'], *n.* the crushed outer part of wheat, oats and other grains separated from the flour and used as food for humans and livestock. **Ex.** *I eat cereal containing bran to increase fiber in my diet.*

branch (1) [brænč'], *n.* 1. a smaller part growing out from the main part of a tree; a limb. **Ex.** *There are several new branches on the tree this year.* 2. any small part going out from a main part like a branch. **Ex.** *This branch of the river flows between the mountains.* 3. a member or part of a larger group or organization. **Ex.** *The Air Force is a branch of the military service.* —*v.* put forth branches; separate into branches. —**branch out,** grow larger. **Ex.** *This department store has branched out to several other cities.*

brand (4) [brænd'], *n.* 1. a particular kind or make. **Ex.** *What brand of flour do you use?* 2. a trade name or mark put on a product by a particular manufacturer or producer. **Ex.** *She was looking for the identifying brand on the can.* —*v.* 1. mark with a particular sign. **Ex.** *They branded the cattle with the mark of the ranch.* 2. mark or point out a person as shameful. **Ex.** *He was branded a thief by the newspaper.*

brandy (5) [bræn'diy], *n.* a liquor made from wine or from the juice of a fruit. **Ex.** *He drank too much apple brandy and has a headache.*

brass (3) [bræs'], *n.* a yellow metal made by melting copper and zinc together. —**brasses,** *n.* in music, the instruments made of brass. **Ex.** *The brasses drowned out the violins.*

brave (2) [breyv'], *adj.* possessing or showing courage. **Ex.** *The brave young boy saved the child from the burning house.* —*v.* meet or face with courage. **Ex.** *The early settlers braved cold, hunger and violence.* —**brav·er·y,** *n.* courage. **Ex.** *She was praised for her bravery.*

brawl (5) [brɔ:l'], *n.* noisy quarrel or fight. **Ex.** *The brawl in the street could be heard in the houses nearby.* —*v.* fight angrily and noisily. **Ex.** *The two men were brawling in the bar.*

bray (5) [brey'], *n.* the loud cry of a mule or donkey. —*v.* make a sound like that of a mule or donkey. **Ex.** *The donkey brayed and pulled back.*

brazen (5) [brey'zən], *adj.* 1. made of or like brass in appearance or sound. **Ex.** *Inside the temple was a great brazen figure.* 2. shameless. **Ex.** *The brazen woman laughed loudly at the judge who sentenced her.*

breach (5) [briyč'], *n.* 1. the act or result of breaking; a break. **Ex.** *Their differing views created a breach between the business partners.* 2. an opening made by breaking. **Ex.** *The pounding of the sea made a breach in the stone wall along the shore.* 3. a breaking of a law or of any promise. **Ex.** *His failure to pay was a breach of contract.* —*v.* make a breach in. **Ex.** *The soldiers breached the enemy lines.*

bread (1) [bred'], *n.* 1. an article of food made by mixing flour, water, yeast, etc., and baking. **Ex.** *She cut the bread and gave each child a piece.* 2. the food needed to live. **Ex.** *One must work to earn one's bread.*

breadth (4) [bredθ'], *n.* 1. distance from one side of a thing to the other; width. **Ex.** *They measured the length and breadth of the field.* 2. largeness; extent. **Ex.** *He has an unusual breadth of understanding.*

break (1) [breyk'], *v.* 1. cause to become pieces by hitting or placing a strain on. **Ex.** *He had to break the window to enter the house.* 2. hurt; damage; injure. **Ex.** *Did he break his arm when he fell?* 3. fail to follow or obey. **Ex.** *Those who break the law will be punished.* 4. force one's way in, out or through. **Ex.** *He could not break through the crowd.* 5. stop for a short time; interrupt. **Ex.** *When does your school break for spring vacation?* 6. go beyond; do better than; change. **Ex.** *She is* *trying to break herself of smoking.* —*n.* 1. a crack or opening. **Ex.** *The dog escaped through a break in the fence.* 2. the action of forcing a way in or out. **Ex.** *The prisoner made a break for freedom.* 3. a brief stop; a time for rest or change; a pause. **Ex.** *Let us meet during the lunch break.* —**break away, in** or **out,** move away, into or out with force. **Ex.** *The lion was able to break out of his cage very easily.* —**break down,** stop operating or functioning as usual. **Ex.** *If the car breaks down, we will walk.* —**break off,** stop. **Ex.** *Why does she want to break off their friendship?* —**break up,** cause to become pieces; cause to stop. **Ex.** *He has decided to break up the company.*

breakfast (2) [brek'fəst], *n.* the first meal of the day. **Ex.** *What did you have to eat for breakfast?* —*v.* eat the first meal of the day. **Ex.** *She breakfasted in bed.*

breast (2) [brest'], *n.* 1. one of the parts of the body of human or animal females from which their babies get milk. **Ex.** *The mother's breasts were full of milk.* 2. the chest or upper part of the front of the body.

breath (2) [breθ'], *n.* air drawn into the body through the nose and mouth and then out. **Ex.** *She smelled onions on his breath.*

breathe (2) [briyð'], *v.* draw in and let out air. **Ex.** *Open the windows wide so we can breathe some fresh air.*

bred (5) [bred'], *v.* past tense and participle of **breed.** **Exs.** *He bred roses as a hobby. These horses were bred on my father's farm.*

breed (4) [briyd'], *v.* 1. produce young by the mating of animals. **Ex.** *Rabbits breed frequently.* 2. raise animals such as cattle, sheep and horses. **Ex.** *He breeds racehorses.* 3. produce. **Ex.** *Dirt breeds disease.* —*n.* a particular kind of animal or plant. **Ex.** *What breed of cattle do they raise on this farm?*

breeze (3) [briyz'], *n.* a light, gentle wind. **Ex.** *There is usually a cool breeze here in the evening.*

brew (5) [bruw'], *v.* 1. make beer. 2. prepare a beverage or a liquid by placing the ingredients in water that has come to a boil. **Ex.** *Please brew me some tea.* 3. be forming or beginning. **Ex.** *The police were called in because trouble was brewing.* —*n.* that which is brewed. **Ex.** *If you are making coffee, I like a strong brew.*

---

a, far; æ, am; e, get; ey, late; i, in; iy, see; ɔ, all; ow, go; u, put; uw, too; ə, but, ago; ər, fur; aw, out; ay, life; oy, boy; ŋ, ring; θ, think; ð, that; ž, measure; š, ship; j, edge; č, child.

bribe (4) [brayb'], *n*. a gift or favor given or promised to influence a person to do something that he should not or may not want to do. **Ex.** *The judge was accused of taking a bribe to free the prisoner.* —*v*. give a bribe to; influence by a bribe. **Ex.** *He was bribed to keep silent.* —**brib'er·y,** *n*. the act of giving or accepting bribes.

brick (3) [brik'], *n*. a block of clay hardened by baking in the sun or fire and used as a building material. —*v*. cover with brick. **Ex.** *They bricked up the opening where the window used to be.*

bride (3) [brayd'], *n*. a woman newly married or about to be married. **Ex.** *The bride looked beautiful.* —**brid'al,** *adj*.

bridegroom [brayd'gruwm'], *n*. a man newly married or about to be married. **Ex.** *The bridegroom looked handsome.*

bridge (1) [brij'], *n*. 1. a structure built over a river, road, railroad, etc., used as a path or road. 2. anything like a bridge. **Ex.** *They were trying to build a bridge of friendship between the two countries.* 3. a game of cards for four players. —*v*. build or make a bridge on or over. **Ex.** *It was difficult to bridge the river.*

BRIDGE 1

bridle (4) [bray'dəl], *n*. 1. the leather bands and metal pieces that are put about the head of a horse and used to control and guide it. 2. anything that slows down or controls. —*v*. 1. put a bridle on. **Ex.** *He bridled the horse.* 2. control. **Ex.** *You must learn to bridle your temper.*

brief (2) [briyf'], *adj*. short; using few words. **Ex.** *He had time only to give a brief report.* —*v*. instruct on how to do a piece of work. **Ex.** *He briefed the men on their duties.* —**brief'ly,** *adv*.

briefcase [briyf'keys], *n*. a container made of cloth, plastic or leather for carrying papers, books, etc. **Ex.** *She put a portable calculator in her briefcase.*

brier (5) [bray'ər], *n*. 1. a woody plant with thorns on its stem. 2. a thorn. **Ex.** *He scratched his leg on a brier.*

bright (1) [brayt'], *adj*. 1. shining; giving or having much light. **Ex.** *The sun is bright today.* 2. happy. **Ex.** *Her bright eyes showed her pleasure.* 3. of a brilliant color. **Ex.** *The box was painted a bright red.* 4. intelligent; quick-witted. **Ex.** *His* *school record shows he is bright.* —**bright'en,** *v.* —**bright'ly,** *adv.* —**bright'ness,** *n.*

brilliant (3) [bril'yənt], *adj.* 1. shining very brightly. **Ex.** *His eyes are a brilliant blue.* 2. very intelligent. **Ex.** *The young lawyer has a brilliant mind.* —**bril'liance,** *n.*

brim (4) [brim'], *n.* 1. the upper edge of anything hollow. **Ex.** *The cup was filled to the brim.* 2. an edge that extends out. **Ex.** *The wide brim of her hat protected her from the sun.* —*v.* be full to the brim. **Exs.** *That coffee cup is brimming over. The children were brimming over with laughter.* — **brim'ful,** *adj.* full up to the brim.

bring (1) [briŋ'], *v.* come with, carry or lead to. **Ex.** *Bring me a glass of water, please.* 2. make happen; cause to come or come about. **Ex.** *I could not bring myself to see her again.* —**bring about,** cause to happen. **Ex.** *He will bring about many changes.* —**bring around,** persuade; convince. **Ex.** *I will bring him around to my way of thinking.* —**bring to,** revive a person who has fainted. **Ex.** *The fresh air may bring him to.* —**bring up,** raise. **Ex.** *His grandmother brought him up.*

brink (5) [briŋk'], *n.* 1. the edge of a steep place. **Ex.** *He fell over the brink of the cliff.* 2. the point just before. **Ex.** *The scientists were at the brink of success in their experiment.*

brisk (5) [brisk'], *adj.* 1. active; lively. **Ex.** *He likes to take a brisk walk every morning.* 2. sharp and cool. **Ex.** *The brisk winter weather made me hungry.* —**brisk'ly,** *adv.* —**brisk'ness,** *n.*

bristle (4) [bris'əl], *n.* one of the short, stiff, coarse hairs of certain animals, or something like them, used especially to make brushes. **Ex.** *My brush has nylon bristles.* —*v.* 1. rise or stand stiff or erect. **Ex.** *He was so frightened that his hair seemed to bristle.* 2. be roused up or stirred. **Ex.** *He bristled with anger.* —**brist'ly,** *adj.*

brittle (5) [brit'əl], *adj.* easily broken. **Ex.** *The brittle glass shattered on the table.* —**brit'tle·ness,** *n.*

broad (1) [brɔ:d'], *adj.* 1. very wide. **Ex.** *We watched the boats pass each other on the broad river.* 2. covering a large area. **Ex.** *The farmer planted broad fields of wheat.* 3. general; not limited. **Ex.** *He is a man of broad interests.* —**broad'ly,** *adv.* —**broad'en,** *v.* —**broad'-mind'ed,** *adj.* willing to listen to the ideas of others; tolerant. **Ex.** *People respect him for his broad-minded approach to problems.*

broadcast (3) [brɔːd'kæst'], *v.* send messages, speeches, music, etc. by radio or television. *Ex. That station broadcasts educational programs.* —*n.* a radio or television program. *Ex. We listened to the news broadcast.* —**broad'cast·er,** *n.*

broil (5) [broyl'], *v.* cook under or over a flame or other high heat. *Ex. I am going to broil the meat for dinner.* —**broil'er,** *n.* the part of a stove used for broiling.

broke (1) [browk'], *v.* past tense of *break*. *Ex. The boy fell and broke his arm.*

broken (1) [brow'kən], *v.* past participle of *break*. *Ex. The boy has broken his arm.* —*adj.* 1. not whole; in pieces. *Ex. This broken dish cannot be replaced.* 2. not kept. *Ex. A broken promise ended their friendship.* 3. not working or operating as intended. *Ex. The broken radio needs to be repaired.*

bronze (4) [branz'], *n.* a reddish-brown metal made by melting copper and tin together. *Ex. That statue is made of bronze.* —*adj.* the color of bronze. —*v.* give a bronze color to something.

brood (4) [bruwd'], *n.* young birds hatched or cared for together. *Ex. How many chickens are in the brood? —v.* think steadily and moodily about something. *Ex. She brooded on her past mistakes so much that she became ill.*

brook (2) [bruk'], *n.* a small stream of water. *Ex. The younger children were playing in the brook.*

broom (3) [bruwm'], *n.* a device for sweeping, with a stiff brush and a long handle.

brother (1) [brəð'ər], *n.* 1. a boy or man with the same parents as another person. *Ex. She has two older brothers and one younger brother.* 2. one of the same race or group or of the human race. *Ex. All men are brothers.* —**broth'er·ly,** *adj.*

brother-in-law [brəð'ərinlɔː'], *n.* the husband of one's sister; the brother of one's husband or wife.

BROOM

brought (1) [brɔːt'], *v.* past tense and participle of *bring*. *Exs. They brought a friend home with them. She had brought the gifts to the house earlier.*

brow (3) [braw'], *n.* 1. hair growing above the eye. 2. the forehead. *Ex. His cap covered his brow.* 3. the upper part of a hill; the edge of a steep place. *Ex. He disappeared over the brow of the hill.*

BROW

brown (1) [brawn'], *n.* the dark color made by mixing red, black and yellow; the color of coffee. —*adj.* having the color brown. **Ex.** *He has brown eyes.* —*v.* to make brown by cooking. **Ex.** *The meat is browning in the oven.*

bruise (4) [bruwz'], *v.* 1. injure by striking, without breaking the skin, often causing a black and blue mark. **Ex.** *He bruised his arm when he hit it on the stone.* 2. injure or hurt other than physically. **Ex.** *That sharp answer bruised her feelings.* —*n.* the injury; the mark left by such an injury. **Ex.** *The bruise became black and blue.* —**bruis'ing,** *adj.*

brunette [bruw'net], *adj.* a female with brown hair. **Ex.** *Her older daughter is a brunette.*

brush (2) [brəš'], *n.* a device consisting of stiff or soft hairs, fibers, etc. attached to a handle, used for painting, cleaning, scrubbing, etc. —*v.* 1. sweep, rub, clean or polish with a brush. **Ex.** *She brushed her hair before going to bed.* 2. touch lightly in passing. **Ex.** *The cat brushed against her leg.*

brush (2) [brəš'], *n.* 1. a thick growth of bushes, small trees, and low woody plants. **Ex.** *Brush was growing along the roadside.* 2. small branches cut from trees. **Ex.** *He raked the brush into a pile.*

brute (4) [bruwt'], *n.* 1. a beast. **Ex.** *The bear was a great brute.* 2. a cruel, unfeeling person. **Ex.** *Unfortunately, she married a brute.* —*adj.* 1. of or like a brute. 2. purely physical. **Ex.** *He pulled the tree out of the ground by brute force.* —**bru'tal, brut'ish,** *adj.* like a brute; cruel. **Ex.** *He is a brutal man.* —**bru·tal'i·ty,** *n.* savageness; cruelty.

bubble (3) [bəb'əl], *n.* 1. a small ball of air or gas in a liquid. **Ex.** *Many bubbles appeared in the boiling water.* 2. a small ball of air or gas in a thin liquid cover. **Ex.** *Children like to make bubbles with soap and water.* —*v.* rise in or form bubbles; foam. **Ex.** *When a liquid boils, it bubbles.* —**bub'bling,** *adj.*

buck (4) [bək'], *n.* the male of a deer, goat, rabbit, and certain other animals. **Ex.** *The deer hunters had shot a fine buck.* —*v.* suddenly jump upward, with the head low. **Ex.** *The horse bucked, but the rider managed to stay on its back.*

---

a, far; æ, am; e, get; ey, late; i, in; iy, see; ɔ, all; ow, go; u, put; uw, too; ə, but, ago; ər, fur; aw, out; ay, life; oy, boy; ŋ, ring; θ, think; ð, that; ž, measure; š, ship; J, edge; č, child.

bucket (4) [bək'ət], *n.* a vessel for holding or carrying water or other liquid; a pail. —**buck'et·ful**, *n.* the amount contained in a bucket.

BUCKET

buckle (5) [bək'əl], *n.* 1. a fastening, often of metal, for holding together the ends of a belt. 2. a similar device used as an ornament, as on women's shoes. —*v.* fasten with a buckle. **Ex.** *He buckled his belt.*

BUCKLE 1

bud (3) [bəd'], *n.* a blossom or leaf of a plant before it opens. **Ex.** *The rose already has a few pink buds.* —*v.* form buds. **Ex.** *The trees are budding early this spring.*

budget (4) [bəj'ət], *n.* a plan or estimate of expected income and expense for a period of time. **Ex.** *They planned a monthly budget for their family.* —*v.* make a plan for using money, time, goods, etc. **Ex.** *If you wish to get all of your work done, you must budget your time.*

buffalo (5) [bəf'əlow], *n.* a kind of wild ox with short horns, a large hairy head and a humped back, such as the American wild buffalo.

buffet (5) [bəf'ət], *n.* a blow with the hand; any blow. **Ex.** *The buffets of fate were almost more than he could bear.* —*v.* hit; strike repeatedly. **Ex.** *The ship was buffeted by the waves.*

buffet (5) [bəfəy'], *n.* 1. a piece of furniture for holding dishes, silver, etc. 2. dishes of food placed on a table or buffet so that guests may serve themselves. **Ex.** *Please help yourself from the buffet.* —*adj.* served in buffet style. **Ex.** *They were invited to a buffet supper.*

bug (1) [bəg'], *n.* any small insect. **Ex.** *A bug was crawling on the wood.*

bugle (4) [byuw'gəl], *n.* a brass horn used especially for military signals. —**bu'gler**, *n.*

build (1) [bild'], *v.* 1. join materials together to make something. **Ex.** *They used wood to build the house.* 2. establish; develop. **Ex.** *It took several years to build the business.* —**build'er**, *n.*

BUGLE

building (1) [bil'diŋ], *n.* 1. anything built for use

as a house, store, factory, etc. 2. the work of one who builds. **Ex.** *Building is his trade.*

built (1) [bilt'], *v.* past tense and participle of *build.* **Exs.** *He built his own house. They had built their house of stone.* —**built'-up'**, *adj.* filled with houses. **Ex.** *This built-up area used to be a large farm.*

bulb (4) [bəlb'], *n.* 1. a thick, ball-shaped root of certain plants. **Ex.** *We planted these tulip bulbs last fall.* 2. something in the shape of a bulb. **Ex.** *We need a new electric light bulb.* —**bul'bous**, *adj.*

bulge (5) [bəlj'], *n.* a part that swells out. **Ex.** *The bag of candy made a bulge in the child's pocket.* —*v.* extend; swell out. **Ex.** *His suit bulged in several places.* —**bulg'ing**, *adj.*

bulk (3) [bəlk'], *n.* 1. greatness of size. **Ex.** *We saw the ship's bulk through the fog.* 2. the greatest or major part. **Ex.** *The bulk of the debt was already paid.* 3. large quantities of some product not packaged or bottled. **Ex.** *This store has flour, rice and sugar for sale in bulk.* —**bulk'y**, *adj.* extremely large; large and of awkward shape. **Ex.** *She was wearing a bulky sweater.*

bull (3) [bul'], *n.* the male animal of the ox family. **Ex.** *The bull was protecting the cows.*

bull's-eye [bulz'ay`], *n.* the center of a target used in practice shooting; any shot that hits it. **Ex.** *He hit the bull's-eye with his first shot.*

bullet (4) [bul'it], *n.* a small piece of metal that is shot from a gun. **Ex.** *He was killed by a single bullet.*

bulletin (4) [bul'ətən], *n.* 1. a brief public notice or announcement of news. **Ex.** *A bulletin on the radio warned of the spreading forest fire.* 2. a magazine or paper published by an organization. **Ex.** *The company issues a monthly bulletin for its employees.* —**bul'le·tin board'**, *n.* a piece of wood or other material on which bulletins are posted.

bully (4) [bul'iy], *n.* a person who is cruel to others who are weaker. **Ex.** *At last the class bully was beaten.* —*v.* try to control others by threats, cruelty or violence. **Ex.** *He bullies his younger brother unmercifully.*

bulwark (5) [bul'wərk], *n.* 1. a solid, wall-like structure of any material built around a place for purposes of defense. **Ex.** *The soldiers kept their heads down behind the bulwark.* 2.

anything that protects. **Ex.** *His health insurance was a bulwark against the expense of illness.*

bump (4) [bəmp'], *v.* come suddenly into contact with something; strike roughly against. **Ex.** *He bumped into the wall.* —*n.* 1. a blow made by striking against something or someone. **Ex.** *The airplane landed with a bump.* 2. a swelling, often sore, resulting from a heavy blow. **Ex.** *She has a large bump on her head.* 3. a raised place. **Ex.** *The bump in the road caused many traffic accidents.* —**bump'y,** *adj.* —**bump'er,** *n.* a bar across the front or back of a car to protect it from damage when bumped.

bun [bən'], *n.* 1. a small round roll. **Ex.** *We need buns for the hamburgers.* 2. a small, round sweet roll. **Ex.** *She served buns with the coffee.*

bunch (3) [bənč'], *n.* a collection of similar things grouped together. **Ex.** *She picked a bunch of flowers.* —*v.* collect or gather in a group. **Ex.** *The cows were bunched together in the shed.*

bundle (3) [bən'dəl], *n.* a number of things tied or rolled together. **Ex.** *She carried a bundle of clothes.* —*v.* tie or wrap in a bundle. **Ex.** *Please bundle these newspapers.* —**bundle up,** dress warmly. **Ex.** *They bundled up to protect themselves from the cold.*

bungalow (5) [bəŋ'gəlow], *n.* a small house, usually having only one floor.

burden (3) [bər'dən], *n.* 1. a load; that which is carried. **Ex.** *The elephant was carrying a heavy burden.* 2. difficulty, worry or responsibility that a person must endure. **Ex.** *Supporting his family was a great burden for him.* —*v.* load heavily; load too heavily. **Ex.** *I am sorry to burden you with these packages.*

bureau (3) [byur'ow], *n.* 1. a government department or office. **Ex.** *The weather bureau says there will be rain tonight.* 2. a business office. **Ex.** *He found work through an employment bureau.* 3. a chest of drawers for holding clothes. **Ex.** *There is a mirror hanging above the bureau.* —**bu·reau'cra·cy,** *n.* system of government administration noted for many, often complicated rules, which are strictly followed. —**bu'reau·crat',** *n.* government official or worker in a bureaucracy. —**bu'reau·crat'ic,** *adj.* strict in following rules; like a bureaucrat.

burglar (5) [bər'glər], *n.* a person who forcibly enters a house, store, etc. to steal. **Ex.** *The burglar was caught by the police.*

burial (5) [ber'iyəl], *n.* act of burying. **Ex.** *The burial of the dead sailor was performed at sea.*

burn (1) [bərn'], *v.* 1. be on fire. **Ex.** *This hard wood will burn a long time.* 2. destroy by fire or heat. **Ex.** *The house burned to the ground.* 3. be injured by heat. **Ex.** *She burned her hand on the stove.* 4. give light. **Ex.** *The electric lights burned all night.* —*n.* 1. a burned place. **Ex.** *There was a burn in the rug.* 2. an injury caused by fire, extreme cold, electricity, etc. **Ex.** *He suffered a burn on his hand.*

burrow (5) [bər'ow], *n.* a tunnel in the ground made by an animal as a place to live. **Ex.** *Rabbits live in burrows.* —*v.* dig a tunnel in the earth. **Ex.** *Rats burrowed under the floor of the house.*

burst (2) [bərst'], *v.* 1. break open or into pieces suddenly. **Ex.** *The bubble burst.* 2. come, enter, appear, start, etc., suddenly and with force. **Ex.** *The angry man burst into the room.* —*n.* 1. act of bursting. **Ex.** *A burst of laughter interrupted the speaker.* 2. a sudden display of activity. **Ex.** *He passed the other man with a burst of speed.*

bury (2) [ber'iy], *v.* 1. put into the ground and cover with earth. **Ex.** *The dog was burying a bone in the garden.* 2. put a dead body into the ground or into the sea, often with a ceremony. **Ex.** *He was buried next to his wife.*

bus (1) [bəs'], *n.* a motor coach. —**bus'es, bus'ses,** *n.* more than one bus.

bush (2) [buš'], *n.* a low plant with many branches, like a small tree. **Ex.** *The children hid in the bushes.* —**bush'y,** *adj.*

BUS

bushel (3) [buš'əl], *n.* 1. a dry measure equal to thirty-two dry quarts. **Ex.** *He bought a bushel of apples from the farmer.* 2. a container which holds this quantity. **Ex.** *The farmer put the apples into a bushel.* See **Weights and Measures.**

business (1) [biz'nəs], *n.* 1. one's work; an occupation. **Ex.** *His business is farming.* 2. buying and selling; trade; commerce. **Ex.** *Business was good last year, and we made a profit.* 3. an industrial or commercial company, establishment or enterprise. **Ex.** *He and his father own the business.* 4. one's personal concern. **Ex.** *My affairs are none of your business.* —**busi·ness·like,** *adj.*

a, far; æ, am; e, get; ey, late; i, in; iy, see; ɔ, all; ow, go; u, put; uw, too; ə, but, ago; ər, fur; aw, out; ay, life; oy, boy; ŋ, ring; θ, think; ð, that; ž, measure; š, ship; j, edge; č, child.

bust (4) [bəst'], *n.* the head, neck, and shoulders of a person, shaped in clay, wood, metal, etc. **Ex.** *He made a bust of her in marble.*

bustle (4) [bəs'əl], *v.* move about busily and with a great show of energy. **Ex.** *The waitress bustled about serving the customers.* —*n.* noisy activity; stir. **Ex.** *In the bustle of their departure, one lady forgot her coat.*

busy (1) [biz'iy], *adj.* 1. doing something; not idle. **Ex.** *Their mother was busy cleaning the house.* 2. full of activity. **Ex.** *The busy street was filled with cars, bicycles, and people.* —**bus'i·ly**, *adv.*

but (1) [bət'], *conj.* 1. however; yet. **Ex.** *He went but I did not.* 2. except. **Ex.** *I will go anywhere but to the mountains.* —*prep.* except; other than. **Ex.** *No one knows this but me.* —*adv.* only; just. **Ex.** *There is but one answer to your question.*

butcher (3) [buč'ər], *n.* 1. one whose work is preparing animals for use as food. **Ex.** *The butcher was sharpening his knives.* 2. one who sells meat. —*v.* skin and cut up, as a butcher does. **Ex.** *We butchered a pig in the fall.*

butt (5) [bət'], *n.* the thicker end of anything. **Ex.** *He struck him with the butt of his gun.* —*v.* strike or hit with force, especially with the head or horns. **Ex.** *The goat butted the boy and knocked him down.*

butter (1) [bət'ər], *n.* the solid, yellow fat gotten by beating cream for some time. **Ex.** *He spread butter on his bread.* —*v.* put butter on. **Ex.** *She buttered her bread.*

butterfly (4) [bət'ərflay'], *n.* an insect with large, broad wings, usually bright in color.

button (2) [bət'ən], *n.* 1. a small, usually round, piece of metal, glass, etc. pushed through an opening to fasten clothing parts together. 2. a small device like a button. **Ex.** *Press the button to start the machine.* —*v.* fasten clothing. **Ex.** *Button your coat.*

BUTTON 1

buy (1) [bay'], *v.* get by paying a price, usually money. **Ex.** *I will buy a new dress when I have enough money.* —**buy'er**, *n.*

buzz (4) [bəz'], *v.* make a long, low, steady sound like that made by bees; murmur or whisper excitedly. **Ex.** *The whole town is buzzing about their marriage.* —*n.* a long, low, steady sound like that made by bees. **Ex.** *He was awakened by the* *buzz of a mosquito.* **—buz'zer,** *n.* that which makes a buzzing sound. **Ex.** *Why didn't you answer the buzzer?*

by (1) [bay'], *prep.* 1. near; at. **Ex.** *He sat by my side.* 2. during. **Ex.** *They traveled by night.* 3. according to a fixed measurement. **Ex.** *They bought oranges by the dozen.* 4. not later than. **Ex.** *They were home by midnight.* 5. through the means of. **Ex.** *They traveled by train.* 6. in measurements. **Ex.** *The table top is three feet by five feet.* **—adv.** 1. near. **Ex.** *We stood by and watched.* 2. to a point and on to the far side of; past. **Ex.** *Several cars drove by.* **—by and by,** after some time. **Ex.** *He will be home by and by.* **—by the way,** also; in passing. **Ex.** *By the way, I am leaving on Monday.*

bypass [bay'pæs], *n.* a road which avoids something by going around it, especially a busy area. **Ex.** *We took the bypass to escape the city traffic.* **—v.** avoid. **Ex.** *I do not like this highway because it bypasses all the interesting little towns.*

by-product [bay'prad'əkt], *n.* something which is made as the result of making something else; an added result. **Ex.** *Will this process yield any useful by-products?*

C

C, c, [siy'], *n.* The third letter of the English alphabet.

cab (4) [kæb'], *n.* an automobile in which the passengers pay a fare; a taxicab. **Ex.** *He took a cab to the airport.*

cabbage (4) [kæb'ij], *n.* a vegetable with many curved leaves forming a round, firm head. **Ex.** *Are we going to have boiled cabbage with the baked ham?*

CABBAGE

cabin (3) [kæb'en], *n.* 1. a small house; a hut. **Ex.** *The pioneers built a log cabin in the clearing.* 2. one of the private rooms on a ship where officers or passengers sleep. **Ex.** *We returned to our cabin after breakfast.*

cabinet (3) [kæb'ənit], *n.* 1. a piece of furniture with drawers or shelves and doors for storing or displaying articles. **Ex.** *We will need at least three file cabinets in this office.* 2. a group of advisers to the chief executive of a government, made up of the heads of different departments. **Ex.** *The President is meeting with his cabinet.*

cable (3) [key'bəl], *n.* 1. a strong, thick rope, often made of wire. **Ex.** *The bridge was suspended from cables.* 2. a waterproof bundle of wires used for sending electricity. **Ex.** *The telephone repairmen were working on the damaged cable.* 3. a message sent under the ocean by means of such bundles of wires. **Ex.** *They sent a cable from London to New York.* —*v.* send a message by cable. **Ex.** *They cabled us the news.* —**ca'ble·gram,** *n.* a cable.

cactus [kæk'təs], *n.* a leafless plant which grows in the desert and has sharp points on fleshy stems and branches. **Ex.** *There are pretty pink blossoms on that cactus.*

CACTUS

café (3) [kæ`fey'], *n.* a coffeehouse, restaurant or bar. **Ex.** *They stopped at a sidewalk café for lunch.*

cafeteria [kæf`ətiy'riyə], *n.* a public place where one selects and buys food and drink from a counter to carry to a table. **Ex.** *We often have our breakfast at a cafeteria near the office.*

cage (3) [keyǰ'], *n.* a boxlike room or space, with sides made of wire or bars, in which animals are kept. **Ex.** *The bird escaped from its cage.* —*v.* put or confine in a cage. **Ex.** *They caged their pet until the guests had left.*

cagey [keyǰ'iy], *adj.* cunning; tricky. **Ex.** *His cagey answers do not tell us much.*

cake (1) [keyk'], *n.* 1. a sweet food made of flour, sugar, eggs and milk and baked in an oven. **Ex.** *My mother is baking a birthday cake for my brother.* 2. any mass, usually one shaped like a cake. **Ex.** *Great cakes of ice were cut from the pond.*

calamity (5) [kəlæm'ətiy], *n.* bad fortune, either personal or public. **Ex.** *The flood was a great calamity for the village.*

calcium (5) [kæl'siyəm], *n.* a soft, white chemical element found in bone, chalk, lime, marble, etc. **Ex.** *Calcium is needed by the body to build bones and teeth.*

calculate (4) [kæl'kyəleyt'], *v.* 1. add, subtract, multiply or divide to obtain information. **Ex.** *They calculated how much it had cost to build the house.* 2. plan in advance. **Ex.** *His remarks were calculated to win the banker's confidence.* 3. estimate. **Ex.** *He calculated that the cost would be high.* —**cal'cu·lat'ing,** *adj.* 1. that performs calculations. **Ex.** *Each person in our office has a calculating machine.* 2. shrewd; scheming. **Ex.** *Do not trust such a calculating person.* —**cal'cu·la'tion,** *n.* the use of mathematics in solving a problem; the result. —**cal'cul·la'tor,** *n.* a person who or machine that calculates.

calendar (3) [kæl'əndər], *n.* a chart showing the days, weeks, months and years. **Ex.** *Here is a calendar for the coming year.*

calf (4) [kæf'], *n.* 1. the young of the cow and of certain other animals. **Ex.** *The calf soon learned to drink milk from a pail.* 2. the fleshy part at the back of the human leg below the knee. **Ex.** *After running, he had a cramp in his right calf.*

call (1) [kɔ:l'], *v.* 1. cry out in a loud voice. **Ex.** *He called my name.* 2. give a name to; name. **Ex.** *We have decided we will call the baby "Mary."* 3. telephone. **Ex.** *I am going to call her tomorrow.* —*n.* 1. a cry or shout. **Ex.** *We heard a call in the night.* 2. a summons or signal. **Ex.** *That is the first call for dinner.* 3. a telephone conversation. **Ex.** *We have been expecting your call.* —**call for,** request. **Ex.** *He called for help.* —**call off,** decide against doing, having, etc. **Ex.** *He called off the trip.* —**call on,** 1. visit. **Ex.** *We called on them at their home.* 2. ask to do. **Ex.** *We called on him to make a contribution.* —**call up,** 1. telephone. **Ex.** *Call her up tonight.* 2. order one to come for military duty. **Ex.** *During the emergency, I was called up by the army.*

calm (2) [ka:m'], *n.* a period of quiet and stillness. **Ex.** *A great calm followed the storm.* —*adj.* 1. peaceful; quiet. **Ex.** *It was a calm evening with no wind.* 2. undisturbed by passion or emotion; not excited. **Ex.** *She spoke in a calm voice.* —*v.* make peaceful or quiet; soothe. **Ex.** *She calmed the weeping girl.* —**calm'ly,** *adv.* —**calm'ness,** *n.*

calorie [kæl'əriy], *n.* 1. a unit measuring the amount of energy that food produces; a unit for measuring heat. **Ex.** *She will have to reduce the calories in her diet or she will put on weight.*

a, far; æ, am; e, get; ey, late; i, in; iy, see; ɔ, all; ow, go; u, put; uw, too; ə, but, ago; ər, fur; aw, out; ay, life; oy, boy; ŋ, ring; θ, think; ð, that; ž, measure; š, ship; j, edge; č, child.

calves (4) [kævz'], *n.* plural of *calf.* **Ex.** *This cow has had two calves so far.*

came (1) [keym'], *v.* past tense of *come.* **Ex.** *They came to our house.*

camel (4) [kæm'əl], *n.* a large animal that can go for long periods without water, used in many desert regions for carrying goods or for riding.

camera (4) [kæm'(ə)rə], *n.* a device for taking photographs. **Ex.** *I need some film for my camera.*

CAMEL

camp (2) [kæmp'], *n.* a place where soldiers or other people live in tents or simple buildings placed close together. **Ex.** *The young soldier soon became accustomed to life in the camp.* —*v.* 1. establish a camp. **Ex.** *The army camped for the night.* 2. live, usually for a short time, in a tent or out of doors. **Ex.** *The children camped in the woods.* —**camp'er,** *n.* 1. a person who camps. 2. a vehicle like a car equipped for camping.

campaign (3) [kæm'peyn'], *n.* 1. a connected series of military actions in a war to gain a certain result. **Ex.** *The old general had seen many campaigns.* 2. the competition by opposing political candidates for public office. **Ex.** *The President's campaign to get reelected began several months ago.* —*v.* serve in or go on a campaign. **Ex.** *He campaigned by visiting the home of each voter in his district.* —**cam·paign'er,** *n.* one who campaigns.

campus (5) [kæm'pəs], *n.* the main buildings and grounds of a college or school. **Ex.** *Many students live on the campus.*

can (1) [kæn'], *v.* used with another verb to show: 1. know how to; be able to. **Ex.** *She can swim very well.* 2. have the right to. **Ex.** *He can vote.* 3. may; have permission. **Ex.** *You can go now.*

can (1) [kæn'], *n.* 1. a small, sealed, metal container for fruit, vegetables, milk, etc. **Ex.** *She opened a can of corn.* 2. a large container of metal or other strong material for water, waste material, etc. **Ex.** *He carried out the ash can.* —*v.* preserve food in cans. **Ex.** *That factory buys and cans fruit.* —**canned',** *adj.* preserved in cans. **Ex.** *While they were camping, they ate a lot of canned food.*

canal (3) [kənǽl'], *n.* a man-made waterway used by boats or ships. **Ex.** *The Panama Canal connects the Caribbean Sea with the Pacific Ocean.*

cancel (5) [kǽn'səl], *v.* 1. strike or cross out with lines or marks. **Ex.** *The stamps on a letter are canceled to show that they have been used.* 2. decide not to join in a planned activity or not to have such an activity take place. **Ex.** *The singer canceled his concert.* —**can'cel·la'tion,** *n.*

cancer (5) [kǽn'sər], *n.* a dangerous disease in which certain cells grow at a rapid rate and destroy healthy parts of the body. **Ex.** *Her father, who died of cancer, had been a heavy smoker.*

candidate (3) [kǽn'dədeyt], *n.* one who seeks or is suggested for an office or an honor. **Ex.** *He had been a candidate for office three times.* —**can'di·da·cy,** *n.* the state or fact of being a candidate.

candle (3) [kǽn'del], *n.* a stick of wax or similar material, with a string running through it, that gives light when burned. **Ex.** *The garden was lit by candles.* —**can'dle·stick',** *n.* a holder for a candle.

candy (2) [kǽn'diy], *n.* a sweet food made mostly of sugar, often with the addition of flavoring, nuts, fruits, etc. **Ex.** *The children had eaten too much candy.*

cane (4) [keyn'], *n.* 1. a stick used as an aid in walking. **Ex.** *He leaned heavily on his cane.* 2. a plant having a jointed stem with either a hollow or soft, spongy center. **Ex.** *This sugar is made from the juice of sugar cane.*

cannon (4) [kǽn'ən], *n.* a large gun fastened to a base or wheels. **Ex.** *The cannon thundered out a message of death.*

CANNON

cannot [kǽn'at], *v.* negative form of *can.* **Ex.** *He cannot come today.*

canoe (3) [kənuw'], *n.* a light, narrow boat moved by paddles. —*v.* ride in a canoe. **Ex.** *The boys canoed on the lake.*

CANOE

can't (1) [kænt'], short form, contraction of *cannot.* **Ex.** *I can't go now.*

canvas (4) [kǽn'vəs], *n.* a strong, heavy cloth made of cotton or other fibers used for tents, sails, oil paintings, etc. **Ex.** *The artist showed us three of his canvases.*

canyon (5) [kæn'yən], *n.* a deep valley with high, steep sides and often with water flowing through it. **Ex.** *It was a great adventure to climb down the side of the canyon.*

cap (2) [kæp'], *n.* 1. a small, closely fitting covering for the head, often with a projecting edge in front. 2. anything like a cap, such as a top or lid. **Ex.** *Put the cap on the soda bottle.* —*v.* put a cap on. **Ex.** *The trees were capped with snow.*

capable (3) [key'pəbəl], *adj.* having skill; fit; able to do something well. **Ex.** *She is a capable teacher.* —**ca`pa·bil·i·ty,** *n.* —**ca·pa·bly,** *adv.* —**capable of,** able or ready to. **Ex.** *He is capable of doing good work.*

capacity (3) [kəpæs'ətiy], *n.* 1. the space for receiving or containing. **Ex.** *The capacity of this bottle is one gallon.* 2. ability to do or become. **Ex.** *He has the capacity to become a doctor.* 3. position. **Ex.** *She worked in the capacity of nurse.*

cape (3) [keyp'], *n.* 1. a sleeveless garment that fastens at the neck and hangs over the shoulders covering the arms. **Ex.** *She wore a long cape over her dress.* 2. a narrow piece of land that extends out into the sea. **Ex.** *The fisherman lived on the cape.*

capital (2) [kæp'ətəl], *n.* 1. the city or town in which the government is located. **Ex.** *Washington, D.C., is the capital of the United States.* 2. money, buildings, land and machines owned and used by businesses, people or the government to make more money. **Ex.** *He saved his money and used it as capital to start his own business.* —**cap·i·tal·ism,** *n.* an economic system in which most of the means for producing goods and services are owned and operated for profit by individuals or private companies. **cap·i·tal·ist,** *n.* a person who owns much capital or supports capitalism. —**cap`i·tal·is'tic,** *adj.*

capital (2) [kæp'ətəl], *adj.* 1. referring to the large form of letters of the alphabet. **Ex.** *In this sentence, the first word begins with a capital* I. 2. punishable by death. **Ex.** *Murder is a capital offense.* —**cap·i·tal·ize,** *v.* write in capital letters. **Ex.** *In "Mary," the letter "M" is capitalized.*

Capitol [kæp'itəl], *n.* the building where the United States Congress meets in Washington, D.C.; the building where the lawmakers of a state meet. **Ex.** *We saw many interesting statues in the capitol.*

capsule [kæp'səl], *n.* 1. a case of gelatin containing a dose of medicine that dissolves after swallowing. **Ex.** *You are to take* *two capsules a day, one in the morning and one at night.* 2. the section of a spacecraft in which the astronauts carry on their work, eat, sleep, etc. **Ex.** *The capsule returned to earth safely.*

captain (1) [kǽp'tən], *n.* 1. one in authority over others; a chief; leader. **Ex.** *That boy is the captain of the team.* 2. an army officer ranking above a first lieutenant. 3. a navy officer ranking above a commander. 4. the commander or master of a ship. **Ex.** *The captain ordered his crew to abandon ship.*

captive (4) [kǽp'tiv], *n.* a prisoner, especially in war. **Ex.** *The captives were not released until the end of the war.* **—cap·tiv'i·ty,** *n.* state of being held or of not being free. **Ex.** *They suffered greatly during their captivity.*

capture (3) [kǽp'čər], *v.* take by force or by surprise; take prisoner; seize. **Exs.** *The hunters captured the wild animal with a strong rope net. The idea captured his imagination.* **—n.** the act of capturing. **Ex.** *The capture was made at dawn.*

car (1) [kar'], *n.* 1. an automobile. **Ex.** *Four of us are going in his car.* 2. anything on wheels used for carrying passengers, goods, etc., especially over rails. **Ex.** *There were 55 freight cars in that train.*

caravan (5) [kǽr'əvæn`], *n.* a company of persons traveling together, often for safety, as across a desert or through dangerous country. **Ex.** *A caravan of cars made its way to the camping grounds.*

carbon (4) [kar'bən], *n.* 1. a non-metallic chemical element found in all living matter. **Ex.** *Diamonds are pure carbon, while coal is a form of carbon that is not pure.* 2. a kind of paper coated with carbon, which is placed between sheets of paper, coated side down, so that what is written on the top sheet also appears on the other sheets; the copy itself. **Ex.** *Bring me the original and two carbons of the letter.*

carcass (5) [kar'kəs], *n.* the body of a dead animal. **Ex.** *The men were cooking the carcass of a sheep over a wood fire.*

card (2) [kard'], *n.* 1. a piece of heavy, stiff paper, either blank or printed. **Ex.** *Hold up the card so we can see what is written on it.* 2. One of a set of cards with spots, figures, pictures,

a, far; æ, am; e, get; ey, late; i, in; iy, see; ɔ, all; ow, go; u, put; uw, too; ə, but, ago; ər, fur; aw, out; ay, life; oy, boy; ŋ, ring; θ, think; ð, that; ž, measure; š, ship; j, edge; č, child.

etc., used in playing games. **Ex.** *He likes to play cards at least once a week.* 3. a piece of stiff paper bearing a greeting. **Ex.** *She received many birthday cards.*

cardboard [kard'bɔrd`], *n.* a heavy paper used to make boxes, signs, etc. **Ex.** *The box was made of cardboard.* —*adj.* made of cardboard.

cardinal (5) [kar'dənəl], *n.* 1. a high-ranking church official. 2. an American songbird with red feathers. —*adj.* of the highest importance; chief; principal. **Ex.** *Exercise is of cardinal importance in his health program.*

care (1) [ke:r'], *n.* 1. serious attention. **Ex.** *She took good care of the baby.* 2. worry; anxiety. **Ex.** *Her friends told her to forget her cares.* 3. protection; charge. **Ex.** *She is under a doctor's care.* —*v.* 1. wish; like. **Ex.** *Would you care to go to the theater?* 2. feel anxiety, worry or interest. **Ex.** *I do not care where we go this evening.* 3. watch; take charge of. **Ex.** *They cared for the children during the parents' absence.* 4. love. **Ex.** *They care very much for each other.* —**care'ful,** *adj.* acting so as not to harm, make mistakes, etc. **Ex.** *Be careful when you cross the street.* —**care'ful·ness,** *n.* —**care'ful·ly,** *adv.* —**care'less,** *adj.* acting without care. —**care'less·ly,** *adv.* —**in care of,** at the address of. **Ex.** *While I'm away, please send my mail in care of my mother.*

career (3) [kəri:r'], *n.* profession; life's work; progress in a profession or public life. **Ex.** *He is preparing for a career as a lawyer.*

caress (4) [kəres'], *n.* a gentle touch, kiss or embrace. **Ex.** *The mother's caresses calmed the child.* —*v.* touch or stroke tenderly. **Ex.** *Soft music caressed their ears.* —**ca·ress'ing,** *adj.* —**ca·ress'ing·ly,** *adv.*

caretaker [ke:r'teyk`ər], *n.* one who is employed to take care of a building or place. **Ex.** *The caretaker unlocked the apartment door.*

careworn [ke:r'wɔrn`], *adj.* tired from worry and concern. **Ex.** *She looked careworn.*

cargo (4) [kar'gow`], *n.* a load of articles carried by a ship or plane. **Ex.** *A cargo of tea arrived from India.*

carpenter (3) [kar'pəntər], *n.* a workman who builds or repairs wooden objects or structures such as houses. **Ex.** *The carpenter built a porch on the house.*

carpet (3) [kar'pət], *n.* 1. a thick, heavy material used as a floor covering. **Ex.** *The carpet on the hall floor is red.* 2. a carpetlike covering. **Ex.** *The grass was a green carpet.* —*v.* 1. cover with a carpet. **Ex.** *They want to carpet the bedroom.* 2. cover like a carpet. **Ex.** *Snow carpeted the ground.*

carriage [kær'iǰ, ker'iǰ], *n.* any wheeled vehicle for carrying people or objects. **Ex.** *If you are careful, you may wheel your baby sister in her carriage.*

CARRIAGE

carrot (5) [kær'ət, ker'ət], *n.* a plant with a long, pointed, orange-colored root eaten as a vegetable. **Ex.** *She served peas and carrots with the roast beef.*

carry (1) [kær'iy], *v.* take from one place and bring to another; move while supporting. **Ex.** *Two men carried the heavy box into the house.* —**car'ri·er,** *n.* 1. a person or thing that carries people or goods. **Ex.** *Who controls the rates for public carriers?* 2. a person or thing that passes on a disease without suffering the effects of the disease. **Ex.** *He did not realize that he was a carrier.* —**carry on,** do or continue. **Ex.** *Carry on the work while I am away.* —**carry out,** 1. follow. **Ex.** *He would not carry out her orders.* 2. a small shop in which food is prepared to be taken out to eat. **Ex.** *We got some lunch from the carry out to take back to the office.*

cart (3) [kart'], *n.* a light, small wagon used for transporting articles, or carrying people. **Ex.** *The farmer took his vegetables to market in a cart.* —*v.* carry in a cart. **Ex.** *The farmer carted the hay to the barn.*

carton (5) [kar'tən], *n.* a box made of heavy, stiff paper. **Ex.** *They bought a carton of eggs.*

cartoon [kar'tuwn], *n.* 1. a drawing, the purpose of which is to show in an amusing way the folly of some person or thing of interest in the news. **Ex.** *The first thing that he looks at in the paper is the cartoon on the editorial page.* 2. a motion picture made from a series of drawings. **Ex.** *An amusing cartoon was shown before the featured film.*

cartridge (5) [kar'triǰ], *n.* 1. a case, usually of metal, for holding the gunpowder and the bullet, for a rifle, gun, etc. **Ex.** *The soldier placed a cartridge in his gun.* 2. a case or holder like this.

carve (3) [karv'], *v.* 1. shape by cutting. **Ex.** *He carved the figure out of stone.* 2. cut meat. **Ex.** *His father carved the meat for us.* —**carv'er,** *n.*

case (1) [keys'] *n.* 1. a paricular instance; a single happening. **Ex.** *I would say that this was a case of laziness.* 2. a problem to be handled by the police or tried in a court of law. **Ex.** *The judge decided the case in our favor.* 3. someone with a problem, such as sickness. **Ex.** *The doctor is treating several cases of this disease.* 4. the true facts. **Ex.** *He said that he was hit by a car, but that is not the case.* —**in case,** in the event that. **Ex.** *Wear your raincoat in case it rains.*

case (1) [keys'], *n.* 1. a container. **Ex.** *The goods shipped by train were packed in cases.* 2. a box with its contents. **Ex.** *To save money I buy canned food by the case.*

cash (2) [kæš'], *n.* coins or paper money. **Ex.** *I paid by check because I did not have any cash with me.* —*v.* give or get money for. **Ex.** *Please cash this check for me.*

cashier (5) [kæ'ši:r'], *n.* a person who receives and pays money. **Exs.** *He works as a cashier at a bank. Pay the cashier, not the waiter.*

cassette [kæset'], *n.* a small container holding either magnetic tape or film. **Ex.** *This cassette has a recording of French songs.*

cast (4) [kæst'], *v.* 1. throw away, out or down. **Ex.** *The boy was casting stones into the water.* 2. direct; send in a certain direction. **Ex.** *The lamp cast a bright light on the table.* 3. shape melted metal by pouring into a hollow form. **Ex.** *The statue was cast in bronze.* —*n.* the actors in a play. **Ex.** *This play has a cast of twelve.* —**cast one's vote,** vote. **Ex.** *For which candidate did you cast your vote?*

castle (2) [kæs'əl], *n.* a large, strong building or group of buildings; the home of a nobleman. **Ex.** *A king once lived in that mountain castle.*

casual (4) [kæž'uwəl], *adj.* 1. happening by chance; not planned. **Ex.** *It was not a business appointment, just a casual meeting with a friend.* 2. without a definite purpose. **Ex.** *After giving the book a casual glance, he put it down.* —**cas'u·al·ty,** *n.* one hurt or killed. **Ex.** *There were twelve casualties in the train wreck.*

cat (2) [kæt'], *n.* a small, furry animal kept as a pet and useful for catching rats and mice.

CAT

catalog, catalogue (4) [kæt'ələg'], *n.* 1. a paper or book, usually containing descriptions and pictures of items for sale. **Ex.** *Since she was a very busy person, she did much of her shopping by catalog.* 2. an alphabetical record on cards of the books in a library or of things in other collections. **Ex.** *You can find the title of the book you want in the card catalog.*

catastrophe (5) [kətæs'trəfiy'], *n.* a sudden happening that causes great damage, loss or suffering. **Ex.** *The flood was a catastrophe.* —**cat'a·stroph'ic,** *adj.*

catch (1) [kæč'], *v.* 1. seize after a chase; capture. **Ex.** *Did they catch the horse that ran away?* 2. stop the motion of and seize in the hands. **Ex.** *Catch the ball.* 3. get by a hook or trap. **Ex.** *How many fish did you catch?* 4. get an illness. **Ex.** *He catches cold easily.* —*n.* 1. the act of taking, holding or seizing. **Ex.** *The ballplayer made a good catch.* 2. something taken or captured. **Ex.** *The fishermen said their catch was good today.* —**catch up,** 1. reach those ahead. **Ex.** *Walk slowly, and I will catch up with you.* 2. become current, up-to-date. **Ex.** *I must catch up on my work.*

caterpillar (4) [kæt'ərpil'ər], *n.* the worm-like stage in the life of an insect such as the butterfly.

CATERPILLAR

cathedral (5) [kəθiy'drəl], *n.* an important large church. **Ex.** *France has many famous cathedrals.*

cattle (2) [kæt'əl], *n.* the family of farm animals that includes cows, bulls, steers and oxen. **Ex.** *The animals in that field are beef cattle.*

caught (1) [kɔ:t'], *v.* past tense of *catch.* **Ex.** *The boy caught the ball with both hands.*

cause (1) [kɔ:z'], *n.* 1. the thing or person that produces a result. **Ex.** *What was the cause of the fire?* 2. a reason for an action. **Ex.** *You have good cause to be angry.* 3. an aim or purpose. **Ex.** *They fought for the cause of freedom.* —*v.* make happen; be the cause of. **Ex.** *He did not want to cause trouble.*

---

a, far; æ, am; e, get; ey, late; i, in; iy, see; ɔ, all; ow, go; u, put; uw, too; ə, but, ago; ər, fur; aw, out; ay, life; oy, boy; ŋ, ring; θ, think; ð, that; ž, measure; š, ship; j, edge; č, child.

caution (3) [kɔː'šən], *n.* 1. watchfulness in regard to danger; carefulness. **Ex.** *Proceed with caution when crossing the street.* 2. a warning against danger or evil. **Ex.** *Let his experience serve as a caution to you.* —*v.* give warning; advise of danger. **Ex.** *The lifeguards cautioned the swimmers to stay close to the shore.*

cautious (3) [kɔː'šəs], *adj.* careful to avoid danger or trouble. **Ex.** *He was a cautious driver.* — **cau'tious·ly,** *adv.*

cavalry (4) [kæv'əlriy], *n.* soldiers who fight on horseback. **Ex.** *The cavalry rode into the city.*

cave (3) [keyv'], *n.* a hollow place in the earth, usually in a hill or mountain. **Ex.** *Pictures were painted on the walls of the cave.* —**cave in,** sink or fall in. **Ex.** *The roof caved in because of the heavy snow.*

caveman [keyv'mæn'] *n.* a human who lived long ago in caves.

cavern (5) [kæv'ərn], *n.* a large cave. **Ex.** *The children were lost in the cavern.* —**cav'ern·ous,** *adj.* large, like a cavern. **Ex.** *We were ushered into a cavernous room.*

cavity (5) [kæv'ətiy], *n.* hole; hollow place. **Ex.** *She had the cavity in her tooth filled.*

cease (2) [siys'], *v.* stop; end. **Ex.** *Suddenly she ceased crying.* —**cease'less,** *adj.* going on without end. —**cease'less·ly,** *adv.*

cedar (4) [siy'dər], *n.* an evergreen tree with sweet-smelling wood. **Ex.** *We bought a cedar chest in which to store woolen clothes.*

ceiling (3) [siy'liŋ], *n.* the overhead surface of a room, opposite the floor. **Ex.** *A light hung from the middle of the ceiling.*

celebrate (4) [sel'əbreyt'], *v.* honor an event with special activity. **Ex.** *I will celebrate my birthday tomorrow.* —**cel'e·bra'tion,** *n.* the act of celebrating. —**ce·leb'ri·ty,** *n.* a famous or well-known person.

celery (5) [sel'(ə)riy], *n.* a green vegetable that grows in stalks with a leafy top. **Ex.** *She made a salad of celery, nuts and apples.*

cell (2) [sel'], *n.* 1. a room in a prison. **Ex.** *The prisoner was locked in a cell.* 2. the basic part of the stucture of all living matter. **Ex.** *Every plant and animal is made up of one or more cells.*

cellar (3) [sel'ər], *n.* an underground area,

CELERY

usually under a building, often used for storage. **Ex.** *The potatoes were stored in the cellar.*

cement (4) [siment'], *n.* 1. a grayish-white powdery substance made from lime and clay that, when mixed with water and often sand and allowed to dry, becomes hard like stone. **Ex.** *The basement floor is made of cement.* 2. any paste or thick liquid which hardens when it dries and is used to hold things together or to fill holes. —*v.*

cemetery (3) [sem'əter`iy], *n.* a burial ground; graveyard. **Ex.** *The family went to the cemetery to put flowers on his grave.*

censure (5) [sen'šər], *n.* act of finding fault or condemning as wrong. **Ex.** *His actions deserve severe censure.* —*v.* find fault with; condemn as wrong. **Ex.** *You must not censure him until you know the whole story.*

census (5) [sen'səs], *n.* an official count of the population of a country, city or town that usually includes details about age, sex, occupation, etc. **Ex.** *In the United States there is a census every ten years.*

cent (1) [sent'], *n.* a United States coin worth one one-hundredth of a dollar; a penny. See **Weights and Measures.**

center (2) [sen'tər], *n.* 1. the middle point; a place in the middle. **Ex.** *This building is at the center of town.* 2. a place that is the main point of some kind of activity. **Ex.** *The public library was a center of interest for everyone in the town.* 3. the middle point of a circle or sphere. —*v.* 1. place on or near a center. **Ex.** *He centered the picture on the wall.* 2. concentrate. **Ex.** *Their interests centered on their home.*

centigrade [sen'təgreyd`], *adj.* referring to a temperature scale divided into one hundred parts, zero (0) being the point at which water freezes and one hundred (100) being the point at which water boils. **Ex.** *What is the centigrade reading on the thermometer?*

central (3) [sen'trəl], *adj.* 1. in, at or near the center. **Ex.** *They live in the central area of the city.* 2. main; principal. **Ex.** *What is the central idea of this program?* —**cen'tral·ize,** *v.* bring to or put in a center or one place. **Ex.** *Many powers are centralized in the federal government.*

century (1) [sen'čəriy], *n.* a period of 100 years. **Ex.** *That happened almost a century ago.*

cereal (4) [sir'(i)yəl], *n.* 1. any grass yielding grain used for food; the grain produced from such grass. **Ex.** *Wheat and rice are cereals.* 2. a food made from grain. **Ex.** *What kind of cereal would you like for breakfast?*

ceremony (3) [ser'əmow'niy], *n.* 1. an act or series of acts done in a particular way established by custom. **Ex.** *His parents attended the graduation ceremony.* 2. very polite formal behavior. **Ex.** *They were received with great ceremony.* —**cer`e·mo'ni·al**, *adj.* —**cer·e·mo'ni·ous·ly**, *adv.*

certain (2) [sərt'ən], *adj.* 1. having no doubt; confident. **Ex.** *I am certain that my information is correct.* 2. sure to happen. **Ex.** *Spring is certain to follow winter.* 3. definite but not named. **Ex.** *Certain people are aware of the facts in the case.* —**cer'tain·ly**, *adv.* surely. —**cer'tain·ty**, *n.*

certificate (4) [sərtif'əkət], *n.* an official statement declaring that something is true. **Ex.** *You can use your birth certificate as proof of your age.* —**cer'ti·fy`**, *v.* officially declare that something is true: guarantee.

chain (2) [čeyn'], *n.* 1. a connected series of rings or links, usually of metal. **Ex.** *They pulled the automobile with a heavy chain.* 2. a series of connected things. **Ex.** *That incident was the first in a chain of events.* —*v.* fasten or secure with a chain. **Ex.** *The dog was chained to the fence.*

chair (1) [če:r'], *n.* a piece of furniture for one person to sit on.

chairman (4) [čer'mən], **chairwoman**, [čer'wum`ən], **chairperson**, [čer'pər'sən], *n.* a person in charge of a meeting or any organized group. **Ex.** *She was asked to be the chairman of the committee.*

CHAIR

chalk (4) [čɔ:k'], *n.* a soft, white, powdery material, sometimes made from shells. **Ex.** *I need a piece of chalk to write the homework assignment on the blackboard.* —**chalk'y**, *adj.*

challenge (3) [čæl'ənj], *n.* a call to a contest of skill or strength. **Ex.** *He thought of his new job as a challenge.* —*v.* 1. call or summon to a contest. **Ex.** *He challenged him to a bicycle race.* 2. question. **Ex.** *She challenged her friend's decision.*

chamber (5) [čeym'bər], *n.* 1. a room. 2. a group of people organized for a business purpose. **Ex.** *The chamber of commerce is encouraging new businesses to locate here.*

champion (3) [čæm'piyən], *n.* 1. the winner; the one who holds first place. **Ex.** *He is a boxing champion.* 2. one who fights for or defends a person or cause. **Ex.** *Our mayor is a champion of the poor.* —*adj.* victorious over all others; the best of its kind. **Ex.** *That is a champion racehorse.*

chance (1) [čæns'], *n.* 1. an opportunity. **Ex.** *Now is your chance to escape.* 2. unknown cause of an event; fortune; luck. **Ex.** *Chance played a part in his success.* 3. how possible or probable it is that something will happen. **Ex.** *The doctor said the patient has a good chance to recover.* 4. a happening resulting from an unknown cause. **Ex.** *We met by chance.* —*adj.* due to chance; accidental. **Ex.** *A chance remark helped solve the problem.*

change (1) [čeynj'], *v.* 1. put or take another in place of. **Ex.** *He changed into a clean shirt before dinner.* 2. become or make different; vary. **Ex.** *If you do not like this picture, it can be changed.* 3. give one for another; exchange. **Ex.** *They changed seats.* —*n.* 1. act of changing; alteration. **Ex.** *He suggested several changes in the plan of the house.* 2. variety; substitution. **Ex.** *The change in jobs was good for him.* 3. the amount returned when payment is more than the amount owed. **Ex.** *She handed him his change.* 4. small coins. **Ex.** *Please give me change for this one-dollar bill.* —**change'a·ble**, *adj.* —**change'less**, *adj.*

channel (5) [čæn'əl], *n.* 1. a narrow body of water that joins two larger bodies of water. **Ex.** *He sailed the boat out into the channel.* 2. a long cut, groove, tube or other path through which something may flow, pass, etc. **Ex.** *Can your television set receive that channel?* —*v.* 1. make a channel. **Ex.** *After the flood, the river channeled a new course.* 2. direct toward or into some particular course. **Ex.** *He channeled all of his energy into fixing his house.*

chant (4) [čænt'], *n.* 1. a song, especially a short, simple tune in which many words are sung or shouted in repeated tones. **Ex.** *We often use chants in our religious services.* 2. words shouted over and over to a regular beat. **Ex.** *We heard the chant of the strikers, "Health care! Health care!" before we saw them.* —*v.* sing or shout in a chant. **Ex.** *The worshipers chanted a prayer.*

chaos (5) [key'as'], *n.* lack of order; complete confusion. **Ex.** *The thieves left the house in chaos.* —**cha·ot'ic**, *adj.*

chap (5) [čæp'], *v.* crack or roughen and redden the skin. **Ex.** *My hands are chapped from the cold.*

chapel (5) [čæp'əl], *n.* a small or private place of prayer or worship. **Ex.** *The wedding was held in the chapel.*

chapter (2) [čæp'tər], *n.* any of the main divisions of a book. **Ex.** *This novel has twenty chapters.*

character (1) [kær'iktər], *n.* 1. all the qualities by which a person is judged; his strengths and weaknesses. **Ex.** *As he grew older, his character changed greatly.* 2. those qualities in a person considered to be morally good. **Ex.** *We hope that a person of character will be appointed.* 3. the qualities that distinguish one person or thing from others. **Ex.** *The character of the country changed as we traveled south.* 4. person in a play or story. **Ex.** *The most important character in the story is a young doctor.* —**char`ac·ter·i·za'tion,** *n.* —**char'ac·ter·ize`,** *v.*

characteristic (3) [kær`iktəris'tik], *adj.* belonging to a person or thing as part of its nature; typical. **Ex.** *Burning leaves have a characteristic smell.* —*n.* a distinguishing feature or quality. **Ex.** *A green color is a characteristic of that type of apple.*

charcoal (5) [čar'kowl'], *n.* 1. a black, coal-like material made from burning wood in a container that has little air. **Ex.** *We cooked our food over charcoal.* 2. a stick for drawing made of this material; the drawing made. **Ex.** *He did the portrait in charcoal.*

charge (1) [čarǰ'], *v.* 1. set a price for. **Ex.** *How much do you charge for this bread?* 2. delay payment until a later date. **Ex.** *She was able to charge the furniture she bought.* 3. rush. **Ex.** *He charged toward the door to escape.* 4. put the blame upon; accuse. **Ex.** *They charged him with murder.* —*n.* 1. an accusation. **Ex.** *A criminal charge has been made against him.* 2. care; management. **Ex.** *He has charge of the horses.* 3. price; cost. **Ex.** *Their charge for the work was high.* 4. a quantity of electricity. **Ex.** *What electric charge is carried by that battery?* —**in charge of,** have control of or responsibility for. **Ex.** *He is in charge of the office.* —**charge card,** *n.* —**charge plate,** *n.* a card, issued by a store, bank, etc., usually of plastic, which makes it possible for the holder to charge purchases.

charity (3) [čær'ətiy], *n.* 1. help or money given to those in need. **Ex.** *Their family had to depend on charity for clothing.* 2. kindness; willingness to forgive. **Ex.** *They treated even their enemies with charity.* 3. an organized fund or institution for giving help to those in need. **Ex.** *The Red Cross is a well-known charity.* —**char'i·ta·ble,** *adj.* —**char'i·ta·bly,** *adv.*

charm (2) [čarm'], *n.* 1. some quality or feature which delights or attracts. **Ex.** *Her voice had great charm.* 2. an act, thing or word which is believed to have magic power to do good or evil. **Ex.** *He believed a charm could prevent him from becoming ill.* —*v.* please greatly. **Ex.** *She charmed them with her dancing.* —**charm'er,** *n.* —**charm'ing,** *adj.*

chart (4) [čart'], *n.* 1. an arrangement of facts in the form of a list or drawing so that it may be read at a glance. **Ex.** *This sales chart shows how many sales were made last week compared to other weeks.* 2. a map used to show distances at sea, military operations or weather conditions. **Ex.** *The course of the ship was marked on the chart.* —*v.* 1. draw or show on a chart. 2. plan a course of action.

charter (4) [čar'tər], *n.* 1. an official paper giving rights or privileges to a person, business group, association, etc. **Ex.** *The charter permits the bank to open an office here.* 2. an official paper that contains the aims of a group or organization. **Ex.** *He has a framed copy of the United Nations Charter hanging on his office wall.* 3. rent or hire for private use, such as a boat, airplane, etc. **Ex.** *This bus is available for charter.* —*v.* 1. establish by charter. **Ex.** *The university was chartered two hundred years ago.* 2. hire for private use. **Ex.** *The group chartered a boat for the day.*

chase (3) [čeys'], *v.* 1. pursue in order to seize. **Ex.** *The police chased the thief.* 2. cause to run away. **Ex.** *The dog chased them from the house.* —*n.* act of chasing; pursuit.

chaste (5) [čeyst'], *adj.* virtuous; pure in matters relating to sex. **Ex.** *She was a chaste young woman.* —**chas'ti·ty,** *n.* state of being chaste; virginity.

chat (4) [čæt'], *v.* talk informally in a light, familiar manner. **Ex.** *The women chatted on the telephone for an hour.* —*n.* a relaxed conversation. **Ex.** *They had a nice chat at lunch.*

chatter (5) [čæt'ər], *v.* 1. make a series of rapid, speechlike sounds that cannot be understood. **Ex.** *The squirrels chattered among themselves.* 2. talk idly and rapidly. **Ex.** *She chattered on foolishly.* —*n.* 1. light, quick noises or voices. 2. idle or foolish talk. —**chat'ter·er,** *n.*

chauffeur (5) [šow'fər, šowfə:r'], *n.* the paid operator of a private automobile. **Ex.** *They rented a car with a chauffeur for the day.*

cheap (2) [čiyp'], *adj.* 1. inexpensive; bought or sold at a low price. **Ex.** *These are good shoes and were very cheap.* 2. poor in quality; of no great value. **Ex.** *Cheap material was used in the building.* 3. unworthy of respect. **Ex.** *He felt cheap when he considered his actions.* —**cheap'en,** *v.*

cheat (3) [čiyt'], *n.* one who does not act honestly or who deceives. **Ex.** *That boy who copied my work is a cheat!* —*v.* deceive; obtain something by a trick. **Ex.** *The man was cheated out of his money by a stranger.*

check (2) [ček'], *n.* 1. a written order, usually on a printed form, directing a bank to pay money from an account. **Ex.** *He wrote a check for the amount he owed me.* 2. examination; search. **Ex.** *The health inspector made a check of the bakery.* 3. a paper which shows how much is owed in a café or restaurant. **Ex.** *Ask the waiter for our check so we can pay and leave.* 4. a mark (√) put before each thing in a list as it is examined. **Ex.** *He put a check before our names when he saw we were present.* —*v.* 1. examine; compare. **Ex.** *Check your list to see if you have forgotten anything.* 2. control; stop. **Ex.** *The dam checked the flow of water.* 3. leave in the care of another, in a public place. **Ex.** *Check your hat at the door, please.* —**check in,** place your name on a list as a guest, a member, etc. **Ex.** *He checked in at the hotel.* —**check out,** 1. pay one's bill at a hotel and leave. **Ex.** He checked out of the hotel last night. 2. have a record made of something borrowed. **Ex.** *How many books did you check out of the library today?*

checkbook [ček'buk'], *n.* a book of printed forms used for writing orders for withdrawing money from an account with a bank.

checking account [ček'iŋ əkawnt'], *n.* a bank account from which the depositer can take money by writing a check. **Ex.** *The balance in my checking account is very low right now.*

checkroom [ček'ruwm'], *n.* a room in a public place where one can leave one's hat, coat, etc. for a brief time.

checkup [ček'əp'], *n.* an examination to establish the condition of someone or something. **Ex.** *He went to his doctor for a checkup.*

cheek (3) [čiyk'], *n.* either side of the face below the eye. **Ex.** *She kissed him on the cheek.*

cheer (2) [či:r'], *n.* 1. a shout of approval or joy. **Ex.** *A cheer rose from the crowd as they heard the news.* 2. that which gives joy or gladness. **Ex.** *His words of cheer brought relief to* *the anxious people.* —v. 1. greet with shouts or other sounds of approval. **Ex.** *The crowd cheered at the football game.* 2. make glad. **Ex.** *His friends cheered the sick man with visits.* —**cheer'ful,** *adj.* full of cheer. —**cheer'ful·ly,** *adv.* —**cheer up,** make or become happier. **Ex.** *His funny stories cheered us up.*

cheese (3) [čiyz'], *n.* a solid food made from the thick, soft substance that separates from milk when it becomes sour. **Ex.** *He ate bread and cheese for lunch.*

chemical (3) [kem'ikəl], *n.* a substance made by, or used in, the science of chemistry. —*adj.* concerned with chemistry. **Ex.** *For his term project he is studying the chemical structure of certain compounds.* —**chem'i·cal·ly,** *adv.*

chemistry (3) [kem'əstriy], *n.* the science in which substances are studied to discover what they are made of, how they act under different conditions and how they combine or separate to form other substances. **Ex.** *Plastics were developed through chemistry.* —**chem'ist,** *n.* a person who studies and works in the field of chemistry.

cherish (4) [čer'iš], *v.* 1. treat with love and tenderness. **Ex.** *He cherishes his wife.* 2. keep in mind. **Ex.** *She cherished the memory of her parents.*

cherry (3) [čer'iy], *n.* 1. a small, round edible fruit, usually red, that has a small pit at its center. **Ex.** *These cherries would make a delicious pie.* 2. the tree on which the fruit grows; a tree of the same family that does not bear edible fruit. **Ex.** *The cherries are in blossom now at the Tidal Basin in Washington, D.C.*

CHERRY

chest (2) [čest'], *n.* 1. the upper front part of the body within the ribs. **Ex.** *With your hand on your chest, you can feel your heart beating.* 2. a box, often large and strong, with a lid. **Ex.** *The carpenter took a hammer from his tool chest.*

chew (3) [čuw'], *v.* bite and crush with the teeth. **Ex.** *My dog likes to chew bones.* —**chew'ing gum,** *n.* a substance, flavored and sweetened, suitable for long chewing.

---

a, far; æ, am; e, get; ey, late; i, in; iy, see; ɔ, all; ow, go; u, put; uw, too; ə, but, ago; ər, fur; aw, out; ay, life; oy, boy; ŋ, ring; θ, think; ð, that; ž, measure; š, ship; j, edge; č, child.

chicken (2) [čǐk'ən], *n.* the common farm bird raised for its eggs and meat. **Ex.** *We are having fried chicken for dinner.*

CHICKEN

chief (1) [čǐyf'], *n.* the head or leader of a group of people. **Ex.** *The oldest man in the tribe was the chief.* —*adj.* 1. highest in rank or authority. **Ex.** *The chief clerk will see that the work is done.* 2. most important. **Ex.** *What are the chief points of this plan?* —**chief'ly,** *adv.* almost entirely. —**chief'tain,** *n.* a chief.

child (1) [čayld'], *n.* a baby; a young boy or girl. **Ex.** *The child is just learning to talk.* —**child'ish,** *adj.* like a child. **Ex.** *The man's behavior was childish.* —**child'ish·ness,** *n.*

childhood (1) [čayld'hud'], *n.* state or time of being a child. **Ex.** *She had a happy childhood.*

children (1) [čǐl'drən], *n.* plural of *child.* **Ex.** *All of her children are in school.*

chili [čǐl'iy], *n.* 1. a powdered spice, made from the pod of various pepper plants, that makes food taste hot. **Ex.** *This recipe calls for two tablespoons of chili.* 2. a dish of meat and usually dried beans seasoned with chili. **Ex.** *We are making chili for the picnic.*

chill (3) [čǐl'], *n.* feeling of coldness. **Ex.** *There is a chill in the air now that winter is approaching.* —*adj.* 1. rather cold. **Ex.** *A chill wind blew.* 2. without warmth of feeling. **Ex.** *He gave her a chill greeting.* —*v.* 1. cool; make cold. **Ex.** *Chill the wine before serving it.* 2. cause to feel a chill. **Ex.** *The thought of the battle chilled the soldier.* —**chill'y,** *adj.*

chimney (3) [čǐm'niy], *n.* an outlet for smoke from a stove or furnace, especially an outlet on the roof of a building. **Ex.** *The chimney of the factory produced clouds of smoke.*

chin (3) [čǐn'], *n.* the part of the face below the mouth; the point of the lower jaw. **Ex.** *Your chin moves when you speak.*

china [čay'nə], *n.* 1. dishes and decorative pieces made of earthenware, porcelain, etc. **Ex.** *Do you carry this pattern of china?* 2. porcelain. **Ex.** *This is the china we use when we have company.*

chip (4) [čǐp'], *n.* 1. a small piece broken or cut off something. **Ex.** *She swept up the chips from the broken cup.* 2. a place where a small piece has been broken off. **Ex.** *There is a chip on* *his front tooth.* —*v.* break off small pieces. **Ex.** *Be careful not to chip the dishes when you wash them.* —**chipped,** *adj.*

chirp (5) [čərp'], *v.* make a short, sharp sound, as small birds and some insects do. **Ex.** *As the sun rose, the birds began to chirp.* —*n.* a short, sharp sound.

chisel (5) [čiz'əl], *n.* a long, flat tool with a sharp edge used for cutting or shaping wood or stone. —*v.* cut with a chisel. **Ex.** *He chiseled a groove in the wood.*

CHISEL

chivalry (5) [šiv'əlriy], *n.* the ideal qualities of a gentleman, such as honor, generosity and bravery. **Ex.** *He was admired for his chivalry.* —**chiv'al·rous,** *adj.*

chocolate (3) [čɔk'lət], *n.* 1. a dark brown food substance made from the ground beans of a certain tree, often used in sweets and desserts. **Ex.** *Shall I use chocolate in the cake?* 2. candy made of chocolate. **Ex.** *He brought her a box of chocolates.* —*adj.* 1. anything made with chocolate. 2. a reddish-brown color.

choice (2) [čoys'], *n.* 1. act of selecting; the right to select. **Ex.** *The students had a choice of languages to study.* 2. thing or person selected. **Ex.** *She was his choice for the leading role.*

choir (5) [kwayr'], *n.* a group of trained singers, usually in a church. **Ex.** *Members of the choir are practicing for the holiday concert.*

choke (3) [čowk'], *v.* 1. cause to be unable to breathe by pressing the throat or by stopping the supply of air. **Ex.** *The murderer choked his victim.* 2. have difficulty breathing. **Ex.** *He was choking on a piece of meat.* 3. stop the growth of. **Ex.** *Weeds were choking the garden.* —**choke back,** hold back. **Ex.** *He choked back his tears and tried to smile.*

cholesterol [kəles'tərɔl], *n.* a substance occurring in the fatty tissues of animals. **Ex.** *We are watching our diets to see that we do not eat too much cholesterol.*

choose (1) [čuwz'], *v.* make a choice; select. **Ex.** *In a democracy, the people choose their leaders.*

chop (3) [čap'], *v.* 1. cut by striking with something sharp, as an ax. **Ex.** *He chopped down the tree.* 2. cut into small pieces. **Ex.** *She chopped the onions before browning them.* —*n.* 1. act of chopping. 2. a slice of meat with a piece of bone in it. **Ex.** *We had lamb chops for dinner.* —**chop'py,** *adj.* rough. **Ex.** *During the storm, the sea was choppy.*

chorus (4) [kɔr'əs], *n.* 1. a group of people singing together. 2. the part of the song repeated after each verse. **Ex.** *Everyone joined in singing the chorus.*

chose (2) [čowz'], *v.* past tense of *choose.* **Ex.** *The teacher chose two boys and two girls to represent the class.*

chosen (2) [čow'zən], *v.* past participle of *choose.* **Ex.** He was chosen to be the leader.

chronic (5) [kran'ik], *adj.* continuing for a long time. **Ex.** *She is suffering from a chronic illness.*

chuckle (5) [čək'əl], *v.* laugh quietly. **Ex.** *He chuckled at the amusing way things were happening.* —*n.* a soft, quiet laugh. **Ex.** *His chuckle was barely heard.*

church (1) [čərč'], *n.* a building for public worship. **Ex.** *That is the church we attend on Sunday.*

cigar (3) [sigar'], *n.* tightly packed roll of tobacco leaves for smoking.

cigarette (1) [sig'əret', sig'ərət'], *n.* finely cut tobacco in a long, thin paper tube for smoking.

cinder (5) [sin'dər], *n.* a partly burned piece of coal, wood, etc. that is not flaming. **Ex.** *The fire had reduced itself to cinders.*

circle (1) [sər'kəl], *n.* 1. a closed curve that has all of its points at an equal distance from its center. 2. a group of people having the same interests. **Ex.** *She has a wide circle of friends.* —*v.* surround; move around in a circle. **Ex.** *The group of dancers joined hands and circled the leader.*

CIRCLE 1

circuit (4) [sər'kət], *n.* 1. act of moving, or revolving around, as in a circle. **Ex.** *The moon makes a complete circuit around the earth in a little more than twenty-nine days.* 2. a regular movement from place to place, as a part of one's occupation. **Ex.** *The judge made his circuit from one court to another throughout his district.* 3. the path through which an electric current flows.

circular (4) [sərk'yələr], *adj.* round like a circle; of a circle. **Ex.** *He made a circular motion with his hand.* —*n.* a notice or letter written or printed for general distribution. **Ex.** *We received a circular advertising a new restaurant.*

circulate (5) [sərk'yəleyt'], *v.* 1. move in a circle or move around a path returning to the starting point. **Ex.** *The blood circu-*

lates through the body. 2. pass from place to place or person to person. **Ex.** *The story circulated quickly.* —**cir`cu·la'tion**, *n.*

circumference (5) [sərkəm'f(ə)rəns], *n.* the outside line of or distance around a circle or any curved area. **Ex.** *They walked around the circumference of the lake.*

circumstances (2) [sər'kəmstæns`ez], *n.* 1. the conditions, facts or events connected with another fact or event. **Ex.** *He explained the circumstances that caused him to be late.* 2. financial condition. **Ex.** *He lived in very comfortable circumstances.* —**cir`cum·stan'tial**, *adj.* having to do with the circumstances of a situation. **Ex.** *The circumstantial evidence against him was very convincing.*

circus (4) [sər'kəs], *n.* a traveling show of entertainment staged in a large, level space, often in a tent. **Ex.** *The children enjoyed seeing the trained animals at the circus.*

cite (5) [sayt'], *v.* 1. refer to as a proof, an example or an illustration of an argument. **Ex.** *To prove your statement you must cite your references.* 2. summon to appear before a court. **Ex.** *He was cited for drunken driving.* 3. give honorable mention to. **Ex.** *The soldier was cited for bravery.* —**ci·ta'tion**, *n.*

citizen (2) [sit'əzən], *n.* a member of a country or state by birth or by law. **Ex.** *A citizen of a country enjoys certain rights and has certain obligations to it.* —**cit'i·zen·ship`**, *n.* having the rights and duties of a citizen.

city (1) [sit'iy], *n.* any important, large town. **Ex.** *They are moving into the city.*

city hall [sit'iy hɔ:l'], *n.* the building in which a city government is located.

civil (3) [siv'əl], *adj.* 1. of or relating to citizens, their rights and affairs. **Ex.** *Exercising civil rights is important in a democracy.* 2. well-mannered; gentlemanly. **Ex.** *He received a civil answer to his question.* —**ci·vil'ian**, *n.* a person not in the military forces. —**civil service**, all parts of the national government except the military; the people, chosen on the basis of special examinations, who work in those parts of the government. —**civil war**, war within a country between groups of citizens.

a, far; æ, am; e, get; ey, late; i, in; iy, see; ɔ, all; ow, go; u, put; uw, too; ə, but, ago; ər, fur; aw, out; ay, life; oy, boy; ŋ, ring; θ, think; ð, that; ž, measure; š, ship; j, edge; č, child.

civilization (3) [siv'ələzey'šən], *n.* 1. culture and manner of living of a people, period or nation. **Ex.** *Modern civilization is strongly influenced by science.* 2. the relative progress in government, art, education, etc., that a nation or people has made. **Ex.** *The ancient Romans reached a high degree of civilization.* **—civ'i·lize,** *v.* bring to a higher state of culture.

claim (2) [kleym'], *v.* 1. ask for or demand something as belonging to one. **Ex.** *He claimed a share of the family property.* 2. state as fact. **Ex.** *She claimed that she was the best student in the class.* **—n.** 1. a demand for something that belongs to one. **Ex.** *He submitted a claim to his insurance company.* 2. a title or right to something. **Ex.** *He has no claim to special attention.* 3. something claimed, especially land. **Ex.** *The settler put a wooden marker at each corner of his claim.* **—claim'ant,** *n.* one who makes a claim.

clam (5) [klæm'], *n.* an animal from the sea enclosed in a hard double shell. **Ex.** *Some clams are good to eat, either raw or cooked.*

clamor (5) [klæm'ər], *n.* continual shouting and noise. **Ex.** *The speaker could hardly be heard above the clamor of the crowd.* **—v.** demand noisily. **Ex.** *The children clamored for candy.*

clamp [klæmp'], *n.* a device used to hold two or more things tightly together. **—v.** hold together with a clamp. **Ex.** *We clamped the corners of the picture frame together until the glue dried.*

clan (5) [klæn'], *n.* a group of families related by blood. **Ex.** *The people living in that valley are all members of one clan.* **—clan'nish,** *adj.* of a clan; staying together and keeping out or ignoring others. **Ex.** *The families in this village are very clannish.*

clang (5) [klæŋ'], *n.* a loud, ringing sound like that of a bell. **Ex.** *We heard the clang of the dinner bell.*

clap (4) [klæp'], *v.* 1. strike the hands together to show approval or enjoyment. **Ex.** *The audience clapped after the speech.* 2. put or place suddenly. **Ex.** *She clapped her hand over her mouth.* **—n.** 1. the striking of the hands together. 2. a loud noise. **Ex.** *A clap of thunder followed the lightning.*

clarify (5) [klær'əfay'], *v.* make or become clearer. **Ex.** *His answers to our questions helped to clarify the problem.* **—clar'i·fi·ca'tion,** *n.*

clarity [klær'ə·tiy], *n.* clearness. **Ex.** *She expressed her ideas with remarkable clarity.*

clash (4) [klæš'], *n.* 1. a loud, unpleasant noise, often of metal striking against metal. **Ex.** *A clash was heard as the cars crashed.* 2. opposition; conflict. **Ex.** *There is a clash of views about the election.* —*v.* 1. hit with a clash. 2. conflict. **Ex.** *Their opinions always clashed.*

clasp (3) [klæsp'], *n.* 1. a grasping of hands in a handshake; an embrace. **Ex.** *She gave him a firm handclasp.* 2. a hook or catch used to fasten two things together. **Ex.** *The clasp on her string of pearls is made of silver.* —*v.* hold tightly in the arms; hold hands tightly. **Ex.** *The dancers clasped hands and formed a circle.*

class (1) [klæs'], *n.* 1. a group of persons or things similar to one another. **Ex.** *He is a member of the professional class.* 2. a group of students taught together. **Ex.** *He and I were in the same English class.* 3. a division based on grade or quality. **Ex.** *Very few of the passengers are traveling first class.* —*v.* put in a group; classify. **Ex.** *They were classed as liberals.* —**class'room,** *n.* a room in which students are taught.

classic (4) [klæs'ik], *n.* a work, especially of music, literature, or art, of great excellence. **Ex.** *That book could become a classic.* —**clas'si·cal,** *adj.*

classified ad [klæs'əfayd æd'], *n.* an advertisement, usually short, placed in a special section of a newspaper by someone wanting to sell, buy, rent, etc. **Ex.** *He looked in the classified ads to see what jobs were available.*

classify (5) [klæs'əfay'], *v.* 1. arrange in classes or groups. **Ex.** *They classified the children according to age.* 2. declare information or mark documents confidential, secret, etc. **Ex.** *This document is classified SECRET.* —**clas'si·fi·ca'tion,** *n.*

clatter (5) [klæt'ər], *n.* crashing, clashing sounds. **Ex.** *The clatter of dishes was heard from the kitchen.* —*v.* move with or make a clatter. **Ex.** *The horse's shoes clattered on the stones.*

clause (5) [klɔːz'], *n.* 1. a part of a sentence that has a subject and verb of its own. **Ex.** *In the sentence, "I knew him when he was a boy," the clause, "when he was a boy," depends on the clause "I knew him."* See **A Brief Explanation of English Grammar.** 2. an article in a contract, law, etc. **Ex.** *The first clause in the law explained its purpose.*

claw (4) [klɔː'], *n.* a sharp, hooked nail on the foot of a bird or animal. **Ex.** *The cat scratched the chair with her claws.* —*v.* tear or scratch. **Ex.** *The lion clawed its trainer.*

clay (3) [kley'], *n.* a kind of stiff, muddy earth that hardens after drying. **Ex.** *Clay is used to make bricks.*

clean (1) [kliyn'], *adj.* free from dirt. **Ex.** *The windows were very clean.* —*v.* make free from dirt. **Ex.** *She cleaned the floor with soap and water.* —**clean'er,** *n.* a person or thing that cleans. —**clean'li·ness,** *n.* the state of being clean; regularly keeping clean. **Ex.** *His cleanliness made a good impression on the interviewer.*

cleanser [klen'zər], *n.* something special, such as a powder or liquid, used for removing dirt. **Ex.** *You will need to use cleanser on that dirty sink.* —**cleanse',** *v.* make clean or pure.

clear (1) [kli:r'], *adj.* 1. easily understood; plain. **Ex.** *His explanation was clear.* 2. bright; uncloudy, **Ex.** *The sky is clear today.* 3. free from doubt; certain. **Ex.** *It was a clear case of murder.* 4. free of anything that might block. **Ex.** *The road is clear.* —*v.* 1. remove persons or things; empty. **Ex.** *She is the one who clears the table after meals.* 2. prove or declare innocent. **Ex.** *The lawyer's defense cleared the accused man.* 3. become clear. **Ex.** *The weather will clear in the afternoon.* —**clear'ance,** *n.* the act of clearing; the result of being cleared. **Ex.** *they received clearance to start work.* —**clear'ness,** *n.* the state of being clear. —**clear'ly,** *adv.* —**clear'ing,** *n.* land where there are no trees. —**clear out,** make a cleared place. **Ex.** *He cleared out the room.* —**clear up,** 1. make clear or plain. **Ex.** *He cleared up the mystery.* 2. make neat. **Ex.** *He cleared up the room.*

clench (5) [klenč'], *v.* press closely together. **Ex.** *She clenched her teeth in pain.*

clergy (4) [klər'jiy], *n.* the men and women who are authorized by their religious group to serve as leaders. **Ex.** *She was studying to become a member of the clergy.* —**cler'i·cal,** *adj.* relating to the clergy.

clerk (3) [klərk'], *n.* an office worker who keeps records, writes letters, etc.; a person who keeps the records of a court, city council, etc.; a salesman or saleswoman in a store. **Ex.** *The file clerk put the papers in the cabinet.* —*v.* act as a clerk. **Ex.** *She clerks in a department store.* —**cler'i·cal,** *adj.* of or relating to clerks or their work.

clever (2) [klev'ər], *adj.* 1. quick-thinking; intelligent. **Ex.** *He was clever enough to solve the problem.* 2. skillful. **Ex.** *The ring had been made by a clever workman.* —**clev'er·ly,** *adv.* —**clev'er·ness,** *n.*

click (4) [klik'], *n.* a light, sharp sound like that of a key turning in a lock. **Ex.** *We heard the click of a woman's heels on the sidewalk.* —*v.* make or cause to click. **Ex.** *The lock clicked as I shut the door.*

client (4) [klay'ənt], *n.* one who employs the services of a professional person. **Ex.** *The lawyer advised her client that he should not make any statements without her approval.*

cliff (4) [klif'], *n.* high, steep rock. **Ex.** *He was hurt in a fall from a cliff.*

climate (2) [klay'mət], *n.* the general weather conditions of a place over a period of time. **Ex.** *The doctor advised a move to a warm, dry climate.* —**cli·mat'ic,** *adj.*

climax (5) [klay'mæks'], *n.* the strongest idea or event in a series; the point of most interest or excitement in a story. **Ex.** *The climax of the story occurred when the hero died.* —**cli·mac'tic,** *adj.*

climb (2) [klaym'], *v.* 1. go up or down something by using the feet and sometimes the hands. **Ex.** *To reach the roof he climbed a ladder.* 2. grow upward. **Ex.** *The vine climbed the wall.* —*n.* the act of going up or down. —**climb'er,** *n.* one who or that which climbs.

cling (4) [kliŋ'], *v.* stick to; hold tightly. **Ex.** *Mud is clinging to your shoes.*

clinic [klin'ik], *n.* a part of a hospital or a place connected with a hospital that offers medical treatment by specialists for patients who usually do not stay in the hospital overnight. **Ex.** *I'm going to the eye clinic to learn whether I need new glasses.*

clip (4) [klip'], *v.* cut short; cut off or out. **Ex.** *The barber clipped the boy's hair.* —**clipp'ers,** *n.* a tool for cutting or trimming. —**clip'ping,** *n.* that which is cut off or out.

clip (4) [klip'], *n.* a device used to fasten things together. **Ex.** *The papers were fastened together with a clip.* —*v.* fasten or clasp together.

cloak (5) [klowk'], *n.* 1. a long, loose outer garment, often without sleeves but covering the shoulders and arms. **Ex.** *She wore a black velvet cloak over her evening gown.* 2. that which hides or conceals like a cloak. **Ex.** *He used fine words*

as a cloak for his deceitful actions. —*v.* hide, conceal. **Ex.**
A heavy fog cloaked the city.

clock (1) [klak'], *n.* a device which measures and
shows time. —*v.* measure the time taken to
do something. **Ex.** *We clocked the horse as he
ran around the track.* —**clock'wise,** in the direction clock hands move.

CLOCK

clog [klag'], *v.* prevent passage; stop up, block.
Ex. *Too much grease caused the sink to clog.*

close (1) [klows'], *adj.* near in space or time. **Ex.** *The school is
close to my house.* 2. near in relationship. **Ex.** *We are close
friends.* 3. needing fresh air. **Ex.** *Open the window, please;
this room is very close.* 4. with little difference; almost even.
Ex. *The test results were very close.* —*adv.* in a position near
to. **Ex.** *We walked close to the wall.* —**close call,** *n.* something serious that almost happened but did not. **Ex.** *He had a
close call when the wall fell near him.* —**close'ly,** *adv.* with
attention. **Ex.** *The teacher watched the boy closely.*

close (1) [klowz'], *v.* 1. shut. **Ex.** *Close the door.* 2. come to an
end. **Ex.** *The program closed with the school song.* —*n.* the
end. **Ex.** *At the close of the meeting, everyone left quickly.*

closet (3) [klaz'ət], *n.* an enclosed space for storing things. **Ex.**
He kept all his clothes in one closet.

cloth (1) [klɔ:θ'], *n.* material made from the threads of cotton,
wool, silk, etc. **Ex.** *She bought cloth for a dress.*

clothe (2) [klowŏ'], *v.* provide with clothes. **Ex.** *The Red Cross
helped to clothe the flood victims.*

clothes (1) [klowz', klowŏz'], *n., pl.* garments for the body such
as suits, coats, etc. **Ex.** *Pack your clothes in this suitcase.*
—**cloth'ing,** *n.* garments of any type. **Ex.** *He needs some new
winter clothing.*

cloud (1) [klawd'], *n.* 1. a mass of tiny drops of water floating
in the air. **Ex.** *The sun is hidden by a cloud.* 2. mass of steam,
smoke or dust. **Ex.** *A cloud of dust arose as the horseman
passed.* —*v.* fill with clouds. **Ex.** *The sky is clouding over.*
—**cloud'y,** *adj.* —**cloud'i·ness,** *n.*

clover (5) [klow'vər], *n.* small, low-growing plant almost always
having three leaves. **Ex.** *The cows like to eat clover.*

clown [klawn'], *n.* a person who entertains by telling jokes, performing tricks and often dressing in a funny costume. **Ex.**

The children always enjoy the clowns in the circus. —*v.* act like a clown. **Ex.** *This a serious matter; please do not clown around.*

club (2) [kləb'], *n.* 1. a group of persons associated for a common purpose. **Ex.** *She belongs to the garden club.* 2. a heavy wooden stick: a weapon. **Ex.** *The policeman swung his club as he walked.* —*v.* beat with a club.

clue (5) [kluw'], *n.* anything that leads to the solution of a problem or a mystery. **Ex.** *The police have found several clues.*

clumsy (4) [kləm'ziy], *adj.* awkward; without grace. **Ex.** *The boy was a clumsy dancer.* —**clum'si·ly,** *adv.* —**clum'si·ness,** *n.*

clung [kləŋ], *v.* past tense and past participle of *cling.* **Exs.** *She clung to the railing to keep from falling. He has always clung to his old-fashioned ways.*

cluster (4) [kləs'tər], *n.* similar things growing or grouped together. **Ex.** *A cluster of men and women waited at the door.* —*v.* gather together. **Ex.** *They clustered around the fire.*

clutch (4) [kləč'], *v.* 1. seize or grip tightly. **Ex.** *He clutched the knife.* 2. try to reach and grasp. **Ex.** *She clutched at the railing as she fell.* —**clutch'es,** *n.,pl.* control or power. **Ex.** *The man was in the clutches of a moneylender.*

co- (3) [kow], *prefix.* 1. together with; at the same time. **Ex.** *He is a co-worker.* 2. equal. **Ex.** *He is a co-owner of the house.*

coach (3) [kowč'], *n.* 1. a railroad passenger car. **Ex.** *The coach was so crowded that many people were standing.* 2. a large, closed carriage, usually pulled by horses. **Ex.** *The queen came to the ceremony in a coach.* 3. a teacher of sports. **Ex.** *We have a new coach for the football team this year.* —*v.* teach; train. **Ex.** *His father coached him in English.*

coal (2) [kowl'], *n.* 1. a black, hard substance that burns and gives off heat. **Ex.** *This house used to be heated with coal.* 2. a piece of burning substance. **Ex.** *A coal fell from the stove and burned the rug.*

coarse (3) [kɔrs'], *adj.* 1. in relatively large pieces; not fine. **Ex.** *The path was covered with coarse sand.* 2. rough to the touch. **Ex.** *Her dress was made of coarse wool.* 3. lacking good manners; indelicate. **Ex.** *His conversation was coarse.* —**coars'en,** *v.* make coarse; become coarse. **Ex.** *Hard work had coarsened her hands.*

coast (2) [kowst'], *n.* the seashore; the land next to the sea. **Ex.** *His house is on the coast.* —*v.* 1. slide or glide down a hill. **Ex.** *The children coasted down the snowy slope.* 2. move along without effort. **Ex.** *If you continue to coast along, you will fail this course.* —**coast'al,** *adj.* near the seashore.

coat (1) [kowt'], *n.* 1. an outer garment with sleeves. **Ex.** *He wore a long black coat.* 2. the hair or fur of an animal. **Ex.** *The dog's coat was dirty.* 3. a covering or outside layer. **Ex.** *The house needs a coat of paint.* —*v.* cover with something. **Ex.** *The table is coated with dust.*

coax (4) [kowks'], *v.* ask gently and repeatedly for something. **Ex.** *The children coaxed their parents to let them play outside.* —**coax'ing,** *adj.* —**coax'ing·ly,** *adv.*

cocaine [kow'keyn], *n.* a narcotic drug that is illegal except for medical use. **Ex.** *He died from an overdose of cocaine.*

cock (5) [kak'], *n.* the male of various birds, especially of chickens. **Ex.** *The cock crowed at dawn.* —*v.* tilt to one side. **Ex.** *His hat was cocked over one eye.*

cockpit [kak'pit], *n.* in a small plane, the place where the pilot and sometimes passengers sit; in a large plane, the place where the pilot, copilot and sometimes others sit.

cockroach [kak'rowč], *n.* a large oval-shaped brown or black insect with long feelers that is a common household pest. **Ex.** *Although we keep our house clean, we set out traps for cockroaches.*

cocktail [kak'teyl], *n.* a mixed drink usually made with liquor.

cocoa (5) [kow'kow`], *n.* 1. a powder made from the ground beans of a South American tropical tree and having a chocolate flavor. 2. a hot drink made by mixing this powder with milk, water and sugar. **Ex.** *Would you like some cocoa before you go to bed?*

coconut [kow'kənət`], *n.* a large brown palm nut with an edible sweet white flesh, the hollow center of which is filled with a drinkable milklike liquid. **Ex.** *She frosted the cake and then scattered shredded coconut on top.*

code (4) [kowd'], *n.* 1. any system of laws or rules. **Ex.** *The city building code limits the height of new buildings.* 2. a system of signals for sending messages. **Ex.** *The sailors used flags to send a message in code.* 3. a system of words used to send secret messages. —*v.* put into the symbols of a code.

coffee (2) [kɔ:f'iy], *n.* a drink made from the roasted seeds of a certain tree that have been crushed into fine pieces. **Ex.** *He likes to drink hot coffee.*

coffin (5) [kɔ:f'ən], *n.* a box in which a dead person is buried. **Ex.** *They lowered the coffin into the grave.*

coil (4) [koyl'], *v.* wind in the shape of circles. **Ex.** *The snake coiled itself around the man's arm.* —*n.* a circle, or series of circles, made by winding something around and around. **Ex.** *The sailor made a coil of rope.*

COIL

coin (2) [koyn'], *n.* a piece of metal marked and issued by a government authority for use as money. **Ex.** *She took several coins from her purse.* —**coin'age,** *n.* act of making coins.

coincide (5) [kow'insayd'], *v.* 1. correspond exactly; agree. **Ex.** *Their stories of what happened coincide.* 2. occur at the same time or occupy the same place. **Ex.** *His arrival and my departure coincided.* —**co·in'ci·dence,** *n.* a chance occurrence of two or more events at the same time. —**co·in'ci·den'tal,** *adj.*

cold (1) [kowld'], *adj.* 1. low in temperature; not warm. **Ex.** *Winter nights here are often cold.* 2. experiencing a feeling of cold. **Ex.** *He was cold without his coat.* 3. unemotional; unfriendly. **Ex.** *He is a cold person.* —*n.* 1. low temperature; lack of heat. **Ex.** *She suffered from the cold.* 2. a common illness that affects the throat and nose. **Ex.** *How did you catch cold?* —**cold'ly,** *adv.* —**cold'ness,** *n.*

cold-blooded [kowld'bləd'əd], *adj.* lacking in feeling or warmth. **Ex.** *He is a cold-blooded killer.*

cold war [kowld' wɔ:r'], *n.* strong differences between two countries that lead to a strained political relationship without actual war. **Ex.** *The cold war was damaging to both countries.*

coleslaw [kowl'slɔ:], *n.* a salad of raw cabbage, thinly sliced or finely chopped and mixed with oil and vinegar or mayonnaise and salt and pepper. **Ex.** *Who is going to make the coleslaw for the picnic?*

collapse (4) [kəlæps'], *v.* 1. fall to pieces; fall down. **Ex.** *The roof of the house collapsed.* 2. fold into a smaller space. **Ex.** *He collapsed the umbrella when the rain stopped.* —*n.* act of collapsing; failure. **Ex.** *The collapse of the company ruined him.* —**col·laps'i·ble,** *adj.*

collar (3) [kal'ər], *n.* 1. the part of a shirt, coat, etc. that is around the neck. **Ex.** *He buttoned his collar.* 2. a leather neckpiece worn by some animals such as a dog, horse, etc. **Ex.** *He tied a rope to the dog's collar.*

colleague (5) [kal'iyg`], *n.* an associate in office or professional work. **Ex.** *His colleagues gave him a gift when he retired.*

collect (2) [kəlekt'], *v.* 1. gather together and take away. **Ex.** *The teacher always collects the homework.* 2. demand and obtain payment of. **Ex.** *Income taxes are collected yearly.* 3. come together. **Ex.** *The people collected in the marketplace.* 4. bring objects together for pleasure or study. **Ex.** *He collects old coins.* —**col·lec'tion,** *n.* the things collected. —**col·lec'tor,** *n.* a person who collects. —**col·lec'tive,** *adj.* as a group. **Ex.** *We made a collective effort to finish the work.* —**col·lec'tive·ly,** *adv.*

college (1) [kal'ij], *n.* an educational institution beyond high school, often one of several schools forming a university. **Ex.** *He went to high school but not to college.* —**col·le'gi·an,** *n.* a college student. —**col·le'gi·ate,** *adj.*

collide [kə'layd], *v.* hit against someone or something with force. **Ex.** *She was severely injured when her car collided with the telephone pole.* —**col·li'sion,** *n.*

colonel (3) [kər'nəl], *n.* an army officer above the rank of major and below the rank of general. **Ex.** *While the colonel was away, the major was in charge of the men.*

colony (2) [kal'əniy], *n.* 1. a group of people who form a settlement in a new land but remain under the rule of their native country. **Ex.** *In 1607, the English established a colony in North America.* 2. a group of people in the same occupation or with the same interests. **Ex.** *There is a colony of artists near the seashore.* 3. a group of animals, plants, etc. living in one place. —**col'o·nist,** *n.* —**col'o·nize,** *v.* —**co·lo'ni·al,** *adj.*

color (1) [kəl'ər], *n.* 1. the effect of light on the eye. **Ex.** *Everything we see has color.* 2. appearance; look. **Ex.** *He had a healthy color after his vacation.* 3. coloring matter; paint. **Ex.** *You have a pleasing color on your walls.* —*v.* put color on; print. **Ex.** *The child was coloring a picture book.* —**col'or·ed,** *adj.* having color.

color-blind [kəl'ərblaynd'], *adj.* not able to see color or certain colors.

colossal (5) [kəlas'əl], *adj.* huge; enormous. **Ex.** *There are colossal mountains in the north.*

colt (4) [kowlt'], *n.* a young horse. **Ex.** *The colt followed its mother.*

column (3) [kal'əm], *n.* 1. an upright support or decoration for a building. 2. anything suggesting an upright support. **Ex.** *A column of smoke rose from the camp fire.* 3. a line of soldiers or ships, one behind another. **Ex.** *A column of soldiers marched down the street.* 4. the printed sections of a page of a book, newspaper or magazine. **Ex.** *That article is continued on page nine, column one.* 5. articles appearing regularly in a newspaper, magazine, etc., usually by the same author. **Ex.** *That writer has an interesting daily column.* —**col'um·nist,** *n.* one who writes a column for a newspaper, magazine, etc.

COLUMN 1

comb (2) [kowm'], *n.* an instrument used for smoothing and arranging the hair. —*v.* arrange the hair with a comb. **Ex.** *The girl combed her hair.*

COMB

combat (4) [kambæt'], *v.* fight; struggle; oppose. **Ex.** *Both candidates for mayor promise to combat crime.* —**com'bat,** *n.* a battle. **Ex.** *The soldier was wounded in combat.* —**com·bat'ant,** *n.* one who fights.

combine (2) [kəmbayn'], *v.* mix; bring together. **Ex.** *The color blue can be combined with yellow to make green.* —**com'bi·na'tion,** *n.* something made by mixing two or more things together.

come (1) [kəm'], *v.* 1. move toward; approach. **Ex.** *Come here.* 2. arrive. **Ex.** *When did you come to this town?* 3. take or have its place in a series. **Ex.** *Six comes after five.* 4. be related to. **Ex.** *Jack comes from a good family.* 5. be caused by; the result of. **Ex.** *Success often comes from hard work.* 6. is available. **Ex.** *This hat comes in three colors.* 7. extend; reach. **Ex.** *Her dress comes to her ankles.* —**come about,** happen. **Ex.** *How did it come about?* —**come over,** happen to. **Ex.** *What has come over you?* —**come to,** become conscious. **Ex.** *The water helped him to come to.* —**come up,** be mentioned. **Ex.** *When did the matter come up?*

comedy (4) [kam'ədiy], *n.* a light and amusing play or movie with a happy ending. —**co·me'di·an,** *n.* 1. an actor in a comedy. 2. a performer who amuses people by doing or saying funny things.

comet (5) [kam'ət], *n.* a bright body seen in the sky, usually with a tail of light. **Ex.** *Comets move around the sun.*

comfort (2) [kəm'fərt], *v.* cheer; give strength and hope. **Ex.** *The mother comforted her crying child.* —*n.* 1. consolation. **Ex.** *Her children were a great comfort to the widow.* 2. freedom from pain or worries. **Ex.** *She lived in comfort with her parents.* —**com'fort·a·ble,** *adj.*

comic [kam'ik], *adj.* funny; amusing; causing laughter. **Ex.** *Although it was a serious play, there were some comic moments.* —*n.* a person who amuses people; a comedian. **Ex.** *Your friend is quite a comic.* —**com'ics, com'ic strip,** *n.* a series of drawings that relate a story or an incident, usually with the words spoken by the characters shown as coming from their mouths. **Ex.** *What is your favorite comic strip?*

command (2) [kəmænd'], *v.* 1. order. **Ex.** *He commanded the soldiers to fire.* 2. have authority over. **Ex.** *That officer commands a ship.* —*n.* 1. order; direction. **Ex.** *The soldiers obeyed the command.* 2. control. **Ex.** *He is in command of the situation.* —**com·mand'ment,** *n.* a law.

commander [kəmæn'dər], *n.* an officer in the U.S. navy above the rank of lieutenant and below the rank of captain. **Ex.** *The sailors saluted the commander.*

commence (4) [kəmens'], *v.* start; begin. **Ex.** *The school day commences with physical exercises.* —**com·mence'ment,** *n.* 1. a beginning. 2. the ceremony at which a school or college gives degrees.

commend (5) [kəmend'], *v.* praise. **Ex.** *The student was commended for his good work.* —**com·mend'a·ble,** *adj.* —**com'men·da'tion,** *n.*

comment (3) [ka'ment'], *n.* words, spoken or written, that explain or express an opinion. **Ex.** *His comments about the book were favorable.* —*v.* make remarks. **Ex.** *Everyone commented on her new dress.* —**com'men·ta'tor,** *n.* one who comments. **Ex.** *Which news commentator do you prefer?*

commerce (3) [ka'mərs], *n.* trade; buying and selling, especially on a large scale and between different places. **Ex.** *He is engaged in commerce.* —**com·mer'cial,** *adj.* —*n.* an advertisement on radio or television. **Ex.** *There are so many commercials that it is hard to follow this program.* —**com·mer'cial ·ize,** *v.*

commission (3) [kəmiš'ən], *n.* 1. a group of individuals entrusted with certain business or public duties. **Ex.** *He was appointed to the commission studying health problems.* 2. the authority by which one holds or acts in a position of responsibility. **Ex.** *He has received a commission as a naval officer.* 3. money paid to the person who sells an item, usually a percentage of the sales price. **Ex.** *We paid a 6 percent commission to the company that sold our house for us.* —*v.* give a commission; appoint to do. **Ex.** *The artist was commissioned to paint a picture of the building.*

commissioner (3) [kəmiš'ənər], *n.* the chief of a government department of public service. **Ex.** *The commissioner of education was once a schoolteacher.*

commit (3) [kəmit'], *v.* 1. give in trust; place in the charge of. **Ex.** *The boy was committed to the care of his aunt.* 2. do something bad. **Ex.** *He committed a robbery.* —**com·mit'ment,** *n.* a promise; pledge.

committee (2) [kəmit'iy], *n.* a group of people appointed to do a certain thing. **Ex.** *A committee was formed to plan the new school.*

commodity (4) [kəmad'ətiy], *n.* a thing that is useful or of value, especially an article of commerce or trade. **Ex.** *What agricultural commodities are doing well on the market today?*

common (2) [kam'ən], *adj.* 1. shared by all of a group. **Ex.** *Our common interest in art brought us together.* 2. often found or experienced. **Ex.** *These white flowers are very common.* 3. ordinary; not special. **Ex.** *The package was wrapped in common brown paper.* —**com'mon·ly,** *adv.* —**commonplace,** *adj.* usual; frequent; ordinary. —**common sense,** *n.* practical intelligence.

commotion [kə·mow'šən], *n.* very noisy confusion; disturbance. **Ex.** *What is causing the commotion outside?*

---

a, far; æ, am; e, get; ey, late; i, in; iy, see; ɔ, all; ow, go; u, put; uw, too; ə, but, ago; ər, fur; aw, out; ay, life; oy, boy; ŋ, ring; θ, think; ð, that; ž, measure; š, ship; j, edge; č, child.

communicate (3) [kəmyuwn'əkeyt`], v. 1. make known; give information. **Ex.** *Radio, television and newspapers quickly communicate news to all parts of the world.* 2. pass from one person to another. **Ex.** *How is this disease communicated?* —**com·mu·ni·ca·ble,** *adj.* readily passed to others. **Ex.** *A cold is a very communicable disease.*

communication (3) [kəmyuwn`əkey'šən], n. 1. exchange of information, ideas, etc. **Ex.** *Communication can be difficult when people do not speak the same language.* 2. the news, message or information sent. **Ex.** *We received your communication.* —**com·mu·ni·ca'tions,** *n.* the various means or ways of communicating. **Ex.** *Communications were interrupted by the storm.*

communism (4) [kam'yəniz`əm], n. a system and program of common ownership of the means for producing goods and services and of governmental control of economic and political activities. **Ex.** *Communism was the system practiced in the former Soviet Union.* —**com'mu·nist,** *n.* one who believes in communism. —**com'mu·nist, com`mu·nis'tic,** *adj.*

community (2) [kəmyuwn'ətiy], n. a group of people living in a particular city, town, etc. **Ex.** *Our community has its own library.*

commute [kə'myuwt], v. travel regularly a long way back and forth between one's home and one's place of work. **Ex.** *Because he commutes to work, he has to start out early in the morning.*

compact (4) [kəmpækt', kam'pækt`], adj. 1. packed tightly together. **Ex.** *The saleswoman tied the customer's purchases into a compact bundle.* 2. brief; without unnecessary words. **Ex.** *His report was clear and compact.* —*n.* a small, flat, usually metal container with a mirror in the lid, for face powder.

companion (2) [kəmpæn'yən], n. a person who goes with another; a friend; an associate. **Ex.** *They were companions on the journey.* —**com·pan'ion·ship,** *n.* friendship.

company (1) [kəm'pəniy], n. 1. a business. **Ex.** *He is the president of a manufacturing company.* 2. the state or condition of being companions. **Ex.** *The boy was good company on the long trip.* 3. any number of guests. **Ex.** *What time is the company coming?*

compare (2) [kəmpe:r'], v. 1. examine similarities or differences. **Ex.** *She compared the ideas to see if they agreed.* 2. consider or describe as the same or equal to. **Ex.** *The quality* *of these two coats can be compared.* —**com·pa·ra·ble,** *adj.* of approximately the same kind; equal to. **Ex.** *This metal is comparable to iron in strength.* —**com·par'a·tive,** *adj.* relative; nearly the same. **Ex.** *After many hardships, he now lives in comparative ease.* —**com·par'i·son,** *n.* an examination to learn similarities or differences. **Ex.** *A comparison was made between the two machines to learn which would be more effective.*

compass (3) [kəm'pəs], *n.* 1. an instrument for determining directions, having a needle which always points north. 2. an instrument for drawing circles and for measuring distances.

COMPASS 2

compel (2) [kəmpel'], *v.* force. **Ex.** *My sense of duty compels me to do this.*

compensate (4) [kam'pənseyt'], *v.* 1. repay; substitute for. **Ex.** *Nothing can compensate them for the loss of their children.* 2. pay. **Ex.** *We will compensate you for your work.* —**com'pen·sa' tion,** *n.*

compete (3) [kəmpiyt'], *v.* be in rivalry for. **Ex.** *Three men competed for the prize.* —**com'pe·ti'tion,** *n.* the act of competing for. —**com·pet'i·tor,** *n.* one who competes. —**com·pet'i·tive,** *adj.*

competence (3) [kam'pətəns], *n.* ability. **Ex.** *Her competence as a teacher is known to everyone at the school.* —**com'pe·tent** *adj.* capable; skillful. **Ex.** *He is a very competent doctor.* —**com'pe·tent·ly,** *adv.*

complain (2) [kəmpleyn'], *v.* 1. express pain, dissatisfaction, annoyance, etc. **Ex.** *She complained about having to work late.* 2. report a wrong. **Ex.** *He complained to the police about the noise in his neighborhood.* —**com·plaint',** *n.* —**com·plain' ant,** *n.* one who makes a complaint, as in court.

complete (1) [kəmpliyt'], *adj.* 1. whole; full. **Ex.** *We bought a complete set of dishes.* 2. ended or finished. **Ex.** *The book is not complete yet.* 3. perfect. **Ex.** *We have complete trust in you.* —*v.* finish; bring to an end. **Ex.** *They completed the journey.* —**com·plete'ly,** *adv.* —**com·plete'ness, com·ple'tion,** *n.*

complex (3) [kəmpleks', kam'pleks`], *adj.* made of many parts that are difficult to understand; not simple; complicated. **Ex.** *The engine of an airplane is very complex.* —**com·plex'i·ty,** *n.*

complexion (5) [kəmplek'šən], *n.* 1. appearance and color of the skin, in particular of the face. **Ex.** *He has a healthy complex-*

ion. 2. general appearance; nature. **Ex.** *Machines have changed the complexion of modern life.*

complicate (3) [kam'pləkeyt'], *v.* make or become complex or difficult. **Ex.** *The birth of a son delighted them but also complicated their lives.* **—com'pli·ca'tion,** *n.* **com'pli·cat'ed,** *adj.*

compliment (4) [kam'pləmənt], *n.* an expression of praise or admiration. **Ex.** *The girl enjoyed the compliment.* **—v.** praise or express approval. **Ex.** *He complimented her on her voice.* **—com'pli·men'tary,** *adj.* 1. praising or admiring. 2. without charge; free. **Ex.** *I was just given some complimentary tickets to tonight's concert.*

compose (3) [kəmpowz'], *v.* 1. combine to form. **Ex.** *This substance is composed of many chemicals.* 2. calm oneself. **Ex.** *He composed himself after the accident.* 3. write; create. **Ex.** *She composes beautiful music.* **—com·pos'er,** *n.* the one who composes. **—com'po·si'tion,** *n.* that which is composed, especially a piece of writing or music.

compound (3) [kam'pawnd'], *n.* 1. a mixture; anything made of two or more parts. 2. a chemical substance of two or more elements. **Ex.** *Salt is a compound of two chemical elements.* **—adj.** made of two parts or more. **Ex.** *"Horseback" is a compound word.* **—v.** combine; make up; added to. **Ex.** *His problems were compounded by the cold weather.*

comprehend (5) [kam'prihend'], *v.* understand. **Ex.** *She cannot comprehend the problem.* **—com'pre·hen'si·ble,** *adj.* capable of being understood. **Ex.** *This poem is not comprehensible to me.* **—com'pre·hen'sive,** *adj.* complete; including much. **Ex.** *He gave a comprehensive description of the criminal.* **—com' pre·hen'sion,** *n.*

compress (5) [kəmpres'], *v.* press into a small size. **Ex.** *The clay was compressed into bricks.* **—com·pres'sion,** *n.* **—com·pres' sor,** *n.*

compromise (4) [kam'prəmayz'], *n.* the settlement of an argument by each side yielding some of what it wants. **Ex.** *The disagreement about the boundary between the two countries was settled by compromise.* **—v.** resolve by compromise.

compute (5) [kəmpyuwt'], *v.* determine by mathematics. **Ex.** *He is computing his yearly taxes.* **—com·pu'ter,** *n.* 1. a person who determines an amount by using mathematics. 2. a machine which performs mathematical and other operations, especially by electricity and at a high speed. **Ex.** *He used a computer to write his report.* **—com·put'er·ize,** *v.* place a computer or computers in position for use in managing an operation, department, company, etc. **Ex.** *The records at the hospital were computerized two years ago.*

comrade (3) [kam'ræd`], *n.* companion; good friend. **Ex.** *They were comrades at school.*

conceal (3) [kənsiyl'], *v.* 1. hide. **Ex.** *He concealed himself behind a large tree.* 2. keep secret. **Ex.** *There was no way that he could conceal what had happened.* **—con·ceal'ment,** *n.*

concede (5) [kənsiyd'], *v.* 1. admit as true or just in a dispute. **Ex.** *We concede your rights to this property.* 2. yield. **Ex.** *The employer conceded to the workers' demand for more pay.*

conceit (5) [kənsiyt'], *n.* flattering judgment of oneself. **Ex.** *Her conceit about her beauty annoyed many people.* **—con·ceit'ed,** *adj.*

conceive (3) [kənsiyv'], *v.* 1. invent; think of and develop an idea. **Ex.** *The author conceived a plan for a novel in four parts.* 2. understand. **Ex.** *I cannot conceive how he did such a foolish thing.* 3. become pregnant. **—con·ceiv'a·ble,** *adj.*

concentrate (4) [kan'səntreyt`], *v.* 1. give one's whole attention to. **Ex.** *You must concentrate on your work.* 2. gather together closely. **Ex.** *The business area of that town is concentrated in about six square blocks.* **—n.** a substance which has been made thicker and stronger by removing some of the water from it. **Ex.** *She bought three cans of grape juice concentrate.* **—con`cen·tra'tion,** *n.* deep thought and close attention.

concept (4) [kan'sept`], *n.* a notion; an idea. **Ex.** *The judge had a clear concept of justice.* **—con·cep'tion,** *n.* 1. the act of conceiving an idea. **Ex.** *His conception of what the building should look like was entirely different from mine.* 2. an idea concerning. **Ex.** *He has no conception of what it is like to be a doctor.* 3. the beginning of pregnancy.

concern (2) [kənsərn'], *v.* 1. relate to; interest. **Ex.** *The election of officials should concern every citizen.* 2. trouble; worry. **Ex.** *Their son's difficulties in school concerned them greatly.*

—*n.* 1. matter or affair of importance to one. **Ex.** *The situation is of great concern to me.* 2. anxiety; great care. **Ex.** *She expressed concern for their safety.* 3. a business firm. **Ex.** *From what concern do you usually buy farm equipment?* —**con·cer'ning,** *prep.* regarding; about.

concert (3) [kan'sərt], *n.* a musical performance. **Ex.** *We are going to a piano concert tonight.*

concerted (3) [kənsərt'ed], *adj.* agreed upon; acting together; combined. **Ex.** *They made a concerted effort to win.*

concession (5) [kənseš'ən], *n.* the act of yielding or admitting as true. **Ex.** *To reach an agreement, you and I both must make concessions.*

conclude (2) [kənkluwd'], *v.* 1. finish; end. **Ex.** *The president concluded the meeting with an announcement.* 2. arrange; settle; reach an agreement. **Ex.** *The two countries concluded an economic agreement.* 3. decide. **Ex.** *He concluded that they had gone.*

conclusion (3) [kənkluw'žən], *n.* 1. the end; the final part. **Ex.** *At the conclusion of the talk, we asked the speaker questions.* 2. a reasoned judgment. **Ex.** *He thought about the problem carefully before reaching a conclusion.* —**con·clu·sive,** *adj.* answering doubts and questions; convincing; final. **Ex.** *The evidence against him was conclusive.*

concrete (4) [kan'kriyt'], *n.* building material made by mixing crushed stone, cement and water. **Ex.** *The workmen poured the concrete for the road.* —*adj.* 1. real; specific. **Ex.** *The professor supported each statement with a concrete example.* 2. made of concrete.

condemn (3) [kəndem'], *v.* 1. say a person or thing is bad. **Ex.** *Do not condemn me just because I do not agree with you.* 2. judge guilty; sentence. **Ex.** *The judge condemned the man to ten years in prison.* 3. declare not suitable or fit for use. **Ex.** *The building was condemned as too dangerous to occupy.* —**con'dem·na'tion,** *n.*

condense (3) [kəndens'], *v.* 1. reduce to fewer words. **Ex.** *Can you condense your report into two pages?* 2. concentrate; make more compact. **Ex.** *They condensed the work of three days into two.* 3. reduce from a gas or vapor to a liquid. **Ex.** *The cold condensed the steam into water.* —**con'den·sa'tion,** *n.*

condition (1) [kəndiš'ən], *n.* 1. state of a person or thing. **Ex.** *The road was in good condition.* 2. state of affairs or circumstances. **Ex.** *Economic conditions are not favorable just now.* —*v.* put into order or good condition for use. **Ex.** *Please condition the car for a long trip.* —**on condition that,** provided that. **Ex.** *You may go on condition that you finish your homework first.*

condominium [kan'dəmin'iyəm], *n.* a unit, such as an apartment, a house or an office in an apartment building, a development or an office building, individually owned together with a share of the common property, such as the halls, grounds, etc. **Ex.** *He preferred to buy a condominium rather than pay rent for an apartment.*

conduct (2) [kan'dəkt'], *n.* the way one acts; behavior. **Ex.** *Her conduct in school was poor.* —**con·duct'**, *v.* 1. behave; act. **Ex.** *He conducted himself with dignity.* 2. guide; lead. **Ex.** *The teacher conducted his students through the museum.* 3. manage; direct. **Ex.** *He conducted the meeting well.* 4. serve as a channel for heat, electricity, etc. **Ex.** *Pipes conducted heat through the building.* —**con·duc'tor**, *n.* 1. leader of an orchestra, chorus, band, etc. 2. person who collects fares on a train or streetcar. 3. something through which heat or electricity will pass.

cone (5) [kown'], *n.* 1. a form that narrows from a circular base to a point. 2. anything cone shaped. **Ex.** *The children wanted ice cream cones.* 3. the cone-shaped fruit of the pine tree and some other trees. **Ex.** *They made a beautiful wreath of pine cones.*

CONE 1

confer (3) [kənfə:r'], *v.* 1. grant; give. **Ex.** *The university conferred a high honor upon the scientist.* 2. exchange opinions; meet to consult or discuss. **Ex.** *The principal conferred with the teachers.* —**con'fer·ence**, *n.* a meeting for discussion purposes. **Ex.** *The president met with newsmen for a conference.*

confess (3) [kənfes'], *v.* 1. admit a crime or tell one's faults. **Ex.** *He confessed that he had stolen the money.* 2. admit what one really thinks. **Ex.** *I confess I do not like this city.* —**con·fes'sion**, *n.* 1. act of confessing. 2. a statement, especially written, of something confessed.

confide (5) [kənfayd'], *v.* 1. tell in trust. **Ex.** *He confided the whole story to his wife.* 2. entrust or commit to. **Ex.** *He confided the child to his mother's care.*

confidence (2) [kan'fədəns], *n.* 1. complete trust. **Ex.** *She has confidence in her daughter.* 2. self-reliance; a belief in one's own ability. **Ex.** *She has confidence in herself.* —**con'fi·dent**, *adj.* sure; certain. **Ex.** *He is confident that he will succeed.* —**con'fi·den'tial**, *adj.* secret. **Ex.** *The contents of that letter are confidential.* —**in confidence**, in secret. **Ex.** *I told him that in confidence.*

confine (3) [kənfayn'], *v.* 1. keep within limits. **Ex.** *Confine yourself to the facts when you tell the story.* 2. hold against one's will, such as in a prison. **Ex.** *He will be confined for ten years.* —**con·fine'ment**, *n.*

confirm (3) [kənfərm'], *v.* 1. strengthen; make sure. **Ex.** *The new facts confirmed his opinion.* 2. assure the truth of. **Ex.** *He would not confirm the report.* —**con·firmed'**, *adj.* established in one's habits. **Ex.** *He was a confirmed smoker.* —**con'fir·ma'tion**, *n.*

confiscate [kan'fiskeyt'], *v.* seize something officially without paying for it. **Ex.** *The police confiscated the robber's gun.*

conflict (3) [kənflikt'], *v.* be in opposition to. **Ex.** *His ideas conflict with mine.* —[kan'flikt], *n.* 1. a fight; a battle, especially a long one. **Ex.** *The conflict had completely destroyed the countryside.* 2. a sharp contest of opposing opinions or ideas. **Ex.** *The conflict was over who should lead the people.*

conform (5) [kənfɔrm'], *v.* 1. obey. **Ex.** *A citizen is expected to conform to the laws of his country.* 2. become or make similar; agree. **Ex.** *Children like to conform to the customs of their group.* —**con·form'i·ty**, *n.*

confront [kənfrənt'], *v.* 1. meet; come face to face with. **Ex.** *Still another task confronted her.* 2. face with hostility, boldness or threats. **Ex.** *The bully confronted him on the playground.* —**con'fron·ta'tion**, *n.*

confuse (3) [kənfyuwz'], *v.* 1. produce a mental condition in which one is unable to decide or act. **Ex.** *The complicated directions confused me.* 2. mistake one person or thing for another. **Ex.** *He confused me with my brother.* —**con·fu'sion**, *n.*

congratulate (4) [kəngræč'əleyt'], *v.* express pleasure on a person's success or good fortune. **Ex.** *Friends congratulated him on his marriage.* —**con·grat'u·la'tions**, *n.*

congregation (5) [kaŋ'grəgey'šən], *n.* a group of people gathered for religious worship. **Ex.** *How large is your congregation?*

—**con·gre·gate,** *v.* gather. **Ex.** *A crowd congregated in the street.*

Congress (2) [kaŋ'grəs], *n.* the group of persons elected by the people of each state to make the laws of the United States of America. **Ex.** *The Congress of the United States meets in Washington, D.C.* —**con·gres'sion·al,** *adj.*

conjunction (4) [kənǰəŋk'šən], *n.* a word that joins together sentences, phrases or groups of words. **Ex.** *In the sentence "She and I will go, but he will not,"* and *and* but *are conjunctions.* See **A Brief Explanation of English Grammar.**

connect (2) [kənekt'], *v.* 1. join or unite one thing to another; put together. **Ex.** *Connect the two wires.* 2. associate or be associated with. **Ex.** *I do not wish to be connected with him in any way.* —**con·nec'tion,** *n.*

conquer (3) [kaŋ'kər], *v.* 1. get by using force. **Ex.** *They quickly conquered the new territory.* 2. overcome; defeat. **Ex.** *She was able to conquer her fear of flying.* —**con'quer·or,** *n.*

conquest (5) [kan'kwest'], *n.* 1. the act of gaining by force. **Ex.** *Rockets helped to make possible the conquest of space.* 2. that which is conquered or gained by force.

conscience (3) [kan'šəns], *n.* a sense of what is right and wrong; a feeling of obligation to do right or be good. **Ex.** *His conscience kept him from stealing.* —**con·sci·en'tious,** *adj.* 1. careful to do what is right. **Ex.** *He is conscientious about returning the things he borrows.* 2. acting with great care and attention to detail. **Ex.** *She is known as a conscientious researcher.*

conscious (3) [kan'šəs], *adj.* 1. aware of oneself and the people and things around one. **Ex.** *She was conscious of someone's presence.* 2. awake; mentally active. **Ex.** *The injured man was still conscious.* 3. with purpose; deliberate. **Ex.** *He made a conscious effort to improve his work.* —**con'scious·ly,** *adv.* —**con'scious·ness,** *n.*

consent (2) [kənsent'], *n.* agreement; permission. **Ex.** *Her parents gave their consent to the marriage.* —*v.* agree; give approval. **Ex.** *He consented to let me go.*

consequence (3) [kan'səkwens'], *n.* 1. result. **Ex.** *The consequences of his acts were serious.* 2. importance. **Ex.** *His* *comments were of no consequence.* —**con·se·quent·ly** *adv.* as a result of; therefore. **Ex.** *He left before I arrived; consequently I wasn't able to speak to him.*

conservative (4) [kənsər'vətiv'], *adj.* 1. opposed to change; wanting to preserve existing conditions. **Ex.** *He is conservative in his views about government.* 2. careful about taking risks; not extreme. **Ex.** *He is very conservative in his dress.* —**con·serv' a·tism**, *n.*

conserve (5) [kənsərv'], *v.* preserve; keep from being wasted. **Ex.** *Conserve your strength for the difficult work ahead.* —**con·ser·va'tion**, *n.* a protecting from waste, loss or harm; conserving. **Ex.** *We have a program for the conservation of our national forests.*

consider (1) [kənsid'ər], *v.* 1. think carefully about; examine. **Ex.** *Consider all the costs before you buy a house.* 2. believe to be; regard as. **Ex.** *They consider him a good teacher.* 3. be thoughtful of. **Ex.** *She considers others before herself.* —**con·sid'er·ate**, *adj.* —**con·sid·er·a'tion**, *n.*

considerable (1) [kənsid'ərəbəl], *adj.* 1. much; rather large. **Ex.** *We had considerable rain this summer.* 2. worth regarding as important. **Ex.** *He was a man of considerable talent.* —**con·sid' er·a·bly**, *adv.*

consist (2) [kənsist'], *v.* be made of. **Ex.** *This plan consists of three parts.* —**con·sis'tent**, *adj.* 1. always acting in accord with the same principles, ideas, etc. **Ex.** *He was consistent in his views.* 2. in agreement. **Ex.** *Her story is consistent with the evidence.* —**con·sist'en·cy**, *n.* 1. a state of always acting in accord with the same principles, ideas, etc. **Ex.** *His consistency in opposing any change in the plans makes progress difficult.* 2. state of thickness, stickiness or firmness. **Ex.** *The consistency of this mixture is too stiff.*

console (3) [kənsowl'], *v.* comfort. **Ex.** *The grieving woman was consoled by her friends.* —**con·so·la'tion**, *n.*

consonant [kan'sənənt], *n.* a speech sound in which the breath is partly or completely stopped by the tongue, teeth or lips; all the letters other than the vowels *a,e,i,o,u* and sometimes *y* are consonants. **Ex.** *In the words sat and you the letters s, t and y are consonants.*

conspicuous (5) [kənspik'yuwes], *adj.* noticeable; attracting attention. **Ex.** *He was conspicuous because of his height.* —**con·spic'u·ous·ly**, *adv.*

conspire (5) [kənspayr'], *v*. 1. plot; plan together in secret to do something unlawful or evil. **Ex.** *The two men conspired to rob a bank.* 2. act together. **Ex.** *All things conspired to make the day a happy one.* —**con·spir'a·tor,** *n*. one who conspires. —**con·spir'a·cy,** *n*. the act of conspiring.

constant (3) [kan'stənt], *adj*. 1. unchanging; always present. **Ex.** *There is a constant need for affordable housing in this city.* 2. firm in belief; faithful. **Ex.** *He was a constant friend.* —**con'stant·ly,** *adj*. always.

constitute (3) [kan'stətuwt', kan'stətyuwt'], *v*. 1. compose; form. **Ex.** *The farm and the cattle constitute his entire fortune.* 2. appoint. **Ex.** *He constituted himself their guide.* 3. establish a law, a government, etc. **Ex.** *These rules were constituted by lawful authority.*

constitution (2) [kan'stətuw'šən, kan'stətyuw'šən], *n*. 1. the structure or form of a person, animal or thing. **Ex.** *With his strong constitution, he is not often sick.* 2. the fundamental principles, often written, according to which a nation, state or group is governed. **Ex.** *There are procedures for amending the Constitution of the United States.* —**con·sti·tu'tion·al,** *adj*. of or from a constitution. **Ex.** *He has a constitutional right to speak.* —**con·sti·tu'tion·al'i·ty,** *n*. agreement with the constitution.

construct (3) [kənstrəkt'], *v*. build. **Ex.** *These workmen are constructing a road.* —**con·struc'tion,** *n*. —**con·struc'tive,** *adj*. helping to improve; helpful. **Ex.** *He made constructive suggestions.*

consul (5) [kan'səl], *n*. an official appointed by a government to live in a foreign city to look after the interests of his own country. —**con'su·lar,** *adj*. —**con'su·late,** *n*. the office of the consul.

consult (3) [kənsəlt'], *v*. 1. seek information or advice from. **Ex.** *He consulted a lawyer about his problem.* 2. confer with. **Ex.** *Two doctors consulted about the patient.* —**con·sult'ant,** *n*. a specialist who gives advice. —**con·sul·ta'tion,** *n*. the act of consulting.

consume (4) [kənsuwm', kənsyuwm'], *v*. 1. use up. **Ex.** *Business consumed all of his time.* 2. eat or drink. **Ex.** *Your family consumes a lot of food.* 3. destroy, as by fire. **Ex.** *Fire consumed the house.* —**con·sum'er,** *n*. one who consumes. —**con·sump'tion,** *n*. act or process of consuming.

contact (3) [kan'tækt`], *n.* 1. a touching. **Ex.** *The contact of two electric wires caused the fire.* 2. a meeting or association. **Ex.** *I have few contacts with him, though we work in the same building.* 3. a friend or person who can be of help. **Ex.** *He will be a useful contact if you want to join the club.* —*v.* get in touch with. **Ex.** *I'll contact him about the meeting tomorrow.*

contact lens [kan'tækt` lenz'], a small eyeglass that fits directly over the front of the center of the eyeball to improve vision.

contagious [kentey'jəs], *adj.* 1. spread from one person to another. **Exs.** *His cold was so contagious that the whole family caught it. Her contagious cheerfulness made everyone begin to smile.* 2. able to spread disease. **Ex.** *The doctor said that the patient was no longer contagious.*

contain (1) [kənteyn'], *v.* 1. hold; include. **Ex.** *This book contains ten short stories.* 2. control. **Ex.** *She was so angry that she could hardly contain her feelings.* —**con·tain'er,** *n.* a box, barrel, bottle, etc. used to hold something.

contaminate [kəntæm'əneyt`], *v.* make dirty, impure or unfit for use; pollute by mixing with something poisonous or not clean. **Ex.** *The smoke from the factory was contaminating the air.* —**con·tam`i·na'tion,** *n.* —**con·tam'i·na`ted,** *adj.* **Ex.** *The contaminated food made her ill.*

contemplate (4) [kan'təmpleyt`], *v.* 1. think about seriously. **Ex.** *He needed time to contemplate what he should do before making a decision.* 2. intend; have as a purpose. **Ex.** *They do not contemplate building a house this year.* —**con·tem·pla'tion,** *n.*

contemporary (4) [kəntem'pərer`iy], *adj.* 1. living or happening in the same era. 2. belonging to the present. **Ex.** *They collect contemporary art.* —*n.* a person living during the same time as another. **Ex.** *He was a contemporary of my grandfather.* —**con·tem`po·ra'ne·ous,** *adj.*

contempt (4) [kəntempt'], *n.* scorn; the feeling a person has for that which is unworthy. **Ex.** *He looked at the thief with contempt.* —**con·tempt'i·ble,** *adj.* deserving scorn. —**con·temp'tu·ous,** *adj.* scornful.

contend (5) [kəntend'], *v.* 1. struggle against. **Ex.** *Early settlers in America had to contend with many hardships.* 2. argue; claim. **Ex.** *He contends that he is innocent.* —**con·tend'er,** *n.* a competitor. —**con·ten'tion,** *n.* the act of contending.

content (2) [kən'tent], *n.* 1. the subject matter, ideas or meaning of a speech, article, book, work of art, etc. **Ex.** *Some people have objected to the content of this novel.* 2. the amount contained. **Ex.** *The metallic content of this rock is high.* —**con'tents,** *n.* 1. all that is contained. **Ex.** *We examined the contents of the box.* 2. a listing of things with which a particular piece of written material is concerned. **Ex.** *He looked at the table of contents of the magazine.*

content (2) [kəntent'], *adj.* satisfied; pleased with one's position or circumstances. **Ex.** *He is content to live in a small house.* —*v.* satisfy; make happy. **Ex.** *The baby contented herself with the new toy.* —**con·tent'ed·ly,** *adv.* —**con·tent'ment,** *n.*

contest (3) [kan'test'], *n.* a competition or a game in which the players struggle to win. **Ex.** *We held a contest to see who could run fastest.*

contest (3) [kantest'], *v.* dispute; try to prove the opposite. **Ex.** *He contested our claim to ownership of the house.* —**con·test'ant,** *n.* a person who takes part in a contest; a person involved in a dispute.

continent (2) [kan'tənənt], *n.* any of the seven great land divisions of the world: Africa, Antarctica, Asia, Australia, Europe, North America and South America. —**con·ti·nen'tal,** *adj.* of or relating to a continent; European. **Ex.** *His manners are very continental.* —**the Continent,** *n.* Europe.

continue (1) [kəntin'yuw], *v.* 1. keep doing or being. **Ex.** *The rain continued all week.* 2. proceed after an interruption. **Ex.** *We will continue our meeting after lunch.* 3. last; endure. **Ex.** *The government was not able to continue in power.* —**con·tin'u·al,** *adj.* —**con·tin'u·al·ly,** *adv.* happening again and again. —**con·tin'u·ous,** *adj.* —**con·tin'u·ous·ly,** *adv.* without a break in space or time. —**con·tin'u·ance,** *n.* the act of continuing or putting off until a future time. —**con·tin'u·a'tion,** *n.* something which continues from something else. —**con·tin·u'i·ty,** *n.* a state of continuing without interruption.

contract (2) [kan'trækt'], *n.* an agreement, especially one that is written and legally binding. **Ex.** *They signed a contract to buy the house.* —**con·tract',** *v.* agree by contract. **Ex.** *They contracted to pay cash for the house.* —**con'tract·or,** *n.* a person or company providing material or services at an agreed price. **Ex.** *We talked to the contractor about the grade of lumber that he was supplying.*

contract (2) [kantrækt'], *v.* 1. reduce in size; become smaller or shorter. **Ex.** *Most metals contract when they cool.* 2. get; acquire. **Ex.** *He contracted a fatal disease.* —**con·trac'tion,** *n.*

contradict (kan`trədikt'], *v.* state the opposite to be true; deny positively. **Ex.** *He contradicted everything she said.* —**con`tra·dic'tion,** *n.*

contrary (3) [kan'trer`iy], *adj.* opposite; not agreeing with. **Ex.** *My opinion is contrary to yours.* —*n.* the opposite. **Ex.** *He said that no one is hungry, but the contrary is true.*

contrast (3) [kan'træst`], *v.* 1. compare so that the differences are shown. **Ex.** *The teacher contrasted the hot climate of one country with the cold climate of another.* 2. exhibit differences when compared. **Ex.** *The heights of the boys contrasted with the heights of the girls* —*n.* 1. a difference between things which are compared. **Ex.** *The contrast between his words and his actions is disappointing.* 2. a person who or thing which shows a difference when compared. **Ex.** *There is quite a contrast between that tall man and his shorter brother.*

contribute (3) [kəntrib'yət], *v.* 1. give to some fund or charity. **Ex.** *They have contributed a lot of money to charity.* 2. write articles, stories, etc., for a newspaper or magazine. **Ex.** *My favorite author contributes regularly to this magazine.* —**con·trib'u·tor,** *n.* one who contributes. —**con·tri·bu'tion,** *n.* that which is contributed. —**con·trib'u·tor·y,** *adj.*

contrive (5) [kəntrayv'], *v.* plan cleverly; scheme; plot; manage to succeed by scheming. **Ex.** *The prisoner contrived to escape.*

control (1) [kəntrowl'], *v.* 1. manage or direct. **Ex.** *The lights controlled the traffic.* 2. keep in check; have command over. **Ex.** *You must control your excitement.* —*n.* 1. power to manage or direct. **Ex.** *He lost control of the car, and it went off the road.* 2. act of keeping in check. **Ex.** *She brought her temper under control.*

controversy (5) [kan'trəvər`siy], *n.* dispute or argument. **Ex.** *There was a controversy about the location of the new school.* —**con·tro·ver'sial,** *adj.*

convalesce [kan`vəles'], *v.* recover gradually from an illness. **Ex.** *She is convalescing at home.* —**con`va·les'cence,** *n.* the act or period of convalescing. Ex. *His convalescence is taking a long time.* —con`va·les'cent, *adj.* recovering from an illness. Ex. *The doctor prescribed several convalescent aids to make things easier for the patient.* —*n.* a person gradually recovering from an illness.

convenience (2) [kənviyn'yəns], *n.* anything that makes work or life easier. Ex. *A car is a great convenience.*

convenient (2) [kənviyn'yənt], *adj.* 1. easy to use or reach. Ex. *Put the table in a convenient place.* 2. causing little trouble. Ex. *Is it convenient for you to meet me?* —con·ven'ient·ly, *adv.*

convent (4) [kan'vent`], *n.* 1. a community of women devoted to a religious life. 2. the place where they live.

convention (4) [kənven'šən], *n.* 1. a large meeting for a particular purpose. Ex. *He is attending the national convention of his party.* 2. a custom or general rule that is accepted because of common usage. Ex. *It is the convention in many countries for people to shake hands when they are introduced.* —con·ven'tion·al, *adj.*

conversation (2) [kan`vərsey'šən], *n.* talk between two or more people. Ex. *I enjoyed the conversation we had this afternoon.*

converse (2) [kənvərs'], *v.* talk. Ex. *We will converse in English.*

convert (3) [kənvərt'], *v.* 1. change from one substance or state to another. Ex. *In that factory, iron is converted into steel.* 2. adopt or cause to adopt a different belief or religion. Ex. *His professor converted him to a new educational philosophy.* —con·ver'sion, *n.* —con·ver'ti·ble, *adj.* able to be converted. Ex. *Our convertible couch turns into a comfortable double bed.* —*n.* a car that has a folding and/or removable roof.

convey (4) [kənvey'], *v.* 1. carry or bear from one place to another. Ex. *A truck conveyed my furniture to my new home.* 2. make known; give. Ex. *This book conveys the author's meaning very well.* —con·vey'ance, *n.* anything used to convey, such as a car or train. —con·vey'er, *n.*

convict (5) [kənvikt'], *v.* prove or declare guilty of a crime. Ex. *The prisoner was convicted of robbery.* —con'vict, *n.* a person sent to prison for committing a crime. Ex. *The convict was locked in a cell.*

conviction [kənvik'šən], *n.* 1. a finding that a person is guilty. Ex. *As a result of his conviction, he was sentenced to six* *months in jail.* 2. a deeply held belief. **Ex.** *Because of his religious convictions, he would not fight in the war.*

convince (3) [kənvins'], *v.* persuade by argument; satisfy by proof. **Ex.** *You have convinced me that I should go.* —**con·vinc' ing,** *adj.* —**con·vinc'ing·ly,** *adv.*

cook (1) [kuk'], *v.* prepare food by using heat. **Ex.** *The rice was cooked in a large pot.* —*n.* one who prepares food to be eaten.

cookie (2) [kuk'iy], *n.* a small, crisp, sweet cake. **Ex.** *The child wanted cookies with her milk.*

cool (1) [kuwl'], *adj.* 1. somewhat cold; not too hot. **Ex.** *A cool breeze was blowing.* 2. comfortable. **Ex.** *The house is cool in summer.* 3. calm. **Ex.** *He stayed cool during the argument.* 4. unfriendly. **Ex.** *He was cool toward us.* —*v.* make or become cool. **Ex.** *The evening breeze cooled the room.* —**cool'ly,** *adv.* —**cool'ness,** *n.*

cooler [kuw'lər], *n.* a container or a device in which to make or keep something cool. **Ex.** *We packed our food and drinks for the picnic in the cooler.*

cooperate (2) [kowap'əreyt'], *v.* act or work together to accomplish something. **Ex.** *All members must cooperate to make this group a success.* —**co·op·er·a'tion,** *n.* —**co·op'er·a·tive,** *adj.* willing to act or work with others; acting together. **Ex.** *This was a cooperative effort.*

cooperative [kowap'ərətiv], *n.* 1. an organization whose members are joint owners of it and who work and act together for their mutual economic benefit. **Ex.** *The cooperative transported the farmer's daily milk production to the processing plant.* 2. an apartment building and the land on which it is built, divided into shares owned by the purchasers. **Ex.** *You will have to obtain the permission of the board of directors of the cooperative before selling your shares.*

coordinate (5) [kowɔr'dəneyt'], *v.* bring into proper relation; cause to agree in timing, manner of performance, etc. for greater efficiency. **Ex.** *Have you coordinated these plans with all the people concerned?* —**co·or·di·na'tion,** *n.*

copper (3) [kap'ər], *n.* a reddish metal that is one of the best conductors of heat and electricity. **Ex.** *The lamp wire is made of copper.*

copy (2) [kap'iy], *n.* 1. an imitation or likeness of an original work. **Ex.** *That is a copy of a famous painting.* 2. one of a number of the same book, newspaper, magazine, etc. **Ex.** *I bought a copy of your book.* —*v.* 1. make a copy of. **Ex.** *Copy this letter.* 2. imitate. **Ex.** *She copies her sister's style of dress.* —**cop'ier,** *n.* an office machine that makes copies.

coral (5) [kɔr'əl], *n.* a hard, shell-like substance, usually white or red, consisting of the bones of very small sea animals. **Ex.** *These beads are made of coral.* —*adj.* made of coral; like coral in color.

cord (3) [kɔrd'], *n.* 1. a string or small rope. **Ex.** *Tie a cord around the box.* 2. a rubber-covered wire used to conduct electricity.

cordial (4) [kɔr'jəl], *adj.* warm and friendly. **Ex.** *He gave us a cordial welcome.* —**cor'dial·ly,** *adv.*

core (5) [kɔːr'], *n.* 1. the tough center part containing the seeds of apples, pears and some other fruits. 2. the most important part of anything. **Ex.** *The core of the city's problem is a lack of affordable housing.*

cork (5) [kɔrk'], *n.* the outer bark of a type of oak tree; a piece of this bark shaped to fill the opening of a bottle. —*v.* fill a hole of a bottle with a cork. **Ex.** *He corked the bottle after pouring us drinks.*

corn (1) [kɔrn'], *n.* 1. a common grain grown in America and eaten by people and animals. **Ex.** *How many ears of corn shall I cook for you?*

CORN

corner (1) [kɔr'ner], *n.* 1. the place where two sides or surfaces of a thing meet. **Ex.** *There is a chair in one corner of the room.* 2. the place where two streets come together. **Ex.** *He was standing on the street corner.* —*v.* force into or keep in a place or position from which it is difficult to escape. **Ex.** *The police cornered the robber in a shed.* —*adj.* at, on or in a corner. —**cut corners,** save time or money.

corporal [kɔr'pərəl,], *n.* a lower-ranking enlisted military person above a private first class and below a sergeant. **Ex.** *The corporal brought his squad to attention.*

corporation (3) [kɔr`pərey'šən], *n.* a group of persons permitted by law to act as one person when managing a business. **Ex.**

---

a, far; æ, am; e, get; ey, late; i, in; iy, see; ɔ, all; ow, go; u, put; uw, too; ə, but, ago; ər, fur; aw, out; ay, life; oy, boy; ŋ, ring; θ, think; ð, that; ž, measure; š, ship;], edge; č, child.

Those men are organizing a corporation to sell machines.
—**cor'po·rate**, *adj.*

corps (5) [kɔːr'], *n.* 1. a special branch or section of a service, usually the military. **Ex.** *He is a member of the Marine Corps.* 2. a group of persons working together. **Ex.** *The corps of dancers traveled from city to city.*

corpse (5) [kɔrps'], *n.* the dead body of a human being. **Ex.** *His sister identified his corpse.*

correct (2) [kərekt'], *adj.* 1. free from mistakes; true. **Ex.** *He gave the correct answer.* 2. agreeing with what is considered proper. **Ex.** *His manners are always correct.* —*v.* 1. change to what is right; rid of mistakes. **Ex.** *You must correct your grammar.* 2. direct attention to the mistake of; punish for mistakes. **Ex.** *We do not like to correct our children in front of company.* —**cor·rect'ly**, *adv.* —**cor·rect'ness**, *n.* —**cor·rec'tion**, *n.* a correcting. **Ex.** *He made corrections in what he had written.* —**cor·rec'tive**, *adj.* designed or intended to correct.

correspond (3) [kɔr'əspand'], *v.* 1. match; agree with. **Ex.** *Your words do not correspond with your actions.* 2. be equal or similar to. **Ex.** *A captain in the U.S. Navy corresponds to a colonel in the U.S. Army.* 3. communicate with someone by letters. **Ex.** *They correspond with each other regularly.* —**cor·re·spond'ence**, *n.* —**cor·re·spond'ent**, *n.* 1. one who communicates by letter. 2. a person who is paid to supply news from a distant area to a newspaper, magazine, television station, etc.

corridor (4) [kɔr'ədər], *n.* a passageway or long hall that connects rooms or parts of a building. **Ex.** *I met him in the corridor on the way to my office.*

corrode [kərowd'], *v.* eat away or destroy gradually by chemical action. **Ex.** *The iron fence was being corroded by rust.* —**cor·ro·sion**, *n.*

corrupt (4) [kərəpt'], *adj.* dishonest, usually to gain money. **Ex.** *The corrupt judge accepted money to let the prisoner go unpunished.* —*v.* cause to be dishonest, usually by giving money. **Ex.** *He was corrupted by evil companions.* —**cor·rup'tion**, *n.*

cosmetic [kazmet'ik], *n.* a preparation such as face powder, rouge, nail polish, etc., intended to make the user more beautiful. **Ex.** *She applies her cosmetics with a skillful and subtle touch.* —*adj.*

cost (1) [kɔːst'], *n.* 1. the amount paid or asked for something. **Ex.** *The cost of adding a room to the house was too high for us.* 2. loss; sacrifice. **Ex.** *The father saved his son's life at the cost of his own.* —*v.* 1. be priced at. **Ex.** *That car costs a lot of money.* 2. cause the loss or sacrifice of. **Ex.** *The experiment cost him his life.* —**cost'ly,** *adj.* expensive; not cheap. **Ex.** *She was wearing costly furs.* —**at all costs,** by whatever means necessary. **Ex.** *At all costs, stop them from leaving!*

costume (3) [ka'stuwm, ka'styuwm], *n.* 1. clothing characteristic of a class, time or place. **Ex.** *The guides at the museum were dressed in eighteenth-century costumes.* 2. the clothes actors and actresses wear in a play. **Ex.** *The costumes in this play are very colorful.*

cot (4) [kat'], *n.* a light, narrow bed, especially a folding one.

cottage (3) [kat'iǰ], *n.* a small house.

cottage cheese [kat'iǰ čiyz'], *n.* a soft, white, lumpy mild cheese made from sour skim milk. **Ex.** *For lunch she ate a salad of cottage cheese and fruit.*

cotton (2) [kat'ən], *n.* 1. soft, white threadlike substance that grows around the seeds of the cotton plant. 2. thread or cloth made of this substance. **Ex.** *This shirt is made of pure cotton.*

couch (3) [kawč'], *n.* a sofa; a piece of furniture to sit or lie on.

cough (3) [kɔːf'], *v.* force air through the throat noisily. —*n.* 1. the act or sound of coughing. **Ex.** *The boy's cough attracted the girl's attention.* 2. a condition of frequent coughing. **Ex.** *You have a bad cough.*

COUCH

could (1) [kud'], *v.* 1. past tense of the verb *can.* **Ex.** *Last year only two people could go.* 2. should be or would be able. **Ex.** *He could help you if he wanted to.*

couldn't [kud'nt], short form, contraction of *could not.* **Ex.** *He couldn't find his hat anywhere.*

council (4) [kawn'səl], *n.* 1. people meeting together to give advice or make plans. **Ex.** *The political party held a council to decide on future actions.* 2. a group of people chosen or elected to make laws or rules. **Ex.** *The city council is in conflict with the mayor.* —**coun'cil·lor,** *n.*

counsel (4) [kawn'səl], *n.* 1. advice; opinion. **Ex.** *I sought the lawyer's counsel.* 2. a lawyer who is handling a case. **Ex.** *He* *is the counsel for the defense.* —*v.* give advice; advise. **Ex.** *His adviser counseled him very wisely.* —**coun'se·lor,** *n.* 1. an adviser. 2. a lawyer.

count (1) [kawnt'], *v.* 1. say numbers in regular order. **Ex.** *The child can count to ten.* 2. get the total by numbering. **Ex.** *The teacher counted the students in the room.* 3. be important; have value. **Ex.** *Everything you do counts in this world.* 4. take or be taken into account. **Ex.** *Because he cheated, his score will not count.* —*n.* a total by numbering; a counting. **Ex.** *A count showed that thirty people were present.* —**count on,** rely on; depend upon. **Ex.** *Can I count on your help?* —**count up,** add. **Ex.** *Count up what I owe you.*

countdown [kawnt'dawn], *n.* the act of counting backwards from a given time to zero to let people know how much time remains before something is to begin. **Ex.** *Because of a mechanical difficulty, the countdown for the launching of the spaceship was halted at four.*

countenance (5) [kawn'tənəns], *n.* 1 face; features; expression showing one's nature or feelings. **Ex.** *The old man had a noble countenance.* 2. approval or support. —*v.* support; approve. **Ex.** *I cannot countenance such behavior.*

counter (4) [kawn'tər], *n.* 1. a long table in a store at which business is done. **Ex.** *The clerk stood behind the glove counter.* 2. a work surface, often up against a wall and/or on top of a cabinet or cabinets. **Ex.** *She put the bag of groceries on the kitchen counter.*

counter (4) [kawn'tər], *v.* make a move, statement, etc. in opposition to another move, statement, etc. **Ex.** *She countered my argument.*

counter- (4) [kawn'tər], *prefix.* against; opposite; in response. **Exs.** *act, counteract; proposal, counterproposal; intelligence, counterintelligence.*

counterfeit [kawn'tərfit], *v.* make a copy or imitation of something, usually in order to deceive or cheat someone. **Ex.** *The criminal had counterfeited ten-dollar bills.* —*n.* something that has been copied or imitated in order to deceive someone. **Ex.** *The diamond ring he sold her was a counterfeit.* —*adj.* not real; false. **Ex.** *This is a counterfeit quarter.* —**coun'ter·feit`er,** *n.* one who does counterfeiting.

country (1) [kən'triy], *n.* 1. the territory of a nation. **Ex.** *Canada is a very large country.* 2. land with farms and very small towns; land outside of the large cities. **Ex.** *Do you prefer to live in the city or in the country?* 3. a particular area of land. **Ex.** *That is very hilly country.* 4. the entire nation, especially the people. **Ex.** *The President asked the country to make sacrifices.*

countryside (2) [kən'triysayd'], *n.* land outside the city. **Ex.** *We will drive out into the countryside.*

county (4) [kawn'tiy], *n.* in the United States, one of the parts into which a state is divided for purposes of government.

couple (2) [kəp'əl], *n.* 1. two things of the same kind together. **Ex.** *He ate a couple of eggs for breakfast.* 2. a man and a woman together. **Ex.** *They are a handsome couple.*

coupon [kuw'pan], *n.* 1. a ticket entitling one to a service, reduction in price, etc. **Ex.** *I have a coupon worth one dollar off on this laundry soap.* 2. a ticket for use in ordering some item, entering a contest, etc. **Ex.** *She filled out the coupon to obtain some travel pamphlets.*

courage (2) [kər'ij], *n.* bravery; the ability to face danger or difficulties without fear. **Ex.** *You will need courage to try again after your defeat.* —**cou·ra'geous,** *adj.* —**cou·ra'geous·ly,** *adv.*

course (1) [kɔrs'], *n.* 1. moving from one point to the next; progress. **Ex.** *We watched a floating log in its course down the river.* 2. the way or direction in which something should move. **Ex.** *Our ship was off its course because of bad weather.* 3. an entire series of studies or any one of these studies. **Ex.** *What course are you taking at the university?* —**in the course of,** while; during. **Ex.** *In the course of my life, I have seen many strange things.* —**of course,** certainly. **Ex.** *Of course, I will go with you.*

court (2) [kɔrt'], *n.* 1. a place where disputes are settled according to law. **Ex.** *The man accused of the crime was brought to court.* 2. judges and officials of the court. **Ex.** *The proceedings of the court will now begin.* 3. an area outdoors or indoors prepared and marked for certain games such as basketball and tennis. **Ex.** *He's waiting for you at the tennis court.* 4. an open area partly or entirely enclosed by walls or buildings; courtyard. 5. the palace of a ruler. 6. the attendants and relatives of a ruler. —*v.* seek the affection or favor of. **Ex.** *He courted her for a year before they were married.*

courtesy (4) [kər'təsiy], *n.* 1. good manners; polite way of acting. **Ex.** *He was admired for his courtesy.* 2. a favor; polite act. **Ex.** *Please do me the courtesy of answering my question.* —**cour·te·ous,** *adj.* —**cour·te·ous·ly,** *adv.*

courthouse [kɔrt'haws'], *n.* a building in which courts of law meet.

courtroom [kɔrt'ruwm'], *n.* a room in which a court of law meets.

courtship [kɔrt'šip'], *n.* the courting of a woman for marriage.

courtyard [kɔrt'yard'], *n.* an area open to the sky but enclosed by buildings and or walls. **Ex.** *They ate dinner in the courtyard.*

cousin (2)[kəz'ən], *n.* the child of one's uncle or aunt.

cover (1) [kəv'ər], *v.* 1. put a layer of something on. **Ex.** *She covered the table with a cloth.* 2. hide. **Ex.** *He covered the coin with his hand.* 3. extend over. **Ex.** *His farm covers two hundred acres.* 4. get news. **Ex.** *The reporter covered the fire.* —*n.* 1. anything that covers, such as a lid or blanket. **Ex.** *In winter, she liked to have at least two covers on her bed.* 2. shelter; protection. **Ex.** *The prisoner escaped under cover of the night.*

cow (2) [kaw'], *n.* a large farm animal that gives milk. **Ex.** *He has a herd of sixty cows.*

coward (4) [kaw'ərd], *n.* a person who lacks courage. **Ex.** *No one wishes to be thought a coward.* —**cow'ard·ly,** *adj.* **Ex.** *He behaved in a cowardly fashion.* —**cow'ard·ice,** *n.* **Ex.** *Everyone knew of his cowardice.*

COW

cowboy [kaw'boy'], *n.* a man who works with cattle, often in the American West.

cowhide [kaw'hayd'], *n.* the skin of a cow; leather made from cowskin.

cozy [kow'ziy], *adj.* sheltered and warm; snug and comfortable. **Ex.** *Your house has a very cozy atmosphere.*

crab [kræb'], *n.* an often edible broad, flat, hard-shelled sea animal with five pairs of legs. **Ex.** *We feasted on crabs last night.*

CRAB

crack (3) [kræk'], *v.* 1. break, with or without separating, into parts. **Ex.** *The cup was cracked.* 2. make a sharp, sudden sound as of something breaking. **Ex.** *The driver cracked the whip over the horses' heads.* —*n.* 1. a break without complete separation. **Ex.** *There was a crack in the mirror.* 2. a sharp, sudden sound, as of something breaking. —**cracked'**, *adj.*

crackdown [kræk'dawn], *n.* the act of becoming more strict in enforcing rules, laws, etc. **Ex.** *The police are continuing with their crackdown on drug dealers.* —**crack down,** *v.*

cracker (5) [kræk'er], *n.* a thin, crisp biscuit. **Ex.** *She gave the child some crackers and milk.*

cradle (4) [kreyd'əl], *n.* a baby's bed., usually on rockers. —*v.* hold in the arms and rock as in a cradle. **Ex.** *She cradled the child in her arms.*

craft [kræft'], *n.* any boat, ship or other vessel, including aircraft, taken singly or as a group. **Ex.** *In such a storm, no craft could keep to its course.*

craft (4) [kræft'], *n.* 1. any kind of skilled work done with the hands. **Ex.** *We are studying the arts and crafts of the country in order to understand its culture.* 2. cunning; skill in tricking others. **Ex.** *By craft he got the property away from his brothers and sisters.* —**craft'y**, *adj.* —**craft'i·ly**, *adv.*

cram [kræm'], *v.* 1. force or push into a space that is almost too small; fill too full. **Ex.** *We were crammed into the bus until the door could hardly close.* 2. stuff with food. **Ex.** *He crammed himself with cookies.* 3. study very intently for a relatively short time to prepare for a test. **Ex.** *He did not join us because he is cramming for his final examination.*

cramp [kræmp'], *n.* a sudden, severe pain in a muscle or muscles making movement difficult. **Ex.** *The cramp in her hand made her drop the pen.* —**cramps'**, *n.* severe pains in the abdomen. **Ex.** *While she was swimming, she had an attack of cramps.*

cranberry [kræn'ber'iy], *n.* a small, round, tart, edible red berry that grows on shrubs in swampy ground. **Ex.** *At Thanksgiving dinner we always have a sauce made from cranberries.*

crane [kreyn'], *n.* 1. a machine having a strong, thick wire rope attached to a movable arm used for moving and lifting heavy objects. **Ex.** *The crane moved the steel beam into position.* 2. a tall wading bird with long legs, a long neck and a long beak. —*v.* stretch one's neck in order to be able to see something or someone better. **Ex.** *He craned his neck to look over the wall.*

crank (5) [kræŋk'], *n.* a handle that forms a right angle and is fastened to the shaft of a machine in order to turn it. **Ex.** *Turn the crank to start the motor.* —*v.* turn a crank.

crash (2) [kræš'], *n.* 1. a hitting against something with force by which damage is caused. **Ex.** *Many people died in the airplane crash.* 2. a loud noise like something breaking. **Ex.** *He heard the crash of a falling tree.* 3. a sudden financial loss or failure; a sudden and steep fall in the stock market. **Ex.** *He lost thousands of dollars in the last crash.* —*v.* 1. hit. **Ex.** *The two cars crashed into each other.* 2. make a sudden loud noise. **Ex.** *Thunder crashed in the sky.* 3. fall suddenly and steeply, as in stocks and bonds. **Ex.** *When the market crashed, he lost a fortune.*

crate [kreyt'], *n.* a container or supporting frame, often made of wood, used for packing and shipping items such as fruit, bottled drinks, furniture, etc. **Ex.** *Where shall I put these crates of eggs?*

crave (5) [kreyv'], *v.* 1. want very much. **Ex.** *She craves his company.* 2. beg. **Ex.** *He craved forgiveness.* —**crav'ing,** *n.*

crawl (3) [krɔːl'], *v.* 1. move slowly on one's hands and knees. **Ex.** *The wounded soldier crawled to safety.* 2. move slowly. **Ex.** *The cars crawled through the traffic.*

crazy (2) [krey'ziy], *adj.* 1. sick in mind. **Ex.** *She has gone crazy from grief.* 2. not practical; very foolish. **Ex.** *He has crazy ideas.*

creak (5) [kriyk'], *v.* make a sharp, thin, high sound. **Ex.** *The floor creaked as he stepped on a loose board.* —*n.* the sound of a creak. —**creak'y,** *adj.*

cream (2) [kriym'], *n.* 1. the rich, buttery part of milk that rises to the top. **Ex.** *Do you like cream in your coffee?* 2. any soft, thick substance which resembles cream. **Ex.** *She uses face cream to soften her skin.* —*v.* make into a smooth mixture like cream. **Ex.** *She creamed the butter and sugar before adding the eggs.* —**cream'y,** *adj.*

create (2) [kriy`eyt'], *v.* 1. bring into being; make; form. **Ex.** *Building the new road created many jobs.* 2. produce as a work of thought or imagination. **Ex.** *That artist created many beautiful pictures.* —**cre·a'tion,** *n.* that which is created. —**cre·a'tor,** *n.* one who creates. —**cre·a'tive,** *adj.*

creature (2) [kriy'čər], *n.* any living being; any animal or person. **Ex.** *It was a small, furry four-legged creature.*

credit (3) [kred'ət], *n*. 1. belief that something is true; trust. **Ex.** *He put no credit in the statement.* 2. honor; recognition. **Ex.** *The boy received credit for his hard work.* 3. reputation for paying one's bills. **Ex.** *My credit is good at this store.* 4. an amount of money in a bank account. **Ex.** *His bank balance shows a credit.* —*v*. 1. believe; accept as the truth. **Ex.** *The woman did not credit the boy's story.* 2. add to an account. **Ex.** *The bank credited the deposit to his account.* 3. regard as owing to or caused by. **Ex.** *The old man credited his long life to his regular habits.* —**cred'i·ble,** *adj*. believable. —**cred·i·bil' i·ty,** *n*. —**cred'i·tor,** *n*. one to whom money is owed. —**credit to** or **with,** attribute to or recognize someone for. **Ex.** *The invention is credited to him.* —**do credit to,** bring praise or honor to. **Ex.** *The painting would do credit to a great artist.* —**on credit,** with a promise to pay later. **Ex.** *They bought their car on credit.*

credit card [kred'ət kard], a small card, usually plastic, which permits one to charge to one's account purchases, services, etc. and pay for them later. **Ex.** *She had ten credit cards in her wallet.*

creed (5) [kriyd'], *n*. a statement of the principal beliefs of a religion, an organization, etc.; guiding principles in science, politics, etc. **Ex.** *It was part of his creed to try to do a good deed each day.*

creek (3) [kriyk', krik'], *n*. stream of water smaller than a river. **Ex.** *The boys like to play in the creek during the summer.*

creep (3) [kriyp'], *v*. 1. crawl; move with the body close to the ground. **Ex.** *A baby creeps before it walks.* 2. move slowly, quietly and carefully. **Ex.** *The thief was creeping outside the building in the dark.* 3. grow along the ground or over a wall. **Ex.** *The vine is creeping up the side of the house.* —**creep'y,** *adj*. causing fear. **Ex.** *They heard creepy noises.*

crept (3) [krept'], *v*. past tense and participle of *creep*. **Exs.** *The boy crept quietly through the dark house. She had crept out of bed before anyone else was awake.*

crescent [kres'ənt], *n*. 1. the shape of the moon during the first and last quarters of its revolution around the earth, when only a thin curve of the moon can be seen. **Ex.** *The gleaming crescent of the moon could be seen in the sky.* 2. anything

CRESCENT

a, far; æ, am; e, get; ey, late; i, in; iy, see; ɔ, all; ow, go; u, put; uw, too; ə, but, ago; ər, fur; aw, out; ay, life; oy, boy; ŋ, ring; θ, think; ð, that; ž, measure; š, ship; J, edge; č, child.

shaped like this such as a roll, a row of houses on a curved street, etc.

crest (4) [krest'], *n.* 1. a bunch of hair, feathers or fur on the head of a bird or animal. 2. anything like a crest. **Ex.** *The crest of the mountain rose above us.*

crew (3) [kruw'], *n.* 1. the men working on a ship, plane or train. **Ex.** *The ship had a small crew.* 2. a group of persons working together. **Ex.** *A crew of workmen painted the building.*

crib [krib'], *n.* a baby's or small child's bed with high sides that can be moved up and down to keep the child from falling out. **Ex.** *The baby is sound asleep in her crib.*

cried [krayd'], *v.* past tense and participle of *cry.* **Exs.** *She cried as she waved good-bye to him. The baby had cried most of the night.*

crime (2) [kraym'], *n.* a wrong act forbidden by law. **Ex.** *Murder is a very serious crime.*

criminal (2) [krim'ənəl], *n.* a person who has committed a crime. **Ex.** *The criminal was sent to jail.* —*adj.* relating to crime. **Ex.** *He had studied criminal law.*

crimson (5) [krim'zən], *n.* a deep red color. —*adj.* of a deep red color. **Ex.** *His hands were crimson with blood.*

cripple (4) [krip'əl], *n.* a person or animal that is without the normal use of some part of the body. **Ex.** *He became a cripple when he lost his leg in the war.* —*v.* damage; take away the use of any part. **Ex.** *The automobile accident crippled her.*

crisis (4) [kray'səs], *n.* 1. a decisive or extremely important stage in a series of events. **Ex.** *The sick man passed the crisis and began to regain his strength.* 2. a time of difficulty or danger. **Ex.** *Scarcity of food caused a crisis in the nation.*

crisp (4) [krisp'], *adj.* 1. hard but easily broken. **Ex.** *He had crisp, buttered toast for breakfast.* 2. firm and fresh. **Ex.** *The salad vegetables were crisp.* 3. sharp; clear. **Ex.** *She had a crisp manner of speaking.* 4. pleasantly cool. **Ex.** *The air was crisp.* —**crisp'ly,** *adv.* —**crisp'ness,** *n.*

critic (3) [krit'ik], *n.* 1. a person skilled in judging books, music, plays, art, etc. **Ex.** *I saw the music critic of the newspaper at the concert.* 2. a person who objects or complains without reason. **Ex.** *He is a critic of everyone's actions but his own.* —**crit'i·cism,** *n.* the judgment expressed. —**crit'i·cize,** *v.*

critical (3) [krit'ikəl], *adj.* 1. tending to complain about another's actions or to judge severely. **Ex.** *I do not like people who are too critical.* 2. extremely dangerous; at a very important stage. **Ex.** *The most critical battle of the war occurred near that town.* —**crit'i·cal·ly,** *adj.*

crooked (4) [kruk'əd], *adj.* 1. bent; curved; twisted; not straight. **Ex.** *It was hard to drive along the crooked road in the dark.* 2. not honest. **Ex.** *He was involved in some very crooked business.*

crop (2) [krap'], *n.* produce of the soil such as grain, fruit or vegetables. **Ex.** *The farmer raised a wheat crop.* —*v.* cut or bite short. **Ex.** *The cattle cropped the grass in the field.*

cross (1) [krɔːs'], *v.* 1. go across; extend from one side to the other side. **Ex.** *We crossed the street.* 2. draw a line through. **Ex.** *Be sure to cross your t's when you write.* —*n.* 1. a structure having an upright post with a bar across it close to the top. 2. any mark made by putting one line directly across another, such as an x, to show a particular location. —*adj.* mean; angry. —**cross'ing,** *n.* a place at which to cross.

cross-examine [krɔs'igzæm'ən], *v.* examine one already examined for further information. **Ex.** *The lawyer cross-examined the witness.*

cross-purpose [krɔs'pər'pəs], *n.* an opposite purpose or reason. **Ex.** *Instead of working together, we are working at cross-purposes.*

cross-reference [krɔs' ref'rəns], *n.* a referral to another part of a book, paper, etc. **Ex.** *The cross-references helped him to learn more about the subject.*

crossroad [krɔs'rowd], *n.* a road that crosses another or leads from one main road to another. **Ex.** *Turn right at the next crossroad.* —**cross'roads,** *n.* 1. a point at which two or more roads cross one another. **Ex.** *The traffic was held up at the crossroads.* 2. a point at which one has to make an important decision. **Ex.** *She was at a crossroads in her career.*

cross section [krɔs' sek'šən], 1. a section or part of something that shows what the whole thing is like. **Ex.** *He spoke with a cross section of the group.* 2. a thin flat section or slice made by cutting an object at right angles to its length; such a section or a picture of it.

crouch (4) [krawč'], *v.* stoop low with bent knees. **Ex.** *The hunter crouched in the long grass.* —*n.* act of stooping or bending low.

crow (4) [krow'], *n.* 1. a large bird, usually black, with shiny feathers and an unpleasant shrieking cry. 2. the loud cry made by a rooster. —*v.* make such a cry. **Ex.** *The rooster crowed at dawn.*

crowd (1) [krawd'], *n.* a large number of people in a group. **Ex.** *A crowd collected to hear the speaker.* —*v.* 1. push together. **Ex.** *People crowded into the bus.* 2. gather together in a crowd. **Ex.** *People crowded to see the President.*

crown (2) [krawn'], *n.* 1. a head covering for a king or queen. **Ex.** *The gold crown was covered with jewels.* 2. royal power. **Ex.** *After the revolt, the crown passed to another.* 3. anything like a crown. **Ex.** *Let's walk up to the crown of the hill.* 4. a ring of flowers or leaves for the head worn as a sign of victory or honor. —*v.* place a crown upon. **Ex.** *She was crowned apple blossom queen.*

crude (3) [kruwd'], *adj.* 1. not polished; lacking grace. **Ex.** *His manners were crude.* 2. in a natural state; raw; not ready for use. **Ex.** *Crude oil was piped to the refinery.* 3. looking unfinished; made without skill. **Ex.** *The merchant was offering crude carvings for sale.* —**crude'ly,** *adv.* —**crude'ness,** *n.*

cruel (2) [kruw'əl], *adj.* 1. liking to cause pain for others; without mercy or pity. **Ex.** *The cruel boy threw stones at the children.* 2. causing suffering. **Ex.** *The cruel heat of the desert sun prevented them from traveling during the day.* —**cru'el·ly,** *adv.* —**cru'el·ty,** *n.*

cruise (5) [kruwz'], *v.* ride or sail from place to place; go on a long trip by ship for pleasure. **Ex.** *They cruised through the Mediterranean.* —*n.* a ship voyage, especially one for pleasure and with stops at many ports. —**cruis'er,** *n.* 1. a fairly large ship designed to take passengers on pleasure trips. 2. a medium-sized battleship. 3. a police car.

crumb (4) [krəm'], *n.* a very small bit of bread, cake, etc. **Ex.** *She fed crumbs to the birds.*

crumble (5) [krəm'bəl], *v.* 1. break into crumbs, such as bread, cake, etc. 2. fall into decay. **Ex.** *The bricks and mortar of their house crumbled from lack of care.* —**crum'bly,** *adj., adv.*

crusade (5) [kruw`seyd'], *n.* 1. any campaign or fight for a good cause or against a bad cause. **Ex.** *The citizens are having a crusade for better housing.* 2. any of the religious wars fought during the eleventh, twelfth, and thirteenth centuries. —*v.* engage in a crusade. **Ex.** *Women in the United States crusaded for the right to vote.* —**cru·sad'er,** *n.*

crush (2) [krəš'], *v.* 1. press together with force so as to break, hurt or change the shape of. **Ex.** *She crushed her hat when she sat on it.* 2. break into fine pieces as by pounding. **Ex.** *The machine crushed the stones into a fine powder.* 3. defeat completely. **Ex.** *The revolt was crushed.* —*n.* 1. the act of crushing; strong pressure. 2. many people or things crowded together. **Ex.** *We lost sight of each other in the crush of people at the door.*

crust (4) [krəst'], *n.* 1. the hard outer part of bread. **Ex.** *He had only a crust of bread for supper.* 2. the shell or covering of a pie. 3. any hard outer shell. **Ex.** *She walked over the crust of the snow.* —**crus'ty,** *adj.*

crutch (5) [krəč'], *n.* a support used by a lame person to help in walking.

cry (1) [kray'], *v.* 1. call in a loud voice; shout. **Ex.** *He was crying for help.* 2. weep. **Ex.** *What is making your mother cry?* —*n.* 1. a loud call or shout. **Ex.** *He heard the cry, "Fire! Fire!"* 2. weeping; sound made by one in pain or grief. **Ex.** *We heard the cries of the injured boy.* 3. call of an animal or bird. **Ex.** *The hunter heard the cry of the wounded animal.* 4. appeal. **Ex.** *The cry of the people was for food.*

CRUTCH

crystal (3) [kris'təl], *n.* 1. a hard, clear, glasslike rock; also a piece of this material used as an ornament. 2. glass of superior brilliancy; articles made of this glass. **Ex.** *Crystal was sparkling on the table.* 3. the shapes of many substances when they become solid. **Ex.** *The crystals of snow were beautiful.* 4. the clear, thin covering over the face of a watch. —*adj.* made of or like crystal; clear. **Ex.** *The crystal water was icy cold.* —**crys'tal·lize,** *v.* 1. form into crystals. **Ex.** *The melted sugar crystallized on the fruit.* 2. give form to something. **Ex.** *His plans crystallized into action.*

cub (5) [kəb'], *n.* the young of some animals, such as the fox, bear and lion. **Ex.** *The lioness was playing with her cub.*

cube (5) [kyuwb'], *n.* a solid having six square sides, all equal in size. —**cu'bic,** *adj.*

CUBE

cuff (4) [kəf'], *n.* 1. a band around the lower part of a sleeve. 2. the turned-up fold around the bottom of the legs of trousers. **Ex.** *I don't want any cuffs on these trousers.*

culprit [kəl'prit], *n.* one who is guilty of a wrongdoing or a criminal act. **Ex.** *The culprit hung his head in shame.*

cult [kəlt'], *n.* a special system of religious worship, of fashion or style, of principles, etc. and the people who follow it. **Exs.** *That cult has attracted the attention of the police. The professor had studied the cult of the tea ceremony in Japan.*

cultivate (3) [kəl'təveyt'], *v.* 1. loosen the soil around plants to help them grow; prepare and use land for raising crops. **Ex.** *The farmer was cultivating his fields.* 2. help and protect the growth of; improve; develop, as by education. **Ex.** *He cultivated his mind by reading.* —**cul·ti·va'tion,** *n.*

culture (3) [kəl'čər], *n.* 1. the particular ideas, arts and way of life of a people or nation. **Ex.** *We have learned much from the culture of ancient Greece.* 2. the result in an individual or a society of an interest in and understanding of that which is highly valued in behavior, ideas, the arts, literature and scholarship. **Ex.** *She came from a home of refinement and culture.* 3. a specially prepared material in which bacteria and cells will grow, used in scientific experiments. —**cul'tur·al,** *adj.* —**cul'tur·al·ly,** *adv.*

cunning (3) [kən'iŋ], *adv.* 1. clever in cheating; deceiving. **Ex.** *He was not as strong as the other fighter, but he was more cunning.* 2. clever; skillful. **Ex.** *This clock was made by a cunning workman.* —*n.* skill in tricking others. **Ex.** *He used cunning to take the land away from his partner.* —**cun'ning·ly,** *adv.*

cup (1) [kəp'], *n.* 1. a small container with a handle, usually in the shape of a bowl, used for drinking. 2. a unit of measure equal to eight ounces; the amount a cup will hold. **Ex.** *I used two cups of flour to make the cake.* —*v.* form a cup shape. **Ex.** *He cupped his hands and dipped water from the brook.*

CUP 1

cupboard (3) [kə'bərd], *n.* a closet or piece of furniture with shelves for storing food, dishes, etc.

curb (4) [kerb'], *n.* 1. the raised edging of stone or concrete along a street. **Ex.** *He stepped off the curb into the traffic.* 2. that which controls. **Ex.** *He resolved to put a curb on his spending.* —*v.* control. **Ex.** *He was told to curb his temper.*

cure (2) [kyu:r'], *n.* 1. any remedy or method of treatment that makes a sick person healthy. **Ex.** *The doctors were searching for a cure for her disease.* 2. restoration to health. **Ex.** *The child's cure was immediate.* —*v.* 1. restore to health; make well. **Ex.** *The medicine helped to cure her cold.* 2. stop from doing or remove something bad. **Ex.** *Her burned finger cured her of playing with matches.* —**cur'a·ble,** *adj.*

curious (2) [kyur'iəs], *adj.* 1. strange; odd; unusual; peculiar. **Ex.** *We saw some curious birds today.* 2. eager to learn; desiring knowledge. **Ex.** *He has the curious mind of a student.* 3. interested in things that do not concern one. **Ex.** *The curious girl listened to our private conversation.* —**cu'ri·os'i·ty,** *n.* 1. a desire to know. **Ex.** *Her curiosity led her to pursue further studies.* 2. a curious thing. **Ex.** *He brought home many curiosities from his travels.* —**cu'ri·ous·ly,** *adv.*

curl (2) [kərl'], *v.* 1. form or twist into rings. **Ex.** *She curls her hair every night.* 2. bend into curves. **Ex.** *Smoke curled from the burning paper.* —*n.* 1. arrangement of the hair in rings. 2. anything in the shape of curves or rings. **Ex.** *Curls of smoke rose from the chimney.* —**curl'y,** *adj.*

currency (4) [kər'ənsiy], *n.* money in use in a country, both coins and paper. **Ex.** *The currency of the country is sound.*

current (2) [kər'ənt], *adj.* belonging to the present time. **Ex.** *This is the current issue of the magazine.* —*n.* the flow of water or air. **Ex.** *The current carried the boat downstream.* 2. movement of electricity in a wire. **Ex.** *There is not enough current in your home for all the electrical equipment you have.*

curriculum [kərik'yələm], *n.* all of the courses offered for study at a school, college, etc. **Ex.** *That university's curriculum does not offer all the courses that I need.*

curse (2) [kərs'], *n.* 1. a wish that evil might happen to another. **Ex.** *He placed a curse upon his enemy.* 2. something that causes evil or trouble. **Ex.** *His jealousy was a curse to him.* 3. evil words; bad language. **Ex.** *In his anger, he shouted curses.* —*v.* 1. use evil language. **Ex.** *He cursed his bad luck.* 2. wish evil or harm upon. **Ex.** *She cursed her enemies.*

curtain (2) [kər'tən], *n.* a cloth which is hung at a window or in front of a stage to decorate, hide, cover or separate one place from another. **Ex.** *She made curtains for the kitchen windows.*

curve (2) [kərv'], *n.* a bending line, as in part of a circle. **Ex.** *The road had many curves.* —*v.* bend in a curve. **Ex.** *The road curved away from the river.*

cushion (4) [kuš'ən], *n.* 1. a soft pillow to sit on or lean against. **Ex.** *Here is a cushion for your chair.* 2. anything that acts like a pillow in softening or protecting against a blow or shock. **Ex.** *His medical insurance was a cushion against the expenses of his illness.* —*v.* 1. provide with cushions or cushionlike pads. **Ex.** *We cushioned the bench in the hall.* 2. give some protection against a blow or shock. **Ex.** *His heavy clothing cushioned his fall.*

custody [kəs'tədiy], *n.* 1. caring for or keeping someone or something; guardianship. **Ex.** *The grandparents were given custody of the orphan.* 2. the state of being held or guarded, especially by the police. **Ex.** *The stolen goods were in the custody of the police.*

custom (2) [kəs'təm], *n.* 1. a long-established habit or habits having almost the force of law. **Ex.** *They were strangers and did not know our customs.* 2. a usual action; habit. **Ex.** *It was his custom to take a bath before going to bed.* —**cus'tom·ar·y,** *adj.* usual. —**cus'toms,** *n.* taxes paid to the government on things brought from a foreign country; the government agency collecting these taxes.

customer (3) [kəs'təmər], *n.* a person who buys from another. **Ex.** *This store has thousands of customers.*

cut (1) [kət'], *v.* 1. make a hole, narrow opening, wound, etc. with a knife or other sharp-edged tool. **Ex.** *He cut himself while shaving.* 2. divide into parts using such a tool; carve. **Ex.** *Please cut me a slice of bread.* 3. make or form by cutting. **Ex.** *She cut out a dress.* 4. shorten by trimming. **Ex.** *He cut the grass.* 5. lower; reduce. **Ex.** *They had to cut expenses.* —*n.* 1. the result of cutting; a wound. **Ex.** *He received a cut on his hand.* 2. a reduction. **Ex.** *There was a cut in prices.* —**cut back,** shorten; reduce in size. **Ex.** *He cut back the rose bush.* —**cut down,** reduce; lessen. **Ex.** *I must cut down on what I eat.* —**cut in,** move between; interrupt. **Ex.** *He cut in on their conversation.* —**cut short,** stop without finishing. **Ex.** *He cut short his visit.*

cute [kyut'], *adj.* charmingly pretty; appealing. **Ex.** *How cute your little girl is!*

-cy (3) [siy], *suffix*. 1. quality; condition; state. **Exs.** *Hesitant, hesitancy; frequent, frequency.* 2. rank; position. **Exs.** *President, presidency; captain, captaincy.*

cycle [say'kəl], *n*. 1. a series of events occurring in a regular order time after time. **Ex.** *His life seems to have been a cycle of success and failure.* 2. the period of time needed for completion of such a series. **Ex.** *The rinse cycle of our washing machine takes about fifteen minutes.*

cyclone [say'klown], *n*. an extremely violent wind that moves very quickly in a circle around a calm central area, often accompanied by a severe storm. **Ex.** *House after house had its roof ripped off by the cyclone.*

cylinder (5) [sil'əndər], *n*. a round object with two flat ends; a roller-shaped object which may be hollow or solid. **—cy·lin'dri·cal,** *adj*.

CYLINDER

D

D, d [diy'], *n*. the fourth letter of the English alphabet.

dad (3) [dæd'], *n*. a familiar term for father. **—dad'dy,** *n*. a child's word for father.

daffodil [dæf'ədil'], *n*. an early spring plant with long leaves and yellow or white flowers which have bell-shaped centers. **Ex.** *She arranged a bunch of daffodils in a glass bowl.*

dagger (5) [dæg'ər], *n*. a short knife with a pointed blade used as a weapon. **Ex.** *The murderer had used a dagger.*

DAFFODIL

daily (1) [dey'liy], *adj.* every day. **Ex.** *How many daily newspapers do you read?* —*adv.*

dainty (4) [deyn'tiy], *adj.* of delicate beauty and charm. **Ex.** *The tea was served in dainty little cups.* —**dain·ti·ly,** *adv.* —**dain'ti ·ness,** *n.*

dairy (4) [de:r'iy], *n.* 1. a place where milk and cream are stored or are made into butter and cheese. **Ex.** *In this dairy, the milk from the cows is stored in a stainless steel tank.* 2. a store or company that sells milk, butter, cheese, ice cream, etc. —*adj.* —**dair'y farm,** *n.* a farm on which cows are kept and milk is the chief product.

daisy [dey'siy], *n.* a flower with leaflike divisions of white, yellow or pink around a yellow center. **Ex.** *White daisies were scattered through the tall grass.*

DAISY

dam (4) [dæm'], *n.* a wall built across a river to hold back flowing water. **Ex.** *Dams are essential to our flood-control program.* —*v.* hold back by means of a dam. **Ex.** *Engineers are going to dam the river three miles north of the city.*

damage (2) [dæm'ij], *n.* harm; hurt; loss due to injury. **Ex.** *The damage to the finish of the table was caused by cleaning it with soap and water.* —*v.* harm; hurt; injure. **Ex.** *The fire damaged everything in the store.* —**dam'a·ges,** *n.pl.* money asked or paid for harm or damage done. **Ex.** *The judge ordered him to pay the damages claimed.*

damn (4) [dæm'], *v.* 1. condemn as bad, not legal or wicked. **Ex.** *The critics damned his new play.* 2. curse. **Ex.** *In his anger, he damned his friend.* —*n.* the use of the word damn as a curse. —**dam·na'tion,** *n.*

damp (3) [dæmp'], *adj.* slightly wet; moist. **Ex.** *She put a damp cloth on his forehead.* —**damp'en,** *v.* 1. make moist. **Ex.** *The light rain dampened our clothes.* 2. slow; decrease; make dull. **Ex.** *The bad news dampened their enthusiasm.* —**damp'ly,** *adv.* —**damp'ness,** *n.*

dance (1) [dæns'], *v.* 1. move the feet and body, usually to music or the beat of a drum, either alone or with others. 2. move in a lively way. **Ex.** *She danced with joy at the good news.* —*n.* 1. a series of steps, usually in time to music. **Ex.** *Everyone wants to learn the latest dance.* 2. a party where people dance.

Ex. *With whom are you going to the dance?* —**danc'er,** *n.* a person who dances.

dandelion [dæn'dəlay'ən], *n.* a small, edible, bright yellow wildflower with long leaves. **Ex.** *She uses the leaves of dandelions to make salad and the flowers to make wine.*

danger (1) [deyn'jər], *n.* 1. a situation in which great harm, injury or loss is possible. **Ex.** *The ship was in danger of sinking during the storm.* 2. something that may cause harm. **Ex.** *In spite of the great danger, there was no loss of life.* **dan'ger·ous,** *adj.*

DANDELION

dare (1) [de:r'], *v.* 1. have courage; be bold; meet bravely. **Ex.** *Do you dare climb that mountain alone?* 2. tell someone to do something to show he or she is not afraid; challenge. **Ex.** *He dared his brother to jump from the tree.* —*n.* a challenge. **Ex.** *He was too wise to accept the dare.* —**dar'ing,** *adj.* brave; fearless.

dark (1) [dark'], *adj.* 1. without light. **Ex.** *The room was completely dark.* 2. not light colored. **Ex.** *She wore a dark blue dress.* —*n.* lack of light; a dark place or time. **Ex.** *The child did not like the dark.* —**dark'en,** *v.* make dark or darker. **Ex.** *The sky darkened before the storm.* —**dark'ly,** *adv.* —**dark'ness,** *n.*

darling (3) [dar'liŋ], *n.* one who is dearly loved. **Exs.** *What time are you coming home, darling? Their only child is their darling.* —*adj.* dearly loved. **Ex.** *He is a darling baby.*

darn (4) [darn'], *v.* fix a hole in cloth by sewing threads over it. **Ex.** *His wife darned the hole in his sweater.* —*n.* the place fixed in this way. **Ex.** *The darn could hardly be seen.*

dart (3) [dart'], *n.* a short, pointed weapon or toy, either shot or thrown. **Ex.** *They were playing a game of darts.* —*v.* suddenly begin to run fast. **Ex.** *The child darted away from his mother.*

dash (3) [dæš'], *n.* 1. a mark (—) used in writing or printing. 2. a small amount. **Ex.** *The soup needs a dash of pepper.* 3. a short race. **Ex.** *He won the 100-yard dash.* —*v.* 1. run fast. **Ex.** *The boy dashed for the bus.* 2. throw or scatter a liquid. **Ex.** *The waves dashed against the rocks.* 3. break or throw with violence. **Ex.** *In her anger, she dashed the glass to the floor.* —**dash'ing,** *adj.* colorful; lively. **Ex.** *They are a dashing couple.*

data (5) [dey'tə, dæt'ə], *n.* facts or information, often expressed in numbers, used in reaching conclusions, making decisions, etc. **Ex.** *He is gathering data about birds for a scientific study.*

date (1) [deyt'], *n.* 1. a statement of time. **Ex.** *The date of the meeting was set for next Friday.* 2. an agreement to see a friend at a certain time. **Ex.** *I have a date with my friend tomorrow.* —*v.* 1. note the time of writing or doing. **Ex.** *Please date all of your letters.* 2. give the date at which something happened or existed. **Ex.** *Historians date the event as occurring in the eleventh century.* 3. belong to a specific time. **Ex.** *This house dates back to 1800.* —**dat'ed,** *adj.* 1. not current; out-of-date; 2. marked with a date.

date (1) [deyt'], *n.* the sweet fruit of a type of palm tree. **Ex.** *This cake calls for one cup of chopped dates.*

daughter (1) [dɔ:'tər], *n.* a female child considered in relation to her father, her mother or both parents. **Ex.** *She is the older daughter.*

daughter-in-law (3) [dɔ:'tərinlɔ:'], *n.* the wife of one's son. **Ex.** *She was very fond of her daughter-in-law.*

daunt (5) [dɔ:nt'], *v.* frighten; discourage. **Ex.** *He was not daunted by the threat to his life.* —**daunt'less,** *adj.* fearless.

dawn (2) [dɔ:n'], *n.* 1. sunrise. **Ex.** *We started our trip at dawn.* 2. the beginning. **Ex.** *Since the dawn of time, man has struggled with nature.* —*v.* become light. **Ex.** *The day dawned bright and sunny.*

day (1) [dey'], *n.* 1. a twenty-four-hour period. **Ex.** *He will be gone for three days.* 2. the time of light; the time between sunrise and dark.

daydream [dey'driym'], *n.* a time of dreamy thinking while awake. **Ex.** *He leaned back in his chair and gave way to daydreams.* —*v.* have daydreams.

daylight [dey'layt], *n.* 1. the light of day; the time between sunrise and sunset. **Ex.** *This is work that I need to do in daylight.* 2. the break of day; dawn. **Ex.** *We started our trip at daylight.*

daze (5) [deyz'], *v.* confuse or stun by a blow or shock. **Ex.** *He was dazed by the fall.* —*n.* condition of being dazed. **Ex.** *The injured girl was in a daze after the accident.*

dazzle (5) [dæz'əl], *v.* 1. confuse with a very bright light. **Ex.** *Coming out of the dark theater, we were dazzled by the* *bright sunlight.* 2. surprise; cause admiration. **Ex.** *He was dazzled by the girl's beauty.* —**daz'zling,** *adj.*

de- (1) [diy], *prefix.* 1. do the reverse; undo. **Exs.** *Frost, defrost; increase, decrease.* 2. take away. **Exs.** *Vein, devein; inflate, deflate.*

dead (1) [ded'], *adj.* 1. no longer alive. **Ex.** *The patient is dead.* 2. not now in use. **Ex.** *Dead languages are still studied in school.* —*n.* a dead person or persons. **Ex.** *We put flowers on the graves of the dead.* —**dead'en,** *v.* make dead; lessen feeling. **Ex.** *The doctor gave him medicine to deaden his pain.* —**dead'ly,** *adj.* 1. able to cause death. **Ex.** *A deadly poison is made from this plant.* 2. like death. **Ex.** *Her face grew deadly pale.* —**dead'end'** 1. a street, passage, pipe, etc. closed at one end. **Ex.** *This street is a dead end.* 2. a situation, job, etc. which is leading nowhere. **Ex.** *His research proved to be a dead end.*

deadline [ded'layn`], *n.* the time by which it is necessary that something be done. **Ex.** *The deadline for completing this work is five o'clock Monday afternoon.*

deadlock [ded'lak`], *n.* a point in a dispute, struggle, etc., at which both sides are equally strong and neither can win. **Ex.** *The two leaders were at a deadlock in their discussion, and neither would make any concessions.*

deaf (3) [def'], *adj.* 1. unable to hear; unable to hear properly. **Ex.** *He was deaf and could not hear the noise.* 2. unwilling to hear. **Ex.** *He was deaf to my pleading.* —**deaf'en,** *v.* —**deaf'ness,** *n.*

deal (1) [diyl'], *v.* 1. treat; be concerned with; give attention to. **Ex.** *You must learn to deal with your problems.* 2. act or behave. **Ex.** *That lawyer deals honorably with everyone.* 3. do business in or with; buy or sell. **Ex.** *We deal directly with the farmers for our vegetables.* 4. deliver; give. **Ex.** *The fighters were dealing each other severe blows.* —**deal'er,** *n.* a person whose business it is to buy and sell. **Ex.** *Buy your car from a dependable automobile dealer.*

dealt [delt'], *v.* past and past participle of *deal.* **Exs.** *He dealt five cards to each person. Why haven't you dealt with this matter yet?*

a, far; æ, am; e, get; ey, late; i, in; iy, see; ɔ, all; ow, go; u, put; uw, too; ə, but, ago; ər, fur; aw, out; ay, life; oy, boy; ŋ, ring; θ, think; ð, that; ž, measure; š, ship; ǰ, edge; č, child.

dean (5) [diyn'], *n.* an official of a college or school who is in charge of students or teachers. **Ex.** *He is dean of men.*

dear (1) [di:r'], *adj.* 1. loved very much. **Ex.** *He is a dear friend of mine.* 2. highly respected; a polite form of address. **Ex.** *He began the letter with the words Dear Sir.* —*n.* a person who is loved. **Ex.** *Your mother is a dear.* —**dear'ly,** *adv.*

death (2) [deθ'], *n.* the ending of life; act of dying. **Ex.** *After his death, his body was sent home to be buried.* —**death'ly,** *adj., adv.* like death. **Exs.** *There was a deathly silence after his announcement. The house was deathly cold.*

debate (4) [dibeyt'], *v.* give arguments for or against something. **Ex.** *The people of the town debated whether to build a new road.* —*n.* a public argument for and against a question; a discussion. **Ex.** *The high school students are having a debate today.* —**de·bat'a·ble,** *adj.* —**de·bat'er,** *n.*

debris [dəbriy'], *n.* unwanted, broken or destroyed remains; rubbish; trash. **Ex.** *They had begun to clear up the debris from the storm.*

debt (2) [det'], *n.* 1. something that is owed. **Ex.** *His debts are more than he can pay.* 2. the obligation to pay; the condition of owing. **Ex.** *He is in debt to his brother.* —**debt'or,** *n.* one who owes a debt.

decade [dek'eyd], *n.* a period of ten years. **Ex.** *Decades of neglect had reduced the house to ruins.*

decay (3) [dikey'], *v.* 1. rot; spoil; become bad. **Ex.** *The wood in this fence is decaying.* 2. lose health and strength; pass gradually from a good condition to a poor one. **Ex.** *His strength is decaying with old age.* —*n.* 1. a gradual decline; a falling into ruin. **Ex.** *The beautiful old house had fallen into decay.* 2. state of being rotten. **Ex.** *There were no signs of decay in the tooth.*

deceit (5) [disiyt'], *n.* the act or practice of deceiving or lying. **Ex.** *Those merchants used deceit in their business dealings.* —**de·ceit'ful,** *adj.*

deceive (3) [disiyv'], *v.* lead into error; cause someone to believe what is not true. **Ex.** *He deceived his friends about his income.* —**de·ceiv'er,** *n.* —**de·ceiv'ing,** *adj.*

December (1) [disem'bər], *n.* the twelfth and last month of the year.

decent (3) [diy'sənt], *adj.* 1. proper; respectable; modest. **Ex.** *He always uses decent language.* 2. moderate but sufficient. **Ex.** *He earns a decent salary.* —**de'cen·cy,** *n.* —**de'cent·ly,** *adv.*

deception (5) [disep'šən], *n.* that which deceives; the act of deceiving. **Ex.** *His deception led us to believe he had gone.* —**de·cep'tive,** *adj.*

decide (1) [disayd'], *v.* 1. choose to do after thinking carefully. **Ex.** *He decided to leave home.* 2. end a contest by selecting one side as the victor; settle; judge. **Ex.** *The jury will decide the case tomorrow.*

decimal [des'əməl], *adj.* based on the number ten. **Ex.** *The decimal system is the basis for counting money in the United States.* —*n.* a fraction expressed in terms of ten or multiples of ten. **Ex.** *The fraction 7/10 expressed as a decimal is .7.* —**dec'i·mal point',** *n.* a dot preceding the number expressed as a decimal.

decision (3) [disiž'ən], *n.* 1. a settling; the act of resolving a problem by giving a judgment on the matter; the conclusion arrived at. **Ex.** *I made a decision to accept the job offer.* 2. the personal qualities of firmness and determination. **Ex.** *He is a man of decision.*

decisive [diysays'iv], *adj.* 1. having the power to make a final determination. **Ex.** *The matching fingerprint was the decisive factor in the jury's verdict.* 2. acting with firmness and determination. **Ex.** *His decisive manner helped him to get the job.* 3. without doubt or question. **Ex.** *The election was a decisive defeat for the opposition.* —**de·ci'sive·ly,** *adv.*

deck (2) [dek'], *n.* 1. the floor or floors of a ship. **Ex.** *The ship had seven decks.* 2. a set of playing cards. **Ex.** *There are fifty-two cards in the deck.*

declare (2) [dikle:r'], *v.* say positively; cause to be known; proclaim. **Ex.** *"I refuse to go," he declared.* —**dec'la·ra' tion,** *n.*

decline (2) [diklayn'], *v.* 1. refuse. **Ex.** *They declined the invitation.* 2. become less, as in strength, power, value. **Ex.** *His health is declining.* —*n.* 1. a lessening in power, health, value, etc.; the period when this is happening. **Ex.** *There was a decline in the sale of automobiles this month compared to last month.* 2. a descending slope. **Ex.** *The car rolled down the decline.*

decorate (3) [dek'əreyt'], v. 1. put ornaments on; make more pleasing by adding to. **Ex.** *We decorated the hall with flags.* 2. select the colors and furnishings of a house. **Ex.** *They decorated their house in a Spanish style.* 3. give a medal, a ribbon, etc. as an honor. **Ex.** *The soldier was decorated for his heroism.* —**dec'o·ra·tor,** n. one who decorates. —**dec'o·ra'tion,** n. anything used to decorate. —**dec'o·ra·tive,** adj.

decrease (3) [dikriys'], v. cause to become less; gradually become smaller in size, number, etc. **Ex.** *We will decrease the size of the group from thirty to twenty.* —n. 1. a lessening. **Ex.** *There was a decrease in sales this week.* 2. amount of lessening. **Ex.** *The decrease in price was 10 percent.*

decree (5) [dikriy'], n. an official government order or decision. **Ex.** *By decree, tomorrow has been declared a day of mourning.* —v. decide or order by decree. **Ex.** *The judge decreed that a divorce be granted.*

dedicate (4) [ded'əkeyt'], v. 1. devote to a special or sacred purpose. **Ex.** *The statue was dedicated to the soldiers who had died in battle.* 2. give or devote. **Ex.** *He had dedicated his life to serving others.* 3. honor a person by putting his name at the beginning of a book, poem, etc. **Ex.** *The author's latest book was dedicated to his father.* —**ded'i·ca'tion,** n.

deduct [diydəkt'], v. take away from a total; subtract. **Ex.** *How much can we deduct for medical expenses on our tax return?* —**de·duc'tion,** n., the act of deducting; the amount deducted.

deed (2) [diyd'], n. an act; that which is done. **Ex.** *His deeds did not reflect his words.* 2. a paper which shows ownership of property. **Ex.** *After he had paid for the house, he was given the deed to it.*

deem (5) [diym'], v. believe; think; judge. **Ex.** *He deems it wise to remain silent.*

deep (1) [diyp'], adj. 1. going far down. **Ex.** *The ocean is deep here.* 2. going from front to back. **Ex.** *This stage is only twenty-five feet deep.* 3. extreme. **Ex.** *He is in deep trouble.* 4. low in tone. **Ex.** *He has a deep voice.* 5. strong and dark in color. **Ex.** *Dried blood is a deep red in color.* 6. felt strongly. **Ex.** *You have my deep sympathy.* 7. greatly absorbed. **Ex.** *They were in deep conversation.* —n. 1. a deep thing or place. **Ex.** *The great fish disappeared into the deep.* 2. the most extreme part. **Ex.** *The cold is most* *severe in the deep of winter.* —*adv.* to or at a depth. **Ex.** *They must dig deep for water.* —**deep'en,** *v.* —**deep'ly,** *adv.*

deer (3) [di:r'], *n.* a wild animal with horns and hoofs.

defeat (2) [difiyt'], *v.* 1. overcome; cause to lose in a battle or struggle. **Ex.** *We defeated the enemy.* 2. make hopeless. **Ex.** *Our plans for the trip were defeated by the weather.* —*n.* failure; state of having lost. **Ex.** *After his defeat in the elections, he returned to his former business.*

DEER

defect (4) [diy'fekt`, difekt'], *n.* a fault; a weakness; something not perfect. **Ex.** *The car was unsafe because of a defect in construction.* —**de·fec'tive,** *adj.*

defect (4) [diyfekt'], *v.* leave one's cause, group or country for another. **Ex.** *He defected because he no longer believed in the policies of his government.* —**de·fec'tion,** *n.* —**de·fec'tor,** *n.*

defend (2) [difend'], *v.* 1. protect; keep safe; guard. **Ex.** *The dog defended his master from the attack.* 2. act, speak or write in favor of something under attack. **Ex.** *He wrote a letter to the newspaper defending his actions.* —**de·fend'ant,** *n.* a person against whom legal action is brought. —**de·fend'er,** *n.* one who defends. —**de·fen'sive,** *adj.*

defense (3) [difens'], *n.* 1. act of defending; resistance against attack. **Ex.** *The army's defense of the city was successful.* 2. argument in support of one's actions. **Ex.** *The president gave a speech in defense of his policies.* 3. that which is used to protect. **Ex.** *High walls were their only defense against the enemy.*

defer (5) [difər'], *v.* delay until a later time. **Ex.** *The ship deferred its sailing because of bad weather.* —**de·fer'ment,** *n.*

defer (5) [difər'], *v.* yield to the judgment or opinion of another. **Ex.** *I will defer to your greater experience in matters of this kind.* —**def'er·ence,** *n.*

defiance (5) [difay'əns], *n.* the act of defying. **Ex.** *He showed his defiance by walking away.* —**de·fi'ant,** *adj.* showing defiance. **Ex.** *His defiant attitude surprised us.*

deficiency [difi'šənsiy], *n.* a shortage or lack of something needed; lack. **Ex.** *She has a calcium deficiency.* **de·fi'cient,** *adj.* lacking; having an absence or shortage of. **Ex.** *The plan was deficient in detail.*

deficit [def'əsit], *n.* the amount by which money spent is greater than money coming in; the amount by which the money on hand is less than that required; shortage. **Ex.** *Taxes are going to be raised to compensate for the budget deficit.*

defile (5) [difayl'], *v.* 1. make dirty or impure. **Ex.** *The river was defiled by the wastes poured into it.* 2. bring dishonor upon. **Ex.** *His shameful acts defiled his family's name.*

define (4) [difayn'], *v.* 1. give the meaning of; explain. **Ex.** *A dictionary defines words.* 2. fix the limits of. **Ex.** *The treaty defined the boundary between the two countries.* **—def·i·ni'tion,** *n.* meaning. **Ex.** *What is the definition of that word?*

definite (3) [def'ənət], *adj.* 1. clear; exact. **Ex.** *His meaning is very definite.* 2. limiting; determining; fixed. **Ex.** *This work must be completed within a definite period of time.* **—def'i·nite·ly,** *adv.*

defy (4) [difay'], *v.* 1. dare; challenge to do something that is difficult or not possible. **Ex.** *I defy you to solve this problem.* 2. refuse to obey; pay no attention to. **Ex.** *The driver of the car was defying the law by speeding.* 3. withstand; resist successfully. **Ex.** *The beauty of this scene defies description.*

degree (1) [dəgriy'], *n.* 1. a step or stage in a series. **Ex.** *The country reached a high degree of civilization.* 2. a unit used in measuring temperature. 3. one 360th of a circle. (The sign for degree in temperature measurements or parts of a circle is °. **Ex.** *90°.*) 4. the rank given by a university to a student who fulfills certain requirements or to a person as an honor. **Ex.** *He received a graduate degree this past June.*

dejected [diyjekt'id], *adj.* low in spirit; depressed; sad. **Ex.** *She was dejected because she was not going to the dance.* **—de·jec'tion,** *n.*

delay (2) [diley'], *v.* 1. decide to do at a later time. **Ex.** *He has delayed his trip for two weeks.* 2. cause to be late; stop for a time. **Ex.** *The accident delayed the train.* **—n.** a wait; a length of time before something happens or someone appears. **Ex.** *There will be a delay of two hours because of engine trouble.*

delegate (3) [del'əgeyt], *n.* one sent to act for another; one who represents another. **Ex.** *Delegates have been sent by three countries.* **—v.** 1. send to represent. **Ex.** *We delegated one of our most able men to go.* 2. transfer authority or responsibility to another.

Ex. *He delegated some of the work to his assistant.* **—del'e·ga'tion,** *n.* 1. the act of delegating. 2. a group of delegates.

deliberate (4) [dəlib'ərət], *adj.* 1. intentional; for a specific purpose. **Ex.** *The man gave me a deliberate push.* 2. slow and careful in deciding what to do. **Ex.** *She was very deliberate in her actions.* **—de·lib'er·ate·ly,** *adv.* **—de·lib`er·a'tion,** *n.*

deliberate [dəlib'əreyt`], *v.* consider carefully before deciding. **Ex.** *The jury deliberated for several hours before declaring the accused guilty.*

delicate (2) [del'əkət], *adj.* 1. pleasing because of fineness. **Ex.** *The wine has a delicate flavor.* 2. finely made; fine in quality. **Ex.** *The box was decorated with delicate carvings.* 3. easily broken; not strong. **Ex.** *They drank from delicate glasses.* 4. requiring careful handling. **Ex.** *The teacher handled the delicate problem with understanding.* **—del'i·cate·ly,** *adv.* **—del'i·ca·cy,** *n.* 1. condition of being delicate. 2. fine or unusual food.

delicatessen [del`ikətes'ən], *n.* a store or section of a store that sells cooked dishes, cold meats, salads, etc. **Ex.** *Instead of preparing a meal for our guests, we bought some food at the delicatessen.*

delicious (3) [dəliš'əs], *adj.* very pleasing to the taste; delightful. **Ex.** *The food was delicious.*

delight (1) [dilayt'], *n.* 1. great joy or pleasure. **Ex.** *She felt great delight at meeting her old friends again.* 2. something that gives pleasure. **Ex.** *My flower garden has been a delight this spring.* *—v.* 1. please greatly. **Ex.** *Their gift delighted her.* 2. feel great pleasure. **Ex.** *They were delighted to hear the good news.* **—de·light'ful,** *adj.*

delinquency [diylin'kwənsiy], *n.* 1. behavior, particularly by young people, that does not conform to accepted social and legal standards. **Ex.** *His repeated delinquencies had brought him to court.* 2. failure to meet one's obligations, especially to pay bills. **Ex.** *His delinquency in paying the rent has resulted in his eviction from his apartment.* **—de·lin'quent,** *adj.* *—n.* a delinquent person.

deliver (2) [diliv'ər], *v.* 1. carry and give to someone. **Ex.** *Please deliver this package to my mother.* 2. speak. **Ex.** *He delivered an excellent speech.* 3. strike. **Ex.** *The boxer delivered a blow to the other boxer's head.* 4. help to give birth. **Ex.** *The doctor delivered the child.* 5. set free; release; save from danger. **—de·liv'er·ance,** *n.* the act of saving; the state of being saved from danger. **Ex.** *They prayed for the deliverance of the trapped miners.* **—de·liv'ery,** *n.* the act of delivering.

delusion (5) [diluw'žən], *n.* a mistaken belief, often a sign of mental illness. Ex. *He was under the delusion that he was a king.* —de·lude, *v.* deceive; mislead. Ex. *Don't delude yourself into thinking that you can pass this course without working.*

demand (1) [dimænd'], *v.* 1. request as a right. Ex. *He demanded to be heard.* 2. request with authority. Ex. *The policeman demanded our names.* 3. require; need. Ex. *The man's wound demanded immediate attention.* —n. 1. act of demanding. Ex. *He stated his demand in a loud voice.* 2. an expressed desire for ownership or use. Ex. *The great demand for cotton cloth raised the price.*

democracy (2) [dəmak'rəsiy], *n.* a system of government in which the people hold the ruling power by electing certain persons to make the laws and to do the work of governing.

democrat (2) [dem'əkræt], *n.* 1. a person who believes that a country should be governed by and for the people. 2. a member of the Democratic party, one of the two main political parties in the United States. —dem'o·crat'ic, *adj.*

demolish (5) [dimal'iš], *v.* destroy; tear down; ruin. Ex. *The building was demolished by the wreckers.* —dem'o·li'tion, *n.* the act of destroying.

demonstrate (4) [dem'ənstreyt'], *v.* 1. prove by facts. Ex. *The scientist demonstrated the correctness of his theory.* 2. explain by using examples. Ex. *The teacher demonstrated by showing the students pictures.* 3. make a public show of opinions or feelings. Ex. *Hundreds demonstrated to protest the tax.* —dem'on·stra'tion, *n.* —de·mon'stra·tive, *adj.* showing feelings openly. Ex. *Her demonstrative ways embarrassed him.*

den (5) [den'], *n.* 1. a place where a wild animal lives. Ex. *The hunter followed the lion to its den.* 2. a small private room used for reading or studying. Ex. *The professor worked in his den until midnight.*

denial (5) [dinay'əl], *n.* 1. refusal of a request, right, opportunity, etc. Ex. *The denial of her request upset her.* 2. act of declaring that a statement is not true. Ex. *He made a denial of any connection with the crime.*

denounce (5) [dinawns'], *v.* 1. state a dislike for. Ex. *He denounced the man as a coward.* 2. inform against; accuse. Ex. *She denounced him to the police.*

dense (4) [dens'], *adj.* 1. thick; crowded; close together. Ex. *Dense smoke filled the room.* 2. slow to understand; dull;

stupid. **Ex.** *When I tried to explain the new proposal to her, she seemed very dense.* —**dense'ly,** *adv.* —**dense'ness, den'si·ty,** *n.*

dent [dent'], *n.* a place lower than the surface around it; a hollow, made by a blow or pressure. **Ex.** *He escaped from the accident with only a couple of dents in his car.* —*v.* make such a place by a blow or pressure. **Ex.** *His car dented mine in the accident.*

dental (5) [den'təl], *adj.* concerning teeth or the work of dentists. **Ex.** *He needs dental care.* —**den'tist,** *n.* a doctor whose work is caring for teeth. —**den'tis·try,** *n.* the work of dentists.

deny (2) [dinay'], *v.* 1. declare to be untrue. **Ex.** *He denied that he took the book.* 2. refuse to fulfill a request, allow an opportunity, etc. **Ex.** *His employer denied him an increase in salary.*

depart (4) [dipart'], *v.* 1. leave; go away. **Ex.** *He said good-by and departed.* 2. make a change. **Ex.** *The radio station departed from its usual program.* —**de·par'ture,** *n.*

department (2) [dipart'mənt], *n.* a separate part of a government, business or other organization. **Ex.** *This college has an excellent history department.* —**de'part·men'tal,** *adj.*

department store [dipart'mənt stɔ:r'], *n.* a large store, organized into departments, selling many different things and services.

depend (2) [dipend'], *v.* 1. rely on for help or support. **Ex.** *The children depend upon their father to wake them up in the morning.* 2. be controlled by. **Ex.** *Whether or not we go on the trip depends on the weather.* —**de·pend'ent,** *adj.* relying on or controlled by. —*n.* one who depends upon another. —**de·pend' ence,** *n.* state of being dependent.

deport (2) [dipɔrt'], *v.* force to leave the country. **Ex.** *He was deported from the United States.* —**de'por·ta'tion,** *n.*

deposit (3) [dipaz'ət], *v.* 1. put down; place. **Ex.** *Deposit the package on the table.* 2. place in a bank account. **Ex.** *He deposited part of his salary in the bank.* 3. give as part of total payment. **Ex.** *He deposited a small amount of money toward the purchase of the car.* —*n.* 1. money paid to or in a bank account. 2. a part payment on a purchase. 3. a quantity of a mineral, such as oil or gas, found in nature. **Ex.** *The country has large oil deposits.*

depression (3) [dipreš'ən], *n.* 1. a place lower than the surface around it. **Ex.** *The heavy rains filled the depression in the road.* 2. low spirits. **Ex.** *The man had feelings of depression because of his illness.* 3. a period of reduced business activity during which many people lose their jobs. **Ex.** *There was a severe depression in the 1930s.* —**de·press'**, *v.* cause to feel unhappy. **Ex.** *The news depressed him.* —**de·press'ing**, *adj.*

deprive (5) [diprayv'], *v.* keep from using, having, enjoying, etc.; take away from. **Ex.** *Death deprived the young children of their parents.* —**dep'ri·va'tion**, *n.*

depth (3) [depθ'], *n.* 1. measurement down from the surface; deepness. **Ex.** *The depth of the river at this point is twenty feet.* 2. measurement from the front to the back or from the top to the bottom. **Ex.** *What is the depth of that box?*

deputy (4) [dep'yuwtiy], *n.* a person appointed to act in place of another; an assistant. **Ex.** *The sheriff appointed a deputy.* —**dep'u·tize**, *v.*

derive (3) [dirayv'], *v.* take; get; obtain; receive. **Ex.** *He derives pleasure from books.* —**der'i·va'tion**, *n.* the source of something. —**de·riv'a·tive**, *adj.* derived from. —*n.* that which is derived.

descend (3) [disend'], *v.* go or come down. **Exs.** *The woman descended the stairs. The business will descend to my son.* —**descend from**, have as an ancestor. **Ex.** *He is descended from a famous writer.* —**de·scend'ant**, *n.* one who is related to a particular ancestor. —**de·scent'**, *n.* act of descending.

describe (2) [diskrayb'], *v.* give an account of. **Ex.** *He described his sister to me.* —**de·scrip'tion**, *n.* written or spoken words used to tell about a person, place, happening, etc. **Ex.** *His description of the child's grief saddened everyone.* —**de·scrip'tive**, *adj.*

desert (2) [dez'ərt], *n.* a dry area, usually sandy, with little or no plant life. **Ex.** *He was almost overcome by the heat of the desert.*

desert (2) [dizərt'], *v.* 1. abandon; fail when needed. **Ex.** *He deserted his wife.* 2. leave military duty without permission. **Ex.** *The soldier deserted his post and fled to a nearby town.* —**de·sert'er**, *n.* —**de·ser'tion**, *n.*

deserve (2) [dizərv'], *v.* be worthy of; merit; earn. **Ex.** *Their efforts deserve to be rewarded.*

design (2) [dizayn'], *v.* 1. plan; intend; scheme. **Ex.** *Her questions were designed to make me angry.* 2. make plans for. **Ex.** *She designed and made the dress that she is wearing.* —*n.* 1. a sketch; a plan for a house, a city, a bridge, etc. **Ex.** *Have they approved the design for the store yet?* 2. an artistic arrangement; a pattern. **Ex.** *The material has a beautiful design of flowers.*

desire (1) [dizayr'], *v.* want very much. **Ex.** *They desire to have their son become a doctor.* —*n.* a want; the thing wanted. **Ex.** *His greatest desire is to be able to sleep.* —**de·sir'a·ble,** *adj.* worthy of wanting; valuable. **Ex.** *The house is in a desirable location.*

desk (2) [desk'], *n.* a piece of furniture like a table, usually with drawers, which is used for writing, studying, etc. **Ex.** *She was sitting at her desk and going over the household accounts.*

desolate (4) [des'ələt], *adj.* 1. not lived in; deserted; ruined. **Ex.** *A desolate house stood in the deserted mining town.* 2. unhappy; miserable; lonely. **Ex.** *She has led a desolate life since his death.* —*v.* ruin; lay waste. **Ex.** *The fire desolated a large part of the city.* —**des'o·late·ly,** *adv.* —**des'o·la'tion,** *n.*

despair (2) [dispe:r'], *n.* state of hopelessness. **Ex.** *He was in despair when his father died.* —*v.* lose hope; be without hope. **Ex.** *They despaired of being rescued.*

desperate (3) [des'pərət], *adj.* 1. despairing; almost without hope. **Ex.** *The enemy attack left them in a desperate situation.* 2. reckless; extreme. **Ex.** *He took a desperate chance.* —**des'per·ate·ly,** *adv.* —**des'per·a'tion,** *n.*

despise (3) [dispayz'], *v.* dislike very much; scorn. **Ex.** *He despises people who lie.* —**des·pi'ca·ble,** *adj.*

despite (3) [dispayt'], *prep.* in spite of; regardless. **Ex.** *He went despite my warning.*

dessert (3) [dəzərt'], *n.* a sweet dish or fruit served at the end of a meal. **Ex.** *Apple pie is a favorite American dessert.*

destine (4) [des'tən], *v.* be fated for. **Ex.** *He was destined to become a great president.* —**destined for,** going toward as planned. **Ex.** *The ship was destined for South America.* —**des'ti·na'tion,** *n.*

destiny (4) [des'təniy], *n.* 1. that which is certain to happen. **Ex.** *It was his destiny to die young.* 2. a course of events often thought of as detemined in advance and impossible to change. **Ex.** *Destiny directed him toward the life of a soldier.*

destroy (1) [distroy'], *v.* 1. break into pieces; ruin. **Ex.** *Fire destroyed his house.* 2. kill. **Ex.** *They destroyed the enemy.* —**de·stroy'er**, *n.* 1. one who destroys. 2. a small, speedy ship of war.

destruction (3) [distrək'šən], *n.* the act of destroying or being destroyed; ruin. **Ex.** *The destruction of their house left them no place to live.* —**de·struc'tive**, *adj.*

detach (5) [ditæč], *v.* part; separate. **Ex.** *The engine was detached from the rest of the train.* —**de·tach'a·ble**, *adj.* —**de·tached'**, *adj.* —**de·tach'ment**, *n.* 1. a separation. 2. a group of soldiers separated from the others for a special purpose. **Ex.** *He took a detachment up the hill.*

detail (2) [diy'teyl`, di'teyl'], *n.* one small part of a whole. **Ex.** *Each detail of the picture was carefully painted.*

detain (5) [diteyn'], *v.* delay; keep from proceeding. **Ex.** *The accident detained us for an hour.*

detect (4) [ditekt'], *v.* 1. discover the true character of. **Ex.** *He detected a slight degree of fear in her manner.* 2. sense the presence, existence or fact of. **Ex.** *We detected an odor of food in the room.* —**de·tec'tion**, *n.* the act of detecting. —**de·tec'tive**, *n.* a police offficer or private investigator whose work is to collect evidence and information in connection with crimes. —*adj.* concerning police or private investigation work.

detergent [diytərj'ənt], *n.* a substance made from chemicals for washing. **Ex.** *We are trying out a new detergent in our dishwasher.*

determine (2) [ditər'mən], *v.* 1. decide. **Ex.** *The judge will determine who is telling the truth.* 2. resolve. **Ex.** *I am determined to go.* 3. establish accurately. **Ex.** *We must determine the boundaries of our property.* —**de·ter'mi·na'tion**, *n.* —**de·ter'mined**, *adj.*

detour [diy'tuwr], *n.* a way for going around. **Ex.** *Taking the detour made our trip fifteen minutes longer.* —*v.* go around or cause to gc around. **Ex.** *We had to detour because of construction on the main road.*

develop (2) [divel'əp], *v*. 1. cause to grow by gradual change. **Ex.** *Sun and rain help to develop plants.* 2. make or become larger, better, more advanced, more knowledgeable, etc. **Ex.** *He developed his mind by study.* 3. use a section of land in a certain way by constructing buildings, roads, etc. **Ex.** *They are developing this land for a shopping mall.* 4. treat film to make photgraphs. **Ex.** *You can have your film developed at this shop.* —**de·vel'op·ment,** *n*.

device (1) [divays'], *n*. 1. a tool or machine designed for a special purpose. **Ex.** *The steering device on my car is broken.* 2. a plan or scheme used to produce a certain result. **Ex.** *The child's tears were a device to get attention.*

devil (2) [dev'əl], *n*. an evil spirit; the chief evil spirit. **Ex.** *The devil appeared to him in a dream.* —**dev'il·ish,** *adj*.

devise (4) [divayz'], *v*. plan; invent. **Ex.** *He devised a new method of doing the work.*

devote (2) [divowt'], *v*. give one's time completely to some person, purpose or service. **Ex.** *The mother devoted herself to caring for her sick child.* —**de·vo'tion,** *n*.

devour (4) [divawr'], *v*. 1. eat hungrily or greedily. **Ex.** *The starving man devoured the food.* 2. destroy; ruin. **Ex.** *Flames devoured the barn.* 3. take in eagerly by the senses or the mind. **Ex.** *His eyes devoured the contents of the letter.*

dew (3) [duw', dyuw'], *n*. water from the air that condenses on cool surfaces, especially at night. **Ex.** *There was a heavy dew on the grass early this morning.* —**dew'y,** *adj*.

diabetes [day'əbiy'tis], *n*. a disease in which the body is unable to use sugar normally. **Ex.** *The doctor has put him on a special diet because he has diabetes.* —**di·a·bet'ic,** *adj*.

diagnose [day'əgnows'], *v*. discover or identify what is medically wrong by examination and a study of symptoms. **Ex.** *The doctors have not yet been able to diagnose her illness.* —**di· ag·no'sis,** *n*.

diagonal [dayæg'ənəl], *n*. a straight line going from one corner to the opposite corner of a square or rectangle. —*adj*. running in a slanting direction. **Ex.** *Her gray tweed skirt has a pattern of thin red diagonal stripes.* —**di·ag'o·nal·ly,** *adv*.

diagram [166] **diet**

diagram [day'əgræm], *n.* a plan, drawing or outline showing or describing the parts of a thing, how to put them together and, if necessary, how they work. **Ex.** *I find this diagram difficult to follow.* —*v.* explain by means of a plan, drawing or outline.

dial [day'əl], *n.* 1. a face, such as that on a clock or compass, with numbers and one or two pointers by means of which measurements are shown. **Ex.** *He turned the dial of the radio to get a different station.* 2. a disk on a telephone with numbered holes that one moves with a finger in making a call. **Ex.** *Please turn on the light so I can see the dial.* —*v.* 1. get or tune in to a radio station or a television channel. **Ex.** *I am dialing the public television channel.* 2. make a telephone call by dialing. **Ex.** *What number did you dial?* —**dial tone,** *n.* the tone that one hears after picking up the telephone signaling that one may go ahead and dial.

diamond (2) [day'mənd], *n.* 1. a crystallized mineral; one of the hardest substances known. **Ex.** *A clear, pure diamond is a jewel of great value.* 2. a figure with four equal sides but with unequal angles.

DIAMOND 2

diary (5) [day'əriy], *n.* a daily record, especially of personal observations and experiences. **Ex.** *The traveler kept a diary of his trip.*

dictate (4) [dik'teyt`], *v.* 1. read or say something for another to write. **Ex.** *He dictated a letter to his secretary.* 2. command with authority; order. **Ex.** *Terms are dictated to the conquered.* —*n.* a command; a rule. **Ex.** *He followed the dictates of his heart.* —**dic·ta'tion,** *n.* —**dic'ta·tor,** *n.* a ruler who has unlimited power. **Ex.** *The country was ruled by a dictator for many years.* —**dic`ta·to'ri·al,** *adj.*

dictionary (3) [dik'šəner`iy], *n.* a reference book in which the words of a language are arranged from *A* to *Z* and for which meanings are given. **Ex.** *You are now using* The New Horizon Ladder Dictionary.

did (1) [did'], *v.* past tense of *do.* **Ex.** *He did the work yesterday.*

didn't [did'ənt], short form, contraction of *did not.* **Ex.** *You didn't hear me, did you?*

die (1) [day'], *v.* 1. cease living. **Ex.** *My father died two years ago.* 2. decrease; become less. **Ex.** *The music died away.*

diet (3) [day'ət], *n.* 1. usual daily food and drink. **Ex.** *Bread is an important part of my diet.* 2. a special selection of food eaten for one's health. **Ex.** *The doctor recommended a diet without salt.* —*v.* be on a diet, especially to lose weight. **Ex.** *She has been dieting for two weeks.* —**di·e·tar`y,** *adj.*

differ (3) [dif'ər], *v.* 1. be unlike; be different. **Ex.** *She differs from her sister in character.* 2. do not agree. **Ex.** *Their opinions about politics differ.*

difference (1) [dif'rəns], *n.* the way in which things are not alike. **Ex.** *One difference between my brother and me is that I like sports.* —**make a difference,** cause a change in a situation; be important. **Ex.** *Liking your work can make a difference in how you do it.*

different (1) [dif'rənt], *adj.* 1. partly or totally unlike. **Ex.** *His ideas were different from mine.* 2. not the same. **Ex.** *Three different people came to see you while you were away.* 3. unusual. **Ex.** *His style of painting is different.* —**dif'fer·ent·ly,** *adv.* —**dif·fer·en'ti·ate,** *v.* see or describe a difference. **Ex.** *He could not differentiate one color from another.*

difficult (1) [dif'əkəlt`], *adj.* not easy. **Ex.** *Sewing is difficult for me.* —**dif'fi·cul`ty,** *n.* 1. that which is not easy to do or to understand. 2. trouble. **Ex.** *He is in difficulty with the law.*

dig (2) [dig'], *v.* 1. open or loosen earth; make a hole in the ground. **Ex.** *The boys were digging a hole.* 2. bring to the surface by digging. **Ex.** *The miners were digging coal.*

digest (3) [diǰest'], *v.* change food in the stomach into a form that the body can use. **Ex.** *Chew your food well so it can be digested properly.* —*n.* a short form of a long book, story, etc. —**di·ges'tion,** *n.* the process of changing food in the stomach into a form that the body can use.

dignify (4) [dig'nəfay`], *v.* cause to seem honorable, worthy and admirable. **Ex.** *They dignified her job by giving her a special title.* —**dig'ni·fied,** *adj.* having dignity or honor; assured and serious in manner.

dignity (2) [dig'nətiy], *n.* 1. a quality of goodness and honor that is admired and deserves respect. **Ex.** *No matter what the circumstances, she always behaved with dignity.* 2. assurance and seriousness of manner or style. **Ex.** *What could have been an embarrassing situation was handled with dignity.*

dim (3) [dim'], *adj.* 1. not bright; not clear. **Ex.** *There was only a dim light.* 2. unclear in seeing or understanding. **Ex.** *The old man's eyes were dim with tears.* —*v.* make or become less bright. **Ex.** *He dimmed his lights as he approached an oncoming car.* —**dim'ly,** *adv.* —**dim'ness,** *n.*

dime (5) [daym'], *n.* a United States coin worth ten cents; one tenth of a dollar. See **Weights and Measures.**

dimension (5) [dimen'šən], *n.* 1. a measurement in length, width or height. **Ex.** *What are the dimensions of the room?* 2. extent; importance. **Ex.** *They hesitated to start a project of such large dimensions.* —**di·men'sion·al,** *adj.*

diminish (4) [dimin'iš], *v.* make less; become smaller in size, amount or importance; lessen; reduce. **Ex.** *As their food supply diminished, they began to lose hope of surviving.* —**di·min'ish·ing,** *adj.*

dine (2) [dayn'], *v.* 1. eat dinner. **Exs.** *We always dine at seven. They invited their friends to dine with them.* —**din'er,** *n.* 1. one who dines. 2. a car on a railroad train where meals are served; a restaurant built to look like this.

dinner (1) [din'ər], *n.* 1. the large meal of the day. **Ex.** *We always eat dinner at night, but he eats it at noon.* 2. a special meal in honor of some person or occasion. **Ex.** *This evening we are going to a dinner to honor our doctor.*

dip (3) [dip'], *v.* 1. plunge into any liquid, completely or partly, and lift out. **Ex.** *She dipped her hand in the cool water.* 2. lift liquid, as with a spoon or cup. **Ex.** *He dipped soup from the pot for each of the children.* —*n.* 1. the act of dipping; a brief plunge. **Ex.** *They went for a dip in the ocean.* 2. a liquid into which something is dipped. —**dip'per,** *n.* a container with a long handle used for dipping.

diploma [diplow'mə], *n.* a document issued by an educational institution certifying that a student has finished a particular course of study or has earned a degree. **Ex.** *The doctor's framed diplomas hung on his office wall.*

diplomatic (5) [dip'ləmæt'ik], *adj.* 1. relating to the management of affairs between two countries. **Ex.** *The diplomatic service represents our government in foreign capitals.* 2. having the ability to deal with others without giving offense. **Ex.** *His diplomatic remarks satisfied everyone.* —**dip'lo·mat,** *n.* a person who represents his country in dealing with another country. —**di·plo'ma·cy,** *n.*

direct (1) [dərekt'], *v.* 1. manage; control. **Ex.** *The policeman directed traffic.* 2. command; order. **Ex.** *The teacher directed* *us to sit quietly.* 3. point or aim toward. **Ex.** *He directed his eyes at the girl.* 4. tell or show the way or road. **Ex.** *Can you direct me to the hotel?* —*adj.* 1. not through some other person or thing; personal; immediate. **Ex.** *He was in direct contact with the president of the company.* 2. proceeding in a straight line or by the shortest course. **Ex.** *This is the most direct road to the city.* 3. frank; honest. **Ex.** *Please give me a direct answer.* —**di·rec'tion,** *n.* the way in which or the place toward which someone or something is directed. **Ex.** *He went in that direction.* —**directions,** *n.* instructions. **Ex.** *Where are the directions for putting this toy together?* —**di·rec'tor,** *n.* one who directs. —**di·rec'tory,** *n.* a book that lists names and addresses, etc. —**di·rect'ly,** *adv.* straight; immediately; **Ex.** *Go directly home.*

dirt (2) [dərt'], *n.* 1. anything that is not clean, such as dust, mud, etc. **Ex.** *She washed the dirt from her hands.* 2. loose or packed earth; soil. **Ex.** *He was in the garden digging in the dirt.* —**dir'ty,** *adj.* not clean; soiled by dirt. **Ex.** *He wore a dirty shirt.* —*v.* make dirty; soil. **Ex.** *Try not to dirty your new clothes.*

dis- (2) [dis], *prefix.* 1. reversal or undoing of an act. **Exs.** *Belief, disbelief; appear, disappear.* 2. stop; refuse to. **Exs.** *Agree, disagree; obey, disobey.* 3. not. **Exs.** *Honest, dishonest; pleased, displeased.*

disappear (2) [dis'əpi:r'], *v.* 1. become unseen. **Ex.** *The ship disappeared in the distance.* 2. be lost; cease to exist. **Ex.** *The old houses have all disappeared from this street.* —**dis'ap·pear' ance,** *n.*

disappoint (2) [dis'əpoynt'], *v.* fail to satisfy the hopes, expectations or wishes of. **Ex.** *The boy's failure at school disappointed his parents.* —**dis'ap·point'ment,** *n.* —**dis'ap·point'ing,** *adj.* **Ex.** *His work was disappointing.*

disaster (4) [dizæs'tər], *n.* sudden and extraordinary bad fortune. **Ex.** *The flood was a disaster for the village.* —**dis·as'trous,** *adj.* causing disaster.

discard [diskard'], *v.* throw away; cast aside; get rid of or reject as useless. **Ex.** *Why did you discard this pretty sweater?*

discern (5) [disərn'], *v.* see or understand clearly through the senses or mental powers; distinguish; recognize. **Ex.** *In the*

a, far; æ, am; e, get; ey, late; i, in; iy, see; ɔ, all; ow, go; u, put; uw, too; ə, but, ago; ər, fur; aw, out; ay, life; oy, boy; ŋ, ring; θ, think; ð, that; ž, measure; š, ship; j, edge; č, child.

darkness I could not discern his face. **—dis·cern'i·ble**, *adj.* **—dis·cern'ment**, *n.*

discharge (3) [dis'čarǰ', dis'čarǰ], *v.* 1. relieve from work or responsibility. **Ex.** *He was discharged from his job.* 2. unload. **Ex.** *The bus discharged the children at the school.* 3. shoot; fire a gun. **Ex.** *The gun discharged with a loud noise.* 4. set at liberty. **Ex.** *The patient was discharged from the hospital.* 5. set forth; let out. **Ex.** *The broken pipe was discharging water into the street.* **—n.** 1. act of discharging. **Ex.** *His discharge from the army left him free to return to school.* 2. that which is discharged. **Ex.** *The doctor looked to see whether there was any discharge from the wound.*

discipline (4) [dis'əplin], *n.* 1. strict training of mind and body to obey rules and control one's behavior. **Ex.** *Military schools are known for their discipline.* 2. orderly conduct; self-control. **Ex.** *This poorly organized paper shows your lack of discipline.* **—v.** 1. train in obedience and control. **Ex.** He disciplined himself by walking two miles every day. 2. punish. **Ex.** *They disciplined the children by sending them to bed early.* **—dis'ci·pli·nar'y**, *adj.*

disclose [dis'klowz'], *v.* show; reveal; open. **Ex.** *He disclosed to us that he was leaving his job.* **—dis·clo'sure**, *n.*

discord (5) [dis'kɔrd'], *n.* 1. lack of agreement; conflict. **Ex.** *There was discord over what should be done.* 2. an unpleasant combination of sounds. **Ex.** *They shut their ears to the discord.*

discount [dis'kawnt'], *n.* the amount or percentage by which a price is lowered. **Ex.** *Buy now and get a 20 percent discount from the usual price.* **—v.** 1. give an amount off. **Ex.** *We are discounting the price 20 percent today.* 2. believe only in part. **Ex.** *Discount half of what he says.*

discourage [diskər'ij], *v.* cause to give up hope or lose confidence. **Ex.** *His father's criticism discouraged the boy.*

discourse (5) [dis'kɔrs'], *n.* 1. an orderly expression of ideas in speech or writing. **Ex.** *The judge's talk was a discourse on international law.* 2. conversation; talk. **Ex.** *In their discourse after dinner, they talked about politics.* **—v.** talk; express ideas in an orderly way. **Ex.** *They discoursed on the subject of the election.*

discover (1) [diskəv'ər], *v.* find or learn something for the first time. **Ex.** *Columbus discovered America in 1492.* **—dis·cov'ery**, *n.*

discreet (5) [diskriyt'], *adj.* showing good judgment in conduct; careful in action and speech. **Ex.** *He is very discreet in his choice of friends.* —**dis·creet'ly,** *adv.* —**dis·cre'tion** *n.*

discriminate [diskrim'əneyt'], *v.* 1. Regard and treat a person or a group better or worse because of prejudice. **Ex.** *He discriminated against the women in his office.* 2. differentiate; distinguish. **Ex.** *He is learning how to discriminate between imitation and genuine antiques.* —**di·scrim'i·na'tion,** *n.*

discuss (2) [diskəs'], *v.* consider by presenting various ideas and opinions; talk about. **Ex.** *The business partners discussed their plans for the coming year.* —**dis·cus'sion,** *n.*

disdain (5) [disdeyn'], *v.* regard as unworthy; scorn. **Ex.** *He disdains work of any kind.* —*n.* scorn. **Ex.** *She spoke to the poor young man with disdain.* —**dis·dain'ful,** *adj.*

disease (2) [diziyz'], *n.* sickness; illness. **Ex.** *A person with that disease will have a fever.*

disgrace (4) [disgreys'], *n.* 1. loss of honor and respect; shame. **Ex.** *His use of drugs led to his disgrace.* 2. cause of shame; that which makes one lose honor. **Ex.** *His actions were a disgrace to his family.* —*v.* cause to be shamed. **Ex.** *She disgraced her family by her shocking conduct.* —**dis·grace'ful,** *adj.* —**dis·grace'ful·ly,** *adv.*

disguise (4) [disgayz'], *v.* 1. change the dress or appearance in order not to be known or in order to appear as someone else. **Ex.** *He was disguised as an old man.* 2. hide the true nature or character of. **Ex.** *He disguised his greed with generous words.* —*n.* 1. clothing or costume that changes appearance. **Ex.** *No one recognized her in her disguise.* 2. that which conceals the real nature or character of a person or thing. **Ex.** *His smiling face was a disguise for a very unfriendly nature.*

disgust (4) [disgəst'], *n.* a very strong feeling of dislike that often makes one feel sick. **Ex.** *The smell of the rotten meat filled her with disgust.* —*v.* cause to feel disgust. **Ex.** *Her bad behavior disgusted him.* —**dis·gust'ing,** *adj.*

dish (1) [diš'], *n.* 1. a plate, bowl or cup in which food is served or from which food is eaten. **Ex.** *Please put the dishes on the table.* 2. the food served in a dish; any particular food. **Ex.** *Fried chicken is his favorite dish.*

dishwasher [diš'wɔːš'ər], *n.* a person or machine that washes dishes. **Ex.** *Have you finished loading the dishwasher yet?*

disillusion [dis'iluw'žən], *v.* free from a false idea. **Ex.** *The results of the election disillusioned him.* —**dis·il·lu'sioned,** *adj.* filled with unpleasant feelings and unhappy as a result of having been freed from an illusion. **Ex.** *She was disillusioned when she heard that he was married.*

disinfect [disinfəkt'], *v.* clean by use of a substance that will destroy germs. **Ex.** *I felt a stinging sensation when the nurse disinfected the cut on my hand.* —**dis'in·fect'ant,** *n.* a chemical substance that destroys germs. **Ex.** *They washed the floor with disinfectant.*

disk [disk'], *n.* a thin, flat round plate or an object that appears like this, such as a record, the sun, etc. **Ex.** *This computer has a powerful hard disk.*

dismal (5) [diz'məl], *adj.* dark and cheerless; sorrowful. **Ex.** *The rain made the autumn day dismal.* —**dis'mal·ly,** *adv.*

dismay (4) [dismey'], *v.* cause fear or dread so that one is unable to act; frighten; alarm. **Ex.** *He was dismayed by the sight of the burning house.* —*n.* sudden loss of hope and self-confidence. **Ex.** *The sight of the damaged car filled her with dismay.*

dismiss (4) [dismis'], *v.* send someone away; allow to go. **Ex.** *The children at the school were dismissed and told to go home.* 2. discharge; remove from office, service or employment. **Ex.** *He was dismissed because he was always late for work.* 3. refuse to consider further. **Ex.** *The matter was so unimportant that she dismissed it from her thoughts.* —**dis·miss'al,** *n.*

disorder [disɔr'dər], *n.* 1. confusion; absence of order. **Ex.** *His papers were in disorder.* 2. disturbance; riot. **Ex.** *Police quieted the disorder.* —**dis·or'der·ly,** *adj.*

dispatch (4) [dispæč], *v.* 1. send off. **Ex.** *They dispatched a telegram.* 2. get something done effectively and quickly. **Ex.** *He dispatched his business in a few hours.* —*n.* 1. promptness and effectiveness. **Ex.** *He did his work with dispatch.* 2. a written message. **Ex.** *The dispatch contained important news.* —**dis·patch'er,** *n.* a person working for a transportation company who directs the departure of trains, buses, etc. according to a schedule.

dispense (5) [dispens'], *v.* give out in portions; distribute. **Ex.** *The nurse was dispensing medicine.* —**dis·pen'sa·ry,** *n.* a place where medicines are prepared and distributed. —**dispense with,**

do without; do away with. **Ex.** *We can dispense with further discussion.*

disperse (5) [dispərs'], *v.* 1. cause to break apart and go different ways; scatter. **Ex.** *The crowd dispersed when the rain fell.* 2. spread. **Ex.** *News of the family's need for help was quickly dispersed throughout the neighborhood.* 3. cause to disappear or vanish. **Ex.** *The hot sun will disperse the fog.* —**dis·pers'al,** *n.*

displace [displeys'], *v.* 1. force or compel to move from the usual or proper place. **Ex.** *The flood temporarily displaced them from their homes.* 2. take the place of. **Ex.** *On the farm, the tractor has displaced the horse.*

display (2) [displey'], *v.* 1. spread out; exhibit. **Ex.** *They display the flag on national holidays.* 2. show or reveal. **Ex.** *When questioned, they displayed their ignorance of the matter.* —*n.* an exhibit; a show. **Ex.** *We enjoyed the interesting displays at the fair.*

dispose (3) [dispowz'], *v.* 1. get rid of; do away with. **Ex.** *They disposed of the paper by burning it.* 2. arrange or settle matters finally. **Ex.** *We were not able to dispose of the problem.* —**dis·pos'al,** *n.* 1. the getting rid of something. **Ex.** *Garbage disposal is a serious problem throughout the country.* 2. availability for use. **Ex.** *Our guest room is at your disposal while you are here in town.*

disposition [dis'pəziš'ən], *n.* general way of behaving, acting or feeling; usual mood. **Ex.** *He has a lazy disposition.*

dispute (3) [dispyuwt'], *v.* 1. oppose by argument; quarrel. **Ex.** *The villagers are disputing the building of a new road through the center of town.* 2. doubt the truth of; question. **Ex.** *He disputed my word.* —*n.* an argument; a quarrel. **Ex.** *They had a bitter dispute about money.*

disrupt (4) [disrəpt'], *v.* create a disturbance; cause a speech, a meeting, a plan, etc. to be interrupted in a disorderly way. **Ex.** *The noisy students disrupted the class.*

dissent [disent'], *n.* disagreement; difference of opinion. **Ex.** *There was very little dissent to the proposed plan.* —*v.* **dis·sen'sion,** *n.* strong disagreement or difference of opinion. **Ex.** *The dissension in the organization caused it to split into two groups.*

dissolve (3) [dizalv'], *v.* 1. mix evenly in a liquid. **Ex.** *He dissolved some sugar in his coffee.* 2. end. **Ex.** *The two men dissolved their partnership.* 3. disappear; fade away. **Ex.** *Their fears dissolved with the coming of day.*

distance (1) [dis'təns], *n.* the amount of space between two locations or objects. **Ex.** *The distance from my house to yours is two miles.*

distant (1) [dis'tənt], *adj.* 1. separated; away. **Ex.** *The town is two miles distant.* 2. not near; far; separated in space, time or other scale. **Ex.** *The stars are more distant from the earth than the moon is.* 3. not friendly. **Ex.** *Her manner is distant because she is not at ease with most people.* —**dis'tant·ly**, *adv.*

distinct (3) [distiŋkt'], *adj.* 1. unlike; different; individual. **Ex.** *My cat has characteristics distinct from yours.* 2. clear; plain. **Ex.** *His handwriting was very distinct.* —**dis·tinct'ly**, *adv.* —**dis·tinc'tion**, *n.*

distinguish (3) [distiŋ'gwiš], *v.* 1. recognize one thing from or among others; recognize as different. **Ex.** *I was able to distinguish my friend in the crowd.* 2. perceive clearly. **Ex.** *The night was too dark to distinguish the man's face.* 3. make oneself famous or well known. **Ex.** *The man distinguished himself as an author.* —**dis·tin'guished**, *adj.* well-known and respected; dignified. **Ex.** *She is a distinguished scientist.*

distract (5) [distrækt'], *v.* 1. have one's mind or attention drawn away from what one is doing. **Ex.** *She was distracted from her work by a noise.* 2. confuse to the point that one is unable to think. **Ex.** *He was distracted by the many instructions he had received.* —**dis·trac'tion**, *n.* anything which distracts, either pleasantly or unpleasantly.

distress (3) [distres'], *n.* 1. physical or mental suffering; pain; trouble. **Ex.** *The sick woman was in great distress.* 2. a state of danger. **Ex.** *The ship was in distress and called for help.* —*v.* cause suffering or worry. **Ex.** *The bad news distressed them.*

distribute (3) [distrib'yət], *v.* divide among many. **Ex.** *Please distribute the books to the students.* —**dis'tri·bu'tion**, *n.*

district (2) [dis'trikt], *n.* 1. a definite portion of a city or state. **Ex.** *He was elected to represent his district.* 2. any portion of an area; a region. **Ex.** *They live in a farming district.*

disturb (3) [distərb'], v. 1. bother; interrupt. **Ex.** *The doctor is busy; you must not disturb him.* 2. make uneasy; worry; trouble. **Ex.** *His unfriendly manner disturbs me.* 3. change the correct or normal condition of. **Ex.** *The wind disturbed the papers on the desk.* —**dis·turb'ance**, n.—**dis·turb'ing**, adj.

ditch (3) [dič'], n. a narrow channel, usually long, dug in the earth. **Ex.** *The workmen dug a ditch beside the road to drain the water away.*

dive (4) [dayv'], v. 1. jump into water, especially headfirst. **Ex.** *The swimmers dived from the side of the boat.* 2. plunge into, physically or mentally. **Ex.** *The rabbit dived into the hole.* 3. plunge downward. **Ex.** *The plane dived toward the earth.* —n. 1. a plunge into water. 2. a plunge down or a sudden plunge. —**div'er**, n.

divert (5) [divərt'], v. 1. turn aside or in a different direction. **Ex.** *The river was diverted from its channel by the engineers.* 2. turn away from business or study; amuse; entertain. **Ex.** *The children diverted themselves by playing games.* —**di·vert'ing**, adj. —**di·ver'sion**, n.

divide (1) [divayd'], v. 1. separate; keep apart. **Ex.** *A fence divides his property from mine.* 2. share; separate into portions and distribute. **Ex.** *The four men divided the money among themselves.* 3. separate by feelings or ideas. **Ex.** *A difference of opinion divided the family.*

divine (3) [divayn'], adj. 1. of a god. **Ex.** *People thought that the storm was a divine punishment.* 2. holy; religious. **Ex.** *Divine services are held once a week.*

division (3) [diviž'ən], n. 1. the act of dividing. **Ex.** *The division of the property will be taken care of by the lawyers.* 2. one of the parts into which something is divided. **Ex.** *This work is handled by another division of the business.*

divorce (3) [divɔrs'], n. the legal ending of marriage. **Ex.** *His wife asked him for a divorce.* —v. 1. separate by divorce. **Ex.** *She has been divorced for a year.* 2. separate. **Ex.** *It is difficult to divorce politics from government.*

dizzy (4) [diz'iy], adj. affected with a spinning or unsteady feeling. **Ex.** *She became dizzy from the heat and fainted.* —**diz'zi·ly**, adv. —**diz'zi·ness**, n.

do (1) [duw'], v. 1. perform. **Ex.** *They do their work well.* 2. put forth effort. **Ex.** *Do your best.* 3. take care of. **Ex.** *My sister and I do the housework.* 4. be satisfactory. **Ex.** *This coat will* *not do for the winter.* 5. bring about; cause. **Ex.** *A rest will do you good.* 6. fare; prosper. **Ex.** *How do you do?* (The verb *do* has some special uses that have no definite meaning: 1. in asking questions. **Ex.** *Do you like English?* 2. in emphasizing a verb. **Ex.** *You say you do not have the book, but you do have it.* 3. in taking the place of a verb, to avoid repeating it. **Ex.** *She walks the way I do.* —**do away with,** get rid of. **Ex.** *We can do away with these old papers.* —**have to do with,** be about; be on the subject of. **Ex.** *What has this to do with me?* —**make do,** manage. **Ex.** *We will make do with the money we have.*

dock (4) [dak'], *n.* 1. a platform built along the shore or out over the water, at which ships load or unload. 2. a space between two piers for a ship. —*v.* come into a dock. **Ex.** *The ship docked early in the morning.*

doctor (1) [dak'tər], *n.* 1. a person trained in medicine to treat sick or injured people. 2. the holder of an advanced academic degree. **Ex.** *He is a doctor of philosophy.*

doctrine (5) [dak'trən], *n.* that which is taught as the principles in any branch of knowledge. **Ex.** *Every religion has its own doctrine.* —**doc'trin·al,** *adj.*

document (4) [dak'yəmənt], *n.* an original or official paper relied upon as proof or support of something. **Ex.** *The Declaration of Independence is an important document of American history.* —*v.* provide or prove with documents. **Ex.** *The lawyer documented his arguments very well.* —**doc'u·men'ta·ry,** *adj.* having, using or being documents. —**doc'u·men·ta'tion,** *n.*

dodge (4) [daj'], *v.* 1. move quickly to one side. **Ex.** *The man jumped aside to dodge the car.* 2. avoid some duty or responsibility by a trick. **Ex.** *He dodged the question by pretending not to hear it.* —*n.* 1. the action of dodging. 2. a skillful trick.

does (1) [dəz'], *v.* present tense of *do,* used with singular nouns and pronouns such as *he, she,* and *it.* **Ex.** *The boy does his work well.*

doesn't [dəz'ənt], short form, contraction of *does not.* **Ex.** *This book doesn't answer my questions.*

dog (1) [dɔːg'], *n.* a meat-eating animal often kept as a pet.

doll (2) [dal'], *n.* a figure of a baby or other human used as a toy. **Ex.** *The little girls were playing with dolls.*

dollar (1) [dal'ər], *n.* a unit of money in

DOG

the United States equal to 100 cents. (The sign for dollar is $.
Ex. *$1.00*.) **Ex.** *That book will cost you eight dollars.* See
Weights and Measures.

-dom (2) [dəm], *suffix.* 1. rank; office; area. **Exs.** *King, kingdom;
official, officialdom.* 2. state of being. **Exs.** *Free, freedom; bore,
boredom.*

domain (5) [dow'meyn'], *n.* 1. a territory under the rule of; an
estate. **Ex.** *The king was respected throughout his domain.* 2.
a field of thought or action. **Ex.** *Chemistry is that scientist's
domain.*

dome (4) [dowm'], *n.* a round roof shaped like
an upside-down bowl.

DOME

domestic (3) [dəmes'tik], *adj.* 1. of the household
and family. **Ex.** *Of all the domestic tasks I
have to do, I like cooking best.* 2. of or manufactured in one's own country; not foreign. **Ex.**
*I prefer to buy domestic rather than foreign
products.* 3. accustomed to being with people. **Ex.** *The only
domestic pet we have is a cat.* —**do·mes'ti·cate,** *v.* tame or
train an animal to live with people. —**do'mes·ti'ci·ty,** *n.* life
at home.

dominate (4) [dam'əneyt'], *v.* 1. rule or control by power
or authority; govern. **Ex.** *The boy was dominated by his
older brother.* 2. hold a commanding position over. **Ex.**
The building on the hill dominates the city. —**dom'i·na'
tion,** *n.*

dominion (4) [dəmin'yən], *n.* 1. supreme authority; power of
governing. **Ex.** *Few countries now hold dominion over distant
lands.* 2. the territory governed.

donate [dow'neyt], *v.* give as gift; contribute. **Ex.** *We are donat-
ing these clothes to the flood victims.* —**do·na'tion,** *n.* the act
of giving or contributing; that which is given or contributed.
Ex. *Our organization is dependent upon donations of money
to finance its operations.*

done (1) [dən'], *v.* past participle of *do.* **Ex.** *He has done his
work well.*

a, far; æ, am; e, get; ey, late; i, in; iy, see; ɔ, all; ow, go; u, put; uw, too;
ə, but, ago; ər, fur; aw, out; ay, life; oy, boy; ŋ, ring; θ, think; ð, that;
ž, measure; š, ship; ĵ, edge; č, child.

donkey (4) [dɔŋ'kiy], *n.* an animal somewhat like a small horse with long ears.

DONKEY

don't (1) [downt'], short form, contraction of *do not*. **Ex.** *Don't be late.*

doom (4) [duwm'], *n.* 1. fate or destiny, especially an unhappy or tragic one; ruin; death. **Ex.** *Her car carried her over the cliff to her doom.* 2. a judgment or sentence against the accused. **Ex.** *The prisoner heard his doom pronounced.* —*v.* sentence to some fate. **Ex.** *The criminal was doomed to death.*

door (1) [dɔ:r'], *n.* a piece of wood, metal or other material for opening or closing an entrance to a building, room, car, etc.

doorway [dɔ:r'wey'], *n.* the opening in which a door is located. **Ex.** *I could see a young girl standing in the doorway of the kitchen.*

DOOR

dormitory [dɔr'mətɔriy], *n.* 1. a building at a college or university in which there are bedrooms for students. **Ex.** *During his freshman year, he lived in a dormitory.* 2. a large room having a number of beds for sleeping. **Ex.** *There was a dormitory for the waitresses working at the summer resort.*

dose [dows'], *n.* the amount of medicine given or to be taken at one time. **Ex.** *What was the dose that the doctor prescribed?*

dot (2) [dat'], *n.* 1. a very small round mark (·). **Ex.** *He made a dot on the paper with his pencil.* 2. a small spot, usually round. **Ex.** *Her dress is red with white dots.* —*v.* mark with or as with a dot or many dots. **Ex.** *The grass was dotted with tiny flowers.*

double (1) [dəb'əl], *adj.* 1. twice in size, quantity, etc. **Ex.** *The bigger boys received double portions of food.* 2. consisting of two parts or layers. **Ex.** *The double doors led to the dining room.* —*n.* twice as much; twice as many. **Ex.** *He is earning double your salary.* —*v.* make or become double in size, quantity, etc. **Ex.** *The merchant doubled his last month's sales.* —**dou'bly,** *adv.* —**double up,** 1. fold over or bend. **Ex.** *The pain caused him to double up.* 2. form into twos. **Ex.** *Double up that line of men.*

doubt (1) [dawt'], *v.* be uncertain about; not trust; question. **Ex.** *I doubt that he will come.* —*n.* a condition of being uncertain or unsure. **Ex.** *We are in doubt about the results.*

dough (5) [dow'], *n.* a mixture of flour, water or milk and other materials for baking. **Ex.** *He shaped the dough into loaves of bread.*

doughnut [dow'nət'], *n.* sweet dough formed into a small cake, usually round with a hole in the middle, and fried in a deep container of liquid fat **Ex.** *They stopped to have coffee and doughnuts.*

dove [dəv'], *n.* 1. a bird like a pigeon but usually not as large with a small head, a broad body and short legs. 2. a white-colored bird of this variety used as a symbol of peace. **Ex.** *That antiwar organization uses a drawing of a white dove on its stationery.* 3. someone who is opposed to war. **Ex.** *He sided with the doves on the question of military aid.*

down (1) [dawn'], *adv.* 1. at, in or toward a lower position. **Ex.** *He lay down on the bed.* 2. to a lesser quantity or amount. **Ex.** *The price of food is down this month.* 3. from a past time to the present. **Ex.** *Down through the years, the styles have changed.* 4. in cash, usually a part payment. **Ex.** *You can buy it for ten dollars down and ten dollars each week.* —*prep.* 1. from a higher to a lower place. **Ex.** *Water runs downhill.* 2. along. **Ex.** *We walked down the road.* —**down and out,** poor; having bad luck. **Ex.** *We were helped by friends when we were down and out.*

downcast [dawn'kæst'], *adj.* 1. very sad. **Ex.** *He seems downcast today.* 2. toward the ground. **Ex.** *His downcast eyes made him seem shy.*

downfall [dawn'fɔ:l'], *n.* 1. a loss of position or power. **Ex.** *Excessive drinking led to his downfall.* 2. a heavy fall of rain or snow, often sudden. **Ex.** *He was delayed when the light snow turned into a downfall.*

downgrade [dawn'greyd'], *v.* lower the value of or the importance of; lower the regard for. **Ex.** *They downgraded his job.*

downhearted [dawn'har'təd], *adj.* unhappy. **Ex.** *Why are you so downhearted today?*

downpour [dawn'pɔ:r'], *n.* a heavy rain. **Ex.** *I was caught in a downpour without my umbrella.*

downstairs [dawn'ste:rz], *adv.* on, to or toward a lower floor; down the stairs. **Exs.** *Who is that downstairs? She ran downstairs to answer the bell.*

downtown (3) [dawn'tawn'], *adv.* to, toward or in the business center of a town. **Ex.** *My father goes downtown every day.*

doze [dowz'], *v.* sleep lightly; nap. **Ex.** *He was dozing in front of the fire.*

dozen (2) [dəz'ən], *n.* a set of twelve. **Ex.** *We need a dozen eggs.*

draft (3) [dræft'], *n.* 1. a current of air. **Ex.** *There's a cold draft coming from the open window.* 2. the choosing of people for military service. **Ex.** *He was not accepted for the draft because of poor eyesight.* 3. a plan or sketch of something to be done; an outline or a rough version of a piece of writing. **Ex.** *He is reworking the first draft of his novel.* —*v.* 1. make a plan or sketch of; write out. **Ex.** *He drafted plans for a house.* 2. select for some special purpose, as for military service. **Ex.** *He was drafted into the army.* —**draft'y**, *adj.* having a current of air.

drag (2) [dræg'], *v.* slowly pull a heavy thing. **Ex.** *The little boy dragged the large box up the hill.*

drain (3) [dreyn'], *v.* 1. draw off a liquid gradually; draw off completely. **Ex.** *The wetland was drained of water so houses could be built on it.* 2. empty of wealth, strength, etc. by drawing from it gradually; exhaust. **Ex.** *Her energy was drained away by overwork.* 3. empty into. **Ex.** *This river drains into the sea.* —*n.* a pipe or other means of draining. **Ex.** *The drain in the kitchen sink is not working.* —**drain'er**, *n.* a device made of wire, plastic, wood, etc. in which to place dishes after washing so that water can drain from them. —**drain'age**, *n.* a means of draining or that which is drained off.

drama (4) [dra'mə, dræm'ə], *n.* a story, sometimes in verse, written to be acted on a stage; a play. —**dra·mat'ic**, *adj.* exciting, like a drama. **Ex.** *He spoke in a dramatic way.* —**dram'a·tist**, *n.* one who writes dramas. —**dram'a·tize**, *v.* 1. make into a drama. **Ex.** *He dramatized his own book for the movie based on it.* 2. present in a dramatic way. **Ex.** *Pictures of the hungry children dramatized the need for food.*

drank (2) [dræŋk'], *v.* Past tense of *drink*. **Ex.** *He drank a glass of water and asked for another.*

drastic [dræs'tik], *adj.* strong and sudden; extreme; harsh. **Ex.** *They are taking drastic action to solve the drug problem.* —**dras'ti·cal·ly**, *adv.* **Ex.** *My home town has changed drastically since I was a boy.*

draw (2) [drɔ:'], *v.* 1. form a picture with a pencil, paint, etc. **Ex.** *That artist draws beautiful flowers.* 2. pull. **Ex.** *A horse* *was needed to draw the wagon.* 3. attract. **Ex.** *This speaker always draws a large crowd.* 4. pull out; take out. **Ex.** *I saw him draw the gun from his pocket.* —**draw'ing,** *n.* 1. a picture that has been made with a pencil or pen. 2. something decided by a chance selection of a name, number, etc. —**draw out,** make more lengthy. **Ex.** *He draws out his speeches so much that people get tired.* —**draw up,** prepare in written form. **Ex.** *A lawyer will draw up the legal papers that will give you ownership of the house.*

drawback [drɔː'bæk'], *n.* a thing or condition that halts or holds back. **Ex.** *His poor speaking voice is a drawback to his success.*

drawer (3) [drɔːr'], *n.* a boxlike container, part of a larger piece of furniture, that slides in and out and is used for storage.

DRAWER 1

drawn (2) [drɔːn'], *v.* past participle of *draw.* **Ex.** *The cart was drawn by two horses.* —*adj.* looking very tired; pale. **Ex.** *His drawn face showed that he had not slept well.*

dread (3) [dred'], *v.* fear greatly; look forward to with fear and terror. **Ex.** *He dreaded the day he would have to leave home.* —*n.* great fear. **Ex.** *She has a dread of snakes.*

dream (1) [driym'], *n.* 1. a series of thoughts, pictures or emotions that occur during sleep. **Ex.** *I had a disturbing dream last night.* 2. something like a dream that one keeps in mind when awake. **Ex.** *It was her dream to live on an island someday.* —*v.* have a dream. —**dream'er,** *n.* —**dream'i·ly,** *adv.* —**dream'y,** *adj.*

dreary (4) [drir'iy], *adj.* cheerless; without joy; dull. **Ex.** *The rain made the house seem dreary.* —**drear'i·ly,** *adv.* —**drear'i·ness,** *n.*

dress (1) [dres'], *n.* 1. an outer garment, worn by women or girls, that covers the body from the shoulders to the knees or below. **Ex.** *She wore a pretty dress.* 2. clothing in general. **Ex.** *I knew that he was a stranger by his unusual dress.* —*v.* 1. put on clothes. **Ex.** *The mother dressed her children quickly.* 2. put on medicine and bandages. **Ex.** *The doctor dressed the sore on her arm.* —**dress'y,** *adj.* stylish; fancy; suitable for an occasion where established customs are followed. **Ex.** *Is this too dressy to wear to work?*

---

a, far; æ, am; e, get; ey, late; i, in; iy, see; ɔ, all; ow, go; u, put; uw, too; ə, but, ago; ər, fur; aw, out; ay, life; oy, boy; ŋ, ring; θ, think; ð, that; ž, measure; š, ship; j, edge; č, child.

dressing [dres'iŋ], *n.* 1. a cloth placed on a sore. **Ex.** *The doctor put a new dressing on the wound.* 2. a sauce, usually for salads. **Ex.** *He made an oil and vinegar dressing for the salad.* 3. a mixture placed inside a chicken, duck, etc., when roasting it. 4. the act of putting on clothing. **Ex.** *Dressing the children takes me a long time.*

drew (2) [druw'], *v.* past tense of *draw.* **Exs.** *The boy drew a picture of a tree. The horse drew the wagon along the street.*

dried (1) [drayd'], *v.* past tense and participle of *dry.* **Exs.** *Mother dried the clothes outside. Have you dried the dishes yet?*

drift (3) [drift'], *v.* 1. carry or be carried by currents. **Ex.** *The boat drifted toward the shore.* 2. going along without knowing or caring where one is going. **Ex.** *He drifted from one town to another.* 3. heap or be heaped up by the wind. **Ex.** *The snow drifted across the road.* —*n.* 1. the act of drifting; the amount of drift. **Ex.** *They mapped the drift of the ocean current.* 2. anything that has been piled up or driven by wind or water. **Ex.** *They built fences to control the drifts of sand.* —**drift'er,** *n.*

drill (4) [dril'], *n.* 1. a tool for making holes. 2. the act or exercise of training soldiers, especially in marching. **Ex.** *The troops have drill twice a week.* —*v.* 1. make a hole using a drill. **Ex.** *He drilled a hole in the board.* 2. go through exercises, physical or mental, to learn. **Ex.** *The teacher drills us on the multiplication tables every day.* 3. train soldiers. **Ex.** *The soldiers were drilling on the field in the rain.*

drink (1) [drink'], *v.* 1. swallow water or any liquid. **Ex.** *We drink coffee with our dinner.* 2. take alcoholic liquors. **Ex.** *What will you have to drink? I am having wine.* —*n.* 1. any liquid swallowed. **Ex.** *She wants a drink of water.* 2. liquor containing alcohol. **Ex.** *He went into the bar for a drink.* —**drink'er,** *n.* —**drink to,** drink as an offering of good wishes. **Ex.** *I drink to your health.*

drip (4) [drip'], *v.* fall or let fall in drops. **Ex.** *When the roof leaked, water dripped from the ceiling.* —*n.* the falling of a liquid drop by drop. **Ex.** *We heard the drip of water outside the window.* —**drip'pings,** *n.* the liquid that falls from cooking meat. **Ex.** *The drippings added a delicious flavor to the gravy.*

drive (1) [drayv'], *v.* 1. go or take in a motor car. **Ex.** *They drive to work every morning.* 2. push or urge forward, back or away from. **Ex.** *The boy was driving the sheep to the shed.* 3.

control and direct the movement of an automobile, wagon, etc. **Ex.** *He drives a bus.* —*n.* 1. a journey in an automobile. **Ex.** *They would like to go for a drive.* 2. a road to drive on. **Ex.** *The road is called Riverside Drive because it follows the river.* 3. an organized effort by a group of people; a campaign. **Ex.** *They had a drive to raise money for charity.* —**driv'er,** *n.* —**drive at,** mean; intend. **Ex.** *I know what he is driving at when he says that.*

driven [driv'ən], *v.* past participle of *drive.* **Ex.** *Have you driven on the new freeway?*

droop (3) [druwp'], *v.* 1. hang, sink or bend down from hunger, exhaustion, etc. **Ex.** *The flowers are drooping because they need water.* 2. be low in spirits or sad. **Ex.** *Our spirits drooped when we heard we could not go.* —*n.* a sloping down; a drooping. **Ex.** *The droop of his shoulders showed his despair.*

drop (1) [drap'], *n.* 1. the small quantity of liquid that falls in one round mass. **Ex.** *A drop of rain struck his cheek.* 2. a sudden fall. **Ex.** *The child's drop from the roof injured him.* 3. the distance of the fall. **Ex.** *It was a drop of five feet.* —*v.* 1. fall; let fall. **Ex.** *The man dropped to the ground.* 2. go lower; sink. **Ex.** *Prices dropped sharply.* —**drop in,** visit. **Ex.** *Why don't you drop in tomorrow?* —**drop out,** stop being part of; quit. **Ex.** *He dropped out of school.*

drought (5) [drawt', drɔːt'], *n.* a prolonged period of dry weather, with little or no rain. **Ex.** *Many trees died during the long drought.*

drove [drowv'] *v.* past tense of *drive.* **Ex.** *He drove from coast to coast.* —*n.* a group moving together or being driven. **Ex.** *A drove of cattle blocked the road.*

drown (3) [drawn'], *v.* die or kill by keeping the head under water or other liquid. **Ex.** *They were drowned when the ship sank.*

drowsy (5) [draw'ziy], *adj.* sleepy; half-asleep. **Ex.** *Put the drowsy child to bed.* —**drowse',** *v.* —**drow'si·ly,** *adv.* —**drow'si·ness,** *n.*

drug (3) [drəg'], *n.* 1. anything used as a medicine to treat a disease or in making medicines. **Ex.** *Drugs should be used only at the direction of a doctor.* 2. any of various substances used to relieve pain, bring about sleep, stimulate the senses, etc., which may be harmful and addictive; narcotic. **Ex.** *The young dealer in drugs was shot by a rival.* —*v.* put to sleep or make dull by the use of drugs. **Ex.** *He walked as if he were drugged.* —**drug'gist**, *n.* one who makes or sells drugs legally.

drugstore [drəg'stɔːr], *n.* a store which sells medicines, drugs and often, in addition, cosmetics, magazines, films, household paper products, candy, etc. and sometimes light meals. **Ex.** *While you are at the drugstore, get me a ballpoint pen, please.*

drum (2) [drəm'], *n.* 1. a hollow musical instrument that is played by beating upon the flat ends with sticks or with the hands. **Ex.** *We heard the roll of the drums in the distance.* 2. a covered or closed container shaped like this. **Ex.** *Be careful! That is a drum of gasoline.* —*v.* beat or play on a drum. —**drum'mer**, *n.* one who plays a drum.

drumstick [drəm'stik'], *n.* 1. a stick for playing a drum. 2. the lower part of the leg of a chicken or other bird, when cooked.

drunk (4) [drəŋk'], *v.* past participle of *drink.* **Ex.** *He said he had drunk too much.* —*adj.* overcome by or behaving as if overcome by alcoholic liquor. **Ex.** *He was drunk and did not know what he was doing.* —**drunk, drunk'ard**, *n.* one who is frequently drunk. —**drunk'en**, *adj.* —**drunk'en·ly**, *adv.*

dry (1) [dray'], *adj.* 1. not wet. **Ex.** *The clothes are dry.* 2. thirsty. **Ex.** *His throat was very dry after working in the sun.* 3. not interesting; dull. **Ex.** *His lecture was dry.* —*v.* make or become dry. **Ex.** *He hung his clothes on the line to dry.* —**dry'ly, dri'ly**, *adv.* —**dry'ness**, *n.* —**dry up**, become dry; lose water. **Ex.** *Now that the well has dried up, where are we going to get water?*

dry-clean [dray'kliyn'], *v.* clean clothes with a liquid other than water. —**dry cleaning**, *n.* the cleaning of materials without water. —**dry cleaner**, *n.* one whose business is to clean clothes. **Ex.** *You should send your silk dress to the dry cleaner.*

dryer [dray'ər], *n.* a machine that dries by the use of heat or forced air. **Ex.** *She put the wet clothes in the dryer.*

dry measure [dray' mez'ər], *n.* a measure of dry things. See **Weights and Measures.**

duck (1) [dək'], *n.* a flat-billed, swimming bird with a short neck and legs, often raised for its meat. **Ex.** *She prepared the roast duck with an orange sauce.* —**duck'ling**, *n.* a baby duck; a young duck.

duck (1) [dək'], *v.* move or lower the head or body, usually to avoid being hit, seen, etc. **Ex.** *He ducked when I tried to hit him.*

due (1) [duw'], *adj.* 1. owed as a debt, right or matter of politeness. **Ex.** *This money is due me for the work I did.* 2. expected. **Ex.** *The plane is due any minute now.* —*n.* that which is rightfully owed. **Ex.** *Give the man his due; he is a good writer.* —*adv.* directly. **Ex.** *The ocean is due east of us.* —**due to,** caused by. **Ex.** *The closing of school was due to the snow.* —**dues,** *n. pl.* a charge for membership in a club or organization. **Ex.** *The club has just increased its membership dues.*

dug (3) [dəg'], *v.* past tense and participle of *dig.* **Exs.** *The dog dug up the bone. Have you ever dug a ditch?*

dull (2) [dəl'], *adj.* 1. tiring; boring; uninteresting. **Ex.** *That is a dull book.* 2. not cheerful; not colorful. **Ex.** *A rainy day is likely to be dull.* 3. not sharp; not clear or distinct. **Ex.** *The knife is so dull that it will not cut.* 4. stupid; slow to understand. **Ex.** *He is a dull child.* —**dull'ness,** *n.*

dumb (3) [dəm'], *adj.* 1. stupid. **Ex.** *What a dumb remark!* 2. unable or briefly unable to speak. **Ex.** *She was struck dumb by the sight.*

dump (4) [dəmp'], *v.* throw down; unload. **Ex.** *The workmen dumped the dirt into the hole.* —*n.* a place for dumping things that are not wanted.

dump truck [dəmp' trək'], *n.* a truck with a back part that can be raised and slanted to permit dumping.

dumpy [dəmp'iy], *adj.* short and fat. **Ex.** *She has a pretty face but a dumpy figure.*

dungarees [dəŋ'gəriyz'], *n.* a pair of pants made from heavy cloth, usually blue cotton, worn for outside work and leisure-time activities; jeans. **Ex.** *If he goes to the office on Saturday, he usually wears dungarees.*

duplicate [duw'pləkeyt'], *v.* make an exact copy. **Ex.** *Please duplicate this letter.* —**du'pli·cate** *n.* an exact copy; something that is the same. **Ex.** *She wore a dress to the party that was a duplicate of mine.* —*adj.* exactly like something else. **Ex.** *Here is a duplicate key to use while you are staying with us.*

durable [duwr'əbəl], *adj.* long-lasting; able to stand up under hard use. **Ex.** *In spite of the children, this furniture has proved to be very durable.*

---

a, far; æ, am; e, get; ey, late; i, in; iy, see; ɔ, all; ow, go; u, put; uw, too; ə, but, ago; ər, fur; aw, out; ay, life; oy, boy; ŋ, ring; θ, think; ð, that; ž, measure; š, ship; j, edge; č, child.

during (1) [dur'iŋ, dyur'iŋ], *prep.* 1. through the whole time. **Ex.** *He studied hard during his college years.* 2. in the course of. **Ex.** *Come sometime during the evening.*

dusk (1) [dəsk'], *n.* 1. the time just before dark. **Ex.** *He always works in the garden until dusk.* 2. shadowy darkness. **Ex.** *The old man sat in the dusk of his room.* —**dusk'y,** *adj.*

dust (2) [dəst'], *n.* fine, dry, powdery earth; fine powder of any kind. **Ex.** *Dust from the road covered the car.* —*v.* remove or wipe dust from. **Ex.** *We dust the furniture every day.* —**dust'y,** *adj.*

duty (1) [duw'tiy, dyuw'tiy], *n.* 1. what one does because it is moral, right or just. **Ex.** *It is our duty to obey our country's laws.* 2. the respect one should show parents, older people, etc. **Ex.** *He recognized his duty to his family.* 3. that which one has to do as part of one's work. **Ex.** *What are your duties as a teacher?* —**du'ti·ful,** *adj.* —**du'ti·ful·ly,** *adv.*

dwarf (5) [dwɔrf'], *n.* a human being, animal or plant much smaller than the normal size of its kind. —*adj.* of unusually small size. **Ex.** *A dwarf apple tree grew in the flower pot.*

dwell (5) [dwel'], *v.* live. **Ex.** *Some bats dwell in caves.* —**dwell'ing,** *n.* a house in which people live. —**dwell on,** think, write or speak about continually. **Ex.** *Please do not dwell on unimportant matters.*

dye (4) [day'], *n.* coloring matter used to color cloth, hair, etc. —*v.* color with a dye. **Ex.** *She dyed her hair red.*

dynamite [day'nəmayt], *n.* a substance that causes a powerful explosion. **Ex.** *They used dynamite to remove the tree stumps from the field.*

E

E, e [iy'], *n.* the fifth letter of the English alphabet.

each (1) [iyč'], *adj.* every one by itself of two or more. **Ex.** *Each man has his own opinion.* —*pron.* every one. **Ex.** *Each will be asked one question.* —*adv.* to, of, by or for every person or thing. **Ex.** *They gave the boys an apple each.* —**each other,** *adv.* each the other. **Ex.** *That man and woman love each other.*

eager (2) [iy'gər], *adj.* want very much. **Ex.** *He is eager to open the box to see what is inside.* —**ea'ger·ness,** *n.* —**ea'ger·ly,** *adv.*

eagle (3) [iy'gəl], *n.* a large bird noted for its strength, keenness of sight and power of flight.

EAGLE

ear (1) [i:r'], *n.* 1. either of the two parts of the body with which human beings and mammals hear. 2. the seed bearing portion of various cereal plants, such as corn and wheat. **Ex.** *We picked a dozen ears of corn for lunch.*

EAR

early (1) [ər'liy], *adj.* 1. at or near the beginning of. **Ex.** *They discovered the disease in its early stages.* 2. before the usual or set time. **Ex.** *He was early for his appointment.* —*adv.* 1. near the beginning. **Ex.** *He left early in the morning.* 2. before the usual or set time. **Ex.** *He arrived fifteen minutes early.*

earn (2) [ərn'], *v.* 1. receive as pay for work or service. **Ex.** *He earns money by working in the factory.* 2. deserve or get. **Ex.** *The fearless soldier earned a medal for bravery.* —**earn'ings,** *n.* wages; salary.

earnest (3) [ər'nist], *adj.* serious; not joking. **Ex.** *He has an earnest attitude toward his work.* —**ear'nest·ness,** *n.* —**ear'nest·ly,** *adv.*

earth (1) [ərθ'], *n.* 1. the planet on which humans live. **Ex.** *The earth travels around the sun.* 2. ground; soil; dirt. **Ex.** *He planted the seeds in the earth.* —**earth·ly,** *adj.* concerning the earth, not heaven. **Ex.** *The poor man's only earthly possessions were the clothes he wore.* —**earth·y,** *adj.* 1. of or like the earth. **Ex.** *He liked the earthy smell of the garden.* 2. not refined; crude. **Ex.** *She was embarrassed by his earthy jokes.* —**earth·en,** *adj.* made of earth or baked clay earth.

earthquake (5) [ərθ'kweyk'], *n.* a shaking of the earth's surface caused by changes in the position of rocks or by other disturbances underground. **Ex.** *Many buildings were damaged by the earthquake.*

ease (2) [yz'], *n.* 1. state of being comfortable; freedom from pain, want or discomfort. **Ex.** *The rich family lived a life of ease.* 2. without difficulty; naturalness. **Ex.** *The famous actor spoke with ease.* —*v.* make less painful, difficult, etc. **Ex.** *This medicine will ease your pain.*

east (1) [iyst'], *n.* 1. the direction to the right of one facing north; one of the four points of the compass. **Ex.** *The sun rises in the east.* 2. regions or countries lying to the east; that part of the United States lying east of the Mississippi River. **Ex.** *He spent several years in the East.* —*adv.* toward the east. **Ex.** *This train goes east.* —*adj.* 1. toward, in or at the east. **Ex.** *He lives on the east side of the island.* 2. from the east. **Ex.** *An east wind is blowing.* —**east'ern,** *adj.* characteristic of the east or East; in, of, to or from the east. **Ex.** *He has an eastern accent.* —**east'ern·er,** *n.* a person from the east.

easy (1) [iy'ziy], *adj.* 1. not difficult. **Ex.** *He left the easy work for last.* 2. comfortable; not hurried. **Ex.** *When he retires, he expects to lead an easy life.* —**eas'i·ly,** *adv.* without difficulty. **Ex.** *He did the work easily.*

eavesdrop [iyvz'drap], *v.* listen to something one is not intended to hear; listen secretly. **Ex.** *She has been known to eavesdrop.* —**eaves'drop'per,** *n.*

eat (1) [iyt'], *v.* take food into the body; have a meal. **Ex.** *My children like to eat cake.* —**eat'a·ble,** *adj.* suitable to eat. —**eat'er,** *n.* one who eats. **Ex.** *Is he a meat eater?*

echo (3) [ek'ow], *n.* a sound heard a second time as a result of reflected sound waves. **Ex.** *He heard the echo of his voice from the other side of the valley.* —*v.* sound again. **Ex.** *The room echoed with music.*

ecology [ikal'əjiy], *n.* the scientific study of persons, animals and plants and their relationship to one another and to the environment. —**e·col'o·gist,** *n.* one who studies ecology.

economic (2) [ek'ənam'ik, iy'kənam'ik], *adj.* of or concerned with the economy. **Ex.** *There are many serious economic problems facing this city.* —**e·co·nom'ics,** *n.* the science concerned with the production, distribution and use of income and wealth. **Ex.** *He is majoring in economics in college.*

economy (2) [iykan'əmiy], *n.* 1. the management of the money and other resources of a nation, community, etc. **Ex.** *The development of railroads had a tremendous effect on the country's economy.* 2. a way of doing something so as not to waste. **Ex.** *Her economies in preparing the family's meals cut expenses.* —**e·co·nom'i·cal,** *adj.* —**e·co·nom'i·cal·ly,** *adv.* —**e·con'o·mize,** *v.*

ecstasy (5) [ek'stəsiy], *n.* a strong emotion, especially of joy or delight. **Ex.** *The beautiful music filled them with ecstasy.* —**ec·stat'ic,** *adj.*

-ed (1) [id, d, t], *suffix.* 1. past action of a verb. **Exs.** *He headed the city government. She tried on several hats. We walked two miles yesterday.* 2. past participle ending. **Exs.** *Fade, faded; load, loaded.* 3. characterized by. **Exs.** *beard, bearded; wing, winged.*

edge (1) [ej'], *n.* 1. the line at which something ends or begins. **Ex.** *He sat at the edge of the river and put his feet in the water.* 2. the thin cutting side of the blade of an instrument. **Ex.** *He sharpened the edge of his axe.* —*v.* 1. put a border on. **Ex.** *She edged the neck of the dress with white.* 2. move sideways, little by little. **Ex.** *The man edged his way through the crowd.* —**edg'y,** *adj.* tense; nervous. **Ex.** *He has been rather edgy lately.* —**on edge,** tense; nervous. **Ex.** *She seems on edge today.*

edible (3) [ed'ibəl], *adj.* suitable for eating. **Ex.** *This meat is no longer edible.*

edit (3) [ed'it], *v.* 1. prepare a piece of writing to be published by making changes, corrections, etc. **Ex.** *He corrected errors in grammar and spelling when he edited the manuscript.* 2. manage and direct the preparation of a newspaper, magazine, etc. **Ex.** *He edits the village newspaper.* —**ed'i·tor,** *n.*

edition (4) [ədiš'ən], *n.* 1. the form in which a literary work is published. **Ex.** *He bought an illustrated edition of the book.* 2.

a, far; æ, am; e, get; ey, late; i, in; iy, see; ɔ, all; ow, go; u, put; uw, too; ə, but, ago; ər, fur; aw, out; ay, life; oy, boy; ŋ, ring; θ, think; ð, that; ž, measure; š, ship; j, edge; č, child.

one of several printings of the same work, issued at different times and differing from the others by changes or additions. **Ex.** *I prefer this edition of the book to the earlier one.*

editorial (4) [ed`ɔtɔr'iyəl], *n.* an article in a newspaper or magazine giving the opinions or views of the editor or publishers. **Ex.** *The editorial was critical of the court's ruling.* —*adj.* of or relating to an editor. **Ex.** *How large is the editorial staff of this magazine?*

educate (2) [ej'ukeyt`], *v.* develop the mind or character by training; teach. **Ex.** *He was educated in good schools.* —**ed`u·ca`tor**, *n.* one who educates. —**ed`u·ca`tion**, *n.* the act of educating; the things learned from being educated. —**ed`u·ca`tion·al**, *adj.*

-ee [iy], *suffix.* 1. someone to whom something is done or given. **Exs.** *pay, payee; appoint, appointee.* 2. someone who is or is doing. **Exs.** *devote, devotee; stand, standee.*

effect (2) [əfekt'], *n.* 1. a result caused by something. **Ex.** *The effects of the storm could now be seen.* 2. a mental impression. **Ex.** *The drums had an effect on the animals like that of thunder.* —*v.* cause; accomplish. **Ex.** *He effected many changes.* —**ef·fec'tive**, *adj.* successful in producing an intended or desired effect. **Ex.** *Water is effective in stopping some kinds of fires.* —**ef·fec'tive·ness** *n.*

efficient (4) [ifiš'ənt], *adj.* producing the desired result with the least waste. **Ex.** *An automobile is more efficient for rapid travel than a horse.* —**ef·fi'cient·ly**, *adv.* —**ef·fi'cien·cy**, *n.*

effort (1) [ef'ərt], *n.* 1. the work required to do something; struggle. **Ex.** *With great effort, they pulled the car out of the mud.* 2. an attempt. **Ex.** *He will make an effort to visit you.*

egg (1) [eg'], *n.* 1. the roundish shell or skin-covered body produced by female birds, fish, etc. from which the young later come out. **Ex.** *In a robin's nest we saw two blue eggs.* 2. the hen's egg eaten as food. **Ex.** *I need four eggs for this cake.*

EGG

eggplant [eg'plænt], *n.* a large, egg-shaped vegetable with skin that is usually purple but is sometimes white and with flesh that is greenish white and that has many small edible seeds. **Ex.** *We like eggplant prepared with onions, green peppers and tomatoes.*

EGGPLANT

eight (1) [eyt'], *n., adj.* the number between seven and nine; the number *8.* —**eighth,** *n.* one of eight parts; —*adj.* coming after seven others. **eight'een,** *n., adj.* the number *18.* **eight'eenth,** *n., adj.* coming after seventeen others. —**eight'y,** *n., adj.* the number *80.* —**eight'i·eth,** *n., adj.* coming after seventy-nine others.

either (1) [iy'ðər], *adj.* 1. one of two but not the other. **Ex.** *Take either book.* 2. each of two. **Ex.** *There are seats on either side of the room.* —*pron.* one or the other of two. **Ex.** *Either of the dresses is suitable.* —*conj.* one or the other of two. **Ex.** *Either give it back to him or pay him for it.*

elaborate (4) [əlæb'ərət], *adj.* complicated; with much detail; developed with great care. **Ex.** *Elaborate plans were made for the party.*

elaborate (4) [əlæb'əreyt`], *v.* 1. develop carefully and in detail. **Ex.** *He elaborated his theory in the book he wrote.* 2. explain with more details. **Ex.** *He refused to elaborate on his original statement.* —**e·lab'o·rate·ly,** *adv.*

elastic (5) [əlæs'tik], *adj.* able to return to its original shape or size after being stretched. **Ex.** *A rubber ball bounces because it is elastic.* —*n.* a material containing rubber or similar threads that make it stretchable. **Ex.** *She used elastic in the waist of the skirt.* —**e·las`tic'i·ty,** *n.*

elbow (2) [el'bow], *n.* the joint between the upper and lower arm, enabling the arm to bend. **Ex.** *He held her elbow and guided her across the street.*

elder (3) [el'dər], *adj.* older. **Ex.** *My elder brother is three years older than I am.* —*n.* a person who is older. **Ex.** *The children listened to the advice of their elders.* —**el'der·ly,** *adj.* rather old. —**el'dest,** *n., adj.* oldest.

elect (2) [ilekt'], *v.* select or choose for an office by vote. **Ex.** *The people elected him President.* —**e·lec'tion,** *n.* the act of choosing or selecting by vote. **Ex.** *We have a presidential election every four years.*

electric (1) [ilek'trik], *adj.* concerned with electricity. —**e·lec'tri·cal,** *adj.* —**e·lec'·tri·cal·ly,** *adv.* —**e·lec'tri'cian,** *n.* one who puts in wiring, places electrical equipment in position for use, repairs and sometimes operates it. **Ex.** *The electrician said, after examining the wiring, that it was worn out and had to be replaced.*

electricity (1) [ilek'tris'ətiy, iy'lektris'ətiy], *n.* a form of power that travels through wires to produce light, heat, etc. **Ex.** *That lamp uses very little electricity.*

electronics [i'lektran'iks], *n.* the division of industry that makes technical devices such as television, radios, etc.; such technical devices. —**e·lect·tron'ic,** *adj.*

elegant (3) [el'əgənt], *adj.* 1. having the qualities of richness, fineness and dignity combined for a pleasing effect. **Ex.** *The furnishings of the palace were elegant.* 2. having good manners and taste; showing that one can appreciate what is beautiful. **Ex.** *She always had an elegant air about her.* —**el'e·gant·ly,** *adv.* —**el'e·gance,** *n.*

element (2) [el'əment], *n.* 1. one of the more than 100 basic substances known to scientists that cannot be separated chemically into substances of other kinds. **Ex.** *Iron is an element.* 2. one of the basic principles or necessary parts of something. **Ex.** *He has mastered the elements of the English language.* —**el'e·men'tal,** *adj.* simple; basic.

elementary (3) [el'əmen't(ə)riy], *adj.* dealing with the first, most simple facts about a subject. **Ex.** *The elementary principles of mathematics are taught in the lower grades at school.*

elementary school [el'ələmen't(ə)riy skuwl'], a school of the first six or eight years of education.

elephant (2) [el'əfənt], *n.* a huge, heavy, gray-skinned animal with a long tubelike nose, which is called a trunk.

ELEPHANT

elevate (4) [el'əveyt'], *v.* lift up; raise. **Ex.** *The platform was elevated to a height of five feet.* —**el'e·va'tion,** *n.* 1. a raised place; a high piece of ground. **Ex.** *The house was on a wooded elevation.* 2. height above sea level. **Ex.** *Santa Fe, New Mexico, has an elevation of almost 7,000 feet.*

elevator (5) [el'əvey'tər], *n.* a cage or platform for carrying persons or goods from one level to another in a building. **Ex.** *This elevator goes only to the sixth floor.*

eleven (2) [əlev'ən, ilev'ən], *n., adj.* the number between ten and twelve; the number *11.* —**e·lev'enth,** *n.,* one of eleven parts. *adj.* coming after ten others.

eligible [el'ijibəl], *adj.* 1. qualified for. **Ex.** *He is eligible to compete in the race.* 2. worthy of being chosen; desirable, especially for marriage. **Ex.** *My brother is a very eligible bachelor.*

eliminate (4) [əlim'əneyt', ilim'əneyt'], *v.* remove; get rid of; leave out. **Ex.** *Part of the program was eliminated to save time.* —**e·lim'i·na'tion**, *n.*

elm (5) [elm'], *n.* a tall, leafy, shade tree with a spreading top. **Ex.** *They enjoyed resting in the shade of the elm tree.*

ELM

eloquence (5) [el'əkwəns], *n.* language used with grace and force so that it influences the thinking and feeling of people. **Ex.** *The speaker was noted for his eloquence.* —**el'o·quent**, *adj.* —**el'o·quent·ly**, *adv.*

else (1) [els'], *adj.* 1. instead of; in the place of; other. **Ex.** *If he cannot go; someone else must.* 2. in addition to. **Ex.** *I am leaving; who else is?* —*adv.* 1. in a different place, time or manner. **Ex.** *How else could he have managed?* 2. otherwise. **Ex.** *Dress warmly or else you will be cold.*

elsewhere [els'hwe:r'], *adv.* at, to or in some other place. **Ex.** *It may be quieter elsewhere.*

embargo [embar'gow], *n.* a government order forbidding trade. **Ex.** *There is an embargo on the import of certain kinds of guns.* —*v.* place an embargo on.

embarrass (4) [embær'əs], *v.* cause to feel uncomfortable about one's appearance, actions, etc. **Ex.** *They were embarrassed because there was not enough food for all the guests.* —**em·bar' rass·ment**, *n.*

embassy [em'bəsiy], *n.* all the staff of the office headed by an ambassador and representing a government abroad; the building in which the staff works and the ambassador sometimes lives. **Ex.** *My sister works at the United States Embassy in London.*

embrace (3) [embreys'], *v.* hold in one's arms to show love or fondness. **Ex.** *The groom embraced his bride.*

emerge (4) [imərj'], *v.* come into view; appear; become known. **Ex.** *After the rain, the sun emerged from the clouds.* —**e·mer' gence**, *n.*

a, far; æ, am; e, get; ey, late; i, in; iy, see; ɔ, all; ow, go; u, put; uw, too; ə, but, ago; ər, fur; aw, out; ay, life; oy, boy; ŋ, ring; θ, think; ð, that; ž, measure; š, ship; j, edge; č, child.

emergency (3) [imər'jənsiy], *n.* an unexpected circumstance or occurrence requiring immediate action. **Ex.** *The fire at the hospital created a serious emergency.* —**e·mer'gen·cy room`**, *n.* an area in a hospital where emergency cases are treated.

emigrate (5) [em'əgreyt`], *v.* leave one's own country or region to settle in another. **Ex.** *In the nineteenth century, many Europeans emigrated to America.* —**em'i·gra'tion,** *n.*

eminent (5) [em'ənənt], *adj.* ranking above many others in talent, worth, etc.; famous; distinguished. **Ex.** *An eminent scientist is teaching at our university.* —**em'i·nent·ly,** *adv.* —**em'i·nence,** *n.*

emotion (2) [imow'šən], *n.* a strong feeling of any kind; a particular feeling. **Ex.** *She felt a rush of many emotions— love, hate and fear all at once.* —**e·mo'tion·al,** *adj.*—**e·mo'tion·al·ly,** *adv.*

emperor (3) [em'pərər], *n.* the ruler of an empire. —**em'press**, *n.* wife of an emperor; the female ruler of an empire.

emphasis (3) [em'fəsəs], *n.* 1. special attention given because of importance. **Ex.** *Our school places great emphasis on mathematics.* 2. stress given to particular words, parts of words or phrases in speaking. **Ex.** *In pronouncing the word* travel, *the emphasis is on the syllable* trav. —**em'pha·size,** *v.*—**em·phat'ic,** *adj.* spoken or done with emphasis.

empire (2) [em'payr], *n.* a group of countries or states controlled by a single ruler. **Ex.** *The United States was once part of the British Empire.*

employ (2) [employ'], *v.* 1. give work to for wages; hire. **Ex.** *That store employs many people.* 2. use. **Ex.** *The methods he employed were very practical.* —**em·ploy'ment,** *n.* 1. the state of being employed. 2. that on which one is employed. —**em·ploy'er,** *n.* one who employs another. **Ex.** *That employer pays his workers good wages.*

employee (5) [employ'iy, em'ployiy`], *n.* one who works for wages or salary in the service of another.

empty (2) [emp'tiy], *adj.* 1. having nothing inside. **Ex.** *I need an empty box for packing the dishes.* 2. not occupied. **Ex.** *Is this seat empty?* 3. having no purpose; without meaning. **Ex.** *Her life seemed empty now that he was gone.* —*v.* 1. make or become empty; pour out; take out. **Ex.** *She emptied the water from the pail.* 2. discharge; flow out or into. **Ex.** *That stream empties into the river.* —**emp'ti·ness,** *n.*

en- (1) [en], *prefix*. 1. put on or into; surround; close in. **Exs.** *case, encase; circle, encircle.* 2. make. **Exs.** *able, enable; large, enlarge.* 3. add strength to a meaning. **Exs.** *liven, enliven; snare, ensnare.*

-en (1) [ən], *suffix*. 1. make or become. **Exs.** *Deep, deepen; sick, sicken; fat, fatten.* 2. made of; like. **Exs.** *Gold, golden; wool, woolen; wood, wooden;* 3. gain; cause to have. **Exs.** *Haste, hasten; strength, strengthen; length, lengthen.*

enamel (5) [inæm'əl], *n.* 1. a hard, shiny substance baked on the surface of metal. **Ex.** *The kitchen sink is covered with enamel.* 2. a paint used to give a surface a smooth, shiny finish. 3. the hard, white outer covering of the teeth.

-ence (2) [əns], *suffix*. act of, state of or quality of. **Exs.** *Prefer, preference; differ, difference; excel, excellence.*

enchant (5) [enčænt'], *v.* charm; delight greatly. **Ex.** *The audience was enchanted by the grace of the dancer.* —**en·chant' ment,** *n.*

enclose [inklow'z], *v.* 1. surround on all sides with a fence, wall, etc. **Ex.** *The garden behind the house was enclosed by a fence on either side and a hedge across the back.* 2. put something inside an envelope together with a letter. **Ex.** *I am enclosing some snapshots of the children with this letter.* —**en·clo'sure,** *n.*

encounter (3) [enkawn'tor], *v.* meet, often unexpectedly. **Ex.** *While out walking, we encountered an old friend* —*n.* 1. a meeting, often unexpected. **Ex.** *The encounter surprised him.* 2. a battle. **Ex.** *That bloody encounter was the beginning of the war.*

encourage (2) [enkər'ij], *v.* 1. give hope, courage or confidence to. **Ex.** *The teacher's praise encouraged the boy to study.* 2. help the development of; aid. **Ex.** *The sun encouraged the growth of the plants.* —**en·cour'age·ment.** —*n.* the giving of hope or confidence.

encyclopedia [ênsay`kləpiy'diyə], *n.* a reference book which contains articles giving information on various subjects, sometimes in a variety of fields, sometimes in one. **Ex.** *My parents gave me an encyclopedia of music for my birthday.*

end (1) [end'], *n.* 1. the part that comes last. **Ex.** *The end of the story was more interesting than the beginning.* 2. the furthest point. **Ex.** *My house is at the end of the road.* 3. aim; purpose; objective. **Ex.** *What end does he have in mind? —v.* bring or come to an end; stop; finish. **Ex.** *The road ended at the river.*

endeavor (3) [endev'ər], *v.* make an effort; try very hard. **Ex.** *They endeavored to find a home for him. —n.* an effort; an attempt. **Ex.** *He made an endeavor to save the drowning girl.*

endorse [endɔrs'], *v.* 1. sign one's name on the back of a check, money order, etc. **Ex.** *You forgot to endorse your check.* 2. make public one's approval or support. **Ex.** *The senator has endorsed his party's candidate for governor.* —**en·dorse' ment,** *n.*

endow (4) [endaw'], *v.* 1. give money or property to provide continuing support for. **Ex.** *The rich man endowed a new school for special studies in medicine.* 2. provide with a quality or ability. **Ex.** *She was endowed with great charm.* —**en·dow'ment,** *n.*

endure (2) [enduːr', endyuːr'], *v.* 1. serve patiently; bear. **Ex.** *The early settlers endured great hardships.* 2. continue for a long time; last. **Ex.** *Those ancient buildings have endured for centuries.* —**en·dur'ance,** *n.*

enemy (1) [en'əmiy], *n.* 1. an unfriendly person; one who is opposed to an idea, cause, etc. **Ex.** *The quarrel made them enemies.* 2. a person or persons opposed to one in war. **Ex.** *The enemy attacked during the night. —adj.* of or about the enemy.

energy (2) [en'ərjiy], *n.* 1. strength or force of action. **Ex.** *He used his energy to work for peace.* 2. the capacity of certain natural forces to do work. **Ex.** *Sunlight and electricity are both forms of energy.* —**en'er·get'ic,** *adj.* full of energy; active. **Ex.** *He is an energetic worker.*

enforce [enfɔrs'], *v.* cause or compel to obey; put or keep in force. **Ex.** *The rule against smoking in public buildings is being strictly enforced.* —**en·force'ment,** *n.*

engage (2) [engeyj'], *v.* 1. occupy the attention or time of. **Ex.** *She is engaged in writing a book.* 2. promise to marry. **Ex.** *They became engaged yesterday.* 3. employ; hire. **Ex.** *They engaged workmen to paint the house.* —**en·gage·ment,** *n.* 1. an agreement to marry. **Ex.** *Their engagement was announced recently.* 2. an appointment to meet at a particular time and place. **Ex.** *He could not see me because he had another engagement.*

engine (2) [en'jən], *n.* 1. a machine that uses energy to cause motion or to do work. **Ex.** *Most cars have gasoline engines.* 2. the car of a railroad train that pulls the load. **Ex.** *The engine pulling the railroad cars used electricity for power.*

engineer (2) [en`jəni:r], *n.* one who is trained to plan and build roads, bridges, etc. **Ex.** *Many engineers worked together to design this bridge.* —*v.* —**en`gi·neer'ing,** *n.* the science of designing and building engines, roads, bridges, etc.

English (1) [iŋ'gliš], *n.* 1. the main language spoken in England, the United States, Canada, Australia and some other countries. 2. the people of England. —*adj.* of or having to do with England, its people or its language.

enjoy (1) [enjoy'], *v.* receive pleasure from. **Ex.** *She enjoyed her vacation.* —**en·joy'ment,** *n.* —**en·joy'able,** *adj.* pleasurable. **Ex.** *He had an enjoyable time at the party.*

enlighten [enlayt'ən], *v.* inform; provide knowledge. **Ex.** *The book enlightened him about life in colonial times.*

enlist (5) [enlist'], *v.* 1. join a cause or group, especially by one's own wish. **Ex.** *He enlisted in the army.* 2. secure the help or support of. **Ex.** *May we enlist your help?* —**en·list'ment,** *n.* —**en·list'ed man,** *n.* soldier; any man in the armed forces except commissioned officers and warrant officers.

enormous (3) [inɔːr'məs], *adj.* extremely large; huge. **Ex.** *The enormous building was over 100 stories high.* —**e·nor'mous·ly,** *adv.*

enough (1) [ənəf', inəf'], *adj.* as many or as much as required or desired; sufficient. **Ex.** *We have enough chairs to seat everyone.* —*n.* the amount required or desired. **Ex.** *Did you have enough?* —*adv.* as much as necessary or desired. **Ex.** *Is the water hot enough to make the tea?*

enroll [enrowl'], *v.* become a group member, such as a student in a course, a voter in an election, etc. usually by writing one's name; register or become registered as a member of. **Ex.** *How many students are enrolled in your history class?* —**en·roll'ment,** *n.*

ensign [en'sən], *n.* the lowest ranking commissioned officer in the navy; a naval officer one grade below a lieutenant junior grade.

ensue (5) [ensuw'], *v.* 1. follow; come afterward. **Ex.** *We met and a long conversation ensued.* 2. happen as a consequence. **Ex.** *After some angry words, a fight ensued.*

-ent (3) [ənt], *suffix.* 1. being or acting in a particular way. **Exs.** *Differ, different; urge, urgent.* 2. one who, or that which, acts in a particular way. **Exs.** *Depend, dependent; preside, president.*

enter (1) [en'tər], *v.* 1. come or go into. **Ex.** *He entered the house.* 2. become a member; join. **Ex.** *He entered the army last week.*

enterprise (3) [en'tərprayz'], *n.* 1. a business or project, especially one that requires boldness and hard work. **Ex.** *Building the dam was a worthwhile enterprise.* 2. the quality or character that leads one to begin new and difficult projects. **Ex.** *The man who built the steel factory was a man of enterprise.*

entertain (3) [en'tərteyn'], *v.* 1. hold the attention of; amuse. **Ex.** *Her jokes and stories entertained everyone.* 2. have as a guest. **Ex.** *We entertained friends for lunch.* --**en·ter·tain'er**, *n.* one who amuses or entertains as a profession. —**en·ter·tain'ment** *n.* the act of entertaining or that which entertains.

enthusiasm (3) [enθuw'ziyæz'əm], *n.* keen interest; strong liking. **Ex.** *The work that he likes he does with enthusiasm.* —**en·thu'si·as'tic**, *adj.* **en·thu'si·as'ti·cal·ly**, *adv.*

entire (2) [entayr'], *adj.* whole; complete; all. **Ex.** *The walls supported the entire weight of the roof.* —**en·tire·ly**, *adv.* —**en·tire'ty**, *n.*

entitle (3) [entay'təl], *v.* give a right or claim to. **Ex.** *This ticket entitles you to attend the concert without charge.* —**en·ti'tle·ment**, *n.*

entrance (2) [en'trəns], *n.* 1. a place through which one enters; door; gate. **Ex.** *We went into the house through the front entrance.* 2. act of entering. **Ex.** *Everyone in the courtroom rose at the entrance of the judge.*

entreat (5) [entriyt'], *v.* earnestly plead; beg. **Ex.** *He entreated her to marry him.* —**en·treat'y**, *n.*

entry (4) [en'triy], *n.* 1. act of entering. **Ex.** *The general made a grand entry into the city.* 2. a passage or hallway through which one enters. **Ex.** *There is a closet for your coat in the entry.* 3. each item entered in a list. **Ex.** *They checked the entries in the account books.*

envelope (3) [en'vəlowp`, an'vəlowp'], *n*. a folded piece of paper in which a letter or something similar is placed for mailing; any covering like this. **Ex.** *Please put a stamp on this envelope.* —**en·vel'op,** *v*. wrap or cover completely. **Ex.** *The city was enveloped in flames.*

environment (4) [envay'rənmənt], *n*. all the surrounding things, conditions and influences that affect the development of a person, animal or plant. **Ex.** *The teacher blamed the boy's difficulties on his environment.* —**en·vi'ron·men'tal,** *adj*.

envy (3) [en'viy], *n*. 1. dislike or jealousy caused by something another person has or can do. **Ex.** *His sudden wealth filled me with envy.* 2. the person or thing that causes such feeling. **Ex.** *His new bicycle was the envy of his friends.* —*v*. feel envy at, toward or because of. **Ex.** *He envied his friend's success in business.* —**en'vi·ous,** *adj*. full of envy. —**en'vi·ous·ly,** *adv*.

epidemic [ep'idem'ik], *n*. the rapid spread of a particular disease or of something that spreads like a disease. **Exs.** *Our high school has been closed because there is an epidemic of flu. There has been an epidemic of robberies in our neighborhood.*

episode (5) [ep'əsowd`], *n*. an important happening or incident in a story or history. **Ex.** *The episode of the rescue was the most exciting part of the book.*

equal (1) [iy'kwəl], *adj*. 1. the same in amount, size, number, etc. **Ex.** *One half is equal to the other half.* 2. having the same rights, abilities, etc. **Ex.** *All people are equal before the law.* —*n*. a thing or person that is equal. **Ex.** *It will be hard to find his equal as a teacher.* —*v*. be equal to; match. **Ex.** *The runner equaled the world's record.* —**e·qual'i·ty,** *n*. —**e'qual·ly,** *adv*.

equator (2) [ikwey'tər], *n*. an imaginary line around the world that is equal in distance from the north and south poles; zero degrees latitude. **Ex.** *Quito, Ecuador, is a little south of the equator.* —**e·qua·tor'i·al,** *adj*. of, at or near the equator.

equip (3) [ikwip'], *v*. provide or furnish what is needed. **Ex.** *He equipped himself for a hunting trip.* —**e·quip'ment,** *n*. the things needed for some special purpose. **Ex.** *What other camping equipment will you need beside your tents?*

equivalent (4) [ikwiv'ələnt], *adj*. equal or same in quantity, value or meaning. **Ex.** *One half dozen is equivalent to six.* —*n*. that which is equal to something else. **Ex.** *You may pay me in cash or give me the equivalent in merchandise.*

-er (1) [ər], *suffix.* 1. a person or thing that does something. **Exs.** *Listen, listener; teach, teacher; read, reader.* 2. a person concerned with. **Exs.** *Law, lawyer; bank, banker; engine, engineer.* 3. a person who resides in or on. **Exs.** *Island, islander; New York, New Yorker.* 4. more. **Exs.** *Cold, colder; fast, faster.* See **A Brief Explanation of English Grammar.**

era (4) [i:r'ə], *n.* a period of history associated with an important event or person. **Ex.** *We are living in the atomic era.*

erase (5) [ireys'], *v.* rub out; wipe clean; remove. **Ex.** *The student erased the spelling mistakes in his composition.* —**e·ras'er**, *n.* something that erases. —**e·ras'·ure**, *n.* something that has been erased.

erect (3) [irekt'], *adj.* straight up; not leaning or slanted. **Ex.** *He stood proud and erect to receive the medal.* —*v.* 1. build; construct. **Ex.** *They will erect a building here.* 2. put in an upright position. **Ex.** *They erected a flagpole.* —**e·rec'tion**, *n.*

erode [irowd'], *v.* 1. wear away by washing, rubbing or carrying away; eat away. **Ex.** *The heavy rains have eroded the garden.* 2. be or become eaten or worn away. **Ex.** *Our iron fence is rapidly eroding.* —**e·ro'sion**, *n.*

err (4) [ə:r'], *v.* make an error; do or be wrong. **Ex.** *He erred when he said that the earth was flat.*

errand (4) [e:r'ənd], *n.* a short trip to perform a special task. **Ex.** *Her mother sent her on an errand to buy bread.*

error (2) [e:r'ər], *n.* 1. an incorrect act or belief; a mistake. **Ex.** *He made an error in addition.* 2. the condition of believing or doing what is not correct. **Ex.** *You are in error about her age.* —**er·ro'ne·ous**, *adj.* — **er·ro'ne·ous·ly**, *adv.*

erupt [irupt'], *v.* burst or break out suddenly with great force. **Exs.** *When the volcano erupted, the villagers fled from their homes. The students erupted into laughter at the teacher's mistake.* —**e·rup'tion**, *n.*

-ery (2) [əriy], *suffix.* 1. place where something is done. **Exs.** *Bake, bakery; refine, refinery.* 2. act, art or occupation of. **Exs.** *Mock, mockery; rob, robbery.* 3. quality or condition **Exs.** *Brave, bravery; slave, slavery.* 4. things collectively. **Ex.** *Jewel, jewelry.*

escalate [es'kəleyt'], *v.* 1. increase in size, strength of feeling, seriousness, etc. **Ex.** *Fights among backers of the two teams soon escalated into a riot.* 2. raise or rise. **Ex.** *Food prices are continuing to escalate.* —**es'ca·la'tion** *n.*

escalator [es'kəleytər], *n.* a set of moving steps that carries people from one floor to another; a moving stairway or staircase. **Ex.** *Shall we take the escalator or the elevator?*

escape (1) [eskeyp'], *v.* 1. get free; run away from. **Ex.** *Two prisoners escaped last night.* 2. keep from being harmed or injured; avoid. **Ex.** *He escaped being hurt in the fall.* 3. come gradually out of a closed place. **Ex.** *Gas was escaping from the pipe.* —*n.* 1. act or fact of escaping. **Ex.** *The prisoner's escape was not noticed until morning.* 2. the leaking or flowing out of something. **Ex.** *The escape of so much gas was dangerous.*

escort (4) [es'kort], *n.* a person or group accompanying another or others to protect or show honor. **Ex.** *An escort was waiting for the distinguished visitor.* —**es·cort'**, *v.* accompany to protect or show honor. **Ex.** *He escorted her home.*

-ese (2) [iyz], *suffix.* of or from a certain place. **Exs.** *China, Chinese; Japan, Japanese.*

especially (1) [espeš'əliy], *adv.* unusually; particularly. **Ex.** *He is an especially good student in history.*

-ess (1) [es], *suffix.* female. **Exs.** *Lion, lioness; actor, actress.*

essay (5) [es'ey], *n.* a short piece of writing on a single subject that gives the writer's personal ideas. **Ex.** *The students wrote essays about the importance of education.* —**es'say·ist**, *n.* one who writes essays.

essence (5) [es'əns], *n.* the essential quality of a thing; the most important quality or part. **Ex.** *The essence of his success in teaching is patience.*

essential (3) [əsen'čəl], *adj.* 1. extremely important; necessary. **Ex.** *Food and water are essential to life.* 2. of, belonging to or constituting the inner character of something; basic. **Ex.** *Sympathy is an essential part of her nature.* —*n.* something important, necessary or basic. **Ex.** *We took only essentials on the trip.* —**es·sen'ti·al·ly**, *adv.*

-est (2) [əst], *suffix.* most. **Exs.** *Warm, warmest; pretty, prettiest; soon, soonest.* See **A Brief Explanation of English Grammar.**

establish (2) [əstsæb'liš], *v.* 1. make permanent; settle; set firmly. **Ex.** *They established themselves in the community.* 2. begin a

a, far; æ, am; e, get; ey, late; i, in; iy, see; ɔ, all; ow, go; u, put; uw, too; ə, but, ago; ər, fur; aw, out; ay, life; oy, boy; ŋ, ring; θ, think; ð, that; ž, measure; š, ship; j, edge; č, child.

school, group, nation, etc. **Ex.** *He plans to establish a new business.* 3. prove to be true. **Ex.** *They established their ownership of the property.* —**es·tab'lish·ment,** *n.* 1. act of establishing. 2. the thing established.

estate (3) [əsteyt'], *n.* 1. everything owned by a person, including land, money and other types of property. **Ex.** *He left a small estate when he died.* 2. a large area of land with a big, luxurious house. **Ex.** *They lived on a large estate.* —**real estate,** *n.* land with its natural resources and any man-made improvements.

esteem (4) [estiym'], *v.* respect; consider highly; value greatly. **Ex.** *His writing is much esteemed.* —*n.* respect. **Ex.** *They held him in high esteem.* —**es'ti·ma·ble,** *adj.* deserving respect.

estimate (3) [es'təmeyt'], *v.* make a careful guess about the value, amount, size, etc. **Ex.** *They estimated that the trip would take two hours.*

estimate (3) [es'temit'], *n.* a careful guess about the value, amount, size, etc. **Ex.** *They submitted an estimate of building costs.* —**es'ti·ma'tion,** *n.* 1. the act of estimating. 2. opinion; estimate. **Ex.** *In your estimation, is he qualified for the job?*

et cetera (3) [etset'ərə], a Latin phrase meaning "and other things of that kind." **Ex.** *The hammers, nails, et cetera which you ordered have arrived. Et cetera* is frequently shortened to *etc.* in writing.

eternal (3) [itər'nəl], *adj.* 1. with neither beginning nor end; never ending. **Ex.** *He said that his religion is based on eternal truths.* 2. seeming to continue forever. **Ex.** *His years as a prisoner of war seemed eternal.* —**e·ter'nal·ly,** *adv.* —**e·ter'ni·ty,** *n.*

ethics [eθ'iks], *n.* a general system of moral principles and their study. **Ex.** *The senator felt that voting for the bill would be contrary to his ethics.* —**eth'i·cal,** *adj.*

ethnic [eθ'nik], *adj.* having to do with a cultural, national, racial, religious or tribal group. **Ex.** *At the festival many interesting ethnic dances were performed.*

etiquette [et'iket], *n.* the collected rules of correct social behavior or correct behavior within a special group, such as the military. **Ex.** *He believes that etiquette requires a man to rise when a lady enters the room.*

evacuate [iyvæk'yuweyt'], *v.* empty or cause to be empty; move out or away from; take out or away from; remove or cause to be removed. **Ex.** *Everyone was safely evacuated from the flooded area of town.* —e·vac`u·a'tion, *n.*

evaluate [ivæl'yuweyt`], *v.* examine, fix or judge the value of. **Ex.** *A committee is evaluating the effectiveness of the remedial reading program.* —e·val`u·a'tion, *n.*

evaporate (5) [ivæp'əreyt`], *v.* 1. change from a liquid into a vapor. **Ex.** *Water evaporates when boiled.* 2. vanish; disappear. **Ex.** *When she saw that her children were safe, her fears for them evaporated.* —e·vap`o·ra'tion, *n.*

eve (4) [iyv'], *n.* evening or day before some special day or event. **Ex.** *December thirty-first is New Year's Eve.*

even (1) [iy'vən], *adj.* 1. not higher or lower; level; smooth; flat. **Ex.** *The top of the table has an even surface.* 2. equal in size, number or quantity. **Ex.** *Each of the children got an even share of the candy.* —*adv.* 1. just or exactly. **Ex.** *Even as he spoke, the clock struck twelve.* 2. unlikely as it may seem. **Ex.** *Even his brother hated him.* 3. still; in comparison. **Ex.** *It was even later than we thought.* —e'ven·ly, *adv.* —e'ven·ness, *n.* —**get even with,** obtain revenge. **Ex.** *She got even with him by giving him the wrong answers.*

evening (1) [ivy'niŋ], *n.* the time of the day between sunset and the early part of night. **Ex.** *Children usually go to bed early in the evening.*

event (2) [ivent'], *n.* 1. that which happens, especially a happening of importance. **Ex.** *The party was an important social event.* 2. an item or contest in a program of sports. **Ex.** *My brother is running in the next event.* —e·vent'ful, *adj.* full of happenings. —**in any event,** regardless of what happens. **Ex.** *We will go in any event.* —**in the event of,** if a particular event occurs. **Ex.** *In the event of a fire, leave by the stairs.*

eventual (5) [iven'čuwəl], *adj.* coming after the passing of time or as a result of. **Ex.** *They hoped for the eventual success of their plans.* —e·ven'tu·al·ly, *adv.* —e·ven'tu·al'i·ty, *n.* something that might happen. **Ex.** *They are prepared for any eventuality.*

ever (1) [ev'ər], *adv.* at any time. **Ex.** *Have you ever seen him before?*

every (1) [ev'riy], *adj.* each one, not leaving out any. **Ex.** *Every time I saw him, he was smiling.* —**every other,** every second one. **Ex.** *Every other book in the row was red.*

everybody [ev'riybad'iy], *pron.* all persons. **Ex.** *Everybody in the school came to the party.*

everyday [ev'riydey], *adj.* 1. characteristic of every day; daily. **Ex.** *One of my everyday tasks is making my bed.* 2. not special; ordinary; common. **Ex.** *You had better wear your everyday coat because it's snowing.*

everyone [ev'riywən'], *pron.* all persons. **Ex.** *Everyone in the class passed the test.* —**eve'ry one'**, each person. **Ex.** *Every one had a different opinion.*

everything [ev'riyθiŋ], *pron.* all things. **Ex.** *He put everything away before he left.*

everywhere [ev'riyhwe:r'], *adv.* to or in every place. **Ex.** *We looked everywhere for you.*

evict [ivikt'], *v.* put out from an apartment, house, land, etc. by legal means. **Ex.** *They were evicted from their house because they did not pay their rent for three months.*

evidence (2) [ev'ədəns], *n.* indication; a reason for believing; proof. **Ex.** *Based on the evidence, the police believe two people committed the crime.*

evident (3) [ev'ədənt], *adj.* not difficult to understand or see; clear; plain. **Ex.** *It was evident they were brothers.* —**ev'i·dent·ly,** *adv.*

evil (2) [iy'vəl], *n.* anything which results in harm or suffering. **Ex.** *Although he treated me badly, I wish him no evil.* —*adj.* 1. not good; harmful; injurious. **Ex.** *Smoking is an evil habit.* 2. morally bad; sinful. **Ex.** *The criminal led an evil life.*

evolve (5) [ivalv'], *v.* develop gradually. **Ex.** *Their plan evolved by trial and error.* —**ev'o·lu'tion,** *n.* gradual development.

ewe [yuw'], *n.* a female sheep. **Ex.** *That ewe had a lamb this past spring.*

ex- (1) [eks], *prefix.* earlier; former. **Exs.** *President, ex-President; teacher, ex-teacher.*

exact (2) [egzækt'], *adj.* without error; having no mistakes; correct. **Ex.** *Make an exact copy of this letter.* —**ex·act'ly,** *adv.* in a way that is exact. **Ex.** *You have done this job exactly as I wanted it done.*

exaggerate (4) [egzæʝ'əreyt'], *v.* speak of something as larger, more important or greater than it is. **Ex.** *The fisherman exaggerated the size of the fish he had caught.* —**ex·ag'ger·a'tion,** *n.*

exalt (5) [egzɔ:lt'], *v.* 1. raise in rank, honor, etc.; praise. **Ex.** *The hero was exalted in song.* 2. fill with pride or joy. **Ex.** *They were exalted by their son's success.* —**ex·al·ta'tion**, *n.*

examine (2) [egzæm'ən], *v.* 1. look at with care. **Ex.** *The doctor examined my sore eye.* 2. test the truth or knowledge of. **Ex.** *The teacher examined the students on the previous lesson.* —**ex·am'in·er**, *n.* one who examines. —**ex·am'i·na'tion**, *n.* 1. the act of looking at closely and carefully. 2. a test of what one has learned.

example (2) [egzæm'pəl], *n.* 1. a part that shows what the rest of a thing or group is like. **Ex.** *This painting is an example of the artist's work.* 2. model or pattern to be followed. **Ex.** *His essay was used as an example for the class.*

exceed (3) [eksiyd'], *v.* 1. be or go beyond the limit of. **Ex.** *Don't exceed the speed limit.* 2. be greater or better than. **Ex.** *His skill exceeds that of the other carpenters.* —**ex·ceed'ing·ly**, *adv.*

excellent (2) [ek'sələnt], *adj.* better than others; of great worth. **Ex.** *He is an excellent student.* —**ex·cel'**, *v.* be better. **Ex.** *He excels at sports.* —**ex'cel·lence**, *n.*

except (1) [eksept'], *prep.* other than; but. **Ex.** *He works every day except Sunday.* —**ex·cep'tion**, *n.* 1. the act of leaving out. **Ex.** *Everyone must be here; there will be no exceptions.* 2. something or someone that is left out or is different. **Ex.** *That case is an exception to the rule.* —**ex·cep'tion·al**, *adj.* different; unusual. —**take exception to,** object to; argue against. **Ex.** *I took exception to what he had said.*

excess (4) [ek'ses'], *adj.* more than necessary, allowed or desirable. **Ex.** *She must eat less to lose her excess weight.* —*n.* extra amount; the amount over that needed. **Ex.** *He is spending in excess of his income.* —**ex·ces'sive**, *adj.* beyond the limit. —**ex·ces'sive·ly**, *adv.*

exchange (2) [eksčeynj'] *v.* give or receive something for something else; trade. **Ex.** *He exchanged the box for a larger one.* —*n.* 1. a giving of something for something else; a trade. **Ex.** *He gave her two pictures in exchange for a book.* 2. the act of exchanging. **Ex.** *There was an exchange of ideas between the two leaders.* 3. a place of business where things are bought and sold. **Ex.** *He lost a fortune on the stock exchange.*

---

a, far; æ, am; e, get; ey, late; i, in; iy, see; ɔ, all; ow, go; u, put; uw, too; ə, but, ago; ər, fur; aw, out; ay, life; oy, boy; ŋ, ring; θ, think; ð, that; ž, measure; š, ship; j, edge; č, child.

excite (2) [iksayt'], *v.* cause strong feelings or mental or physical activity. **Exs.** *The remark excited his anger. The fire excited the animals.* —**ex·cit'ing,** *adj.* causing strong feelings. —**ex·cit' a·ble,** *adj.* easily excited. —**ex·cite'ment,** *n.*

exclaim (3) [ekskleym'], *v.* cry out or speak suddenly with emotion. **Ex.** *"She is hurt!" he exclaimed.* —**ex·cla·ma'tion,** *n.* a word or sentence that exclaims. —**ex·cla·ma'tion mark** or **point,** the mark (!) used after words or sentences to show strong or sudden feeling.

exclude (4) [ekskluwd'], *v.* keep out; shut out; refuse to consider or think about. **Exs.** *He was excluded from the meeting. I excluded that idea from my thoughts.* —**ex·clu'sion,** *n.* the act or state of being excluded.

exclusive (5) [ekskluw'siv], *adj.* limited or belonging to a particular individual or group. **Ex.** *I have the exclusive right to sell these houses.* —**ex·clu'sive·ly,** *adv.*

excursion [ekskər'žən], *n.* a short round trip made for a special purpose, sometimes available at a reduced fare; a trip of this type made for pleasure. **Ex.** *Six of us are going on an excursion to the beach this weekend.*

excuse (2) [ekskyuwz'], *v.* 1. pardon or forgive; overlook a fault. **Ex.** *Please excuse me for being late.* 2. free from blame; be an apology for. **Ex.** *Her sleepiness did not excuse her lack of attention.* 3. release from a duty or promise. **Ex.** *The teacher excused him from attending class.*

excuse (2) [ekskyuws'], *n.* a reason, real or pretended, given for being excused. **Ex.** *He had a good excuse for being absent.*

execute (4) [ek'əkyuwt`], *v.* 1. complete; put into effect. **Ex.** *The lawyer executed the dead man's will.* 2. put to death according to law. **Ex.** *The spy was executed this morning.* —**ex'e·cu'tion,** *n.* —**ex'e·cu'tion·er,** *n.* one who kills those sentenced by law to die.

executive (3) [egzek'yətiv], *n.* 1. any of the persons who manage and direct a business or organization. **Ex.** *He is an executive of a steel company.* 2. any of the persons who put the laws of a nation into effect. **Ex.** *The President is the chief executive of the United States.* —*adj.* concerning the operation or management of a company or the governing of a country. **Ex.** *The new manager is noted for his executive ability.*

exercise (2) [ek'sərsayz'], *n.* 1. physical effort for the purpose of improving the body or staying healthy. **Ex.** *He enjoys walking for exercise.* 2. a series of movements done regularly to strengthen muscles. **Ex.** *He does exercises every morning.* 3. problems done for training or improving the mind. **Ex.** *The class did a written exercise each day.* —*v.* use physical effort or do a series of regular movements to improve or train the body. **Ex.** *He exercised his muscles every day.*

exert (4) [egzərt'], *v.* vigorously use. **Ex.** *He exerted all his strength to lift the heavy trunk.* —**ex·er'tion,** *n.*

exhale (4) [eksheyl'], *v.* force air out from the lungs; breathe out. **Ex.** *He held his breath for a moment before he exhaled.*

exhaust (3) [egzɔːst'], *v.* 1. tire very much. **Ex.** *The hard work exhausted him.* 2. use completely. **Ex.** *They had exhausted all their money.* —*n.* the hot gas produced by a gasoline engine; the pipe through which this gas escapes. —**ex·haus'tion,** *n.*

exhibit (3) [egzib'it], *v.* 1. show; display. **Ex.** *The paintings were exhibited at the art gallery.* 2. reveal. **Ex.** *She never exhibited her emotions.* —*n.* the act of showing; a display. **Ex.** *We attended an exhibit of photographs.* —**ex'hi·bi'tion,** *n.* a display. —**ex·hib'i·tor,** *n.* one who exhibits something.

exile (4) [eg'zayl', ek'sayl'], *v.* force a person to leave his home and country. **Ex.** *The political leaders were exiled to an island.* —*n.* 1. a person who is exiled. **Ex.** *The exile lived a lonely life.* 2. state of being exiled. **Ex.** *While in exile, he wrote long letters.*

exist (2) [egzist'], *v.* 1. be; have material being. **Ex.** *These mountains have existed for ages.* 2. live. **Ex.** *We need air and water to exist.* —**ex·ist'ence,** *n.* —**ex·ist'ent,** *adj.*

exit (5) [eg'zit], *n.* 1. a place through which to go out. **Ex.** *He left the building through the rear exit.* 2. the act of going out. **Ex.** *The thief made a quick exit through the window.* —*v.* go out. **Ex.** *Please exit through the rear door.*

expand (4) [ekspænd'], *v.* 1. make or grow larger. **Ex.** *The balloon expanded as it was filled with air.* 2. develop the details of. **Ex.** *He expanded his short story into a novel.* —**ex·pan'sion,** *n.*

expect (1) [ekspekt'], *v.* look forward to; look for confidently; anticipate. **Ex.** *He expects her to come on Friday.* —**ex·pect'ant,** *adj.* —**ex'pec·ta'tion,** *n.*

expedition (3) [ek`spədiš'ən], *n*. 1. a journey for some special purpose such as trade, exploration, or war. **Ex.** *The boy dreamed of going on an expedition to discover an unknown land.* 2. the group of people, ships, etc. that makes such a journey. **Ex.** *There were twenty-five people in the expedition.*

expel (5) [ekspel'], *v*. 1. drive or force out. **Ex.** *They used pumps to expel water from the ship.* 2. force to leave as punishment. **Ex.** *The student was expelled from college.*

expend (4) [ekspend'], *v*. spend; use. **Ex.** *He had expended much time and effort on the experiment.* —**ex·pen'di·ture,** *n*. anything spent. **Ex.** *His expenditures went beyond his income.* —**ex·pend'a·ble,** *adj*. that can be consumed in use without concern. **Ex.** *The paper is expendable, but the books are not.*

expense (2) [ekspens'], *n*. 1. the cost; the money paid out. **Ex.** *He could not afford the expense of a new car.* 2. the cause of spending. **Ex.** *Food and rent were his chief expenses.* —**ex·pen'sive,** *adj*. costing much; very high-priced. **Ex.** *The gold watch is more expensive than the silver one.*

experience (1) [ekspir'iyəns], *n*. 1. the act of living through an event or events; something that one has done or lived through. **Ex.** *His first ride in an airplane was an exciting experience.* 2. the knowledge or skill gained from work or practice. **Ex.** *He is a teacher of wide experience.* —*v*. live through; feel. **Ex.** *He experienced many troubles when he was younger.*

experiment (2) [eksper'əmənt], *n*. a test or trial made to prove a theory true or false or to discover something. **Ex.** *The purpose of the experiment is to determine whether this material will burn.* —*v*. test or make a trial in order to find out. **Ex.** *The doctors are experimenting with a new medicine.* —**ex·per`i·men'tal,** *adj*. — **ex·per`i·men'tal·ly,** *adv*.

expert (3) [ek'spərt], *n*. a person who has special skill or knowledge in some particular subject; an authority. **Ex.** *He is an expert in the field of international law.* —*adj*. 1. very skillful; having much training, knowledge and experience. **Ex.** *He is an expert driver.* 2. coming from an expert. **Ex.** *He gave us expert advice.* —**ex·pert'ly,** *adv*.

expire (5) [ekspayr'], *v*. cease; die; terminate. **Ex.** *The agreement expired yesterday.* —**ex·pi·ra'tion,** *n*.

explain (1) [ekspleyn'], *v*. 1. tell what the meaning is. **Ex.** *After the teacher had explained the lesson, the children understood it.* 2. make plain; make clear; tell about. **Ex.** *He explained how* *the machine worked.* 3. give reasons for. **Ex.** *Please explain your lateness.* —**ex·plan·a'tion,** *n.* —**ex·plan'a·to'ry,** *adj.*

explode (2) [eksplowd'], *v.* burst with a loud noise. **Ex.** *A bomb exploded today and killed many people.* —**ex·plo'sion,** *n.* —**ex·plo'sive,** *adj.*

exploit (4) [eks'ployt], *n.* a bold, heroic act or deed. **Ex.** *The soldier was decorated for his exploits.*

exploit (4) [eksployt'], *v.* 1. use in a practical way; get the full value from. **Ex.** *The new dam did much to exploit the water power resources of the area.* 2. make unfair use of; use for one's own advantage or profit. **Ex.** *The strikers complained that they were being exploited by the company.* —**ex'ploi·ta'tion,** *n.*

explore (2) [eksplɔ:r'], *v.* 1. travel in a place that is not well known to discover more about it. **Ex.** *Humans are now exploring space.* 2. make a careful search; examine closely. **Ex.** *He explored every possibility before making a decision.* —**ex'plo·ra'tion,** *n.* the act of exploring. —**ex·plor'er,** *n.* one who explores.

export (3) [ek'spɔrt`, eksport'], *v.* send goods made in one country to be sold in another. **Ex.** *Japan exports a large number of cars to the United States.* —*n.* 1. the act of sending goods from one country for sale in another. **Ex.** *American farmers raise wheat and rice for export.* 2. the article exported. **Ex.** *Machinery is one of our most important exports.* —**ex·port'er,** *n.* one who exports.

expose (3) [ekspowz'], *v.* 1. leave unprotected. **Ex.** *The child was exposed to the sun too long.* 2. uncover; make known; reveal. **Ex.** *The crime of the official was exposed by a reporter.* —**ex·pos'ure,** *n.*

express (2) [ekspres'], *v.* 1. say clearly; state. **Ex.** *She expressed her ideas very well.* 2. reveal; show one's feelings. **Ex.** *He expressed his anger by shouting.* —*adj.* 1. for one purpose only. **Ex.** *He went for the express purpose of seeing his friend.* 2. in the quickest or shortest way; without stopping. **Ex.** *The express train does not stop at any station between here and the city.* —**ex·pres'sion,** *n.* 1. an outward sign of how one feels or thinks. **Ex.** *Their cheers were an expression of their approval.* 2. a putting into words. **Ex.** *This story is an expression of the author's ideas.* —**ex·pres'sive,** *adj.*

expressway [ekspres'wey`], *n.* a divided road built for fast driving. **Ex.** *If we take the expressway, we'll save a couple of hours' driving time.*

exquisite (5) [eks'kwizət, ikskwiz'ət], *adj.* 1. made with great care and skill; of rare and delicate beauty. **Ex.** *The diamond pin was an exquisite work of art.* 2. of the finest quality; excellent. **Ex.** *The table was set with exquisite dishes and silver.* —**ex·qui'site·ly,** *adv.*

extend (2) [ekstend'], *v.* 1. stretch or be stretched out in area or in length. **Ex.** *The railroad has been extended for another twenty miles.* 2. continue for a longer time. **Ex.** *They extended their visit for two more days.* 3. give; offer. **Ex.** *We extend our sympathy on the death of your mother.* —**ex·ten'sion,** *n.* —**ex·ten'sive,** *adj.* covering a large area; including much or many.

extent (3) [ekstent'], *n.* 1. size, amount, length, etc. to which a thing is extended. **Ex.** *He opened the window to its full extent.* 2. degree; measure. **Ex.** *The extent of his knowledge astonished his students.*

exterior (5) [ekstiyr'iyər], *adj.* outer. **Ex.** *The exterior surface of the house was bleached by the sun.* —*n.* the outer surface or part. **Ex.** *The exterior of the house was brick.*

external (4) [ekstər'nəl], *adj.* 1. on, coming from or applied to the outside; outer. **Ex.** *This medicine is for external use only.* 2. relating to foreign nations. **Ex.** *The country's external problems concerned its frontiers with neighboring countries.* —**ex·ter'nal·ly,** *adv.*

extinct (5) [ekstiŋkt'], *adj.* no longer living or in existence. **Ex.** *Many animals that lived thousands of years ago are now extinct.* —**ex·tinc'tion,** *n.*

extinguish [ekstiŋ'wiš], *v.* put out, such as a fire or light. **Ex.** *They extinguished their fire on the beach by pouring water on it.* —**ex·tin'guish·er,** *n.* a container filled with chemicals that are sprayed on small fires to put them out.

extra (2) [eks'trə], *adj.* greater than ordinary, expected or necessary; additional. **Ex.** *He received more money for the extra work he did.* —*adv.* more than usually. **Ex.** *Such a big man needs extra-large clothes.*

extract (5) [ekstrækt'], *v.* pull out, usually with effort. **Ex.** *He had two teeth extracted.* —**ex·trac'tion.** *n.* 1. the act of extracting. **Ex.** *The extraction of her tooth was very painful.* 2. origin; line of descent. **Ex.** *He is of Italian extraction.*

extract (5) [eks'trækt], *n.* 1. a substance taken out which is the essential part. Ex. *She flavored the cake with lemon extract.* 2. a section taken from a written work, often for the purpose of quoting. Ex. *She read an extract from my favorite poem.*

extraordinary (3) [ekstrɔr'dənə:r`iy], *adj.* not ordinary; not usual. Ex. *That painter has extraordinary talent.* —**ex'tra·or·di·nar`i·ly,** *adv.*

extravagance (5) [ekstræv'əgəns], *n.* wastefulness; spending more money than is necessary. Ex. *Buying a second car was an extravagance.* —**ex·trav'a·gant,** *adj.*

extreme (3) [ekstriym'], *adj.* 1. greatest; to the utmost. Ex. *He uses extreme care when driving in the snow.* 2. farthest away. Ex. *He lives in the house at the extreme end of the street.* 3. going beyond the usual or accepted. Ex. *That candidate has very extreme political ideas.* —*n.* either of two things as different or as far apart as possible. Ex. *The weather went from one extreme to the other.* —**ex·treme'ly,** *adv.* —**ex·trem'ist,** *n.* one who has extreme ideas. —**ex·trem'i·ty,** *n.* the point farthest removed; the end. —**ex·trem'i·ties,** *n.* the feet and or hands.

eye (1) [ay'], *n.* 1. the part of the body with which people and animals see. 2. power of seeing; sight; vision. Ex. *He has a good eye for color.* 3. something that looks like an eye. Ex. *I need a needle with a large eye.* —*v.* look at steadily; stare. Ex. *She eyed the man silently.* —**eye'less,** *adj.* without eyes; blind. —**catch one's eye,** attract one's attention. —**keep an eye on** or **out,** watch closely. Ex. *Keep an eye out for cars when crossing the street.*

eyeball [ay'bɔ:l'], *n.* the whole of an eye inside the eyelid. Ex. *He had a bit of dirt on his right eyeball.*

eyebrow [ay'braw`], *n.* the curved line of hair above each eye. Ex. *She raised her eyebrows in surprise.*

eyeglass [ay'glæs'], *n.* a piece of special glass used to improve vision. —**eye'glass·es,** *n.* two of such pieces of glass in a frame.

EYE 1

eyelash [ay'læš'], *n.* each of the hairs growing on the edge of the eyelid.

eyelid [ay'lid`], *n.* the skin that covers and uncovers the eyeball as one opens or closes one's eyes. Ex. *She closed her eyelids and tried to sleep.*

EYEGLASSES

eyesight [aysayt'], *n.* the ability or power to see. **Ex.** *Because of his poor eyesight he has to wear very thick glasses.*

eyesore [ay'sɔːrˋ], *n.* anything not pleasant to look at. **Ex.** *The neglected old houses were eyesores.*

eyewitness [ay'wit'nəs], *n.* a person who saw something him- or herself, not someone who was only told about it. **Ex.** *He was an eyewitness to the accident.*

F

F, f [ef'], *n.* the sixth letter of the English alphabet.

fable (4) [fey'bəl], *n.* a short story that explains a moral, especially one in which animals speak and act like people. **Ex.** *He read to the child from an old book of fables.* —**fab'u·lous**, *adj.* hardly believable; astonishing.

fabric (4) [fæb'rik], *n.* cloth; material. **Ex.** *She chose a satin fabric for her wedding dress.* —**fab'ri·cate**, *v.* 1. make by assembling parts. **Ex.** *He fabricated a car with the parts he had collected.* 2. invent. **Ex.** *He fabricated the story.*

face (1) [feys'], *n.* 1. the front part of the head from the forehead to the chin. **Ex.** *She has a pretty face.* 2. something resembling a face. **Ex.** *It is too dark to see the face of the clock.* —*v.* 1. look toward; be turned toward. **Ex.** *The teacher faced the class.* 2. meet with courage. **Ex.** *They could not face their accusers.* —**fa'cial**, *adj.* of or for the face. **Ex.** *She bought some facial cream.* —**in the face of,** 1. in the presence of. **Ex.** *He showed his courage in the face danger.* 2. despite. **Ex.** *He completed the work in the face of many difficulties.* —**make a face,** twist one's face to show feeling. **Ex.** *When he tasted the bitter medicine, he made a face.* —**on the face of it,** from what can be seen or known. **Ex.** *On the face of it, your plan seems good.*

facility (4) [fəsil'ətiy], *n.* 1. ease or skill in doing, acting, working, etc. **Ex.** *We admired his facility in playing the piano.* 2. that which makes it easier to do something. **Ex.** *This kitchen has the latest facilities for cooking.* —**fa·cil'i·tate,** *v.* make easier. **Ex.** *It would facilitate matters if you could stay an hour longer.*

fact (1) [fækt'], *n.* 1. a thing known to be true or to have really happened. **Ex.** *He gave the police all the facts.* 2. truth; reality. **Ex.** *In fact, he just left.* 3. something said to be true or supposed to have happened. **Ex.** *Are you sure of your facts?* —**fac'tu·al,** *adj.* based on fact. **Ex.** *His factual report made a good impression upon his listeners.*

faction (5) [fæk'šən], *n.* a group of people within a larger group differing from it in certain aims or beliefs. **Ex.** *He belongs to the liberal faction of his political party.*

factor (5) [fæk'tər], *n.* any one of the causes of a result. **Ex.** *Mechanical failure was the chief factor in causing the wreck.*

factory (2) [fæk'təriy], *n.* a building or group of buildings where goods are manufactured. **Ex.** *We have a shoe factory in our town.*

faculty (4) [fæk'əltiy], *n.* 1. any of the physical powers of the body, such as hearing, sight, etc.; any special ability or talent. **Ex.** *The old man still had all his faculties.* 2. all those who teach in a school or college; all the persons who teach in a department of a college or university. **Ex.** *He is a member of the college faculty.*

fade (3) [feyd'], *v.* 1. lose or cause to lose color or brightness. **Ex.** *The sun has faded the curtains.* 2. die away. **Ex.** *The sound faded into the night.* 3. lose strength and freshness. **Ex.** *Those flowers have faded.*

Fahrenheit [fær'ənhayt'], *adj.* referring to a temperature scale with 32 being the point at which water freezes and 212 the point at which water boils. **Ex.** *We were very uncomfortable today with the temperature at 95° Fahrenheit.*

fail (1) [feyl'], *v.* 1. not succeed; not reach. **Ex.** *He failed today's test.* 2. not do; neglect. **Ex.** *She failed to answer the letter.* 3. be of no use or help; disappoint. **Ex.** *He failed us when we needed him most.* 4. become weaker. **Ex.** *His health has been* *failing.* —**fail'ure,** *n.* —**without fail,** certainly; surely. **Ex.** *I will come without fail.*

faint (2) [feynt'], *adj.* weak; without brightness, strength, etc. **Exs.** *We heard a faint cry for help. She felt faint.* —*v.* lose consciousness. **Ex.** *She fainted when she heard the news.* —*n.* loss of consciousness. **Ex.** *She fell in a faint.* —**faint'ly,** *adv.*

fainthearted [feynt'har'təd], *adj.* not brave; lacking confidence. **Ex.** *He was too fainthearted to ask her to marry him.*

fair (1) [fe:r'], *adj.* 1. just; honest. **Ex.** *They received a fair share of the money.* 2. ordinary; average; not very good or very bad. **Ex.** *He is a fair student.* 3. not dark; light-colored. **Ex.** *She has blonde hair and very fair skin.* 4. sunny; not stormy. **Ex.** *The weather is fair today.* —**fair'ly,** *adv.*

fair (1) [fe:r'], *n.* a gathering of people to buy and sell goods, show products, etc. **Ex.** *A fair is held in the village every Saturday.*

fairy (3) [fe:r'iy], *n.* an imaginary being in children's stories that is supposed to look like a tiny human with wings and to have powers of magic. **Ex.** *The fairy promised to grant the child's wish.*

faith (2) [feyθ'], *n.* 1. believing without proof; trust. **Ex.** *He has complete faith in his lawyer.* 2. religion or belief. **Ex.** *There are people of many faiths in the United States.* —**faith'ful,** *adj.* loyal; honest. —**faith'ful·ly,** *adv.* —**faith'ful·ness,** *n.*

fake [feyk'], *n.* something or someone that is not what it, he or she seems, appears, claims or is claimed to be. **Ex.** *According to the experts, this statue is a fake.* —*v.* pretend, appear or claim falsely. **Ex.** *That student faked a note from his mother excusing his absence.* —*adj.* pretending to be real; false. **Ex.** *She always wears fake pearls.*

fall (1) [fɔ:l'], *v.* 1. drop; go down; descend. **Ex.** *The snow started to fall last night.* 2. suddenly drop or come down from a standing position. **Ex.** *Be careful on the ice or you will fall.* 3. be killed or wounded. **Ex.** *I saw him fall in battle.* 4. hit; land; strike. **Ex.** *Where did the blow fall?* 5. become less in number or lower in degree; decrease. **Ex.** *In summer, the price of fresh fruit will fall.* 6. pass suddenly into a new state or condition; become. **Ex.** *I often fall asleep while reading.* —*n.* 1. the act of falling or dropping. **Ex.** *The fall hurt the child's leg.* 2. a steep fall of water from a dam, cliff, etc.; waterfall. **Ex.** *They walked up beside the river to see the falls.*

2. the season between summer and winter; autumn. Ex. *My brother will be going to college this fall.* —**fall'en,** adj. Ex. *The fallen tree blocked the road.* —**fall back,** retreat. Ex. *The soldiers will have to fall back if the heavy enemy gunfire continues.* —**fall back on,** turn to or go to for help. Ex. *She had to fall back on her family.* —**fall behind,** 1. drop back as in a race or other effort. Ex. *He is falling behind in his work.* 2. be late in paying. Ex. *Why are you falling behind in paying your bills?* —**fall off,** drop off; decrease. Ex. *Sales are falling off because of the extremely cold weather.* —**fall out,** 1. step out of a line. Ex. *The soldiers were told to fall out after the march.* 2. quarrel. Ex. *They are friends, but they often fall out.* 3. anything that falls. —**fall through,** fail to develop; fail. Ex. *Why did your plans fall through?*

false (2) [fɔːls'], adj. 1. not true; incorrect. Ex. *She had a false idea of what she was to be paid.* 2. dishonest; lying. Ex. *She made a false statement.* 3. not real. Ex. *He has false teeth.* —**false'ly,** adv. —**fal'si·fy`,** v. —**false'hood,** n. lie.

falter (5) [fɔːl'tər], v. 1. be unsteady or unsure; stumble; hesitate. Ex. *She began to falter in her beliefs.* 2. stumble or hesitate in moving. Ex. *The old man faltered as he walked.*

fame (2) [feym'], n. public reputation, especially a very favorable one. Ex. *Her fame does not seem to have changed her basic friendliness.*

familiar (2) [fəmil'yər], adj. 1. well-known; common. Ex. *His voice is familiar to radio listeners.* 2. well-acquainted; friendly. Ex. *He was familiar with my family.* —**fa·mil'i·ar'i·ty,** n. 1. a thorough knowledge of. 2. friendliness, usually not wanted. Ex. *She objected to his familiarity.* —**fa·mil'iar·ize,** v. make well known; become acquainted. Ex. *He familiarized himself with the strange city.* —**fa·mil'iar·ly,** adv.

family (1) [fæm'(ə)liy], n. 1. the group consisting of children and their parents. Ex. *There are seven in my family.* 2. a group of people related to one another. Ex. *The whole family, including my cousins, came to my wedding.* 3. a group of related animals or plants. Ex. *The lion and the tiger belong to the same family.*

famine (4) [fæm'in], n. a great scarcity of food resulting in starvation. Ex. *If the crops fail, there will be a famine this year.*

famous (1) [fey'məs], adj. very well-known. Ex. *He is a famous writer.*

fan (3) [fæn'], *n.* a device used to create currents of air, usually to cool. **Ex.** *In the summer, we use an electric fan.* —*v.* make a current of air, as with a fan; blow air toward. **Ex.** *He fanned the fire until it grew stronger.*

FAN

fan [fæn'], *n.* a person who is a strong admirer or supporter of something or someone, such as a sport, an actor or actress, etc. **Ex.** *The singer's fans crowded into the theater.*

fanatic [fənæt'ik], *n.* a person who is extreme and unreasonable in his enthusiasm for a cause, a person, etc., particularly in religion or politics. **Ex.** *She is a fanatic about keeping her house spotless.*

fancy (1) [fæn'siy], *n.* 1. the power of forming mental pictures of things that are not present; imagination. **Ex.** *The idea of travel appealed to her fancy.* 2. the things imagined; an image. **Ex.** *She had wild fancies of fame and wealth.* 3. a liking. **Ex.** *He took a fancy to her.* —*adj.* 1. of better than ordinary quality. **Ex.** *They bought some fancy fruits for their sick friend.* 2. having complicated design and much ornament; not plain. **Ex.** *She wore a fancy dress to the party.* —*v.* 1. imagine; picture to oneself. **Ex.** *The senator's assistant fancied himself a great politician.* 2. like. **Ex.** *She fancied the dress and bought it.*

fantastic (5) [fæn'tæs'tik], *adj.* 1. beyond belief. **Ex.** *She told fantastic stories about her trip.* 2. wildy fanciful. **Ex.** *The wall was covered with fantastic designs.* —**fan'ta·sy,** *n.* imagination; unreal dreams, stories, etc. **Ex.** *In his fantasy, he imagined he was a famous writer.*

far (1) [fa:r'], *adv.* 1. at, to or from a great distance. **Ex.** *Do you live far from here?* 2. to or at a certain distance or degree. **Ex.** *How far up did the plane go?* 3. very much or a great deal. **Ex.** *He is a far better writer than his brother.* —*adj.* 1. distant; not near. **Ex.** *He came from a far country.* 2. farther away. **Ex.** *He lives on the far side of the mountain.* —**as far as, so far as,** to the extent or degree that. **Ex.** *As far as I know, he has not come.* —**by far, far and away,** greatly. **Ex.** *He is far and away the better swimmer.* —**so far, thus far,** to this place, time, etc. **Ex.** *He has not arrived so far.*

faraway [fa:r'əwey'], *adj.* distant; seeming to be distant. **Ex.** *As she read his letter, she had a faraway look in her eyes.*

fare (3) [fe:r'], *n*. 1. the price of a ride. **Ex.** *How much is the fare on this bus?* 2. a person who pays to use transportation. **Ex.** *The taxi picked up two fares at the corner.* 3. food. **Ex.** *The fare we tasted was good.* —*v*. get along; manage; do. **Ex.** *How did you fare on your trip?*

farewell (3) [fe:r'wel'], *interj*. good-bye. **Ex.** *Farewell, my friends.* —*n*. leave-taking; departure; good wishes at departure. **Ex.** *Their farewell was sad.* —*adj*. parting. **Ex.** *They gave him a farewell party.*

farm (1) [farm'], *n*. land used for raising crops or animals. **Ex.** *They grow very good corn on their farm.* —*v*. raise crops or animals. **Ex.** *He farmed the land himself.* —**farm'er,** *n*. one who farms.

farsighted [fa:r'say'tid], *adj*. 1. able to see things at a distance. **Ex.** *She wears glasses because she is farsighted.* 2. able to plan wisely for the future. **Ex.** *If you had been more farsighted, you would have expected this problem.*

farther (2) [far'ðər], *adv*. at or to a greater distance or degree. **Ex.** *I can swim farther than you can.* —*adj*. more distant. **Ex.** *The farther hill is ten miles away.*

fascinate (5) [fæs'əneyt'], *v*. 1. attract strongly; charm. **Ex.** *Her beauty fascinated him.* 2. hold motionless by a strong power, such as fear. **Ex.** *The child was fascinated by the snake.* —**fas'ci·na'tion,** *n*.

fashion (2) [fæš'ən], *n*. 1. manner; way. **Ex.** *He talked in a childish fashion.* 2. dress, way of living, etc. that is popular. **Ex.** *She always wore the latest fashions.* —*v*. make; shape; form. **Ex.** *He fashioned a figure out of clay.* —**fash'ion·a·ble,** *adj*. in style. **Ex.** *She wears fashionable clothes.*

fast (1) [fæst'], *adj*. 1. moving or working at high speed; quick; rapid. **Ex.** *The boy is a fast runner.* 2. indicating a time ahead of the correct time. **Ex.** *His watch is fast.* —*adv*. 1. quickly; rapidly. **Ex.** *His car will not go very fast.* 2. tightly. **Ex.** *Hold fast to my hand.* 3. completely. **Ex.** *He is fast asleep.*

fast (1) [fæst'], *v*. go without food. **Ex.** *They are fasting today for religious reasons.* —*n*. a time of fasting. **Ex.** *He ate no solid food during his fast.*

a, far; æ, am; e, get; ey, late; i, in; iy, see; ɔ, all; ow, go; u, put; uw, too; ə, but, ago; ər, fur; aw, out; ay, life; oy, boy; ŋ, ring; θ, think; ð, that; ž, measure; š, ship; j, edge; č, child.

fast food [fæst' fuwd'], *n*. food that is prepared rapidly and served quickly, such as hamburgers, pizza, etc. **Ex.** *When I'm very busy, I order fast food for lunch.*

fasten (3) [fæs'ən], *v*. 1. attach securely to something; join. **Ex.** *He fastened the papers together with a paper clip.* 2. fix firmly in place by closing or locking. **Ex.** *Fasten the back door before you go to bed.* —**fas'ten·er,** *n*. that which fastens. —**fas'ten·ing,** *n*. anything used to fasten.

fat (1) [fæt'], *n*. an oily substance, white or yellowish, found especially in animals. **Ex.** *She melted the fat and fried potatoes in it.* —*adj.* 1. fleshy; heavy. **Ex.** *He is a fat but healthy baby.* 2. thick; well filled. **Ex.** *She was carrying a fat pocketbook.* —**fat'ten,** *v.* —**fatty,** *adj.*

fatal (3) [fey'təl], *adj.* deadly. **Ex.** *He was in a fatal accident.* 2. causing ruin or destruction. **Ex.** *The delay was fatal to their plan.* —**fa'tal·ly,** *adv.* —**fa·tal'i·ty,** *n.* a death.

fate (2) [feyt'], *n.* 1. a force or power thought to determine in advance what is going to happen. **Ex.** *He blamed fate for his failure in life.* 2. the events that happen as though controlled by this force or power. **Ex.** *It was their fate to meet and marry.* —**fat'ed,** *adj.* decided in advance by fate. **Ex.** *He was fated to lead his country.* —**fate'ful,** *adj.* having an important meaning for the future. **Ex.** *It was a fateful day when we met.*

father (1) [fɑ'ðər], *n.* 1. male parent. **Ex.** *That man is my father.* 2. founder; creator. **Ex.** *George Washington was the father of our country.* 3. a title for a priest. —*v.* be the father of **Ex.** *He fathered eight children.* —**fa'ther·ly,** *adj.*

father-in-law [fɑ'ðərənlɔ:'], *n.* the father of one's wife or husband.

fatigue (4) [fətiyg'], *n.* weariness. **Ex.** *After a hard day's work, they were overcome by fatigue.* —*v.* make or become weary or tired. **Ex.** *Working in the hot kitchen fatigued her.*

faucet [fɔ:w'sit], *n.* a device for starting, stopping and controlling the flow of water or other liquids from a pipe or container. **Ex.** *I hear water dripping; did you turn off the faucet in the kitchen?*

FAUCET

fault (2) [fɔ:lt'], *n.* 1. imperfection. **Ex.** *His greatest fault is laziness.* 2. blame. **Ex.** *Whose fault is it that the window was broken?* —**fault'y,** *adj.* —**find fault with,** point to the weaknesses of. **Ex.** *She finds fault with everything he does.*

favor (1) [fey'vər], *n.* 1. liking; approval. **Ex.** *He is in favor of your plan.* 2. a kind, helpful action. **Ex.** *He did me a favor.* 3. special treatment. **Ex.** *The teacher showed some favor to the younger children.* —*v.* 1. like; approve. **Ex.** *The President favored a small tax increase.* 2. show preference; give special treatment. **Ex.** *That teacher favors the boys.*

favorable (3) [fey'v(ə)rəbəl], *adj.* 1. approving; friendly. **Ex.** *He is favorable to our plan.* 2. giving help. **Ex.** *We will leave as soon as we have favorable weather.* —**fa'vor·a·bly,** *adv.*

favorite (3) [fey'v(ə)rət], *n.* a person or thing liked best or preferred. **Ex.** *She is her father's favorite.* —*adj.* preferred; liked best. **Ex.** *Blue is my favorite color.* —**fa'vor·it·ism,** *n.* an act of showing preference for one person. **Ex.** *The teacher's display of favoritism toward one girl angered the other students.*

fawn (5) [fɔːn'], *n.* a deer less than one year old.

fawn (5) [fɔːn'], *v.* try to win favor or notice by acting in a humble and flattering way. **Ex.** *He fawned on her only to borrow money.*

FAWN

fear (1) [fiːr'], *n.* 1. a feeling one has when danger, trouble, evil, etc. is close. **Ex.** *He felt fear when he heard the sudden noise.* 2. an uneasy or anxious feeling; anxiety. **Ex.** *Fear for the future kept her awake.* 3. a particular cause of fear. **Ex.** *Her greatest fear was being alone.* —*v.* 1. be afraid. **Ex.** *He fears nothing.* 2. feel anxious. **Ex.** *I fear that he may be hurt.* —**fear'ful,** *adj.* causing fear; feeling fear.

feast (2) [fiyst'], *n.* a large meal with many dishes prepared for some special occasion. **Ex.** *We enjoyed the wedding feast.* —*v.* eat much food. **Ex.** *They feasted for three days during the king's visit.*

feat (5) [fiyt'], *n.* a deed of great courage, skill or strength. **Ex.** *The first flight into space was a brilliant feat.*

feather (2) [feð'ər], *n.* a light, thin outgrowth from a bird's skin that forms a covering. **Ex.** *There was a small, bright red feather in the band of his hat.* —*v.* supply or cover with feathers. **Ex.** *The bird feathered a nest for its young.* —**feath'er·y,** *adj,* like feathers.

FEATHER

feature (2) [fiy'čər], *n.* 1. a part of the face such as the eyes, nose, mouth or chin. **Ex.** *Her mouth is her best feature.* 2. a notable quality. **Ex.** *One desirable feature of this house is its convenient location.* 3. the main attraction of a program; a special article or story in a newspaper or magazine. **Ex.** *There is an interesting feature about world peace in this magazine.* —*v.* present as especially important. **Ex.** *They featured him as the novelist of the year.*

February (1) [feb'ruwer'iy], *n.* the second month of the year.

fed (2) [fed'], *v.* past tense and participle of feed. **Exs.** *The children were fed first. Have you fed the animals yet?*

federal (3) [fed'(ə)rəl], *adj.* of or relating to a union of states which give up some of their individual powers to a central government. **Ex.** *The United States has a federal government.* —**fed'er·al·ism,** *n.* the principle of such a union. —**fed'er·al·ist,** *n.* one who supports the federal principle. **Ex.** *Federalists wanted the central government to be strong.* —**fed'er·ate`,** *v.* form a union of states. —**fed'er·a'tion,** *n.* 1. a union of states, nations or other groups which give up some of their individual powers to a central government. 2. the act of forming a federation.

fee (4) [fiy'], *n.* a payment required for a service or privilege. **Ex.** *The fee for admission was expensive.*

feeble (4) [fiy'bəl], *adj.* weak; without strength. **Ex.** *He was too feeble to lift the chair.* —**fee'ble·ness,** *n.* —**fee'bly,** *adv.*

feed (1) [fiyd'], *v.* 1. give food to. **Ex.** *Feed the baby first.* 2. eat. **Ex.** *The chickens are feeding in the yard.* —*n.* food, especially for animals. **Ex.** *The farmer is carrying a bag of feed.*

feel (1) [fiyl'], *v.* 1. experience an emotion. **Ex.** *She feels happy because of his success.* 2. think; believe. **Ex.** *He feels you should go.* 3. know or be aware of through the sense of touch. **Ex.** *She could feel the rain on her cheeks.* 4. examine by touching; test. **Ex.** *Feel his forehead to see if he has a fever.* —*n.* sense of touch; becoming aware of by the sense of touch. **Ex.** *This material has a silky feel.* —**feel'ing,** *n.* 1. an emotion; pleasure, pain, etc. experienced within oneself. **Ex.** *When she saw the jewel, she had a sudden feeling of desire.* 2. attitude; belief. **Ex.** *My feeling is that he will make a good president.* 3. the act of being aware by touch; the sense of touch. **Ex.** *Since his injury, he has had no feeling in his left arm.* —**feel'ing·ly,** *adv.* —**feel'ings,** *n.* the capacity for being affected by outside influences. **Ex.** *Her feelings were hurt by what he had said.*

feet (1) [fiyt'], *n.* plural of *foot.* **Ex.** *We heard the sound of marching feet.*

fell (1) [fel'], *v.* past tense of *fall.* **Ex.** *He fell from the tree.*

fell (1) [fel'], *v.* 1. knock down. **Ex.** *He was felled by one blow.* 2. cut down. **Ex.** *A woodsman will fell the tree for us.*

fellow (1) [fel'ow], *n.* a male; a companion. **Ex.** *He went with two other fellows.* —*adj.* being a comrade, associate, etc. **Ex.** *We are fellow students.*

fellowship [fel'owšip'], *n.* 1. friendliness; comradeship. **Ex.** *She enjoyed the fellowship of living in a dormitory.* 2. money given to graduate students to help them continue their studies. **Ex.** *My brother, who is working for a Ph.D. in history, has been awarded a fellowship.*

felt (1) [felt'], *v.* past tense and participle of *feel.* **Exs.** *He felt better yesterday than he does today. How long has she felt ill?*

felt (1) [felt'], *n.* cloth made by rolling and pressing together a mass of wool, hair or fur. **Ex.** *His winter hat is made of felt.*

female (2) [fiy'meyl'], *n.* 1. woman or girl. **Ex.** *Only one female works in our office.* 2. an animal of the sex that brings forth young or lays eggs. **Ex.** *Hens and cows are females.* —*adj.* 1. of a woman or girl. **Ex.** *This gym class is for female students only.* 2. of an animal of the sex that brings forth young or lays eggs. **Ex.** *The female deer has no horns.*

feminine (5) [fem'ənin], *adj.* of or like a woman or a girl. **Ex.** *The pink lace dress looked very feminine.* —**fem'i·nin'i·ty,** *n.* the quality of being like a woman or a girl. —**fem'i·nism',** *n.* a basic belief that women should have the same opportunities and rights as men; the movement based on this belief. —**fem'i·nist,** *n.* a believer in feminism. —*adj.*

fence (1) [fens'], *n.* railing, wall or other means of keeping people or animals in or out; a means of marking a boundary. **Ex.** *They have a fence around their house.* —*v.* put a fence around. **Ex.** *They fenced the field.* —**on the fence,** not on one side or the other. **Ex.** *He is on the fence about this question.*

fend (5) [fend'], *v.* resist; force away. **Ex.** *She fended off the dog with a stick.* —**fend'er,** *n.* the metal guard over each wheel of a car. —**fend for oneself,** take care of oneself without help.

a, far; æ, am; e, get; ey, late; i, in; iy, see; ɔ, all; ow, go; u, put; uw, too; ə, but, ago; ər, fur; aw, out; ay, life; oy, boy; ŋ, ring; θ, think; ð, that; ž, measure; š, ship; j, edge; č, child.

fern (5) [fərn'], *n.* a plant that has delicate, feathery leaves but no flowers. **Ex.** *He put green ferns in with the bunch of roses.*

ferry (4) [fer'iy], *v.* carry or be carried from place to place, usually over a small body of water. **Ex.** *We ferried the goods across the river.* —*n.* a boat which carries goods or people across a river or other small body of water; a ferryboat. **Ex.** *We go by ferry to work every day.*

FERN

fertile (4) [fər'təl], *adj.* 1. producing plentiful crops. **Ex.** *His land is fertile.* 2. able to produce seeds, fruit or young. **Ex.** *The rabbit is a very fertile animal.* —**fer·til'i·ty.** *n.* —**fer'ti·lize,** *v.* make fertile. —**fer'til·liz·er,** *n.* anything which when added to the soil, increases its fertility.

festive (4) [fes'tiv], *adj.* joyous; gay; merry; suitable for a feast. **Ex.** *His birthday was a festive occasion.* —**fes'tiv·al; fes·tiv'i·ty,** *n.*

fetch (3) [feč'], *v.* go and get; bring. **Ex.** *Please fetch me a glass of water.* —**fetch'ing,** *adj.* pleasing; attractive. **Ex.** *She wore a fetching hat.*

feud (5) [fyuwd'], *n.* a long and deadly quarrel, especially between families. **Ex.** *Because of the family feud, they did not speak when they met.* —*v.* carry on a feud. **Ex.** *They have been feuding for thirty years.*

feudal (5) [fyuw'dəl], *adj.* of or having to do with the way of life when kings and lords owned all land and granted the use of it to others in return for goods and services. **Ex.** *That family has owned its land since feudal times.*

fever (2) [fiy'vər], *n.* 1. a high body temperature, usually due to illness. **Ex.** *Her high fever indicated that she was very sick.* 2. an excited, restless condition. **Ex.** *He was in a fever of excitement over the news.* —**fe'ver·ish,** *adj.*

few (1) [fyuw'], *adj.* not many. **Ex.** *A few friends came for dinner.* —*n.* a small number. **Ex.** *A few of the people who came to the party were business acquaintances.*

fiber (4) [fay'bər], *n.* the threadlike structures of a plant or animal. **Ex.** *The fibers of cotton make this cloth strong.*

fiberglass [fay'bərglæs'], *n.* a material made of fine threadlike fibers of glass, sometimes mixed with plastics. **Ex.** *These curtains are made of fiberglass.*

fiction (5) [fik'šən], *n.* 1. a piece of writing about imaginary persons and events. **Ex.** *His novels are fiction at its best.* 2. something imagined or invented. **Ex.** *What she told us was pure fiction.* —**fic'tion·al**, *adj.*

field (1) [fiyld'], *n.* 1. a piece of open land with few or no trees, especially land on which crops can be grown or animals fed. **Ex.** *The farmer is plowing his fields.* 2. a piece of land used for some special purpose or yielding some special product. **Ex.** *This ball field is part of the school playground.* 3. an area of activity, interest or opportunity. **Ex.** *Science is his field of study.*

fiend (5) [fiynd'], *n.* 1. a devil; an evil spirit. **Ex.** *The fiends in his dreams frightened him.* 2. a very wicked, cruel person. **Ex.** *We will catch the fiend who committed these murders.* —**fiend'ish**, *adj.*

fierce (2) [fiyrs'], *adj.* savage; furious in anger or cruelty; of a nature to inspire terror. **Ex.** *The fierce dog frightened the stranger away.* 2. raging; violent. **Ex.** *The fierce fire destroyed several houses.* 3. eager; very strong. **Ex.** *A fierce ambition drove him on.* —**fierce'ly**, *adv.* —**fierce'ness**, *n.*

fiery [fay'əriy], *adj.* 1. containing or consisting of fire. **Ex.** *We were fascinated by the fiery volcano.* 2. like a fire in appearance or in intensity of heat. **Ex.** *His fiery temper often got him into difficulties.* 3. causing a burning or hot feeling. **Ex.** *This food is delicious but it's too fiery for my digestive system.*

fifteen (1) [fif'tiyn'], *n., adj.* the number between fourteen and sixteen; the number *15.* —**fif'teenth'**, *n., adj.* coming after fourteen others.

fifth (1) [fifθ'], *n., adj.* coming after four others.

fifty (1) [fif'tiy], *n., adj.* the number between forty-nine and fifty-one; the number *50.* —**fif'tieth**, *n., adj.* coming after forty-nine others.

fig (4) [fig'], *n.* a small, soft, sweet fruit with many small seeds; the tree on which figs grow. **Ex.** *I think figs are delicious fresh or dried.*

FIG

fight (1) [fayt'], *v.* 1. struggle with, using force; attempt to defeat or destroy an enemy; battle. **Ex.** *He was fighting with his brother.* 2. try to overcome. **Ex.** *He has been fighting his illness*

figure [224] **fill out**

for a long time. —*n.* 1. use of force to gain victory; battle. **Ex.** *The fight was long and hard.* 2. struggle; contest. **Ex.** *The fight against this disease will be won in time.*

figure (1) [fig'yər], *n.* 1. a symbol for a number. **Ex.** *The figure #1 is the number for the word* one. 2. amount. **Ex.** *The cost figure he gave for the work was too high.* 3. pattern; design; drawing. **Ex.** *Her dress was made of blue cloth with small figures in red.* 4. form; outline; shape. **Ex.** *She saw the figure of a man ahead of her.* 5. a person or character. **Ex.** *He is one of the great figures in history.* 6. a carved, painted or drawn representation. **Ex.** *In the garden were many stone figures.* —*v.* use numbers to find the answer to a problem. **Ex.** *He figured what the cost of the house would be.* —**figure out,** find an answer or solution to. **Ex.** *I figured out a way of doing it.*

figurehead [fig'yərhed'], *n.* 1. a person in an important position controlled by someone else who has the real power. **Ex.** *The queen can't help because she is only a figurehead.* 2. a carved figure or part of a figure attached to the front part, or prow, of a ship. **Ex.** *The museum has a large collection of figureheads.*

file (3) [fayl'], *n.* 1. a place for keeping papers in order; a set of papers kept in order. **Ex.** *The lawyer had a separate file on each of his cases.* 2. a row of people or things. **Ex.** *A long file of people was waiting for the bus.* —*v.* 1. put away in order. **Ex.** *The clerk filed the cards alphabetically.* 2. march or move in a line. **Ex.** *The children filed out of the classroom.*

file (3) [fayl'], *n.* a steel tool with many small ridges for smoothing rough surfaces. —*v.* rub smooth with a file. **Ex.** *The workman filed the rough edges of the lock.*

fill (1) [fil'], *v.* 1. put or pour into until no more can be contained; make full; become full. **Ex.** *He filled the pail with water.* 2. supply what is needed; satisfy. **Ex.** *They filled the order.* 3. occupy or put someone into an office or job. **Ex.** *No one was found to fill that job.* —*n.* a complete supply; satisfaction. **Ex.** *He has had his fill of cake.* —**fill'ing,** *n.* something used to fill something else. **Exs.** *What kind of filling do you want for your sandwich? The dentist had to replace a filling in my tooth.* —**fill in,** 1. make complete. **Ex.** *Fill in all the spaces on the form.* 2. act as a substitute. **Ex.** *Will you fill in for me at the office tomorrow?* —**fill out,** 1.

become rounder or fatter. **Ex.** *Her good cooking filled him out.* 2. make complete by writing. **Ex.** *Please fill out this form.* —**fill up,** make full. **Ex.** *Fill up the bottle with water.*

filling station [fi'iŋ stey'šən], a place to buy gas, oil, etc. for cars, trucks, etc. **Ex.** *We need to stop at the next filling station for gas.*

film (2) [film'], *n.* 1. a roll or sheet covered with a coating that is changed by light and used in making photographs. **Ex.** *He took the roll of film out of his camera.* 2. a motion picture; a movie. **Ex.** *There is a new film being shown at the theater.* 3. a very thin surface. **Ex.** *There is a film of ice on the lake.* —*v.* make a motion picture. **Ex.** *They are filming a famous novel.*

filter (5) [fil'tər], *n.* a device using a substance such as cloth or sand through which water, air, etc. is passed to remove something not wanted. **Ex.** *We need to change the filter in the air conditioner.* —*v.* pass through a device or substance in order to strain out something. **Ex.** *They filtered the water through a cloth to remove the dirt.*

filth (5) [filθ'], *n.* a foul or dirty substance. **Ex.** *The deserted house was full of filth.* —**filth'y,** *adj.*

final (2) [fay'nəl], *adj.* 1. at the end; last. **Ex.** *The final test was the hardest one of the year.* 2. not to be changed. **Ex.** *The ruling of the principal was final.* —**fi'nal·ly,** *adv.*

finance (3) [fay'næns, fənæns'], *n.* the management of money. **Ex.** *He studied banking and finance at the university.* —*v.* provide money for. **Ex.** *The bank financed his purchase of a house.* —**fi'nan·ces,** *n.* funds; money; income. —**fi·nan'cial,** *adj.* —**fin'an·cier',** *n.* a manager of large amounts of money.

find (1) [faynd'], *v.* 1. discover by accident. **Ex.** *Where did you find the money?* 2. discover by searching. **Ex.** *Did he find the book for which he was looking?* 3. observe; declare as being. **Ex.** *We find it will be impossible for us to go with you.* 4. arrive at; reach. **Ex.** *Water finds its own level.* —*n.* something of value that is found. **Ex.** *That painting is an important find.* —**find'er,** *n.* one who or that which finds. —**find out,** learn; discover. **Ex.** *Did you find out what they are doing?*

fine (1) [fayn'], *adj.* 1. very good; excellent. **Ex.** *He goes to a fine school.* 2. very small; not coarse; very thin. **Ex.** *The* *beach is covered with fine sand.* 3. made with care. **Ex.** *She must be very skilled to do such fine sewing.* —**fine'ly,** *adv.* —**fine'ness,** *n.*

fine (1) [fayn'], *n.* money paid as a punishment for an offense. **Ex.** *There is a fine for crossing the street against the light.* —*v.* cause to pay money as punishment. **Ex.** *The judge fined him fifty dollars for speeding.*

finger (1) [fiŋ'gər], *n.* 1. one of the five end parts of the hand. **Ex.** *Her second finger was cut.* 2. anything shaped or used like a finger. **Ex.** *The fingers of this glove are torn.* —*v.* touch or feel with the fingers. **Ex.** *She fingered the soft material.*

fingernail [fiŋ'gərneyl'], *n.* the hard covering at the end of each finger. **Ex.** *She was painting her fingernails.*

fingerprint [fiŋ'gərprint'] *n.* the mark made by the lines of the inner end of a finger or thumb on a surface. **Ex.** *All employees in this company are required to have their fingerprints taken when they are hired.* —*v.*

FINGERPRINT

finish (1) [fin'iš], *v.* 1. end; complete. **Ex.** *She has already finished the work she had to do.* 2. use all there is or was. **Ex.** *We finished the cake at supper.* 3. give a surface to. **Ex.** *He finished the table with red paint.* —*n.* 1. the end. **Ex.** *We saw the finish of the race.* 2. the way in which a surface is treated with oil, paint, etc. **Ex.** *The chair had a dark finish.* —**finish up,** 1. end. 2. use all. **Ex.** *If you finish up the candy, I will buy more.*

fir (5) [fər'], *n.* a tree that belongs to the pine family and remains green all year. **Ex.** *They planted a fir tree on either side of the doorway.*

fire (1) [fayr'], *n.* 1. the fact of burning, as shown by light and heat; something burning, as in a stove. **Ex.** *They built a fire to keep warm.* 2. the discharge from a gun. **Ex.** *We could hear the gunfire of the hunters.* 3. strong spirit or feeling. **Ex.** *The young actor spoke his lines with fire.* —*v.* shoot. **Ex.** *The soldiers fired their guns.* —**catch fire,** start burning. —**on fire,** burning. —**open fire,** start shooting. —**set fire to,** cause to burn. —**under fire,** being attacked.

FIR

firearm [fayr'arm'], *n.* any weapon that fires or shoots bullets and can be carried; a gun.

firecracker [fayr'kræk'ər], *n.* paper with powder inside that explodes when it is lighted and burns. **Ex.** *The firecrackers exploded rapidly, one after the other.*

fire engine [fayr'en'jən], *n.* a firefighter's truck with equipment needed to put out a fire. **Ex.** *The fire engines raced down the street with sirens screaming.*

fire extinguisher [fayr' extiŋ'gwišər], a container filled with chemicals which are sprayed on small fires to put them out.

firefighter [fayr'fayt'ər], *n.* a person who fights fires either as an employee of a city, town or village, or as a volunteer. **Ex.** *The firefighter sprayed great quantities of water on the burning building.*

fireplace [fayr'pleys'], *n.* an open place at the bottom of a chimney for an indoor fire; hearth; any structure in or on which a fire is built. **Ex.** *They lit a fire in the fireplace.*

fireproof [fayr'pruwf], *adj.* not easily burned. **Ex.** *The school was built of fireproof materials.* —*v.* make fireproof by treating with chemicals or other methods.

fire station [fayr' stey'šən], *n.* a place where fire engines are kept and firefighters on duty stay when not fighting fires.

firetrap [fayr'træp'], *n.* a building that is dangerous because it could burn easily.

fireworks [fayr'wərks], *n.* a series of firecrackers and other explosive devices making a loud noise or a display of light. **Ex.** *Fireworks lighted the night sky with brilliant color.*

firm (1) [fərm'], *adj.* 1. not easily moved or changed. **Ex.** *He has very firm ideas.* 2. strong and steady in character. **Ex.** *She is firm yet kind.* 3. solid and unyielding. **Ex.** *The house is on firm ground.* —*n.* a business partnership.

first (1) [fərst'], *adj.* coming before any other. **Ex.** *The first letter I opened was from my sister.* —*adv.* 1. before any other person or thing. **Ex.** *He always arrives first.* 2. the first time. **Ex.** *When did you first meet?* 3. rather; before. **Ex.** *I will not pay the money; I will go to jail first.* —*n.* 1. that which is first. **Ex.** *We are the first on the list.* 2. the beginning; start. **Ex.** *I liked him from the first.*

first aid [fərst' eyd'], treatment given to injured or sick people while waiting for the doctor. **Ex.** *The injured man was given first aid and then taken to the hospital.*

firsthand [fərst'hænd'], *adj., adv.* direct from the person who saw or did something. **Ex.** *We heard a firsthand account of the meeting from a man who was there.*

first person [fərst' pər'son], *n.* the form of a *pronoun* or *verb* referring to the speaker. **Exs.** I, me *and* we *are first person pronouns.* Am *is the first person singular form of the verb* be.

first-rate [fərst'reyt'], *adj.* best quality; very good. **Ex.** *This is a first-rate book.*

fiscal [fisk'əl], *adj.* having to do with the financial affairs of a government, institution or business. **Ex.** *The cabinet will be discussing several fiscal matters at today's meeting.*

fish (1) [fiš'], *n.* an animal, usually with scales, that lives and can breathe in water. —*v.* catch or attempt to catch fish. **Ex.** *They fished from a boat.* —**fish'y,** *adj.* smelling or tasting of fish. —**fisherman,** *n.* one who fishes. **Ex.** *He earns his living as a fish·er·man.*

FISH

fist (3) [fist'], *n.* the hand closed tightly, as it is in fighting. **Ex.** *He raised his fist and threatened to hit me.*

fit (1) [fit'], *adj.* 1. suited to or suitable for a special purpose; right; proper. **Ex.** *Is that book fit for young people to read?* 2. ready; prepared. **Ex.** *The soldiers are fit for battle.* 3. in good health. **Ex.** *You are looking fit.* —*v.* 1. be the proper size, shape, or quality. **Ex.** *These shoes fit my feet very comfortably.* 2. make a person ready or qualified. **Ex.** *Training will fit you for this work.* 3. make the right size. **Ex.** *The dressmaker had to shorten the coat to make it fit me.* 4. provide with; equip. **Ex.** *These doors have been fitted with new locks.* —*n.* the manner in which a thing fits. **Ex.** *That suit is a perfect fit.*

fit (1) [fit'], *n.* 1. a sudden attack of a disease. **Ex.** *He fell to the floor in a fit.* 2. a sudden expression of emotion or feeling. **Ex.** *She left in a fit of anger.*

fitting [fit'iŋ], *adj.* proper; suitable. **Ex.** *Flowers would be a fitting gift for her birthday.* —*n.* trying on clothes to see if they are the right size. **Ex.** *I had to have two fittings by the dressmaker before the clothes looked right.*

five (1) [fayv'], *n., adj.* the number between four and six; the number 5.

fix (1) [fiks'], *v.* 1. attach firmly. **Ex.** *They fixed the sign to the wall.* 2. settle definitely; determine. **Ex.** *Fix a date for the* meeting. 3. repair. **Ex.** *He will fix the broken table.* 4. prepare; get ready. **Ex.** *My wife will fix dinner for us.* 5. direct and hold steady. **Ex.** *Fix your eyes on that sign.*

flag (2) [flæg'], *n.* a piece of cloth with colored designs used as a symbol of a country, group, etc. —*v.* signal with, or as if with, a flag. **Ex.** *They flagged the train.* —**flag down,** cause to stop by waving something. **Ex.** *He flagged down a passing car.*

FLAG

flake (4) [fleyk'], *n.* a small, very thin piece. **Ex.** *The snow was falling in large flakes.* —*v.* break away or split into small, thin pieces. **Ex.** *Paint was flaking from the ceiling.* —**flak'y,** *adj.*

flame (2) [fleym'], *n.* 1. the brightly colored light of a fire. **Ex.** *The flame of the burning candle was yellow.* 2. a state `of burning brightly and strongly. **Ex.** *Suddenly the entire building was in flames.* 3. a strong passion or emotion. **Ex.** *The flames of love had died.* —*v.* flame; burn brightly. **Ex.** *Fire flamed from the burning house.* —**fla'ming,** *adj.* burning with a flame. **Ex.** *He threw water on the flaming papers.* —**flam'ma·ble,** *adj.* easy to catch fire and burn quickly. **Ex.** *Paper is very flammable.*

flank (4) [flænk'], *n.* 1. the side of an animal between the ribs and the upper part of the legs. **Ex.** *The horse's flanks were wet.* 2. the right or left side of anything. **Ex.** *The enemy attacked both our flanks.* —*v.* go around; stand or be placed at the side or sides. **Ex.** *Trees flanked the garden.*

flap (4) [flæp'], *v.* 1. swing loosely and noisily. **Ex.** *The curtain flapped in the wind and woke me.* 2. move up and down as in beating. **Ex.** *The birds flapped their wings as they flew over the beach.* —*n.* 1. anything broad, flat and thin that hangs loosely, attached at one side only. **Ex.** *She sealed the flap of the envelope.* 2. The motion or sound produced by something that flaps. **Ex.** *We heard the flap of the sails above our heads.*

flare (4) [fle:r'], *v.* 1. burn with an unsteady, swaying flame or with a sudden burst of flame. **Ex.** *The candle flared in the wind.* 2. spread out in a bell shape. **Ex.** *Her full skirt flared as she walked.* 3. become excited or angry. **Ex.** *His temper* flared at their remarks. —*n.* 1. a short, bright, swaying flame. **Ex.** *We saw a flare of light.* 2. a flaming light used as a signal. **Ex.** *They placed flares by the hole to warn of the danger.* —**flare'-up,** *n.* a sudden burst, breaking out or return of flames, trouble, violent emotion, pains of illness, etc. **Ex.** *What caused the flare-up of his old knee injury?*

flash (2) [flæš'], *n.* 1. a sudden, brief light. **Ex.** *There was a flash of lightning in the sky.* 2. a sudden, brief show of emotion, wit, etc. **Ex.** *We saw a flash of anger in her eyes.* 3. the time occupied by a flash of light; an instant. **Ex.** *He returned in a flash.* —*v.* 1. light suddenly. **Ex.** *The electric sign flashed on and off.* 2. move quickly. **Ex.** *The car flashed past us.* 3. gleam; sparkle. **Ex.** *His eyes flashed with anger.*

flashlight [flæš'layt'], *n.* a battery-powered electric light that is small enough to be easily carried. **Ex.** *We used a flashlight to find the keyhole.*

flat (2) [flæt'], *adj.* 1. not curved; smooth and level or nearly so. **Ex.** *His farm is on flat land.* 2. thin; not deep. **Ex.** *Put the cake on a flat plate.* 3. not interesting. **Ex.** *The food tasted flat.* —*adv.* at full length; spread out. **Ex.** *Put the map flat on the table.* —*n.* the flat surface or part of anything. **Ex.** *She set it on the flat of her hand.* —**flat'ten,** *v.* cause to become flat.

flatter (3) [flæt'ər], *v.* 1. seek to please by attention, false praise or by more praise than deserved. **Ex.** *He flatters those who can help him.* 2. make to appear better than is actually so. **Ex.** *This picture flatters her.* 3. be pleased **Ex.** *I am flattered that you came.* —**flat'ter·er,** *n.* one who flatters. —**flat'ter·y,** *n.* act of flattering.

flavor (3) [fley'vər], *n.* 1. taste, especially distinct in character. **Ex.** *What gives the soup such a good flavor?* 2. something which has its own special taste. **Ex.** *I like the lemon flavor of this cake.* 3. the special quality of a thing. **Ex.** *This novel has the flavor of city life.* —*v.* give flavor to. **Ex.** *His colorful style flavors the story.* —**fla'vor·ing,** *n.* something which is added to give a special taste.

flaw [flɔ:'], *n.* some small thing, such as a tear, crack, stain, etc., that spoils the perfection of something; a fault; a defect. **Exs.** *Because there are some slight flaws in this material, its price has been considerably reduced. Despite his flaws, he is a very likeable person.*

fled (3) [fled'], *v.* past tense and participle of *flee.* **Exs.** *They fled from the burning house. The thieves had fled before the police came.*

flee (3) [fliy'], *v.* run away from something. **Ex.** *As the bombs dropped, people began to flee to shelters.*

fleece (5) [fliys'], *n.* the coat of wool that covers a sheep or a similar animal; the wool cut from such a coat. **Ex.** *His warm coat was lined with fleece.* —*v.* 1. cut the wool from a sheep or similar animal; shear. **Ex.** *It will soon be time to fleece the sheep.* 2. take money or possessions by a trick. **Ex.** *He was fleeced of his savings by two strangers.*

fleet (2) [fliyt'], *n.* 1. a number of war vessels under a single command; the navy of a country. **Ex.** *The fleet is in the harbor.* 2. any group, such as vessels and airplanes, that moves together or operates under a single control. **Ex.** *He owns a fleet of trucks.*

fleet (2) [fliyt'], *adj.* swift in motion; fast. **Ex.** *He is so fleet flooted that I thought he would win the race.* —**flee'ting,** *adj.* passing rapidly; very brief. **Ex.** *For a fleeting moment I thought he was someone I knew.*

flesh (2) [fleš'], *n.* 1. the soft muscular and fatty parts of the body under the skin and over the bones of a person or animal. **Ex.** *The knife cut into the flesh of his arm.* 2. meat; those parts of an animal which are eaten. **Ex.** *When we were abroad, we ate goat's flesh.* 3. the soft parts of fruits and vegetables. **Ex.** *The flesh of the apple was sweet.* —**flesh'y,** *adj.* fat. **Ex.** *He had a fleshy look about the face and neck.*

flew (2) [fluw'], *v.* past tense of *fly.* **Ex.** *The bird flew away.*

flexible (5) [flek'səbəl], *adj.* 1. able to bend or be bent easily. **Ex.** *This fishing rod is strong and flexible.* 2. ready to yield to influence; easily led; easily changed. **Exs.** *He has a flexible nature. I am working at home so my hours are flexible.*

flicker (4) [flik'ər], *v.* 1. burn unsteadily; shine with an unsteady light. **Ex.** *The fire flickered and died.* 2. move like a flame. **Ex.** *The shadows flickered on the wall.* —*n.* 1. an unsteady light or flame. **Ex.** *They saw the flicker of candles.* 2. a brief movement or feeling. **Ex.** *A flicker of hope showed in her eyes.*

flier (1) [flay'ər], *n.* 1. one who flies an airplane. **Ex.** *That flier has been up in every kind of plane.* 2. a printed sheet of paper announcing or advertising something and given out by hand. **Ex.** *We received a flier telling about the school next Saturday.*

flight (2) [flayt'], *n.* 1. movement through the air; the act or manner of flying. **Ex.** *We watched the birds in flight.* 2. the distance covered or the course followed in flying. **Ex.** *This flight takes us over the ocean.* 3. a stairway or set of steps. **Ex.** *His room is two flights above us.*

flight (2) [flayt'], *n.* the act of running away. **Ex.** *The dog put the robbers to flight.* —**flight'y,** *adj.* not serious; not responsible. **Ex.** *Her flighty behavior cost her her job.*

fling (4) [fliŋ'], *v.* throw. **Ex.** *The boys were flinging stones into the pond.* —*n.* 1. the act of throwing. **Ex.** *He gave his hat a fling into the air.* 2. a time of fun and pleasure. **Ex.** *After his fling, he settled down to study.*

flint (5) [flint'], *n.* a hard kind of stone that produces a spark when it is hit by steel. **Ex.** *A spark from a flint was used to start the fire.*

flip (5) [flip'], *v.* throw or toss with a sudden, sharp movement. **Exs.** *The fish flipped itself back into the water. He flipped a coin to decide what to do.*

flirt (5) [flərt'], *v.* 1. play at love. **Ex.** *She flirted with many men but loved only one.* 2. consider lightly. **Ex.** *He flirted with the idea of living abroad.* —*n.* a person who flirts. **Ex.** *She has a reputation of being a flirt.*

flit (5) [flit'], *v.* fly or move lightly and swiftly. **Ex.** *We watched the bee flit from flower to flower.*

float (2) [flowt'], *v.* 1. be on a liquid without sinking into it. **Ex.** *Is that a log floating on the water?* 2. move or be moved gently, as on water or through the air. **Ex.** *The falling leaves floated to the ground.* —*n.* an object that rests on the surface of a liquid or holds something up in a liquid. **Ex.** *He climbed out of the water and rested on the float.*

flock (2) [flak'], *n.* a number of birds or animals, usually of one kind, that travel or are herded together. **Ex.** *The flock of birds all flew to one tree.* —*v.* gather in a large group. **Ex.** *The students flocked around the teacher after class.*

flood (2) [fləd'], *n.* 1. flowing of water from a river, lake, etc. over the land along the banks. **Ex.** *The flood destroyed many homes on the shore.* 2. any great outpouring. **Ex.** *A flood of memories came back to her.* —*v.* 1. overflow; cover with water. **Ex.** *The river flooded the town.* 2. fill to overflowing. **Ex.** *The sunlight flooded the room.*

floor (1) [flɔːr'], *n.* 1. the bottom or lower part of a room. **Ex.** *He walked across the floor.* 2. a level of a building. **Ex.** *He lives on the third floor.* 3. the lowest surface of anything. **Ex.** *We are discovering many things about the ocean floor.* —*v.* 1. cover with a floor. **Ex.** *He floored the house with oak.* 2. knock down. **Ex.** *He floored his attacker with a single blow.*

floral [flɔːr'əl] *adj.* of or having to do with flowers. **Exs.** *That is a lovely floral arrangement. We chose wallpaper with a floral pattern.*

florist [flɔː'rist], *n.* a person who sells flowers and house plants. **Ex.** *I ordered a dozen roses from the florist.*

flour (2) [flaw'ər], *n.* a finely ground grain, usually white and powdery, such as wheat flour. **Ex.** *I will need more flour to make two loaves of bread.*

flourish (3) [flər'iš], *v.* 1. grow in a strong, healthy way; be healthy or successful. **Ex.** *Flowers will flourish in this rich soil.* 2. make bold and sweeping movements; wave. **Ex.** *He flourished a gun at us.* —*n.* a bold, sweeping movement. **Ex.** *The officer made a flourish with his sword.*

flow (2) [flow'], *v.* 1. move like a liquid. **Ex.** *This river flows to the sea.* 2. fall or hang loose. **Ex.** *Her long hair flowed down over her shoulders.* —*n.* 1. the act, manner, or quantity of flowing. **Ex.** *They could not stop the flow of blood from the wound.* 2. anything that moves steadily and easily like a stream of liquid. **Ex.** *The flow of mail is heaviest during holidays.*

flower (1) [flaw'ər], *n.* 1. the blossom or part of any plant bearing the seed. **Ex.** *The bees are flying from flower to flower.* 2. state of being in bloom. **Ex.** *Her garden is in flower.* —*v.* produce flowers. **Ex.** *The rose bushes are flowering.*

FLOWER 1

flown (2) [flown'], *v.* past participle of *fly.* **Ex.** *The birds have flown away.*

flu [fluw'], *n.* a disease, caused by a virus, that is somewhat similar to a bad cold but much more severe and often accompanied by fever. **Ex.** *He is feeling very weak after a bout with flu.*

---

a, far; æ, am; e, get; ey, late; i, in; iy, see; ɔ, all; ow, go; u, put; uw, too; ə, but, ago; ər, fur; aw, out; ay, life; oy, boy; ŋ, ring; θ, think; ð, that; ž, measure; š, ship; j, edge; č, child.

fluid (2) [fluw'id], *n.* anything that can flow such as water, gas, air, etc. **Ex.** *Blood is an important body fluid.* —*adj.* 1. able to flow in the form of a liquid or gas. **Ex.** *He poured two fluid ounces of the medicine into the glass.* 2. changing easily; not fixed. **Ex.** *Our plans are fluid enough to be changed quickly.*

flung (3) [fləŋ], *v.* past tense and participle of *fling*. **Exs.** *He flung his coat onto the chair. The children had flung their toys all around the room.*

fluorescent [fluwəres'ənt], *adj.* showing or being able to show a bright white light when subject to electric radiation. **Ex.** *We need a new tube for the fluorescent light in the kitchen.*

flush (4) [fləš'], *n.* 1. a red coloring of the skin. **Ex.** *A flush of embarrassment colored her cheeks.* 2. a sudden flow or rush of emotion. **Ex.** *She experienced a flush of pleasure at seeing him.* —*v.* 1. to glow or redden. **Ex.** *His face flushed with anger.* 2. flood with water in order to clean. **Ex.** *Water trucks flush our city streets every morning.*

flush (4) [fləš'], *adj.* even or level; making an even surface with. **Ex.** *The door is flush with the wall.*

flute (5) [fluwt'], *n.* a musical instrument in the shape of a long, thin tube with a series of holes along the side and an opening at one end through which one blows. —**flut'ist,** *n.* one who plays the flute.

FLUTE

flutter (3) [flət'ər], *v.* 1. move back and forth quickly; wave. **Ex.** *The flag fluttered in the breeze.* 2. move wings rapidly without flying. **Ex.** *The little bird fluttered its wings.* 3. tremble; shake. **Ex.** *Her heart fluttered when she saw him.* —*n.* a rapid movement back and forth: a quivering. **Ex.** *They heard a flutter of wings.*

fly (1) [flay'], *v.* 1. move through the air on wings, as a bird or an airplane. **Ex.** *She is flying home tomorrow.* 2. operate an airplane. **Ex.** *He is learning to fly.* 3. wave in the air. **Ex.** *The flag is flying in the wind.* 4. move or pass rapidly. **Ex.** *How time flies!* 5. run from danger. **Ex.** *He was forced to fly from his home.* —**fly into,** pass suddenly into some condition. **Ex.** *She is likely to fly into a temper if you disagree with her.*

FLY

fly (1) [flay'], *n.* a winged insect, especially the common housefly.

foam (4) [fowm'], *n.* a white mass of bubbles formed on liquids. **Ex.** *The wind whipped the waves into foam.* —*v.* gather or form bubbles. **Ex.** *The fresh milk foamed in the pail.*

focus (5) [fow'kəs], *n.* a central point; a center of activity, attention, etc. **Ex.** *The pretty girl was the focus of all eyes.* —*v.* 1. center the mind on one thing or subject. **Ex.** *Please focus your attention on the speaker.* 2. bring into clear view by adjusting the lens of the eye, of a camera, etc. **Ex.** *He was so tired he could not focus his eyes on the book.* —**in focus,** clear. —**out of focus,** unclear; blurred.

foe (4) [fow'], *n.* an enemy; one who holds ill feelings against a person, idea, etc. **Ex.** *He is a formidable foe of drug dealers.*

fog (3) [fag', fɔ:g'], *n.* 1. a cloud lying near the ground. **Ex.** *A heavy fog is preventing planes from landing.* 2. a state of mental confusion. **Ex.** *These days she seems to be walking around in a fog.* —*v.* 1. cover or surround with fog. **Ex.** *Steam fogged his glasses.* 2. confuse. **Ex.** *Doubts fogged his mind.* —**fog'gy,** *adj.*

foil (5) [foyl'], *v.* prevent the success of; stop. **Ex.** *The police foiled his plan to commit a murder.*

foil (5) [foyl'], *n.* 1. a very thin sheet of metal, such as gold or tin. **Ex.** *The pieces of chocolate candy were wrapped in foil.* 2. any person or thing that serves to set off another to advantage by contrast. **Ex.** *That black dress is a perfect foil for your diamond pin.*

fold (2) [fowld'], *v.* 1. double or bend over upon itself. **Ex.** *She folded the paper carefully.* 2. bring together and clasp. **Ex.** *She folded her arms and waited for him to speak.* —*n.* a part that is doubled or bent over another part. **Ex.** *The tablecloth had six folds.* —**fold'er,** *n.* 1. one who folds. 2. a folded heavy paper or cardboard container used to hold other papers.

-fold (2) [fowld'], *suffix.* 1. having a stated number of parts. **Ex.** *There was a threefold screen in the living room.* 2. multiplied by. **Ex.** *His wealth had increased tenfold.*

foliage (5) [fow'liyij], *n.* the leaves of a plant or tree or of a number of plants or trees. **Ex.** *In summer, the house next door is hidden by foliage.*

folk (2) [fowk'], *n.* 1. a group of related people forming a tribe or nation. **Ex.** *The folk who settled this valley came from the north.* 2. people; persons. **Ex.** *Folks around here are friendly.*

—*adj.* having to do with the customs of a people or country. **Ex.** *We enjoyed watching the folk dances.*

follow (1) [fal'ow], *v.* 1. come after in natural order. **Ex.** *Night follows day.* 2. accept the authority of; obey. **Ex.** *He followed his father's advice.* 3. engage in or observe an occupation, profession, activity, etc. **Ex.** *He followed the law as his father had before him.* 4. pursue. **Ex.** *He followed and caught the thief.* 5. travel on or along. **Ex.** *Follow this road for four miles.* —**fol'low·er,** *n.* one who follows. —**fol'low·ing,** *n.* 1. a body of followers. **Ex.** *That writer has a large following.* 2. things that follow. **Ex.** *I need the following: eggs, sugar, butter and milk.* —*adj.* coming after; next after. **Ex.** *He is leaving the following week.*

folly (3) [fal'iy], *n.* 1. condition of being unwise or foolish; lack of good sense. **Ex.** *If you are careless about your health, you will pay for your folly.* 2. a foolish act or idea. **Ex.** *It is folly to drive fast on icy roads.*

fond (3) [fand'], *adj.* 1. having an affection or liking for. **Ex.** *She is fond of horses.* 2. affectionate; tender and loving. **Ex.** *He gave her a fond glance.* —**fond'le,** *v.* touch in a fond way. —**fond'ly,** *adv.* —**fond'ness,** *n.*

food (1) [fuwd'], *n.* 1. that which is taken in by an animal or plant to supply the material for strength and growth. **Ex.** *Milk is the baby's chief food.* 2. that which is taken in as a solid rather than a liquid. **Ex.** *They offered us food and drink.* 3. anything that sustains or develops. **Ex.** *Those ideas are food for thought.*

food processor [fuwd' pras'es·ər], *n.* a small machine designed to slice, shred, mix, etc. food. **Ex.** *I chopped the vegetables for this salad in the food processor.*

food stamps [fuwd' stæmps'], *n.* stamps with which to buy food given by the United States government to people of low income. **Ex.** *By the last week of the month, the family had used up its food stamps.*

fool (1) [fuwl'], *n.* 1. a person who is silly or lacks sense; a person who is made to appear this way. **Ex.** *She acted like a fool.* 2. a person who amuses or entertains people by silly actions. **Ex.** *He enjoyed playing the fool.* —*v.* trick; deceive. **Ex.** *He fooled them into believing that he was wealthy.* —**fool'ish,** *adj.*

foot (1) [fut'], *n.* 1. a measurement of length. **Ex.** *There are twelve inches in a foot.* See **Weights and Measures.** 2. that part of the leg below the ankle on which a person or animal stands and walks. **Ex.** *He put his right foot in the water.* 3. something like a foot in position or use; the bottom; the lowest part. **Ex.** *Wait for me at the foot of the stairs.* —**foot'step'**, *n.* a step made by the foot; a sound made by walking or running. **Ex.** *We heard footsteps in the dark.* —**on foot**, walking. **Ex.** *He came in the car; I came on foot.* —**un'der'foot**, in the way. **Ex.** *The children are always underfoot when I want to clean.*

football (3) [fut'bɔːl'], *n.* a leather ball filled with air; a game using such a ball and played on a long field. **Ex.** *In American football, the ball is egg shaped.*

foothill [fut'hil'], *n.* a low hill near the bottom of mountains. **Ex.** *Do you have enough energy to go walking in the foothills today?*

foothold [fut'howld'], *n.* a place for the foot that is safe, as in climbing. **Ex.** *The cracks between the rocks were good footholds as we made our way to the top.*

footnote [fut'nowt'], *n.* a note, usually at the bottom of a page, that gives an explanation of something on the page or refers to another page, book, etc. **Ex.** *In a footnote, the author gave additional information about an individual only named in the text.*

for (1) [fɔːr'], *prep.* 1. in order to gain or attain the object or purpose in mind. **Ex.** *He is saving money for a car.* 2. in place of; instead of; in exchange. **Ex.** *I gave him a quarter for an apple.* 3. in the interest of; to the benefit or support of. **Ex.** *He is working for himself.* 4. obliging someone to do; requiring action. **Ex.** *I have work for him to do.* 5. showing the cause or reason. **Ex.** *He was punished for being late.* 6. intended to be used or received by. **Ex.** *This note is for my sister.* 7. intending to go to. **Ex.** *He is leaving for the city.* 8. extending or lasting. **Ex.** *We waited for an hour.* 9. in respect to; in regard to; concerning. **Ex.** *It is warm for this time of year.*

forbid (3) [fərbid'], *v.* command someone not to do something; prohibit. **Ex.** *I forbid you to see him again.* —**for·bid'den**, *adj.* not permitted. **Ex.** *Smoking is forbidden in this room.*

a, far; æ, am; e, get; ey, late; i, in; iy, see; ɔ, all; ow, go; u, put; uw, too; ə, but, ago; ər, fur; aw, out; ay, life; oy, boy; ŋ, ring; θ, think; ð, that; ž, measure; š, ship; ǰ, edge; č, child.

force (1) [fɔrs'], *n.* 1. power; strength; energy. **Ex.** *The force of the wind closed the door.* 2. strength used against a person or an object. **Ex.** *He entered the house by force.* 3. the military power of a nation; a large group of soldiers; any group of persons prepared to do some special work. **Ex.** *He hopes to become a member of the police force.* —*v.* 1. compel to do something; make do something by the use of strength or power. **Ex.** *He forced me to give him the money.* 2. break open, into or through, obtain, get, etc. by using strength. **Ex.** *We forced our way through the crowd.* —**for'ci·ble,** *adj.* —**for'ci·bly,** *adv.* in a compelling manner; using strength with force. **Ex.** *The angry man was forcibly removed from the room.*

ford (5) [fɔrd'], *n.* a place in a river or stream where the water is shallow enough so that one may cross by walking or riding. **Ex.** *The ford in this river is a busy place.* —*v.* cross a river at a shallow spot by walking or riding. **Ex.** *Cars can ford the river at this point.*

fore (3) [fɔr'], *n.* the front. **Exs.** *The idea of space travel came to the fore in the 1950s.*

fore- (3) [fɔr'], *prefix.* before; in advance; front. **Exs.** *Warn, forewarn; paw, forepaw.*

forearm [fɔr'arm'], *n.* the arm from elbow to wrist.

forecast [fɔr'kæst'], *v.* tell in advance what will or is likely to happen; predict. **Ex.** *Using his knowledge of the political situation, he forecast the outcome of the election.* —*n.* prediction. **Ex.** *What's the weather forecast for tomorrow?*

forefather [fɔr'fa·ðər], *n.* ancestor. **Ex.** *His forefathers came from Africa.*

forefinger [fɔr'fin·gər], *n.* the finger next to the thumb.

forefront [fɔr'frənt'], *n.* the very front; the most important or active place. **Ex.** *He was always in the forefront of the battle.*

foregoing [fɔr'gow'iŋ], *adj.* appearing before. **Ex.** *See the foregoing page for an explanation.*

foreground [fɔr'grawnd'], *n.* the front part of a scene or picture. **Ex.** *In the foreground there is a large tree.*

forehead (2) [fɔr'hed', fɔr'id], *n.* the part of the face above the eyes and below the hair. **Ex.** *A lock of hair fell over his forehead.*

foreign (1) [fɔːr'ən], *adj.* 1. outside of one's own place or country. **Ex.** *He often travels to foreign countries.* 2. not from one's own place or country. **Ex.** *He enjoys foreign wines.* 3. relating to or dealing with other countries. **Ex.** *That company is engaged in foreign trade.* —**for'eign·er,** *n.* a person from another country.

foreman [fɔːr'mən], *n.* one in charge of a group of workers. **Ex.** *His father was a foreman in a steel factory.*

foremost (3) [fɔːr'mowst'], *adj.* first in place, order, time, etc. **Ex.** *He was the foremost statesman of that era.*

forerunner [fɔːr'rən`ər], *n.* someone or something that goes before; a sign of something to come or happen later. **Ex.** *He was a forerunner of today's pilots.*

forest (1) [fɔːr'əst], *n.* a large area of land with many trees; the trees themselves. **Ex.** *The farmers cut down the forest and planted crops.* —**for'est·ry,** *n.* the science of growing forests.

forever (1) [fɔːrev'ər], *adv.* for an unlimited time. **Ex.** *I will not live forever.* 2. always. **Ex.** *He is forever talking about the war.*

forfeit [fɔːr'fit], *v.* lose something or have it taken away as the result of breaking a law, failing to do something, making a mistake, etc. **Ex.** *They had to forfeit the land because they did not pay the taxes on it.*

forgave [fɔːrgeyv'], *v.* past tense of *forgive.* **Ex.** *She forgave his coming home late to dinner when she saw how upset he was.*

forge (4) [fɔːrj'], *n.* a furnace or a place with a furnace in which metal is shaped by beating and hammering. **Ex.** *The children watched horseshoes being made at the forge.* —*v.* 1. form by heating and hammering; force into shape. **Ex.** *The settlers forged a new nation.* 2. copy or imitate to deceive, especially handwriting. **Ex.** *He forged my name on the letter.* —**forg'er,** *n.* —**for'ger·y,** *n.* the crime of copying and pretending the copy is the original. **Ex.** *He was found guilty of forgery.*

forget (1) [fərget'], *v.* 1. not remember. **Ex.** *Who is he? I forget his name.* 2. leave undone because of not remembering; neglect. **Ex.** *He keeps forgetting to visit his elderly aunt.* —**for·get'ful,** *adj.* likely to forget.

forgive (2) [fərgiv'], *v.* pardon; stop feeling anger or a desire to punish. **Ex.** *He will forgive you if you apologize.* —**for·give'ness,** *n.*

forgiven [fɔːrgiv'ən], *v.* past participle of *forgive*. **Ex.** *They had finally forgiven him for what he did years ago.*

forgo [fɔːr'gow'], *v.* go without; not take. **Ex.** *I will forgo dessert.*

forgot (2) [fərgat'], *v.* past tense of *forget*. **Ex.** *He forgot to lock the door.*

forgotten [fɔːrgat'ən], *v.* past participle of *forget*. **Ex.** *I had forgotten he was coming.*

fork (3) [fɔrk'], *n.* 1. an instrument with two or more long points used to pick up food. 2. a farming tool that looks like an eating fork. **Ex.** *He picked up the hay with a pitchfork.* 3. division of anything into two or more parts; place where such a division occurs. **Ex.** *He turned left at the fork in the road.* —*v.* divide into two or more branches. **Ex.** *The river forks a mile north of here.*

FORK 1

form (1) [fɔrm'], *n.* 1. kind; sort; way. **Ex.** *Ice and snow are forms of water.* 2. shape; figure. **Ex.** *The form of a man appeared in the doorway.* 3. a card or sheet of paper with blank spaces to be filled out with required information. **Ex.** *He was given several forms to complete.* 4. any of the different uses or spellings into which a word is changed. **Ex.** Broke *is the past form of the verb* break. —*v.* 1. take the shape of; make. **Ex.** *Form a circle and join hands.* 2. train; develop. **Ex.** *Part of the purpose of this camping program is to help form the child's character.* —**for·ma'tion,** *n.* the act of forming. **Ex.** *The father had a great influence on the formation of his son's mind.* 2. that which has been formed. **Ex.** *The tourists stopped to admire the rock formation.* 3. an arrangement in particular order of groups of people, vehicles, etc. **Ex.** *The members of the band are now in marching formation.* —**for'ma·tive,** *adj.* developing.

formal (4) [fɔr'məl], *adj.* 1. following society's rules or customs exactly; according to a fixed form. **Ex.** *You must write a formal acceptance to this invitation.* 2. ceremonial; concerned with form or appearance. **Ex.** *Guests at the wedding wore formal clothes.* —**for·mal'i·ty,** *n.* —**for'mal·ly,** *adv.*

former (2) [fɔr'mər], *adj.* 1. previously but not now; earlier in time. **Ex.** *He is a former teacher.* 2. the first of two. **Ex.** *I like the red coat and the blue one, but I prefer the former.* —**for'mer·ly,** *adv.*

formidable (4) [fɔr'mədəbəl], *adj.* 1. causing fear or dread; alarming. **Ex.** *The army made a formidable show of strength.* 2. very difficult. **Ex.** *They had a formidable job to do.*

formula (4) [fɔr'myələ], *n.* 1. a special combination of words or symbols used to express a rule, fact or principle. **Ex.** *H_2O is the chemical formula for water.* 2. a method or set of directions for doing something. **Ex.** *He could give no easy formula for success.*

formulate (5) [fɔr'myələyt'], *v.* organize according to a system. **Ex.** *Formulate your ideas before you begin to write.*

forsake [fɔrseyk'], *v.* stop helping; desert. **Ex.** *His friends will not forsake him.*

fort (3) [fɔrt'], *n.* a place with strong walls protected by guns; any armed place surrounded by walls or other means of defense and occupied by troops. **Ex.** *There was a fort at the mouth of the river.*

forth [fɔrθ'], *adv.* 1. forward; onward. **Ex.** *The army marched forth to battle.* 2. out of concealment. **Ex.** *The rabbit jumped forth from behind the bush.*

forthright [fɔrθ'rayt'], *adv.* honest and direct. **Ex.** *He is a forthright speaker.*

forthwith [fɔrθ'wiθ', fɔrθ'wið'], *adv.* immediately; without delay. **Ex.** *He gave his answer forthwith.*

fortify (5) [fɔr'təfay'], *v.* strengthen; make stronger. **Exs.** *A hot meal fortified him against the cold. They fortified the town against an attack.*

fortune (2) [fɔr'čən], *n.* 1. chance; luck. **Ex.** *Fortune did not favor him.* 2. the future; one's fate. **Ex.** *She had her fortune told.* 3. very great wealth. **Ex.** *He received a large fortune when his uncle died.* —**for'tu·nate,** *adj.* lucky. —**for'tu·nate·ly,** *adv.*

forty (1) [fɔr'tiy], *n., adj.* the number between thirty-nine and forty-one; the number *40.* —**for'ti·eth,** *adj.* coming after thirty-nine others.

forward (1) [fɔr'wərd], *adj.* 1. near, at or of the front part of anything. **Ex.** *The forward cars of the train are already in the* station. 2. bold; rude; not modest. **Ex.** *That child is too forward.* **—adv.** toward the front. **Ex.** *They slowly moved forward.* **—v.** send onward. **Ex.** *Please forward my mail to my new address.*

fought (2) [fɔ:t'], *v.* past tense and participle of *fight.* **Exs.** *They fought a bloody battle. They had fought all night.*

foul (3) [fawl'], *adj.* 1. dirty; offending the senses. **Ex.** *The room had a foul smell.* 2. choked up with dirt. **Ex.** *The old well was foul with leaves.* 3. hateful; evil. **Ex.** *He was guilty of a foul crime.* 4. not favorable; stormy. **Ex.** *Foul weather prevented them from leaving.* 5. not permitted by the rules of the game. **Ex.** *The batter hit a foul ball.* **—foul'ly,** *adv.*

found (1) [fawnd'], *v.* past tense and participle of *find.* **Exs.** *He found the book for which he was looking. She had finally found the missing papers.*

found (1) [fawnd'], *v.* 1. start or establish. **Ex.** *He helped to found the university.* 2. base; build on a base. **Ex.** *He founded his business on the principle of giving customers their money's worth.* **—found'er,** *n.* one who establishes something.

foundation (2) [fawn'dey'šən], *n.* 1. the act of founding or establishing. **Ex.** *The foundation of a college was his dream.* 2. that on which something rests or is built; a base. **Ex.** *The foundation of the house was stone.* 3. an institution that is established to spend money for educational purposes, pay for research, etc. **Ex.** *The work of the Ford Foundation is known worldwide.*

fountain (2) [fawn'tən], *n.* a place or device from which water rises or is forced to rise. **Exs.** *There is a drinking fountain in the hall. Visitors admire the beautiful display of lighted fountains in the park.*

FOUNTAIN

fountain pen [fawn'tən pen'], *n.* a pen with a container of ink, filled from an outside source, which automatically flows to the writing point when the pen is in use. **Ex.** *He signed his name with an expensive fountain pen.*

four (1) [fɔːr'], *n., adj.* the number between three and five; the number *4.* **—fourth',** *n., adj.* coming after three others. **—four'teen',** *n., adj.* the number *14.* **—four'teenth',** *n., adj.* coming after thirteen others.

fowl (4) [fawl'], *n.* birds, especially farm birds, such as chickens raised for eating; the meat of such birds. **Ex.** *I prefer the taste of chicken to that of other kinds of fowl.*

fox (3) [faks'], *n.* a flesh-eating wild animal of the dog family, similar to a wolf but smaller. 2. the fur of a fox. **Ex.** *Her coat is trimmed with fox.*

FOX 1

fraction (4) [fræk'šən], *n.* 1. a part of anything, especially a small part. **Ex.** *He saves only a fraction of his salary.* 2. one of several parts of a whole. **Ex.** *Two examples of fractions are ½ and ⅔.* —**frac'tion·al,** *adj.*

fracture (5) [frækčər], *n.* a break or crack, especially of a bone. **Ex.** *She suffered a fracture of the left leg.* —*v.* crack or break. **Ex.** *He fractured his right heel.*

fragile (5) [fræj'əl], *adj.* easily broken; delicate. **Ex.** *That glass dish is very fragile.* — **fra·gil'i·ty,** *n.*

fragment (3) [fræg'mənt], *n.* 1. a part broken off or separated. **Ex.** *She was cut by a fragment of glass.* 2. a part that is incomplete. **Ex.** *He read me a fragment of the letter.* —**frag'men·tar'y,** *adj.*

fragrance (4) [frey'grəns], *n.* a sweet or pleasant smell. **Ex.** *The fragrance of baking bread reminds me of home.* —**fra'grant,** *adj.*

frail (4) [freyl'], *adj.* weak; easily damaged or broken. **Ex.** *He was too frail to play games outdoors.* —**frail'ty,** *n.* weakness. **Ex.** *She worried about the frailty of her mother.*

frame (2) [freym'], *n.* 1. a border which encloses something, such as a picture or mirror. **Ex.** *The mirror has a silver frame.* 2. the part of anything that gives it shape and holds it up; an open structure. **Ex.** *The brick house was built on a wood frame.* 3. the structure of the body. **Ex.** *He had a large frame.* —*v.* 1. put in a frame. **Ex.** *I am going to frame this picture.* 2. imagine, as ideas; plan; compose. **Ex.** *The Founding Fathers framed the Constitution of the United States.* —**fram'er.** *n.* —**frame of mind,** a particular mental state; a mood. **Ex.** *She is in a bad frame of mind.*

framework [freym'wərk], *n.* a structure that gives something its shape and holds it up; supporting frame. **Ex.** *The copper statue was built over a framework of plywood.*

frank (3) [fræŋk'], *adj.* unreserved and honest in speaking one's thoughts and feelings. **Ex.** *He liked the boy's frank way of speaking.* —**frank'ly,** *adv.* in an unreserved, honest manner. **Ex.** *Speaking frankly, I don't like her.* —**frank'ness,** *n.* openness. **Ex.** *His frankness sometimes made people uncomfortable.*

frankfurter [fræŋk'fərtər], *n.* a kind of mildly spiced sausage, usually reddish in color. **Ex.** *We are having frankfurters, boiled cabbage, and fried potatoes for dinner tonight.*

frantic (4) [fræn'tik], *adj.* wild with excitement, fear, pain, etc. **Ex.** *Frantic efforts were made to escape the sinking ship.* —**fran'ti·cal·ly,** *adv.* wildly. **Ex.** *He called frantically for help.*

fraud (4) [frɔːd'], *n.* an act of trickery, lying or cheating. **Ex.** *They took his property from him by fraud.* —**fraud'u·lent,** *adj.* by trickery, lying or cheating. **Ex.** *He obtained the money by fraudulent means.*

free (1) [friy'], *adj.* 1. having political and civil rights; not enslaved; not imprisoned. **Ex.** *They were fighting to make their country free.* 2. permitted or able to do something at will; not limited by rules. **Ex.** *You are free to leave when you choose.* 3. without cost or charge. **Ex.** *These books are free.* 4. not tied down; not fastened; loose. **Ex.** *He took the free end of the line.* 5. not burdened; not worried; not blocked; etc. **Ex.** *The road is free from snow.* 6. not in use; not occupied. **Ex.** *When you are free, I would like to speak with you.* —*v.* release; make free. **Ex.** *I would like to free the bird from the cage.* —*adv.* without paying. **Ex.** *The children were admitted to the theater free.* —**free'dom,** *n.* —**free'ly,** *adv.*

freeway [friy'wey'], *n.* a wide road with few stops which is designed for fast driving. **Ex.** *We can travel on the freeway for most of the trip.*

freeze (2) [friyz'], *v.* 1. harden by cold into ice or a similar solid. **Ex.** *The river freezes in the winter.* 2. cause to be or become very cold. **Ex.** *Please close the window before I freeze.* 3. make or become very still as a result of fear, horror, etc. **Ex.** *The sight of the wreck made her freeze with horror.* 4. preserve food by bringing its temperature down to below thirty-two degrees Fahrenheit. **Ex.** *I am going to freeze the pie that we didn't finish tonight at dinner.* —**freez'er,** *n.* a place to freeze food or to keep frozen food.

freight (3) [freyt'], *n.* 1. transportation of goods by truck, train or plane. **Ex.** *Send the furniture by freight.* 2. goods that are transported. **Ex.** *This train carries no freight.* 3. the price paid for transporting goods. **Ex.** *The freight was more than I could pay.* —**freight'er,** *n.* a ship which transports goods and sometimes a few passengers.

frenzy (5) [fren'ziy], *n.* an uncontrolled outburst of emotion. **Ex.** *He was in a frenzy because he had missed his plane.* —**fren'zied,** *adj.* in a state of uncontrolled emotion. **Ex.** *The frenzied woman rushed to the hospital.*

frequent (2) [friy'kwənt], *adj.* occurring often. **Ex.** *The train made frequent stops.* —*v.* visit often. **Ex.** *The actors frequent an eating place near the theater.* —**fre'quen·cy,** *n.* —**fre'quent·ly,** *adv.* often. **Ex.** *I ride the bus quite frequently.*

fresh (1) [freš'], *adj.* 1. newly made or gathered; recent. **Ex.** *These eggs are fresh.* 2. not salty. **Ex.** *The sailor was glad to wash in fresh water again.* 3. rested; looking healthy and young. **Ex.** *Do that work while you are still fresh.* 4. new; different. **Ex.** *This writer has fresh ideas about the problem.* 5. having just arrived; not experienced. **Ex.** *He is just fresh from college.* 6. pure and cool. **Ex.** *This country air is fresh.* —**fresh'en,** *v.* make fresh. **Ex.** *She opened the window to freshen the room.* —**fresh'ly,** *adv.* —**fresh'ness,** *n.*

freshman [freš'mən], *n.* a person in his or her first year of high school or college; a beginner at anything. **Ex.** *He is a freshman in the Senate.*

fret (5) [fret'], *v.* make or become worried and restless. **Ex.** *She fretted at the delay.* —**fret'ful,** *adj.*

Friday (1) [fray'diy], *n.* the day between Thursday and Saturday; the sixth day of the week.

fried [frayd'], *v.* past tense and participle of *fry.* **Exs.** *I fried two eggs for your breakfast. We have fried some chicken for the picnic.*

friend (1) [frend'], *n.* 1. a person one likes and is close to. **Ex.** *His friend was almost like a brother to him.* 2. a person who believes in and supports a group, cause, etc. **Ex.** *He is a friend of labor.* —**friend'ly,** *adj.* kindly. **Ex.** *She is always friendly when I see her.*

fright (2) [frayt'], *n.* sudden great fear. **Ex.** *Fright caused her to run.* —**fright'en,** *v.* fill with fear. **Ex.** *The dog frightened the rabbit.*

a, far; æ, am; e, get; ey, late; i, in; iy, see; ɔ, all; ow, go; u, put; uw, too; ə, but, ago; ər, fur; aw, out; ay, life; oy, boy; ŋ, ring; θ, think; ð, that; ž, measure; š, ship; j, edge; č, child.

frigid [frij'id], *adj.* 1. very cold. **Ex.** *During the frigid weather last month, our heating bill soared.* 2. icy or cold and distant in behavior. **Ex.** *His frigid manner makes it difficult to work with him.* —**fri·gid'i·ty,** *n.* —**frig'id·ly,** *adv.*

fringe (4) [frinj'], *n.* 1. a border of lengths of cord, thread, etc. **Ex.** *The fringe of the rug is badly worn.* 2. anything that suggests a border or edge. **Ex.** *They live on the fringe of town.* —*v.* 1. furnish with a fringe. **Ex.** *I fringed this scarf with two-inch lengths of yarn.* 2. serve as a fringe for. **Ex.** *Suburbs fringed the city.*

FRINGE 1

frog (3) [frag', frɔːg'], *n.* a small animal without a tail that lives on land or in water.

FROG

from (1) [frəm'], *prep.* 1. having some person, place or thing as its beginning, source or cause. **Ex.** *Where is the note from your teacher?* 2. at a place separated, distant or not near. **Ex.** *We are far from home.* 3. because of. **Ex.** *He is suffering from a cold.* 4. out of. **Ex.** *He took some money from his pocket.*

front (1) [frənt'], *n.* 1. the forward part; the opposite of back. **Ex.** *The front of the house faces the park.* 2. the beginning; the first part. **Ex.** *The writer's picture is in the front of the book.* 3. a place before a person or a thing. **Ex.** *A tree is growing in front of the house.* —*v.* face toward. **Ex.** *The house fronted on the river.* —**front'al,** *adj.* of the front. **Ex.** *The enemy made a frontal attack on our troops.*

frontier (4) [frən'tiːr'], *n.* 1. that part of a country which borders another country. **Ex.** *There are not many guards along the frontier.* 2. the outer area of a settled region lying next to a wilderness. **Ex.** *There are few frontiers remaining in the United States.* 3. a new or not completely developed field of knowledge. **Ex.** *There are many frontiers in science to be explored.*

frost (3) [frɔːst'], *n.* 1. temperature cold enough to cause freezing. **Ex.** *There is frost in the air.* 2. light covering of ice formed by dew or water vapor freezing on a surface. **Ex.** *There was frost on the window.* —*v.* 1. cover with frost. **Ex.** *The windows are frosted.* 2. cover a cake with a topping made of sugar, butter, flavoring, etc. **Ex.** *She frosted the* *cake with chocolate icing.* —**frost'ing,** *n.* a covering for cake; icing. —**frost'y,** *adj.* of a temperature cold enough to cause freezing; cold; chilly. **Ex.** *The frosty night air was refreshing.*

frostbite [frɔst'bayt`], *n.* damage to a part of the body caused by freezing. **Ex.** *The skier was suffering from frostbite.*

frown (3) [frawn'], *v.* 1. draw the eyebrows together as in worry or anger. **Ex.** *She frowned as she heard the news.* 2. show that one does not like or disapproves of something. **Ex.** *His employer frowned upon his request to leave early.* —*n.* the look one has when frowning. **Ex.** *There was a frown on her face.*

froze (2) [frowz'], *v.* past tense of *freeze.* **Ex.** *Our water pipes froze during the last cold spell.*

frozen [frow'zən], *v.* past participle of *freeze.* **Ex.** *When we awoke, we saw that the water in the pool had frozen.*

frugal (5) [fruw'gəl], *adj.* 1. without waste; thrifty. **Ex.** *She is frugal in managing her money.* 2. cheap; very simple. **Ex.** *They could afford only a frugal meal.* —**fru'gal·ly,** *adv.* —**fru·gal'i·ty,** *n.*

fruit (1) [fruwt'], *n.* 1. the parts of some trees and plants, consisting of the seeds and the surrounding flesh, that can be eaten. **Ex.** *What kind of fruit do you want: apples, oranges or bananas?* 2. the product of study, work, effort, etc. **Ex.** *The fruits of his research have helped many people.*

frustrate (3) [frəs'treyt`], *v.* cause to have no effect; keep from doing or obtaining what one wishes; disappoint one's hopes, wishes, etc. **Ex.** *The weather frustrated our attempts to climb the mountain.* —**frus·tra'tion,** *n.*

fry (3) [fray'], *v.* cook in fat over a flame. **Ex.** *She will fry eggs for our breakfast.*

fuel (4) [fyuw'əl], *n.* 1. any substance that is burned to make heat or power. **Ex.** *What kind of fuel do you use to heat your house?* 2. anything that causes an emotion to become stronger. **Ex.** *Her unkind words added fuel to his anger.* —*v.* supply with or take in fuel. **Ex.** *The cook fueled the fire with more wood.*

fugitive (5) [fyuw'jətiv], *n.* one in the act of running away. **Ex.** *He is a fugitive from the police.* —*adj.* escaping; fleeing. **Ex.** *The fugitive criminal was captured.*

-ful (1) [fəl], *suffix.* 1. *full of.* **Exs.** *Care, careful; beauty, beautiful.* 2. tending or likely to. **Exs.** *Wake, wakeful; harm, harmful.* 3. a quantity sufficient to fill. **Exs.** *Hand, handful; cup, cupful.*

fulfill (2) [fulfil'], *v.* carry out; make real; cause to happen. **Ex.** *By completing college, he fulfilled his mother's dreams.*

full (2) [ful'], *adj.* 1. filled with as much as a thing or person can hold. **Ex.** *I drank a full glass of water.* 2. containing a plentiful supply; enough for one's needs. **Ex.** *His pockets are always full of money.* 3. with something or someone occupying it. **Ex.** *Every seat in the theater was full.* 4. being at its greatest size or highest development. **Ex.** *There is a full moon tonight.* 5. complete in number, quantity, length, etc. **Ex.** *We waited for a full hour.* 6. filled out; rounded. **Ex.** *With her sails full, the ship moved rapidly.* —*n.* the greatest extent or highest degree. **Ex.** *He enjoyed his vacation to the full.* —*adv.* entirely; completely. **Ex.** *He turned full around to face us.* —**ful'ly,** *adv.* completely, entirely. **Ex.** *He was fully satisfied with their work.* —**in full,** entirely; completely. **Ex.** *He paid his debt in full.*

full-blown [ful'blown'], *adj.* in full bloom; fully developed. **Ex.** *The plain little girl had become a full-blown beauty.*

full dress [ful' dres'], formal dress. **Ex.** *Full dress is required at the ball.*

fumble (5) [fəm'bəl], *v.* feel about for; handle with a lack of skill or ease. **Ex.** *He fumbled for the lock in the dark.*

fume (5) [fyuwm'], *n.* strong-smelling vapor from smoke, gas, paint, etc. that may be irritating and/or harmful. **Ex.** *The gasoline fumes made her sick.* —*v.* 1. throw off fumes. **Ex.** *The chimney was fuming clouds of smoke.* 2. show anger. **Ex.** *He fumed because he had missed the train.*

fun (2) [fən'], *n.* 1. pleasure; amusement. **Ex.** *The young people had fun at the dance.* 2. playfulness. **Ex.** *He is always happy and full of fun.* —**make fun of,** joke about. **Ex.** *They made fun of the way he spoke.*

function (3) [fəŋk'šən], *n.* 1. the natural or special action or activity of a person or thing. **Ex.** *The function of a watch is to keep time.* 2. any public ceremony, gathering, etc. **Ex.** *The mayor had to attend many political functions.* —*v.* act; operate; carry out normal work. **Ex.** *His car does not function as it should.* —**func'tion·al,** *adj.* useful; practical. **Ex.** *The plan for this kitchen is not functional.*

fund (3) [fənd'], *n*. 1. a sum of money set aside for a special purpose. **Ex.** *That fund is for entertainment.* 2. a store or stock of something. **Ex.** *He has a fund of information about famous people.* —**funds,** *n*. available money. **Ex.** *His funds for food are limited.*

fundamental (3) [fən'dəmen'təl], *adj*. of or relating to a foundation; basic; essential. **Ex.** *They had fundamental differences of opinion.* —*n*. a principle, rule or law that serves as a basis of a system. **Ex.** *In college he had studied the fundamentals of government.* —**fun'da·men'tal·ly,** *adv*.

funeral (2) [fyuw'n(ə)rəl], *n*. services, often religious, held after a person has died before burial or burning. **Ex.** *People came from great distances to attend his funeral.*

funny (2) [fən'iy], *adj*. amusing; causing laughter. **Ex.** *Everyone laughed at his funny stories.*

fur (2) [fə:r'], *n*. 1. the skin of an animal, covered with soft, thick hair. **Ex.** *The fur of a bear is very warm.* 2. an article of clothing made of fur. **Ex.** *This store sells furs.* —*adj*. made of fur. **Ex.** *She has two fur coats.* —**fur'ry,** *adj*.

furious (4) [fyur'iyəs], *adj*. 1. full of fury or rage. **Ex.** *He was furious when he heard the news.* 2. violent; fierce. **Ex.** *A furious storm sank the boat.* —**fur'i·ous·ly,** *adv*.

furnace (3) [fər'nəs], *n*. a closed structure in which heat is produced for warming a house, melting metals, etc. **Ex.** *An oil furnace heats our school building.*

furnish (2) [fər'niš], *v*. 1. supply with furniture or equipment. **Ex.** *It took months to furnish their house.* 2. provide or supply. **Ex.** *The hotel furnished clean sheets and towels every day.* —**fur'nish·ings,** *n*. furniture and equipment in a house, office, etc.

furniture (2) [fər'ničər], *n*. the movable things, such as tables, chairs, beds and desks, in a house, office, store, etc. **Ex.** *Their furniture fits comfortably in the new house.*

furrow (5) [fər'ow], *n*. 1. a long, narrow cut made in the earth by a plow for the purpose of planting. **Ex.** *The farmer was proud of his straight furrows.* 2. a long, narrow depression in any surface. **Ex.** *There were deep furrows on the old man's* *forehead.* —*v.* make furrows; plow land. **Ex.** *Care furrowed his brow.*

further (1) [fər'ðər], *adj.* 1. at a greater distance. **Ex.** *He is at the further end of the field.* 2. added or more. **Ex.** *We are waiting for further word about the weather.* —*adv.* 1. at or to a greater distance; farther. **Ex.** *He will go further in life than his brother.* 2. to a greater degree or extent; more. **Ex.** *He questioned the teacher further.* —*v.* help forward; advance; promote. **Ex.** *To further peace, we need better understanding among nations.*

furthermore [fər'ðərmɔ:r'], *adv.* also; in addition. **Ex.** *I cannot go, and furthermore I will not go.*

fury (1) [fyuwr'iy], *n.* 1. rage or wild anger. **Ex.** *He was in a terrible fury.* 2. violence; fierceness. **Ex.** *The fury of the storm frightened the children.*

fuse (5) [fyuwz'], *n.* 1. the string or similar material which is lighted to make something explode. **Ex.** *Twenty seconds after he lit the fuse, the bomb burst.* 2. a safety device containing a wire that melts when the electric current becomes too strong and thus stops the flow of electricity. **Ex.** *When he replaced the fuse, the light went on again.* —*v.* combine by melting together; melt. **Ex.** *The two metals fused into one.*

fuss (4) [fəs'], *n.* an unnecessary worry or bother; nervous action about something unimportant. **Ex.** *She made a big fuss about a spot on her dress.* —*v.* worry about unimportant things. **Ex.** *He fusses about everything.* —**fuss'y,** *adj.*

futile (5) [fyuw'təl], *adj.* 1. useless; not possible of success. **Ex.** *He made futile efforts to rescue the child.* 2. not important; valueless. **Ex.** *He wasted his time in futile talk.* —**fu·til'i·ty,** *n.*

future (1) [fyuw'čər], *n.* 1. the time that is to come. **Ex.** *They are planning for the future.* 2. a condition in the time to come. **Ex.** *His future in business seemed promising.* —*adj.* 1. in the time that is to come. **Ex.** *I am looking forward to seeing you at a future time.* 2. expressing the time to come. **Ex.** Will go *is the future tense of the verb* go.

-fy (3) [fay], *suffix.* 1. make; become. **Exs.** *Clear, clarify; intense; intensify.* 2. cause to feel or have. **Exs.** *Terror, terrify; glory, glorify.*

G

G, g [jiy'], *n.* the seventh letter of the English alphabet.

gain (1) [geyn'], *v.* 1. obtain; win; earn. **Ex.** *Her kindness gained her many friends.* 2. obtain or add as an increase. **Ex.** *He gained weight.* 3. become better; improve. **Ex.** *The patient is gaining strength.* —*n.* 1. money made in business; profit. **Ex.** *His gains were greater than his losses.* 2. increase; improvement. **Ex.** *He has shown some gains since he changed schools.* —**gain'ful,** *adj.* profitable. —**gain'ful·ly,** *adv.* profitably.

gale (4) [geyl'], *n.* 1. a strong wind. **Ex.** *The gale blew down a tree.* 2. a sudden loud burst, as of sound. **Ex.** *His funny story caused a gale of laughter from the audience.*

gallant (4) [gæl'ənt], *adj.* 1. brave; noble. **Ex.** *The gallant soldier died to save his friend.* 2. polite and attentive. **Ex.** *The handsome gentleman was gallant to all the ladies.* —**gal'lant·ly,** *adv.*

gallery (3) [gæl'(ə)riy], *n.* 1. a room or building where works of art are shown or sold. **Ex.** *We visited a gallery of modern art.* 2. a long, narrow platform built out from the wall of the upper part of a room from which one can see the activities below. **Ex.** *They sat in the gallery and watched the dancers.*

gallon (3) [gæl'ən], *n.* a measure of liquids; four quarts. **Ex.** *The tank of this car holds seventeen gallons of gas.* See **Weights and Measures.**

gallop (3) [gæl'əp], *v.* ride or run very fast. **Ex.** *The horse galloped to victory.* —*n.* 1. the fastest manner in which a horse runs when all four feet are off the ground at the same time. **Ex.** *The race horse had a beautiful gallop.* 2. a ride at this speed. **Ex.** *We went for a gallop.*

GALLOP 1

gallows (5) [gæl'owz], *n.* a high wooden

frame with a rope from which criminals were hanged. **Ex.** *The murderer died on the gallows.*

gamble (4) [gæm'bəl], *v.* 1. play any game of chance for money or other things of value; bet. **Ex.** *He gambled away a fortune at the horse races.* 2. risk anything of value; take a chance. **Ex.** *Drive carefully and don't gamble with your life.* —*n.* a matter involving risk. **Ex.** *Putting money into that failing business is a gamble.* —**gam'bler,** *n.* one who gambles.

game (1) [geym'], *n.* 1. any contest played according to rules in which persons or teams compete against each other. **Ex.** *She enjoys a game of cards.* 2. any form of amusement or play. **Ex.** *What games did the children play at the party?* 3. wild animals that are hunted. **Ex.** *He is hunting game in the woods.* —*adj.* of animals, including fish and birds, that are hunted. **Ex.** *A forest fire destroyed the nests of the game birds.*

gang (3) [gæŋ'], *n.* 1. a group of people gathered together for some reason. **Ex.** *The gang of small boys was playing ball.* 2. a group of criminals. **Ex.** *A gang of robbers broke into the store.*

gangplank [gæŋ'plæŋk'], *n.* a movable walk used to go on or off a ship. **Ex.** *She held the rail tightly as she walked down the gangplank.*

gangster (5) [gæŋ'stər], *n.* a person in a criminal gang. **Ex.** *The gangster was arrested by the police.*

gap (4) [gæp'], *n.* 1. a break or opening, as in a wall; a mountain pass. **Ex.** *The cows went through a gap in the fence.* 2. a vacant space or interval. **Ex.** *The mother's death left a gap in the lives of her children.*

garage (4) [gəra:ž', gəra:j'], *n.* a building for sheltering, servicing or repairing automobiles, trucks, etc. **Ex.** *My car is in the garage for repairs.*

garbage (5) [gar'bij], *n.* waste; unwanted or spoiled food. **Ex.** *Leave your garbage in a can outside your door.*

garden (1) [gar'dən], *n.* a piece of ground where plants are grown for beauty or for food. **Ex.** *They have a rose garden behind their house.* —*v.* work in a garden. **Ex.** *She likes to garden.* —**gar'den·er,** *n.* one who gardens.

garment (3) [gar'mənt], *n.* any article of clothing. **Ex.** *These garments are made of 100 percent wool.*

garrison (4) [gær'əsən], *n.* a fort or town where soldiers are stationed, sometimes for purposes of protection; also the body of troops stationed there. **Ex.** *The garrison is on the hill.*

gas (2) [gæs'], *n.* 1. any substance that is neither solid nor liquid. **Ex.** *Air is a gas.* 2. any such substance which burns and provides heat or light. **Ex.** *Our home is heated by gas.* 3. gasoline. **Ex.** *The car needed ten gallons of gas.* —**gas'e·ous**, *adj.*

gash (5) [gæš'], *n.* a deep, long cut. **Ex.** *He was taken to the hospital with a gash in his head.* —*v.* make a deep, long cut. **Ex.** *She gashed her hand with a knife.*

gasoline (3) [gæs'əliyn`, gæs`əliyn'], *n.* a liquid used as fuel for automobiles and other engines. **Ex.** *His car gets twenty miles to a gallon of gasoline.*

gasp (3) [gæsp'], *n.* a sudden, sharp intake of air, made with the mouth open. **Ex.** *She gave a gasp of surprise when she saw him.* —*v.* 1. struggle to get air with the mouth open. **Ex.** *He gasped for air as he ran from the smoke-filled room.* 2. speak with gasps. **Ex.** *She gasped out her story.*

gate (1) [geyt'], *n.* the part of a fence, wall or passageway that opens and closes like a door; entrance. **Ex.** *There was a guard at the gate of the factory.*

gather (1) [gæð'ər], *v.* 1. bring together into one group or place; assemble. **Ex.** *The guests gathered around the fire.* 2. collect, as a harvest. **Ex.** *The farmer gathered the crops.* 3. learn from observation. **Ex.** *I gather that he did not like my ideas.* —**gath'er·ing**, *n.* a crowd; a coming together.

gave (1) [geyv'], *v.* past tense of give. **Ex.** *He gave me the book.*

gay (2) [gey'], *adj.* 1. full of joy; expressing happiness. **Ex.** *The orchestra played gay dance music.* 2. bright and colorful. **Ex.** *Gay flags decorated the hall.* —**gai'e·ty**, *n.* —**gai'ly**, *adv.*

gaze (2) [geyz'], *v.* look long and steadily; look with wonder. **Ex.** *He gazed lovingly into her eyes.* —*n.* a long, steady look. **Ex.** *Her gaze was fixed on the moon.*

a, far; æ, am; e, get; ey, late; i, in; iy, see; ɔ, all; ow, go; u, put; uw, too; ə, but, ago; ər, fur; aw, out; ay, life; oy, boy; ŋ, ring; θ, think; ð, that; ž, measure; š, ship; j, edge; č, child.

gear (5) [giːr'], *n.* 1. in a mechanical device, a wheel with teeth that fit together with similar parts of another wheel, so that the movement of one wheel causes the other to move; a particular arrangement of such wheels. **Ex.** *When a car is in gear, the motor begins to turn the wheels.* 2. the equipment used for a particular occupation. **Ex.** *Several pieces of the sailor's gear were missing.*

GEAR 1

geese (3) [giys'], *n.* plural of *goose.* **Ex.** *The wild geese were flying high above us.*

gelatin [jel'ətin], *n.* 1. an almost tasteless, odorless, jellylike substance made by boiling the bones, skin, etc. of animals in water and used in making jellies, desserts, glue, etc.; a similar substance made from vegetables. **Ex.** *This recipe calls for two tablespoons of powdered gelatin.* 2. a dish made with this substance as its base. **Ex.** *For dessert we are having a fruit gelatin served with whipped cream.*

gem (3) [jem'], *n.* 1. a rare and beautiful stone; a jewel. **Ex.** *The crown sparkled with gems.* 2. something as rare and valuable as a gem. **Ex.** *That painting is the gem of the collection.*

gene [jiyn'], *n.* one of the tiny particles in the cell of a plant or an animal, inherited from its parents, that controls the development of its characteristics.

general (1) [jen'(ə)rəl], *adj.* 1. not detailed; not definite. **Ex.** *I have a general idea of what he means.* 2. not local; widespread. **Ex.** *A general election will be held this fall.* 3. affecting or including all. **Ex.** *These rules are for the general good.* 4. not specialized. **Ex.** *He is taking a course in general science.* —*n.* any high-ranking army officer above a colonel. —**gen'er·al·ly,** *adv.* usually. —**gen'er·al'i·ty,** *n.* —**gen'eral·ize,** *v.*

generate (3) [jen'əreyt'], *v.* produce; make. **Ex.** *The motor generated steam.* —**gen'era'tor,** *n.* a machine that produces power. **Ex.** *Because of the increased demand for electricity, the company is buying a new generator.* —**gen·er·a'tion,** *n.* the act of producing, making or bringing into being. **Ex.** *The generation of electric power will have to be increased to meet customer needs.*

generation (3) [jĕn`ərey'šən], *n.* 1. all persons born about the same time. **Ex.** *This generation could be called the computer age generation.* 2. the average period of a generation, commonly accepted as thirty years. **Ex.** *It happened two generations ago.*

generic [jənər'ik], *adj.* characteristic or representative of an entire class of things; general; not protected by a trademark. **Ex.** *We try to buy the less expensive generic drugs instead of those with trademarks.*

generous (2) [jĕn'ərəs], *adj.* 1. ready to give; willing to share. **Ex.** *He is generous to his friends.* 2. free from meanness of character; noble of mind. **Ex.** *It was generous of him to admit his mistake.* 3. plentiful; large. **Ex.** *They always serve generous portions of food.* —**gen'er·ous·ly,** *adv.* —**gen`er·os'i·ty,** *n.*

genius (3) [jiyn'yəs], *n.* 1. extraordinary natural mental and creative ability; any great ability. **Ex.** *The teacher recognized the boy's musical genius.* 2. a person who has a great mental ability. **Ex.** *She is recognized as a genius.*

gentle (1) [jĕn'təl], *adj.* 1. not rough or violent. **Ex.** *He has a gentle manner.* 2. moderate; mild. **Ex.** *A gentle breeze was blowing.* —**gen'tle·ness,** *n.* **gent'ly,** *adv.*

gentleman (1) [jĕn'təlmən], *n.* 1. a man of culture, good manners and honor. **Ex.** *A gentleman would not have behaved that way.* 2. any man. **Ex.** *It belongs to the gentleman in the brown suit.*

genuine (4) [jĕn'yuwən], *adj.* 1. not imitation; real. **Ex.** *It is a genuine gold ring.* 2. sincere; true. **Ex.** *He proved himself a genuine friend.* —**gen'u·ine·ly,** *adv.* —**gen'u·ine·ness,** *n.*

geography (4) [jiyag'rəfiy], *n.* 1. the science of the areas of the earth in regard to nations, climate, plants, people, etc. **Ex.** *The children need updated maps for their study of geography.* 2. the hills, lowlands, etc. of a particular area or place. **Ex.** *We are studying the geography of our town.* —**ge·og'ra·pher,** *n.* one who studies geography. —**ge`o·graph'ic,** *adj.*

germ (4) [jərm'], *n.* a plant or animal so tiny that it cannot be seen by the eye alone, especially such a plant or animal which produces disease. **Ex.** *The wound must be kept clean so that germs do not infect it.*

gerund (5) [jer'ənd], *n.* a verb form, ending in *ing*, that is used as a noun. **Exs.** *In the sentence, "Winning the race was important to him,"* winning *is a gerund. In the sentence, "He angered his friend by speaking rudely,"* speaking *is a gerund.*

gesture (3) [jes'čər], *n.* 1. a movement of the body, hands, face, etc. that expresses a feeling or thought. **Ex.** *She held out her hand in a gesture of welcome.* 2. something done only to be polite. **Ex.** *His offer of help was only a gesture.* —*v.* make gestures. **Ex.** *She gestured to attract our attention.*

get (1) [get'], *v.* 1. obtain; gain; acquire. **Ex.** *I expect to get some money soon.* 2. go and bring back. **Ex.** *Get some bread at the store.* 3. carry; take; remove. **Ex.** *We could not get the fallen tree out of the road.* 4. prepare; make ready. **Ex.** *I have to get dinner now.* 5. cause to happen. **Ex.** *When can you get this finished?* 6. persuade. **Ex.** *Can I get you to do something for me?* 7. be; become. **Ex.** *He gets sick very easily.* 8. arrive; reach. **Ex.** *When will we get to town?* —**get along,** 1. be friendly; work well with. **Ex.** *He gets along well with young people.* 2. progress; succeed. **Ex.** *How are you getting along in business?* 3. grow older. **Ex.** *He is getting along in years.* —**get by,** 1. pass. **Ex.** *The faulty work did not get by the inspector.* 2. just manage. **Ex.** *I'll get by, with your help.* —**get down to,** *start.* **Ex.** *After lunch, he will get down to work.* —**get in,** enter; receive; arrive. **Ex.** *When does the bus get in?* —**get off,** 1. come off; remove. **Ex.** *Get the dog off the rug while I clean it.* 2. leave. **Ex.** *I want to get off to the country early.* —**get over,** recover from. **Ex.** *He is getting over his illness.* —**get through,** finish. **Ex.** *Hurry and get through with your work so we can leave.* —**get up,** rise. **Ex.** *He didn't get up when she entered the room.*

ghastly (5) [gæst'liy], *adj.* 1. causing horror or terror. **Ex.** *The murder was a ghastly crime.* 2. ghostlike; without color. **Ex.** *After a sleepless night, she looked ghastly.* —**ghast'li·ness,** *n.*

ghost (3) [gowst'], *n.* 1. the soul of a dead person imagined as wandering about among living persons in the form of a pale shadow. **Ex.** *Ghosts are said to appear in this cemetery at night.* 2. a shadow or slight suggestion of something. **Ex.** *He does not have a ghost of a chance.* —**ghostly,** *adj.*

giant [jay'ənt], *n.* 1. an imaginary being in human form but of unusually large size and great power. **Ex.** *Our children like stories about giants.* 2. a person or thing of unusual importance, ability, etc. **Ex.** *He is one of the giants of the newspaper world.* —*adj.* very large. **Ex.** *The child dreamed of a giant cat.*

gift (1) [gift'], *n.* 1. a present; something that is given without cost to the receiver. **Ex.** *Her gift to him was a book.* 2. a special ability. **Ex.** *He has a gift for music.* —**gift'ed,** *adj.*

gigantic (4) [ĵay`gæn'tik], *adj.* very large; huge in size. **Ex.** *That football player is gigantic.*

giggle (5) [gig'əl], *v.* laugh in a light, silly way. **Ex.** *The young girls giggled among themselves.* —*n.* a light, silly laugh. **Ex.** *The teacher heard giggles in the back of the room.*

gin (5) [ĵin'], *n.* a strong alcoholic liquor, flavored with a special kind of berry and usually like water in color. **Ex.** *He likes drinks made with gin.*

gin (5) [ĵin'], *n.* a machine for separating cotton from its seeds. **Ex.** *The cotton gin was invented in 1793.*

ginger (4) [ĵin'ĵər], *n.* a sharply flavored plant root used for seasoning food and drinks and for medicinal purposes. **Ex.** *My favorite cake is one flavored with ginger.* —**gin'ger ale,** *n.* a nonalcoholic drink made of ginger-flavored soda water. **Ex.** *This ginger ale is very refreshing.*

gingerly [ĵin'ĵərliy], *adv.* very carefully; cautiously. **Ex.** *She opened the door gingerly because she didn't know what to expect.*

girdle (5) [gər'dəl], *n.* 1. a woman's lightweight undergarment which supports the abdomen. **Ex.** *The doctor told her to wear a girdle.* 2. any encircling band, especially a belt or cord worn about the waist. **Ex.** *In the play she wore a long black dress and a girdle with a silver clasp.* —*v.* encircle as with a belt. **Ex.** *The mountain peak was girdled with clouds.*

girl (1) [gərl'], *n.* a female child; a young unmarried woman. **Ex.** *The girls were playing with their dolls.*

give (1) [giv'], *v.* 1. hand to another to keep. **Ex.** *I want to give you this book.* 2. grant; state; make public. **Ex.** *Give me your opinion, please.* 3. perform; do. **Ex.** *Give the screw another turn.* 4. hand; pass to; lend. **Ex.** *Please give me your pencil.* 5. yield to pressure. **Ex.** *We pushed until the door began to give.* 6. be the cause or source of; produce. **Ex.** *The new system is giving good results.* 7. sacrifice; pay with. **Ex.** *He was willing to give his life for his friends.* —**give in,** stop opposing. **Ex.** *Will he give in to her and buy the car?* —**give off,** send out. **Ex.** *What is giving off that terrible smell?* —**give out,** make known; distribute. **Ex.** *The press secretary will give out the information.* —**give up,** 1. stop. **Ex.** *He is trying to* *give up smoking.* 2. hand over; surrender. **Ex.** *He is giving himself up to the police.*

given [giv'ən], *v.* past participle of *give.* **Ex.** *What has he given you?*

given name [giv'ən neym'], *n.* one's first name. **Ex.** *George Washington's given name was George.*

glad (1) [glæd'], *adj.* 1. pleased; happy. **Ex.** *We were glad to see her.* 2. showing or causing pleasure. **Ex.** *He brought us glad news.* 3. willing. **Ex.** *We will be glad to help.* —**glad'den,** *v.* —**glad'ly,** *adv.* —**glad'ness,** *n.*

glamour (5) [glæm'ər], *n.* strong attraction; charm; fascination. **Ex.** *The glamour of the life of an actress made other careers seem dull to her.* —**glam'or·ous,** *adj.*

glance (2) [glæns'], *v.* 1. look quickly or briefly. **Ex.** *She glanced in the mirror as she passed.* 2. strike and go off in a slanting direction. **Ex.** *The stone struck the car and glanced off.* —*n.* a quick or brief look. **Ex.** *She cast a glance in his direction.*

glare (3) [gle:r'], *n.* 1. a steady, brilliant light. **Ex.** *The glare of the sun was almost blinding.* 2. a staring, angry look. **Ex.** *Her glare silenced him.* 3. smooth, glassy surface. **Ex.** *The road was a glare of ice.* —*v.* 1. shine with a strong, almost blinding light. **Ex.** *The electric sign glared through my bedroom window at night.* 2. look at with anger in one's eyes. **Ex.** *The old woman glared at the noisy children.* —**glar'ing,** *adj.* 1. too bright. 2. obvious; very noticeable.

glass (1) [glæs'], *n.* 1. a hard, easily broken material through which one can see. **Ex.** *These windows are made of nonbreakable glass.* 2. something made of glass, such as a window pane or mirror. **Ex.** *She looked at herself in the glass.* 3. the quantity contained in a drinking glass. **Ex.** *He drank a glass of wine before dinner.* —**glass'es,** *n.* eyeglasses. —**glass'y,** *adj.* like glass; hard, clear and shiny.

glaze (5) [gleyz'], *v.* 1. cover with glass or with something which looks like glass. **Ex.** *The road was glazed with a thin coat of ice.* 2. produce a glassy surface on dishes, baked goods, etc. **Ex.** *The cook glazed the cake with sugar.* —*n.* a glassy surface. **Ex.** *The glaze on these dishes does not crack easily.*

gleam (3) [gliym'], *n.* 1. a slight or brief glow, ray or beam of light. **Ex.** *A gleam of light shone through the partly open* *door.* 2. a soft, shining light reflected from a polished surface. **Ex.** *The gleam of copper pans brightened the kitchen.* 3. a faint suggestion or hint. **Ex.** *There was a gleam of laughter in her eyes.* —*v.* send out a gleam. **Ex.** *A light gleamed in the distance.*

glide (3) [glayd'], *v.* move smoothly and easily along. **Ex.** *They glided across the ice.* —*n.* act of gliding. —**glid'er,** *n.* an airplane with no engines that glides on air.

glimpse (3) [glimps'], *n.* 1. a brief view; a quick look. **Ex.** *We had a glimpse of the lake as we flew over it.* 2. a faint idea; a suggestion. **Ex.** *We see glimpses of other writers' styles in his book.* —*v.* look at briefly; glance at; see only briefly. **Ex.** *We glimpsed a running figure.*

glisten (4) [glis'ən], *v.* shine with a sparkling light; glitter. **Ex.** *The snow glistened in the sunlight.*

glitter (3) [glit'ər], *v.* sparkle with a brilliant light. **Ex.** *The diamonds in her ring glittered.* —*n.* brilliant, sparkling light; splendor. **Ex.** *They prefer the quiet of their home to the glitter of society.*

globe (3) [glowb'], *n.* 1. the earth; the world. **Ex.** *They have traveled around the globe.* 2. a round ball with a map of the earth on it. **Ex.** *The teacher pointed out the continents on the globe.* 3. a round or ball-shaped object. **Ex.** *An electric globe hung from the ceiling.* —**glo'bal,** *adj.* 1. concerning the entire earth; worldwide. **Ex.** *The purpose of the conference was to promote global peace.* 2. complete; including much. **Ex.** *The doctor took a global approach in treating the patient's illness.*

gloom (4) [gluwm'], *n.* 1. darkness; dimness; deep shade. **Ex.** *They dreaded the gloom of approaching night.* 2. low spirits; sadness. **Ex.** *Gloom descended upon the family when they heard the news.* —**gloom'y,** *adj.*

glory (2) [glɔ:r'iy], *n.* 1. praise or honor given for doing something good, worthy, special, etc. **Ex.** *His acts of courage brought him glory.* 2. beauty; that which is splendid. **Ex.** *They stood silent before the glory of the sunset.* —**glor'i·fy,** *v.* —**glor'i·ous,** *adj.*

glossary (1) [glas'əriy, glɔ:s'əriy], *n.* a list of words and terms with an explanation of their meanings. **Ex.** *The author has provided a glossary at the end of the book.*

glove (2) [gləv'], *n.* a covering for the hand, with a separate place for each finger.

glow (2) [glow'], *n.* 1. light that comes from a heated substance. **Ex.** *The glow of the fire lighted the room.* 2. brightness of color. **Ex.** *There was a rosy glow in her cheeks.* 3. warm feeling; emotion. **Ex.** *There was a glow of happiness in his eyes.* —*v.* 1. give bright light because of heat. **Ex.** *The dying coals glowed.*

GLOVE

2. shine. **Ex.** *The headlights of the car glowed in the distance.* 3. show strong, bright color. **Ex.** *The children's faces glowed as they played in the snow.* 4. show emotion. **Ex.** *They glowed with excitement when they heard the news.*

glue (3) [gluw'], *n.* a thick substance used for sticking things together. **Ex.** *He used glue to repair the binding of the book.* —*v.* join or fasten with glue. **Ex.** *The carpenter glued the leg to the chair.*

gnaw (4) [nɔː'], *v.* 1. wear away or remove by biting little by little; chew. **Ex.** *The dog gnawed the bone.* 2. make by chewing. **Ex.** *The rat gnawed a hole in the door.*

go (1) [gow'], *v.* 1. move from one location to another. **Ex.** *We go this way to town.* 2. leave; depart from. **Ex.** *You should go now.* 3. move about, be or do in a certain way. **Ex.** *It is too cold to go without a coat.* 4. be or remain in a particular condition. **Ex.** *She let the children go hungry.* 5. move for some purpose. **Ex.** *She has to go and get dinner ready.* 6. do at a future time; intend to do. **Ex.** *He is going to come here tomorrow.* 7. reach; reach a certain state; become. **Ex.** *I will go mad if that noise doesn't stop.* 8. be in operation; run; work. **Ex.** *Can you make this clock go?* 9. fit; be suited to; belong. **Ex.** *Those colors go well together.* —**go on,** continue. **Ex.** *Why does he go on talking about his problems?* —**go by,** 1. pass. **Ex.** *We go by that house every morning.* 2. obey; follow. **Ex.** *I will go by the rules in doing the work.* —**go out,** 1. cease; end. **Ex.** *The fire will go out if you don't add more wood.* 2. attend a party, dinner, movie, etc. **Ex.** *Are you going out tonight?* —**go off,** 1. leave. **Ex.** *Don't go off without me.* 2. explode; fire. **Ex.** *Did you hear the gun go off?* —**go over,** look at closely. **Ex.** *Go over the work and see if it is correct.* —**go through,** experience; suffer. **Ex.** *I could not bear to go through anything like that again.* —**go without,** deprive oneself; sacrifice. **Ex.** *Their mother sometimes goes* *without food so that they can eat.* **—let oneself go,** express one's true self. **Ex.** *At the party he let himself go and broke into a wild dance.*

goal (4) [gowl'], *n.* 1. aim or end; that toward which effort is directed. **Ex.** *His goal in life is to be a children's doctor.* 2. the end of the journey or race. **Ex.** *The goal of our hike was the lake.* 3. the line or net a ball must reach or cross in certain games in order to score. **Ex.** *In football, one scores when one carries or kicks the ball past the goal.*

goat (3) [gowt'], *n.* a horned animal related to the sheep.

god (1) [gad'], *n.* a spirit that is worshiped for the special powers he is believed to have. **Ex.** *They prayed to God for help.* **—god-dess,** *n.* a female spirit that is worshiped

GOAT

for the special powers she is believed to have. **Ex.** *There is a statue of the goddess in this museum.*

goes (2) [gowz'], *v.* present tense of the verb *go* used with singular nouns and pronouns such as he, she and it. **Exs.** *He goes to work early. If she goes to the store, I will go with her.*

gold (1) [gowld'], *n.* 1. a precious yellow metal. **Ex.** *The rings were made of gold.* 2. coins made from gold; money. **Ex.** *He cares more for gold than for what it will buy.* 3. something compared to this metal in value, brightness, color, etc. **Ex.** *She has a heart of gold.* **—adj.** of or like gold. **Ex.** *He has a gold watch.* **—gold'en,** *adj.* 1. made of or having the color of gold; bright yellow. **Exs.** *The prize was a golden apple. The child had golden hair.* 2. very useful; very good. **Ex.** *This is a golden opportunity to travel.*

golf (5) [gɔːlf'], *n.* a game, played on a grassy field, in which a small ball is hit with special clubs into a series of holes. **Ex.** *Do you like golf better than swimming?* **—v.** play the game of golf. **Ex.** *He golfs every Wednesday afternoon.* **—golfer,** *n.* one who plays golf.

gone (1) [gɔːn'], *v.* past participle of *go.* **Ex.** *The train has gone.*

GOLFER

good (1) [gud'], *adj.* 1. better than average. **Ex.** *Her schoolwork is always good.* 2. suitable; qualified.

Ex. *He is a good man for this job.* 3. generous; friendly; kind. **Ex.** *His parents were very good to him.* 4. agreeable; pleasant. **Ex.** *We had a good time during our vacation.* 5. morally proper; well behaved. **Ex.** *She was always a good child.* 6. honorable; well regarded. **Ex.** *He has a good name in business.* 7. strong; sound. **Ex.** *You must have good eyes to be able to read such small print.* 8. considerable; fairly great in amount. **Ex.** *He has read a good many books.* —*n.* 1. that which is good. **Ex.** *He is not old enough to know good from bad.* 2. benefit; advantage. **Ex.** *She is doing it for your own good.* —*interj.* an expression of agreement or satisfaction. **Ex.** *Good! I am glad you can go.* —**good'ness,** *n.* —**as good as,** almost; equal to. **Ex.** *The work is as good as done.* —**for good,** forever. **Ex.** *He has gone for good.* —**good for,** will continue or last for. **Ex.** *Our supply of firewood is good for the rest of the winter.*

good-bye, good-by (1) [gud'bay'], *interj.* farewell, an expression used when parting. **Ex.** *Oh! Here's my bus. Good-bye.* —*n.* **Ex.** *I just have time to say good-bye.* —**good af'ter·noon', good morn'ing, good night,** *interj.* greetings or farewells proper for the times of day stated.

good-looking [gud'luk'iŋ], *adj.* pleasing in appearance; attractive. **Ex.** *What a good-looking brother you have!*

goods (2) [gudz'], *n.* 1. things one owns that can be moved. **Ex.** *Are these all of your household goods?* 2. things offered for sale. **Ex.** *The store had a wide selection of goods.* 3. cloth. **Ex.** *Do you sell cotton goods?*

good turn [gud' tərn'], a helpful act. **Ex.** *He did me a good turn by carrying that box.*

good will [gud' wil'], a friendly feeling. **Ex.** *By helping her with her work, we gained her good will.*

goose (2) [guws'], *n.* 1. a bird that can swim and is similar to a duck but is larger and has a longer neck. 2. the meat of this bird.

gorge (5) [gɔrj'], *n.* a narrow passageway through hills, with high walls of rock on each side. **Ex.** *The boat trip through the river gorge is difficult.* —*v.* eat too much food. **Ex.** *He gorged himself at dinner.*

GOOSE

gorgeous (4) [gɔr'jəs], *adj.* splendid in appearance or coloring. **Ex.** *She was wearing a gorgeous evening gown.* —**gor'geous·ly,** *adv.*

gorilla [gəril'ə], *n.* a strong, hairy animal belonging to the monkey family, with a large body, short legs and long arms but without a tail; a large ape. **Ex.** *At the zoo the children stared at the family of gorillas in their cage.*

gossip (4) [gas'əp], *n.* 1. useless and sometimes harmful talk, which may not be true, about other people. **Ex.** *Her letter was filled with gossip about her neighbors' troubles.* 2. a person who gossips. **Ex.** *I avoided her because she was such a gossip.* —*v.* talk in a useless and sometimes harmful way about others. **Ex.** *He was gossiping about his boss.*

got (1) [gat'], *v.* past tense and participle of *get.* **Exs.** *He got some water from the well. What have you got in that bag?* —**got'ten,** *v.* past participle of *get.* **Ex.** *Have you gotten a letter from her?*

govern (1) [gəv'ərn], *v.* 1. rule by authority. **Ex.** *The President, together with Congress, governs our country.* 2. be guided by; influence. **Ex.** *He was governed by his father's ideas.* —**gov'ern·or,** *n.* one who governs, usually a state. **Ex.** *The governor proposed a new sales tax.*

government [gəv'ərnmənt], *n.* 1. the people and organization in power; the rulers. **Ex.** *The government has just increased taxes.* 2. the form of government. **Ex.** *Our country has a democratic form of government.*

gown (3) [gawn'], *n.* 1. a woman's dress or robe. **Ex.** *She bought an evening gown for the party.* 2. a long, loose outer garment worn at official events. **Ex.** *The students, wearing caps and gowns, received their university degrees.*

GOWN

grab (4) [græb'], *v.* take hold of suddenly; seize. **Ex.** *She grabbed the stair rail when she slipped.* —*n.* the act of taking hold of suddenly. **Ex.** *The thief made a grab for the woman's purse.*

grace (3) [greys'], *n.* 1. beauty of form or motion. **Ex.** *She danced with grace.* 2. charm; a pleasing manner. **Ex.** *His speech was full of grace and wit.* —**grace'ful,** *adj.* —**gra'cious,** *adj.* charming. —**in the good graces of,** liked by; favored. **Ex.** *What can I do to stay in her good graces?*

grade (2) [greyd'], *n.* 1. a step or degree in an order or series based on quality, progress, etc. **Ex.** *That store sells only the best grade of meat.* 2. a division of a school arranged according to the progress of the students, usually one year long. **Ex.**

He is in the eleventh grade. 3. score showing the quality of work done, as on a test at school. **Ex.** *All her grades were high.* 4. the slope or slant of a road. **Ex.** *That road has a steep grade.* —*v.* 1. arrange in grades. **Ex.** *The farmer graded the eggs from the largest to smallest.* 2. give a score to. **Ex.** *The teacher graded the test papers.*

grade school [greyd' skuwl'], school of the first six or eight years of study.

gradual (2) [græj'uwəl], *adj.* happening or changing by small degrees. **Ex.** *The doctor noticed a gradual improvement in his patient.* —**grad'u·al·ly**, *adv.*

graduate (3) [græj'uwət], *n.* one who has completed a course of study. **Ex.** *He is a university graduate.* —*adj.* having been graduated; of or for a graduate. **Ex.** *He is working for a graduate degree.* —*v.* 1. give or receive a degree upon completion of a course of study. **Ex.** *He graduated from college last year.* 2. divide into degrees or a series. **Ex.** *The rate of the income tax is graduated according to the amount of income.* —**grad'u·a'tion**, *n.*

graft (5) [græft'], *n.* the part of a plant or tree put into a cut in another plant or tree to grow there; the portion of living skin, bone, etc. removed from one part of a person's body and put into another part or into another person's body. **Ex.** *The badly burned boy was given a skin graft.* —*v.* put a graft on a plant or a part of the body. **Ex.** *The doctor grafted new skin onto the girl's leg.*

graft (5) [græft'], *n.* the dishonest use of one's position to get money; money obtained in this way. **Ex.** *The mayor went to prison because he was guilty of graft.*

grain (1) [greyn'], *n.* 1. the seed of certain plants, such as wheat and corn, that may be eaten; the plants themselves. **Ex.** *The farmers are harvesting the grain.* 2. a very small piece. **Ex.** *A few grains of sugar fell on the floor.* 3. a very small amount. **Ex.** *There is not a grain of truth in what he says.* 4. a pattern of natural markings such as those in wood, marble, leather, etc. **Ex.** *This piece of wood has a beautiful grain.*

gram (5) [græm'], *n.* a unit of weight in the metric system. See **Weights and Measures.**

grammar (3) [græm'ər], *n.* 1. a study of words, their form and their use in sentences; the rules for using a language. **Ex.** *He is studying English grammar.* 2. a book describing rules of language. **Ex.** *This grammar is easy to understand.* 3. speaking or writing considered in relation to rules of language. **Ex.** *She uses poor grammar.* —**gram·mat'i·cal**, *adj.* concerning or in agreement with rules of grammar. —**gram·mat'i·cal·ly**, *adv.* **Ex.** *He always speaks grammatically correct English.*

grand (2) [grænd'], *adj.* 1. large; expensive; splendid. **Ex.** *They live in a grand house.* 2. having great dignity; fine; noble. **Ex.** *He was a grand old man.* 3. most important; main; principal. **Ex.** *They had dinner in the grand dining room of the hotel.* —**grand'ly**, *adv.* —**grand'ness**, *n.*

grandchild [græn(d)'čayld'], *n.* one's grandson or granddaughter.

granddaughter [græn(d)'dɔ:t'ər], *n.* daughter of one's son or daughter.

grandfather [græn(d)'fa`ðər], *n.* father of one's father or mother.

grandmother [græn(d)'məðər], *n.* mother of one's father or mother.

grandparent [græn(d)'pe:r'ənt], *n.* one's grandmother or grandfather.

grandson [græn(d)'son'], *n.* son of one's son or daughter.

granite (4) [græn'ət], *n.* a very hard rock containing various minerals which give it different colors such as gray, pink, red and green. **Ex.** *That building is faced with polished granite.*

grant (2) [grænt'], *v.* 1. give that which is requested; agree to. **Ex.** *He granted their request to hold a meeting.* 2. agree as to truth. **Ex.** *I grant that he was there.* —*n.* the act of giving; that which is given; a gift. **Ex.** *The university received a large grant of money from a former student.* —**take for granted,** 1. regard as true; expect confidently. **Ex.** *He took it for granted that I knew the answer.* 2. undervalue. **Ex.** *They took their brother's help for granted.*

grape (2) [greyp'], *n.* a juicy, smooth-skinned, small fruit that grows in bunches; the vine that bears this fruit. **Ex.** *He made wine from the grapes.*

grapefruit [greyp'fruwt], *n.* a round, juicy, yellow-skinned fruit, larger than an orange, that grows on a tree and tastes slightly sour. **Ex.** *I think a half grapefruit is a refreshing start to breakfast.*

GRAPES

graph [266] **gravitate**

graph [græf'], *n.* a drawing or diagram that shows the numerical relationships of particular facts. **Ex.** *This graph compares the consumption of electricity in the city this year to that of last year.*

GRAPH

grasp (2) [græsp'], *v.* 1. seize and hold with the fingers, hand, etc.; try to seize. **Ex.** *The drowning man grasped at the rope.* 2. understand. **Ex.** *The child heard the words but did not grasp their meaning.* —*n.* 1. a firm, strong hold. **Ex.** *His grasp hurt my arm.* 2. understanding. **Ex.** *That teacher has a good grasp of his subject.*

grass (2) [græs'], *n.* a plant with long, narrow, green, bladelike leaves. **Ex.** *The cattle were eating the grass in the field.*

grasshopper (5) [græs'hap`ər], *n.* a winged insect that can hop or leap a long distance.

grateful (2) [greyt'fəl], *adj.* thankful; appreciative. **Ex.** *We are grateful for your help.* —**grate'ful·ly,** *adv.*

GRASSHOPPER

gratify (4) [græt'əfay`], *v.* give pleasure to; satisfy. **Ex.** *The large audience gratified the speaker.*

gratitude (5) [græt'ətuwd`, græt'ətyuwd`], *n.* the feeling of being grateful for a gift, help or kindness. **Ex.** *They showed their gratitude by sending her flowers.*

grave (1) [greyv'], *adj.* 1. thoughtful; dignified. **Ex.** *He had a grave look on his face.* 2. serious, important. **Ex.** *We have some grave matters to discuss.* 3. dangerous. **Ex.** *The condition of the patient was grave.* —**grave'ly,** *adv.*

grave (1) [greyv'], *n.* a place where a dead person is buried. **Ex.** *We put flowers on her grave.*

gravel (4) [græv'əl], *n.* small stones, often mixed with coarse sand. **Ex.** *The path to the house was covered with gravel.*

gravity (4) [græv'ətiy], *n.* 1. the force that pulls things toward the center of the earth and prevents objects on the earth from being thrown into space. **Ex.** *The spaceship needed tremendous power to escape the force of gravity.* 2. seriousness; importance; state of being grave. **Ex.** *The hush in the room indicated the gravity of the situation.* —**grav'i·tate`,** *v.* move or be attracted to or toward. **Ex.** *We gravitated toward the speaker.*

gravy (5) [grey'viy], *n.* a sauce made by mixing flour with the juices that come from cooking meat. **Ex.** *The boy liked gravy on his potatoes.*

gray (1) [grey'], *adj.* 1. of a color made by mixing black and white. **Ex.** *She wore a gray dress.* 2. cheerless; dull. **Ex.** *It is a gray day.* —*n.* a color made by mixing black and white. **Ex.** *When I wear gray, I usually add a touch of brightness with a red scarf or a green pin.*

graze (4) [greyz'], *v.* feed on grass and other growing plants. **Ex.** *The cows are grazing in the field.*

graze (4) [greyz'], *v.* touch or scratch in passing. **Ex.** *The pitcher threw a wild ball that grazed the batter's arm.*

grease (4) [griys'], *n.* 1. the melted fat of animals. **Ex.** *She spilled grease on the stove while cooking.* 2. any fatty, oily matter. **Ex.** *His clothes were stained with grease from the car.* —*v.* put grease on; oil. **Ex.** *Grease the pan well before frying the eggs in it.* —**greas'y,** *adj.*

great (1) [greyt'], *adj.* 1. very large or more than usual in size, number, etc. **Ex.** *More than eight million people live in this great city.* 2. important; famous; remarkable. **Ex.** *Our country's first President was a great man.* 3. extreme; much more than the usual. **Ex.** *He is a great friend of mine.* 4. older or younger by a generation, used with a (-) mark. **Ex.** *My great-grandfather is the father of my grandfather.* —**great'ness,** *n.* —**great'ly,** *adv.*

greed (2) [griyd'], *n.* a great desire to take and have things for oneself without thinking of others. **Ex.** *Although he had many toys, his greed made him want more.* —**greed'y,** *adj.* —**greed'i·ly,** *adv.*

green (1) [griyn'], *adj.* 1. of a color made by mixing blue and yellow; of the color of growing leaves and grass. **Ex.** *She bought a green hat.* 2. not ripe; not ready to be eaten. **Ex.** *Eating green apples made the little boy sick.* 3. not experienced; untrained. **Ex.** *The new workmen were too green to do a good job.* —*n.* the color green. —**greens,** *n. pl.* green leafy vegetables.

greenhouse [griyn'haws'], *n.* a building made mostly of glass in which flowers and plants are grown.

greet (2) [griyt'], *v.* 1. speak to upon meeting; welcome. **Ex.** *She opened the door and greeted me by saying "hello."* 2. receive in a special way. **Ex.** *The angry man greeted him with insults.* —**greet'ing,** *n.* the act or words of someone who greets.

grew (1) [gruw'], *v.* past tense of grow. **Ex.** *I grew accustomed to their being here.*

grief (2) [griyf'], *n.* great sorrow or sadness, such as one feels when a loved one dies. **Ex.** *It was difficult for him to express his grief.*

grieve (3) [griyv'], *v.* feel or cause to feel grief. **Ex.** *He grieved over the death of his son.* —**griev'ance,** *n.* a wrong about which one feels troubled or angry. **Ex.** *Long hours of work without extra pay was their grievance.* —**griev'ous,** *adj.* 1. causing great sadness. 2. very serious; harmful. —**griev'ous·ly,** *adv.*

grill [gril'], *n.* an open metal frame used to cook meat, fish, vegetables, etc. over an open fire. **Ex.** *As soon as the fire is hot enough, you can put the hamburgers on the grill.* —*v.* cook on a grill. **Ex.** *We are going to grill chicken, corn and potatoes in the backyard tonight.*

grim (4) [grim'], *adj.* 1. severe; stern; not yielding. **Ex.** *The judge had a grim look on his face.* 2. shocking; frightful; cruel. **Ex.** *The dead men were a grim sight.* —**grim'ly,** *adv.* —**grim'ness,** *n.*

grin (4) [grin'], *v.* smile broadly by drawing back the lips to show the teeth. **Ex.** *The boy grinned when he saw the dog.* —*n.* a big smile. **Ex.** *The girl's broad grin showed her delight.*

grind (4) [graynd'], *v.* 1. reduce to small, fine pieces by crushing. **Ex.** *We buy coffee beans and grind them ourselves.* 2. sharpen; make smooth; shape by rubbing. **Ex.** *The old man had made his living by grinding scissors and knives.* 3. press or rub two things against each other. **Ex.** *He grinds his teeth in his sleep.* —**grind'er,** *n.*

grindstone [grayn(d)'stown'], *n.* a round, flat stone used for sharpening various things such as axes, chisels, knives, etc.

grip (3) [grip'], *n.* 1. a firm hold, as with the hands. **Ex.** *He had a grip on my shoulder.* 2. a small suitcase. **Ex.** *He packed his grip for the journey.* —*v.* seize firmly. **Ex.** *He gripped the boy by the arm.*

groan (3) [grown'], *n.* a low, sad sound of pain or grief. **Ex.** *We could hear the groans of the injured man.* —*v.* make such a sound. **Ex.** *The sick woman groaned.*

grocery (3) [grows'(ə)riy], *n.* a store where food and other supplies for home use are sold. **Ex.** *We bought sugar and flour at the grocery.* —**gro'cer·ies,** *n.* the items sold at a grocery. **Ex.** *I bought enough groceries for the week.* —**gro'cer,** *n.* the owner, manager or clerk at a grocery.

groom (4) [gruwm'], *n.* 1. person who tends horses. **Ex.** *The groom was brushing the horse.* 2. a man newly married or about to be married. **Ex.** *The bride and groom cut the wedding cake together.* —*v.* 1. make clean and neat. **Ex.** *The boy groomed himself carefully.* 2. prepare or get someone ready. **Ex.** *He was groomed to run for mayor.*

groove (5) [gruwv'], *n.* a long, thin depression or cut in a surface. **Ex.** *He cut a groove in the wood with a chisel.*

grope (5) [growp'], *v.* feel about with the hands, as in the dark; search for blindly. **Ex.** *He groped for the light switch.*

gross (4) [grows'], *n.* twelve dozen; 144. **Ex.** *He ordered a gross of pencils.* —*adj.* 1. very noticeable; extreme. **Ex.** *The accident was caused by gross negligence.* 2. improper; indelicate; coarse. **Ex.** *A gentleman does not use gross language.*

ground (1) [grawnd'], *n.* land; the earth's surface; soil. **Ex.** *They planted the seeds in the ground.* —*adj.* on, at or near the surface of the earth. **Ex.** *He lives on the ground floor of the building.* —*v.* 1. place, put or keep on the ground. **Ex.** *The airplane was grounded by bad weather.* 2. fix firmly; establish. **Ex.** *His defense was grounded on shaky evidence.* 3. run onto the ground. **Ex.** *The boat is grounded on the sand and won't be able to move until high tide.* —**grounds,** *n. pl.* 1. the area around a building or buildings; land for a special use. **Ex.** *They have a gardener to take care of the grounds.* 2. reason; foundation; proof. **Ex.** *What grounds do they have for such a conclusion?* 3. the very small pieces of coffee that remain in the pot after the coffee has been poured. **Ex.** *We put our used coffee grounds in the flower bed.* —**cover ground,** travel a considerable distance; make progress. **Ex.** *He had only fifteen minutes but covered a lot of ground in his speech.* —**gain or lose ground,** move forward or fall back. —**ground'less,** *adj.* without cause or basis in fact. **Ex.** *The rumor proved to be groundless.*

ground (4) [grawnd'], *v.* past tense and participle of **grind**. **Exs.** *The butcher ground the meat. Have you ground the coffee yet?*

groundwork [grawnd'wərk'], *n.* foundation; basis. **Ex.** *His experience as a journalist was excellent groundwork for his job as press secretary for the President.*

---

a, far; æ, am; e, get; ey, late; i, in; iy, see; ɔ, all; ow, go; u, put; uw, too; ə, but, ago; ər, fur; aw, out; ay, life; oy, boy; ŋ, ring; θ, think; ð, that; ž, measure; š, ship; j, edge; č, child.

group (1) [gruwp'], *n.* 1. a gathering of persons or things taken as a unit; a collection. **Ex.** *There were ten people in the group.* 2. a number of similar persons or things placed or considered together. **Ex.** *That is an interesting group of paintings.* —*v.* place together in a group. **Ex.** *The children grouped themselves around their parents.*

grove (3) [growv'], *n.* a small woods or group of trees. **Ex.** *There are one hundred orange trees in that grove.*

grow (1) [grow'], *v.* 1. become larger in size, number, etc. **Ex.** *The boy is growing rapidly.* 2. develop; become older. **Ex.** *That plant needs water to grow.* 3. gradually become. **Ex.** *The children are growing tired.* 4. cultivate; raise. **Ex.** *The farmer grows potatoes in this field.* —**growth'**, *n.* act of growing; an increase. —**grow on,** become more likable. **Ex.** *The boy's charm grows on you.* —**grow up,** become an adult.

growl (4) [grawl'], *v.* 1. make a deep threatening sound in the throat. **Ex.** *The dog growled at the stranger.* 2. talk in low and angry tones. **Ex.** *The impatient man growled an answer to the question.* —*n.* the act of growling. **Ex.** *The growls of the dog frightened the children.*

grown (1) [grown'], *v.* past participle of *grow.* **Ex.** *The boy has grown rapidly.* —*adj.* having reached one's full growth. **Ex.** *He does not look like a grown man.*

grown-up [grown'əp'], *n.* an adult. **Ex.** *The grown-ups watched the children play.* —*adj.* of or for adults. **Ex.** *He acts grown-up.*

grudge (4) [grəǰ'], *n.* a feeling of resentment toward someone because of a past wrong. **Ex.** *He had a grudge against his noisy neighbor.* —*v.* give or allow unhappily. **Ex.** *He grudged his landlord the rent.* —**grudg'ing,** *adj.* —**grudg'ing·ly,** *adv.*

grumble (4) [grəm'bəl], *v.* 1. complain in a low unpleasant manner or voice. **Ex.** *He is always grumbling about his boss.* 2. make low, unpleasant sounds. **Ex.** *His stomach grumbled with hunger.* —**grum'bler,** *n.* a person who grumbles.

grunt (4) [grənt'], *v.* 1. make a deep noise, as the sound of a pig. **Ex.** *The pigs were grunting as they ate.* 2. express with a grunt. **Ex.** *The sullen man grunted a reply.* —*n.* the sound of a pig; a sound like this.

guarantee (4) [gær'əntiy'], *n.* a promise that something will satisfy in a certain way. **Ex.** *This guarantee lets me return the television set within ten days if its reception is not good.* —*v.* promise satisfaction, according to terms agreed upon. **Ex.** *The merchant guaranteed that the color of the material would not fade.*

guard (1) [gard'], *v.* 1. watch a person, place or thing to make sure no one harms, steals, etc.; protect. **Ex.** *The dog guards our house well.* 2. act so as to prevent, control, etc. **Ex.** *They tried to guard against illness.* —*n.* 1. the act of guarding. **Ex.** *He was on guard all night.* 2. a person, group or thing that guards or protects. **Ex.** *There is an armed guard at the gate of the military camp.* —**guard'ian,** *n.* —**on guard,** careful; alert. **Ex.** *He was told to be on guard against strangers.*

guerrilla [gəril'ə], *n.* a member of a group of soldiers who attack superior forces unexpectedly in small numbers. **Ex.** *The government troops surprised a band of guerrillas near the edge of town.* —*adj.* of or like guerrillas and their methods of fighting. **Ex.** *This unit of soldiers has just completed a course in guerrilla warfare.*

guess (1) [ges'], *v.* 1. form an opinion without many facts. **Ex.** *He guessed that it would rain.* 2. form an opinion that is correct but which was arrived at by chance. **Ex.** *You guessed my age correctly.* 3. think; believe. **Ex.** *I guess you will want to rest after your long trip.* —*n.* an opinion formed by guessing.

guest (2) [gest'], *n.* 1. a person invited to go somewhere or do something at the expense of the inviter. **Ex.** *We are having guests at our house for dinner tonight.* 2. a person who pays for food at an eating place or for a room at a hotel. **Ex.** *How long was he a guest at the hotel?*

guide (1) [gayd'], *v.* 1. lead; direct; show the way. **Ex.** *He guided them around the city.* 2. direct the opinions or acts of; influence. **Ex.** *Let his words guide you.* —*n.* 1. one who shows the way. **Ex.** *A guide led us through the mountains.* 2. that which guides or directs. **Ex.** *That book was a helpful guide to the sights of the city.*

guild (5) [gild'], *n.* a group organized for some special purpose. **Ex.** *The ladies' guild raised money for the hospital.*

guilt (2) [gilt'], *n.* the fact or feeling of having done something wrong, bad, or not legal. **Ex.** *His guilt was proven by his fingerprints.* —**guilt'y,** *adj.* 1. having committed a wrong. **Ex.** *He was guilty of breaking the window.* 2. judged in court to have committed a crime. **Ex.** *The jury decided that the man was guilty of stealing.* 3. showing or caused by a feeling that one has done wrong. **Ex.** *He had a guilty look on his face.* —**guilt'i·ly,** *adv.*

guitar [gitar'], *n.* a musical instrument, with a long neck and a body shaped like but larger than a violin, having six or more strings which are plucked with the fingers. **Ex.** *The sound of the guitar brought back memories of her travels.*

GUITAR

gulf (2) [gəlf'], *n.* 1. a large part of an ocean or sea extending into the land. **Ex.** *Fishing boats were out in the gulf.* 2. a wide separation, as of wealth, education, etc. **Ex.** *There is a great gulf between the very rich and the very poor.*

gulp (5) [gəlp'], *v.* 1. swallow eagerly or hurriedly. **Ex.** *The thirsty man gulped the cold water.* 2. hold back with a swallowing motion. **Ex.** *She tried to gulp back her tears.* —*n.* the amount swallowed at one time. **Ex.** *The dog ate the meat in one gulp.*

gum (3) [gəm'], *n.* 1. a gluelike substance or liquid that comes from some plants and trees. **Ex.** *The gum from rubber trees has many uses.* 2. a flavored and sweetened substance suitable for long chewing. **Ex.** *The boy asked for a piece of chewing gum.* —*v.* cover something with gum or glue in order to make it stick to something; stick together with gum or glue. **Ex.** *He gummed the labels on the packages.* —**gummy,** *adj.* sticky; like gum.

gum (3) [gəm'], *n.* the fleshy part of the mouth that covers the roots of the teeth. **Ex.** *My gum hurt after the tooth was pulled out.*

gun (1) [gən'], *n.* 1. a large metal tube from which a ball of lead or similar object is shot by an explosion of gunpowder; a cannon; a shotgun, rifle or pistol. **Ex.** *The guns destroyed the enemy's buildings across the river.* 2. any device that sprays liquid in a fine mist. **Ex.** *They used a spray gun to kill the insects.* —*v.* hunt or shoot with a gun. **Ex.** *They gunned down the man-eating lion.* —**gun'ner,** *n.* one who fires or shoots a gun.

gush (5) [gəš'], *v.* 1. flow or pour suddenly and in great amounts. **Ex.** *Blood gushed from the wound.* 2. express too much emotion in a rush of words so that what one says seems a little foolish and sometimes false. **Ex.** *She gushed to her hostess about how delicious the meal had been.* —**gush'ing,** *adj.*

gust (5) [gəst'], *n.* a brief, sudden rush of air, wind, smoke, etc. **Ex.** *A gust of wind blew off his hat.* —**gust'y,** *adj.*

gutter (5) [gət'ər], *n.* 1. a narrow ditch or depression along the side of a street which drains the water from the street. **Ex.** *The gutters filled with water during the heavy rain.* 2. narrow metal or tile channels fastened to the lower edges of a roof for guiding off water. **Ex.** *The leaves in the gutter caused the roof to leak.*

gym (5) [jĭm'], **gymnasium** [jĭm`ney'ziyəm], *n.* 1. a room or building equipped with special apparatus for body building exercises and sports. **Exs.** *She goes to her office an hour early so that she can work out at the gym. On rainy days the students play games in the gymnasium.* 2. a school course, usually required, in which students learn how to exercise and take part in various sports; physical education. **Ex.** *He is changing into his sports clothes for gym.*

H

H, h [eyč'], *n.* the eighth letter of the English alphabet.

habit (2) [hæb'ĭt], *n.* 1. an act repeated so often that it is difficult to change or stop. **Ex.** *Smoking was a habit that was difficult for him to break.* 2. custom; a regular practice. **Ex.** *He has a habit of rising early.* —**ha·bit'u·al,** *adj.* —**ha·bit'u·al·ly,** *adv.*

habitation (5) [hæb`itey'šen], *n.* 1. the act of inhabiting or occupying a dwelling place. **Ex.** *That old house is not fit for habitation.* 2. a place where people live; a dwelling. **Ex.** *He walked for miles and saw no signs of habitation.* —**hab'it·a·ble,** *adj.* able to be lived in.

had (2) [hæd'], *v.* past tense and participle of *has.* **Exs.** *He had no money. We have had no word from her.*

hadn't [hæd'ənt], short form, contraction of *had not.* **Ex.** *He hadn't answered my letter, so I called him long distance.*

haggard [hæg'ərd], *adj.* having a thin, worn, exhausted look in the face as from suffering or anxiety. **Ex.** *He looked haggard after a sleepless night.*

hail (3) [heyl'], *v.* greet with a shout; praise. **Ex.** *The king was hailed by his people.*

hail (3) [heyl'], *n*. small pieces of ice that fall during a storm. **Ex.** *For a short time the ground was covered with hail* —*v.* fall as hail. **Ex.** *Suddenly bullets began to hail all around us.* —**hail'stone`**, *n*. a small hard ball of hail.

hair (1) [he:r'], *n*. fine, threadlike growths form-ing the fur of animals or growing from the skin of human beings, especially from the head; also one of these threadlike growths. **Ex.** *Her hair is long and thick* —**hair'y**, *adj*. having a lot of hair on the body. **Ex.** *He has a hairy chest.*

HAIR

half (1) [hæf'], *n*. one of the parts of anything divided equally in two. **Ex.** *The two brothers each received half of the money.* —*adj.* forming one of two equal parts. **Ex.** *He owns a half share of this land.* —*adv.* partly. **Ex.** *This meat is only half cooked.*

hall (1) [hɔ:l'], *n*. 1. a passage at the doorway of a building or between rooms in a building. **Ex.** *The kitchen is at the end of this hall.* 2. a large room or building for public meetings. **Ex.** *The lecture was held in the town hall.*

halt (3) [hɔ:lt'], *v*. come or cause to come to a stop for a short time. **Ex.** *The marching soldiers halted.* —*n.* a stop; a pause. **Ex.** *They came to a halt at the corner and looked both ways.*

halve [hæv'], *v*. 1. divide into two equal parts. **Ex.** *She halved the apple and gave one piece to her brother.* 2. reduce by half. **Ex.** *We halved our expenses by using this machine.* —**halves**, *n. pl.* plural of *half*.

ham (4) [hæm'], *n*. one of the rear legs of a pig, either fresh or salted and smoked, eaten as meat. **Ex.** *They had ham and eggs for breakfast.*

hamburger [hæm'bərgər], *n*. ground beef; a round, flat cake made of ground beef, often served in a roll. **Ex.** *How many hamburgers do you think you can eat?*

hammer (3) [hæm'ər], *n*. a tool with a head set on a handle and used for pounding nails. —*v.* pound with a hammer. **Ex.** *He hammered a nail into the piece of wood.* 2. beat on something. **Ex.** *She hammered on the door until someone heard her.* —**hammer away**, work to complete. **Ex.** *He hammered away at the problem.*

HAMMER

hamper (5) [hæm'pər], v. hold back; make difficult; get in the way of. **Ex.** *Heavy clothing hampered the movements of the climbers.* —n. a basket, usually with a cover. **Ex.** *They took a hamper of food with them on their journey.*

hand (1) [hænd'], n. 1. a part of the body at the end of the arm including the fingers and thumb. 2. something similar to a hand in shape or use. **Ex.** *The hands of the clock pointed to twelve.* 3. control; care. **Ex.** *The child is in the hands of her aunt.* —v. give by hand; pass. **Ex.** *The nurse handed the doctor the instruments.* —**at hand,** near. **Ex.** *She was at hand when he needed her.* —**by hand,** with the hands rather than by a machine. **Ex.** *She sewed the seams by hand.* —**change hands,** change ownership. **Ex.** *That building has changed hands several times in the last two years.* —**from hand to mouth,** without anything such as food or money to spare. **Ex.** *During the depression many people lived from hand to mouth.* —**hand down,** 1. pass along as from older to younger. **Ex.** *My trousers were usually handed down to me from my older brother.* 2. give a legal decision. **Ex.** *The judge handed down his ruling last Monday.* —**hand in glove,** together; closely. **Ex.** *The banker and the builder were working hand in glove to get around the housing laws.* —**hand in hand,** holding hands. **Ex.** *The boys and girls were walking hand in hand down the street.* —**hand to hand,** in fighting, one against one; at close quarters. **Ex.** *They fought street by street and hand to hand.* —**in hand,** under control. **Ex.** *The firemen have the fire in hand.* —**on hand,** ready for use. **Ex.** *They always keep extra food on hand for unexpected guests.* —**upper hand,** position of advantage. **Ex.** *They have the upper hand in this election.*

HAND 1

handbag [hænd'bæg'], n. a purse; a small suitcase. **Ex.** *She took some money from her handbag.*

handbook [hænd'buk'], n. a small book of instructions. **Ex.** *The handbook explained how to set the clock radio.*

handgun [hænd'gən'], n. a small gun that can be fired using one hand; a pistol. **Ex.** *He was killed by a shot from a handgun.*

handicap (4) [hænd'ikæp'], n. anything that is a disadvantage or makes success difficult. **Ex.** *Lack of a high school education was a handicap for her in getting a job.* —v. make things more difficult for. **Ex.** *His illness handicaps him in his work.*

handily [hænd'əliy], *adv.* easily. **Ex.** *He won the race handily.*

handiness [hænd'inəs], *n.* skill in using the hands. **Ex.** *Her handiness in sewing was useful to us.*

handkerchief (2) [hæŋ'kərčif], *n.* a square piece of cloth carried on the person for wiping the nose. **Ex.** *Do you have a clean handkerchief?*

handle (2) [hæn'dəl], *n.* that part of an object by which it is held in the hand. **Ex.** *The handle of the pot is hot.* —*v.* 1. touch or feel with the hand. **Ex.** *Handle this delicate silk carefully.* 2. control; manage. **Ex.** *She knows how to handle children.*

handsome (2) [hæn'səm], *adj.* 1. of fine or admirable appearance; good-looking. **Exs.** *He is a handsome boy. That is a handsome piece of furniture.* 2. large; generous. **Ex.** *He left a handsome fortune.* —**hand'some·ly,** *adv.* generously; in a proper manner. **Ex.** *They were handsomely rewarded for their efforts.*

handwriting (3) [hænd'rayt`iŋ], *n.* 1. writing done by hand rather than typed or printed. **Ex.** *Printing is easier for me to read than handwriting.* 2. the way a person writes. **Ex.** *His handwriting is improving.*

handy [hæn'diy], *adj.* 1. easily reached; not far away. **Ex.** *This store is handy to our house.* 2. helpful; easy to use. **Ex.** *This can opener is very handy.*

hang [hæŋ'], *v.* 1. fasten to a nail, hook, rope, etc. and let fall loosely. **Ex.** *Hang your coat in the closet.* 2. put or be put to death by swinging from a rope around the neck. **Ex.** *The criminal was hanged in the prison yard.* —**hang'er,** *n.* a shaped support of wire, wood, etc. for hanging a piece of clothing. —**hang back,** be reluctant to go forward. **Ex.** *The others are eager to go, but she is hanging back for some reason.* —**hang on,** continue to hold. **Ex.** *Hang on to this rope, and I will pull you up with it.* —**hang out,** extend out; lean out. **Ex.** *The boy was hanging out of the window.* —**hang up.** 1. put on a hanger. **Ex.** *Hang up your clothes before you go out to play.* 2. end a telephone conversation. **Ex.** *Why did she hang up so suddenly?*

hangar [hæŋ'ər], *n.* a large shed or building in which planes are kept. **Ex.** *The plane taxied out from the hangar.*

happen [hæp'ən], *v.* 1. occur; take place. **Ex.** *They told us everything that had happened on their trip.* 2. occur by chance rather than by plan. **Ex.** *They happened to meet on the street.* —**hap'pen·ing,** *n.*

happy [hæp'iy], *adj.* 1. pleased; contented; joyful. **Ex.** *We are happy to see you.* 2. fortunate; lucky. **Ex.** *He made a happy decision when he went into business.* —**hap'pi·ly,** *adv.* —**hap'pi·ness,** *n.*

harass [hərǽs'], *v.* repeatedly bother, annoy, torment, or cause to worry. **Ex.** *The clerk was harassed by impatient customers.* —**har'ass·ment,** *n.* the act of harassing. **Ex.** *She brought charges of harassment against her employer.*

harbor (2) [har'bər], *n.* a place where ships may safely anchor; a port. **Ex.** *The ship docked in the harbor.* —*v.* give shelter to. **Ex.** *Unknowingly they were harboring a thief.*

hard (1) [hard'], *adj.* 1. firm and solid; not soft. **Ex.** *The bread was too hard to eat.* 2. difficult. **Ex.** *This is a hard problem to solve.* 3. working steadily and with energy. **Ex.** *He is a hard worker.* 4. severe; stern. **Ex.** *She has a hard face.* —*adv.* with great energy or force. **Ex.** *He is studying hard.* —**hard and fast,** not changeable. **Ex.** *These are hard and fast rules, and you will have to obey them.* —**hard of hearing,** not able to hear well.

hard-boiled [hard'boyld'], *adj.* 1. of an egg that is boiled until it has become hard. **Ex.** *There is a hard-boiled egg in your lunch box.* 2. apparently unfeeling; unsympathetic. **Ex.** *Our English professor is also the author of hard-boiled detective stories.*

hardly (2) [hard'liy], *adv.* 1. almost none. **Ex.** *There was hardly any food in the house.* 2. possible but not likely. **Ex.** *They would hardly start on a trip in this rain.*

hardship (3) [hard'šip'], *n.* anything that causes difficulty, suffering or pain. **Ex.** *Bathing in salt water was a hardship for the new sailors.*

hardware [hard'we:r'], *n.* objects made of metal, such as nails, tools, etc. **Ex.** *He bought a hammer, hinges and other hardware at the store.*

hardy (5) [har'dy], *adj.* able to live under bad conditions; strong. **Ex.** *Only hardy plants will survive this cold winter.*

harm (2) [harm'], *n.* 1. damage; hurt. **Ex.** *His delay did great harm to our plans.* 2. evil; wrong. **Ex.** *He meant no harm by his remarks.* —*v.* injure; damage. **ex.** *My dog won't harm you.* —**harm'ful,** *adj.*

harmony (4) [har'məniy], *n.* 1. agreement in feeling, ideas, manners, etc. **Ex.** *There was always harmony in the family.* 2. pleasing combination of parts, sounds or colors. **Ex.** *The different styles of furniture in the room were in harmony.* —**har·mo·ni·ous,** *adj.* —**har'mo·nize,** *v.*

harness (3) [har'nis], *n.* 1. a device made of long pieces of leather and metal rings with which a horse or other work animal is fastened to a wagon or plow. 2. a device like this used to support a baby. **Ex.** *Is your little brother's harness tightly fastened?* —*v.* 1. put such a device on an animal. **Ex.** *Have you harnessed the pony yet?* 2. control something to make use of its power. **Ex.** *This dam harnesses the water power of the river.*

harp (4) [harp'], *n.* a stringed musical instrument played with the fingers. —**harp'ist,** *n.* one who plays the harp.

harsh (4) [harš'], *adj.* 1. rough, unpleasant or sharp to the senses. **Ex.** *He has a harsh voice.* 2. cruel; severe; stern. **Ex.** *Her parents were very harsh to her.* —**harsh'ly,** *adv.* —**harsh'ness,** *n.*

HARP

harvest (2) [har'vəst], *n.* 1. the gathering in of crops. **Ex.** *Many men were needed to help with the harvest.* 2. the crop itself. **Ex.** *The harvest was plentiful this year.* —*v.* gather crops. **Ex.** *The farmer harvested his wheat.* —**har'vest·er,** *n.* 1. a person who harvests. 2. a machine for harvesting.

has (1) [hæz'], *v.* present tense of *have* used with he, she, it and singular nouns. **Ex.** *The girl has more interesting ideas than he has.*

hasn't [hæz'ent], short form, contraction of *has not.* **Ex.** *Once again she hasn't done her homework.*

haste (3) [heyst'], *n.* a hurry; a rush. **Ex.** *They left in haste for the airport.* —**hast'en,** *v.* move or act quickly; hurry. **Ex.** *He hastened home to his sick wife.* —**hast'y,** *adj.* 1. hurried; quick. **Ex.** *He made a hasty telephone call.* 2. too quickly. **Ex.** *His hasty decision got him into financial difficulties.* —**make haste,** hurry. **Ex.** *Make haste or we will miss our bus.*

hat (1) [hæt'], *n.* a covering for the head. —**pass the hat,** ask for money, especially for a deserving cause. **Ex.** *They passed the hat for victims of the fire.* —**take one's hat off to,** admire; express approval. **Ex.** *I take my hat off to those who arranged this meeting.*

HAT

hatch (4) [hæč'], *v.* 1. bring forth young from an egg or eggs. **Ex.** *The hen hatched ten chickens.* 2. create a plan or scheme. **Ex.** *The prisoners hatched a plan to escape.*

hatch (4) [hæč'], *n.* an opening in the deck of a ship. **Ex.** *If there is a storm, we will have to close the hatches.*

hatchet (6) [hæč'ət], *n.* a small, short-handled ax that can be used with one hand.

HATCHET

hate (2) [heyt'], *v.* 1. have strong feelings against; regard as an enemy. **Ex.** *Why do you hate him?* 2. be unwilling; not like. **Ex.** *I hate to trouble you with my problems.* —*n.* a strong feeling against. **Ex.** *She had mixed feelings of love and hate for his stern parents.* —**ha'tred,** *n.* a strong dislike. **Ex.** *His hatred of the government drove him from his native land.*

haughty (5) [hɔ:'tiy], *adj.* having too much pride; thinking little of others and too much of oneself. **Ex.** *She gave him a haughty look.* —**haugh'ti·ly,** *adv.* —**haugh'ti·ness,** *n.*

haul (4) [hɔ:l'], *v.* 1. move by pulling or dragging with force. **Ex.** *They hauled the small boat up on the beach.* 2. move or carry from one place to another in a truck, wagon, etc. **Ex.** *That company hauls furniture at a reasonable rate.* —*n.* 1. the act of pulling, dragging or moving. **Ex.** *They were very tired after such a heavy haul.* 2. that which is pulled, dragged or moved. **Ex.** *He returned from the market with quite a haul.* 3. the distance something is dragged, hauled or moved. **Ex.** *It was a long haul from the station to the hotel.*

haunt (3) [hɔ:nt'], *v.* 1. visit often, especially as a ghost. **Ex.** *That old house is said to be haunted by the spirit of its first owner.* 2. return often to the mind. **Ex.** *Memories of poverty still haunted her.* —*n.* a place where one spends or has spent much time; a favorite spot. **Ex.** *The museum is his favorite haunt.* —**haunt'ing,** *adj.* returning to or remaining in one's thoughts. **Ex.** *She has a haunting beauty.*

have (1) [hæv'], *v.* 1. possess; own; hold. **Ex.** *Does he have a car?* 2. contain. **Ex.** *A day has twenty-four hours.* 3. get; receive; take. **Ex.** *Will you have dinner now?* 4. experience; engage in; perform. **Ex.** *We were having a good time swimming when it began to rain.* 5. hold in the mind or memory; feel. **Ex.** *We have some doubts about him.* —**have on,** be wearing. **Ex.** *The clothes I have on are dirty.* —**have to,** must. **Ex.** *I have to go now.*

haven't [hæv'ənt], short form, contraction of *have not*. **Ex.** *I haven't heard from him recently.*

havoc [hæv'ɔːk], *n.* far-reaching damage or destruction; confusion; disorder. **Exs.** *The flood brought havoc to the valley. The cut in their budget played havoc with their well-planned program.*

hawk (4) [hɔːk'], *n.* 1. any of the large family of birds that lives by eating other birds and small animals. **Ex.** *The chickens were frightened by the hawk.* 2. someone who believes in using military force to achieve political ends. **Ex.** *He voted with the hawks to increase military spending.* —*v.* sell merchandise on the street or from house to house, often calling out to attract attention to one's wares. **Ex.** *He was hawking magazines and newspapers.*

hay (3) [hey'], *n.* grass cut and dried for use as feed for animals. **Ex.** *The hay was stored in the barn.*

hazard (5) [hæz'ərd], *n.* danger; peril; risk. **Ex.** *The ice on the roads is a hazard when driving.* —*v.* 1. dare to offer. **Ex.** *May I hazard a suggestion?* 2. risk. **Ex.** *The pilot hazarded his life for the safety of the passengers.* —**haz'ard·ous,** *adj.*

haze [heyz'], *n.* fine particles of dust, smoke, mist, etc. held in the air. **Ex.** *We could not see the distant mountains because of the haze.* —**haz'y,** *adj.*

he (1) [hiy'], *pron.* a male person or animal that has already been mentioned or that is understood. **Ex.** *My brother is not here; he is at work.*

head (1) [hed'], *n.* 1. the upper part of the human body and the upper or front part of the body of most animals, containing the brain, mouth, eyes, ears, etc., and joined to the rest of the body by the neck. **Ex.** *He stood head and shoulders above the rest of the crowd.* 2. a position of leadership or command; chief. **Ex.** *He is the head of the school.* 3. the top part of anything. **Ex.** *Hit the nail on the head.* 4. the front; the highest position. **Ex.** *She is at the head of her class.* 5. mind; intelligence. **Ex.** *He has a good head for science.* —*v.* 1. lead; command. **Ex.** *He heads the city government.* 2. go to or be at the front, head or top of. **Ex.** *Your name heads the list.* 3. move in a certain direction. **Ex.** *We headed home.* —**head off,** get ahead of and stop. **Ex.** *Head him off before he falls in the hole.*

—keep or lose one's head, keep or lose control of one's thoughts and actions. **Ex.** *He lost his head during the argument.* **—over one's head,** too difficult to understand, manage, do, etc. **Ex.** *Their discussion was over my head.* **—turn one's head,** make one feel too proud. **Ex.** *Their flattery turned her head.*

headache [hed'eyk`], *n.* a pain in the head. **Ex.** *I have a terrible headache this morning because I didn't sleep well last night.*

headlight [hed'layt`], *n.* a light on the front of a car, truck, train, etc. **Ex.** *It's dark enough to need the headlights now.*

headline [hed'layn`], *n.* large words printed at the top of a story in a newspaper. **Ex.** *He usually reads the headlines first.*

headlong [hed'lɔ:ŋ`], *adj., adv.* with the head first; at a great speed; without thought. **Exs.** *He took a headlong plunge into the water. She rushed headlong into the crowd.*

head-on [hed`an'], *adj., adv.* with the front part forward. **Exs.** *Both drivers were killed in the head-on crash. The cars hit each other head-on.*

headquarters (5) [hed'kwɔr`tərz], *n.* any center from which orders are issued. **Ex.** *Many policemen work here at police headquarters.*

headstrong [hed'strɔ:ŋ`], *adj.* doing what one wants to despite what others may advise. **Ex.** *He is so headstrong that he often gets into trouble.*

headway [hed'wey`], *n.* forward movement; progress. **Ex.** *Because of the snow we made little headway.*

heal (2) [hiyl'], *v.* 1. return to good health; cure. **Ex.** *The doctor healed the sick man.* 2. become well. **Ex.** *The cut healed quickly.*

health (1) [helθ'], *n.* 1. the condition of being free from sickness. **Ex.** *He has regained his health.* 2. general condition of the body and mind. **Ex.** *She is in poor health.* **—health'y,** *adj.* having or showing good health. **Ex.** *What a healthy baby you have!*

heap (3) [hiyp'], *n.* a number of things lying one on top of the other; a pile. **Ex.** *A heap of stones blocked the road.* **—v.** 1. gather, put or throw in a heap; pile. **Ex.** *She heaped the clothes together.* 2. give in great quantities. **Ex.** *The mother heaped the child's plate with food.*

---

a, far; æ, am; e, get; ey, late; i, in; iy, see; ɔ, all; ow, go; u, put; uw, too; ə, but, ago; ər, fur; aw, out; ay, life; oy, boy; ŋ, ring; θ, think; ð, that; ž, measure; š, ship; ĵ, edge; č, child.

hear (1) [hi:r'], *v.* 1. notice or perceive by ear. **Ex.** *Do you hear a strange sound?* 2. listen to; pay attention to. **Ex.** *He did not hear my explanation.* 3. receive news or information. **Ex.** *Did you hear about the fire?* —**hear'ing,** *n.* 1. the sense by which one receives sound; the ability to hear. **Ex.** *His hearing is poor.* 2. the distance at which one can hear or be heard. **Ex.** *You can safely speak; no one else is within hearing.* 3. an examination in a court of law before a judge. **Ex.** *The hearing of this case starts tomorrow.* —**hearing aid,** a device to help improve the hearing. **Ex.** *She wears a hearing aid in each ear.*

heard [hərd'], *v.* past tense and participle of *hear.* **Exs.** *We heard about your accident. Have you heard yet when she's returning?*

heart (1) [hart'], *n.* 1. an organ that pumps blood through all parts of the body. **Ex.** *We will have to perform surgery on your heart.* 2. this organ considered as a center of life, thought and honest feeling. **Ex.** *He spoke from the heart.* 3. the breast. **Ex.** *She pressed the child to her heart.* 4. the center or middle part of anything. **Ex.** *They live in the heart of town.* 5. the most important part. **Ex.** *Your words go to the heart of the matter.* —**at heart,** in the center of one's feelings. **Ex.** *At heart, she was still a child.* —**by heart,** by memorizing; from memory. **Ex.** *He knew the words of the song by heart.* —**change of heart,** change of mind or view. **Ex.** *She had a change of heart and went with us.* —**take heart,** become encouraged or hopeful. **Ex.** *We took heart when we heard you were coming.* —**take to heart,** be very serious about. **Ex.** *We are taking his advice to heart.*

hearth (4) [harθ'], *n.* 1. the floor of a fireplace, usually made of brick or stone. **Ex.** *The fire was burning on the hearth.* 2. home; the fireside. **Ex.** *They spent the holidays at the family hearth.*

hearty [hart'iy], *adv.* 1. enthusiastic; welcoming; vigorous. **Ex.** *He responded to my funny story with a hearty laugh.* 2. large; generous. **Ex.** *They served hearty meals at camp.* —**heart'i·ly,** *adv.* enthusiastically; vigorously. **Ex.** *The old sailor greeted us heartily.*

heat (1) [hiyt'], *n.* 1. great warmth. **Ex.** *The heat of the sun dried the wet clothes.* 2. very warm weather or climate. **Ex.** *They do not mind the summer heat.* 3. warmth of feeling. **Ex.** *He said sharp words in the heat of the argument.* 4. warmth supplied for a room or a house. **Ex.** *We use gas for heat.* —*v.* cause to be warm or hot; become warm or hot. **Ex.** *The water heated rapidly.* —**heat'er,** *n.* a device using oil, gas or electricity to produce warmth.

heat wave [hiyt' weyv'] a period of very hot weather. **Ex.** *The summer before this we had a heat wave which lasted six weeks.*

heave (4) [hiyv'], *v.* 1. raise or lift with great effort. **Ex.** *The fat man heaved himself to his feet.* 2. utter with great effort or as if in pain. **Ex.** *She heaved a sigh of relief.* 3. rise and fall as the chest does in heavy breathing. **Ex.** *Her body heaved with sobs.*

heaven (1) [hev'ən], *n.* in most religions, the place where God or a god and spirits are said to dwell. **Ex.** *He believed he would go to heaven when he died.* —**heav'en·ly,** *adj.* —**the heavens,** the sky. **Ex.** *Millions of stars seemed to be shining in the heavens.*

heavy (1) [hev'iy], *adj.* 1. of great weight; not easy to lift. **Ex.** *The heavy load caused him to walk unsteadily.* 2. of great amount or force. **Ex.** *A heavy rain fell today.* 3. difficult to bear; burdensome. **Ex.** *Heavy taxes drove them from the city.* 4. full of sorrow. **Ex.** *Her heart was heavy because of the death of her husband.* —**heav'i·ly,** *adv.* —**heav'i·ness,** *n.*

hectic [hek'tic], *adj.* typically marked by feverish activity with much confusion and excitement. **Ex.** *The three weeks before the wedding were more hectic than anyone had imagined.*

he'd [hiyd'], short form, contraction of *he had* and *he would.* **Exs.** *He'd better leave right now. He'd like to join you tomorrow.*

hedge (4) [hej'], *n.* 1. a row of bushes that forms a fence. **Ex.** *There was a hedge in front of the house.* 2. a kind of protection, especially against financial loss; insurance. **Ex.** *He invested in rental property as a hedge against inflation.* —*v.* 1. fence with a hedge. **Ex.** *They hedged their backyard.* 2. avoid being honest and direct. **Ex.** *She hedged when I asked her age.*

heel (2) [hiyl'], *n.* 1. the part of the foot that is below and in back of the ankle. **Ex.** *His painful heel made running difficult.* 2. that part of a sock, stocking or shoe that covers the heel. **Ex.** *There is a hole in the heel of your sock.*

height (1) [hayt'], *n.* distance upward from the ground; distance from bottom to top. **Ex.** *His height is six feet three inches.* 2. a high point; a high place. **Ex.** *Some people are afraid of heights.* 3. highest point; peak. **Ex.** *He died at the height of his career.*

heir (4) [e:r'], **heiress** [e:r'es], *n.* the person who receives or has the right to receive another person's property when that person dies. **Ex.** *When he died, his son was his only heir.*

held (1) [held'], *v.* past tense and participle of *hold*. **Exs.** *He held her hand tightly. She had held on as long as she could.*

helicopter [hel'əkop'tər], *n.* an aircraft with rotating blades attached above it that keep it in the air. **Ex.** *A helicopter took the wounded man from the ship to a hospital.*

hell (2) [hel'], *n.* 1. in some religions, a place or state for punishment of the wicked after death; a place where evil spirits are thought to dwell. **Ex.** *The road to hell is said to be paved with good intentions.* 2. any state of great pain or suffering. **Ex.** *He found it was a hell on earth to live with a guilty conscience.* —**hell'ish,** *adj.*

he'll [hiyl'], short form, contraction of *he will*. **Ex.** *He'll be here for dinner.*

hello (1) [helow', həlow'], *interj.* a word used to greet someone or attract attention. **Ex.** *Hello, sir; I am glad to see you.*

helmet (4) [hel'mət], *n.* a covering to protect the head, made of metal, leather, or other strong material. **Ex.** *All bicycle riders in the race were required to wear helmets.*

help (1) [help'] *v.* 1. aid; assist. **Ex.** *Please help me with this work.* 2. give relief to. **Ex.** *This medicine will help to cure your illness.* 3. prevent; avoid. **Ex.** *He could not help arriving late.* 4. serve; wait on. **Ex.** *The waiter helped us to the meat.* —*n.* aid; assistance. **Ex.** *I came to offer my help.* —**help'er,** *n.* one who helps. —**help'ful,** *adj.* of help; useful. **Ex.** *Your suggestion was very helpful.* —**help'ing,** *n.* a serving or portion of food for one person. **Ex.** *Please have another helping of meat and vegetables.* —**help out,** assist. **Ex.** *She helped out when we were very busy.*

hem (4) [hem'], *n,* a folded edge on a garment made by turning back the material and sewing it in place. **Ex.** *This skirt should have a narrow hem.* —*v.* 1. make a hem in. **Ex.** *The dress was hemmed by hand.* 2. block on all sides; surround. **Ex.** *His car was hemmed in by the traffic.*

hemisphere [hem'isfiyr'], *n.* one half of a globe; one half of the earth, especially as divided by the equator. **Ex.** *The United States is in the Northern Hemisphere.*

hen (3) [hen'], *n.* a female chicken. **Ex.** *We raised hens so we could have fresh eggs.*

her (1) [hə:r'], *pron.* 1. form of *she* used as the object of a verb or preposition. **Ex.** *She is not at home now; please call her* *later*. 2. form of *she* used to show ownership. **Ex.** *That is her book*.

herb (4) [ərb', hərb'], *n.* one of a group of plants used in medicine or in flavoring food. **Ex.** *We like to use herbs in cooking*.

herd (3) [hərd'], *n.* a number of large animals gathered together. **Ex.** *The herd of cattle is in the back field now.* —*v.* 1. cause to move in a group. **Ex.** *He herds his sheep from one place to another*. 2. go in a herd. **Ex.** *The people herded together for safety*.

here (1) [hi:r'], *adv.* 1. in this place. **Ex.** *The book is right here.* 2. to this place. **Ex.** *Please come here.* —*n.* this place. **Ex.** *It is not in here*.

hereafter [hi:r'æf'tər], *adv.* after this time. **Ex.** *Hereafter, I will do the work myself*.

hereby [hi:r'bay'], *adv.* by means of this letter, these words, etc. **Ex.** *I hereby give you my permission*.

here's [hiyrz'], short form, contraction of *here is*. **Ex.** *Here's the book I wanted*.

heritage (5) [he:r'ətij], *n.* that received from one's ancestors, such as traditions, ideals and rights. **Ex.** *Free education is an American heritage*.

hermit (4) [hər'mət], *n.* one who leaves society and lives alone, especially for reasons of religion. **Ex.** *A hermit lives in that forest*.

hero (2) [hi:r'ow], *n.* 1. a man or boy of great courage; a man or boy who has done a brave deed. **Ex.** *He was a war hero.* 2. one greatly admired by others; one looked upon as a model. **Ex.** *The father was a hero to his son.* 3. the principal male character in a story, poem, play, etc. **Ex.** *The hero of this novel is a doctor.* —**he·ro'ic**, *adj.* —**her'o·ism**, *n.*

heroin [her'owin], *n.* an illegal, habit-forming drug. **Ex.** *He was arrested for selling heroin*.

heroine [her'owin], *n.* 1. a woman or girl of great courage; a woman or girl who has done a brave deed. **Ex.** *She was a war*

a, far; æ, am; e, get; ey, late; i, in; iy, see; ɔ, all; ow, go; u, put; uw, too; ə, but, ago; ər, fur; aw, out; ay, life; oy, boy; ŋ, ring; θ, think; ð, that; ž, measure; š, ship; j, edge; č, child.

heroine. 2. one greatly admired by others; one looked upon as a model. **Ex.** *The mother was a heroine to her daughter.* 3. the principal female character in a story, poem, play, etc. **Ex.** *The heroine of this novel is a doctor.*

herring (5) [her'iŋ], *n.* a small fish caught in the North Atlantic and used for food. **Ex.** *Do you like pickled herring?*

hers (1) [hərz'], *pron.* belonging to her. **Ex.** *This book is hers.*

herself (2) [hərself'], *pron.* 1. her own self. **Ex.** *She fell and hurt herself.* 2. her usual self. **Ex.** *She is behaving strangely; she is not herself today.*

he's [hiyz'], short form, contraction of *he is.* **Ex.** *He's leaving tomorrow.*

hesitate (3) [hez'əteyt`], *v.* wait, as if uncertain; pause because of doubts. **Ex.** *He hesitated before crossing the street.* —**hes'i·tant,** *adj.* —**hes'i·ta'tion,** *n.*

hid (2) [hid'], *v.* past tense of *hide.* **Ex.** *She hid the money in a book.*

hidden [hid'ən], *v.* past participle of *hide.* **Ex.** *The treasure had been hidden long ago.*

hide (2) [hayd'], *v.* 1. place something where it cannot be seen or found; conceal. **Ex.** *The child was hiding under the bed.* 2. keep secret. **Ex.** *She tried to hide her feelings from everyone.*

hide (2) [hayd'], *n.* the skin of an animal. **Ex.** *How many pairs of shoes can be made from this hide?*

hideous (4) [hid'iyəs], *adj.* extremely ugly; frightening; morally shocking. **Ex.** *That was a hideous crime.* —**hid'e·ous·ly,** *adv.* —**hid'e·ous·ness,** *n.*

high (1) [hay'], *adj.* 1. tall; extending far upward. **Ex.** *The table was high above the little girl's reach.* 2. at some distance above the ground. **Ex.** *The plane flew high above the city.* 3. sharp; raised in tone. **Ex.** *She spoke in a high voice.* 4. of superior rank, character or kind. **Exs.** *He is a very high official. She has very high principles.* 5. more than usual; greater in degree. **Exs.** *The child has a high fever. The automobile was traveling at a high speed.* 6. very serious; grave. **Ex.** *The official was removed for high crimes against the state.* 7. expensive. **Ex.** *He paid a high price for the car.* —*adv.* at or to a high place, level, rank or degree. **Ex.** *The airplane* *flew high above the clouds.* —**high'ly,** *adv.* 1. in or to a high degree; greatly. **Ex.** *Her story was highly unlikely.* 2. with high praise. **Ex.** *They spoke highly of his work.* 3. at or in a high position, rank, price, etc. **Exs.** *He is a highly placed officer. She is a highly paid writer.*

highhanded [hay`hæn'dəd], *adj.* misusing one's authority; acting without the advice of others. **Ex.** *He acted in a very high-handed way.*

highlight [hay'layt`], *v.* point out; feature. **Ex.** *He highlighted the picture by placing it over the fireplace.* —*n.* the important or best part. **Ex.** *They described the highlights of their trip.*

high rise [hay' rayz'], *n.* a tall building with many floors. **Ex.** *We took the elevator to the thirty-second floor of the high rise.* —**high-rise,** *adj.*

high school [hay' skuwl'], *n.* a school of the tenth, eleventh and twelfth years of study and sometimes the ninth. **Ex.** *Their oldest girl is in high school.*

high seas [hay' siyz'], *n.* that part of the sea or ocean that does not belong to any country. **Ex.** *They were on the high seas when the storm broke.*

high-strung [hay`strəŋ'], *adj.* very nervous or tense. **Ex.** *She is a very high-strung child.*

highway (3) [hay'wey`], *n.* an important road; a main road. **Ex.** *That highway crosses the entire country.*

hijack [hay'jæk`], *v.* rob goods in transit from a vehicle such as a train, truck, etc. **Ex.** *The robbers hijacked the payroll money from the armored car as it left the bank.* 2. gain control of a moving vehicle or aircraft by use of force. **Ex.** *The plane was hijacked two hours into its flight.* —**hi'jack`er,** *n.* —**hi'jack`ing,** *n.*

hike (4) [hayk'], *v.* walk a great distance, especially in the woods, country or mountains. **Ex.** *The boys hiked for three hours before stopping for lunch.* —*n.* a walk of some distance, especially in the woods, country or mountains. **Ex.** *Their hike took them up into the hills.* —**hik'er,** *n.* one who hikes.

hill (1) [hil'], *n.* high rounded land that is not as high as a mountain. **Ex.** *The mountain was surrounded by low hills.* —**hill'y,** *adj.* having many hills. **Ex.** *It's very hilly around here.*

him (1) [him'], *pron.* form of *he* used as the object of a verb or preposition. **Ex.** *He was away at the time we wanted to speak to him.*

himself (2) [himself'], *pron.* 1. his own self. **Ex.** *He looked at himself in the mirror.* 2. his usual self. **Ex.** *He is very unhappy today; he is not himself.*

hind (3) [haynd'], *adj.* located toward or the back or rear. **Ex.** *The horse rose on its hind legs.*

hinder (4) [hin'dər], *v.* 1. interrupt; delay. **Ex.** *The constant ringing of the telephone hindered my work.* 2. stop; prevent from acting. **Ex.** *There is nothing to hinder you from leaving now.* —**hin'drance,** *n.*

hindsight [hayn(d)'sayt'], *n.* knowing what should have been done when it is too late. **Ex.** *Hindsight did not help him to recover the money he had lost.*

hinge (4) [hinj'], *n.* a joint, usually of metal, used on a door to enable it to open and shut and on a box, trunk, etc., to allow the top or lid to be raised and lowered. —*v.* furnish with a hinge or hinges. **Ex.** *The door had been hinged so that it would open outward.*

HINGE

hint (3) [hint'], *n.* 1. indirect suggestion. **Ex.** *He ignored her hints that he leave.* 2. slight trace; slight suggestion. **Ex.** *There was a hint of winter in the air.* —*v.* make an indirect suggestion. **Ex.** *He hinted that he needed money.*

hip (4) [hip'], *n.* that part of the human body projecting on both sides just below the waist and above the upper legs. **Ex.** *She fell and broke her right hip.*

hire (2) [hayr'], *v.* obtain for pay the services of a person or the use of a thing. **Ex.** *They hired several new workers.* —*n.* the act of hiring. **Ex.** *This car is for hire.*

his (1) [hiz'], *pron.* form of *he,* used to show ownership. **Ex.** *That brown hat is his.*

hiss [his'], *v.* make a sound like a long, continuing *s,* often to express scorn, disapproval, anger, etc. **Ex.** *The air hissed from the tire as it went flat.* —*n.* a sound like a long, continuing *s.* **Ex.** *We heard the angry hiss of the goose as the boy tried to pet it.*

history (1) [his't(ə)riy], *n.* 1. the written record of the past. **Ex.** *Abraham Lincoln is a famous person in American history.* 2. the branch of knowledge that records and explains past events. **Ex.** *She is studying American history.* 3. a long story or tale. **Ex.** *He told us the history of that old house.* —**his·to'ri·an,** *n.* one who writes about or is an expert in history. —**his·tor'ic,** *adj.* important in history. **Ex.** *That is a historic building.* —**his·tor'i·cal,** *adj.* concerned with the study of history; representing a fact or facts of history. **Ex.** *That historical play was very interesting.*

hit (1) [hit'], *v.* 1. strike; give a blow. **Ex.** *The boy hit his little brother.* 2. strike with force. **ex.** *The speeding car hit the tree.* 3. reach or strike by throwing or shooting. **Ex.** *A piece from the bursting shell hit his shoulder.* —*n.* 1. a blow, shot, etc., especially one that reaches the object aimed at. **Ex.** *The gunner made more hits than misses.* 2. something that is very successful, such as a play, song, etc. **Ex.** *His first novel was a hit.* —**hit it off,** get along.

hitch (5) [hič'], *v.* tie; fasten as with a rope. **Ex.** *He hitched the horse to the post.*

hive (5) [hayv'], *n.* a box or covering for honeybees. **Ex.** *Bees were swarming around the hive.* 2. a colony of honeybees living in such a box or covering. **Ex.** *The farm has three hives of bees.*

hoard (5) [hord'], *n.* an accumulation or a supply of something for future use, especially a secret one. **Ex.** *He had a hoard of paintings in the attic.* —*v.* pile up or keep in large amounts for future use. **Ex.** *They hoarded sugar and coffee when those items were scarce.* —**hoard'er,** *n.* one who hoards.

hoarse (5) [hors'], *adj.* rough and deep in sound, as the voice of a person with a cold. **Ex.** *He shouted until he was hoarse.* —**hoarse'ly,** *adv.* —**hoarse'ness,** *n.*

hobby (5) [hab'iy], *n.* an activity done in one's spare time for pleasure. **Ex.** *Stamp collecting was his hobby.*

hoe (5) [how'], *n.* a long-handled tool with a flat blade at one end for digging in the garden. —*v.* use the hoe. **Ex.** *She was hoeing the vegetables when I arrived.*

HOE

hog (4) [hag', hɔ:g'], *n.* a large, fully grown pig raised for its meat. **Ex.** *The hogs were feeding in the pigpen.*

---

a, far; æ, am; e, get; ey, late; i, in; iy, see; ɔ, all; ow, go; u, put; uw, too; ə, but, ago; ər, fur; aw, out; ay, life; oy, boy; ŋ, ring; θ, think; ð, that; ž, measure; š, ship; j, edge; č, child.

hoist (4) [hoyst'], *v.* raise or lift, especially by a mechanical device. **Ex.** *The ship hoisted anchor.* —*n.* a mechanical device for lifting heavy things. **Ex.** *We need a hoist to lift the boat out of the water.*

hold (1) [howld'], *v.* 1. grasp and keep in the hands or arms. **Ex.** *Please hold this package.* 2. keep in a certain position. **Ex.** *Please hold the door open.* 3. possess; keep. **Ex.** *I am holding this land for my children.* 4. contain. **Ex.** *This bottle holds one quart.* 5. have; occupy. **Ex.** *He holds the rank of captain.* 6. engage in; conduct. **Ex.** *They are holding a meeting today.* 7. keep with an effort. **Ex.** *The soldiers managed to hold the fort against attack.* —*n.* 1. the act of holding or grasping. **Ex.** *Get a good hold on this rope.* 2. a controlling force; a strong influence. **Ex.** *The general has a powerful hold over the country.* 3. the lower part of a ship in which the load is carried. **Ex.** *The hold was filled with bags of sugar.* —**hold forth,** talk for a long time. **Ex.** *He used to hold forth about guns for hours.* —**hold off,** keep away. **Ex.** *The soldiers could not hold off the enemy.* —**hold on,** continue to hold, keep in one place. **Ex.** *Hold on to him while I call the police.* —**hold up,** 1. prevent from falling. **Ex.** *The fence needs some new posts to hold it up.* 2. rob. **Ex.** *Two men tried to hold up the bank at noon yesterday.*

holdings [howld'iŋz], *n. pl.* anything that one owns, such as land, stocks and bonds, etc. **Ex.** *He has large holdings abroad.*

hole (1) [howl'], *n.* a torn or broken place in something; a tear. **Ex.** *There is a hole in your dress.* 2. a hollow place in the ground. **Ex.** *The rabbit went into his hole.* 3. an opening into or through something, usually serving a purpose. **Ex.** *There were three small holes through which he oiled the pump.*

holiday (2) [hal'ədey'], *n.* 1. any day on which one is not required to work; vacation. **Ex.** *We spent our holiday at the seashore.* 2. a day on which no business is done in honor of some event or person. **Ex.** *New Year's Day is a legal holiday in the United States.* —*adj.* joyful; gay. **Ex.** *People were in a holiday mood.*

hollow (2) [hal'ow], *adj.* 1. have a hole within; empty. **Ex.** *The fox hid in the hollow tree.* 2. having a depression or low place. **Ex.** *The car bumped over the hollow spot in the road.* 3. having a dull sound; empty sounding. **Ex.** *The barrels made a hollow sound when tapped.* 4. with no real meaning;

empty; false. **Ex.** *She gave her rival hollow praise.* —*n.* a hole in or within something; a depression. **Ex.** *The boys were playing in the hollow.* —**hollow out,** make or become hollow. **Ex.** *He hollowed out a stick of wood to make a whistle.*

holy (2) [how'liy], *adj.* 1. reserved for purposes of religion or worship. **Ex.** *This building is a holy place.* 2. pure in heart; saintly. **Ex.** *He is a holy man.* —**ho'li·ness,** *n.*

homage (5) [ham'ij, am'ij], *n.* respect or honor shown or given to another. **Ex.** *Our homage is due the men who died for us in battle.*

home (1) [howm'], *n.* 1. the place where a person lives. **Ex.** *Do you own your home?* 2. the family group. **Ex.** *He comes from a happy home.* 3. one's native country or place; the place where one was born or brought up. **Ex.** *Her home is the United States.* —*adj.* connected with the home; domestic. **Ex.** *He enjoyed home life after living in a hotel.* —*adv.* to, toward or at home. **Ex.** *She will be home all evening.*

homely (4) [howm'liy], *adj.* not good-looking; ugly. **Ex.** *She is a homely woman.* —**home'li·ness,** *n.*

homesick (3) [howm'sik'], *adj.* longing for home. **Ex.** *She was homesick when she first went away to college.* —**home'sick·ness,** *n.*

homework [howm'wərk], *n.* work assigned in school to be done at home rather than in school. **Ex.** *He finished his homework in two hours.*

honest (2) [an'əst], *adj.* 1. truthful; able to be trusted. **Ex.** *He is an honest person.* 2. having or giving full worth or value. **Ex.** *She always does an honest day's work.* 3. open and frank. **Ex.** *The boy has an honest face.* —**hon'est·ly,** *adv.* —**hon'es·ty,** *n.*

honey (2) [hən'iy], *n.* 1. a sweet, thick fluid produced by bees from the liquid they gather from flowers. **Ex.** *The children like bread and honey.* 2. darling; a term of affection. **Ex.** *Honey, do you know where my glasses are?*

honeymoon [hən'iymuwn'], *n.* a trip taken by newly married persons soon after their wedding. **Ex.** *They went to the mountains for their honeymoon.*

honk [hɔːŋk'], *n.* the loud, harsh sound made by one goose calling to another; any sound like this. **Ex.** *I was awakened by the honk of a car.* —*v.* make this loud, harsh sound. **Ex.** *The geese were honking as they made their way across the grass.*

honor (1) [an'ər], *n.* fame; glory; public respect. **Ex.** *He held a place of honor in his town.* 2. something given as a sign or mark of respect. **Ex.** *The soldier was given a medal of honor.* 3. good reputation. **Ex.** *He was a man of honor.* 4. source of credit or glory. **Ex.** *She was an honor to the school.* 5. a title of respect given to public officials. **Ex.** *His Honor, the judge, is entering the courtroom.* 6. a strong sense of right to which one is true. **Ex.** *Her honor kept her from accepting the gift.* —*v.* 1. hold in high respect. **Ex.** *We should honor our parents.* 2. give honor to. **Ex.** *They honored the returning hero.* 3. keep a promise. **Ex.** *The store honored its sales agreement.* —**hon·or·a·ble**, *adj.* —**hon·or·ar·y**, *adj.* given as an honor. **Ex.** *The university gave him an honorary degree.*

hood (4) [hud'], *n.* 1. a soft covering for the head and neck, sometimes attached to a coat or jacket. **Ex.** *She put her hood up to protect her hair from the snow.* 2. anything that covers. **Ex.** *She lifted the hood of the car engine to see what was wrong.*

-hood (2) [hud], *suffix.* 1. members of a group. **Exs.** *Priest, priesthood; brother, brotherhood.* 2. state of being. **Exs.** *Mother, motherhood; child, childhood.*

hoof (3) [huf'], *n.* the foot or the hard covering on a foot of an animal such as horses, cows, pigs and some other animals. **Ex.** *There was a small stone in the horse's hoof.*

hook (2) [huk'], *n.* a curved piece of metal, wood, etc. for catching or holding something. —*v.* fasten or catch with a hook. **Ex.** *He hooked a big fish out of the stream.*

hop (3) [hap'], *v.* 1. take short, quick jumps on one foot. **Ex.** *The children hopped down the street.* 2. move by jumps. **Ex.** *The bird hopped about on the ground.* —*n.* a short jump.

HOOK

hope (1) [howp'], *n.* 1. a desire that one expects will be fulfilled. **Ex.** *He has great hopes of success.* 2. a person or thing on which one bases hope. **Ex.** *This plan is our last hope for an agreement.* 3. the thing hoped for. **Ex.** *His hope is to go to college.* —*v.* desire something with confidence that it will happen; expect. **Ex.** *I hope you will come again soon.* —**hope'ful**, *adj.* feeling or causing hope. **Ex.** *The fact that she can now eat solid food is a hopeful sign.*

horizon (3) [həray'zən], *n.* 1. the line where the sky and earth appear to meet. **Ex.** *We saw a ship on the horizon.* 2. limit of knowledge or experience. **Ex.** *Your son says he is seeking new horizons.*

horizontal (3) [hər`əzan'təl], *adj.* sideways; not up and down; parallel to the ground or horizon. **Ex.** *The horizontal lines on this paper are an inch apart.* —**hor'i·zon'tal·ly,** *adv.*

horn (2) [hɔrn'], *n.* 1. hard, bonelike growths, which are often curved and pointed, on the heads of cattle, goats and many other animals. **Ex.** *The deers locked horns.* 2. anything made of horn. **Ex.** *His eyeglass frames are made of horn.* 3. a musical instrument, usually made of brass, played by blowing air through it. 4. any device that makes a loud sound as a warning. **Ex.** *We stepped back when we heard the auto-mobile horn.*

HORN 1

HORN 3

horrible (3) [hɔr'əbəl, har'əbəl], *adj.* 1. causing great fear; dread-ful. **Ex.** *He had a horrible cut on his face.* 2. ugly; unpleasant; disagreeable. **Ex.** *That was a horrible experience.*

horrid (5) [hɔːr'əd, har'əd], *adj.* terrible; shocking; dreadful. **Ex.** *She said some horrid things to him.*

horror (3) [hɔːr'ər, har'ər], *n.* 1. a painful feeling of great fear or shock. **Ex.** *She drew back in horror at the sight.* 2. anything that causes such a feeling. **Ex.** *He had not forgotten the horrors of war.* 3. a painful or very strong feeling of not liking. **Ex.** *She had a horror of heights.* —**hor'ri·fy,** *v.* cause great shock or fear; fill with horror. **Ex.** *The sight of the plane crashing to earth horrified her.*

horse (1) [hɔrs'], *n.* a large four-footed animal used by people for working and riding. **Ex.** *The old horse was sleeping on its feet.*

horsepower (hɔrs'pawr`), *n.* a measure of the power of engines, enough to raise 33,000 pounds one foot in one minute. **Ex.** *This car has a 200-horsepower engine.*

HORSE

hose (5) [howz'], *n.* 1. an easily bent tube, usually of rubber or plastic, through which liquid can flow. **Ex.** *Water from the fire hoses poured into the burning house.* 2. a covering for the legs and feet; stockings

or socks. **Ex.** *This shop sells men's accessories, including hose.*
—*v.* water or wash by means of a hose. **Ex.** *The boy hosed the garden.*

hospital (2) [has'pitəl], *n.* a place where sick or injured people are given medical care. **Ex.** *The sick man was sent to the hospital.* —**hos'pi·tal·ize`**, *v.* put in a hospital.

hospitality (5) [has'pətæl'ətiy], *n.* kind and generous treatment of guests. **Ex.** *They are known for their hospitality.* —**hos·pi'ta·ble**, *adj.*

host, hostess (3) [howst', hows'tis], *n.* one who receives guests in his or her home. **Ex.** *They are wonderful hosts.*

hostage [has'tij], *n.* a person held by force so that his safe release can be used for bargaining purposes. **Ex.** *They have killed one hostage and are threatening to kill the rest if their demands are not met.*

hostile (4) [has'təl], *adj.* 1. ready for war; in a warlike manner. **Ex.** *A hostile attack is expected during the night.* 2. unfriendly. **Ex.** *The student was hostile to the teacher.* —**hos·til'i·ty**, *n.* —**hos·til'i·ties**, *n. pl.* acts of war. **Ex.** *Hostilities between the two countries broke out in the spring and are still continuing.*

hot (1) [hat'], *adj.* 1. extremely warm. **Ex.** *The tea is too hot to drink.* 2. burning to the taste. **Ex.** *This is a hot red pepper!* 3. quick; excitable; full of passion. **Ex.** *He has a hot temper.*

hotbed [hat'bed'], *n.* a place or condition which favors the rapid growth or development of something, usually bad. **Ex.** *Areas of poor housing are sometimes hotbeds of crime.*

hot dog [hat' dɔːg'], *n.* a kind of mildly spiced sausage, reddish in color, served in a split roll with mustard, ketchup and/or relish, if desired. **Ex.** *He sells hot dogs at the football stadium.*

hotel (2) [howtel'], *n.* an establishment or building where room and usually food are provided to travelers for payment. **Ex.** *We stayed at some very nice hotels on our trip.*

hotheaded [hat'hed'əd], *adj.* quick to anger; acting thoughtlessly and too quickly. **Ex.** *He is so hotheaded that he is always in trouble.* —**hot'head'**, *n.* one who is quick to anger; one who acts thoughtlessly and too quickly.

hothouse [hat'haws'], *n.* a building made mostly of glass in which plants and flowers are grown.

hound (4) [hawnd'], *n.* 1. a dog with a sharp sense of smell, used in hunting. **Ex.** *They went hunting with the hounds.* 2. any dog. **Ex.** *He is just a hound.* —*v.* hunt with hounds or as with hounds; pursue without stopping. **Ex.** *His creditors were hounding him for money.*

hour (1) [awr'], *n.* 1. sixty minutes. **Ex.** *The trip will take two hours.* 2. a particular or appointed time. **Ex.** *At what hour did you see him?* 3. the time. **Ex.** *The hour was late when he returned.* —**hour'ly,** *adv.* every hour. **Ex.** *You must take this medicine hourly.*

house (1) [haws'], *n.* 1. a building in which people live. **Ex.** *They live in a large brick house.* 2. a structure for sheltering or storing something, such as goods or animals. **Ex.** *The boys are building a doghouse.* —*v.* provide with shelter. **Ex.** *The horses were housed in a new stable.*

housebreaking [haws'breyk'iŋ], *n.* the act of entering the house of another for the purpose of robbery or some other crime. **Ex.** *He was sent to prison for housebreaking.* —**house'break'er,** *n.*

household (2) [haws'howld'], *n.* all of the people, as a group, who live together in one house. **Ex.** *The household was awake at seven in the morning.* —*adj.* referring to things of the house; domestic. **Ex.** *The household expenses were high.* —**house'hold'er,** *n.* one who lives in his or her own house or apartment.

housekeeper [haws'kiyp'ər], *n.* one who is hired to manage a house. **Ex.** *Since the mother is a business executive, she employs a housekeeper.*

House of Representatives [haws' əv rep'rizen'tətivz], the lower and larger branch of the United States Congress; the lower branch of some state legislatures.

housewife [haws'wayf'], *n.* the female head of a household; a woman who manages her own home. **Ex.** *She is an excellent housewife.*

housing [hawz'iŋ], *n.* 1. the act of providing a place to live. **Ex.** *The housing of such a large group will be difficult.* 2. houses; a place to live. **Ex.** *Housing is expensive in this city.*

how (1) [haw'], *adv.* 1. in what way or manner. **Ex.** *Do you know how to swim?* 2. to what extent, degree or amount. **Ex.** *How much time do we have?* 3. in what condition. **Ex.** *How are you?*

however (1) [haw'ev'ər], *conj.* nevertheless; yet; in spite of that. **Ex.** *He does not think he will succeed; however, he will try.* —*adj.* in what way; by what means. **Ex.** *However can I repay you?*

howl (3) [hawl'], *v.* 1. make a long, loud, sad cry, as the cry of a wolf or a dog. **Ex.** *The dogs were howling at the moon.* 2. make a similar cry in anger, pain, etc. **Ex.** *The baby is howling for food.* 3. make a sound like an animal or human howling. **Ex.** *The wind howled outside.* —*n.* a long, loud, sad cry. **Ex.** *We heard the howl of wolves in the distance.*

huddle (5) [həd'əl], *v.* 1. crowd together. **Ex.** *Four people were huddled under one umbrella.* 2. draw oneself in as though to make oneself smaller. **Ex.** *She was huddled in the corner of a big chair.* —*n.* a confused heap or crowd. **Ex.** *There was a huddle of people at the entrance.*

hue (5) [hyuw'], *n.* a color; a shade of a color. **Ex.** *The room was decorated in various hues of blue, ranging from light to dark.*

hug (4) [həg'], *v.* hold tightly in the arms; embrace. **Ex.** *The mother hugged the crying child* —*n.* a tight hold with the arms; a close embrace. **Ex.** *She gave him a sisterly hug.*

huge (2) [hyuwj'], *adj.* of great size. **Ex.** *The huge building seemed to touch the sky.*

hum (4) [həm'], *v.* 1. make a low, steady sound like that of a bee flying. **Ex.** *The sewing machine hummed as she sewed.* 2. sing with closed lips and without forming words. **Ex.** *He hummed as he worked.* —*n.* wordless murmur; a low, steady sound. **Ex.** *We heard the hum of voices in the next room.*

human (1) [hyuw'mən], *n.* a man, woman or child; a person. *adj.* 1. of, like or referring to a man, woman or child. **Ex.** *A human body needs care.* 2. being a person; consisting of persons. **Ex.** *The human race includes all persons.* —**hu'man·ly,** *adv.* —**hu·man'i·ty,** *n.* 1. all human beings; the human race. **Ex.** *The balance between man and nature is of concern to all humanity.* 2. kindness. **Ex.** *They treated the prisoners with humanity.* —**hu·man'i·tar'i·an,** *n.* one who is concerned with and tries to improve the lives of human beings. —*adj.* —**human being,** *n.* a person.

humble (2) [həm'bəl], *adj.* 1. of low rank or position; plain; simple. **Ex.** *She came from a humble home.* 2. modest; without false pride; not proud. **Ex.** *He was a humble man.* —*v.*

bring low; lower oneself in importance, dignity or condition. **Ex.** *She humbled herself and asked forgiveness.* —**hum'bly,** *adv.*

humid [hyuw'mid], *adj.* filled with moisture; damp. **Ex.** *It's so humid that my clothes feel wet.* —**hu·mid'i·ty,** *n.* the amount of moisture in the air; dampness. **Ex.** *It wouldn't seem so hot if the humidity weren't so high.* —**hu·mid'i·fy`,** *v.* add moisture to dry air. **Ex.** *Your throat would not feel so dry if you humidified the room.*

humiliate (5) [hyuwmil'iyeyt`], *v.* cause to lose pride and self-respect, especially in the presence of others. **Ex.** *Her daughter's rudeness humiliated her.* —**hu·mil'i·a'tion,** *n.*

humor (2) [hyuw'mər], *n.* 1. the quality of causing amusement. **Ex.** *This story is full of humor.* 2. the way one feels; mood. **Ex.** *He is in a bad humor today.* 3. the ability to understand, enjoy or express what is funny or amusing. **Ex.** *It takes a sense of humor to be able to laugh at oneself.* —*v.* agree with every wish of a person. **Ex.** *Because she is sick we have to humor her.* —**hu'mor·ist,** *n.* a person who is able to use humor with skill in writing, acting, etc. —**hu'mor·ous,** *adj.*

hump [həmp'], *n.* a raised, rounded place on the back or shoulders. **Ex.** *Some camels have one hump and some have two humps.*

hundred (1) [hən'drəd], *n., adj.* the number that comes after ninety-nine; the number *100.* —**hun'dredth,** *adj.* coming after ninety-nine others.

hung (2) [heŋ'], *v.* past tense and participle of *hang.* **Exs.** *She hung the clothes on the line to dry. He had hung his coat in the closet.*

hunger (1) [heŋ'gər], *n.* 1. the unpleasant feeling or weakness caused by the need for food. **Ex.** *He was so aware of his hunger that he could not study.* 2. the need for food. **Ex.** *He died of hunger.* 3. a strong desire. **Ex.** *She felt a hunger for good music.* —*v.* 1. need food; be hungry. **Ex.** *They hungered for a bit of bread.* 2. have an eager desire. **Ex.** *He hungered for fame.* —**hun'gry,** *adj.* 1. needing food; feeling hunger. **Ex.** *The child was hungry.* 2. desiring strongly; eager. **Ex.** *They are hungry for knowledge.* —**hun'gri·ly,** *adv.*

a, far; æ, am; e, get; ey, late; i, in; iy, see; ɔ, all; ow, go; u, put; uw, too; ə, but, ago; ər, fur; aw, out; ay, life; oy, boy; ŋ, ring; θ, think; ð, that; ž, measure; š, ship; ǰ, edge; č, child.

hunt (1) [hənt'], *v.* 1. search for wild animals or birds to catch or kill them. **Ex.** *The men are hunting deer.* 2. try to find; search for; seek. **Ex.** *They are still hunting for the lost child* —*n.* the act of hunting wild animals; the act of searching. **Ex.** *Are you going to join the hunt on Saturday morning?* —**hunt'er,** *n.*

hurl (4) [hərl'], *v.* 1. throw or cast with great force. **Ex.** *A rock was hurled at the car.* 2. say with great force. **Ex.** *She hurled insults at him.*

hurrah (4) [hərɑ:'], *interj.* an exclamation of joy; a cheer. **Ex.** *Hurrah for our team!*

hurricane [hər'əkeyn'], *n.* a storm with violent, rapidly moving winds and a great deal of rain. **Ex.** *The threat of a hurricane forced the evacuation of the oceanfront town.*

hurry (1) [hə:r'iy], *v.* 1. move or act quickly or rapidly. **Ex.** *They hurried home.* 2. cause to move or act more rapidly. **Ex.** *We tried to hurry them on their way.* —*n.* act of hurrying; haste; need for hurrying. **Ex.** *Don't bother me now; I am in a hurry!*

hurt (1) [hərt'], *v.* 1. cause bodily injury, pain or suffering. **Ex.** *He hurt himself when he fell.* 2. damage; harm. **Ex.** *Nothing will hurt this plastic tablecloth.* 3. cause mental pain; distress. **Ex.** *I don't want to hurt her feelings.* —*n.* pain; injury; harm.

husband (1) [həz'bənd], *n.* a man who is married. **Ex.** *They are husband and wife.*

hush (3) [həš'], *v.* become quiet or still; make quiet. **Ex.** *The children hushed their voices as their father spoke.* —*n.* silence or quiet, especially after noise. **Ex.** *A hush fell upon the city at midnight.*

hustle (5) [həs'əl], *v.* 1. push along quickly and energetically; crowd roughly or rudely. **Ex.** *The crowd hustled into the train.* 2. force roughly or quickly. **Ex.** *The guards hustled the prisoner into the car.* —*n.* noisy, busy activity. **Ex.** *She was glad to be out of the hustle of the busy store.* —**hustle and bustle,** busy, energetic activity. **Ex.** *They enjoyed the hustle and bustle of the holiday season.*

hut (5) [hət'], *n.* a small, rough house; a cabin. **Ex.** *They passed a hut in the forest.*

hydrogen (5) [hay'drəjən], *n.* a gas that has no color or smell and that burns with a very hot flame. **Ex.** *Hydrogen combines chemically with oxygen to form water.*

hymn (4) [him'], *n.* a song in honor or praise of a god, nation, etc. **Ex.** *The people joined together in singing a hymn.*

hyphen [hay'fən], *n.* a mark (-) used to join parts of words or two or more words. **Ex.** Sister-in-law *is a word with two hyphens.* —**hy'phe·nate`**, *v.* join or write with a hyphen.

hypodermic [hay`pədər'mik], *adj.* of or related to a kind of hollow needle used to inject a solution under the skin. **Ex.** *He became infected from a used hypodermic needle.* —*n.*

I

I, i [ay'], *n.* the ninth letter of the English alphabet.

I (1) [ay'], *pron.* the person speaking, thinking, writing, etc. **Ex.** *I want to leave now.*

-ible (1) [əbəl], *suffix.* that is possible; that can be done. **Exs.** *Eat, edible; divide, divisible.*

-ic (1) [ik], *suffix.* 1. of the nature of; like. **Ex.** *Metal, metallic.* 2. in the manner of. **Ex.** *Artist, artistic.* 3. consisting of; containing; related to. **Ex.** *History, historic.*

ice (1) [ays'], *n.* frozen water. **Ex.** *Is the ice thick enough to walk on?* —**i'cy**, *adj.* very cold; like ice. **Ex.** *Your hands are icy.* —**i'ci·cle**, *n.* a long, pointed, hanging piece of ice formed by water that freezes as it runs or falls down in drops. **Ex.** *Icicles had formed on the rocky hillside.*

ice cream (3) [ays' kriym'], *n.* a frozen food made of cream and/or milk, sugar, flavoring and sometimes eggs. **Ex.** *We like to have ice cream for dessert.* —**ice cream cone,** a cookie formed into a cone shape which holds ice cream.

icing [ay'sing], *n.* a mixture of sugar, butter or a butter substitute, a liquid, flavoring and sometimes eggs used to spread over the top of a cake and decorate it. **Ex.** *She wrote "Happy Birthday" with icing on the cake.*

I'd [ayd'], short form, contraction of *I had* and *I would*. **Exs.** *I'd left before he arrived. I'd help her if she asked me.*

idea (1) [aydiy'ə], *n.* 1. a thought; a mental picture. **Ex.** *She has a strange idea of happiness.* 2. opinion; belief; plan. **Ex.** *He has definite ideas on every subject.*

ideal (3) [aydiy'əl], *n.* 1. an idea of something that is perfect. **Ex.** *Peace and justice are ideals.* 2. something or someone thought of as perfect. **Ex.** *The pilot was the boy's ideal —adj.* perfect. **Ex.** *We think that the seashore is an ideal spot for a vacation.* —i·de·al·ly, *adv.* —i·de·al·ism, *n.* the practice of forming ideals; a strong belief in ideals. —i·de·al·ist, *n.* a person who believes in and lives by ideals. —i·de·al·ize, *v.* act or plan as if a person, thing or action is perfect. **Ex.** *He idealized his wife.*

identify (3) [ayden'təfay'], *v.* recognize as being a particular person or thing; prove as the same. **Ex.** *She identified the things that were stolen from her house.* 2. associate closely; consider as the same. **Ex.** *Though they themselves are no longer poor, they can still identify with the problems of the poor.* —i·den·ti·fi·ca'tion, *n.*

identity [ayden'tətiy], *n.* 1. the qualities taken as a whole by which a person or thing is known and recognized. **Ex.** *The identity of the body has not yet been discovered.* 2. the personality. **Ex.** *He felt that he would lose his identity if he worked for such a large company.* 3. sameness; the likeness of one thing to another. **Ex.** *The identity of the handwriting proved that she had written the letter.* —i·den'ti·cal, *adj.* 1. exactly alike. **Ex.** *The sisters always wore identical clothes even though they were not twins.* 2. the same. **Ex.** *I know three people whose birthdays are identical to mine.*

idiot (5) [id'iyət], *n.* 1. a very foolish or very stupid person. **Ex.** *He is behaving like an idiot.* 2. one who is not able to learn because of the condition of his brain. —id'i·ot'ic, *adj.* foolish; stupid. **Ex.** *Driving without a license was an idiotic thing to do.*

idle (3) [ay'dəl], *adj.* 1. doing nothing; not busy. **Ex.** *She spent an idle hour watching boats on the river.* 2. lazy. **Ex.** *The idle boy did not prepare his class assignment.* —v. 1. do nothing. **Ex.** *Although there was a great deal of work to be done, they idled the day away.* 2. operate a motor at low speed so that the machine does not actually move or expend much energy. **Ex.** *He idled the motor while waiting for his wife.* —i'dle·ness, *n.* —i'dly, *adv.*

idol (4) [ay'dəl], *n.* 1. an image or object that people worship. **Ex.** *A stone idol stood at the entrance to the village.* 2. any person admired to the point of adoration. **Ex.** *Her idol is a movie actor.* —**i'dol·ize,** *v.* adore; worship.

if (1) [if'], *conj.* 1. on condition that; provided. **Ex.** *I will help you if you come early.* 2. in case that; in the event that. **Ex.** *He will come if you need him.* 3. supposing that; granted that. **Ex.** *If both suits cost the same, I will take the blue one.* 4. whether. **Ex.** *We wondered if you were ill.* —**even if,** though; although. **Ex.** *We will go even if it rains.*

-ify (3) [əfay], *suffix.* make; form into; cause to become. **Exs.** *Class, classify; solid, solidify.*

ignore (3) [ignɔ:r'], *v.* refuse to notice or recognize. **Ex.** *She ignored the warning sign.* —**ig'no·rance,** *n.* lack of knowledge; the condition of being ignorant. **Ex.** *His ignorance of the subject was evident when he spoke.* —**ig'no·rant,** *adj.* lacking in knowledge. **Ex.** *He was ignorant of the danger.*

il- (3) [il], *prefix.* not. **Exs.** *Literate, illiterate; legal, illegal.*

ill (1) [il'], *adj.* 1. not well; sick. **Ex.** *He is very ill.* 2. bad. **Ex.** *Her ill manners cost her many friends.* —*n.* sickness; trouble; harm; evil. **Ex.** *He suffered all the ills of the tropics.* —**ill'ness,** *n.* sickness.

ill- (1) [il], *prefix.* poorly; badly. **Exs.** *Kept, ill-kept; mannered, ill-mannered.*

I'll [ayl'], short form, contraction of *I shall* and *I will.* **Exs.** *I'll telephone him immediately. I'll be ready soon.*

illegal (5) [iliy'gəl], *adj.* not legal; unlawful. **Ex.** *He was arrested for the illegal sale of guns.* —**il·le'gal·ly,** *adv.* —**il'le·gal'i·ty,** *n.*

illegitimate [il'ijit'əmit], *adj.* 1. not legal. **Ex.** *The department head ignored the illegitimate use of its funds.* 2. born to a mother who is not married. **Ex.** *When she was sixteen, she had an illegitimate daughter.*

illiterate [ilit'erit], *adj.* not able to read or write. **Ex.** *He had difficulty getting a job because he was illiterate.* —**il·lit'er·a·cy,** *n.*

illuminate (4) [iluw'məneyt'], *v.* 1. supply with light. **Ex.** *The lamp illuminated the room.* 2. explain; enlighten, as with knowledge. **Ex.** *The professor illuminated the problem for his students.* —**ill·lu'mi·na'tion,** *n.*

illusion (4) [iluw'žən], *n.* 1. something which seems to be real or true but is not. **Ex.** *The sun shining on the sand produced the illusion that there was a lake in the distance.* 2. a false impression, belief or idea. **Ex.** *She had illusions about her chances for a career in the movies.*

illustrate (3) [il'əstreyt'], *v.* 1. explain by examples, figures, etc. **Ex.** *He illustrated his point with a story about his youth.* 2. provide with pictures, as in a book or magazine. **Ex.** *The book was illustrated with drawings and maps.* —**il'lus·tra'tor,** *n.* one who makes illustrations for books, magazines, etc. —**il'lus·tra'tion,** *n.* the act of illustrating; that which illustrates.

ill will [il' wil'], bad feeling. **Ex.** *His actions earned him much ill will.*

im- (2) [im], *prefix.* 1. not. **Exs.** *Mature, immature; moral, immortal.* 2. in; into; on. **Exs.** *Migrate, immigrate; peril, imperil.*

I'm [aym'], short form, contraction of *I am.* **Ex.** *Guess where I'm going today.*

image (3) [im'ij], *n.* 1. a likeness of a person or thing in the form of a painting, drawing or, especially, a statue. **Ex.** *The artist carved an image of her in wood.* 2. the picture reflected by a mirror. **Ex.** *In the mirror he saw an image of himself.* 3. a mental picture; an idea. **Ex.** *He tried to create in people's minds an image of himself as a friendly, generous man.* 4. a copy; a person or thing closely resembling another. **Ex.** *She is the image of her mother.*

imagine (2) [imæj'ən], *v.* 1. form a picture or idea in the mind. **Ex.** *I imagine you are tired after your trip.* —**i·mag'in·a·ble,** *adj.* that can be imagined. **Ex.** *It was the happiest time imaginable for us.* —**i·mag'i·nar·y,** *adj.* not real. —**i·mag'i·na'tion,** *n.* the ability to imagine. **Ex.** *That child has a wonderful imagination.* —**i·mag'i·na·tive,** *adj.* having or showing imagination. **Ex.** *The story included an imaginative description of life in a castle.*

imitate (3) [im'əteyt'], *v.* 1. copy in action or manner. **Ex.** *Boys often imitate their sports heroes.* 2. resemble. **Ex.** *The wood was painted to imitate marble.* —**im'i·ta'tion,** *n.* 1. a product or result of imitating. **Ex.** *These pearls are only imitations.* 2. the act of copying. **Ex.** *The entertainer did imitations of famous people.* —**im'i·ta'tive,** *adj.* like someone or something else. **Ex.** *His style is imitative of other artists.*

immediate (2) [imiy'diyit], *adj.* 1. without delay; instant. **Ex.** *We must have an immediate reply.* 2. very near in time or place. **Ex.** *Our immediate plan is to sell the store.* 3. direct; directly related. **Ex.** *Heart failure was the immediate cause of death.* —**im·me'di·ate·ly,** *adv.*

immense (3) [imens'], *adj.* 1. very large; vast; huge; very big. **Ex.** *She was left an immense fortune.* 2. boundless; not able to be measured. **Ex.** *He watched the bird until it was lost in the immense heavens.* —**im·men'si·ty,** *n.*

immigrant (4) [im'əgrənt], *n,* a person from a foreign land who enters a country for the purpose of making his home there permanently. **Ex.** *He came to the United States as an immigrant when he was a young boy.* —**im'mi·grate,** *v.* —**im' mi·gra'tion,** *n.* the act of immigrating.

immortal (5) [imor'təl], *adj.* not mortal; never dying; everlasting. **Ex.** *He enjoyed reading the legends about immortal heroes.* —*n.* a person whose fame is enduring. **Ex.** *His writings have made him an immortal.* —**im'mor·tal'i·ty,** *n.* unending life.

immune [imyuwn'], *adj.* 1. inheriting protection against disease-causing agents such as germs or acquiring protection against a particular disease by inoculation. **Ex.** *We were given shots to make us more immune to the flu.* 2. protected. **Ex.** *He was promised that he would be immune from prosecution if he cooperated.* 3. not affected by. **Ex.** *The ballplayer was immune to the shouts of the crowd.* —**im'mu'nize,** *v.* —**im·mu'ni·ty,** *n.* the state of being immune. —**im'mu·ni·za'tion,** *n.* the act of making immune.

impact (4) [im'pækt], *n.* 1. the striking of one object or body against another; the act of coming together with force. **Ex.** *The force of the impact threw the driver out of the car.*

impeach [impiyč'], *v.* bring a charge of an illegal act against a public official who is then tried before the United States Congress or a state legislature. **Ex.** *President Andrew Johnson was impeached but was acquitted by one vote in 1868.*

imperial (4) [impi:r'iyəl], *adj.* of or suitable to an empire or the rulers of an empire. **Ex.** *There was a ceremony to welcome* *their imperial majesties.* —**im·pe'ri·al·ism**, *n.* 1. the policy of gaining control of territories to build an empire. 2. the policy by which a powerful nation gains political and economic control over a poorer nation.

implement (4) [im'pləmənt], *n.* an object used for a particular task; a tool; an instrument used in performing work. **Ex.** *The plow was one of his most important farm implements.* —*v.* carry out; ensure completion. **Ex.** *Money is needed to implement the program.*

implore (5) [implɔːr'], *v.* ask for earnestly and with feeling; ask for help or mercy; beg; plead. **Ex.** *We implored him to act before it was too late.* —**im·plor'ing**, *adj.* begging; pleading. **Ex.** *She gave him an imploring look.*

imply (4) [implay'], *v.* say indirectly; hint; suggest something without actually saying it. **Ex.** *Your manner implies that you are not pleased with me.* —**im'pli·ca'tion**, *n.* the act of implying; that which is implied. **Ex.** *What was the implication of his remark?*

import (3) [impɔrt', im'pɔrt], *v.* bring commercial goods in from a foreign country. **Ex.** *That merchant imports wine.* —*n.* 1. a product brought in from another country. **Ex.** *Imports during the year were greater than exports.* 2. meaning. **Ex.** *What is the import of the president's remarks?* —**im·port'er**, *n.* one who brings in goods from a foreign country. —**im'por·ta'tion**, *n.* the act of importing.

important (1) [impɔr'tənt], *adj.* having great meaning, value, power, etc. **Ex.** *He has an important position with this company.* —**im·por'tance**, *n.* great meaning, value, power, etc. **Ex.** *This is a meeting of considerable importance.*

impose (4) [impowz'], *v.* 1. subject to a tax, penalty or other burden. **Ex.** *The judge imposed a heavy fine on the lawbreaker.* 2. force oneself or one's company upon others; take advantage of. **Ex.** *He imposed on his friends by visiting them too often.* —**im'po·si'tion**, *n.* that which imposes; the act of imposing. **Ex.** *It was an imposition for her to ask for your help.* —**im·pos'ing**, *adj.* grand in size, manner, appearance, etc. **Ex.** *The new museum is an imposing building.*

impossible (2) [impas'əbəl], *adj.* that cannot be, exist or happen; not possible. **Ex.** *It is impossible for me to see you tomorrow.* —**im·pos'si·bil'i·ty**, *n.*

impress (2) [impres'], *v.* 1. have a strong effect on the thinking or feelings; influence. **Ex.** *My talk with the president impressed me deeply.* 2. fix firmly in the mind. **Ex.** *His employer impressed on him the importance of getting to work on time.* 3. produce a mark by pressing. **Ex.** *The writing paper is impressed with the school seal.* —**im·pres'sion,** *n.* 1. a strong effect on the mind or feelings. **Ex.** *The boy made a good impression by his hard work.* 2. a general feeling; an uncertain belief. **Ex.** *It is my impression that they have met before.* 3. mark made by pressing. **Ex.** *The impression of the seal on the wax was very clear.* —**im·pres'sion·a·ble,** *adj.* easily impressed. **Ex.** *The child was very impressionable.* —**im·pres'sive,** *adj.* making a strong impression; admirable.

improve (2) [impruwv'], *v.* 1. become better. **Ex.** *His health is improving.* 2. make better. **Ex.** *She improved her reading ability by practice.* —**im·prove'ment,** *n.*

impulse (3) [im'pəls], *n.* 1. a sudden desire to do something. **Ex.** *Acting on impulse, she quit her job.* 2. the force that starts an action. **Ex.** *An electrical impulse started the motor.* —**im·pul'sive,** *adj.* acting without thinking; not thought out.

in (1) [in'], *prep.* 1. held by; contained by; surrounded by; covered by. **Ex.** *They walked home in the rain.* 2. during. **Ex.** *He will be away in April.* 3. within the limits of; not beyond. **Ex.** *They are visiting in the city.* 4. showing; affected by; influenced by. **Ex.** *In her haste, she forgot the money.* 5. according to; with regard to. **Ex.** *In her mind, he is guilty.* 6. by means of; by the use of. **Ex.** *The design was done in colored wool.* 7. belonging to; being a part of. **Ex.** *There are three girls in the group.* 8. having as a location; affecting. **Ex.** *He has a pain in his stomach.* 9. working at; occupied by. **Ex.** *He is now in business.* —*adv.* inside; toward the inside. **Ex.** *Bring your friend in.*

in- (2) [in], *prefix.* 1. in; into; within; toward. **Exs.** *Side, inside; born, inborn; coming, incoming.* 2. not; without. **Exs.** *Attention, inattention; action, inaction; correct, incorrect; definite, indefinite.*

inasmuch as [in‘əzməč' æz'], because; since. **Ex.** *Inasmuch as you're busy, I will come back later.*

inaugurate (5) [inɔː'gyəreyt`], v. 1. begin. Ex. *A French language course was inaugurated in school this year.* 2. place in office with ceremony. Ex. *The President of the United States is elected in November of one year and inaugurated in January of the following year.* —in·au`gu·ra'tion, n. —in·au'gu·ral, adj.

incense (4) [in'sens], n. a substance producing a pleasing odor when burned. Ex. *There was the fragrance of incense in their home.*

incense (4) [insens'], v. enrage; fill with anger. Ex. *The official was incensed at the lack of respect shown him.*

incessant (5) [inses'ənt], adj. continuous; apparently endless; unceasing. Ex. *The incessant barking of the dog kept her awake.* —in·ces'sant·ly, adv.

inch (1) [inč'], n. a unit of length which is one twelfth of a foot. Ex. *That piece of wood is three inches wide.* See **Weights and Measures.**

incident (3) [in'sədənt], n. something that happens or takes place; an event. Ex. *He told of many incidents that had occurred when he was in the army.* —in'ci·dence, n. the regularity with which something happens. Ex. *The incidence of car accidents at the entrance to the bridge is increasing.* —in'ci·den'tal, adj. of lesser importance; secondary. Ex. *The taxi fare to the station was an incidental expense of the trip.* —in'ci·den'tal·ly, adv.

incite [insayt'], v. 1. excite, urge or provoke someone to have a strong feeling or to take action. Ex. *He incited the angry crowd to storm city hall.* 2. direct or provoke some strong feeling or action. Ex. *He incited a rebellion against the government.*

incline (3) [inklayn'], v. 1. slope; lean. Ex. *The path inclined down to the river.* 2. bend the head or body. Ex. *The mother inclined her head to hear the child's words.* —n. slope; slant. Ex. *They had to walk up a steep incline.* —in·clined', adj. having a preference for or tendency to. Ex. *I am inclined to go since the weather is nice.* —in·cli·na'tion, n. 1. a preference; choice. Ex. *He went to college against his inclination.* 2. a sloping, bending or leaning position. Ex. *He recognized her with an inclination of the head.*

include (3) [inkluwd'], v. 1. contain as part of a whole. Ex. *This book includes all of his poems.* 2. place with others in a group. Ex. *We shall include her name on the list of guests.* —in·clu'sion, n. —in·clu'sive, adj.

income (3) [in'kəm], *n.* money received as salary, earnings, profit from business, etc. **Ex.** *He has a very high income.*

increase (1) [inkriys'], *v.* 1. make greater, larger or more numerous; add to. **Ex.** *He increased his efforts.* 2. become greater or more numerous; grow. **Ex.** *The number of people living in the city is increasing rapidly.* —**in'crease,** *n.* the growth or amount of growth in size, number, etc. **Ex.** *There has been an increase in the tax rate.* —**in·creas'ing,** *adj.* becoming greater, larger, etc. —**in·creas'ing·ly,** *adj.*

incredible (5) [inkred'əbəl], *adj.* not believable. **Ex.** *He told me an incredible story.* —**in·cred'i·bil'i·ty,** *n.* —**in·cred'i·bly,** *adv.*

incriminate [inkrim'əneyt'], *v.* accuse of or connect someone with a crime or wrongdoing. **Ex.** *He was incriminated in the bank robbery.*

indeed (1) [indiyd'], *adv.* really; in fact; in truth; very much. **Ex.** *It is indeed a pleasure to be here.*

independence (3) [in'dəpən'dəns], *n.* freedom from the rule or control of others. **Ex.** *Many countries gained their independence in the 1960s.* —**in'de·pend'ent,** *adj.* not influenced, controlled by, or dependent upon others. **Ex.** *She is an independent thinker.* —**Independence Day,** the day on which a country became independent from another. **Ex.** *Independence Day in the United States is the Fourth of July, the day the United States declared its independence from England.*

index (4) [in'deks], *n.* an alphabetical list or table of subjects, names, etc. at the back of a book telling on what pages they may be found. **Ex.** *The teacher taught the children how to use the index of their textbook.* —*v.* provide with an index. **Ex.** *He is indexing a history book.* —**index finger,** *n.* the finger next to the thumb.

indicate (2) [in'dəkeyt'], *v.* 1. be a sign of. **Ex.** *The red traffic light indicates stop.* 2. show; point. **Ex.** *Please indicate on the map where the city is.* 3. make known. **Ex.** *He indicated that he wanted to leave.* —**in'di·ca'tion,** *n.* a sign or signal. **Ex.** *There had been no indication that she was ill.* —**in·dic'a·tive,** *adj.*

indict [indayt'], *v.* make a formal charge or accusation against someone of committing a crime. **Ex.** *She was indicted for fraud.* —**in·dict'ment,** *n.*

indignant (4) [indig'nənt], *adj.* full of anger about an action which is unfair, unjust or cruel. **Ex.** *He was indignant that the* convicted man was given such a light sentence. —in·**dig'nant·ly**, adv. —in·**dig·na'tion**, n. anger caused by that which is unfair, unjust or cruel.

individual (2) [in'dəviǰ'uwəl], adj. 1. single; one; separate from others. **Ex.** They each received an individual letter from the company. 2. of a single person; different from others. **Ex.** The students' rooms reflected their individual interests. 3. about, by or for one person. **Ex.** The members of the committee gave individual reports. —n. single human being. **Ex.** She is a happy individual. —in·**di·vid'u·al·ly**, adv. —in·**di·vid'u·al·ism**, n. 1. the idea or belief that individuals and their interests are more important than the group or common interest. 2. individuality. —in·**di·vid'u·al'i·ty**, n. the quality or qualities of a person or thing that are different from those of another. **Ex.** She showed her individuality in the style of her dress.

indoors (5) [in'dɔrz', in'dɔrz`], adv. in or into a building. **Ex.** They play indoors during the bad weather. —**in'door, in·door'**, adj. **Ex.** There are many indoor activities they enjoy.

induce (4) [induws', indyuws'], v. 1. lead into doing something; persuade. **Ex.** Nothing would induce him to change his mind. 2. effect; cause. **Ex.** His poor health was induced by smoking. —in·**duce'ment**, n. that which persuades. **Ex.** The offer of a higher salary was an inducement for her to change jobs.

indulge (4) [indəlǰ'], v. 1. yield to. **Ex.** He indulged his desire for rich food to a harmful extent. 2. grant the wishes of. **Ex.** Those parents indulge their children too much. —in·**dul'gence**, n. —in·**dul'gent**, adj. —in·**dul'gent·ly**, adv.

industrious (3) [indəs'triyəs], adj. hardworking. **Ex.** He is an industrious student.

industry (1) [in'dəstriy], n. 1. any business that produces goods or services. **Ex.** He works in the automobile industry. 2. business and manufacturing as a whole. **Ex.** The President asked the leaders of industry for advice. 3. hard work. **Ex.** You have the ability to be successful, but you are not showing enough industry. —in·**dus'tri·al**, adj. —in·**dus'tri·al·ize'**, v. develop industries. **Ex.** The country is trying to industrialize in order to improve its economy. —in·**dus'tri·al·ist**, n. an owner or a manager of an important industry.

inevitable (4) [inev'ətəbəl], adj. not avoidable or escapable; certain. **Ex.** Increasing the amount of the budget made an increase in taxes inevitable. —in·**ev'i·ta·bly**, adv.

infamous [in'fəməs], *adj.* of very bad reputation; known to be wicked. **Ex.** *He is an infamous liar.*

infant (4) [in'fənt], *n.* a very, very young child; a baby. **Ex.** *The woman was carrying an infant in her arms.* —*adj.* 1. of or referring to a baby. 2. in a very early stage of growth or development. **Ex.** *Infant industries sometimes need government help.* —**in'fan·cy,** *n.* —**in'fan·tile,** *adj.* childish.

infantry (4) [in'fəntriy], *n.* soldiers who fight on foot; the branch of the military consisting of these soldiers. **Ex.** *When he was in the infantry, he often marched long distances.*

infect (5) [infekt'], *v.* 1. make ill with something that produces disease. **Ex.** *Dirt infected his wound.* 2. spread one's feelings or moods to others. **Ex.** *Her enthusiasm infected all of them.* —**in·fec'tion,** n. a condition produced in the body by the entry of a disease. **Ex.** *An infection caused his death.* —**in·fec'tious,** *adj.* caused by or causing infection; spreading rapidly.

inferior (4) [infi:r'iyər], *adj.* 1. lower in rank, importance, etc. **Ex.** *The rank of captain is inferior to that of a general.* 2. low or lower in quality, excellence, estimation, etc.; poor or poorer when compared to someone or something else. **Ex.** *The builder used inferior material in that house.* —*n.* one lower in rank or importance. **Ex.** *He was always courteous to his inferiors as well as superiors.* —**in·fe`ri·or'i·ty,** *n.*

infinite (4) [in'fənit], *adj.* 1. too great to measure; vast. **Ex.** *The sky is infinite in size.* 2. endless; without limit. **Ex.** *His father has infinite patience.* —**in'fi·nite·ly,** *adv.* —**in·fin'i·ty,** *n.* that which is without end.

infinitive (5) [infin'ətiv], *n.* a simple form of a verb, usually preceded by *to.* **Exs.** *In the sentence "I want to see him tomorrow,"* to see *is an infinitive. In the sentence "He had me wait,"* wait *is an infinitive.*

inflammation (5) [in`fləmey'šən], *n.* a painful, often hot and red, swelling of some part of the body. **Ex.** *The inflammation of his left knee made it difficult for him to walk.* —**in·flame',** *v.* 1. swell and become painful and often hot and red. **Ex.** *Her right eye was inflamed.* 2. anger or incite. **Ex.** *His speech inflamed the people to rebel.* —**in·flam'ma·ble,** *adj.* easily catching fire. **Ex.** *That material is highly inflammable.* —**in·flam'ma·tor'y,** *adj.*

causing anger or excitement. **Ex.** *She wrote an inflammatory magazine article that resulted in many letters to the editor.*

inflate (5) [infleyt'], *v.* 1. cause to swell by filling with air or gas. **Ex.** *He inflated the life preserver.* 2. make larger or greater than is proper or usual. **Ex.** *Scarcity has inflated the price of fruit.* **—in·fla'tion,** *n.* 1. the act of filling with air or gas. 2. a period in which there is a general rise in prices; a lessening of the buying power of money. **Ex.** *Because of inflation, they had to spend more money for food.*

inflict (5) [inflikt'], *v.* 1. give a blow; cause to suffer pain, wounds, etc. **Ex.** *The enemy artillery inflicted many wounds upon our soldiers.* 2. put on as a punishment, tax, etc. **Ex.** *The government inflicted heavy taxes on the people.*

influence (2) [in'fluwəns], *n.* 1. the act or power to persuade or affect. **Ex.** *He had a great influence upon his students.* 2. a person or thing that affects. **Ex.** *The bad weather influenced them to stay home.* 3. the power that comes from wealth, authority, etc. **Ex.** *Do you know anyone with influence who can help us?* —*v.* have an effect upon; affect; change. **Ex.** *She was not influenced by the promise of riches.* **—in'flu·en'tial,** *adj.* of or having influence.

inform (2) [infɔrm'], *v.* 1. tell; give knowledge to. **Ex.** *The repairman informed me that the work was completed.* 2. give evidence or information, especially against someone. **Ex.** *The spy informed on members of his group.* **—in·form'ant,** *n.* one who gives information. **—in·form'er,** *n.* one who gives information against others.

information (2) [in'fərmey'šən], *n.* 1. knowledge; facts; news. **Ex.** *She got the information she needed from the library.* 2. the act of informing or becoming informed. **Ex.** *For your information, I will be away on Friday.* **—in·form'a·tive,** *adj.* providing knowledge. **Ex.** *This book is very informative.*

-ing (1) [iŋ], *suffix.* 1. continuing action of a verb. **Ex.** *When I came, he was eating.* 2. the act of one who does what the verb describes. **Exs.** *Fish, fishing; dream, dreaming; run, running.* 3. the product or result of an action. **Exs.** *Draw, drawing; offer, offering.* 4. material for. **Exs.** *Roof, roofing; flavor, flavoring.*

ingenious (5) [inǰiyn'yəs], *adj.* 1. showing cleverness of planning or design. **Ex.** *The door was fastened with an ingenious lock.* 2. talented; clever. **Ex.** *The ingenious boy won a prize for his invention.* **—in·gen'ious·ly,** *adv.* **—in'ge·nu'i·ty,** *n.* **Ex.** *Her ingenuity never ceases to amaze me.*

ingredient (4) [ingriy'diyənt], *n.* one of the parts of a mixture or combination. **Ex.** *Chocolate is one of the ingredients I need to make this cake.*

inhabit (3) [inhæb'it], *v.* have as a home; live in. **Ex.** *Wild animals once inhabited much of this land.* —**in·hab'it·a·ble,** *adj.* suitable for living. —**in·hab'it·ant,** *n.* one who inhabits.

inhale (4) [inheyl'], *v.* draw into the lungs, breathe in. **Ex.** *He stood at the open window and inhaled deeply.*

inherit (4) [inher'it], *v.* 1. receive something upon the death of the former owner. **Ex.** *She inherited land and money from her uncle.* 2. have at birth from one's parents. **Ex.** *The baby inherited his mother's blue eyes.* —**in·her'i·tance,** *n.*

initial (4) [iniš'əl], *adj.* first; of the beginning. **Ex.** *He failed in his initial attempt.* —*n.* the first letter of a person's name or names. **Ex.** *President Franklin Delano Roosevelt's initials were F.D.R.* —*v.* sign with one's initials. **Ex.** *She initialed the correction to show that she had approved it.* —**i·ni'tial·ly,** *adv.* at first; at the beginning. **Ex.** *Initially I was favorably impressed.*

initiative (5) [iniš'ətiv], *n.* 1. an introductory act or step. **Ex.** *They took the initiative in getting acquainted with their neighbors.* 2. willingness and ability to get things started. **Ex.** *In the absence of the owner of the shop, the clerk showed his initiative.* —**i·ni'ti·ate`,** *v.* 1. begin; start. **Ex.** *We will initiate the new schedule next Monday.* 2. introduce a new member into an organization, activity, etc. **Ex.** *We are going to initiate three new members at the next club meeting.*

inject [injekt'], *v.* force a liquid by means of a needle underneath the skin into a muscle, vein, etc. **Ex.** *Before the bone x-ray was taken, the nurse injected a dye in the pateint's vein.* —**in·jec'tion,** *n.*

injure (3) [in'jər], *v.* harm; hurt; wound. **Ex.** *He injured his right leg when he fell.* —**in·ju'ri·ous,** *adj.* —**in'ju·ry,** *n.* damage or harm done or received. **Ex.** *Her injury prevented her from participating in sports that summer.*

ink (4) [ink'], *n.* a fluid used for writing or printing. **Ex.** *This pen has no ink in it.* —*v.* mark with ink.

inland [in'lænd], *adv.* toward the interior of a country; away from the border or coast of a country. **Ex.** *He took the train inland.* —*adj.* of or concerning the interior of a country;

away from the border or coast. **Ex.** *There is a lot of tourist travel on this inland waterway.*

in-law (3) [in'lɔ:'], *n.* relative by marriage. **Ex.** *Have you met my brother-in-law, my wife's brother?*

inlet [in'let'], *n.* a narrow body of water going into the land or between islands. **Ex.** *They entered the inlet just before dark.*

inmate [in'meyt'], *n.* a person held in a prison or mental hospital. **Ex.** *The inmates were allowed to have visitors on Sunday.*

inn (5) [in'], *n.* a place that provides bedrooms and food for travelers; a small hotel; a place that serves food and drink, often in the country. **Ex.** *The village has only one inn.*

inner [in'ər], *adj.* 1. inside; farther in. **Ex.** *She works in an inner office next to mine.* 2. nearest to the center. **Ex.** *He has good contacts in the inner circles of the state government.*

innocent (3) [in'əsənt], *adj.* 1. not guilty, especially legally; free from moral wrong; pure. **Ex.** *A person is innocent until proven guilty.* 2. not intending to do wrong; harmless. **Ex.** *They joined in the innocent pleasures of the country people.* 3. simple; knowing no evil. **Ex.** *She was an innocent young girl.* —**in'no·cent·ly,** *adv.* —**in'no·cence,** *n.*

innumerable [inuw'mərəbəl], *adj.* too many to be counted. **Ex.** *There have been innumerable requests for her to make one more stage appearance.*

inoculate [inak'yəleyt'], *v.* introduce into the body of a person or an animal a weakened form of a virus or germ that causes a particular disease in order to develop a protection against that disease; vaccinate. **Ex.** *My children had to be inoculated against several childhood diseases before they were allowed to enter school.* —**in·oc'u·la'tion,** *n.*

inquire (2) [inkwayr'], *v.* ask; request information. **Ex.** *They inquired about his past experience.* —**in·quir'ing,** *adj.* showing an interest in or desire for knowledge, information, etc.; curious. **Ex.** *Her teachers noted with pleasure her inquiring mind.* —**in·qui'ry,** *n.* a question.

inquisitive [inkwiz'ətiv], *adj.* 1. eager to learn; curious. **Ex.** *He has an inquisitive mind.* 2. interested in things which do not concern one; too curious; prying. **Ex.** *I resented her inquisitive manner.*

insane (5) [inseyn'], *adj.* 1. not sane; mentally very ill. **Ex.** *After being insane for many years, she regained her sanity.* 2. very foolish; senseless. **Ex.** *The idea of a trip to the moon was once considered insane.* —**in·san'i·ty,** *n.*

inscription (5) [inskrip'šən], *n.* a message or note written in a book, carved in stone, etc.; a dedication. **Ex.** *The inscription on the ancient monument was hard to read.*

insect (2) [in'sekt], *n.* a very small animal, usually with three pairs of legs and two pairs of wings.

INSECT

insert (5) [insərt'], *v.* put in. **Ex.** *The secretary inserted the letter in the envelope.* —**in'sert,** *n.* that which is inserted. —**in·ser'tion,** *n.* the act of inserting.

inside (1) [in'sayd`], *n.* the inner side; the surface, part, etc. that is within. **Ex.** *The inside of the box is painted red.* —*adj.* 1. on or in the inside. **Ex.** *He preferred an inside job to an outside one.* 2. private; secret. **Ex.** *He has inside information about the company's plans.* —*prep.* within; in or into the interior. **Ex.** *Have you been inside the new theater?* —*adv.* on the inside; within; to the inside. **Ex.** *Wait for me inside.* —**in·sid'er,** *n.* a person who is inside, as inside a group, and has special knowledge. **Ex.** *Insiders say that the President will soon propose a new tax program.*

insight [in'sayt`], *n.* special understanding. **Ex.** *Her insight into the problem will be helpful to us.*

insist (2) [insist'], *v.* 1. demand firmly. **Ex.** *I insist that he go today.* 2. be firm in holding an opinion or position. **Ex.** *She insisted that she was right.* —**in·sis'tent,** *adj.* —**in·sis'tent·ly,** *adv.* —**in·sis'tence,** *n.*

inspect (4) [inspekt'], *v.* 1. view closely; examine. **Ex.** *They inspected several new car models before deciding which one to buy.* 2. view officially. **Ex.** *The mayor inspected the new waterworks.* —**in·spec'tion,** *n.* the act of inspecting. —**in·spec'tor,** *n.* one who inspects.

inspire (3) [inspayr'], *v.* 1. have an influence upon; cause to act. **Ex.** *His brother's success inspired the boy to work harder.* 2. produce a feeling. **Ex.** *His words inspired confidence in us.* —**in·spi·ra'tion,** *n.* —**in·spi·ra'tion·al,** *adj.*

a, far; æ, am; e, get; ey, late; i, in; iy, see; ɔ, all; ow, go; u, put; uw, too; ə, but, ago; ər, fur; aw, out; ay, life; oy, boy; ŋ, ring; θ, think; ð, that; ž, measure; š, ship; j, edge; č, child.

install (4) [instɔːl'], *v.* place in position for service or use. **Ex.** *They are installing the electric wiring in the new house now.* —**in·stal·la·tion,** *n.* the act of putting in place; that which has been put in place.

installment [instɔːl'mənt], *n.* 1. one of a series of payments to be made at regular intervals until a debt is paid. **Ex.** *The washing machine is to be paid for in twenty monthly installments.* 2. one part of a novel, play, etc. that appears or is presented in a series until the story is completed. **Ex.** *I can hardly wait for the next installment of this television show.* —**in·stall'ment plan,** *n.* a plan by which a person can buy something and pay for it over a period of time in installments. **Ex.** *My brother is buying his car on the installment plan.*

instance (2) [in'stəns], *n.* 1. occasion; case. **Ex.** *There were many instances of courage during the terrible fire.* 2. example; something given as proof. **Ex.** *Can you give an instance of the boy's ability?*

instant (2) [in'stənt], *n.* 1. a moment; a very short period of time. **Ex.** *It was over in an instant.* 2. a particular moment or point in time. **Ex.** *Come here this instant.* —*adj.* 1. happening in a moment or without delay. **Ex.** *The play was an instant success.* 2. ready for quick preparation. **Ex.** *She fixed us some instant coffee.*

instead (1) [insted'], *adv.* 1. in the place of; taking the place of. **Ex.** *They came by train instead of by plane because of the storm.* 2. in its place; rather. **Ex.** *They ordered coffee but were served tea instead.*

instinct (3) [in'stiŋkt], *n.* 1. a natural, unlearned tendency or feeling in persons or animals. **Ex.** *Fear of the unknown is a common instinct.* 2. natural ability or talent. **Ex.** *She has an instinct for saying the right thing.* —**in·stinc'tive,** *adj.* of or concerning instinct. **Ex.** *His instinctive reaction was to go to their help.* —**in·stinc'tive·ly,** *adv.* resulting from instinct. **Ex.** *Instinctively she drew back.*

institution (2) [in'stətuw'šen, in'stətyuw'šen], *n.* 1. an organization, such as a school, hospital or church, which does some special kind of work. **Ex.** *She is planning to leave money to several educational institutions when she dies.* 2. established law, custom, etc. **Ex.** *Marriage is a basic institution in most societies.* 3. the act of starting or establishing. **Ex.** *The children benefited from the institution of some new summer pro-*

grams. **—in'sti·tute,** v. start or establish. **Ex.** *They instituted new rules for use of the clubhouse.* **—n.** an organization or society set up for a special purpose, such as education or research. **Ex.** *My daughter is studying at the art institute.* **—in·sti·tu'tion·al,** *adj.*

instruct (2) [instrəkt'], v. 1. teach; train; educate. **Ex.** *He instructed the students in history.* 2. direct; command. **Ex.** *The doctor instructed her patient to remain in bed.* **—in·struc'tion,** n. 1. the act of instructing; the knowledge or information given. 2. an order; advice. **—in·struc'tor,** n. one who instructs.

instrument (2) [in'strəmənt], n. 1. a tool or device, especially for exact work. **Ex.** *These instruments must be kept absolutely clean.* 2. a device for producing musical sounds. **Ex.** *He wants to play a brass instrument such as the horn.*

insulate [in'səleyt'], v. put a layer of material on, over or inside of something in order to prevent the passage of electricity, heat or sound. **Ex.** *This house is expensive to heat because it is not well insulated.* **—in·su·la'tion,** n. the act of insulating; the material used to insulate. **Ex.** *We have just had insulation put in under the roof.*

insult (3) [in'səlt], n. an act or remark which is rude or injures another's feelings. **Ex.** *Your refusal to believe my story is an insult.* **—in·sult',** v. act or speak rudely; offend. **Ex.** *He insulted the speaker by leaving before the lecture ended.* **—in·sult'ing,** *adj.*

insure (3) [inšu:r'], v. 1. make sure; make certain. **Ex.** *They sent a car for him in order to insure his presence at the meeting.* 2. protect or secure against damage or loss. **Ex.** *They deposited the money in the bank to insure that it would not be lost or stolen.* 3. buy or obtain insurance. **Ex.** *He had insured his house against wind damage.* **—in·sur'ance,** n. 1. a contract giving protection against monetary loss in case of fire, accident, theft, etc. **Ex.** *Did she have insurance on the stolen jewelry?* 2. the amount for which someone or something is insured. **Ex.** *The insurance on their house is $350,000.*

integrate (5) [in'təgreyt'], v. 1. open to the use of all races; do away with segregation. **Ex.** *The schools in this city have been integrated.* 2. bring together to form a whole. **Ex.** *He integrated ideas from several philosophers into his own personal philosophy.*

integrity (5) [integ'rətiy`], *n.* 1. honesty; trustworthiness. **Ex.** *She is known as a person of integrity.* 2. soundness; freedom from faults or defects. **Ex.** *The integrity of the airplane engine was in question.* 3. wholeness; completeness. **Ex.** *During the Civil War, the integrity of the United States was in danger.*

intellect (5) [in'təlekt`], *n.* 1. the power of the mind by which one knows and reasons; understanding. **Ex.** *His ease in solving that problem showed the depth of his intellect.* 2. a person possessing great powers of the mind. **Ex.** *She is one of this century's great intellects.* —**in·tel·lec'tu·al,** *adj., n.*

intelligence (3) [intel'əjəns], *n.* 1. the ability to think, reason and understand. **Ex.** *His intelligence is remarkable.* 2. news; information, especially that which concerns secrets of another country, business organization, etc. **Ex.** *No intelligence about the flood victims has reached us.* —**in·tel'li·gent,** *adj.* having or showing intelligence. —**in·tel'li·gent·ly,** *adv.* in a reasoned way; wisely.

intend (2) [intend'], *v.* 1. plan; have as a purpose. **Ex.** *I intend to buy a new suit today.* 2. design for a particular purpose. **Ex.** *We intended this room for the baby.*

intense (4) [intens'], *adj.* 1. very strong; great. **Ex.** *The intense heat exhausted him.* 2. earnest; serious. **Ex.** *She is an intense worker.* —**in·tense'ly,** *adv.* —**in·ten'si·ty,** *n.* —**in·ten'si·fy`,** *v.*

intent (3) [intent'], *n.* purpose; aim. **Ex.** *What is your intent in asking these questions?* —*adj.* giving full attention. **Ex.** *He was so intent upon his reading that he did not hear the bell.* 2. firmly decided; determined. **Ex.** *They were intent upon revenge.* —**in·tent'ly,** *adv.* with full attention. —**in·ten'tion,** *n.* purpose; plan. **Ex.** *It was his intention to invite her to dinner.* —**in·ten'tion·al,** *adj.* on purpose. —**in·ten'tion·al·ly,** *adv.* purposely.

inter- (2) [intər], *prefix.* 1. among; between; together. **Exs.** *Mix, intermix; mingle, intermingle.* 2. between; among. **Exs.** *Continental, intercontinental; national, international; American, inter-American.*

intercourse (5) [in'tərkɔrs`], *n.* 1. activity or actions between persons or nations; exchange of ideas, products, etc. **Ex.** *There was a great deal of commercial intercourse between the two countries.* 2. physical relations between the sexes; sexual relations.

interest (1) [in't(ə)rest], *n.* 1. a desire to give special attention to someone or something; attraction toward. **Ex.** *He had a great* *interest in music.* 2. the ability to cause such a desire. **Ex.** *The question of the origin of humans is of unending interest to humankind.* 3. the object of one's attention or feelings. **Ex.** *Gardening is one of her many interests.* 4. benefit; advantage. **Ex.** *It will be to your interest to get more education.* 5. a share in ownership of a business. **Ex.** *They bought an interest in a shoe factory.* 6. regular payments for the use of money borrowed. **Ex.** *They pay their interest on the loan monthly.* —*v.* 1. draw or excite the attention or curiosity of. **Ex.** *Foreign stamps interest him.* 2. cause to be concerned in; involve. **Ex.** *He interested his friend in outdoor sports.* —**in'ter·est·ed,** *adj.* having an interest in; concerned. **Ex.** *He is an interested party in this case.* —**in'ter·est·ing,** *adj.* of interest. **Ex.** *This is an interesting book.*

interfere (4) [in'tərfi:r'], *v.* 1. get in the way of; work against. **Ex.** *The noise interfered with his sleep.* 2. take a part in the affairs of others, especially when not asked to do so. **Ex.** *She knew she should not interfere in other people's arguments.* —**in·ter·fer'ing,** *adj.* —**in·ter·fer'ence,** *n.*

interior (3) [inti:r'iyər], *n.* 1. the inside; the inner part. **Ex.** *The interior of the house is cool.* 2. the inland part of a country; any place located at a distance from the coast or border. **Ex.** *The hunters went deep into the interior.* —*adj.* 1. being within something; referring to the inside. **Ex.** *He is studying interior decorating.* 2. far from the boundaries or shores of a country; inland. **Ex.** *The interior regions have not been developed.*

interjection (5) [in'tərjek'šən], *n.* a word or words used to show feeling or emotion with no grammatical relation to the rest of the sentence; an exclamation. **Exs.** *Oh! Ah! Well! Alas!* See **A Brief Explanation of English Grammar.**

internal (4) [intər'nəl], *adj.* 1. inner; of or for the interior. **Ex.** *This medicine is not for internal use.* 2. within a country; domestic. **Ex.** *His office is concerned with internal affairs.* —**in'ter'nal·ly,** *adv.*

international (3) [in'tərnæš'ənəl], *adj.* concerning relations between or among nations. **Ex.** *So far six nations have signed that international trade agreement.* —**in·ter·na'tion·al·ly,** *adv.*

a, far; æ, am; e, get; ey, late; i, in; iy, see; ɔ, all; ow, go; u, put; uw, too; ə, but, ago; ər, fur; aw, out; ay, life; oy, boy; ŋ, ring; θ, think; ð, that; ž, measure; š, ship; ĵ, edge; č, child.

interpret (4) [intər'prət], *v.* tell or explain the meaning of something. Ex. *Please interpret this message for me.* 2. translate from one language to another. Ex. *She interpreted for the foreign visitors.* —**in·ter'pre·ta'tion,** *n.* the act of interpreting; explanation. Ex. *What is your interpretation of the poem?* —**in·ter'pre·ter,** *n.* one who interprets.

interrupt (2) [in'tərəpt'], *v.* stop for a short time. Ex. *They interrupted the meeting for lunch.* 2. break into; prevent. Ex. *A shot interrupted the quiet.* 3. stop another's action, conversation, etc. temporarily, especially with questions or remarks. Ex. *Their conversation was interrupted by a telephone call.* —**in'ter·rup'tion,** *n.*

intersect [in'tərsekt'], *v.* 1. cut across or divide by passing through. Ex. *The railroad intersected the town.* 2. meet and cross as roads, streets, highways, etc. Ex. *This road and the main highway intersect at the next traffic light.* —**in·ter·sec'tion,** *n.* the place where roads, streets, etc. meet and cross. Ex. *Traffic moves very slowly at this intersection.*

interval (3) [in'tərvəl], *n.* the time between two events; space or distance between two things. Ex. *In the interval between his departure and return, there was a reorganization in the office.* —**at intervals,** 1. occasionally. Ex. *At intervals she looked out the window.* 2. with space or periods of time in between. Ex. *Trees were planted at intervals of twenty feet.*

intervene (5) [in'tərviyn'], *v.* 1. come or happen between. Ex. *Only an instant intervened between the flash of lightning and the thunder.* 2. come between in order to settle or solve. Ex. *He intervened in the quarrel between the two brothers.* —**in'ter·ven'tion,** *n.*

interview (3) [in'tərvyuw'], *n.* 1. a meeting of two person to discuss something. Ex. *Every new student has an interview with a guidance counselor.* 2. a conversation between a journalist or a writer and another person or persons to obtain information, usually to be published or broadcast. Ex. *The President and his wife granted an interview about life in the White House.* —**in'ter·view'er,** *n.* one who interviews.

intimate (3) [in'təmit], *adj.* 1. very close or familiar. Ex. *They are intimate friends.* 2. private; very personal. Ex. *We do not discuss intimate matters with strangers.* 3. resulting from a thorough study of or familiarity with. Ex. *He has an intimate knowledge of that problem.* —**in'ti·mate·ly,** *adv.* —**in'ti·ma·cy,** *n.*

intimate (3) [in'təmeyt'], *v.* suggest; hint. **Ex.** *He intimated by a glance at his watch that it was time for us to leave.* —**in·ti·ma'tion,** *n.*

into (1) [in'tuw], *prep.* 1. from being outside toward being within a place or thing. **Ex.** *Come into the house.* 2. showing a change of state from one kind of thing or condition to another. **Ex.** *Spring changed into summer.*

intoxicate (5) [intak'səkeyt'], *v.* 1. lose or cause to lose mental and physical control as the result of the use of alcohol or drugs. **Ex.** *Because the whiskey had intoxicated him, he did not drive his car.* 2. excite. **Ex.** *They were intoxicated by the bright lights and music.* —**in·tox'i·ca'tion,** *n.* a condition of being intoxicated.

intra- (2) [intrə], *prefix.* within; inside. **Exs.** *State, intrastate; vein, intravenous.*

intrigue (5) [intriyg'], *v.* 1. plan in a secret way; plot; scheme. **Ex.** *They are intriguing against the government.* 2. excite the curiosity or interest of. **Ex.** *The story of your adventures intrigues me.* —*n.* a plot; a scheme. **Ex.** *They were accused of being involved in a political intrigue.* —**in·tri'guing,** *adj.*

introduce (2) [in'trəduws', in'trədyuws'], *v.* 1. make known; present; acquaint. **Ex.** *She introduced her friend to her mother.* 2. bring to notice; bring into use. **Ex.** *New electrical products are continually being introduced.* 3. bring forward for consideration; propose. **Ex.** *Several plans were introduced at the meeting.* 4. bring a person or persons to a first knowledge of something; make familiar with. **Ex.** *The children were introduced to a foreign language in the fifth grade.* —**in'tro·duc'tion,** *n.*

intrude (5) [intruwd'], *v.* push, force or come in without being asked or wanted. **Ex.** *Their neighbors intruded upon them during dinner.* —**in·trud'er,** *n.* one who intrudes. —**in·tru'sion,** *n.* the act of intruding.

invade (4) [inveyd'], *v.* 1. enter in order to seize or conquer. **Ex.** *Enemy troops invaded the country.* 2. rush in; crowd into. **Ex.** *On the first day of the season, hundreds of city dwellers invaded the beach.* —**in·vad'er,** *n.* one who invades. —**in·va'sion,** *n.* the act of invading.

invalid [in'vəlid], *n.* a person weakened by illness; a sickly person; a person unable to take care of him- or herself because of illness or injury. **Ex.** *The invalid waved weakly from the couch where she was resting.*

invent (2) [invent'], *v.* 1. plan and make something never made before. **Ex.** *Who invented the telephone?* 2. create in the mind. **Ex.** *He invented an excuse for not having done his homework.* —**in·ven'tion,** *n.* the act of inventing; the thing invented. —**in·ven'tor,** *n.* one who invents.

invest (4) [invest'], *v.* 1. put money into a business enterprise, real estate, etc. to earn a profit. **Ex.** *He invested his money in a store.* 2. devote one's time or energy. **Ex.** *He invested his time in learning to paint.* 3. put in office with ceremony. **Ex.** *The judge was invested with the robes of office.* —**in·vest'ment,** *n.* the act of investing; the money, time, etc. invested. —**in·ves'tor,** *n.* one who invests.

investigate (3) [inves'təgeyt'], *v.* examine officially; search or inquire into. **Ex.** *The police investigated the murder.* —**in·ves'ti·ga'tion,** *n.* official examination; search; inquiry. **Ex.** *They are making an investigation of the charge that funds were misused.* —**in·ves'ti·ga·tor,** *n.* one who investigates.

invisible [inviz'əbəl], *adj.* not capable of being seen; hidden; not visible. **Ex.** *From the road the house was invisible behind the trees.*

invite [invayt'], *v.* 1. ask as one's guest. **Ex.** *They invited us to go to the theater.* 2. attract; tend to cause. **Ex.** *His behavior invited unfavorable comment.* —**in·vi·ta'tion,** *n.* an act of asking as one's guest. **Ex.** *She sent us a written invitation to dinner.* —**in·vit'ing,** *adj.* having a quality which attracts. **Ex.** *The hot food looked inviting.*

involve (3) [invalv'], *v.* 1. include as a necessary part. **Ex.** *Her work involves a great deal of travel.* 2. bring into difficulty or trouble; be connected with. **Ex.** *She became involved in her neighbors' quarrel.* —**in·volved',** *adj.* 1. complicated; confusing; difficult to understand. **Ex.** *His explanation was too involved for us.* 2. much occupied with; closely connected with. **Ex.** *She was so involved with her young friends that we seldom saw her.* —**in·volv'ment,** *n.*

-ion (1) [ən], *suffix.* act of; condition of; result of. **Exs.** *Collect, collection; correct, correction; connect, connection.*

-ior (3) [iyər], *suffix.* 1. state or quality of. **Ex.** *Behave, behavior.* 2. one who. **Ex.** *Save, savior.*

-ious (2) [əs, iyəs], *suffix.* having or characterized by; full of. **Exs.** *Space, spacious; victory, victorious; vary, various.*

ir- (3) [ir], *prefix.* not. **Exs.** *Rational, irrational; responsible, irresponsible.*

iron (1) [ay'ern], *n.* 1. a strong, hard metal used in making tools and machines. **Ex.** *The plow was made of iron.* 2. something hard, strong and unyielding. **Ex.** *He has a grip of iron.* 3. an electrical device used for pressing or smoothing cloth. **Ex.** *Be careful; the iron is hot.* —*adj.* made of iron. **Ex.** *There is an iron fence around the building.* 2. like iron; strong. **Ex.** *Because of his iron fists, he seldom loses a fight.* —*v.* press; make smooth with an iron. **Ex.** *Please iron this shirt.* —**ironing board,** a board, usually on a stand, on which clothing, linens, etc. are placed in order to be ironed.

IRON 3

irregular (5) [ireg'yələr], *adj.* 1. not having a regular or even shape, arrangement or order. **Ex.** *Train schedules were irregular during the flood.* 2. occurring at an uneven or unequal rate. **Ex.** *The sick woman's heartbeat was irregular.* 3. not according to the usual rule or to the accepted principle or method. **Ex.** *He kept irregular accounts.* —**ir·reg'u·lar·ly,** *adv.* —**ir·reg`u·lar'i·ty,** *n.*

irritate (4) [i:r'əteyt`], *v.* 1. make nervous, impatient or angry. **Ex.** *When she has a headache, the slightest noise irritates her.* 2. cause to become red or sore. **Ex.** *The rough cloth irritated the child's tender skin.* —**ir'ri·ta·ble,** *adj.* easily irritated. —**ir`ri·ta'tion,** *n.*

is (1) [iz'], *v.* present of *be* used with he, she, it and singular nouns. **Ex.** *He is a doctor.*

-ish (2) [iš], *suffix.* 1. like. **Exs.** *Devil, devilish; girl, girlish.* 2. somewhat; rather. **Exs.** *Tall, tallish; yellow, yellowish.* 3. of; belonging to. **Exs.** *England, English; Spain, Spanish.*

island (1) [ay'lənd], *n.* a section of dry land entirely surrounded by water. **Ex.** *The island can be reached only by boat.*

isle (3) [ayl'], *n.* a small island; an island. **Ex.** *We visited the isles off the coast.*

a, far; æ, am; e, get; ey, late; i, in; iy, see; ɔ, all; ow, go; u, put; uw, too;

-ism (3) [izəm], *suffix*. 1. the act of; the result of. **Exs.** *Terrorize, terrorism; criticize, criticism.* 2. the state, condition or quality of. **Exs.** *Defeat, defeatism; hero, heroism.* 3. theory; belief. **Exs.** *National, nationalism; real, realism.*

isn't [iz'ənt], short form, contraction of *is not.* **Ex.** *Why isn't she coming?*

isolate (4) [ay'səleyt`], *v.* set apart; separate; cause to be alone. **Ex.** *He isolated himself in order to study.* —**i'so·la'tion,** *n.* —**i'so·la'tion·ist,** *n.* one who favors his or her country's keeping out of international involvements.

issue (2) [iš'uw, iš'yuw], *n.* 1. printed material such as a newspaper or magazine, usually part of a series. **Ex.** *The latest issue of the newspaper contains a story about my accident.* 2. a matter of interest or discussion. **Ex.** *Limiting land use is a current issue before the city council.* —*v.* 1. send out; publish. **Ex.** *That magazine is issued once a month.* 2. give out; distribute. **Ex.** *Food and clothing were issued to the flood victims.* —**at issue,** being discussed or argued about. **Ex.** *Where to build was the question at issue.*

-ist (2) [ist], *suffix.* 1. one who practices; one whose profession is. **Exs.** *Art, artist; science, scientist.* 2. one who believes in. **Exs.** *Nationalism, nationalist; socialism, socialist.*

it (1) [it'], *pron.* 1. a thing, place, happening, idea, etc. that has already been mentioned or is mentioned later. **Ex.** *He saw a house that he liked and bought it.* 2. a word used to make the sentence complete. **Exs.** *It is raining. It is cold. It's too bad he couldn't come.*

itch [itč'], *n.* 1. a stinging feeling or a tickling sensation that makes one want to scratch or rub the affected area. **Ex.** *I don't know why I have an itch in my ankle.* 2. a feeling of restlessness because of some desire. **Ex.** *He had an itch to travel abroad.* —*v.* 1. feel a stinging or tickling sensation. **Ex.** *His hands itched after he touched the poisonous vine.* 2. feel a restless desire. **Ex.** *He itched to be in school again.*

item (3) [ay'təm], *n.* 1. a separate article or thing in a list or group. **Ex.** *Beef, bread and potatoes were three of the items on her shopping list.* 2. a piece of news or information. **Ex.** *He read an item about his friend in the newspaper.* —**i'tem·ize,** *v.* list things one by one. **Ex.** *Please itemize your expenses.*

it'll [it'əl], short form, contraction of *it will* and *it shall*. **Ex.** *When do you think it'll be ready? It'll go badly for you if you are late.*

its (1) [its'], *pron.* of or belonging to it. **Ex.** *The cat is playing with its tail.*

it's [its'], short form, contraction of *it is*. **Ex.** *It's too late to go now.*

itself (2) [itself'], *pron.* its own self. **Exs.** *The dog hurt itself. Death itself held no fears for him.*

-ity (2) [ətiy, itiy], *suffix.* state; quality. **Exs.** *Real, reality; regular, regularity; active, activity.*

-ive (2) [iv], *suffix.* having the quality of; likely; tending to. **Exs.** affirm, affirmative; express, expressive; support, supportive.

I've [ayv'], short form, contraction of *I have*. **Ex.** *I've attended to it already.*

-ize (3) [ayz], *suffix.* 1. make into or like; become. **Exs.** *Human, humanize; crystal, crystallize.* 2. act in a certain way; engage in. **Exs.** *Theory, theorize; sympathy, sympathize.* 3. treat; combine with; subject to the action of. **Exs.** *Critic, criticize; drama, dramatize.*

J

J, j [jey'], *n.* the tenth letter of the English alphabet.

jacket (2) [jæk'it], *n.* 1. an outer garment worn on the upper part of the body; a short coat. 2. an outer covering such as the skin of a potato.

jail (4) [jeyl'], *n.* a prison for those awaiting trial or for those who have been convicted of minor crimes. **Ex.** *The judge sent him to jail*

JACKET 1

for sixty days. —*v.* take into or hold in jail. **Ex.** *He was jailed for stealing a car.* —**jail'er,** *n.* a person who is charge of a jail.

jam (4) [jæm'], *v.* 1. push together; crowd in together. **Ex.** *The returning workers jammed into the buses.* 2. cause to become stuck; force in so that something will not move. **Ex.** *The key is jammed in the lock.* —*n.* a crowding together; a being crowded together. **Ex.** *There is a traffic jam in the city streets every morning.*

jam (4) [jæm'], *n.* a food made of fruit and sugar cooked together until thick. **Ex.** *He spread jam on his bread.*

January (1) [jæn'yuwe:r'iy], *n.* the first month of the year.

jar (2) [ja:r'], *n.* a container, usually round and made of glass, with a wide opening at the top.

jar (2) [ja:r'], *v.* cause to shake; shock. **Ex.** *The sudden stop that the bus driver had to make jarred the passengers.*

JAR

jaw (4) [jɔ:'], *n.* one of the two bones that hold the teeth and form the frame of the mouth. **Ex.** *The meat was so tough that her jaws hurt from chewing it.*

jazz [jæz'], *n.* a kind of American music originating around 1900 with a strong rhythm, played by a group of musicians who create variations on the basic melody as they perform individually. **Ex.** *We are going to attend an annual jazz festival next weekend.*

jealous (3) [jel'əs], *adj.* 1. fearful of losing love or favor to another. **Ex.** *The little boy was jealous of his baby sister.* 2. angry or sad because someone else has what one wants. **Ex.** *She was jealous of her neighbor's good fortune.* —**jeal'ous·y,** *n.*

jeans [jiynz'], *n.* a pair of pants made from heavy blue cotton cloth, worn for outside work and leisure-time activities; dungarees. **Ex.** *Most of the students were wearing jeans.*

jeep [jiyp'], *n.* a small, strong car with all four wheels connected to the source of driving power which can travel over poor roads and rough land and is often used by the military. **Ex.** *During the heavy snowstorm, jeeps were used to transport workers and staff members to the hospital.*

jelly (4) [jel'iy], *n.* a food, usually sweet, made by boiling sugar and fruit juice together until the mixture is thick and partly clear. **Ex.** *We had toast and jelly at breakfast.* —**jell'**, *v.* cause to become semisolid like jelly.

jerk (4) [jərk'], *n.* a quick, sharp movement. **Ex.** *He stopped the car with a jerk, and we were thrown forward.* —*v.* give a sudden push, pull or twist to. **Ex.** *She jerked open the door.* —**jerk'y,** *adj.* —**jerk'i·ly,** *adv.* with sudden starts and stops.

jet (3) [jet'], *n.* 1. a burst of liquid or gas forced from a small opening. **Ex.** *A jet of water came from the hole in the pipe.* 2. an airplane powered by a streams of hot air and gases that are forced out through the engine.

jewel (2) [juw'əl], *n.* a gem; a valuable stone such as a diamond. **Ex.** *The green jewel in her ring sparkled.* —**jew'el·er,** *n.* a person who makes, sells or repairs jewelry. —**jew'el·ry,** *n.* valuable ornaments, often made of precious metals, such as gold and silver, as well as gems; jewels.

job (1) [jab'], *n.* 1. work; employment. **Ex.** *His job pays him just enough money to live on.* 2. a piece of work; a duty. **Ex.** *My mother has many different jobs to do at home after she returns from the office.*

jog [jag'], *v.* 1. run at a slow, even pace for exercise; ride a horse at a slow steady trot. **Ex.** *He likes to jog for half an hour in the morning before going to work.* 2. shake, shove or push slightly with the elbow, hand, etc. **Ex.** *You jogged my hand and made me spill my coffee.* —*n.* 1. a slight shake, shove or push. 2. a slow, even pace. —**jog'ger,** *n.* one who jogs.

join (1) [joyn'], *v.* 1. become a member of. **Ex.** *She joined the Girl Scouts.* 2. bring or put together; combine; connect. **Ex.** *The carpenter joined the two pieces of wood with glue.* 3. come together; meet. **Ex.** *There is a stop sign at the point where the two roads join.* 4. be a part of. **Ex.** *We are going for a walk; will you join us?*

joint (3) [joynt'], *n.* 1. the place at which two things are joined. **Ex.** *The joints of the chair were loose.* 2. the place where two bones of the body are joined. **Ex.** *His right knee joint is swollen.* —*adj.* shared by two or more; affecting two or more. **Ex.** *The men were joint owners of the land.* —**joint'ed,** *adj.* having joints. —**joint'ly,** *adv.*

a, far; æ, am; e, get; ey, late; i, in; iy, see; ɔ, all; ow, go; u, put; uw, too;
ə, but, ago; ər, fur; aw, out; ay, life; oy, boy; ŋ, ring; θ, think; ð, that;
ž, measure; š, ship; j, edge; č, child.

joke (2) [jowk'], *n.* something done or said to cause laughter or amusement. Ex. *The jokes she told made everybody laugh.* —*v.* speak or act in an amusing or playful way. Ex. *Though he had been badly hurt, he just joked about his accident.* —**jok'er,** *n.* a person who jokes.

jolly (4) [jal'iy], *adj.* gay; joyful; in good spirits. Ex. *Everyone at the party was very jolly.*

jolt (5) [jowlt'], *v.* shake roughly. Ex. *The car jolted over the rocky road.* —*n.* a rough movement; a sudden shock. Ex. *The bad news gave us a jolt.*

journal (3) [jər'nəl], *n.* 1. a written account of what happens daily. Ex. *During his trip, he kept a journal of his experiences.* 2. a newspaper published daily; any regular publication. Ex. *She writes for a business journal.* —**jour'nal·ism,** *n.* the business of managing or writing news for a journal, radio, etc. —**jour'nal·ist,** *n.* one who writes for a newspaper, radio, etc. Ex. *The President was asked questions by several journalists.*

journey (1) [jər'niy], *n.* trip. Ex. *We are making a journey abroad this summer.*

joy (1) [joy'], *n.* 1. great delight, pleasure or happiness. Ex. *They were filled with joy at the good news.* 2. that which causes joy. Ex. *Their daughter is their pride and joy.* —**joy'ful, joy'ous,** *adj.* feeling, showing or causing great happiness. —**joy'ful·ly, joy'ous·ly,** *adv.*

judge (1) [jəj'], *n.* 1. a public official who settles problems of law in a court. Ex. *The judge sentenced the thief to two years in prison.* 2. a person appointed to decide the winner of a contest. Ex. *The judges could not agree on who had won the race.* —*v.* 1. form an opinion; estimate the quality of. Ex. *The critics judged the play to be a success.* 2. think; believe. Ex. *We judge the problem to be serious.* —**judg'ment,** *n.* 1. a judge's decision; a verdict. 2. the ability to decide wisely. Ex. *He used good judgment in returning to school.* 3. an opinion. Ex. *In my judgment, she should not be allowed to stay out so late.*

jug (5) [jəg'], *n.* a container with a handle, used to hold liquids. Ex. *She filled the jug with water.*

juice (2) [juws'], *n.* the fluid part of fruit, vegetables or meat. Ex. *He drank a glass of orange juice at breakfast.* —**juic'y,** *adj.* having much juice.

JUG

July (1) [julay'], *n.* the seventh month of the year.

jump (1) [jəmp'], *v.* 1. leap or spring into the air. **Ex.** *She jumped to catch the ball.* 2. leap or spring down from. **Ex.** *The people jumped from the burning building.* 3. pass from one place to another by a leap. **Ex.** *He jumped over the hole in the street.* 4. move suddenly because of a surprise, shock, etc. **Ex.** *She jumped when the telephone rang.* 5. rise suddenly. **Ex.** *Last month, food prices jumped because of the dry season.* —*n.* 1. a leap; the act of jumping. 2. a sudden rise in price, amount, etc. —**jump'y,** *adj.* nervous.

junction (5) [jənk'šen], *n.* 1. the act of joining; the state of being joined. **Ex.** *The two rivers make their junction near the sea.* 2. a place of joining or crossing. **Ex.** *There is a store at the junction of the two roads.*

June (1) [juwn'], *n.* the sixth month of the year.

jungle (4) [jəŋ'gəl], *n.* land covered with a tangled growth of trees, vines and bushes. **Ex.** *They saw many kinds of wild animals as they traveled through the jungle.*

junior (3) [juwn'yər], *adj.* 1. of or concerning the younger of two; of the son of a father when both have the same name, usually written *Jr.* **Ex.** *Thomas Smith, Jr., is the son of Thomas Smith, Sr.* 2. of lower rank. **Ex.** *This training course is for junior officers.* —*n.* 1. a person younger in age or lower in rank. **Ex.** *He is my junior by two years.* 2. a student in the second year of a three-year high school or in the third year of a four-year high school or college. **Ex.** *She is a junior in college this year.*

junior college [juwn'yər kal'ij], a two-year school offering courses at the level of the first two years of college. **Ex.** *After junior college, I will go to the university for two years and get a degree.*

junior high school [juwn'yər hay' skuwl'], a school of the seventh, eighth and ninth years of study.

junk (5) [jəŋk'], *n.* old or worthless material such as used metal, paper, broken glass, etc. **Ex.** *They took the junk to the city dump.* —**junk food,** food, the contents of which give one little or no nourishment.

jury (3) [ju:r'iy], *n.* 1. a group of persons, usually twelve, who are selected to decide what is true in a court of law. **Ex.** *The jury decided that the man on trial was guilty.* 2. a group of persons who decide who is best, what is best, etc. in a contest. **Ex.** *The jury gave prizes to two of his paintings.* —**ju'ror,** *n.* one who is a member of a jury.

just (1) [jəst'], *adv.* 1. at the same time. **Ex.** *He left just as I came in.* 2. barely. **Ex.** *We had just enough food for two days.* 3. only. **Ex.** *Help me for just a minute.* 4. very shortly before or after the present moment. **Ex.** *She just arrived.* 5. exactly. **Ex.** *That is just what I want.*

just (1) [jəst'], *adj.* 1. fair; acting for fair and truthful reasons. **Ex.** *The teacher was always just in her treatment of the students.* 2. fair and right. **Ex.** *He has a just claim to the property.* —**just'ly,** *adv.*

justice (2) [jəs'tis], *n.* 1. the quality of being fair, just or right. **Ex.** *In the interests of justice, a new trial was ordered.* 2. proper punishment or reward. **Ex.** *The injured man demanded justice.* 3. a judge. **Ex.** *The new justice is said to be liberal in his thinking.*

justify (5) [jəs'təfay'], *n.* 1. prove to be just. **Ex.** *The results justified the expense.* 2. excuse; free from blame. **Ex.** *The accused tried to justify his actions.* —**jus'ti·fi`a·ble,** *adj.* capable of being proved just. —**jus'ti·fi·ca'tion,** *n.* that which shows something to be just.

K

K, k [key'], *n.* the eleventh letter of the English alphabet.

keen (3) [kiyn'], *adj.* 1. very sharp. **Ex.** *This ax has a very keen blade.* 2. quick to understand, see or hear. **Exs.** *She has a keen mind. The eagle has keen sight.* —**keen'ly,** *adv.*

keep (1) [kiyp'], *v.* have for one's own use; possess. **Ex.** *This book is yours to keep.* 2. fulfill. **Ex.** *He always keeps his promise.* 3. prevent. **Ex.** *They could not keep her from going.* 4. remain; stay as it is. **Ex.** *How long will this milk keep?* 5. save for later use. **Ex.** *Keep the cake until tomorrow.* 6. have the care of. **Ex.** *He keeps horses on the farm.* —**keep'er,** *n.* one who has the care of people, animals or things. **Ex.** *She* *is our housekeeper.* —**keep company,** associate with; be a friend of. **Ex.** *I do not like the company you keep.* —**keep to oneself,** stay away from others. **Ex.** *The quiet boy kept to himself most of the time.* —**keep track of,** stay informed. **Ex.** *Did you keep track of what they were doing?* —**keep up with,** stay equal to or beside; be aware. **Ex.** *They are always trying to keep up with their neighbors.*

kept (1) [kept'], *v.* past tense and particle of *keep.* **Exs.** *The clerk kept us waiting. If you had kept that coin, it would be worth a lot of money now.*

kerosene (5) [ke:r'əsiyn`, ke:r'əsiyn'], *n.* an oil burned in lamps and stoves for cooking and heating; coal oil. **Ex.** *This stove burns kerosene.*

ketchup [keč'əp], *n.* a thick red sauce, made of tomatoes, sugar, vinegar and spices, used to flavor meat. **Ex.** *He poured ketchup on his hamburger.*

kettle (3) [ket'əl], *n.* 1. a covered container for boiling water used for making tea or for other purposes; a teakettle. 2. a covered container for boiling or cooking; a pot. **Ex.** *She put the soup in the kettle to heat.*

KETTLE 1

key (2) [kiy'], *n.* 1. a metal device for opening or closing a lock. 2. that which solves, explains, etc. **Ex.** *He believed that the key to success was hard work.* 3. flat pieces on a piano, typewriter, etc. which one presses or strikes to operate. **Ex.** *The keys of the piano were worn from use.* —*adj.* of chief importance. **Ex.** *The key point in our program is safety.* —**key' hole,** *n.* a hole in which to place the key in a lock.

KEY 1

keyboard [kiy'bord], *n.* a row or rows of small bars or buttons which are pressed in order to operate a musical instrument, typewriter, etc. **Ex.** *She sat down at the keyboard and began to play a popular song.*

keynote [kiy'nowt'], *n.* the most important idea of a talk, written aritcle, etc. **Ex.** *The keynote of the president's speech was safeguarding freedom.*

a, far; æ, am; e, get; ey, late; i, in; iy, see; ɔ, all; ow, go; u, put; uw, too; ə, but, ago; ər, fur; aw, out; ay, life; oy, boy; ŋ, ring; θ, think; ð, that; ž, measure; š, ship; j, edge; č, child.

kick (2) [kik'], *v.* strike or give a blow to with the foot. **Ex.** *The horse kicked the boy in the leg.* —*n.* the act of kicking; a blow or thrust with the foot. —**kick'er,** *n.* a person who kicks.

kidnap [kid'næp'], *v.* carry away by force and hold, usually for payment of some kind; abduct. **Ex.** *They kidnapped the child and are holding her for ransom.* —**kid'nap·per,** *n.*

kill (1) [kil'], *v.* take the life of a person, animal, plant, etc.; cause to die. **Ex.** *He killed the lion with a single shot.* —**kill time,** help to make time pass. **Ex.** *She killed time until his arrival by reading the newspaper.* —**kill'er,** one who or that which kills.

kilogram [kil'əgræm], *n.* basic measure of weight in the metric system, equal to a little more than two pounds. See **Weights and Measures.**

kin (5) [kin'], *n.* any or all of one's relatives. **Ex.** *His aunts, uncles and other kin came to the wedding.* —**next of kin,** the closest living relative or relatives. **Ex.** *His father is his next of kin.*

kind (1) [kaynd'], *n.* class; sort; type. **Ex.** *What kind of dog is that?*

kind (1) [kaynd'], *adj.* 1. gentle; friendly. **Ex.** *She is kind to her neighbor's children.* 2. showing goodness. **Ex.** *Helping that old lady with her packages was a kind thing to do.* —**kind'ly,** *adv.* in a gentle, friendly way. **Ex.** *She spoke kindly to the old man.* —**kind'ness,** *n.*

kindergarten [kin'dərgart`ən], *n.* a preschool program for five- and six-year-old children to help them develop socially, physically and mentally and to prepare them for grade school. **Ex.** *My five-year-old daughter now goes to kindergarten.*

kindle (4) [kin'dəl], *v.* 1. start a fire; cause to burn. **Ex.** *We kindled the fire in the stove.* 2. inflame, excite. **Ex.** *His speech kindled their interest.* —**kin'dling,** *n.* bits of material such as dry wood used for starting a fire.

king (1) [kiŋ'], *n.* a male ruler whose position usually passes from father to son. —**king'dom,** *n.* a country ruled by a king or queen. —**king'ly,** *adj.* of or that which is suitable to a king. **Ex.** *Everyone was impressed by the actor's kingly appearance.*

kiss (1) [kis'], *v.* touch with the lips in love or respect. **Ex.** *The man kissed his wife good-bye.* —*n.* the act of kissing.

kit (5) [kit'], *n*. 1. a set of tools, instruments, supplies, etc. **Ex.** *A kit of tools came with the car.* 2. the case for such equipment; the case with its contents. **Ex.** *He packed a shaving kit in his suitcase.*

kitchen (1) [kič'ən], *n*. a room where food is prepared. **Ex.** *He is in the kitchen cooking dinner.*

kite (4) [kayt'], *n*. a frame of wood or metal, covered with paper or cloth and flown in the wind at the end of a long string.

KITE

kitten (3) [kit'ən], *n*. the young of the cat family. **Ex.** *The cat has just had six kittens.*

knee (2) [niy'], *n*. the part of the leg that joins the upper leg to the lower leg and enables the leg to bend.

KNEE

kneel (4) [niyl'], *v*. fall or rest on the knees or one knee. **Ex.** *She was kneeling beside the bed.*

knelt [nelt'], *v*. past tense and participle of *kneel*. **Exs.** *He knelt down to comfort her. During the marriage ceremony they had knelt before the altar.*

knew (1) [nuw', nyuw'], *v*. past tense of *know*. **Ex.** *The boy knew his lesson well.*

knife (2) [nayf'], *n*. a sharp blade for cutting attached to a handle. —*v*. cut with a knife. **Ex.** *He was knifed in the back by the robber.*

knit (3) [nit'], *v*. 1. make sweaters, socks, etc. by locking wool threads together in stitches using special needles. **Ex.** *She knitted her husband a scarf.* 2. grow firmly together; unite. **Ex.** *The broken bones in his leg are knitting nicely.*

KNIFE

knives [nayvz'], *n*. plural of *knife*. **Ex.** *All her kitchen knives are very sharp.*

knob (5) [nab'], *n*. a rounded handle of a door, drawer, television, etc. **Ex.** *She turned the knob to open the door.* 2. a rounded, raised place at the end of something. **Ex.** *He grasped the knob of the cane.*

knock (2) [nak'], *v*. 1. strike a blow with a closed hand on a surface, such as a door, to attract attention. **Ex.** *She heard* *someone knock on the door.* 2. make or do by striking or pounding on with tools. **Ex.** *They knocked out an opening in the wall for a window.* 3. cause to break or fall by striking. **Ex.** *He was knocked down by a horse.* 4. strike against something while moving. **Ex.** *He knocked into the chair in the dark.* —*n.* a loud, sharp blow on a surface, such as a door, to attract attention. **Ex.** *I came as soon as I heard your knock.* —**knock out,** cause to lose consciousness by hitting. **Ex.** *The boxer knocked him out and won the fight.*

knot (3) [nat'], *n.* 1. the joined ends of a rope, cord, etc.; the point at which there is a tie in ropes, cords, etc. **Ex.** *Tie the knots of your package tightly.* 2. a hard swelling or lump at the point where a limb or branch connects with the trunk of a tree. **Ex.** *There were many knots in the pine boards.* —*v.* tie a cord, rope, etc, into a knot. **Ex.** *Knot the thread once more.*

KNOT

know (1) [now'], *v.* 1. be certain of. **Ex.** *Do you know how much money you have spent today?* 2. recognize; be acquainted with. **Ex.** *Do you know that man?* 3. understand and be able to use. **Ex.** *She knows English well enough to write letters.* 4. be able to see that things are different; be able to judge. **Ex.** *We expect him to know right from wrong.* 5. realize; be aware. **Ex.** *They know they must study hard.* —**know'ing,** *adj.* well-informed; wise. **Ex.** *He gave her a knowing look.* —**know'ing·ly,** *adv.* purposely. **Ex.** *He did it knowingly.*

know-how [now'haw'], *n.* expert knowledge and practical ability in doing something. **Ex.** *She has considerable business know-how.*

knowledge (2) [nal'ij], *n.* 1. that which is known; understanding. **Ex.** *Do you have enough knowledge of engines to fix that car?* 2. wide learning or understanding. **Ex.** *The old man was respected for his knowledge.* 3. all that humans know. **Ex.** *Knowledge increases with every generation.*

known (1) [nown'], *v.* past participle of *know.* **Ex.** *He had known her for several years.*

knuckle (5) [nək'əl], *n.* the joint between sections of a finger and between a finger and the hand that enables the finger to bend and the hand to open and close. **Ex.** *The knuckles on her hands are swollen.*

L

L, l [el'], *n.* the twelfth letter of the English alphabet.

label (5) [ley'bəl], *n.* a slip of paper or other material fastened to something to show what it is, who owns it, who made it, etc. **Ex.** *She read the label on the jar carefully.* —*v.* 1. put a label on. **Ex.** *This bottle is labeled "poison."* 2. describe as; call. **Ex.** *He was labeled a "thief" because of a youthful mistake.*

labor (1) [ley'bər], *n.* 1. hard work. **Ex.** *He spent the summer doing physical labor.* 2. workers as a group. **Ex.** *Skilled labor was scarce.* —*v.* work hard; toil. **Ex.** *The men labored from dawn to dark.* —**la·bor·or**, *n.* —**la·bo·ri·ous**, *adj.* requiring great effort. —**Labor Day**, *n.* a national holiday, observed the first Monday in September, to honor the working force. **Ex.** *We are going for a ride in the country on Labor Day.*

laboratory (3) [læb'(ə)rətɔːr'iy], *n.* a room or building where experiments in science are performed. **Ex.** *That university has a good physics laboratory.*

labor union [ley'bər yuwn'yən], a group of workers organized to better wages, working conditions, health benefits, etc. **Ex.** *He and his brother belong to the labor union at the plant where they work.*

lace (3) [leys'], *n.* 1. threads made into a delicate patterned cloth with many openings like those in a net. 2. cord or string put through the holes in a shoe to draw the edges together. **Ex.** *Here is a new pair of laces for your shoes.* —*v.* fasten or draw together by a lace. **Ex.** *Lace your shoes.* —*adj.* made of delicately patterned threads. **Ex.** *What a beautiful lace tablecloth that is!* —**lac'y,** *adj.* like lace.

LACE 1

LACE 2

---

a, far; æ, am; e, get; ey, late; i, in; iy, see; ɔ, all; ow, go; u, put; uw, too; ə, but, ago; ər, fur; aw, out; ay, life; oy, boy; ŋ, ring; θ, think; ð, that; ž, measure; š, ship; ǰ, edge; č, child.

lack (2) [læk'], *n*. a shortage or absence of something needed. **Ex.** *The farmers worried about the lack of rain.* —*v.* be without. **Ex.** *They lacked the courage to name the murderer.*

lad (4) [læd'], *n*. a boy; a youth. **Ex.** *They lived on a farm when he was a lad.*

ladder (1) [læd'ər], *n*. a structure, made of metal, wood, rope, etc., consisting of two side pieces beween which a series of crosspieces or rungs are set, used for climbing. 2. anything that helps a person to rise or climb higher. **Ex.** *Education was her ladder to success.*

LADDER 1

lady (1) [ley'diy], *n*. 1. a woman of good family; a woman with good manners and a sense of honor. **Ex.** *She is always a lady.* 2. any woman. **Ex.** *He began his speech with the usual, "Ladies and gentlemen . . ."*

lag (5) [læg'], *v*. move slowly; fall behind. **Ex.** *The child lagged behind the others.* —*n.* a falling behind. **Ex.** *There was a lag in the sale of cars this past month.*

laid (1) [leyd'], *v*. past tense and participle of *lay*. **Exs.** *He laid the magazine on the table. She had laid the table for dinner before we arrived.*

lain [leyn'], *v*. past particle of *lie*. **Ex.** *He had lain on the bed for two hours without being able to fall asleep.*

lake (1) [leyk'], *n*. a large body of water surrounded by land. **Ex.** *They went sailing on the lake.*

lamb (2) [læm'], *n*. 1. a young sheep. **Ex.** *The lambs were playing on the hillside.* 2. the meat of a young sheep. **Ex.** *They had roast lamb for dinner.*

lame (3) [leym'], *adj*. 1. having an injured leg or foot that makes walking difficult. **Ex.** *The lame boy walked slowly.* 2. stiff and sore. **Ex.** *Cold weather bothered her lame back.* 3. Not good; poor. **Ex.** *His lame excuse was not accepted.* —**lame'ly**, *adv.* —**lame'ness**, *n*.

lament (4) [ləment'], *v*. mourn; weep; feel or express sorrow. **Ex.** *They lamented the death of their father.* —*n.* the sound or expression of grief or sorrow; weeping. **Ex.** *They heard the lament of the mourners as they entered the church.*

lamp (2) [læmp'], *n*. a device for making light.

LAMP

land (1) [lænd'], *n* 1 the part of the earth's surface not covered by water; the ground. **Ex.** *Some traveled by land and others by sea.* 2. a region; a country. **Ex.** *They visited many lands during their travels.* 3. property. **Ex.** *They own land in the West.* —*v.* 1. arrive at or on land from the sea or air. **Ex.** *His airplane landed an hour ago.* 2. come to the ground. **Ex.** *He was thrown from the horse but landed on his feet.* —**land'ing**, *n.* 1. the act of arriving on land. **Ex.** *Their landing was delayed because of the weather.* 2. a place where people or goods are put on shore from a ship or boat. **Ex.** *We waited at the landing for them to arrive.* 3. the floor at the bottom or top of a flight of stairs or a space partway up. **Ex.** *She was waiting for me on the landing.*

landlady [læn(d)'ley'diy], *n.* a woman who owns and rents land, houses, rooms, etc. **Ex.** *The landlady just raised the rent.*

landlocked [lænd'lakt'], *adj.* surrounded or nearly surrounded by land; unable to reach the sea by way of water. **Ex.** *The nearest port to this landlocked city is 100 miles away.*

landlord [læn(d)'lord'], *n.* a man who owns and rents land, houses, rooms, etc. **Ex.** *The landlord had to put a new furnace in our house.*

landmark [læn(d)'mark'], *n.* a well-known statue, building or other object by which a person can tell where he is. **Ex.** *The White House is a landmark in Washington, D.C.*

landscape [lænd'skeyp'], *n.* 1. a wide view of the country scene. **Ex.** *She enjoyed watching the landscape as it changed from season to season.* 2. a painting, photograph, etc. of such a scene. **Ex.** *His landscapes have won many prizes.* —*v.* improve the appearance of an area surrounding a house, building, etc. or of open spaces by planting trees, flowers, shrubs, etc. and sometimes by making artificial bodies of water. **Ex.** *Gardeners are landscaping the grounds around the new apartment building.*

lane (3) [leyn'], *n.* 1. a narrow road between fences, trees, houses, etc. **Ex.** *The children were playing in the lane.* 2. part of a highway for traffic moving in one line. **Ex.** *There is a four-lane highway between the two cities.*

language (1) [læŋ'gwij], *n.* 1. speech; writing that represents speech. **Ex.** *Language must have meaning as well as sound.* 2. the speech of a particular country, nation, group, etc. **Ex.** *English is the language most commonly spoken in the United States.*

lantern (4) [læn'tərn], *n.* a container of glass or other material protecting a light-giving flame from the wind, rain or snow.

lap (3) [læp'], *n.* the front of the body from the waist to the knees when one sits down. **Ex.** *The child sat on his mother's lap.*

lap (3) [læp'], *v.* 1. wash against with a slapping sound, as water. **Ex.** *The waves lapped gently against the shore.* 2. take up liquid with the tongue. **Ex.** *The cat lapped the milk from its dish.*

LANTERN

large (1) [larǰ'], *adj.* big; being of more than the usual size, amount or number. **Ex.** *He lives in a large house.* —**large'ly,** *adv.* mainly. **Ex.** *She is largely responsible for the change.* —**at large,** free; not held. **Ex.** *The robber escaped and is still at large.*

laser [ley'zər], *n.* a device that produces an extremely powerful ray or narrow beam of light. **Ex.** *The sugeon is going to use the beam from a laser in this operation.*

lash [læš], (4) *n.* 1. the part of a whip that bends, especially its tip. **Ex.** *As he swung the whip, the lash made a loud crack.* 2. a blow with the whip. **Ex.** *In his anger, he tried to give the boy a lash with his whip.* 3. the hair on the edge of the lid of the eye; eyelash. **Ex.** *She has long, thick lashes.* —*v.* 1. beat or drive with a whip. **Ex.** *He lashed the horses until they ran.* 2. beat against. **Ex.** *The waves lashed against the wall.* 3. move quickly and suddenly from side to side or back and forth. **Ex.** *The cow lashed her tail at the flies.*

last [læst', last'], (1) *adj.* placed after all others. **Ex.** *December is the last month of the year.* 2. most recent. **Ex.** *These last few days have been cold.* 3. the only one remaining. **Ex.** *You look as if you had lost your last friend.* —*adv.* 1. after all others. **Ex.** *The letter z comes last in the alphabet.* 2. on the most recent occasion. **Ex.** *She looked well when I last saw her.* —*v.* 1. continue. **Ex.** *The rain lasted all day.* 2. continue in the same condition. **Ex.** *This furniture will last for a lifetime.* 3. be enough. **Ex.** *This money must last until next payday.* —*n.* the end; the final part. **Ex.** *She ate the last of the cake.* —**last'ly,** *adv.* finally; in conclusion. **Ex.** *Lastly, I want to discuss the problem of housing.*

late (1) [leyt'], *adj.* 1. after the correct time. **Ex.** *He was late in arriving at school.* 2. not early; toward the end. **Ex.** *It hap-*

pened in the late eighteenth century. 3. recently ended or dead. **Ex.** *I knew your late father.* **—adv.** 1. not in time. **Ex.** *Help came too late to save the dying boy.* 2. not early. **Ex.** *She came late in the afternoon.* **—late'ly,** *adv.* recently; not long ago. **Ex.** *I have not seen her lately.* **—late'ness,** *n.*

Latin [lǽt'in], *n.* 1. the language spoken by the ancient Romans. **Ex.** *I took Latin in high school.* 2. anyone who comes from a country in which the language is derived from Latin, such as Italian, Spanish, French or Portuguese. **—adj.** 1. having to do with Latin. 2. having to do with the people or countries that use a language derived from Latin. **Ex.** *The president is meeting with representatives from several Latin American countries.*

latitude (4) [lǽt'ətuwd, lǽt'ətyuwd], *n.* 1. distance measured in degrees north or south of the equator. **Ex.** *One degree of latitude on the earth's surface equals almost seventy miles.* 2. freedom from narrow rules or limits. **Ex.** *That girl is given too much latitude in her choice of friends.*

latter (2) [lǽt'ər], *adj.* 1. near; near the end. **Ex.** *He was here in the latter part of May.* 2. being the second of the two previously mentioned. **Ex.** *The latter fire was more serious than the former one.*

laugh (1) [lǽf'], *v.* 1. make sounds that show one is merry, amused or happy. **Ex.** *The man laughed loudly at the joke.* 2. make fun of; scorn. **Ex.** *They laughed at his mistake.* **—n.** the act or sound which shows merriment, happiness, amusement, scorn, etc. **—laugh'a·ble,** *adj.* causing laughs; foolish. **—laugh'ter** *n.* the act of laughing; the sound of laughing. **Ex.** *Shouts of laughter greeted his remarks.*

launch (4) [lɔ:nč'], *n.* a motorboat used to carry people and supplies between a ship and the shore. **Ex.** *The launch came alongside the ship.* **—v.** 1. cause to float. **Ex.** *The new ship was launched to the cheers of the crowd.* 2. send up into space. **Ex.** *A new spaceship was launched yesterday.* 3. start; begin. **Ex.** *They launched the attack at midnight.*

launch pad [lɔ:nč' pæd'], the starting place from which a spaceship goes into space. **Ex.** *The launchpad for the moon flight was at Cape Kennedy, Florida.*

---

a, far; æ, am; e, get; ey, late; i, in; iy, see; ɔ, all; ow, go; u, put; uw, too; ə, but, ago; ər, fur; aw, out; ay, life; oy, boy; ŋ, ring; θ, think; ð, that; ž, measure; š, ship; J, edge; č, child.

laundry (5) [lɔn'driy], *n.* a place where clothes and linen are washed, dried and sometimes ironed. **Ex.** *They send their sheets and towels to the laundry.* 2. clothes and linens that have been or are to be washed. **Ex.** *She gathered the dirty laundry together.* —**laun'der,** *v.* wash. —**laun'dro·mat`,** *n.* a place where one uses coin-operated machines to wash and dry one's laundry.

lava [la'və], *n.* 1. rock that has melted into a very hot liquid and then explodes from a volcano. **Ex.** *Most of the villagers escaped the river of flowing lava.* 2. the rock that re-forms after the melted lava has cooled and hardened. **Ex.** *They walked over the field of lava.*

law (1) [lɔ:'], *n.* 1. any one or all of the rules made by a government. **Ex.** *Everyone is expected to obey the law.* 2. the profession or study of these rules. **Ex.** *He intends to study law.* —**law'ful,** *adj.* according to the law; legal.

lawn (3) [lɔ:n'], *n.* land covered with grass kept closely cut, as near or around a house. **Ex.** *He is cutting the lawn.*

lawsuit [lɔ:'suwt`], *n.* a claim brought into court for a legal decision. **Ex.** *In this lawsuit, the claimant is asking to be paid for damage to his car.*

lawyer (2) [lɔ:'yər], *n.* a person trained in the law; a person who practices the law by advising about and representing people in legal matters. **Ex.** *I had a lawyer represent me in court.*

lay (1) [ley'], *v.* 1. put or place so as to rest on or against something. **Ex.** *Lay the book on the table.* 2. put or place. **Ex.** *The story is laid in a foreign country.* 3. put down to be buried. **Ex.** *We saw them lay the body to rest.* 4. produce and bring forth. **Ex.** *Our hens lay many eggs.* 5. construct as a base. **Ex.** *They were laying a foundation for a new house.* 6. place or put over something else so that it will lie flat or in a certain position. **Ex.** *Will you please help me to lay the rug?* —**lay away,** save; set aside for later use. **Ex.** *She had the clerk lay away a dress that she wanted to purchase.* —**lay off,** cause a worker to stop being employed for a period of time. **Ex.** *They are going to lay people off until there is more work to do.* —**lay out,** set things out where they can be seen, worn or used. **Ex.** *She is laying out the clothes that he is going to wear this evening.* —**lay over,** stop for a period of time during travel. **Ex.** *How long do we have to lay over in New York on this trip?*

lay (1) [ley'], *v.* past tense of *lie.* **Ex.** *He lay down and slept.*

lay (1) [ley'], *adj.* not of the clergy. **Ex.** *A layman conducted part of the church service.*

layer (2) [ley'ər], *n.* 1. one thickness or fold. **Ex.** *The cake has three layers.* 2. a thin covering. **Ex.** *There was a layer of dust on the desk.*

lazy (3) [ley'ziy], *adj.* not willing to work or be active. **Ex.** *She is a lazy student.* —**la'zi·ly,** *adv.* slowly; not eagerly. —**la'zi·ness,** *n.*

lead (1) [liyd'], *v.* 1. guide; show the way. **Ex.** *You lead and I will follow.* 2. be in the first place; be at the head of. **Ex.** *He leads his class.* 3. command; direct. **Ex.** *The general will lead the army into battle.* 4. live; experience. **Ex.** *He leads a busy life.* —**lead up to,** get ready; bring to. **Ex.** *We knew what he was leading up to after his first question.*

lead (1) [led'], *n.* 1. a heavy gray metal that is easily melted. **Ex.** *That pipe is made of lead.* 2. a black substance used in pencils. **Ex.** *The lead in this pencil is too soft.* —*adj.* made of lead. —**lead'en,** *adj.* 1. made of lead. 2. the color of lead. 3. heavy. **Ex.** *He walked with a leaden step.*

leader (1) [liy'dər], *n.* one who guides, directs or leads. **Ex.** *The president is the leader of our country.*

leaf (3) [liyf'], *n.* one of the green parts that grows from the stems or branches on trees, plants and bushes. **Ex.** *She watched the leaf fall slowly to the ground.*

league [liyg'], *n.* a group of people, countries, teams, etc. that have joined together to promote or work for a common interest. **Ex.** *The League of Nations was formed in 1920 to promote world peace.*

leak (3) [liyk'], *n.* an opening, hole or crack that accidentally lets something in or out. **Ex.** *There is a leak in the roof.* —*v.* come out through a crack or opening. **Ex.** *Gas is leaking from the stove.* —**leak'y,** *adj.* having a leak or leaks. **Ex.** *Several of the water pipes in the house were leaky.*

lean (2) [liyn'], *v.* 1. bend the upper part of the body. **Ex.** *She leaned out of the window to see what was happening.* 2. rest against; place at a slant. **Ex.** *Lean your umbrella against the wall.*

lean (2) [liyn'], *adj.* with little or no fat. **Ex.** *He eats only lean meat.*

leap (4) [liyp'], *n.* a jump; a springing up. **Ex.** *The boy made a high leap over the gate.* —*v.* 1. jump. **Ex.** *He leaped when the bell rang.* 2. jump over. **Ex.** *The dog leaped over the fence.*

leap year [liyp' yi:r'], a year, occurring every fourth year, that has 366 days instead of 365. **Ex.** *The extra day in a leap year is February twenty-ninth.*

learn (1) [lərn'], *v.* 1. gain skill or knowledge of. **Ex.** *She is learning to dance.* 2. come to know a fact or facts. **Ex.** *We have just learned where he is staying.* —**learn'ed,** *adj.* having much knowledge. —**learn'ing,** *n.* great knowledge through study.

lease (4) [liys'], *n.* a written agreement giving the right to use property for a certain length of time in exchange for rent. **Ex.** *They signed a one-year lease for the house.* —*v.* rent under a written agreement. **Ex.** *I leased the rental car for one week.*

least (1) [liyst'], *adj.* littlest; the smallest in size, quantity, etc. **Ex.** *He did the work without the least difficulty.* —*adv.* to the smallest extent, amount, degree, etc. **Ex.** *He liked that book least of all.*

leather (2) [leð'ər], *n.* the prepared skin or hide of certain animals. **Ex.** *His shoes were made of leather.* —*adj.* made of the prepared skin or hide of certain animals. **Ex.** *A wide leather belt would go well with that dress.*

leave (1) [liyv'], *v.* 1. go away. **Ex.** *Did you see him leave?* 2. go away from. **Ex.** *She leaves home early in the morning.* 3. allow to remain behind or in some place. **Ex.** *You may leave your books here.* 4. let remain in a particular condition. **Ex.** *Leave the window open an inch.* 5. let someone else do; trust someone with. **Ex.** *Leave the rest of the work for me.* —*n.* permission to be absent from work or military duty; the period of such absence. **Ex.** *She is on leave for two weeks.*

leaves (3) [liyvz'], *n.* plural of *leaf.*

lecture (3) [lek'čər], *n.* 1. a speech or talk given to a class or group. **Ex.** *The professor gave a lecture on modern art.* 2. a solemn speech about something wrong that the listener has done. **Ex.** *Whenever she stayed out late, she had to listen to a lecture from her parents.* —*v.* give a speech or talk to a class or group. **Ex.** *When are you going to lecture again?* 2. give a solemn speech about something wrong that the listener has done. **Ex.** *His father lectured him about using the family car without permission.*

led [led'], *v.* past tense and participle of *lead.* **Exs.** *He led them out of the forest. He had led the band for two years.*

ledge (4) [lej'], *n.* a flat, narrow projection on which something can be placed. **Ex.** *He put his pipe on the window ledge.* 2. a ridge of rock. **Ex.** *They seated themselves on the ledge facing the lake.*

left (1) [left'], *v.* past tense and participle of *leave.* **Exs.** *He left just a few minutes ago. Be sure you haven't left anything behind.*

left (1) [left'], *adj.* 1. of or on the side of the body which is to the west when one is facing north. **Ex.** *She writes with her left hand.* 2. desiring basic changes in government; favoring liberal, democratic, socialistic, etc. ideas in politics. **Ex.** *He belongs to the left wing of the party.* —*n.* 1. the side that is to the left. **Ex.** *When you're driving north, their house is on the left.* 2. groups, parties, etc. that favor liberal political ideas and basic changes in government. **Ex.** *Her political ideas are to the left of center.* —*adv.* toward the left. **Ex.** *Walk two blocks and turn left.* —**left'ist,** *n.* one who favors the left in politics.

left-hand [left'hænd'], *adj.* on or toward the left. **Ex.** *Make a left-hand turn at the next corner.* —**left'-hand'ed,** *adj.* tending to prefer to use the left hand. **Ex.** *Both of my children are left-handed.*

leg (1) [leg'], *n.* 1. one of the lower parts of the human body that is used in standing or walking. **Ex.** *She has shapely, slender legs.* 2. one of the lower parts of the body of an animal used in standing or walking. **Ex.** *Insects have six legs.* 3. anything shaped or used like a leg. **Ex.** *One of the table legs is loose.* 4. the part of a garment that covers the leg. **Ex.** *The left leg of his trousers is torn.*

legal (3) [liy'gəl], *adj.* 1. lawful. **Ex.** *In some towns it is not legal to keep stores open on Sunday.* 2. of the law. **Ex.** *She is a member of the legal profession.* —**le'gal·ly,** *adv.* in a way that is lawful. —**le·gal'i·ty,** *n.* —**le'gal·ize,** *v.*

legend (4) [lej'ənd], *n.* 1. a story coming down from the past that many believe but which may not be true. **Ex.** *My grandfather knew many old legends.* 2. what is written on a coin, a medal, a picture, a map, etc. **Ex.** *I could not read the legend on the coin.* —**leg'end·ar'y,** *adj.*

legible [leʲ'əbəl], *adj.* able to be read, especially easily. **Ex.** *Your handwriting is both beautiful and legible.*

legislate (4) [leʲ'isleyt'], *v.* make laws. **Ex.** *The Congress of the United States has the power to legislate.* —**leg'is·la'tor**, *n.* a member of a lawmaking body. —**leg'is·la'tion**, *n.* 1. the act of making laws. 2. the laws made. **Ex.** *This legislation concerns education.* —**leg'is·la'ture**, *n.* a lawmaking group. —**leg'is·la'tive**, *adj.*

legitimate (4) [leʲit'əmit], *adj.* 1. right; lawful. **Ex.** *They have a legitimate claim to the property.* 2. born of parents who are married to each other. **Ex.** *He is their legitimate child.* 3. expected; reasonable. **Ex.** *Her request was a legitimate one.* —**le·git'i·ma·cy**, *n.*

leisure (4) [liy'žər], *n.* free time in which one may rest, amuse oneself and do things one enjoys doing. **Ex.** *He had no leisure for his favorite sport.* —**lei'sure·ly**, *adj.* taking plenty of time. **Ex.** *They enjoyed a leisurely walk.* —*adv.* slowly; without hurrying. **Ex.** *The cow moved leisurely out of the way of the car.* —**at one's leisure,** when one is not busy. **Ex.** *Do this at your leisure.*

lemon (3) [lem'ən], *n.* an oval-shaped sour, juicy fruit which is light yellow in color and grows in warm climates. **Ex.** *The juice of a lemon will add flavor to this salad.* —*adj.* pale yellow. —**lem'on·ade'**, *n.* a refreshing drink made from lemon juice, sugar and water. **Ex.** *A glass of iced lemonade would be welcome on a hot day like this.*

lend (2) [lend'], *v.* 1. permit someone else to use for a time something that one owns. **Ex.** *I asked him to lend me his car.* 2. make a loan of money. **Ex.** *The bank lends money as part of its regular business.* —**lend'er**, *n.* —**lend a hand,** help. **Ex.** *Please lend me a hand with this typing.* —**lend itself to,** be suitable for. **Ex.** *That chair lends itself to use in the bedroom, dining room or living room.*

length (1) [leŋkθ', lenθ'], *n.* 1. the distance from one end to the other. **Ex.** *The length of this rope is ten feet.* 2. the measure of how long something lasts. **Ex.** *The length of the school year is ten months.* 3. the longest side of any object. **Ex.** *The table is six feet in length.* —**length'y**, *adj.* long; too long. **Ex.** *His speech was very lengthy.* —**length'en**, *v.* make longer; become or grow longer. **Ex.** *She lengthened her dress.* —**at length,** 1. after a long time; finally. **Ex.** *They talked for some time, and* *at length he told her the purpose of his visit.* 2. in detail; completely. **Ex.** *She described the work at length.* —**go to any lengths,** do everything necessary. **Ex.** *He will go to any lengths to get her back.*

lenient [liy'niyənt], *adj.* 1. showing kindness or mercy in judgment; forgiving. **Ex.** *The judge was lenient and sentenced the convicted man to community service.* 2. not strict; permissive. **Ex.** *The principal was very lenient in disciplining the students.* —**le'·ni·ence,** *n.* —**le'ni·en·cy,** *n.*

lens (5) [lenz'], *n.* 1. a specially shaped piece of glass in eyeglasses, cameras and certain instruments used for viewing. **Ex.** *He needed powerful lenses in his glasses.* 2. the part of the eye that focuses the light entering the eye.

lent (2) [lent'], *v.* past tense and participle of *lend.* **Exs.** *He lent me his book. I had lent him some money before and he did not pay me back.*

less (1) [les], *adj.* smaller in amount or extent. **Ex.** *He owns less land than his brother.* —*adv.* not so much. **Ex.** *The weather is less cold today than it has been.* —*n.* a smaller amount or part. **Ex.** *She gave me less than she gave him.* —**less·en,** *v.* become or make less.

-less (1) [lis], *suffix.* 1. without. **Exs.** *Fear, fearless; home, homeless.* 2. unable to; unable to be. **Exs.** *Help, helpless; count, countless.*

lesson (2) [les'ən], *n.* 1. that which must be learned; a part of a course of study. **Ex.** *The teacher explained the history lesson.* 2. a useful piece of wisdom; something learned for one's own good. **Ex.** *The accident was a lesson to him to drive more carefully.*

let (1) [let'], *v.* 1. permit, allow. **Ex.** *I let him have the money.* 2. command; request. **Ex.** *Let us go there now.* —**let alone,** 1. do not bother. **Ex.** *Let him alone; he is reading.* 2. without reference to; not to mention. **Ex.** *They haven't got enough money to buy food, let alone a car.* —**let down,** disappoint. **Ex.** *She let us down by not coming.*

let's [lets'], shortened form, contraction of *let us.* **Ex.** *Let's go to a movie tonight.*

letter (1) [let'ər], *n.* 1. one of the symbols of the alphabet. **Ex.** *A and B are the first two letters of the English alphabet.* 2. a written or printed message. **Ex.** *He wrote a letter to his friend.*

letter-perfect [let'ərpə:r'fikt], *adj.* completely correct in every detail. **Ex.** *She always does letter-perfect work.*

lettuce (5) [let'əs], *n.* a garden vegetable with green leaves, used in salads. **Ex.** *She made a bacon, lettuce, and tomato sandwich for her lunch.*

level (2) [lev'əl], *adj.* 1. flat; smooth; even. **Ex.** *The floor is not level.* 2. even with something else. **Ex.** *The two pictures are not level.* —*n.* 1. the height to which a thing rises or reaches. **Ex.** *The flood waters rose to a level of more than twenty feet.* 2. a certain position; rank. **Ex.** *He rose to the level of ambassador.* —*v.* make smooth and flat. **Ex.** *The builder leveled the ground for a parking lot.*

lever [lev'ər, liy'ver], *n.* 1. a bar that does not bend easily used to raise a heavy object or to pry open an object. **Ex.** *If you have a knife, I can use it as a lever to remove the cap from this bottle.* 2. a bar or handle attached to an appliance or machine which, when pulled or pushed, causes the appliance to start or stop.

levy (5) [lev'iy], *v.* force the payment of; collect money by taxing. **Ex.** *A tax was levied to raise money for a new school building.* —*n.* a raising of or collecting by authority or force. **Ex.** *A levy was needed to pay for a new road.*

liable (4) [lay'əbəl], *adj.* responsible; required by law to pay. **Ex.** *He stated that he would not be liable for his son's debts.* 2. likely to happen, especially with undesirable or unpleasant results. **Ex.** *If you take the back road, your car is liable to get stuck in the snow.* —**li·a·bil'i·ty**, *n.* 1. a responsibility to pay a debt; the amount of debt. **Ex.** *What is the total of your liabilities?* 2. an unfavorable condition. **Ex.** *Lack of education was a distinct liability for her.*

liar (1) [lay'ər], *n.* one who tells an untruth, knowing it is not the truth. **Ex.** *Because he was such a liar, she did not believe anything he told her.*

liberal (3) [lib'ərəl], *adj.* 1. generous; more than enough. **Ex.** *He gave the waiter a liberal tip.* 2. open to new ideas; not limited. **Ex.** *They want their children to have a liberal education.* 3. favorable to individual freedom and political and social progress and betterment. **Ex.** *He is liberal in his views on government.* —*n.* a person whose principles and views favor individual freedom and political and social progress and betterment. **lib'er·al·ism**, *n.* —**lib'er·al·ize**, *v.*

liberty (2) [lib'ərtiy], *n.* 1. freedom from the will of a master or from an absolute ruler or government. **Ex.** *He dreamed of bringing liberty to his country.* 2. freedom from being held against one's will. **Ex.** *She opened the cage and gave the bird its liberty.* 3. freedom of choice; freedom to act, speak, think, etc. as one chooses. **Ex.** *The boy did not have the liberty of choosing his school.* —**lib'er·ate**, *v.* make free. **Ex.** *The prisoners of war were liberated.* —**at liberty,** not held against one's will; free; not busy. **Ex.** *I am at liberty to go with you.*

library (2) [lay'brer`iy], *n.* a room or building where a collection of books is kept; a collection of books. **Ex.** *Our school has a large library.* —**li·brar'i·an**, *n.* one who is in charge of or works in a library.

license (4) [lay'səns], *n.* legal written permission to do something. **Ex.** *He always carries his driver's license.* —*v.* permit by law. **Ex.** *She is licensed to practice medicine.* —**license plate,** a sign, usually made of metal and attached to the front and rear of a car, having letters and numbers which indicate that the car has been officially registered.

lick (4) [lik'], *v.* 1. pass the tongue over. **Ex.** *The dog licked my hand.* 2. pick up with the tongue. **Ex.** *The cat licked the milk from its dish.* —*n.* 1. the act of passing the tongue over. **Ex.** *She gave the ice cream cone a lick.* 2. a small amount. **Ex.** *He hasn't done a lick of his homework yet.*

lid (3) [lid'], *n.* 1. a removable cover; a top. 2. a cover of skin that is moved in opening and closing the eye; the eyelid.

LID 1

lie (1) [lay'], *v.* 1. have one's body extended on the ground, on a bed or on some other flat place. **Ex.** *They lie down for a rest every afternoon.* 2. rest or remain on a flat place. **Ex.** *Why is that newspaper lying on the floor?* 3. be in a certain place. **Ex.** *New York City lies north of Washington, D.C.*

lie (1) [lay'], *v.* say something one knows to be untrue. **Ex.** *He lied about the amount of money he had spent.* —*n.* an untrue statement. **Ex.** *She told a lie to explain her absence.*

---

a, far; æ, am; e, get; ey, late; i, in; iy, see; ɔ, all; ow, go; u, put; uw, too; ə, but; ago; ər, fur; aw, out; ay, life; oy, boy; ŋ, ring; θ, think; ð, that; ž, measure; š, ship; ǰ, edge; č, child.

lieutenant (4) [luw'ten'ənt], *n*. 1. an army officer ranking below a captain. 2. a naval officer three ranks below a captain. 3. one who acts for or assists a superior. **Ex.** *The lieutenant governor attended the meeting in place of the governor.*

life (1) [layf'], *n*. the state of living; the state of being alive. **Ex.** *They could not tell if there was still life in the tree.* 2. the time of being alive; the time between being born and dying. **Ex.** *She worked hard all her life.* 3. a living being; a person. **Ex.** *Five lives were lost in the fire.* 4. living things of any kind. **Ex.** *There seems to be no life on the moon.* 5. a way of living. **Ex.** *We find city life interesting.* 6. the story of someone's life. **Ex.** *He is writing a life of our first president.*

life belt [layf' belt'], *n*. a special belt to help a person stay afloat in water.

lifeboat [layf'bowt'], *n*. one of the small boats, carried on a ship, to be used in case the ship is sinking or is in other danger. **Ex.** *They were in a lifeboat for three days before being rescued.*

LIFE BELT

lifeguard [layf'gard], *n*. an expert swimmer whose duty it is to protect the safety of other swimmers, bathers, etc. **Ex.** *He has a job this summer as a lifeguard.*

life jacket [layf' jæk'it], *n*. a jacket without sleeves which can be inflated so that the person wearing it can float and not drown. **Ex.** *At the beginning of our flight across the Atlantic, we were shown a film explaining how to use a life jacket.*

life preserver [layf' prəzər'vər], *n*. a device, such as a jacket or a ring, that helps a person to stay afloat in water. **Ex.** *The passengers were shown how to use the life preservers.*

life-sized [layf'sayzd'], *adj*. same in size as the thing or person represented. **Ex.** *They made a life-sized statue of him.*

lifetime [layf'taym], *n*. the length that one lives or that a thing lasts. **Ex.** *He had many interesting experiences during his lifetime.* —*adj*.

lift (1) [lift'], *v*. 1. raise; take or bring to a higher place. **Ex.** *The man lifted the heavy load.* 2. rise and go; go away. **Ex.** *When the fog lifts, we shall try again.* —*n*. 1. the act of raising. **Ex.** *He gave his son a lift into the air.* 2. a free ride. **Ex.** *Thank you for giving me a lift home.* 3. a feeling of pleasure or happiness. **Ex.** *It gave him a lift to know that he had passed the examination.*

lift-off [lift'ɔ:f'], *n.* the moment at which a spacecraft leaves the launch pad on its flight. **Ex.** *The crowd held its breath as the countdown for lift-off began.*

light (1) [layt'], *n.* 1. a form of energy that affects the eyes so that one is able to see. **Ex.** *The sun is the source of our light.* 2. that which gives light, such as a lamp. **Ex.** *He saw a light in the window.* —*adj.* 1. having light; bright; clear. **Ex.** *This is a nice, light room.* 2. pale in color. **Ex.** *She has light brown hair.* —*v.* 1. set fire to; burn. **Ex.** *Please light the fire.* 2. give light to. **Ex.** *You will need at least three lamps to light this room properly.* —**light'er**, *n.* that which starts a fire. —**in light of**, with knowledge of. **Ex.** *In light of the bad weather report, we should leave early.*

light (1) [layt'], *adj.* 1. not heavy; having little weight. **Ex.** *He was wearing a light coat.* 2. less than usual in amount or force. **Ex.** *We had only a light rain.* 3. not serious. **Ex.** *She enjoys light reading.* —**light'ly**, *adv.* —**light'ness**, *n.*

light bulb [layt' bəlb'], *n.* a sealed glass container, shaped like some plant bulbs, in which there is a threadlike wire that glows when an electric current passes through it. **Ex.** *Where do you keep your spare light bulbs?*

LIGHT BULB

lighthearted [layt'har'təd], *adj.* gay; happy; without worries. **Ex.** *The good news made her feel very lighthearted.*

lighthouse [layt'haws'], *n.* a tower or structure resembling a tower with a strong light to warn ships of danger. **Ex.** *The lighthouse was on a small island offshore.*

lightning (2) [layt'niŋ], *n.* a flash of electricity in the sky. **Ex.** *Lightning is usually followed by thunder.*

like (1) [layk'], *prep.* 1. almost the same as; similar to. **Ex.** *Our house looks like theirs.* 2. showing the same qualities; in the same way. **Ex.** *Some other animals bark like dogs.* 3. typical of; with a special quality. **Ex.** *How like her to be late!* 4. almost certain to; as if about to happen. **Ex.** *It looks like snow today.* 5. in a state of mind for. **Ex.** *I feel like going to the movies.* —**like'ness**, *n.* 1. the fact of being similar. **Ex.** *Her likeness to her mother is very strong.* 2. a picture; an image. **Ex.** *That likeness of her has been displayed at several art shows.*

like (1) [layk'], *v.* 1. have affection for. **Ex.** *They liked the neighbor's children very much.* 2. take pleasure in; enjoy. **Ex.**

She likes to swim. 3. choose; prefer. **Ex.** *What would you like to do?* —**lik'a·ble,** *adj.* —**lik'ing,** *n.* a preference for. **Ex.** *She has a liking for cake.*

-like (3) [layk], *suffix.* similar to. **Exs.** *Life, lifelike; child, childlike.*

likewise [layk'wayz'], *adv.* in a similar way. **Ex.** *She has studied the lesson carefully and you must do likewise.*

likely (1) [layk'liy], *adj.* seeming about to happen. **Ex.** *A rise in prices seems likely.* 2. probable; believable. **Ex.** *That is not a very likely story.* —*adv.* probably. **Ex.** *Very likely you are right.*

lily (3) [lil'iy], *n.* a tall plant with horn-shaped flowers, often white, grown from a bulb. **Ex.** *The bride carried lilies.*

limb (3) [lim'], *n.* 1. an arm or a leg. **Ex.** *He lost a limb in the accident.* 2. a branch of a tree. **Ex.** *He cut off the dead limb of the tree.*

lime [laym'], *n.* 1. a small round or oval greenish-yellow fruit that grows on a tree, is juicy and usually tastes sour. **Ex.** *Have you any limes so that I can make a pie for dessert?* 2. a powder, formed by burning a special kind of rock or seashell, which is used as a fertilizer and in making cement, mortar, etc. **Ex.** *Before the spring planting, the farmer spread lime on his field.*

limit (2) [lim'it], *n.* 1. the farthest edge; the boundary line. **Ex.** *They live beyond the city limits.* 2. as far as a person or thing can go. **Ex.** *They stretched the rope to its limit.* 3. the greatest amount, number, etc. permitted. **Ex.** *He was arrested for driving beyond the speed limit.* —*v.* keep within bounds; set a limit to. **Ex.** *She limited her telephone conversation to three minutes.* —**lim'i·ta'tion,** *n.* a limiting; something that limits. **Ex.** *His lack of a college degree was a limitation on his professional advancement.*

limousine [lim'ə·ziyn], *n.* any of various large, luxurious automobiles, particularly in which the driver's seat is separated by a glass partition from the back of the car where the passengers sit. **Ex.** *They hired several limousines to take the members of the wedding party to the church.*

limp (4) [limp'], *adj.* lacking stiffness; not firm. **Ex.** *The flowers were limp from lack of water.* —**limp'ly,** *adv.* —**limp'ness,** *n.*

limp (4) [limp'], *v.* walk unevenly because of an injury. **Ex.** *He limped across the street.* —*n.* an uneven step or walk. **Ex.** *She walked with a limp.*

line (1) [layn'], *n.* 1. a row of letters, things, words, etc. **Ex.** *A line of people waited to get on the bus.* 2. a mark drawn by pencil, pen, etc. **Ex.** *The child was learning to draw a straight line.* 3. any mark like that made by a pencil or pen. **Ex.** *The old woman's face was covered with lines.* 4. a division; a limit. **Ex.** *He drove across the city line.* 5. wires or pipes used to carry electricity, gas, etc. **Ex.** *A telephone line is now being put in place.* —*v.* 1. make lines on; mark with lines. **Ex.** *Care lined the old man's face.* 2. form a row or line along. **Ex.** *Crowds lined the street to see the marching soldiers.* —**draw a line,** limit. **Ex.** *You must draw a line with children and tell them what they cannot do.* —**hold the line,** keep a firm position; resist. **Ex.** *We must hold the line on prices and keep them from rising.* —**line up,** get into or form a line. **Ex.** *Boys will line up on this side.* —**read between the lines,** find hidden meanings in written or spoken words. **Ex.** *She wrote that she was fine, but reading between the lines I knew that she was having problems.*

line (1) [layn'], *v.* place covering on the inside of. **Ex.** *Her coat was lined with silk.* —**lin'ing,** *n.* an inside covering.

lineman [layn'mən], *n.* one who fixes telephone or electric wires.

linen (3) [lin'ən], *n.* cloth or thread made from the stems of a particular plant. **Ex.** *She bought three yards of linen for a tablecloth.* —**lin'ens,** *n. pl.* articles, such as sheets, pillow-cases, etc., once made of linen but now often made of cotton and other materials. **Ex.** *We bought some linens on sale.*

-ling (3) [liŋ], *suffix.* 1. small; lesser. **Exs.** *Duck, duckling; prince, princeling.* 2. of. **Ex.** *Earth, earthling; world, worldling.*

linger (3) [liŋ'gər], *v.* stay as if unwilling to leave; leave or move slowly. **Ex.** *She told him not to linger on his way home from school.*

link (4) [liŋk'], *n.* 1. one ring or loop of a chain; any of the joined sections of something like a chain. **Ex.** *A chain is only as strong as its weakest link.* 2. anything that joins as a link joins. **Ex.** *The photographs were a link to the past.* —*v.*

connect or unite with a link or as with a link. **Ex.** *The railroad cars were linked together.*

linoleum [linow'liyəm], *n.* a washable, sometimes plastic-coated covering for floors and countertops which is made by mixing ground cork and special oils and spreading the mixture on a backing of canvas or similar material. **Ex.** *We are going to replace the linoleum in our kitchen.*

lion (2) [lay'ən], *n.* a large, yellowish-brown, flesh-eating member of the cat family, found in Africa and Asia. **—li'on·ess,** *n.* female lion.

LION

lip (2) [lip'], *n.* 1. either of the two edges of the mouth. 2. anything like a lip. **Ex.** *A drop of water remained on the lip of the cup.*

lip-read [lip'riyd'], *v.* learn what another is saying by watching that person's lips form the words. **Ex.** *The deaf boy can lip-read what we say.*

LIP 1

lipstick [lip'stik'], *n.* a cosmetic in the form of a short waxlike stick to color the lips in any of various shades of red. **Ex.** *Why aren't you wearing any lipstick?*

liquid (2) [lik'wid], *n.* a substance that is neither a solid nor a gas. **Ex.** *Water and milk are liquids.* **—adj.** in the form of a liquid. **Ex.** *The sick man could take only liquid food.* **—liq'ue·fy,** *v.* change into a liquid.

liquor (2) [lik'ər], *n.* a drink containing alcohol. **Ex.** *Does this restaurant have a license to serve liquor?*

list (1) [list'], *n.* 1. a series of separate items, names, etc. written in order. **Ex.** *He forgot to bring his list of the people he had called.* 2. the condition of leaning to one side. **Ex.** *The list of the ship was very noticeable.* **—v.** 1. make a list of. **Ex.** *She listed the articles she was going to buy.* 2. lean to one side. **Ex.** *The ship was listing badly.*

listen (1) [lis'ən], *v.* 1. try to hear. **Ex.** *They were listening to the car radio.* 2. give one's attention to. **Ex.** *You must listen to your teacher.* **—lis'ten·er,** *n.* one who listens. **Ex.** *People like her because she is such a good listener.*

lit (4) [lit'], *v.* past tense and participle of *light.* **Exs.** *She placed some candles on the table and lit them. The fire had been lit before we arrived.*

liter (4) [liy'tər], *n.* the basic unit of measure of liquids in the metric system, equal to a little more than one quart. See **Weights and Measures.**

literacy [lit'ərəsiy], *n.* the ability to read and write. **Ex.** *Before he was hired, he was given a test to determine his literacy.* —**lit·er·ate,** *adj.* able to read and write. **Ex.** *My grandfather became literate when my grandmother taught him to read.*

literal (4) [lit'ərəl], *adj.* 1. following the exact meaning of the words. **Ex.** *He explained the literal meaning of the phrase.* 2. according to the facts; correct. **Ex.** *The newspaper gave a literal account of the accident.* —**lit·er·al·ly,** *adv.*

literary (3) [lit'ərer'iy], *adj.* 1. of or about literature. **Ex.** *He is reading a book of literary criticism.* 2. knowing about literature; well-read. **Ex.** *She is a literary person.* 3. doing writing; having writing as a profession. **Ex.** *As an editor, she is familiar with many people in the literary world.*

literature (2) [lit'(ə)rəčər, lit'(ə)rəčur], *n.* 1. all of the poems, stories and writings of a period or country, especially those considered of enduring value because of their excellence of style or thought. **Ex.** *He was studying American literature.* 2. the written material on a certain subject. **Ex.** *The library has a collection of literature on nineteenth-century French art.* 3. any kind of printed material. **Ex.** *Here is some literature on the work our organization is doing.*

litter (5) [lit'ər], *n.* 1. things left or scattered about carelessly. **Ex.** *They cleaned up the litter after the party.* 2. young animals born of the same mother at the same time. **Ex.** *There were six kittens in the litter.* —*v.* scatter things about carelessly. **Ex.** *The picnickers had littered the grass with paper.*

little (1) [lit'əl], *adj.* 1. not tall; not big; small in size. **Ex.** *We have a little house in the country.* 2. a small quantity of; a small degree of. **Ex.** *May I have a little water, please?* 3. short in time or distance. **Ex.** *Let's go for a little walk.* —*adv.* in or to a small quantity or degree. **Ex.** *You look a little tired.*

live (1) [liv'], *v.* 1. have one's home. **Ex.** *The boy lived with his aunt and uncle.* 2. be alive; exist. **Ex.** *My father lived to be ninety.* 3. spend one's time in a certain manner. **Ex.** *They live quietly.* —**liv'a·ble,** *adj.* 1. suitable for living in. **Ex.** *This is a livable house.* 2. worth living; endurable. **Ex.** *He felt that life was no longer livable.* —**liv'ing,** *adj.* having life. —*n.* the means with which to carry on life. **Ex.** *What does he do for a* living? —**live down,** by actions cause people to forget or forgive something wrong that one has done. **Ex.** *By working hard, he lived down his youthful mistakes.* —**live up to,** keep up to what is expected of one. **Ex.** *By becoming a doctor, she lived up to her parents' hopes for her.*

live (1) [layv'], *adj.* having life; alive. **Ex.** *They brought back live animals.* —**live'ly,** *adj.* 1. full of energy. **Ex.** *The band played a lively march.* 2. exciting. **Ex.** *We had a lively evening at the theater.* —*adv.* with energy. **Ex.** *You had better step lively if you expect to make your train.* —**live'li·ness,** *n.*

livelihood [layv'liyhud'], *n.* the means by which or the resources with which one supports life. **Ex.** *She earned her livelihood as a teacher.*

liver (4) [liv'ər], *n.* a large, reddish-brown organ of the body that helps to change the food one eats into body-building material.

livestock [layv'stak], *n.* four-footed animals, such as cattle, sheep, pigs, horses and goats, raised on a farm or ranch. **Ex.** *It was his job to feed the livestock every morning before he went to school.*

living room [liv'iŋ ruwm'], the main room of a house where guests are received and most activities except eating and sleeping occur. **Ex.** *We need a new couch in the living room.*

lizard [liz'ərd], *n.* any of various reptiles that have a long body, sometimes covered with scales, four feet and a long tail. **Ex.** *The children saw a lizard eat an insect in the garden.*

LIZARD

load (2) [lowd'], *n.* 1. that which is carried or to be carried. **Ex.** *In the wagon was a load of wood.* 2. something which weighs down or burdens. **Ex.** *The load of work was too great for him.* —*v.* 1. fill; put something on or in. **Ex.** *They loaded the cart with dirt.* 2. prepare a gun for firing. **Ex.** *He loaded the gun.*

loaf (4) [lowf'], *n.* 1. a shaped mass of bread baked in one piece. **Ex.** *On her way home she bought a loaf of brown bread.* 2. any food baked in the shape of bread. **Ex.** *We ate meat loaf for dinner.*

loaf (4) [lowf'], *v.* spend time idly. **Ex.** *He does nothing but loaf all day.* —**loaf'er,** *n.*

loan (2) [lown'], *n.* 1. a lending; permission to use for a time. **Ex.** *May I have the loan of your book?* 2. that which is lent. **Ex.** *He got a loan from the bank.* —*v.* make a loan; lend. **Ex.** *The bank loaned money to the farmer.*

loaves [lowvz'], *n. pl.*, plural of *loaf.* **Ex.** *She baked six loaves of bread.*

lobby (5) [lab'iy], *n.* 1. an entrance hall of a building. **Ex.** *He waited for me in the lobby of the theater.* 2. a group of people working to influence lawmakers to vote for legislation favoring its cause. **Ex.** *He works for the dairy lobby.* —*v.* influence lawmakers to vote for legislation favoring a particular cause. **Ex.** *They are lobbying for a medical-care bill.* —**lob'by·ist,** *n.*

local (2) [low'kəl], *adj.* 1. concerning or having to do with one place. **Ex.** *We have a daily local newspaper in our town.* 2. making all or almost all stops. **Ex.** *The local train makes twenty stops on its way to the city.* —**lo'cal·ly,** *adv.* —**lo·cal'i·ty,** *n.* a place and its surrounding area. **Ex.** *For what is this locality famous?*

locate (2) [low'keyt], *v.* 1. find the place or position of. **Ex.** *We located the leak in the gas pipe.* 2. show where something is. **Ex.** *Please locate that city on the map for me.* —**lo·ca'tion,** *n.* the place where something is. **Ex.** *Is this a good location on which to build?*

lock (2) [lak'], *n.* a device for fastening doors, chests, drawers, etc., especially one that operates with a key. —*v.* 1. fasten or be fastened with a lock. **Ex.** *Is the gate locked?* 2. shut inside or outside by means of a lock. **Ex.** *The dog was locked in the house.* —**lock'er,** *n.* a chest, box, narrow closet, etc. which can be locked. **Ex.** *The student put the books in his locker when he went to lunch.*

lock (2) [lak'], *n.* a curl or bunch of hair. **Ex.** *A lock of hair hung over her forehead.*

locomotive [low'kəmow'tiv], *n.* an engine that runs on a track and pulls railroad cars; a railroad engine. **Ex.** *The locomotive was pulling a long line of freight cars.*

lodge (3) [laj'], *n.* 1. a small house or cottage, especially one used in connection with outdoor activities. **Ex.** *On our vacation we stayed at a hunting lodge.* 2. the local branch of a large group. **Ex.** *My lodge meets once a month.* —*v.* 1. live in a rented room or rooms in the house of another, usually for a short time. **Ex.** *He lodged with my family for several weeks.* 2. get stuck in a place. **Ex.** *A small piece of chicken bone was lodged between his teeth.* —**lodg'er,** *n.* a person who rents a room in the house of another. —**lodg'ing,** *n.* a place to rest or stay for a short time. **Ex.** *His brother offered him lodging while he looked for work.* —**lodg'ings,** *n.* a rented room or rooms in the house of another. **Ex.** *She found lodgings near her work.*

lofty (4) [lɔf'tiy], *adj.* 1. extending or rising very high. **Ex.** *Snow covered the lofty mountain peaks.* 2. high in ideals, spirit, etc. **Ex.** *He was a poet of lofty sentiments.*

log (2) [lɔːg'], *n.* 1. length of wood cut from a tree. **Ex.** *He put another log on the fire.* 2. the record of a ship's voyage. **Ex.** *The captain kept the ship's log.* —*adj.* made from logs. **Ex.** *They lived in a log cabin.* —*v.* record; write in a log. **Ex.** *She logged the names of those in attendance.*

logic (4) [laʤ'ik], *n.* 1. the science of reasoning. **Ex.** *He studied logic in college.* 2. good sense; sound and reliable thinking. **Ex.** *Her arguments showed logic.* —**log'i·cal,** *adj.*

loiter [loy'tər], *v.* spend time standing around idly, often on street corners; loaf; move slowly and idly; linger. **Exs.** *The policeman asked the two men why they were loitering about at midnight. The little boy loitered on his way to school looking at the spring flowers.*

lone (1) [lown'], *adj.* alone; without company; apart from others. **Ex.** *A lone traveler passed by.* —**lone'ly,** *adj.* 1. feeling oneself alone and longing for company. **Ex.** *The old man led a lonely life.* 2. visited by few or no people. **Ex.** *The house was in a lonely place.* —**lone'li·ness,** *n.* —**lone'some,** *adj.* having or causing a lonely feeling. **Ex.** *She had a lonesome look on her face.*

long (1) [lɔːŋ'], *adj.* 1. measuring more than usual from beginning to end; not short. **Ex.** *She has long hair.* 2. in length. **Ex.** *This board is eight feet long.* —*adv.* 1. for much time. **Ex.** *I have long thought about such a trip.* 2. from the beginning to the end. **Ex.** *He was away at school all winter long.* —**as long as, so long as,** since; as. **Ex.** *As long as you are going, why not take me with you?* —**before long,** soon; in a short time. **Ex.** *We will leave before long.*

longhand [lɔŋ'hænd'], *n.* ordinary handwriting with the words spelled out in full. **Ex.** *He wrote his name in longhand.*

longitude (4) [lɔn'jətuwd', lɔn'jətyuwd'], *n.* a distance on the earth's surface, measured in degrees east or west of an imaginary north–south line labeled zero degrees, drawn through Greenwich, England.

longshoreman [lɔŋ'šɔr'mən], *n.* a man who works at putting cargo on or taking it off a ship in port.

long-winded [lɔŋwin'did], *adj.* speaking or writing for so long as to be dull. **Ex.** *I fell asleep listening to the long-winded speaker.*

look (1) [luk'], *v.* 1. turn the eye toward in order to see; turn the attention toward or away from. **Ex.** *Hearing a noise, he looked toward the door.* 2. search; hunt for. **Ex.** *The dog looked for rabbits in the bushes.* 3. seem to be; present an appearance of. **Ex.** *The woman looked tired.* —*n.* 1. the act of looking at or examining. **Ex.** *After one look, I knew he was someone I had seen before.* 2. appearance. **Ex.** *She had a sad look on her face.* —**look after,** watch; guard. **Ex.** *Look after the children for me.* —**look back,** consider past events; remember. **Ex.** *She looked back at what had happened and tried to determine what had gone wrong.* —**look down on,** think of as less than oneself. **Ex.** *She looks down on people who work with their hands.* —**look forward to,** wait for eagerly. **Ex.** *I look forward to resting tomorrow.* —**look on,** 1. regard; consider. **Ex.** *I look on her as a sister.* 2. watch. **Ex.** *I looked on while they played.* —**look out,** watch for. **Ex.** *Look out for falling rocks.* —**look over,** examine. **Ex.** *Look over the books and choose one that you would like.* —**look to,** depend on. **Ex.** *I look to him for help.* —**look up,** search or hunt for in a book, newspaper, etc. **Ex.** *Look up her number in the telephone book, please.* —**look up to,** admire. **Ex.** *She looks up to her older brother.*

looking glass [luk'iŋ glæs'], a mirror.

loop (4) [luwp'], *n.* the rounded opening made by curving a thread, cord, rope, etc. back so that it crosses itself. —*v.* form a loop. **Ex.** *The old road looped around the lake.*

LOOP

loose (2) [luws'], *adj.* 1. not fastened or tied; free. **Ex.** *The horse is loose.* 2. not firmly set or fastened in. **Ex.** *The leg of the table is loose.* 3. not tightly fitting. **Ex.** *He wore a long,* loose coat. 4. not firm or packed down. **Ex.** *This plant grows best in loose soil.* —**loos'en,** *v.* make or become loose; untie. **Ex.** *He loosened his shoelaces.* —**loose'ly,** *adv.* —**loose'ness,** *n.* —**break loose,** become free. **Ex.** *He broke loose from the jail.* —**set loose,** turn loose; free. **Ex.** *He set the dog loose to run.*

lord (1) [lord'], *n.* a ruler; a person with power. **Ex.** *He obeyed no lord or king.* —**Lord,** *n.* God. —**lord'ly,** *adj.* in the manner of a lord.

lose (1) [luwz'], *v.* 1. have no longer because of accident or death. **Ex.** *It makes me sad to lose such a good friend.* 2. have no longer and not be able to find. **Ex.** *She is always losing her pen.* 3. fail to keep. **Ex.** *He loses his temper easily.* 4. be defeated. **Ex.** *Our team is losing the game.* 5. suffer a loss. **Ex.** *They are losing money on the sale of their house.* —**lose oneself,** be so interested as not to be aware of what else is happening. **Ex.** *The boy loses himself in his books.*

loss (1) [lo:s'], *n.* the act of losing. **Ex.** *The loss of the ship marked the end of the battle.* 2. failure to keep, get or win. **Ex.** *The loss of the ball game disappointed them.* 3. the person, thing or amount lost. **Ex.** *Their losses in the business were caused by poor planning.* —**at a loss,** unsure; uncertain. **Ex.** *He was at a loss about what he should do next.*

lost (1) [lo:st'], *v.* past tense and participle of *lose.* **Exs.** *He lost his hat yesterday. She did not know where she had lost her ring.*

lot (1) [lat'], *n.* 1. a great many; a great amount; a great deal. **Ex.** *He has a lot of friends.* 2. a section of land. **Ex.** *He owns a small lot in the country.* —*adv.* to a great extent. **Ex.** *She feels a lot better.*

lotion (4) [low'šən], *n.* a liquid used on the skin to smooth, heal or cleanse. **Ex.** *She uses lotion on her hands.*

lottery [lat'əriy], *n.* a gambling game in which numbered tickets are sold, certain ones are selected by chance and the holders of these are awarded prizes, frequently money. **Ex.** *They haven't yet heard from the person holding the winning number in the lottery.*

loud (1) [lawd'], *adj.* 1. having or making a strong, powerful sound. **Ex.** *The firing of the gun made a loud noise.* 2. full of sound or noise. **Ex.** *She spoke in a loud voice.* —**loud'ly,** *adv.* —**loud'ness,** *n.*

loudspeaker [lawd'spiyk'ər], *n.* a device that changes electrical signals into sound and also makes the sound louder.

lounge (5) [lawnj'], *v.* stand, walk, sit or lie easily and lazily. **Ex.** *They lounged on the beach all day.* —*n.* a room in which one can be comfortable and at ease. **Ex.** *They met in the main lounge of the club.*

LOUDSPEAKER

love (1) [ləv'], *n.* 1. a strong feeling of affection; fond and tender attachments. **Ex.** *They show their love for their children in many ways.* 2. a strong sexual feeling for another. **Ex.** *Their love for each other was obvious.* 3. a strong liking for. **Ex.** *He has always had a love of learning.* —*v.* 1. have a strong feeling of affection for. **Ex.** *They loved their parents very much.* 2. have a strong liking for. **Ex.** *She loves music.* —**lov'a·ble,** *adj.* attracting strong affection. **lov'ing,** *adj.* feeling or showing strong affection. —**lov'er,** *n.* —**in love,** in a state of loving. **Ex.** *He has fallen in love with her.* —**make love,** kiss, embrace, etc. as lovers do.

lovely (2) [ləv'liy], *adj.* 1. beautiful. **Ex.** *Your dress is lovely.* 2. having admirable qualities. **Ex.** *She is a lovely person.* 3. enjoyable. **Ex.** *We had a lovely day.* —**love'li·ness,** *n.*

low (1) [low'], *adj.* 1. not high; not tall. **Ex.** *Their house was a long, low building.* 2. below the normal height; closer to the earth than usual. **Ex.** *The airplane seemed to be very low.* 3. below the usual level; below the general level of the earth's surface. **Ex.** *The land near the mouth of the river is quite low.* 4. smaller than usual in amount, degree, value or power. **Ex.** *Our supply of flour is very low.* 5. near the bottom of the musical scale; deep in pitch. **Ex.** *He sings the low notes very well.* 6. not loud. **Ex.** *They spoke in low tones.* 7. not high in rank or position; humble. **Ex.** *He holds a very low position in that office.* —*adv.* in a low manner; to a low place or degree. **Ex.** *The sun sank low in the west.*

lower (1) [low'ər], *v.* 1. reduce in amount, price, force, etc. **Ex.** *Prices were lowered to sell the goods quickly.* 2. cause loss of respect. **Ex.** *He lowered himself in the eyes of others by his actions.* 3. bring down. **Ex.** *They lowered the flag at sundown.* —*adj.* less than another; below another. **Ex.** *That store charges lower prices.*

loyal (3) [loy'əl], *adj.* faithful to family, friends, etc. **Ex.** *As a loyal citizen, he expressed his support of the government's policy.* —**loy'al·ty**, *n.*

luck (2) [lək'], *n.* 1. fortune; something that happens by chance. **Ex.** *If my luck does not change, I will not be able to buy a house.* 2. good fortune. **Ex.** *I had luck in finding a good job.* —**luck'y**, *adj.* —**luck'i·ly**, *adv.*

luggage [ləg'ij], *n.* the baggage of a traveler, usually suitcases, boxes, etc. **Ex.** *She had four pieces of luggage.*

lull (5) [ləl'], *v.* calm; soothe. **Ex.** *The mother lulled the baby to sleep by singing to her.* —*n.* a short period of quiet after noise or activity. **Ex.** *There was a lull in the battle.* —**lul'la·by**, *n.* a song sung to put a baby to sleep.

lumber (3) [ləm'bər], *n.* wood cut into timber, boards, etc. **Ex.** *They bought some lumber to make a fence.* —**lum'ber·yard'**, *n.* a place of business where lumber is cut and sold.

lump (5) [ləmp'], *n.* 1. a piece or mass of no particular shape. **Ex.** *He threw some lumps of coal on the fire.* 2. a swelling. **Ex.** *The lump on her head was caused by a fall.* —*v.* form into a lump. **Ex.** *The sugar lumped in the damp weather.* —**lump'y**, *adj.* having lumps.

lunar [luw'nər], *adj.* to, from, of or concerning the moon. **Ex.** *The lunar landing by the astronauts on July 20, 1969, was a thrilling event.*

lunch (2) [lənč'], *n.* a light meal, usually in the middle of the day. **Ex.** *What did you have for lunch?*

lung (4) [ləŋ'], *n.* either of the two breathing organs in the chest of humans and many other animals.

LUNG

lure (4) [luwr', lyuwr'], *n.* 1. an attraction. **Ex.** *The lure of the sea took him away from home.* 2. something to attract fish. **Ex.** *The fisherman had some bright-colored lures.* —*v.* lead or attract with something that seems desirable. **Ex.** *They lured the dog into the house by offering it meat.*

lust (5) [ləst'], *n.* 1. eagerness to enjoy. **Ex.** *He was possessed by a lust for gold.* 2. a strong desire for sex. **Ex.** *His dreams were full of lust.* —*v.* have a strong desire. **Ex.** *She lusted for fame and fortune.* —**lust'y**, *adj.* full of life and spirit. **Ex.** *The baby gave a lusty yell.* —**lust'i·ly**, *adv.*

luster (4) [ləs'tər], *n.* 1. a bright shine on a surface; brilliance. **Ex.** *He shined his shoes to a high luster.* 2. fame; glory. **Ex.** *The luster of his achievements did not dim with the passing years.*

luxury (3) [lək'šəriy, ləg'žəriy], *n.* 1. the physical comforts and richness of life beyond that which is necessary. **Ex.** *They were wealthy enough to live in luxury.* 2. something which one is not usually able to afford. **Ex.** *They considered going to theater a luxury.* —**lux·u'ri·ate**, *v.* enjoy with delight and freedom. —**lux·u'ri·ous**, *adj.* giving a feeling of luxury. —**lux·u'ri·ant**, *adj.* growing thickly and richly. **Ex.** *He had a luxuriant head of hair.*

-ly (1) [liy], *suffix.* 1. in a certain way. **Exs.** *Happy, happily; gradual, gradually.* 2. each; every. **Exs.** *Week, weekly; day, daily.* 3. like; similar. **Exs.** *Man, manly; woman, womanly.*

lyric (5) [li:r'ik], *adj.* 1. suitable for singing. **Ex.** *It was a lyric piece of music.* 2. having to do with poems describing inner feelings. **Ex.** *She is a lyric poet.* —*n.* A short poem expressing personal emotion. —**lyr'ics**, *n. pl.* the words of a song. **Ex.** *The lyrics suit the music.* —**lyr'i·cal**, *adj.*

M

M, m [em'], *n.* the thirteenth letter of the English alphabet.

macaroni [mæk'ərow'niy], *n.* a kind of pasta shaped in short tubes which are prepared for eating by boiling. **Ex.** *We'd like some macaroni and cheese for lunch.*

machine (1) [məšiyn'], *n.* a device with moving parts used to do work. **Ex.** *My mother has a sewing machine.* —*adj.* 1. having to do with machines. **Ex.** *Machine parts are made in this factory.* 2. produced by machines. **Ex.** *This is a machine-made rug.* —**ma·chin'ist**, *n.* a skilled operator and repairer of machines.

machinery (2) [məšiyn'(ə)riy], *n.* a group of machines, as in a factory; the parts of a machine. **Ex.** *The machinery in this factory needs to be modernized.*

mad (1) [mæd'], *adj.* 1. not in one's right mind; mentally ill; crazy. **Ex.** *The man had suddenly gone mad.* 2. extremely excited. **Ex.** *At the sight of the fire, the horses became mad with fear.* 3. senseless and foolish. **Ex.** *The girl had a mad desire to become a singer.* 4. angry. **Ex.** *The two children were mad at each other.* 5. very interested in; having a strong liking for. **Ex.** *The whole family was mad about old cars from the 1920s and 1930s.*

madam (3) [mæd'əm], *n.* a respectful term used in speaking to or of a woman. **Ex.** *The clerk asked, "May I help you, madam?"*

made (1) [meyd'], *v.* past tense and participle of *make.* **Exs.** *She made a cake. She has finally made up her mind to sell her house.*

magazine (2) [mæg'əziyn], *n.* a collection of stories, pictures and articles published at regular intervals. **Ex.** *I like to read a weekly news magazine as well as a daily newspaper.*

magic (3) [mæǰ'ik], *n.* 1. the art of seeming to make things happen outside of the laws of nature. **Ex.** *Some people still believe in magic.* 2. an extraordinary influence. **Ex.** *The magic of the singer's voice charmed them all.* 3. the art of performing tricks that deceive the eye. **Ex.** *The children enjoyed watching the tall man perform magic.* —*adj.* as if produced by magic; as if producing magic. **Ex.** *The words of the general had a magic influence on his tired soldiers.* —**mag'i·cal**, *adj.* strangely mysterious or charming. **Ex.** *She had spent a magical evening with him.* —**mag'i·cal·ly**, *adv.* —**ma·gi'cian**, *n.* one who performs magic.

magistrate (4) [mæǰ'istreyt', mæǰ'istrit'], *n.* the holder of an office with the power to enforce laws. **Ex.** *The magistrate found the defendant guilty.*

magnet (5) [mæg'nit], *n.* any substance or device that has the power to attract iron and steel. **Ex.** *She used a magnet to pick up the pins.* —**mag·net'ic**, *adj.* —**mag'net·ism**, *n.* 1. the power of a magnet. 2. the power to attract. —**mag'net·ize**, *v.*

magnificent (2) [mægnif'əsent], *adj.* splendid; unusually fine; rich. **Ex.** *The house has a magnificent view.* —**mag·nif'i·cent·ly**, *adv.* —**mag·nif'i·cence**, *n.*

magnify (5) [mæg'nəfay'], *v*. cause to appear larger. **Ex.** *This lens will magnify the small print on that piece of paper.* —**mag·ni·fy·ing glass**', a lens that makes that which is seen through it appear larger than it actually is.

magnitude (5) [mæg'nətuwd', mæg'nətyuwd'], *n*. 1. greatness of size, quantity, etc. **Ex.** *A crowd of great magnitude attended the President's inauguration.* 2. greatness; importance. **Ex.** *He had not realized the magnitude of the problem.*

maid (2) [meyd'], *n*. a girl or woman servant. **Ex.** *A maid cleaned our hotel room.*

maiden (3) [meyd'ən], *n*. a girl or young woman who is not married. **Ex.** *She is a pretty maiden of sixteen.* —*adj*. 1. unmarried. **Ex.** *She is my maiden aunt.* 2. first. **Ex.** *It is the ship's maiden voyage.*

maiden name [meyd'ən neym'], *n*. a woman's family name before she is married. **Ex.** *After her marriage to Mr. Smith, Helen Jones became Helen Smith; Jones is her maiden name.*

mail (1) [meyl'], *n*. 1. letters, papers, parcels, etc. sent through a post office. **Ex.** *There is no mail today because it is Sunday.* 2. the service by which letters, packages, etc. are sent, carried and delivered. —*v*. send by mail. **Ex.** *He mailed the letter yesterday.* —**mail' order**', an order placed by mail for goods; a buying and selling of goods through the mail. **Ex.** *What percentage of their business is mail order?*

mailbox [meyl'baks'], *n*. a public box on the street into which letters are placed to be picked up and sent through the mail; a box at one's residence where mail is delivered.

mailman [meyl'mæn'], *n*. a person who delivers mail.

main (2) [meyn'], *adj*. most important; largest; principal. **Ex.** *Most of the stores in our town are on the main street.* —**main'ly**, *adv*.

main (2) [meyn'], *n*. a principal pipe or cable in a system for carrying water, gas, electricity, etc. to the users. **Ex.** *The street was flooded when the water main broke.*

mainland (5) [meyn'lænd', meyn'lənd], *n*. a single mass of land of a country or a continent considered apart from its islands. **Ex.** *The islanders often go to the mainland.*

a, far; æ, am; e, get; ey, late; i, in; iy, see; ɔ, all; ow, go; u, put; uw, too; ə, but, ago; ər, fur; aw, out; ay, life; oy, boy; ŋ, ring; θ, think; ð, that; ž, measure; š, ship; j, edge; č, child.

mainstream [meyn'striym], *n.* the general course or direction in which the principal ideas, actions, etc. in a particular field are flowing. **Ex.** *Her novels were not in the mainstream of her day.*

maintain (5) [meynteyn'], *v.* 1. keep; preserve; continue. **Ex.** *He maintained a steady speed on the highway.* 2. keep in a certain manner or condition. **Ex.** *The city maintains the parks.* 3. provide with means of support. **Ex.** *His salary was too small to maintain a family of five.* 4. declare to be true; say positively. **Ex.** *She maintains that she is innocent.*

maintenance (5) [meyn'tənəns], *n.* 1. support; repair. **Ex.** *Taxes pay for the maintenance of this road.* 2. a means of support. **Ex.** *Insurance provided maintenance for his family during his illness.*

majesty (3) [mæj'əstiy], *n.* 1. dignity; nobility; greatness. **Ex.** *They were inspired by the majesty of the mountains.* 2. a title used in speaking to or of a king or queen. **Ex.** *Her Majesty is a guest of the United States.* —**ma·jes'tic,** *adj.*

major (2) [mey'jər], *adj.* greater in size, extent, importance, amount, etc. **Ex.** *He spent the major part of his salary for rent and food.* —*n.* 1. an army officer ranking next above a captain. 2. the main subject that a student studies in college. **Ex.** *The major of most of the students that we met was history.* —*v.* specialize in a particular study. **Ex.** *He majored in chemistry.*

majority (3) [məjɔːr'ətiy], *n.* the greater part of a quantity or number; more than half. **Ex.** *To win the election, a candidate will need to have the majority of votes.*

make (1) [meyk'], *v.* 1. build; produce; bring into existence. **Ex.** *They will make a camp near the river.* 2. become; have the qualities needed for. **Ex.** *Dry wood makes a good fire.* 3. cause to be or become. **Ex.** *The hot weather makes some people sleepy.* 4. cause to do; force to do. **Ex.** *The rain and sun make the grass grow.* 5. do; perform. **Ex.** *He will make a trip to town tomorrow.* 6. think about. **Ex.** *She is making plans to go away.* 7. be equal to; add to. **Ex.** *Two and two make four.* —**make believe,** pretend. **Ex.** *Don't stop talking; just make believe I am not here.* —**make out,** 1. write on a form. **Ex.** *He was told to make out an application for the job.* 2. see or recognize. **Ex.** *He could not make out who was standing in the doorway.* —**make over,** change; redo. **Ex.** *The* *new owner made over the house.* **—make up,** 1. invent; tell an untruth. **Ex.** *Why did you make up such a story?* 2. form; join. **Ex.** *He is trying to make up a party of eight to go on the trip.* 3. pay for a loss. **Ex.** *I will make up for your losses.* 4. become friends again. **Ex.** *We often quarrel but we always make up.* 5. decide. **Ex.** *You should make up your mind to work harder.*

make-up [meyk'əp'], *n.* 1. all of the various preparations such as powder, rouge, lipstick, etc. that are intended to make the user more beautiful; cosmetics. **Ex.** *She rushed out of the house without putting on her make-up.* 2. similar preparations used when appearing on the stage, television, in films, etc. **Ex.** *I did not recognize the actress without her make-up.* **—make up,** apply cosmetics to the face.

mal- (3) [mæl'], *prefix,* badly; ill. **Exs.** *Adjusted, maladjusted; content, malcontent.*

malady (5) [mæl'ədiy], *n.* illness; sickness. **Ex.** *He's suffering from a strange malady.*

malaria (5) [məle:r'iyə], *n.* a disease of the blood caused by the bite of a certain mosquito, which causes the patient to have chills and fever. **Ex.** *An attack of malaria made her weak.*

male (2) [meyl'], *n.* a man; a boy. **Ex.** *There are two males among the children in that family.* 2. an animal belonging to the sex that fathers young. **Ex.** *The males of some birds have bright feathers.* **—adj.** 1. belonging to the male sex. **Ex.** *We saw the male lion first.* 2. consisting of men or boys. **Ex.** *That is an excellent male singing group.*

malignant [məlig'nənt], *adj.* 1. having an evil nature; intentionally causing harm or suffering. **Ex.** *The villain in the play was truly a malignant character.* 2. of an abnormal growth that is apt to spread and cause death. **Ex.** *The doctor explained that the tumor was malignant but could be treated.*

mall [mɔːl'], *n.* 1. a public walking area shaded by trees. **Ex.** *On a hot day like this, it is still pleasant to go walking on the mall.* 2. a large outdoor or indoor area lined with shops, often on both sides, made inviting with trees, flowers, plants, etc. **Ex.** *She enjoyed going to the mall to window-shop.*

mammal (3) [mæm'əl], *n.* an animal, the female of which produces milk to feed its young. **Ex.** *Humans, cows, dogs and cats are all mammals.*

man (1) [mæn'], *n.* 1. an adult male person. **Ex.** *The boy grew into a fine young man.* 2. the human race. **Ex.** *Man has a highly developed brain.* 3. a person in general; anyone. **Ex.** *Any man would be glad to have this opportunity.* 4. a male employee; a person in the military service of low rank. **Ex.** *An officer and one man looked over the area.* 5. husband. **Ex.** *They are now man and wife.* —*v.* 1. supply with men. **Ex.** *The ship is fully manned.* 2. take one's place for action. **Ex.** *Man the guns!* —**man'ly,** *adj.*

-man [mæn], *suffix.* 1. a person of, from or born in. **Exs.** *English, Englishman; country, countryman.* 2. a person working in or at. **Exs.** *Fire, fireman; business, businessman.* 3. a person who uses. **Exs.** *Boat, boatman; rifle, rifleman.*

manage (2) [mæn'ij], *v.* 1. direct; lead; supervise. **Ex.** *He manages a large factory.* 2. control; guide; handle. **Ex.** *She could not manage the horses.* 3. succeed in accomplishing. **Ex.** *They managed to stay afloat by clinging to a large piece of wood.* —**man'age·a·ble,** *adj.* —**man'age·ment,** *n.* 1. the act or manner of directing or controlling. **Ex.** *Improved management could solve many of your problems.* 2. the person or persons managing. **Ex.** *Labor and management do not always agree.* —**man'ag·er,** *n.* one who manages.

mankind (3) [mæn'kaynd', mæn'kaynd'], *n.* the human race; all human beings. **Ex.** *The library has several good histories of mankind.*

manner (1) [mæn'ər], *n.* the way in which something is done or happens; a way of acting or behaving. **Ex.** *He spoke in a friendly manner.* —**man'ners,** *n. pl.* socially correct behavior. **Ex.** *Sometimes she seems to have no manners.* —**man'ner·ism,** *n.* a distinctive way of doing something. **Ex.** *He has a strange mannerism of always clearing his throat before he asks a question.*

mansion (5) [mæn'šən], *n.* a very large house, usually that of a wealthy family. **Ex.** *That old mansion has more than thirty rooms.*

manual [mæn'yuwəl], *adj.* done with or by the hands. **Ex.** *In the manual training class, the boy made a small table.* —*n.* a booklet giving instructions for and information about something. **Ex.** *She studied the manual carefully before she began to use the computer.*

manufacture (2) [mæn'yəfæk'čər], *n.* the making of goods in large quantities, usually by machine. **Ex.** *The manufacture of shoes* *is the chief business of this town.* —*v.* make or produce goods in large quantities, usually by machine. **Ex.** *That factory manufactures automobiles.* —**man·u·fac'tur·er,** *n.* one who makes or produces goods in large quantities, usually by machine. **Ex.** *He is the largest manufacturer of toys in the country.*

manure (5) [mənuwr', menyuwr'], *n.* waste matter of animals; any substance put in soil to provide food for plants to help them grow. **Ex.** *The farmer spread manure on the field.*

manuscript (4) [mæn'yəskript'], *n.* a letter, article or book in unpublished form, especially an author's copy that is sent to an editor or printer. **Ex.** *His manuscript was accepted for publication.*

many [men'iy], *adj.* a large number of; numerous. **Ex.** *Many people were at the party.* —*n.* a large number. **Ex.** *Many of those women are my friends.* —*pron.* many persons or things. **Ex.** *Many came who were not invited.*

map (2) [mæp'], *n.* a drawing of the earth's surface or part of it. —*v.* 1. make a drawing of the earth's surface or part of it. **Ex.** *Most parts of the world have been mapped.* 2. plan carefully. **Ex.** *They mapped out a work plan for the week.*

MAP

maple (5) [mey'pəl], *n.* 1. a shade tree grown for its wood and the sweet liquid that some varieties produce. **Ex.** *We have a maple in our yard.* 2. the hard, light-colored wood of this tree. **Ex.** *This table is made of maple.* 3. the flavor of the liquid or sap from the tree; the flavor of the sugar made from the sap. **Ex.** *We flavored the cake with maple.*

marble (3) [mar'bəl], *n.* 1. a hard stone, either white or colored, that can be highly polished and is used in making statues or in building. **Ex.** *The front of that building is covered with marble.* 2. a small ball of glass or stone, used in games. **Ex.** *The boys were trading marbles.* —*adj.* of marble. **Ex.** *That table has a marble top.*

march (1) [marč'], *v.* 1. walk with measured steps, as soldiers do. **Ex.** *The boys marched around the playground.* 2. cause to

---

a, far; æ, am; e, get; ey, late; i, in; iy, see; ɔ, all; ow, go; u, put; uw, too; ə, but, ago; ər, fur; aw, out; ay, life; oy, boy; ŋ, ring; θ, think; ð, that; ž, measure; š, ship; j, edge; č, child.

walk in that way. **Ex.** *The teacher marched the children out of the burning building.* —*n.* 1. the act of marching. **Ex.** *The troops were on the march.* 2. the distance marched; the kind of march. **Ex.** *They made a twenty-mile march.* 3. music to accompany marching. **Ex.** *The band played a march.* —**march' er,** *n.*

March (1) [marč'], *n.* the third month of the year.

mare (4) [me:r'], *n.* a female horse. **Ex.** *Their only farm animal was an old mare.*

margarine [mar'jərin'], *n.* a substitute for butter usually made of vegetable oils, milk, water, salt and a coloring agent. **Ex.** *She spread the bread for the children's sandwiches with margarine.*

margin (4) [mar'jin], *n.* the blank space around the writing or printing on a page. **Ex.** *Leave a margin of one inch on the left side of your paper.* 2. an amount allowed or available beyond what is necessary. **Ex.** *You should include in your budget a 10 percent margin for unexpected expenses.* —**mar'gin·al,** *adj.* of low or minimal value, standards, profits, etc.

marijuana [mær'əwa'nə], *n.* a plant, the leaves and flowers of which are used to produce a habit-forming, illegal drug. **Ex.** *He was arrested for selling marijuana.*

marine (4) [məriyn'], *adj.* of the sea; found in the sea. **Ex.** *Many kinds of marine life are found along this section of the coast.* —*n.* a soldier trained for duty both on land and at sea. **Ex.** *The marines landed on the island.* —**mar'i·ner,** *n.* a sailor.

mark (1) [mark'], *n.* 1. a line, spot, scratch, stain or other impression; an effect upon something. **Ex.** *Several dirty marks were on the wall.* 2. a seal, letter or number put on by an official, teacher, etc. to show quality or approval. **Ex.** *The girl always received high marks for her work.* 3. something which guides or shows the limits or important points. **Ex.** *We could see no landmarks that would help us to find our way.* 4. goal; target. **Ex.** *He was able to hit the mark the first time.* —*v.* 1. make a line, spot, effect, etc. **Ex.** *The little girl marked the wall with a pencil.* 2. show approval, price, quality, etc. **Ex.** *The teacher marked the students' papers.* 3. show clearly. **Ex.** *His manner marked him as a man from the country.* —**make one's mark,** succeed; become known. **Ex.** *He made his mark as a writer.* —**mark down,** 1. lower a price. **Ex.** *The twenty-dollar book was marked down to ten dollars.* 2. write something on paper. **Ex.** *Mark down the date before* *you forget it.* —**mark time,** 1. move the feet as in marching but without moving forward. **Ex.** *They marked time to the music.* 2. make no progress. **Ex.** *She is only marking time in her present job.* —**mark up,** raise the price. **Ex.** *They marked up the price of many foods just before the holidays.*

market (1) [mar'kit], *n.* 1. a place where goods are bought, sold or traded. **Ex.** *She buys her fruits and vegetables at the farmers' market.* 2. a demand. **Ex.** *There is a good market in the city for fresh fruit.* —*v.* present for sale. **Ex.** *That farmer markets his vegetables in the city.* —**mar·ket·ting,** *n.* the act of shopping for or buying, especially food. **Ex.** *Mother does her marketing on Friday.* —**be in the market for,** want to buy. **Ex.** *I am in the market for a new car.* —**put on the market,** present for sale. **Ex.** *They put their house on the market.*

marriage (3) [mæ:r'ij], *n.* 1. the act of living legally together as husband and wife. **Ex.** *Their marriage is a happy one.* 2. the act of marrying; a wedding. **Ex.** *The marriage was performed in the morning.*

marry (1) [mæ:r'iy], *v.* 1. join as husband and wife. **Ex.** *They asked the judge to marry them.* 2. take as husband or wife. **Ex.** *He hopes to marry her.* 3. become husband and wife. **Ex.** *They will marry in June.*

marsh (4) [marš'], *n.* soft wet land. **Ex.** *Rice is grown in those marshes.* —**marsh'y,** *adj.*

marshal (4) [mar'šəl], *n.* an officer of a United States court with duties similar to a sheriff; an officer of a local police or firefighting force. **Ex.** *United States marshals were sent to enforce the court order.* —*v.* 1. arrange in proper order. **Ex.** *The lawyer marshaled the facts in the case.* 2. lead or guide. **Ex.** *He marshaled the troops for a drill.*

martial [mar'šəl], *adj.* warlike; of or having to do with the armed forces. **Exs.** *A martial spirit had swept over the country. The Marine Corps band was playing martial music.* —**mar'tial law',** rule by the military according to its laws. **Ex.** *No one was allowed on the street after dark without a pass when the city was under martial law.*

marvel (2) [mar'vəl], *n.* something unexpected, wonderful or astonishing. **Ex.** *Space travel is one of the marvels of our time.* —*v.* be filled with wonder. **Ex.** *They marveled at the speed of the train.* —**mar'vel·ous,** *adj.* surprising and wonderful. **Ex.** *She has a marvelous memory.*

masculine (5) [mæs'kyəlin], *adj.* 1. being strong, brave, manly, etc.; suitable for a man. **Ex.** *He has a very masculine voice.*

mash [mæš'], *v.* make into a soft mixture by mixing or crushing with a fork or other kitchen tool. **Ex.** *After you have mashed the potatoes, add a little warm milk and butter to them.*

mask (4) [mæsk'], *n.* a covering to hide or protect the face. **Ex.** *The workman wore a mask to protect his face from the sparks.* —*v.* hide; conceal. **Ex.** *She masked the real purpose of her visit.*

mass (2) [mæs'], *n.* 1. a quantity of matter of no definite shape, usually of a large size. **Ex.** *A mass of snow blocked the door.* 2. a large number or quantity. **Ex.** *The garden was a mass of flowers.* 3. the majority; the principal part. **Ex.** *The great mass of people elected him president.* 4. size; bulk. **Ex.** *The mass of the load made it difficult to handle.* —*v.* gather or form in a mass or masses. **Ex.** *The troops were massed for an attack.* —*adj.* 1. of, concerning or for a large mass of people. **Ex.** *Mass education is a nationwide policy.* 2. produced in great quantities. **Ex.** *Mass production of cars has lowered their price.* —**mass'es**, *n.* ordinary or working people as a group.

massacre (5) [mæs'əkər], *n.* the cruel, random killing of people in great numbers. **Ex.** *More than a thousand people were killed in the massacre.* —*v.* kill at random great numbers of people in a cruel way. **Ex.** *The enemy massacred the citizens of the town.*

massive (4) [mæs'iv], *adj.* large; weighty. **Ex.** *The house was built on a massive rock.*

mass media [mæs' miy'diyə], *n.* the various means of communication, such as newspapers, radio and television, through which information, news and opinions are directed to the public. **Ex.** *The defeated senator said that the unfair reporting by the mass media had caused him to lose the election.*

mast (3) [mæst'], *n.* a long pole of wood, steel, etc. fixed in an upright position on a ship or boat to which sails and ropes are fastened. **Ex.** *The sailor climbed up the mast.*

MAST

master (1) [mæst'ər], *n.* 1. a person who rules or commands people, animals or things. **Ex.** *The dog followed his master.* 2. a man skilled in some work or art. **Ex.** *That carpenter is a master at his work.* —*v.* 1. control; conquer.

Ex. *He tried to master his temper.* 2. become skillful at. **Ex.** *She has mastered several languages.*

mastermind [mæs'tərmaynd'], *n.* a person of unusual executive ability who plans and leads others in some project. **Ex.** *She was the mastermind of the reorganization plan.* —*v.* plan and direct. **Ex.** *He masterminded the bank robbery.*

masterpiece [mæs'tərpiys'], *n.* something of the greatest excellence; the best one has created. **Ex.** *All of his later paintings were considered masterpieces.*

mat (4) [mæt'], *n.* a flat piece of material, often coarse, made of grass, straw, etc. and used for a covering or for protection. **Ex.** *He wiped his shoes on the floor mat near the door.* —*v.* cover as with a mat; stick together in a mass. **Ex.** *The walls were matted with vines.*

match (2) [mætč'], *n.* a short, thin piece of wood or heavy paper tipped with a mixture that catches fire when rubbed on a rough surface. **Ex.** *He had to use three matches before the fire was lit.*

MATCH

match (2) [mætč'], *n.* 1. someone or something that is exactly alike, similar to or equal to another. **Ex.** *She has a button that is a perfect match for the one you lost.* 2. a person or thing that is suitable for another. **Ex.** *His suit, tie and socks were a good match.* 3. a contest. **Ex.** *They went to a boxing match.* —*v.* 1. find or make something just like another. **Ex.** *She matched the glove she had lost.* 2. be alike or equal to. **Ex.** *Her dress matched the color of her eyes.*

mate (3) [meyt'], *n.* 1. one of a pair. **Ex.** *He could not find the mate to his shoe.* 2. male or female of a pair. **Ex.** *His wife is a good mate for him.* 3. companion. **Ex.** *They are schoolmates.* —*v.* 1. bring two animals together to make a pair or to breed. **Ex.** *The two horses were mated.* 2. join as a pair; unite in marriage. **Ex.** *They are happily mated.*

material (1) [məti:r'iyəl], *n.* 1. the substance, substances or matter of which something is made or from which something can be made. **Ex.** *Probably 95 percent of the material in this*

a, far; æ, am; e, get; ey, late; i, in; iy, see; ɔ, all; ow, go; u, put; uw, too; ə, but, ago; ər, fur; aw, out; ay, life; oy, boy; ŋ, ring; θ, think; ð, that; ž, measure; š, ship; ǰ, edge; č, child.

house is wood. 2. anything that may be worked upon or be developed into something else. **Ex.** *His own life provided the material for his novel.* —*adj.* 1. of or consisting of matter or things of substance. **Ex.** *His material needs were few.* 2. important. **Ex.** *She was a material witness to what had happened.* —**ma·te'ri·al·ly,** *adv.*

mathematics (2) [mæθ'əmæt'iks], *n.* the science concerned with quantities, sizes, shapes and their relationships, as defined by numbers and signs. **Ex.** *His knowledge of mathematics was useful to him in his engineering studies.* —**math'e·mat'i·cal,** *adj.* —**math'e·mat'i·cal·ly,** *adv.* —**math'e·ma·ti'cian,** *n.* a person who studies and works in the field of mathematics.

matter (1) [mæt'ər], *n.* 1. something happening; something thought about or talked about. **Ex.** *An important matter caused him to stay in town.* 2. difficulty; trouble. **Ex.** *What is the matter with the sick child?* 3. anything that can be seen or felt; that which things are made of; substance. **Ex.** *The student was surprised to learn that gas is a kind of matter.* —*v.* be of importance; have meaning. **Ex.** *What people think matters to him.*

mattress (4) [mæ'tris], *n.* a case of cloth stuffed with hair, cotton, straw, etc. on which to sleep. **Ex.** *I like to sleep on a firm mattress.*

mature (4) [mətyu:r', mətu:r'], *adj.* 1. ripe; arrived at full growth; fully developed. **Ex.** *She seems to be a mature person.* 2. carefully planned or thought out. **Ex.** *He is not able to give a mature opinion.* —*v.* come to full growth. **Ex.** *This fruit has not matured enough to be picked.* —**mat·tur'i·ty,** *n.*

maximum (4) [mæk'səməm], *n.* the greatest quantity allowed, attainable, etc. **Ex.** *Her luggage weighed more than the maximum permitted.* —*adj.* the greatest possible or allowed. **Ex.** *He drove at the maximum speed.*

may (1) [mey'], *v.* used with another verb to mean: 1. allow; permit. **Ex.** *May I come in?* 2. possibly; likely. **Ex.** *The sun may shine again this afternoon.* 3. desire; wish. **Ex.** *May you always be successful.*

May (1) [mey'], *n.* the fifth month of the year.

maybe (2) [mey'biy], *adv.* perhaps. **Ex.** *Maybe we will go tomorrow.*

mayonnaise [mey'əneyz'], *n.* a thick sauce or dressing, usually made of olive oil, egg yolks, vinegar and/or lemon juice and salt and pepper. **Ex.** *I like to serve fresh sliced tomatoes with mayonnaise.*

mayor (3) [mey'ər], *n.* the chief government official of a city, town or village. **Ex.** *He was elected mayor.*

me (1) [miy'], *pron.* the form of *I* used as the object of a verb or preposition. **Exs.** *Give me the ball. He brought the book to me.*

meadow (5) [med'ow], *n.* a field where grass grows, often used for growing hay or for pasturing animals. **Ex.** *The cows are in the meadow.*

meal (2) [miyl'], *n.* 1. food eaten at one time to satisfy hunger. **Ex.** *When did you have your last meal?* 2. one of the regular times for eating. **Ex.** *Dinner is the meal that our family eats together.*

meal (2) [miyl'], *n.* grain, roughly ground. **Ex.** *We have corn ground into meal at the mill.*

mean (1) [miyn], *v.* 1. plan; want to do; intend. **Ex.** *He did not mean to hurt her.* 2. be a sign of; indicate; say. **Exs.** *What does this word mean? Those dark clouds mean it will rain soon.* **—mean'ing,** *n.* what is intended by a word or act. **Exs.** *He did not know the meaning of the word. What was the meaning of her leaving so suddenly?*

mean (1) [miyn], *adj.* 1. unpleasant; unkind. **Ex.** *She is mean to her little brother.* 2. not generous. **Ex.** *He was too mean to pay his workers well.* **—mean'ness,** *n.*

mean (1) [miyn], *n.* the middle point. **Ex.** *His own views were a mean between the extreme views of the others.* **—means,** *n. pl.* 1. that by which something is done or gained. **Ex.** *He would use any means to win.* 2. riches; money. **Ex.** *He has the means with which to buy that expensive car.*

meant (2) [ment'], *v.* past tense and participle of *mean.* **Exs.** *He meant what he said. I had not meant to hurt her feelings.*

meantime (3) [miyn'taym'], *n.* the time between. **Ex.** *I was out shopping for a couple of hours, and in the meantime the dog got out.* **—adv.** 1. during the time between. **Ex.** *He left at four o'clock and returned at seven; meantime she wrote letters.* 2. at the same time. **Ex.** *She set the table; meantime lunch was cooking.*

meanwhile (3) [miyn'hwayl], *adv.* 1. during the time between. **Ex.** *We have three hours before they come; meanwhile I am* *going to take a nap.* 2. at the same time. **Ex.** *She was working in the garden; meanwhile he washed the car.*

measure (1) [mež'ər], *n.* 1. the extent, size, quantity or capacity of something. **Ex.** *The tailor took the man's measure for a suit.* 2. anything used to find size, quantity, etc. **Ex.** *The farmer filled the measure with grain.* 3. a standard, system or unit of measurement. **Ex.** *What do you use as a measure of a student's work?* 4. an action intended to accomplish a purpose. **Ex.** *The city has taken measures to repair the streets.* —*v.* 1. learn the extent, quantity, etc. **Ex.** *She measured her waist.* 2. be of a certain size, quantity, etc. **Ex.** *This rug measures nine feet by twelve feet.* 3. compare with a standard. **Ex.** *A man's worth as a person should not be measured by his wealth.* —**meas'ure·ment,** *n.* the act of measuring; the size, height, etc. of something learned by measuring. **Ex.** *Do you know the measurements of this room?*

meat (1) [miyt], *n.* animal flesh, other than fish, considered as food. **Ex.** *What kind of meat are you serving for dinner?* —**meat'y,** *adj.* of, like, or having meat. **Ex.** *The soup has a meaty flavor.*

mechanic (3) [mekæn'ik], *n.* a worker skilled in repairing or working with machinery. **Ex.** *That is the mechanic who repaired our car.* —**me·chan'i·cal,** *adj.* 1. of, like or related to machinery. **Ex.** *He is a mechanical engineer.* 2. operated by machinery. **Ex.** *The child has a number of mechanical toys.* —**me·chan'i·cal·ly,** *adv.* —**me·chan'ism,** *n.* the parts of a machine that cause it to work. **Ex.** *The mechanism needs to be repaired.*

medal (3) [med'əl], *n.* a small, distinct piece of metal with a design and some words on it, used to honor or reward. **Ex.** *The professor was given a medal for his scientific discovery.*

media [miy'diyə], *n.* See **mass media.**

mediate [miy'diyeyt'], *v.* bring about agreement, peace, etc. between two opposing sides through the services of an individual who is not on either side. **Ex.** *Whom do you think would be acceptable to both parties to mediate this dispute?* —**me'di·a'tion,** *n.* the act of mediating. —**me'di·a'tor,** *n.* one who mediates.

medicare [med'i`kær], *n.* a government program basically designed to provide medical care for people sixty-five and older.

Ex. *Part of the expenses of her operation were paid for by medicare.*

medicine (2) [med'əsən], *n.* 1. a substance, drug, etc. used in treating disease or given to relieve pain. **Ex.** *She took the medicine which the doctor had ordered for her.* 2. the science and art of curing disease or improving health. **Ex.** *He is studying medicine.* —**med'i·cal**, *adj.* of or concerning medicine. **Ex.** *She went to medical school.*

medium (4) [miy'diyəm], *n.* 1. something not at either extreme of a scale. **Ex.** *He tried to achieve a happy medium between study and play.* 2. that through which something acts, something is done or an effect is made. **Ex.** *Money is a medium of exchange.* 3. the substance, element, condition, etc. in which something or someone lives, does his work, etc. **Ex.** *That author's medium is the mystery novel.* —*adj.* having a position in the middle in degree, size, amount, etc. **Ex.** *He usually buys suits in the medium price range.*

meek [miyk'], *adj.* willing to yield to others; submissive; patient and humble. **Ex.** *He seemed so meek that I never expected him to express his opinion publicly.*

meet (1) [miyt'], *v.* 1. see one another; come together. **Ex.** *We often meet in the street.* 2. be introduced to; become acquainted with. **Ex.** *I have not yet had a chance to meet him.* 3. wait for and welcome; come together according to a plan. **Ex.** *We will meet her at the train station.* 4. satisfy. **Ex.** *Will anything here meet your needs?* —**meeting**, *n.* a gathering of two or more people. **Ex.** *A teachers' meeting was held this morning.*

mellow (4) [mel'ow], *adj.* 1. having a good flavor from aging or ripening. **Ex.** *The wine from that old bottle is mellow.* 2. made kind and gentle by age. **Ex.** *The years have made him mellow.* 3. not coarse; not rough; full and pure. **Ex.** *The horns have a mellow tone.* —*v.* 1. make or become mellow. **Ex.** *The wine mellowed with age.* 2. make kind and gentle by age. **Ex.** *My parents mellowed with the passing years.* —**mel'low·ness**, *n.*

melody (4) [mel'ədiy], *n.* the musical sounds of a song; a sweet or pleasing arrangement of sounds. **Ex.** *I remember the melody but not the words of that song.* —**me·lod'ic**, *adj.*

a, far; æ, am; e, get; ey, late; i, in; iy, see; ɔ, all; ow, go; u, put; uw, too; ə, but, ago; ər, fur; aw, out; ay, life; oy, boy; ŋ, ring; θ, think; ð, that; ž, measure; š, ship; ǰ, edge; č, child.

melon (3) [mel'ən], *n.* a large, rounded, sweet, juicy, edible fruit that grows on a vine.

melt (2) [melt'], *v.* 1. become liquid by heat. **Ex.** *The sun melted the snow.* 2. dissolve; disappear gradually. **Ex.** *The sugar melted in my tea.* 3. soften. **Ex.** *The child's smile melted her mother's anger.*

MELON

meltdown [melt'dawn], *n.* a very serious accident at a nuclear plant as a result of which the central part of a nuclear reactor could or does melt. **Ex.** *The meltdown caused a massive leak of atomic radiation.*

melting point [mel'tiŋ poynt'], *n.* the temperature at which a solid substance melts.

member (1) [mem'bər], *n.* one of a group. **Ex.** *She is a member of the historical society.* —**mem'ber·ship,** *n.* 1. state of being a member. **Ex.** *He would like a membership in our club.* 2. all the people who belong to the group. **Ex.** *The entire membership was at the meeting.*

memory (2) [mem'əriy], *n.* 1. the power to keep in the mind; the ability to remember. **Ex.** *He has a good memory for dates.* 2. the thing remembered. **Ex.** *She has happy memories of her childhood.* —**mem'o·ra·ble,** *adj.* important or enjoyable enough to remember. **Ex.** *It was a memorable day!* —**me·mo'ri·al,** *n.* something to preserve the memory of a person or event. —**Me·mo·ri·al Day,** *n.* a national holiday in the United States in memory of its service people who died in all American wars, celebrated on May thirtieth in most states. —**mem'o·rize`,** *v.* learn and keep in one's memory. **Ex.** *We have two poems to memorize for English class.*

men (1) [men'], *n.* plural of *man.* **Ex.** *Three men were seated at the table.*

menace (4) [men'is], *n.* a threat; something that could cause harm. **Ex.** *Forest fires are a menace during the dry season.* —*v.* **Ex.** *Frost menaced the orange crop.* —**men'ac·ing,** *adj.*

mend (3) [mend'], *v.* 1. make whole again; repair. **Ex.** *She is mending the hole in the boy's shirt.* 2. improve; make or become better. **Ex.** *The sick girl is mending under the doctor's care.* —*n.* a part that has been mended. **Ex.** *The mend in the dress can hardly be seen.* —**on the mend,** improving; getting better. **Ex.** *He has been sick but is on the mend.*

-ment [mənt], *suffix.* 1. result of; act of. **Exs.** *Develop, development; advance, advancement.* 2. means of; things used for. **Exs.** *Entertain, entertainment; accompany, accompaniment.* 3. condition; state of being. **Exs.** *Astonish, astonishment; disappoint, disappointment.*

mental (2) [men'təl], *adj.* 1. of, in or concerning the mind. **Ex.** *He has great mental ability.* 2. having sickness of the mind. **Ex.** *She is a mental patient.* —**men·tal'i·ty,** *n.* powers of the mind; ability to think. **Ex.** *Though an adult, he has only the mentality of a child.* —**men'tal·ly,** *adv.*

mention (2) [men'šən], *v.* refer to briefly; speak about. **Ex.** *Your name was mentioned only once during the conversation.* —*n.* a brief reference. **Ex.** *Mention was made of the accident.*

menu (3) [men'yūw], *n.* a list of food available at an eating place. **Ex.** *I asked the waiter for the dinner menu.*

merchandise (4) [mər'čəndayz'], *n.* goods that are offered for sale. **Ex.** *This store has a large stock of merchandise.*

merchant (2) [mər'čənt], *n.* a person who buys and sells goods. **Ex.** *That merchant has enlarged his store.* —*adj.* commercial; used in buying and selling. **Ex.** *Merchant ships crowded the harbor.*

mercy (2) [mər'siy], *n.* 1. kindness or forgiveness toward those who have been found guilty of breaking the law, who are enemies, etc. **Ex.** *They showed mercy by freeing the prisoners they had taken in battle.* 2. the power to be kind or forgive. **Ex.** *He was dependent upon the mercy of the judge.* —**at the mercy of,** be completely in the power of. **Ex.** *They were at the mercy of the storm.*

mere (2) [mi:r'], *adj.* nothing more than; only. **Ex.** *His mother died when he was a mere child.* —**mere'ly,** *adv.*

merge [mərj'], *v.* combine or join and become one. **Exs.** *As we sat talking, daylight merged into dusk. Several rivers merge with the Mississippi River.* —**merg'er,** *n.* the joining of two or more businesses. **Ex.** *When the merger occurred, quite a large number of employees lost their jobs.*

merit (3) [me:r'it], *n.* 1. excellence; worth; that which deserves praise. **Ex.** *His work has a great deal of merit.* 2. the real fact or quality, whether good or bad. **Ex.** *The court will judge the case on its merits.* —*v.* deserve. **Ex.** *She merits the prize that she won.* —**mer'i·to'ri·ous,** *adj.*

merry (2) [me:r'iy], *adj.* gay; joyful; full of fun. **Ex.** *Her birthday party was a merry occasion.* —**mer'ri·ly**, *adv.* —**mer'ri·ment**, *n.*

mess (4) [mes'], *n.* 1. a condition of being dirty or not neat. **Ex.** *Her clothes were a mess.* 2. a state of confusion; disorder. **Ex.** *His business affairs were in a mess.* —*v.* make dirty; make confused. **Ex.** *The children messed up their playroom.* —**mess'y**, *adj.*

message (2) [mes'ij], *n.* news, information, a request, etc., either written or spoken, sent from one person to another. **Ex.** *I received a message from my brother through a friend.*

messenger (2) [mes'inǰər], *n.* one who carries a message or goods. **Ex.** *The messenger delivered the dress from the shop.*

met (1) [met'], *v.* past tense and participle of *meet*. **Ex.** *We met where we had met before.*

metal (2) [met'l], *n.* 1. any chemical element that is shiny when pure or polished, that can be melted and combined with something else and that can conduct heat and electricity. **Ex.** *Iron, gold and silver are well-known metals.* 2. a mixture of these elements. **Ex.** *Brass is a metal made from copper and zinc.* —*adj.* made from metal. **Ex.** *He was drinking from a metal cup.* —**me·tal'lic**, *adj.* of or like metal. **Ex.** *That cloth has a metallic appearance.*

meter (4) [miy'tər], *n.* the basic measure of length in the metric system, equal to a little more than three feet. See **Weights and Measures.** —**met'ric**, *adj.* concerning a meter or the metric system of measurement.

meter (4) [miy'tər], *n.* a device for measuring the amount of something used. **Ex.** *A man came to read the electric meter today.*

method (1) [meθ'əd], *n.* 1. a definite way of doing something. **Ex.** *He has his own method of doing his work.* 2. an orderly and regular way of doing something. **Ex.** *Method is needed to do that job well.* —**me·thod'i·cal**, *adj.* orderly; organized. —**me·thod'i·cal·ly**, *adv.* in a careful, organized way. **Ex.** *She prepared her lessons methodically.*

metric system [met'rik sis'təm], *n.* a system of measurement, based on units of ten, that is used throughout most of the world. See **Weights and Measures.**

metro [met'row], *n.* a system of trains operating underground, such as in Washington, D.C.; subway. **Ex.** *Where can I take the metro?*

metropolitan [me'trəpal'itən], *adj.* of the areas neighboring or near a large, busy city. **Ex.** *The Washington D.C. metropolitan area includes parts of Maryland and Virginia.*

mice (3) [mays'], *n.* plural of *mouse.* **Ex.** *He caught two mice in the trap.*

microphone [may'krəfown'], *n.* an instrument that picks up sound waves and changes them into electrical waves used in broadcasting, telephones, etc., and in increasing the volume of sound. **Ex.** *Please speak directly into the microphone.*

microscope (5) [may'krəskowp'], *n.* an instrument with a piece of special glass, a lens, or a combination of lenses, that causes very tiny things to appear large enough so that they become visible for study. —**mi'cro'scop'ic,** *adj.*

MICROSCOPE

microwave [may'krə'weyv], *n.* a short electrical wavelength used in sending radio messages, cooking, etc. **Ex.** *We find that cooking by microwave is a great time saver.* —**mi'cro'wave ov'en,** *n.* an oven that uses the deeply penetrating heat of the microwave so that food is cooked inside at the same time that it is being cooked outside.

mid- (2) [mid], *prefix.* middle of; halfway through. **Exs.** *Winter, midwinter; way, midway.*

middle (1) [mid'əl], *n.* the place or time equally distant from either end or side; the center. **Ex.** *The table was in the middle of the room.* —*adj.* 1. in the center; equally distant from both ends. **Ex.** *The middle window is open.* 2. neither great nor small; between the extremes of size, quantity, etc. **Exs.** *Our teacher is a man of middle age. The middle class is neither rich nor poor.*

midnight (2) [mid'nayt'], *n.* twelve o'clock at night. **Ex.** *The party ended at midnight.* —*adj.* 1. of or at midnight. **Ex.** *They took a midnight swim.* 2. like midnight; very dark. **Ex.** *He bought a midnight blue suit.*

midst (3) [midst'], *n.* the middle; the part in the center. **Ex.** *There is a small house in the midst of the trees.*

might (1) [mayt'], *v.* 1. past tense of *may* but in meaning sometimes less likely or less definite than *may*. **Ex.** *If she had been stronger, she might have recovered.* 2. Used with another verb to show possibility. **Ex.** *He might be able to help you.*

might (1) [mayt'], *n.* power; force; physical strength. **Ex.** *He tried with all his might to lift the heavy weight.* —**might'y,** *adj.* large in size; having great power.

migrate (5) [may'greyt], *v.* 1. move from one place in order to settle in another. **Ex.** *His parents migrated to the United States when he was a small child.* 2. go from one region to another with the change in seasons. **Ex.** *The birds have begun to migrate south.* —**mi'grant,** *n.* a person, animal or bird that migrates from place to place. —**mi·gra'tion,** *n.* the act of migrating. —**mi'gra·tor`y,** *adj.* migrating.

mild (3) [mayld'], *adj.* 1. calm; gentle. **Ex.** *She is a very mild person.* 2. not cold or stormy. **Ex.** *The climate is very mild.* 3. not strong or sharp in taste. **Ex.** *She likes mild cheeses.* —**mild'ly,** *adv.* —**mild'ness,** *n.*

mile (1) [mayl'], *n.* a unit for measuring distance, equal to 5,280 feet. **Ex.** *The nearest village is four miles away.* See **Weights and Measures.**

military (2) [mil'əter`iy], *adj.* 1. referring to the armed services or to the affairs of war. **Ex.** *Military training is offered to both men and women at this college.* 2. of, by or for people of the armed services. **Ex.** *The band played a military march.* —*n.* the armed services; the men and women in the armed services. **Ex.** *Their son is serving in the military.*

milk (1) [milk'], *n.* 1. the white liquid produced by female animals to feed their young. **Ex.** *The milk of cows and goats is used in making cheese.* 2. any liquid or juice like milk. **Ex.** *The milk from the rubber tree is used to make rubber.* —*v.* take milk from a cow, goat, etc. **Ex.** *The farmer milks his cows twice a day.* —**milk'y,** *adj.* having milk; white like milk. —**milk shake,** a drink made of milk, ice cream and flavoring mixed together.

mill (2) [mil'], *n.* 1. a place where grain is made into flour or meal. **Ex.** *The farmer took his grain to the mill to be ground.* 2. a place where goods are manufactured; a factory. **Ex.** *My*

---

father works in a steel mill. —*v.* crush, shape or prepare in a mill. **Ex.** *The wheat was milled into flour for bread.* —**mill'er**, *n.* one who keeps or operates a mill where grain is ground.

milligram [mil'əgræm'], *n.* a measure of weight in the metric system; 1/1000 of a gram. See **Weights and Measures**.

millimeter [mil'əmiy`tər], *n.* a measure of length in the metric system, equal to 1/1000 of a meter. See **Weights and Measures**.

million (1) [mil'yən], *n., adj.* one thousand times one thousand; the number 1,000,000.

millionaire (4) [mil'yəne:r', mil'yəne:r'], *n.* a person who has a million dollars or more; a very rich person. **Ex.** *That millionaire owns his own airplane.*

mind (1) [maynd'], *n.* 1. the thinking, feeling, etc. part or center of a person. **Ex.** *His mind is busy with many affairs.* 2. that which one thinks, believes or desires. **Ex.** *We could not get her to speak her mind.* 3. mental ability; intelligence. **Ex.** *He has lost his mind.* 4. a person of great intelligence. **Ex.** *He is one of our great minds.* —*v.* 1. object to; be offended by. **Ex.** *Would you mind not smoking, please?* 2. pay attention to; observe; be careful of. **Ex.** *Mind what you are doing.* 3. obey. **Ex.** *That child will not mind his mother.* —**bear in mind**, remember. **Ex.** *Bear in mind that I have already been there.* —**have a mind to**, be inclined to. **Ex.** *I have a mind not to go with you.* —**have in mind**, be thinking of. **Ex.** *I have in mind a plan to take care of that problem.* —**make up one's mind**, decide. **Ex.** *He made up his mind to leave early.* —**never mind**, do not think about it. **Ex.** *Never mind; I will do it myself.* —**of one mind**, agreed. **Ex.** *We are of one mind about what to do next.* —**out of one's mind**, mentally ill. **Ex.** *He acts as if he were out of his mind.*

mine (1) [mayn'], *pron.* that which belongs to me. **Ex.** *This house is mine.*

mine (1) [mayn'], *n.* 1. a man-made hole in the earth from which useful substances are removed. **Ex.** *Several new coal mines have been opened in this area.* 2. a bomb placed under the surface of land or water so that it cannot be seen. **Ex.** *They were killed by an enemy mine.* —*v.* 1. dig in the earth for coal, metals, etc. **Ex.** *The men are mining for gold.* 2. lay military mines. **Ex.** *That land was mined during the war.* —**min'er**, *n.* a worker in the mine. —**min'ing**, *n.* 1. the act of taking metals, coal, etc. from the ground. 2. the act of laying mines.

mineral (2) [min'(ə)rəl], *n.* a substance with a definite chemical structure found in nature; a substance which is neither animal nor plant. **Ex.** *Coal and iron are important minerals.* —*adj.* of or containing minerals. **Ex.** *Some people drink mineral water for their health.*

mingle (3) [min̦'gəl], *v.* 1. combine, mix. **Ex.** *Her happiness was mingled with sadness.* 2. join with; unite. **Ex.** *We mingled with the crowd in the market.*

miniature (5) [min'ičər, min'iyəčər], *n.* 1. a copy in a very small size. **Ex.** *The child looked like her mother in miniature.* 2. a very small painting. **Ex.** *He had several miniatures of family members.* —*adj.* copied in a very small size. **Ex.** *A miniature car was on the table.*

minimize (4) [min'əmayz'], *v.* make very small; make seem very small. **Ex.** *He modestly minimized the importance of his work.*

minimum (4) [min'əməm], *n.* the least possible or permitted amount. **Ex.** *Some plants grow well with a minimum of care.* —*adj.* smallest, lowest or least permitted. **Ex.** *Those employees are paid only a minimum wage.*

minister (2) [min'istər], *n.* 1. a person who conducts the services in a church. **Ex.** *The minister lives next door to the church.* 2. in some countries, a high ranking official who heads a department of government. **Ex.** *The Indian Minister of Education is on a visit to the United States.* —*v.* take care of; give service, care or aid to. **Ex.** *The nurse ministered to the needs of her patient.* —**min·is·te·ri·al,** *adj.* —**min'is·try,** *n.* 1. act of ministering. 2. in some countries, a department of government. 3. profession of a minister of a church.

minor (4) [may'nər], *adj.* small in size, extent, importance, etc. **Ex.** *There are only minor objections to the plan.* —*n.* a person under the legal age of responsibility. **Ex.** *Minors cannot vote.* —**mi·nor'i·ty,** *n.* 1. the smaller number. **Ex.** *We went, although a minority voted to stay home.* 2. a small part of the population that differs in race, religion, etc. from the majority. —*adj.*

mint (5) [mint'], *n.* 1. a place where coins and paper money are officially made by the government. **Ex.** *The mint issued a new coin this week.* 2. a great supply. **Ex.** *He has a mint of ideas.* 3. one of a variety of plants with a pleasant, fresh smell, the leaves of which are used for flavoring. **Ex.** *She made a sauce with mint leaves to serve with the lamb.* —*v.* make coins. **Ex.**

Where was this gold coin minted? —adj. new; like new. **Ex.** *The car is in mint condition.*

minus (4) [may'nəs], *prep.* decrease by; subtract. **Ex.** *Six minus two is four. —adj.* less than zero; showing subtraction. **Ex.** *The temperature is minus ten degrees.* **—minus sign:** (–). **Ex.** *6 – 2 = 4.*

minute (1) [min'it], *n.* 1. one of the sixty equal parts of an hour; sixty seconds. **Ex.** *He will return in ten minutes.* 2. a short time. **Ex.** *I will see her in a minute.* 3. a particular point in time; an instant. **Ex.** *Please give him this message the minute that you see him.* **—min'utes,** *n. pl.* an official record of the proceedings of a meeting of a committee, society, etc. **Ex.** *The secretary read the minutes of the previous meeting.*

minute (1) [maynuwt', maynyuwt'], *adj.* 1. very, very small. **Ex.** *The doctor removed a minute piece of dust from the patient's eye.* 2. including every little fact about something. **Ex.** *She described her vacation in minute detail.* **—mi·nute'ly,** *adv.* in great detail. **Ex.** *He went into the matter minutely.*

miracle (4) [mi:r'əkəl], *n.* 1. an event that cannot be explained by the known laws of nature. **Ex.** *Her being able to see again seemed to be a miracle.* 2. something marvelous. **Ex.** *We hear about new miracles of science every day.* **—mi·rac'u·lous,** *adj.*

mirror (3) [mi:r'ər], *n.* a piece of glass coated on the back with a reflecting substance, used for looking at oneself. **Ex.** *He shaved in front of a mirror. —v.* reflect; reflect as a mirror does. **Ex.** *The stars were mirrored in the still water.*

MIRROR

mirth (5) [mərθ'], *n.* amusement; gladness as shown by laughter. **Ex.** *The joke caused a great deal of mirth among the children.*

mis- (3) [mis], *prefix.* wrongly; poorly; bad. **Exs.** *Lead, mislead; spent, misspent; fortune, misfortune.*

miscarry [miskæ:r'iy], *v.* 1. not succeed; fail. **Ex.** *His plans miscarried.* 2. lose a baby before it is born. **Ex.** *His wife miscarried because of her illness.* **—mis·car'riage,** *n.*

mischief (4) [mis'čif], *n.* 1. an act done innocently or in fun that causes harm or trouble. **Ex.** *Tipping over the table was his*

a, far; æ, am; e, get; ey, late; i, in; iy, see; ɔ, all; ow, go; u, put; uw, too; ə, but, ago; ər, fur; aw, out; ay, life; oy, boy; ŋ, ring; θ, think; ð, that; ž, measure; š, ship; j, edge; č, child.

latest piece of mischief. 2. harm or damage. **Ex.** *She apologized for the mischief her false story had caused.* 3. a playful mood. **Ex.** *The children are full of mischief today.* —**mis' chie·vous,** *adj.*

miser (5) [may'zər], *n.* a person who has money but does not like to spend it. **Ex.** *The old miser starved himself to death.* —**mi'ser·ly,** *adj.*

misery (3) [miz'(ə)riy], *n.* 1. state of great unhappiness or suffering. **Ex.** *His illness caused her great misery.* 2. that which causes great unhappiness or suffering. **Ex.** *The misery of the poor should concern us all.* —**mis'er·a·ble,** *adj.*

misgiving (3) [misgiv'iŋ], *n.* a feeling of doubt, worry, concern, etc. **Ex.** *The mother had misgivings about letting the child play outside.*

mislay [misley'], *v.* put in a place and not remember; lose. **Ex.** *Try not to mislay this letter.*

miss (1) [mis'], *v.* 1. fail to hit, find, reach, see, etc. **Ex.** *He ran but missed the train.* 2. fail to attend, do, etc. **Ex.** *She missed several classes.* 3. feel or discover the absence of. **Ex.** *The child misses her mother.* —**miss'ing,** *adj.* lost; absent. **Ex.** *My book is missing.*

miss (1) [mis'], *n.* 1. a title of respect for a girl or an unmarried woman. **Ex.** *I want you to meet my friend, Miss Martin.* 2. a form of address to an unnamed female. **Ex.** *What are you doing, miss?*

missile (4) [mis'əl], *n.* any weapon that can be thrown, hurled, pushed, fired, etc. through the air. **Ex.** *There are missiles that can go thousands of miles into space.*

mission (4) [miš'ən], *n.* 1. a group of people sent by a government, church, etc. for a special purpose. **Ex.** *The trade mission visited six countries.* 2. the special purpose for which the group is sent. **Ex.** *The nurses went on a mission of mercy.* 3. the station or headquarters of the group. **Ex.** *The mission is in that office building across the street.* 4. special purpose in life. **Ex.** *A doctor's mission is to save lives.*

missionary (5) [miš'əne:r'y], *n.* a person sent on a mission, usually by a church to spread its religion. **Ex.** *He is going abroad as a missionary.*

mist (4) [mist'], *n.* a cloud of very fine drops of water in the air. **Ex.** *It was difficult to see the house through the mist.* —*v.*

form a mist; become dim or less clear. **Ex.** *Her eyes misted with tears.*

mistake (2) [misteyk'], *n.* an error; an expression, act, etc. that is wrong. **Ex.** *It was a mistake for us to start our trip in this storm.* —*v.* 1. regard something or somebody as something or somebody else. **Ex.** *Hę always mistakes my overcoat for his.* 2. fail to understand. **Ex.** *You mistake my meaning.* —**mis·tak'en,** *adj.* wrong; in error; judging wrongly. **Ex.** *He was mistaken about the time of the meeting.* —**mis·tak'en·ly,** *adv.*

mister (1) [mis'tər], *n.* 1. a title of respect for a man, usually written *Mr.* **Ex.** *Mr. Jones is here to see you.* 2. a form of address to an unnamed man. **Ex.** *Where are you going, mister?*

mistook [mistuwk'], *v.* past tense of *mistake.* **Ex.** *I mistook her for someone I knew.*

mistress (5) [mis'tris], *n.* 1. a woman who has authority or control over. **Ex.** *She is headmistress of the school my daughter attends.* 2. a woman who lives with a man without being married to him. **Ex.** *The king's mistress had great influence over him.*

mitten (5) [mit'ən], *n.* a kind of glove with one part for the thumb and another for the four fingers.

mix (2) [miks'], *v.* 1. put together or combine in such a way as to make one. **Ex.** *The painter mixed blue and yellow paint to make green.* 2. prepare by putting different things together. **Ex.** *The cook mixed a chocolate cake.* 3. join in company with. **Ex.** *He likes to mix with people.* —*n.* a group of things combined or

MITTEN

put together; a mixture. **Ex.** *There are many prepared cake mixes on the market today.* —**mix'ture,** *n.* a product of mixing; a combination. **Ex.** *This mixture is too thin.* —**mix up,** confuse. **Ex.** *She was so mixed up by the noise that she couldn't think.* —**mixed company,** men and women together in a group. **Ex.** *He acts differently in mixed company.*

moan (4) [mown'], *n.* 1. a long, low sound indicating pain or sorrow. **Ex.** *A moan came from the room of the sick man.* 2. any similar sound. **Ex.** *We heard the moan of the wind as it blew through the trees.* —*v.* make moans. **Ex.** *The girl moaned in pain.*

mob (3) [mab'], *n.* 1. a large group of excited people. **Ex.** *The speaker was threatened by an angry mob.* 2. an organized gang of criminals. **Ex.** *The police believe that the mob ordered last night's killing.* —*v.* crowd about someone to admire or attack. **Ex.** *The actor was mobbed by his admirers.* —**mob'ster,** *n.* a member of an organized gang of criminals.

mobile (4) [mow'bəl], *adj.* movable; moving easily; easy to move. **Ex.** *The new lightweight furniture is very mobile.* —**mo·bil'i·ty,** *n.* —**mo'bil·ize,** *v.* organize and make ready for action, as for war. **Ex.** *Because of the danger of enemy attack, the country was mobilized.* —**mo'bil·i·za'tion,** *n.*

mock (3) [mak'], *v.* 1. treat with scorn. **Ex.** *People once mocked the idea that the earth is round.* 2. make fun of by copying or imitating in an unkind way. **Ex.** *The boy should not have mocked his teacher.* —*adj.* not real; imitation. **Ex.** *The soldiers staged a mock battle.* —**mock'er·y,** *n.* —**mock'ing,** *adj.* scornful. —**mock'ing·ly,** *adv.*

mode (4) [mowd'], *n.* manner of being or doing; method. **Ex.** *His mode of living is different from mine.*

model (2) [mad'əl], *n.* 1. a thing or person that is worth copying; an example. **Ex.** *He looked upon the teacher as his model.* 2. an object or figure, often small, made to show how something looks or will look. **Ex.** *The designer made this chair as a model for the manufacturer.* 3. design; style. **Ex.** *His car is the latest model.* 4. a person whose work is to wear and display clothing. **Ex.** *The models walked around the room, stopping before each customer to tell about the clothes that they were wearing.* —*v.* form or make; follow a model. **Ex.** *The boy modeled himself after his father.* —*adj.* 1. suitable to be copied or followed; excellent. **Ex.** *She is a model student.* 2. made to show how something looks or will look. **Ex.** *He has a collection of model trains.*

moderate (3) [mad'ərət], *adj.* 1. kept or keeping within reasonable limits; not extreme. **Ex.** *He drinks a moderate amount of coffee.* 2. average in quality, amount or extent. **Ex.** *The play was a moderate success.* —*n.* a person who takes a position in the middle. **Ex.** *They preferred a moderate for mayor.* —**mod'er·ate·ly,** *adv.* —**mod'er·a'tion,** *n.* state of being moderate.

moderate (3) [madəreyt'], *v.* 1. make less strong. **Ex.** *The wind moderated the heat.* 2. act as leader of a discussion or debate. **Ex.** *Who is going to moderate the labor dispute?* —**mod'er·a'tor,**

n. one who leads a discussion. **Ex.** *The moderator allowed each person five minutes to speak.*

modern (1) [mad'ərn], *adj.* 1. of the present or a very recent time. **Ex.** *That pianist plays the music of modern composers.* 2. recent; of the most improved type. **Ex.** *Their house has many modern conveniences.* —**mod'ern·ize,** *v.* make modern.

modest (3) [mad'əst], *adj.* 1. making little of one's own capabilities, achievements, etc. **Ex.** *He was modest about the heroic rescue he had made.* 2. not luxurious, large, etc.; simple. **Ex.** *They live in a modest home.* 3. not offending, especially in dress; retiring in manner. **Ex.** *She wore a dress of modest length.* —**mod'est·ly,** *adv.* —**mod'es·ty,** *n.*

modify (4) [mad'əfay'], *v.* 1. change slightly. **Ex.** *He modified his plans because of the weather.* 2. make less extreme; moderate. **Ex.** *The judge modified the prisoner's sentence.* 3. in grammar, change the quality of, limit the quantity of or describe a word. **Ex.** *In the sentence, "She wore a green hat," the adjective* green *modifies the noun* hat. —**mod'i·fi'er,** *n.* 1. a word or group of words describing another word or group of words. See **A Brief Explanation of English Grammar.** 2. one who or that which changes, moderates, etc. —**mod'i·fi·ca'tion,** *n.* the act of modifying; a change.

moist (2) [moyst'], *adj.* somewhat wet; damp. **Ex.** *These plants grow best in moist surroundings.* —**moist'en,** *v.* make somewhat wet; dampen. **Ex.** *She moistened his forehead with a wet cloth.* —**mois'ture,** *n.* liquid in the form of small condensed drops.

molasses (5) [məlæs'iz], *n.* the thick, brown, sticky liquid which is a by-product of manufacturing sugar. **Ex.** *My brother likes molasses on bread.*

mold (4) [mowld'], *n.* a hollow form in which something soft or liquid is shaped as it hardens; the thing shaped. **Ex.** *The dessert had been made in a mold.* —*v.* form into a desired shape or condition. **Ex.** *The artist molded the clay into a figure of a child.*

mold (4) [mowld'], *n.* a woolly-looking growth that appears on damp or decaying vegetable or animal substances. **Ex.** *Mold has spoiled the bread.* —*v.* become covered with mold. **Ex.** *The cheese has molded.* —**mold'y,** *adj.*

a, far; æ, am; e, get; ey, late; i, in; iy, see; ɔ, all; ow, go; u, put; uw, too; ə, but, ago; ər, fur; aw, out; ay, life; oy, boy; ŋ, ring; θ, think; ð, that; ž, measure; š, ship; j, edge; č, child.

mole (5) [mowl'], *n.* a dark-colored spot or growth, usually brown. **Ex.** *She has a small mole on her cheek.*

mole (5) [mowl'], *n.* a small, soft, furry animal that lives mostly underground. **Ex.** *A mole is digging tunnels under our lawn.*

MOLE

molecule (3) [mal'əkyuwl'], *n.* the smallest fragment of a chemical compound that retains its chemical characteristics. **Ex.** *A molecule of water is composed of two atoms of hydrogen and one atom of oxygen.*

moment (1) [mow'ment], *n.* 1. a very short period of time. **Ex.** *Please wait a moment.* 2. a particular point of time. **Ex.** *The doctor is not here at the moment.* 3. the right time for an action. **Ex.** *Now is the moment to ask her your question.* 4. importance. **Ex.** *They are discussing matters of great moment.* —**mo'men·tar·y,** *adj.* lasting only a very short time. —**mo'men·tar'i·ly,** *adv.* —**mo'men'tous,** *adj.* important.

monarch (4) [man'ərk, man'ark`], *n.* a ruler by right of royal descent, such as an emperor, empress, king, queen, etc. **Ex.** *The band played for the visiting monarch.* —**mon'arch·y,** *n.* government by a monarch.

Monday (1) [man'diy], *n.* the second day of the week.

money (1) [mən'iy], *n.* 1. government stamped metal coins and printed paper bills that are issued for use in buying and selling. **Ex.** *He is saving money to buy a car.* 2. property; wealth. **Ex.** *She seems to have money.*

monitor (5) [man'ətər], *n.* a person or thing that watches and warns or reminds. **Ex.** *The monitor flashed a red warning signal.* —*v.* listen to; watch; look at and follow closely. **Ex.** *They monitored the flight of the spaceship.*

monk (4) [məŋk'], *n.* a member of a religious organization who devotes himself to prayer and religious activities. **Ex.** *He left his successful business to study to become a monk.*

monkey (4) [məŋ'kiy], *n.* a tree-climbing animal with a long tail and with paws that look like human hands.

monopoly (5) [mənap'əliy], *n.* sole or complete control of the production and/or sale of a product or service. **Ex.** *Railroads are government monopolies in some countries.* —**mo'nop·o·lize`,** *v.* gain or have complete control of. **Ex.** *He always monopolizes the conversation.*

MONKEY

monotony (5) [mənat'əniy], *n.* a lack of change; tiring sameness. **Ex.** *He found the monotony of the factory job difficult to bear.* —**mo·not'o·nous,** *adj.* of a sameness; having little or no change. **Ex.** *His speech was monotonous.* —**mon'o·tone`,** *n.* an unchanging tone of voice.

monster (4) [man'stər], *n.* any animal or plant that is unnatural or extreme in shape or size or that is very ugly. **Ex.** *The monster had a head larger than its body.* 2. a very wicked or cruel person. **Ex.** *That monster is head of a crime ring.* —**mon'strous,** *adj.* horrible; shocking.

month (1) [menθ'], *n.* one of the twelve portions into which a year is divided. **Ex.** *He was born in the month of December.* —**month'ly,** *adj.* done, happening or appearing each month. **Ex.** *He makes monthly payments on his house.* —*n.* something published each month. **Ex.** *This magazine is a monthly.* —*adv.* one time in each month. **Ex.** *We pay our rent monthly.*

monument (3) [man'yəmənt'], *n.* 1. something erected in memory of a person or event. **Ex.** *That statue is a monument to the discoverer of America.* 2. any great literature, art, structure, etc. that endures. **Ex.** *His writings are monuments of the culture of his time.* —**mon'u·men'tal,** *adj.* 1. like a monument. **Ex.** *He built a monumental home to house his art treasures.* 2. larger than life size. **Ex.** *There is a monumental bronze head of him in the museum.* 3. significant and enduring; great in amount, degree, etc. **Ex.** *They spent a monumental amount of money on the project.*

mood (3) [muwd], *n.* a state of mind; the way one feels about oneself. **Ex.** *He was usually in a happy mood.* —**mood'y,** *adj.* having frequent changes of mood. **Ex.** *She's very difficult to live with when she's moody.*

moon (1) [muwn'], *n.* a heavenly body that circles the earth once in about every twenty-nine days. **Ex.** *The moon is very bright tonight.* —**moon'light,** *n.* light from the moon. **Ex.** *The garden was bright in the moonlight.*

mop (5) [map'], *n.* materials such as a sponge, coarse strings, rags, cloth, etc. fastened at the end of a stick for cleaning or removing liquid from floors. **Ex.** *This mop needs to be washed before it is used again.* —*v.* clean or wipe with a mop. **Ex.** *He mopped the kitchen floor.*

moral (2) [mɔːr'əl, mar'əl], *adj.* 1. concerned with the principles of right and wrong in character and conduct. **Ex.** *She has* *high moral standards.* 2. of good character; right or proper in conduct. **Ex.** *A teacher should be a moral person.* —*n.* a lesson about what is right or wrong as shown in a story. **Ex.** *What is the moral of this story?* —**morals,** *n.* *pl.* character; principles of conduct; standards of behavior. **Ex.** *He is a man of high morals.* —**mo·ral'i·ty,** *n.* 1. a set of morals by which one is guided. 2. the quality of being moral. —**mor'al·ly,** *adv.* in a moral way.

more (1) [mɔːr'], *adj.* 1. greater in size, amount, etc. **Ex.** *She does more work than you do.* 2. greater in number. **Ex.** *We will need two more men for this work.* 3. additional, further. **Ex.** *You can get more information tomorrow.* —*n.* a greater number, amount or degree. **Ex.** *Won't you have some more?* —*adv.* 1. in or to a greater extent or degree. **Ex.** *A plane travels more rapidly than a train.* 2. in addition; again. **Ex.** *Tell me the story once more.*

moreover (3) [mɔrow'vər], *adv.* also; besides; in addition. **Ex.** *He is a quick worker; moreover, he is careful.*

morning (1) [mɔr'niŋ], *n.* the early part of the day, ending at noon; from midnight to noon. **Ex.** *Where were you yesterday morning?* —*adj.* of or happening in the morning. **Ex.** *Morning classes begin at eight o'clock.*

morsel (5) [mɔr'səl], *n.* a very small amount. **Ex.** *The hungry children did not leave a morsel of food on their plates.*

mortal (3) [mɔr'təl], *adj.* 1. certain to die. **Ex.** *Man is mortal.* 2. causing death. **Ex.** *The soldier received a mortal wound in battle.* —*n.* man; a human being. **Ex.** *We are mortals, not gods.* —**mor·tal'i·ty,** *n.* 1. the condition of being mortal. **Ex.** *Whatever he did, he did without thought of his mortality.* 2. the death rate. **Ex.** *The mortality rate for infants in this city is above the national average.* —**mor'tal·ly,** *adv.* in a way that kills. **Ex.** *He was mortally knifed.*

mortar [mɔr'tər], *n.* a mixture of lime, cement, sand and water used for holding bricks or stones together in buildings, walls, etc. **Ex.** *Before laying the bricks, the workmen mixed the mortar.*

mortgage (4) [mɔr'gij], *n.* a claim to property given as an assurance for the repayment of a cash loan. **Ex.** *The bank holds a $100,000 mortgage on the house.* —*v.* give a lender a claim to one's property in case a debt is not paid when due. **Ex.** *They mortgaged their house in order to obtain money to* *pay their hospital bills.* —**mort·ga·gee'**, *n.* a person to whom property is mortgaged; the lender of money. —**mort·ga·gor'**, *n.* one who borrows money and gives a mortgage in return.

mosquito (5) [məskiy'tow], *n.* a small flying insect, the female of which bites humans and animals. **Ex.** *Some mosquitoes carry disease.*

moss (4) [mɔs'], *n.* very small, soft green plants that grow close together on the ground, rocks, trees, etc. **Ex.** *The stones were covered with moss.*

MOSQUITO

most (1) [mowst'], *adj.* 1. greatest in number, amount or degree. **Ex.** *This is the most cake I have ever eaten.* 2. almost all. **Ex.** *Most schools in this area open in September.* —*adj.* in or to the greatest degree or extent; very. **Ex.** *He was most willing to help us.* —*n.* the greatest amount or degree. **Ex.** *We invited the whole class and most of the members came.* —**most'ly**, *adv.* mainly; chiefly. **Ex.** *The children mostly wanted to play.* —**at most,** at the most, not more than. **Ex.** *At most, five of us will go.* —**for the most part,** mainly; chiefly. **Ex.** *Their experiences for the most part were very pleasant.* —**make the most of,** use to full advantage. **Ex.** *While we wait, let's make the most of our time by reading.*

motel [mowtel'], *n.* a hotel for travelers who are driving, usually built so that each room can be entered directly from a parking lot and often located outside cities on main highways. **Ex.** *We stopped driving so late that there was only one room vacant at the motel.*

moth (5) [mɔ:θ], *n.* a winged insect, related to the butterfly, that flies mainly at night.

mother (1) [məð'ər], *n.* 1. a female parent. **Ex.** *The mother was washing the baby.* 2. the origin, source or cause of something. **Ex.** *We can learn a great deal from Mother Nature.* —*v.* act as a mother to; care for. **Ex.** *It was strange to see the dog mother a baby duck.* —*adj.* of, like or as if from a mother. **Ex.** *Her mother love overcame her anger at the way he had acted.* —**moth'er·ly**, *adj.*

MOTH

mother-in-law [məð'ərinlɔ'], *n.* the mother of one's wife or husband.

motion (2) [mow'šən], *n.* movement; change of position or place. **Ex.** *The ship's motion made some of the passengers feel seasick.* —*v.* make a meaningful movement, as of the hand or the head. **Ex.** *The police motioned the car to stop.*

motion picture [mow'šən pik'čər], *n.* movie; photographic pictures seen so quickly, one after another, that the things in them appear to move. **Ex.** *That motion picture is playing at our neighborhood theater.*

motive (3) [mow'tiv], *n.* a thought or feeling that makes one act; a reason for acting in a certain manner. **Ex.** *What was his motive for taking them on that trip?* —**mo'tiv·ate,** *v.* give or provide a motive. **Ex.** *I was motivated to go there by what I had heard about the place.*

motor (2) [mow'tər], *n.* an engine that makes a machine run. **Ex.** *An electric motor makes the fan turn.* —*adj.* run by a motor. **Ex.** *They made that trip in a motorcar.* —*v.* travel by automobile. **Ex.** *They motored to town.* —**mo'tor·ist,** *n.* a person who drives an automobile.

motorcycle [mow'tərsay`kəl], *n.* a two-wheeled machine similar in appearance to a bicycle but much heavier and powered by an engine. **Ex.** *Police on motorcycles rode ahead of the visiting official's car.*

motto (4) [mat'ow], *n.* a short saying to guide one's actions. **Ex.** *His motto is "Live and let live."*

mound (5) [mawnd'], *n.* a small hill; a raised bank of earth, stone, sand, etc. **Ex.** *It was a tribal custom to build mounds over the dead.*

mount (2) [mawnt'], *v.* 1. go up; climb. **Ex.** *He mounted the steps.* 2. get up on. **Ex.** *She mounted her horse.* 3. rise; increase. **Ex.** *Prices are mounting rapidly.* 4. fasten in a proper setting or frame. **Ex.** *The photograph was mounted on white paper.* —*n.* a horse for riding. **Ex.** *She chose a gentle mount.*

mount (2) [mawnt'], *n.* a mountain or hill, called so generally only in poems or as part of a name. **Ex.** *Mount Everest is the highest mountain in the world.*

mountain (1) [mawn'tən], *n.* a part of the earth's surface that rises very high above the area around it. **Ex.** *The mountains* were topped with snow. —*adj.* of mountains. **Ex.** *The mountain air was fresh and clear.* —**moun'tain·ous,** *adj.* like a mountain; full of mountains. **Ex.** *He lived in a mountainous area.*

mourn (3) [mɔrn'], *v.* feel or express sorrow or grief. **Ex.** *They mourned the death of their father.* —**mourn'er,** *n.* —**mourn'ful,** *adj.* sad; sorrowful. —**mourn'ing,** *n.* the showing of sorrow over someone's death or a loss. **Ex.** *As a sign of mourning, his widow is wearing black.*

mouse (3) [maws'], *n.* a small animal found in fields or in houses.

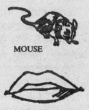

MOUSE

mouth (1) [mawθ'], *n.* 1. the opening in the face of a person or animal through which food and drink are taken in and from which sounds come out; the space containing the tongue and teeth. **Ex.** *He raised the glass to his mouth.* 2. an opening resembling the mouth or acting like a mouth. **Ex.** *There were many fish at the mouth of the river.*

MOUTH 1

—**mouth'ful,** *n.* as much as the mouth will hold; as much as is usually put into the mouth. **Ex.** *He took a mouthful of food.*

move (1) [muwv'], *v.* 1. change the position or place of. **Ex.** *She moved the chair from one side of the room to the other.* 2. change the place where one lives. **Ex.** *They moved to another town two months ago.* 3. put or keep in motion. **Ex.** *The wind moved the leaves along the street.* 4. go. **Ex.** *The train moved slowly.* 5. stir or excite the feelings. **Ex.** *The speech moved her so that she cried.* —*n.* 1. the act of moving. **Ex.** *He made a sudden move toward the door.* 2. a change in the place that one lives. **Ex.** *Their move to a new home was made yesterday.*

movement (1) [muwv'mənt], *n.* 1. the act or activity of moving; a way of moving. **Ex.** *The movements of the dancer were beautiful to watch.* 2. a series of acts or efforts for a definite purpose. **Ex.** *A movement was begun to stop the sale of harmful drugs.*

movie (2) [muw'viy], *n.* 1. a motion picture. **Ex.** *Did you enjoy the movie you saw last night?* 2. the place where motion pictures are shown. **Ex.** *There is a movie just around the corner from us.*

mow [mow'], *v.* cut down grass, wheat, etc. with a sharp-bladed instrument or a machine. **Ex.** *The farmer wasn't able to mow* *his hay because of the heavy rains.* —**mow'er,** *n.* a machine for mowing. **Ex.** *The lawn mower will have to be sharpened before you can use it.*

Mr. (1) [mis'tər], *n.* the shortened form of mister, used before a man's last name or full name. **Ex.** *Mr. Jones just arrived.*

Mrs. (1) [mis'iz], *n.* the shortened form of mistress, used before the last or full name of a married woman. **Ex.** *Mrs. Jones is returning Thursday.*

much (1) [məč'], *adj.* great in amount or degree. **Ex.** *Does she have much work to do?* —*adv.* to a great extent or degree. **Ex.** *He is much taller than his brother.* —*n.* a great part or amount. **Ex.** *Much of his story is not true.*

mud (1) [məd], *n.* soft, sticky, wet earth. **Ex.** *A lot of mud was sticking to our shoes.* —**mud'dy,** *adj.* covered with mud.

muffin [məf'in], *n.* a kind of bread, sometimes slightly sweetened, baked in small cup-shaped portions. **Ex.** *We had hot muffins with butter and jam for breakfast.*

muffle (5) [məf'əl], *v.* wrap something with a covering to make it quieter. **Ex.** *She muffled the bell so that it would not awaken the family.* —**muf'fler,** *n.* 1. a device for lessening the sound of a machine. 2. a scarf worn around the neck. **Ex.** *It's so cold outside you'll need to wear a muffler.*

mug (5) [məg'], *n.* a large, heavy drinking cup with a handle. **Ex.** *The child was drinking milk from a mug.*

mule (3) [myuwl'], *n.* an animal born from the union of a donkey and horse.

multi- (3) [məlti, məltə], *prefix.* containing many; consisting of many; having many of. **Exs.** Millionaire, multimillionaire; colored, multicolored.

multiple [məl'təpəl], *adj.* having or consisting of many parts, elements, etc. **Ex.** *He has had multiple problems while working on this project.*

MULE

multiply (3) [məl'təplay'], *v.* 1. add the same number as many times as stated. **Ex.** *Five multiplied by four equals twenty.* $5 \times 4 = 20$. 2. increase in number or amount. **Ex.** *The population of the city is multiplying rapidly.* —**mul'ti·pli·ca'tion,** *n.*

multitude (4) [məl'tə'tuwd', məl'tətyuwd'], *n.* 1. a great number. **Ex.** *There were a multitude of reasons for not going.* 2. a crowd. **Ex.** *Multitudes came to see the games.*

mumble (5) [məm'bəl], *v.* speak indistinctly, as one does when the lips are partly closed. **Ex.** *I could not understand what the old man mumbled.* —*n.* low, indistinct words.

municipal (4) [myuwnis'əpəl], *adj.* of or concerning the affairs or laws of a city, town or village. **Ex.** *The mayor's office is in the municipal building.* —**mu·nic'i·pal'i·ty,** *n.* a town, city, village, etc. with powers of local self-government.

murder (2) [mər'dər], *n.* the crime of purposely killing a person. **Ex.** *The man was guilty of murder.* —*v.* purposely kill a human being unlawfully. **Ex.** *He murdered his wife.* —**mur'der·er,** *n.* —**mur'der·ous,** *adj.* of or having to do with murder; very dangerous.

murmur (4) [mər'mər], *n.* 1. a soft, low, continuous sound of voices or anything like voices. **Ex.** *We heard the murmur of a stream.* 2. softly spoken words of complaint or discontent. **Ex.** *The child went to bed without a murmur.* —*v.* speak in a soft low tone, especially continuously; complain in a low voice. **Ex.** *The children murmured among themselves.*

muscle [məs'əl], *n.* the tissue in the body that tightens or stretches to move a part of the body. **Ex.** *He injured the muscles of his arm lifting a heavy weight.* —**mus'cu·lar,** *adj.*

museum (3) [myuwziy'əm], *n.* a building where objects of permanent interest in the arts, sciences, etc. are preserved and shown. **Ex.** *They took the children to the art museum.*

mushroom (5) [məš'ruwm], *n.* a small, quick-growing plant that has a stalk topped by an umbrella-shaped cap.

MUSHROOM

music (1) [myuw'zik], *n.* 1. the art of creating, writing or producing pleasing or meaningful sound patterns for singing or playing on musical instruments. **Ex.** *He is studying music.* 2. such arrangements in written form. **Ex.** *The pianist brought his music with him.* 3. pleasing sounds such as those made by singing voices or musical instruments. **Ex.** *Hearing her voice was music to my ears.* —**mu·si'cian,** *n.* a person skilled at writing or playing music. —**mu'si·cal,** *adj.* like or containing music.

must (1) [məst'], *v.* used with another verb to mean: 1. be necessary; be required to. **Ex.** *Man must eat to live.* 2. be certain to; may reasonably be supposed to. **Ex.** *She must have arrived there by now.* —*n.* that which is required or necessary. **Ex.** *Getting plenty of sleep is a must if you are to do this job well.*

mustache (5) [məš'tæš', məstæš'], *n.* hair that grows on a man's upper lip. **Ex.** *He has a black mustache.*

mustard [məs'tərd], *n.* 1. plant with small yellow flowers that have many tiny seeds. 2. a hot-tasting powder made by grinding these seeds; a paste made by mixing this powder with water, oil, vinegar, and other spices. **Ex.** *Did you bring the mustard for the hot dogs and hamburgers?*

mustn't [məs'ənt], short form, contraction of *must not.* **Ex.** *You mustn't go out in this heat.*

mutter (3) [mət'ər], *v.* utter words indistinctly, especially to oneself or in partly hidden disapproval. **Ex.** *The boy muttered something we could not hear.*

mutton (4) [mət'ən], *n.* the flesh of a fully grown sheep used as food. **Ex.** *I prefer lamb to mutton.*

mutual (4) [myuw'čuwəl], *adj.* 1. done or felt by each of two toward the other. **Ex.** *They are mutual friends.* 2. shared together. **Ex.** *They have a mutual interest in the theater.* —**mu·tu·al·ly,** *adv.*

muzzle (5) [məz'əl], *n.* 1. nose, mouth and jaws of a four-footed animal. **Ex.** *The dog put his muzzle through a hole in the fence.* 2. a cover made of wire or leather to put over an animal's mouth to keep it from biting. **Ex.** *In this town dogs are required to wear muzzles.* 3. the open front end of a rifle, cannon, etc. **Ex.** *He pointed the muzzle of the gun toward me.* —*v.* 1. put a muzzle on an animal to prevent it from biting. 2. keep someone from giving his opinions. **Ex.** *The university tried to muzzle the student newspaper.*

my (1) [may'], *pron.* of or belonging to me. **Ex.** *That is my hat.*

myself (2) [mayself'], *pron.* 1. my own self. **Ex.** *I cut myself on some broken glass.* 2. I, not someone else. **Ex.** *I myself will carry the message.* 3. my usual self. **Ex.** *I do not feel like myself today.*

mystery (2) [mis'təriy], *n.* 1. something that is not or cannot be explained or understood; something kept secret which arouses interest. **Ex.** *The disappearance of the ship is a mystery.* 2. a short story, novel or play about a crime that is difficult to solve. **Ex.** *He likes to read murder mysteries.* —**mys·te'ri·ous,** *adj.*

mystic (5) [mis'tik], *n.* a person who believes that he learns special truths through experiences of the spirit. **Ex.** *The leader of their group is a mystic.* —*adj.* referring to mysticism. **Ex.** *Mystic symbols are used in most religions.* —**mys'ti·cal·ly,** *adv.* —**mys'ti·cism`,** *n.* an attempt to understand special truths through prayer and spiritual experiences.

myth (5) [miθ'], *n.* 1. a traditional story used to explain the origin or existence of something. **Ex.** *There are many myths about how the world began.* 2. an imaginary person or thing. **Ex.** *The girl's handsome lover was a myth.* —**myth'i·cal,** *adj.* imaginary; not real.

N

N, n [en'], *n.* the fourteenth letter of the English alphabet.

nag [næg'], *v.* disturb by continually complaining, blaming, finding fault, etc. **Ex.** *My wife has been nagging me to buy a new suit for weeks.*

nail (2) [neyl'], *n.* 1. a thin pin of metal, pointed at one end, which is used for hammering into wood or walls. 2. the hard growth on the ends of fingers and toes. *v.* fasten with a nail or nails. **Ex.** *He nailed the two boards together.*

NAIL 1

naive [naiyv'], *adj.* 1. lacking experience; unaffected; innocent. **Ex.** *She was less naive than she appeared to be.* 2. lacking understanding and judgment. **Ex.** *His remarks about foreign policy were very naive.*

NAIL 2

naked (2) [ney'kid], *adj.* 1. unclothed; bare. **Ex.** *Naked boys were swimming in the river.* 2. without usual or natural covering. **Ex.** *Cold weather caused the leaves to fall and left the trees naked.* —**na·ked·ness**, *n.* the condition of being naked.

name (1) [neym'], *n.* word or words by which a person, animal, place or thing is known or called. **Ex.** *The man's name is John Henry Brown.* —*v.* 1. give a name to. **Ex.** *They have not yet named the new baby.* 2. mention by name; tell the name or names of. **Ex.** *He learned to name the months of the year in school.* —**first name, middle name, last name,** the parts of a person's full name. **Ex.** *John Henry Brown's first name is John; his middle name is Henry and his last name is Brown.* —**in the name of,** by the authority of. **Ex.** *Surrender in the name of the law!*

namesake [neym'seyk'], *n.* a person given the same name as another, especially as an honor. **Ex.** *Among his children, John loves his namesake, John Jr., best.*

nap (4) [næp'], *n.* a brief sleep. **Ex.** *The children take a nap every afternoon.* —*v.* take a brief sleep. **Ex.** *He often naps in his chair.*

napkin (3) [næp'kin], *n.* a piece of paper or cloth used during a meal to keep clothing clean and to wipe the lips and fingers. **Ex.** *Please place a napkin to the left of each fork on the dining room table.*

narcotic [narkat'ik], *n.* a drug that taken in small doses brings about sleep or reduces pain while dulling the senses and when taken in more than prescribed doses becomes habit forming and dangerous. **Ex.** *He was suspected of selling narcotics.* —*adj.*

narrate (5) [næreyt'], *v.* tell a story; give an account of. **Ex.** *He narrated the important events of his trip.* —**nar·ra'tion, nar'ra·tive,** *n.* a telling of a story or a description of an event. —**nar'ra·tor,** *n.* one who tells a story or describes an event.

narrow (2) [nær'ow], *adj.* 1. not wide; not broad. **Ex.** *This road is too narrow for two cars to pass each other.* 2. limited in size or amount. **Ex.** *We were offered a narrow choice of food.* 3. close. **Ex.** *We had a narrow escape from death.* —*v.* decrease in width or range. **Ex.** *The railroad narrowed to a single track in the mountains.* —**nar'row·ly,** *adv.* —**nar'row·ness,** *n.*

narrow-minded [nær'owmayn'dəd], *adj.* not trying to understand the ideas of others; not tolerant. **Ex.** *His narrow-minded ideas made him unpopular with the students.*

nasty (5) [næs'tiy], *adj.* 1. offensive; disgusting; dirty. **Ex.** *The spoiled meat had a nasty smell.* 2. not decent; not proper. **Ex.** *The drunken man used nasty language.* 3. unpleasant; mean; disturbing. **Ex.** *The weather was cold and nasty.* 4. dangerous; serious; painful. **Ex.** *She was in a nasty accident.* —**nas'ti·ly,** *adv.* —**nas'ti·ness,** *n.*

nation (1) [ney'šən], *n.* a group of people united under one government. **Ex.** *The United States of America is one nation.* —**na'tion·al,** *n.* a citizen of a nation. **Ex.** *He is an American national.* —*adj.* of a nation as a whole. **Ex.** *All schools are closed on national holidays.* —**na'tion·al·ly,** *adv.* in a national way. —**na'tion·al·ism,** *n.* strong feelings of love for or loyalty to one's country's interests. —**na'tion·al'i·ty,** *n.* citizenship. **Ex.** *He is of American nationality.* —**na'tion·al·ize,** *v.* place a private business, a piece of land, etc. under government ownership.

native (2) [ney'tiv], *adj.* 1. relating to the place where one was born. **Ex.** *America is my native land.* 2. belonging naturally to a particular place. **Ex.** *Palm trees are native to warm climates.* 3. belonging to a person from birth; inborn. **Ex.** *Her talent for languages seems to be a native ability.* —*n.* a person who is born in a particular place. **Ex.** *He is not a native of this city.*

nature (1) [ney'čər], *n.* 1. the world and everything in, on and around it. 2. the force or forces that seem to control or guide the physical world. **Ex.** *Nature governs the weather.* 3. whatever in a thing or animal is common to its kind. **Ex.** *It is in the nature of mothers to defend their children.* 4. anything not made by people or changed by people. **Ex.** *She loved the wild flowers found in nature.* 5. the special manner of a person; the unlearned ways which direct conduct. **Ex.** *His father's nature was gentle.* —**nat'u·ral,** *adj.* 1. not learned or acquired; common to its kind. **Ex.** *It is natural for parents to love their children.* 2. true to nature; normal; usual. **Ex.** *Although she was angry, she tried to speak in a natural manner.* 3. concerning nature; existing in nature; dealing with the forces of nature. **Ex.** *He teaches the natural sciences.* —**nat'u·ral·ly,** *adv.* in a normal manner. —**nat'u·ral·ist,** *n.* a student of nature, especially animals and plants. —**nat'u·ral·ize,** *v.* make someone a citizen of a country who was not born a citizen of that country. **Ex.** *He was born in France and naturalized in this country.*

naughty (4) [nɔːˈtiy], *adj.* 1. not obeying; behaving badly. **Ex.** *The mother punished her naughty little girl.* 2. not nice or proper. **Ex.** *She shocked her father by telling a naughty joke.* —**naugh'ti·ly,** *adv.* —**naugh'ti·ness,** *n.*

naval (5) [neyˈvəl], *adj.* of or for a navy. **Ex.** *At present three ships are engaged in naval operations in this area.*

navigate (5) [nævˈəgeyt'], *v.* guide or direct the course of a boat, ship or plane. **Ex.** *The sick captain was still able to navigate the ship.* —**nav'i·ga'tion,** *n.* the act of navigating. —**nav'i·ga'tor,** *n.* one who navigates. —**nav'i·ga·ble,** *adj.* deep and wide enough for ships to pass. **Ex.** *These waters are navigable for a boat the size of yours.*

navy (3) [neyˈviy], *n.* the sea force of a nation, including all ships, officers, men and supplies. **Ex.** *The navy defends our country's shores and seas.*

navy blue [ney'viy bluw'], a dark shade of blue. **Ex.** *In the fall the sailors changed to their navy blue uniforms.*

near (1) [niːr'], *adv.* 1. not far; at a close distance. **Ex.** *As we got near, we saw flames.* 2. soon; close in time. **Ex.** *Our vacation is drawing near.* —*adj.* 1. not distant. **Ex.** *The swimmers will gather on the near side of the pool.* 2. closely related; personal. **Ex.** *Only near relatives attended the wedding.* —*prep.* close in place or time. **Ex.** *We live near the ocean.* —*v.* draw close; approach. **Ex.** *At last, we neared home.* —**near'ness,** *n.*

nearby [niːr'bay'], *adj.* not far away; near. **Ex.** *She lives in a nearby house.* —*adv.* not far; at a close distance. **Ex.** *He lives nearby.*

nearly (1) [niːr'liy], *adv.* almost. **Ex.** *I nearly missed the train.*

nearsighted [niːr'say'tid], *adj.* able to see clearly only what is very near. **Ex.** *Because you are nearsighted, you will have to wear glasses when you drive a car.*

neat [niyt'], *adj.* 1. clean and orderly. **Ex.** *The child was taught to keep her room neat.* 2. careful and orderly in detail. **Ex.** *He kept neat records.* 3. able and willing to keep oneself and one's things clean and in order. **Ex.** *She is a very neat housekeeper.* 4. pleasing and tasteful in design and appearance. **Ex.** *She was wearing a neat dress.* —**neat'ly,** *adv.* —**neat'ness,** *n.*

necessary (1) [nes'əse:r'iy], *adj.* needed; required; essential. **Ex.** *Food is necessary for life.* —**nec·es·sar·i·ly,** *adv.* —**ne·ces·si·ty,** *n.* that which is necessary. **Ex.** *They gave the old man food and other necessities.*

neck (1) [nek'], *n.* the part of the body that connects the head with the shoulders. **Ex.** *She wore a thin gold chain around her neck.*

necklace [nek'lis], *n.* a string of beads, shells, attractive pieces of enamel, etc. or chains of gold, silver, etc. worn around the neck for decoration. **Ex.** *She was wearing a beautiful pearl necklace.*

necktie (3) [nek'tay'], *n.* a narrow strip of cloth worn, usually by men, around the neck under the collar and tied in front.

NECKTIE

need (1) [niyd'], *n.* 1. a condition in which something is necessary; a lack of something; a desire for something; a reason for. **Ex.** *The need for rest made him stop his work for a few moments.* 2. the thing needed. **Ex.** *Food and clothing are their most important needs right now.* 3. a condition of want; poverty. **Ex.** *He helped me find a job when I was in need.* —*v.* 1. require; want. **Ex.** *The baby needs his milk now.* 2. be forced; be compelled; be obliged. **Ex.** *We need not go there today.* —**need'y,** *adj., n.* very poor. **Exs.** *The needy family was given food. They are collecting clothing for the needy.*

needle (1) [niy'dəl], *n.* 1. a thin sewing tool, sharp at one end and with a hole at the other end through which to pass a thread. 2. the needle-shaped leaf of some trees. **Ex.** *The ground was covered with pine needles.* 3. a thin steel pointer on a compass or other instrument. **Ex.** *The needle of the compass pointed north.* 4. a slender, hollow, pointed doctor's instrument for forcing medicine through the skin to inner parts of the body such as a vein or muscle. **Ex.** *He hardly felt the doctor's needle.*

NEEDLE 1

negative (3) [neg'ətiv], *adj.* 1. expressing refusal; disagreeing. **Ex.** *Her negative reply meant I could not go with my friends.* 2. lacking firm or positive qualities. **Ex.** *The unhappy man has a negative attitude toward life.* —*n.* 1. an expression which denies, refuses or disagrees. **Ex.** *She was very angry because her request was answered in the negative.* 2. the image on a film or plate used for printing a photograph. **Ex.** *The photographer developed the negative.* —**neg·a·tive·ly,** *adv.*

neglect (3) [nəglekt'], *v.* 1. give too little care to; fail to perform duties. **Ex.** *She was unhappy because he neglected her.* 2. leave undone through carelessness or forgetfulness. **Ex.** *The boy had bad teeth because he neglected to brush them.* —*n.* the act of neglecting; the condition of being neglected. **Ex.** *Their yard was a mess because of their neglect.*

negotiate [nigow'šiyeyt'], *v.* talk together in order to bring about an agreement. **Exs.** *He successfully negotiated the sale of his business to his competitors. Our country is trying to negotiate an arms agreement.* —**ne·go'ti·a'tion,** n. —**ne·go'ti·a'tor,** *n.*

Negro [niy'grow], *n.* a member of one of the racial divisions of humanity, having brown or black skin.

neighbor (1) [ney'bər], *n.* 1. a person who lives nearby. **Ex.** *My nearest neighbor lives across the street.* 2. any person, group, etc. that is near. **Ex.** *Our country has good relations with its neighbors.* —**neigh'bor·ing,** *adj.* close to each other. **Ex.** *The United States and Mexico are neighboring countries.* —**neigh'bor·ly,** *adj.* friendly; acting as good neighbors should.

neighborhood (3) [ney'bərhud'], *n.* 1. a small section of a city or town. **Ex.** *They live in a neighborhood of small homes.* 2. an area near some place or thing. **Ex.** *They live in the neighborhood near the high school.* 3. the people living in a particular locality. **Ex.** *The whole neighborhood attended the dance.*

neither (1) [niy'ðər], *conj.* not either. **Ex.** *He neither drinks nor smokes.* —*adj.* not one or the other of two. **Ex.** *Neither statement is true.* —*pron.* not one or the other. **Ex.** *Neither of the boys will be able to go.*

neon [niy'an], *n.* an inactive gaseous element without color that makes up a very, very small fraction of the air. —*adj.* of or using neon. **Ex.** *Large, bright neon signs add color to the downtown area at night.*

nephew (2) [nef'yuw], *n.* the son of one's brother or sister. **Ex.** *I have two nephews, one six and one nine.*

nerve (1) [nərv'], *n.* 1. a threadlike structure or bundle of such structures connecting the brain with other parts of the body, through which actions of the body are controlled. 2. control of one's feelings; courage. **Ex.** *His outside work on tall buildings requires nerve.* —*v.* arouse strength and courage. **Ex.** *She nerved herself for the dangerous task.* —**nerv'ous**, *adj.* 1. of or having to do with the nerves. 2. easily excited; restless. **Ex.** *She becomes nervous after a long day's work.* 3. anxious; feeling fear. **Ex.** *His fast driving makes me nervous.* —**nerv'ous·ly**, *adv.* —**nerv'ous·ness**, *n.* —**get on one's nerves**, make one nervous, impatient or angry. **Ex.** *The baby's crying sometimes gets on my nerves.*

-ness (1) [nis, nəs], *suffix.* quality or state of being. **Exs.** *Good, goodness; kind, kindness; ill, illness.*

nest (2) [nest'], *n.* a home built by birds and other creatures, such as mice, squirrels and some insects, in which to have and raise their young. —*v.* build or have a nest. **Ex.** *There are birds nesting in that tree.*

NEST

net (2) [net'], *adj.* remaining after all necessary expenses are paid. **Ex.** *The net profit of the business was small.* —*v.* earn as a profit. **Ex.** *They netted a large profit on the sale of their house.*

net (2) [net'], *n.* 1. material made of string, cord, thread, etc. tied, twisted or woven together so that open spaces are left. **Ex.** *The skirt of her evening dress was covered with net.* 2. a device made of such material used to catch fish, insects, etc.

NET 2

network (5) [net'wərk'], *n.* 1. any combination of things that cross and join many times like a net. **Ex.** *A network of roads connected the city and the surrounding towns.* 2. a group of radio or television stations in different cities and towns connected by a communications system that permits all of them to broadcast the same program. **Ex.** *On which network is that program going to appear?*

neutral (4) [nuw'trəl], *adj.* 1. not on either side in a dispute. **Ex.** *He remained neutral in the argument between his two friends.*

a, far; æ, am; e, get; ey, late; i, in; iy, see; ɔ, all; ow, go; u, put; uw, too; ə, but, ago; ər, fur; aw, out; ay, life; oy, boy; ŋ, ring; θ, think; ð, that; ž, measure; š, ship; ǰ, edge; č, child.

2. of no notable kind, quality, color, etc. **Ex.** *She chose a gray suit because she wanted something in a neutral color.* —*n.* a person, country, etc. that does not support either side in a dispute. **Ex.** *In neither of the two world wars did the United States remain a neutral.* —**neu·tral'i·ty,** *n.*

never (1) [nev'ər], *adv.* not ever; at no time. **Ex.** *He has never been at our house.*

nevertheless (2) [nev'ərðəles'], *adv.* however; in spite of that; yet. **Ex.** *He did not like the man but helped him nevertheless.*

new (1) [nuw', nyuw'], *adj.* 1. not existing before; not known before. **Ex.** *She often prepares food in new ways.* 2. recently made, built, bought, grown, etc. **Ex.** *He bought a new suit.* 3. another. **Ex.** *After resting, we made a new attempt to lift the heavy stone.*

news (1) [nuwz', nyuwz'], *n.* 1. information about any recent happenings or events, especially as reported on the radio, in the newspapers, etc. **Ex.** *We watched the news on television.* 2. new or unfamiliar information. **Ex.** *That she had been married before was news to me.*

newscaster [nuwz'cæstər], *n.* a person who broadcasts the news on radio or television. **Ex.** *Who is your favorite newscaster?*

newspaper [nuwz'pey·pər, nyuwz'pey·pər], *n.* a daily or weekly publication that reports the latest news. **Ex.** *Our neighbor's son delivers the daily newspaper.*

next (1) [nekst'], *adj.* 1. coming immediately after. **Ex.** *We hope to see you next week.* 2. nearest to; closest to. **Ex.** *He's in the next room.* —*adv.* 1. the first time after this. **Ex.** *I'll tell him when next I see him.* 2. in the place, time or position that is nearest. **Ex.** *Your name has been placed next on the list.* —**next door,** in the house, building, etc. that is nearest. **Ex.** *This house is number one; number three is next door.*

nice (1) [nays'], *adj.* 1. pleasant; agreeable. **Ex.** *We had a nice time at the party.* 2. thoughtful; kind. **Ex.** *Giving her flowers was a nice thing to do.* —**nice'ly,** *adv.*

nickel (5) [nik'əl], *n.* 1. a hard, silver-white metal that is combined with other metals because of its strength and resistance to moisture. **Ex.** *Nickel and copper combine well.* 2. a United States coin worth five cents; the twentieth part of a dollar.

nickname (5) [nik'neym`], *n.* a name, other than the name given to one at birth, by which one is called. **Ex.** *Because his hair is red, George has the nickname "Red."*

niece (1) [niys`], *n.* the daughter of one's brother or sister. **Ex.** *What college is your niece attending?*

night (1) [nayt`], *n.* the time from sunset to sunrise when there is little or no light. **Ex.** *I slept all night.* —*adj.* at, for or of night. **Ex.** *He goes to night school and works at an office during the day.* —**night'ly**, *adv.* every night.

nightclub [nayt'kləb`], *n.* a place where people go at night to listen to music, dance, eat, drink, etc. **Ex.** *That nightclub is popular with people who like jazz.*

nightfall [nayt'fɔːl`], *n.* the end of the day, immediately after the sun has set. **Ex.** *They waited until nightfall before going outside.*

nightmare (5) [nayt'meːr`], *n.* 1. a dream which causes fear or dread. **Ex.** *The child had a nightmare and woke up crying.* 2. any experience which causes great fear or dread. **Ex.** *The automobile accident was a nightmare.*

nine (1) [nayn`], *n.* the number between eight and ten; the number 9. —**ninth`**, *n.*, *adj.* coming after eight others.—**nine'teen`**, *n.*, *adj.* the number *19.* —**nine'teenth`**, *n.*, *adj.* coming after eighteen others. —**nine'ty**, *adj.* the number *90.* —**nine'ti·eth**, *n.*, *adj.* coming after eighty-nine others.

nitrogen (5) [nay'trəjən], *n.* a colorless, odorless, tasteless gas that occurs as part of all animal and vegetable matter. **Ex.** *The air is composed of about 80 percent nitrogen.*

no (1) [now`], *adv.* 1. used to express a denial or refusal. **Ex.** *No, you may not go with them.* 2. not so. **Ex.** *No, I don't agree with you.* 3. not at all. **Ex.** *She is no better today.* —*adj.* not any; not at all. **Ex.** *He has no friends and is lonely.* —*n.* a denial; a refusal. **Ex.** *Your no to my request surprises me.*

noble (2) [now'bəl], *adj.* 1. honorable; generous; showing dignity or excellence of character. **Ex.** *Giving his life to save the drowning child was a noble thing to do.* 2. of high birth or rank. **Ex.** *The owner of that castle is a member of a noble family.* —**no·bil'i·ty**, *n.* —**no'bly**, *adv.*

nobody [now'bad`iy], *pron.* no one; not anyone; no person. **Ex** *Nobody was willing to help me.*

nod (2) [nad'], *v.* 1. bend the head forward slightly as a sign of agreement or greeting. **Ex.** *The teacher nodded her approval.* 2. let the head fall forward in going to sleep. **Ex.** *The old man nodded in his chair.* —*n.* the act of bending the head forward in agreement or greeting. **Ex.** *Seeing her neighbor, she gave her a nod.*

noise (1) [noyz'], *n.* sound, especially when loud, confused or unpleasant. **Ex.** *The children are making too much noise.* —**nois'i·ly**, *adv.* —**nois'y**, *adj.*

nominate (4) [nam'əneyt'], *v.* 1. name as a candidate in an election. **Ex.** *Her party nominated her to run for mayor.* 2. propose or offer for a position. **Ex.** *The president nominated him to be an ambassador.* —**nom'i·na'tion**, *n.* the act of nominating, the state of being nominated. —**nom'i·nee'**, *n.* the person nominated.

non- [nan], *prefix.* not. **Exs.** *Member, nonmember; owner, nonowner.* A mark (-), called a hyphen, is placed after "non" when it is used with a word beginning with a capital letter. **Exs.** *African, non-African; Swiss, non-Swiss.*

none (1) [nən'], *pron.* 1. not one; no one. **Ex.** *None would offer his help.* 2. not any; no part. **Ex.** *None of her work is done.* —*adj.* not at all; to no extent. **Ex.** *He came none too soon.*

nonsense (3) [nan'sens], *n.* 1. words, ideas or acts that are not understandable. **Ex.** *The fool is talking nonsense.* 2. foolish conduct. **Ex.** *Their parents were very strict and permitted no nonsense from them.* —**non·sen'si·cal**, *adj.*

noodle [nuwd'əl], *n.* a flat piece of dough, made from flour, eggs and water, which is usually dried in strips and cooked by boiling. **Ex.** *My mother makes a delicious noodle pudding with eggs, milk, sugar and raisins.*

noon (1) [nuwn'], *n.* the middle of the day; twelve o'clock in the daytime. **Ex.** *We always eat lunch at noon.*

no one [now'wən], *pron.* not anyone; nobody; no person. **Ex.** *No one knew where the teacher was.*

nor (1) [nɔːr'], *conj.* and not; or not; usually used with the word "neither" to show the second of two negatives. **Ex.** *She has neither father nor mother.*

normal (2) [nɔr'məl], *adj.* regular, usual; standard. **Ex.** *Snow is normal for this month.* —*n.* the usual condition, amount, state, etc.; the average. **Ex.** *His temperature is above normal.*

—**nor·mal·ly**, *adv.* usually; regularly. **Ex.** *She normally leaves for the office every morning about this time.*

north (1) [nɔrθ'], *n.* 1. the direction to the left of a person facing east; one of the four points of the compass. **Ex.** *A cold wind blew from the north.* 2. those regions or countries lying to the north; that part of the United States that is north of Maryland, the Ohio River and Missouri. **Ex.** *American winters are colder in the North.* —*adj.* toward, in or at the north. **Ex.** *They live on the north side of the city.* 2. from the north. **Ex.** *A cold north wind is blowing today.* — *adv.* toward the north. **Ex.** *They are going north for the summer.* —**north'ern**, *adj.* characteristic of the north; in, of, to or from the north. —**north'er·ner**, *n.* one from the North.

nose (1) [nowz'], *n.* the part of the face just above the mouth, through which one breathes and smells.

nostril (4) [nas'trəl], *n.* either of the two openings in the nose. **Ex.** *He put some medicine in each nostril.*

NOSE

not (1) [nat'], *adv.* in no way; to no degree. **Ex.** *His story is not true.*

notable (4) [now'təbəl], *adj.* worthy of notice or attention; remarkable; distinguished. **Ex.** *His lecture was a notable success.* —*n.* a person or thing of distinction. **Ex.** *All the notables of the city came to the opening of the new museum.*

notation (5) [nowtey'šən], *n.* 1. a system of symbols and numbers representing words, facts, etc. used in special fields. **Ex.** *He made extensive notations about the experiment he was performing.* 2. a brief note to help one remember something, often written in the margin. **Ex.** *She made notations in the margin of the student's essay as she read it.*

note (1) [nowt'], *n.* 1. a word or words written down to help one's memory. **Ex.** *He took notes on the talk.* 2. careful attention. **Ex.** *Take note of what your teacher says and remember it for the examination.* 3. a short letter. **Ex.** *She wrote a note of thanks for the gift.* 4. a musical tone; the symbol for a musical tone. 5. hint; indication; sug-

NOTE 4

a, far; æ, am; e, get; ey, late; i, in; iy, see; ɔ, all; ow, go; u, put; uw, too; ə, but, ago; ər, fur; aw, out; ay, life; oy, boy; ŋ, ring; θ, think; ð, that; ž, measure; š, ship; ǰ, edge; č, child.

gestion. **Ex.** *A note of sadness was in her voice.* —*v.* 1. notice; pay attention to; observe. **Ex.** *The policeman noted the footprints in the soft earth.* 2. write down as a thing to remember. **Ex.** *Please note the address.* —**not'ed,** *adj.* famous. **Ex.** *His father is a noted writer.*

notebook [nowt'buwk], *n.* a book containing blank pages on which notes can be written. **Ex.** *While the professor talked, the students wrote busily in their notebooks.*

nothing (1) [nəθ'iŋ], *n.* 1. not anything; no thing. **Ex.** *There is nothing in the box.* 2. that which is of no importance or value. **Ex.** *I cut my finger, but it is really nothing.* 3. zero. **Ex.** *Zero plus zero equals nothing.* —*adv.* in no way; not at all. **Ex.** *He works nothing like he used to work.*

notice (1) [now'tis], *v.* see; observe; pay attention to. **Ex.** *He noticed that she was wearing a new hat.* —*n.* 1. attention. **Ex.** *Bring this letter to his notice.* 2. warning; announcement; information. **Ex.** *The notice on the wall of the house said "For Sale."* 3. a warning that one will end an agreement with another at a certain time. **Ex.** *You should give two weeks' notice before quitting your job.* —**no'tice·a·ble,** *adj.* easily seen. —**no'tice·a·bly,** *adv.* —**give notice,** give advance warning of one's intentions. **Ex.** *He is going to give notice to his landlord that he is moving next month.*

notify (3) [now'təfay], *v.* inform; tell. **Ex.** *We will notify you when the books arrive.*

notion (3) [now'šən], *n.* 1. an impression; a vague idea. **Ex.** *He had no notion of the difficulties he was to encounter.* 2. an opinion or belief; a view. **Ex.** *It was her notion that planes were safer than trains.*

notorious (5) [nowtɔːr'iyəs], *adj.* 1. widely known for something bad. **Ex.** *The notorious criminal was caught yesterday.* 2. generally known. **Ex.** *He was notorious for being late.* —**no·to'ri·ous·ly,** *adv.* —**no·to·ri'e·ty,** *n.*

noun (5) [nawn'], *n.* in grammar, a word that is used as the name of a person, place or thing. **Ex.** *In the sentence, "John has a new ball," the words* John *and* ball *are nouns.* —**common noun,** *n.* the name of one kind of person, place or thing. **Exs.** *boy, town, game.* —**proper noun,** *n.* the name of a particular person, place or thing beginning with a capital letter. **Exs.** *John, Alice; America; English.* See **A Brief Explanation of English Grammar.**

nourish (4) [nəːrˈiš], *v.* feed; help to grow; support. **Ex.** *The mother used her own milk to nourish the baby.* **—nourˈishˈment,** *n.* food; that which nourishes. **Ex.** *We stopped along the way for some nourishment.*

novel (2) [navˈəl], *n.* a story of book length that tells of imaginary people and events. **Ex.** *This novel is about a young man's struggle to become a doctor.* **—novˈelˈist,** *n.* one who writes novels.

novel (2) [navˈəl], *adj.* different; new; strange. **Ex.** *His new car had a novel appearance.* **—novˈelˈty,** *n.* 1. something new and strange or unusual. **Ex.** *Snow is usually a novelty to people in hot countries.* 2. newness; strangeness. **Ex.** *The novelty of the new toy did not last long.*

November (1) [nowvemˈbər], *n.* the eleventh month of the year.

now (naw'), *adv.* at the present time; at this moment; immediately. **Ex.** *She is here now.* **—n.** the present; this time. **Ex.** *Now is the time to sell your house.* **—conj.** since. **Ex.** *I need not stay now that you are here.* **—now and then, now and again,** at one time or another; sometimes. **Ex.** *I see him now and again.*

nowhere (now'hweːr'), *adv.* not in, to or at any place. **Ex.** *This road leads nowhere.*

n't [ənt], short form, contraction of *not.* **Ex.** *Either he hasn't been here or I didn't see him.*

nuclear [nuwˈkliyər], *adj.* of, having to do with or using the central part of an atom, such as in the atom bomb, atomic energy, etc. **Ex.** *Our class has been studying how nuclear energy has changed the world.*

nude [nuwd'], *adj.* without clothing or covering; bare. **Ex.** *We saw the nude branches of the trees against the winter sky.* **—n.** 1. a work of art showing the figure of a person without clothing or cover. 2. the state of being nude.

nuisance (4) [nuwˈsəns, nyuwˈsəns], *n.* an act, thing or person that causes trouble, annoys or offends. **Ex.** *It is a nuisance to have a cold.*

numb [nəm'], *adj.* being without the power to feel or move. **Ex.** *My legs had become numb from sitting so long.* **—v.** become or make numb. **Ex.** *Time had helped to numb her sense of loss.*

number (1) [nəm'bər], *n.* 1. words or symbols used to show the order or quantity of things in a series. **Exs.** *The number between the numbers 1 and 3 is the number 2. What is the serial number on your dollar bill?* 2. a quantity; total. **Ex.** *A large number of books lay on the desk.* —*v.* have a number; give a number to. **Ex.** *She numbered the pages from 1 to 100.*

numeral [nyuw'mərəl], *n.* a symbol, such as a letter or figure, that represents a number. **Ex.** *In the Roman numeral system the letters MCMXC represent 1990.* See **Roman Numerals.**

numerical (2) [nuwme:r'ikəl, nyuwme:r'ikəl], *adj.* having to do with numbers. **Ex.** *Each card has a number, and the cards are arranged in numerical order.*

numerous (2) [nuw'mərəs, nyuw'mərəs], *adj.* consisting of many. **Ex.** *He has numerous problems.*

nun (5) [nən'], *n.* a member of a religious organization devoting her life to prayer and religious activities. **Ex.** *That nun is a teacher.*

nurse (2) [nərs'], *n.* 1. a person trained to care for the sick and the injured. **Ex.** *Several nurses assisted the doctor.* 2. a woman employed to take care of a child or children. **Ex.** *The nurse took the children for a walk in the park.* —*v.* 1. take care of; tend a sick person. **Ex.** *She nursed him back to health.* 2. feed a baby milk from the mother's breasts. **Ex.** *She nursed her son until he was six months old.* —**nursing home,** *n.* a place where nurses and others care for old or sick people. **Ex.** *Her eighty-five-year-old mother is in a nursing home.*

nursery (5) [nər's(ə)riy], *n.* 1. a room for the use of a baby or small children. **Ex.** *The children had supper in the nursery.* 2. a school for young children, usually less than five years old; a place where children are placed while their parents are busy elsewhere. **Ex.** *The youngest child spent every morning at a nursery.* 3. a place where trees and plants are grown and sold. **Ex.** *He bought some strong, young trees at the nursery.*

nursery rhyme [nər's(ə)riy raym'], *n.* a very short story in the form of a poem for children. **Ex.** *The children love to recite nursery rhymes.*

nursery school [nər's(ə)riy skuwl'], *n.* a school for young children, usually less than five years old. **Ex.** *He learned to count in nursery school.*

nut (2) [nət], *n.* 1. a dry fruit in a hard, woodlike shell; the fruit of certain trees. **Ex.** *She offered us a bowl of nuts with our drinks.* 2. a piece of metal which has a threaded hole that screws on a bolt.

NUT 2

nutrition [nuwtriš'ən], *n.* 1. the action of providing or being provided with food or nourishment. **Ex.** *A specialist in nutrition talked to the children about their diets.* 2. the process by which people, plants and animals take in and use food. **Ex.** *We try to choose foods that are good for our children's nutrition.*

nylon (3) [nay'lan], *n.* a strong man-made material which can be formed into thread, cloth, etc. **Ex.** *Her umbrella is made of nylon.* —**ny'lons,** *n.* a pair of stockings made of nylon.

O

O, o [ow'], *n.* the fifteenth letter of the English alphabet.

oak (2) [owk], *n.* 1. a large hardwood tree that bears bitter nuts called acorns. **Ex.** *A great oak stood in front of the house.* 2. the wood of this tree, which is used in building, making furniture, etc. **Ex.** *This desk is made of oak.*

oar (3) [ɔːr'], *n.* a pole with a broad, flat end used to row a boat.

oat (4) [owt'], *n.* the grain of a tall cereal grass; the cereal grass. **Ex.** *The horses are eating their oats.* —**oat'meal,** *n.* a cereal made from rolled oats. **Ex.** *We had oatmeal for breakfast today.*

OAR

a, far; æ, am; e, get; ey, late; i, in; iy, see; ɔ, all; ow, go; u, put; uw, too; ə, but, ago; ər, fur; aw, out; ay, life; oy, boy; ŋ, ring; θ, think; ð, that; ž, measure; š, ship; J, edge; č, child.

oath (4) [owθ'], *n.* 1. a serious promise or pledge, often calling upon a god, person or thing one honors. **Ex.** *He placed his hand on the Bible as he took the oath of office.* 2. a curse; the name of a god or other sacred person or thing spoken in anger or for emphasis. **Ex.** *In his rage, he uttered terrible oaths.* **—take an oath,** promise in a formal ceremony to do something. **Ex.** *The witness had to take an oath to tell the truth before he could testify.* **—under oath,** obliged or required by oath. **Ex.** *The judge reminded the witness that he was under oath to tell the truth.*

obedience (4) [owbiy'diyəns], *n.* submitting to authority or law; obeying. **Ex.** *They demanded obedience from their children.* **—o·be'di·ent,** *adj.*

obey (2) [owbey'], *v.* 1. act as one is ordered to act. **Ex.** *The soldier obeyed the command immediately.* 2. be ruled, controlled or guided by. **Ex.** *He was reminded that he must obey the laws of the country he was visiting.*

object (1) [əbjekt'], *v.* 1. show that one does not like or approve; protest. **Ex.** *She objected to the way he drove the car.* 2. give reasons for being against something. **Ex.** *He objected that our plans were too dangerous.* **—ob·jec'tion,** *n.* a statement of disapproval or protest. **Ex.** *He stated his objection to the new idea at the meeting.* **—ob·jec'tion·able,** *adj.* not pleasant; not polite. **Ex.** *Her manner was objectionable.* **—ob·jec'tor,** *n.* one who objects.

object (1) [ab'jikt], *n.* 1. something that can be seen or touched; something that can be known through the senses. **Ex.** *She handed me a small, round object.* 2. purpose; aim; end. **Ex.** *His only object in life was to become rich.* 3. in grammar, the person or thing that receives the action of the verb; the person or thing that is the object of a preposition. **Ex.** *In the sentence, "He gave the book to her,"* book *is the object of the verb* gave, *and* her *is the object of the preposition* to. See **A Brief Explanation of English Grammar.** **—ob·jec'tive,** *n.* aim or purpose of what one does. **Ex.** *Her objective was to become a doctor.* **—adj.** not favorable to one more than another; fair. **Ex.** *Let him decide who is right; he will be objective.*

oblige (2) [əblayj'], *v.* 1. compel to do by law, promise or duty. **Ex.** *Parents are obliged by law to send their children to school.* 2. feel bound or in debt to another because of a favor. **Ex.** *I am very much obliged to you for helping me with my lesson.*

—**ob·li·ga'tion,** *n.* that which one is required to do. **Ex.** *He has an obligation to feed his children.* —**ob·lig'a·tor·y,** *adj.* required. —**o·blig'ing,** *adj.* helpful; ready and glad to be of assistance. **Ex.** *He has always been most obliging to everyone in the office.*

oblong [ab'lɔːŋ`], *n.* a four-sided figure, the straight sides of which form four right angles, with one pair of opposite sides longer than the other pair; anything with this general shape. **Ex.** *I prefer a room to be an oblong, not a square.* —*adj.*

obscure (4) [əbskyuːr'], *adj.* 1. not well-known. **Ex.** *He is an obscure poet.* 2. not easily noticed or seen; hidden. **Ex.** *We had difficulty finding the obscure path through the woods.* 3. not understood; not clear. **Ex.** *The meaning of his lengthy explanation was obscure.* 4. dark; dim. **Ex.** *Heavy curtains made the room obscure.* —*v.* hide; conceal; make dim. **Ex.** *The fog obscured the road.* —**ob·scur'i·ty,** *n.*

observe (2) [əbzərv'], *v.* 1. watch; notice; look at carefully. **Ex.** *He observed a man leaving by the rear door.* 2. keep; honor. **Ex.** *We observed the New Year by visiting old friends.* 3. obey; follow. **Ex.** *She was careful to observe the speed limit.* —**ob·serv'ance,** *n.* keeping; honoring. **Ex.** *We joined in several activities in observance of Independence Day.* —**ob·ser·va'tion,** *n.* 1. the act of noticing. **Ex.** *My observation of the river told me that it was rising rapidly.* 2. the habit or ability of noticing. **Ex.** *Her powers of observation were very keen.* 3. remark. **Ex.** *I did not agree with the critic's observations about the play.* —**ob·serv'ant,** *adj.* quick to notice; watchful. —**ob·serv'er,** *n.* one who observes.

obstacle (4) [ab'stikəl], *n.* something that blocks or stops progress. **Ex.** *An obstacle in the road prevented us from going forward.*

obstinate (5) [ab'stənit], *adj.* stubbornly holding to one's opinion or purpose. **Ex.** *The obstinate girl refused to go with us.* —**ob'stin·a·cy,** *n.* —**ob'sti·nate·ly,** *adv.*

obstruct (4) [abstrəkt'], *v.* prevent passage or progress. **Ex.** *A fallen tree is obstructing the road.* —**ob·struc'tion,** *n.* something that stops passage or progress. —**ob·struc'tive,** *adj.*

obtain (2) [əbteyn'], *v.* acquire; get; gain by effort. **Ex.** *He obtained an education by working during the day and going to school at night.*

obvious (3) [ab'viyəs], *adj.* clear; evident; easily seen or understood. **Ex.** *It was obvious that he had not heard the warning until it was too late.* —**ob'vi·ous·ly**, *adv.*

occasion (2) [əkey'žən], *n.* 1. a particular time when a certain thing happens. **Ex.** *We last saw her on the occasion of her marriage.* 2. an important event. **Ex.** *The college president's reception was quite an occasion.* 3. a favorable time; a good chance; an opportunity. **Ex.** *When the occasion presents itself, I will ask him for his help.*

occasional (3) [əkey'žənəl], *adj.* not happening, appearing, used, etc. regularly. **Ex.** *He is only an occasional visitor to our home.* —**oc·ca'sion·al·ly**, *adv.*

occupation (2) [ak`yəpey'šən], *n.* 1. one's regular business, trade, profession or work. **Ex.** *He said that his occupation was that of a student.* 2. the act of occupying; the state of being occupied. **Ex.** *Our occupation of the house was delayed while it was being painted.* 3. the taking and holding of a building, land, etc. by force. **Ex.** *The occupation of the defeated nation lasted three years.* —**oc·cu·pa'tion·al**, *adj.*

occupy (2) [ak'yəpay`], *v.* 1. fill space. **Ex.** *The new office building occupies an entire block.* 2. engage the time or attention of. **Ex.** *Her mind was occupied with her own troubles.* 3. take and hold by force. **Ex.** *The enemy occupied the fort.* 4. live in. **Ex.** *We occupy the house next to yours.* 5. hold or have an office or a job. **Ex.** *What position does he occupy in the company?* —**oc'cu·pan·cy**, *n.* act of occupying. —**oc'cu·pant**, *n.* one who occupies.

occur (2) [əkə:r'], *v.* 1. happen. **Ex.** *The accident occurred last Friday.* 2. found to exist. **Ex.** *Iron occurs in combination with many other elements.* 3. come to mind. **Ex.** *It did not occur to her to be afraid.* —**oc·cur'rence**, *n.* the act of occurring; a happening; an event. **Ex.** *The occurrence of so many accidents caused alarm.*

ocean (1) [ow'šən], *n.* the body of salt water that covers almost three fourths of the earth's surface; any of the five main divisions of this water: the Atlantic, Pacific, Indian, Arctic and Antarctic oceans. **Ex.** *We crossed the ocean in five days.* —**o·ce·an'ic**, *adj.*

o'clock (1) [əklak'], *adv.* of the clock; according to the clock. **Ex.** *He left at ten o'clock.*

October (1) [ak`tow'bər], *n.* the tenth month of the year.

odd (2) [ad'], *adj.* 1. strange; unusual; not normal. **Ex.** *As a foreigner, he found the sound of English odd.* 2. not one of a pair; lacking a mate. **Ex.** *I am going to throw away this odd glove.* 3. having one remaining when divided by two. **Ex.** *Three, seven and eleven are odd numbers.* —**odd'ly,** *adv.* —**odd'ity,** *n.*

odds (5) [adz'], *n.* 1. a difference that gives one the advantage over another. **Ex.** *The smaller army struggled against great odds.* 2. in gambling, the relationships between the chances that something will or will not happen, is or is not true, etc. **Ex.** *The odds against the horse's winning were five to one.* —**at odds,** disagreeing. **Ex.** *The two boys were at odds as to which of them had seen the money first.* —**odds and ends,** scraps; small quantities of different kinds of things. **Ex.** *The child had a box containing bottle caps, small stones and other odds and ends.*

odor (3) [ow'dər], *n.* 1. a smell; a fragrance. **Ex.** *There was an odor of roses and other flowers in the air.* 2. an unpleasant smell. **Ex.** *The odor of the spoiled meat made her sick.*

of (1) [əv', av'], *prep.* 1. made from. **Ex.** *This chair is made of wood.* 2. belonging to. **Ex.** *The cover of this dish is broken.* 3. containing. **Ex.** *She drank a glass of water.* 4. at a distance from; away from. **Ex.** *Our house is within three miles of the city.* 5. about; concerning. **Ex.** *He likes to talk of his adventures.* 6. by; produced by. **Ex.** *Is this one of that writer's books?* 7. with; having. **Ex.** *He is a man of great strength.* 8. included among. **Ex.** *He is one of my friends.* 9. before. **Ex.** *It is five minutes of nine.*

off (1) [ɔːf'], *adv.* 1. away; to a distance. **Ex.** *The bird flew off.* 2. away from the top or outside. **Ex.** *She took her hat off.* 3. away in future time. **Ex.** *Our holidays are still a month off.* 4. so that something is no longer in operation, continuing, etc. **Ex.** *He turned the lights off.* 5. away from work. **Ex.** *I am taking time off this afternoon.* —*prep.* 1. not on; not attached to; removed from; distant from; away from. **Ex.** *The train is off the track.* 2. not doing; not occupied with. **Ex.** *The soldiers are off duty after three o'clock.* —*adj.* 1. not on; removed. **Ex.** *His coat was off.* 2. not on, connected, continuing, etc. **Ex.** *The electricity is off.* 3. going; on the way. **Ex.** *They are* *off to the theater.* **—be off,** leave. **Ex.** *I must be off now.* **—off and on,** occasionally; sometimes. **Ex.** *He is not a regular visitor, but he comes here off and on.* **—take off,** 1. leave. **Ex.** *I must take off for home.* 2. go into the air. **Ex.** *I watched the plane take off.*

offend (3) [əfend'], *v.* 1. anger; cause displeasure to; hurt the feelings of. **Ex.** *He offended me by the way he spoke.* 2. be unpleasant to the sense of sight, sound, etc. **Ex.** *The papers scattered around the yard next door offended his sight.* **—of·fen'der,** *n.* one who commits an offense. **Ex.** *The judge sentenced the offender to two years in prison.*

offense (3) [əfens'], *n.* 1. a wrong; a sin; a breaking of the law. **Ex.** *He was arrested for the offense of stealing.* 2. something that angers, displeases or hurts the feelings of. **Ex.** *He said he had intended no offense by his remarks.* 3. the act of attacking. **Ex.** *The enemy's offense had been carefully planned.* **—of·fen'sive,** *adj.* 1. having to do with attacking. **Ex.** *Their army has modern offensive weapons.* 2. unpleasant to the senses. **Ex.** *There was an offensive smell in the room.* **—n.** movement or position of attack. **Ex.** *He took the offensive.*

offer (1) [ɔf'ər], *v.* 1. present for acceptance or refusal. **Ex.** *He offered her his chair.* 2. show willingness to do. **Ex.** *The boy offered to carry my packages.* 3. bid or propose as a price. **Ex.** *She offered twenty dollars for the table.* **—n.** the act of offering; a proposal; that which is offered. **Ex.** *We were pleased by his offer.*

offhand [ɔ:f'hænd'], *adv.* without having to consult notes or references; without considering. **Ex.** *Do you know offhand what the population of this city is?* **—adj.** done without consideration. **Ex.** *It was just an offhand remark.*

office (1) [ɔ:f'is, af'is], *n.* 1. a place in which business or work is done. **Ex.** *The doctor has someone in his office.* 2. a public position to which someone is elected. **Ex.** *He holds the office of governor of the state.*

officeholder [ɔ:f'howl`dər], *n.* one who has a government position.

officer (2) [ɔ:f'əsər, af'əsər], *n.* 1. a person in the armed forces in a command position. **Ex.** *He hopes to be an army officer.* 2. any policeman. **Ex.** *The officer told the boys to stop making noise.* 3. a person in an important position. **Ex.** *To which officer of the company did you write?*

official (3) [əfiš'əl], *n.* a person who is in a position of authority. **Ex.** *The President is our most important government official.* —*adj.* 1. of or concerning an office. **Ex.** *He came here on official business.* 2. issued with or by authority. **Ex.** *The official report will be distributed tomorrow.* —**of·fi'cial·ly,** *adv.*

offset [ɔf'set'], *v.* balance; compensate for. **Ex.** *The money he won partly offset his losses.*

offspring [ɔf'spriŋ'], *n.* children; descendants. **Ex.** *He is the oldest of his parents' offspring.*

off-the-record [ɔf'ðərek'ərd], *adj.* not official; not to be published. **Ex.** *The Senator was angry that his off-the-record remarks were published.*

often (1) [ɔːf'ən], *adv.* many times; frequently. **Ex.** *I often see her at the office.*

oh (1) [ow'], *interj.* exclamation of surprise, pain or any emotion. **Exs.** *Oh, how worried we were about you! Oh, you are not going?*

oil (1) [oyl'], *n.* 1. a fatty liquid that does not mix with water and that burns easily. **Ex.** *What kind of oil do you use for cooking?* 2. a yellow or black liquid taken from the ground and used as a fuel or to make machine parts move easily; petroleum. **Ex.** *We need to change the oil in the car.* —*v.* put oil on or in to make machinery move easily. **Ex.** *She oiled the sewing machine.* —**oil'y,** *adj.*

oil slick [oyl' slik'], *n.* a thin coating of oil on the surface of water, particularly as caused by oil leaking from an oil tanker which has had an accident. **Ex.** *There was tremendous damage to marine wildlife and the fishing industry as a result of the oil slick.*

O.K., OK, okay (3) [ow'key'], *adj.* correct; all right. **Ex.** *I have checked your work carefully and it is O.K.* —*v.* approve. **Ex.** *Will you O.K. my request for a loan?* —*n.* approval. **Ex.** *She has my O.K. to continue.*

old (1) [owld'], *adj.* 1. not young; having lived for many years. **Ex.** *My parents are old.* 2. of age; in age. **Ex.** *The baby is one year old.* 3. not new; made, built, done, etc. a long time ago. **Ex.** *This old building was built two hundred years ago.* 4. used, worn or owned for a long time. **Ex.** *My old shoes need to be repaired.* —*n.* 1. a time long past. **Ex.** *They hunted with bows and arrows as in the days of old.* 2. old people, as a group. **Ex.** *Money was set aside for housing for the old.*

olive (3) [al'iv], *n.* a tree which bears small green or black fruit; the fruit itself. **Ex.** *The cooking oil she uses is made from pressed olives.* —*adj.* a greenish-yellow color. **Ex.** *She bought an olive coat.*

omit (3) [owmit'], *v.* leave out; fail to include. **Ex.** *He was not invited because his name was accidentally omitted from the guest list.* —**o·mis'sion,** *n.*

on (1) [an', ɔːn'], *prep.* 1. above and held up by; touching the upper surface of. **Ex.** *The book is on the table.* 2. located in; covering or touching any surface. **Ex.** *A black mark was on the side of the box.* 3. at the time when; within the period of. **Ex.** *He began his new job on Monday.* 4. in a state of; in the condition of. **Ex.** *The house was on fire.* —*adv.* 1. in or into a position of touching, covering or being fastened to. **Ex.** *He put his gloves on.* 2. to a working condition; into operation. **Ex.** *She turned the lights on.* —*adj.* in a working condition; in operation. **Ex.** *The machine is on.* —**on time,** at the appointed time. **Ex.** *We were worried when he did not appear on time.* —**on and on,** for a long time; continuously. **Ex.** *He talked on and on.*

once (1) [wəns'], *adv.* 1. at a time past; formerly. **Ex.** *I once attended that school.* 2. a single time. **Ex.** *My aunt and uncle visit us once a year.* —*conj.* if ever; whenever; as soon as. **Ex.** *Once you have heard the song, you will never forget it.* —*n.* one time; a single time. **Ex.** *Once is enough.* —**all at once,** 1. all at the same moment. **Ex.** *Add the milk to the mixture all at once.* 2. suddenly. **Ex.** *He turned out the lights and all at once there was a shot.* —**at once,** immediately. **Ex.** *They came at once when I called for help.* —**once upon a time,** long ago. **Ex.** *Once upon a time there was a beautiful home here.*

oncoming [an'kəm`iŋ], *adj.* moving nearer. **Ex.** *He ran to escape the oncoming train.*

one (1) [wən'], *n.* 1. the number *1*; a single unit. **Ex.** *Although he is only three years old, he can count from one to ten.* 2. a single person or thing. **Ex.** *The children arrived one at a time.* —*pron.* 1. a certain person or thing. **Ex.** *One of the men smiled.* 2. any person or thing. **Ex.** *One must work to earn one's living.* —*adj.* 1. of a single unit, person or thing; not two or more. **Ex.** *They have only one child.* 2. united; undivided. **Ex.** *The crowd answered with one voice.* 3. of an unnamed time in the future or the past. **Exs.** *You will understand what I mean one day. She saw him one day last week.*

oneself, one's self (1) [wən'self', wenz'self'], *pron.* one's own self. **Ex.** *There were no directions on the box for putting it together oneself.*

one-sided [wən'say'did], *adj.* having, happening, showing, etc. one side; partial; not objective. **Ex.** *He told a very one-sided story about the quarrel with his friend.*

onion (3) [ən'yən], *n.* a plant with a strong smell and taste; the edible bulb of the plant. **Ex.** *We were served slices of fried onion with the meat.*

ONION

only (1) [own'liy], *adj.* 1. being the single one or ones. **Ex.** *She is their only daughter.* 2. alone by reason of being the best. **Ex.** *For your purposes this is the only kind to buy.* —*adv.* just; merely. **Ex.** *He bought only three books.*

onrush [an'reš', ɔn'rəš], *n.* a rushing forward. **Ex.** *He was caught in the onrush of traffic.*

onset [an'set', ɔn'set'], *n.* a beginning. **Ex.** *He was here at the onset of the trouble.*

onto (2) [an'tuw, ɔn'tuw], *prep.* to a position on. **Ex.** *He dropped the book onto the floor.*

onward (3) [an'wərd, ɔn'wərd], *adv.* forward; ahead. **Ex.** *The soldiers marched onward.* —*adj.* moving in a forward direction. **Ex.** *The army continued its onward march.*

open (1) [ow'pən], *adj.* 1. not shut; allowing free entry. **Ex.** *She walked through the open door.* 2. not hidden; not concealed; not secret. **Ex.** *He was very open about his feelings.* 3. used by all; entered freely. **Ex.** *The meeting is open to all who wish to attend.* 4. ready for business. **Ex.** *The office is open from 9:00 a.m. to 5:00 p.m.* 5. not filled; available. **Ex.** *We still have one position for an English teacher open.* —*v.* 1. cause to be no longer closed. **Ex.** *Please open the door.* 2. make or become ready for business. **Ex.** *The new store will open today.* 3. spread out. **Ex.** *Open your books to the first page.* 4. begin; start. **Ex.** *The president opened the meeting by asking the secretary to speak.* —**o'pen·er**, *n.* a tool used to open containers. **Ex.** *He removed the caps from the bottles with a bottle opener.* —**o'pen·ing**, *n.* —**o'pen·ly**, *adv.*

open-handed [ow'pənhæn'did], *adj.* generous. **Ex.** *He was noted for his open-handed support of the opera company.*

open-minded [ow'pənmayn'did], *adj.* willing to listen to and try to understand new ideas. **Ex.** *Her open-minded approach to art made her art history classes interesting.*

opera (3) [ap'(ə)rə], *n.* a play that is sung, usually with accompaniment by an orchestra. **Ex.** *Our neighbor is appearing in an opera.* —**op'er·at'ic**, *adj.* —**op'er·et'·ta**, *n.* a short opera, often humorous.

operate (2) [ap'əreyt'], *v.* 1. do work or run, as a machine does. **Ex.** *This machine operates very well.* 2. control or use. **Ex.** *She operates a sewing machine in the clothing factory.* 3. perform surgery. **Ex.** *That doctor operated on my brother this morning.* —**op·er·a'tion**, *n.* —**op'er·a·tor**, *n.* 1. one who operates a machine. 2. a person who works at a central point in a telephone system and gives assistance, when needed, to persons making calls. **Ex.** *Operator, please give me the telephone number of the mayor's office.*

opinion (1) [əpin'yən], *n.* 1. a belief based on one's own ideas and thinking and not on certain knowledge. **Ex.** *In my opinion, he will win the race.* 2. impression; judgment. **Ex.** *He has a good opinion of your ability.* 3. expert belief. **Ex.** *They asked for the doctor's opinion about the condition of the patient.*

opponent (4) [əpcw'nənt], *n.* a person who is on the other side in a fight, discussion, etc. **Ex.** *He could not match the skill of his opponent.*

opportunity (2) [ap'ərtuw'nətiy, ap'ərtyuwn'ətiy], *n.* a favorable time or occasion; a good chance. **Ex.** *The meeting provided a good opportunity for them to discuss their problems.*

oppose (2) [əpowz'], *v.* be against; fight against; resist. **Ex.** *He opposed all my ideas for change.* —**op'po·si'tion**, *n.* 1. the act of being or fighting against. **Ex.** *There was much opposition to increasing taxes.* 2. a political party or group that opposes the party or person in power. **Ex.** *The opposition attempted to overthrow the ruling general.*

opposite (2) [ap'əzit], *adj.* 1. against; exactly at the other extreme; different; contrary. **Ex.** *They held opposite views on the subject.* 2. facing each other; on the other side; on the other end. **Ex.** *Her house is on the opposite side of the street from mine.* —*n.* that which is very different or at the other extreme. **Ex.** *Happy people and sad people are opposites.* —*prep.* facing. **Ex.** *We sat opposite each other at the table.*

oppress (4) [əpres'], *v.* 1. worry; burden the mind. **Ex.** *His troubles oppressed him.* 2. control by the use of unjust and cruel force or authority. **Ex.** *The government of that country oppresses its people.* —**op·pres'sor,** *n.* one who oppresses. —**op·pres'sion,** *n.* the act of oppressing or being oppressed. —**op·pres'sive,** *adj.*

optical [ap'tikəl], *adj.* 1. of or having to do with sight. **Ex.** *We realized that what we thought we saw was an optical illusion.* 2. intended to help, improve or correct sight. **Ex.** *What optical instruments will your staff need for this project?*

optician [aptiš'ən], *n.* a person who makes and sells eyeglasses. **Ex.** *The optician said my glasses would be ready tomorrow.*

optimism (5) [ap'təmiz'əm], *n.* a feeling that things will turn out for the best. **Ex.** *The candidate's optimism about his chances of winning the election encouraged his supporters.* —**op'ti·mist,** *n.* one who believes that things will turn out for the best. —**op'ti·mis'tic,** *adj.* —**op'ti·mis'tic·al·ly,** *adv.*

option [ap'šən], *n.* 1. the right or freedom to choose; the act of choosing. **Ex.** *We are renting this house with an option to buy in two years.* 2. that which is chosen or is available for choice. **Ex.** *In this situation what options do I have?*

or (1) [ɔːr'], *conj.* 1. introducing the second of two choices. **Ex.** *Do you want to return or stay here?* 2. introducing the last of a series of choices. **Ex.** *You may have tea, coffee or milk.*

-or [ər], *suffix.* the person or thing doing something. **Exs.** *Act, actor; distribute, distributor; govern, governor; elevate, elevator.*

oral [ɔ'rəl], *adj.* 1. spoken, not written; of or using speech. **Ex.** *She gave me oral instructions before she left.* 2. of or having to do with the mouth. **Ex.** *The dentist may have to perform some oral surgery on that patient.* —**o'ral·ly,** *adv.* 1. by mouth. **Ex.** *This medicine is to be taken orally.* 2. spoken. **Ex.** *He gave his report orally.*

orange (2) [ɔːr'iŋ], *n.* 1. a round, reddish-yellow fruit which grows on a tree and is sweet and full of juice. 2. a reddish-yellow color. —*adj.* of the color orange. **Ex.** *She wore an orange dress.* 2. of an orange. **Ex.** *He drank a glass of orange juice.*

ORANGE 1

orator (5) [ɔːr'ətər, ar'ətər], *n.* a skillful and forceful public speaker. **Ex.** *To become a member*

of our high school debating team, you must be a good orator.
—**o·rate'**, *v.* 1. deliver a formal speech. 2. speak too seriously
and with too much feeling. **Ex.** *We became bored when he
continued to orate about his political beliefs.* —**o·ra'tion,** *n.* a
formal speech given on a special occasion such as a holiday,
a dedication, etc.

orbit [ɔr'bit], *n.* the curved path of a planet or other body
moving in space around another body. **Ex.** *The moon travels
in an orbit around the earth.* —*v.* travel in space around the
earth, moon or other heavenly bodies. **Ex.** *The spaceship
orbited the moon before making a landing on it.*

orchard (4) [ɔr'čərd], *n.* a large area of ground on which fruit
trees are grown; a collection of such trees. **Ex.** *These apples
come from an orchard near here.*

orchestra (3) [ɔr'kistrə], *n.* a large group of people who play
musical instruments together, including stringed instruments;
the instruments they play. **Ex.** *Our city has a famous symphony orchestra.*

ordeal [ɔr'diyəl], *n.* a very difficult, severe or trying experience
or test. **Ex.** *Seeing their house destroyed by fire was a terrible
ordeal.*

order (1) [ɔr'dər], *n.* 1. a command; a direction. **Ex.** *The troops
received orders to attack.* 2. a request for goods or services.
Ex. *She gave the company an order for forty copies of the
book.* 3. the goods requested. **Ex.** *Your order should reach
you soon.* 4. the arrangement of people or things one after
the other. **Ex.** *Put these in order according to number.* —*v.* 1.
give an order, direction or command to. **Ex.** *The general
ordered his men to advance.* 2. ask for something one wants;
give an order for. **Ex.** *She ordered food from the store.* —**in
order,** a proper, customary arrangement. **Ex.** *Have you put
your room in order?* —**out of order,** not in working condition.
Ex. *No one answered because the front door bell is out of
order.* —**in order that,** so that. **Ex.** *They used the loudspeaker
system in order that everyone would be able to hear.* —**in
order to,** for the purpose of. **Ex.** *He lit a candle in order to
see.* —**to order,** especially made or fitted. **Ex.** *His clothes fit
him well because he has them made to order.*

orderly (1) [ɔr'dərliy], *adj.* 1. in order; neat. **Ex.** *His books were
arranged in an orderly way.* 2. well-behaved. **Ex.** *The crowd
was quiet and orderly.* —**or'der·li·ness,** *n.* state of being
orderly.

ordinary (2) [ɔr'dənɛːr`iy], *adj.* 1. usual; common. **Ex.** *This is not an ordinary day; it's your birthday!* 2. average; neither good nor bad. **Ex.** *The food at this restaurant is just ordinary.* —**or`di·nar'i·ly,** *adv.*

ore (4) [ɔːr'], *n.* material taken from the ground for the purpose of obtaining the metal that it contains. **Ex.** *This ore will yield a good grade of iron.*

organ (3) [ɔr'gən], *n.* a part of a plant or animal performing certain work. **Ex.** *The heart is the organ that pumps blood throughout the body.* —**or·gan'ic,** *adj.* 1. of or concerning the body. **Ex.** *This is an organic disease.* 2. of having to do with living things or things that have been living. **Ex.** *We use fallen leaves and other organic matter to help enrich the soil in our garden.* 3. fruits, vegetables, etc. raised without the use of chemicals. **Ex.** *This store specializes in selling organic food.*

organ (3) [ɔr'gən], *n.* a large instrument that makes musical sounds when air is sent through its set of pipes. **Ex.** *The music of the organ filled the church.* —**or·gan·ist,** *n.* a musician who plays the organ.

ORGAN 2

organization (3) [ɔr'gənəzey'šən], *n.* 1. a group of people joined together for a common purpose. **Ex.** *The United Nations is a large organization.* 2. the act of coming together in a single body or group for a common purpose. **Ex.** *Were you here at the time of the organization of this club?*

organize (2) [ɔr'gənayz`], *v.* 1. bring together into a group to work for a common purpose; start. **Ex.** *They are trying to organize a new political party.* 2. arrange or place according to a system; put in order. **Ex.** *This book of poems is organized according to author.* —**or·gan·ized,** *adj.* planned; orderly. **Ex.** *He is a very organized person.*

origin (2) [ɔːr'əjin], *n.* the place where something starts; the source. **Ex.** *The origin of this river is a stream in the mountains.*

original (2) [ərij'ənəl], *adj.* 1. first; belonging to the beginning. **Ex.** *The original settlers came to the island long ago.* 2. new; done for the first time; not copied. **Ex.** *That is an original approach to the problem.* 3. being the one of which a copy or copies are made. **Ex.** *She made six copies of the original letter.* —*n.* a thing which is not a copy. **Ex.** *Her dress is an original that she designed and made herself.* —**o·rig'i·nal·ly,** *adv.* at the beginning; at first. — **o·rig'i·nal'i·ty,** *n.* the ability to do original work.

originate (2) [ərij'əneyt'], *v.* begin; invent; create. **Ex.** *The idea for the new book originated at a meeting of teachers.* —**o·rig'i·na'tor,** *n.*

ornament (3) [ɔr'nəmənt], *n.* something that decorates and adds beauty. **Ex.** *There were carved ornaments on top of the desk.* —*v.* decorate with ornaments. **Ex.** *Pearls were used to ornament the neckline of her evening gown.* —**or'na·men'tal,** *adj.*

orphan (4) [ɔr'fən], *n.* a child whose parents are both dead. **Ex.** *The orphan went to live with his aunt.* —*adj.* of or for orphans. **Ex.** *Eighty children lived in the orphan home.* —*v.* make an orphan of. **Ex.** *The child was orphaned at the age of eight.* —**or'phan·age,** *n.* a home for orphans.

other (1) [əð'ər], *adj.* 1. additional. **Ex.** *Only a few people are here now, but other people will come later.* 2. different. **Ex.** *Have you any other problems to discuss?* 3. the one of two or more not yet mentioned, seen, found, etc. **Ex.** *He was looking for his other glove.* —*pron.* 1. the other one. **Ex.** *Each blamed the other.* 2. an additional person or thing. **Ex.** *Two went while the others stayed home.* —*adv.* in a different way; otherwise. **Ex.** *I cannot do other than agree with you.* —**every other,** every second one. **Ex.** *She always works at our house every other Monday.* —**the other day,** a recent day. **Ex.** *I saw his new car the other day.*

otherwise (2) [əð'ərwayz'], *adv.* 1. in a different way. **Ex.** *He had no choice and could not do otherwise.* 2. in all other ways. **Ex.** *He is slow, but otherwise he is a good worker.* 3. under other circumstances; if not. **Ex.** *You must obey the order; otherwise you will be punished.* —*adj.* different. **Ex.** *I was there and know that the facts are otherwise.*

ouch [awč'], *interj.* an expression of pain or shock. **Ex.** *Ouch, that really hurt!*

ought (1) [ɔ:t'], *v.* used with the simple form, the infinitive, of another verb to show that 1. there is a duty or obligation. **Ex.** *You ought to take your parents' advice.* 2. it is advisable or proper. **Ex.** *I wonder if we ought to stay longer.* 3. it is very likely; it is expected. **Ex.** *It ought to rain soon.*

ounce (3) [awns'], *n.* 1. a unit of weight equal to 1/16 of a pound. **Ex.** *This package weighs five ounces.* 2. a unit of measure for fluids. **Ex.** *A measuring cup filled with liquid usually contains eight ounces.* See **Weights and Measures.**

our (1) [awr', ar'], *pron.* used as an adjective, of or belonging to us. **Ex.** *We left our coats at home.*

ours (2) [awrz', arz'], *pron.* that or those which belong to us. **Ex.** *Their children stay up late, but ours go to bed early.*

ourselves (2) [awrselvz', arselvz'], *pron.* 1. our own selves. **Ex.** *We bought ourselves a new car.* 2. we, not someone else. **Ex.** *We ourselves painted the house.*

-ous (3) [əs], *suffix.* the person or thing has, is full of or is like. **Exs.** *Ambition, ambitious; anxiety, anxious; fame, famous.*

out (1) [awt'], *adv.* 1. forth from; into the open. **Ex.** *Take the dog out.* 2. away from the inside. **Ex.** *He looked out of the window.* 3. away from the home, office or other place where one usually is. **Ex.** *She has stepped out for a minute.* 4. to the point of not existing. **Ex.** *The fire burned out during the night.* 5. reaching beyond the usual limit. **Ex.** *The shop sign extends out over the sidewalk.* —*adj.* 1. absent; away from work, school, etc. **Ex.** *Several students are out because of illness.* 2. no longer hidden; no longer concealed. **Ex.** *Their secret is out.* 3. not working; not on. **Ex.** *The lights are out.* —**out of,** away from the inside; away from. **Ex.** *The bird flew out the window.* —**out to,** trying to. **Ex.** *He is out to win the race.*

out- (1) [awt], *prefix.* 1. greater or better than in quality or action. **Exs.** *Do, outdo; talk, outtalk.* 2. away from the center; outward in direction. **Exs.** *Bound, outbound; break, outbreak.* 3. located or set near or beyond. **Exs.** *Door, outdoor; side, outside.*

outage [awt'ij], *n.* a temporary suspension or failure of electric power. **Ex.** *During the last power outage, all the food in our refrigerator spoiled.*

outcome [awt'kəm], *n.* result. **Ex.** *What was the outcome of the race?*

outdoors [awt'dɔrz'], *n.* the area in the open air; not inside a building. **Ex.** *Living in the outdoors was a welcome change for the city children.* —*adv.* outside a building; in the open air. **Ex.** *The dog ran outdoors.* —**out'door`,** *adj.* of, in or to the outdoors. **Ex.** *They enjoy outdoor games.*

outer (1) [awt'ər], *adj.* being at, on or near the outside. **Ex.** *The fort was protected by an outer wall.*

outer space [awt'ər speys'], *n.* that part of space which is beyond the earth's atmosphere.

outfit (4) [awt'fit'], *n.* 1. a set of clothing or other things needed for a special purpose. **Ex.** *His parents bought him a baseball outfit for his birthday.* 2. a group of people who work together, especially in a military unit. **Ex.** *The soldier returned to his outfit.* —*v.* supply what is necessary; equip. **Ex.** *The men were outfitted for their fishing trip.* —**out'fit·ter**, *n.*

outing [awt'iŋ], *n.* a short pleasure trip; an excursion; a picnic; etc. **Ex.** *Our class is going on an outing to the art museum next Friday.*

outlaw [awt'lɔ:'], *n.* a person who habitually commits crimes and has not been caught by the police. **Ex.** *The police are seeking that outlaw.* —*v.* 1. prohibit something. **Ex.** *Smoking within the hospital has been outlawed.* 2. declare someone a criminal.

outlet (4) [awt'let'], *n.* 1. the opening by which anything is let out. **Ex.** *This room has four electrical outlets.* 2. a means or way of expressing emotion, energy, etc. **Ex.** *Playing the piano is an outlet for her when she is sad.* 3. a market for goods. **Ex.** *A nearby canning factory was the outlet for the farmer's corn crop.*

outline (4) [awt'layn'], *n.* 1. a bordering line showing the shape of an object. **Ex.** *In the dim light, I could see only the outline of a man's figure.* 2. a drawing made of such lines. **Ex.** *He drew an outline of the child's head.* 3. a brief report giving the main parts but not the details of a speech, piece of writing, etc. **Ex.** *He showed his publisher an outline of the book he wanted to write.* —*v.* make, give or draw an outline of. **Ex.** *He outlined his plans to the voters.*

outlook [awt'luk'], *n.* the way one looks at or thinks about the world, life, etc. **Ex.** *He has a cheerful outlook about the future.* 2. prospect; probability. **Ex.** *What is the outlook for house sales for the next three months?*

outpatient [awt'pey`šənt], *n.* a person needing medical attention who is treated at a hospital but not kept there overnight. **Ex.** *I received treatment for my broken arm as an outpatient.*

output (4) [awt'put'], *n.* the amount produced in a given time. **Ex.** *The company has not matched last year's output.*

outrage (4) [awt'reyj`], *n.* a very wicked or evil act. **Ex.** *Many outrages were committed during the war.* 2. an act that shocks or hurts the feelings. **Ex.** *It was an outrage for him to ignore their call for help.* —*v.* shock; greatly disturb. **Ex.** *He outraged the community by his violent acts.* —**out·ra'geous,** *adj.* —**out·ra'geous·ly,** *adv.*

outset [awt'set`], *n.* a beginning, a start. **Ex.** *He was here at the outset of the expedition.*

outside (1) [awt'sayd'], *n.* the outer side, surface or part. **Ex.** *They painted the outside of the house.* —*adv.* on or to the outer side, surface or part. **Ex.** *Step outside and see if we need to wear coats.* —*prep.* on, to or near the outside. **Ex.** *They stood outside the door.* —*adj.* 1. of, at or concerning only the outer side, surface or part. **Ex.** *All the outside doors have locks.* 2. being, acting or coming from beyond the outer limits of an area, group, etc. **Ex.** *They did not want their children to be affected by outside influences.* —**out·sid'er,** *n.* one who does not belong; a stranger. **Ex.** *Outsiders cannot attend this meeting, which is for members only.* —**outside of,** except for. **Ex.** *Outside of her, no one is going.*

outstanding (4) [awt'stæn'diŋ], *adj.* 1. well-known; important; excellent. **Ex.** *That is his most outstanding book.* 2. unpaid. **Ex.** *His bill is still outstanding.*

outwit [awtwit'], *v.* be more clever or cunning. **Ex.** *He tried to catch her, but she outwitted him and escaped.*

oval (3) [ow'vəl], *adj.* having a shape like an egg but with both ends the same. **Ex.** *They have a oval table in the dining room.*

oven (3) [əv'ən], *n.* an enclosed space for baking, heating, roasting or drying. **Ex.** *Bread is baking in the oven.*

over (1) [ow'vər], *prep.* 1. above. **Ex.** *They have a light over the door.* 2. on; upon. **Ex.** *She put her coat over her shoulders.* 3. across; on or to the other side. **Ex.** *The boy jumped over the wall.* —*adv.* 1. above. **Ex.** *He heard a plane flying over.* 2. again. **Ex.** *She had to do the work over.* 3. to another side; to a particular place; across. **Ex.** *They sailed over to see the island.* —**all over,** 1. in, on or to every place. **Ex.** *He has traveled all over the world.* 2. finished. **Ex.** *The excitement was all over when we arrived.* —**over and above,** in addition

a, far; æ, am; e, get; ey, late; i, in; iy, see; ɔ, all; ow, go; u, put; uw, too; ə, but, ago; ər, fur; aw, out; ay, life; oy, boy; ŋ, ring; θ, think; ð, that; ž, measure; š, ship; j, edge; č, child.

to. **Ex.** *His work was over and above what was required of him.* —**o'ver·ly,** *adv.* very; too. **Ex.** *She is overly conscientious in her work.*

over- (1) [ow'vər], *prefix.* 1. above in place, quality, position, etc. **Exs.** *Look, overlook; see, oversee.* 2. across or beyond. **Exs.** *Seas, overseas; clouded, overclouded.* 3. too much; to a great degree. **Exs.** *Do, overdo; eat, overeat.* 4. become upside down; cause to fall. **Exs.** *Turn, overturn; throw, overthrow.*

overall [ow'vərɔːl], *adj.* 1. from one end to the other, usually in measurement. **Ex.** *The overall length of the table is six feet.* 2. including everything. **Ex.** *What was the overall cost of the house?*

overboard [ow'vərbɔrd'], *adv.* over the side of a ship. **Ex.** *He fell overboard.*

overcame [ow'vərkeym'], *v.* past tense of *overcome.* **Ex.** *He overcame many difficulties to graduate from high school.*

overcast [ow'vərkæst'], *adj.* cloudy; gloomy. **Ex.** *Yesterday was a rainy, overcast day.*

overcoat [ow'vərkowt'], *n.* a heavy coat worn in cold weather over a suit or other ordinary clothing for added warmth. **Ex.** *You had better wear an overcoat; the temperature is dropping.*

overcome (3) [ow'vərkəm'], *v.* 1. defeat; conquer. **Ex.** *The early settlers had many difficulties to overcome.* 2. make weak or helpless. **Ex.** *He was overcome by the heat.*

overhear (3) [ow'vərhiːr'], *v.* hear something that one is not supposed to hear. **Ex.** *She overheard the quarrel.*

overlook (3) [ow'vərluk'], *v.* 1. fail to see; miss. **Ex.** *In her hurry, she overlooked one important item.* 2. ignore; excuse. **Ex.** *Please overlook his rudeness; he's very upset.* 3. view from above. **Ex.** *The house overlooked the valley.*

override [ow'vərrayd'], *v.* set aside what others have done or decided; disregard the wishes of others. **Ex.** *Congress may override the President's veto.* —**o'ver·rid'ing,** *adj.* of first place in regard to all considerations. **Ex.** *This matter is of overriding importance and must be taken care of now.*

overrule [ow'vərruwl'], *v.* decide the reverse of what a lesser authority decided. **Ex.** *The principal overruled the teacher's decision.*

overseas [ow'vərsiyz'], *adv.* across, beyond or over the seas; abroad. **Ex.** *My brother was overseas in the army.* —*adj.* located overseas; foreign. **Ex.** *Would you like an overseas assignment?*

overtake (3) [ow'vərteyk'], *v.* reach. **Ex.** *He ran to overtake his friend.*

overtime [ow'vər'taym], *n.* 1. time beyond the regular time such as working hours, playing time in a game, etc. **Ex.** *The basketball game went into overtime.* 2. payment for time worked in addition to one's regular hours. **Ex.** *How much overtime did you earn last week?* —*adv.* beyond the regular time. **Ex.** *We are all working overtime tonight.*

overthrow (5) [ow'vərθrow'], *v.* defeat and remove from power; end by force. **Ex.** *They tried to overthrow the government but failed.* —*n.* the act of overthrowing.

overturn [ow'vərtərn], *v.* upset; turn so that the bottom side is up. **Ex.** *His car was overturned in the accident.*

overwhelm (5) [ow'vərhwelm'] *v.* 1. defeat or overcome by great force or numbers; crush. **Ex.** *The attackers overwhelmed the city.* 2. cover completely; bury. **Ex.** *A snow slide overwhelmed the village.* 3. overcome the feelings and reason. **Ex.** *She was overwhelmed by their kindness.* —o·ver·whelm'ing, *adj.*

overwrought (5) [ow'vərrɔ:t], *adj.* extremely nervous or excited; strained. **Ex.** *His overwrought nerves required complete rest and quiet.*

owe (2) [ow'], *v.* 1. be in debt for; be obliged to pay. **Ex.** *They still owe a large sum on their house.* 2. feel obliged or want to do, give, etc. **Ex.** *I owe you an explanation.* 3. be indebted for. **Ex.** *He owes his life to the doctor's skill.* —ow'ing, *adj.* remaining to be paid; due. **Ex.** *He worked extra hours to pay the money owing on his doctor's bill.*

owl (3) [awl'], *n.* a night-flying, hunting bird with a large head and eyes. —owl'ish, *adj.* like an owl, particularly with regard to the eyes. **Ex.** *He gave her an owlish look.*

OWL

own (1) [own'], *adj.* belonging completely to oneself. **Ex.** *Is that his own horse, or is it borrowed?* —*v.* possess; have for oneself. **Ex.** *They own a very big house.*

—**own'er**, *n*. —**hold one's own,** succeed in resisting difficulties; keep one's position. **Ex.** *The small group of defenders held their own against the attack.*

ox (2) [aks'], *n.* a male animal of the cattle family, usually full-grown and used as a work animal. —**ox'en,** *n. pl.* more than one ox. **Ex.** *Two oxen pulled the plow.*

OX

oxygen (3) [ak'sǝjǝn], *n.* a gas without color or taste that is necessary to life and makes up one fifth of the air. **Ex.** *The patient was given oxygen.*

oyster (5) [oy'stǝr], *n.* any of a variety of small, boneless sea animals having a soft body enclosed in two rough shells, some varieties of which produce pearls and some varieties of which have edible flesh. **Ex.** *They started their meal with oysters.*

OYSTER

P

P, p [piy'], *n.* the sixteenth letter of the English alphabet.

pace (3) [peys'], *n.* 1. a step; the length of a step in walking, about two and one half to three feet. **Ex.** *The winning runner finished several paces ahead of the others.* 2. the rate of movement, development, etc. **Ex.** *The man worked at a slow pace.* —*v.* walk back and forth. **Ex.** *The anxious parents paced the floor waiting for the telephone to ring.*

pacify (4) [pæs'ǝfay'], *v.* calm; make peaceful; quiet. **Ex.** *She pacified the crying child by giving him milk.* —**pa·cif'ic,** *adj.* calm; peaceful. **Ex.** *His pacific approach reduced the strain of the situation.* —**pac'i·fi·er,** *n.* one who or that which calms. **Ex.** *She gave the baby a pacifier.* —**pac'i·fism,** *n.* a strong belief that all disputes between nations should be solved peacefully; opposition to military preparation and readiness. —**pac'i·fist,** *n.* one strongly opposed to war.

pack (2) [pæk'], *v.* 1. put things together in a container for carrying or storing. **Ex.** *He packed a suitcase for the trip.* 2. press or crowd closely together. **Ex.** *People packed the room for the meeting.* —*n.* 1. a bundle or large package for carrying on the back. **Ex.** *The camper had cooking equipment in his pack.* 2. a group of animals, especially those that hunt together. **Ex.** *A pack of wolves was seen in the forest.* 3. a set; a package containing a number of items. **Ex.** *He took a pack of cards from his pocket.* —*adj.* used for carrying burdens. **Ex.** *In the mountains we had several mules as pack animals.*

package (2) [pæk'ij], *n.* a thing or things packed for storage, carrying, sending, etc. **Ex.** *We mailed the package to him.* —*v.* put into a wrapping or container. **Ex.** *They packaged the rice in two-pound boxes.*

packet (5) [pæk'it], *n.* a small package. **Ex.** *She tied a ribbon around the packet of letters.*

pact (5) [pækt'], *n.* an agreement. **Ex.** *The two countries signed a peace pact.*

pad (3) [pæd'], *n.* 1. a case filled with soft material and used for comfort or protection; a cushion. **Ex.** *An attractive pad was on the seat of the chair.* 2. a number of sheets of paper fastened together at one end. **Ex.** *He wrote the message on a pad.* —*v.* line or fill with soft material; protect or soften with a pad. **Ex.** *The inside of the jewel box was padded with cotton.* —**pad'ding,** *n.* soft material used to pad something.

paddle (4) [pæd'əl], *n.* 1. a short pole with a wide blade at one or both ends, used for moving a canoe through the water. 2. a board shaped like a paddle used to mix, beat, stir, etc. **Ex.** *She shaped the butter into small balls using two short paddles.* —*v.* move a boat or canoe with a paddle. **Ex.** *He paddled down the river.* 2. punish by beating, as with a paddle. **Ex.** *The mother paddled the bad child.*

PADDLE 1

a, far; æ, am; e, get; ey, late; i, in; iy, see; ɔ, all; ow, go; u, put; uw, too; ə, but, ago; ər, fur; aw, out; ay, life; oy, boy; ŋ, ring; θ, think; ð, that; ž, measure; š, ship; j, edge; č, child.

page (1) [peyǰ'], *n.* one side of a sheet of paper in a book, magazine, etc.; the printing on the paper. **Ex.** *I have read forty pages of this book.*

page (1) [peyǰ'], *n.* a person who carries messages and performs other small services in a hotel, an office, etc. **Ex.** *The pages were dressed in neat uniforms.* —*v.* try to find a person by calling his name. **Ex.** *A messenger paged the doctor in the hotel dining room.*

paid (1) [peyd'], *v.* past tense and participle of *pay.* **Exs.** *He paid for the things he bought in cash. She felt that she had paid too much for the coat.*

pail (3) [peyl'], *n.* a round container with a handle, used for carrying liquids.

pain (1) [peyn'], *n.* 1. a hurting or suffering somewhere in the body. **Ex.** *He was in great pain when he was ill.* 2. mental or emotional suffering. **Ex.** *The news of her death caused them great pain.* —*v.* cause to suffer; hurt. **Ex.** *The wound pained him.* —**pain'ful,** *adj.* causing pain; unpleasant. **Ex.** *The painful memory upset her.* —**pain'ful·ly,** *adv.* —**take pains,** take special care. **Ex.** *He was taking pains to impress his new employer.*

PAIL

painstaking [peynž'teyk`iŋ], *adj.* taking or requiring extreme care. **Ex.** *He said that repairing watches was a painstaking job.*

paint (1) [peynt'], *n.* a liquid coloring substance applied to protect or beautify a surface or to make pictures. **Ex.** *He put bright paint on the wall with a roller.* —*v.* 1. cover with liquid color. **Ex.** *They painted the chairs red.* 2. make a picture of someone or something with liquid color. **Ex.** *The artist painted several pictures of the girl.* 3. describe clearly. **Ex.** *The speaker painted an exciting picture of his travels.* —**paint'er,** *n.* one who paints. —**paint'ing,** *n.* 1. act of covering with liquid color. 2 a picture made with liquid color. **Ex.** *They have two beautiful oil paintings hanging in their living room.*

pair (1) [pe:r'], *n.* 1. two things of a kind used together. **Ex.** *She bought a pair of gloves.* 2. a single thing made with two similar parts. **Ex.** *He has only one pair of trousers.* 3. two humans or animals that are related, mated or teamed together. **Ex.** *That man and his wife are a happy pair.* —*v.* arrange in pairs. **Ex.** *The two of them were paired at the dinner party.* —**pair off,** form or arrange in a pair or pairs.

pajamas (3) [pəʃa'məz, pəʃæm'əz], *n.* clothing consisting of a loose jacket and trousers worn for sleeping.

palace (2) [pæl'əs], *n.* official home of a ruler. **Ex.** *They were building a new palace for the emperor.*

PAJAMAS

pale (2) [peyl'], *adj.* 1. without much color. **Ex.** *The face of the sick girl was very pale.* 2. very weak in color; dim. **Ex.** *I could hardly see in the pale moonlight.* —*v.* 1. make or become pale. **Ex.** *He paled at the sight of the dead man.* 2. make or become less important, exciting, etc. **Ex.** *Our problems paled when we considered those of the people who had suffered in the flood.* —**pale'ness,** *n.*

palm (3) [pam'], *n.* the inside of the hand, not including the fingers. **Ex.** *She put a coin in the palm of the beggar's hand.* —**palm'ist,** *n.* a person who tells fortunes by reading palms.

palm (3) [pam'], *n.* a tall tree with large leaves at the top that grows in warm climates.

pamphlet (5) [pæm'flit], *n.* a small book, usually with a paper cover and only a few pages. **Ex.** *Several free pamphlets were available at the museum.* —**pam·phlet·eer',** *n.* a person who writes persuasive pamphlets, usually on political subjects.

PALM

pan (2) [pæn'], *n.* a broad, shallow cooking dish, usually of metal and sometimes having a handle. —*v.* wash small stones and sand in a pan to find gold. **Ex.** *The men were panning for gold in the creek.*

PAN

pancake [pæn'keyk`], *n.* a thin, flat cake, made of a mixture of flour, eggs, milk and butter, which is cooked in a pan on the stove. **Ex.** *Let's have pancakes and syrup for breakfast.*

PAN

pane (4) [peyn'], *n.* a piece of glass in a window or door. **Ex.** *The broken pane in the window was replaced.*

panel (4) [pæn'əl], *n.* 1. a flat piece of wood or other material, used in a door, ceiling or wall, which is set off from the surrounding parts. **Ex.** *The panels of the cabinet doors were carved.* 2. a section containing controls or indicators in airplanes, automobiles and many other machines. **Ex.** *He checked* *his instrument panel to see if he had enough gas.* 3. a group of people selected for some special purpose such as judging a contest, serving on a jury or joining in a discussion. **Ex.** *We heard a panel of experts discuss this problem.* —*v.* decorate or cover with panels. **Ex.** *The walls of the dining room are paneled in walnut.* —**pan·el·ing,** *n.* the panels of a wall or the material of which the panels are made. —**pan·el·ist,** *n.* a person who is a member of a panel.

pang (4) [pæŋ'], *n.* a sudden, sharp feeling of pain or mental suffering. **Ex.** *Pangs of hunger reminded him that he had not eaten that day.*

panic (4) [pæn'ik], *n.* a sudden, strong fear that cannot be controlled and often spreads rapidly from one person to another. **Ex.** *The rapid rise of the flood waters caused panic among the townspeople.* —*v.* fill with uncontrollable fear. **Ex.** *The falling bombs panicked the people.* —**pan'ick·y,** *adj.* —**pan'ic-strick'en,** *adj.* filled with panic.

pansy [pæn'ziy], *n.* a low plant having small velvety flowers made up of five leaflike divisions; the flower itself, which grows in a variety of colors. **Ex.** *The blooming pansies looked to her like smiling faces.*

PANSY

pant (5) [pænt'], *v.* breathe hard and quickly or in a labored manner. **Ex.** *The runner panted after the race.* —*n.* a gasp; a quick labored breath.

pantry (4) [pæn'triy], *n.* a small room in which food, dishes and other kitchen supplies are stored. **Ex.** *She brought the cake in from the pantry.*

pants (2) [pænts'], *n.* trousers.

paper (1) [pey'pər], *n.* 1. material made from rags and wood, in the form of thin sheets for writing, printing, drawing, wrapping, etc. 2. a newspaper. **Ex.** *The paper is delivered early in the morning.* 3. a written or printed record of proof. **Ex.** *Have you any papers showing that you are the owner of the car?* 4. an article, report, etc. **Ex.** *The professor read his paper at the meeting.* —*adj.* made of paper. **Ex.** *The children made paper flowers.*

PANTS

paperback [pey'pərbæk'], *n.* a book bound with a soft cover made of heavy paper.

paper boy [pey'pər boy'], *n.* a person who delivers or sells newspapers.

paper clip [pey'pər klip'], *n.* a device made of a thin piece of wire curved into a shape to hold papers together. **Ex.** *I fastened the check to the bill with a paper clip.*

PAPER CLIP

parachute [pær'əšuwt'], *n.* a large umbrella-shaped, cloth device, fastened by cords to a person, package, etc., that is dropped from a great height, usually from an airplane, to permit a slow fall and safe landing. **Ex.** *Food and medical supplies were dropped by parachute to the survivors of the earthquake.* —*v.* to drop or fall from an aircraft using a parachute. **Ex.** *We watched as the soldiers parachuted from the sky during a training exercise.*

parade (4) [pəreyd'], *n.* a march or procession. **Ex.** *Three school bands were among the groups in the parade.* —*v.* march with ceremony. **Ex.** *Soldiers and sailors paraded before the President.*

paradise (3) [paer'ədays', pær'ədayz'], *n.* 1. heaven. **Ex.** *A person as good as he is deserves to go to paradise.* 2. a place having an unusual amount of a desired quality such as beauty, perfect weather, etc. **Ex.** *The island was a paradise of birds and flowers.*

paragraph (3) [pær'əgræf'], *n.* one or more sentences developing one idea and forming a distinct portion of a piece of writing. **Ex.** *A new paragraph always begins on a new line.*

parallel (4) [pær'əlel'], *adj.* 1. being the same distance apart at all points and therefore never meeting. **Ex.** *Those two streets are parallel.* 2. similar. **Ex.** *They have parallel ideas about what to do to solve this problem.* —*n.* 1. something similar to something else. **Ex.** *His experience was a parallel to mine.* 2. a comparison of things. **Ex.** *The critic drew a parallel between the two plays.* —*v.* 1. be parallel to. **Ex.** *The new highway parallels the old road.* 2. be or find something similar or equal to. **Ex.** *He could not parallel his father's achievements.*

PARALLEL 1

paralyze (4) [pær'əlayz'], *v.* 1. cause loss of the ability to move or feel. **Ex.** *The accident paralyzed his arm.* 2. make inactive or helpless. **Ex.** *Their fear paralyzed them.* —**pa·ral'y·sis,** *n.* the condition of being paralyzed.

a, far; æ, am; e, get; ey, late; i, in; iy, see; ɔ, all; ow, go; u, put; uw, too; ə, but, ago; ər, far; aw, out; ay, life; oy, boy; ŋ, ring; θ, think; ð, that; ž, measure; š, ship; J, edge; č, child.

parcel (4) [par'səl], *n.* a package; something that is wrapped. **Ex.** *She addressed the parcel for mailing.*

pardon (2) [par'dən], *n.* 1. forgiveness. **Ex.** *I beg your pardon for being late.* 2. a release from punishment. **Ex.** *The governor reviewed the case and granted the prisoner a pardon.* —*v.* 1. excuse or forgive. **Ex.** *Please pardon this interruption.* 2. free from punishment. **Ex.** *The governor pardoned the criminal.*

parent (2) [par'ənt], *n.* 1. a father or mother. **Ex.** *Her parents went to visit her at college.* 2. a plant or animal that produces another. **Ex.** *The parents were feeding their young birds.* —**pa·ren'tal,** *adj.*

park (2) [park'], *n.* an area of trees, grass, etc. set apart for people to enjoy. **Ex.** *The children were playing in the park.*—*v.* put or leave an automobile, a bicycle, etc. in a particular place for a time. **Ex.** *You may park your car on this street for two hours.*

parking lot [par'kiŋ lat'], *n.* a place to park automobiles. **Ex.** *The parking lots in the city charge a high price.*

parking meter [park'iŋ miy'tər], *n.* a device mounted on a pole, usually placed on the sidewalk next to the street, into which one places a coin or coins to pay for the length of time one wants to park. **Ex.** *Put four quarters into the parking meter so that we can park for two hours.*

parkway [park'wey'], *n.* a road made beautiful with trees and grass. **Ex.** *They went for a pleasant drive on the parkway.*

PARKING
METER

parliament (3) [par'ləmənt], *n.* the national law-making body in certain countries such as the United Kingdom. **Ex.** *The queen is going to address parliament next week.* —**par'lia·men'ta·ry,** *adj.* 1. of, about or like a parliament; having a parliament. **Ex.** *That country has a parliamentary form of government.* 2. in accordance with the rules of a parliament. **Ex.** *The group follows parliamentary procedures in its meetings.*

parlor (3) [par'lər], *n.* 1. formerly a room for receiving or entertaining guests; a living room. **Ex.** *The parlor of their house is nicely furnished.* 2. a room furnished and equipped for a particular purpose, such as a beauty parlor or a pizza parlor.

parrot (5) [pær'ət], *n.* a brightly colored bird with a hooked bill, valued as a pet because some varieties can learn to talk. **Ex.** *Unexpectedly the parrot spoke.*

part (1) [part'], *n.* 1. something less than a whole; a section. **Ex.** *She was not hungry and ate only part of her lunch.* 2. a piece of something. **Ex.** *The automobile needed several new parts.* 3. a share of effort or work. **Ex.** *Each one must do his part.* 4. a character or role in a play. **Ex.** *He played the part of the hero in the school play.* —*v.* 1. divide or break into parts; separate. **Ex.** *The crowd parted to let us pass.* 2. go away from; leave. **Ex.** *He was sorry to part from his friend.* 3. comb the hair so that there is a line dividing it. **Ex.** *His hair is too short to part.* —*adj.* not entire. **Ex.** *She made a part payment on the car.* —**part'ly,** *adv.* not entirely; to some extent. **Ex.** *It is partly my fault.* —**for the most part,** mostly. **Ex.** *For the most part, what he says is true.* —**in part,** to some extent. **Ex.** *You are right in part.* —**part with,** separate from. **Ex.** *I hate to part with this book, but I will give it to you.* —**take part,** join in. **Ex.** *He was taking part in the game.*

partial (1) [par'šəl], *adj.* 1. not complete; of a part. **Ex.** *He suffered a partial loss of hearing.* 2. favoring one over the other or others. **Ex.** *She was partial to her youngest son.* —**par·ti·al'i·ty,** *n.* the act of favoring one over the other or others. **Ex.** *The teacher showed partiality to the less troublesome students.* —**par'tial'ly,** *adv.* to some extent. **Ex.** *The snow has partially melted.*

participate (3) [partis'əpeyt'], *v.* be a part of; join with others. **Ex.** *Most of the students participated in the discussion.* —**par·tic'i·pant,** *n.* one who participates. —**par·tic'i·pa'tion,** *n.* the act of participating.

participle (5) [par'təsip'əl], *n.* a verb form which can be used 1. as an adjective with certain qualities of a verb 2. as a part of a verb phrase with forms of *be* and *have*. **Ex.** *The smiling boy had not been smiling when we saw him yesterday.* The first use of the participle *smiling* is as an adjective; the second use of the participle *smiling* is as a verb with *had been.* Present participles end in *-ing.* **Exs.** *Walk, walking; jump, jumping.* **Ex.** *After we had parted, I watched him through the parted curtains.* The first use of the participle *parted* is as a verb with *had;* the second use of the participle *parted* is as an adjective. Most past participles end in *-ed, -en, -d, -t* or *-n.* **Exs.** *Talk, talked; speak, spoken; say, said; spend, spent; grow, grown.* See **A Brief Explanation of English Grammar.**

particle (4) [par'tikəl], *n.* a very small part of a whole; a tiny piece or amount. **Exs.** *A particle of dirt was in his eye. There is not a particle of truth in what he said.*

particular (2) [pərtik'yələr], *adj.* 1. concerning one single person, thing, etc.; specific. **Ex.** *That particular chair belonged to my father.* 2. very careful; detailed; special. **Ex.** *She paid particular attention to her hair.* —*n.* a small fact or detail. **Ex.** *This report agrees with yours in every particular.* —**par·tic'u·lar·ly,** *adv.* especially.

partisan (5) [par'təzən], *n.* 1. a devoted follower of a cause, person, etc. **Ex.** *His partisans worked eagerly for his election.* 2. a member of a small band of fighters, not part of a regular army, who fight behind enemy lines. **Ex.** *The partisans interfered with the supply line of the invading army.* —*adj.*

partition (4) [partiš'ən], *n.* 1. division into parts, sections or shares. **Ex.** *The partition of the country into two parts caused many problems.* 2. that which divides; a wall. **Ex.** *The partition we installed made two rooms out of one.* —*v.* 1. divide into parts, sections or shares. **Ex.** *They partitioned the farm among their three sons.* 2. divide by a wall. **Ex.** *They partitioned the room to form two offices.*

partner (3) [part'nər], *n.* 1. one who joins or works with another in an enterprise. **Ex.** *This store is owned by two partners.* 2. either one of a couple dancing together. **Ex.** *When the music stopped, everyone changed partners.* 3. one who plays on the same side in a game, as in cards or tennis. **Ex.** *He and his partner won the game.* —**part'ner·ship,** *n.* the condition or state of being partners in an enterprise; an association of partners. **Ex.** *The three friends formed a business partnership.*

party (1) [par'tiy], *n.* 1. a group of people gathered together for enjoyment. **Ex.** *We went to a dinner party last night.* 2. an organized group of people sharing similar political ideas who work together to promote them and to elect to office the people they have chosen. **Ex.** *The United States has a two-party political system.* 3. a group of people coming together for a particular purpose. **Ex.** *A search party hunted for the lost child.*

pass (1) [pæs'], *v.* 1. go by or move past something. **Ex.** *I passed his car on the road.* 2. cause or allow to go, move, proceed, etc. **Ex.** *Please pass the sugar.* 3. successfully meet the requirements of an examination, a trial period, etc. **Ex.** *She passed her history test.* 4. give legal force to; enact. **Ex.** *Congress passed a new education bill last week.* 5. proceed;

move along. **Ex.** *The parade just passed down the street.* 6. go away; come to an end. **Ex.** *The storm has passed and the sun is shining.* 7. change from one form, condition, owner, etc. to another. **Ex.** *The property will pass from father to son.* 8. throw. **Ex.** *He passed the ball to me.* —*n.* 1. a narrow way through which one can go. **Ex.** *The pass is between those mountains.* 2. a permit to enter or leave. —**pass'a·ble,** *adj.* 1. capable of being crossed or used. **Ex.** *In spite of the heavy rain, the road was passable.* 2. acceptable; adequate. **Ex.** *His dancing is not very good, but it is passable.* —**pass'ing,** *adj.* quick; without much thought. **Ex.** *He made a passing comment I did not hear.* —**in passing,** without serious thought; without emphasis. **Ex.** *He made the remark only in passing.* —**pass away,** die; end. **Ex.** *She passed away in her sleep.* —**pass over,** ignore; fail to include. **Ex.** *He was passed over when they chose the team.*

passage (3) [pæs'ij], *n.* 1. a part of a book or other writing, speech, etc. **Ex.** *He read them passages from several books.* 2. The act of passing. **Ex.** *We didn't notice the passage of time.* 3. a way or means of passing. **Ex.** *The passage between the two houses was blocked.* 4. a journey by sea or air; passenger space on such a journey. **Ex.** *He was given passage on a morning flight.*

passenger (2) [pæs'ənjər], *n.* one other than the driver or operator who travels in a car, train, bus, ship, etc. **Ex.** *This ship can carry seven hundred passengers.*

passion (2) [pæs'ən], *n.* 1. a strong emotion such as love, hate or anger. **Ex.** *The young people could not hide the passion they felt for each other.* 2. strong liking; enthusiasm. **Ex.** *He had a passion for sailing.* —**pas'sion·ate,** *adj.* —**pas'sion·ate·ly,** *adv.*

passport (5) [pæs'pɔrt'], *n.* an official government document identifying a citizen, permitting him to leave his country to travel abroad and giving him the protection of his government. **Ex.** *The immigration official examined the traveler's passport.*

past (1) [pæst'], *adj.* 1. gone by in time; finished. **Ex.** *He had thought his troubles were past.* 2. recent; immediately before. **Ex.** *He had not been well for the past few days.* 3. former. **Ex.** *The past president of the club welcomed his successor.* —*n.* 1. the time gone by; the time before. **Ex.** *The past seemed more real to her than the present.* 2. one's earlier life or history. **Ex.** *His exciting past made his present job* *seem dull.* —*adv.* to a point and beyond; by. **Ex.** *The soldiers marched past.* —*prep.* 1. after; later than. **Ex.** *It is past noon.* 2. beyond; farther than. **Ex.** *My house is past the school.*

pasta [pæs'tə], *n.* a food, made from a mixture of flour, water and often eggs, which is shaped into various forms and then usually dried before being cooked in boiling water and served with a sauce or cheese. **Ex.** *I have made a tomato and mushroom sauce for the pasta.*

paste (4) [peyst'], *n.* 1. a mixture of flour and water or other substances used to make paper or other thin materials stick together. **Ex.** *She sealed the envelope with paste.* 2. any mixture that is thick, soft, smooth and moist. **Ex.** *She added tomato paste to the sauce.* —*v.* fasten or stick together with paste. **Ex.** *She pasted the pictures in a photograph album.*

pasteurize [pæs'čərayz'], *v.* 1. treat milk and other foods by heating them to a sufficiently high temperature for a given length of time in order to destroy bacteria and germs. **Ex.** *Has this imported cheese been pasteurized?* —**pas·tur·i·za'·tion,** *n.*

pastry (4) [peys'triy], *n.* 1. pies and other sweet baked goods, made with a shell of flour, butter or oil and water; all fancy baked goods. **Ex.** *We had some delicious pastries with our coffee.* 2. the mixture of flour, butter or oil and water used in making pies, cakes, etc. **Ex.** *She rolled the pastry out until it was a large thin circle.*

pasture (3) [pæs'čər], *n.* 1. ground covered with grass or other plants suitable for the feeding of cows, sheep, etc. **Ex.** *The boy took the cows to the pasture every morning.* 2. the grass or other plants that animals eat. **Ex.** *How many acres of pasture does he own?* —*v.* feed animals on growing grass and plants. **Ex.** *He pastured the sheep on the hill.*

pat (2) [pæt'], *n.* 1. a light, friendly stroke, usually with the hand. **Ex.** *The child gave the dog a pat on the head.* 2. a small piece of something. **Ex.** *She spread a pat of butter on her bread.* —*v.* touch gently; give a pat. **Ex.** *Her mother patted her on the back in encouragement.*

patch (3) [pæč'], *n.* 1. a piece of material used to cover a hole or a weak spot. **Ex.** *She sewed patches on the elbows of his jacket.* 2. a covering put over a wound, sore or injured eye. **Ex.** *He wore a black patch over his left eye.* 3. a small section of land. **Ex.** *We have a vegetable patch beside our house.* —*v.* put a patch on; mend. **Ex.** *The mother patched the boy's* *trousers.* —**patch'work'**, *adj.* made of small different-colored pieces of cloth in varied shapes sewn together. **Ex.** *She made a patchwork covering for the bed.*

patent (5) [pæt'ənt], *n.* 1. government protection giving an inventor the sole right to make, use or sell his invention for a certain number of years. **Ex.** *He has applied for a patent on his latest invention.* 2. the official paper granting this right. —*v.* get the sole rights to an invention. **Ex.** *He patented a new process for making fresh water from salt water.*

path (2) [pæθ'], *n.* 1. a narrow way made by the walking of animals or people. **Ex.** *She followed the path up the hill.* 2. a course along which something moves. **Ex.** *He jumped out of the path of the approaching car.*

pathetic (5) [pəθet'ik], *adj.* arousing feelings of pity, sorrow, tenderness or sympathy. **Ex.** *We could not bear to listen to the sick child's pathetic cries.* —**pa·thet'ic·al·ly**, *adv.*

patience (2) [pey'šəns], *n.* 1. the ability to endure pain, troubles, delays, etc. calmly, with understanding and without complaining. **Ex.** *She endured the long delay with patience.* 2. the ability to work with extreme care and to continue to work despite difficulties. **Ex.** *He showed great patience in making model ships.*

patient (2) [pey'šənt], *adj.* 1. showing patience. **Ex.** *He was patient despite the long wait.* 2. showing self-control and understanding. **Ex.** *She was patient with the children.* 3. continuing to make an effort despite difficulties. **Ex.** *After weeks of patient search, he found an answer to his question.* —*n.* a person being cared for by a doctor. **Ex.** *The doctor asked the patient to take a deep breath.*

patriot (4) [pey'triyət], *n.* a person who deeply loves and defends his country. **Ex.** *The patriot died while fighting in the war for independence.* —**pa'tri·ot'ic**, *adj.* —**pa'tri·ot·ism**, *n.* a deep love for and willingness to defend one's country. **Ex.** *His patriotism was unquestioned.*

patrol (5) [pətrowl'], *v.* make regular, repeated trips around or through an area as a guard or policeman. **Ex.** *Policemen patrol the city day and night.* —*n.* 1. a person or group of persons whose duty it is to guard. **Ex.** *The patrol consisted of three armed men.* 2. the act of patrolling. **Ex.** *They were on patrol.*

patron (4) [pey'trən], *n.* 1. one who buys regularly at a certain store; a regular customer. **Ex.** *She has been a patron of this* *store for many years.* 2. a person who gives his approval and support to a person, art or cause. **Ex.** *The patrons contributed the money for the new wing of the museum.* —**pa'tron·ize**, *v.* 1. be a regular customer of. **Ex.** *She always patronizes this store.* 2. support; be a patron of. 3. behave toward another as if he were an inferior. **Ex.** *He resents the way she patronizes him.* —**pa'tron·iz'ing**, *adj.* behaving as if another were an inferior. **Ex.** *He spoke to her in a patronizing manner.* —**pa'tron·age**, *n.* 1. the aid given by a patron. 2. customers; the act of patronizing. **Ex.** *The store owner appreciated her patronage.* 3. authority to appoint government officials or grant political favors. **Ex.** *He received his government job through patronage.*

pattern (2) [pæt'ərn], *n.* 1. a model or plan to be copied in making something. **Ex.** *She bought a pattern for an evening dress.* 2. a design used to decorate. **Ex.** *What is the pattern of your dishes?* —*v.* make, using a pattern or model. **Ex.** *He patterned himself after his father.*

pause (2) [pɔːz'], *n.* a brief stop or hesitation. **Ex.** *There was a pause in the program while the scenery was changed* —*v.* make a brief stop; hesitate. **Ex.** *He paused to take a drink of water and then continued speaking.*

pave (4) [peyv'], *v.* 1. cover a road with a mixture of small stones, concrete or other materials that hardens like stone as it dries. **Ex.** *Traffic was delayed while the new road was being paved.* 2. prepare the way. **Ex.** *His research helped to pave the way for the invention of the automobile.* —**pave'ment**, *n.* the covering of a road. **Ex.** *To avoid the mud, he walked on the pavement.*

paw (3) [pɔː'], *n.* the foot of an animal which has claws or nails. **Ex.** *The dog lifted its two front paws.* —*v.* hit, dig, or touch with the paws or feet. **Ex.** *The bull pawed the ground.*

pay (1) [pey'], *v.* 1. give money for something or for services obtained. **Ex.** *How much did you pay for that suit?* 2. give money to settle a debt or claim. **Ex.** *He had to pay bills from several stores.* —*n.* wages; salary. **Ex.** *He asked for a raise in pay.* —**pay'ment**, *n.* 1. the act of paying. 2. that which is paid. —**pay'a·ble**, *adj.* due for payment. **Ex.** *The bill is payable today.*

payroll [pey'rowl'], *n.* a list of people working for an organization and the amount each earns; the total amount of the money earned by all the people on the list. **Ex.** *They will not let you start work until you are on the payroll.*

pea (3) [piy'], *n.* a tall, climbing plant which produces green seeds in cases. 2. the seeds or the seed cases of this plant eaten as a vegetable. **Ex.** *May I serve you some peas?*

PEA

peace (1) [piys'], *n.* 1. quiet; freedom from war, fighting or noise. **Ex.** *The war ended and the country was at peace.* 2. an agreement to end a war. **Ex.** *They made peace with their enemies.* 3. law and order. **Ex.** *He was arrested for disturbing the peace.* —**peace'ful**, *adj.* quiet. —**peac'a·ble**, *adj.* preferring peace; peaceful.

peach (3) [piyč'], *n.* 1. a round, juicy, orange-yellow fruit which grows on a tree. **Ex.** *Would you like some cream on your sliced peaches?* 2. orange-yellow color. **Ex.** *This sweater comes in peach, pale blue and white.*

peak (3) [piyk'], *n.* 1 a pointed top, as of a cap, mountain, etc. **Ex.** *A bird sat on the peak of the roof.* 2. highest or greatest point. **Ex.** *Running for president was the peak of his career.*

PEACH 1

peanut [piy'nət], *n.* an edible nutlike, oily seed that comes from a pod which grows under the ground. **Ex.** *Won't you try these honey-roasted peanuts?* —**pea'nut but'ter**, a spread made of ground roasted peanuts, sometimes smooth and sometimes with small pieces of peanuts in it. **Ex.** *The children like peanut butter and jelly sandwiches.*

PEANUT

pear (3) [pe:r'], *n.* a soft fruit, yellow, green or brown in color, round at one end and narrowing toward the stem; the fruit of the pear tree. **Ex.** *We are having baked pears for dessert.*

PEAR

pearl (3) [pərl'], *n.* a smooth, hard, usually white, cream or bluish-gray round stone formed within some shellfish and used as a gem. **Ex.** *That is a beautiful string of pearls!* — *adj.* made of pearl. —**pearl'y**, *adj.* like pearls.

---

a, far; æ, am; e, get; ey, late; i, in; iy, see; ɔ, all; ow, go; u, put; uw, too; ə, but, ago; ər, fur; aw, out; ay, life; oy, boy; ŋ, ring; θ, think; ð, that; ž, measure; š, ship; ǰ, edge; č, child.

peasant (3) [pez'ənt], *n*. in some countries, the owner of a small farm or a farm laborer. **Ex.** *The peasants were planting rice.*

pebble (4) [pəb'əl], *n*. a very small, smooth and rounded piece of rock. **Ex.** *The storm washed many pebbles onto the beach.* —**peb'bly**, *adj*. having many pebbles. **Ex.** *The pebbly road was hard to walk on.*

pecan [pikan'], *n*. a thin-shelled, oval-shaped nut that grows on a large tree. **Ex.** *I am shelling pecans for the pie that mother is going to make.* —*adj*.

peck (4) [pek'], *n*. a dry measure equal to eight quarts. **Ex.** *She bought a peck of potatoes.* See **Weights and Measures.**

peck (4) [pek'], *v*. strike with the bill or something pointed, as a bird does. **Ex.** *The bird pecked at the bark of the tree.*

peculiar (3) [pikyuwl'yər], *adj*. 1. unusual; strange; odd. **Ex.** *We heard a peculiar noise.* 2. special; in one person, group, etc. **Ex.** *That problem is peculiar to this area.* —**pe·cul'iar·ly**, *adv*. —**pe·cu'li·ar'i·ty**, *n*.

pedal (5) [ped'əl], *v*. cause to move or work by pushing down on a footrest attached to a wheel. **Ex.** *He pedaled his bicycle up the hill.* —*n*. a footrest pushed down by the foot when pedaling.

peddle (5) [ped'əl], *v*. go from place to place selling, usually small articles. **Ex.** *He peddles his wares from town to town.* —**ped'dler**, *n*. one who peddles. **Ex.** *The dogs barked at the peddler selling fruit.*

pedestrian [pədes'triyən], *n*. a person who moves about on foot; a walker. **Ex.** *As soon as the light turned green, the pedestrian started across the street.*

peel (4) [piyl], *n*. the outer skin of fruits and vegetables. **Ex.** *She used some orange peel to flavor the cake.* —*v*. 1. cut or pull away the outer skin. **Ex.** *She was peeling onions.* 2. come off in layers. **Ex.** *Paint was peeling from the wall.*

peep (4) [piyp'], *v*. make a small, high sound like that of a young chicken or other bird. **Ex.** *The baby birds peeped at their mother.* —*n*. a small, high sound like that of a young bird or chicken. **Ex.** *The baby chicken uttered peeps.*

peep (4) [piyp'], *v*. look through a small hole; look without being seen. **Ex.** *The child peeped at the guests through the partly opened door.* 2. appear partially. **Ex.** *A flower peeped through the grass.* —*n*. a brief or secret look. **Ex.** *He took a peep at the hidden gifts.*

peer (3) [piːr'], *n.* 1. a person or thing that is equal to another in some way. **Ex.** *As a lawyer, this man has no peer.* 2. a nobleman. **Ex.** *Her grandfather was a peer.*

peer (3) [piːr'], *v.* look at closely in an effort to see more clearly. **Ex.** *The old woman peered at the girl.*

peg (5) [peg'], *n.* a short piece of wood or metal used to hold parts together, hang things on, etc. **Ex.** *He hung his hat on the top peg.* —*v.* put or drive a peg into; fasten with a peg. **Ex.** *The furniture maker pegged rather than nailed this antique chair.*

pen (2) [pen'], *n.* a pointed instrument used with fluid for writing. —*v.* write with a pen. **Ex.** *He penned a letter to his friend.*

pen (2) [pen'], *n.* 1. an enclosed place in which animals are kept. **Ex.** *The boy drove the sheep into the pen.* 2. any enclosed space. **Ex.** *The baby is in the playpen.* —*v.* put into a pen. **Ex.** *The animals were penned for the night.*

penalty (3) [pen'əltiy], *n.* 1. punishment for committing a crime or breaking the law. **Ex.** *The penalty for his offense was five years in prison.* 2. something paid for breaking an agreement or a rule in a contest. **Ex.** *He had to pay a 10 percent penalty because his bill was overdue.* —**pe'nal,** *adj.* concerned with punishment. —**pe'nal·ize,** *v.* give a penalty. **Ex.** *His team was penalized because he struck a member of the opposing team.*

pencil (3) [pen'səl], *n.* a round, slender piece of wood with a center of lead used for writing or drawing. **Ex.** *He sharpened his pencils before class.* —*v.* write, draw or mark with a pencil. **Ex.** *The artist penciled the outline of the model's face.*

penetrate (4) [pen'ətreyt'], *v.* 1. enter; force a way into or through. **Ex.** *The bullet penetrated the door.* 2. spread through. **Ex.** *The smell of paint penetrated the entire house.* —**pen'e·trat·ing,** *adj.* keen; intelligent. **Ex.** *The teacher had a penetrating mind.* —**pen'e·tra'tion,** *n.*

peninsula (5) [pənin'sələ], *n.* a piece of land surrounded on three sides by water. **Ex.** *Spain is a peninsula.*

penmanship [pen'mənšip'], *n.* art of handwriting. **Ex.** *His penmanship is difficult to read.*

penny (2) [pen'iy], *n.* a United States coin worth one cent; the one hundredth part of a dollar. —**pen'ni·less,** *adj.* without any money. **Ex.** *Her illness had left her penniless.*

pension (4) [pen'šən], *n.* a regular payment of money, based on length of service and previous salary, to a person who has retired because of age or illness. **Ex.** *He will start receiving a pension when he retires at age sixty-five.* —*v.* grant a pension. **Ex.** *He was pensioned by the government.* —**pen'sion·er**, *n.* one who receives a pension.

people (1) [piy'pəl], *n.* 1. human beings; any groups of persons. **Ex.** *Ten people live in this house.* 2. all the persons of a particular nation, religion, race, etc. **Ex.** *The President spoke to the American people.* 3. the persons living in the same area, having the same interests, doing the same work, etc. **Ex.** *Farming people depend upon the harvest for their income.* 4. ordinary citizens; voters. **Ex.** *The mayor was popular with the people.* —*v.* populate. **Ex.** *The town was peopled with miners.*

pepper (3) [pep'ər], *n.* 1. a black and white hot-tasting season-ing made by crushing the berries of a certain plant. **Ex.** *This sauce needs more pepper.* 2. a plant that bears sweet or hot, red, green, yellow, white or black fruits that are eaten as vegetables. **Ex.** *She cut up a sweet red pepper to put into the salad.* —*v.* put pepper on. **Ex.** *The cook salted and peppered the meat.* —**pep'per·y**, *adj.* hot to taste.

pepper shaker [pep'ər šey'kər], *n.* a container for pepper, with holes in the top, from which the pepper is shaken. **Ex.** *She used the pepper shaker to season the salad.*

perceive (3) [pərsiyv'], *v.* 1. gain knowledge of or discover through one of the five senses. **Ex.** *He could not perceive any difference between the twins.* 2. understand; comprehend. **Ex.** *He finally perceived what the actual situation was.*

percent (2) [pərsent'], *n.* one part of or in every hundred. **Ex.** *Twenty-five percent equals 25/100ths; one hundred percent equals all. Percent is often written %.* —**per·cent'age**, *n.* a part of a quantity expressed as a percent. **Ex.** *What percent-age of your salary do you spend for rent?*

perception (4) [pərsep'šən], *n.* the capacity for or the act of perceiving. **Ex.** *She showed a keen perception of the problem.* —**per·cep'tive**, *adj.*

perch (4) [pərč'], *n.* 1. a place where a bird rests, such as the branch of a tree or the bar in a cage. **Ex.** *The bird flew down from its perch.* 2. any raised seat or position. **Ex.** *The boy looked down from his perch in the tree.* —*v.* rest on or place on, as on a perch. **Ex.** *The bird perched on the woman's shoulder.*

perfect (1) [pər'fikt], *adj.* 1. having no faults or weaknesses. **Ex.** *Each movement of the dancer was perfect.* 2. complete in all respects. **Ex.** *Her accounts were in perfect order.* 3. total; complete. **Ex.** *He was a perfect stranger.* 4. exact; correct. **Ex.** *The blue of her eyes and that of her dress were a perfect match.* —**per·fect'**, *v.* complete; improve as much as possible. **Ex.** *He is working to perfect his invention.* —**per·fec'tion**, *n.* —**per'fect·ly**, *adv.*

perform (2) [pərfôrm'], *v.* 1. do. **Ex.** *He always performs his work with care.* 2. entertain by acting, dancing, singing, etc. **Ex.** *All the actors performed their parts well.* —**per·form'er**, *n.* one who performs.

perfume (4) [pər'fyuwm, pərfyuwm'], *n.* 1. a sweet smell. **Ex.** *The perfume of roses filled the room.* 2. a liquid used to give a pleasant odor to body or clothing. **Ex.** *She bought a small bottle of perfume.* —**per·fume'**, *v.* scent with perfume. **Ex.** *The pine trees perfumed the mountain air.*

perhaps (1) [pərhæps'], *adv.* possibly; maybe. **Ex.** *Perhaps the letter will come today.*

peril (3) [pe:r'əl], *n.* 1. a condition of very great danger. **Ex.** *The ship was in peril from the storm.* 2. something dangerous. **Ex.** *The explorer was exposed to many perils.* —**per'il·ous**, *adj.* —**per'il·ous·ly**, *adv.*

period (1) [pi:r'iyəd], *n.* 1. a dot (.) used as a punctuation mark in writing and printing. See **Appendix I.** 2. a portion of time marked by certain events, developments, conditions, etc. **Ex.** *During the early period of her life, she lived abroad.* 3. any of the portions of time into which a game, a school day, etc. is divided. **Ex.** *He did his history assignment during a study period.* —**pe·ri·od'ic**, **pe·ri·od'i·cal**, *adj.* happening regularly or from time to time. —**pe·ri·od'i·cal·ly**, *adv.* —**pe·ri·od'i·cal**, *n.* a magazine or other publication that appears regularly but not every day.

perish (3) [pe:r'iš], *v.* die, especially as a result of violence, lack of food or fire. **Ex.** *More than a hundred people perished in the fire.* —**per'ish·able**, *adj.* likely to spoil quickly, as some food. **Ex.** *On the camping trip, we kept our perishable food in an ice chest.*

permanent (3) [pər'mənənt], *adj.* lasting indefinitely or for a very long time; enduring. **Ex.** *Brick walls are more permanent than wooden fences.* —**per·ma·nence,** *n.* the state of being permanent. —**per·ma·nent·ly,** *adv.*

permanent, *n.* **permanent wave** [pər'mənənt weyv'], a wave in the hair put in by means of heat or a chemical and lasting for several months.

permission (2) [pərmiš'ən], *n.* consent; act of permitting. **Ex.** *He asked his parents for their permission to use the car.* —**per·mis·si·ble,** *adj.* allowed; permitted. —**per·mis'sive,** *adj.* allowing much or too much freedom. **Ex.** *Their permissive attitude has created problems with their children.*

permit (2) [pərmit'], *v.* 1. allow to do. **Ex.** *Please permit the boy to leave class early.* 2. enable; make it possible. **Ex.** *Such small windows do not permit enough light to enter.* —**per'mit,** *n.* a written order allowing someone to do something. **Ex.** *You must have a permit to learn how to drive.*

perpendicular (5) [pər`pəndik'yələr], *adj.* 1. at a ninety-degree angle. **Ex.** *A square has four ninety-degree angles made by its four perpendicular sides.* 2. exactly straight up. **Ex.** *The flagpole was raised to a perpendicular position.* —*n.* a line at a ninety-degree angle to another line. **Ex.** *After the storm, the flagpole was no longer on a perpendicular.*

perpetual (4) [pərpeč'uwəl], *adj.* 1. continuing forever; for an unlimited time. **Ex.** *He has a perpetual calendar on his desk.* 2. continuing without interruption. **Ex.** *The perpetual quarreling made her nervous.* —**per·pet'u·al·ly,** *adv.* —**per·pet'u·ate,** *v.* cause to continue or to be remembered. **Ex.** *They erected a statue to perpetuate his memory.*

perplex (4) [pərpleks'], *v.* make a person uncertain or unsure; confuse. **Ex.** *She was perplexed by his strange behavior.* —**per·plex'i·ty,** *n.*

persecute (5) [pər'səkyuwt'], *v.* 1. cause to suffer constantly, especially for religious or political beliefs. **Ex.** *Some early religious leaders were persecuted by their enemies.* 2. cause distress by constantly bothering. **Ex.** *They were persecuted by unwelcome telephone calls day and night.* —**per·se·cu'tion,** *n.* the act of persecuting. —**per'se·cu·tor,** *n.* one who persecutes.

persist (4) [pərsist', pərzist'], *v.* 1. to be insistent on having one's own way in some activity. **Ex.** *The children persist in tracking mud into the house.* 2. continue steadily despite difficulties or resistance. **Ex.** *He persisted in the experiment until he was successful.* 3. remain; endure. **Ex.** *In spite of many washings, the stains persisted.* —**per·sist'ence**, *n.* —**per·sist'ent**, *adj.* —**per·sist'ent·ly**, *adv.*

person (1) [pər'sən], *n.* 1. a man, woman or child; a human being. **Ex.** *Four persons saw her leave.* 2. the body or its outward appearance. **Exs.** *There was no money on his person. That actor is appearing in person.* 3. in grammar any of three classes of pronouns. **Ex.** I *and* we *are pronouns in the first person;* you *is a pronoun in the second person;* he, she, it, *and* they *are pronouns in the third person.* See **A Brief Explanation of English Grammar.** —**per'son·a·ble**, *adj.* of pleasing appearance or personality. **Ex.** *She is a personable young lady.* —**per'son·i·fy**, *v.* 1. represent an idea or thing as a person or having the qualities of a person. **Ex.** *They personified their country as the motherland.* 2. think of a person as representing a quality, idea, etc. **Ex.** *To the boy, his mother personified goodness.* —**per'son·age**, *n.* a person, especially an important one. **Ex.** *The Vice President and other political personages are going to speak.*

personal (2) [pər'sənəl], *adj.* 1. private; of a particular person. **Ex.** *His secretary does not open his personal mail.* 2. having to do with the character, habits, conduct, etc. of a person. **Ex.** *His teacher gave him a good personal recommendation.* 3. done by oneself without help. **Ex.** *He made a personal effort to settle the quarrel.* 4. of the body, dress, etc. **Ex.** *She was very careful about her personal appearance.* 5. in grammar, describing the person speaking, the one spoken to, or the person or thing spoken about. **Ex.** You *and* I *are personal pronouns.* —**per'son·al·ly**, *adv.* by, of or as oneself. **Ex.** *I answered him personally.*

personality (2) [pər'sənæl'ətiy], *n.* 1. the characteristics of a person that make him or her different from everyone else. **Ex.** *I can see the writer's personality in what he writes.* 2. personal qualities that attract. **Ex.** *She was elected class president because of her personality.* 3. a person, especially one who is famous or unusual. **Ex.** *She invited personalities from the theater world to the party.*

personnel (pər'sənel'], *n.* the entire group of people employed by or working for an organization, company, etc.; the office concerned with their affairs such as policy, pay, records, etc. **Ex.** *The personnel in our company have very good health benefits.*

perspire [pərspayr'], *v.* give out moisture through the skin; sweat. **Ex.** *He perspired because he was dressed too warmly.* —**per'spi·ra'tion,** *n.* the act of giving out moisture through the skin; the moisture given out through the skin. **Ex.** *His shirt was soaked with perspiration.*

persuade (3) [pərsweyd'], *v.* 1. cause a person to do something, especially by reasoning, urging and advising. **Ex.** *They persuaded him to stay.* 2. cause to believe. **Ex.** *He persuaded me that he was right.* —**per·sua'sion,** *n.* —**per·sua'sive,** *adj.* able to persuade. **Ex.** *She has a persuasive way of talking.*

pessimism [pes'əmiz'əm], *n.* a feeling that the worst will always happen. **Ex.** *His pessimism depressed those around him.* —**pes'si·mist,** *n.* one who usually approaches everything with a gloomy or pessimistic outlook. —**pes'si·mis'tic,** *adj.* —**pes'si·mis'ti·cal·ly,** *adv.*

pest (5) [pest'], *n.* a troublesome person or thing, especially a harmful insect or small animal. **Ex.** *Garden pests were destroying the roses.* —**pest'er,** *v.* annoy; bother; trouble. **Ex.** *They pestered their mother to buy them ice cream cones.*

pet (3) [pet'], *n.* 1. a tame animal kept as a friend. **Ex.** *The children wanted a rabbit as a pet.* 2. a person treated with special kindness and affection. **Ex.** *The baby was the pet of the family.* —*adj.* 1. kept or treated as a pet. **Ex.** *He has a pet rooster.* 2. especially liked; favorite. **Ex.** *Politics is his pet subject.* —*v.* stroke gently. **Ex.** *She petted the cat.*

petition (4) [pətiš'ən], *n.* a request, carefully prepared, signed by a number of people and addressed to someone in authority. **Ex.** *Hundreds of citizens signed a petition to stop destruction of the town's historic buildings.* —*v.* 1. address a petition to. **Ex.** *The town petitioned the federal government for help after the flood.* 2. pray for; request earnestly. **Ex.** *The prisoner petitioned the governor for mercy.* —**pe·ti'tion·er,** *n.*

petroleum (5) [pətrow'liyəm], *n.* a natural oil found in the earth in certain parts of the world. **Ex.** *Gasoline and other fuels are made from petroleum.*

petty (4) [pet'iy], *adj.* 1. small; of little worth; not important. **Ex.** *Their quarrel began over a petty problem.* 2. narrow-minded;

mean. Ex. *None of us could endure his petty behavior.*
—**pet'ti·ness,** *n.*

pharmacist [far'məsist], *n.* a person who is trained to prepare
and dispense drugs and medicines. Ex. *She asked the pharmacist
if he could suggest something for her sore throat.* —**phar'ma·cy,**
n. a place where drugs and medicines are sold. Ex. *He took
his prescription to the pharmacy to be filled.*

phase (4) [feyz'], *n.* 1. a stage of development. Ex. *Primary
school is a phase in a child's education.* 2. one of the number
of views presented by something to the eye or the mind;
aspect; side. Ex. *He consulted an expert on each phase of the
problem.*

phenomenon (5) [fənam'ənan'], *n.* 1. any fact or happening
which can be observed or known through the senses. Ex.
*Students were studying the phenomenon of lightning in their
science class.* 2. anyone or anything that is extraordinary. Ex.
*When he was able to read at the age of three, he was regarded
as a phenomenon.* —**phe·nom'en·a,** *n.,pl.* —**phe·nom'en·al,** *adj.*

philosophy (3) [filas'əfiy], *n.* 1. the study that attempts to understand the basic principles of human thought about the meaning of life, the relationship of mind to matter and the problems
of right and wrong. Ex. *All first-year students at this college
are required to take a course in philosophy.* 2. a system of
principles derived from such study. Ex. *His philosophy was
based on the goodness of man.* — **phi·los'o·pher,** *n.* one who
teaches or understands philosophy. —**phil·o·soph'i·cal,** *adj.*
—**phil·o·soph'i·cal·ly,** *adv.*

phone (3) [fown'], *n.* telephone. Ex. *We talk on the phone every
day.* —*v.* talk to, using a telephone. Ex. *She phoned him
yesterday.*

photograph (2) [fow'təgræf'], *n.* a picture made with a camera.
Ex. *He showed us several photographs of his baby.* —*v.* make
a picture of, using a camera. Ex. *He photographed the building.* —**pho·tog'ra·pher,** *n.* one who takes photographs, especially as a profession. —**pho·to·graph'ic,** *adj.* —**pho·tog'ra·phy,**
n. the art and practice of taking photographs.

phrase (2) [freyz'], *n.* a group of related words found within many
sentences which by themselves do not form a complete sentence.

a, far; æ, am; e, get; ey, late; i, in; iy, see; ɔ, all; ow, go; u, put; uw, too;
ə, but, ago; ər, fur; aw, out; ay, life; oy, boy; ŋ, ring; θ, think; ð, that;
ž, measure; š, ship; j, edge; č, child.

Ex. *In the sentence, "There were many things to buy in the store,"* to buy *and* in the store *are both phrases.* —v. express in words. **Ex.** *He phrased his answer to the judge's question carefully.*

physical (2) [fiz'ikəl], *adj.* of the body. **Ex.** *The doctor's examination showed that the boy was in excellent physical condition.* 2. of nature; of matter; material; natural. **Ex.** *They are studying the physical features of the earth in their science class.* —**phys·i·cal·ly,** *adv.*

physician (3) [fiziš'ən], *n.* a doctor of medicine. **Ex.** *He consulted a second physician about the need for surgery.*

physics (3) [fiz'iks], *n.* the science of motion, matter and energy (heat, light, mechanics, electricity, etc.). **Ex.** *The students are learning about sound waves in their study of physics.* —**phys'i·cist,** *n.* a person who specializes in the study of physics.

piano (2) [piyæn'ow], *n.* a large musical instrument that gives out sound when wire strings are struck by small hammers operated from a keyboard. —**pi·an'ist,** *n.* one who plays the piano.

PIANO

pick (1) [pik'], *v.* 1. choose; select. **Ex.** *Pick any book you want.* 2. take up with the finger and thumb. **Ex.** *She picked a thread from her dress.* 3. gather; harvest. **Ex.** *They picked all the apples on the tree.* 4. open a lock with some instrument other than a key. **Ex.** *She picked the lock with a pin.* 5. empty secretly, as by a thief. **Ex.** *He had his pocket picked in a crowd.* —n. 1. the act of choosing; the thing chosen; a choice. **Ex.** *They went to the sale early to have their pick of the items.* 2. the best; those most desired. **Ex.** *The pick of his herd were prize-winning cows.* —**pick at,** eat with little appetite. **Ex.** *Because she was not hungry, she just picked at her lunch.* —**pick out,** identify; find. **Ex.** *She quickly picked out her son in the crowd.* —**pick up,** 1. raise in one's hand. **Ex.** *Pick up that book from the floor.* 2. learn; discover. **Ex.** *Where did you pick up that information?* 3. increase. **Ex.** *The car quickly picked up speed.* 4. clean up. **Ex.** *He picked up the room before we arrived.*

pick (1) [pik']), *n.* 1. a hand tool with a heavy curved head pointed at one or both ends which is used to break up the ground. 2. any tool or instrument for breaking, removing, etc. **Ex.** *He broke off a piece of ice with the ice pick.*

PICK 1

picket [pik'it], *n.* 1. a person who walks, usually carrying a sign, outside a business, factory etc. to protest something and often, if there is a strike, to prevent customers and nonstriking employees from entering. **Ex.** *The line of pickets almost blocked the sidewalk.* 2. a pointed piece of wood joined with like pieces by a horizontal bar and attached to a post, driven into the ground at either end, to form a fence. **Ex.** *The pickets in the fence around their house are three feet high.* —*v.* walk around or back and forth outside a business, factory, etc. to protest something.

pickle (4) [pik'əl], *n.* a vegetable or fruit preserved in salt water or vinegar and flavored with herbs, spices and sometimes sugar. **Ex.** *She served pickles with the cold sliced meat.* —*v.* preserve in flavored salt water or vinegar. **Ex.** *Is your mother going to pickle peaches this summer?*

picnic (4) [pik'nik], *n.* a meal planned for eating outdoors; a trip with such a meal. **Ex.** *They had their picnic beside the river.* —*v.* have a picnic. **Ex.** *We picnicked in the woods.* —**pic'nick·er,** *n.* one who picnics. **Ex.** *After lunch, the picknickers chose teams for a game of baseball.*

picture (1) [pik'čər], *n.* 1. a painting, drawing or photograph. **Ex.** *That picture of the President is often seen in the newspaper.* 2. that which strongly resembles another; an image. **Ex.** *She is the picture of her mother.* 3. a description. **Ex.** *The author gives a lively picture of his life as a sailor.* 4. a motion picture; a movie. **Ex.** *The whole family enjoyed the picture we saw last night.* —*v.* describe. **Ex.** *The speaker pictured the scene in colorful words.* —**pic·tor'i·al,** *adj.*

pie (2) [pay'], *n.* a baked dish consisting of a thin shell, and sometimes a cover, made of flour, water and cooking oil and filled with fruit, meat, etc. **Ex.** *She put the pie in the oven to bake.*

piece (1) [piys'], *n.* 1. an amount or part considered as an individual unit. **Ex.** *May I have a piece of candy, please?* 2. a part taken away from something larger. **Ex.** *She cut the pie into six pieces.* 3. a coin. **Ex.** *Can you change this fifty-cent piece?* —*v.* join together; make whole. **Ex.** *She pieced the broken dish together.* —**go to pieces,** become upset or excited. **Ex.** *He goes to pieces when I disagree with him.*

piecemeal [piys'miyl'], *adv.* one part at a time; piece by piece. **Ex.** *He put the machine together piecemeal in his spare time.*

piecework [piys'wərk'], *n*. work paid for by the number of pieces finished instead of by the amount of time taken to finish them. **Ex.** *She does piecework at home.*

pier (3) [pi:r'], *n*. a structure built over the water and used as a landing place for ships and boats. **Ex.** *The ship is at Pier Seven.*

pierce (4) [pi:rs'], *v*. 1. break into or through. **Ex.** *The knife had pierced the wall.* 2. make a hole or opening in. **Ex.** *The girls have been begging me to let them have their ears pierced.* 3. force a way through. **Ex.** *They tried to pierce the enemy's defenses.* 4. deeply or sharply affect the senses or feelings. **Ex.** *The sight of the hungry child pierced my heart.*

pig (2) [pig'], *n*. a farm animal with a broad nose and fat body, raised for its meat.

pigeon (3) [pij'ən], *n*. a bird with a small head, a broad body and short legs.

PIG

pile (2) [payl'], *n*. a number of things or a quantity of something placed or thrown together. **Ex.** *They put all the wood in a pile.* —*v*. form a pile or heap; come together. **Ex.** *The snow piled in front of the door.*

pilgrim (5) [pil'grim], *n*. one who travels to a holy place for religious purposes. **Ex.** *The pilgrims entered the church to pray.* —**Pil'grim**, *n*. one of the members of an English religious group that founded a colony in Massachusetts in 1620. —**pil'grim·age**, *n*. the travels of a pilgrim. **Ex.** *The holy men traveled many miles on their pilgrimage to the sacred city.*

PIGEON

pill (4) [pil'], *n*. medicine in a small rounded mass to be swallowed whole. **Ex.** *She took the pills and drank a glass of water.*

pillar (4) [pil'ər], *n*. a slender, upright structure used as a support, decoration or monument. **Ex.** *The roof of the porch was supported by brick pillars.*

pillow (2) [pil'ow], *n*. a bag filled with feathers, cotton, etc. used to support the head while resting or sleeping. **Ex.** *She sleeps with two pillows.* —**pil'lowcase,** *n*. a cloth covering, made of cotton, cotton and polyester, etc. and closed on three sides, for protecting a pillow. **Ex.** *She changed the sheets and pillowcases on all the beds.*

PILLAR

pilot (3) [pay'lət], *n*. 1. a person who controls an airplane while it is flying. **Ex.** *The pilot landed the airplane safely in spite of the fog.* 2. a person who steers a ship into or out of a harbor or through difficult places. —*v*. act as a pilot. **Ex.** *He skillfully piloted the ship into the harbor.* —*adj*. serving as a test or trial. **Ex.** *If the pilot sales project is successful, we will expand our sales area.*

pin (3) [pin'], *n*. 1. a short, sharp piece of wire with a round or flat head used for a fastening. **Ex.** *She used a pin to attach the flower to her dress.* 2. an ornament for the clothing fastened with a pointed wire and a clasp. **Ex.** *He gave her a jeweled pin for her birthday.* —*v*. 1. fasten or attach with a pin. **Ex.** *She pinned the pieces of the dress together and then tried it on.* 2. hold firmly in one position. **Ex.** *The fallen tree pinned the man to the ground.* —**pin down,** force to tell what actually happened, is planned, is wanted, etc. **Ex.** *We must pin him down about how the money was spent.*

pinch (4) [pinč'], *v*. 1. force together the tips of the finger and thumbs; press upon from opposite sides in any way. **Ex.** *He pinched the fruit to see if it was soft.* 2. press upon in a painful manner. **Ex.** *The door pinched her finger.* —*n*. the forcing together between the tips of the thumb and a finger; a pressing upon from opposite sides. **Ex.** *She gave her little brother a pinch.*

pine (2) [payn'], *n*. a tree that is green throughout the year and has leaves shaped like needles. **Ex.** *The ground was covered with needles shed from the pine trees.*

pineapple (5) [payn'æp'əl], *n*. a large, oval-shaped, sweet, juicy tropical fruit with a rough, prickly skin.

PINEAPPLE

pinecone [payn'kown'], *n*. the cone-shaped fruit of the pine tree.

ping-pong [piŋ' paŋ], *n*. a variation of the game of tennis, played on a special table divided by a low net over which the players hit a small ball back and forth using short paddles. **Ex.** *Let's see if you and I can beat my two brothers at a game of ping pong.*

PINE CONE

a, far; æ, am; e, get; ey, late; i, in; iy, see; ɔ, all; ow, go; u, put; uw, too; ə, but, ago; ər, fur; aw, out; ay, life; oy, boy; ŋ, ring; θ, think; ð, that; ž, measure; š, ship; j, edge; č, child.

pink (2) [piŋk'], *n.* pale red. Ex. *The artist used a lot of pink in her picture of the small girls.* —*adj.* pale red. Ex. *Her favorite flower is a pink rose.*

pinpoint [pin'poynt'], *v.* point to the exact place. Ex. *On the map he pinpointed the places where we were going.*

pint (3) [paynt'], *n.* a measure of volume which equals half a quart; two cups. Ex. *We have less than a pint of milk left.* See **Weights and Measures.**

pioneer (3) [pay'əni:r'], *n.* 1. one who leads the way; the first settler in a new region. Ex. *The early pioneers encountered many dangers.* 2. one who leads the way in any field or activity. Ex. *John Glenn was one of the pioneers in space travel.* —*v.* open a way for others to follow; act as a pioneer. Ex. *Those who pioneer in space travel are greatly admired.*

pipe (2) [payp'], *n.* 1. a tube of metal, glass, etc., used to carry liquids and gases from one place to another. Ex. *The water froze in the pipes during the cold weather.* 2. a tube with a bowl at one end in which tobacco is smoked. Ex. *His father smokes a pipe.* —*v.* send through pipes. Ex. *Water and gas are piped into the house.*

pirate (4) [pay'rət], *n.* one who robs at sea. Ex. *The pirates attacked the merchant ship.* —*v.* illegally copy and publish or use the work of another. Ex. *His book was pirated in several countries.* —**pi'ra·cy,** *n.* the act of pirating.

pistol (4) [pis'təl], *n.* a small gun held and fired with one hand. Ex. *The robber had a pistol hidden under his coat.*

pit (3) [pit'], *n.* 1. a hole in the ground. Ex. *Men are digging sand from a pit near the road.* 2. any hole or low place in a surface. Ex. *The rust had made pits in the metal.* —*v.* make a low place in a surface. Ex. *The ship's anchor was pitted by rust.*

pit (3) [pit'], *n.* the hard, stony center containing the seed in peaches, plums and similar fruit; a stone. Ex. *This device can be used to remove the pits from cherries or olives.* —*v.* remove the hard stony center from fruit. Ex. *She bought some canned cherries that had been pitted to make a pie filling.*

pitch (3) [pič'], *v.* 1. set up and make ready for occupation. Ex. *We pitched our tent under the trees.* 2. throw; toss. Ex. *He pitched the hay onto the wagon.* 3. throw a ball in a ball game. Ex. *The team needs someone who can pitch.* 4. rise and fall by turns; plunge. **Ex.** *The ship pitched violently in the storm.* —*n.* 1. the act of throwing, as a ball. **Ex.** *The first pitch of the game was very fast.* 2. a rising and falling motion; a plunge. **Ex.** *The sudden pitch of the ship knocked him off his feet.* 3. a point or degree. **Ex.** *Feelings are at a high pitch of excitement.* 4. the degree of slope or slant. **Ex.** *The pitch of the roof was very steep.* —**pitch'er,** *n.* one who throws or pitches, especially in a ball game. **Ex.** *The pitcher raised his arm to pitch the ball.*

pitcher (5) [pič'ər], *n.* a container with a handle for holding and pouring liquids. **Ex.** *She put a pitcher of iced tea on the table.*

PITCHER

pitfall [pit'fɔl'], *n.* hidden or unexpected danger or problem. **Ex.** *There are many pitfalls in his plan.*

pity (2) [pit'iy], *n.* 1. sorrow or sadness for the suffering of another. **Ex.** *She felt pity for the starving people.* 2. a reason for sorrow or regret. **Ex.** *What a pity it is that you missed him!* —*v.* feel sorrow or sympathy for another. **Ex.** *We pitied the sick child.* —**have pity on, take pity on,** feel pity for. **Ex.** *Have pity on the poor boy.*

pizza [piyt'sə], *n.* a usually round, flat shell of dough baked with a filling of cheese, tomato sauce and sometimes a variety of other things, such as small pieces of spiced meat, mushrooms, olives, etc. **Ex.** *We had pizza for lunch at a fast-food restaurant.*

place (1) [pleys'], *n.* 1. space; region; area. **Ex.** *There are still many places about which we know very little.* 2. location; the portion of space occupied by a person or thing. **Ex.** *The place for those books is on the second shelf.* 3. a country, city or other particular region. **Ex.** *Write the name of the place where you were born.* 4. a house, apartment or other dwelling. **Ex.** *They have a pleasant place in the country.* 5. a building or other area used for a particular purpose. **Ex.** *There are many nice little eating places near our office.* 6. a position or location previously occupied or used by another; a space not occupied. **Ex.** *This building will be torn down and another built in its place.* 7. job; rank; position. **Ex.** *People in high places are concerned about this problem.* 8. a particular point or part. **Ex.** *He complained of a sore place on his arm.* —*v.* 1. put in a particular spot, position, etc. **Ex.** *She placed her hand on his shoulder.* 2. entrust. **Ex.** *She placed her confi-*

dence in him. **—in place of,** for; instead of. **Ex.** *I went in place of him.* **—take place,** happen; occur. **Ex.** *When is the wedding going to take place?*

plague (4) [pleyg'], *n.* 1. a disease that spreads rapidly and causes much sickness and death. **Ex.** *Thousands of people died during the plague.* 2. something that causes terrible trouble or suffering. **Ex.** *Floods have been a plague in this region for years.* —*v.* trouble; cause to suffer. **Ex.** *A cough plagued her all winter.*

plain (1) [pleyn'], *adj.* 1. having little or no decoration. **Ex.** *She wore a plain black dress.* 2. not rich; simple. **Ex.** *The food was plain but good.* 3. not handsome; not pretty. **Ex.** *She was a very plain girl.* 4. ordinary. **Ex.** *He was a plain working man.* 5. easy to do; simple. **Ex.** *She can do plain sewing.* 6. frank; honest. **Ex.** *His plain remarks sometimes offend people.* 7. easy to understand. **Ex.** *Her meaning was perfectly plain.* 8. easy to see. **Ex.** *The house was in plain sight.* —*n.* a large unbroken area of fairly flat land. **Ex.** *A great deal of wheat is grown on these plains.* **—plain'ly,** *adv.* obviously; clearly; simply. **—plain'ness,** *n.* lack of ornament; frankness.

plan (1) [plæn'], *n.* 1. a previously thought-out method of doing something. **Ex.** *Our plan is to go to the mountains.* 2. a drawing showing the shape or relation between the parts of anything. **Ex.** *The plans for the new building are ready.* —*v.* 1. consider a method of doing something. **Ex.** *She carefully planned each detail of the party.* 2. make a drawing showing the shape of or relation between the parts of anything. **Ex.** *He planned the streets of the new town.* 3. intend; have as a purpose. **Ex.** *She plans to go on to college after finishing high school.* **—plan'ner,** *n.* one who plans.

plane (3) [pleyn'], *n.* 1. level of development or progress. **Ex.** *Their civilization reached a very high plane.* 2. airplane. **Ex.** *He flies his own plane.*

planet [plæn'it], *n.* one of the nine large heavenly bodies revolving around the sun. **Ex.** *He had hoped to discover evidence of living beings on another planet.* **—plan'e·tar·y,** *adj.*

plank (4) [plæŋk'], *n.* 1. a long, flat, thick piece of wood. **Ex.** *The bridge was made of rough planks.* 2. a principle of a political party. **Ex.** *The candidate explained each plank in his party's platform.*

plant (1) [plænt'], *n.* 1. a life form that is usually held to the ground by roots, does not have feelings and makes food from soil, water and air. **Ex.** *He could name almost any kind of plant from grasses to trees.* 2. any small form of vegetable life with a stem softer than that of a tree or bush. **Ex.** *She had many kinds of plants in the garden.* 3. the machines, buildings, etc. of a factory, business or institution. **Ex.** *Automobiles are made in that plant.* —*v.* put into the ground to grow. **Ex.** *He planted vegetables in his garden.* —**plant'er**, *n.* 1. one who plants. 2. owner of a plantation.

PLANT 2

plantation (5) [plæntey'šən], *n.* a large farm or estate where crops such as bananas, coffee or rice are grown and where the workers often live on the estate. **Ex.** *He managed a cotton plantation.*

plaster (4) [plæs'tər], *n.* a soft mixture of powdered stone, sand and water that hardens as it dries and is used for coating walls and ceilings. **Ex.** *The walls cannot be painted until the plaster is dry.* —*v.* cover, as with plaster; spread over thickly. **Ex.** *They plastered the walls with announcements of coming shows.* —**plas'ter·er**, *n.* one who plasters.

plastic (3) [plæs'tik], *n.* a mixture made from chemicals that can be shaped and hardened into many useful things. **Ex.** *That toy car is made of plastic.* —*adj.* 1. made of plastic. **Ex.** *They took plastic dishes on their camping trip.* 2. capable of being molded or shaped. **Ex.** *Students in the art class began by shaping figures from plastic material.* 3. having to do with molding or forming. **Ex.** *This statue is a good example of plastic art.*

plate (2) [pleyt'], *n.* 1. a shallow, usually round, dish from which food is eaten or served. 2. a smooth, flat thin piece of metal, usually one on which words have been carved. **Ex.** *His name is on a brass plate on the door.* 3. a thin sheet of metal used to cover a surface. **Ex.** *This tray is not solid silver; it is only plate.* 4. a sheet of metal used in the process of printing words or pictures. —*v.* cover with a thin layer of metal. **Ex.** *These cups are plated with gold.*

PLATE 1

plateau (4) [plætow'], *n.* a wide, level stretch of land higher than the surrounding area. **Ex.** *The airport was built on a plateau.*

platform (3) [plæt'fɔrm'], *n.* 1. a flat, raised surface usually for speakers, actors, etc. **Ex.** *The president stood on the platform to give his speech.* 2. the statement of policy or plans which a political party presents at elections. **Ex.** *The candidate explained his party's platform.*

play (1) [pley'], *v.* 1. amuse oneself; have fun; engage in sports or games. **Ex.** *The children were playing outside the school.* 2. take part in a game. **Ex.** *The boys played ball.* 3. act in a show. **Ex.** *She played his sister in that show.* 4. perform on a musical instrument. **Ex.** *He plays the drums.* —*n.* 1. amusement; sport. **Ex.** *The children must have some time for play.* 2. a story written in conversational form to be acted on a stage. **Ex.** *The actor's performance in the play was a great success.* —**play'er,** *n.* one who plays. —**play'ful,** *adj.* joking; full of fun. —**play down, play up,** make something appear less or more important. **Ex.** *He played down his role in solving the problem.* —**play into someone's hands,** act in a way that gives someone else an advantage. **Ex.** *Getting angry played into her hands.* —**play on, play upon,** take unfair advantage of another's weakness or feelings. **Ex.** *He played on her love for the child to get money from her.* —**playground,** *n.* a park; a place especially prepared for children to play in. —**playmate,** *n.* a friend with whom a child plays. **Ex.** *His playmate could not come out today.*

plea (4) [pliy'], *n.* an appeal; an earnest request. **Ex.** *An old friend answered their plea for help.* 2. something said in defense; an excuse. **Ex.** *She stayed at home with the plea that she had a headache.* 3. the answer made in court by an accused person concerning the charge against him. **Ex.** *The murderer's plea was self-defense.*

plead (3) [pliyd'], *v.* 1. ask earnestly; beg. **Ex.** *He pleaded for mercy.* 2. answer in court a charge against one. **Ex.** *The accused woman pleaded not guilty.*

pleasant (1) [plez'ənt], *adj.* 1. nice; enjoyable, happy. **Ex.** *We had a pleasant visit with our friend.* 2. having a nice or friendly look, manner, etc. **Ex.** *He was always very pleasant when we met.* —**pleas'ant·ly,** *adv.* —**pleas'ant·ness,** *n.*

please (1) [pliyz'], *v.* 1. give enjoyment to; make one happy. **Ex.** *They did everything they could to please their guests.* 2. desire; wish; choose. **Ex.** *You may do what you please with your own* *money*. 3. be so good as to; be so kind as to. **Ex.** *Please open the door.* **—pleas'ing,** *adj*.

pleasure (1) [plež'ər], *n*. 1. state of being delighted or satisfied. **Ex.** *He found pleasure in listening to music.* 2. anything that gives delight, enjoyment or a satisfying feeling. **Ex.** *Going to the theater was one of her many pleasures.* 3. that which satisfies the senses. **Ex.** *He lives only for pleasure.* **—plea'sur·a·ble,** *adj*.

pledge (3) [plej'], *n*. 1. a serious promise or agreement. **Ex.** *I give my pledge that I will help you.* 2. anything given as security or as a sign that something will be done. **Ex.** *He gave his watch as a pledge to the moneylender.* *—v.* 1. promise to give. **Ex.** *Each person at the dinner pledged a sum of money for the new hospital wing.* 2. make a serious promise. **Ex.** *He pledged to marry her when he returned.*

plenty (2) [plen'tiy], *n*. all that is needed; a large enough amount. **Ex.** *They had plenty of money for their trip.* **—plen'ti·ful,** *adj*.

pliers [play'ərz], *n*. a tool made of two crossed, joined pieces of metal with the two longer ends acting as handles and the two shorter ends acting as a pair of jaws for holding things tightly or bending or cutting them. **Ex.** *He twisted the wires together with the pliers.*

plight (5) [playt'], *n*. a difficult or dangerous situation. **Ex.** *The freezing weather made their plight more serious.*

PLIERS

plot (3) [plat'], *n*. 1. a secret plan to do something wrong or unlawful. **Ex.** *The policeman learned of a plot to bomb the courthouse.* 2. the main story in a novel, play, etc. **Ex.** *This mystery story has an exciting plot.* 3. a small piece of ground. **Ex.** *He intends to build a house on this plot.* *—v.* 1. make secret plans. **Ex.** *The men were plotting to rob a bank.* 2. make a plan or map of. **Ex.** *Some of the islands had not been plotted before.*

plow (2) [plaw'], *n*. a farm tool used to loosen and turn up soil for planting. *—v.* 1. turn up the soil with a plow. **Ex.** *Late in the fall, the farmer began to plow his fields.* 2. move through anything with difficulty, in the manner of plowing. **Ex.** *The ship plowed through the stormy sea.*

PLOW

pluck (3) [plək'], v. 1. pull off or out; pick. Ex. *She plucked a rose from the bush.* 2. pull the feathers out of. Ex. *She was plucking a chicken.* —n. 1. courage. Ex. *It took pluck for him to express his opinion.* 2. a pull. Ex. *He felt a pluck at his sleeve.*

plug (5) [pləg'], n. 1. an object used to block or close a hole. Ex. *He pulled the plug in the sink to let the water out.* 2. a device used to connect a lamp, iron, etc. to a source of electricity. Ex. *That lamp needs a new plug.* 3. an upright and closed pipe on a street from which water can be taken to fight a fire, to water the street, etc.; fire plug. —v. block or close with something. Ex. *They plugged the leak in the boat with a rag wound around a piece of wood.*

PLUG 2

plum (4) [pləm'], n. 1. a juicy, smooth-skinned round fruit having a small pit. Ex. *She bought a pound of red plums.* 2. the purplish-red color of some plums. Ex. *She wore a plum-colored dress.*

plumbing (4) [pləm'iŋ], n. the pipes and connections for water and waste in a building. Ex. *The plumbing is not working, so we have no water in the house.* —**plumb'er**, n. one whose work is installing and repairing plumbing.

plume (4) [pluwm'], n. 1. a feather, especially a long or soft full one. Ex. *Some birds used to be hunted for their plumes.* 2. an ornament made of feathers. Ex. *She trimmed her hat with a plume.* —v. 1. straighten or smooth its feathers. Ex. *The bird plumed itself.* 2. feel pride in; be satisfied with oneself. Ex. *He plumed himself on his excellent record.* —**plum'age**, n. a bird's feathers.

plump (4) [pləmp'], adj. rounded in form; somewhat fat. Ex. *The girl had a plump figure.* —v. make or become rounded or fat. Ex. *She plumped the feather pillows.* —**plump'ness**, n.

plunder (4) [plən'dər], v. rob or take by force. Ex. *Enemy troops plundered the town.* —n. 1. the act of robbing by force. Ex. *Guards were on duty to prevent plunder.* 2. goods taken by force. Ex. *The thieves divided the plunder among themselves.* —**plun'der·er**, n. one who plunders.

plunge (2) [plənj'], v. 1. thrust or throw into suddenly. Ex. *He plunged the red-hot metal into the water.* 2. bring suddenly to some condition. **Ex.** *The news plunged the family into sadness.* 3. leap; throw oneself. **Ex.** *At the sound of the starting gun, the horse plunged forward.* 4. rush; move recklessly. **Ex.** *He plunged through the window.* —*n.* 1. the act of plunging. **Ex.** *He made a plunge for the door.* 2. a swim. **Ex.** *We like to take a plunge in the ocean before breakfast.* — **plung'er,** *n.* 1. any device that operates with a plunging motion. 2. one who plunges.

plural (5) [plu:r'əl], *adj.* more than one. **Ex.** *The plural form of a word in English often ends in* s *or* es. —*n.* the form of the word showing that more than one is meant. **Ex.** *The plural of* man *is* men.

plus (4) [pləs'], *prep.* 1. increased by; added to. **Ex.** *Two plus five equals seven.* 2. in addition. **Ex.** *Her willingness to work plus her pleasing personality made her a nice addition to the staff.* —*adj.* more than zero; added to. **Ex.** *This shows as a plus three on the chart.* —*n.* in mathematics, the plus sign: +. **Ex.** *2 + 5 = 7.*

plywood [play'wud], *n.* a wide, strong board made of several thin layers of wood, each placed at right angles to the next, glued and then pressed together. **Ex.** *He covered the back of the bookcase with a sheet of plywood.*

pneumonia [nuwmow'niyə], *n.* a disease in which the lungs become inflamed and it is difficult for the patient to breathe. **Ex.** *She almost died of pneumonia.*

pocket (2) [pak'it], *n.* a small, open bag sewed into a garment for carrying small articles, money, etc. **Ex.** *He carried a comb in his coat pocket.* —*v.* 1. put into a pocket. **Ex.** *She pocketed her money.* 2. take something not one's own. **Ex.** *He pocketed some of his employer's money.* —*adj.* small enough to be carried in a pocket. **Ex.** *He often carried a pocket dictionary.*

pocketbook (pak'itbuk'), *n.* 1. a woman's handbag or purse. **Ex.** *She took a lipstick from her pocketbook.* 2. a small paperback book. **Ex.** *He bought several pocketbooks to read during the trip.*

pod [pad'], *n.* the long narrow case containing the seeds of certain plants such as beans. **Ex.** *We like to serve pea pods as a vegetable with roast chicken.*

a, far; æ, am; e, get; ey, late; i, in; iy, see; ɔ, all; ow, go; u, put; uw, too; ə, but, ago; ər, fur; aw, out; ay, life; oy, boy; ŋ, ring; θ, think; ð, that; ž, measure; š, ship; j, edge; č, child.

poem (2) [pow'əm], *n.* a special arrangement of words and sounds that expresses strong feeling and appeals to the imagination. **Ex.** *He wrote many short poems.*

poet (2) [pow'it], *n.* one who writes poems. **Ex.** *She read several of her poems to us.* —**po·et'ic,** *adj.* 1. having the qualities of poetry. 2. referring to a poet or poem.

poetry (2) [pow'itriy], *n.* 1. the art of writing poems. **Ex.** *The teacher praised the student's efforts at poetry.* 2. poems or verse taken as a whole. **Ex.** *A volume of her poetry has just been published.* 3. something like poetry in quality or feeling. **Ex.** *His painting captured the poetry of the bird's flight.*

point (1) [poynt'], *n.* 1. the sharp tip of anything that becomes smaller toward the end. **Ex.** *This pencil has a sharp point.* 2. exact place or position. **Ex.** *My house is at the point where the road turns.* 3. a particular degree; a limit. **Ex.** *The water was brought to the boiling point.* 4. a unit of counting or scoring. **Ex.** *Our team won three points to their two.* 5. the most important idea or fact. **Ex.** *I did not understand the point of his story.* 6. a piece of land which extends out into the water. **Ex.** *Many small boats were near the point.* —*v.* 1. direct one's finger toward. **Ex.** *Point to the one you want.* 2. aim. **Ex.** *The boys were told never to point the gun at anyone.* —**poin'ted,** *adj.* 1. having a sharp end. **Ex.** *A pointed stick can be dangerous.* 2. directed at. **Ex.** *He made pointed comments about her.* —**point'er,** *n.* 1. one who points. 2. anything, such as a stick, used for pointing. **Ex.** *The teacher placed the pointer on the map at the place where the first settlers had landed.* —**beside the point,** not concerned with the subject being discussed. **Ex.** *His remarks were beside the point.* —**make a point of,** treat as important; stress. **Ex.** *He made a point of inviting her to speak.* —**on the point of,** about to do something. **Ex.** *I was on the point of leaving when you arrived.* —**stretch a point,** make an exception to the rule. **Ex.** *Her parents stretched a point and allowed her to stay up beyond her bedtime.*

point-blank [poynt'blæŋk'], *adj.* 1. aimed directly at and very close to the target, as with a gun. **Ex.** *The gun was fired at point-blank range.* 2. stated in very clear, blunt terms. **Ex.** *His answer was a point-blank no.*

point of view [poynt' əv vyuw'], a way in which or a position from which something is looked at or considered. **Ex.** *From my point of view, living this far from the city is impractical.*

poise (4) [poyz'], *n.* 1. assurance; dignity; self-control. **Ex.** *He has great poise as a public speaker.* 2. balance; steadiness. **Ex.** *The performers in the high-wire act at the circus displayed amazing poise.* —*v.* 1. balance or be balanced. **Ex.** *The girl poised the basket on her head.* 2. support in a motionless state; seem to be supported. **Ex.** *The eagle was poised in the air.*

poison (2) [poy'zən], *n.* 1. a substance which can destroy life or injure health. **Ex.** *They used poison to kill the rats.* 2. anything that harms, damages or destroys. **Ex.** *The poison of jealousy ruined their relationship.* —*v.* 1. damage or destroy with poison; put poison into. **Ex.** *The dead man had been poisoned.* 2. harm; damage; destroy. **Ex.** *She poisoned her son's mind against his wife.* —**poi'son·ous,** *adj.* able to cause death; able to harm, damage or destroy. —**poi'son·er,** *n.* one who poisons.

poke (4) [powk'], *v.* 1. push or thrust sharply against or into with something. **Ex.** *He poked me in the ribs with his elbow.* 2. cause by pushing or thrusting something. **Ex.** *He accidentally poked a hole in the thin wall.* —*n.* 1. act of poking; thrust. **Ex.** *She gave me a poke to wake me up.* 2. one who moves or acts slowly. **Ex.** *Don't be such a poke!* —**pok'er,** *n.* 1. a metal rod for stirring a fire. 2. a game of cards. —**poke along,** move slowly. **Ex.** *He poked along all day and did not finish his work.* —**poke around,** search in a disorganized way. **Ex.** *She poked around under the bed looking for her shoes.* —**poke fun at,** tease; ridicule. **Ex.** *They poked fun at the way he walked.*

pole (2) [powl'], *n.* 1. a long, slender piece of wood or other material. **Ex.** *We took our fishing poles with us.* 2. either end of an imaginary line that goes through the center of a round body, such as the earth, and around which the body turns. **Ex.** *The earth has a north pole and a south pole.* —*v.* push with a pole. **Ex.** *We poled the boat through the shallow water.* —**po'lar,** *adj.* of or having to do with the North Pole or the South Pole. **Ex.** *They returned from their polar journey in good health.*

police (2) [pəliys'], *n.* 1. the department of government, the duty of which is to guard the public, keep order, make certain that people obey the law, etc. **Ex.** *This is a matter for the police.* 2. the members of such a department. **Ex.** *The police are looking for the killer.* —*v.* control; protect with police. **Ex.** *We will have to police this area more closely.*

policeman [pəliys'mən], *n*. **policewoman** [pəliys'wum`ə`n], *n*. a member of the police force.

policy (2) [pal'əsiy'], *n*. 1. a course of action adopted and followed by a government, a political party, a club, etc. **Ex.** *He is writing a book about the foreign policy of his country.* 2. method or principle of doing things. **Ex.** *The policy of this store is to please the customer.* 3. a written insurance contract. **Ex.** *If he dies, his family will get $100,000 from his life insurance policy.*

polish (3) [pal'iš], *v*. 1. make clean and shiny by rubbing. **Ex.** *We polished the furniture before the guests arrived.* 2. improve. **Ex.** *He polished the story before sending it to his publishers.* —*n*. 1. a substance used to give smoothness and shine. **Ex.** *I need a can of silver polish.* 2. smoothness and shine. **Ex.** *The shoes of that marine always have a fine polish.* 3. correct or elegant manners and speech. **Ex.** *That charming young girl speaks with polish.*

polite (2) [pəlayt'], *adj*. 1. showing thoughtfulness for others in manners and speech. **Ex.** *She was polite to everyone she met.* 2. cultured; possessing fine taste. **Ex.** *Music, literature and art are valued in polite society.* —**po·lite'ly**, *adv*. in a manner showing thoughtfulness for others. **Ex.** *He politely held the door open for the ladies.* —**po·lite'ness**, *n*.

political science [pəlit'ikəl say'əns], *n*. the science of government. **Ex.** *He studied political science at the university.*

politics (2) [pal'ətiks'], *n*. 1. the science dealing with the different forms of government. **Ex.** *He is a student of politics.* 2. the affairs and activities of those who are in public office or who seek such an office; the profession of those engaged in government. **Ex.** *The President has spent most of his life in politics.* —**po·lit'i·cal**, *adj*. —**po·lit'i·cal·ly**, *adv*. —**pol'i·ti·cian**, *n*. a person holding or seeking public office whose career is in politics.

poll (4) [powl'], *n*. 1. the voting at an election. **Ex.** *The poll showed him to be the winner.* 2. the number of votes cast. **Ex.** *The poll in this election was the largest ever recorded.* 3. a list of persons, such as voters, taxpayers, etc. **Ex.** *His name was listed on the poll.* 4. an opinion survey. **Ex.** *A poll was taken to learn which morning television news program was the most popular.* —*v*. 1. record votes. **Ex.** *An unusually large number of votes was polled.* 2. receive a certain number of votes. **Ex.** *The winner polled more than two thirds of the votes.* 3. ask people their opinions. **Ex.** *They polled the store customers about their favorite brand of laundry soap.* —**polls'**, *n.* a place where people go to vote.

pollute [pəluwt'], *v.* make dirty or impure; release harmful, dangerous or unpleasant waste matter into the air, soil or water. **Ex.** *Gasoline fumes pollute the city air.* —**pol·lu'tion**, *n.*

polyester [pal`iyəs'tər], *n.* a man-made fiber, sometimes combined with natural fibers such as cotton and wool, used in making cloth that wears well and does not wrinkle easily. **Ex.** *I always buy sheets and pillowcases made of cotton and polyester.*

pond (2) [pand'], *n.* a pool; a body of water smaller than a lake. **Ex.** *The boys went fishing in the pond.*

ponder (5) [pan'dər], *v.* think about deeply; consider seriously. **Ex.** *They pondered their next move.*

pony (3) [pow'niy], *n.* a kind of horse that is small even when fully grown. **Ex.** *The children liked to ride the pony.*

pool (2) [puwl'], *n.* 1. a small amount of any spilled liquid. **Ex.** *A pool of water formed on the floor under the leak.* 2. a small body of water, such as a pond. **Ex.** *They planted water lilies in the pool.* 3. a tank for swimming. **Ex.** *We ate lunch beside the pool.*

pool (2) [puwl'], *n.* a group of people, machines, supplies, etc. used in common. **Ex.** *Until we can find a permanent secretary for you, someone from the pool will be assigned to you.* —*v.* collect into a group for use in common. **Ex.** *They pooled their money to buy a birthday gift.*

poor (1) [pu:r'], *adj.* 1. lacking money, goods or means of support. **Ex.** *Her family is poor and needs help.* 2. not of good quality; bad. **Ex.** *The harvest is small because the soil is poor.* 3. unfortunate. **Ex.** *The poor child is tired.* —*n.* people with little or no money. **Ex.** *They gave generously to the poor.* —**poor'ly**, *adv.*

pop (4) [pap'], *v.* 1. make a short, quick sound like a gunshot. **Ex.** *The balloon popped loudly as it burst.* 2. move, come in or go out suddenly. **Ex.** *He popped in for a moment and then* *left.* —*n.* 1. short, quick sound like a gunshot. **Ex.** *We heard a pop as the cork came out of the bottle.* 2. a bubbling drink that is not alcoholic; flavored soda water. **Ex.** *He bought a bottle of orange pop.*

popcorn [pap'kɔrn'], *n.* the dried seeds from the ear of a special kind of corn which, when heated, puff up into a soft white mass. **Ex.** *The children bought some popcorn to eat while they watched the movie.*

popular (2) [pap'yələr], *adj.* 1. well-liked; having many friends. **Ex.** *He is one of the most popular boys in the school.* 2. generally favored among the public. **Ex.** *She enjoys popular music.* 3. of, representing or engaged in by the mass of people. **Ex.** *His newspaper articles created popular interest in the need for better schools.* 4. suited to the means of ordinary people. **Ex.** *The tickets were sold at popular prices.* —**pop·u·lar·ly**, *adv.* by people in general. **Ex.** *It is popularly accepted that he will win the election.* —**pop·u·lar'i·ty**, *n.* condition of being well liked. **Ex.** *Her popularity was due to her friendly manner to everyone.*

population (2) [pap'yəley'šən], *n.* the total number of persons living in a country, place, etc. **Ex.** *The world population is growing very fast.*—**pop'u·late**, *v.* provide with people. **Ex.** *Factory workers populated the town.*—**pop'u·lous**, *adj.* having many people. **Ex.** *China is a very populous country.*

porcelain [pɔr'səlin], *n.* 1. a high-quality, hard thin pottery with a glasslike finish through which some light can pass. 2. any of various objects made of this kind of pottery. **Ex.** *We were given several pieces of porcelain as wedding gifts.*

porch (2) [pɔrč'], *n.* 1. a covered approach to a house or other building. **Ex.** *We stood on the porch to greet our guests.* 2. a screened or open room attached to the main building. **Ex.** *They had lunch on the side porch.*

pore (5) [pɔ:r'], *v.* study or look at with deep and steady attention. **Ex.** *He pored over the map for hours.*

pore (5) [pɔ:r'], *n.* a very tiny opening in the skin, a leaf, etc. through which water or air can pass. **Ex.** *The hot bath opened his pores and caused him to sweat.*

pork (3) [pɔrk'], *n.* the flesh of a pig used as food. **Ex.** *They had roast pork for dinner.*

port (2) [pɔrt'], *n.* 1. a city, town, etc. where ships load or unload. **Ex.** *The sailor had visited many ports.* 2. a harbor; a place along the coast where ships may stop for safety in a storm. **Ex.** *The storm forced the ship into port.* 3. the side of the ship on one's left when one is facing the front. **Ex.** *He turned the ship to port.*

portable [pɔr'təbəl], *adj.* small enough to be easily carried. **Ex.** *He brought a portable radio with him.*

porter (4) [pɔr'tər], *n.* 1. one employed to carry a traveler's suitcases at railroad stations, airports, etc. **Ex.** *The hotel porter brought their bags to their room.* 2. an attendant on a train. **Ex.** *The porter made up the passenger's bed.*

porthole [pɔrt'howl'], *n.* an opening or window in the side of a ship for light and air. **Ex.** *She could see the stars through her porthole.*

portion (2) [pɔr'šən], *n.* 1. part or share. **Ex.** *Her portion of the family property was the largest.* 2. one serving of food. **Ex.** *She gave him a large portion of pie.* —*v.* divide into shares; distribute as shares. **Ex.** *He portioned out the food.*

portrait (4) [pɔr'treyt', pɔr'trit], *n.* 1. a picture of a person, especially of the face. **Ex.** *She had her portrait painted by a famous artist.* 2. a description; a picture in words. **Ex.** *The writer painted a brilliant portrait of society life.*

portray (5) [pɔrtrey'], *v.* 1. represent by a drawing, statue, etc. **Ex.** *The artist portrayed liberty in his painting as a woman carrying a gleaming light.* 2. represent in a stage play. **Ex.** *My brother portrayed the hero.* 3. describe in words. **Ex.** *The author in his latest novel portrayed the life of a teacher.*

pose (4) [powz'], *v.* 1. hold or place in a suitable position for a photographer or artist. **Ex.** *They posed for a photograph in front of their house.* 2. represent oneself to be what one is not. **Ex.** *He posed as a doctor.* 3. present for consideration. **Ex.** *Their unexpected arrival posed a problem of what to feed them for dinner.* —*n.* 1. attitude or position held for a picture. **Ex.** *The artist told his model to hold her pose a minute longer.* 2. act of pretending to have a quality which one does not have. **Ex.** *His unfriendly manner is a pose to hide his shyness.*

position (1) [pəziš'ən], *n.* 1. place; location. **Ex.** *The captain checked the ship's position.* 2. the way of holding the body. **Ex.** *She sat in a comfortable position.* 3. the way in which a thing is set or placed. **Ex.** *He placed the books in an upright position.* 4. job; employment. **Ex.** *She hopes to find a teaching position.* 5. social or professional rank. **Ex.** *The judge holds a position of trust in our community.* 6. attitude; point of view. **Ex.** *What is her position concerning the new taxes?*

positive (3) [paz'ətiv], *adj.* 1. expressed with certainty; clear and definite. **Ex.** *The guard has positive instructions not to admit anyone.* 2. very sure; certain. **Ex.** *He is positive that he saw them.* 3. real; practical; worth the time or effort needed. **Ex.** *We are hoping for some positive results from our work.* —**pos'i·tive·ly,** *adv.*

possess (2) [pəzes'], *v.* 1. have; own. **Ex.** *They no longer possess much land.* 2. have as a part or quality of self. **Ex.** *Our dog possesses a keen sense of smell.* 3. control; be controlled by; get or have power over. **Ex.** *Anger possessed him.* —**pos·ses'sion,** *n.* 1. ownership. 2. that which is possessed. —**pos·ses'sive,** *adj.* desiring to keep or own something; acting like an owner. **Ex.** *Her attitude toward him was very possessive.* —**pos·ses'sor,** *n.* one who possesses.

possessive case [pəzes'iv keys'], in English grammar, the form of a noun which shows ownership, usually shown by adding *'s* to the noun. **Ex.** *In the sentence, "John's clothes are new,"* John's *is the possessive case of* John. The following are personal possessive pronouns: *my, mine; your, yours; his, hers; our, ours; their, theirs; and its.* See **A Brief Explanation of English Grammar.**

possible (1) [pas'əbəl], *adj.* 1. capable of being done. **Ex.** *There are two possible ways of getting here.* 2. capable of being or happening; likely to happen. **Ex.** *Rain is possible this afternoon.* —**pos'si·bly,** *adv.* —**pos'si·bil'i·ty,** *n.*

post- (2) [powst'], *prefix.* after; following. **Exs.** *War, postwar; graduate, postgraduate.*

post (2) [powst'], *n.* 1. a long, strong piece of wood or other material used as a support. **Ex.** *The fence posts were set ten feet apart.* 2. a job, office or position. **Ex.** *He holds an important government post.* 3. the place or station of a person on duty. **Ex.** *The guard cannot leave his post.* 4. a camp; a fort. **Ex.** *A wall surrounds the army post.* —*v.* 1. place in a mail box. **Ex.** *These letters must be posted today.* 2. put a sign or notice on a post, wall, etc. **Ex.** *Announcements of* *the show were posted everywhere.* 3. assign as a guard; assign to a particular position. **Ex.** *A soldier was posted at the door of the President's office.* **—post'al,** *adj.* of mail or the mail service. **Ex.** *The two countries signed a postal agreement.*

postage (5) [pows'tij], *n.* the charge for sending a letter or other matter by mail. **Ex.** *How much did the postage cost?*

postage stamp [pows'tij stæmp'], *n.* a small piece of paper with a design that one buys and fastens to a letter to pay for mailing.

post card [powst' kard'], *n.* a commercially produced card often with a picture on one side and space on the other for a message, an address and a postage stamp. **Ex.** *Please don't forget to send me a post card while you're away on vacation.*

poster [pow'stər], *n.* a large printed notice or sign displayed for the public to see. **Ex.** *That is a beautiful poster announcing the coming art exhibition.*

postman [powst'mən], *n.* a person who delivers mail or works in a post office.

postmark [powst'mark`], *n.* a mark placed on a letter that shows the date and place of mailing.

postmaster [powstmæs`ter], *n.* **postmistress** [powst'mis'tris], *n.* a person in charge of a post office.

post office [powst' ɔːf'is], *n.* a place where one can mail letters and packages, buy stamps, etc.

postpaid [powst'peyd'], *adj.* with the cost of mailing already paid. **Ex.** *We will send the package to you postpaid.*

postpone (5) [powstpown'], *v.* delay action until a later time. **Ex.** *They postponed their trip because of bad weather.* **—post·pone'ment,** *n.*

posture [pas'čər], *n.* the way in which one typically holds one's body when standing, walking or sitting. **Ex.** *He always has an erect posture.*

pot (1) [pat'], *n.* 1. a deep, round vessel, usually made of metal, which is used for cooking. **Ex.** *She had a pot of soup cooking on the stove.* 2. any vessel of a similar shape. **Ex.** *A pot of flowers had been placed beside the door.* **—v.** put into a pot. **Ex.** *She potted the plant.*

---

a, far; æ, am; e, get; ey, late; i, in; iy, see; ɔ, all; ow, go; u, put; uw, too; ə, but, ago; ər, fur; aw, out; ay, life; oy, boy; ŋ, ring; θ, think; ð, that; ž, measure; š, ship; ǰ, edge; č, child.

potato (2) [pətey'tow], *n.* one of the thick rounded parts growing underground on the roots of certain vegetables, usually having light brown or red skin and a white edible inner part. —**sweet potato,** *n.* a yellow root growth, similar to a white potato, grown in warm climates.

POTATO

potent (5) [pow'tənt], *adj.* 1. powerful; mighty. **Ex.** *He was a potent ruler in control of a large state.* 2. producing a strong effect. **Ex.** *His potent arguments won support for his proposal.* —**po'ten·cy,** *n.* strength. **Ex.** *What is the potency of that drug?*

potential (5) [pəten'šəl], *adj.* possible, though not yet actually in existence or fully in use. **Ex.** *Education will help her to develop her potential abilities.* —*n.* something that is capable of being developed. **Ex.** *He seems to have potential as a leader.*

pothole [pat'howl], *n.* a hole in the surface of a street, road, etc. caused by heavy usage and weather conditions. **Ex.** *The drivers in this city are plagued by potholes.*

pottery [pat'əriy], *n.* plates, cups, saucers, bowls, pots and decorative pieces, formed from clay, which is then baked to make it hard. **Ex.** *What artist made that beautiful pottery vase?*

pouch (5) [pawč'], *n.* 1. a bag, a sack. **Ex.** *He kept his tobacco in a leather pouch.* 2. a fold of skin or flesh shaped like a bag. **Ex.** *The squirrel filled its cheek pouches with nuts.*

poultry (4) [powl'triy], *n.* domestic farm birds, such as chickens, ducks and geese, raised for food. **Ex.** *That market has fresh poultry for sale.*

pound (2) [pawnd'], *n.* a unit of weight equal to sixteen ounces. **Ex.** *She bought a pound of butter.* See **Weight and Measures.**

pound (2) [pawnd'], *v.* 1. strike repeatedly with great force. **Ex.** *He pounded a nail into the wall.* 2. break, crush or soften by beating. **Ex.** *She pounded the meat to make it tender.* 3. beat heavily. **Ex.** *His heart pounded.*

pour (2) [pɔːr'], *v.* 1. cause to flow continuously. **Ex.** *She poured milk from the container into the glasses.* 2. flow as if in a continuous stream. **Ex.** *People poured out of the office building.* 3. rain heavily. **Ex.** *It has been pouring all morning.*

poverty (3) [pa'vərtiy], *n.* 1. the state or condition of being poor and needy. **Ex.** *Because of their poverty, they often did not* *have enough to eat.* 2. a scarcity or lack of something needed. **Ex.** *The poor crops were due to the poverty of the soil.*

powder (2) [paw'dər], *n.* a dry material in the form of fine, loose pieces. **Ex.** *She bought some face powder.* —*v.* 1. apply powder or something in a powdered form. **Ex.** *She powdered her nose.* 2. crush or grind into fine, loose pieces. **Ex.** *She powdered nuts for use in the cake frosting.* —**pow'der·y,** *adj.*

power (1) [paw'ər], *n.* 1. ability to act. **Ex.** *Most birds have the power to fly.* 2. force; energy in use. **Ex.** *The power of the hammer blows shaped the hot metal.* 3. authority; influence. **Ex.** *They voted to give the police more power.* 4. force or energy applied or that can be applied to work. **Ex.** *Water power turned the mill wheel.* 5. a person, group, etc. that has authority, strength or influence. **Ex.** *That nation is a world power.* —*v.* provide power to. **Ex.** *This saw is powered by electricity.* —**pow'er·ful,** *adj.* strong. —**pow'er plant', pow'er sta'tion,** the machinery or a building with its machinery used for creating power, especially electricity.

practical (2) [præk'tikəl], *adj.* 1. useful. **Ex.** *Her clothes were more practical than elegant.* 2. able to be used; that will work. **Ex.** *His plan was interesting but not practical.* 3. trained by or gained from practice; learned through experience or doing. **Ex.** *He has no practical experience in the business.* —**prac'ti·cal·i·ty,** *n.* —**prac'ti·cal·ly,** *adv.* 1. in a practical manner. **Ex.** *If we approach the problem practically, we will have a better chance of success.* 2. almost; in effect. **Ex.** *The work is practically finished.*

practice (2) [præk'tis], *v.* 1. do again and again in order to learn or become skilled. **Ex.** *He is practicing the typing exercises.* 2. do or use often. **Ex.** *Those people practice strange customs.* 3. work at or follow a profession or occupation. **Ex.** *Her mother practices law.* —*n.* 1. doing repeatedly in order to learn or become skilled. **Ex.** *He spends an hour at music practice daily.* 2. something done regularly or often. **Ex.** *It is our practice to have dinner early.* 3. actual performance. **Ex.** *She knew that the practice of medicine would require many years of training.*

prairie (5) [pre:r'iy], *n.* an almost treeless piece of level, grassy ground with good soil. **Ex.** *The prairie seemed ideal for growing wheat.*

praise (2) [preyz'], *n.* an expression of approval or admiration in words; an expression of worship. **Ex.** *His efforts are worthy of* *high praise.* —*v.* 1. express approval or admiration. **Ex.** *They praised his honesty.* 2. worship. **Ex.** *The people of the tribe praised their god in song.*

pray (2) [prey'], *v.* make a request to a god or spirit. **Ex.** *They prayed for rain.*

prayer (2) [pre:r'], *n.* 1. a request to a god or spirit. **Ex.** *She felt that her prayers had been answered.* 2. a set of words used in worship. **Ex.** *The children learned their prayers from their parents.*

pre- (2) [priy], *prefix.* before in time, position, rank, etc. **Exs.** *Dawn, predawn; arrange, prearrange; pay, prepay.*

preach (3) [priyč'], *v.* 1. give a speech or talk devoted to religion. **Ex.** *Many people went to church to hear him preach.* 2. advise or urge, especially when the advice is not requested. **Ex.** *He felt that his teachers preached too much.* —**preach'er,** *n.*

precaution (5) [prikɔː'šən], *n.* something to do to avoid future accidents, danger or trouble. **Ex.** *They took heavy coats with them as a precaution against the possibility of cold weather.* —**pre·cau'tion·ar·y,** *adj.*

precede (4) [priysiyd'], *v.* be first before another in position, time or importance. **Ex.** *A long dry spell preceded the rain.* —**pre'ced·ence,** *n.* that which is before another in position, time or importance. **Ex.** *The need for food took precedence over everything else.* —**prec'e·dent,** *n.* a previous decision, act, etc. that is used as a guide in later action. **Ex.** *The precedents all indicated that the judge should send him to jail.* —**pre·ced'ing,** *adj.* being or going first. **Ex.** *Turn to the preceding page and read paragraph one.*

precious (2) [preš'əs], *adj.* 1. of great price or value; expensive. **Ex.** *The ring was set with precious stones.* 2. loved; dear. **Ex.** *She had precious memories of her childhood.*

precipice (5) [pres'əpis], *n.* a very high, steep, almost vertical cliff or ledge. **Ex.** *He fell over the precipice and was killed.* —**pre·cip'i·tous,** *adj.* extremely steep; like a precipice.

precise (4) [prisays'], *adj.* 1. exact; definite. **Ex.** *He gave a precise account of how much money he had spent.* 2. extremely careful in following rules. **Ex.** *The principal was very precise in his administration of the school.* —**pre·cise'ly,** *adv.* exactly. **Ex.** *She said precisely what she meant.* —**pre·ci'sion,** *n.* exactness.

predecessor (5) [pred'əses'ər], *n.* one who goes before another. **Ex.** *His predecessor left because he was not happy in the job.*

predict (5) [pridikt'], *v.* tell in advance what will or is likely to happen. **Ex.** *He predicted rain for tomorrow.* —**pre·dic'tion,** *n.* the act of predicting; the thing predicted. **Ex.** *The sales predictions for the next six months are optimistic.* —**pre·dict'able,** *adj.* able to be predicted. **Ex.** *It was predictable that she would want to go.*

preface (3) [pref'əs], *n.* an introduction to a book or speech. **Ex.** *In the preface, the author explained why he had written the book.* —*v.* provide with an introduction. **Ex.** *He prefaced his lecture with a humorous story.*

prefer (2) [prifə:r'], *v.* want one thing more than one wants another or others; have a higher regard for. **Ex.** *I prefer oranges to bananas.* —**pref'er·a·bly,** *adv.* —**pref'er·ence,** *n.* —**pref'er·en'tial,** *adj.* showing, giving, etc. partiality or favor. **Ex.** *The boys complained about preferential treatment being given to the girls.*

prefix (5) [priy'fiks'], *n.* a letter or letters placed before or joined to the beginning of a word which affects or changes the meaning of that word. **Ex.** *The letters -dis, co-, inter- and ex- are common prefixes.*

pregnant (5) [preg'nənt], *adj.* bearing a child within the body; expecting to give birth to a baby or babies. **Ex.** *She gained too much weight when she was pregnant.* —**preg'nan·cy,** *n.*

prehistoric [priy'histɔ:r'ik], *adj.* concerned with or of ancient times before history was recorded. **Ex.** *Many kinds of prehistoric animals no longer exist.*

prejudice (4) [prej'ədis], *n.* an opinion, usually unfavorable, formed without sufficient knowledge, thought or reason. **Ex.** *He had a prejudice against popular music.* —*v.* 1. cause to have a prejudice. **Ex.** *The judge warned the lawyer not to prejudice the jury.* 2. damage. **Ex.** *His carelessness prejudiced his chances for advancement.* —**prej'u·di'cial,** *adj.*

preliminary (5) [prilim'əner'iy], *adj.* coming before or preparing for the main event. **Ex.** *We must make some preliminary plans for the graduation program.* —*n.* anything done before or in preparation for. **Ex.** *As a preliminary, he assembled the necessary tools.*

premature [priy'mǝtyu:r', priy'mǝču:r'], *adj*. happening or being done before the proper time. **Ex.** *It is premature to say now who will win the election.*

premier (5) [primiyr'], *n*. the chief official of certain governments. **Ex.** *The people cheered the new premier.*

preoccupy [priyak'yǝpay'], *v*. have one's mind concerned with one thing to the exclusion of others. **Ex.** *What is preoccupying him?*

prepare (1) [pripe:r'], *v*. 1. make ready. **Ex.** *The farmer prepared the ground for planting.* 2. complete; put together. **Ex.** *She was preparing dinner.* —**prep'a·ra·tion,** *n*. 1. the act of preparing. **Ex.** *The preparations took a long time.* 2. the thing prepared. **Ex.** *He used his own preparation to polish the furniture.* – **pre·par'a·to·ry,** *adj*.

preposition (5) [prep'ǝziš'en], *n*. a word with a meaning of relationship, position, direction, time, etc. which is used to join a noun or pronoun to some other word in the sentence. A prepositional phrase may be used as an adjective or adverb. **Ex.** *In the sentence, "The man with the suitcase went into the station,"* with *and* into *are prepositions.* The prepositional phrase *with the suitcase* is used as an adjective to describe the man, while the phrase *into the station* is used as an abverb to describe where he went. —**prep'o·si'tion·al,** *adj*. See **A Brief Explanation of English Grammar.**

prescribe (4) [priskrayb'], *v*. direct the use of as a treatment or cure. **Ex.** *The doctor prescribed some medicine for her cold.* —**pre·scrip'tion,** *n*. that which is prescribed.

present (1) [prez'ǝnt], *adj*. 1. being at a certain place; being in view. **Ex.** *He was present at the meeting.* 2. now; for now. **Ex.** *My present teacher is a woman.* —*n*. the present time. **Ex.** *She is not here at present but will return next week.* —**pres'ent·ly,** *adv*. 1. soon, in a short period of time from now. **Ex.** *He will be home presently.* 2. now; at present. **Ex.** *She is presently visiting friends.* —**pres'ence,** *n*. 1. the fact of being present; attendance. **Ex.** *Your presence is requested at the dinner.* 2. the area where a person is. **Ex.** *They did not want to argue in the presence of their children.*

present (1) [prizent'], *v*. 1. offer for consideration. **Ex.** *No new ideas were presented at the meeting.* 2. introduce. **Ex.** *They presented their friends to their houseguest.* 3. show; display; exhibit. **Ex.** *The man presented his ticket at the door and was* *allowed to enter.* —**pres'ent,** *n.* a gift. **Ex.** *She bought a birthday present for her sister.*

preserve (2) [prizerv'], *v.* 1. keep from injury or harm. **Ex.** *His quick thinking preserved his life.* 2. keep in good condition. **Ex.** *The city decided to preserve the beautiful old building as a museum.* 3. keep; save. **Ex.** *Even though she was poor, she was able to preserve her dignity.* 4. prepare food to resist spoiling by canning, salting, etc. **Ex.** *She preserved many jars of fruit this past summer.* —*n.* a place set apart for the protection of animals, trees, etc. **Ex.** *We saw many deer in the preserve.* —**pre·serves',** *n.* fruit cooked with sugar to prevent spoiling. **Ex.** *She gave us a jar of her homemade peach preserves.* —**pres'er·va'tion,** *n.* —**pre·serv'a·tive,** *n.* something, usually a chemical, used to prevent spoiling. **Ex.** *She added a preservative to the vegetables she was canning.*

preside (5) [prizayd'], *v.* 1. have the place of authority at a meeting; be in charge of a meeting. **Ex.** *The mayor presided over the town meeting.* 2. direct; control. **Ex.** *His grandmother presided over the family.*

president (1) [prez'ədənt], *n.* 1. the chief officer of a republic. **Ex.** *He is the President of the United States.* 2. the chief officer of a club, a business firm, etc. **Ex.** *He was elected president of his company.* —**pres'i·den·cy,** *n.* office or position of president. **Ex.** *George Washington was the first man elected to the presidency of the United States.*

press (1) [pres'], *v.* 1. act upon by weight or force; push. **Ex.** *He pressed the button and waited for the door to open.* 2. take the juice from by using weight or force. **Ex.** *They were pressing grapes to make wine.* 3. hold close; embrace. **Ex.** *The frightened mother pressed the child to her heart.* 4. make clothes smooth and flat by heat and weight. **Ex.** *The tailor pressed the suit.* 5. urge; insist on. **Ex.** *They pressed us to stay for dinner.* 6. push against each other. **Ex.** *Hundreds of people pressed into the theater.* —*n.* 1. the act of pressing or being pressed; pressure. **Ex.** *Because of the press of business, he hired more help.* 2. any machine for pressing. **Ex.** *The apple juice flowed from the press.* 3. a place where printing is done. **Ex.** *There are several commercial presses in this area.* 4. newspapers, magazines, etc. and those who write for them considered as a group. **Ex.** *The press was well represented at the meeting.*

pressure (3) [preš'ər], *n.* 1. the act of pressing or being pressed; force of weight. **Ex.** *The pressure of his shoe became painful.*

2. demands; burden; strain. **Ex.** *The pressure of her work made her neglect many other things.* 3. the force with which air, steam, water, etc. pushes against a certain area. **Ex.** *The air pressure at sea level is nearly fifteen pounds per square inch.* —**pres'sur·ize,** *v.* maintain air pressure at a desired level, as in airplanes at high altitude.

prestige (5) [prestiyž', prestiyj'], *n.* reputation or influence gained from success, rank, character, etc. **Ex.** *The doctor had great prestige among the members of his profession.*

presume (4) [prizuwm'], *v.* 1. suppose; assume. **Ex.** *I presume you are tired after your long trip.* 2. do something without authority or permission; be too bold; dare. **Ex.** *The stranger presumed to call me by my first name.* —**pre·sum'a·bly,** *adv.* probably; it is reasonable to suppose that. **Ex.** *Presumably he will come with us.* —**pre·sump'tion,** *n.* that which is supposed or assumed. **Ex.** *His plans are based on the presumption that it will not rain tomorrow.* —**pre·sump'tu·ous,** *adj.* too bold; too forward.

pretend (3) [pritend'], *v.* act as if something not real is real; imagine. **Ex.** *The children pretended they were on a ship.* 2. make a false appearance of; claim falsely. **Ex.** *He pretended to be asleep.* —**pre'tense,** *n.* act of pretending. **Ex.** *She made a pretense of working.* —**pre·ten'tious,** *adj.* claiming or demanding a position, an importance, a recognition, etc. that one does not deserve. **Ex.** *Her pretentious behavior offended her fellow workers.*

pretty (1) [prit'iy], *adj.* delicate, graceful and pleasing in appearance. **Ex.** *The young men watched the pretty girls walking by.*

prevail (3) [priveyl'], *v.* 1. triumph; succeed. **Ex.** *He believed his cause would prevail against all opposition.* 2. become common; exist generally. **Ex.** *He refuses to work under the conditions that now prevail.* —**pre·vail'ing,** *adj.* current; most frequent. **Ex.** *The prevailing wind is from the south.* —**prevail upon,** persuade. **Ex.** *He prevailed upon his son to stay in school.*

prevalent (4) [prev'ələnt], *adj.* existing in many places; occurring often. **Ex.** *Rainy weather has been prevalent throughout the month.* —**prev'a·lence,** *n.*

prevent (2) [privent'], *v.* 1. keep something from occurring. **Ex.** *A heavy rain prevented the fire from spreading.* 2. keep from doing or happening. **Ex.** *The arrival of unexpected guests* *prevented us from leaving.* —pre·ven'tion, *n.* —pre·ven'tive, *adj.* planned to prevent something such as illness. Ex. *They took preventive measures against the spread of the disease.*

preview [priy'vyuw'], *n.* a showing before the time that something will be shown generally; that which gives information about what will happen later. Ex. *Before the movie was shown to the students, there was a preview for the teachers.*

previous (3) [priy'viyəs], *adj.* coming or occurring before something else. Ex. *We had met on a previous occasion.* —pre'vi·ous·ly, *adv.*

prey (5) [prey'], *n.* 1. an animal sought and seized for food by another animal. Ex. *The tiger leaped upon its prey.* 2. a person or thing unable to resist someone or something harmful. Exs. *The rich widow was an easy prey for fortune hunters. The old house fell prey to rot and insects.* —v. 1. seek for and take by force. Ex. *The wolves preyed upon the sheep.* 2. disturb or trouble greatly. Ex. *Her debts preyed upon her mind.*

price (1) [prays'], *n.* 1. the amount of money for which anything is bought, sold or offered for sale. Ex. *What is the price of that book?* 2. the amount of effort, feeling, etc. needed to obtain something. Ex. *Loneliness was the price of his success.* —v. set the amount of money that one wants to receive for something. Ex. *The merchant priced the oranges at five for a dollar.* —price'less, *adj.* having very great value. Ex. *That is a priceless work of art.*

prick (4) [prik'], *v.* 1. pierce with something sharp so as to make a small hole. Ex. *She pricked her finger on a thorn.* 2. have or cause a sharp mental pain. Ex. *The memory of cheating on his examination pricked his conscience.* —n. 1. a small hole made by a needle, pin or some similar sharp thing. Ex. *The pricks in the leather formed a pattern.* 2. the feeling of being stuck with something sharp. Ex. *The prick of the needle made her cry in pain.* —prick up one's ears, 1. in the case of animals, raise the ears to listen. 2. in the case of humans, give full attention to something being said or heard. Ex. *The boy pricked up his ears when he heard the word candy.*

pride (2) [prayd'], *n.* 1. self-respect. Ex. *I had too much pride to ask for help.* 2. a pleasant, rewarding feeling of doing or having done something of value. **Ex.** *She takes pride in doing good work.* 3. the belief that one's importance or worth is greater than it truly is. **Ex.** *Pride kept him from doing any work with his hands.* —*v.* 1. have a feeling of self-respect; take pleasure in doing something well. **Ex.** *They prided themselves on their reputation for honesty.* 2. give in to the belief that one's importance or worth is greater than it truly is. **Ex.** *They prided themselves on their wealth.*

priest (3) [priyst'], *n.* one who devotes his life to the service of a god within a formal religious organization. **Ex.** *A priest conducted the church service.* —**priest'ly,** *adj.* —**priest'hood,** *n.* the occupation of being a priest.

primarily (2) [praymer'əliy, pray'mer`əliy], *adv.* originally; mainly. **Ex.** *The book was written primarily for children.*

primary (3) [pray'mer`iy, pray'məriy], *adj.* 1. chief; principal; most important. **Ex.** *His primary reason for studying was to get a better job.* 2. first in order, position or time; preparatory for something else. **Ex.** *My younger brother attends primary school.* —*n.* an election within a political party to choose candidates for a later general election. **Ex.** *He won the nomination in the Democratic primary.*

prime (5) [praym'], *adj.* 1. requiring attention before all else. **Ex.** *Safety is a matter of prime importance in this factory.* 2. best in excellence or quality. **Ex.** *That restaurant serves only prime beef.* —*n.* the period of greatest activity or strength; the age when one is most healthy, strong, etc. **Ex.** *He was in the prime of life.* —*v.* make ready; prepare. **Ex.** *They primed the wood with a first coat of paint.*

prime minister [praym' min'əstər], *n.* the head of government in countries with a parliamentary system.

primer [prim'ər], *n.* a book which gives basic information in a very simple way for children or for those who are first learning about a subject. **Ex.** *This book is a primer on how to repair automobiles.*

primitive (5) [prim'ətive], *adj.* 1. of or concerning the earliest times before recorded history. **Ex.** *Primitive people often lived in caves.* 2. having qualities like those of the earliest times; not developed; simple. **Ex.** *He was born in a primitive log cabin.* —**prim'i·tive·ly,** *adv.*

prince (2) [prins'], *n.* 1. the son of a king or queen. **Ex.** *The young prince will someday become king.* 2. a male ruler. **Ex.**

The prince ruled his people fairly. —**prince'ly,** *adj.* like that of a prince. Ex. *The rich man lived in a princely style.*

princess (2) [prin'ses], *n.* 1. the daughter of a king or queen. Ex. *The princess will become queen if her parents die without having a son.* 2. the wife of a prince.

principal (2) [prin'səpəl], *adj.* first in importance; highest in rank or value; chief. Ex. *Our principal needs are food, water, clothing and shelter.* —*n.* 1. the head of a school. Ex. *The principal called a meeting of the teachers.* 2. a sum of money loaned, saved or borrowed on which one receives or pays interest. Ex. *They have paid off almost all of the principal of the loan on their house.* 3. one who is important or most important. Ex. *Who are the principals in this play?* —**prin'ci-pal-ly,** *adv.* mostly.

principle (2) [prin'səpəl], *n.* 1. a custom or rule that guides the way one acts. Ex. *It is against her principles to smoke.* 2. a truth or ideal upon which a system or method is based. Ex. *The students are studying the principles of democracy.* 3. a law of nature; a law by which something operates. Ex. *The flow of water in a river can be explained by the principle of gravity.*

print (2) [print'], *v.* 1. press a block of metal, wood, etc. on paper so as to make a copy of the marks or letters that are on the block appear on the paper. Ex. *This dictionary was first printed in the United States.* 2. write in letters that look as if they were printed. Ex. *He slowly printed his name.* 3. publish. Ex. *News about the fire was printed in the morning paper.* 4. make photographic pictures. Ex. *Will you please print this roll of film as soon as possible?* —*n.* 1. letters made by printing. Ex. *Can you read the small print?* 2. a copy of a picture or design made by printing on paper, cloth, etc. Ex. *I have prints of that artist's paintings.* 3. a mark made by pressing. Ex. *His fingerprints are on the glass.* —**print'er,** *n.* 1. one whose work or business is printing. 2. a machine that prints. —**print'ing,** *n.* the making of printed material. —**in print,** published; available for sale. Ex. *I see that your book is still in print.* —**out of print,** no longer available for sale. Ex. *His book has been out of print for several years.* —**printing press,** *n.* a machine that prints.

prior (4) [pray'ər], *adj., adv.* earlier than in time, position, rank, etc. Ex. *They lived abroad prior to the war.* —**pri-or'i-ty,** *n.* 1. the right to receive attention, service, etc. ahead of others. Ex.

People with physical difficulties have priority in boarding this plane. 2. condition requiring attention, consideration, etc., ahead of others. **Ex.** *You will have to decide which of these problems has first priority.*

prison (2) [priz'ən], *n.* a public place where one is kept while awaiting trial or to which one is sent as punishment. **Ex.** *The thief was sent to prison for five years.* —**pris'on·er**, *n.* 1. one who is held in prison. **Ex.** *The prisoners were permitted to see visitors once a month.* 2. a military person taken by the enemy; one held against his will. **Ex.** *The captured soldiers were prisoners of war.*

private (2) [pray'vit], *adj.* 1. belonging to a particular person or group. **Ex.** *This garden is private property.* 2. personal. **Ex.** *I do not discuss private matters in front of strangers.* 3. not in public life. **Ex.** *He has left the government and become a private citizen.* 4. secret. **Ex.** *He told no one his private thoughts.* —*n.* an enlisted military person of the lowest rank. **Ex.** *The general began his military life as a private.* —**pri'vate·ly**, *adv.* —**pri'va·cy**, *n.* the condition of being private.

private school [pray'vit skuwl'], *n.* any school not owned and controlled by the federal, state or local government in the United States. **Ex.** *Although it's expensive, they send their children to a private school.*

privilege (2) [priv'əlij], *n.* special advantage, benefit or favor enjoyed by an individual or group. **Ex.** *The oldest son was given the privilege of borrowing the family car.* —**priv'i·leged**, *adj.* enjoying a special favor, benefit or advantage. **Ex.** *We are privileged to have a distinguished guest with us tonight.*

prize (2) [prayz'], *n.* 1. something offered or won in a contest. **Ex.** *The boy received a prize for his painting.* 2. anything worth making a great effort to obtain; anything highly desirable. **Ex.** *That house with its view of the sea is considered a prize.* —*adj.* worthy of a prize; having received a prize. **Ex.** *He has written a prize novel.* —*v.* value highly. **Ex.** *There is one stamp in her collection that she prizes more than the others.*

prize fight [prayz' fayt'], *n.* a boxing contest. —**prize'fight·er**, *n.* one who boxes for pay.

pro- (3) [prow], *prefix.* for; in favor of; in place of. **Exs.** American, pro-American; noun, pronoun.

probable (1) [prab'əbəl], *adj.* likely to be or occur; possible. **Ex.** *A storm is probable today.* —**prob'a·bly**, *adv.* —**prob'a·bil'i·ty**, *n.*

probe (5) [prowb'], *n*. an examination into the facts concerning something. **Ex.** *The tax department is making a probe into his financial activities.* —*v*. examine; question or search thoroughly. **Ex.** *They probed his former political activities.*

problem (1) [prab'ləm], *n*. 1. a difficult question or situation, the answer or solution to which is not known or certain. **Ex.** *The city discussed the problem of low-income housing.* 2. a question given for solution. **Ex.** *The mathematics teacher gave the children five problems to solve.*

procedure (3) [prəsiy'jər], *n*. a particular way of acting or doing something. **Ex.** *The new secretary learned the office procedures very quickly.*

proceed (2) [prəsiyd', prow'siyd], *v*. 1. move or go forward again. **Ex.** *They proceeded on their journey after lunch.* 2. begin and continue an activity. **Ex.** *They proceeded rapidly with the work.* —**pro·ceed'ing**, *n*. activity; activities. **Ex.** *The proceeding at the school was a brief one.* —**pro·ceed'ings**, *n.pl.* action taken against someone in a court of law. **Ex.** *He started proceedings to regain possession of the house.*

proceeds [prow'siydz], *n.pl.* profits resulting from a business or a money-raising activity. **Ex.** *The proceeds from the benefit dinner and dance were enough to fund two scholarships.*

process (2) [pras'es], *n*. 1. a method of producing something in a series of operations. **Ex.** *The process of making rubber was developed many years ago.* 2. a continuous series of natural changes. **Ex.** *His illness had delayed the process of his growth.* 3. a continuous series of actions directed toward a particular result. **Ex.** *They are just beginning the process of learning a foreign language.* 4. course; passing of time. **Ex.** *We are now in the process of moving to a new house.* —*v*. 1. treat or prepare by some process. **Ex.** *Both butter and cheese are processed at that plant.* 2. manage papers, records, etc. by organizing and reviewing them, noting actions taken, etc. **Ex.** *Not all of the students' applications have been processed yet.*

procession (3) [prəseš'ən], *n*. persons or things in a group moving forward in an orderly and formal manner. **Ex.** *We were among those in the wedding procession.*

a, far; æ, am; e, get; ey, late; i, in; iy, see; ɔ, all; ow, go; u, put; uw, too; ə, but, ago; ər, fur; aw, out; ay, life; oy, boy; ŋ, ring; θ, think; ð, that; ž, measure; š, ship; j, edge; č, child.

pro-choice [prow'čoys'], *adj.* favoring the right of a female to have free choice in the matter of birth control and abortion. **Ex.** *The senator was asked whether or not he was pro-choice.*

proclaim (3) [prowkleym'], *v.* announce officially and publicly. **Ex.** *Many former colonies have proclaimed their independence.* —**proc·la·ma'tion,** *n.* a public statement announcing something officially.

procure (4) [prowkyu:r'], *v.* 1. obtain by care or effort; get. **Ex.** *They procured the money needed to build the hospital.* 2. cause; bring about. **Ex.** *The lawyer procured the man's release.* —**pro·cure'ment,** *n.*

produce (1) [prəduws', prədyuws'], *v.* 1. bear; bring forth; yield. **Ex.** *These vines produce good grapes.* 2. make; create; cause. **Ex.** *Boiling water produces steam.* 3. manufacture. **Ex.** *Our company produces automobile tires.* 4. show; exhibit. **Ex.** *She produced a letter to prove her statement.* 5. prepare and bring before the public a play, television program, etc. **Ex.** *He produced two movies last year.* —**pro'duce,** *n.* that which is produced; a product. **Ex.** *The farmers took their produce to market.* —**pro·duc'er,** *n.* a person or thing that produces, causes, yields, etc.

product (2) [prad'əkt], *n.* anything produced by growth, labor, study, etc. **Ex.** *What product does that company manufacture?*

production (3) [prədək'šən], *n.* 1. the act of making or producing something. **Ex.** *Production at the factory increased when working conditions were improved.* 2. that which is produced, such as a play, movie, etc. **Ex.** *A new production will open at this theater next week.* —**pro·duc'tive,** *adj.* capable of producing much; producing much. **Ex.** *The conference was productive of many new ideas.* —**pro·duc·tiv'·ty,** *n.* act or condition of being productive. **Ex.** *The large amount of food grown this year is a result of the productivity of the soil.*

profess (5) [prəfes'], *v.* 1. declare openly or freely. **Ex.** *He professed his love for her.* 2. pretend. **Ex.** *She professed great admiration for her employer.* 3. declare a belief; be a member or follower of. **Ex.** *What religion does he profess?*

profession (3) [prəfešən], *n.* 1. an occupation, such as law or medicine, requiring special knowledge or training. **Ex.** *He is preparing for the teaching profession.* 2. all the persons engaged in such a field of work. **Ex.** *He was known by the profession as a brilliant lawyer.* 3. an open declaration. **Ex.**

He made a public profession of his faith. —**pro·fes'sion·al,** *adj.* 1. of, connected with, preparing or engaged in a profession. **Ex.** *The doctor's professional duties kept him working long hours.* 2. engaged for profit in an activity people usually perform as a sport or for relaxation. **Ex.** *He is a professional card player.* —*n.* 1. one who belongs to a profession. **Ex.** *As a professional, he had little patience with untrained workers.* 2. one who earns his living by playing or teaching a sport or some similar activity. **Ex.** *Everyone enjoyed watching the professionals play ball.* —**pro·fes'sion·al·ly,** *adv.*

professor (2) [prəfes'ər], *n.* a teacher of the highest rank in a university or college. **Ex.** *He is an excellent history professor.*

profit (2) [praf'it], *n.* 1. the money gained from a business activity after the payment of all expenses. **Ex.** *That company made a profit last year.* 2. a benefit; a gain. **Ex.** *There is no profit in discussing the matter further.* —*v.* 1. gain money. **Ex.** *He profited from the sale of his house.* 2. benefit; gain. **Ex.** *You would profit from talking with him.* —**prof'it·able,** *adj.* producing a profit, benefit, etc. —**prof'it·ab·ly,** *adv.*

profound (4) [prəfawnd'], *adj.* 1. characterized by great thought or knowledge. **Ex.** *The professor has written a profound book.* 2. very deep; complete. **Ex.** *The exhausted man fell into a profound sleep.* 3. extreme; intense. **Ex.** *I have a profound admiration for her.*

program (2) [prow'græm, prow'grəm], *n.* 1. the different events of an entertainment, meeting, etc. **Ex.** *The program included a comedy act performed by the students.* 2. a paper on or booklet in which the events of an entertainment or meeting are described. **Ex.** *We read the program while we waited for the play to begin.* 3. a plan of action. **Ex.** *The health program for the coming year will help to lessen the number of absent workers.* 4. a system or series of systems for certain tasks to be performed by a computer. **Ex.** *This new program will enable you to prepare your tax returns using your computer.* —*v.* 1. arrange to include in a series of events, activities, etc. **Ex.** *They programmed the first race to start at 9:00 a.m.* 2. create a series of instructions for a computer so that it will be able to perform a particular task or a number of tasks. **Ex.** *The computer was programmed to search for misspelled words.*

progress (2) [prag'res, prow'gres], *n.* 1. development; betterment. **Ex.** *The progress of the students in their reading ability* *is remarkable.* 2. forward movement. **Ex.** *We made slow progress through the crowd.*

progress (2) [prəgres'], *v.* 1. proceed; move forward. **Ex.** *The work progressed rapidly.* 2. develop; advance. **Ex.** *New methods are helping them to progress economically.* —**pro·gres'sion,** *n.* —**pro·gres'sive,** *adj.* 1. making or showing development, forward movement, etc. **Ex.** *We are concerned about the traffic problems caused by the progressive development of the business district.* 2. characterized by new ideas and reform. **Ex.** *He made many progressive changes in the school.*

prohibit (4) [prowhib'it], *v.* 1. forbid, with threat of punishment. **Ex.** *The rules prohibit smoking in this hospital.* 2. stop; prevent. **Ex.** *Ill health prohibited him from swimming.*

prohibition (4) [prowəbiš'ən], *n.* 1. a law that forbids the manufacture and sale of alcoholic liquors. **Ex.** *Prohibition was in effect in the United States from 1920 to 1933.* 2. the act of forbidding or stopping; an order or law forbidding or stopping anything. **Ex.** *In this city there is a prohibition against constructing buildings more than ten stories high.*

project (3) [praj'ekt], *n.* a plan being considered or in progress. **Ex.** *The road-building project was discussed at the meeting.*

project (3) [prəjekt'], *v.* 1. plan. **Ex.** *New housing is projected for that area of the city.* 2. throw or thrust forward. **Ex.** *The bow projected the arrow into the air.* 3. throw onto a surface using a beam of light. **Ex.** *The movie was projected on a small screen.* 4. make sound heard at a distance. **Ex.** *The actor had difficulty projecting his voice to the back of the theater.* 5. extend out. **Ex.** *The roof of the house projects over the window.* —**pro·jec'tile,** *n.* something made to be thrust forward such as a bullet, rocket, etc. —**pro·ject'or,** *n.* a machine that projects pictures on a screen.

pro-life [prow'layf'], *adj.* opposing birth control and favoring the protection of any conceived human life against abortion. **Ex.** *The candidate was asked whether or not he was pro-life.*

prolong (4) [prəlɔːŋ'], *v.* extend the time in which something occurs; make longer in time. **Ex.** *The old woman's life was prolonged by good care.*

prominent (5) [pram'ənənt], *adj.* 1. well-known; famous. **Ex.** *Several prominent people were present at the meeting.* 2. especially noticeable; easy to see. **Ex.** *The flower on her hat was quite prominent.* —**prom'i·nent·ly,** *adv.* —**prom'i·nence,** *n.*

promise (1) [pram'is], *n.* 1. an agreement or assurance that one will do or will not do something. **Ex.** *He gave us his promise that he would go.* 2. a reason for hoping for or expecting something; an indication of future excellence. **Ex.** *This child shows great promise as a pianist.* —*v.* 1. agree to do or not to do something. **Ex.** *He promised to come again the next day.* 2. give reason to expect. **Ex.** *The dinner promises to be a success.* —**prom·is·ing,** *adj.* likely to develop well; giving reason to hope or expect. **Ex.** *She is a promising young pianist.*

promote (4) [prəmowt'], *v.* 1. advance in rank or position. **Ex.** *The lieutenant was recently promoted to captain.* 2. encourage or help something to happen. **Ex.** *They are trying to promote the sale of a new kind of cheese by giving out samples of it at the store.* —**pro·mot'er,** *n.* one who promotes. —**pro·mo'tion,** *n.* the act of promoting or being promoted.

prompt (3) [prampt'], *adj.* 1. not late; on time. **Ex.** *He was prompt in paying his bills.* 2. ready and quick to act when necessary; done without delay. **Ex.** *His prompt action prevented serious trouble.* —*v.* cause to act. **Ex.** *The clouded sky prompted him to take his umbrella.* —**prompt'ly,** *adv.* —**prompt'ness,** *n.*

pronoun (5) [prow'nawn], *n.* a word used instead of a noun. **Ex.** *In the sentence, "The visitor left his hat here, but he later returned for it,"* his, he *and* it *are pronouns.* See **A Brief Explanation of English Grammar.**

pronounce (3) [prənawns'], *v.* 1. speak the sound of; utter. **Ex.** *The teacher pronounced each word slowly and distinctly.* 2. declare seriously or officially. **Ex.** *The judge will pronounce sentence upon the guilty man tomorrow.* —**pro·nounced',** *adj.* definite; distinct. **Ex.** *Age has made a pronounced change in his appearance.* —**pro·nounce'ment,** *n.* an official or formal statement.

pronunciation (4) [prənən'siyey'šən], *n.* the act or way of saying the sound of. **Ex.** *His pronunciation of that word is not correct.*

proof (3) [pruwf'], *n.* 1. anything that proves that something is true; evidence. **Ex.** *The man was freed when his lawyer provided proof that he was innocent.* 2. trial; test. **Ex.** *One proof of a diamond is that it will cut glass.* —*adj.* protected against. **Ex.** *This wall is not soundproof.*

propaganda (4) [prap'əgæn'də], *n.* a spreading of facts and ideas to inform and change opinions; the ideas or beliefs spread in such a way whether true or false. **Ex.** *The soldiers did not believe the enemy's propaganda.*

propel [prəpel'], *v.* cause to move, drive or push forward. **Ex.** *What propelled you into politics?* —**pro·pel'ler,** *n.* a device, consisting of blades mounted on the head of a shaft which is turned rapidly by an engine, used to move an aircraft or ship forward. **Ex.** *The ship was delayed in leaving port because its propeller had to be repaired.*

proper (2) [prap'ər], *adj.* 1. suitable; right; fit. **Ex.** *She put the book in its proper place on the shelf.* 2. polite; well-mannered. **Ex.** *It is proper to write a thank-you note to the hostess after attending a dinner party.* —**prop'er·ly,** *adv.*

proper noun [prap'ər nawn'], the name of a particular person, place, or thing, beginning with a capital letter. **Ex.** John *is a proper noun.* See **A Brief Explanation of English Grammar.**

property (2) [prap'ərtiy], *n.* 1. anything owned. **Ex.** *These books are the property of a friend.* 2. land. **Ex.** *He bought some property near the river.* 3. a characteristic quality of anything. **Ex.** *One property of steel is its hardness.*

prophet (5) [praf'it], *n.* 1. one who speaks for or delivers messages for a god; a religious leader. **Ex.** *The prophet warned that the world would soon end.* 2. one who tells what is to happen in the future. **Ex.** *He had been the town weather prophet for many years.* —**proph'e·cy,** *n.* the prediction of a happening in the future. **Ex.** *His prophecy was that they would become rich.* —**proph'e·sy,** *v.* tell what will happen; predict. —**pro'phet'ic,** *adj.*

proportion (3) [prəpɔr'šen], *n.* 1. the relation of the size, weight or number of one kind of thing to the size, weight or number of another. **Ex.** *The proportion of sunny days to rainy days last month was four to one.* 2. a part; a section. **Ex.** *Only a small proportion of that land can be farmed.*

propose (2) [prəpowz'], *v.* 1. present to others for consideration. **Ex.** *They proposed a plan for a new school.* 2. plan; intend. **Ex.** *We propose to leave for the city tomorrow.* 3. suggest; make an offer of marriage. **Ex.** *He proposed to her last night.* —**pro·pos'al,** *n.* 1. the act of proposing. 2. a plan or idea offered for consideration. 3. an offer of marriage. —**prop'o·si'tion,** *n.* 1. a plan offered for consideration. 2. a business proposal.

proprietor (4) [prəpray'ətər], *n.* owner. **Ex.** *I would like to speak to the proprietor of this store.* —**proprietary,** *adj.* of, like or concerned with ownership. **Ex.** *He has a proprietary interest in that company.*

prose (4) [prowz'], *n.* language spoken or written in an ordinary way; writing not in the form of poetry. **Ex.** *That newspaper reporter always writes clear, simple prose.* —**pro·sa'ic,** *adj.* ordinary; dull; not poetic. **Ex.** *The speaker presented his ideas in a very prosaic manner.*

prosecute (5) [pras'ikyuwt'], *v.* seek punishment of a person in a court by trying to prove guilt. **Ex.** *The men were prosecuted for stealing state funds.* —**pros·e·cu'tion,** *n.* 1. the act of prosecuting. 2. those who are working together to prove the guilt of a person in court. **Ex.** *She is a witness for the prosecution.* —**pros'e·cu·tor,** *n.* one who prosecutes.

prospect (3) [pras'pekt], *n.* 1. the expectation of something; the thought of something to come. **Ex.** *The prospect of being without water began to worry us.* 2. buyer; candidate. **Ex.** *Have you a prospect for the car you are selling?* 3. a wide or unlimited view of a scene. **Ex.** *The city lay below us, a fascinating prospect.* —*v.* search for oil, gas, gold, silver or other valuable minerals. **Ex.** *Men are prospecting for gold in those hills.* —**pro·spec'tive,** *adj.* expected; probable. **Ex.** *Our prospective trip should be an exciting one.* —**pros`pec·tor,** *n.* a person who searches for valuable minerals. —**pros'pects,** *n. pl.* possibilities for advancement, success, etc. **Ex.** *Her prospects in the company are very good.*

prosper (3) [pras'pər], *v.* be successful; grow in a healthy way; become rich. **Ex.** *His business prospered at its new location.* —**pros·per'i·ty,** *n.* —**pros'per·ous,** *adj.*

protect (2) [prətekt'], *v.* defend; guard; shield. **Ex.** *The soldiers protected the city.* —**pro·tec'tion,** *n.* the act of protecting; the condition of being protected; that which protects. **Ex.** *His thin jacket was no protection against the cold.* —**pro·tec'tor,** *n.* one who protects. —**pro·tec'tive,** *adj.* —**pro·tec'tive·ly,** *adv.*

protest (2) [prow'test], *n.* objection; complaint. **Ex.** *Our neighbor's protests about the noise caused us to end the party.* —**pro·test',** *v.* 1. speak against; object; complain. **Ex.** *They protested against the new tax.* 2. declare strongly. **Ex.** *He protested that he was innocent.* —**under protest,** unwillingly; with spoken objections. **Ex.** *She did what she was told to do under protest.*

proud (1) [prawd'], *adj.* 1. well pleased; feeling pride in. **Ex.** *You must be very proud of your daughter's success.* 2. having self-respect. **Ex.** *He was too proud to ask for a loan.* 3. feeling too much pride; setting too high a value on oneself; vain. **Ex.** *They were too proud to speak to their neighbors.* —**proud'ly,** *adv.*

prove (1) [pruwv'], *v.* 1. show to be true or real. **Ex.** *Can you prove where you were yesterday evening?* 2. show something is true by experiment. **Ex.** *One taste proved that the milk was sour.*

proverb (5) [prav'ərb], *n.* an old, well-known, wise saying. **Ex.** *"Don't put all your eggs in one basket," is an often-quoted proverb.* —**pro·ver'bial,** *adj.* like a proverb. 2. well-known.

provide (2) [prəvayd'], *v.* 1. furnish; supply. **Ex.** *The farm provided them with all the food they needed.* 2. prepare for in advance; get before needed. **Ex.** *We must provide for a cold winter by getting more blankets.* —**pro·vid'ed,** *conj.* on condition that; if. **Ex.** *I shall go provided that the weather is clear.*

province (3) [prav'ins], *n.* 1. in some countries, a large division having its own government. **Ex.** *From which province in Canada do you come?* 2. a field of knowledge or activity. **Ex.** *What you want to know does not come within my province.* —**pro·vin'cial,** *adj.* 1. of or having to do with a province. 2. interested only in local affairs; narrow in thinking. **Ex.** *His approach to the problem was very provincial.*

provision (3) [prəviž'ən], *n.* 1. preparation made for the future. **Ex.** *Provision will have to be made for five extra people at dinner tomorrow.* 2. a part of a written agreement, contract, treaty or other legal record. **Ex.** *There is a provision in the Constitution concerning the right of free speech.* —**pro·vi'sions,** *n. pl.* things provided or prepared; food. **Ex.** *We carried our provisions with us.*

provoke (4) [prəvowk'], *v.* 1. cause to feel anger; bother. **Ex.** *Interruptions provoked him.* 2. bring into being; cause. **Ex.** *Her questions provoked an interesting discussion.* —**pro·vok'ing,** *adj.* annoying; bothersome. —**prov'o·ca'tion,** *n.* —**pro·voc'a·tive,** *adj.* exciting; stimulating.

prow (5) [praw'], *n.* the front part of a ship.

prowl (5) [prawl'], *v.* wander about quietly and secretly in search of something. **Ex.** *The cat*

PROW

prowled around the cellar looking for mice. —**prowl'er,** *n.* one who prowls; a person who moves about in secret with the intent to rob or steal.

prudence (5) [pruw'dəns], *n.* carefulness in speaking and acting; practical wisdom. **Ex.** *As an ambassador, he acted with prudence.* —**pru'dent,** *adj.* —**pru'dent·ly,** *adv.*

prune (4) [pruwn'], *n.* a dried plum. **Ex.** *We soaked the prunes before boiling them.*

prune (4) [pruwn'], *v.* cut off branches, roots or other parts from a plant, tree, etc. in order to shape it or make it grow better. **Ex.** *The gardener is pruning the hedges.*

pry (5) [pray'], *v.* examine closely and curiously somebody else's private affairs. **Ex.** *She is always prying into other people's affairs.*

pry (5) [pray'], *v.* raise, open or move by placing one end of a bar under a surface or edge and moving the other end of the bar. **Ex.** *The burglar pried open the window.*

psychology (4) [saykal'əjiy], *n.* 1. the science concerned with the study of the mind and its processes. **Ex.** *Child psychology is a required course in teacher training.* 2. the mental and emotional processes that determine how an individual or group behaves. **Ex.** *As a good salesman, he understood the psychology of his customers.* —**psy·cho·log'i·cal,** *adj.* —**psy·cho·log'i·cal·ly,** *adv.* —**psy·chol'o·gist,** *n.* one who specializes in psychology.

public (1) [pəb'lik], *adj.* 1. of or having to do with the people as a whole. **Ex.** *Public interest in building a new school is very strong.* 2. open to use by all. **Ex.** *He borrowed two books from the public library.* 3. engaged in the service of the people. **Ex.** *The mayor is an honored public servant.* 4. known to most people. **Ex.** *The news was made public.* —*n.* the people as a whole. **Ex.** *The public wants to know more about that matter.* —**pub'lic·ly,** *adv.* —**in public,** in a place where all can see, hear, etc. **Ex.** *He spoke in public.*

public-address system [pəb'lik ədres' sis'təm], *n.* a device for making sound louder so that it can be heard at a distance. **Ex.** *We heard a scream over the public-address system.*

a, far; æ, am; e, get; ey, late; i, in; iy, see; ɔ, all; ow, go; u, put; uw, too; ə, but, ago; ər, fur; aw, out; ay, life; oy, boy; ŋ, ring; θ, think; ð, that; ž, measure; š, ship; j, edge; č, child.

publication (3) [pəb'likey'šən], *n.* 1. something such as a book or magazine that is printed. **Ex.** *The publication that he wanted was a book about agriculture.* 2. the informing of or the giving to the public. **Ex.** *The report received wide publication through the newspaper.*

publicity (4) [pəblis'ətiy], *n.* 1. the attention of the public. **Ex.** *His rescue of the child from the burning house brought him much publicity.* 2. information or activities planned to bring a person, place or thing to the attention of the public. **Ex.** *Publicity about the play appears in today's newspaper.*

public relations [pəb'lik riley'šenz], actions planned to cause the public to approve of a business, group, individual, etc.

public school [pəb'lik skuwl'], a government-controlled school that one does not pay to attend and that is availabe to all. **Ex.** *I studied in the public schools.*

public servant [pəb'lik sər'vənt], a person who is appointed or elected to a government position.

public service [pəb'lik sər'vis], 1. government employment. 2. a free service for the benefit of the public. **Ex.** *The weather report was broadcast as a public service.*

public-spirited [pəb'likspi:r'itid], *adj.* interested in the problems of the community; working to improve the community. **Ex.** *A greater number of public-spirited citizens is needed to make this city more livable.*

public utility [pəb'lik yutil'ətiy], a government-regulated business or industry providing a basic product or service such as electricity, gas, water, etc. to the public. **Ex.** *The telephone company is a public utility.*

publish (2) [pəb'liš], *v.* 1. print and offer a newspaper, book, song, etc. for distribution or sale to the public. 2. make known to the public. **Ex.** *Yesterday's newspapers published a detailed account of the latest space flight.* —**pub'lish·er**, *n.*

pudding (3) [pud'iŋ], *n.* a soft, sweet, cooked dessert usually made with milk, eggs and flour or other cereal. **Ex.** *They served rice pudding for dessert.*

puddle [pəd'əl], *n.* a small, shallow pool of water or other liquid. **Exs.** *The boys were beating the puddle with sticks to make waves in the water. There was a puddle of milk in the saucer.*

puff (5) [pəf'], *n.* 1. a short, quick blast of air, steam, smoke, etc. **Ex.** *A sudden puff of wind blew the papers from her desk.* 2. a small, soft, light pad used for applying powder. —*v.* 1. blow short, quick blasts of air. **Ex.** *The wind puffed about the house.* 2. breathe hard. **Ex.** *The boy was puffing as he rushed into school.* 3. give out smoke, steam, etc. in short blasts; move while giving out puffs. **Ex.** *The engine puffed into the railroad station.* —**puff up,** fill with air in puffs. **Ex.** *The balloon puffed up as he blew into it.*

pull (1) [pul'], *v.* 1. apply force to cause movement toward the person or thing applying the force. **Ex.** *The horse pulled the wagon along the road.* 2. remove from a fixed place; draw out. **Ex.** *They were pulling weeds in the garden.* 3. tear; cause to come apart. **Ex.** *The cat pulled the pillow to pieces.* —*n.* the applying of force; the effort of pulling. **Ex.** *It was a hard pull for the horses.* —**pull oneself together,** make oneself calm and self-controlled after being upset. **Ex.** *After crying for a long time, she began to pull herself together.*

pulley [pul'iy], *n.* a wheel, attached to a frame, with a groove over which a rope or chain is passed to aid in raising or lowering heavy objects. **Ex.** *He used a rope and pulley to lift the buckets of mortar to the bricklayers on the second floor.*

PULLEY

pulp (5) [pəlp'], *n.* 1. the part of a fruit containing the juice. **Ex.** *We ate the pulp of the orange and threw away the skin and seeds.* 2. a mixture of materials such as ground wood, used paper and rags, softened by liquids and chemicals, that is used to make paper. **Ex.** *The trees were cut down for pulp.*

pulpit (5) [pul'pit], *n.* a raised place in a church from which a minister or other speaker talks to the people. **Ex.** *The minister was speaking in the pulpit.*

pulse (4) [pəls'], *n.* the regular beating of the heart as it pumps blood through the body. **Ex.** *The doctor felt the patient's pulse.* —*v.* beat regularly, as a pulse. **Ex.** *The city was pulsing with life.*

pump (3) [pəmp'], *n.* a machine that raises or moves water or other liquids, especially by forcing them through a pipe. **Ex.** *The pump supplied water from a deep well.* —*v.* 1. raise or move with a pump. **Ex.** *Water for the fields was pumped from the river.* 2. operate or move as a pump does. **Ex.** *The heart pumps blood through the body.*

pumpkin [pəmp'kin], *n.* a large round orange-yellow fruit, grown on a vine, with a hard, thick outer skin and an interior of firm edible flesh and seeds. **Ex.** *This pumpkin is large enough to make the filling for several pie shells.*

PUMPKIN

punch (4) [pənč'], *n.* a quick, hard blow with the fist. **Ex.** *In his anger, he gave his brother a punch in the nose.* —*v.* strike or hit with a quick, hard blow of the fist. **Ex.** *During the fight, he was punched in the eye.*

punch (4) [pənč'], *n.* a tool used to make holes or cut a design in materials. **Ex.** *The holes in his belt were made with a punch.* —*v.* cut a design or make holes as with a punch. **Ex.** *The shoemaker punched a hole in the leather.*

punctual (5) [pəŋk'čuwəl], *adj.* prompt; on time; not tardy. **Ex.** *He was always punctual in keeping appointments.* —**punc'tu·al·ly**, *adv.* —**punc'tu·al'i·ty**, *n.*

punctuation (3) [pəŋk'čuwey'šen], *n.* the system of making writing easier to understand by using periods and other such marks to end sentences or break them into shorter parts. **Ex.** *The punctuation in that sentence is not correct.* —**punc'tu·ate**, *v.* —**punctuation mark**, a mark used to punctuate. See **Marks, Signs and Symbols.**

punish (2) [pən'iš], *v.* 1. cause pain, loss, suffering, etc. for doing a bad thing. **Ex.** *The mother punished the child by not allowing him to have any dessert with his dinner.* 2. set as a penalty for a crime. **Ex.** *Some states punish murderers by putting them to death.* —**pun'ish·ment**, *n.* 1. act of punishing. 2. the penalty a person is given for doing wrong.

pup, puppy (5) [pəp, pəp'iy], *n.* a young dog. **Ex.** *The puppy was two months old.*

pupil (2) [pyuw'pəl], *n.* one who studies under the direction of a teacher. **Ex.** *Only ten pupils are in my class.*

pupil (2) [pyuw'pəl], *n.* the dark center of the eye through which light enters the eye and which becomes smaller in bright light and larger in dim light. **Ex.** *The doctor put drops in the patient's eyes to enlarge the pupils for examination.*

purchase (2) [pər'čis], *v.* buy with money or with something of equal value. **Ex.** *She purchased a new dress.* —*n.* 1. the act of buying. **Ex.** *They are saving their money for the purchase of a house.* 2. something obtained by buying. **Ex.** *Her pur-*

chases were delivered to her home. —**pur'chas·er**, *n*. one who buys.

pure (1) [pyu:r'], *adj*. 1. free from anything which is different or which lessens the value. **Ex.** *Her dress was made of pure silk.* 2. free from anything unclean or unhealthful; clean. **Ex.** *High on the mountain they found pure water to drink.* 3. innocent; not evil. **Ex.** *The young girl, still pure in heart, could not understand why anyone would do such an evil thing.* —**pure'ly**, *adv*. —**pu'ri·fy**, *v*. make pure.

purple (2) [pər'pəl], *n*. a color made from mixing blue and red together. **Ex.** *That artist likes to use purple in his paintings.* —*adj*. of a bluish-red color. **Ex.** *The grapes were turning purple on the vine.*

purpose (1) [pər'pəs], *n*. 1. what one decides to do; the objective of or reason for one's action; intention. **Ex.** *The purpose of his trip was to visit a new factory.* 2. the use; the result intended. **Ex.** *What is the purpose of this machine?* —**pur'pose·ly**, *adv*. with a purpose; intentionally. **Ex.** *He purposely knocked against the man.* —**on purpose**, intentionally. **Ex.** *She broke my toy on purpose.*

purr [pə:r], *n*. a soft, low, continuous sound that a cat makes when it is contented or happy; a sound like that. **Ex.** *The engine of the expensive car made a gentle purr.* —*v*. make such a sound. **Ex.** *The cat purred as I held it in my arms.*

purse (3) [pərs'], *n*. 1. a woman's handbag, used for carrying money, powder, comb, etc.; a small bag with a clasp for carrying money. **Ex.** *Her brown purse matched her shoes.* 2. a sum of money offered as a prize. **Ex.** *The owner of the winning horse won a large purse.* —*v*. draw together tightly. **Ex.** *She pursed her lips in an expression of dislike.*

pursue (3) [pərsuw'], *v*. 1. follow someone quickly with the purpose of catching. **Ex.** *The policeman pursued the thief.* 2. follow in order to obtain or accomplish. **Ex.** *He is pursuing a career as a pianist.* —**pur·su'er**, *n*. one who pursues. —**pur·suit'**, *n*. 1. the act of pursuing; a chase. **Ex.** *The hunters were in pursuit of the fox.* 2. an activity which one follows or is involved in for pleasure. **Ex.** *Fishing is his favorite pursuit.*

---

a, far; æ, am; e, get; ey, late; i, in; iy, see; ɔ, all; ow, go; u, put; uw, too; ə, but, ago; ər, fur; aw, out; ay, life; oy, boy; ŋ, ring; θ, think; ð, that; ž, measure; š, ship; j, edge; č, child.

push (1) [puš'], *v*. 1. use force against something for the purpose of moving it. **Ex.** *He pushed his bicycle up the hill.* 2. move oneself by using force against that which stops one from moving. **Ex.** *He pushed his way through the crowd.* 3. try very hard to do something; urge. **Ex.** *He pushed the men to increase their sales.*

push-up [puš'əp'], *n*. an exercise done by lying flat on the floor, face down, and, while keeping the body straight, raising the body by pushing up with the arms. **Ex.** *He does twenty push-ups every morning before showering.*

put (1) [put'], *v*. 1. cause to be in a certain place; set in a position. **Ex.** *He put the money in his pocket.* 2. cause to be in a condition or state. **Ex.** *She put the baby to sleep by singing softly.* 3. attach; assign; join to. **Ex.** *He put too high a price on the book.* 4. express; say. **Ex.** *He wanted to go with them but could not put his wish into words.* **—put aside,** set aside; save for later consideration, use; etc. **Ex.** *They put aside a little money each week.* **—put away,** store in a proper place; save for future use. **Ex.** *She washed the dishes and put them away.* **—put down.** 1. defeat. **Ex.** *The government put down the revolt.* 2. write. **Ex.** *He put his ideas down on a piece of paper.* **—put forth,** extend out; grow out; offer. **Ex.** *She put forth several good ideas.* **—put off,** cause to wait; delay. **Ex.** *He has put off making a decision until tomorrow.* **—put on,** 1. dress. **Ex.** *She put on her coat.* 2. produce a performance. **Ex.** *He is putting on a new play.* **—put out,** 1. stop a fire or light. **Ex.** *They used water to put out the fire.* 2. place outside or in a forward position. **Ex.** *She put out her hand.* **—put through.** 1. cause to be completed, effected, accepted, etc. **Ex.** *They put through a new law.* 2. conduct a demonstration; subject to. **Ex.** *He put the car through a severe test.* **—put together;** place different pieces together to make a whole; assemble. **Ex.** *How do you put this lamp together?* **—put up,** 1. make available; offer. **Ex.** *The land has been put up for sale.* 2. build. **Ex.** *He put up that house last year.* 3. preserve vegetables, fruits, etc. **Ex.** *She put up twelve jars of green beans.* 4. provide a place to sleep. **Ex.** *They put us up for the night.* **—put up with,** suffer without complaining; endure. **Ex.** *He puts up with a lot of noise from his students.*

puzzle (2) [pəz'əl], *n*. 1. a person or matter difficult to understand; a problem difficult to solve. **Ex.** *She has always been a puzzle to me.* 2. a game or other device that tests one's intelligence or skill. **Ex.** *They tried to put the puzzle together.*

—*v.* 1. be difficult to understand; confuse. **Ex.** *His absence puzzles me.* 2. think deeply about some difficult problem in order to solve it. **Ex.** *They puzzled over the question for some time.*

pyramid (5) [piːrˈəmidʼ], *n.* a structure that is usually square at the bottom with triangular sides that come together at the top in a point. **Ex.** *We slowly climbed to the top of the pyramid.*

PYRAMID

Q, q [kyuwʼ], *n.* the seventeenth letter of the English alphabet.

quaint (5) [kweyntʼ], *adj.* strange or unusual but pleasing because of past customs, dress, etc. recalled. **Ex.** *She put on one of her grandmother's quaint dresses.* —**quaint'ly**, *adj.* —**quaint'ness**, *n.*

qualify (3) [kwalˈəfayʼ], *v.* 1. make or become fit or able. **Ex.** *He qualified for the job by studying at night.* 2. give or obtain legal power or rights. **Ex.** *He will be qualified to vote when he is eighteen.* 3. decrease the strength of; limit. **Ex.** *He qualified his earlier remarks.* —**qual'i·fi·ca'tion**, *n.* 1. act of qualifying. 2. that which qualifies. **Ex.** *What are your qualifications for the job?*

quality (2) [kwalˈətiy], *n.* 1. that which something is known to have or be; an attribute. **Ex.** *An important quality of steel is its strength.* 2. excellence; value. **Ex.** *The furniture that store sells is known for its quality.* 3. degree of excellence. **Ex.** *Only materials of the highest quality were accepted.*

quantity (2) [kwanˈtətiy], *n.* 1. an amount. **Ex.** *A small quantity of salt was in the box.* 2. a large amount. **Ex.** *She always buys canned goods in quantity.*

quarrel (2) [kwɔ:r'əl, kwar'əl], *n.* 1. an argument; a dispute. **Ex.** *We have not spoken to each other since our quarrel.* 2. reason for opposing or arguing. **Ex.** *I have no quarrel with what he says.* —*v.* argue or dispute in anger. **Ex.** *The children seldom quarrel.*

quarry (5) [kwɔ:r'iy, kwar'iy], *n.* a large hole in the ground or a cut into a hillside from which marble and other stones are taken. **Ex.** *The men are working in the quarry.* —*v.* obtain stone from a large hole in the ground or a cut in a hillside. **Ex.** *They are quarrying marble.*

quarry (5) [kwɔ:r'iy, kwar'iy], *n.* the animal or person being pursued. **Ex.** *The hunter's quarry was a rabbit.*

quart (3) [kwɔrt'], *n.* 1. a liquid measure equal to two pints. **Ex.** *Our family drinks four quarts of milk a day.* 2. a dry measure equal to two pints. **Ex.** *They picked a quart of berries.* See **Weights and Measures.**

quarter (1) [kwɔr'tər], *n.* 1. one of the four equal divisions of anything; one fourth (¼). **Ex.** *We each ate a quarter of the orange.* 2. a United States coin worth one fourth of a dollar; twenty-five cents. **Ex.** *He had two quarters in his pocket.* 3. one fourth of an hour; fifteen minutes. **Ex.** *We went home at a quarter after four.* 4. one fourth of a year; a period of three months. **Ex.** *We pay our taxes every quarter.* 5. any place or direction. **Exs.** *People come to New York from all quarters of the world. Help came from an unexpected quarter.* —*v.* 1. divide into four equal parts. **Ex.** *Quarter the apple and give each child a section.* 2. provide a place to live. **Ex.** *The family was quartered in a hotel.* —*adj.* equal to one fourth. **Ex.** *He ran in the quarter-mile race.* —**quar·ter·ly,** *adj.* appearing or happening four times a year. **Ex.** *It was a quarterly meeting.* —*adv.* four times a year. **Ex.** *The report comes out quarterly.* —*n.* a magazine published four times a year. **Ex.** *He writes for that quarterly.* —**quar·ters,** *n.* a place where one lives or stays. **Ex.** *He went to his quarters to change his clothes.* —**at close quarters,** very near to each other. **Ex.** *They were fighting at close quarters.*

quartz [kwɔrtz'], *n.* a common glasslike mineral that occurs in many different forms, such as crystals, semiprecious stones and the chief part of sand. **Ex.** *My watch keeps exact time because a tiny piece of quartz controls the battery current.*

queen (1) [kwiyn'], *n.* 1. wife of a king. **Ex.** *The young king did not yet have a queen.* 2. a female ruler. **Ex.** *The queen* *ordered us to come to the castle.* —**queen'ly,** *adj.* of, like, for or suited for a queen. **Ex.** *She walked in a queenly manner.*

queer (2) [kwi:r'], *adj.* not ordinary; unusual. **Ex.** *There was something queer about the way her voice sounded on the telephone.*

quench (5) [kwenč'], *v.* 1. satisfy. **Ex.** *The water quenched his thirst.* 2. stop; put out. **Ex.** *The campers quenched the fire by throwing water on it.*

query (5) [kwi:r'iy], *n.* question. **Ex.** *In answer to my query, he said that the theater was closed.* —*v.* 1. ask questions. **Ex.** *She queried me about my work.* 2. create a question about; express doubt about. **Ex.** *They queried the need for a new school.*

question (1) [kwes'čən], *n.* 1. a sentence or word used in asking for information. **Ex.** *He answered my questions willingly.* 2. a problem; a matter to be discussed. **Ex.** *The question of how to raise the money to build a new road was discussed at the meeting.* 3. a matter of uncertainty. **Ex.** *There is some question about who wrote the book.* —*v.* 1. ask questions of. **Ex.** *The man was questioned about where he had been.* 2. doubt. **Ex.** *We questioned the wisdom of her actions.* —**beyond question,** without question, having no doubt. **Ex.** *Beyond question, he is the best one for the job.*

questionnaire [kwes'čəne:r'], *n.* a series of questions on a printed form, usually given to a number of people to provide information for a survey. **Ex.** *This questionnaire is being mailed to all high school English teachers in the city to find out which books have been most popular among their students.*

quick (1) [kwik'], *adj.* 1. rapid; fast. **Ex.** *They had a quick lunch of bread and cheese.* 2. prompt in action; ready. **Ex.** *His quick reply surprised everyone.* 3. easily angered or excited. **Ex.** *She had a quick temper.* —**quick'ly,** *adv.* —**quick'ness,** *n.*

quiet (1) [kway'ət], *adj.* 1. making little or no noise; silent. **Ex.** *The children became quiet when the teacher started to talk.* 2. having little or no movement; calm. **Ex.** *The boat moved slowly over the quiet water.* 3. not excited; gentle. **Ex.** *He spoke in a quiet voice.* 4. restful; peaceful. **Ex.** *They spent a quiet afternoon together.* —*v.* make or become quiet; calm.

Ex. *His arrival quieted her fears.* —*n.* a condition of silence, calmness or peacefulness. **Ex.** *A loud noise suddenly broke the quiet.* —**qui'et·ly,** *adv.*

quilt (5) [kwilt'], *n.* a warm covering for a bed made by placing cotton or other soft material between two large pieces of cloth and sewing the whole together with tiny stitches in such a way that the threads make a pattern. **Ex.** *In the winter we use quilts on the beds.* —*v.* make a quilt. **Ex.** *The farmers' wives often used to quilt at winter parties.*

quit (3) [kwit'], *v.* 1. stop doing something; cease. **Ex.** *The doctor told his patient that for the sake of her health she had to quit smoking.* 2. leave; depart. **Ex.** *He had to quit college and get a job.* —**quit'ter,** *n.* one who quits easily.

quite (1) [kwayt'], *adv.* 1. entirely; completely. **Ex.** *She was quite certain of the date.* 2. rather; somewhat. **Ex.** *He was quite tired.*

quiver (3) [kwiv'ər], *v.* shake slightly but rapidly; tremble. **Ex.** *The little dog quivered with fright.* —*n.* the act of quivering; a trembling. **Ex.** *There was a quiver of excitement in the crowd.*

quiver (3) [kwiv'ər], *n.* a container for carrying arrows. **Ex.** *He pulled an arrow from his quiver.*

QUIVER

quiz [kwiz], *n.* a short test. **Ex.** *In our history class we have a quiz every day at the beginning of class.* —*v.* ask questions of; examine closely. **Ex.** *The robbery suspect was quizzed by the police.*

quota [kwow'tə], *n.* 1. the amount or share of something a person is allowed to have or is expected to produce. **Exs.** *Mother said that you have had your quota of cookies for today. This factory has not met its monthly production quota.* 2. the greatest number of people allowed during a particular period to enter a country, group, college or university, etc. **Ex.** *Our club has already accepted its quota of new members for this year.*

quote (3) [kwowt'], *v.* repeat exactly the written or spoken words of another. **Ex.** *He quoted from a speech by the president of the university.* —**quo·ta'tion,** *n.*

R

R, r [a:r'], *n.* the eighteenth letter of the English alphabet.

rabbit [ræb'it], *n.* a small animal with long ears and a short tail.

race (1) [reys'], *n.* 1. a contest to see who or what can move at a faster or the fastest speed. **Ex.** *Which horse won the race?* 2. any contest. **Ex.** *Three candidates have entered the race for mayor.* —*v.* 1. be or cause to be in a contest of speed. **Ex.** *The contestants raced the last hundred yards at very fast speeds.* 2. move very quickly; move at a very fast speed. **Ex.** *The children raced out of the front door.* —**rac'er,** *n.*

RABBIT

race (1) [reys'], *n.* a group of people with common physical characteristics; a group of people sharing a common background of history, language, customs, etc. **Ex.** *People of many races settled in the United States.* —**ra'cial,** *adj.* —**rac'ism,** *n.* the unproved belief that one race of people is better than another.

racetrack [reys'træk], *n.* a course, usually oval or round, where horses, dogs, cars, etc. run races. **Ex.** *A friend of ours has a horse running at the racetrack tomorrow.*

rack (3) [ræk'], *n.* a framework of shelves or bars on which articles or materials are placed, hung or carried. **Ex.** *He put the suitcases on the luggage rack.*

rack (3) [ræk'], *v.* cause to suffer greatly. **Ex.** *His body was racked with pain.*

racket (4) [ræk'it], *n.* a loud, confused noise. **Ex.** *The students made a big racket as they left the school.*

RACKET

racket (4) [ræk'it], *n.* a rounded wooden frame, crossed by strings and having a handle that is used to hit a ball in certain games such as tennis.

radar [rey'dar], *n.* a method of sensing the presence of distant objects and determining their position, size, speed, etc. by the use of reflected radio waves; the equipment required to do this; ra(dio) d(etecting) a(nd) r(anging). **Ex.** *Radar indicated that an unknown aircraft was approaching.*

radiant (4) [rey'diyənt], *adj.* 1. giving forth rays of heat or light; bright; shining. **Ex.** *The radiant moon lighted our path.* 2. bright with joy, health, etc. **Ex.** *The news made her radiant with happiness.* —**ra'di·ance,** *n.* —**ra'di·ate,** *v.* 1. give forth rays of heat or light. 2. come out from a central point in rays like the spokes of a wheel. —**ra'di·a'tion,** *n.* the rays given out.

radiator [rey'diyey'tər], *n.* 1. a device for heating air by means of a series of pipes through which steam or hot water circulates. **Ex.** *This room is very cold; have you turned on the radiator?* 2. a cooling device in an engine consisting of a series of pipes through which a cooling agent passes. **Ex.** *The engine is overheating; something must be wrong with the radiator.*

radical (4) [ræd'ikəl], *adj.* 1. fundamental; basic. **Ex.** *There were radical differences between the two systems.* 2. extreme; favoring great changes. **Ex.** *His ideas are too radical to be acceptable to most people.* —*n.* a person who has extreme ideas for change. **Ex.** *In his time, he was called a radical.* —**rad'i·cal·ism,** *n.* —**rad'i·cal·ly,** *adv.*

radio (2) [rey'diyow], *n.* 1. a system of sending and receiving signals or sounds through the air without wires. **Ex.** *The news was sent by radio.* 2. a device for receiving radio broadcasts. **Ex.** *They listened to the President's speech on the radio.* —*adj.* used in radio; sent by radio. **Ex.** *What radio programs do you listen to regularly?* —*v.* send by radio. **Ex.** *Can we radio for help?*

radioactivity [rey'diyowæktiv'ətiy], *n.* the giving off of energy in the form of certain rays, usually harmful to living things, caused by spontaneous or intentionally planned atomic changes. **Ex.** *The workers' clothing was tested for any traces of radioactivity.* —**ra'di·o·ac'tive,** *adj.*

radium [rey'diyəm], *n.* a rare, very bright, shining white, highly radioactive metal that is used in the treatment of cancer. **Ex.** *She will be receiving radium treatments five days a week over a period of several weeks for breast cancer.*

raffle [ræf'əl], *n.* a sale, often benefiting a charity, of a prize such as a car, a house, or a diamond ring, etc., in which tickets are sold and one ticket is drawn as the winning one. **Ex.** *We've won a trip for two to Europe in the club raffle!* —*v.* sell in a raffle. **Ex.** *The firemen's benefit fund is raffling off a turkey for Thanksgiving.*

raft (5) [ræft'], *n.* a platform made of rubber, logs fastened together, etc. and used as a boat. **Ex.** *Rafts were lowered from the sinking ship.*

rag (3) [ræg'], *n.* a torn piece of cloth without value; any piece of cloth used for washing, cleaning, etc. **Ex.** *He wiped his boots with an old rag.* —**rags'**, *n. pl.* old worn and torn clothing. **Ex.** *The beggar was dressed in rags.* —**rag'ged,** *adj.*

rage (3) [reyj'], *n.* 1. a great anger. **Ex.** *When he found that they had gone without him, he flew into a rage.* 2. a popular fashion, usually not lasting long. **Ex.** *The handsome new singer quickly became the rage.* —*v.* 1. feel or express great anger. **Ex.** *She raged when she heard the news of her rival's success.* 2. act with great violence. **Ex.** *As the storm raged, the waves grew higher and higher.* 3. spread at great speed. **Ex.** *The fire raged through the woods.*

raid (4) [reyd'], *n.* 1. a sudden attack made as an act of war or for the purpose of seizing or stealing something. **Ex.** *The radio was destroyed in the raid.* 2. a forcible entry by the police in order to make arrests, stop something unlawful or seize goods as evidence. **Ex.** *In an early-morning raid, the police found the stolen articles.* —*v.* make a sudden attack. **Ex.** *Thieves raided the store last night.* —**raid'er,** *n.* one who raids.

rail (2) [reyl'], *n.* 1. a piece of wood or metal used as a part of a fence or as a protection at the side of a ship or along a stair. **Ex.** *He leaned over the boat rail to look at the water.* 2. one of the two metal bars on which trains run. **Ex.** *The train stopped because a rail was broken ahead.* 3. railroad. **Ex.** *Are you traveling by air or rail?*

RAIL 1

railing [rey'liŋ], *n.* a fence or protective device made of rails. **Ex.** *We need a railing on the porch so that our two-year-old can play there.*

railroad (2) [reyl'rowd'], *n.* 1. a road for trains with two rails on which the trains travel. **Ex.** *A railroad ran through the center of town.* 2. the company which manages such a road, its stations, equipment, managers, etc. **Ex.** *My father worked for the railroad for many years.*

rain (1) [reyn'], *n.* 1. water falling from the sky in drops. **Ex.** *Three inches of rain had made the ground soft.* 2. the falling of water; a shower. **Ex.** *Were you out in the rain?* 3. the falling of something in the manner of rain. **Ex.** *There was a rain of letters to the editor of the newspaper on that subject.* —*v.* 1. fall in drops of water. **Ex.** *It rained all day yesterday.* 2. fall in the manner of rain. **Ex.** *Friends and family rained gifts upon her for her twenty-first birthday.* —**rain'y,** *adj.*

rainbow (4) [reyn'bow'], *n.* a part of a circle of various colors seen in the sky when the sun shines through raindrops. **Ex.** *After the storm, a rainbow formed in the sky.*

raincoat [reyn'kowt], *n.* a coat made of cloth that has been treated to be waterproof or water resistant. **Ex.** *I'm glad that I was wearing my raincoat when I was caught in that heavy shower.*

raise (1) [reyz'], *v.* 1. lift up; move to a higher position. **Ex.** *He raised his hand and waved.* 2. excite; awaken. **Ex.** *The good news raised their hopes for success.* 3. cause to grow; grow. **Ex.** *They are raising corn in that field.* 4. increase in amount, rank, etc. **Ex.** *He was raised from clerk to manager.* —*n.* an increase in amount, especially of pay. **Ex.** *He received a small raise in recognition of his good work.*

raisin (2) [rey'zən], *n.* a dried grape. **Ex.** *Mother added raisins to the cake.*

rake (4) [reyk'], *n.* a garden tool with a long handle and a set of short hooks or teeth used for gathering hay, leaves, etc. —*v.* prepare, gather or remove with a rake. **Ex.** *He raked the soil carefully before planting.*

RAKE

rally (5) [ræl'iy], *v.* 1. bring together or into order again. **Ex.** *The scattered soldiers were rallied for the next attack.* 2. gather or call persons together for some united effort; come in order to help. **Ex.** *After putting out the fire, the neighbors rallied to provide food.* 3. improve one's health or strength. **Ex.** *As the medicine took effect, the patient began to rally.* —*n.* a meeting or gathering for a special purpose. **Ex.** *We are going to a political rally tonight.*

ram (4) [ræm'], *n.* 1. a male sheep. **Ex.** *One old ram led the flock.* 2. any long, heavy object used to break open gates, doors, etc. **Ex.** *They used a tree trunk as a ram to break down the wall.* —*v.* strike or push against with great force. **Ex.** *The boat rammed into the pier.*

ramp [ræmp'], *n.* a man-made incline or slope connecting one level to another or providing an entrance or an exit to a freeway. **Ex.** *The accident happened on the ramp in the parking garage.*

ran (1) [ræn'], *v.* past tense of *run.* **Ex.** *The boy ran all the way home.*

ranch (4) [rænč'], *n.* a very large farm, especially one on which large numbers of animals are raised. **Ex.** *The children spent the summer on a cattle ranch.* —*v.* work on or run a ranch. —**ranch'er,** *n.* one who owns or runs a ranch.

random (5) [ræn'dəm], *adj.* made, done, etc. without definite aim, plan or purpose. **Ex.** *The rooms were filled with a random selection of furniture.*

rang (3) [ræŋ'], *v.* past tense of *ring.* **Ex.** *The telephone rang while you were away from your desk.*

range (2) [reynǰ'], *n.* 1. the limit or reach of something; the greatest distance to which anything such as sound, a moving object, etc. can travel. **Ex.** *Everyone within range of his voice heard the remark and laughed.* 2. the extent of a series of variations or possibilities within a group. **Ex.** *This chair is available in a wide range of materials and colors.* 3. a row, line, series or chain. **Ex.** *A range of mountains separates the two countries.* 4. a large area of grassy land where animals move about and feed. **Ex.** *He rode over the range looking for some lost cows.* 5. a stove for cooking. **Ex.** *They have an electric range.* 6. an area for firing and testing guns, rifles and other weapons. **Ex.** *How many days did you spend at the rifle range this summer?* —*v.* 1. vary within certain limits. **Ex.** *The children ranged in age from three to ten years old.* 2. wander freely through an area. **Ex.** *With his pack on his back, he ranged over the neighboring countryside.* 3. place persons or things in order or in rows. **Ex.** *Bottles and glasses were ranged on the table.* —**rang'er,** *n.* 1. a member of a body of special troops who protect a certain area of the country. 2. a guard to protect a forest or wild animal and plant life. **Ex.** *Many rangers work in the national forests.*

rank (2) [ræŋk'], *n.* 1. a grade in military forces. **Ex.** *He has the rank of a major.* 2. relative position in a group of professional or talented people. **Ex.** *He is an artist of the first rank.* —*v.* 1. place in a higher or lower position. **Ex.** *His examination paper was ranked the best in his class.* 2. arrange in a formation. **Ex.** *The men were ranked according to their height.* —**rank'ing**, *adj.* of the highest rank. **Ex.** *The ranking officer will take charge of the meeting.*

ransom (5) [ræn'səm], *n.* 1. money demanded or paid to free a person. **Ex.** *A large ransom was demanded for the safe return of the child.* 2. the release of a person in return for payment of money. **Ex.** *The ransom of the prisoner was accomplished during the night.* —*v.* obtain release by paying a price demanded. **Ex.** *The merchant was ransomed by his son.*

rap (4) [ræp'], *n.* a sharp, quick knock or blow. **Ex.** *We heard a rap on the door.* —*v.* strike or tap sharply. **Ex.** *Who is rapping on the table?*

rapid (2) [ræp'id], *adj.* fast; quick; swift. **Ex.** *The rapid growth of the city surprised us.* —**rap'id·ly**, *adv.* —**rap'ids**, *n. pl.* a part of a river that flows swiftly, usually over rocks. —**ra·pid'i·ty**, *n.* swiftness.

rapture (4) [ræp'čər], *n.* a feeling of great joy or delight. **Ex.** *The beauty of the sunset filled everyone with rapture.*

rare (3) [re:r'], *adj.* unusual; uncommon; infrequent. **Ex.** *Horses are rare in cities.* —**rare'ly**, *adv.* —**rare'ness**, *n.* the quality of being rare. —**rar'i·ty**, *n.* something unusual; the condition of being rare.

rare (3) [re:r'], *adj.* only slightly cooked. **Ex.** *He likes his beef very rare.* —**rare'ness**, *n.*

rascal (4) [ræs'kəl], *n.* 1. a person without principles; a person who is not honest. **Ex.** *Two rascals tricked the old man out of his money.* 2. a lively child who causes trouble while doing something in fun. **Ex.** *The little rascal ran outside.*

rash (5) [ræš'], *adj.* acting thoughtlessly and too quickly. **Ex.** *He often makes rash promises.* —**rash'ly**, *adv.* —**rash'ness**, *n.*

rash (5) [ræš'], *n.* red spots on the skin, sometimes indicating illness. **Ex.** *They don't know what is causing the rash on his arm.*

raspberry [ræz'beriy], *n.* small, sweet, red or black fruit with many seeds, which grows on a thorny bush. **Ex.** *I picked a handful of raspberries and immediately ate them.*

RASPBERRY

rat (3) [ræt'], *n.* a long-tailed animal similar to a mouse but larger. **Ex.** *Many countries have programs to get rid of rats because they spread disease.*

RAT

rate (2) [reyt'], *n.* 1. an amount measured in relation to something else; speed. **Ex.** *She types our letters at the rate of 100 words a minute.* 2. the price of a unit of anything or service that is bought or sold. **Ex.** *He is paid at the rate of five dollars an hour.* —*v.* place a price on. **Ex.** *Her jewelry is rated at twice the price she paid.* 2. consider to be in a certain rank or class. **Ex.** *She is rated among the best ice skaters in the country.* —**at any rate,** anyhow; anyway. **Ex.** *I will write or phone you; at any rate we will be in touch.* —**rat'ing,** *n.* the position of a person or thing in comparison to others regarding quality, reliability, popularity, usefulness, etc.

rather (1) [ræð'ər], *adv.* 1. in or to some degree; somewhat. **Ex.** *It is rather cold today.* 2. more willingly; more gladly; preferably. **Ex.** *I would rather go today than tomorrow.* 3. more accurately. **Ex.** *They had a discussion, or rather a quarrel.*

ratio (4) [rey'šow, rey'šiyow], *n.* the relation of one thing to another expressed in numbers or degree. **Ex.** *The ratio of successful candidates to applicants was one in five.*

ration (5) [ræš'ən, rey'šən], *n.* 1. a fixed allowance of food or other supplies allotted a person in times of scarcity. **Ex.** *She used her sugar ration to make jam.* 2. the daily food allowance for a member of the armed forces. **Ex.** *Each soldier was given three rations before the battle.* —*v.* divide or distribute as rations. **Ex.** *Water is rationed during the dry season.*

rational (5) [ræš'ənəl], *adj.* 1. sensible; reasonable. **Ex.** *Does he have a rational explanation for his behavior?* 2. sane; able to reason. **Ex.** *Last night she had a high fever and was not rational.* —**ra'tion·al·ly,** *adv.* —**ra'tion·al·ize`,** *v.* give a logical reason or explanation for something without appearing to know that it is not the actual reason. **Ex.** *He rationalized his failure in the examination by saying that the teacher did not like him.*

a, far; æ, am; e, get; ey, late; i, in; iy, see; ɔ, all; ow, go; u, put; uw, too; ə, but, ago; ər, fur; aw, out; ay, life; oy, boy; ŋ, ring; θ, think; ð, that; ž, measure; š, ship; j, edge; č, child.

rattle (5) [ræt'əl], *v.* 1. make or cause to make short, sharp rapid sounds. **Ex.** *The windows rattle when the wind blows.* 2. move while making a succession of such sounds. **Ex.** *The old car rattled along the road.* —*n.* 1. a series of short, sharp, rapid sounds. **Ex.** *He was awakened by the rattle of stones against the window.* 2. a baby's toy that makes a series of short, sharp, rapid sounds.

rave (5) [reyv'], *v.* talk wildly; speak in a confused manner. **Ex.** *Because of his high fever, the sick man raved and could not be understood.* 2. praise with great enthusiasm. **Ex.** *The girls raved about the new singer.* —**rav'ing,** *adj.* wild; raging.

raw (2) [rɔː'], *adj.* 1. uncooked. **Ex.** *We like to eat raw fruit.* 2. not yet treated or processed. **Ex.** *The raw cotton is picked and then weighed.* 3. sore, with skin scraped off. **Ex.** *His hands were raw from working in the fields.* 4. untrained. **Ex.** *He held the enemy off with a few raw soldiers.*

ray (2) [rey'], *n.* 1. a narrow line of light. **Ex.** *A ray of light came though a hole in the door.* 2. a slight promise; a small amount. **Ex.** *The new medicine gave him a ray of hope.* 3. energy coming from some source. **Ex.** *Rays of heat from the stove soon warmed the room.*

rayon (5) [rey'an], *n.* a manufactured cloth, made from chemically treated plant cells, that sometimes looks and feels similar to silk. **Ex.** *Her dress was made of rayon.*

razor (5) [rey'zər], *n.* an instrument with a sharp edge for shaving hair from the face. **Ex.** *He put a new blade in his razor.*

re- [riy, ri], *prefix.* 1. again. **Exs.** *Read, reread; state, restate.* 2. back. **Exs.** *Pay, repay; act, react.*

reach (1) [riyč'], *v.* 1. arrive at; come to. **Ex.** *The boat reached shore safely.* 2. extend a hand, foot, etc. toward. **Ex.** *The boy reached for an apple.* 3. touch, strike or grasp with the hand or with some object. **Ex.** *The child could not reach the bell.* 4. extend to; stretch out as far as. **Ex.** *His land does not reach the river.* —*n.* the act of reaching; the power to reach; the extent of the reach. **Ex.** *The boy made a quick reach for the ball.*

react [riyækt'], *v.* 1. act as a result of. **Ex.** *He reacted to my question with surprise.* 2. return to an earlier condition; act in an opposite way. **Ex.** *When meat prices increased, people reacted by not buying meat.* —**re·ac'tor,** *n.* a person or thing that reacts.

reaction (3) [riyæk'šən], *n.* 1. something that is a response or a result. **Ex.** *Did you see his reaction to her arrival?* 2. a return to an earlier thing or state. **Ex.** *The forces of reaction have again gained political power.* —**re·ac'tion·ar'y**, *adj.* of, showing, or favoring a return to an earlier condition. **Ex.** *He is a reactionary in his views on education.*

read (1) [riyd'], *v.* 1. look at and understand the meaning of printed or written words, letters and numbers. **Ex.** *He reads the newspaper every morning.* 2. speak written or printed words. **Ex.** *She likes to read to the children.* —**read'er**, *n.* 1. one who reads. 2. a book for teaching how to read. —**read'ing**, *n.* the act of looking at and understanding the meaning of printed or written words and numbers.

read [red'], *v.* past tense and participle of *read*. **Exs.** *I read the book last week. I have read all the letters you sent me.*

readable [riyd'əbəl], *adj.* easy to read; enjoyable; interesting. **Ex.** *Her style of writing is very readable.*

readily (3) [red'əliy], *adv.* 1. quickly; easily; promptly. **Ex.** *One can readily see that he will succeed.* 2. willingly. **Ex.** *We gave him the money readily.*

ready (1) [red'iy], *adj.* 1. prepared; completed; arranged. **Ex.** *Dinner is ready.* 2. willing. **Ex.** *They are always ready to help.* —*v.* prepare. **Ex.** *They readied the house for visitors.* —**read'i·ness**, *n.*

real [riyl'], *adj.* 1. true; actual. **Ex.** *What was his real reason for not coming with us?* 2. not false. **Ex.** *This a real diamond.* —**re'al·ism**, *n.* an understanding of things as they actually are. **Ex.** *Realism tells us that some criminals are incurable.* —**re'al·ist**, *n.* one who see things as they actually are. **Ex.** *Realists admit many things cannot be changed overnight.* —**re'al·is'tic**, *adj.* —**re·al'i·ty**, *n.* the state of being real. **Ex.** *In reality, nothing happened.* —**re'al·ly**, *adv.* truly; actually. **Ex.** *Spring is really here.*

real estate [riyl' əsteyt'], property in the form of land together with its buildings, trees, crops, water, mineral rights, man-made improvements, etc. **Ex.** *We have been looking at different kinds of real estate for investment purposes.*

realize (1) [riyəlayz'], *v.* 1. understand clearly; be aware of. **Ex.** *He did not realize how cold it was until he went outside.* 2. make real; cause to become true. **Ex.** *She realized her dreams when she became a doctor.* —**re'al·i·za'tion**, *n.*

realm (4) [relm'], *n*. a country ruled by a king or queen. **Ex.** *The queen visited every town in her realm.* 2. an area over which some influence or activity extends. **Ex.** *He has read many books about the realm of magic.*

reap (4) [riyp'], *v*. 1. cut and harvest grain. **Ex.** *The farmers reaped their wheat.* 2. receive as a result of effort or behavior. **Ex.** *The man reaped a fortune from his invention.* —**reap'er,** *n*. 1. a machine for cutting grain. 2. a person who cuts grain.

rear (2) [ri:r'], *n*. the back part; the farthest end of something. **Ex.** *The people in the rear of the room could not hear the speaker.* —*adj*. at the back. **Ex.** *The rear window of the car was dirty.*

rear (2) [ri:r'], *v*. 1. raise; aid in growing. **Ex.** *When their parents died, an aunt reared the two boys.* 2. rise up on the back legs, as a four-legged animal; lift up. **Ex.** *The horse reared at the sight of the snake.*

reason (1) [riy'zən], *n*. 1. cause for a belief or act; purpose. **Ex.** *What is the reason for this meeting?* 2. something said that explains; an excuse. **Ex.** *He could give no reason for being in the building.* 3. the power to think or decide. **Ex.** *A man of reason is needed in this situation.* 4. good judgment; sound thinking. **Ex.** *He was too excited to listen to reason.* —*v*. to think or argue in a way that uses sound thinking. **Ex.** *His friends tried to reason with him.* —**rea·son·a·ble,** *adj*. having or showing reason. **Ex.** *She is a reasonable person.*

rebel (3) [reb'əl], *n*. 1. one who resists or fights the government of his own country. **Ex.** *The rebels finally had to admit defeat.* 2. one who resists any kind of control. **Ex.** *As a schoolboy, he was considered a rebel.*

rebel (3) [ribel'], *v*. 1. rise up against one's government. **Ex.** *The people rebelled and overthrew the dictator.* 2. resist authority; refuse to obey. **Ex.** *The students rebelled against the rules of required dress.* 3. have a strong feeling of distaste. **Ex.** *He rebelled at the idea of eating raw meat.* —**re·bel'lion,** *n*. —**re·bel'lious,** *adj*.

rebuke (5) [riybyuwk'], *v*. blame sharply. **Ex.** *The manager rebuked the clerk for his mistake.* —*n*. a sharp criticism of one's actions. **Ex.** *Her face burned with anger at the unjustified rebuke.*

recall (4) [rikɔ:l'], *v*. 1. remember. **Ex.** *He tried to recall where they had met before.* 2. ask to return. **Ex.** *She was recalled to*

the hospital for more treatment. 3. take back; cancel. **Ex.**
These stamps were recalled because of mistakes in printing.
—*n.* the act of recalling.

receipt (4) [risiyt'], *n.* 1. the act of receiving. **Ex.** *Please notify
me upon your receipt of the package.* 2. a written statement
saying that one has received money, a package, etc. **Ex.** *He
signed a receipt for the money.* —**re·ceipts,** *n. pl.* the amount
of money received in a business. **Ex.** *She counted the receipts
for the day.*

receive (1) [risiyv'], *v.* 1. take something that is offered, given,
sent, etc.; get; accept. **Ex.** *I received several books on art for
my birthday.* 2. welcome; greet. **Ex.** *They received their guests
at the door.* —**re·ceiv'er,** *n.* 1. one who receives. 2. a device
for receiving radio waves or similar electric impulses; a radio
set; the part of a telephone through which one hears. **Ex.** *She
picked up the telephone receiver and heard a voice say, "Hello."*

recent (2) [riy'sənt], *adj.* done or occurring not very long ago.
Ex. *Recent news confirms last week's report that he is alive.*
—**re·cent·ly,** *adv.*

reception (3) [risep'šən], *n.* 1. the act of receiving or greeting.
Ex. *She was pleased by the critic's reception of her book.* 2. an
entertainment or party to greet or honor someone. **Ex.** *After
the wedding ceremony, a reception was held in the garden.* 3. the
receiving of radio waves and similar electrical impulses. **Ex.**
The quality of our television reception varies with the weather.

recess (4) [riy'ses, rises'], *n.* 1. an open or hollow space in a wall.
Ex. *There was a small statue in the recess of the wall.* 2. an
inner place. **Ex.** *The treasure was found in a recess at the back
of the cave.* —*v.* set back into an open or hollow place. **Ex.**
The windows were deeply recessed.

recess (4) [riy'ses, rises'], *n.* a short period of rest from work or
study. **Ex.** *During the recess, the children played in the school
yard.* —*v.* rest from work or study for a time. **Ex.** *Congress
recessed for the holiday.*

recession [riyse'šən], *n.* a slowdown, usually brief, of economic
activity, happening during a period of overall healthy growth.
Ex. *During the recession the company's planned expansion
had to be delayed.*

a, far; æ, am; e, get; ey, late; i, in; iy, see; ɔ, all; ow, go; u, put; uw, too;
ə, but, ago; ər, fur; aw, out; ay, life; oy, boy; ŋ, ring; θ, think; ð, that;
ž, measure; š, ship; ǰ, edge; č, child.

recipe (4) [res'əpiy], *n.* a list of things needed and directions for preparing something to eat or drink. **Ex.** *I would like your recipe for this delicious dessert.*

recipient [risip'iyənt], *n.* one who receives; a receiver. **Ex.** *The recipient of the award was loudly cheered.*

recite (4) [risayt'], *v.* 1. repeat or say aloud from memory. **Ex.** *Several children on the program recited poems.* 2. tell something; give a detailed account of. **Ex.** *She recited all her troubles of the last year when I saw her yesterday.* —**re·cit'al**, *n.* 1. the act of reciting or telling; that which is recited. 2. a musical or dance performance, often by only one person. **Ex.** *We went to a piano recital last night.* —**rec'i·ta'tion**, *n.* 1. the act of reciting. 2. the thing recited.

reckless (3) [rek'lis], *adj.* dangerously thoughtless; rashly careless. **Ex.** *She was arrested for reckless driving.* —**reck'less·ly**, *adv.* —**reck'less·ness**, *n.* a rashly careless act. **Ex.** *His recklessness caused the accident.*

recognize (2) [rek'əgnayz'], *v.* 1. know or recall that someone or something was known or seen before. **Ex.** *I recognized him as the same man I had seen yesterday.* 2. know by knowledge or experience already acquired. **Ex.** *The singing teacher recognized the girl's voice as one worth training.* 3. be aware of; accept as true. **Ex.** *He recognized his inability to do the job.* 4. show appreciation and approval. **Ex.** *They recognized his heroism by giving him a medal.* —**rec'og·ni'tion**, *n.*

recollect (5) [rek'elekt'], *v.* remember. **Ex.** *I cannot recollect his name.* —**rec'ol·lec'tion**, *n.* 1. the act of remembering. **Ex.** *According to my recollection, they were married about twenty years ago.* 2. something remembered; memory. **Ex.** *They had many recollections of their trip.*

recommend (2) [rek'əmend'], *v.* 1. state that someone or something is good for a particular position or purpose; praise. **Ex.** *His former employer recommended him.* 2. urge as a wise course; advise. **Ex.** *What do you recommend that I read?* 3. make acceptable or pleasing. **Ex.** *That old house has little to recommend it.* —**rec'om·men·da'tion**, *n.* 1. the act of recommending. 2. a statement, often written, that someone or something is good for a particular position or purpose. 3. advice. **Ex.** *My recommendation was that he should buy it.*

reconcile (4) [rek'ənsayl'], *v.* 1. cause to be friendly again. **Ex.** *A friend reconciled the couple after their quarrel.* 2. settle. **Ex.**

They reconciled their differences. 3. bring into agreement. **Ex.** *We could not reconcile his apparently fine conduct with his bad reputation.* 4. cause one to accept. **Ex.** *They could not reconcile themselves to the loss of their son.* —**rec'on·cil'i·a' tion,** *n.*

record (1) [rikɔrd'], *v.* 1. write down something in order to have it for use at a future time, often in official form or papers. **Ex.** *The teacher recorded the test results.* 2. show by means of a measuring device. **Ex.** *An instrument recorded the amount of electricity used.* 3. put sound into a form that can be kept and heard again. **Ex.** *We recorded the music played by the band.*

record (1) [rek'ərd], *n.* 1. a written account of facts or happenings; writings kept as history. **Ex.** *They kept a record of their expenses.* 2. a round, flat piece of black plastic or other material with fine cuts that reproduce sound. **Ex.** *The young people played records of dance music at the party.* 3. the best performance, amount, rate, etc. **Ex.** *Several swimming records were set this year.* 4. the known facts about and performance of someone or something. **Ex.** *She made a good record in school.* —**break a record,** do better than the previous best. **Ex.** *He ran so fast that he broke the record.* —**off the record,** not to be published or quoted. **Ex.** *The President told the press, off the record, what his plans were.* —**re·cor'ding,** *n.* —**record player,** a machine for playing records.

recover (2) [rikʌv'ər], *v.* 1. get again something lost, stolen or taken away. **Ex.** *The police recovered his stolen watch.* 2. return to health or to a normal condition. **Ex.** *She has finally recovered from her cold.* —**re·cov'er·y,** *n.*

recover (2) [rikʌv'ər], *v.* cover again. **Ex.** *She recovered the chair with striped material.*

recreation (5) [rek'riyey'šən], *n.* 1. a refreshing of one's strength or spirits by some entertainment, exercise or restful activity. **Ex.** *They walked for recreation.* 2. any entertainment, game, etc. that refreshes. **Ex.** *His favorite recreations were reading and playing ball.* —**rec're·a'tion·al,** *adj.*

recruit (4) [rikruwt'], *n.* a new member, especially of the armed forces. **Ex.** *The recruits were issued uniforms.* —*v.* 1. get new people to join the armed forces. **Ex.** *The Navy has been recruiting here recently.* 2. get new members or helpers in the business, political group, etc. **Ex.** *They recruited six new salespersons.* —**re·cruit'er,** *n.* one who recruits.

rectangle [rek'tæŋgəl], *n.* any four-sided figure, the straight sides of which form four right angles. **Ex.** *The garden was divided into rectangles, both oblong and square.* —**rec·tan'gu·lar,** *adj.*

RECTANGLE

recycle [riysay'kəl], *v.* subject something that has been used to physical or chemical action so that it or a part of it can be used again. **Ex.** *We send our empty bottles and the newspapers that we have read to be recycled.*

red (1) [red'], *adj.* having a bright color like that of fresh blood. **Ex.** *He gave her a single red rose.* —*n.* a bright color like that of fresh blood. **Ex.** *Do you like red better than blue?* —**red'den,** *v.* become or make red.

Red Cross [red' krɔːs'], an international organization that cares for those who are sick, wounded, etc. in times of war, disaster, etc.

redeem (5) [ridiym'], *v.* 1. buy back; regain. **Ex.** *He redeemed his ring from the moneylender.* 2. make the final payment on a loan. **Ex.** *She hopes to redeem her loan next month.* 3. keep a pledge; fulfill a promise. **Ex.** *He redeemed his promise to pay half the expenses of the trip.* —**re·demp'tion,** *n.*

red-handed [red'hæn'did], *adj.* in the very act of. **Ex.** *They caught him red-handed stealing the money.*

redhead [red'hed], *n.* a person whose hair is red. **Ex.** *The twins are redheads.* —**red'head'ed,** *adj.*

red tape [red' teyp'], official rules and procedures that cause delay. **Ex.** *He said that there was a lot of red tape when he went to get a building permit.*

reduce (2) [riduws', ridyuws'], *v.* 1. make smaller in amount, number or size. **Ex.** *His salary was reduced because business was slow.* 2. lower in rank or condition. **Ex.** *The major was reduced to captain because of his poor performance.* 3. lose weight by dieting. **Ex.** *The doctor ordered me to reduce.* —**re·duc'tion,** *n.*

reed (4) [riyd'], *n.* 1. a slender, hollow-stemmed grass. **Ex.** *Reeds grew along the river.* 2. a thin piece of reed or wood used in the mouthpiece of some musical instruments. **Ex.** *The musician carried an extra reed in a small case.*

reel (4) [riyl'], *n.* a device on which string, wire, film, etc. is wound and kept. **Ex.** *This movie is on three reels.* —*v.* 1. put on or take off a reel. **Ex.** *He reeled in his fishing line.* 2. move as if hit or when hit; sway. **Ex.** *He reeled from the blows and fell.*

refer (3) [rifər'], *v.* 1. send to for help, information, etc. **Ex.** *She referred me to the library.* 2. go to for information. **Ex.** *He referred to the dictionary for the meaning of the word.* 3. direct attention to; mention. **Ex.** *She often refers to her childhood.*

referee [ref'əriy], *n.* 1. an official who is in charge of certain games and sports, such as basketball and boxing, and sees that the rules are followed. **Ex.** *The football referee called the ball out on the nine-yard line.* 2. a person to whom a dispute or some other matter is referred for settlement. **Ex.** *The referee will not give his decision this week.* —*v.* act as a referee.

reference (3) [ref'ərəns], *n.* 1. the act of referring or consulting. **Ex.** *The journalist kept a card file of information on her desk for easy reference.* 2. a source of information. **Ex.** *References, such as dictionaries, can be found in our school library.* 3. mention of sources from which information was taken or in which similar information may be found. **Ex.** *His book contains many references to previous books on the subject.* 4. written statements about a person's ability, character, etc. **Ex.** *The new worker has good references.*

refine (4) [rifayn'], *v.* improve; make less coarse or rough; make pure. **Exs.** *He refined what he had written. They visited a mill where sugar is refined.* —**re·fined'**, *adj.* 1. made less coarse; made pure. 2. polite and developed by education. **Ex.** *He is both intelligent and refined.* —**re·fine'ment**, *n.* —**re·fin'er·y**, *n.* the place where certain raw products such as oil, sugar, etc. are purified.

reflect (3) [riflekt'], *v.* 1. change the direction in which waves such as those of heat, light or sound are traveling or cause them to return to the place from which they came. **Ex.** *White walls reflect more light than dark walls.* 2. give back an image. **Ex.** *The mirror reflected the other end of the room.* —**re·flec'tion**, *n.* act of reflecting; that which is reflected. **Ex.** *He saw the reflection of his face in the water.*

reflect (3) [riflekt'], *v.* think deeply. **Ex.** *She reflected on her problems.* —**re·flec'tion**, *n.* thought; consideration. **Ex.** *After some reflection, she decided to accept the offer.*

a, far; æ, am; e, get; ey, late; i, in; iy, see; ɔ, all; ow, go; u, put; uw, too; ə, but, ago; ər, fur; aw, out; ay, life; oy, boy; ŋ, ring; θ, think; ð, that; ž, measure; š, ship; ǰ, edge; č, child.

reform (3) [rifɔrm'], v. 1. make something better by changing. **Ex.** *The new President promised to reform the government.* 2. stop doing bad acts; improve. **Ex.** *The criminal tried to reform.* —n. the act of reforming; a change to a better condition. **Ex.** *The governor promised many reforms in the tax laws.* —**ref·or·ma'tion**, n. act of reforming. —**re·form'a·tor·y, reform school**, n. a place where young minor criminals are sent for punishment and training.

refrain (4) [rifrayn'], v. keep oneself from doing. **Ex.** *In order to lose weight, she refrained from eating candy and other sweets.*

refrain (4) [rifrayn'], n. a phrase, line or group of lines in a song or poem repeated at intervals. **Ex.** *After each verse, everyone joined in singing the refrain.*

refresh (3) [rifreš'], v. make fresh or less tired by rest, food, drink, etc. **Ex.** *Cold drinks refreshed the tired travelers.* —**re·fresh'ing**, adj. —**re·fresh'ments**, n. light food and drink. **Ex.** *What refreshments did they serve at the party?*

refrigerator (4) [rifriǰ'ərey'tər], n. a cabinet or room, kept at a cold temperature, for storing food. **Ex.** *She put the meat in the refrigerator.* —**re·frig'er·ate**, v. cause to become cold or remain cold. **Ex.** *They refrigerated the milk immediately after milking.*

refuge (4) [ref'yuwǰ], n. a protected, safe place; shelter from trouble. **Ex.** *The man found a refuge from the rain.* —**ref'u·gee**, n. a person who has fled from cruel treatment, danger, etc. to seek refuge. **Ex.** *The flood created hundreds of refugees.*

refuse (2) [rifyuwz'], v. decline to accept, give or do something. **Ex.** *He refused to give me the money that he owed me.* —**re·fus'al**, n.

refuse (2) [ref'yuwz], n. waste; useless material without value. **Ex.** *There was a box for refuse near the door.*

regard (2) [rigard'], v. 1. think of; consider. **Ex.** *The children regard him with affection.* 2. give careful attention to; show respect for. **Ex.** *She regarded what he had written thoughtfully.* 3. concern. **Ex.** *My talk with him did not regard you.* —n. 1. reference; relation. **Ex.** *I shall speak to him in regard to that matter.* 2. concern; thought. **Ex.** *He had no regard for her feelings.* 3. respect; liking. **Ex.** *We have great regard for that teacher.* —**re·gard'ing**, prep. concerning. —**re·gards**, n. good wishes; affection. **Ex.** *Give my best re-*

gards to your wife. —**re·gard'less,** *adj.* without thought of. **Ex.** *Regardless of how you feel, you must continue.*

regime [režiym', reyžiym'], *n.* a system of governing, ruling or administering. **Ex.** *The whole country voted for a new regime.*

regiment (4) [reǰ'əmənt], *n.* a military unit consisting of a number of companies and usually commanded by a colonel. **Ex.** *The camp of the first regiment is beyond that hill.* —*v.* control by a system of strict rules and orders. **Ex.** *His method of teaching regimented the children.*

region (2) [riy'jən], *n.* 1. a large part of the earth. **Ex.** *They were flying over a region of ice and snow.* 2. a particular area or place. **Ex.** *The wooded region south of the city will become a park.* —**re'gion·al,** *adj.*

register (3) [reǰ'istər], *n.* 1. an official list or book where certain information is recorded. **Ex.** *All visitors must sign the hotel register.* 2. a device used in business for counting and recording. **Ex.** *She put the money in the cash register.* —*v.* 1. enter or have entered in a register. **Ex.** *You are required to register before an election if you want to vote.* 2. show on a scale. **Ex.** *The thermometer registered a temperature below freezing last night.* —**reg'is·tra'tion,** *n.* act of registering. **Ex.** *Registration of new students occurs on Monday.*

regret (3) [rigret'], *v.* feel sorry about something that is done or that is happening. **Ex.** *We regret that he has to leave.* —*n.* sorrow for something; distress; a wish that something might be different. **Ex.** *She felt regret for having spoken unkind words.* —**re·grets',** *n. pl.* an expression of being sorry not to be able to attend. **Ex.** *Some of those invited to dinner sent their regrets.*

regular (2) [reg'yələr], *adj.* 1. following established habit, custom, pattern, etc.; usual. **Ex.** *He returned home at the regular hour.* 2. steady and uniform; happening at fixed intervals. **Ex.** *I could hear the regular breathing of the sleeping man.* 3. formed according to some rule or principle; balanced. **Ex.** *She chose some material with a regular pattern.* 4. recognized; accepted; qualified in the usual way. **Ex.** *He is not a regular member.*

regulate (4) [reg'yəleyt'], *v.* 1. govern or control according to rules or laws. **Ex.** *This department regulates commerce.* 2. cause to operate correctly; set at a certain speed, temperature, etc. **Ex.** *This clock needs to be regulated.* —**reg'u·la'tion,**

n. 1. the act of regulating. 2. a law or rule which regulates. **Ex.** *Regulations establish the age at which a young person can drive a car.* —**reg·u·la·tor,** *n.* that which or one who regulates. —**reg·u·la·tor·y,** *adj.*

rehearse (5) [rihərs'], *v.* practice a play, music, etc. before presenting it to an audience. **Ex.** *We will rehearse the play this afternoon.* —**re·hears'al,** *n.* the act of rehearsing; practice.

reign (3) [reyn'], *n.* the rule of a king or other person; the time of such rule. **Ex.** *The prince was not in the country during his father's reign.* —*v.* 1. have power as a king, queen, etc. **Ex.** *She reigned for many years.* 2. prevail; exist in a wide area. **Ex.** *After three bad harvests, hunger reigned in the country.*

rein [reyn'], *n.* a strip of leather by which a rider or driver controls a horse. —*v.* guide, control or stop by reins or by some other means. **Ex.** *He reined in the team of horses as they approached the river.* —**hold the reins,** be in control. **Ex.** *He holds the reins in that company.*

reject (3) [rijekt'], *v.* refuse to accept, use, believe, etc. **Ex.** *He rejected their offer of help.*

reject (3) [riy'jekt], *n.* something that is refused as damaged, incomplete, not up to standards, not acceptable, etc. **Ex.** *The faulty machine part was sent back to the factory as a reject.*

rejoice (3) [rijoys'], *v.* be or be made very happy. **Ex.** *They rejoiced when they heard he was safe.* —**re·joic'ing,** *n., adj.*

relate (3) [rileyt'], *v.* 1. tell; report. **Ex.** *We listened with interest as he related his adventures.* 2. connect; associate. **Ex.** *It was natural to relate his disappearance to the disappearance of the money.* 3. be concerned with; have reference to. **Ex.** *To what does your problem relate?* —**re·lat'ed,** *adj.* of the same family or group. **Ex.** *They are related by marriage.*

relation (2) [riley'šən], *n.* 1. connection. **Ex.** *Weight has a close relation to health.* 2. a person connected to another by blood or marriage; a member of the same family; a relative. **Ex.** *He is staying with his relations.* —**re·la'tions,** *n. pl.* the various connections between countries, groups, etc. **Ex.** *Relations between Canada and the United States are friendly.* —**re·la'tion·ship,** *n.* state of being related.

relative (3) [rel'ətiv], *n.* a person connected by blood or marriage; a member of the same family; a relation. **Ex.** *She has been visiting her relatives.* —*adj.* having meaning only through a comparison with something else; not absolute. **Ex.** *His family lives in relative comfort.* —**rel'a·tive·ly,** *adv.*

relax (4) [rilæks'], *v.* 1. become less firm, stiff or tight. **Ex.** *His book dropped from his hands as he relaxed into sleep.* 2. rest from work. **Ex.** *They relaxed by going to the movies.* —**re'lax·a'tion,** *n.* the act of relaxing; that which relaxes.

release (3) [riliys'], *v.* 1. free; allow to go. **Ex.** *They released the prisoners.* 2. permit to be known, published or sold. **Ex.** *The full story has not yet been released.*

reliable (4) [rilay'əbəl], *adj.* worthly of trust; dependable. **Ex.** *I believe what he says because he is very reliable.* —**re·li'a·bil'i·ty,** *n.*

relief (2) [riliyf'], *n.* 1. a bringing of aid or comfort; a reduction of pain, strain, etc. **Ex.** *The doctor ordered heat treatments for the relief of the patient's sore arm.* 2. a release from work or duty; the person who takes over the work or duty. **Ex.** *The soldier on guard could see his relief approaching.* 3. a release from work in order to rest. **Ex.** *He worked from noon until dark with no relief.* 4. help given to people in need. **Ex.** *The government provides some relief for poor families.*

relieve (3) [riliyv'], *v.* 1. bring aid and/or comfort; reduce pain and worry. **Ex.** *The medicine relieved her headache.* 2. release someone from duty by taking his place. **Ex.** *The guard at the gate was relieved every four hours.*

religion (2) [rilij'ən], *n.* 1. a belief in or worship of a god or gods. **Ex.** *They are studying the religions of the world.* 2. a particular system of beliefs or worship centered around a god, a philosophy of life, etc. **Ex.** *What is your religion?* —**re·li'gious,** *adj.* 1. devoted to a religion. **Ex.** *She is very religious.* 2. referring to religion. **Ex.** *Religious services are held here every Sunday.* —**re·li'gious·ly,** *adv.* regularly and devotedly. **Ex.** *He reads the financial section of the paper religiously.*

relish (5) [rel'iš], *n.* 1. enjoyment; satisfaction. **Ex.** *The old man watched the game with relish.* 2. sour, salted or sweet foods intended to awaken the desire to eat. **Ex.** *Among the relishes she served were olives and tiny onions in vinegar.* —*v.* enjoy. **Ex.** *He relished the idea of a sea voyage.*

---

a, far; æ, am; e, get; ey, late; i, in; iy, see; ɔ, all; ow, go; u, put; uw, too; ə, but, ago; ər, fur; aw, out; ay, life; oy, boy; ŋ, ring; θ, think; ð, that; ž, measure; š, ship; j, edge; č, child.

reluctant (5) [rilək'tənt], *adj.* unwilling; not inclined. **Ex.** *The mother was reluctant to leave her children alone.* —**re·luc'tant·ly,** *adv.* —**re·luc'tance,** *n.*

rely (4) [rilay'], *v.* depend; trust. **Ex.** *You can rely on me to help you.* —**re·li'ance,** *n.* dependence. **Ex.** *Surely his reliance on his parents for support will have to end sometime.*

remain (4) [rimeyn'], *v.* 1. stay in a place after others go away. **Ex.** *One person must remain in the office while we go out.* 2. stay the same. **Ex.** *She has remained as beautiful as ever.* 3. continue to exist. **Ex.** *After the fire, nothing remained of the house.* 4. be left after part is removed or lost. **Ex.** *Little remained of the food after the boys had eaten.* —**re·mains,** *n. pl.* 1. that which is left. **Ex.** *The remains of a meal were left on the table.* 2. a dead body. **Ex.** *He was asked to identify the remains.* —**re·main'der,** *n.* that which remains. **Ex.** *I used some and gave the remainder to her.*

remark (2) [rimark'], *v.* say; mention. **Ex.** *He remarked that the weather was fine.* —*n.* an observation; a comment. **Ex.** *I did not like his remark about her.*

remarkable (3) [rimar'kəbəl], *adj.* unusual; special enough to deserve mention. **Ex.** *He told me a remarkable story.* —**re·mark'ab·ly,** *adv.*

remedy (3) [rem'ədiy], *n.* 1. a medicine or treatment that cures. **Ex.** *This is a good remedy for a sore throat.* 2. a means of correcting a wrong or an evil. **Ex.** *They built a new school as a remedy for crowded classrooms.* —*v.* cure; improve; correct. **Ex.** *Being sorry will not remedy the damage you have done.* —**re·me'di·al,** *adj.* able to remedy. **Ex.** *Remedial lessons were given to the slower students.*

remember (1) [rimem'bər], *v.* 1. return to the mind. **Ex.** *He could not remember where he had put his eyeglasses.* 2. keep in mind. **Ex.** *Remember that you have an appointment with the doctor tomorrow.* —**re·mem'brance,** *n.* 1. the act of remembering. 2. an object given or kept to remind someone of something.

remind (2) [rimaynd'], *v.* 1. cause one to remember. **Ex.** *Please remind me to take my medicine.* 2. cause one to think of. **Ex.** *The mountains reminded her of home.* —**re·mind'er,** *n.* that which helps one to remember.

remit (5) [rimit'], *v.* 1. send money in payment to a person or place. **Ex.** *Please remit the amount of your bill by check.* 2.

forgive or pardon all or a portion of a debt or punishment. **Ex.** *Because of the boy's age, the judge remitted the prison sentence.* —**re·mit'tance,** *n.* the sending of money; the money sent.

remnant (5) [rem'nənt], *n.* 1. that part which remains of anything. **Ex.** *Remnants of the meal lay on the table when he had finished eating.* 2. a short length of material left from a much larger piece, usually sold for much less than the regular price. **Ex.** *This skirt is made from a remnant.*

remodel [riymad'əl], *v.* rebuild; change the form or design of. **Ex.** *We remodeled our kitchen last year.*

remorse [rimɔrs'], *n.* a deep sense of regret for having done wrong. **Ex.** *She was filled with remorse for having spoken so angrily to her mother.*

remote (4) [rimowt'], *adj.* 1. far away. **Ex.** *The accident occurred in a remote place.* 2. only slightly related or connected. **Ex.** *All members of the family except remote relations were invited.* 3. slight. **Ex.** *There is only a remote possibility that he will be elected.* —**re·mote'ly,** *adv.* —**re·mote'ness,** *n.* —**remote control,** a device for controlling from a distance the operation of various appliances and machinery such as a television set, a garage door, etc.

remove (2) [rimuwv'], *v.* 1. take away or off. **Ex.** *She removed her hat and coat.* 2. get rid of; put an end to. **Ex.** *She could not remove the spot from the carpet.* 3. put out of a position or office. **Ex.** *He was removed from his job because he was not qualified.* —**re·mov'al,** *n.*

render (4) [ren'dər], *v.* 1. make; cause to be or become. **Ex.** *They were rendered homeless by the fire.* 2. do; perform. **Ex.** *That organization renders great service to the community.* 3. present for payment or consideration. **Ex.** *The lawyer has not yet rendered his bill.* —**ren·di'tion,** *n.* a way of performing music, a play, etc; a version. **Ex.** *I liked her rendition of the song.*

renounce (5) [rinawns'], *v.* 1. give up; abandon. **Ex.** *He renounced his citizenship.* 2. refuse to recognize. **Ex.** *Her parents renounced her because of her marriage.* —**re·nun'ci·a'tion,** *n.* act of renouncing.

renovate [ren'əveyt'], *v.* repair; remodel; fix so as to make like new or to return to its original or former condition. **Ex.** *It took them almost two years to renovate their house.*

renown (5) [rinawn'], *n.* fame; high reputation. **Ex.** *He won renown for his courage.*

rent (3) [rent'], *n.* a payment regularly made to an owner for the use of land, a building or other property. **Ex.** *The rent for the house was more than they could afford.* —*v.* use or allow the use of property for which a regular payment is made. **Ex.** *They rented a car for the trip.*

repair (2) [ripe:r'], *v.* 1. fix; mend. **Ex.** *He had his shoes repaired.* 2. correct; make right; remedy. **Ex.** *He tried to repair the wrong he had done.* —*n.* 1. the act or process of repairing. **Ex.** *The repair of the car will take a week.* 2. the state or condition of something. **Ex.** *Your bicycle is in good repair.*

repeal (4) [ripiyl'], *v.* set aside or end officially. **Ex.** *That law was repealed by Congress.* —*n.* the act of officially setting aside or ending. **Ex.** *The repeal of the prohibition law had an immediate effect on the restaurant business.*

repeat (2) [ripiyt'], *v.* 1. say again. **Ex.** *She repeated the accusation.* 2. say from memory. **Ex.** *He repeated the entire poem.* 3. do or make again. **Ex.** *If you repeat that mistake, you will be punished.* —**re·peat'ed**, *adj.* said, done, etc. again and again. —**re·peat'ed·ly**, *adv.*

repel (5) [ripel'], *v.* 1. drive or force back. **Ex.** *The enemy was repelled.* 2. push away; refuse. **Ex.** *She repelled his attempts to be friendly.* 3. cause a strong feeling of dislike. **Ex.** *She was repelled by the odor of the spoiled food.* —**re·pel'lent**, —*n.* that which repels. **Ex.** *She sprayed the room with insect repellent.* —*adj.* repulsive. **Ex.** *They found the idea repellent.*

repent (4) [ripent'], *v.* feel guilt or regret for past conduct. **Ex.** *He repented and confessed his crime.* —**re·pent'ant**, *adj.* —**re·pent'ance**, *n.*

repetition (5) [rep'ətiš'ən], *n.* 1. the act of repeating. **Ex.** *Frequent repetition of the word helped him to remember it.* 2. something that is repeated or is a copy. **Ex.** *The builder's last house is a repetition of his first.* —**rep·e·ti'tious**, *adj.*

replace [ripleys'], *v.* 1. put someone or something into the place of another. **Ex.** *We've replaced our old gas stove with an electric one.* 2. put something back into its original or previous position. **Ex.** *After selecting a pin to wear, she replaced the rest of her jewelry in the drawer.* 3. take the place of someone or something. **Ex.** *Who is going to replace the retiring club president?* —**re·place'ment**, *n.*

reply (1) [riplay'], *v.* answer in words or in writing or by doing something. **Ex.** *When did she reply to your letter?* —*n.* an answer. **Ex.** *He made no reply to my question.*

report (1) [ripɔrt'], *n.* 1. an account of a happening; a statement giving the results of an inquiry or search. **Ex.** *A report of the accident was in the newspapers.* 2. a story or statement told without certainty as to the facts. **Ex.** *I have heard good reports about him.* —*v.* 1. tell about. **Ex.** *The class reported on its trip to the museum.* 2. tell in a formal statement; give the results of a special study. **Ex.** *The committee reported on housing conditions in the city.* 3. tell officials that someone has not acted properly. **Ex.** *She reported him to the police.* 4. appear; arrive at. **Ex.** *Report to my office.* —**re·port'er,** *n.* one who reports, especially for a newspaper, magazine, etc. —**report card,** a written statement about the progress of a student, usually expressed in letters or numbers.

repose (5) [ripowz'], *n.* 1. rest; sleep. **Ex.** *His brief repose was interrupted by her arrival.* 2. calm; peace. **Ex.** *There was an air of repose in the village.* —*v.* lie at rest. **Ex.** *Many soldiers killed in battle repose in foreign soil.*

represent (2) [rep'rizent'], *v.* 1. express by some symbol or sign; symbolize. **Ex.** *On this map, the color blue represents water.* 2. show; picture. **Ex.** *This painting represents the artist's boyhood home.* 3. act in place of or as a substitute for. **Ex.** *Since I cannot go, he will represent me.* 4. serve as an example of. **Ex.** *She represents the modern businesswoman.* —**rep·re·sen·ta'tion,** *n.* act of representing or being represented. —**rep·re·sent'a·tive,** *n.* 1. one who represents another or others. 2. a member of the House of Representatives, the lower of the two legislative groups that make up the United States Congress, or a member of a similar body in certain state legislatures. —*adj.* representing another or others.

repress (5) [ripres'], *v.* 1. control; keep back. **Ex.** *She repressed her tears in public.* 2. control completely by authority; crush. **Ex.** *That country's government represses all those who try to speak freely.* 3. force out of one's awareness. **Ex.** *She repressed her fear of the dark.* —**re·pres'sion,** *n.* —**re·pres'sive,** *adj.*

reprisal [riprayz'əl], *n.* an act of paying back others for something damaging done, often by doing something worse. **Ex.**

The warship shelled the town in reprisal for the bombing of the embassy.

reproach (4) [riprowč], *v.* blame; find fault with. **Ex.** *She reproached him for staying out so late.* —*n.* 1. the act of blaming; words of blame. **Ex.** *Her mother's reproaches make her unhappy.* 2. the cause for shame or blame. **Ex.** *The poor reading ability of the student was a reproach to the school system.*

reproduce (5) [riy`prəduws', riy'prədyuws'], *v.* 1. show or produce again. **Ex.** *He reproduced the letter from memory.* 2. copy or imitate. **Ex.** *I reproduced the report on the computer.* 3. among animals and plants, produce one's kind. **Ex.** *Humans can reproduce in nine months.* —**re·pro·duc'tion,** *n.* 1. the act of reproducing. 2. the thing reproduced.

reprove (5) [ripruwv'], *v.* blame or find fault with in a gentle way. **Ex.** *She reproved the maid for breaking the dish.* —**re·proof',** *n.* act of reproving.

reptile (4) [rep'til, rep'tayl], *n.* any cold-blooded animal that creeps or crawls, such as a snake or turtle. **Ex.** *Most reptiles that lived in the prehistoric era are now extinct.*

republic (3) [ripəb'lik], *n.* a form of government in which people elect others to represent them and do the work of the government. **Ex.** *The president of our republic is chosen every four years.* —**re·pub'li·can,** *adj.* —**Re·pub'li·can,** *n.* a member of the Republican party, one of the two main political parties of the United States. **Ex.** *Dwight D. Eisenhower, the thirty-fourth President of the United States, was a Republican.*

repulse (5) [ripəls'], *v.* 1. drive back or push away an attacker. **Ex.** *The enemy was repulsed.* 2. refuse or turn away from in an unfriendly manner. **Ex.** *She repulsed her neighbor's offer of help.* —*n.* 1. the act of driving back. **Ex.** *The quick repulse of his army surprised the general.* 2. refusal. **Ex.** *He was hurt by her repulse of his friendship.* —**re·pul'sive,** *adj.* causing a feeling of disgust or strong dislike. —**re·pul'sion,** *n.* act of repulsing; a strong dislike. **Ex.** *She felt repulsion as the drunken men approached her.*

reputation (3) [rep`yətey'šən], *n.* the opinion which people generally have about a person or thing. **Ex.** *That hotel has a reputation for good service.* —**re·pute',** *n.* reputation. —**rep'u·ta·ble,** *adj.* well thought of; reliable; having a good reputation.

request (2) [rikwest'], *n.* 1. the act of asking for. **Ex.** *He would not listen to my request.* 2. the thing asked for. **Ex.** *The old* *woman's dying request was granted.* —v. 1. ask for something. **Ex.** *The boy requested permission to leave school early.* 2. ask someone to do something. **Ex.** *She requested me to write a letter of recommendation.*

require (1) [rikwayr'], v. 1. need. **Ex.** *The sick man required constant attention.* 2. demand, as by right or authority. **Ex.** *The school required a record of his past studies.* —**re·quire'ment,** n. something needed or demanded. **Ex.** *Successful completion of the basic course is a requirement for admission to this course.*

rescue (3) [res'kyuw], v. make free from danger, evil, etc.; save. **Ex.** *The passengers were rescued from the sinking ship.* —n. the act of saving. **Ex.** *The rescue of the flood victims was accomplished rapidly.* —**res'cu·er,** n. one who rescues.

research (3) [risərč', riy'sərč], n. careful study to discover correct information. **Ex.** *Scientists are continuing research on peaceful uses of atomic energy.* —v. study carefully to discover correct information. **Ex.** *He has not researched that aspect of the situation yet.* —**re·search'er,** n. one who does research.

resemble (3) [rizem'bəl], v. be or look like or similar to. **Ex.** *Her voice resembles her mother's.* —**re·sem'blance,** n. a similarity; a likeness. **Ex.** *There's a strong resemblance between the two brothers.*

resent (3) [rizent'], v. feel bitterness or anger at. **Ex.** *She resented his remarks about her poor driving.* —**re·sent'ment,** n.

reservation [rez'ərvey'šən], n. 1. that which is set aside for one's use. **Ex.** *We have a room reservation at that hotel for Friday night.* 2. certain lands set aside by the United States government as a place for Indian tribes to live. 3. doubt; uncertainty. **Ex.** *I have some reservations about whether he is capable of doing the work.*

reserve (3) [rizərv'], v. 1. save for future use. **Ex.** *They reserved some of the corn to use as seed.* 2. have set aside for one's use. **Ex.** *We reserved a hotel room for tonight.* 3. hold or keep for oneself. **Ex.** *He reserved the right to approve the illustrations for his book.* —n. 1. something set aside for future use or a particular purpose. **Ex.** *The city's reserve of water is low.* 2. public land set aside for a particular use. **Ex.** *This park is one of the national forest reserves.*

reservoir (5) [rez'ərvwar`, rez'ərvɔ:r'], n. 1. a large tank or lake for storing water; a large tank for storing liquids. **Ex.** *Most of* *the city's water comes from this reservoir.* 2. a supply of anything held back or available for later use. **Ex.** *His reservoir of strength helped him to recover.*

reside (3) [rizayd'], *v.* 1. have as one's home; live in a place. **Ex.** *Where do you reside now?* 2. be located in or at. **Ex.** *The power to enact laws resides in the legislature.* —**res'i·dence,** *n.* a place where one lives. —**res'i·dent,** *n.* one who resides. —**res'i·den'tial,** *adj.* of or consisting of homes. **Ex.** *He lives in a residential area near the lake.*

resign (3) [rizayn'], *v.* quit one's position, job, etc. **Ex.** *She resigned from her job because of illness.* —**res'ig·na'tion,** *n.* the act of quitting.

resist (3) [rezist'], *v.* 1. oppose; fight to prevent. **Ex.** *The thief resisted arrest.* 2. prevent oneself from doing. **Ex.** *He could not resist laughing at her mistake.* —**re·sist'ance,** *n.* —**re·sist'ant,** *adj.*

resolute (5) [rez'əluwt], *adj.* having an unchanging purpose; constant. **Ex.** *Despite the opposition to his plan, he remained resolute.*

resolution (5) [rez'əluw'šən], *n.* 1. a formal agreement by a group of people. **Ex.** *A resolution to support the government program was voted on by the legislature.* 2. the resolving of something. **Ex.** *The resolution of the problem was a difficult process.* 3. decision on a way of acting. **Ex.** *He made a resolution to be more generous.* 4. condition of being firm and unchanging in purpose. **Ex.** *Her resolution to overcome all obstacles made her succeed.* 5. condition of having arrived at an answer to a problem. **Ex.** *Their resolution of the border dispute was praised.*

resolve (3) [rizalv'], *v.* 1. decide or determine to do something. **Ex.** *He resolved to quit smoking.* 2. express a group opinion or decision by voting. **Ex.** *The group resolved to oppose the proposed highway.* 3. solve. **Ex.** *Most of the problems were resolved at the last meeting.* —*n.* something definitely decided; intention. **Ex.** *His resolve to be a doctor has not changed.*

resort (3) [rizɔrt'], *v.* go to for help. **Ex.** *He resorted to asking his friends for money.* —*n.* 1. a place that people visit for a rest or vacation. **Ex.** *They went to a resort in the mountains last summer.* 2. a person or thing from whom or which one seeks help. **Ex.** *He was her last resort.*

resource (4) [risɔrs', riy'sɔrs], *n*. 1. a reserve or source of supply, support or assistance. **Ex.** *This country has many natural resources.* 2. skill or talent in handling difficulties. **Ex.** *A person of great resource was needed to accomplish the job.* —**re·source'ful**, *adj*. able or skillful in handling difficulties.

respect (2) [rispəkt'], *v*. 1. regard with honor. **Ex.** *We respect him as a great artist.* 2. show consideration or concern for. **Ex.** *They respected his right to differ with them.* —*n*. 1. regard, admiration and honor. **Ex.** *We have great respect for your opinion.* 2. concern or consideration for. **Ex.** *He always shows respect for his elders.* 3. aspect; detail; way. **Ex.** *In many respects, he is more capable than his brother.* —**re·spect'able**, *adj*. highly regarded; correct and acceptable. —**pay one's respects**, show regard formally. **Ex.** *They attended the reception to pay their respects to the new college president.*

respective (5) [rispek'tiv], *adj*. of or for each individual or thing; particular. **Ex.** *Each went his respective way.*

respond (4) [rispand'], *v*. 1. reply; answer. **Ex.** *She did not respond to my question.* 2. act as a result of; show an effect. **Ex.** *The sick man responded to the new medicine.*

response (4) [rispans'], *n*. 1. an answer; a reply. **Ex.** *I am awaiting your response to my letter.* 2. the reaction produced as a result of. **Ex.** *The doctor was pleased with the patient's response to the treatment.* —**re·spon'sive**, *adj*. being an answer or reaction; willing to respond. **Ex.** *She was very responsive to my suggestions.*

responsible (2) [rispan'səbəl], *adj*. 1. having a duty to do or to take care of; accountable for something that should be done. **Ex.** *Who is responsible for turning out the lights?* 2. being the cause or producer. **Ex.** *Which driver was responsible for the accident?* 3. deserving of trust. **Ex.** *You can depend upon him; he is a responsible person.* 4. involving important obligations. **Ex.** *He holds a responsible position in the bank.* —**re·spon'si·bly**, *adv*. —**re·spon'si·bil'i·ty**, *n*. that for which one is responsible. **Ex.** *Locking the doors is his responsibility.*

rest (1) [rest'], *v*. 1. become refreshed by sitting, sleeping, etc. **Ex.** *She rested for half an hour.* 2. lean; lie; be set; be supported. **Ex.** *He rested his left arm on the table.* —*n*. 1. a period of doing no work and of being inactive; a period of sleeping, sitting, etc. **Ex.** *Have a rest and you will not feel so tired.* 2. absence of motion. **Ex.** *The ball came to rest at his feet.* —**rest'ful,** *adj.* quiet; able to give rest. **Ex.** *The park is a restful place.* —**res'tive,** *adj.* not resting; disturbed. **Ex.** *The students were restive while he talked.* —**rest'less,** *adj.* without rest; not able to rest. **Ex.** *She was restless as she waited for him to return.* —**rest'less·ly,** *adv.*

rest (1) [rest'], *n.* 1. that which is left; the remainder. **Ex.** *Eat the rest of your dinner.* 2. those that remain; the others. **Ex.** *The rest of the students are taking the trip next week.*

restaurant (3) [res'tərant'], *n.* a public place where meals are served to customers by a waiter or waitress for money. **Ex.** *They ate dinner at the best restaurant in town.*

restore (4) [ristɔːr'], *v.* 1. return to an original, usual or former condition. **Ex.** *After a long sickness, his health was restored.* 2. return. **Ex.** *The thief restored the jewels he had stolen.* —**res'to·ra'tion,** *n.* 1. the act of restoring or rebuilding. 2. that which is restored or rebuilt.

restrain (4) [ristreyn'], *v.* hold under control; limit action. **Ex.** *She could not restrain the children from running into the street.* —**re·straint',** *n.* 1. the act or means of restraining. **Ex.** *They had to put temporary restraints on the disturbed man.* 2. reserve; self-control. **Ex.** *His restraint in not showing his anger was admirable.*

restrict (5) [ristrikt'], *v.* limit; confine. **Ex.** *The sale of liquor in this city is restricted to people twenty-one years old and over.* —**re·stric'tion,** *n.* —**re·stric'tive,** *adj.* limiting. **Ex.** *The rules are very restrictive here.*

rest room [rest' ruwm'], *n.* a room in a public place such as a theater, restaurant, etc. equipped with one or more toilets for eliminating bodily wastes and one or more wash basins for washing the hands. **Ex.** *The rest rooms are downstairs.*

result (1) [rizəlt'], *n.* that which follows or is produced by a cause; an effect. **Ex.** *I became ill as a result of my long journey.* —*v.* happen or arise from a cause. **Ex.** *His broken leg resulted from a fall.* —**re·sult'ant,** *adj.*

resume (5) [rizuwm'], *v.* 1. continue after a stop. **Ex.** *Classes resumed yesterday after the end of spring vacation.* 2. occupy again. **Ex.** *After speaking, he resumed his seat.* —**re·sump'tion,** *n.*

résumé (3) [rez`umey', rez'umey`], *n.* 1. a short report of the contents of something longer. Ex. *Give me a five-minute résumé of her talk.* 2. a short report of one's working experience submitted when one is applying for a job. Ex. *He mailed copies of his résumé to several possible employers.*

retail (5) [riy'teyl], *n.* the sale of goods in small quantities to the actual user. Ex. *Most people buy meat and groceries at retail.* —*adj.* having to do with selling at retail. Ex. *This is a retail store.* —**re'tail'er**, *n.* one who sells at retail; a store owner.

retain (3) [riteyn'], *v.* 1. continue to possess; hold. Ex. *They still retain their big house.* 2. remember. Ex. *She tried to retain all the rules of English grammar that she had learned.* 3. hire or engage the services of by paying a sum of money. Ex. *Is she the lawyer the accused retained for his defense?*

retard (5) [ritard'], *v.* slow progress; delay. Ex. *Lack of money retarded the program.* —**re·tard'ed**, *adj.* slow or behind in some way. Ex. *Mentally retarded people need special help to learn.*

retire (3) [ritayr'], *v.* 1. leave one's job because of long service, age, poor health, etc. Ex. *He retired from his job several years ago.* 2. go to bed. Ex. *She did not retire until midnight.* 3. draw apart from to be alone or quiet. Ex. *There was so much noise in the living room that he retired to the study.* —**re·tir'ing**, *adj.* shy; withdrawn. Ex. *She is very retiring with strangers.* —**re·tire'ment**, *n.* 1. the act of retiring. 2. the period after one has retired.

retort (4) [ritort'], *v.* answer quickly in a sharp or clever way. Ex. *He retorted that her questions were not worth answering.* —*n.* a sharp or clever reply. Ex. *She was not amused by his retort.*

retouch [riytəč], *v.* change small parts to improve the whole. Ex. *He retouched the old painting to eliminate cracks.*

retreat (3) [ritriyt'], *v.* 1. go away or apart from in order to gain privacy. Ex. *She retreated to her bedroom during her parents' argument.* 2. move back and away from action. Ex. *The troops retreated from the hill.* —*n.* 1. the act of moving back. Ex. *The army's retreat was not expected.* 2. a quiet place in which to be alone. Ex. *A shaded corner of the garden was his favorite retreat.*

return (1) [ritərn'], *v.* 1. go or come back to or from. Ex. *We returned home by car.* 2. bring, give, send or put back. Ex.

Please return these books to her. —n. 1. the act of going or coming **back** to or from a place. **Ex.** *We met him on his return from school.* 2. the act of bringing, putting, sending or paying back; that which is returned. **Ex.** *If you help me, I will help you in return.* —adj. of or for a return. **Ex.** *They have tickets for their return trip.*

reveal (2) [riviyl'], *v.* 1. tell or make known something either not known or secret. **Ex.** *Her aunt revealed what had happened in the house years ago.* 2. show plainly; display. **Ex.** *He opened the door and revealed the garden.* —**rev'e·la'tion,** *n.* act of revealing; something revealed. **Ex.** *That she could cook was a revelation to her new husband.*

revenge (3) [rivenj], *v.* harm or injure as payment for real or imagined harm or injury done. **Ex.** *He revenged the wrong done to his family.* —n. 1. the act of harming or injuring in repayment. **Ex.** *They set fire to their neighbor's house in revenge.* 2. the desire for revenge. **Ex.** *His mind was filled with thoughts of revenge.*

revenue (4) [rev'ənuw', rev'ənyuw'], *n.* money received from any source such as profit, taxes, income, etc., especially the taxes and other money collected by governments. **Ex.** *The new tax will be an added source of revenue.*

revere (5) [rivi:r'], *v.* feel great honor, respect and affection toward. **Ex.** *The students revered the old professor.* —**rev'er·ence,** *n.* feeling of great respect. —**rev'er·ent,** *adj.* —**rev'er·ent·ly,** *adv.* —**Rev'er·end,** *n.* a respectful title for a member of the clergy.

reverse (4) [rivərs'], *adj.* 1. contrary or opposite in direction; backward; upside down. **Ex.** *He read the numbers in reverse order.* 2. of the opposite to that facing; of the back or rear. **Ex.** *The reverse side of the material won't be seen when the dress is worn.* —n. 1. that which is the opposite or contrary. **Ex.** *He said he would refuse, but he did the reverse.* 2. the back or rear side of anything. **Ex.** *Some words were written on the reverse of the painting.* —v. turn backwards; turn inside out; turn upside down. **Ex.** *To reach town they had to reverse their direction.* —**re·vers'ible,** *adj.* able to be turned or worn inside out. **Ex.** *His raincoat is reversible.*

review (3) [rivyuw'], *v.* 1. examine again; study again. **Ex.** *Review all the facts before you decide.* 2. think of again. **Ex.** *He reviewed the events of the day before.* 3. make a critical examination and judgment of some art or writing. **Ex.** *This* *book has been reviewed favorably in several newspapers.* 4. reconsider the findings of a lower court. **Ex.** *Will a higher court review the judge's decision?* —*n.* 1. the process of looking over, discussing or studying again. **Ex.** *The teacher said that tomorrow there would be a review of what we had studied so far this term.* 2. an article in a magazine or newspaper about a book, painting, etc. **Ex.** *The concert received good reviews.* —**re·view'er**, *n.* one who reviews literature and the arts for a newspaper, magazine, etc.

revise (5) [rivayz'], *v.* 1. change or alter. **Ex.** *When you know the facts, you may revise your opinion.* 2. read carefully to correct errors and make more timely. **Ex.** *They have been asked to revise their book.* —**re·vi'sion**, *n.*

revive (4) [rivayv'], *v.* 1. return or be returned to consciousness. **Ex.** *The quick action of the doctor revived the dying man.* 2. return or be returned to health or an active condition. **Ex.** *The hot tea revived the chilled traveler.* —**re·viv'al**, *n.*

revoke [rivowk'], *v.* call back; put an end to; recall. **Ex.** *His driver's license was revoked after he was convicted of drunken driving.*

revolt (3) [rivowlt'], *n.* 1. rebellion. **Ex.** *The revolt began among a small group of workers.* 2. a protest; a refusal to follow orders or obey authority. **Ex.** *The clothes that young people wear today are often a symbol of revolt.* —*v.* 1. rebel against authority. **Ex.** *They revolted against their foreign ruler.* 2. fill with horror or strong feelings of dislike. **Ex.** *He was revolted by the smell and became ill.*

revolution (3) [rev'əluw'šən], *n.* 1. complete ruin or defeat of an established government or a political system and its replacement by another. **Ex.** *The American Revolution occurred in 1776.* 2. any complete or thorough change. **Ex.** *The invention of modern machines has caused a revolution in the way we live.* 3. the act of revolving one complete turn. **Ex.** *One revolution of the minute hand of the clock takes one hour.* —**rev'o·lu'tion·ar·y**, *adj.* —**rev'o·lu'tion·ize**, *v.* cause a great change. **Ex.** *The airplane revolutionized travel.*

revolve (3) [rivalv'], *v.* turn around or spin on its own center; move in orbit. **Ex.** *The earth revolves around the sun.*

revolver (5) [rival'vər], *n.* a pistol that can be fired several times without reloading because of a revolving part that holds several bullets. **Ex.** *The dead man had been shot in the chest several times with a revolver.*

reward (2) [riwɔrd'], *n.* 1. money or honor given for some special service or performance. **Ex.** *As a reward for his bravery, the soldier was given a medal.* 2. money for the return of lost or stolen property. **Ex.** *A reward was offered for the return of the dog.* —*v.* give a reward to or for. **Ex.** *She rewarded him with a kiss.* —**re·ward'ing,** *adj.* satisfying; worthwhile. **Ex.** *He had always found teaching rewarding work.*

rhyme (4) [raym'], *n.* 1. similarity of sounds at the ends of words or lines of poetry. **Ex.** *The poet used the word* flight *as a rhyme for the word* night. 2. poems in which the sounds at the ends of the lines are similar. **Ex.** *What was your favorite childhood rhyme?* —*v.* 1. sound similar. **Ex.** Dear *rhymes with* near. 2. use a word as a rhyme for another word. **Ex.** *He rhymed* heart *with* part.

rhythm [riðˈəm], *n.* regularly repeated arrangement of sounds or movements such as in music, dance, poetry, speech and natural occurrences. **Exs.** *The rhythm of the piece the band was playing made him want to dance. She enjoyed following the rhythm of the seasons.* —**rhyth'mic,** *adj.*

rib (3) [rib'], *n.* 1. any of the arched bones attached to the backbone and enclosing the chest. **Ex.** *The blow he received broke a rib.* 2. something that looks or feels like a rib. **Ex.** *My umbrella has a bent rib.*

ribbon (2) [rib'ən], *n.* 1. a narrow piece of cloth, plastic or other material used to form bows, tie gift packages, etc. **Ex.** *The girl wore a blue ribbon in her hair.* 2. something that resembles a ribbon. **Ex.** *A ribbon of smoke curled from the chimney.* 3. a narrow, torn piece of something. **Ex.** *The sails of the ship were torn to ribbons by the storm.*

rice (2) [rays'], *n.* the seed or grain from a grassy plant widely grown in warm climates and used as a main food in many parts of the world, especially Asia; the plant itself. **Ex.** *She served rice with the meat.*

rich (1) [rič'], *adj.* 1. having much money or goods. **Ex.** *He is a rich man.* 2. yielding or producing much. **Ex.** *The town is surrounded by rich farmland.* 3. having plenty of. **Ex.** *The* *water from this spring is rich in minerals.* 4. valuable; costly. **Ex.** *Her gown was made of a rich cloth.* 5. full of eggs, milk or cream, butter and sugar. **Ex.** *This cake is so rich that you should serve it in thin slices.* 6. full and strong. **Ex.** *Her rich voice expressed the deep feeling of the song.* —**rich'ness,** *n.*

rid (3) [rid'], *v.* make free or clear of something undesirable; eliminate something from. **Ex.** *He rid the house of rats.* —**get rid of,** get free or clear of. **Ex.** *She got rid of the smell by opening the window.* —**rid'dance,** *n.* a getting rid of.

ridden (1) [rid'ən], *v.* past participle of *ride.* **Ex.** *He has ridden that horse before.*

riddle (5) [rid'əl], *n.* 1. a puzzle in the form of a question. **Ex.** *To the riddle "What walks on four legs in the morning, two legs at noon and three legs in the evening?" the answer is "Man."* 2. any person, place or thing that is mysterious or difficult to understand. **Ex.** *That painting has always been a riddle to me.*

ride (1) [rayd'], *v.* 1. sit on or in and be carried along. **Ex.** *Five people can ride in this car.* 2. sit on and cause to move. **Ex.** *He rides his bicycle to school.* —*n.* a trip in a car, on a horse, etc. **Ex.** *We are going for a boat ride this evening.* —**rid'er,** *n.* one who rides.

ridge (3) [rij], *n.* 1. a range of hills or mountains; the upper part of such a range. **Ex.** *Our camp is just beyond the next ridge.* 2. any raised, narrow strip or line. **Ex.** *Two birds were sitting on the ridge of the roof.*

ridiculous (3) [ridik'yələs], *adj.* deserving of or causing scorn; foolish. **Ex.** *That is a ridiculous way to behave!* —**ri·dic'u·lous·ly,** *adv.* —**rid'i·cule,** *n.* words or actions intended to make a person or thing seem foolish. **Ex.** *His idea was received with ridicule.* —*v.* mock; make fun of. **Ex.** *They ridiculed his strange clothes.*

rifle (3) [ray'fel], *n.* a gun with a long barrel, the inside surface of which has thin, twisted cuts designed to make a bullet spin.

RIFLE

right (1) [rayt'], *adj.* 1. agreeing with the facts; correct. **Ex.** *Most of the students' answers were right.* 2. of or on the side of the body on which the hand is usually stronger, more skillful and quick; on the side of the body toward the east when facing north. **Ex.** *He held the pencil in his right hand.* 3.

suitable to the situation; fit. **Ex.** *Is this dress right to wear to a wedding?* 4. done according to law or according to one's duty or conscience; just; good. **Ex.** *She always did what she believed to be right.* 5. meant to be seen or placed toward the outside. **Ex.** *Which is the right side of this material?* —*n.* 1. that which is lawful or proper. **Ex.** *He is old enough to know right from wrong.* 2. something to which a person has a legal and proper claim. **Ex.** *The rights of the people are protected by law.* 3. in politics, those least desirous of change and most anxious to keep things as they are. **Ex.** *The right does not want a new tax.* 4. the right hand or side. **Ex.** *An old friend was sitting on my right.* —*adv.* 1. according to law, duty or conscience; correctly. **Ex.** *We must try to do it right.* 2. in a straight line; directly. **Ex.** *She went right home after school.* 3. exactly. *Put it right there.* 4. toward the right. **Ex.** *Turn right at the next corner.* —*v.* correct. **Ex.** *They attempted to right an old wrong.*

right angle [rayt' æŋ'gəl], an angle of ninety degrees.

right-hand [rayt'hænd'], *adj.* 1. on or toward the right. **Ex.** *He made a right-hand turn.* 2. chiefly relied upon. **Ex.** *He is my right-hand man.* —**right-handed,** *adj.* tending to prefer

RIGHT ANGLE

to use the right hand. **Ex.** *All of the people in this class happen to be right-handed.*

right of way [rayt əv wey'], 1. the right to move, as in driving a car, before others do. **Ex.** *When the traffic light became green, he had the right of way.* 2. lawful right to go across another's property. **Ex.** *We have a right of way through his farm to the highway.*

rigid (4) [rij'id], *adj.* 1. not easily bent; stiff. **Ex.** *The tent was supported by rigid poles.* 2. severe; strict. **Ex.** *His parents had rigid ideas.* —**rig'id·ly,** *adv.* —**ri·gid'i·ty,** *n.*

rim (4) [rim'], *n.* an edge or border of something rounded or curved. **Ex.** *There was a band of gold around the rim of the cup.*

ring (1) [riŋ'], *n.* 1. a narrow circle of metal, often gold or silver, worn on the finger as an ornament. **Ex.** *She was wearing a diamond engagement ring.* 2. any narrow band of material in the shape of a circle used for holding or fastening things. **Ex.** *He carried six keys on his key ring.* 3. any arrangement of things or persons in a circle. **Ex.** *The dancers stood in a ring.* 4. a group of persons working together for some illegal or evil reason. **Ex.** *A ring of thieves stole the money.* —*v.* surround; form a ring around. **Ex.** *The fort was ringed by enemy forces.*

ring (1) [riŋ'], *v.* 1. give or produce a sound as of a bell. **Ex.** *Did you hear the dinner bell ring?* 2. cause a bell to sound. **Ex.** *Did you ring the bell?* 3. summon or announce with a bell. **Ex.** *Will you please ring for someone to carry my bags?* —*n.* 1. the sound of a bell or something similar to a bell. **Ex.** *I heard the ring of laughter outside.* 2. telephone call. **Ex.** *Give me a ring so that we can talk about the matter.*

ringleader [riŋ'liy'dər], *n.* one who leads or directs a group, usually in illegal activities. **Ex.** *All the members of the ring were caught except the ringleader.*

rinse (3) [rins'], *v.* 1. wash lightly. **Ex.** *She rinsed her hands.* 2. remove the soap from with clean water as a final step in washing. **Ex.** *Did you rinse the dishes thoroughly?* —*n.* the act of rinsing; the liquid in which something is rinsed; a special liquid that adds color or shine to hair. **Ex.** *What kind of a rinse do you use for your hair?*

riot (4) [ray'ət], *n.* 1. a disturbance created by a large group of people whose behavior is noisy, wild and violent. **Ex.** *The police were called to control the riot.* 2. a brilliant and sometimes confusing display. **Ex.** *The flower beds were a riot of color.* —*v.* take part in a riot. **Ex.** *Crowds were rioting in the streets.* —**ri'ot·ous,** *adj.*

rip (4) [rip'], *v.* cut or tear something roughly. **Ex.** *He ripped his shirt on a nail.* —*n.* a torn place. **Ex.** *She mended the rip in her dress.*

ripe (3) [rayp'], *adj.* 1. ready to be eaten. **Ex.** *This apple is ripe.* 2. having reached full development. **Ex.** *The farmer lived to a ripe old age.* —**rip'en,** *v.* become or make ripe.

ripple (4) [rip'əl], *v.* form small waves or movements like waves. **Ex.** *The breeze began to ripple the surface of the lake.* —*n.* a small wave or wavelike form. **Ex.** *The canvas was stretched over the frame without a ripple.*

rise (1) [rayz'], *v.* 1. go upwards; go from a sitting or lying position to a standing position. **Ex.** *She was unable to rise from her seat.* 2. get out of bed; get up after sleeping. **Ex.** *He rises early in the morning.* 3. gain rank, fortune, etc. **Ex.**

a, far; æ, am; e, get; ey, late; i, in; iy, see; ɔ, all; ow, go; u, put; uw, too; ə, but, ago; ər, fur; aw, out; ay, life; oy, boy; ŋ, ring; θ, think; ð, that; ž, measure; š, ship; j, edge; č, child.

Everyone expects him to rise to a top position in the company. 4. become greater, higher or stronger. **Ex.** *His voice began to rise as he became more angry.* —*n.* 1. the act of rising. **Ex.** *His rise to a position of wealth came suddenly.* 2. An increase or advance. **Ex.** *We expect a rise in food prices this winter.* 3. a hill; a piece of ground higher than that surrounding it. **Ex.** *The city was built on a rise.* —**give rise to,** cause; produce. **Ex.** *His words gave rise to doubts concerning his true intentions.*

risen [riz'ən], *v.* past participle of *rise.* **Ex.** *He has risen far in his profession.*

risk (3) [risk'], *n.* the possibility of loss, damage, injury; danger. **Ex.** *There are some risks in every venture of this kind.* —*v.* 1. place in a position of danger. **Ex.** *He risked his life to save the child.* 2. take the chance of. **Ex.** *He was not willing to risk losing any more money.* —**risk'y,** *adj.* dangerous.

rival (3) [ray'vəl], *n.* one who tries to equal or do better than another; one who competes for something. **Ex.** *The two boys were rivals for the first prize.* —*adj.* trying for the same thing; competing. **Ex.** *They worked for rival businesses.* —*v.* 1. try to do better than. **Ex.** *The two teams rivaled each other for first place.* 2. equal; be as good as. **Ex.** *Nothing can rival the beauty of a sunrise.* —**ri'val·ry,** *n.*

river (1) [riv'ər], *n.* a large body of water that flows into another river, a lake or an ocean. **Ex.** *After four weeks of rain, the river had swollen to flood level.*

road (1) [rowd'], *n.* 1. a public way or passage for traveling between places by car, bus, etc. **Ex.** *That road takes you to the city quickly.* 2. way; path; course. **Ex.** *He seems to be on the road to fame and fortune.*

roam (4) [rowm'], *v.* wander; go from place to place without a plan. **Ex.** *The dog roamed the fields.*

roar (2) [rɔːr'], *v.* 1. make a loud, deep cry or sound. **Ex.** *The bull roared in anger.* 2. shout or laugh loudly. **Ex.** *The audience roared at his jokes.* —*n.* a loud, deep sound or noise. **Ex.** *They could hear the roar of the ocean waves.*

roast (3) [rowst'], *v.* cook food, usually without water, fat or oil, by placing it in a hot oven or over a fire. **Ex.** *She roasted a leg of lamb and some potatoes for dinner.* —*n.* a piece of meat cooked or to be cooked in a hot oven or over a fire. **Ex.** *We had a roast for dinner.* —*adj.* prepared by roasting. **Ex.** *We like roast chicken.*

rob (3) [rab'], *v*. take the money or property of another by force; steal. **Ex.** *Their house was robbed last night.* —**rob'ber**, *n*. one who robs. —**rob'ber·y**, *n*. the act of robbing.

robe (3) [rowb'], *n*. 1. a long, loose garment worn over other clothes; a gown. **Ex.** *He wore a robe over his pajamas.* 2. a specially shaped, long gown worn by a judge, a priest, etc. showing rank or office.

robin (5) [rab'in], *n*. a bird with a dark back and a reddish orange breast.

robot [row'bat], *n*. 1. a machine, sometimes with a slightly human appearance, that is able to perform certain tasks that a human can do. **Ex.** *After dinner the robot served coffee in the living room.* 2. a person who performs tasks in a mechanical manner without thinking about what he or she is doing. **Ex.** *I handed her the draft of my letter which she began typing immediately like a robot.*

rock (1) [rak'], *n*. 1. a broken piece of stone. **Ex.** *The boy threw a rock through the window.* 2. a large mass of stone, sometimes forming a cliff. **Ex.** *They climbed up on the rock.* —*v*. move back and forth or from side to side gently; shake strongly. **Ex.** *The boat was rocked by the wind.* —**rock'y**, *adj*. 1. like rock or having many pieces of stone. **Ex.** *The land was very rocky.* 2. moving back and forth; not steady. **Ex.** *The plane ride was somewhat rocky.* —**rock'er**, *n*. 1. one who rocks. 2. something, such as a chair, that rocks.

rock and roll [rak' ænd rowl'], a type of popular dance music, based partly on a special kind of jazz and on folk music, with a very strong loud beat. **Ex.** *The band at their wedding reception played extremely loud rock and roll.*

rock-bottom [rak'bat'əm], *adj*. at the lowest level or limit. **Ex.** *We bought this at a rock-bottom price.* —**rock bottom**, *n*. the lowest level. **Ex.** *His life has hit rock bottom.*

rocket (5) [rak'et], *n*. a tubelike device moved through the air or into space by burning fuel and letting the gas produced escape from the rear or bottom. **Ex.** *Rockets placed the spacecraft in orbit.*

ROCKET

rod (3) [rad'], *n*. a straight thin piece of wood, metal, etc. **Ex.** *She hung the curtains on a rod.*

rode (2) [rowd'], *v.* past tense of *ride*. **Ex.** *The boy rode to school on his bicycle.*

rogue (5) [rowg'], *n.* 1. a person who is not honest and has no principles. **Ex.** *That rogue sold me damaged goods!* 2. a mischievous, fun-loving person. **Ex.** *The little rogue hid my hat.* —**rogu'ish**, *adj.*

role (3) [rowl'], *n.* 1. a part or character which an actor, actress or singer takes in a play, movie, opera, etc. **Ex.** *Her role in that movie gave her a chance to prove her acting ability.* 2. a part or function assumed in life. **Ex.** *His new role as a parent required patience.*

roll (1) [rowl'], *v.* 1. move or be moved like a ball by turning over and over. **Ex.** *The ball rolled down the hill.* 2. move or be moved on wheels. **Ex.** *The train rolled along rapidly.* 3. wind into a ball or into a rounded shape. **Ex.** *She rolled the string into a ball.* 4. move along regularly and evenly. **Ex.** *Great waves rolled toward the shore.* 5. spread out and make flat by pressing with a roller or rollers. **Ex.** *The workers rolled the metal into thin sheets.* —*n.* anything formed into a ball or tube shape. **Ex.** *She bought a roll of wrapping paper.* 2. bread baked in a small, long or rounded portion. **Ex.** *He ate two rolls with his lunch.* 3. a list of names of members of a group. **Ex.** *The teacher called the roll.* —**roll out,** 1. flatten. 2. unwind. —**roll'er,** *n.* 1. a long rounded object that rolls, smooths or crushes. 2. a small wheel. 3. a device for applying paint.

roll call [rowl'kɔ:l'], *n.* a reading aloud of a roll of names in order to learn who is present and who is absent. **Ex.** *He was not present at roll call.*

roller skate [row'lər skeyt'], *n.* a skate with four wheels for skating on hard surfaces other than ice.

romance (3) [rowmæns', row'mæns], *n.* 1. a love affair. **Ex.** *Their romance began in high school.* 2. a story of heroic deeds and exciting scenes appealing to the imagination; a love story. **Ex.** *She enjoyed reading romances.* 3. the quality of excitement and love. **Ex.** *They traveled seeking adventure and romance.* —**ro·man'tic,** *adj.* 1. characteristic of or suggesting romance. 2. not practical; tending to dream. **Ex.** *He has a romantic idea that he might become a ship captain.*

roof (2) [ruwf', ruf], *n.* 1. the outside top cover of a building. **Ex.** *The roof was beginning to leak.* 2. something which in form or position is like a roof. **Ex.** *He slept in the open with the sky as his roof.* —*v.* cover with a roof. **Ex.** *The house was roofed with tin.*

room (1) [ruwm', rum], *n.* 1. an area of a building enclosed by walls and a ceiling. **Ex.** *They ate dinner in the dining room.* 2. space. **Ex.** *There is room in the car for one more person.* 3. opportunity. **Ex.** *There is room for advancement in his job.* —*v.* rent a room or rooms in the house of another. **Ex.** *She rooms with two other girls.* —**room'er,** *n.* one who rents a room in the house of another; a lodger. —**rooming house',** *n.* a house in which rooms can be or are rented. —**room'mate,** *n.* another person with whom one shares a room, apartment, etc. **Ex.** *He and his roommate work in the same office.*

rooster (3) [ruw'stər], *n.* a male chicken.

root (2) [ruwt', rut'], *n.* 1. the part of a plant that is under the ground and takes food from the soil. **Ex.** *Trees have large roots.* 2. a part of a tooth, hair, etc. which is under the skin. **Ex.** *The root of the tooth had to be removed.* 3. cause; origin. **Ex.** *An unbalanced diet was the root of her trouble.* —*v.* 1. send out roots and begin to grow. **Ex.** *This plant is difficult to root.* 2. dig up or search for something. **Ex.** *The pigs rooted in the straw with their noses.*

ROOSTER

rope (2) [rowp'], *n.* a strong cord made of twisted smaller cords. **Ex.** *He led the cow by a rope around her neck.* —*v.* catch and hold with a rope. **Ex.** *The men are out roping wild horses.*

ROPE

rose (2) [rowz'], *v.* past tense of *rise.* **Ex.** *They rose early in the morning.*

rose (2) [rowz'], *n.* 1. a bush having sweet-smelling flowers on stems with thorns; the flower itself. **Ex.** *Red roses were growing in the garden.* 2. a pinkish-red color. —**ros'y,** *adj.* 1. pink or pinkish-red. 2. fresh; healthy. 3. cheerful; happy. **Ex.** *She has a rosy view of life.*

rot (3) [rat'], *v.* 1. become soft and inedible; spoil. **Ex.** *The apples on the ground rotted.* 2. cause to decay or spoil. **Ex.**

a, far; æ, am; e, get; ey, late; i, in; iy, see; ɔ, all; ow, go; u, put; uw, too; ə, but, ago; ər, fur; aw, out; ay, life; oy, boy; ŋ, ring; θ, think; ð, that; ž, measure; š, ship; ǰ, edge; č, child.

Too much rain rotted the roots of the plant. —**rot'ten**, *adj.* spoiled; decayed; very bad. **Exs.** *Those eggs smell as if they are rotten. That was a rotten way to treat someone.*

rotate (5) [row'teyt], *v.* 1. turn around the center; revolve; spin like a wheel. **Ex.** *It takes the earth twenty-four hours to rotate on its axis.* 2. alternate; take turns. **Ex.** *The men rotate at the job so no one gets too tired.* —**ro·ta'tion**, *n.*

rouge [ruwž'], *n.* a cosmetic in the form of powder in a cake or a waxlike substance used to color the cheeks pink or red. **Ex.** *She applied a little rouge to her pale cheeks.*

rough (2) [rəf'], *adj.* 1. uneven; unpolished; not smooth. **Ex.** *The wall was made of rough stone.* 2. not gentle in actions; full of wild activity. **Ex.** *His rough manner frightened her.* 3. raging with storms and winds. **Ex.** *We had a rough sea voyage.* 4. having little comfort or luxury. **Ex.** *The early settlers lived a rough life.* 5. not finished; done in haste and without detail. **Ex.** *He showed us a rough sketch for the painting.* —**rough'en**, *v.* become or cause to become rough. **Ex.** *Work in the garden had roughened her hands.* —**rough'ly**, *adv.*

round (1) [rawnd'], *adj.* 1. having the shape of a ball, ring or circle. **Ex.** *I like to seat my guests at a round table.* 2. curving; not flat. **Ex.** *We could see the round top of the hill above the trees.* —*adv.* around; in a circle. **Exs.** *They gathered round and listened to his stories. The wheel turned round.* —*prep.* 1. enclosing; encircling. **Ex.** *He had a string tied round his finger.* 2. on all sides of. **Ex.** *They gathered round the speaker.* —*n.* 1. a series of events. **Ex.** *They went to a round of parties during the holidays.* 2. movement around a center or in a circle. 3. the act of bursting forth suddenly. **Ex.** *A round of applause greeted the president of our class.* 4. a game; a division of a game or sport. **Ex.** *How many rounds do you think this boxer will last?* 5. a single gunshot; the material needed for the shot. **Ex.** *Each person fired one round.* —*v.* travel around. **Ex.** *The ship rounded the southernmost point of land on March first.* —**rounds,** *n. pl.* a walk, trip, visit, etc. regularly taken in the course of business or duty; routine. **Ex.** *The doctor is making his rounds.* —**round off** or **out,** 1. make round or curved. **Ex.** *They rounded off the sharp corners of the table.* 2. express a number in the nearest number easy to add, subtract, etc. **Ex.** *He had 147 and we rounded it off to 150.* —**round up,** bring together. **Ex.** *Round up the children for supper.*

roundabout [rawnd'əbawt'], *adj.* not direct. **Ex.** *He was late because he went home by a roundabout way.*

round trip [rawnd' trip'], *n.* trip to a destination and back. **Ex.** *How much is the fare for the round trip?*

rouse (4) [rawz'], *v.* 1. awaken. **Ex.** *The noise roused the baby.* 2. excite. **Ex.** *The incident roused the people to protest.*

rout (5) [rawt'], *n.* a complete defeat with great confusion and a forced retreat. **Ex.** *The rout of their army ended the war.* —*v.* cause to flee. **Ex.** *The police routed the attacking mob.*

route (2) [ruwt', rawt'], *n.* 1. a way or road for passage or travel. **Ex.** *He had a choice between the scenic or the more direct route.* 2. a particular area in which a delivery or sales person works. **Ex.** *The boy has a newspaper route.* —*v.* send by a certain way. **Ex.** *The policeman routed the traffic around the accident.*

routine (4) [ruwtiyn'], *n.* way of doing things regularly, daily, etc. because of rules or habit. **Ex.** *She quickly became accustomed to the office routine.* —*adj.* done by routine; not requiring much thought. **Ex.** *He is assigned only routine duties.*

row (1) [row'], *n.* a series of persons or things arranged in a line. **Ex.** *The last two rows of seats were empty.*

row (1) [row'], *v.* move a boat through the water by using two poles with broad flat ends. **Ex.** *He rowed the boat across the lake.*

row (1) [raw'], *n.* a noisy quarrel. **Ex.** *We were awakened by a row next door.*

rowboat [row'bowt'], *n.* a small boat moved by rowing. **Ex.** *They were fishing from a rowboat.*

royal (2) [roy'əl], *adj.* 1. referring to a king, queen, etc. **Ex.** *He is a member of the royal family.* 2. part of or belonging to a royal government or to its ruler. **Ex.** *This is a ship of the royal navy.* —**roy'al·ly**, *adv.* —**roy'al·ty**, *n.* royal persons.

rub (2) [rəb'], *v.* 1. move something over a surface while pressing upon the surface. **Ex.** *He rubbed his sleepy eyes.* 2. move one surface against another with pressure. **Ex.** *Her shoe rubbed the skin on her heel.* 3. spread something by rubbing. **Ex.** *He rubbed the wax over the wood until it shone.* 4. remove by rubbing. **Ex.** *He rubbed the dirt off his shoes.* —**rub'down'**, *n.* a rubbing of the body for health or relaxation. **Ex.** *The nurse gave the patient a rubdown with alcohol.*

rubber (2) [rəb'er], *n*. 1. a commerically prepared substance, made from the thick juice of certain trees growing in hot climates, that can stretch and return to its original shape. **Ex.** *The rubber on my right front tire looks thin.* 2. a thin shoe made of this material that slips over a regular shoe and acts as a protection against rain, snow, etc. **Ex.** *You had better wear your rubbers because it looks like rain.* —*adj.* made of rubber. **Ex.** *The doctor wore rubber gloves.*

rubbish (5) [rəb'iš], *n*. 1. anything useless or without value. **Ex.** *Put the rubbish in the garbage can.* 2. useless or senseless words. **Ex.** *What he said was a lot of rubbish.*

ruby (5) [ruw'biy], *n*. a red stone, highly valued as a jewel. **Ex.** *Her ring has rubies and diamonds set in it.* —*adj.* deep red in color. **Ex.** *The wine was ruby red.*

rude (3) [ruwd'], *adj.* showing intentionally bad manners or lack of respect for others; impolite; crude. **Ex.** *His rude interruptions of the speaker disturbed his supporters.* —**rude'ly**, *adv.* —**rude'ness**, *n*.

ruffle (4) [rəf'əl], *v*. 1. gather or draw into tiny folds and sew down, as in cloth. **Ex.** *She ruffled the material and used it as edging on the curtains.* 2. disturb the arrangement of slightly. **Ex.** *The wind ruffled her hair.* —*n*. a strip of ruffled material.

rug (2) [rəg'], *n*. a single piece of thick material used as a floor covering. **Ex.** *There were several small rugs in the room.*

rugged [rəg'id], *adj.* 1. having a surface, edge or border that is rough; not even or regular. **Ex.** *Pirates used to land their boats on this rugged shoreline.* 2. very strongly built; tough; long wearing; enduring. **Exs.** *The men who built this railroad were rugged fellows. You will find that this oak flooring is very rugged.* 3. difficult to do or endure; rough, severe and unpleasant. **Ex.** *Their rugged training had prepared them well for their assignment.*

ruin (2) [ruw'in], *n*. 1. the remains of a building that has fallen down; anything which has become worthless through damage, age, etc. **Ex.** *We passed the ruin of an old castle.* 2. decay; destruction. **Ex.** *The church had fallen into ruins.* 3. that which is the cause of destruction or decay. **Ex.** *His love of drink was his ruin.* —*v*. 1. spoil; damage. **Ex.** *The rain ruined our plans.* 2. destroy financially. **Ex.** *The loss of his store by fire ruined him.* —**ru'in·a'tion**, *n*. —**ru'in·ous**, *adj.*

rule (1) [ruwl'], *n.* 1. an order; an established guide for conduct. **Ex.** *Students must obey the school rules.* 2. the usual way of doing things; one's regular practice; usual behavior. **Ex.** *It is their rule to eat dinner late.* 3. the government of a king or other person in authority. **Ex.** *His rule over the country lasted thirty years.* —*v.* 1. govern; control. **Ex.** *The queen ruled her country well.* 2. decide officially. **Ex.** *The court ruled that the activities of the accused were punishable.* —**rul'er,** *n.* a person who rules a country. **Ex.** *The country has had only three rulers during this century.* —**rul'ing,** *n.* an official decision. **Ex.** *The court's ruling supported freedom of speech.* —**as a rule,** generally; most often. **Ex.** *As a rule, he will not go to meetings.* —**rule out,** eliminate from consideration. **Ex.** *She ruled out going back to school.*

ruler (1) [ruwl'ər], *n.* a flat strip of wood, metal, etc. with a straight edge used in drawing lines and for measuring. **Ex.** *His ruler showed the width of the page to be six and one half inches.*

rum (5) [rəm'], *n.* a strong alcoholic liquor made from molasses or from the liquid from sugar cane. **Ex.** *He served a cool drink made with rum.*

rumble (4) [rəm'bəl], *n.* a continuous low, heavy sound. **Ex.** *She was awakened during the storm by the rumble of thunder.* —*v.* make a continuous low, heavy sound. **Ex.** *The trucks rumbled over the street.*

rumor (4) [ruw'mər], *n.* a report or story which may or may not be true. **Ex.** *There is a rumor that the president of the company will resign.* —*v.* tell or spread a rumor. **Ex.** *It is rumored that they will marry.*

run (1) [rən'], *v.* 1. move rapidly by steps that are faster than those used in walking. **Ex.** *Because he was late, he had to run to catch the train.* 2. take part in a race or contest. **Ex.** *Who is running for mayor?* 3. be in operation. **Ex.** *We could not get the motor to run.* 4. go to and from. **Ex.** *A boat runs between our town and the one across the lake.* 5. lie; stretch; extend. **Ex.** *The road runs through the woods and along the river.* 6. flow; move in a stream. **Ex.** *Tears were running down her face.* —*n.* the act of running. **Ex.** *He was tired after his long run.* —**run'ner,** *n.* one who moves rapidly by fast steps.

a, far; æ, am; e, get; ey, late; i, in; iy, see; ɔ, all; ow, go; u, put; uw, too; ə, but, ago; ər, fur; aw, out; ay, life; oy, boy; ŋ, ring; θ, think; ð, that; ž, measure; š, ship; j, edge; č, child.

runaway [rən'əwey'], *n.* a person or thing that flees from a place. **Ex.** *The runaway was returned to his family by friends.* —*adj.* of a person or thing that flees. **Ex.** *An engineer finally stopped the runaway train.*

run-down [rən'dawn'], *adj.* in poor health; in need of fixing. **Ex.** *The run-down house needed a new roof and new windows.*

rung (3) [rəŋ'], *v.* past participle of *ring.* **Ex.** *The bells were rung yesterday to mark the holiday.*

rung [rəŋ'], *n.* a crosspiece of a ladder used as a step. **Ex.** *He was standing on the top rung of the ladder when he fell.*

runner-up [rən'ərəp'], *n.* one who finishes a contest just behind the winner; number two. **Ex.** *My brother was the runner-up in the last race.*

running mate [rən'iŋ meyt'], *n.* one who seeks a lower elected office by running with one who seeks a higher office. **Ex.** *It is customary for the presidential candidate to choose his running mate.*

run-of-the-mill [rən'əvðəmil'], *adj.* plain; ordinary. **Ex.** *The excellent actors made the run-of-the-mill play seem interesting.*

runway [rən'wey'], *n.* a hard surfaced road or strip of land from which airplanes take off into the air or on which they land. **Ex.** *The plane had to sit on the runway for thirty minutes before taking off.*

rural (4) [ru:r'əl], *adj.* of farming areas; concerning the country. **Ex.** *They live in a small rural community.*

rush (1) [rəš'], *v.* go, move or send with unusual speed. **Ex.** *The firemen rushed to the burning building.* —*n.* the hurried movement of people or things. **Ex.** *She feared the rush of cars on the street.*

rush hour [rəš' awr'], *n.* a time of much traffic as people go to or return from work. **Ex.** *There are too many cars on the road during rush hour.*

rust (3) [rəst'], *n.* a rough, reddish-brown covering that forms on iron and steel exposed to air and moisture. **Ex.** *The unpainted iron fence was covered with rust.* —*v.* 1. become covered with rust; cause to be covered with rust. **Ex.** *My knife rusted when I left it out in the rain.* 2. spoil or become dull through lack of use. **Ex.** *His talents rusted after he retired.* —**rust'y**, *adj.*

rustle (4) [rəs'əl], *v.* make sounds as of things rubbing softly together. **Ex.** *Her silk dress rustled as she walked.* —*n.* the soft sound of things rubbing together gently while moving. **Ex.** *We heard the rustle of mice in the straw.*

rustle (4) [rəs'əl], *v.* steal cattle. **Ex.** *The cowboy knew who had been rustling the steers.*

rut [rət'], *n.* 1. a long track or groove made in the ground by continual passing of cars, trucks, etc. **Ex.** *The deep ruts in this dirt road make driving difficult.* 2. a set or fixed way of living, working, etc. that has a tiring and uninteresting sameness. **Ex.** *He feels that his present job has put him in a rut.*

rye (5) [ray'], *n.* a grass, the grain of which is used in feeding animals, making flour or whiskey, etc.; the seed or grain from this grass. **Ex.** *What proportion of rye do you use in the feed for your cows?* —*adj.* made of or with rye. **Ex.** *I like toast made from rye bread.*

S

S,s (1) [es'], *n.* the nineteenth letter of the English alphabet.

-s (1) [s, z], *suffix.* plural of many nouns. **Exs.** *Book, books; college, colleges; girl, girls.* —*es, suffix.* plural of many other nouns. **Exs.** *Arch, arches; box, boxes; hero, heroes.*

-s (1) [s, z] *suffix.* present tense of some verbs when speaking of a person or thing. **Exs.** *Run: He runs quickly. Write: She writes clearly.*

-'s (1) [s, z], *suffix.* 1. showing control or ownership. **Ex.** *That is John's book.* 2. short form, contraction of *is.* **Ex.** *She's late.* 3. short form, contraction of *has.* **Ex.** *He's eaten.* 4. short form, contraction of *us.* **Ex.** *Let's start.*

sabotage [sæb'ətaʃ], *n.* use of secret means to weaken a business, company, or in wartime, a country by damaging its buildings, machinery, etc. **Ex.** *The labor union denied that it was responsible for the acts of sabotage.* 2. any use of intentional, secret means to do harm to an effort or plan. **Ex.** *They tapped their rival company's telephone for purposes of sabotage.* —*v.* commit sabotage. **Ex.** *His hopes for promotion were sabotaged by his fellow workers.*

sack (3) [sæk'], *n.* 1. a bag, usually large, made of heavy, rough cloth. **Ex.** *They put the potatoes in a sack.* 2. a bag.

sacred (3) [sey'krid], *adj.* concerned with religion; holy. **Ex.** *The organist played sacred music.*

sacrifice (3) [sæk'rəfays'], *n.* 1. the act of doing without something for the benefit of someone else or for the purpose of obtaining something else. **Ex.** *They made great sacrifices to send their children to college.* 2. the offering of something to a god; that which is offered. **Ex.** *In many religions today, animal sacrifices are no longer offered.* —*v.* do without or give up something for the sake of someone or something else. **Ex.** *They sacrificed their vacation to save money for a down payment on a house.*

sad (1) [sæd'], *adj.* 1. unhappy. **Ex.** *Losing our old friend made us very sad.* 2. causing unhappiness. **Ex.** *The sad news made her cry.* —**sad'den'**, *v.* make unhappy. —**sad'ly**, *adv.* —**sadness**, *n.*

saddle (2) [sæd'əl], *n.* a seat, usually made of leather, that is placed on an animal's back for the use of the rider.

SADDLE

safe (1) [seyf'], *adj.* 1. out of danger; away from harm. **Ex.** *You will be safe from the storm here.* 2. without risk. **Ex.** *His careful driving made it a safe trip.* —*n.* a metal box in which papers, money, jewelry and other valuables are locked. **Ex.** *He had an old safe in his office.* —**safe'ly**, *adv.*

safeguard [seyf'gard'], *n.* anything that protects or increases safety. **Ex.** *The brick walls are a safeguard against fire.* —*v.* protect. **Ex.** *They tried to safeguard the children by installing traffic lights at the streets the children had to cross on the way to school.*

safety (1) [seyf'ty], *n.* freedom from danger or harm. **Ex.** *They had no accidents on the road and reached home in safety.* —*adj.* intended as or providing protection. **Ex.** *Please fasten your safety belt.*

sag [sæg'], *v.* hang, sink or bend down from the normal position. **Exs.** *The couch is sagging on the left side where I usually sit. His energy had sagged in the extremely hot weather.*

said (1) [sed'], *v.* past tense and participle of *say.* **Exs.** *He said yesterday that we would go. Has she said anything about the problem to you?*

sail (1) [seyl'], *n.* a large piece of cloth raised over a boat so that the wind moves the boat. —*v.* 1. travel by boat or ship. **Ex.** *We are sailing to Europe.* 2. start a trip by boat or ship. **Ex.** *The ship sails at midnight.* —**sail'or,** *n.* 1. one who works as a member of the crew of a ship; one who sails a boat. 2. a member of a navy, especially one not an officer.

SAIL

saint (3) [seynt'], *n.* 1. a holy person. **Ex.** *They named their child after a saint.* 2. any person of unusual goodness. **Ex.** *He considered his mother a saint.* —**saint'ly,** *adj.* like a saint.

sake (2) [seyk'], *n.* 1. reason for doing. **Ex.** *He fought for the sake of his country's freedom.* 2. interest; benefit. **Ex.** *Please do this for my sake.*

salad (3) [sæl'əd], *n.* a dish of cold cooked or raw vegetables, fruit or meat prepared with oil and vinegar or a similar sauce. **Ex.** *Potato salad is a summer favorite of mine.*

salary (2) [sæl'əriy], *n.* a payment at regular periods, such as once a week or month, for work done. **Ex.** *His salary will be increased next year.*

sale (2) [seyl'], *n.* 1. the act of selling. **Ex.** *The sale of the house took several months.* 2. a special selling at reduced prices. **Ex.** *She waited until a sale to buy her coat.* —**on sale,** 1. offered for sale. **Ex.** *There is no fish on sale today.* 2. offered for sale at a special price. **Ex.** *Hats are on sale this week.*

saliva [səlay'və], *n.* a clear fluid, produced in the mouth, that moistens the mouth and helps to start digestion. **Ex.** *She wiped the saliva from the baby's lips.*

salmon (4) [sæm'ən], *n.* 1. a large, edible ocean fish which usually lives in salt water but swims to fresh water to lay its eggs. 2. a yellowish-pink color. —**salmon pink,** a reddish-orange color.

saloon (4) [sǝluwn'], *n.* a place where beer, wine, etc. are sold and drunk. **Ex.** *He stopped at the saloon for a drink.*

salt (1) [sɔlt'], *n.* a white substance found in sea water and in the earth, used to season or preserve food. **Ex.** *A little salt made the meat taste better.* —*v.* season with salt. **Ex.** *The cook salted the potatoes lightly.* —**salt'y,** *adj.* containing or tasting of salt.

salt shaker [sɔlt' šey'kǝr], *n.* a container for salt, with holes in the top from which the salt is shaken. **Ex.** *She filled the salt shaker.*

salute (4) [sǝluwt'], *v.* 1. honor by raising the right hand to the forehead. **Ex.** *The children stopped and saluted the flag as they passed it.* 2. greet in a way that shows honor. **Ex.** *He saluted the lady with a bow.* —*n.* an act that honors, such as raising the right hand to the right side of the forehead. **Ex.** *The general returned the private's salute.* —**sal`u·ta'tion,** *n.* an act of greeting; spoken or written words of greeting. **Ex.** *Use "Dear Sir" as the salutation in this business letter.*

salvation (5) [sælvey'šǝn], *n.* the act of saving from danger, difficulty or evil. **Ex.** *She believed that he was not beyond salvation.*

same (1) [seym'], *adj.* 1. not different. **Ex.** *He wears the same suit every day.* 2. like one another. **Ex.** *Our hats are almost exactly the same color.* 3. not changed. **Ex.** *The condition of the sick man is the same as it was yesterday.* —*pron.* a person, place or thing that is not different. **Ex.** *My friend ordered tea, and I ordered the same.* —*adv.* in a way that is not different. **Ex.** *She acts the same as she always did.*

sample (4) [sæm'pǝl], *n.* a small part of something used to show what the whole is like; an example. **Ex.** *She asked for a sample of the dress material.* —*v.* find out by examining or testing a small part of something. **Ex.** *Sample the coffee to see if it is strong enough to drink.*

sanction (5) [sæŋk'šǝn], *n.* 1. authority or approval by someone in authority. **Ex.** *The government gave its sanction to the new building.* 2. anything done by one or more nations to try to force another or others to obey international law. **Ex.** *The sanctions applied against the offending country seriously affected its economic stability.* —*v.* give permission; approve. **Ex.** *I cannot sanction such behavior.*

sand (2) [sænd'], *n.* very tiny, hard pieces of crushed rock found in great quantities in deserts and on many shores. **Ex.** *The children got sand in their shoes.* —*v.* smooth or polish with sand or sandpaper. **Ex.** *The carpenter carefully sanded the wood.* —**sand'y,** *adj.*

sandal (5) [sænd'əl], *n.* a kind of shoe consisting only of a sole held to the foot by narrow strips of leather, cloth, etc.

sandbar [sænd'ba:r'], *n.* a ridge of sand formed in water by the movement of currents or tides. **Ex.** *Because of the sandbar, large ships could not enter the harbor.*

sandpaper [sænd'pey`pər], *n.* a paper with sand attached to it, used for smoothing or polishing when building or making things.

sandwich (3) [sæn(d)'wič], *n.* two or more slices of bread with meat, cheese or other filling between them. **Ex.** *They ate sandwiches for lunch.* —*v.* put between two other things. **Ex.** *Their house was sandwiched between two tall buildings.*

sane (4) [seyn'], *adj.* 1. in good mental health; having a sound mind. **Ex.** *The court judged the man sane and therefore responsible for his acts.* 2. showing good judgment or wisdom; reasonable. **Ex.** *You have made a sane decision.* —**sane'ly,** *adv.* —**san'i·ty,** *n.*

sang (2) [sæŋ'], *v.* past tense of *sing.* **Ex.** *We sang the school song.*

sanitary (5) [sæn'əter`iy], *adj.* 1. of or concerned with health. **Ex.** *The sanitary department of the city is responsible for collecting the trash from this block twice a week.* 2. clean; lacking in dirt or anything that causes sickness. **Ex.** *That restaurant was closed because its food preparation was not sanitary.* —**san`i·ta'tion,** *n.*

sank (2) [sæŋk'], *v.* past tense of *sink.* **Ex.** *The boat sank beneath the water.*

sap (4) [sæp'], *n.* the juice in a plant or tree that carries food and water to its parts. **Ex.** *We made sugar from the sap of the maple trees.*

sap (4) [sæp'], *v.* 1. exhaust gradually; weaken. **Ex.** *The disease sapped her strength.* 2. weaken by digging away at the base; destroy at the base. **Ex.** *The river sapped away the foundation of the house.*

sarcasm [sar'kæz`əm], *n.* sharp, unkind, mocking comments intended to hurt or make fun of something or someone;

cutting remarks that mean the opposite of what is said. **Exs.** *"You must have gotten up very early!" said the teacher with ill-concealed sarcasm to the tardy student. The people who worked for him hated his sarcasm.* —**sar·cas'tic,** *adj.*

sat (1) [sæt'], *v.* past tense of *sit.* **Ex.** *He sat and read the paper.*

satellite (4) [sæt'əlayt`], *n.* 1. a smaller body in space that moves in a regular path around a larger body. **Ex.** *The moon is a satellite of the earth.* 2. a man-made body which is put into space to revolve around the earth or some other planet. **Ex.** *The American satellite could be seen in the sky.* 3. a nation that is controlled, led or greatly influenced by a larger or stronger nation. **Ex.** *Troops from the controlling nation were sent into the satellite to put down civil disturbances there.*

satin (4) [sæt'in], *n.* a fine cloth with a smooth, shiny surface. **Ex.** *Her evening gown was made of satin.*

satisfy (2) [sæt'isfay`], *v.* 1. fulfill the desires, requirements or demands of. **Ex.** *The water satisfied his thirst.* 2. convince. **Ex.** *Your explanation satisfies me.* 3. pay a debt; meet an obligation. **Ex.** *He could not satisfy the terms of the agreement.* —**sat`is·fac'tion,** *n.* —**sat`is·fac'to·ry,** *adj.* —**sat`is·fac'to·ri·ly,** *adv.*

Saturday (1) [sæt'ərdiy], *n.* the seventh day of the week.

sauce (3) [sɔ:s'], *n.* a soft or liquid preparation put on food to flavor it. **Ex.** *The vegetables were served with a cheese sauce.*

saucepan [sɔ:s'pæn'], *n.* a pot with a handle, used for cooking.

saucer (3) [sɔ:s'ər], *n.* a small, round, shallow dish in which a cup is set.

saucy (3) [sɔ:s'iy], *adj.* not polite; not respectful. **Ex.** *She was saucy to her mother.*

sausage (4) [sɔ:s'iʃ], *n.* chopped or ground meat flavored with salt, pepper, herbs, etc. and stuffed into an edible casing or tube. **Ex.** *She cooked sausages for dinner.*

CUP AND SAUCER

savage (3) [sæv'iʃ], *adj.* 1. uncivilized; untamed. **Ex.** *They needed guns to protect themselves from the savage animals.* 2. cruel. **Ex.** *His savage acts quickly turned the people against him.* 3. rough; uncultivated. **Ex.** *The pioneers found the country a savage wilderness.* —*n.* an uncivilized person. **Ex.** *Savages lived in the forest.* —**sav'age·ly,** *adv.* —**sav'age·ness,** *n.* —**sav'age·ry,** *n.*

save (1) [seyv'], *v.* 1. make safe; remove from harm. **Ex.** *They saved the children from the fire.* 2. set apart for future use. **Ex.** *He was saving money to buy a car.* 3. avoid wasting, spoiling, etc. **Ex.** *She saved the remaining meat for another meal.* —**sav'ings,** *n. pl.* money that has been set apart for future use. **Ex.** *Her savings are in the bank.*

savings account [seyv'iŋz əkawnt'], *n.* a bank account in which money is put for future use and on which interest is paid by the bank. **Ex.** *He is going to use the money in his savings account to help pay for his college education.*

saw (1) [sɔ:'], *v.* past tense of *see.* **Ex.** *He saw his aunt yesterday.*

saw (1) [sɔ:'], *n.* a cutting tool that has a thin metal blade with a toothed edge. —*v.* cut with a saw.

say (1) [sey'], *v.* 1. speak. **Ex.** *What did he say?* 2. express in words. **Ex.** *The farmers say that the harvest will be good.* 3. repeat from memory. **Ex.** *Two of the children are going to say some poems.* 4. order. **Ex.** *You must do whatever he says.* —*n.* what one desires to say. **Ex.** *They have had their say.* —**say'ing,** *n.* a well-known statement expressing popular wisdom. **Ex.** *As the saying goes, a bird in the hand is worth two in the bush.*

SAW

scale (2) [skeyl'], *n.* one of the small, hard skin plates that cover the body of fish and some other animals. —*v.* remove scales from. **Ex.** *He scaled the fish.*

scale (2) [skeyl'], *n.* 1. a measuring instrument consisting of a series of regularly spaced marks upon the surface of a piece of wood, metal, etc. which correspond to the units of some system of measurement. **Ex.** *This ruler has a scale in inches.* 2. a relation between the actual size of an object and its size on a drawing or map. **Ex.** *The scale of this map is one inch to sixty miles.* 3. an arrangement of things in a series from low to high. **Ex.** *The scale of wages at this factory is above average.* —*v.* climb. **Ex.** *He scaled the mountain.* —**scales,** *n.* an instrument for weighing.

scan (5) [skæn'], *v.* 1. glance at quickly; read hurriedly. **Ex.** *He scanned the newspaper in a few minutes.* 2. examine carefully and closely. **Ex.** *They scanned the mountainside for any sign of the climbers.*

scandal (4) [skæn'dəl], *n.* 1. a shocking act or circumstance; something that brings shame. **Ex.** *His career was marked by scandals.* 2. shameful talk about others, often not true. **Ex.** *She will not listen to scandal.* —**scan'dal·ize,** *v.* shock by shameful action or talk. —**scan'dal·ous,** *adj.*

scant (5) [skænt'], *adj.* scarcely enough; scarcely sufficient. **Ex.** *He paid scant attention to the children.* —**scant'y,** *adj.* scarcely large enough or sufficient in size, amount, etc. **Ex.** *We were served a scanty supper.* —**scant'i·ly,** *adv.* scarcely sufficient. **Ex.** *I'm sure those scantily clothed children will catch cold.*

scar (4) [ska:r'], *n.* 1. a mark that remains after a wound, burn, etc. heals. **Ex.** *There was a scar on his right cheek.* 2. the effect on the mind of sorrow or grief. **Ex.** *Her brother's death left a scar on her memory.* —*v.* cause a scar or scars. **Ex.** *Illness has scarred his face.*

scarce (2) [ske:rs'], *adj.* 1. not plentiful. **Ex.** *Sugar was scarce during the war.* 2. uncommon. **Ex.** *We lived on a road where travelers were scarce.* —**scarce'ly,** *adv.* 1. hardly. **Ex.** *She scarcely knows him.* 2. definitely not. **Ex.** *I would scarcely have expected to see them here.* —**scar'ci·ty,** *n.* lack. **Ex.** *There is a scarcity of fresh fruit because of the late frost.*

scare (3) [ske:r'], *v.* cause fear; become afraid. **Ex.** *The sudden noise scared her.* —*n.* a sudden fright or alarm. **Ex.** *We had a bad scare last night.* —**scar'y,** *adj.*

scarf (3) [skarf'], *n.* 1. a wide strip of material worn about the neck or shoulders or over the head for warmth, protection or decoration. **Ex.** *Her green scarf matched her gloves.* 2. a long narrow strip of material used to cover the top of a table, bureau, etc. **Ex.** *She put a white scarf on the chest of drawers.*

scatter (2) [skæt'ər], *v.* throw or sprinkle loosely in many directions. **Ex.** *The farmer scattered the grass seed over the field.*

scene (1) [siyn'], *n.* 1. the time and place at which an action occurred or is occurring. **Ex.** *The police quickly reached the scene of the crime.* 2. a part of a play. **Ex.** *The hero appeared in the first scene.* 3. a picture or view. **Ex.** *She likes to paint winter scenes.* —**scen'er·y,** *n.* 1. the surrounding views. **Ex.** *At this season the scenery in the country is green and fresh.* 2. the background on a stage. —**scen'ic,** *adj.* having beautiful scenery.

scent (3) [sent'], *n.* 1. an odor, especially a pleasant one. **Ex.** *The room was filled with the scent of flowers.* 2. an odor left by an animal. **Ex.** *The hunting dogs followed the scent of the fox.* —*v.* smell; give a smell to. **Ex.** *The flowers scented the room.*

schedule (4) [skeǰ'uwl], *n.* 1. a statement of the times at which events are planned to happen. **Ex.** *May I have a bus schedule, please?* 2. the time when something is planned to happen. **Ex.** *The train arrived on schedule.* —*v.* place in or add to a list of things to be done; plan a time at which something is to be done. **Ex.** *When is the next meeting scheduled to take place?*

scheme (3) [skiym'], *n.* 1. a plan of something to be done. **Ex.** *Many schemes for improving the city were offered.* 2. a secret and dishonest plan; a plot. **Ex.** *He had a scheme to get the old man's money.* 3. design; system; arrangement. **Ex.** *She planned a new color scheme for the room.* —*v.* make secret and dishonest plans. **Ex.** *He schemed to get his brother's share of the family money.*

scholar (4) [skal'ər], *n.* 1. a person famous for his learning; a person of great learning. **Ex.** *He was respected as a great scholar in the field of history.* 2. a student. **Ex.** *Only a few of our scholars live at home.* —**schol'ar·ly,** *adj.* 1. of or concerning persons of great learning. **Ex.** *This university has a very scholarly faculty.* 2. showing great learning or careful study. **Ex.** *This book is a very scholarly work.* —**schol'ar·ship,** *n.* 1. financial aid given to support and pay the expenses of a student. **Ex.** *He was given a scholarship to attend the university.* 2. great learning obtained through much reading and study. **Ex.** *His scholarship is evident in his writing.*

school (1) [skuwl'], *n.* 1. a place where people are taught. **Ex.** *Our youngest child will go to school this year.* 2. the students and teachers of such a place. **Ex.** *Nearly half of the school stayed home because of the bad weather.* 3. a period or course of study during which classes are held. **Ex.** *School begins in September.* 4. a department of a college or university; a place where special subjects are taught or where students are prepared for a particular profession. **Ex.** *He is studying at the law school.* —**scho·las'tic,** *adj.* of or having to do with schools.

science (2) [say'əns], *n.* 1. knowledge about nature and the world obtained by study and experiments. **Ex.** *Her interest in science began in biology class.* 2. any branch of such knowledge. **Ex.** *The science of medicine keeps changing rapidly.* —**sci`en·tif`ic**, *adj.* —**sci`en·tist**, *n.*

scissors (3) [siz'ərz], *n.* an instrument with two handles and two blades used for cutting, often called a pair of scissors. **Ex.** *I need a pair of scissors to cut this paper.*

SCISSORS

scoff (5) [skɔ:f'], *v.* mock; show a lack of respect for by using rude language. **Ex.** *They scoffed at his plan to build an airship.* —*n.* a rude, scornful remark. **Ex.** *We ignored the scoffs of the children.*

scold (4) [skowld'], *v.* blame sharply and in anger. **Ex.** *His parents scolded him for returning late.* —*n.* a person who often finds fault. **Ex.** *The woman next door was a terrible scold.*

scope (4) [skowp'], *n.* 1. range of one's freedom to act. **Ex.** *In punishing him, the guard went beyond the scope of his authority.* 2. range of one's understanding. **Ex.** *The ideas of the speaker were beyond the scope of his listeners.* 3. range or extent of material covered. **Ex.** *This book has greater scope than others on the same subject.*

scorch (5) [skɔrč'], *v.* 1. burn only enough to change the color or taste. **Ex.** *The dress had been scorched.* 2. dry up completely; wither. **Ex.** *The sun scorched the grass.*

score (2) [skɔ:r'], *n.* 1. the record of points made in a game. **Ex.** *Our team has the highest score.* 2. a rating on a test or examination. **Ex.** *His score on the English test was 100 percent.* 3. very many. **Ex.** *There are scores of difficulties that must be faced.* 4. twenty of anything. **Ex.** *They have lived here for more than a score of years.* 5. written or printed music showing the parts each musician is to play or sing. **Ex.** *The conductor made some changes in the score.* —*v.* 1. gain points in a game. **Ex.** *We scored ten points late in the game.* 2. give or receive a rating on a test or an examination. **Ex.** *The teacher scored our test papers.*

scorn (3) [skɔrn'], *n.* 1. a feeling of anger and dislike or of low regard. **Ex.** *He felt only scorn for the thief.* 2. the showing of a feeling of anger and dislike or low regard. **Ex.** *She looked at the villagers with scorn.* —*v.* 1. show a feeling of anger and dislike or low regard. **Ex.** *In later life, he scorned his school friends.* 2. refuse to do something because of a feeling of scorn. **Ex.** *She scorned the advice of her teacher.*

scotch tape [skač' teyp'], *n.* a clear or semiclear strip of paper or paperlike material, in a roll, which has a substance on one or both sides that makes it stick to other surfaces, such as when sealing packages, fastening one sheet of paper to another, etc. **Ex.** *He fastened the notice to the door with scotch tape.*

scour (5) [skawr'], *v.* clean or polish by rubbing hard, usually with a rough material. **Ex.** *She scoured the pots and pans.*

scour (5) [skawr'], *v.* search thoroughly for something or someone. **Ex.** *They scoured the town looking for the boy.*

scourge (5) [skərj'], *n.* 1. a cause of pain or great difficulty. **Ex.** *Poverty is still the scourge of many cities.* 2. a whip. **Ex.** *The slaves were driven by the scourge.* —*v.* 1. whip. **Ex.** *Sailors were once scourged for many kinds of offenses.* 2. cause pain or great difficulty. **Ex.** *He was scourged by the memory of his past crimes.*

scout (3) [skawt'], *n.* 1. a soldier, plane, etc. sent out to watch the enemy and get information. **Ex.** *A scout was sent out during the night.* 2. a member of the Boy Scouts or the Girl Scouts, groups in which young people engage in activities to develop skills and good character. **Ex.** *He wants to be a Scout like his older brother.* —*v.* go out to watch and listen. **Ex.** *We scouted the hills beyond the river.*

scowl (4) [skawl'], *n.* an expression of anger, doubt, worry, etc. in which the eyebrows are drawn together and the corners of the mouth with the lips pressed together point down. **Ex.** *He always seemed to have a scowl on his face.* —*v.* draw the eyebrows together and the corners of the mouth down in anger, doubt, worry, etc. **Ex.** *He scowled at me when I asked for more money.*

scramble (5) [skræm'bəl], *v.* 1. climb or crawl quickly, using the hands and feet. **Ex.** *The boys scrambled up into the tree.* 2. struggle or compete with others in a way that is not orderly or quiet. **Ex.** *The children scrambled for the candy.* 3. mix together in a confused way. **Ex.** *His letters were scrambled together on the desk.* 4. fry eggs which have been stirred and mixed. **Ex.** *She scrambled some eggs for our breakfast.* —*n.* 1. a quick climb or crawl using the hands and feet. **Ex.** *We were tired from our scramble up the hill.* 2. a disorderly struggle or fight for something. **Ex.** *The game became a wild scramble for the ball.*

scrap (4) [skræp'], *n.* 1. a small bit of something; a small part. **Ex.** *She wrote the telephone number on a scrap of paper.* 2. old or broken material. **Ex.** *He buys and sells scrap.* —*adj.* in bits or pieces. **Ex.** *In this factory they melt scrap metal and use it again.* —*v.* 1. break into pieces; convert into broken materials. **Ex.** *The owners have decided to scrap the old boat.* 2. throw away something or stop doing something no longer of any value. **Ex.** *Our carefully prepared plan had to be scrapped.* —**scraps'**, *n. pl.* bits of food remaining after eating. **Ex.** *They fed the scraps to the dog.* —**scrap'book'**, *n.* a book of blank pages on which one may paste photographs, postcards, newspaper articles, souvenirs such as a bit of ribbon or a feather, etc. **Ex.** *This is a scrapbook about the last trip that we took.*

scrape (3) [skreyp'], *v.* 1. rub with a sharp tool or rough material to make a smooth or clean surface. **Ex.** *The sailors were scraping the deck of the ship.* 2. remove something by scraping. **Ex.** *We scraped the old paint from the furniture.* 3. rub something against a rough surface accidentally. **Ex.** *She scraped her arm on the rock.* 4. gather slowly and with difficulty. **Ex.** *He scraped together enough money to buy a secondhand car.* —*n.* the act or sound of rubbing with something rough. **Ex.** *We heard the scrape of a window opening.*

scratch (3) [skræč'], *v.* 1. tear or mark a surface with something sharp. **Ex.** *The thorns scratched his arms and legs.* 2. rub with the fingernails. **Ex.** *He scratched his head thoughtfully.* 3. make a sharp, unpleasant noise by rubbing against a surface. **Ex.** *His old pen scratched badly as he wrote.* —*n.* 1. a tear, mark or wound. **Ex.** *There was a deep scratch on the tabletop.* 2. a sharp, unpleasant noise. **Ex.** *We heard only the scratch of the chalk on the blackboard.*

scream (2) [skriym'], *v.* cry out loudly and sharply. **Ex.** *We heard someone scream in fright.* —*n.* a loud, sharp cry. **Ex.** *A scream for help came from inside the building.*

screech (5) [skriyč'], *v.* 1. give a sharp, high scream. **Ex.** *The parrots were screeching in their cages.* 2. make a sharp, high sound. **Ex.** *The car screeched to a sudden stop.* —*n.* a high, sharp sound or scream. **Ex.** *He heard a screech of anger from the old woman.*

screen (3) [skriyn'], *n.* 1. a net or cloth of fine wire or strong thread with small openings through which only extremely small objects can pass. **Ex.** *The windows were covered with screens.* 2. a frame or curtain used to protect or conceal. **Ex.** *During the day the bed was hidden by a screen.* 3. a surface on which movies or other pictures are projected. **Ex.** *The screen was silver colored.* —*v.* 1. protect or conceal. **Ex.** *The bushes screened the hunters from the animals.* 2. separate large pieces from small by sifting through a screen. **Ex.** *He screened the sand to remove pieces of stone.* 3. separate or select people or things by carefully examining them. **Ex.** *The workers were screened to determine their mechanical ability.*

screw (3) [skruw'], *n.* a metal fastener that is forced into place by turning. —*v.* fasten or tighten by using a screw or screws. **Ex.** *The chair was firmly screwed together.*

screwdriver [skruw'dray`vər], *n.* a tool, consisting of a narrow rod with a handle at one end and a flattened or otherwise shaped part at the other end, which fits into the head of a screw and makes it possible to turn the screw. **Ex.** *I need a smaller screwdriver for these screws.*

SCREW

script (5) [skript'], *n.* 1. handwriting. **Ex.** *I recognized my father's careful script.* 2. a written or printed copy of the text of a play, broadcast, etc. **Ex.** *She studied the script until she knew her part.*

scrub (4) [skrəb'], *v.* wash by rubbing hard with a brush or cloth. **Ex.** *She scrubs the kitchen floor every week.*

SCREWDRIVER

sculptor (5) [skəlp'tər], *n.* an artist who makes figures or designs by carving, cutting or modeling. **Ex.** *The sculptor made the statue from a block of white stone.*

sculpture (4) [skəlp'čər], *n.* 1. the art of carving, cutting or modeling figures or designs in various materials such as wood, stone and metal. **Ex.** *She studied both painting and sculpture.* 2. the product of such work. **Ex.** *His sculpture of a horse won first prize.* —*v.* carve, cut or model a sculpture. **Ex.** *He sculptured the head of his wife in copper.*

sea (1) [siy'], *n.* 1. the salt water that covers the greater part of the earth's surface. **Ex.** *This ship has sailed many seas.* 2. any large body of water, smaller than an ocean and partly or entirely enclosed by land. —at sea, on the sea; on the ocean; sailing. **Ex.** *The boat has been at sea for several days.*

seaboard [siy'bɔrd'], *n.* land near or at the edge of the sea or ocean. **Ex.** *There are many villages along the seaboard.*

seacoast [siy'kowst], *n.* land at the edge of the sea or ocean. **Ex.** *Some of the houses along the seacoast were badly damaged by the storm.*

seafood [siy'fuwd'], *n.* fish from the sea eaten as food. **Ex.** *That restaurant serves good seafood.*

sea gull [siy'gəl'], *n.* a rather large bird with long wings and gray and white feathers usually found along the seacoast. **Ex.** *Flocks of seagulls moved along the beach.*

seal (3) [siyl'], *n.* 1. a warm-blooded sea animal living mostly in cold regions. 2. the fur of this animal; sealskin.

SEAL

seal (3) [siyl'], *n.* 1. an impression or design placed on papers, documents, etc. to show that they are official or legal; the device for making such an impression. **Ex.** *The paper had been stamped with the required official seal.* 2. any paper, metal or other device placed upon a closed door, envelope, etc. in such a way that it cannot be opened without breaking the device. **Ex.** *The seal on one of the railroad cars had been broken.* —v. 1. close or fasten tightly. **Ex.** *She sealed the letter.* 2. settle finally; determine definitely. **Ex.** *The decision of the jury sealed the man's fate.*

SEAL 1

sea level [siy' lev'əl], the level of the sea halfway between low and high tides, from which heights and depths are measured. **Ex.** *That hill is five hundred feet above sea level.*

seam (4) [siym'], *n.* the line which indicates where two pieces of cloth, leather, etc. have been joined or sewn together. **Ex.** *The sleeve tore at the seam.*

seaplane [siy'pleyn'], *n.* a plane built to land on water.

search (2) [sərč'], *v.* 1. examine carefully or look for in order to find something or someone. **Ex.** *They searched the house for the lost ring.* 2. examine a person or his personal belongings in order to find evidence of a crime such as a gun, stolen property, etc. **Ex.** *Both of the men were searched by the police.* —*n.* the act of examining or looking for. **Ex.** *He came here in his search for work.*

seashell [siy'šel'], *n.* the hard outer covering of certain forms of sea life. **Ex.** *There were many kinds of seashells on the beach after the storm.*

seashore [siy'šowr], *n.* the land alongside the ocean or a sea. **Ex.** *We are going to the seashore for the weekend.*

seasick [siy'sik'], *adj.* sick because of the rolling movement of a ship on water. **Ex.** *During the storm, he became seasick.*

season (1) [siy'zen], *n.* 1. one of the four parts—winter, spring, summer and autumn or fall—into which the year is divided. **Ex.** *Winter is the coldest season of the year.* 2. a particular time during the year that is noticeably different from other times. **Ex.** *Are you going away during the holiday season?* —**in season,** in the time of year during which something is easily available. **Ex.** *Fresh fruit is in season during the summer.*

season (1) [siy'zən], *v.* change or increase the flavor. **Ex.** *She seasoned the meat with salt and pepper.* —**seasoning,** *n.* flavoring that changes the taste of food. **Ex.** *What seasonings did you use in this dish to make it taste so good?*

seat (1) [siyt], *n.* 1. the thing on which one sits. **Ex.** *There are four hundred seats in this theater.* 2. the part of the chair on which one places the body. **Ex.** *The seat of the chair was broken.* 3. the part of the body or the part of the clothing on which one sits. **Ex.** *The seat of his trousers was torn.* 4. a place to sit or the right to sit there, such as a member of an elected government body has. **Ex.** *He lost his seat in Congress.* 5. the place at which the center of anything is established; the center of government. **Ex.** *This town is the county seat.* —*v.* place on a seat; cause to sit down. **Ex.** *He seated himself beside his friend.* —**be seated, take a seat,** sit. **Exs.** *Please be seated. Please take a seat.*

seat belt [siyt'belt'], *n.* bands or strips of strong and heavy cloth, attached to the seat of a car, airplane, etc., which are worn by a passenger to hold him or her safely in place in case of an accident. **Ex.** *The police said that the injured man was not wearing his seat belt.*

---

a, far; æ, am; e, get; ey, late; i, in; iy, see; ɔ, all; ow, go; u, put; uw, too; ə, but, ago; ər, fur; aw, out; ay, life; oy, boy; ŋ, ring; θ, think; ð, that; ž, measure; š, ship; ǰ, edge; č, child.

seaweed [siy'wiyd'], *n*. any plant in the sea. **Ex.** *His foot was caught in the seaweed.*

second (1) [sek'ənd], *adj*. 1. following after one other. **Ex.** *He arrived on the second bus.* 2. the same or about the same as another; another. **Ex.** *A second bathroom is at the end of the hall.* —*n*. the one following one other in time, place, importance, etc. **Ex.** *You are the second to ask that question.* —*adv*. in the place behind or after the first. **Ex.** *He finished second in the race.* —**sec'ond·ar·y**, *adj*. 1. higher than elementary. **Ex.** *The older children are in secondary school.* 2. having less power or value. **Ex.** *The price of the material was of secondary importance.* —**second-class**, *adj*. not the best or of the best but next to it. **Ex.** *He bought a second-class train ticket.* —**secondhand**, *adj*. 1. not original or direct. **Ex.** *I received a secondhand account of what had happened.* 2. not new; used by another or others. **Ex.** *That secondhand car cost two thousand dollars.* —**second-rate,** *adj*. not of the best; of poor quality. **Ex.** *This is a second-rate hotel.*

second (1) [sek'ənd], *n*. 1. one of the sixty parts into which a minute is divided. **Ex.** *This clock is thirty seconds slow.* 2. a moment; a short time. **Ex.** *For a second he saw a bright light.*

second person [sek'ənd pər'sən], the pronoun *you* or the verb form referring to the person to whom one is speaking. **Ex.** *Are is the second-person form of the verb* be.

secret (2) [siy'krit], *adj*. hidden from others; known only to a few. **Ex.** *He kept some money in a secret place.* —*n*. 1. something known only to a few and purposely hidden. **Ex.** *He cannot be trusted to keep a secret.* 2. something not generally known. **Ex.** *The old man had learned many of the secrets of nature.* 3. the reason for something; the hidden cause. **Ex.** *What was the secret of his success in business?* —**se'cre·cy,** *n*. the act of keeping something secret. —**se'cre·tive.** *adj*. liking to keep secrets.

secretary (2) [sek'rəter`iy], *n*. 1. a person employed to write letters, answer telephones, and manage other details of office business. **Ex.** *His secretary greeted the visitors.* 2. the person in charge of a government department. **Ex.** *A new secretary of labor has recently been appointed.* —**sec're·tar'i·al,** *adj*.

sect (5) [sekt'], *n*. a group of people, usually religious, who, though they follow the same leader or teacher or hold the same basic beliefs, differ in particular ways from other similar groups. **Ex.** *That religion has many sects.*

section (2) [sek'šən], *n.* 1. a division; a separate part. **Ex.** *She cut the orange into sections.* 2. a separate or definite part of a town, city, state, etc. **Ex.** *They live in the old section of the city.* —**sec'tion·al,** *adj.*

secure (2) [sikyu:r'], *adj.* 1. safe from danger; protected against harm. **Ex.** *The fort was secure against any surprise attack.* 2. free from fear or concern. **Ex.** *He was secure in the knowledge that his friends would help him.* 3. fixed firmly; strong. **Ex.** *The house was built upon a secure foundation.* —*v.* 1. fasten firmly in place. **Ex.** *Before the storm, we secured the doors and windows.* 2. get possession of; obtain. **Ex.** *She is hoping to secure a position in the library.* 3. guard; make safe. **Ex.** *A police guard secured the bank against robbery.* —**se·cure'ly,** *adv.*

security (3) [sikyu:r'ətiy], *n.* 1. a feeling of safety; freedom from danger or harm. **Ex.** *They fled to the security of the mountains.* 2. protection. **Ex.** *They put a new lock on the door as security.* 3. something given or promised as a sign that a debt will be paid. **Ex.** *Their house was their security for the loan.* —**se·cur'i·ties,** *n. pl.* stocks and bonds.

see (1) [siy'], *v.* 1. come to know or sense by means of the eyes; have the power of sight. **Ex.** *Can you see the bird in that tree?* 2. understand; know the meaning or manner of. **Ex.** *He could not see how the money had been spent.* 3. find out; learn. **Ex.** *See whether he has arrived yet.* 4. meet. **Ex.** *I sometimes see him on the street.* 5. visit. **Ex.** *She comes to see me every week.*

seed (1) [siyd'], *n.* 1. the part of a plant from which a new plant grows. **Ex.** *This plant grew from a very small seed.* 2. that from which anything grows; a beginning; a source. **Ex.** *The seed of doubt had been planted in his mind.* —*v.* plant with seeds. **Ex.** *Half of the garden has already been seeded.* —**seed'less,** *adj.* without seeds. **Ex.** *These are seedless grapes.*

seek (2) [siyk'], *v.* 1. go in search of. **Ex.** *They were seeking a path through the mountains.* 2. try to obtain; attempt to get. **Ex.** *He is seeking election to the office of mayor.*

seem (1) [siym'], *v.* appear to be; give the impression of. **Ex.** *She seems tired.*

seen (1) [siyn'], *v.* past participle of *see.* **Ex.** *I have seen him before.*

segregate [seg'rəgeyt'], *v.* 1. set aside or apart or separate from the main body or group. **Ex.** *The violent patients were segre-*

gated from the others. 2. set aside or apart from the main body or group on the basis of race, religion, nationality, class, etc. **Ex.** *This university no longer segregates the men from the women in the university dormitories.* —**seg're·ga'tion,** *n.*

seize (2) [siyz'], *v.* 1. take hold of quickly and firmly; grasp. **Ex.** *She seized the child by the arm.* 2. take control of. **Ex.** *The army seized the town.* —**sei'zure,** *n.*

seldom (2) [sel'dəm], *adv.* rarely; not very often. **Ex.** *They are seldom at home.*

select (2) [səlekt'], *v.* choose. **Ex.** *She selected the material carefully.* —*adj.* of fine quality; special; chosen with care. **Ex.** *That shop sells select fruit.* —**se·lec'tion,** *n.* 1. the act of choosing. 2. that which is chosen. —**se·lec'tive,** *adj.* choosing with care. **Ex.** *She is selective about the clothes she buys.* —**se·lec'tive serv'ice,** required military service.

self (1) [self'], *n.* 1. all the qualities that cause one person to be different from others. **Ex.** *He doesn't seem to know his real self.* 2. a part of a person's character. **Ex.** *We see only her worst self in the early morning.* 3. personal interest or advantage. **Ex.** *He did his work with no thought of self.*

self- (1) [self'], *prefix.* used with nouns and adjectives to show that 1. the one performing the act is the one affected by it. **Exs.** Control, self-control; defense, self-defense. 2. the action is done through its own effort or power. **Exs.** *starting, self-starting; closing, self-closing.*

selfish (4) [self'iš], *adj.* caring only for oneself; thinking only of one's own comfort or advantage. **Ex.** *He was too selfish to share his candy.*

selfless [self'les], *adj.* not caring or worrying about oneself; entirely unselfish. **Ex.** *With selfless devotion she nursed him back to health.*

self-made [self'meyd'], *adj.* having become successful due to one's own efforts. **Ex.** *The owner of that business is a self-made man.*

sell (1) [sel'], *v.* 1. give something in exchange for money. **Ex.** *He is trying to sell his house.* 2. offer to give in exchange for money. **Ex.** *That store sells shoes.* 3. be offered for sale; be given in exchange for money. **Ex.** *Fruit sells for a higher price at the beginning of the season.*

semi- (3) [sem'iy], *prefix.* 1. half. **Exs.** *Circle; semicircle; sphere, semisphere.* 2. partly. **Exs.** *Sweet, semisweet; automatic, semiautomatic.* 3. happening twice in a period. **Exs.** *Monthly, semimonthly; annually, semiannually.*

Senate (2) [sen'it]. *n.* the upper and smaller branch of the U.S. Congress. **Ex.** *A new law is being discussed just now by members of the Senate.* **—sen'a·tor,** *n.* a member of the Senate.

send (1) [send'], *v.* 1. cause to go; permit to go. **Ex.** *They hope to send their children to the university.* 2. cause to be carried, taken or directed to or away from a place. **Ex.** *They will send the food to the island by boat.* 3. request someone to come. **Ex.** *When did you send for the doctor?*

senior (4) [siyn'yər], *adj.* 1. older. **Ex.** *He was senior to his brother by ten years.* 2. more advanced in rank; longer in position or service. **Ex.** *The senior executives have a private dining room.* 3. in the final year of study in high school or college. **Ex.** *Their oldest boy is in his senior year.* —*n.* 1. one who is older or holds a higher rank. **Ex.** *He was respectful toward his seniors.* 2. a student in the final year of study in high school or college. **Ex.** *The seniors are planning a dance.* **—sen·ior'i·ty,** *n.* the position of being older, longer in service, etc. **Ex.** *Because of his seniority he received more pay.* **—sen'ior cit'i·zen,** an older person, especially one who is sixty-five or over.

sensation (4) (sensey'šən], *n.* 1. any feeling produced by the sense of touch, sight, hearing, smell or taste. **Ex.** *Touching the hot stove produced a painful sensation.* 2. that which causes excitement. **Ex.** *The show was a sensation for weeks.* **—sen·sa'tion·al,** *adj.* 1. exciting. **Ex.** *Seeing so much wild game was sensational.* 2. intended to shock or cause excitement. **Ex.** *That newspaper prints a great deal of sensational news.*

sense (1) [sens'], *n.* 1. any of the powers by which one sees, hears, tastes, smells or feels. **Ex.** *The old man had lost his sense of hearing.* 2. a feeling produced by one of these powers. **Ex.** *She had a sudden sense of coldness.* 3. understanding; reasoning. **Ex.** *He had a sense of what needed to be done.* 4. ability to feel or appreciate. **Ex.** *He has no sense of humor.* —*v.* become aware of; feel. **Ex.** *She sensed that someone was* *in the room.* —**sense'less,** *adj.* without reason. **Ex.** *That was a senseless thing to do.* —**sen'si·ble,** *adj.* understandable; reasonable. **Ex.** *You made a sensible choice.* —**sen'si·bly,** *adv.* —**make sense,** be understandable, reasonable. **Ex.** *What he says makes sense to me.*

sensitive (4) [sen'sətiv], *adj.* 1. easily or quickly affected by the senses; quick to notice or understand. **Ex.** *As a sensitive teacher, she was aware of the student's difficulties.* 2. too much affected by the senses; easily hurt or offended. **Ex.** *She was so sensitive that she cried when the teacher corrected her.* 3. changing when acted upon by something else. **Ex.** *This chemical is sensitive to light.* —**sen'si·tiv'i·ty,** *n.*

sent (1) [sent'], *v.* past tense and participle of *send.* **Exs.** *I sent a letter to him yesterday. Have you sent her a bill yet?*

sentence (2) [sen'təns], *n.* 1. a group of words, or sometimes a single word, used to state a fact or an opinion, to ask a question, or to express a command or request. **Ex.** *This author's paragraphs usually contain from three to six sentences.* See **A Brief Explanation of English Grammar.** 2. the punishment for committing a crime or breaking the law. **Ex.** *He served a prison sentence for his crime.* —*v.* set the punishment of a guilty person. **Ex.** *The judge sentenced him to two years in prison.*

sentiment (3) [sen'təmənt], *n.* 1. words or thoughts based on feeling rather than reason. **Ex.** *There was no time for sentiment.* 2. gentle, loving feelings that are weak or silly. **Ex.** *The young girls preferred stories full of sentiment.* 3. thoughts combined with feelings. **Ex.** *What are your sentiments about electing a new mayor?* —**sen·ti·men'tal,** *adj.*

sentry [sen'triy], *n.* a person in the military posted at a particular place whose duty it is to keep individuals without authorization from entering, to give the alarm in case of fire, etc.; a guard. **Ex.** *The sentry walked back and forth with his rifle on his shoulder.*

separate (1) [sep'əreyt'], *v.* 1. force apart; keep apart. **Ex.** *The policemen separated the fighters.* 2. keep apart by being between. **Ex.** *A wall separates the two gardens.* 3. part; go away from. **Ex.** *We said good night and separated outside the theater.* 4. divide into parts or groups; set apart. **Ex.** *The farmer's wife separated the cream from the milk.* —**sep·a·ra'tion,** *n.*

separate (1) [sep'ərit], *adj.* 1. not together. **Ex.** *They ate at separate tables.* 2. different; distinct. **Ex.** *Her stories have* *been printed in thirty separate magazines.* 3. independent; existing alone. **Ex.** *In the United States, the church and state are separate.* —**sep'a·rate·ly,** *adv.*

September (1) [septem'bər], *n.* the ninth month of the year.

sequence (5) [siy'kwəns], *n.* 1. the condition of one thing following after another. **Ex.** *Can you remember the sequence of events yesterday?* 2. the order of things in time or position. **Ex.** *The books were arranged in sequence according to author.*

serene (5) [səriyn'], *adj.* 1. calm; peaceful. **Ex.** *She looked serene.* 2. clear, bright. **Ex.** *The morning sky was serene.*

sergeant (4) [sar'jənt], *n.* 1. one of the highest grades of enlisted men. **Ex.** *The sergeant led the troops onto the field.* 2. a police officer below the rank of lieutenant. **Ex.** *A sergeant and two policemen arrived at the scene of the crime.*

series (2) [si:r'iyz], *n.* a number of similar things or events that follow regularly one after another in time, position or order. **Ex.** *She attended all the lectures in the series.* —**se'ri·al,** *adj.* following regularly one after another. **Ex.** *What is the serial number on your dollar bill?* —*n.* a novel, play, etc. which is published or broadcast in short parts until it is completed. **Ex.** *Have you been watching the serial about events in India shortly before it gained its independence?* —**se'ri·al·ize,** *v.*

serious (2) [si:r'iyəs], *adj.* 1. thoughtful, earnest or grave in action and character. **Ex.** *He spoke about the problem in a serious way.* 2. important; needing careful attention. **Ex.** *I am reading a serious book.* 3. dangerous. **Ex.** *He was in a serious automobile accident.* —**se'ri·ous·ly,** *adv.* —**se'ri·ous·ness,** *n.*

sermon (4) [sər'mən], *n.* 1. a talk on a religious subject. **Ex.** *His sermons were always interesting.* 2. a talk about one's morals or manners that bores or angers. **Ex.** *The boy hated his mother's frequent sermons.*

servant (3) [sər'vənt], *n.* a person employed to do household work in the home of another. **Ex.** *They have two servants, a cook and a maid.* —**civil servant,** a person who works for the government. —**public servant,** a person who is appointed or elected to a government position. **Ex.** *John F. Kennedy was a trusted public servant.*

serve (1) [sərv'], *v.* 1. give food and/or drink to. **Ex.** *Let me serve you some pie.* 2. assist; help. **Ex.** *Let me know if I can* *serve you in any way.* 3. work as an official; be employed by the government, especially in the military. **Ex.** *He served his country in the army during two wars.* 4. work as a servant. **Ex.** *She had served the family as a cook for more than twenty years.*

service (1) [sər'vis], *n.* 1. a helpful act; something done for another. **Ex.** *He did me a great service once.* 2. work for money. **Ex.** *He needed the services of a lawyer.* 3. the organized supply of something. **Ex.** *The bus service in this town is good.* 4. the army, navy, air force, etc. **Ex.** *He spent several years in the service.* 5. a religious ceremony. **Ex.** *He went to the early Sunday morning service.* —*v.* keep in good condition or repair. **Ex.** *He has his car serviced every ten thousand miles.* —**serv'ice·a·ble,** *adj.* able to provide good service; long-wearing. —**civil service,** the nonmilitary people, as a body, who work for the government. **Ex.** *She has been in the civil service for many years.*

serviceman [sər'vismæn'], *n.* 1. a male member of the armed forces. **Ex.** *We shared a table with two servicemen in the diner on the train.* 2. a person who repairs or keeps something in good condition, such as household equipment, office machines, cars, etc. **Ex.** *We called a serviceman to repair the washing machine.*

servicewoman [sər'viswum'ən], *n.* a female member of the armed forces. **Ex.** *A servicewoman gave us directions to the parade ground.*

session (4) [seš'ən], *n.* 1. the meeting of a group, court, etc. **Ex.** *He missed the first session of the class.* 2. a series of meetings of a class, group, etc. **Ex.** *He attended the spring session at the university.*

set (1) [set'], *v.* 1. put in place or position. **Ex.** *She set the lamp on the table.* 2. put in some condition. **Ex.** *He set the house on fire.* 3. put into the right condition; put in order. **Ex.** *She set the clock.* 4. assign a time, price or limit to. **Ex.** *We set the time of the meeting for six o'clock.* 5. place a jewel into the metal part of a piece of jewelry. **Ex.** *The diamond was set in a gold ring.* 6. sink below the place where the sky and the earth seem to meet. **Ex.** *The sun sets early in winter.* —*adj.* fixed; established; firm. **Ex.** *School usually begins at a set time.* —*n.* a number of persons, things, activities, etc. that form a group or are related in some way. **Exs.** *She bought a set of dishes. Their meeting resulted from* *a strange set of circumstances.* —**set'ting,** *n.* 1. the act of putting in place, in order. **Ex.** *Setting the table took a good deal of time.* 2. the metal part in which a jewel is fixed. **Ex.** *That ring has a very unusual setting.* 3. the time and place of a play, story, etc.; the stage scenery of a play. **Ex.** *New York City, 1945, is the setting of the play.* 4. the surrounding scene or view. **Ex.** *The house is located in a beautiful setting.* —**set aside,** 1. keep for a purpose; not in use at the time. **Ex.** *He set aside some money for his vacation.* 2. dismiss; reject; in law, rule contrary to another court. **Ex.** *When the lower court decision was set aside, the accused man was freed.* —**set back,** slow or reverse progress. **Ex.** *I was set back in my work by illness.* —**set down,** write on paper. **Ex.** *Set down your ideas before you forget them.* —**set forth,** 1. begin a trip. **Ex.** *He has just set forth on a trip around the world.* 2. explain; present. **Ex.** *She set forth her ideas in a speech.* —**set off,** 1. cause to explode; cause an action. **Ex.** *He set off a firecracker.* 2. begin an action. **Ex.** *He set off for town.* 3. make noticeable by contrast. **Ex.** *The house was set off by tall trees on either side.* —**set on, set upon,** cause to attack; attack. **Ex.** *He was set upon by robbers.* —**set out,** 1. begin an action. **Ex.** *She set out to do some shopping.* 2. place something where it can be noticed. **Ex.** *He set out the photographs on the table.* —**set to,** begin seriously. **Ex.** *He set to work and finished the job quickly.* —**set up,** build; establish. **Ex.** *He is setting up a new company.*

settle (1) [set'əl], *v.* 1. agree upon; decide. **Ex.** *He helped me settle on which car to buy.* 2. put in order; put in place. **Ex.** *She settled her affairs before leaving town.* 3. make a home or homes. **Ex.** *Brave men and women settled the wilderness.* 4. quiet; calm. **Ex.** *His words settled our fears.* 5. move downward; sink. **Ex.** *The boat settled to the bottom of the river.* 6. pay money that is owed. **Ex.** *He settled his bills monthly.* —**set'tle·ment,** *n.* 1. the act of settling. 2. a place where people have recently built homes; a village. **Ex.** *There were few settlements on the plains.* 3. an amount of money paid according to an agreement. —**sett'ler,** *n.*

seven (1) [sev'ən], *n., adj.* the number between six and eight; the number 7. —**sev'enth,** *n., adj.* coming after six others. —**sev'en·teen',** *n., adj.* the number between sixteen and eighteen; the

a, far; æ, am; e, get; ey, late; i, in; iy, see; ɔ, all; ow, go; u, put; uw, too; ə, but, ago; ər, fur; aw, out; ay, life; oy, boy; ŋ, ring; θ, think; ð, that; ž, measure; š, ship; j, edge; č, child.

number *17*. —**sev`en·teenth'**, *n., adj.* coming after sixteen others. —**sev'en·ty**, *n., adj.* the number *70*. —**sev'en·ti·eth`**, *adj., n.* coming after sixty-nine others.

several (1) [sev'(ə)rəl], *adj.* three or more but not many. **Ex.** *There were several people waiting in the office.*

severe (3) [səvi:r'], *adj.* 1. not gentle; cruel; strict. **Ex.** *The man was given a severe punishment.* 2. causing much pain or damage. **Ex.** *They were not prepared for the severe storm.* 3. not bright or lively; plain in appearance. **Ex.** *She wore a severe, dark dress.* —**se·vere'ly**, *adv.* —**se·ver'i·ty**, *n.*

sew (2) [sow'], *v.* 1. join together or unite with needle and thread; mend. **Ex.** *She sewed the button on his coat.* 2. use needle and thread. **Ex.** *She liked to sew.* —**sew'ing**, *n.* 1. the act or work of using needle and thread. 2. something that has been or needs to be sewed. **Ex.** *Her sewing for the day was on the table.*

sewn [sown'], *v.* past participle of *sew*. **Ex.** *A patch had been sewn on the elbow of his sweater.*

sex (3) [seks'], *n.* 1. either the male or female group into which all living things are divided. **Ex.** *Children of both sexes attend this school.* 2. the characteristics of being male or female. **Ex.** *He could tell the sex of the bird by its feathers.* 3. physical relations between the sexes; sexual inter-course. —**sex'u·al**, *adj.* —**sexism**, *n.* the attitude that one sex is superior to the other. —**sexist**, *adj.* having an attitude that one sex is superior to the other.

shabby (4) [šæb'iy], *adj.* 1. faded and ragged from hard wear. **Ex.** *He was wearing a shabby suit.* 2. dressed in faded, ragged clothes. **Ex.** *He looked shabby.* 3. mean; impolite. **Ex.** *They acted in a shabby way.* —**shab'bi·ly**, *adv.* —**shab'bi·ness**, *n.*

shack (5) [šæk'], *n.* a rough or cheaply built hut. **Ex.** *There were several shacks along the railroad tracks.*

shade (1) [šeyd'], *n.* 1. darkness or dimness caused by some-thing which blocks the rays of the sun or of other light. **Ex.** *We sat in the shade of a large tree.* 2. something which is used to cut off the rays of the sun or a lamp. **Ex.** *The window shades had been pulled down.* 3. the amount of darkness in a color. **Ex.** *She chose a light shade of green paint for the walls.* —*v.* 1. prevent light from reaching; darken. **Ex.** *She shaded her head with an umbrella.* 2. in-crease the amount of darkness in a color. **Ex.** *The artist shaded part of the house in his picture.* —**shad'y**, *adj.*

shadow (2) [šæd'ow], *n.* a dark image that is made by something that blocks a source of light. **Ex.** *With the light behind him, his shadow could be seen on the wall.* 2. something present only to a slight degree. **Ex.** *The shadow of a smile could be seen on her lips.* —**shad'ow·y,** *adj.*

shaft (5) [šæft'], *n.* 1. long, slender rod or bar, such as the handle of a spear; the long slender part of a tool or machine. **Ex.** *The broken drive shaft of the car was repaired in the garage.* 2. a narrow opening that goes through the floors of a building. 3. an opening into a mine. **Ex.** *The men go down into the mine through that shaft.*

shake (1) [šeyk'], *v.* 1. move or cause to move back and forth or up and down in short, quick movements. **Ex.** *The two men stopped to shake hands.* 2. throw upon or stir by using such movements. **Ex.** *She was shaking salt and pepper on the roast beef.* 3. tremble. **Ex.** *The frightened boy was shaking with terror.* —*n.* the act of shaking. **Ex.** *He gave an angry shake of his head.* —**shak'er,** *n.* a container in or from which something is shaken. **Ex.** *Have you filled the salt and pepper shakers?* —**shak'y,** *adj.* —**shake hands,** take the hand of another in greeting, farewell or agreement.

shaken [šey'kən], *v.* past participle of *shake.* **Ex.** *The wind had shaken the leaves from the trees.*

shall (1) [šæl'], *v.* used with another verb to 1. show action in the future. **Ex.** *I shall see you tomorrow.* 2. request or suggest. **Ex.** *Shall I open the window?*

shallow (3) [šæl'ow], *adj.* 1. not deep. **Ex.** *The pond was too shallow for swimming.* 2. lacking in depth of feeling or understanding. **Ex.** *She is a very shallow person.*

shame (2) [šeym'], *n.* 1. a painful feeling coming from the knowledge of something wrong or not proper, done by oneself or another. **Ex.** *She felt shame at having been so thoughtless.* 2. a loss of regard or honor. **Ex.** *The boy's stealing brought shame upon his parents.* 3. something that brings a loss of regard, honor, etc. **Ex.** *The unjust laws were the shame of the nation.* —*v.* awaken a painful feeling of guilt, loss of honor, etc. **Ex.** *He was shamed by his own lack of generosity.*

shampoo [šæmpuw'], *n.* a special soap in the form of a liquid or a cream used for washing the hair. **Ex.** *She bought a bottle of shampoo.* —*v.* wash the hair. **Ex.** *He shampoos his hair at the same time that he showers.*

shan't [šænt'], short form, contraction of *shall not*. **Ex.** *Please wait for me; I shan't be long.*

shape (2) [šeyp'], *n.* 1. the form or figure of something, especially in regard to appearance. **Ex.** *An apple and an orange have somewhat the same shape.* 2. something of which only the general form can be seen. **Ex.** *A dim shape appeared at the window.* —*v.* give form to. **Ex.** *She shaped the chopped meat into balls.* —**shape'ly**, *adj.* pleasing in form. **Ex.** *She has shapely legs.*

share (1) [še:r'], *n.* 1. a part belonging to, given to or owned by a single person or group. **Ex.** *Each son received a share of the property.* 2. any of the equal interests or rights into which the ownership of a company is divided. **Ex.** *He owns two hundred shares of the business.* —*v.* 1. distribute in portions. **Ex.** *The children shared the cake equally.* 2. use together. **Ex.** *The two sisters shared a bedroom.* 3. join with others; have a part of. **Ex.** *The two families shared the expenses of the trip.*

shark [šark'], *n.* a large fish having a tough, scaly, grayish or bluish skin and living in the ocean, some varieties of which eat other fish and attack human beings. **Ex.** *People were not allowed to go in swimming because a man-eating shark had been sighted.*

sharp (2) [šarp'], *adj.* 1. having a thin, fine cutting edge or point. **Ex.** *She used a sharp knife to slice the meat.* 2. ending in a point or edge; somewhat pointed. **Ex.** *She had a small face with sharp features.* 3. not gradual; sudden. **Ex.** *There is a sharp curve in the road ahead.* 4. clear; well-defined; distinct. **Ex.** *He saw the sharp outline of a figure in the doorway.* —**sharp'ly**, *adv.* —**sharp'ness**, *n.* —**sharp'en**, *v.* make or become sharp or sharper. **Ex.** *He sharpened the knives.* —**sharp'en·er**, *n.* a device for sharpening. **Ex.** *Where is your pencil sharpener?*

shatter (4) [šæt'ər], *v.* 1. break or burst into small pieces. **Ex.** *The mirror shattered when it fell.* 2. damage; destroy completely. **Ex.** *The telegram shattered their hopes of seeing him alive again.*

shave (3) [šeyv'] *v.* with an instrument having a sharp edge, cut the hair or beard close to the skin. **Ex.** *He sometimes has to shave twice a day.* —*n.* the act of cutting off the beard. **Ex.** *He went to the barbershop for a shave and a haircut.*

shawl (5) [šɔ:l'], *n.* a large scarf or piece of cloth used around the shoulders or over the head. **Ex.** *Her shawl kept her warm.*

she (1) [šiy'], *pron.* a female person or animal that has already been mentioned or is understood. **Ex.** *My sister says she will be late for work.*

shear (5) [ši:r'], *v.* 1. remove from by cutting. **Ex.** *We watched the farmer shear the wool from the sheep.* 2. cut with a sharp instrument. **Ex.** *The machine sheared the steel into strips.* —**shears'**, *n. pl.* a large pair of scissors. **Ex.** *He used the pruning shears to trim the bushes.*

shed (3) [šed'], *n.* a small structure, often with an open side, built for the purpose of sheltering or storing. **Ex.** *The garden tools are in that shed.*

shed (3) [šed'], *v.* 1. pour out; cause to fall or flow; send forth. **Ex.** *The girl shed tears over her loss.* 2. cast off; drop off. **ex.** *Those trees shed their leaves in the autumn.* 3. keep out the rain or moisture. **Ex.** *His old raincoat no longer sheds water.* —**shed light on,** explain; clarify. **Ex.** *His remarks shed new light on the subject.*

she'd [šiyd'], short form, contraction of *she had* and *she would.* **Ex.** *She'd had a tiring day and went to lie down. She'd like to buy a new dress for the party.*

sheep (2) [šiyp'], *n.* a grass-eating animal raised for its flesh and wool. —**sheep'ish,** *adj.* not at ease, as if having done something foolish, stupid or wrong; embarrassed. **Ex.** *His face had a sheepish expression when his lie was discovered.* —**sheep' ish·ly,** *adv.*

SHEEP

sheer (5) [ši:r'] *adj.* 1. thin enough to be seen through. **Ex.** *I could see the garden through the sheer curtains at the window.* 2. complete; absolute. **Ex.** *His story was sheer nonsense.* 3. very steep. **Ex.** *From the top of the cliff to the river was a sheer drop of fifty feet.*

sheet (2) [šiyt'], *n.* 1. a wide piece of cloth, usually made of cotton or cotton and polyester, used in pairs on a bed next to the body. **Ex.** *She put clean sheets on the guest room bed.* 2. a single piece of paper, such as the sizes used for letters or notebook pages. **Ex.** *He wrote a long letter covering three sheets on both sides.* 3. anything with a broad, long, and thin shape. **Ex.** *A sheet of ice covered the lake.*

a, far; æ, am; e, get; ey, late; i, in; iy, see; ɔ, all; ow, go; u, put; uw, too; ə, but, ago; ər, fur; aw, out; ay, life; oy, boy; ŋ, ring; θ, think; ð, that; ž, measure; š, ship; ǰ, edge; č, child.

shelf (3) [šelf'], *n.* 1. a thin piece of wood or other material fastened to a wall or forming part of a piece of furniture that is used to hold things. **Ex.** *That book is on the bottom shelf.* 2. a projecting horizontal surface like a shelf. **Ex.** *The wrecked ship rested on a rocky shelf near the bottom of the sea.*

shell (2) [šel'], *n.* 1. the hard outer covering of eggs, nuts, seeds, and some animals. **Ex.** *We collected many shells on the beach.* 2. a case for holding the powder and other material that is fired from a gun, rifle, etc. **Ex.** *Empty rifle shells were scattered on the ground.* 3. anything similar to a shell. **Ex.** *The house burned until only a shell remained.* —*v.* remove from the shell, covering, etc. **Ex.** *She was shelling peas.*

she'll [šiyl'], short form, contraction of *she will* **Ex.** *She'll join us later.*

shelter (2) [šel'tər], *n.* 1. something that gives protection; a place of safety. **Ex.** *A cave was their shelter for the night.* 2. protection. **Ex.** *They sought shelter from the rain.* —*v.* provide with protection or a place of safety. **Ex.** *A farmer sheltered them in his barn.*

shelve (5) [šelv'], *v.* 1. place on a shelf. **Ex.** *The magazines are shelved on the first floor.* 2. put aside until later. **Ex.** *The question was shelved until the next meeting.* —**shelves'**, *n.* plural of shelf. —**shel'ving**, *n.* shelves or material of which shelves are made. **Ex.** *What kind of wood will you use for the shelving?*

shepherd (5) [šep'ərd], *n.* one who herds sheep. **Ex.** *The shepherd guided his sheep down the hill.*

sheriff (3) [še:r'if], *n.* the chief law officer of a county. **Ex.** *The sheriff brought the captured criminal before the judge.*

she's [šiyz], short form, contraction of *she is.* **Ex.** *She's a very lovely person.*

shield (3) [šiyld'], *n.* 1. a piece of armor usually carried on the left arm and used for defense. **Ex.** *The shield protected him from the blows of his attacker.* 2. anything used as a defense or protection. **Ex.** *His umbrella was a shield against the rain.* —*v.* protect. **Ex.** *She needed her wide hat to shield her face from the sun.*

shift (3) [šift'], *v.* move, transfer or change from one place, person or position to another. **Ex.** *The wind shifted from east to west.* —*n.* 1. a change from one person, thing or position

to another. **Ex.** *A shift in position made her more comfortable.*
2. a period or time of work at a place where not all people
work the same hours. **Ex.** *He works the night shift at the
factory.* —**shift'less,** *adj.* lazy. **Ex.** *He is too shiftless to keep a
steady job.* —**shift'y,** *adj.* not reliable; tricky. **Ex.** *I would
not do business with such a shifty person.*

shine (1) [šayn'], *v.* 1. give out rays of light; glow with light. **Ex.**
The sun is shining. 2. be bright with reflected light. **Ex.** *We
could see the cat's eyes shining in the darkness.* 3. cause to
give off light; direct a light. **Ex.** *Shine the light into that
corner.* —*n.* brightness caused by something that gives or
reflects light. **Ex.** *The shine of the brass nameplate caught my
eye.* —**shin'y,** *adj.*

shingle (5) [šiŋ'gəl], *n.* one of the thin pieces of wood or other
material placed on the roof or sides of a house in rows, with
each row partly covering another. **Ex.** *The sides of the house
were covered with white wooden shingles.* —*v.* cover with
shingles. **Ex.** *They shingled the roof of the house.*

ship (1) [šip'], *n.* 1. a large vessel that travels on the ocean. **Ex.**
The ship was loaded with tons of grain. 2. airplane; spacecraft. —*v.* send or carry by ship, train, truck or airplane.
Ex. *We will ship the goods to you at once.* —**ship'ment,** *n.*
goods shipped at one time. —**ship'per,** *n.*

-ship (1) [šip], *suffix.* 1. state or quality of. **Ex.** *Friend, friendship.*
2. rank. **Ex.** *Judge, judgeship.* 3. art or skill of. **Ex.** *Leader,
leadership.*

shirt (1) [šərt'], *n.* a garment for the upper part of a man's body
having long or short sleeves and usually a collar. **Ex.** *He wore
a white shirt with his blue suit.*

shiver (4) [šiv'ər], *v.* shake or tremble, especially from cold,
excitement or fear. **Ex.** *The boy shivered in the wintry wind.*
—*n.* a tremble; the act of shivering. **Ex.** *A shiver ran down
her spine.*

shock (2) [šak'], *n.* 1. something that greatly disturbs the mind
or emotions; a great disturbance of the mind or emotions.
Ex. *News of his death was a shock to us.* 2. a blow; a violent
shake; a sudden coming together of two forces. **Ex.** *The
shock of the explosion broke the windows.* 3. the effect of
electricity on the body. **Ex.** *He received a shock from an
exposed electric wire.* —*v.* 1. cause to feel astonishment,
horror, etc. **Ex.** *Her appearance shocked us.* 2. give an elec-

tric shock to. **Ex.** *He was badly shocked when he accidentally touched the fallen power line.*

shoe (1) [šuw'], *n.* a covering for the foot, usually made of leather. —**shoe'lace, shoe'string**, *n.* a piece of thin cord or leather used to tighten and fasten a shoe. **Ex.** *He tied his shoelaces.*

SHOE

shone (2) [šown'], *v.* past tense and participle of *shine.* **Exs.** *The sun shone brightly on the lake. If the moon had shone that night, I would not have become lost.*

shook (2) [šuk'] *v.* past tense of *shake.* **Ex.** *He shook with fright.*

shoot (2) [šuwt'], *v.* 1. cause a gun or other weapon to send out something intended to hit or kill. **Ex.** *As the birds rise, the hunters shoot at them.* 2. hit, wound, or kill with small balls of metal or bullets shot from a gun, rifle, etc. **Ex.** *How many rabbits did he shoot?* 3. send or push out. **Ex.** *The plants are shooting out new leaves every day now.*

shop (1) [šap'], *n.* 1. a store; a place for selling goods. **Ex.** *He bought some chocolates at the candy shop.* 2. a place where a special kind of work is done. **Ex.** *She had the chair repaired at the carpenter's shop.* —*v.* buy; go from shop to shop to look at and buy goods. **Ex.** *The two women liked to shop together.* —**shop'per**, *n.* one who shops. **Ex.** *She was a careful shopper.* —**set up shop**, establish or begin a business. **Ex.** *He set up shop as a shoe repairman.*

shoplifter [šap'lif'tər], *n.* one who steals things from a store. **Ex.** *The store owner watched carefully for shoplifters.*

shore (1) [šɔːr'], *n.* land alongside a body of water such as an ocean, lake, etc. **Ex.** *The boat was near the shore.* —**shore·line**, the line where water and shore meet.

short (1) [šɔrt'], *adj.* 1. lasting for only a little while. **Ex.** *I am busy and can stay for only a short time.* 2. having little length. **Ex.** *The string was too short to tie around the package.* 3. having little height. **Ex.** *My younger brother is shorter than I.* 4. rudely brief. **Ex.** *He was very short with me.* 5. not having enough. **Ex.** *When we counted the money, we were short ten dollars.* —*adv.* all of a sudden. **Ex.** *He stopped short when he saw her.* —**short'ly**, *adv.* soon. **Ex.** *They will be here shortly.* —**short'en**, *v.* make shorter. **Ex.** *She shortened her dress.*

—**short'ness,** *n.* the state of being short. —**short'age,** *n.* less than the correct or necessary amount. **Ex.** *There is a shortage of food.* —**shorts',** *n.* 1. short trousers for men or women. 2. short trousers used by men as underwear. —**in short,** briefly. **Ex.** *In short, we went home angry.* —**short for,** a briefer way or form. **Ex.** *Don't is short for do not.* —**short of,** 1. lacking the amount needed. **Ex.** *We are short of butter.* 2. not quite; almost. **Ex.** *We have just short of a quart of milk.*

short circuit [šort' sər'kət], *n.* an accidental failure in an electrical connection that may cause a stoppage in the supply of electricity, a fire or other serious problems.

shortcoming [šort'kəm'iŋ], *n.* weakness. **Ex.** *He is a good man, but he has his shortcomings.*

short cut [šort' kət'], a way of going, doing, etc. that saves time, money, energy etc. **Ex.** *I know a short cut from here to school.*

shortening [šort'niŋ], *n.* any kind of edible fat, such as butter and oil, used in making bread, cakes, cookies, pastry, etc. **Ex.** *I'll need one cup of shortening for this cake.*

shorthand [šort'hænd'], *n.* a system of rapid writing in which signs and symbols are used in place of words or parts of words. **Ex.** *Here are the important parts of the speech, based on notes my secretary took in shorthand.*

short-handed [šort'hæn'did], *adj.* lacking enough help. **Ex.** *We have to work long hours because we are short-handed.*

short-sighted [šort'sayt'id], *adj.* seeing only what is near in space or time; not thinking about future possibilities. **Ex.** *He is too short-sighted to realize the importance of spending money for maintenance.*

short wave [šort'weyv'], a radio signal or wave of less than about sixty meters in length, used for overseas broadcasts and special broadcasting. **Ex.** *He listens to programs from many countries via short wave.*

shot (1) [šat'] *v.* past tense and participle of *shoot.* **Exs.** *The hunter shot two rabbits. They discovered they had shot a man by mistake.*

shot (1) [šat'], *n.* 1. a bullet or small balls of metal used in a gun. **Ex.** *The deer was killed with one shot.* 2. the act of shooting or the sound made by it. **Ex.** *We heard a shot.* 3. a liquid forced by means of a needle underneath the skin into a muscle, vein, etc. **Ex.** *Have you had your shots for the trip yet?* —**long shot,** an effort not likely to succeed. **Ex.** *He has never won before, and it is a long shot that he will now.*

should (1) [šud'], *v.* used with another verb to show: 1. ought to. **Exs.** *She should learn to drive. I should have gone with you.* 2. may happen; likely to happen. **Ex.** *If it should rain, I will close the window.*

shoulder (1) [šowl'dər], *n.* 1. the part of a human body to which an arm is joined. 2. the part of an animal to which a front leg is joined. 3. something similar in shape to a shoulder. **Ex.** *The car ran onto the shoulder of the road.*

shouldn't [šud'ənt], short form, contraction of *should not.* **Ex.** *You shouldn't stay out so late on a school night.*

SHOULDER 1

shout (1) [šawt'], *v.* speak or call very loudly. **Ex.** *She shouted my name.* —*n.* a loud call or cry. **Ex.** *Shouts of laughter came from the crowd.* —**shout someone down,** silence someone by shouting loudly. **Ex.** *The angry crowd shouted down the speaker.*

shove (4) [šev'], *v.* 1. push along by applying force. **Ex.** *She shoved the heavy table against the wall.* 2. force aside, away, through, into, etc. by pushing. **Ex.** *He shoved his way into the room.* —*n.* a push. **Ex.** *He gave the boy a shove.*

shovel (4) [šəv'el], *n.* a tool with a long handle used for lifting and moving loose material. —*v.* lift and throw with a shovel; clear or dig with a shovel. **Ex.** *He shoveled the snow out of the road.*

show (1) [šow'], *v.* 1. allow to be seen; present so as to be seen. **Ex.** *Please show me your new car.* 2. teach; describe; explain. **Ex.** *Please show me how to operate this machine.* 3. guide. **Ex.** *He showed us to our seats.* 4. prove. **Ex.** *Your work shows that you have been careless.* —*n.* 1. act of showing. **Ex.** *He was surprised by her show of grief.* 2. a performance of a movie, play, television program, etc. **Exs.** *They went to the early show. They gave a good show.* 3. an exhibition; a display. **Ex.** *Did you enjoy the flower show?* —**show'y,** *adj.*

SHOVEL

too brightly colored, shiny, etc. **Ex.** *I think this dress is too showy for me to wear to the office.* —**show off,** act in a way to attract attention. **Ex.** *The child was showing off by jumping up and down.* — **show up,** 1. be easily seen. **Ex.** *The house shows up clearly against the sky.* 2. appear; arrive. **Ex.** *I waited an hour before he showed up for our appointment.*

showcase [šow'keys'], *n.* a glass case in a store, museum, etc. in which things are placed so that buyers, viewers, etc. can see them. **Ex.** *The clerk took the watch out of the showcase for the customer.*

shower (2) [šaw'ər], *n.* 1. a fall of rain that lasts only for a short time. **Ex.** *A sudden shower ended the picnic.* 2. a bath taken standing up with water falling on the body from above. **Ex.** *As he stepped into the shower, the telephone rang.* 3. something resembling a rain shower. **Ex.** *He was knocked down by a shower of blows.* —*v.* 1. fall as rain. **Ex.** *Rain showered on the parade.* 2. wash in a spray of water. **Ex.** *He showers every morning.* 3. give generously. **Ex.** *They showered us with gifts.*

shown (1) [šown'], *v.* past participle of *show.* **Ex.** *Have you shown your mother your new dress?*

shrank (4) [šrænk'], *v.* past tense of *shrink.* **Ex.** *He shrank back in fear.*

shred (5) [šred'], *n.* a narrow strip either cut or torn off. **Ex.** *Her dress was torn to shreds.* —*v.* cut or tear into narrow strips. **Ex.** *She shredded vegetables for the salad.*

shrewd (4) [šruwd'], *adj.* keen; sharp; clever; tricky. **Ex.** *He is a shrewd businessman.* —**shrewd'ly,** *adv.* —**shrewd'ness,** *n.*

shriek (3) [šriyk'], *v.* utter or make a sharp, high sound or cry; scream. **Ex.** *She shrieked in horror.* —*n.* a sharp, high cry; a scream. **Ex.** *A shriek of pain came from the wounded man.*

shrill (4) [šril'], *adj.* having or making a high, sharp tone. **Ex.** *She had a shrill voice.* —*v.* make a high, sharp sound. **Ex.** *Insects shrilled in the trees.*

shrimp [šrimp'], *n.* a small sea animal with five pairs of legs and a rather long tail, eaten as a food. **Ex.** *This menu lists twelve different dishes made with shrimp.*

shrine (5) [šrayn'], *n.* a place that is greatly respected for religious or historic reasons. **Ex.** *We visited many historic shrines on our trip to the nation's capital.*

shrink (4) [šriŋk'], *v.* make or become smaller. **Ex.** *This shirt will not shrink when it is washed.* 2. draw away from in horror, pain, disgust, etc. **Ex.** *She still shrinks at the sight of blood.* —**shrink'age**, *n.* the amount lost by shrinking. **Ex.** *Shrinkage of funds made it impossible to expand the business.*

shroud (5) [šrawd'], *n.* 1. something that covers or shelters. **Ex.** *They escaped under the shroud of night.* 2. a cloth in which a dead person is wrapped and buried. **Ex.** *The weeping women brought a shroud* —*v.* cover as with a shroud. **Ex.** *She shrouded her face from curious eyes with a veil.*

shrub (4) [šrəb'], *n.* a bush; a low, woody plant with many branches. **Ex.** *Many shrubs were planted around the house.* —**shrub'ber·y**, *n.* a group of shrubs.

shrug (4) [šrəg'], *v.* raise and draw the shoulders together to show lack of interest, knowledge, concern, etc. **Ex.** *When I questioned him, he only shrugged.* —*n.* the act of raising and drawing the shoulders together. **Ex.** *He denied the accusation with a shrug.*

shrunk (4) [šrəŋk'] *v.* past tense and participle of *shrink.* **Exs.** *The jacket shrunk when it was cleaned. The dress had shrunk one inch.*

shudder (4) [šəd'ər], *v.* shake or tremble suddenly with fear, disgust, etc. **Ex.** *The cold made her shudder.* — *n.* the act of shaking or trembling suddenly from fear, disgust, etc. **Ex.** *A shudder ran through him as he saw a white shape in the darkness.*

shun (4) [šən'] *v.* purposely avoid; stay away from. **Ex.** *He shunned his old friends.*

shut (2) [šət'], *v.* 1. close an opening, especially to keep something in or out. **Ex.** *Shut the window, please.* 2. close by holding or bringing together the parts of. **Ex.** *The teacher shut her book.* —**shut down,** stop working or operating. **Ex.** *The machines were shut down when the electric power failed.* —**shut out,** prevent from entering or being included. **Ex.** *He was shut out of his house when he left the key inside.* —**shut up,** 1. put or keep inside. **Ex.** *They shut up the criminal in a prison cell.* 2. stop talking. **Ex.** *The rude man said that we should shut up.*

shutter (5) [šət'ər], *n.* a wooden cover for a window that may be closed for protection. **Ex.** *They closed the shutters during the storm.*

shuttle [šət'əl], *n.* a train, bus or plane that goes back and forth regularly between the same two points.

SHUTTER

Ex. *I reached the airport just in time to make the ten o'clock shuttle.* —*v.* travel back and forth between the same two points regularly or frequently. **Ex.** *His work requires him to shuttle between the two cities at least twice a week.*

shy (4) [šay'], *adj.* easily frightened; not at ease with others. **Ex.** *She is a shy child.* —*v.* draw back suddenly; start. **Ex.** *The horse started to shy as the car approached.* —**shy'ly,** *adv.* —**shy'ness,** *n.*

sick (1) [sik'], *adj.* 1. ill; suffering from disease. **Ex.** *When she became sick, I called the doctor.* 2. filled with regret or grief. **Ex.** *She is sick about failing the test.* —**sick'en,** *v.* cause to become sick; become sick. **Ex.** *He sickened and died.* —**sick'en·ing,** *adj.* causing sickness or disgust. **Ex.** *The accident was a sickening sight.* —**sick'ly,** *adj.* in poor health; pale; weak. **Ex.** *He had always been a sickly child.* —**sick'ness,** *n.* —**sick of,** tired of. **Ex.** *He was sick of his job.*

side (1) [sayd'], *n.* 1. any of the lines that form the edges of a surface; any of the surfaces of an object. **Ex.** *A square has four equal sides.* 2. one of the two broad surfaces of something very thin. **Ex.** *He wrote on both sides of the paper.* 3. a surface other than the front, back, top or bottom. **Ex.** *A railroad passenger car usually has windows on both sides.* 4. a surface or place in relation to something else. **Ex.** *Our house is here; his house is on the other side of the river.* 5. either half of the human body. **Ex.** *He had a pain in his left side.* 6. an aspect or quality of a person, situation, etc. **Ex.** *She shows only her cheerful side to others.* 7. one of two opposing individuals, groups, etc. **Ex.** *Let us choose sides for the game.* —*adj.* being at, on or of one side. **Ex.** *We entered through a side door.* —*v.* help, favor, etc. one of two sides. **Ex.** *He sided with his brother in the quarrel.* —**side by side,** together. **Ex.** *If we work side by side, we will win.* —**take sides,** support one person or position in an argument. **Ex.** *If you take sides, the others will be angry.*

sideburns [sayd'bərnz'], *n.* the hair in front of the ears on the side of a man's face. **Ex.** *He preferred to let his sideburns grow long.*

a, far; æ, am; e, get; ey, late; i, in; iy, see; ɔ, all; ow, go; u, put; uw, too; ə, but, ago; ər, fur; aw, out; ay, life; oy, boy; ŋ, ring; θ, think; ð, that; ž, measure; š, ship; j, edge; č, child.

side effect [sayd' əfekt'], *n.* an effect that a medicine, treatment or activity has in addition to the desired or intended one, particularly an unpleasant or bad one. **Ex.** *The medicine relieved his pain but made him feel sleepy as a side effect.*

sidestep [sayd'step'], *v.* avoid as by stepping aside. **Ex.** *He sidestepped answering the question by pretending he had not heard it.*

sidewalk [sayd'wɔ:k'], *n.* an area where people walk along the side of a street, usually raised and paved. **Ex.** *At lunch time the sidewalks were filled with crowds of people.*

sideways [sayd'weyz'], **sidewise** [sayd'wayz'], *adv.* seen from one side; with one side facing the viewer; toward one side. **Ex.** *He had to turn sideways to make his way through the narrow opening.*

siding [sayd'iŋ], *n.* boards or other material used to cover the side of a wooden building. **Ex.** *They nailed the wood siding to the frame of the house.*

siege (4) [siyĵ'], *n.* 1. the surrounding of a fort or other defended place in order to force its surrender. **Ex.** *During the long siege, food and water became very scarce.* 2. a long continuing period as of illness, difficulty, etc. **Ex.** *After a siege of three months, the company met union demands.*

sift (4) [sift'], *v.* 1. separate the coarse parts of something from the fine parts by passing it through a screen of fine wire. **Ex.** *She sifted the flour for the cake.* 2. examine closely. **Ex.** *The lawyer sifted the evidence before he agreed to take the case.* —**sift'er,** *n.* a device for separating coarse parts from fine.

sigh (4) [say'], *v.* 1. draw in one's breath and let it out so that it can be heard to express sadness, weariness, etc. **Ex.** *She sighed with relief when she saw him walking toward the house.* 2. make a sound like this. **Ex.** *The wind sighed through the trees.* —*n.* the act or sound of sighing. **Ex.** *He breathed a sigh of weariness as he lifted the load.*

sight (1) [sayt'], *n.* 1. the power or ability to see. **Ex.** *The old man had lost his sight.* 2. the act of seeing. **Ex.** *Our first sight of the city was at night.* 3. a view; something of interest; something worth seeing. **Ex.** *The valley was a beautiful sight.* —*v.* see. **Ex.** *The guard sighted an escaping prisoner.* —**catch sight of,** see briefly; glimpse. **Ex.** *He caught sight of the children running through the woods.* —**sight'see·ing,** *n.* the act of visiting interesting places and things. **Ex.** *Where did you go sightseeing today?*

sign (1) [sayn'], *n*. 1. a card, board or space on which directions, a warning, etc. are written or printed. **Ex.** *The sign says "No Parking."* 2. something that indicates the existence of another thing. **Ex.** *The first robin was a sign of spring.* 3. a motion by which a command is given or a thought expressed. **Ex.** *The traffic policeman made a sign for us to advance.* 4. a symbol representing an idea. **Ex.** *The white flag was their sign of surrender.* —*v*. 1. write one's name. **Ex.** *He signed the letter.* 2. make known by sign language. **Ex.** *She signed to her friend from the window.* —**sign'er**, *n*. one who signs. —**sign language**, *n*. a system of communicating, especially among the deaf, using certain movements of the hands. **Ex.** *They were talking in sign language.* —**sign off**, in radio or television, stop broadcasting for the day. —**sign up**, enlist; be hired. **Ex.** *He signed up for the army.*

signal (2) [sig'nəl], *n*. something that warns, directs, etc. **Ex.** *The sound of the gun was the signal for the start of the race.* —*adj*. use in signaling **Ex.** *The pilot radioed the signal tower for instructions.* —*v*. 1. make a signal to **Ex.** *He signaled the man to stop.* 2. send messages by means of signals. **Ex.** *The ship signaled for help.*

signature (4) [sig'nəčər], *n*. the name of a person as written by his or her own hand. **Ex.** *His signature is difficult to read.*

significance (4) [signif'əkəns], *n*. 1. importance. **Ex.** *He knew the significance of the action he was taking.* 2. meaning. **Ex.** *What was the significance of the look he gave you?* —**sig·nif'i·cant**, *adj*. **sig·nif·i·cant·ly**, *adv*.

signify (5) [sig'nəfay'], *v*. 1. show by sign or action. **Ex.** *If you agree, signify by raising your right hand.* 2. mean. **Ex.** *The fact that they left doesn't signify anything.*

silence (2) [say'ləns], *n*. 1. the state of not speaking or of not making noise. **Ex.** *Students are required to maintain silence in the library.* 2. an absence of noise. **Ex.** *The silence of the falling snow is comforting.* 3. failure or unwillingness to speak out. **Ex.** *The club members were surprised by the president's silence about the case.* —*v*. quiet. **Ex.** *The speaker silenced the crowd.* —**si'lent**, *adj*. —**si'lent·ly**, *adv*.

silk (2) [silk'], *n*. the fine, bright, threadlike substance produced by a certain kind of worm; also, the thread or cloth made from this substance. **Ex.** *She selected blue silk for her dress.* —*adj*. made of silk. **Ex.** *He wore a silk tie.* —**sil'ken, silk'y**, *adj*. made of silk; smooth, soft or shiny like silk.

sill [sil'], *n.* the horizontal piece of wood, stone, etc. that is placed at the bottom of the frame of a door or window. **Ex.** *The bathroom door has a marble sill.*

silly (3) [sil'iy], *adj.* without good sense; foolish. **Ex.** *The children said silly things.* —**sil'li·ness,** *n.*

silver (1) [sil'vər], *n.* 1. a white precious metal that can be shaped easily. **Ex.** *He wore a ring made of silver.* 2. money; coins made of silver. **Ex.** *Give me my change in silver, please.* 3. knives, forks, spoons and other table pieces. **Ex.** *Please put the silver on the table.* —*adj.* made of silver. **Ex.** *She poured the tea from a silver pot.* —**sil'ver·y,** *adj.* like silver in color, tone, etc. **Ex.** *We heard her silvery laughter in the next room.*

silverware (3) [sil'vərwer'], *n.* knives, spoons, forks and other tableware made of silver, silverplate or stainless steel. **Ex.** *Do you have enough silverware for twelve?*

similar (2) [sim'ələr], *adj.* be like something but not exactly the same. **Ex.** *The two men wore similar suits.* —**sim'i·lar·ly,** *adv.* —**sim'i·lar'i·ty,** *n.* likeness. **Ex.** *There were similarities in their education and experience.*

simple (1) [sim'pəl], *adj.* 1. easy to understand; not difficult. **Ex.** *She answered the simple questions without difficulty.* 2. plain. **Ex.** *She wore a simple dress to work.* 3. natural; sincere. **Ex.** *His parents were simple people.* —**sim'pli·fy,** *v.* make simple. —**sim'ply,** *adv.* 1. in a simple way; plainly. **Ex.** *She did the cooking simply and quickly.* 2. merely; just. **Ex.** *He simply walked away from us.* 3. absolutely; completely. **Ex.** *She was simply exhausted.*

simplicity (5) [simplis'ətiy], *n.* 1. the quality of being easy to understand. **Ex.** *The simplicity of his words appealed to the audience.* 2. naturalness. **Ex.** *The child spoke with honesty and simplicity.* 3. plainness; lack of ornament. **Ex.** *The simplicity of her dress was accented by a jeweled pin.*

sin (2) [sin'], *n.* the breaking of a religious law, especially when done purposely; any wrong act. **Ex.** *She had been taught that stealing was a sin.* —*v.* break a religious law; commit a wrong act. **Ex.** *He felt guilty because he had sinned.* —**sin'ner,** *n.* one who sins.

since (1) [sins'], *prep.* from the time stated until now. **Ex.** *I have known him since childhood.* —*conj.* 1. after the time stated. **Ex.** *Since the factory shut down, he has been out of work.* 2. because. **Ex.** *You may take this book since I have read it.*

—*adv.* 1. from a definite time in the past until now. **Ex.** *He joined the club in 1970 and has been a member ever since.* 2. after a certain time in the past and before the present. **Ex.** *She once wanted to be a doctor but has since changed her mind.*

sincere (4) [sinsi:r'], *adj.* 1. honest; showing good faith. **Ex.** *He was a sincere friend.* 2. real; genuine. **Ex.** *She made a sincere effort to improve.* —**sin·cere'ly,** *adv.* —**sin·cer'i·ty,** *n.* honesty. **Ex.** *She spoke with sincerity.*

sing (1) [siŋ'], *v.* 1. use the human voice to make musical sounds with or without words. **Ex.** *He sings popular songs.* 2. make musical sounds. **Ex.** *The birds were singing.* —**sing'er,** *n.*

single (1) [siŋ'gəl], *adj.* 1. one only. **Ex.** *The room was empty except for a single chair.* 2. unmarried. **Ex.** *Is your sister still single?* 3. for the use of one person. **Ex.** *The traveler asked for a single room.* —**sin'gly,** *adv.* alone; one at a time. **Ex.** *The neighbors came singly to offer comfort.*

single file [siŋ'gəl fayl'], a line or row of persons or things, one behind the other. **Ex.** *They marched single file.*

single-handed [siŋ'gəlhæn'did], *adj. adv.* with no help. **Exs.** *Her single-handed efforts provided for the children. He fought his attackers single-handed.*

single-minded [siŋ'gəlmayn'did], *adj.* determined and able to work hard for a single objective until it is achieved. **Ex.** *He is a single-minded man who thinks only about the job he is doing.*

singular (5) [siŋ'gyələr], *adj.* 1. remarkable; unusual. **Ex.** *She is a woman of singular beauty.* 2. strange; odd. **Ex.** *We noticed the man's singular behavior.* 3. in grammar, of a form referring to a single person or thing. **Ex.** *Is is a singular form of the verb be.* —*n.* the form of a word that refers to only one. **Ex** Leaf *is the singular of* leaves.

sink (2) [siŋk'], *v.* 1. go down into water or other fluid. **Ex.** *The ship is filling with water and sinking.* 2. go down or seem to go down slowly. **Ex.** *We watched the sun sink in the west.* 3. become lower. **Ex.** *Sell now; prices are sinking.* —*n.* a basin or container with a drain and usually a water supply. **Ex.** *She washed the dishes in the sink.*

---

a, far; æ, am; e, get; ey, late; i, in; iy, see; ɔ, all; ow, go; u, put; uw, too; ə, but, ago; ər, fur; aw, out; ay, life; oy, boy; ŋ, ring; θ, think; ð, that; ž, measure; š, ship; j, edge; č, child.

sip [sip'], *v.* drink a small amount at a time. **Ex.** *She sipped the hot tea slowly.* —*n.* a very small amount of liquid; a small taste. **Ex.** *Won't you try just a sip of this soup?*

sir (2) [sər'], *n.* respectful term used in speaking or writing to a man. **Ex.** *Is this your hat, sir?*

siren (5) [say'rən], *n.* an instrument for making loud, high, easily heard warning signals. **Ex.** *We heard the siren of a police car.*

sister (1) [sis'tər], *n.* a girl or woman with the same parents as another person. **Ex.** *He has two sisters, both older than he.*

sister-in-law [sis'tərinlɔː'], *n.* wife of one's brother; sister of one's husband or wife.

sit (1) [sit'], *v.* 1. rest on the lower part of the body; be seated. **Ex.** *Sit in this chair.* 2. rest. **Ex.** *Several birds are sitting in the tree.* 3. occupy a place as a member. **Ex.** *He sits in Congress.* —**sitting,** *n.* 1. a period of time during which one is seated and engaged in just one activity. **Ex.** *The painter told her that he would need her for at least three more sittings.* 2. the time allowed to serve a meal to a group of people. **Ex.** *There are two sittings for dinner aboard this ship; the first one is from six o'clock to seven thirty.* 3. a regular meeting of an official body such as a court. **Ex.** *The Supreme Court will consider that case at its next sitting.* —**sit in,** 1. join with others as in a meeting. **Ex.** *He was asked to sit in on the committee's meetings.* 2. protest by sitting as a group in a particular place and refusing to leave. —**sit on,** be a member of a committee or other such group. **Ex.** *She sits on the election committee.* —**sit out,** take a rest from some activity for a period. **Ex.** *She was tired and decided to sit out the next dance.* —**sit up,** 1. move the body into a position where one is sitting. **Ex.** *Can you sit up in bed?* 2. stay awake and not go to bed. **Ex.** *She had been sitting up all night waiting for her son to come home.*

site (4) [sayt'] *n.* location; position. **Ex.** *This is the site of the famous battle about which I was telling you.*

situation (2) [sič'uwey'šən], *n.* 1. the general state of affairs. **Ex.** *The political situation is very complicated.* 2. personal condition; state of affairs; position. **Ex.** *He is in a difficult situation.* —**sit'u·ate,** *v.* locate; place. **Ex.** *Their house is situated near the river.*

six (1) [siks'], *n., adj.* the number between five and seven; the number 6. —**sixth',** *n., adj.* coming after five others. —**six'teen,** *n., adj.* the number between fifteen and seventeen; the num-

ber *16.* —**six'teenth'**, *n., adj.* coming after fifteen others. —**six'ty,**
n., adj. the number *60.* —**six'ti·eth,** *n., adj.* coming after
fifty-nine others.

size (1) [sayz'], *n.* 1. the place occupied by a thing; length, width
and height. **Ex.** *Your house is the same size as ours.* 2. one of
a set of measurements accepted as standard. **Ex.** *What is your
shoe size?* 3. amount, extent, etc. **Ex.** *The size of his debt is
enormous.*

skate (3) [skeyt'], *n.* 1. a blade of metal attached to a shoe,
allowing the wearer to glide over ice. 2. a metal frame with
rollers attached to a shoe, allowing the wearer to roll over a
smooth surface. —*v.* glide on ice or roll over a smooth
surface wearing skates. **Ex.** *The children are skating on the
frozen pond.* —**skat'er,** *n.*

skeleton (4) [skel'ətən] *n.* 1. all the bones of a human or other
animal body in their natural position, serving as a frame for
the flesh. **Ex.** *The explorers discovered a skeleton in the cave.*
2. anything like a skeleton, such as the frame of a building or
a ship. **Ex.** *They could see skeletons of ruined buildings.*
—**skel'e·tal,** *adj.*

skeleton key [skel'ətən kiy'], a specially made key that opens
many different locks.

sketch (3) [skeč'], *n.* 1. a drawing or painting done simply and
quickly. **Ex.** *We liked his sea sketches best.* 2. a rough plan or
design. **Ex.** *His sketch included the main points of his plan.* —*v.*
draw or paint simply and quickly. **Ex.** *He sketched her as she
stood in the doorway.* —**sketch'y,** *adj.* incomplete; lacking detail.
Ex. *He gave us only a sketchy account of what had happened.*

ski [skiy'], *n.* one of a pair of long, thin pieces of wood, metal or
plastic, turned up at the front end, which is attached to a
boot and used to move smoothly and easily over the surface
of the snow. **Ex.** *Did you bring skis with you, or are you
going to rent a pair?* —*v.*

skid [skid'], *v.* slip or slide to the side or forward, especially
after trying to bring a car, truck, etc. to a stop. **Ex.** *The car
skidded out of control on the icy road.* —*n.* the act of slipping
or sliding to the side or forward in a car, truck, etc. **Ex.** *The
bicycle went into a skid and threw the boy riding it to the ground.*

skill (2) [skil'], *n.* 1. the ability that results from training, experience, etc. **Ex.** *He plays the piano with skill.* 2. a particular art
or science, particularly one that requires the use of the hands.

Ex. *Repairing fine furniture is a skill he learned from his father.* —**skilled'**, *adj.* requiring or having a particular skill. **Ex.** *He was skilled at repairing watches.* —**skill'ful,** *adj.* having skill. **Ex.** *He is a skillful surgeon.* —**skill'ful·ly,** *adv.*

skim (4) [skim'], *v.* 1. remove with some instrument that which floats or comes to the top of a liquid. **Ex.** *The cook skimmed the fat from the soup.* 2. read rapidly but not thoroughly. **Ex.** *He skimmed the newspaper.* 3. pass over or cause to pass over quickly and lightly. **Ex.** *The motorboat skimmed over the water.*

skim milk [skim' milk'], milk from which the cream has been skimmed. **Ex.** *She drinks skim milk to help cut down on the fat in her diet.*

skimp [skimp'], *v.* be so economical that one uses or spends less than one needs to. **Exs.** *At the end of the month she always has to skimp on food for the family because she has used up all her food stamps. This house is always cold in winter because the builder skimped on insulation.* —**skimp'y,** *adj.*

skin (1) [skin'], *n.* 1. the outer covering of a human or other animal body. **Ex.** *Her skin was smooth and soft.* 2. the skin of an animal with its fur after it has been removed from the body. **Ex.** *The collar of her coat was made from a fox skin.* 3. the outer covering of some fruits and vegetables. **Ex.** *Don't slip on that banana skin.* —*v.* remove the skin. **Ex.** *The hunter skinned the deer.* —**skin'ny,** *adj.* very thin. **Ex.** *He is a skinny boy.*

skip (4) [skip'], *v.* 1. move from one point to another without touching what is in between. **Ex.** *She skipped chapter two of the book.* 2. move forward by jumping or hopping from one foot to the other. **Ex.** *The children skipped along on their way to school.*

skirt (2) [skərt'], *n.* the lower part of a dress; a separate garment for women and girls that hangs from the waist. —*v.* move around the edge of; avoid. **Ex.** *He skirted the business section of the city to avoid heavy traffic.*

SKIRT

skull (4) [skəl'], *n.* the bony frame of the head that covers and protects the brain. **Ex.** *He was knocked unconscious by a blow on the skull.*

sky (1) [skay'], *n.* the space above the earth; the upper air; the heavens. **Ex.** *There isn't a cloud in the sky.*

SKULL

skylight [skay'layt`], *n.* a window in a roof. **Ex.** *He could see stars through the skylight.*

skyline [skay'layn`], *n.* 1. the line of sight where the earth seems to meet the sky; the horizon. **Ex.** *We watched the airplane until it disappeared beyond the skyline.* 2. the outline of buildings, mountains, etc., seen against the sky. **Ex.** *The skyline of mountains was an inspiring sight.*

skyscraper [skay'skreyp`ər], *n.* a very tall building. **Ex.** *New York is famous for its skyscrapers.*

slacks [slæks`], *n.* an outer garment extending from the waist to the ankles and covering each leg separately; pants; trousers, often worn for relaxed occasions. **Ex.** *Those slacks go well with your jacket.*

slain (3) [sleyn`], *v.* past participle of *slay.* **Ex.** *Thousands were slain in the battle.*

slam (4) [slæm`], *v.* 1. shut violently and noisily. **Ex.** *She slammed the door shut.* 2. throw or place violently and noisily. **Ex.** *She slammed the pans into the sink.*

slander [slændər], *n.* a purposely false spoken comment, statement, etc. that injures a person's good reputation. **Ex.** *He would not listen to the slander against his friend.* —*v.* injure a person's reputation by purposely making false statements. **Ex.** *She never hesitated to slander anyone with whom she was angry.* —**slan'der·er,** *n.* one who slanders. —**slan'der·ous,** *adj.*

slang (5) [slæŋ`], *n.* 1. language that is not considered a part of standard speech or writing. **Ex.** *The city children used interesting slang.* 2. special words used by people in a profession, particular group, etc. **Ex.** *The customer did not understand the slang that the waitress used when she gave his order to the cook.*

slant (3) [slænt`], *v.* be or lie in a direction that is not level or straight up and down but inclines; slope. **Ex.** *Her handwriting slants to the left.* —*n.* a slope; a slanting line or surface. **Ex.** *The roof has a steep slant.*

slap (4) [slæp`], *v.* hit or strike with the open hand or with something flat. **Ex.** *She slapped the child on the cheek.* —*n.* a blow with the open hand or with something flat. **Ex.** *We heard the slap of the waves against the boat.*

a, far; æ, am; e, get; ey, late; i, in; iy, see; ɔ, all; ow, go; u, put; uw, too; ə, but, ago; ər, fur; aw, out; ay, life; oy, boy; ŋ, ring; θ, think; ð, that; ž, measure; š, ship; j, edge; č, child.

slash (5) [slæš'], *v.* 1. make long, quick cuts with something sharp. **Ex.** *He slashed through the high grass with a long knife.* 2. reduce or lower very much. **Ex.** *The store owner slashed prices.* —*n.* the cut or opening made by slashing. **Ex.** *The slash on his cheek was slow to heal.*

slat [slæt'], *n.* a thin strip of wood, metal, etc. used in window blinds, furniture, etc. **Ex.** *One of the slats in this metal blind seems to be bent.*

slate (5) [sleyt'], *n.* hard, flat, blue-gray stone often made into roof tiles or into a flat surface for writing upon with chalk. —*adj.* made of slate. **Ex.** *The repair of the old slate roof was costly.*

slaughter (4) [slɔː'tər], *n.* 1. the killing of animals to be used as food. **Ex.** *The cattle were sent to the city for slaughter.* 2. the violent killing of human beings; the killing of people in large numbers. **Ex.** *The battle became a slaughter.* —*v.* 1. kill animals for food. **Ex.** *The lambs were slaughtered for market.* 2. kill violently or in large numbers. **Ex.** *Hundreds of the enemy were slaughtered.*

slave (2) [sleyv'], *n.* 1. a human being controlled by another as property. **Ex.** *The slaves were working in the fields.* 2. one who is controlled by a habit. **Ex.** *He is a slave to alcohol.* —*v.* work very hard. **Ex.** *He has been slaving away on his book for the last year.* —**slav'er·y,** *n.* 1. the condition of being a slave. **Ex.** *He was born into slavery.* 2. the keeping of slaves. **Ex.** *Slavery was abolished in the United States after the Civil War.*

slay (5) [sley'], *v.* kill violently. **Ex.** *He intended to slay his father's murderer.* —**slay'er,** *n.*

sled (5) [sled'], *n.* a flat wooden frame on metal runners used for carrying people or loads over snow or ice.

SLED

sleep (1) [sliyp'], *n.* a resting of the mind and body with the eyes closed, usually while lying down. **Ex.** *He had a good night's sleep.* —*v.* rest in this way. **Ex.** *I had difficulty going to sleep last night.* —**sleep'er,** *n.* 1. one who sleeps. **Ex.** *She is a sound sleeper.* 2. a car of a train that has beds. **Ex.** *He took a sleeper on his trip across the country.* —**sleep'y,** *adj.* feeling a need for sleep.

sleet [sliyt'], *n.* frozen or partly frozen rain; a mixture of rain and snow. **Ex.** *This sleet will make driving dangerous today.* —*v.* fall in a shower of sleet. **Ex.** *It has been sleeting all afternoon.*

sleeve (3) [sliyv'], *n.* the part of clothing that covers the arm. **Ex.** *The sleeves of his coat were too long.*

slender (3) [slen'dər], *adj.* small in width as compared to height; pleasingly thin. **Ex.** *She was a tall, slender blonde.*

slept (1) [slept'], *v.* past tense and participle of *sleep.* **Exs.** *He slept until noon today. She has not slept at home for the last couple of nights because her apartment is being painted.*

slice (3) [slays'], *n.* a thin, flat piece cut from something. **Ex.** *He ate two slices of bread.* —*v.* make slices by cutting. **Ex.** *Please slice the cake.*

slick (5) [slik'], *adj.* 1. shiny and smooth. **Ex.** *The magazine was printed on slick paper.* 2. slippery. **Ex.** *The roads were slick with ice.*

slid [slid], *v.* past tense and past participle of *slide.* **Exs.** *He slid away while no one was looking. The boat had slid off the shore into the water.*

slide (3) [slayd'], *v.* 1. move or cause to move smoothly over a surface as if on ice. **Ex.** *This window slides up and down easily.* 2. slip and lose balance. **Ex.** *Did you see him slide and fall on the ice?* —*n.* 1. the act of sliding. **Ex.** *She progressed by slips and slides along the icy path.* 2. a piece of playground equipment with a smooth surface, usually metal, for sliding. **Ex.** *The children were taking turns going down the slide.* 3. a piece of film with a picture on it, which can be viewed by passing light through it. **Ex.** *They showed us slides of their trip.* 4. a small piece of glass on which tiny samples are placed to be viewed under a microscope. **Ex.** *The biology teacher had prepared some slides for his class.* 5. a mass of material, such as rock, snow or ice, that falls downhill with great force. **Ex.** *We had to turn back because of a snow slide.*

slight (2) [slayt'], *adj.* 1. small in amount or degree; not important. **Ex.** *She stayed home for a day because of a slight cold.* 2. frail; delicate. **Ex.** *The girl was too slight to carry the heavy bundle.* —*v.* act toward as unimportant; ignore. **Ex.** *She slighted him by speaking to all the others first.* —*n.* act of slighting. **Ex.** *His slights made her cry.* —**slight'ly,** *adv.* in a small degree. **Ex.** *He was only slightly hurt in the accident.*

slim (4) [slim'], *adj.* slender in form; slight. **Ex.** *She has a slim figure.* —*v.* make or become slim. **Ex.** *She slimmed her figure by dieting.*

sling (5) [slin'], *n.* 1. a device, often made of a small piece of leather with two pieces of a cord or rope attached, used for throwing stones. **Ex.** *He put a small stone in his sling, whirled it and let the stone fly.* 2. a loop of rope or other strong material put under heavy objects so that they can be lifted more easily. 3. a bandage which is folded so that the arm is supported in the fold and two ends are tied in a loop around the neck. —*v.* 1. put in a sling to raise or lower; carry by a sling. 2. throw using a sling. 3. throw carelessly or roughly. **Ex.** *He would usually sling his bookbag over his shoulder.*

SLING 1

slingshot [slin'šat'], *n.* a Y-shaped weapon, often made from a forked stick, with an elastic strap attached to the top parts, that throws a stone or other hard object when the elastic strap is released.

slip (2) [slip'], *v.* 1. slide; shift from a position; slide and fall. **Ex.** *She slipped on the ice and broke her hand.* 2. leave quickly and smoothly, as in escaping. **Ex.** *The child slipped out of the house and ran away.* 3. move easily or cause to move easily. **Ex.** *The boat slipped along the river.* —*n.* the act of slipping. **Ex.** *His slip on the stairway resulted in a broken leg.* —**slip one's mind,** be forgotten. **Ex.** *The fact that we had a meeting today slipped my mind.*

slip (2) [slip'], *n.* 1. a small piece of paper. **Ex.** *The clerk gave me a sales slip with my purchase.* 2. a woman's undergarment, extending from the shoulders to the end of the skirt. **Ex.** *The slip she wore was too long.*

slipcover [slip'kəvər], *n.* a removable cover, usually of cloth, put over a chair or sofa to keep it clean.

slipper (4) [slip'ər], *n.* a light shoe that slips on and off easily, usually worn indoors. **Ex.** *He liked to wear slippers in the evening.*

slippery (5) [slip'əriy], *adj.* 1. likely to cause slipping. **Ex.** *Spilled oil had made the floor slippery.* 2. likely to slip easily. **Ex.** *The slippery dish fell from his hands.*

slit (5) [slit'], *v.* 1. cut open along a line. **Ex.** *She slit the envelope open with a knife.* 2. cut into strips. **Ex.** *He slit the banana in two from end to end.* —*n.* a long, narrow cut or opening. **Ex.** *The sunshine entered through a slit between the closed curtains.*

slogan (5) [slow'gən], *n.* a word or phrase used by a group or business to get attention for its ideas or products. **Ex.** *"Votes for Women" was a slogan of the early 1900s.*

slope (3) [slowp'], *v.* incline up or down; lie at an angle or slant. **Ex.** *The ground here slopes down to the water.* —*n.* 1. a surface that has one side higher or lower than the other side; a surface that slants. **Ex.** *We climbed the slope near the camp.* 2. the amount of slant. **Ex.** *The slope of that hill is very steep.*

slot [slat'], *n.* a narrow opening through which a coin, letter, etc. can be put. **Ex.** *How much money did you put in the slot of the parking meter?*

slow (1) (slow'], *adj.* 1. not fast in moving, talking, etc. **Ex.** *She is a slow worker.* 2. using more time than usual. **Ex.** *The trip is two hours longer by the slow train.* 3. not interesting; not lively; not busy. **Ex.** *Business is slow here in August because of vacations.* 4. behind the actual time. **Ex.** *My watch is five minutes slow.* —*v.* become, go, or make slow or slower. **Ex.** *The car slowed to a stop.* —**slow'ly,** *adv.* —**slow'ness,** *n.*

slum (5) [sləm'], *n.* a section of a town or city where many people live crowded together in poor, often dirty and unhealthy conditions. **Ex.** *The government is tearing down the slum and building new housing.*

slumber (5) [sləm'bər], *n.* a sleep. **Ex.** *The bell woke him from his slumber.* —*v.* 1. be asleep. **Ex.** *She slumbered on until midday.* 2. be in a quiet, peaceful state. **Ex.** *Everything came to a halt as the town slumbered underneath a blanket of snow.*

slump (5) [sləmp'], *v.* 1. drop or fall heavily or suddenly. **Ex.** *The wounded man slumped to the ground.* 2. sit, stand or walk in a drooping manner. **Ex.** *The bored children slumped over their desks.* —*n.* a decline in sales, prices, etc. **Ex.** *There was a slump in the sale of cars.*

slung [sləng'], *v.* past tense and past participle of *sling.* **Exs.** *He slung the bag over his shoulder and walked out the door. He picked up the newspaper which the paper boy had slung against the door.*

slur [slər'], *v.* pronounce a word or a part of a word indistinctly. **Ex.** *It's difficult to understand her because she slurs* *her words.* —*n.* 1. a way of speaking in which a word or part of a word is not spoken clearly. **Ex.** *Why do you suppose she has such a slur in her speech?* 2. a remark, comment, etc. which is unjustly damaging or makes someone or something seem unimportant or of little value. **Ex.** *He was furious with the person who had made slurs about his sister.*

sly (4) [slay'], *adj.* 1. cunning and secretive; skillful at tricking. **Ex.** *He is too sly to be trusted.* 2. full of playful tricks. **Ex.** *We enjoyed her sly humor.* —**sly'ly,** *adv.* —**sly'ness,** *n.* —**on the sly,** so as not to be seen. **Ex.** *He took a handful of candy on the sly.*

small (1) [smɔ:l'], *adj.* 1. little in size. **Ex.** *She is small for her age.* 2. little in amount. **Ex.** *He could buy only one apple with the small sum of money he had.* 3. few in number. **Ex.** *A small crowd gathered.* 4. not important. **Ex.** *This is only a small problem.*

small arms [smɔ:l' armz'], guns small enough to be carried in the hands, such as pistols and rifles.

small letter [smɔ:l' let'ər], any letter other than a capital letter. **Ex.** *In* The, h *and* e *are small letters;* T *is a capital letter.*

small-minded [smɔ:'mayn'did], *adj.* not generous; mean; intolerant. **Ex.** *Gossips are often small-minded people.*

small talk [smɔ:l' tɔ:k'] unimportant conversation. **Ex.** *He made small talk about the weather.*

smart (3) [smart'], *adj.* 1. quick to learn; showing intelligence; clever. **Ex.** *Both children are very smart.* 2. clean and neat; well-dressed. **Ex.** *They liked his smart appearance.* 3. very energetic; lively; forceful and severe. **Ex.** *She gave him a smart slap.* —*v.* 1. cause or feel stinging pain. **Ex.** *Her eyes smarted from the smoke.* 2. have hurt feelings. **Ex.** *She smarted from the teacher's criticism of her work.* —**smart'ly,** *adv.* —**smart'ness,** *n.*

smash (3) [smæš], *v.* 1. break or be broken into many pieces by force, often with a crashing sound; crush. **Ex.** *The cup smashed when the girl dropped it.* 2. hit or move with force. **Ex.** *The two cars smashed into each other.* —*n.* a breaking or hitting; the sound of breaking or hitting. **Ex.** *He heard the smash of breaking dishes from the kitchen.* —**smash'up`,** *n.* a bad wreck of a car or train. **Ex.** *His car was destroyed in a smashup.*

smear (5) [smi:r'], *v.* 1. rub, spread or cover with oil, fat, etc. **Ex.** *The children's faces were smeared with dirt.* 2. make or become dirty or stained. **Ex.** *The painter was afraid that the children would smear the sign before it was dry.* 3. **unfairly** damage or hurt the reputation of someone. **Ex.** *Each political party accused the other of smearing its candidates.* —*n.* 1. a mark or spot made by smearing. **Ex.** *There was a smear of jam on his shirt.* 2. an effort to damage or hurt the reputation of. **Ex.** *By the time he was able to disprove the lie, the smear had cost him the election.*

smell (1) [smel'], *v.* 1. sense with the nose; perceive through the nose. **Ex.** *He smelled something burning.* 2. have or give off a characteristic odor that can be sensed by the nose. **Ex.** *The mountain air smelled of pine trees,* —*n.* 1. something sensed by the nose. **Ex.** *The smell of the cooking made them hungry.* 2. the special sense that the nose has by which one notices smells. **Ex.** *Our dog has a keen sense of smell.* —**smell'y,** *adj.* having an unpleasant odor.

smile (1) [smayl'], *n.* an expression of the face that shows happiness, pleasure, amusement, etc. **Ex.** *She met her friends with a smile.* —*v.* show by a facial expression that one is happy, pleased, amused, etc. **Ex.** *He smiled at the funny story.* —**smil'ing,** *adj.* —**smil'ing·ly,** *adv.*

smoke (1) [smowk'], *n.* 1. that which can be seen rising into the air from something burning. **Ex.** *Cigarette smoke filled the room.* 2. the act of using a cigarette, cigar or pipe; the period of time taken to use one. **Ex.** *They stopped their work for a smoke.* —*v.* 1. produce smoke. **Ex.** *The wet wood made the fire smoke heavily.* 2. use cigarettes, cigars or pipes. **Ex.** *She does not smoke, but her husband does.* 3. preserve meat or fish by placing it in a special smoke-filled enclosure. **Ex.** *They cooked some of the fish and smoked the rest.* —**smok'er,** *n.* 1. one who smokes. 2. a device for smoking meat, fish or other food. —**smok'y,** *adj.*

smoke detector [smowk' ditek'tər], a device which can sense the presence of smoke and give an alarm of the possible danger of fire. **Ex.** *A fireman said that having smoke detectors in the house had saved the lives of the occupants.*

smooth (2) [smuwð] *adj.* 1. having an even surface. **Ex.** *There was no wind, and the lake was as smooth as glass.* 2. steady in motion; even. **Ex.** *We had good weather, and our airplane trip was very smooth.* —*v.* 1. cause to have an even surface. **Ex.** *He smoothed his hair.* 2. make easy by removing difficulties or by helping. **Ex.** *Letters of introduction smoothed the*

way in his new venture. —**smooth'ly,** *adv.* —**smooth'ness,** *n.*
—~~smooth~~ **over,** describe as or try to make appear less serious
or bad. **Ex.** *She smoothed over the children's quarrel.*

smother (5) [sməð'ər], 1. prevent from breathing freely; kill by
preventing from breathing. **Ex.** *The victim of the fire had been
smothered by smoke.* 2. put out or deaden a fire by keeping
out the air. **Ex.** *We smothered the fire with sand.*

smuggle (5) [sməg'əl], *v.* 1. bring into or remove from the
country in a manner contrary to the law. **Ex.** *They smuggled
the drugs across the border.* 2. bring in or take out secretly.
Ex. *The boys smuggled a pie out of the house.* — **smug'gler,** *n.*

snack (5) [snæk'], *n.* a small amount of food or drink; a light
meal eaten between regular meals. **Ex.** *He enjoyed a bedtime
snack.* —*v.*

snake (3) [sneyk'], *n.* A cold-blooded, crawling
animal with a long, slender body and no
legs.

SNAKE

snap (3) [snæp'], *v.* 1. make or cause to make
a sharp, sudden sound by breaking, closing,
etc. **Ex.** *The lock snapped shut.* 2. bite;
attempt to bite; seize suddenly and hold. **Ex.** *The dog snapped
at the child.* 3. speak in a sharp, angry way. **Ex.** *He snapped at
the noisy children.* —*n.* 1. a sharp, sudden sound caused by
breaking, closing, etc. **Ex.** *He broke the branch with a snap.*
2. a sudden bite or attempt to bite; a seizing or grasping. **Ex.**
The fish made a snap at the hook. 3. any fastening device that
closes with a snapping sound. **Ex.** *The snap on the dress was
loose.* 4. a thin, hard cookie. **Ex.** *She ate some ginger snaps
with her milk.* —*adj.* made, done, etc. hurriedly and without
much thought. **Ex.** *He made a snap decision to go with us.*

snapshot [snæp'šat'], a photograph taken quickly with a small
camera held in the hand. **Ex.** *He showed us snapshots of his
wife and children.*

snare (5) [sne:r'], *n.* 1. a device for capturing birds or animals.**Ex.**
The hunter set snares in the woods. 2. anything which is used
to trap someone. **Ex.** *The question was a snare to catch him
in a lie.* —*v.* capture with a snare. **Ex.** *He snared several
rabbits.*

snarl (5) [snarl'], *v.* 1. make an angry rolling sound in the throat
while showing the teeth. **Ex.** *The dog snarled at the stranger.*
2. say with an angry voice. **Ex.** *The angry man snarled his*

answer. —n. the sound or act of snarling. **Ex.** *We heard the snarls of the feeding lions.*

snarl (5) [snarl'], *v.* twist and knot; tangle. **Ex.** *The boy had snarled the string of his kite.* —n. a group of unwanted knots and twists; a tangle. **Ex.** *We were caught in a traffic snarl.*

snatch (3) [snæč'], *v.* seize or try to seize suddenly. **Ex.** *The thief snatched the money and ran.* —n. 1. the act of snatching. **Ex.** *He made a snatch at the rope and missed.* 2. very small or brief parts. **Ex.** *She knows snatches of poetry.*

sneak (5) [sniyk'], *v.* move, act, carry, etc. quietly and secretly to avoid being heard or seen. **Ex.** *The girls sneaked a kitten into the house.* —n. a person who is cunning, secretive and not honest. **Ex.** *What sneak ate a piece of the cake I just baked?* —**sneak'y,** *adj.* **sneak'i·ly,** *adv.*

sneaker [sniyk'ər], *n.* a shoe made of strong, heavy cotton cloth, leather, etc. with rubber or rubberlike soles. **Ex.** *What brand of sneakers do you wear?*

sneer (5) [sni:r'], *v.* express a scornful feeling; indicate by a scornful look, remark or gesture that something or someone is worthless. **Ex.** *He sneered at their plans.* —n. a scornful look, remark or gesture. **Ex.** *She answered with a sneer.*

sneeze (5) [sniyz'], *v.* let out the breath from the mouth and nose suddenly with force and noise. **Ex.** *The dust made me sneeze.* —n. the act or sound of sneezing. **Ex.** *He tried to hold back a sneeze.*

sniff (4) [snif'], *v.* 1. draw air into the nose noisily. **Ex.** *He sniffed the cold air.* 2. smell in this manner. **Ex.** *She sniffed the flowers.* —n. the act or sound of sniffing. **Ex.** *The dog took a sniff at the guest's shoes.*

snore (5) [snɔ:r'], *v.* breathe noisily while sleeping. **Ex.** *He snores loudly.* —n. the act or sound of snoring. **Ex.** *His snores often waken her.*

snort (5) [snɔrt'], *v.* 1. force the breath in or out of the nose suddenly and loudly. **Ex.** *The horse snorted as the man approached.* 2. express scorn, anger, etc. by such a sound. **Ex.** *The old man snorted in disgust at the idea.* —n. the act or sound of snorting. **Ex.** *He gave a snort of laughter.*

---

a, far; æ, am; e, get; ey, late; i, in; iy, see; ɔ, all; ow, go; u, put; uw, too; ə, but, ago; ər, fur; aw, out; ay, life; oy, boy; ŋ, ring; θ, think; ð, that; ž, measure; š, ship; j, edge; č, child.

snow (1) [snow'], *n.* 1. soft, white pieces of frozen water that fall from the sky. **Ex.** *Several inches of snow covered the ground.* 2. the fall of such pieces. **Ex.** *We had a light snow yesterday.* —*v.* fall as snow. **Ex.** *It snowed all night.* —**snow-blind,** *adj.* unable to see for a time as a result of sunlight reflected from the snow. —**snowflake,** *n.* a small, thin bit of snow. **Ex.** *The snowflakes were falling so fast that it was hard to see.* —**snow'y,** *adj.*

snug (5) [snəg'], *adj.* 1. sheltered and warm. **Ex.** *The children were snug in their beds.* 2. just large enough to contain; small but comfortable. **Ex.** *They live in a snug little house.*

so (1) [sow'], *adv.* 1. in such a way; in the manner described. **Ex.** *He raised his fist and held it so for a moment.* 2. also; too. **Ex.** *She left early, and so did we.* 3. very. **Ex.** *I am so tired.* 4. to such an extent; of such an amount. **Ex.** *I have so much to tell you and so little time.* 5. as a result; therefore. **Ex.** *He was ill and so could not come.* 6. more or less. **Ex.** *I shall be home in an hour or so.* —*conj.* in order that; for the purpose of. **Ex.** *Come early so that we can discuss our plans* —*interj.* an exclamation of surprise, doubt, etc. **Ex.** *So this is how you spend your evenings!* —**and so on, and so forth,** et cetera. **Ex.** *She gave the children cake, cookies, candy and so forth.*

soak (3) [sowk'], *v.* 1. be in or place in water or some other liquid until thoroughly wet. **Ex.** *She soaked the clothes before washing them.* 2. draw in; suck up. **Ex.** *Use this napkin to soak up the spilled milk.* 3. penetrate or be absorbed through. **Ex.** *The oil soaked through the paper bag.* —*n.* the act of soaking. **Ex.** *Give your injured hand a good soak in hot water.*

soap (2) [sowp'], *n.* a substance for washing and cleaning. **Ex.** *The soap slipped from his hand.* —*v.* rub soap on or over. **Ex.** *She soaped the collar of the shirt.* —**soap'suds`,** *n.* a creamy or bubbly mixture formed by mixing soap with water. —**soap'y,** *adj.*

soar (4) [sɔ:r'], *v.* 1. fly up into the air as a bird; fly at a great height. **Ex.** *The plane soared above us.* 2. rise above the usual level. **Ex.** *Because of the freeze, the price of oranges soared.*

sob (3) [sab'], *v.* cry or weep with gasping sounds. **Ex.** *She sobbed when she heard the terrible news.* —*n.* the sound of sobbing. **Ex.** *She answered with a sob.*

sober (3) [sow'bər], *adj.* 1. not under the influence of alcohol. **Ex.** *The minister was the only sober man at the party.* 2.

moderate, especially in the use of liquor. **Ex.** *He has become more sober with age.* 3. serious; quiet; plain. **Ex.** *Everyone at the funeral wore sober clothing.* —*v.* make or become sober. **Ex.** *The news sobered him.* —**sob·er·ly,** *adv.*

so-called [sow'kɔld], *adj.* commonly named as; known as, often suggesting doubt as to the correctness of the term. **Ex.** *Your so-called friend is spreading lies about you.*

social (2) [sow'šəl], *adj.* 1. of or having to do with people as a group; of or having to do with the community of all human beings. **Ex.** *Housing is a serious social problem in this city.* 2. friendly; liking to be with others. **Ex.** *He is a very social person who entertains frequently.* 3. of or having to do with society, especially persons of wealth and fashion. **Ex.** *That dance was the social event of the season.* 4. of or for companionship. **Ex.** *It was a social meeting so no one discussed business.* —**so'cial·ly,** *adv.* —**so'cial·ize,** *v.* be active socially. **Ex.** *She doesn't like to socialize with her fellow workers.*

socialism (5) [sow'šəlizəm], *n.* a political or economic system in which the means of production are owned by the people in common or by the government. —**so'cial·ist,** *n.* one who believes in and favors socialism; a Socialist Party member. **Ex.** *Socialists want the government to own the factories.* —*adj.* of or having to do with socialism. **Ex.** *He voted for the candidate running on the Socialist ticket.* —**so'cial·ize,** *v.* bring under government or group control or ownership.

social science [sow'šəl say'əns], any of the areas of study which are concerned with society, such as history, government, economics, etc.

social security [sow'šəl sikyur'ətiy], a government plan that provides financial help to those who are old, not able to work because of physical disabilities, etc. and that is paid for by taxes on employers and employees. **Ex.** *He receives a social security check each month.*

social worker [sow'šəl wərk'ər], a person trained to engage in the work of governmental or private organizations established to improve the social conditions of people in a community. **Ex.** *A social worker was helping the family to obtain better housing.*

society (2) [səsay'ətiy], *n.* 1. people with a shared background as a group; the community of all human beings. **Ex.** *Sometimes he found the rules of society difficult to follow.* 2. a group or organization of persons who meet for a special purpose. **Ex.** *He is one of those who helped to establish a stamp collectors' society.* 3. rich and fashionable people. **Ex.** *He knows many people in high society.* 4. friendship and companionship. **Ex.** *She enjoys the society of the opposite sex.*

sock (4) [sak'], *n.* a short stocking. **Ex.** *Put on a pair of clean socks.*

socket [sak'it], *n.* a hollow opening or place into which something fits. **Exs.** *I'm having difficulty getting this light bulb out of the socket. The man's eyes were set in deep sockets.*

sod [sad'], *n.* a piece of grass-covered earth held together by the roots of the grass. **Ex.** *He bought some sod to put in the bare spots of his lawn.* —*v.* cover with sod. **Ex.** *He sodded the land around his house.*

soda (3) [sow'də], *n.* 1. any of the various substances, usually in the form of a white powder and having a common element, that are used in cooking, medicine, etc. **Ex.** *She added baking soda to the cake mixture.* 2. a drink made of water treated with gas which causes the water to bubble. **Ex.** *He poured himself a glass of soda.* 3. a drink containing soda water, flavoring and sometimes ice cream. **Ex.** *The boys ordered chocolate sodas.*

soda cracker [sow'də kræk'ər], a light crisp cracker containing baking soda.

soda fountain [sow'də fawn'tən], a counter at which customers sit on stools on one side to drink sodas or eat ice cram and other light foods prepared on and served from the other side. **Ex.** *They stopped at the soda fountain on their way home from school.*

sofa (3) [sow'fə], *n.* a couch stuffed with soft material and having a back and arms. **Ex.** *She and her husband sat on the sofa.*

soft (1) [sɔft'], *adj.* 1. easily shaped, formed, etc; yielding to the touch or pressure. **Ex.** *She likes to sleep on a soft bed.* 2. not strong, bright, sharp, etc. **Ex.** *A soft wind was blowing.* 3. gentle; tender; full of sympathy. **Ex.** *He spoke roughly to conceal his soft heart.* 4. smooth; delicate. **Ex.** *The baby's skin was very soft.* 5. quiet. **Ex.** *He spoke in a soft voice.* —**soft'en**, *v.* make or become soft. —**soft'ly**, *adv.* —**soft'ness**, *n.*

soft-boiled [sɔft'boyld'], *adj.* of an egg in the shell cooked by boiling in water just enough so that the yellow part is still soft. **Ex.** *He had two soft-boiled eggs with toast for breakfast.*

soft drink [sɔft driŋk], a drink which is sometimes sweet and contains soda water but never alcohol. **Ex.** *I will have a soft drink instead of wine.*

software [sɔft'we:r], *n.* programs or instructions for a computer to follow. **Ex.** *When I bought my computer secondhand, I received a lot of software with it.*

soggy [sag'iy], *adj.* heavy with moisture; soaked; very wet; not firm because of too much moisture. **Ex.** *The bread was too soggy to make sandwiches.*

soil (1) [soyl'], *n.* 1. the top covering of the earth in which plants can grow. **Ex.** *The farmer tilled the soil.* 2. a country; a region. **Ex.** *He died far from home on foreign soil.* 3. a spot, mark or stain. **Ex.** *Washing removed the soil from the dress.* —*v.* make dirty or unclean. **Ex.** *She soiled her hands working in the garden.*

solar (5) [sow'lər], *adj.* to, from, of or concerning the sun. **Exs.** *Solar energy makes the plants grow. The house is heated by solar energy.*

solar system [sow'lər sis'təm], the sun and all of the bodies, including the earth, that circle around the sun.

sold (1) [sowld'], *v.* past tense and participle of *sell.* **Exs.** *He sold his house at a profit. He had sold insurance before he became the mayor.*

soldier (1) [sowl'jər], *n.* one serving in the army, especially one not an officer. **Ex.** *The soldier cleaned his gun.*

sole (3) [sowl'], *n.* 1. the under part of the foot. **Ex.** *The stone cut the sole of his foot.* 2. the under part of a shoe, boot, etc., not including the heel. **Ex.** *He had new soles put on his old shoes.*

sole (3) [sowl'], *adj.* being the only one or ones; belonging to one person or group; only. **Ex.** *He is the sole owner of the store.* —**sole'ly,** *adv.*

solemn (3) [sal'əm], *adj.* 1. formal; serious; sober. **Ex.** *He gave his solemn promise to defend his country.* 2. impressive; inspiring respectful fear and wonder. **Ex.** *They watched the solemn ceremony in the church with awe.* —**sol'emn·ly,** *adv.* —**sol·em'ni·ty,** *n.*

solicit (5) [səlis'it], *v.* request or ask for seriously; appeal to or for. **Ex.** *They solicited money to help the blind.* —**so·lic'it·or,** *n.* one who solicits. —**so·lic'i·tous,** *adj.* attentive; caring; concerned. **Ex.** *He was very solicitous of her health.*

solid (2) [sal'id], *adj.* 1. having a definite shape and volume; not in the form of a liquid or gas. **Ex.** *The water had frozen into a solid block of ice.* 2. not hollow; having no empty spaces within. **Ex.** *That door is made of a solid piece of wood.* 3. strong; firm; dependable. **Ex.** *The mayor is a man of solid character.* 4. of one material, color, etc. **Ex.** *Her dress was solid black.* —*n.* something that is not a liquid or a gas. **Ex.** *After two days on a liquid diet, the patient began to eat solids again.* —**sol'id·ly,** *adv.* —**so·lid'i·fy,** *v.* form into a solid.

solidarity [sal'ədær'ətiy], *n.* a state of being united in common interests, sympathies, responsibilities and purposes, as in a group or series of groups. **Ex.** *The solidarity of the union members enabled them to be successful in their strike.*

solitary [sal'əter'iy], *adj.* 1. away from others; by oneself or itself; alone. **Ex.** *The light of a solitary fishing boat could be seen across the water.* 2. not including anyone or anything else; single. **Ex.** *He is the solitary occupant of the house.*

solitude [sal'ətuwd'], *n.* the state or characteristic of being alone and away from other people. **Exs.** *He likes to spend some time in solitude every day. She enjoys the solitude of her cabin in the hills.*

solo [sow'low], *n.* music composed for one person alone to sing or to play. **Ex.** *She played a beautiful piano solo tonight.* —*adj.* 1. composed for a single person or instrument; sung or played by a single individual. **Ex.** *This opera includes several striking solo passages.* 2. performed by a single person; done alone. **Ex.** *On his first solo dive, he discovered the wreck.*

solution (2) [səluw'šən, səlyuw'šən], *n.* 1. the answer to a problem. **Ex.** *The teacher gave them the correct solution to the mathematics problem.* 2. a mixture made by dissolving a solid substance in a liquid. **Ex.** *He made a solution of salt and water.*

solve (2) [solv'], *v.* find the solution or answer; find an explanation. **Ex.** *Scientists have solved the problem of making drinking water from sea water.*

somber (5) [sam'bər], *adj.* 1. dark; dimly lighted and shadowy. **Ex.** *She was depressed by the somber house.* 2. sad and gloomy. **Ex.** *He was sad, and his thoughts about the future were very somber.* —**som'ber·ly,** *adv.*

some (1) [səm], *adj.* 1. of an amount, number or part not stated. **Ex.** *I bought some apples.* 2. of a certain person or thing unknown or unstated. **Ex.** *Some man called you while you were away.* —*pron.* an unstated number or amount but less than all; a portion. **Ex.** *Some of the people had already gone home.*

somebody [səm'bad`iy], *pron.* an unnamed person. **Ex.** *Will somebody please help me?* —*n.* a person who is well known or of importance. **Ex.** *He is certainly somebody!*

someday [səm'dey], *adv.* at an uncertain time in the future. **Ex.** *She hopes to travel abroad someday.*

somehow [səm'haw`], *adv.* in some way not known. **Ex.** *Don't worry; I will finish the work somehow.*

someone [səm'wən`], *pron.* an unnamed person. **Ex.** *Is someone at the door?*

something [səm'θiŋ`], *pron.* an unnamed thing. **Ex.** *He left something for you.*

sometime [səm'taym], *adv.* at an uncertain time in the past or future. **Exs.** *He saw her sometime last week. Let's have lunch sometime.*

sometimes [səm'taymz`], *adv.* at times; occasionally. **Ex.** *I go there sometimes, but not often.*

somewhat [səm'(h)wət, səm'hwat`], *adv.* a little; to an unknown degree. **Ex.** *He is somewhat tired.*

somewhere [səm'hwe:r`], *adv.* in an unnamed place. **Ex.** *I left my gloves somewhere.*

son (1) [sən`], *n.* a male child considered in relation to his father, his mother or both parents. **Ex.** *Their son is a doctor.*

song (1) [sɔːŋ`], *n.* 1. words and music for singing. **Ex.** *She sang three songs for the school program.* 2. a musical sound like singing. **Ex.** *We heard the song of a bird outside our window.*

son-in-law [sən'inlɔː`], *n.* the husband of one's daughter.

soon (1) [suwn`], *adv.* 1. not long after the present time; in a short time. **Ex.** *We must hurry because our train is leaving soon.* 2. early; not long after the mentioned time. **Ex.** *How soon can you come?* 3. quickly; rapidly. **Ex.** *The children were soon tired of the game.*

soothe (4) [suwð'], *v.* 1. lessen or relieve pain, anxiety, etc. **Ex.** *The presence of friends soothed his grief.* 2. calm or quiet. **Ex.** *She drank a cup of tea to soothe her nerves.*

sophomore [saf'əmɔːr'], *n.* a student in the first year of a three-year high school or the second year of a four-year high school or college. **Ex.** *My daughter is already a sophomore in college.*

sordid (5) [sɔr'did], *adj.* 1. dirty; foul. **Ex.** *They lived in a sordid slum.* 2. morally bad; base; selfish. **Ex.** *The accused had a sordid reputation.* **—sor'did·ly**, *adv.* **—sor'did·ness**, *n.*

sore (2) [sɔːr'], *adj.* 1. physically painful; aching. **Ex.** *His sore leg made walking difficult.* 2. sorrowful; grieving. **Ex.** *She is sore at heart over the loss of her daughter.* 3. causing painful or angry feelings. **Ex.** *The failure of their daughter's marriage is a sore point with them.* **—n.** a spot or place on the body where the flesh is hurt and marked or broken. **Ex.** *The sore on her arm has not yet healed.* **—sore'ly**, *adv.* very much. **Ex.** *The flood victims were sorely in need of food.*

sorrow (2) [sa:r'ow, sɔ:r'ow], *n.* 1. suffering; sadness; grief. **Ex.** *The widow had a look of sorrow on her face.* 2. something that causes suffering, sadness, or grief. **Ex.** *His bad behavior was a great sorrow to his parents.* **—v.** be sad; grieve. **Ex.** *They are still sorrowing for their son, who died two years ago.* **—sor'row·ful**, *adj.* **—sor'row·ful·ly**, *adv.*

sorry (1) [sa:r'iy, sɔ:r'iy], *adj.* 1. feeling sorrow, sympathy, or regret. **Ex.** *I am sorry to hear you have been ill.* 2. pitiful; worthless; poor, etc. **Ex.** *His apartment was in a sorry state.*

sort (1) [sɔrt'], *n.* 1. any class or group of persons or things that are the same or like each other in some way. **Ex.** *What sort of people do you like?* 2. type; character; kind. **Ex.** *We have books of all sorts.* **—v.** separate according to type, size, or class. **Ex.** *The farmer's wife sorted the eggs putting them into baskets marked large, medium and small.*

sought (3) [sɔːt'], *v.* past tense and participle of *seek.* **Ex.** *She sought permission to leave early. He was not the man they had sought.*

soul (3) [sowl'], *n.* 1. in many religions, the center of feeling, thought and action in man, regarded as separate from his physical body; the spirit. **Ex.** *He earned hardly enough to keep body and soul together.* 2. the spirit of man, in relation to a god, believed to be separate from the body and to continue to live after its death. **Ex.** *They were praying for the* *souls of the dead.* 3. man's emotional nature, especially as shown in what he writes, paints, etc. **Ex.** *He put his soul into his work.* 4. a person. **Ex.** *Not a soul offered to help.* —**soul'ful,** *adj.* showing strong emotions. **Ex.** *The dog gave us a soulful look.* —**soul'less,** *adj.* lacking feeling and warmth.

sound (1) [sawnd'], *n.* 1. rapidly moving waves of energy that affect the ear and result in hearing. **Ex.** *How fast does sound travel?* 2. that which is heard. **Ex.** *They heard the sound of the train whistle.* —*v.* 1. make a noise or sound. **Ex.** *The music sounds too loud.* 2. cause to sound. **Ex.** *He sounded the fire alarm.* 3. appear; seem. **Ex.** *His plan sounds practical.*

sound (1) [sawnd'], *adj.* 1. good; in undamaged or healthy condition. **Ex.** *The doctor said that the patient's heart was sound.* 2. safe; secure. **Ex.** *He put his money in a sound business.* 3. showing good judgment. **Ex.** *He has sound ideas.* —**sound'ness,** *n.*

soundproof [sawnd'pruwf'], *adj.* having the quality of preventing sound from going through. **Ex.** *The room is quiet because of the soundproof walls.* —*v.* make soundproof. **Ex.** *They soundproofed the television studio.*

soup (2) [suwp'], *n.* a liquid food made by cooking meat, fish vegetables, etc., depending upon the flavor desired, in water. **Ex.** *We had chicken soup for lunch.*

sour (2) [sawr']. *adj.* 1. having an acid taste like that of fruit not yet ripened. **Ex.** *These grapes taste sour.* 2. changed chemically to an acid or spoiled condition. **Ex.** *She made cheese from the sour milk.* 3. unpleasant; unfriendly. **Ex.** *He greeted me with a sour look.*

source (2) [sɔ:rs'], *n.* 1. a place or thing from which something comes or originates. **Ex.** *This region is an important source of coal.* 2. the beginning or starting place of a stream of water. **Ex.** *The source of the river was in the mountains.* 3. a person, book, etc. that provides information. **Ex.** *What sources did you use in preparing this magazine article?*

south (1) [sawθ'], *n.* 1. the direction to the right of one facing east; one of the four points of the compass. **Ex.** *There is a warm breeze blowing from the south.* 2. regions or countries lying to the south; that part of the United States south of

Pennsylvania and the Ohio River and generally east of the Mississippi including the states of Alabama, Arkansas, Florida, Georgia, Louisiana, Mississippi, North Carolina, South Carolina, Tennessee, Texas and Virginia. **Ex.** *He grew up in the South.* —*adv.* toward the south. **Ex.** *We traveled fifty miles south.* —*adj.* 1. toward, in or at the south. **Ex.** *They live on the south side of the city.* 2. from the south. **Ex.** *The south wind was a welcome change from the cold north winds.* —**south'ern,** *adj.* characteristic of the south; in, of, to, or from the south. **Ex.** *They live in an old southern home.* —**south'ern·er,** *n.* a person from the south.

sovereign (5) [sav'(ə)rin], *n.* a ruler, king or queen. **Ex.** *The sovereign rules the country.* —*adj.* 1. highest in power, authority or rank; supreme. **Ex.** *In that country a general is the sovereign power.* 2. independent of any other state; possessing independent authority. **Ex.** *The members of the United Nations are sovereign states.* —**sov'er·eign·ty,** *n.* state of being independent of others and having independent power.

sow (3) [saw'], *n.* an adult female pig. **Ex.** *The sow had eight little pigs.*

sow (3) [sow'], *v.* 1. plant seed on or in the earth. **Ex.** *The farmer will sow his wheat next week.* 2. plant in the mind. **Ex.** *Enemy agents tried to sow discontent among the people.*

sown (3) [sown], *v.* past participle of *sow.* **Ex.** *The grain was sown in early spring.*

space (1) [speys'], *n.* 1. the unlimited area in which all things are found or located; the area within which the sun, moon, stars, etc. are. **Ex.** *Men traveled through outer space to reach the moon.* 2. the area between or inside things. **Ex.** *As their family increased, they needed a house with more space.* 3. an area used for a particular purpose. **Ex.** *I could not find a parking space.* —*v.* place in an area with space between things; separate. **Ex.** *The trees were spaced ten feet apart.* —**spa'cious,** *adj.* very large; containing much space. **Ex.** *This is a spacious room.*

spacecraft [speys'kræft'], *n.* a vehicle powered by rockets and capable of traveling outside the earth's atmosphere.

space suit [speys' suwt'], a special suit worn by an astronaut in space and having devices for maintaining air pressure and furnishing oxygen.

spade (3) [speyd'], *n.* a tool, usually with a short handle and a flat blade, used for digging. —*v.* dig or take away with a spade. **Ex.** *He spaded the garden.*

spaghetti [spəget'iy], *n.* a food made from a mixture of flour and water, which is formed into long strings that are then dried before being cooked in boiling water and served with a sauce, cheese, etc. **Ex.** *He ordered spaghetti with meatballs.*

SPADE

spank (5) [spænk'], *v.* strike the rounded parts of the lower back with a flat object or with the open hand in punishment. **Ex.** *His father spanked him for coming home late.* —*n.* a single blow given in this manner. **Ex.** *A spank by the doctor started the baby's breathing.* —**spank'ing,** *n.* a series of spanks. **Ex.** *She gave him a spanking for disobeying her.*

spare (2) [spe:r'], *v.* 1. part with; do without. **Ex.** *He could not spare the time for a vacation.* 2. keep from harming or destroying; show mercy; treat gently. **Ex.** *He tried to spare her feelings.* 3. save; use without wasting and with care. **Ex.** *They did not spare expenses when they built their new house.* —*adj.* 1. not being used; extra. **Ex.** *They have a spare room for guests.* 2. free from required activity. **Ex.** *He likes to read in his spare time.* —*n.* that which is extra or not immediately needed or used. **Ex.** *Take my pen; I have a spare.*

spark (3) [spark'], *n.* 1. a tiny glowing piece of material thrown off by something that is burning. **Ex.** *Sparks from the burning house were carried by the wind.* 2. anything like a spark, such as a small flash of electricity. **Ex.** *The broken wire sent out sparks.* 3. a small trace; a suggestion. **Ex.** *A spark of interest showed in his eyes.* —*v.* produce or give out sparks. **Ex.** *The old electric lamp sparked when she touched it.*

sparkle (3) [spark'əl], *v.* 1. produce sparks or sparklike lights. **Ex.** *The lake sparkled in the sunshine.* 2. be attractive, bright or lively. **Ex.** *The conversation at the party sparkled.* —*n.* spark; brilliance. **Ex.** *She admired the sparkle of the diamond.*

spark plug [spark' pləg'], one of the parts in an engine that produces sparks that explode the gasoline. **Ex.** *My car has six spark plugs.*

speak (1) [spiyk'], *v.* 1. say words; talk. **Ex.** *The child began to speak at the age of one and a half.* 2. express one's thoughts; converse; talk with. **Ex.** *Let me speak to him.* 3. give a speech or lecture. **Ex.** *He is going to speak about modern art.* 4. use a language. **Ex.** *Does she speak English?* **—speak out,** speak on a subject publicly or openly. **Ex.** *It is time for us to speak out and tell them what we think.* **—speak up,** speak in a louder voice. **Ex.** *Speak up so I can hear you.* **—speaker,** *n.* 1. one who speaks. 2. loudspeaker.

spear (3) [spi:r'], *n.* a weapon with a long handle and a sharp head or blade for throwing or thrusting. **—v.** thrust into as with a spear. **Ex.** *He speared the meat with his fork.*

spearhead [spi:r'hed'], *n.* 1. the head or point of a spear. 2. a person, group, etc. at the front leading in a fight, campaign, etc. **Ex.** *The police of this city are the spearhead of the effort to control crime.* **—v.**

SPEAR

special (1) [speš'əl], *adj.* 1. of a particular kind; different; unusual. **Ex.** *She has a special way of making bread.* 2. not for general use; having a particular purpose. **Ex.** *There is a special room for dancing.* 3. of an unusual degree; great. **Ex.** *The seriously wounded man needed special care.* **—spe'cial·ist,** *n.* a person who specializes, particularly in medicine. **Ex.** *The patient was advised to see a heart specialist.* **—spe'cial·ize,** *v.* study or practice a particular kind of work. **Ex.** *That teacher specializes in reading problems.* **—spe'cial·ty,** *n.* that in which one specializes or is unusually skillful or talented. **Ex.** *The cook's specialty is desserts.*

species (4) [spiy'šiyz], *n.* a group of animals or plants which have one or more characteristics in common. **Ex.** *The wolf and the dog belong to the same species.*

specific (4) [spəsif'ik], *adj.* definite; particular; precise. **Ex.** *He had specific instructions to follow.* **—spe·cif'i·cal·ly,** *adv.*

specify (5) [spes'əfay], *v.* 1. state exactly or in detail. **Ex.** *Please specify which color you want.* 2. state that something is required. **Ex.** *The contract specifies that brick, not wood, is to be used.* **—spec'i·fi·ca'tion,** *n.* a detailed statement or description of what is wanted or required.

specimen (4) [spes'əmən], *n.* a part or one of a group of things intended to show what the rest is like; an example; a sample. **Ex.** *The doctor took a specimen of the boy's blood.*

speck [spek'], *n.* 1. a small spot or piece. **Ex.** *A few specks of dirt got on the paper.* 2. a bit; a little. **Ex.** *There is just a speck of butter left.*

spectator (5) [spek'teytər], *n.* one who observes but does not take part. **Ex.** *Many spectators watched the ball game.*

speculate (5) [spek'yəleyt`], *v.* 1. think long and carefully about some subject; theorize; guess. **Ex.** *They speculated about the author's hidden meaning.* 2. engage in any business that is risky but that might bring large profits. **Ex.** *He speculated in land.* —**spec'u·la·tor**, *n.* one who speculates. —**spec·u·la'tion**, *n.* the act of speculating. —**spec'u·la'tive**, *adj.*

sped (3) [sped'], *v.* past tense and participle of *speed.* **Exs.** *He sped on his way as soon as he had received his instructions. The car had sped down the street after the accident.*

speech (2) [spiyč'] *n.* 1. a talk given to an audience. **Ex.** *They cheered him after his speech.* 2. the power of speaking. **Ex.** *The illness caused him to lose his speech.* 3. the manner of speaking. **Ex.** *I know from your speech that you do not come from this area.*

speed (2) [spiyd'], *n.* 1. swiftness; rapidity in moving. **Ex.** *The train gained speed after it left the station.* 2. rate of motion. **Ex.** *The airplane flew at a speed of 700 miles an hour.* —*v.* 1. hurry. **Ex.** *Exercise speeded his recovery.* 2. drive very fast or faster than the law allows. **Ex.** *He was speeding when the police stopped him.* —**speed'er**, *n.* one who speeds. —**speed'y**, *adj.* —**speed'i·ly**, *adv.* —**speed up**, increase the speed of.

spell (2) [spel'], *v.* say or write the letters of a word in the proper order. **Ex.** *Can you spell cat?* 2. form a word. **Ex.** *The letters* c-a-t *spell* cat. —**spell'er**, *n.* 1. one who spells. 2. a book used in learning to spell. —**spell'ing**, *n.* saying or writing the letters of a word in the proper order; the form in which words are spelled. **Ex.** *He has difficulty with spelling.*

spell (2) [spel'], *v.* do the work of another, usually so he can rest. **Ex.** *You look tired; let me spell you for a while.* —*n.* a period of time. **Ex.** *We had a long cold spell this past winter.*

spell (2) [spel'], *n.* magic words or actions that influence or control someone. **Ex.** *He seems to be under her spell and*

a, far; æ, am; e, get; ey, late; i, in; iy, see; ɔ, all; ow, go; u, put; uw, too; ə, but, ago; ər, fur; aw, out; ay, life; oy, boy; ŋ, ring; θ, think; ð, that; ž, measure; š, ship; j, edge; č, child.

willing to do whatever she says. **—spell'bound`,** *adj.* fascinated; awed. **Ex.** *We were spellbound by his speech.*

spend (1) [spend'], *v.* give out as payment. **Ex.** *How much money do you spend for food each week?* 2. use. **Ex.** *He spends too much time at play.* 3. pass the time. **Ex.** *We like to spend the holidays at home.* **—spend'thrift',** *n.* an individual who wastes his money.

spent (1) [spent'], *v.* past tense and participle of *spend.* **Exs.** *She spent almost a week's salary for one dress. He had spent two weeks of his vacation in Europe before he came here.*

sphere (3) [sfi:r'], *n.* 1. a round body whose surface at all points is equally distant from the center; a ball; a globe. **Ex.** *The earth is a sphere.* 2. the area within which a person or thing exists, acts or moves. **Ex.** *His new position as manager has enlarged his sphere of influence.* **—spher'i·cal,** *adj.* round. **Ex.** *A ball is a spherical object.*

spice (5) [spays'], *n.* a vegetable substance used to flavor foods. **Ex.** *She used several spices in cooking the meat.* **—***v.* flavor with spices. **Ex.** *The cook spiced the food with hot red peppers.*

spider (3) [spay'dər], *n.* a small creature with eight legs that spins threads to form a web which is a trap for insects. **—spi'der·y,** *adj.* like a spider. **Ex.** *The tall man had long, spidery legs.*

SPIDER

spill (3) [spil'], *v.* 1. cause or allow liquid or any loose material to run or fall from a container. **Ex.** *The child spilled his milk on the floor.* 2. fall or run out. **Ex.** *Water spilled from the fountain.*

spilled [spild'], **spilt** (3) [spilt'] *v.* past tense and participle of *spill.* **Exs.** *They had spilled flour on the table when they were making bread. Who spilt the ink on the rug?*

spin (3) [spin'], *v.* 1. turn or cause to turn rapidly around a center point. **Ex.** *The earth spins on its axis as it moves around the sun.* 2. make threads by drawing out and twisting wool or the threadlike structures of certain plants. **Ex.** *There were hundreds of machines spinning cotton.* 3. form a thread from a substance produced by a creature from its body. **Ex.** *We watched the spider spin its web.* 4. tell at some length, usually imaginatively. **Ex.** *As children, we loved to listen to her spin stories of farm life.*

spinach [spin'ič], *n.* a garden plant, the wide green leaves of which are eaten as either a raw or cooked vegetable. **Ex.** *She added some young spinach to the salad greens.*

spine (4) [spayn'], *n.* the backbone of a human or of an animal, which extends from the head to the tail. **Ex.** *His spine was broken in the accident.* **—spin'al,** *adj.* **—spine'less,** *adj.* 1. of an animal having no spine. 2. weak; without determination or courage. **Ex.** *He was too spineless to be of any help.*

spirit (3) [spir'it], *n.* 1. mood; attitude; general outlook. **Ex.** *She took his advice in the right spirit.* 2. the part of a human being that is not physical; the soul. **Ex.** *Though he is dead, he is with us in spirit.* 3. liveliness; character and energy. **Ex.** *She showed spirit in her replies.* 4. a being that cannot be explained by the laws of nature and that has no physical reality, such as an angel, fairy, devil, etc. **Ex.** *He believes in evil spirits.* 5. alcohol. **Ex.** *He likes strong spirits.* **—v.** carry away secretly and quickly as if by a spirit or spirits. **Ex.** *Someone spirited the child away.* **—spir'it·ed,** *adj.* full of energy; active. **Ex.** *She is a very spirited child.* **—spir'it·u·al,** *adj.* concerning religion. **Ex.** *He takes a spiritual approach to difficulties.*

spit (3) [spit'], *v.* 1. throw out from the mouth. **Ex.** *He spit out the seeds of the orange.* 2. throw out as if spitting. **Ex.** *He spit his words out angrily.* **—n.** the act of spitting; the matter forced out. **Ex.** *She wiped the spit from the corner of the baby's mouth.*

spite [spayt'], *n.* a mean desire to hurt or make a person feel humble and lose self-respect. **Ex.** *She spilled the water on his good suit out of spite.* **—v.** do something because of such a mean desire. **Ex.** *She only spoke about that incident to spite me.* **—in spite of,** without thinking of or considering; even though. **Ex.** *In spite of the cold, he opened both windows wide.*

splash (4) [splæš'], *v.* cause liquid to scatter in all directions by striking or throwing it. **Ex.** *The children were splashing water on each other in the swimming pool.* **—n.** 1. the sound of liquid splashing. **Ex.** *We heard the splash of waves against the boat.* 2. liquid splashed; a spot made by the liquid splashed. **Ex.** *There was a splash of paint on the floor.*

splashdown [splæš'dawn'], *n.* the landing that a spacecraft makes in a body of water. **Ex.** *We waited anxiously for news of the splashdown.*

splendid (2) [splen'did], *adj.* 1. magnificent; elegant; brilliant. **Ex.** *Only a wealthy person could afford such a splendid house.* 2. excellent; distinguished. **Ex.** *The artist painted a splendid picture of my mother.* —**splen'did·ly,** *adv.*

splinter (5) [splin'tər], *n.* a very thin, long piece of wood or other material broken away from a larger piece. **Ex.** *The carpenter got a splinter in his finger.* —*v.* split or break into splinters. **Ex.** *A shot splintered the window.*

split (3) [split'], *v.* 1. break or divide lengthwise from end to end into two or more parts. **Ex.** *He split the wood with an axe.* 2. burst. **Ex.** *The ripe melon split in the sun.* 3. divide into portions or parts. **Ex.** *The boys split the money into shares.* 4. divide into groups. **Ex.** *Our club was split by the argument.* —*n.* 1. the opening made by splitting. **Ex.** *She mended the split in her coat.* 2. a division. **Ex.** *There was a split in the party on the issue of new taxes.* —**split'ting,** *adj.* sharp or painful. **Ex.** *I have a splitting headache.*

spoil (2) [spoyl'], *v.* 1. damage; cause to become useless; rot. **Exs.** *She spoiled the meat by burning it. Milk spoils quickly if it is not kept in a cold place.* 2. damage or weaken the character of by granting every wish. **Ex.** *He was their only son, and they spoiled him.* —**spoil'age,** *n.* act of spoiling; that which is spoiled. —**spoils,** *n. pl.* things taken from another by force, as from the enemy in war.

spoke (1) [spowk'], *n.* one of the bars or rods that goes from the center of the wheel to the rim and acts as a support for the rim. **Ex.** *One of the spokes of your rear bicycle wheel is missing.*

spoke (1) [spowk'], *v.* past tense of *speak.* **Ex.** *He spoke to me about that situation yesterday.*

spoken (2) [spow'kən], *v.* past participle of *speak.* **Ex.** *He had spoken to her about the problem before she left.* —*adj.* 1. said aloud; uttered. **Ex.** *They had a spoken agreement.* 2. speaking in a certain kind of way. **Ex.** *She is a soft-spoken woman.*

spokesman [spowks'mən], *n.* **spokesperson** [spowks'pər·sən]; **spokeswoman** [spowks'wum'ən], *n.* one who speaks as a representative of another or of a group. **Ex.** *At the meeting, a spokesperson for the government gave us the President's views.*

sponge (4) [spənj'], *n.* many tiny animals living together under water as a mass full of holes; the skeleton of this mass or an absorbent material like this used for cleaning, bathing, etc.

Ex. *He cleaned his car with a sponge.* —*v.* clean or soak up as with a sponge. **Ex.** *She sponged the table clean.* —**spong'y,** *adj.* soft and absorbent like a sponge.

sponsor [span'sər], *n.* 1. a person who takes some responsibility for another person who is in need of a recommendation, is in training, etc. **Ex.** *He is one of the sponsors of the junior boys basketball team.* 2. a member of Congress or other legislature who introduces a bill and works for its passage. 3. a business, company, corporation, etc. which provides the money for a program on radio or television, in a museum, etc., usually in return for advertising its name or product. **Ex.** *Who is the sponsor of this art exhibit?* — *v.*

spontaneous (5) [spantey'niyəs], *adj.* 1. proceeding naturally, without plan, effort or thought. **Ex.** *The children's spontaneous laughter charmed the guests.* 2. caused by a force within; independent of anything outside oneself or itself. **Ex.** *A spontaneous fire started in the hay.* —**spon·ta'ne·ous·ly,** *adv.* —**spon'ta·ne'i·ty,** *n.*

spool (5) [spuwl'], *n.* a tube of wood, metal or plastic on which something is wound. **Ex.** *Please hand me the spool of light blue thread.*

spoon (2) [spuwn'], *n.* a tool with a handle and a small bowl used for eating, stirring and serving food.

sport (2) [spɔrt'], *n.* 1. a particular activity performed for exercise, competition or relaxation. **Ex.** *Swimming is her favorite sport.* 2. fun; amusement. **Ex.** *Jumping in the leaves was great sport for the children.* 3. an individual whose reputation is either good or poor depending on whether or not he plays

SPOON

fairly and accepts the rules of the game, behaves well in a difficult situation, etc. **Ex.** *When a penalty was declared against him, he was a good sport and accepted it without complaint.* —*adj.* —**sports,** *adj.* suitable for sports. **Exs.** *He wore a sport shirt. She was wearing a sports dress.* —**sport'ing,** *adj.* fair; like a sportsman. **Ex.** *He gave his rival a sporting chance.* —**sports'man, sports'wom·an,** *n.* 1. one who participates in sports. 2. one who is courteous and obeys the rules of the and obeys the rules of the game without complaining. **Ex.** *She was a sportswoman about losing.*

spot (1) [spat'], *n.* 1. a small mark on or in a surface. **Ex.** *She has a paint spot on her dress.* 2. a particular place; a location. **Ex.** *They are building their house in a beautiful spot.* —*v.* 1. mark or became marked with spots. **Ex.** *The soup spotted his tie.* 2. see; recognize. **Ex.** *I spotted her from across the street.* —**spot'less,** *adj.* without spots or stains. **Ex.** *His record was spotless.* —**spot'ty,** *adj.* having spots; not even or regular. **Ex.** *Her performance at work was spotty.*

spotlight [spat'layt'], *n.* 1. a lamp with a strong ray of light used in theaters to shine on an actor or actress or on the scenery to draw attention. 2. public attention. **Ex.** *Her romance with the governor had put her in the spotlight.*

spouse [spaws'], *n.* the person to whom one is married; a husband or wife. **Ex.** *If you are married, we will need the name of your spouse.*

spout (5) [spawt'], *v.* discharge or throw out a liquid with force. **Ex.** *Gasoline spouted from the hole in the tank.* —*n.* the opening of a pipe or tube through which liquid is discharged. **Ex.** *Steam was coming from the spout of the kettle.*

sprang (3) [spræŋ'], *v.* past tense of *spring.* **Ex.** *At the sound of the alarm, he sprang out of bed.*

spray (3) [sprey'], *n.* 1. water or other liquid scattered in a large mass of tiny drops. **Ex.** *Spray from the high waves hit our faces.* 2. an instrument for scattering liquid in this manner; the liquid so scattered. **Ex.** *He used a spray to kill the insects.* —*v.* discharge spray upon; let fall as spray. **Ex.** *She sprayed the flowers with water.* — **spray'er,** *n.*

spread (1) [spred'], *v.* 1. extend in length and width; open out. **Ex.** *She spread the cloth on the table.* 2. make or become more widely known; scatter or become scattered widely. **Ex.** *The bad news spread quickly.* 3. cover with. **Ex.** *She spread butter on the bread.* —*n.* 1. the act of spreading. **Ex.** *The spread of learning has been furthered by television.* 2. a food soft enough to be spread on bread, crackers, etc. **Ex.** *What kind of spread should I make for the party?* —**spread'er,** *n.* that which spreads. **Ex.** *Please put the butter spreader on the table.*

spring (1) [spriŋ'], *v.* 1. leap; rise suddenly. **Ex.** *The sound of the shot made him spring from his chair.* 2. return to position or shape after being stretched. **Ex.** *He saw the door spring shut.* 3. come into being. **Ex.** *The city seemed to spring up overnight.* **—n.** 1. the season between winter and summer. **Ex.** *The days became warmer when spring arrived.* 2. the act of springing; a leap. **Ex.** *The sudden spring of the lion surprised him.* 3. a place where water rises from the earth. **Ex.** *Their drinking water comes from a spring.* 4. stiff steel, wire, etc. wound in a series of circles that yields when pressed but returns to the original shape when free. **Ex.** *The spring in the old clock is broken.* **—adj.** of or for the spring season. **Ex.** *In April he bought some spring clothes.* **—spring'y,** *adj.*

sprinkle (3) [spriŋ'kəl], *v.* 1. scatter in drops or very small pieces. **Ex.** *He sprinkled salt and pepper on his food.* 2. rain lightly. **Ex.** *Take your umbrella with you; it is sprinkling.* **—n.** a light rain. **Ex.** *It was only a sprinkle, and I did not get very wet.* **—sprink'ler,** *n.* that which sprinkles. **—sprink'ling,** *n.* not very many; a few. **Ex.** *There was only a sprinkling of people in the theater.*

sprung (3) [sprəŋ'], *v.* past participle of *spring.* **Ex.** *He had sprung from the bed when the alarm clock rang.*

spun (4) [spən'], *v.* past tense and participle of *spin.* **Exs.** *He spun around to see who was behind him. She had spun the thread that she later wove into cloth.*

spur (4) [spər'], *n.* 1. a metal device with sharp points put on the heel of a rider's shoe or boot and used to urge a horse to move. **Ex.** *The horse leaped over the fence at the touch of the spur.* 2. anything that resembles or acts as a spur. **Ex.** *The teacher's words were a spur to the girl's imagination.* **—v.** 1. apply spurs to a horse. **Ex.** *He spurred the horse into a gallop.* 2. urge. **Ex.** *Danger spurred him on.*

spy (3) [spay'], *n.* 1. one who watches others secretly to get information. **Ex.** *The manufacturer sent a spy to learn the methods of a rival company.* 2. one employed by a government to obtain secret information about another country. **Ex.** *The spy reported the development of a new weapon.* **—v.** 1. act as a spy. **Ex.** *His job was to spy on the military forces of the neighboring country.* 2. catch sight of; glimpse; see. **Ex.** *She spied her friends walking down the street.*

squad (5) [skwad'], *n.* 1. a small group of soldiers, usually eight or ten people. **Ex.** *The squad marched onto the field.* 2. any small group of people organized for a particular purpose. **Ex.**

A police squad hurried to the scene of the trouble. —**squad' car'**, a car used by police to patrol streets.

squadron (5) [skwad'rən], *n.* a military organization of airplanes or ships that moves as a unit. **Ex.** *Those two pilots formerly flew in the same squadron.*

square (1) [skwe:r'], *n.* 1. a flat shape having four equal sides and four right or ninety-degree angles. 2. an open area in a village, town or city with streets on all four sides. **Ex.** *There were many shops around the square.* 3. the number which results from multiplying one number by itself. **Ex.** *The square of four is sixteen. (4 × 4 = 16.)* —*v.* 1. multiply a number by itself. **Ex.** *If you square four, the result is sixteen.* 2. straighten; make square. **Ex.** *The general told the young soldier to square his shoulders.* 3. fit or agree with **Ex.** *Your story does not square with what others have told us.* —*adj.* 1. shaped like a square. **Ex.** *She was carrying a square box.* 2. having the same length and width. **Ex.** *A square yard is one yard long and one yard wide.* —**square'ly**, *adv.*

SQUARE 1

square root [skwe:r' ruwt'], a number which when multiplied by itself equals a known number. **Ex.** *The square root of four is two.*

squash [skwaš'], *n.* the hard skinned fruits of various vines, the fleshy parts of which are eaten as vegetables. **Ex.** *Today's fresh vegetable is steamed yellow squash.*

squeak [skwiyk'], *n.* a thin, sharp, high cry or sound. **Ex.** *The mouse's squeaks scared her.* —*v.* make a thin, sharp, high sound. **Ex.** *The door squeaked as I opened it.* —**squeak'y**, *adj.* —**squeak'i·ly**, *adv.*

squeeze (4) [skwiyz'], *v.* 1. apply pressure. **Ex.** *He squeezed my hand in greeting.* 2. apply pressure in order to get something out. **Ex.** *She squeezed the juice from several oranges for breakfast.* 3. push one's way into or through a small space. **Ex.** *They squeezed through the crowd.* —*n.* the act of applying pressure. **Ex.** *She gave the child an affectionate squeeze.* —**squeez'er**, *n.* a device for squeezing oranges, lemons, etc.

squirrel (3) [skwər'əl], *n.* a small, bushy-tailed, tree-climbing animal. **Ex.** *The squirrel was busy gathering nuts.*

SQUIRREL

stab (5) [stæb'], *v.* cut into or through with a

pointed weapon; thrust. **Ex.** *He stabbed the man with a knife.* —*n.* the thrust or wound made with a pointed weapon. **Ex.** *He received a stab in the chest.*

stable (3) [stey'bəl], *adj.* 1. firm; not easily shaken; solid. **Ex.** *They built the house on a stable foundation.* 2. remaining the same; unchanging. **Ex.** *Prices have been stable for the last year.* —**sta·bil'i·ty**, *n.* the condition of being stable. —**sta'bi·lize**, *v.* make stable. —**sta'bi·liz·er**, *n.* that which stabilizes. *Ex. Our crossing was very smooth because of the ship's stabilizers.*

stable (3) [stey'bəl], *n.* a building for the housing and feeding of horses or cattle. **Ex.** *He fed the horses in the stable.* —*v.* put or keep in a stable. **Ex.** *They stabled the horses for the night.*

stack (4) [stæk'], *n.* a large pile. **Ex.** *They piled the straw into a stack.* —*v.* pile up in a stack. **Ex.** *She stacked the dirty dishes in the sink.*

stadium [stey'diyəm], *n.* a large area surrounded by rows of seats where people can sit and watch any of various sports, such as baseball and football, being played. **Ex.** *It was difficult to find a parking space near the stadium.*

staff (3) [stæf'], *n.* 1. a group of assistants to a manager, chief, etc. **Ex.** *She explained the new policy to the editorial staff.* 2. a stick used as a support. **Ex.** *The old man leaned on his staff.* —*v.* supply with a staff. **Ex.** *They staffed the school with excellent teachers.*

stage (2) [steyj'], *n.* 1. a platform, raised so that it can be easily seen, on which a play can be acted, a speech given, etc. **Ex.** *When the curtain went up, there were two actors on the stage.* 2. the acting profession. **Ex.** *She wants to go on the stage.* 3. a single step in a process; a period of development. **Ex.** *Your child is at an interesting stage.* —*v.* put on or exhibit as on a stage, in public, etc. **Exs.** *They will stage that play for the first time. The students staged a demonstration.*

stagecoach [steyj'kowč'], *n.* a large carriage, pulled by horses, that was once used for transporting passengers, mail and freight. **Ex.** *We watched a movie about the robbery of a stagecoach.*

stage fright [steyj' frayt'], nervousness felt when going before a group of people to act, speak, etc. **Ex.** *Her stage fright disappeared as soon as she began to speak.*

a, far; æ, am; e, get; ey, late; i, in; iy, see; ɔ, all; ow, go; u, put; uw, too; ə, but, ago; ər, fur; aw, out; ay, life; oy, boy; ŋ, ring; θ, think; ð, that; ž, measure; š, ship; j, edge; č, child.

stagehand [steyj'hænd`], *n.* one who works in a theater fixing the lights, scenery, etc., but does not act.

stagger (4) [stæg'ər], *v.* 1. sway when walking; walk unsteadily. **Ex.** *The drunken man staggered along the road.* 2. shock; affect strongly. **Ex.** *News of the accident staggered him.* —*n.* a swaying, unsteady walk.

stain (3) [steyn']. *n.* 1. a dirty spot; an unwanted spot. **Ex.** *There was a coffee stain on his shirt.* 2. a coloring matter used on wood or other materials. **Ex.** *He rubbed the table with a dark brown stain.* —*v.* 1. discolor; make dirty. **Ex.** *The child stained her dress with berries.* 2. add color; change the color. **Ex.** *The carpenter stained the chair a bright blue.* —**stain'less,** *adj.* 1. spotless; without stains. 2. able to resist staining or rusting. **Ex.** *Our sink is made of stainless steel.*

staircase (5) [ste:r'keys`], *n.* a series of steps including the railing at the sides. **Ex.** *I have always wanted a house with a circular staircase.*

stairs (2) [ste:rz'], *n.* a series of steps used in going up or down from one level to another. **Ex.** *Those stairs go up to the bedrooms.*

stairway [ste:r'wey'], *n.* a series of steps; a staircase. **Ex.** *An outside stairway leads to the garden.*

stake (3) [steyk'], *n.* 1. a pointed post or piece of wood forced into the ground. **Ex.** *Stakes marked his property line.* 2. an interest in something, as money put into a business. **Ex.** *As a partner, he has a stake in that business.* —*v.* mark or identify by stakes. **Ex.** *The settlers staked out their land.* —**stakes',** *n.* something, such as money, risked in a game or contest. **Ex.** *He left the gambling game when the stakes became too high.*

stale (4) [steyl'], *adj.* 1. dry, flat, etc. in taste because of being old. **Ex.** *There was only a piece of stale cake left.* 2. of no more interest; having lost strength, energy or interest in. **Ex.** *She has grown stale in her job and needs a change.*

stalk (3) [stɔ:k'], *v.* 1. follow and approach quietly, in pursuit. **Ex.** *The hunters stalked the lion.* 2. walk stiffly and proudly. **Ex.** *With her head held high, she stalked from the room.*

stalk (3) [stɔ:k'], *n.* the main stem of a plant; any part like this.

STALK

stall (4) [stɔ:l'], *n.* 1. a section of a stable or shed for one animal. **Ex.** *The horse was miss-*

ing from its stall. 2. a small table or section where business is done. **Ex.** *They sell their vegetables at a stall in the farmers' market.* —*v.* come or bring to a stop without intending to. **Ex.** *The motor stalled because the car was out of gas.*

stammer (4) [stæm'ər], *v.* speak in a hesitating way by pausing between words or repeating parts of words. **Ex.** *The frightened girl could only stammer a reply.* —*n.* the act of speaking in this way. **Ex.** *He speaks with a stammer.*

stamp (2) [stæmp], *v.* 1. strike or hit noisily and with force. **Ex.** *He stamped his feet to keep warm.* 2. print on or press into with some mark, design, etc. **Ex.** *The name of the manufacturer was stamped on the box.* —*n.* a small piece of paper put on letters, packages and certain products to show that a fee or tax has been paid. **Ex.** *She put an airmail stamp on the letter.* 2. any device which prints on or presses into; the mark made by such a device. **Ex.** *He has a rubber stamp with his name and address on it.*

stand (1) [stænd'], *v.* 1. move into or be in an upright or erect position in which only the feet are on a surface. **Ex.** *He always stands when older people come into the room.* 2. be or grow into a position. **Ex.** *A tall tree stands in front of the house.* 3. remain; not run away. **Ex.** *You must stand and fight.* 4. bear; endure. **Ex.** *I cannot stand this cold weather.* —*n.* 1. the act of standing firmly; the act of holding a belief or opinion. **Ex.** *What is your stand on that question?* 2. a small table on which something rests. **Ex.** *She put the two brass figures on a stand.* 3. a table on which something is placed for sale. **Ex.** *She stopped at the baked goods stand to buy a cake.* —**stand a chance,** have a prospect or possibility. **Ex.** *With his poor attendance record at practice, he didn't stand a chance of making the team.* —**stand by,** 1. stay or stand near. **Ex.** *She was standing by the door as he passed.* 2. support. **Ex.** *A second doctor was standing by during the operation.* —**stand for,** 1. endure. **Ex.** *I will not stand for this treatment.* 2. be a symbol of. **Ex.** *Our flag stands for our love of country.* 3. seek to be elected. **Ex.** *He is standing for office this year.* —**stand in,** substitute for someone else. **Ex.** *Who is going to stand in for you while you're away?* —**stand out,** be noticeable. **Ex.** *She stands out from the other girls because of her height.* —**stand up,** 1. stand; move into a standing position. **Ex.** *Did you stand up when the women came into the room?* 2. last; continue to operate. **Ex.** *This car will stand up under difficult driving conditions.* —**stand up for,** defend; support. **Ex.** *We are no longer friends because he didn't stand up for me when I was in trouble.*

standard (2) [stæn'dərd], *n.* anything accepted by general agreement as a basis for comparison; a model. **Ex.** *The standards for admission in this school are very high* —*adj.* not special; usual; agreed or established. **Ex.** *We stock standard sizes of shoes in this store.* —**stand'ard·ize,** *v.*

standing army [stæn'diŋ ar'miy], a permanent army. **Ex.** *Our country has a strong standing army.*

standpoint [stænd'poynt'], *n.* a position from which one considers things; viewpoint; point of view. **Ex.** *From your standpoint, what action do you think we should take?*

stanza (5) [stæn'zə], *n.* a group of lines of verse forming a part of a poem or a song. **Ex.** *That poem has four stanzas.*

staple (5) [stey'pəl], *n.* 1. a principal product of a country or area. **Ex.** *Coffee is a staple of Brazil.* 2. a frequently used item of food in a household. **Ex.** *We keep a supply of staples such as flour, sugar and tea in the house at all times.* —*adj.* produced, used or sold in large quantities; principal. **Ex.** *Bread is a staple food in many countries.*

star (1) [star'], *n.* 1. any of the seemingly fixed, light-giving heavenly bodies that appear in the night sky. **Ex.** *It was a dark and stormy night, and not a single star could be seen.* 2. a flat figure, having five or more points, that is often used to represent something. **Ex.** *There is one star in our flag for each of the states.* 3. a brilliant person; a famous actor or actress.

STAR 2

Ex. *She is a movie star.* —*v.* act the most important part in a movie, play, etc. **Ex.** *She starred in that play.* —**star'ry,** *adj.* —**star'light,** *n.* light from the stars.

starch (5) [starč'], *n.* a white, tasteless substance found in certain foods such as potatoes, rice, flour, etc. **Ex.** *When she serves foods containing starch, she balances them with a leafy vegetable and meat, fish or poultry.* 2. a preparation of this substance mixed with water to stiffen cotton and linen materials. **Ex.** *He likes to have a little starch in his shirt collars.* —*v.* stiffen with starch. **Ex.** *She starched her dresses.* —**starch'y,** *adj.*

stare (2) [ste:r'], *v* look long and steadily; gaze. **Ex.** *He stared at the strangely dressed men.* —*n.* a long, steady gaze. **Ex.** *She turned away from his stare.*

stark (5) [stark'], *adj*. 1. complete; absolute. **Ex**. *Stark fear shone in his eyes.* 2. rough; severe; cheerless. **Ex**. *We walked over the stark, frozen fields.* —*adv*. entirely; completely. **Ex**. *The baby was stark naked.* —**stark'ly,** *adv*.

start (1) [start'], *v*. 1. begin. **Ex**. *We are going to start on our trip tomorrow.* 2. cause to begin. **Ex**. *He started the engine of the car.* 3. make a sudden, quick movement because of surprise or fear. **Ex**. *He started when I mentioned your name.* —*n*. a beginning. **Ex**. *She has made a good start on her work.* —**start'er,** *n*. one who or that which starts. —**start out,** begin a trip. **Ex**. *He started out for his office at eight in the morning.*

startle (3) [star'təl], *v*. cause sudden fright; cause to move suddenly in surprise. **Ex**. *Your knock startled me.* —**star'tling,** *adj*. surprising; frightening. **Ex**. *What a startling development that is!*

starve (2) [starv'], *v*. 1. be very hungry for food; suffer from hunger; die from lack of food. **Ex**. *Many animals starved during the snowstorm.* 2. suffer from a lack of something needed. **Ex**. *The children were starving for affection.* —**star·va'tion,** *n*.

state (1) [steyt'] *n*. 1. the condition of a person or a thing. **Ex**. *He was in an angry state.* 2. a group of people under one government; a nation. **Ex**. *Many foreign states were represented at the meeting.* 3. one of the political divisions of some nations. **Ex**. *The United States consists of fifty states.*

state (1) [steyt'], *v*. declare; say. **Ex**. *He stated his views on the subject very clearly.* —**state'ment,** *n*. the act of stating; that which is stated.

stately (4) [steyt'liy], *adj*. majestic; showing great dignity. **Ex**. *We were impressed by her stately appearance.* —**state'li·ness,** *n*.

stateroom [steyt'ruwm'], *n*. a cabin or bedroom for passengers on a ship.

statesman (3) [steyts'mən], *n*. a man who shows ability and wisdom in the affairs of government. **Ex**. *They honored him as their leading statesman.* —**states'man·ship,** *n*. the art of diplomacy or of governing wisely.

a, far; æ, am; e, get; ey, late; i, in; iy, see; ɔ, all; ow, go; u, put; uw, too; ə, but, ago; ər, fur; aw, out; ay, life; oy, boy; ŋ, ring; θ, think; ð, that; ž, measure; š, ship; j, edge; č, child.

station (1) [stey'šən], *n.* 1. a place of special work or duty. **Ex.** *We called the police station for help.* 2. a place for passengers to get on or get off along a train or bus route; the building at such a place. **Ex.** *We bought our tickets at the railroad station.* 3. a place equipped for sending or receiving radio or television broadcasts. **Ex.** *We could see the tower of the radio station.* —*v.* put in a certain place or position. **Ex.** *A guard was stationed at the gate.* —**sta·tion·ar·y,** *adj.* fixed; not changing or moving.

stationery [stey'šəneriy], *n.* materials used for writing, such as writing paper and envelopes, pens, pencils, ink, etc. **Ex.** *Where did you put my business stationery?*

station wagon [stey'šən wæg'ən], a long automobile with three rows of seats, the last two of which can be removed to make room to carry a lot of luggage or various large objects. **Ex.** *When the five of us went on vacation, we were able to fit all our clothes and camping equipment in the station wagon.*

statistics (4) [stətis'tiks], *n. pl.* numbers counted and arranged to express facts; the science of gathering and arranging facts expressed in numbers. **Ex.** *Statistics show that the population of the world is increasing.* — **sta·tis'tic,** *n.* a numerical fact. —**sta·tis'ti·cal,** *adj.* —**sta·tis'tic·al·ly,** *adv.* —**stat'is·tic'ian,** *n.* a person who works with statistics.

statue (3) [stæč'uw], *n.* a figure of a person or an animal, made in metal, carved in wood, etc. **Ex.** *A copper statue of a kneeling woman decorates the municipal building.*

stature (5) [stæč'ər], *n.* 1. height. **Ex.** *The boy did not reach his father's stature of six feet.* 2. growth; development. **Ex.** *The professor is a man of great mental stature.*

status (5) [stey'təs, stæt'əs], *n.* 1. state or condition of affairs. **Ex.** *What is the present status of our foreign relations with that country?* 2. position; rank. **Ex.** *The status of a doctor is very high in this community.*

statute (5) [stæč'uwt], *n.* a rule; a law, especially one passed by a lawmaking body. **Ex.** *The new statute increased the sales tax.* —**stat'u·tor·y,** *adj.*

stay (1) [stey'], *v.* 1. remain in a place; not go. **Ex.** *We stayed there for three hours.* 2. be a guest; live for a time. **Ex.** *Our friends are staying with us for a month.* 3. continue to be. **Ex.** *The children stayed clean most of the day.* —*n.* the act of remaining in a place; a visit. **Ex.** *How long was your stay in the country?*

stead (5) [sted'], *n.* the place of someone or something taken by a substitute. **Ex.** *While I am away, he will act in my stead.*

steady (2) [sted'iy], *adj.* 1. not changing; not stopping; regular. **Ex.** *A steady wind was blowing.* 2. serious; dependable. **Ex.** *His employers know him to be a steady worker.* 3. firm; well-supported. **Ex.** *The table is steady.* —*v.* make or become steady. **Ex.** *Please steady the ladder.* —**stead'i·ly**, *adv.* —**stead'i·ness**, *n.*

steak (3) [steyk'], *n.* meat or fish cut in slices for cooking close to a flame or for frying. **Ex.** *They served steak to their guests.*

steal (2) [stiyl'], *v.* take away unlawfully. **Ex.** *The thief tried to steal my watch.*

steam (2) [stiym'], *n.* 1. the gas that forms when water boils. **Ex.** *Steam rose from the pot.* 2. this gas used under pressure as a source of energy. **Ex.** *This engine is run by steam.* —*v.* 1. produce steam. **Ex.** *The food is steaming.* 2. move or run by steam. **Ex.** *The ship steamed up the river.* 3. cook by steam. **Ex.** *She steamed the vegetables.* —*adj.* using or operating by steam. **Ex.** *They have steam heat in their house.* —**steam'y**, *adj.* —**steam'er**, *n.* 1. a ship powered by steam. 2. a pot used for cooking with steam.

steel (2) [stiyl'], *n.* iron made harder and stronger by mixing it with other substances. **Ex.** *His tools were made of steel.* —*adj.* of or like steel.

steep (3) [stiyp'], *adj.* having a slope or slant almost straight up and down. **Ex.** *The hill was too steep for them to climb.* —**steep'ly**, *adv.* **steep'ness**, *n.*

steer (3) [st:r'], *n.* a young male of the cattle family raised to be eaten; an ox. **Ex.** *The steers were fattened for market.*

steer (3) [sti:r'], *v.* 1. guide or direct the course of a car, ship, etc. **Ex.** *We steered the boat toward land.* 2. be guided or directed. **Ex.** *This car steers easily.*

stem (3) [stem'], *n.* 1. the part of a plant from which the leaves and flowers grow. **Ex.** *She chose roses with long stems.* 2. any thing or part that looks like a stem. **Ex.** *The tall glass had a long, thin stem.*

stenographer [stənag'rəfər], *n.* a person who is able to write down in shorthand what is said. **Ex.** *She called in the stenographer and asked him to take a letter.* —**ste·nog'ra·phy**, *n.* writing in shorthand; the skill of writing in shorthand.

step (1) [step'], *n.* 1. a movement made by lifting one foot and placing it in a new position. **Ex.** *The baby took his first steps today.* 2. a measure of the distance covered in one such movement. **Ex.** *She was walking three steps ahead of me.* 3. the manner of walking. **Ex.** *He walked with a firm step.* 4. that on which one places the foot on going up or down stairs. **Ex.** *She walked up the steps to the front door.* 5. an action, phase, degree or rank in a series. **Ex.** *What steps must I take to obtain a driver's permit?* —*v.* walk; move or go by making a step. **Ex.** *She stepped aside.* —**step down,** 1. go from a higher to a lower position. 2. resign from a job. **Ex.** *The previous president stepped down a year ago.* —**step up,** 1. go from a lower to a higher position. 2. increase. **Ex.** *Because of all the new orders, we have had to step up production.* —**take steps,** do some things to reach an objective. **Ex.** *He is taking steps to prevent such an accident from happening again.*

stepbrother [step'brəð'ər], *n.* the son of one's stepparent by a previous marriage.

stepchild [step'čayld'], *n.* a stepson or stepdaughter.

stepdaughter [step'dɔ:'tər], *n.* the daughter of one's husband or wife by a previous marriage.

stepfather [step'fa:'ðər], *n.* husband of one's mother after she remarries.

stepmother [step'məð'ər], *n.* wife of one's father after he remarries.

stepparent [step'pær'ənt], *n.* stepfather or stepmother.

steppingstone [step'iŋstown'], *n.* 1. a stone on which to step, as in crossing a stream. 2. anything which is a step toward progress in one's career, life, etc. **Ex.** *This job could be a steppingstone to success.*

stepsister [step'sis'tər], *n.* the daughter of one's stepparent by a previous marriage.

stepson [step'sən'], *n.* son of one's husband or wife by a previous marriage.

stereo [ster'iyow'], *n.* an arrangement of two loudspeakers so that sound for a radio, record player, etc. comes from two places at the same time. **Ex.** *Your stereo makes it sound as if we were sitting right in the concert hall.*

stern (3) [stərn'], *adj.* 1. severe; strict. **Ex.** *The judge's face was stern as he spoke.* 2. firm; unchanging. **Ex.** *She made a stern resolve to do better in the future.* —**stern'ly,** *adv.* —**stern'ness,** *n.*

stern (3) [stərn'], *n.* the back part of a ship. **Ex.** *Our cabin was toward the stern of the ship.*

stew (4) [stuw', styuw'], *v.* boil food slowly. **Ex.** *She stewed some fruit for dessert.* —*n.* a dish, somewhat thicker than soup, prepared in this manner. **Ex.** *We had lamb stew for dinner.*

stick (1) [stik'], *n.* 1. a branch or part of a tree or bush when broken or cut off. **Ex.** *The boys picked up the sticks and used them to start a fire.* 2. any long, slender piece of wood. **Ex.** *The children were fighting with sticks.* 3. a long, slender piece. **Ex.** *We bought two sticks of candy.* —*v.* 1. be held or caught and unable to move. **Ex.** *What made the door stick?* 2. push a pointed thing so as to pierce with it. **Ex.** *Be careful or you will stick the needle in your finger.* 3. fasten or be fastened by piercing with a point or by gluing. **Ex.** *May I stick this notice on the wall?* 4. push forward; push into. **Ex.** *Stick this letter in the mailbox, please.* 5. stay with or by; continue doing. **Ex.** *Stick to your work until you finish it.* —**stick'y**, *adj.* 1. sticking because it has glue or something similar on it. **Ex.** *The child's hands were sticky with honey.* 2. hot and damp. **Ex.** *This sticky weather is tiring.* —**stick'i·ness**, *n.* —**stick by**, remain loyal. **Ex.** *His wife is sticking by him, although all of his friends have deserted him.*

stiff (2) [stif'], *adj.* 1. not easily bent; hard. **Ex.** *The paint brush was too stiff to use.* 2. not easily moved. **Ex.** *My neck is stiff.* 3. formal. **Ex.** *She was stiff and unfriendly in her greeting.* 4. strong; severe. **Ex.** *He was given a stiff punishment.* —**stiff'en**, *v.* make or become stiff. —**stiff'ly**, *adv.* —**stiff'ness**, *n.*

stifle (5) [stay'fəl], *v.* 1. cause difficulty in breathing. **Ex.** *We were stifled by the heat.* 2. prevent from doing, happening, etc. **Ex.** *She stifled a sob.* —**sti'fling**, *adj.* lacking fresh air. **Ex.** *This room is stifling.*

stigma (5) [stig'mə], *n.* a mark or stain on one's name or reputation. **Ex.** *The stigma of his crime caused him many difficulties.*

still (1) [stil'], *adj.* 1. not moving; motionless. **Ex.** *The hot summer air was still.* 2. quiet; noiseless; silent. **Ex.** *He asked the shouting children to be still.* —*adv.* 1. up till the present or stated time. **Ex.** *Was he still here when you arrived?* 2.

even yet. **Ex.** *He has a lot of money, but he wants still more.* 3. nevertheless; even so. **Ex.** *She knew the work was hard, but she still wanted to try it.* —**still'ness,** *n.* the state of being motionless or quiet. **Ex.** *The stillness was broken by the sound of thunder.*

stillborn [stil'bɔrn'], *adj.* born dead. **Ex.** *She was grief stricken over the birth of her stillborn child.*

still life [stil'layf'], a picture or painting of nonliving objects, such as fruit or cut flowers, pleasingly arranged. **Ex.** *She bought a still life of oranges and lemons in a blue bowl.*

stimulate (4) [stim'yəleyt'], *v.* cause to become active or more active; excite. **Ex.** *The school travel club stimulates students to read about foreign countries.* —**stim'u·lant,** *n.* something that stimulates. **Ex.** *Coffee is a stimulant.* —**stim·u·la'tion,** *n.* the act of stimulating.

sting (3) [stiŋ'], *v.* 1. cause pain by sticking with something sharp. **Ex.** *Be careful or the bee will sting you.* 2. cause or suffer a sharp, quick pain. **Ex.** *The blow made his face sting.* 3. cause or suffer hurt to the feelings. **Ex.** *His unkind comments sometimes sting.* —*n.* 1. the act of stinging. **Ex.** *The sting of a bee is painful.* 2. the wound or pain caused by the sting. **Ex.** *Put some medicine on the sting.*

stir (2) [stər'], *v.* 1. mix. **Ex.** *She stirred some sugar into her coffee.* 2. move slightly. **Ex.** *The sleeping patient had not stirred for an hour.* 3. excite. **Ex.** *The people were deeply stirred by his rousing speech.* —*n.* a state of excitement. **Ex.** *His appearance caused a stir in the crowd.* —**stir'ring,** *adj.*

stirrup (5) [stər'əp], *n.* a flat-bottomed ring of metal or wood hung from the saddle of a horse to support the rider's foot. **Ex.** *He placed his foot in the stirrup.*

stitch (4) [stič'], *n.* in sewing, a single movement of a threaded needle into and out of the material; a loop of the thread made in this way. **Ex.** *She made a neat row of stitches along the edge of the collar.* —*v.* sew; join together by stitches. **Ex.** *She stitched the two lengths of cloth together.*

stock (1) [stak'], *n.* 1. a supply of goods available. **Ex.** *That store has a large stock of canned goods for sale.* 2. animals kept on a farm. **Ex.** *He got up early to feed the stock.* 3. shares of ownership in a company. **Ex.** *He owns stock in several companies.* —*v.* store away; have available for sale. **Ex.** *Our store stocks this shoe in both black and brown.* —**take stock,** 1.

count, weigh or measure the amount or number of each item in stock. 2. consider all aspects of a situation before acting. **Ex.** *The commander took stock of the situation and then planned his next move.*

stockbroker [stak'brow`kər], *n.* a person who buys and sells shares of stocks, bonds, etc.

stock exchange [stak' ekčeynǰ'], a place where stocks and bonds are bought and sold.

stockholder [stak'howl`dər], *n.* a person who owns shares in a business. **Ex.** *That stockholder owns ten shares.*

stocking (2) [stak'iŋ], *n.* a close-fitting cloth, usually knitted, covering the leg and foot. **Ex.** *She bought three pairs of stockings.*

stock market [stak' mar'kit], a place where stocks and bonds are bought and sold.

stockpile [stak'payl`], *n.* a large amount of an item set aside for later use when that item might be scarce. **Ex.** *The company has a large stockpile of wool for making blankets.*

stockyard [stak'yard`], *n.* a place where animals are kept briefly until they are slaughtered or shipped to another place.

stole (2) [stowl'], *v.* past tense of *steal.* **Ex.** *They are the ones who stole the money.*

stolen [stow'lən], past participle of *steal.* **Ex.** *My car has been stolen.*

stomach (2) [stəm'ək], *n.* 1. the large, baglike organ of the body into which food goes after it is eaten. **Ex.** *He has a pain in his stomach.* 2. the part of the body in which this organ is located. **Ex.** *Lie flat on your stomach.*

stone (1) [stown'], *n.* 1. hard earthy or mineral matter which is not metal; rock. **Ex.** *The house was made of stone.* 2. a small piece of rock. **Ex.** *The stone hit the window.* 3. a gem; a jewel. **Ex.** *Her ring is set with precious stones.* 4. the hard center containing the seed of some fruits such as peaches, plums and cherries; pit. **Ex.** *These olives have had the stones removed.* —*adj.* made of stone. **Ex.** *The building was surrounded by a stone wall.* —*v.* throw stones at. **Ex.** *The boys stoned the strange dog.* —**ston'y,** *adj.* having many stones. **Ex.** *The road was stony.*

stood (1) [stud'], *v.* past tense and participle of *stand.* **Exs.** *My friend stood next to me. The tree had stood there for more than a hundred years.*

stool (4) [stuwl'], *n*. a chair without arms or a back.

stoop (3) [stuwp'], *v*. 1. bend the body forward and down; stand or walk with the shoulders bent forward. **Ex.** *He stooped to pick up the paper.* 2. act beneath one's dignity or position. **Ex.** *He would not stoop to trickery.* —*n*. the act or position of stooping. **Ex.** *She walked with a stoop.*

STOOL

stop (1) [stap'], *v*. 1. cease moving or cause to cease moving. **Ex.** *Stop this car so that I can get out.* 2. come or bring to an end; discontinue. **Ex.** *We stopped talking so that we could hear the music.* —*n*. 1. the act of stopping; the halting of any movement or action. **Ex.** *He put a stop to the noise.* 2. a place at which to stop. **Ex.** *I am getting off the bus at the next stop.* —**stop'per,** *n*. something that stops or closes. **Ex.** *Put a stopper in that open bottle.* — **stop off, stop over,** stop at one place while traveling to another. **Ex.** *Stop off and see us on your way home.* —**stop up,** prevent the flow or passage by filling, blocking, etc. **Ex.** *Rust had stopped up the pipes.*

store (1) [stɔːr'], *n*. 1. any building or place in a building where goods are available for sale; a shop. **Ex.** *She went to the store to buy bread.* 2. a supply of something for future needs. **Ex.** *They kept a large store of food in their kitchen.* —*v*. 1. set aside something for future needs. **Ex.** *They stored the apples in barrels.* 2. put away to keep safe. **Ex.** *She stored the winter clothes in a dry place.* — **stor'age,** *n*. 1. the act of storing; condition of being stored. 2. a place for storing. **Ex.** *This house has a lot of space for storage.*

storm (1) [stɔrm'], *n*. 1. strong winds together with rain or snow; heavy fall of rain or snow. **Ex.** *The boat was lost in the storm.* 2. something like a storm in force. **Ex.** *A storm of shouts greeted the speaker.* —*v*. 1. blow violently with rain, snow, etc. **Ex.** *It stormed last night.* 2. act angrily or violently. **Ex.** *The angry crowd stormed through the streets.*

story (1) [stɔːr'iy], *n*. the telling or writing of some happening, either real or imagined. **Ex.** *He told us the story of his life.* 2. a short tale about imagined happenings. **Ex.** *This book contains many interesting stories.* —**storyteller,** *n*. one who tells stories.

story (1) [stɔːr'iy], *n.* one level of a building with the rooms or space on it. **Ex.** *Most of these houses have only one story.*

stout (3) [stawt'], *adj.* 1. heavily built; fat. **Ex.** *He was too stout to fit into his old clothes.* 2. sturdily made; strong. **Ex.** *He tied the package with a stout cord.* —**stout'ly**, *adv.* —**stout'ness**, *n.*

stove (2) [stowv'], *n.* a heating or cooking device, usually in the kitchen. **Ex.** *The pot of water on the stove is boiling.*

straight (1) [streyt'], *adj.* 1. without a bend, curve or wave. **Ex.** *She drew a straight line.* 2. in good order. **Ex.** *He could not keep his accounts straight.* —*adv.* in a straight line, upright. **Ex.** *Sit up straight.* 2. directly. **Ex.** *Go straight home.* —**straight'en**, *v.* make or become straight; put in order. **Ex.** *Straighten up your room.*

straight face [streyt' feys'], a face that is without expression or emotion. **Ex.** *He told the story with such a straight face that we almost believed him.* —**straight'faced**, *adj.*

straightforward [streyt'fɔr'wərd], *adj.* in a direct, honest way. **Ex.** *He gave us straightforward answers.*

strain (2) [streyn'], *v.* 1. stretch tight; pull with force. **Ex.** *The dog strained at the rope.* 2. injure by stretching. **Ex.** *He strained his back lifting the heavy package.* 3. try as hard as possible. **Ex.** *She strained to get the work finished.* 4. put or force through a netting, often made of metal, to separate. **Ex.** *She strained the soup to remove the pieces of bone.* —*n.* 1. the act of straining; the condition of being strained. **Ex.** *The strain of his work caused him to become ill.* 2. an injury. **Ex.** *The doctor said the pain was caused by a back strain.* —**strain'er**, *n.* any device used to strain for the purpose of separating. **Ex.** *They used cloth as a strainer to separate the juice from the cooked fruit.*

strait (5) [streyt'], *n.* 1. a narrow passage of water connecting two larger bodies of water. **Exs.** *This boat sails through the Strait of Gibraltar. The water is often rough in these straits.* 2. a condition of trouble or distress. **Ex.** *The family was in desperate financial straits.*

strange (1) [streynj'], *adj.* 1. odd; unusual. **Ex.** *I saw a strange sight today.* 2. not known; unfamiliar. **Ex.** *A strange man knocked at the door.* —**strange'ly**, *adv.* —**strange'ness**, *n.*

stranger (1) [streyn'jǝr], *n.* 1. somebody from another place. **Ex.** *Many strangers visit our city.* 2. an unfamiliar or unknown person. **Ex.** *We warned the children not to talk to strangers.*

strap (4) [straep'], *n.* a narrow strip of material, such as leather, used for binding, wrapping or holding things together; any narrow strip like this. **Ex.** *The strap of her purse broke.* —*v.* bind with a strap. **Ex.** *He strapped the books together.*

strategy [straet'ǝjiy], *n.* 1. the science of military operátions, especially those intended to trick or surprise the enemy. **Ex.** *The general was famous for his superior strategy.* 2. plans involving tricks and surprises used in politics, business or personal affairs. **Ex.** *His strategy helped him to win the election.* —**stra·te'gic,** *adj.* 1. of or having to do with strategy. 2. essential or important in strategy.

straw (3) [strɔ:'], *n.* 1. a single dried stem or stalk of grain; these stems or stalks after being cut and dried. **Ex.** *The farmer covered the barn floor with straw.* 2. a hollow paper or plastic tube used for drinking. **Ex.** *She drank her soda through a straw.* —*adj.* made of straw. **Ex.** *She was wearing a straw hat.*

strawberry (5) [strɔ:'ber'iy], *n.* a small, sweet red fruit that grows on a low vine. **Ex.** *We had strawberries and cream for dessert.*

stray (4) [strey'], *v.* go away from a usual or proper place, with no aim in mind; wander. **Ex.** *The child strayed from home.* —*adj.* 1. having wandered and become lost. **Ex.** *They are looking for the stray sheep.* 2. occasional. **Ex.** *Except for a stray remark, he said nothing about his business.* —*n.* a person, animal, or thing that has wandered. **Ex.** *This animal shelter is a home for strays.*

streak [4] [striyk'] *n.* a line or mark differing in color or feel from its background. **Ex.** *He has streaks of gray in his hair.* —*v.* mark; form streaks. **Ex.** *Lightning streaked across the sky.*

stream (1) [striym'], *n.* 1. a current or flow of water such as a brook, river, etc. **Ex.** *They walked along the bank of the stream.* 2. anything that flows steadily; a continuous movement. **Ex.** *A stream of light came through the open door.* —*v.* flow or pour out in a stream or like a stream. **Ex.** *Blood streamed from the cut.*

street (1) [striyt'], *n.* a road in a city or town, usually with sidewalks and buildings on either or both sides. **Ex.** *Our house is on this street.*

streetcar (3) [striyt'kar'], *n.* a public passenger car that travels on rails along the streets. **Ex.** *He rides a streetcar to and from work.*

strength (1) [streŋθ'], *n.* 1. power or force of a body or part of a body. **Ex.** *The sick man was told to eat meat to regain his strength.* 2. mental power; moral power. **Ex.** *Our leader has great strength of character.* 3. force, as measured in size and numbers, as of men, ships, etc. **Ex.** *They did not know the strength of the enemy.* 4. ability to resist breaking, tearing, etc. **Ex.** *They used steel because of its strength.* —**strength'en,** *v.* make or become stronger.

strenuous (5) [stren'yuwəs], *adj.* active; full of energy; requiring much energy. **Ex.** *The pioneers led a strenuous life.* —**stren'u·ous·ly,** *adv.*

stress (4) [stres'], *v.* emphasize. **Ex.** *He stressed the need for understanding between nations.* —*n.* 1. emphasis; the importance placed on something. **Ex.** *His parents placed stress on honesty.* 2. strain; pressure. **Ex.** *He is able to work well under stress.*

stretch (2) [streč'], *v.* 1. extend over a distance. **Ex.** *The forest stretched for miles along the road.* 2. extend the body or a part of the body. **Ex.** *She stretched out on the bed to rest.* 3. pull out to a fuller or greater length. **Ex.** *This material stretches easily.* —*n.* 1. the act of stretching; the state of being stretched. **Ex.** *He stopped and took a stretch.* 2. a continuous space or time. **Ex.** *We met again after a stretch of three years.* 3. the ability to stretch or be stretched. **Ex.** *This rubber band has lost its stretch.*

stricken (4) [strik'ən], *v.* past participle of *strike*. **Ex.** *He has been stricken by a life-threatening disease.* —*adj.* suffering from serious illness, troubles, wounds, etc. **Ex.** *Neighbors helped the stricken family.*

strict (3) [strikt'], *adj.* 1. requiring that rules be obeyed or followed closely. **Ex.** *The teacher was strict.* 2. exact; complete. **Ex.** *He told me this in strict confidence.* —**strict'ly,** *adv.* 1. exactly. **Ex.** *Is that strictly true?* 2. absolutely. **Ex.** *It is strictly forbidden to smoke here.* —**strict'ness,** *n.*

stride (4) [strayd'], *v.* walk with long steps. **Ex.** *I saw him striding down the street.* —*n.* 1. a long step. **Ex.** *He reached* *the door in one stride.* 2. progress. **Ex.** *Great strides have been made in the exploration of space.* —**take in one's stride,** manage without difficulty. **Ex.** *He had encountered similar problems before and took this one in his stride.*

strife (4) [strayf'] *n.* fighting or quarreling. **Ex.** *There had always been strife between the two families.*

strike (3) [strayk'], *v.* 1. hit with a blow; hit against with force. **Ex.** *We saw the car strike the dog and kill it.* 2. attack. **Ex.** *The enemy may strike at any time.* 3. produce a sound by hitting something. **Ex.** *The clock is striking seven.* 4. produce a light, flame, etc. by rubbing. **Ex.** *Strike a match so that we can see.* 5. enter the mind or imagination; impress. **Ex.** *How did that idea strike you?* 6. stop work to compel an employer to meet certain demands. **Ex.** *The men are striking for higher wages.* —*n.* 1. the act of hitting or attacking. **Ex.** *He was not prepared for the snake's sudden strike.* 2. the act of quitting work until certain demands, such as higher wages or better working conditions, have been satisfied. **Ex.** *The workers are on strike for higher pay.* —**strik'er,** *n.* one who goes on strike. —**strike up,** start; begin. **Ex.** *When did they strike up a friendship?*

string (2) [strin'], *n.* 1. a thin cord used to tie or bind things. **Ex.** *Have you some string that I could use to tie this package?* 2. a connected series of things. **Ex.** *He bought her a string of pearls.* 3. wire or cord tightly stretched on a musical instrument to produce a tone. **Ex.** *She tightened the strings of her violin.* —**pull strings,** get what one desires, such as a favor or power, by using influence. **Ex.** *He became director by pulling strings.*

string bean [strin' biyn], *n.* the long green seed case of a bean plant eaten as a vegetable. **Ex.** *These string beans are young and tender and full of flavor.*

strip (2) [strip'], *v.* 1. remove one's clothing. **Ex.** *He stripped to the skin.* 2. remove a covering. **Ex.** *She stripped the sheets from the bed.* 3. remove. **Ex.** *The movers stripped the house of furniture.*

STRING BEAN

strip (2) [strip'], *n.* a long, narrow piece. **Ex.** *He cut the paper into strips one inch wide.*

stripe (4) [strayp'], *n.* a long, narrow strip or band of something different in color, material, etc. from the area on each side of it. **Ex.** *The flag of the United States has seven red stripes and six white ones.*

strive (4) [strayv'], *v.* 1. work hard; make a great effort. **Ex.** *We must strive to finish the job today.* 2. fight; struggle. **Ex.** *She had to strive against her fears.*

strode [strowd'], *v.* past tense of *stride.* **Ex.** *He strode out of the room without saying a word.*

stroke (2) [strowk'] *n.* 1. the act of hitting a blow. **Ex.** *He broke the lock with one stroke of the hammer.* 2. the sound produced by striking. **Ex.** *The stroke of the church bell awakened her.* 3. a movement with an instrument. **Ex.** *He paints his pictures with broad strokes.* 4. a sudden, unexpected act. **Ex.** *She had a stroke of good luck.* —*v.* move the hand over lightly or lovingly. **Ex.** *The children stroked the cat.*

stroll (4) [strowl'], *v.* walk slowly or idly. **Ex.** *The couple strolled arm in arm.* —*n.* a slow, easy walk. **Ex.** *They went for a stroll in the park.* —**stroll'er,** *n.* 1. a person who takes a stroll. 2. a light, chairlike, four-wheeled carriage in which small children are pushed.

strong (1) [strɔːŋ'], *adj.* 1. having great physical or mental strength; forceful. **Ex.** *He has strong arms.* 2. not easily broken or destroyed. **Ex.** *We need a strong chain for the dog.* 3. affecting one of the senses powerfully. **Ex.** *He likes the taste of strong coffee.* —**strong'ly,** *adv.*

strove [strowv'], *v.* past tense of *strive.* **Ex.** *We strove to do our best, but our customers weren't satisfied.*

struck (2) [strək'], *v.* past tense and participle of *strike.* **Exs.** *He struck his head on the corner of the table as he fell. The clock had just struck nine when the doorbell rang.*

structure (3) [strək'čər], *n.* 1. something built or constructed. **Ex.** *The old bridge was an iron structure.* 2. manner of building, forming or organizing. **Ex.** *He is writing about the structure of modern society.* —**struc'tur·al,** *adj.* of or used in making a structure.

struggle (2) [strəg'əl], *v.* 1. fight with. **Ex.** *The two boys were struggling with one another.* 2. use great effort. **Ex.** *They are struggling to learn English.* —*n.* 1. a great effort. **Ex.** *It is often a struggle for me to arrive at work on time.* 2. a contest;

a fight. **Ex.** *There was a court struggle for control of the property.*

stubborn (4) [stəb'ərn], *adj.* 1. insisting on having one's own way; unyielding. **Ex.** *The stubborn child refused to eat.* 2. difficult to treat or work with; resistant. **Ex.** *She has a stubborn cold.* —**stub'born·ly,** *adv.* —**stub'born·ness,** *n.*

stuck (3) [stək'], *v.* past tense and participle of *stick.* **Exs.** *The car was stuck in the mud. The idea has stuck in my mind ever since you mentioned it.*

student (1) [stuw'dənt; styuw'dənt], *n.* one who attends a school; one who studies. **Ex.** *She will be a college student next year.*

studio (4) [stuw'diyow; styuw'diyow], *n.* 1. the workroom of an artist. **Ex.** *The studio was filled with paintings.* 2. a place where motion pictures are made. **Ex.** *We visited a movie studio during our vacation.* 3. a room or rooms from which radio and television programs are broadcast.

study (1) [stəd'iy], *n.* 1. the act of using the mind for the purpose of gaining knowledge. **Ex.** *My college courses require many hours of study.* 2. close examination for the purpose of learning. **Ex.** *A study is being made of the effect of different occupations on the heart.* 3. a room which is set aside for studying. **Ex.** *He is reading in the study.* —*v.* 1. make an effort to gain knowledge by using the mind. **Ex.** *She is studying at the university.* 2. examine carefully. **Ex.** *He studied the picture for several minutes.* 3. read in order to understand. **Ex.** *Study the next lesson in the book.* —**stu'di·ous,** *adj.*

stuff (2) [stəf'], *n.* 1. any unnamed substance. **Ex.** *The shoes were made of some soft stuff that looked like leather.* 2. a number of different things. **Ex.** *The boy emptied all the stuff from his pockets.* —*v.* fill until very full. **Ex.** *The trunk had been stuffed with all sorts of things—old clothing, books, toys and so on.* —**stuff'ing,** *n.* anything used as filling. **Ex.** *She made a bread stuffing for the roast chicken.* —**stuff'y,** *adj.* close; lacking air. **Ex.** *The windows were closed, and the room was stuffy.*

stumble (3) [stəm'bəl], *v.* 1. trip while walking or running. **Ex.** *He stumbled over the stone on the sidewalk.* 2. speak or act unsteadily or in an unsure manner. **Ex.** *The young actor stumbled over his words.* —**stumble on** or **upon,** find unexpectedly. **Ex.** *I stumbled on some old letters of yours in a trunk.*

stump (3) [stəmp'], *n.* 1. the part of a tree trunk that remains in the earth after the main part is cut off. **Ex.** *He sat on the tree* *stump.* 2. the part of anything such as an arm, leg, etc. that remains after the main part is removed.

stun (5) [stən'], *v.* 1. cause loss of strength or consciousness by a fall, a blow or other violence. **Ex.** *The heavy blow stunned him.* 2. shock; astonish. **Ex.** *The bad news stunned us.* —**stun'ning,** *adj.*

stung (3) [stəŋ'], *v.* past tense and participle of *sting.* **Exs.** *The icy wind stung our faces. He had been stung by a bee.*

stunt (5) [stənt'], *v.* slow or stop the growth of; keep from normal growth. **Ex.** *The child's growth had been stunted by a poor diet.*

stunt (5) [stənt'], *n.* a trick or display of strength or skill, especially one done to attract attention. **Ex.** *The skaters performed stunts on the ice.*

stupid (3) [stuw'pid, styuw'pid], *adj.* 1. not bright mentally; not able to learn much; lacking in understanding. **Ex.** *He was not stupid but merely slow.* 2. foolish. **Ex.** *Playing with matches is a stupid thing to do.* —**stu'pid·ly,** *adv.* —**stu·pid'i·ty,** *n.*

sturdy (4) [stər'diy], *adj.* 1. of a strong build; firmly built. **Ex.** *Pack these books in a sturdy box, please.* 2. firm; unyielding. **Ex.** *We had to admire their sturdy refusal to surrender.* —**stur'di·ly,** *adv.* —**stur'di·ness,** *n.*

style (2) [stayl'], *n.* 1. a way or manner of painting, writing, speaking, doing, etc. **Ex.** *That author's style appeals to me.* 2. a way or manner of dressing, living, etc. at a particular time or period. **Ex.** *The dress she is wearing is out of style this year.* 3. a quality of excellence in painting, writing, speaking, etc. **Ex.** *His acting has style.* —*v.* design in a certain way or manner. **Ex.** *Her hair was attractively styled.* —**styl'ish,** *adj.* in the latest fashion.

sub- (3) [səb], *prefix.* 1. almost; nearly; less than. **Exs.** *Human, subhuman; total, subtotal.* 2. below or lower in position, rank, etc. **Ex.** *Soil; subsoil; station, substation.* 3. further divided into smaller parts. **Exs.** *Divide; subdivide; section, subsection.*

subdue (4) [səbduw', səbdyuw'], *v.* 1. conquer. **Ex.** *The attacking forces quickly subdued the guard.* 2. reduce in force or strength; lower. **Ex.** *Voices were subdued in the sickroom.*

subject (1) [səb'jikt], *n.* 1. the person or thing discussed, examined, painted, etc. **Ex.** *What is the subject of his latest* *novel?* 2. a branch of knowledge; a course of study. **Ex.** *He is an expert on the subject of children's diseases.* 3. a person under the control of a government, a ruler or another person. **Ex.** *They were subjects of the king.* 4. the person or thing with which a sentence is concerned. **Ex.** *In the sentence, "The boys went fishing," boys is the subject.* —*adj.* 1. under the power or control of. **Ex.** *The islanders did not want to remain a subject people.* 2. tending to get or have. **Ex.** *The child is subject to colds.* 3. dependent upon. **Ex.** *The sale of the group's land was subject to the members' approval.*

subject (1) [səbjekt'], *v.* 1. bring under control. **Ex.** *The country was subjected to foreign rule.* 2. foolishly expose oneself to. **Ex.** *He went out and subjected himself to the bad weather.* 3. cause to endure. **Ex.** *She was subjected to many tests.* —**sub·jec'tive,** *adj.* showing or affected by personal feelings, background, etc. **Ex.** *His writing is very subjective.*

subject matter [səb'jikt mæt'ər], that with which a piece of writing, talk, etc. is concerned. **Ex.** *Trees are the subject matter of his latest paintings.*

sublime (5) [səblaym'], *adj.* noble; high in thought or feeling. **Ex.** *That poet expresses sublime thoughts in simple language.*

submarine (4) [səb'məriyn'], *n.* a ship that travels under water. **Ex.** *The submarine rose to the surface of the sea.* —*adj.* being, living, etc. deep in the sea. **Ex.** *Fish are one type of submarine life.*

submerge (4) [səbmərj'], *v.* sink; go down into or under water. **Ex.** *She submerged the baby's bottle in boiling water.*

submit (3) [səbmit'], *v.* 1. yield or surrender to the power of another. **Ex.** *They had to submit to the superior force of the enemy.* 2. refer to others for their consideration or judgment. **Ex.** *They submitted their plans to the committee.* — **sub·mis'sion,** *n.* —**sub·mis'sive,** *adj.*

subordinate (5) [səbɔr'dənit], *adj.* in or of a lower rank, position or importance. **Ex.** *As a salesclerk, his position was subordinate to that of the manager.* —*n.* a person who is below another in order, rank or position. **Ex.** *Part of the success of his company is due to his concern for the welfare of his subordinates.* —*v.* place in a lower order, rank or position; consider of less importance. **Ex.** *The mother subordinated her wishes to the needs of her family.*

subordinate clause [səbɔr'dənit klɔːz'], a clause which is not a complete sentence. **Ex.** *In the sentence, "He was reading a* *book which he had borrowed from the library," "which he had borrowed from the library" is a subordinate clause.* See **A Brief Explanation of English Grammar.**

subscribe (5) [səbskrayb'], *v.* 1. order and pay for tickets to a series of entertainments, such as plays and concerts, or for the regular delivery of a newspaper, magazine, etc. **Ex.** *They subscribe to several monthly magazines.* 2. contribute or give to. **Ex.** *They subscribe to the hospital fund.* —**sub·scrib'er,** *n.* one who subscribes. —**sub·scrip'tion,** *n.* 1. payment for tickets to a series of entertainments or for the regular delivery of a newspaper, magazine, etc. for a certain period of time. 2. a contribution or gift to.

subsequent (4) [səb'səkwənt], *adj.* later in time, order or place; following. **Ex.** *That problem is discussed in a subsequent chapter of the book.* —**sub'se·quent'ly,** *adv.*

subsist (5) [səbsist'], *v.* manage or continue to live; exist. **Ex.** *The sick man subsisted on bread and milk.* —**sub·sis'tence,** *n.* 1. act of continuing to live or exist. **Ex.** *His life was a mere subsistence because he was so weak.* 2. a means of support; food. **Ex.** *Their vegetable garden is a source of subsistence for them in the summer.*

substance (2) [səb'stəns], *n.* 1. the actual physical material of which a thing consists. **Ex.** *The match tips were covered with a chemical substance.* 2. the nature of a thing; the main or essential part. **Ex.** *He told me the substance of the discussion.*

substantial (3) [səbstæn'šəl], *adj.* 1. large in amount or size. **Ex.** *He received a substantial payment for his services.* 2. strong. **Ex.** *The walls were substantial and had stood for hundreds of years.* 3. wealthy; rich; important. **Ex.** *He has substantial business interests.* 4. of or having substance; not imaginary. **Ex.** *She has substantial evidence for her claim.* —**sub·stan'tial·ly,** *adv.*

substitute (3) [səb'stətuwt'; səb'stətyuwt'], *n.* a person or thing used in or taking the place of another. **Ex.** *Nylon is used as a substitute for silk in stockings.* —*v.* use in or take the place of another. **Ex.** *She substituted for our regular teacher.* —*adj.* —**sub'sti·tu'tion,** *n.* the act of substituting; the thing substituted.

subtle (4) [set'əl], *adj.* 1. able to perceive, understand or express small differences; mentally keen. **Ex.** *He is a subtle writer.* 2.

showing such small differences that it is difficult to perceive or understand them. **Ex.** *At first the subtle meanings in her words were not clear.* 3. mysterious; faint; delicate. **Ex.** *Her subtle smile made him curious.* —**sub'tle·ty,** *n.*

subtract (3) [səbtrækt'], *v.* reduce in size or amount by taking part away. **Ex.** *If you subtract two from four, the remainder is two. (4 − 2 = 2.)* —**sub·trac'tion,** *n.*

suburb (4) [sʌb'erb], *n.* an area of many homes on the edge of or close to a city. **Ex.** *They would rather live in the suburbs than in the city.* —**sub·ur'ban,** *adj.* —**sub·ur'ban·ite,** *n.* one who lives in a suburb. —**sub·ur'bi·a,** the suburbs.

subway [sʌb'wey'], *n.* a train operating underground in a city. **Ex.** *She goes to work on the subway.*

succeed (1) [səksiyd'], *v.* 1. reach one's object or desire; accomplish one's aim. **Ex.** *He succeeded in reaching home before the rain started.* 2. come next after another; follow. **Ex.** *They must elect someone to succeed the present mayor.*

success (1) [səkses'], *n.* 1. a favorable or satisfactory ending or result. **Ex.** *He met with great success in his work.* 2. a person or thing that succeeds. **Ex.** *She is a success in business.* —**suc·cess'ful,** *adj.* —**suc·cess'ful·ly,** *adv.*

succession (4) [səkseš'ən], *n.* 1. a series of things or persons, each following the other. **Ex.** *After a succession of warm days, the weather became cold.* 2. the act of following another in position or office. **Ex.** *His succession to the throne occurred after the death of his mother, the queen.* —**suc·ces'sive,** *adj.* —**suc·ces'sive·ly,** *adv.* —**suc·ces'sor,** *n.* one who follows another in position or office. **Ex.** *Has his successor been selected yet?*

such (1) [sʌč], *adj.* 1. of this or that sort; of these or those sorts. **Ex.** *Such people are dangerous.* 2. of the same kind as; similar to. **Ex.** *A painting such as this is very expensive.* 3. so great; so much of. **Ex.** *We had such a good time at your party.*

suck (3) [sʌk'], *v.* 1. draw with the mouth. **Ex.** *He sucked his soda through a straw.* 2. draw from with the mouth. **Ex.** *The baby sucked milk from its mother's breast.* 3. eat something in the mouth slowly by passing the tongue over it but without chewing it. **Ex.** *She was sucking a piece of candy.* 4. draw in or from. **Ex.** *A window fan sucked the hot air from the room.* —**suc'tion,** *n.* the act of sucking.

sudden (1) [səd'ən], *adj.* 1. not expected; without warning. **Ex.** *There was a sudden change in the weather.* 2. done or occurring quickly or without preparation. **Ex.** *She made a sudden turn.* —**sud'den·ly**, *adv.* —**sud'den·ness**, *n.* —**all of a sudden**, suddenly. **Ex.** *All of a sudden, the wall fell.*

suds [sədz'], *n.* a creamy or bubbly mixture formed by soap mixed with water; soapsuds.

sue (5) [suw', syuw'], *v.* start a law case against. **Ex.** *They are suing for the money owed them.*

suffer (1) [səf'ər], *v.* 1. feel pain of body or mind. **Ex.** *They are suffering from hunger.* 2. receive or experience pain, grief, etc. **Ex.** *He suffered a broken leg when he fell.* 3. endure; become worse. **Ex.** *She cannot suffer much more pain.* —**suf'fer·ing**, *n.* condition of one who is feeling pain of body or mind.

sufficient (2) [səfiš'ənt], *adj.* enough for the need; adequate. **Ex.** *He bought a sufficient quantity of paint to cover the house.* —**suf·fi'cient·ly**, *adv.* —**suf·fi'cien·cy**, *n.* that which is enough.

suffix (5) [səf'iks], *n.* letters at the end of a word or added to a word that affect or change the meaning or part of speech. **Ex.** *The letters* -er, -ly *and* -ment *are common suffixes.*

sugar (1) [šug'ər], *n.* a sweet substance in crystal or powdered form made from the juice of certain plants. **Ex.** *She stirred some sugar into her coffee.* —**sug'ar·y**, *adj.* like or containing sugar.

suggest (2) [səgjest'], *v.* 1. offer or propose as something to think about. **Ex.** *He suggested they come next week.* 2. cause one to think about something by association or connection of ideas. **Ex.** *His behavior suggests that he is not well.* —**sug·ges'tion**, *n.* 1. the act of suggesting; that which is suggested. **Ex.** *We liked her suggestion that we eat in town.* 2. a slight trace or hint. **Ex.** *There was a suggestion of snow in the air.*

suicide (4) [suw'isayd'], *n.* 1. the act of ending one's own life intentionally. **Ex.** *When her husband died, she felt like committing suicide.* 2. a person who intentionally ends his own life. **Ex.** *The dead man was a suicide.* —**su'i·cid'al**, *adj.*

suit (1) [suwt'], *n.* 1. a set of outer clothing to be worn together. **Ex.** *He put on his new winter suit.* 2. a case in a court of law. **Ex.** *She has started a suit to get the money he owes her.* —*v.* meet the wants or needs of; satisfy. **Ex.** *The house suited their large family.* —**suit'a·ble**, *adj.* fitting; meeting the needs of.

suitcase (3) [suwt'keys`], *n*. a long, flat traveling bag large enough to contain clothing. **Ex.** *He took two suitcases with him on the trip.*

sulfur (5) [səl'fər], *n*. a chemical element of a pale yellow color, used in making gunpowder, matches, medicine, etc. —**sul·fur'ic**, *adj*. containing sulfur. **Ex.** *They are using sulfuric acid in that experiment.* —**sul'fur·ous**, *adj*. of or like sulfur. **Ex.** *The smoke from that plant has a sulfurous smell.*

sullen (4) [səl'ən], *adj*. 1. silent, bitter and unpleasant. **Ex.** *The angry child gave him a sullen look.* 2. dark and gloomy. **Ex.** *The sullen weather made her feel depressed.* —**sul'len·ly**, *adv*. —**sul'len·ness**, *n*.

sultry (5) [səl'triy], *adj*. hot and moist with little air movement. **Ex.** *The day was so sultry that they had hardly any energy.* —**sul'tri·ness**, *n*.

sum (2) [səm'], *n*. 1. an amount, usually of money. **Ex.** *He gave me a large sum in gold.* 2. the number that results from adding two or more numbers or quantities together. **Ex.** *The sum of three and five is eight. (3 + 5 = 8).* **sum up**, give a summary by mentioning the important points. **Ex.** *He summed up the situation in three short sentences.*

summary (5) [səm'əriy], *n*. a brief statement that gives all the important parts of a longer matter. **Ex.** *He gave me a summary of the events that led to the accident.* —*adj*. 1. brief. **Ex.** *He presented a summary account.* 2. done swiftly and without attention to ceremony. **Ex.** *She complained about the summary treatment given her.* —**sum'ma·rize**, *v*.

summer (1) [səm'ər], *n*. the hottest season of the year, occurring between spring and fall. **Ex.** *They have gone to the mountains for the summer.* —*adj*. suitable for or characteristic of summer. **Ex.** *She bought light summer clothes for her trip.*

summit (5) [səm'it], *n*. the top; the highest point. **Ex.** *The mountain climbers reached the summit before dark.*

summon (3) [səm'ən], *v*. 1. formally command to come. **Ex.** *He was summoned to appear in court.* 2. request to come; ask to appear. **Ex.** *They were summoned to the bedside of their dying father.* 3. call forth. **Ex.** *He summoned all his courage to meet the danger.* —**sum'mons**, *n*. an order to appear in court; a request to appear.

sun (1) [sən'], *n*. 1. the light- and heat-giving heavenly body around which the earth and other planets move. **Ex.** *The sun* *rises in the east.* 2. the heat or light received from the sun. **Ex.** *Her wide hat protected her face from the sun.* —**sun'ny,** *adj.* bright.

sunbathe [sən'beyð'], *v.* expose one's body to the sun, especially to acquire a tan.

sunbeam [sən'biym'], *n.* a ray of light from the sun. **Ex.** *Sunbeams came through the open door.*

sunburn [sən'bərn'], *n.* a reddening of the skin caused by exposure to the sun. —*v.*

Sunday (1) [sən'diy], *n.* the first day of the week.

sundry (5) [sən'driy], *adj.* of various kinds. **Ex.** *Sundry problems were discussed.* —**sun'dries,** *n.* various small and less important articles or items. **Ex.** *This store sells dress materials and sundries.*

sung (2) [sən'], *v.* past participle of *sing.* **Ex.** *He had sung the song before.*

sunglasses [sən'glæs'əz], *n.* eyeglasses designed to protect the eyes from the rays of the sun.

sunk (2) [səŋk'], *v.* past participle of *sink.* **Ex.** *The boat had sunk without a trace.* —**sunk'en,** *adj.*

sunlight [sən'layt], *n.* light from the sun. **Ex.** *He opened the blinds to let in the sunlight.*

sunrise [sən'rayz], *n.* the time of day when the sun comes above the horizon in the east. **Ex.** *He always gets up at sunrise.*

sunshine [sən'šayn], *n.* the bright or direct light of the sun. **Ex.** *The hot sunshine made us look for the shade of a tree.*

sunset [sən'sət], *n.* the time of day when the sun goes below the horizon in the west. **Ex.** *The concert will start just after sunset.*

sunstroke [sən'strowk'], *n.* an illness caused by too much exposure to the heat of the sun.

super- (3) [suw'pər], *prefix.* 1. greater in quantity, size, strength, etc.; beyond. **Exs.** *Man, superman; conductor, superconductor; natural, supernatural.* 2. above; added to the top of. **Exs.** *Impose, superimpose; structure, superstructure.*

---

a, far; æ, am; e, get; ey, late; i, in; iy, see; ɔ, all; ow, go; u, put; uw, too; ə, but, ago; ər, fur; aw, out; ay, life; oy, boy; ŋ, ring; θ, think; ð, that; ž, measure; š, ship; j, edge; č, child.

superb (5) [suwpərb'], *adj.* 1. splendid; noble; majestic. **Ex.** *This area of the city has several superb old buildings.* 2. one of the best of one's kind. **Ex.** *He is a superb pianist.* —**su·perb'ly,** *adv.*

superhighway [suw'pərhay'wey], *n.* an extra-wide road used for high-speed traffic. **Ex.** *If we take the superhighway, we will save time but the scenery won't be as interesting.*

superintend (4) [suw'perintend'], *v.* direct; manage. **Ex.** *How many assistants do you need to help you superintend the factory?* —**su'per·in·ten'dent,** *n.* one whose duty is to direct or manage. **Ex.** *He is the superintendent of the hospital.*

superior (2) [səpi:r'iyər, suwpi:r'iyər], *adj.* 1. better or greater in ability, quality, quantity, etc. **Ex.** *The clothing at that shop is expensive but of superior quality.* 2. higher in rank, degree or grade. **Ex.** *The soldiers obeyed their superior officer without question.* 3. showing too much pride; scornful. **Ex.** *She felt superior to her schoolmates.* —*n.* one in a higher position of authority; a person of greater skill. **Ex.** *The secretary is typing letters for his superior.* —**su·per'i·or'i·ty,** *n.* the quality or state of being superior.

supermarket [suw'pərmar'kit], *n.* a large self-service store selling food and household items. **Ex.** *You can probably find everything you need to make this recipe at the supermarket.*

superstition (4) [suw'pərstiš'ən], *n.* belief based on fear rather than reason; belief in magic, spells, etc. **Ex.** *She believes in the superstition that breaking a mirror brings bad luck.* —**su'per·sti'tious,** *adj.* —**su'per·sti'tious·ly,** *adv.*

supervise (5) [suw'pərvayz'], *v.* direct work of others. **Ex.** *The architect supervised the building of the house.* —**su'per·vi'sion,** *n.* the act of supervising. **Ex.** *He works well without supervision.* —**su'per·vi'sor,** *n.* one who supervises. —**su'per·vi'so·ry,** *adj.*

supper (2) [səp'ər], *n.* an evening meal, lighter than a dinner. **Ex.** *The children went to bed after supper.*

supplement (5) [səp'ləmənt], *n.* 1. something added to make up for something that is lacking. **Ex.** *The doctor suggested extra milk as a supplement to her diet.* 2. something added, especially an extra section added to a book, magazine or newspaper to give further information, provide special articles, etc. **Ex.** *Today's newspaper has a supplement on the new automobile models.* —*v.* add to; supply something lacking. **Ex.** *He sup-*

plemented his salary by working at a second job. —**sup`ple·
men'tal,** *adj.* —**sup`ple·men'ta·ry,** *adj.*

supply (1) [səplay'], *v.* give or provide what is needed, asked for
or lacking. **Ex.** *The school supplied the students with books.*
—*n.* the quantity or amount of something one has available.
Ex. *Our supply of flour is very low.*

support (2) [səpɔrt'], *v.* 1. bear the weight of; hold up or in position; keep from falling. **Ex.** *That chair will not support a
heavy person.* 2. provide the needs of a person or a family.
Ex. *He supports his parents.* 3. aid a person, group, cause,
etc. **Ex.** *I will support you in your efforts to win the election.*
4. make more certain; strengthen. **Ex.** *This new evidence
supports my theory.* —*n.* 1. the act of supporting; the condition of being supported. **Ex.** *We are hoping for your support.*
2. one who or that which supports. **Ex.** *She is the main
support of her family.* —**sup·port'er,** *n.* one who or that which
supports. **Ex.** *She is a strong supporter of women's rights.*

suppose (1) [səpowz'], *v.* 1. believe; think; imagine. **Ex.** *I suppose
you are right.* 2. expect; be expected. **Ex.** *It is supposed to snow
tonight.* 3. require. **Ex.** *You are supposed to report for work
at 8:30 a.m.* 4. assume something is true for the purpose of
argument. **Ex.** *Suppose you had the money; would you give it
to me?* —**sup·posed',** *adj.* thought to be true. —**sup·pos'ed·ly,**
adv. —**sup·po·si'tion,** *n.* that which is supposed or assumed.

suppress (4) [səpres'], *v.* 1. subdue by force or authority; crush.
Ex. *The army was called to suppress the revolt.* 2. keep back
from the public; hide. **Ex.** *He suppressed his anger.* —**sup·pres'
sion,** *n.*

supreme (3) [səpriym', suwpriym'], *adj.* 1. highest in authority,
rank or power. **Ex.** *The president is the supreme commander
of the armed forces.* 2. highest in quality, character, importance, etc. **Ex.** *He showed supreme courage in his decision.*
—**su·preme'ly,** *adv.* —**su·prem'a·cy,** *n.*

Supreme Being [səpriym' biy'iŋ], God.

Supreme Court [sepriym' kɔrt'], the highest court in the United
States.

sure (1) [šu:r'], *adj.* 1. confident; convinced; certain. **Ex.** *I am
sure of his honesty.* 2. steady; reliable. **Ex.** *I have known him
all my life and he is a sure friend.* 3. very probable; almost
certain to happen. **Ex.** *You are sure to reach town if you
follow this road.* —**sure'ly,** *adv.* — **sure'ness,** *n.*

sure-footed [šu:r'fut'id], *adj.* unlikely to fall, slip or stumble. **Ex.** *The sure-footed goat was leaping from rock to rock.*

surface (3) [sər'fis], *n.* 1. an outer side of a body or thing. **Ex.** *Leaves were floating on the surface of the pond.* 2. the outer appearance. **Ex.** *On the surface, the men seemed friendly.* —*v.* 1. come from within to a surface. **Ex.** *A fish surfaced from time to time.* 2. provide with a surface. **Ex.** *They surfaced the road with stone.* —*adj.* having little or no depth; of, on or at the surface. **Ex.** *Surface appearances are often deceiving.*

surge (5) [sərǰ'], *n.* 1. a large, rolling movement of water; a large wave. **Ex.** *He watched the surge of the ocean.* 2. a strong rushing movement or feeling. **Ex.** *She felt a surge of anger at the sight of her rival.* —*v.* rise and swell to great volume. **Ex.** *The wave surged over the deck.*

surgeon (3) [sər'ǰən], *n.* a doctor who specializes in surgery.

surgery (3) [sər'ǰəriy], *n.* 1. the science of treating diseases and injuries by cutting, either to remove the diseased part of the body or to repair injuries. **Ex.** *The doctor said that surgery was required to treat her condition.* 2. the room where such treatment is performed. **Ex.** *The doctor is in surgery.* —**sur'gi·cal,** *adj.* of or concerned with surgery.

surmise (5) [sərmayz'], *v.* form an idea or opinion with few supporting facts; guess. **Ex.** *We surmise that she left early this morning.* —*n.* an idea or opinion with few supporting facts. **Ex.** *It is my surmise that he will resign.*

surname (5) [sər'neym'], *n.* the name of one's family; one's last name. **Ex.** *The surname of John Smith is Smith.*

surpass (5) [sərpæs'], *v.* 1. be greater than in amount, extent or degree; be better than. **Ex.** *She surpasses her sister in intelligence.* 2. go beyond; exceed. **Ex.** *He surpassed the speed limit.*

surplus (4) [sər'pləs], *n.* an amount which exceeds that which is needed. **Ex.** *He kept enough corn to feed his cattle and sold the surplus.* —*adj.* being extra; remaining. **Ex.** *She used the surplus material from her dress to make a scarf.*

surprise (1) [sərprayz'], *v.* 1. cause a feeling of wonder because something is not expected. **Ex.** *His sudden appearance surprised us.* 2. discover a person, a thing or an act suddenly or unexpectedly. **Ex.** *The police surprised the man in the act of taking the money.* 3. attack unexpectedly. **Ex.** *They sur-*

prised the enemy and won the battle. —*n.* 1. something unexpected. Ex. *Their visit was a surprise.* 2. the feeling caused by something unexpected. Ex. *We felt some surprise at her strange question.* —sur·pris'ing, *adj.* —sur·pris'ing·ly, *adv.*

surrender (3) [səren'dər], *v.* 1. yield something to another; abandon. Ex. *He surrendered his rights to the property.* 2. deliver oneself to the control of another. Ex. *The hunted man surrendered to the police.* —*n.* the act of surrendering. Ex. *They expect the enemy's surrender soon.*

surround (2) [sərawnd'], *v.* form a circle around. Ex. *Troops surrounded the city.* —sur·round'ings, *n.* all the things and conditions that are around a person or place. Ex. *She works in pleasant surroundings.*

survey (3) [sərvey'], *v.* 1. examine; look carefully at the whole of something. Ex. *He stood on the hill and surveyed the surrounding countryside.* 2. determine the exact location, size and shape of a piece of land by measuring. Ex. *He had the land surveyed before buying it.* —*n.* 1. the act of surveying a piece of land. Ex. *A survey of the property is being made.* 2. a study giving a general view of the whole of a subject. Ex. *The survey shows a need for more housing.* —sur·vey'or, *n.* one who surveys.

survive (4) [sərvayv'], *v.* 1. remain alive despite something. Ex. *A few people survived the flood.* 2. continue to live or exist longer than. Ex. *Few of the old customs survived the war.* —sur·vi'vor, *n.* one who survives. —sur·vi'val, *n.* that which survives; the act of surviving.

suspect (2) [səspekt'], *v.* 1. imagine a person to be guilty, bad, undesirable, etc. without much proof. Ex. *The police suspected him of the crime.* 2. have doubts about. Ex. *They suspect her motive.* 3. imagine to be true or probable; have an uncertain or indefinite idea. Ex. *I suspect we will see him again.* —sus'pect, *n.* one who is suspected. Ex. *Who are the suspects in this case?*

suspend (4) [səspend'], *v.* 1. hang free except for a support from above. Ex. *The swing was suspended from the branch of a tree.* 2. cause to stop for a time. Ex. *The train schedule was suspended until the railroad tracks were repaired.* 3. stop a person from attending or being part of for a time. **Ex.** *The boy was suspended from school for a week.* —**sus·pen'sion,** *n.* the act or condition of being suspended. —**sus·pense',** *n.* a state of doubt or uncertainty; the anxiety resulting from such a state. **Ex.** *She could hardly bear the suspense of waiting for a decision.*

suspicion (3) [səspiš'ən], *n.* the act of suspecting; the state of being suspected. **Ex.** *He is under suspicion of murder.* —**sus·pic'ious,** *adj.* 1. causing suspicion. **Ex.** *The broken lock was suspicious.* 2. feeling or showing distrust. **Ex.** *She was suspicious when she saw that there were no lights on in the house.* —**sus·pi'cious·ly,** *adv.*

sustain (4) [səsteyn'], *v.* 1. support the weight of; hold up. **Ex.** *Large columns sustained the roof.* 2. support; maintain; give strength to. **Ex.** *Thoughts of home sustained their spirits.* 3. undergo; endure. **Ex.** *He sustained a broken arm in the accident.*

swallow (3) [swal'ow], *v.* 1. take into the stomach through the mouth and throat. **Ex.** *He swallowed the hot coffee.* 2. make swallowing movements with the muscles of the throat. **Ex.** *He swallowed before starting to speak.* —*n.* the act of swallowing.

swallow (3) [swal'ow], *n.* a small, swift bird with long wings. **Ex.** *In the early evening, the air was filled with graceful swallows.*

swam (3) [swæm'], *v.* past tense of *swim.* **Ex.** *He swam across the lake.*

swamp (4) [swamp'], *n.* soft land that is almost always wet but not entirely covered with water. **Ex.** *The hunter was lost in the swamp.* —*v.* flood or cover, as with water. **Ex.** *The roads were swamped after the heavy rain.* —**swamp'y,** *adj.*

swarm (4) [swɔrm'], *n.* 1. a group of bees traveling with a queen bee. **Ex.** *The swarm of bees entered the hollow tree.* 2. a large, active group of insects, things, people, etc. **Ex.** *A swarm of people surrounded the car.* —*v.* move or come together in large numbers. **Ex.** *The children swarmed into the park.*

sway (3) [swey'], *v.* 1. move the body back and forth without moving the feet. **Ex.** *The dancers swayed to the music.* 2. move or lean as to one side. **Ex.** *The car swayed to the left as it rounded the corner.* 3. cause to change one's thinking; influence. **Ex.** *We were not able to sway her opinion.*

swear (4) [swe:r'], *v.* 1. declare or promise earnestly, asking a god to be witness to the truth. **Ex.** *He is willing to swear to the truth of this statement.* 2. use bad language; curse. **Ex.** *He often swears when he is angry.*

sweat (3) [swet'], *v.* give out moisture through the skin. **Ex.** *Unloading the truck made him sweat.* —*n.* the moisture given out through the skin. **Ex.** *Sweat dripped from the runner's forehead.* —**sweat'y**, *adj.*

sweater (3) [swet'ər], *n.* a knitted piece of outer clothing for the upper part of the body, either pulled over the head or buttoned like a jacket. **Ex.** *She was wearing a sweater and skirt.*

sweep (2) [swiyp'], *v.* 1. clean or remove dirt from a floor, rug, etc. by using a broom. **Ex.** *She is sweeping the floor.* 2. move or push away by force; destroy. **Ex.** *The storm was sweeping everything before it.* 3. move swiftly and steadily. **Ex.** *We saw her sweep into the room in a long, flowing dress.* —*n.* the act of sweeping; a sweeping movement. **Ex.** *He indicated with a sweep of his hand that we should leave.* —**sweep'ing**, *adj.* 1. of that which sweeps. **Ex.** *He signed his name in large, sweeping letters.* 2. general but including very much; of wide range. **Ex.** *The new president made sweeping changes in the government.*

sweet (1) [swiyt'], *adj.* 1. having the taste of sugar or honey; not salty or bitter; not spoiled. **Ex.** *This cake is very sweet.* 2. pleasant to hear, see, etc. **Ex.** *She has a sweet voice.* 3. pleasing; agreeable; dear. **Ex.** *She is a sweet young lady.* —*n.* something sweet. —**sweet'en**, *v.* —**sweet'en·er**, *n.* something used to sweeten. —**sweet'ly**, *adv.* —**sweet'ness**, *n.* the state of being sweet.

sweetheart [swiyt'hart'], *n.* a person much loved by another. **Ex.** *She was his sweetheart.*

sweet potato [swiyt' pətey'tow], a thick yellow root that is used as a vegetable. **Ex.** *She boiled the sweet potatoes.*

swell (2) [swel'], *v.* grow or increase in size, amount, degree, bulk, etc. **Ex.** *His injured arm began to swell.* —**swel'ling**, *n.* a part on the body that has swelled. **Ex.** *There was a swelling on her leg.*

swept (2) [swept'], *v.* past tense and participle of *sweep.* **Exs.** *He swept up the broken glass. She was swept along by the crowd.*

swerve [swərv'], *v.* turn unexpectedly and suddenly to one side. **Ex.** *The car swerved to avoid hitting the dog.*

swift (3) [swift'], *adj.* 1. moving or able to move with great speed; very fast. **Ex.** *The current of the river is swift.* 2. happening, coming or done in a very short time. **Ex.** *He was swift to act in the emergency.* —**swift'ly,** *adv.* —**swift'ness,** *n.*

swim (2) [swim'], *v.* 1. go forward or backward in water by moving the arms and legs or tail and body. **Ex.** *Fish were swimming in the pond.* 2. move over or across in this way. **Ex.** *He can swim from one side of the river to the other in half an hour.* 3. be in or covered with water or another liquid. **Ex.** *For dessert she served freshly picked berries swimming in cream.* 4. be or cause to be affected by a spinning or unsteady feeling. **Ex.** *His head was swimming.* —*n.* the act of swimming; a period of swimming. **Ex.** *They went for a long swim.* —**swim'mer,** *n.*

swing (2) [swiŋ'], *v.* 1. cause to move back and forth, as something supported from above. **Ex.** *She was swinging the basket, holding it by its handle.* 2. move or cause to move back and forth around a fixed point; turn. **Ex.** *The gate swings open easily.* 3. move with a long, continuous motion. **Ex.** *He tried to swing the bag over his shoulder.* —*n.* a seat hanging from ropes or chains fastened to a strong overhead support on which one rides back and forth for pleasure. **Ex.** *The children were playing on the swings.*

switch (4) [swič'], *n.* 1. the act of turning, shifting or changing. **Ex.** *The city is planning a switch from streetcars to buses.* 2. a device for turning electric current on and off. **Ex.** *He reached for the light switch.* 3. a slender, easily bent stick or branch used for whipping. **Ex.** *The boy's father whipped him with a switch.* 4. a device used to change a train from one track to another. —*v.* 1. turn, shift, change or exchange. **Ex.** *The girls switched hats.* 2. connect or disconnect an electric current by a switch. **Ex.** *He switched on the light.* 3. swing suddenly or sharply. **Ex.** *The horse switched its tail to chase away the flies.*

swollen (2) [swowl'ən], *v.* past participle of *swell.* **Ex.** *Her left ankle is swollen.*

sword (2) [sɔrd'], *n.* a weapon consisting of a long sharp blade and a handle.

swore [swɔːr'], *v.* past tense of *swear.* **Ex.** *He swore that he would not go.*

SWORD

sworn [swɔːrn'], *v.* past participle of *swear.* **Ex.** *She had sworn to tell the story to no one.*

swum (3) [swəm'], *v.* past participle of *swim*. **Ex.** *He has often swum in this river.*

swung (2) [swəŋ'], *v.* past tense and participle of *swing*. **Exs.** *The door swung open. He had swung at the ball and missed.*

syllable (4) [sil'əbəl], *n.* a word or part of a word which is spoken as one sound. **Ex.** *The word* girl *has one syllable, while the word* happiness *has three syllables.*

symbol (3) [sim'bəl] *n.* 1. that which stands for or represents something else. **Ex.** *The color red is a symbol for danger in many countries.* 2. in writing or printing, a sign, letter, mark, etc. used to represent something. **Ex.** *The symbol for cent is* ¢. **—sym·bol'ic,** *adj.* **—sym'bol'ize,** *v.* be a symbol of; represent. **Ex.** *In battle a white flag symbolizes the desire to stop fighting or to surrender.*

sympathy (2) [sim'pəθiy], *n.* 1. a sharing in the feeling of another, particularly one who is sad or in trouble. **Ex.** *They expressed their sympathy by sending flowers.* 2. approval; support. **Ex.** *He was in sympathy with their aims.* **—sym'pa·thize,** *v.* **—sym'pa·thet'ic,** *adj.*

symphony (3) [sim'fəniy], *n.* a long musical composition, usually in four parts, written for a large orchestra. **Ex.** *Today his symphony was performed for the first time.* **—sym·phon'ic,** *adj.*

symptom (4) [simp'təm], *n.* that which is evidence or a sign of the existence of something else. **Ex.** *A lingering cough is sometimes a symptom of a serious disease.* **—symp'to·mat'ic,** *adj.* indicating or showing. **Ex.** *A fever is sometimes symptomatic of an infection.*

syndrome [sin'drowm), *n.* a series or group of symptoms that are typical or characteristic of a general condition or disease. **Ex.** *The scientists will have to do some more testing to determine whether this symptom is a part of the syndrome.*

syrup (5) [sə:r'əp, si:r'əp], *n.* a thick, sweet liquid made by boiling sap or water containing sugar until it becomes thick. **Ex.** *He liked maple syrup on his biscuits.* **—syr'up·y,** *adj.*

system (1) [sis'təm], *n.* 1. a group of related things combined into or working as an organized whole. **Ex.** *A system of*

a, far; æ, am; e, get; ey, late; i, in; iy, see; ɔ, all; ow, go; u, put; uw, too; ə, but, ago; ər, fur; aw, out; ay, life; oy, boy; ŋ, ring; θ, think; ð, that; ž, measure; š, ship; ǰ, edge; č, child.

railroads joins the country's larger cities. 2. an arranged body of facts, ideas, procedures, etc. **Ex.** *What is their system of government?* 3. arrangement; order; method. **Ex.** *He has developed a better system for doing his work.*

systematic (5) [sis'təmæt'ik], *adj.* 1. using a method or system. **Ex.** *They made a systematic search for the lost ring.* 2. well organized; planned. **Ex.** *She was systematic in doing her housework.* —**sys·tem·at'ic·al·ly,** *adv.* —**sys'tem·a·tize,** *v.* organize; make a planned way of doing. **Ex.** *They systematized the procedures for writing the monthly report.*

T

T, t [tiy], *n.* the twentieth letter of the English alphabet.

table (1) [tey'bəl], *n.* 1. a flat surface supported by one or more legs, used as a piece of furniture. **Ex.** *Put the books on the table.* 2. a list of figures, facts or information according to a system. **Ex.** *You will find the titles of the chapters listed in the book's table of contents.*

TABLE 1

tablespoon (4) [tey'bəlspuwn'], *n.* a large spoon used for measuring and serving food; the amount that this spoon will hold. **Ex.** *She mixed two tablespoons of flour with two tablespoons of butter.*

tablet (5) [tæb'lit], *n.* 1. a pad of writing paper consisting of many sheets glued together at the top. **Ex.** *She tore a sheet of paper from her tablet.* 2. a small portion of medicine pressed into a flat, round cake. **Ex.** *The doctor told her to take three tablets a day.*

table tennis [tey'bəl ten'is], a game similar to tennis, played on a table, using paddles instead of rackets; ping-pong.

tack (5) [tæk'], *n.* a short, sharp-pointed nail with a large, flat or rounded head, used to fasten something. **Ex.** *The carpet was fastened to the floor with tacks.* —*v.* fasten or attach with tacks. **Ex.** *They tacked the notice to the door.*

tackle (4) [tæk'əl], *n.* 1. equipment used for a particular sport or activity. **Ex.** *He bought some fishing tackle.* 2. a special arrangement of wheels and ropes for raising and lowering heavy loads. **Ex.** *The tackle broke as they lifted the piano.* 3. the act of seizing or grasping in order to stop, often by forcing or pushing to the ground. **Ex.** *His tackle stopped the man from escaping.* —*v.* 1. seize or grasp and stop. **Ex.** *The policeman tackled the thief.* 2. agree to do; try to do. **Ex.** *He was eager to tackle the job.*

tact (5) [tækt'], *n.* the ability to do and say the right thing without annoying people or making them feel hurt or angry; diplomacy. **Ex.** *Your answer showed tact.* —**tact'ful,** *adj.* having or using tact. **Ex.** *The way he corrected her was very tactful.* —**tact'ful·ly,** *adv.*

tactics (5) [tæk'tiks'], *n. pl.* 1. the science of organizing and using military forces in war. **Ex.** *The colonel's tactics won the battle.* 2. any method of accomplishing an end. **Ex.** *Her tactics brought results.* —**tac'ti·cal,** *adj.*

tag (5) [tæg'], *n.* 1. any small piece of paper, metal, etc. attached to something with markings to show what it is, who owns it, etc. **Ex.** *Each dress in the store had a tag on it showing the price.* 2. a children's game in which the player chosen to be "it" tries to catch and touch one of the other players, who then becomes "it." —*v.* attach a tag to. **Ex.** *All dogs in this town are required to be tagged.*

tail (1) [teyl], *n.* the long, thin, rear part of an animal's body that extends beyond the rest. **Ex.** *The cat's tail stood straight up in the air.* 2. anything like a tail in location or shape; the last part; the back end. **Ex.** *We were seated near the tail of the airplane.* —*adj.* **Ex.** *She is at the tail end of the line.*

TAIL 1

taillight [teyl'layt'], *n.* a light on the rear of a car or truck. **Ex.** *In the dark, he could see two red taillights on the car ahead of him.*

tailor (3) [tey'lər], *n.* a person whose work is making, altering, repairing, etc. suits, coats, etc. **Ex.** *The tailor repaired a hole* *in my trousers.* —*v.* 1. make, fit, repair as a tailor. **Ex.** *He tailored the coat to fit me.* 2. alter, change, form, etc. to meet certain requirements. **Ex.** *The program was tailored for young children.*

take (1) [teyk'], *v.* 1. grasp; hold. **Ex.** *He wanted to take her in his arms.* 2. seize; capture; win. **Ex.** *Did the soldiers succeed in taking the city?* 3. bring; carry; guide. **Ex.** *A bus takes the children to school.* 4. come to possess; get as one's own; assume. **Ex.** *He is taking a job in the city.* 5. occupy. **Ex.** *Please take this chair; it's very comfortable.* 6. use. **Ex.** *He could not take time to see us.* 7. select; choose. **Ex.** *Take the one you like best.* 8. remove. **Ex.** *Why did you take the book?* 9. do; perform. **Ex.** *Shall we take a walk?* 10. need; require. **Ex.** *How long will the trip take?* 11. breathe in; eat; drink; etc. **Ex.** *Please take a drink of water.* 12. board and ride in a car, plane, ship, etc. **Ex.** *She will take the train to the city.* 13. study. **Ex.** *What courses are you taking?* 14. order and pay for the regular delivery of a magazine, newspaper, etc. **Ex.** *We take three daily newspapers.* 15. photograph. **Ex.** *Will you take my picture?* —**take after,** look like; behave like; resemble. **Ex.** *The boy takes after his father.* —**take down,** 1. reduce in position or rank; lower. **Ex.** *They are taking down the flag.* 2. write. **Ex.** *Take down what he says.* —**take for,** think to be, sometimes mistakenly. **Ex.** *Would you take him for a rich man?* —**take in,** 1. receive; admit. **Ex.** *That woman takes in boarders.* 2. make smaller. **Ex.** *The tailor is taking in my coat so that it will fit better.* 3. include. **Ex.** *His speech is going to take in many subjects.* —**take it,** accept; assume. **Ex.** *I take it you do not want to go.* —**take off,** 1. remove. **Ex.** *Take off your shoes.* 2. rise from the ground or a level. **Ex.** *We saw the plane take off.* —**take on,** 1. employ. **Ex.** *We are taking on extra workers.* 2. begin to do or try; assume. **Ex.** *They are taking on the problem.* 3. assume a look, quality, etc. **Ex.** *He is taking on the appearance of an old man.* —**take one's time,** 1. use as much time as necessary. **Ex.** *Take your time and do the job carefully.* 2. go or do more slowly than necessary. **Ex.** *He is taking his time getting here.* —**take over,** assume control of. **Ex.** *The military are taking over the government.*

taken (1) [tey'kən], *v.* past participle of *take.* **Ex.** *He was taken to school by his older sister.*

tale (2) [teyl'], *n.* a story about either imaginary or real events. **Ex.** *The children listened to the old soldier's tales.*

talent (3) [tæl'ənt], *n.* 1. a special and unusual ability or skill. **Ex.** *He is a pianist of great talent.* 2. people of special and unusual ability or skill, considered as a group. **Ex.** *The director of the play engaged the best talent he could find.* —**tal'ent·ed,** *adj.*

talk (1) [tɔːk'], *n.* 1. the act of expressing thoughts in spoken words; conversation. **Ex.** *I had a long talk with my friend.* 2. a speech without ceremony. **Ex.** *She gave a talk on gardening.* 3. a meeting for discussions. **Ex.** *Talks were held to resolve the labor dispute.* —*v.* speak; express thoughts in spoken words; discuss. **Ex.** *The student talked about his problems with his teacher.* —**talk'a·tive,** *adj.* talking very much; liking to talk very much. —**talk back,** answer impolitely. **Ex.** *You should not talk back to your mother.* —**talk down to,** talk simply as if to show that the listener has little understanding. **Ex.** *The manager always talks down to the clerks.*

tall (1) [tɔːl'], *adj.* 1. higher than the average of its kind; not short. **Ex.** *This city has many tall buildings.* 2. having a stated height. **Ex.** *She is five feet tall.*

tame (3) [teym'], *adj.* 1. not wild; taught to be useful or friendly to humans. **Ex.** *He has a tame rabbit.* 2. easy to handle; gentle. **Ex.** *She rode the tame horse.* 3. dull. **Ex.** *Life in the country was too tame for him.* —*v.* 1. teach to obey; train. **Ex.** *They tamed the elephant.* 2. control; make manageable. **Ex.** *She tried to tame her temper.* —**tame'ly,** *adv.*

tan (4) [tæn'], *n.* 1. a light brown color. **Ex.** *She likes tan because it is a neutral color.* 2. a brown color of the skin from exposure to the sun. **Ex.** *He has a tan from spending time on the beach.* —*adj.* light brown. **Ex.** *He wore tan shoes with his brown suit.* —*v.* 1. make leather from the skins of animals by using an acid. **Ex.** *The goat skins were tanned to be used in making coats.* 2. become brown in the sun. **Ex.** *I tan easily.*

tangible (5) [tæn'jəbəl], *adj.* 1. able to be touched. **Ex.** *There was tangible evidence that the car had been in an accident.* 2. having a worth that can be estimated. **Ex.** *A collection of stamps was his only property of any tangible value.* 3. be able to be understood by the mind or given mental form; real; actual. **Ex.** *He found tangible benefits in their plan.*

---

tangle (4) [tæŋ'gəl], *v.* 1. twist or knot together; become twisted or knotted. **Ex.** *He didn't know how he had managed to tangle his fishing line.* 2. involve and hold. **Ex.** *He fell when his feet became tangled in the grass.* —*n.* 1. a twisted and knotted mass. **Ex.** *She combed the tangles out of her hair.* 2. a complicated state or condition. **Ex.** *His business affairs were in a tangle.*

tank (3) [tæŋk'], *n.* 1. a large basin or other container for liquids. **Ex.** *The garage put gas in the tank of the car.* 2. a large, heavy military car with armor and big guns that travels on metal belts instead of wheels. **Ex.** *The tank moved easily over the rough road.*

tanker [tæŋk'ər], *n.* a ship with large tanks used to carry liquids. **Ex.** *The tanker was loaded with oil.*

tap (3) [tæp'], *v.* strike or hit lightly or gently. **Ex.** *He tapped me on the shoulder.* —*n.* a very light or gentle blow; the sound of such a blow. **Ex.** *I heard a tap on the door.*

tap (3) [tæp'], *n.* a device used to start or stop the flow of water or other liquids in a pipe or container. **Ex.** *Hot water flowed from the tap.* —*v.* make a hole or connection through which a liquid, gas, electric current, etc. can flow. **Exs.** *The rubber trees were ready to tap. His telephone was being tapped.*

TAP

tape (5) [teyp'], *n.* 1. a narrow strip of paper, cloth or other material used for binding. **Ex.** *He sealed the package with tape.* 2. a strip of cloth, plastic or metal marked with inches, feet, etc. and used for measuring. **Ex.** *He measured the height of the door with his steel tape.* 3. a strip of material on which sounds are recorded. —*v.* 1. bind with tape. **Ex.** *They taped his injured ankle.* 2. record on tape. **Ex.** *He taped his speech, and we listened to it later.*

taper (5) [tey'pər], *n.* a long, thin candle. **Ex.** *Lighted tapers were on the dining room table.* —*v.* 1. narrow to a point; gradually become thin at one end. **Ex.** *The shoe tapered to a pointed toe.* 2. gradually become less and less and then stop. **Ex.** *His interest tapered off after their first meeting.*

tape recorder [teyp' rikɔr'dər], a device which uses tape to record and reproduce sound.

tar (5) [tar'], *n.* a thick, black, sticky substance made from coal, wood, etc. **Ex.** *The roof was covered with tar.* —*v.* cover or spread with tar. **Ex.** *They tarred the road.*

tardy (5) [tar'diy], *adj.* late; slow. **Ex.** *She was often tardy for work.* —**tar'di·ly,** *adv.* —**tar'di·ness,** *n.*

target (5) [tar'git], *n.* 1. any object, often one marked with circles one around the other, to be aimed at, as in shooting. **Ex.** *He hit the center of the target with his first shot.* 2. that which is aimed at, as in an attack, criticism, etc. **Ex.** *His play was a target of the critics.*

tariff (4) [tær'if], *n.* 1. a system of taxes placed by a government on imports or exports. **Ex.** *The purpose of this tariff is to protect the market for domestic cars.* 2. the rate of tax placed on an imported or exported article. **Ex.** *What is the tariff on watches?*

tart (5) [tart'], *adj.* 1. sharp and biting to the taste; sour. **Ex.** *She used tart apples to make the pie.* 2. stinging; cutting. **Ex.** *She made a tart reply.* —**tart'ly,** *adv.* —**tart'ness,** *n.*

task (2) [tæsk'], *n.* any work or piece of work that it is one's duty to do; burden. **Ex.** *I have some household tasks to do before I can leave.* —**task force,** a group of people brought together to perform a special job, often military. **Ex.** *They set up a task force to interview the members of the new freshman class.*

taste (1) [teyst'], *v.* 1. notice or try the flavor of food or drink by putting it in the mouth. **Ex.** *She tasted the soup to see if it needed salt.* 2. have a certain flavor. **Ex.** *The bread tasted good.* —*n.* 1. the sense by which one learns the flavor of food, drink, etc. **Ex.** *Cigarettes have dulled his taste.* 2. a quality that is perceived by the tongue; flavor. **Ex.** *The fruit had a sweet taste.* 3. appreciation. **Ex.** *He has a taste for music.* 4. a feeling for what is proper, beautiful, etc. **Ex.** *She shows good taste in her clothing.* —**tast'y,** *adj.* flavorful. **Ex.** *We have had some tasty meals at her house.* —**in good** or **bad taste,** proper or improper. **Ex.** *Her questions were in bad taste.* —**taste'ful,** *adj.* in good taste.

taught (2) [tɔ:t'], *v.* past tense and participle of *teach.* **Exs.** *She taught school for seventeen years. How long had he taught?*

taunt (5) [tɔnt'], *v.* bother or annoy by mocking talk; blame bitterly or scornfully. **Ex.** *They taunted him for losing the race.* —*n.* a bitter or mocking remark. **Ex.** *The taunts angered him.*

tavern (4) [tæv'ərn], *n.* 1. a place where people buy and drink liquor; a bar. **Ex.** *They met at the tavern for a drink.* 2. a small hotel. **Ex.** *He found a room for the night at a tavern.*

tax (2) [tæks'], *n*. 1. an amount of money that one is required to pay to meet the costs of government, usually a fixed percent of income, property, etc. **Ex**. *The government has increased the tax on cigarettes.* 2. a heavy strain. **Ex**. *His many duties were a tax on his strength.* —*v*. 1. require the payment of to help support the government. **Ex**. *In this town personal property is taxed.* 2. place a heavy strain upon. **Ex**. *The heavy work had taxed her heart.* —**tax·a'tion**, *n*. the act of taxing.

taxi (3) [tæk'si], *n*. an automobile which carries passengers for money. **Ex**. *He took a taxi to his office.* —*v*. 1. travel by taxi. **Ex**. *We taxied to the railroad station.* 2. roll along the ground before rising into the air or after landing. **Ex**. *The plane was taxiing down the runway.*

tea (3) [tiy'], *n*. 1. a plant grown chiefly in various countries of Asia, Africa and South America for its leaves; the dried leaves of this plant. **Ex**. *That is tea growing on those hills.* 2. a drink made by pouring boiling water over the dried leaves of this plant. **Ex**. *May I please have a cup of tea?* 3. a party in the afternoon at which tea, coffee, cakes, sandwiches, etc. are served. **Ex**. *She gave a tea for the members of her club.*

teach (1) [tiyč'], *v*. 1. show how to do; train. **Ex**. *My father is teaching me to hunt.* 2. give lessons in; give instructions to. **Ex**. *She teaches music.* 3. supply with knowledge; cause to understand. **Ex**. *His illness may teach him the dangers of smoking.* 4. work as a teacher. **Ex**. *He teaches at our school.* —**teach'er**, *n*. one who teaches. —**teach'ing**, *n*. the act of training, instructing, etc.

team (2) [tiym'], *n*. 1. persons working, playing or acting together as a group. **Ex**. *The company employed a team of experts to improve manufacturing methods.* 2. two or more animals harnessed together for work. **Ex**. *A team of horses pulled the plow.* —*v*. join together for some purpose. **Ex**. *Each new man teamed with an experienced one to learn the job.*

teamwork [tiym'wərk'], *n*. an effort in which everyone cooperates to accomplish a particular thing. **Ex**. *Excellent teamwork enabled us to finish the job quickly.*

tear (1) [te:r'], *v*. 1. pull apart; rip; split. **Ex**. *Be careful or you will tear your coat on that branch.* 2. cause a rip or split by pulling apart. **Ex**. *How did you tear your shirt?* 3. pull off, out, etc.; remove by force. **Ex**. *Please tear the top from this* *box.* 4. move or act with violence or haste. **Ex.** *He went tearing out of the house.* —*n.* a place where something has been pulled apart. **Ex.** *There is a tear in his trousers.*

tear (1) [ti:r']. *n.* a drop of the salty fluid that keeps the eyes moist and that flows from the eyes when a person is crying. **Ex.** *Her eyes filled with tears.*

tear gas [ti:r' gæs'], a gas which, when released into the air, pains the eyes and causes tears to flow. **Ex.** *The police used tear gas to scatter the crowd.*

tease (4) [tiyz'], *v.* 1. mock or joke for the purpose of causing someone to be upset or bothered. **Ex.** *His sister teased him about his sweetheart.* 2. beg in a way that bothers for the purpose of obtaining. **Ex.** *The boy teased his mother for some cookies.*

teaspoon (4) [tiy'spuwn'], *n.* a small spoon for measuring and for eating food; the amount that this spoon will hold. **Ex.** *He stirred two teaspoons of sugar into his coffee.*

technical (4) [tek'nikəl], *adj.* 1. concerning the mechanical or practical arts or skills. **Ex.** *He is studying automobile repair at a technical school.* 2. used in a trade, profession, science, etc.; specialized. **Ex.** *He read many technical books while studying to become an engineer.* —**tech'ni·cal·ly,** *adv.*

technician [tekniš'ən], *n.* one who is skilled in the performance of any specialized technical task. **Ex.** *She is a laboratory technician.*

technique (5) [tekniyk'], *n.* the method and skill used in performing artistic work, scientific operations, etc. **Ex.** *We admired the technique of the pianist.*

technology (5) [teknal'əjiy], *n.* the science of industry and the mechanical or practical arts. **Ex.** *Space flights require advanced technology.* —**tech'no·log'i·cal,** *adj.*

tedious (5) [tiy'diyəs, tiyjəs], *adj.* tiring; boring. **Ex.** *The long wait at the airport was tedious.*

teem (5) [tiym'], *v.* be full; overflow. **Ex.** *His mind teemed with ideas.*

-teen (1) [tiyn'], *suffix.* ten. **Ex.** *Three, thirteen (3, 13); four, fourteen (4, 14); five, fifteen (5, 15).*

a, far; æ, am; e, get; ey, late; i, in; iy, see; ɔ, all; ow, go; u, put; uw, too; ə, but, ago; ər, fur; aw, out; ay, life; oy, boy; ŋ, ring; θ, think; ð, that; ž, measure; š, ship; ǰ, edge; č, child.

teens (1) [tiynz'], *n. pl.* the years when one is thirteen through nineteen years of age. **Ex.** *The girl was in her teens.* —**teen'age, teen'aged,** *adj.* in, of or for the teens. **Ex.** *We watched the teenage dancers.* —**teen'ag`er,** *n.* a person in his or her teens.

teeth (2) [tiyθ'], *n.* plural of *tooth.* **Ex.** *He brushes his teeth morning and night.* —**teethe',** *v.* grow teeth. **Ex.** *The baby is crying because she's teething.*

telegram (3) [tel'əgræm], *n.* a message sent by means of electric signals. **Ex.** *The telegram told him of his mother's death.*

telegraph (4) [tel'əgræf'], *n.* a device or system for sending messages by electric signals. —*v.* send a message by electric signals. **Ex.** *We telegraphed him to come home immediately.*

telephone (2) [tel'əfown'], *n.* an electric device or system for sending sounds, especially the voice, over distances by wire. **Ex.** *There is a telephone in the hall.* —*v.* communicate or speak with by telephone. **Ex.** *She telephoned him at his office.*

telephone book [tel'əfownbuk'], a directory listing names with addresses and telephone numbers.

telescope (4) [tel'əskowp'], *n.* an instrument for making distant objects, such as stars, seem closer and larger through the use of pieces of curved glass and mirrors. **Ex.** *He was studying the moon through the telescope.* —**tel`e·scop'ic,** *adj.*

television (3) [tel'əviž`ən], *n.* 1. a system of sending and reproducing a view or scene, using a device that changes light rays into electric waves and then changes these back into light rays which are seen as a picture. **Ex.** *The schools in this city use television in teaching.* 2. a device for receiving television broadcasts. **Ex.** *We just bought a new television.* 3. the programs, advertisements, etc. that can be viewed on this device. **Ex.** *Did you watch television last night?* —*adj.* —**tel'e·vise,** *v.* send pictures by television.

tell (1) [tel'], *v.* 1. make known by speech or writing; inform. **Ex.** *Can you tell me where he lives?* 2. relate; give an account of. **Ex.** *She was telling the children a story.* 3. express; reveal; show. **Ex.** *Her smile tells me she is happy.* 4. order; command. **Ex.** *Tell him to come back later.* 5. understand; decide; determine. **Ex.** *No one can tell what will happen.* —**tell'er,** *n.* 1. one who tells or gives an account of. **Ex.** *She is a delightful storyteller.* 2. a bank clerk whose job is to receive and give out money. **Ex.** *I handed the teller my deposit slip together with a check.*

telltale [tel'teyl'], *adj.* 1. showing plainly. **Ex.** *From the telltale blood on the floor, we knew that there had been a fight.* 2. revealing what is not meant to be known. **Ex.** *From his telltale downcast look, she knew that something was wrong.*

temper (2) [tem'pər], *n.* 1. anger; the inclination to anger. **Ex.** *The child displayed a mean temper.* 2. state or frame of mind; mood. **Ex.** *She was in a good temper yesterday and smiled all day.* 3. self-control; calm disposition. **Ex.** *He lost his temper easily and started shouting.* —*v.* 1. soften; make less strong. **Ex.** *The judge tempered justice with mercy.* 2. condition to a proper degree of hardness. **Ex.** *The metal was plunged into cold water to temper it.*

temperament (5) [tem'prəment], *n.* 1. the individual nature of a person determined by his mental and physical characteristics. **Ex.** *He has the quiet, serious temperament of a scholar.* 2. an easily excited nature. **Ex.** *The painter showed his temperament by shouting at anyone who offered the least criticism of his work.* —**tem·per·a·men'tal**, *adj.* easily disturbed; emotional. **Ex.** *The conductor handled the temperamental opera star tactfully.*

temperate (4) [tem'pərit], *adj.* 1. keeping proper control of one's actions, emotions, appetite, etc; self-controlled. **Ex.** *He is a man of temperate habits.* 2. neither too hot nor too cold. **Ex.** *The United States has a temperate climate.*

temperature (2) [tem'p(ə)rəčər], *n.* 1. the degree of heat or cold, measured on a scale. **Ex.** *What is the temperature of this room?* 2. the degree of heat above normal of a person's body; fever. **Ex.** *The patient had a high temperature.*

tempest (4) [tem'pəst], *n.* 1. a violent windstorm, usually accompanied by rain. **Ex.** *The tempest forced the ship onto the rocks.* 2. a violent disturbance. **Ex.** *His speech caused a political tempest.*

temple (2) [tem'pəl], *n.* a building used for worship. **Ex.** *The people went to the temple to pray.*

temple (2) [tem'pəl], *n.* the flat part of the head on either side of the forehead. **Ex.** *He had a cut on his right temple.*

temporary (4) [tem'pəre:r'iy], *adj.* limited; for only a short time; not permanent. **Ex.** *He has a temporary job which ends in two weeks.* —**tem'po·rar'i·ly**, *adv.*

tempt (4) [tempt'], *v.* 1. try to get one to do something wrong by making it seem attractive or desirable. **Ex.** *The boys tried to* *tempt him to smoke.* 2. attract one to want or do something; **be attractive or desirable** to. **Ex.** *The chocolate cake tempted her even though she was dieting.* —**temp·ta'tion**, *n.*

ten (1) [ten'], *n., adj.* the number between nine and eleven; the number *10.* —**tenth'**, *adj.* coming after nine others. —*n.* one of ten equal parts of something; *1/10.* **Ex.** *One tenth of the property belongs to me.*

tenant (4) [ten'ənt], *n.* one who occupies or uses a room, land or buildings he does not own, usually for periodic rental payments. **Ex.** *The former tenant of that house has just moved away.* —**ten'an·cy**, *n.* period of time during which one occupies a place as a tenant. **Ex.** *His tenancy of the house is for one year.*

tend (2) [tend'], *v.* be likely to; lean toward; go or move in the direction of. **Ex.** *He tends to be lazy.*

tend (2) [tend'], *v.* take care of; guard. **Ex.** *She tended the baby while his mother was at work.*

tendency (3) [ten'dənsiy], *n.* an inclination to act, go or move in a certain way or direction. **Ex.** *She has a tendency to talk too much.*

tender (2) [ten'dər], *adj.* 1. gentle; loving. **Ex.** *She has a tender nature.* 2. easily harmed or hurt. **Ex.** *The rough material hurt the child's tender skin.* 3. soft; easily cut or chewed; not tough. **Ex.** *They enjoyed the tender steak.* —**ten'der·ly**, *adv.* —**ten'der·ness**, *n.* —**ten'der·ize**, *v.* make tender. **Ex.** *He tenderized the beef by pounding it.*

tenderfoot [ten'dərfut`], *n.* a beginner. **Ex.** *The tenderfoot had much to learn.*

tenderhearted [ten'dərhar'tid], *adj.* easily moved by suffering; quick to sympathize. **Ex.** *The tenderhearted child wept over the dead bird.*

tennis (4) [ten'is], *n.* a game played in which rackets are used to hit a ball back and forth over a net stretched across the center of a court. **Ex.** *The children are learning to play tennis.*

tense (5) [tens'], *adj.* stretched tightly; strained. **Ex.** *Her nerves were tense from waiting.* —*v.* stretch; make tight; strain. **Ex.** *The runner tensed his muscles.* —**tense'ly**, *adv.* —**tense'ness**, *n.*

tense (5) [tens'], *n.* a form of a verb showing when the action or being occurs. **Ex.** Will study *is the future tense of the verb* study.

tension (5) [ten'šən], *n.* 1. the condition caused by stretching, tensing or straining. **Ex.** *Too much tension caused the steel cable to break.* 2. mental strain; a feeling of anxiety. **Ex.** *He was under great tension during the examination.* 3. a strained relationship between people, governments, etc. **Ex.** *A series of talks relieved the tension between the two countries.*

tent (2) [tent'], *n.* a light shelter of cloth supported by poles and fastened to the ground. **Ex.** *The campers lived in a tent.* 2. something resembling this. **Ex.** *An oxygen tent was placed over the patient.* —*v.* live in a tent. **Ex.** *They tented on the old campground.*

term (2) [tərm'], *n.* 1. a fixed period or length of time. **Ex.** *This is her third term in office.* 2. a word or an expression used in a special sense. **Ex.** *This author uses many medical terms.* —**terms'**, *n. pl.* 1. special conditions of a sale, agreement, etc. **Ex.** *The terms of the contract are fair.* 2. relations between people. **Ex.** *They are on friendly terms.*

terminal (5) [tər'mənəl], *adj.* 1. of the end; final. **Ex.** *They made the terminal payment on their bank loan today.* 2. of an illness leading to death. **Ex.** *The doctor has told his family that the disease is terminal.* —*n.* a station at either end of or at a major point along a railroad, bus, air, or other transportation line. **Ex.** *We have to be at the terminal an hour before our flight leaves.*

terminate (5) [tər'məneyt'], *v.* end; stop; bring to a close. **Ex.** *They terminated the agreement.* —**ter'mi·na'tion**, *n.* ending.

terrace (4) [te:r'is], *n.* a flat, raised piece of land, often in a series one above the other, on a slope or a hillside. **Ex.** *The terrace behind the house was covered with brick.* —*v.* form into a terrace. **Ex.** *The hills were terraced for growing rice.*

terrible (3) [te:r'əbəl], *adj.* 1. causing terror or horror. **Ex.** *The terrible fire filled the sky with flames.* 2. severe; very bad. **Ex.** *I have a terrible cold.* —**ter'ri·bly**, *adv.*

terrify (4) [te:r'əfay'], *v.* cause terror or great fear. **Ex.** *The armed man terrified the crowd.* —**ter·rif'ic**, *adj.* 1. causing terror or great fear; extremely bad. **Ex.** *He had a terrific pain in his right arm.* 2. very good; wonderful; excellent; marvelous; astonishing. **Ex.** *She did a terrific job!*

territory (2) [te:r'ətɔr'iy], *n.* 1. a large area of land. **Ex.** *Much of the territory of this state has been set aside for parks.* 2. the land under the rule and control of. **Ex.** *The territory of this nation extends from one ocean to another.* 3. an area in which a person travels or works. **Ex.** *Each salesman has his own territory.* 4. that part of a country or empire which does not have a fully independent government. **Ex.** *Those two states were territories until recently.* —**ter'ri·to'ri·al,** *adj.*

terror (2) [te:r'ər], *n.* 1. extreme fear; great fright. **Ex.** *The sight of the knife filled him with terror.* 2. that which causes great fear. **Ex.** *Poverty was a terror that never left her.* —**ter'ror·ize,** *v.* —**ter'ror·ism,** *n.* an act of planned violence, sometimes used as a way of governing, of trying to destroy a government or of gaining politicals ends. —**ter'ror·ist,** *n.* one who engages in terrorism.

test (2) [test'], *n.* 1. a set of questions, problems, etc. to determine a person's knowledge, fitness or ability; an examination. **Ex.** *She passed her foreign language test.* 2. an attempt to learn or prove what something is like, why something happens, etc. by examining, watching, etc. **Ex.** *They are making a test of the new engine today.* —*v.* measure how something will perform, act, etc. by watching, examining, doing, etc. **Ex.** *The automobile tires were tested by driving on a rocky road.* —**test'er,** *n.*

testify (4) [tes'təfay'], *v.* give evidence, especially in court. **Ex.** *He testified that he had seen the accident.*

testimony (5) [tes'təmow'niy], *n.* 1. the statement of a witness, especially in court. **Ex.** *His testimony helped to prove the guilt of the accused.* 2. serious declaration. **Ex.** *Her testimony at the meeting made a strong impression.*

test tube [test' tuwb', test' tyuwb'], a tall, thin glass tube used in making medical or chemical tests. **Ex.** *The scientist filled the test tube with chemicals.*

text (4) [tekst'], *n.* 1. the printed matter of a book or magazine, not including notes, pictures, etc. **Ex.** *The text of that book is printed in large type.* 2. the original words of an author or speaker. **Ex.** *The newspaper printed the text of the governor's speech in full.* 3. a piece taken from a book, poem, play, etc.

which a speaker or writer uses as a starting point in expressing his own ideas. **Ex.** *He quoted the text and then discussed its meaning.*

textbook [teks'buk`], *n.* a book used for instruction and study, especially one used in school. **Ex.** *The students did not have to pay for their textbooks unless they lost them.*

textile (5) [teks'tayl, teks'til], *n.* cloth made by weaving, such as cotton, silk or wool. **Ex.** *Have you seen the beautiful display of handwoven textiles at the museum?* —*adj.* having to do with cloth made by weaving. **Ex.** *Rayon fabrics are made at that textile factory.*

texture (5) [teks'čər], *n.* the way a surface or material appears or the way it feels when touched. **Ex.** *This wall has a rough texture.*

-th (1) [θ'], *suffix.* 1. a state or quality of being or having. **Exs.** *True, truth; warm, warmth; wide, width.* 2. the order or place of a number in a series. **Exs.** *Six, sixth; four, fourth; eight, eighth.*

than (1) [ðæn'], *conj.* 1. in comparison with. **Ex.** *He is younger than his brother.* 2. but; except; besides. **Ex.** *No one called other than your sister.*

thank (1) [θæŋk'], *v.* say that one has warm feelings toward another because of some act, kindness, etc. **Ex.** *Thank you for your help.* —**thanks'**, *n. pl.* an expression of gratefulness. **Ex.** *They accepted the gift with thanks.* —*interj.* I thank you. **Ex.** *Thanks for the ride.*

Thanksgiving [θæŋks'giv`iŋ], *n.* a national holiday in the United States, observed on the fourth Thursday in November, both to give thanks to God for a year in which things have gone well and to feast. **Ex.** *We spent the four-day weekend of Thanksgiving with friends at their beach home.*

that (1) [ðæt'], *adj.* indicating a particular person, place or thing, usually further from the person speaking than would be indicated by the word *this.* **Ex.** *That woman is his wife.* —*pron.* 1. a particular person, place or thing, usually further from the speaker than would be indicated by the word *this.* **Ex.** *That is my friend.* 2. a previously mentioned fact, idea or thing. **Ex.** *That is what he said.* 3. who; whom; which. **Ex.** *The man that I saw wore a brown suit.* —*conj.* introducing a dependent clause used as: 1. the subject or object of the sentence. **Exs.** *That he denied the story surprises me. I know* *that he was here.* 2. introducing a dependent clause showing cause, purpose or result. **Ex.** *He worked so hard that he became ill.* —*adv.* to the degree indicated. **Ex.** *I cannot walk that fast.*

that's [ðæts'], short form, contraction of *that is.* **Ex.** *That's the one I want.*

thaw (5) [θɔ:'] *v.* 1. melt; become liquid. **Ex.** *The ice in the river will thaw in the spring.* 2. reach a temperature that causes the melting of ice and snow. **Ex.** *It will probably thaw tomorrow.* 3. become less cold in manner. **Ex.** *He began to thaw under the warmth of her personality.* — *n.* 1. the act of thawing. **Ex.** *There has been a thaw in the relations between the two countries.* 2. weather sufficiently warm to melt ice and snow. **Ex.** *The spring thaw came early this year.*

the (1) [ðiy', ðə'], *adj.* 1. referring to one particular person or thing. **Ex.** *I know the man who just entered the room.* 2. referring to a well-known person or thing. **Ex.** *Men have now traveled to the moon.* 3. referring in a general way to every person or thing of a class or group. **Ex.** *The horse is a useful animal.* 4. giving emphasis to; indicating the best one. **Ex.** *She is the person to ask.* —*adv.* that much. **Ex.** *She likes him the better for his frankness.*

theater (2) [θiy'ətər], *n.* 1. a public place where movies are shown, plays are performed, lectures are given, etc. **Ex.** *What is the movie being shown at the theater tonight?* 2. the art of acting in or producing plays; all the people connected with this art. **Ex.** *She has many friends in the world of the theater.* 3. the scene of action or events. **Ex.** *The general visited the theater of war.* —**the·at'ri·cal,** *adj.*

theft (5) [θeft'], *n.* the act of robbing or stealing. **Ex.** *They reported the theft to the police.*

their (1) [ðe:r'], *adj.* of them; owned by or belonging to them. **Ex.** *They left their coats in the car.* —**theirs',** *pron.* the one or ones belonging to them. **Ex.** *Our children stay up late, but theirs do not.*

them (1) [ðem'], *pron.* form of the pronoun *they* used as the object of a verb or preposition. **Ex.** *I will see them tomorrow.*

theme (4) [θiym'], *n.* 1. the main subject or topic of a composition, lecture, etc. **Ex.** *The theme of his talk was the need* *for better education.* 2. a written composition on a given subject. **Ex.** *The teacher had the children write themes about their vacations.*

themselves [ðemselvz'], *pron.* 1. their own selves. **Ex.** *They saw the accident themselves.* 2. their usual selves. **Ex.** *They are not acting like themselves.*

then (1) [ðen'], *adv.* 1. at that time. **Ex.** *They were only young girls then.* 2. next in order of occurrence or happening. **Ex.** *He had dinner and then read the newspaper.* 3. in that case; therefore. **Ex.** *If you like it, then you may have it.* —*adj.* existing or being at the time. **Ex.** *My brother, then a soldier, told me the story.* —*n.* that time. **Ex.** *We had not seen him until then.*

theory (2) [θiy'əriy], *n.* 1. a reasonable but not yet proven explanation of why something exists or how something happens, based on experiments or ideas. **Ex.** *People were slow to accept the theory that the earth revolves around the sun.* 2. the general principles or methods of a science or an art as distinguished from its practice. **Ex.** *He is studying the theory of music.* 3. a guess; an idea. **Ex.** *It is my theory that the money was lost.* —**the'o·rize,** *v.* —**the'o·ret'i·cal,** *adj.*

there (1) [ðe:r'], *adv.* 1. in that place or position. **Ex.** *Who was there yesterday?* 2. to or toward that place. **Ex.** *He is going there now.* 3. on that point; in that matter. **Ex.** *I agree with you there.* 4. used in place of a subject at the beginning of sentence in which the subject follows the verb. **Ex.** *There are three books on the table.* —*interj.* an exclamation used to show pleasure, sympathy, relief, etc. **Ex.** *There, there! You will be all right.* —*n.* that place. **Ex.** *We left there on Sunday.*

thereafter [ðeræf'tər], *adv.* from that time forward; after that. **Ex.** *He went abroad and we did not hear from him thereafter.*

therefore (1) [ðe:r'for'], *adv.* as a result; consequently; for this reason or purpose. **Ex.** *She left home late and therefore missed the bus.*

there's [ðe:rz'], short form, contraction of *there is.* **Ex.** *There's a letter for you.*

---

a, far; æ, am; e, get; ey, late; i, in; iy, see; ɔ, all; ow, go; u, put; uw, too; ə, but, ago; ər, fur; aw, out; ay, life; oy, boy; ŋ, ring; θ, think; ð, that; ž, measure; š, ship; ǰ, edge; č, child.

thermometer (4) [θərmam'ətər], *n.* an instrument for measuring temperature. **Ex.** *The thermometer shows that it is very cold.*

thermostat [θər'məstæt'], *n.* a device for keeping a room, refrigerator, etc. at a particular temperature. **Ex.** *It's so warm in here; please turn down the thermostat.*

these (1) [ðiyz'], *pron.* plural of *this*. **Ex.** *These are the books I wanted.* —*adj.* plural of *this*. **Ex.** *These books are the ones I want.*

THERMOMETER

they (1) [ðey'], *pron.* plural of *he, she or it*. **Ex.** *Our friends said they would visit us next month.* 2. people in general. **Ex.** *They say it will be a cold winter.*

they'd [ðe:d'], short form, contraction of *they had* and *they would*. **Exs.** *They'd expected to leave earlier than they did. They'd like to spend a week here.*

they'll [ðe:l'], short form, contraction of *they will*. **Ex.** *They'll be here soon.*

they're [ðeyr'], short form, contraction of *they are*. **Ex.** *They're coming later.*

they've [ðeyv'], short form, contraction of *they have*. **Ex.** *They've written to us, but they didn't say when they'll be arriving.*

thick (1) [θik'], *adj.* 1. relatively large in size from one surface to the opposite surface. **Ex.** *He ate a thick slice of bread.* 2. measured from opposite surfaces. **Ex.** *The board is two inches thick.* 3. having its parts close together; crowded. **Ex.** *He has thick hair.* 4. not thin; heavy. **Ex.** *The thick smoke made it difficult to breathe.* —*adv.* in a manner to produce something thick; close together. **Ex.** *The blows came thick and fast.* —**thick'ness,** *n.* —**thick'en,** *v.*

thick-skinned [θik'skind'], *adj.* not easily bothered by criticism or unkindness. **Ex.** *The thick-skinned executive laughed at the unpleasant things said about her.*

thief (3) [θiyf'], *n.* one who steals; a robber. **Ex.** *They saw the thief climbing through the window.* —**thieves',** *n. pl.*

thigh (5) [θay'], *n.* the upper part of the leg above the knee. **Ex.** *The fisherman's rubber boots came up to his thighs.*

thin (1) [θin'], *adj.* 1. small in size from one surface to the opposite surface. **Ex.** *This is a very thin book.* 2. not fat;

lean. **Ex.** *He is a thin man.* 3. watery; of little substance. **Ex.** *The sick woman took only some thin soup.* 4. not close together; not heavy. **Ex.** *The old man's hair is thin.* 5. high and weak; not deep and full. **Ex.** *Her thin voice could not be heard above the music.* —*v.* 1. make or become less thick. **Ex.** *She thinned the sauce with milk.* 2. make or become less crowded; reduce in number. **Ex.** *The crowd thinned out until only we were left.* —**thin'ly,** *adv.* **thin'ness,** *n.*

thin-skinned [θin'skind'], *adj.* very easily bothered by criticism or unkindnesses. **Ex.** *The thin-skinned author smarted from the critic's unfavorable comments.*

thing (1) [θiŋ'], *n.* any physical object. **Ex.** *A book is just the thing to give her.* 2. any idea, proposal, project, etc. **Ex.** *That is the thing to decide.* 3. any act, deed, event, etc. **Ex.** *The thing to do is to ask your parents' advice.* —**things',** *n. pl.* goods, clothing, tools, toys, etc. **Ex.** *Pick up your things and put them away.*

think (1) [θiŋk'], *v.* 1. produce thoughts; form in the mind. **Ex.** *I often think of home.* 2. reason; consider. **Ex.** *He is thinking about the problem.* 3. believe; have faith in. **Ex.** *He thinks he can do it.* 4. judge; conclude. **Ex.** *I think that is a good book.* —**think better of,** 1. consider or regard more favorably than before. **Ex.** *Now that I am familiar with his work, I think better of him.* 2. change one's intentions or judgment. **Ex.** *After I realized how expensive the trip would be, I started to think better of going.* —**think nothing of,** consider to be unimportant or easy to do. **Ex.** *He thought nothing of walking ten miles.* —**think over,** consider. **Ex.** *Think over my offer before you sell to anyone else.*

third (1) [θərd'], *adj.* coming after two others. —*n.* 1. the third person or thing. **Ex.** *He is the third in line.* 2. one of three equal parts of anything; ⅓. **Ex.** *He received one third of the money.*

third person [θərd' pər'sən], the form of a pronoun or verb used to indicate the person or thing spoken about. **Exs.** *He, him, she, her, it, they, them, this, these, that and those are third person pronouns.*

thirst (3) [θərst'], *n.* 1. the need of the body for liquids; the dry feeling in the mouth and throat caused by such a need. **Ex.** *He died of thirst.* 2. any great longing for anything. **Ex.** *He had a great thirst for knowledge.* —*v.* 1. feel the need to drink. **Ex.** *They thirsted for water.* 2. have a longing for. **Ex.** *He thirsted for revenge.* —**thirst'i·ly,** *adv.* —**thirst'y,** *adj.*

thirteen (1) [θər'tiyn'], *n., adj.* the number between twelve and fourteen; the number *13.* —**thir'teenth',** *n., adj.* coming after twelve others.

thirty [θər'tiy], *n., adj.* the number between twenty-nine and thirty-one; the number *30.* —**thir'ti·eth,** *n., adj.* coming after twenty-nine others.

this (1) [ðis'], *adj.* indicating a particular person, place or thing, usually nearer the speaker than would be indicated by the word *that.* **Ex.** *This boy is my brother.* —*pron.* 1. a particular person, place or thing, usually nearer the speaker than would be indicated by the word *that.* **Ex.** *I like this better than that.* 2. a fact, idea, statement, etc. that is to be presented or explained. **Ex.** *Listen to this.*

thorn (3) [θɔːrn'], *n.* 1. a needlelike point on a plant. **Ex.** *The stems of these roses have many thorns.* 2. a plant or tree with many needlelike points. 3. something that worries or causes discomfort or problems. **Ex.** *His laziness was a thorn in her side.* —**thorn'y,** *adj.*

thorough (3) [θəːr'ow, θəːr'ə], *adj.* 1. having done all that ought to be done; complete and careful in every detail. **Ex.** *She did a thorough job of cleaning.* 2. complete; absolute. **Ex.** *He is a thorough fool.* —**thor'ough·ly,** *adv.* —**thor'ough·ness,** *n.*

thoroughfare [θəːr'əfeːr'], *n.* a main street open at both ends. **Ex.** *His store is on a main thoroughfare.*

those (1) [ðowz'], *pron.* plural of *that.* **Ex.** *Those are difficult problems.* —*adj.* plural of *that.* **Ex.** *Those apples are harder to reach than these.*

though (1) [ðow'], *conj.* 1. granting the fact that; although. **Ex.** *Though they started early, they arrived late.* 2. still; yet. **Ex.** *They were late, though not too late for dinner.* —*adv.* however. **Ex.** *We did not buy the car; we liked it, though.*

thought (1) [θɔːt'], *n.* 1. a single product of the act of thinking; an idea. **Ex.** *The thought of her visit made him happy.* 2. the act or process of thinking. **Ex.** *He seemed to be in deep thought.* 3. consideration; attention. **Ex.** *A lot of thought should be given to that problem.* 4. a way of thinking; the ideas of a certain group, period, etc. **Ex.** *Science is one of the concerns of modern thought.* —**thought'ful,** *adj.* 1. giving deep thought to. Ex. *She presented a thoughtful plan.* 2. considering the needs, wants, etc. of others. Ex. *It was thoughtful of him to write.* —**thought'less,** *adj.* uncaring; inconsiderate. Ex. *It was thoughtless of her to forget your birthday.*

thought (1) [θɔːt'], *v.* past tense and participle of *think.* Exs. *He thought he heard a noise. She had thought about the problem for a long time.*

thousand (1) [θaw'zənd], *n., adj.* ten hundreds; the number *1,000.*

thrash (4) [θræš'], *v.* 1. beat or whip in punishment or anger. Ex. *The father thrashed the boy for running away.* 2. move the body in a restless, unplanned way. Ex. *He thrashed about in bed all night.*

thread (2) [θred'], *n.* 1. a fine string made by spinning slender bits of cotton, wool, etc. Ex. *She used silk thread in sewing her dress.* 2. the central thought or idea that connects the parts of a story, speech, etc. Ex. *The interruption made her lose the thread of the conversation.* 3. the thin raised line that winds around a bolt or a screw and that holds it in place. —*v.* prepare for sewing by putting a thread through a needle. Ex. *Please thread this needle for me.* 2. pass or make one's way through something with difficulty. Ex. *He threaded his way through the crowd.*

threat (2) [θret'], *n.* 1. a promise or warning that one will do harm, depending upon certain conditions. Ex. *Your threats will not stop me from going.* 2. an indication that something harmful or not desired probably will happen. Ex. *The threat of rain drove us inside.* —**threat'en,** *v.* 1. warn that one will do harm, depending on certain conditions. Ex. *They threatened to kill him if he did not go with them.* 2. indicate that something harmful will probably happen; be a possible danger or threat. Ex. *The rising flood waters threatened the town.*

three (1) [θriy'], *n., adj.* the number between two and four; the number *3.*

threshold (4) [θreš'(h)owld], *n.* 1. the piece of wood, stone, etc. which extends from one side of the door frame to the other beneath the door. Ex. *He carried his bride over the threshold.* 2. the entering or beginning point of something. Ex. *She was on the threshold of a new career.*

---

a, far; æ, am; e, get; ey, late; i, in; iy, see; ɔ, all; ow, go; u, put; uw, too; ə, but, ago; ər, fur; aw, out; ay, life; oy, boy; ŋ, ring; θ, think; ð, that; ž, measure; š, ship; j, edge; č, child.

threw (1) [θruw'], *v.* past tense of *throw*. **Ex.** *They threw their hats into the air.*

thrift (5) [θrift'], *n.* economy; careful use of resources to avoid waste. **Ex.** *Her thrift saved them enough money to make the down payment on a house.* —**thrift**'y, *adj.*

thrill (3) [θril'], *v.* 1. feel or cause to feel sudden emotion or excitement. **Ex.** *The music thrilled them.* 2. shake or shiver because of excitement. **Ex.** *Her voice thrilled with delight.* —*n.* 1. a shiver caused by emotion. **Ex.** *Meeting with the president gave him a thrill.* 2. something that causes a shiver of excitement. **Ex.** *Piloting a plane was a new thrill for her.* —**thrill**'er, *n.* something thrilling, especially an exciting novel, play, etc.

thrive (5) [θrayv'], *v.* 1. prosper; grow rich; succeed. **Ex.** *His new business is thriving.* 2. grow with vigor and strength. **Ex.** *That plant will thrive with daily watering.*

throat (2) [θrowt'], *n.* the passage leading from the mouth to a tube through which food goes to the stomach. **Ex.** *The dry bread was stuck in my throat.*

throb (5) [θrab'], *v.* beat or pound with unusual force or speed, as the heart does when one has been running. **Ex.** *His injured leg throbbed with pain.* —*n.* a throbbing or pounding. **Ex.** *They could feel the throb of the engines as the plane started.*

throne (3) [θrown'], *n.* 1. the special chair on which a ruler or high official sits during certain ceremonies. **Ex.** *The throne had been used by kings for hundreds of years.* 2. the authority that a ruler has; also the ruler himelf. **Ex.** *The throne expressed its disapproval.*

throng (4) [θrɔːŋ'], *n.* a large gathering of people; a crowd. **Ex.** *A throng of admirers awaited him.* —*v.* move into, around, etc. in large numbers. **Ex.** *People thronged into the park to hear the president.*

through (1) [θruw'], *prep.* 1. in at one end and out at the other; from front to back; from top to bottom. **Ex.** *The dog ran through the garden.* 2. by means of; with the help of. **Ex.** *He got his job through a friend.* 3. during. **Ex.** *We talked all through dinner.* 4. by way of. **Ex.** *He went through the hall into the bedroom.* —*adv.* 1. from beginning to end. **Ex.** *He read the letter through.* 2. entirely; completely. **Ex.** *Her clothes were wet through by the rain.* — *adj.* finished. **Ex.** *Are you through with your work?*

throughout (3) [θruwawt'], *prep.* entirely through; everywhere in. **Ex.** *They traveled throughout the country.* — *adv.* entirely, everywhere. **Ex.** *The bowl is silver throughout.*

throw (1) [θrow'], *v.* 1. cause to go through the air by a movement of the arm. **Ex.** *The boys were throwing the ball to one another.* 2. place in a certain position or situation, often suddenly and with force; hurl. **Exs.** *They decided to throw more soldiers into action. The storm may throw the ship against the rocks.* 3. put on carelessly or hastily. **Ex.** *As soon as he could throw his coat on, he rushed out.* 4. send; direct. **Ex.** *Throw the light over here.* —*n.* the act of throwing. **Ex.** *His first throw was too high.* —**throw away, throw out,** dispose of. **Ex.** *Please throw away the empty cans.* —**throw off,** 1. free oneself from. **Ex.** *He could not throw off his cold.* 2. send out. **Ex.** *The fire was throwing off a lot of smoke.* —**throw up,** become sick and force food from the stomach up through the mouth. **Ex.** *He was trying not to throw up his dinner.*

thrown [θrown'], *v.* past participle of *throw.* **Ex.** *She was thrown from her horse.*

thrust (3) [θrəst'], *v.* 1. push with force. **Ex.** *She thrust the door open.* 2. cause to pass into or through. **Ex.** *He thrust the oar into the water.* —*n.* 1. a quick, hard push. **Ex.** *He knocked the man down with a thrust of his elbow.* 2. the act of causing to pass into or through. **Ex.** *The hunter killed the animal with one thrust of the knife.*

thumb (3) [θəm'], *n.* 1. the short, thick finger opposite the other four. **Ex.** *He accidentally hit his thumb with the hammer.* 2. the part of the glove that covers the thumb. **Ex.** *Your glove has a hole in the thumb.*

thumbtack [θəm'tæk'], *n.* a short tack with a large flat head, which can be used to fasten things to a surface by pressing with the thumb.

thump (4) [θəmp'], *n.* the sound of a blow made by a heavy or thick object. **Ex.** *I heard a thump as he fell.* —*v.* 1. hit so as to make a dull, heavy sound. **Ex.** *The dog thumped his tail on the floor.*

thunder (2) [θən'dər], *n.* 1. a loud, heavy rolling sound that usually follows a flash of lightning. **Ex.** *The thunder woke the children.* 2. any loud, heavy rolling sound. **Ex.** *We heard the distant thunder of the guns.* —*v.* produce a loud, heavy rolling sound. **Ex.** *The trucks thundered over the road.* —**thun'der·ous,** *adj.*

thunderbolt [θən'dərbowlt'], *n.* a flash of lightning accompanied by thunder.

thundershower [θən'dəršaw'ər], *n.* a brief rainfall with lightning and thunder.

thunderstorm [θən'dərstɔrm'], *n.* a heavy rainstorm with lightning and thunder.

Thursday (1) [θərz'diy], *n.* the fifth day of the week.

thus (2) [ðəs'], *adv.* 1. in this or that way; in the following way. **Ex.** *The money thus obtained was spent for food.* 2. therefore; consequently. **Ex.** *The bus broke down; thus, I was late for work.* 3. to this or that degree, point or time. **Ex.** *Thus far he has done the work alone.*

tick (4) [tik'], *n.* a light, sharp repeated sound as of a clock. **Ex.** *The silence was broken only by the tick of the clock.* —*v.* make a ticking sound. **Ex.** *The watch ticked loudly.*

ticket (2) [tik'it], *n.* 1. a piece of paper, cardboard, etc., that shows the holder has a right to a seat in a theater, on a train, etc., usually because he has paid for it. **Ex.** *He had just enough money for the price of his plane ticket.* 2. a small piece of paper or cardboard attached to an article for sale showing its price, size, etc. **Ex.** *According to the ticket, the price of the dress had been reduced.* 3. a list of candidates chosen by a political party to run for election. **Ex.** *He voted for all the candidates on his party's ticket.* — *v.* issue or attach a ticket to. **Ex.** *The clerk ticketed the coats.*

tickle (4) [tik'əl], *v.* 1. touch lightly on the body with a finger, a feather, etc., so as to cause a pleasantly exciting sensation; feel this sensation. **Ex.** *She tickled the baby.* 2. excite agreeably; delight. **Ex.** *The dog's trick tickled the children and made them laugh.* —*n.* a light, slightly stinging or tingling sensation. **Ex.** *He felt a tickle in his throat.* —**tick'lish,** *adj.*

tide (2) [tayd'], *n.* 1. the daily rising and falling of the surface of oceans and the bodies of water connected with them, caused by the attraction of the moon and sun, occurring about every twelve hours. **Ex.** *They like to walk along the beach at low tide.* 2. any such current or movement of water. **Ex.** *The tide carried the boat out to sea.* 3. a tendency, flow, etc. **Ex.** *The tide of public opinion went against him.* —*v.* help until a time of difficulty has passed. **Ex.** *Here's some money to tide you over until payday.* —**tid'al,** *adj.*

tidings (5) [tay'diŋz], *n.* a message; information; news. **Ex.** *He brought sad tidings.*

tie (1) [tay'], *v.* 1. secure, bind or fasten, as with a string. **Ex.** *Please tie this package tightly.* 2. form a knot in order to fasten. **Ex.** *She tied the ribbon into a pretty bow.* 3. limit; restrict. **Ex.** *Caring for the children ties her down.* 4. even or equal the score of a game. **Ex.** *Our team tied the score.* —*n.* 1. anything which unites, binds or joins. **Ex.** *Business ties brought them together.* 2. a narrow cloth worn around the neck by men. **Ex.** *He was wearing a blue and white striped tie.* 3. a contest in which the score is equal at some point or remains equal. **Ex.** *The game ended in a tie.* —**tie up,** 1. tie. **Ex.** *He tied up the package.* 2. keep from action; delay **Ex.** *The traffic tied us up for hours.*

tiger (3) [tay'gər], *n.* a large, strong cat with fur of dark yellow marked with narrow black bands. **Ex.** *The tiger leaped upon the deer.* —**ti'gress,** *n.* female tiger.

TIGER

tight (2) [tayt'], *adj.* 1. firmly and closely fixed in place; not easily moved; secure. **Ex.** *Each joint of the chair was tight and strong.* 2. too closely fitting. **Ex.** *The left shoe is tight.* 3. built so that water or air cannot pass through. **Ex.** *They put a tight roof on the house.* —*adv.* firmly; securely. **Ex.** *Hold tight to the rope.* —**tight'en,** *v.* —**tight'ness,** *n.* —**tight'ly,** *adv.* —**tights',** *n. pl.* tight-fitting clothing worn on the legs and hips by certain athletes, dancers, etc.

tightfisted [tayt'fis'tid], *adj.* not willing to give or spend; miserly. **Ex.** *He is very tightfisted with his money.*

tile (4) [tayl], *n.* a thin piece of stone or baked clay used for roofs, floors, etc.; pipes and hollow blocks of such materials. **Ex.** *Some of the roof tiles were broken.* —*v.* place tiles on. **Ex.** *They tiled the bathroom floor.*

till (1) [til'], *prep.* 1. up to the time of; until. **Ex.** *Wait till tomorrow.* 2. before. **Ex.** *I cannot leave till five o'clock.* —*conj.* up to the time that; until. **Ex.** *He waited till she arrived.*

---

till (1) [til'], *v.* work land in order to produce crops by plowing, seeding, etc. **Ex.** *He has tilled the soil all his life.* —**till'er**, *n.*

till (1) [til'], *n.* a drawer, box, etc. where money is kept in a store, restaurant, etc. **Ex.** *The manager counted the money in the till.*

tilt (4) [tilt'], *v.* incline; slope; slant. **Ex.** *He tilted the chair back too far and fell.* —*n.* any slanting, sloping or leaning to one side. **Ex.** *The floor of the old house has a noticeable tilt.*

timber (3) [tim'bər], *n.* 1. wood suitable for building houses, ships, etc.; lumber. **Ex.** *What kind of timber was used for the frame of the house?* 2. growing trees; wooded land. **Ex.** *There were several acres of fine timber on the farm.* 3. a heavy, single piece of wood forming part of a structure. **Ex.** *Heavy timbers supported the roof.*

time (1) [taym'], *n.* 1. the particular or exact moment, hour, day, etc. **Ex.** *What time shall I come?* 2. a particular period. **Ex.** *I was away at the time he was sick.* 3. the number of minutes, hours, days, etc. that something continued or endured. **Ex.** *We will be gone only a short time.* 4. the number of occasions on which something is repeated; frequency. **Ex.** *She visited us several times.* 5. opportunity. **Ex.** *Can you find time to help me?* —*v.* 1. measure or record the length of time, the rate of speed, etc. **Ex.** *She timed his speech.* 2. choose or arrange a suitable moment or occasion. **Ex.** *He timed his visit to suit her convenience.* —**times'**, *v.* multiplied by. **Ex.** *Two times five is ten.* —**time'ly**, *adj.* occurring at the proper or needed time. **Ex.** *He gave us timely advice.* —**at one time,** 1. together. **Ex.** *They all arrived at one time.* 2. at a time in the past. **Ex.** *At one time, there was a house on this spot.* —**at the same time,** 1. together. **Ex.** *They all laughed at the same time.* 2. nevertheless; however. **Ex.** *We want to go, but at the same time we do not want to fly.* —**behind the times,** old-fashioned. **Ex.** *Your ideas of dress are behind the times.* —**from time to time,** occasionally. **Ex.** *We see her from time to time.* —**in time,** 1. early enough. **Ex.** *We rushed the child to the doctor in time to save her life.* 2. eventually. **Ex.** *In time, you will understand what I mean.* —**on time,** 1. at the right time. **Ex.** *He arrived at work on time.* 2. with payments to be made at agreed upon periods of a month, week, etc. **Ex.** *He bought the car on time.*

timekeeper [taym'kiyp`ər], *n.* one who measures or records the time. **Ex.** *The timekeeper said that I was the fastest runner in the race.*

timetable [taym'tey`bəl], *n.* a schedule of arrival and departure times for trains, buses, etc. **Ex.** *Look at the timetable and see when the train is scheduled to arrive.*

timid (4) [tim'id], *adj.* lacking in confidence; cautious; fearful. **Ex.** *The timid child would not greet the guests.* —**tim'id·ly**, *adv.* —**ti·mid'i·ty**, *n.*

tin (2) [tin'], *n.* 1. a soft, silver-colored metal that is easily shaped. **Ex.** *A tin can is made of steel protected by a coating of tin.* 2. a container for baking, sometimes made partly of this metal. **Ex.** *She washed the bread tins.* —*adj.* of tin. **Ex.** *The house has a tin roof.*

tinge (5) [tinj'], *v.* 1. color slightly. **Ex.** *The sky at sunset was tinged with pink.* 2. give a slight trace of color, odor, taste, etc. **Ex.** *Her happiness was tinged with doubt.* —*n.* a slight trace. **Ex.** *There was a tinge of gray in her hair.*

tingle (5) [tiŋ'gəl], *v.* cause or have a stinging sensation as from excitement, noise, cold, etc. **Ex.** *Her ears tingled at the sound of the whistle.*

tinkle (5) [tiŋ'kəl], *v.* make or cause to make a series of short, light ringing sounds. **Ex.** *The little bells tinkled.* —*n.* a short, light ringing sound. **Ex.** *We heard the tinkle of ice in their glasses.*

tint (4) [tint'], *n.* a light shade of a color; a pale, delicate color. **Ex.** *There was a tint of red in her cheeks.* —*v.* color slightly. **Ex.** *She tints her hair.*

tiny (2) [tay'niy], *adj.* very small. **Ex.** *The baby put his tiny hand in mine.*

-tion (1) [šən'], *suffix.* 1. act of. **Exs.** *Accuse, accusation; register, registration.* 2. state of. **Exs.** *Relate, relation; starve, starvation.* 3. result of. **Exs.** *Perfect, perfection; connect, connection.*

tip (2) [tip'], *n.* 1. the pointed or rounded end of something. **Ex.** *The tip of his nose was sunburned.* 2. a cap or small part of metal, rubber, etc. placed on the end of something. **Ex.** *My shoelace had lost its tip.* —*v.* cover the end of. **Ex.** *His cane is tipped with rubber.*

tip (1) [tip'], *v.* 1. incline something so that it falls over; upset. **Ex.** *The child tipped over the glass of milk.* 2. Place on an incline; slant. **Ex.** *He tipped his hat as he passed me.*

tip (1) [tip'], *v.* give a small sum of money to someone for a special service provided. **Ex.** *He tipped the waiter generously.*

—*n.* a small gift of money for services provided. **Ex.** *She gave a tip to the taxi driver.* —**tip'per,** *n.* one who tips.

tiptoe [tip'tow'], *v.* walk quietly by rising on one's toes. **Ex.** *He tiptoed up the stairs.*

tire (2) [tayr'], *v.* 1. lessen the strength of by work, exercise, etc.; become weary or exhausted. **Ex.** *She tires easily.* 2. bore. **Ex.** *Hearing the same story again and again tires me.* —**tired',** *adj.* —**tire'some,** *adj.* causing weariness or boredom. —**tire'less,** *adj.* without becoming tired. **Ex.** *He's a tireless worker.*

tire (2) [tayr'], *n.* a solid or air-filled tube or band made of rubber or something similar that is placed on the wheel of a bicycle, car, truck etc. **Ex.** *There is a spare tire in the trunk of the car.*

tissue (4) [tiš'uw], *n.* 1. a group of cells forming a particular kind of structural material in a plant or animal. **Ex.** *Nerve tissue in his arm was damaged as a result of the accident.* 2. a soft, thin paper that takes in moisture. **Ex.** *Here is a tissue; blow your nose.* 3. a thin light paper used for wrapping and packing. **Ex.** *She wrapped the gift in blue tissue and tied it with white ribbon.*

title (2) [tay'təl], *n.* 1. the name given to a book, picture, movie, etc. **Ex.** *Have you chosen a title for your story?* 2. a word describing the rank, occupation, etc. of a person, which is usually used with the person's name. **Ex.** *We all address him by his title of "Doctor."* 3. a legal right to the possession of property; evidence of ownership. **Ex.** *We have the title to this house.* —**ti'tled,** *adj.* having a title, especially of nobility such as "king," "queen," "lord," etc.

to (1) [tuw'], *prep.* 1. showing the direction of an action; showing the place toward which an action is directed. **Ex.** *He ran to the door.* 2. showing the ending in time of an action; until. **Ex.** *He works from nine to six.* 3. pointing to the result of an action. **Ex.** *To her surprise, they arrived early.* 4. belonging with; involved with. **Ex.** *I want this room to myself.* 5. when compared with. **Ex.** *His income is equal to mine.* 6. showing the person or thing for whom or which an action is performed. **Ex.** *Give the book to him.* —used before the simple, or infinitive, form a verb. **Ex.** *I have to leave now.*

toad (4) [towd'], *n.* a small animal that looks like a frog but lives most of its life on land. **Ex.** *A greenish-brown toad lived in the corner of our garden.*

toadstool [towd'stuwl'], *n.* a mushroom, particularly a poisonous one. **Ex.** *He died from eating a toadstool by mistake.*

toast (3) [towst'], *v.* brown by placing over or before a fire or hot surface. **Ex.** *She toasted some bread for breakfast.* —*n.* bread browned over or before a fire or hot surface. **Ex.** *How many slices of toast do you want?* — **toast'er**, *n.* a device for browning bread.

toast (3) [towst'], *n.* the raising of glasses and drinking as an expression of honor toward someone or something. **Ex.** *At the dinner they drank a toast to the president of the organization.* —*v.* drink to the honor of someone or something. **Ex.** *They toasted the newly married couple.* — **toast'mas'ter**, *n.* one who proposes toasts and introduces speakers at dinners, banquets, etc.

tobacco (2) [təbæk'ow], *n.* a plant, the leaves of which are dried for smoking in cigarettes, cigars, etc.; the dried, prepared leaves of this plant. **Ex.** *He put some tobacco in his pipe and lighted it.*

today (1) [tədey'], *adv.* 1. on this present day. **Ex.** *Write the letter and mail it today.* 2. at or in the present time or period. **Ex.** *Today some airplanes travel faster than sound.* —*n.* 1. the present day. **Ex.** *The lesson for today is easy.* 2. this present time or period. **Ex.** *The women of today have more freedom than those of yesterday.*

toe [tow'], *n.* 1. one of the five end parts of the foot. **Ex.** *Someone stepped on my toe in the crowded bus.* 2. the portion of a stocking or shoe that covers these five parts of the foot. **Ex.** *She has a hole in the toe of her stocking.*

together (1) [təgeð'ər], *adv.* 1. in or into one group or place. **Ex.** *The boys were brought together for a meeting.* 2. at the same time; at one time. **Ex.** *They all left the building together.* 3. in or into contact with each other. **Ex.** *The swift current smashed the two boats together.* 4. by combined action; in cooperation. **Ex.** *They worked together to make the plan a success.*

toil (3) [toyl'], *v.* 1. do difficult, tiring work. **Ex.** *They toiled in the fields.* 2. move with difficulty. **Ex.** *They toiled up the mountain.* —*n.* tiring work. **Ex.** *His back was bent by toil.* —**toil'er**, *n.*

a, far; æ, am; e, get; ey, late; i, in; iy, see; ɔ, all; ow, go; u, put; uw, too; ə, but, ago; ər, fur; aw, out; ay, life; oy, boy; ŋ, ring; θ, think; ð, that; ž, measure; š, ship; ǰ, edge; č, child.

toilet (4) [toy'lit], *n.* a bowl with a seat and lid connected to a plumbing system, used for the disposal of body waste. **Ex.** *The youngest child has not yet learned how to use the toilet.*

token (4) [tow'kən], *n.* 1. a sign; something kept for memory's sake. **Ex.** *This gift is a token of our respect for you.* 2. a piece of stamped metal used in place of money, especially for bus and train fare. **Ex.** *The price of bus tokens has increased again.*

told (1) [towld'], *v.* past tense and participle of *tell.* **Exs.** *She told him to leave. Had you told her you were going to be late?*

tolerant (5) [tal'ərənt], *adj.* having a fair and liberal attitude toward those who differ in opinion, race, religion, politics, etc. **Ex.** *His travels in foreign countries had helped to make him tolerant.* —**tol'er·ant·ly,** *adv.* —**tol'er·ate`,** *v.* 1. allow; permit. **Ex.** *The principal would not tolerate smoking in the school building.* 2. endure; bear. **Ex.** *She tolerates him for the gifts he brings.* —**tol'er·ance,** *n.* —**tol'er·a·tion,** *n.*

toll (4) [towl'], *v.* 1. ring a large, heavy bell with single strokes, slowly and evenly, especially to announce a death. **Ex.** *He tolled the church bell.* 2. sound or announce by tolling. **Ex.** *The bell tolled midnight.* —*n.* the sound of a bell struck in this manner. **Ex.** *We heard the mournful toll of the bell.*

toll (4) [towl'], *n.* 1. a payment for some privilege given, such as traveling over a road, or for some service performed, such as making a long-distance telephone call. **Ex.** *Cars have to pay a toll to cross that bridge.* 2. the amount of loss resulting from an accident, fire, flood, etc. **Ex.** *The fire took a heavy toll.*

tomato (3) [təmey'tow, təma'tow], *n.* a plant bearing a red or yellow fruit which is used as a vegetable; the fruit itself. **Ex.** *She served sliced tomatoes with the main course.*

tomb (4) [tuwm'], *n.* a hole dug in the earth, an opening made in a rock or a building constructed to receive a dead body; a grave. **Ex.** *When their leader died, the people placed his body in a large tomb.*

tomorrow (1) [təma:r'ow, təmɔ:r'ow], *adv.* 1. on the day following this present day. **Ex.** *This work must be completed tomorrow.* 2. of or at a future time or period. **Ex.** *Tomorrow men may live in outer space.* —*n.* 1. the day after this present day. **Ex.** *Today is Sunday; tomorrow will be Monday.* 2. a future time or period. **Ex.** *We dream of a tomorrow with no wars.*

ton (3) [tən'], *n.* a unit of weight equal to 2,000 pounds. **Ex.** *How many tons of coal does this mine produce yearly?* See **Weights and Measures.**

tone (2) [town'], *n.* 1. a sound; the quality of a sound. **Ex.** *I like the tone of this piano.* 2. a manner of speaking or writing that expresses feeling. **Ex.** *She spoke to him in a friendly tone.* 3. the condition of the body and its parts. **Ex.** *Swimming will improve your muscle tone.* 4. a quality of color. **Ex.** *I like that tone of red.* —*v.* improve or strengthen the quality or condition of. **Ex.** *He toned his body by exercising.* —**tone down,** make less noisy, colorful, harsh, etc. **Ex.** *I toned down the angry language of the letter.*

tongue (2) [təŋ'], *n.* 1. the movable organ in the mouth with which one speaks or tastes. **Ex.** *The hot soup burned his tongue.* 2. a language. **Ex.** *He speaks the English tongue.* 3. the manner or tone of speech. **Ex.** *She has a sharp tongue.* —**hold one's tongue,** avoid or refrain from speaking. **Ex.** *I asked her to hold her tongue.* —**lose one's tongue,** not be able to speak. **Ex.** *Was it fright that caused you to lose your tongue?* —**tongue'-tied',** *adj.* not able to speak well because of a physical defect or because of embarrassment, shyness, etc. **Ex.** *The tongue-tied boy was too frightened to speak.*

tonight (2) [tənayt'], *n.* the night of this present day. **Ex.** *Tonight is the only night they will be here.* —*adv.* on this present or coming night. **Ex.** *Sleep well tonight.*

too (1) [tuw], *adv.* 1. also; in addition to. **Ex.** *I, too, have heard from him.* 2. extremely. **Ex.** *It is too bad you cannot come with us.* 3. more than enough. **Ex.** *He ate too much.*

took (1) [tuk'], *v.* past tense of *take.* **Ex.** *The trip took two hours.*

tool (2) [tuwl'], *n.* 1. anything such as hammers, saws or mechanical devices made of metal, wood, etc. and used to do a special kind of work. **Ex.** *He owns several electric tools.* 2. anything or anyone used to accomplish work. **Ex.** *Words are the writer's most important tools.*

tooth (2) [tuwθ'], *n.* 1. one of the hard, bony parts growing in the mouth that is used for biting. **Ex.** *His aching tooth kept him awake all night.* 2. anything which suggests a tooth in shape. **Ex.** *A tooth of the saw is broken.*

toothpaste [tuwθ' peyst'], *n.* a paste for cleaning the teeth. **Ex.** *Where did you put the new tube of toothpaste that you bought today?*

toothpick [tuwθ'pik'], *n.* a thin, short piece of wood used for removing food stuck between the teeth.

top (1) [tap'], *n.* 1. the upper part, edge or surface; the highest point. **Ex.** *They walked up to the top of the hill.* 2. that which serves as a covering, a lid, etc. **Ex.** *Where did you put the bottle top?* 3. the stem and green parts of a plant above the ground. **Ex.** *The top of that plant cannot be eaten but the root can.* 4. the highest rank or degree reached. **Ex.** *In school he was at the top of his class.* —*adj.* at or concerning the highest. **Ex.** *Eggs are selling at top prices now.* —*v.* 1. cover or be covered at the top; crown. **Ex.** *The mountains are topped with snow.* 2. be more than or exceed in height, weight, amount, etc. **Ex.** *He topped his brother's height by three inches.* 3. be the highest in rank, grade, etc.; lead. **Ex.** *He topped his class in mathematics.*

topic (4) [tap'ik], *n.* the subject matter of a conversation, a piece of writing, etc. **Ex.** *We discussed several topics at the meeting.* —**top'i·cal,** *adj.* concerned with topics in the news, currently being discussed, etc.; timely. **Ex.** *Coming at this time, his talk on gun control was topical.*

torch (4) [torč'], *n.* a hand-carried burning light, such as a piece of wood soaked with some substance that burns easily. **Ex.** *The Statue of Liberty holds a torch in her right hand.*

tore (1) [to:r'], *v.* past tense of *tear.* **Ex.** *She tore her dress when she fell.*

torment (4) [torment'], *v.* 1. cause great physical or mental suffering. **Ex.** *She was tormented by fears.* 2. bother greatly. **Ex.** *The child tormented his mother with questions.* —**tor'ment,** *n.* 1. great physical or mental suffering. **Ex.** *He was in torment from his wound.* 2. that which causes suffering, concern or trouble. **Ex.** *Unpaid bills were a torment to them.*

torn (2) [torn'], *v.* past participle of *tear.* **Ex.** *His coat was torn at the shoulder.*

tornado [torney'dow], *n.* a whirling column of air that moves violently at an extremely high speed, usually destroying everything on the ground in its path. **Ex.** *Every house in the northern section of town was flattened by the tornado.*

torrent (5) [tɔːrˈənt], *n.* 1. a violent, rapidly flowing stream of water. **Ex.** *The heavy rain turned the stream into a torrent.* 2. any similar violent, rapid flow or fall. **Ex.** *He replied with a torrent of curses.* —**tor·ren'tial,** *adj.*

torrid [tɔrˈid], *adj.* extremely hot. **Ex.** *The torrid weather completely exhausted her.*

torture (3) [tɔrˈčər], *n.* 1. the act of causing severe physical or mental pain in order to punish, be cruel to or acquire information from. **Ex.** *The torture made him confess to crimes he had not committed.* 2. severe physical or mental pain. **Ex.** *It was torture for the sick man to be moved.* —*v.* cause severe physical or mental pain. **Ex.** *The prisoners were tortured.*

toss (3) [tɔːsˈ], *v.* 1. throw something lightly, without much force. **Ex.** *He tossed his hat on the chair.* 2. throw or be thrown from side to side or back and forth. **Ex.** *The ship was tossed by the waves.* 3. raise with a sudden sharp motion. **Ex.** *She tossed her head angrily.* —*n.* the act of tossing. **Ex.** *The running player caught the football on a long toss.*

total (2) [towˈtəl], *adj.* 1. entire. **Ex.** *What is the total amount of the bill?* 2. complete. **Ex.** *As a result of the fire, the building was a total loss.* —*n.* the result of adding; the entire amount. **Ex.** *Add these numbers and tell me the total.* —*v.* add; learn the whole amount by adding the parts together. **Ex.** *The clerk totaled the bill.* —**to'tal·ly,** *adv.* entirely. **Ex.** *She was totally confused.*

totalitarian (4) [towtælˈətəːrˈiyən], *adj.* concerning a government in which the ruling party has complete control and allows no other parties to exist. **Ex.** *The country is ruled by a totalitarian government.* —*n.* one who supports such a government. —**to·tal·i·tar'i·an·ism',** *n.* belief in such a government.

totter (5) [tatˈər], *v.* sway in an unsteady way. **Ex.** *The building tottered and fell.* 2. move with unsteady steps. **Ex.** *The old man tottered to his chair.*

touch (1) [təčˈ], *v.* 1. place a finger, hand, etc. on or in something to feel it; come or bring into physical contact with something. **Ex.** *She burned her finger when she touched the hot stove.* 2. affect so as to influence or impress. **Ex.** *The child's suffering touched my heart.* 3. refer to slightly; mention briefly; concern with. **Ex.** *We only touched on the subject of money in our talks.* 4. handle or use. **Ex.** *The children were not allowed to touch those dishes.* —*n.* 1. state of touching or being touched. **Ex.** *I felt the touch of a hand on my shoulder.* 2. the sense through which the body perceives or becomes aware of something by contact with it. **Ex.** *One touch told her he had a high fever.* 3. the sensation one gets when feeling something. **Ex.** *The baby's skin had a soft touch.* 4. small amount. **Ex.** *The meat needs a touch of salt.* —**touch'ing,** *adj.* having an effect on one's feelings. **Ex.** *The ragged boy was a touching sight.* —**touch'y,** *adj.* quick to become angry, annoyed, etc. **Ex.** *He is very touchy in the morning.* —**touch off,** cause; start. **Ex.** *He touched off the explosion with a match.* —**touch up,** improve or repair something by making small changes. **Ex.** *The photograph was much clearer after it had been touched up.*

tough (3) [təf'], *adj.* 1. strong and long-lasting; not easily torn. **Ex.** *His shoes are made of tough leather.* 2. not easily cut or chewed. **Ex.** *This meat is tough.* 3. able to endure much without becoming sick or quitting. **Ex.** *Soldiers have to be tough.* —**tough'en,** *v.* make or become tough. —**tough'ness,** *n.*

tour (4) [tuwr'], *n.* a long trip from place to place within a city, country, etc. **Ex.** *They went on a world tour last year.* —*v.* travel from place to place; go on a tour of. **Ex.** *They are touring several countries.* —**tour'ist,** *n.* one who travels for pleasure or education rather than business.

tournament (5) [tər'nəmənt], *n.* games or contests among individuals or teams for the purpose of winning a championship. **Ex.** *Are you entering the tennis tournament?*

tow (5) [tow'], *v.* draw along, as by a rope or chain. **Ex.** *They towed the wrecked car to the garage.* —*n.* a towing; that which is towed. **Ex.** *The car would not start so we got a tow.*

toward (1) [tɔrd', tow'ərd], **towards** [tɔrdz', tow'ərdz], *prep.* 1. in the direction of. **Ex.** *They walked toward the lake.* 2. with respect to; about. **Ex.** *How do you feel toward him?* 3. leading to; for. **Ex.** *They are working toward a better understanding.* 4. shortly before. **Ex.** *It happened toward the end of the day.*

towel (4) [taw'əl], *n.* a cloth or paper used to make things dry by wiping. **Ex.** *May I please have a clean towel to dry the dishes?* —**tow'el·ing,** *n.* material from which towels are made.

tower (2) [taw'ər], *n.* a structure which is very much taller than it is wide and is usually part of a building. **Ex.** *The bell in the church tower was ringing.* —*v.* be much taller than; rise far above other objects or people. **Ex.** *The tall building towered above its neighbors.*

town (1) [tawn], *n.* 1. a center where many people live, larger than a village but not as large as a city. **Ex.** *He lives in the middle of town.* 2. the people of the town. **Ex.** *The whole town came to hear him.* 3. a city. **Ex.** *Where is your hometown?* 4. the center or shopping district of a town or city. **Ex.** *We are going to town this afternoon.*

town hall [tawn' hɔ:l'], the building in which a town government is located, where licenses are obtained, etc. —**town'ship,** *n.* the area governed by a city or town government.

toy (2) [toy'], *n.* something for play rather than work, usually a child's game, doll, stuffed animal, etc. **Ex.** *The children put their toys away before going to bed.* —*adj.* like a toy; made for play. **Ex.** *The children were playing with toy cars.* —*v.* treat or consider lightly, without serious thought or intent. **Ex.** *The sick man toyed with his food.*

trace (2) [treys'], *n.* 1. a mark or other evidence left behind which shows that someone or something has passed. **Ex.** *Sorrow had left its traces on her face.* 2. an almost unnoticeable quantity of something. **Ex.** *There were traces of poison in the cup.* —*v.* 1. follow by finding the trail of marks or other evidence left behind. **Ex.** *The police traced the thief to his hiding place.* 2. follow the course, development, etc. of. **Ex.** *That book traces the history of the Democratic Party.* 3. go back from a particular time, place, etc. to find the origins of. **Ex.** *He traced his family to Ireland.* 4. copy a painting or picture by a placing a thin piece of paper over it and marking the lines seen through the paper. **Ex.** *The children traced the pictures in the book.*

track (2) [træk'], *n.* 1. a mark left behind by anything that has passed. **Ex.** *The hunters saw the tracks of a bear.* 2. a path or trail made by the feet of men or animals. **Ex.** *That track leads to a stream.* 3. the lines of steel rails on which railroad trains move. **Ex.** *The children crossed the railroad tracks on their way to school.* 4. a course laid out for some particular purpose, as for sports. **Ex.** *They spent the day at the racetrack.* —*adj.* having to do with sports performed on a track. **Ex.** *The runner was wearing his track shoes.* —*v.* 1. follow the tracks of. **Ex.** *The dogs tracked the fox to its hole.* 2. leave as marks something such as dirt, snow, etc. carried on the feet. **Ex.** *The children tracked mud into the house.* —**keep track of,** continue to have current knowledge of. **Ex.** *Did you keep track of any of your schoolmates after you left school?* —**lose track of,** not continue to have current knowledge of. **Ex.** *When did you lose track of him?*

tract (4) [trækt'], *n.* an area of land; a region. **Ex.** *During the spring floods, some tracts of land were under water.*

tractor (4) [træk'tər], *n.* a motor-driven piece of farm equipment used to do the work formerly done by horses or oxen, such as plowing or pulling heavy loads. **Ex.** *The farmer attached the plow to the tractor.*

trade (1) [treyd'], *n.* 1. the act or business of buying and selling; commerce. **Ex.** *Trade between the two countries has increased this year.* 2. the exchange of one thing for another. **Ex.** *I gave him a piece of candy in trade for a piece of gum.* 3. those engaged in the same business considered as a group. **Ex.** *That news was of interest to the automobile trade.* 4. an occupation using the hands which requires special training and ability. **Ex.** *The young man is learning the shoemaker's trade.* —*v.* 1. buy and sell; be engaged in commerce. **Ex.** *This country trades with most other countries of the world.* 2. exchange. **Ex.** *Please trade seats with me.* —**trad'er,** *n.* one who buys, sells and trades goods.

trademark [treyd'mark'], *n.* a mark, design or word put on a product to distinguish it and identify the maker. **Ex.** *"JS" is the trademark that appears on all medicines the Jones-Smith Company makes.*

tradition (3) [trədiš'ən], *n.* customs and beliefs which have been followed for generations and which have been passed from the elders to the young people, usually by speech or example. **Ex.** *It is a tradition in that family for the sons to study medicine.* —**tra·di'tion·al,** *adj.*

traffic (3) [træf'ik], *n.* 1. the flow of persons, cars, ships, etc. along a street, river, etc. **Ex.** *There is heavy traffic on this street.* 2. the business of transportation. **Ex.** *That shipping company has doubled its passenger traffic in the past year.* 3. the business of buying, selling and trading, often of an illegal kind. **Ex.** *The increase in drug traffic is a very serious problem for this country.* —*adj.* —*v.* buy, sell and trade, often illegally. **Ex.** *He was accused of trafficking in stolen goods.*

traffic light [træf'ik layt'], a red, green or yellow electric road light that directs and controls traffic by telling drivers when to stop, go or proceed with caution; a set of such lights. **Ex.** *We have to turn right at the next traffic light.*

TRAFFIC LIGHT

tragedy (3) [træĵ'ədiy], *n.* 1. a serious play concerned with extremely sad events, such as the death of a hero. **Ex.** *The audience wept at the tragedy.* 2. an extremely sad event. **Ex.** *Her sudden death was a tragedy.*

tragic (3) [træĵ'ik], *adj.* 1. concerned with tragedy. **Ex.** *He was a famous tragic actor.* 2. involving much suffering or death; terrible. **Ex.** *There was a tragic accident on the highway yesterday.* —**trag'i·cal·ly,** *adv.*

trail (2) [treyl'], *n.* 1. drag or allow to drag behind; flow behind. **Ex.** *Her long evening dress trailed on the floor.* 2. follow the scent, marks or path left behind by someone or something. **Ex.** *The hunters trailed the animal to its den.* 3. be or follow behind. **Ex.** *One bicyclist trailed far behind the other riders.* 4. weaken; fade. **Ex.** *Her voice trailed off into silence.* —*n.* 1. that which follows behind. **Ex.** *The departing train left a trail of smoke.* 2. a path. **Ex.** *They followed the trail back to camp.* 3. marks or other evidence of passage left behind. **Ex.** *The wounded animal left a trail of blood.* —**trail'er,** *n.* a vehicle with no motor that is pulled by a car or truck.

train (1) [treyn'], *n.* 1. an engine and the series of connected cars which it pulls over railroad tracks. **Ex.** *He likes to travel by train.* 2. a line of persons, animals, etc. moving along together. **Ex.** *Early settlers often traveled together in wagon trains.*

train (1) [treyn'], *v.* 1. teach ways of living, acting, etc. **Ex.** *They trained their children to use good manners.* 2. prepare for a particular kind of work. **Ex.** *The men were trained to fly.* —**train'er,** *n.* a person who gives training. —**train'ee,** *n.* one who is being trained. —**train'ing,** *n.* the act of preparing; instruction. **Ex.** *He is in training to become a teacher.*

trait (5) [treyt'], *n.* a feature or quality which distinguishes one from another; a characteristic. **Ex.** *The boy has many of his father's traits.*

a, far; æ, am; e, get; ey, late; i, in; iy, see; ɔ, all; ow, go; u, put; uw, too; ə, but, ago; ər, fur; aw, out; ay, life; oy, boy; ŋ, ring; θ, think; ð, that; ž, measure; š, ship; ĵ, edge; č, child.

traitor (4) [trey'tər], *n.* one who helps the enemies of his country; one who betrays a confidence or trust. **Ex.** *The traitor sold military secrets to a foreign country.* —**trai'tor·ous,** *adj.*

tramp (3) [træmp'], *v.* 1. walk or march with a firm, heavy step. **Ex.** *The soldiers tramped along the street.* 2. bring one's foot down heavily and noisily. **Ex.** *He tramped on my foot.* 3. walk; wander for fun or exercise. **Ex.** *The boys tramped through the forest.* —*n.* 1. a firm, heavy step. **Ex.** *We heard the tramp of his feet on the stairs.* 2. a long, wandering walk. **Ex.** *He went for a tramp on the beach.* 3. a homeless wanderer who begs for food or a little money. **Ex.** *The tramp had slept in the barn.*

trample (4) [træmpəl], *v.* step heavily and roughly upon in a way that breaks, crushes, etc. **Ex.** *The cows trampled the garden.*

tranquil (5) [træŋ'kwil], *adj.* peaceful; undisturbed. **Ex.** *She enjoyed the tranquil country life.* —**tran·quil'i·ty,** *n.* —**tran'quil·ly,** *adv.*

trans- (3) [træns, trænz], *prefix.* over; across; through. **Exs.** *Arctic, transarctic; oceanic, transoceanic; Alantic; transatlantic.*

transaction (5) [trænsæk'šən, trænzæk'šən], *n.* the act of doing and completing business. **Ex.** *Buying a car was an important transaction for them.* —**trans·act',** *v.* accomplish business. **Ex.** *We do not transact any business on the weekend.*

transfer (3) [trænsfər', træns'fər], *v.* 1. move or be moved from one location, position, etc. to another. **Ex.** *He has been transferred to another job.* 2. change from one bus, train, etc. to another. **Ex.** *He was able to ride all the way home on the bus without having to transfer.* —*n.* 1. the act of transferring or being transferred. **Ex.** *He has asked for a transfer to a larger office.* 2. a slip of paper stating that a passenger can transfer from one bus, train, etc. to another. **Ex.** *I asked for a transfer when I boarded the bus.* —**trans·fera·ble,** *adj.* giving the right to change the possession of something from one person to another. **Ex.** *This ticket is not transferable.*

transform [trænsform'], *v.* change the shape, appearance or nature of. **Ex.** *The dress transformed the girl into a young lady.* —**trans'for·ma'tion,** *n.*

transistor [trænzis'tər], *n.* a very small electronic device used to vary the electric current in radios, television sets, computers and other equipment. **Ex.** *The repairman said we need to replace the transistor in the radio.*

transit (5) [træn'sit, træn'zit], *n.* 1. the passage from one place to another over or through. **Ex.** *My point of transit to Europe will be New York.* 2. the process of carrying things or persons or of being carried. **Ex.** *That city has several systems of transit.*

translate (3) [trænsleyt', trænz'leyt], *v.* 1. express the meaning of the words of one language in those of another. **Ex.** *He translated the poem into English.* —**trans·la'tion,** *n.* the act of translating; the result of translating. **Ex.** *I have read an excellent translation of his book.* —**trans'la·tor,** *n.* one who translates.

transmit (5) [trænsmit, trænzmit'], *v.* 1. pass from one person or place to another. **Ex.** *Her illness was transmitted to other members of the family.* 2. allow to pass through. **Ex.** *These walls are too thick to transmit sound.* 3. send out a signal by means of radio waves. **Ex.** *His message was transmitted by radio.* —**trans·mit'ter,** *n.* the equipment by which the signals are actually sent. **Ex.** *The radio station transmitter is located on top of that mountain.* —**trans·mis'sion,** *n.* the transmitting process.

transparent (4) [trænspær'ənt, trænspe:r'ənt], *adj.* 1. admitting the passage of light because of thinness, clearness, etc. so that what is on the other side, or beyond, may be seen. **Ex.** *For privacy, they changed the clear glass in the front door for some less transparent glass.* 2. light and thin; not convincing; obvious. **Ex.** *His excuse for being late was a transparent lie.*

transplant [trænsplænt'], *v.* 1. move a plant from one location to another and put it into the soil again. **Ex.** *We transplanted these bushes on either side of the door from the back garden.* 2. move an organ, piece of skin, etc. from one part of the body to another or from one person to another; perform similar operations on animals. **Ex.** *The doctor transplanted skin to the burned areas.* —*n.* the act or operation of transplanting. **Ex.** *He has been told that he needs a heart transplant.*

transport (3) [trænsport'], *v.* carry from one place to another. **Ex.** *Were the goods transported by rail or by truck?* —**trans'por·ta'tion,** *n.* the means or business of transporting. **Ex.** *We have both bus and subway transportation in this area.*

trap (3) [træp'], *n.* 1. a device used for catching animals, especially by hunters. **Ex.** *He put the meat in the trap to attract the lion.* 2. a device, trick or situation prepared for attracting and catching or deceiving someone. **Ex.** *The police set a trap to catch the escaped prisoner.* —*v.* catch or deceive by a trap. **Ex.** *She was trapped by the lawyer's clever questions.*

trash [træš], *n.* 1. waste; useless material; refuse. Ex. *The trash is picked up twice a week in this neighborhood.* 2. something that is of little worth or poor quality. Ex. *His latest novel is simply trash.*

travel [træv'əl], *v.* 1. go on a journey; move about on a trip. Ex. *He travels a good deal in his work.* 2. pass through or over. Ex. *We usually travel this road on our way to work.* 3. move. Ex. *How fast can this car travel?* —*n.* the act of traveling. Ex. *She enjoys travel.* —**trav'els,** *n. pl.* journey. Ex. *The explorer told us about his travels in the far north.* —**trav'el·er,** *n.* one who travels.

tray [trey'], *n.* a flat surface of wood, metal, etc. with slightly raised edges, used for carrying or holding something. Ex. *She brought the cups and saucers on a tray.*

treachery (4) [treč'əriy], *n.* disloyalty; betrayal. Ex. *They could not believe he would be guilty of treachery.* —**treach'er·ous,** *adj.* 1. not faithful; not to be trusted. Ex. *His treacherous behavior broke her heart.* 2. dangerous because of a false appearance of safety. Ex. *The rocks beneath the surface of the river make it treacherous.*

tread (5) [tred'], *v.* walk or step on; trample. Ex. *She was afraid he would tread on her feet.* —*n.* 1. a stepping or walking; the manner of doing this. Ex. *We heard the tread of marching feet.* 2. the part of a step in a staircase on which one places one's foot. 3. the deeply patterned part of a tire. Ex. *The tread of your right rear tire is badly worn.*

treason (4) [triy'zən], *n.* the act of fighting against one's own country, helping its enemies or revealing national secrets to another country. Ex. *He was found guilty of treason.* —**trea'son·ous,** *adj.*

treasure (2) [trež'ər], *n.* 1. a large collection of money, jewels or other things of great value. Ex. *They were diving for sunken treasure.* 2. something or someone greatly loved or appreciated. Ex. *Her children were her treasures.* —*v.* guard, care for or regard as if a treasure. Ex. *She treasured his letters.* —**treas'ur·er,** *n.* one who takes care of the money of a government, group, etc. —**treas'ur·y,** *n.* the money or funds an organization has. —**Treas'ur·y,** *n.* the department of government which manages the finances of the United States.

treat (2) [triyt'], *v.* 1. handle, regard or act toward in a certain way. Ex. *He treated the old man with respect.* 2. attempt to cure, heal or relieve a disease or an illness by means of medicine, surgery, etc. **Ex.** *The doctor is treating my fever.* 3. discuss a subject in writing or speech. **Ex.** *The author treats that matter very thoroughly.* 4. subject to some physical or chemical action. **Ex.** *This material has been treated to prevent its shrinking.* 5. give or provide without cost something that pleases, such as drinks, entertainment, etc. **Ex.** *She treated the children to ice cream.* —*n.* 1. the act of providing and paying for another's food, drinks, etc.; the things so provided. **Ex.** *We bought her the theater tickets as a treat.* 2. that which gives great pleasure. **Ex.** *It was a treat to eat at a restaurant for a change.* —**treat'ment**, *n.* 1. the act or manner of treating. 2. the use of medical means to try to heal or cure. **Ex.** *The doctor's treatment made her feel better.*

treaty (3) [triy'tiy], *n.* an agreement or contract between two or more nations. **Ex.** *That trade treaty was signed by five countries.*

tree (1) [triy], *n.* a tall, woody plant with a single main stem and with branches growing from the stem, usually at some height above the ground. **Ex.** *A large tree shaded the house.*

TREE

tremble (2) [trem'bəl], *v.* shake because of fear, excitement, cold, wind, etc. **Ex.** *She trembled when she heard the good news.*

tremendous (3) [trimen'dəs], *adj.* causing awe because of greatness, size, etc. **Ex.** *The President of the United States has tremendous responsibilities.* —**tre·men'dous·ly**, *adv.* greatly. **Ex.** *She helped me tremendously.*

trench (4) [trenč'], *n.* a long, deep ditch. **Ex.** *The farmer dug trenches to drain the fields.*

trend (5) [trend'], *n.* a general course, direction or tendency. **Ex.** *The trend in medicine seems to be for doctors to specialize.*

trespass [tres'pæs], *v.* enter property unlawfully or without permission. **Ex.** *We did not realize we were trespassing when we went walking in the woods.*

tri- (3) [tray], *prefix.* 1. having three. **Ex.** *Angle, triangle.* 2. happening every third time. **Ex.** *Weekly, tri-weekly.*

---

a, far; æ, am; e, get; ey, late; i, in; iy, see; ɔ, all; ow, go; u, put; uw, too; ə, but, ago; ər, fur; aw, out; ay, life; oy, boy; ŋ, ring; θ, think; ð, that; ž, measure; š, ship; j, edge; č, child.

trial (2) [tray'əl], *n.* 1. an examination of a matter in a law court to determine whether a charge or claim is true. **Ex.** *The trial proved him guilty.* 2. the act of testing or attempting. **Ex.** *After a series of trials, the design of the car was changed.* —*adj.* for or used in a test or trial. **Ex.** *He was the pilot during the trial flight.*

triangle (5) [tray'æŋ'əl], *n.* a figure consisting of three straight lines which meet to form three angles; anything shaped like this. **Ex.** *She cut the sandwiches into triangles.* —**tri·an'gu·lar,** *adj.*

TRIANGLE

tribe (3) [trayb'], *n.* a group of families living under and being ruled by a common chief or leader. **Ex.** *Members of that tribe settled along the river.* —**trib'al,** *adj.*

tributary (5) [trib'yəter'iy], *n.* 1. a flow of water, such as a stream, river, etc., that contributes water to a larger body of water. **Ex.** *The Mississippi River has many tributaries.* 2. a nation that is forced to contribute money or other wealth to a more powerful nation. **Ex.** *The Roman Empire had many tributaries.* —*adj.* 1. flowing into a larger body of water. **Ex.** *That lake is fed by a tributary river.* 2. under another nation's power and required to contribute to it. **Ex.** *After its defeat in the war, it had become a tributary nation.*

tribute (4) [trib'yuwt], *n.* 1. a statement of praise, a gift, etc. given to show respect or appreciation. **Ex.** *The statue was a tribute to the explorer's courage.* 2. that which one nation is forced to contribute to a more powerful nation. **Ex.** *Each year a larger tribute was demanded.*

trick (2) [trik'], *n.* 1. an action or practice done to mislead, cheat, etc. **Ex.** *His call to the guard for help was a trick.* 2. a clever performance or act of skill that puzzles. **Ex.** *The tricks of the magician delighted the children.* —*v.* cheat; mislead. **Ex.** *They tricked the old woman into giving them her money.* —**trick'er·y,** *n.* the act of using tricks or cheating. —**trick'ster,** *n.* one who tricks another. —**trick'y,** *adj.* —**play a trick,** fool. **Ex.** *They played a trick on her.*

trickle (5) [trik'əl], *v.* flow in a small, thin stream; flow in drops. **Ex.** *The water trickled from the tap.* —*n.* a small, thin flow. **Ex.** *The stream was reduced to a mere trickle.*

tried (1) [trayd'], *v.* past and participle of *try.* **Exs.** *He tried to be good. Have you tried this brand of coffee?*

tries (1) [trayz'], *v.* present tense of *try,* used with *he, she* and *it.* **Ex.** *She tries to be good.*

trifle (4) [tray'fəl], *n.* 1. something of small importance or value. **Ex.** *He had no time for trifles.* 2. a small amount or sum of money. **Ex.** *This cost only a trifle.* 3. a small amount. **Ex.** *The soup needs a trifle more pepper.* —*v.* treat lightly or carelessly; treat without respect. **Ex.** *It is dangerous to trifle with a man in his position.* —**trif'ling,** *adj.* not of much value or importance.

trigger (5) [trig'ər], *n.* a device which, when pressed, starts an action. **Ex.** *He accidentally pressed the trigger of the gun and shot his friend.* —*v.* start or be the immediate cause of an action. **Ex.** *The young man's death triggered the riot.*

trim (3) [trim'], *v.* 1. make neat by cutting, clipping, etc. **Ex.** *The gardener trimmed the dead branches from the trees.* 2. remove something not needed, wanted, etc. by cutting. **Ex.** *She trimmed her nails.* 3. decorate. **Ex.** *The hat was trimmed with ribbon.* —*n.* 1. good shape, health or condition. **Ex.** *The fighter kept in trim by exercise and diet.* 2. the act of trimming, especially by cutting. **Ex.** *The barber gave him a good trim.* 3. decorative edging. **Ex.** *The trim of the house is dark blue.* —*adj.* in good condition; neat; well-designed. **Ex.** *The house has a trim appearance.* —**trim'ming,** *n.* materials used to decorate. —**trim'mings,** *n. pl.* all the other dishes, gravy, etc. that go with the main course of a dinner. **Ex.** *They celebrated with a steak dinner and all the trimmings.*

trip (1) [trip'], *v.* 1. strike the foot against something while walking and fall or nearly fall. **Ex.** *I tripped on the step and fell.* 2. make a mistake. **Ex.** *He tripped on the last question.*

trip (1) [trip'], *n.* a movement from one place to another, usually some distance away; journey. **Ex.** *We took a trip to the mountains.*

triple (5) [trip'əl], *adj.* 1. made up of three parts. **Ex.** *She could see the sides as wll as the front of her face in the triple mirror.* 2. three times as many or as much. **Ex.** *There were triple locks on the front door.* —*n.* an amount and two more equal amounts. **Ex.** *He sold the land for triple the price he had paid for it.* —*v.* increase to three times the given amount. **Ex.** *His business has tripled during the last year.*

triumph (3) [tray'əmf], *n.* 1. the act or condition of winning or being successful. **Ex.** *His triumph over poverty was an exam-*

ple to others. 2. a state of happiness and rejoicing over success. **Ex.** *The returned heroes paraded in triumph through the streets.* —*v.* be successful; win. **Ex.** *They triumphed over their opponents.* —**tri·um'phal,** *adj.* marking a victory.—**tri·um'phant,** *adj.* having won a victory; rejoicing in a victory.

trivial (5) [triv'iyəl], *adj.* of little importance. **Ex.** *The guests at dinner last night spoke only of trivial matters.* —**triv'i·al'i·ty,** *n.* anything not important; a small matter. **Ex.** *You don't have time to waste on such a triviality.* —**triv'i·a,** *n. pl.* things of little importance; trivialities.

trod (5) [trad'], *v.* past tense and participle of *tread.* **Exs.** *He trod on her foot while they were dancing. I walked on the street where the enemy soldiers had trod.*

troop (2) [truwp'], *n.* a crowd or company of persons. **Ex.** *A troop of soldiers ran along the path.* —**troops',** *n. pl.* soldiers; police; other such forces. **Ex.** *The commanding general reviewed the troops.* —*v.* gather or move in great numbers. **Ex.** *People trooped in and out of the building all day.* —**troop'er,** *n.* 1. a soldier or policeman on horseback. 2. a state policeman.

trophy (5) [trow'fiy], *n.* something taken in war or hunting, especially when kept as a remembrance; something awarded or kept as a symbol or evidence of victory or success. **Ex.** *The hunter's room was decorated with animal heads, silver cups and other trophies.*

tropical (4) [trap'ikəl], *adj.* of, in, or like the tropics. **Ex.** *Bright-colored birds fed on the tropical fruit.*

tropics (4) [trap'iks], *n. pl.* the area bordered by two imaginary lines running east and west around the earth, one about 23½° north of the equator and the other about 23½° south. **Ex.** *She was exhausted by the hot climate of the tropics.*

trot (4) [trat'], *n.* 1. the manner, general speed or movement of a horse which is going forward by lifting a front leg and the opposite hind leg at the same time. **Ex.** *The horse was running at a trot.* 2. a slow, even way of running. **Ex.** *At the corner, the boys broke into a trot.* —*v.* move in a slow, running way. **Ex.** *The dog trotted along beside its master.* —**trot'ter,** *n.* a horse that trots.

trouble (1) [trəb'əl], *v.* 1. worry; concern; disturb. **Ex.** *He was troubled by the bad news.* 2. cause inconvenience to; annoy; bother. **Ex.** *He did not trouble himself to write.* —*n.* 1. misfortune; difficulty. **Ex.** *She has lost her job and is in great* *trouble*. 2. that which causes worry, bother or inconvenience. **Ex.** *Your visit will be no trouble for us.* —**trou'ble·some**, *adj.* giving trouble. —**take the trouble,** try; make an effort. **Ex.** *Thank you for taking the trouble to call me.*

trousers (2) [traw'zərz], *n. pl.* an outer garment extending from the waist to the ankles and covering each leg separately. **Ex.** *These trousers need to be pressed.*

TROUSERS

truce (5) [truws'], *n.* a time during a war, quarrel, etc. when the fighting stops for a limited time by agreement of all parties. **Ex.** *A five-day truce was declared at the New Year.*

truck (3) [trək'], *n.* 1. a heavy, motor-powered vehicle with space for carrying loads, used especially on highways. **Ex.** *The truck carrying their furniture arrived at the new house.* 2. a wheeled frame pushed by a person and used for small, heavy objects. **Ex.** *The porter took their suitcases to the train on a truck.* —*v.* move things by truck. **Ex.** *The farmer trucked the cows to market.* —**truck'ing**, *n.* the business of moving things by truck for payment. —**truck farm, truck garden,** a farm where vegetables are grown for market.

trudge (5) [trəj'], *v.* walk wearily or with effort. **Ex.** *The children trudged through the snow to school.*

true (1) [truw'], *adj.* 1. correct; not false. **Ex.** *Is the story in the newspaper true?* 2. according to rule or law; real. **Ex.** *I can prove I am the true owner of this land.* 3. faithful. **Ex.** *He has been a true friend for many years.* —**tru'ly**, *adv.* —**truth'**, *n.* that which is true; not a lie. **Ex.** *He told us the truth.*

trumpet (4) [trəm'pit], *n.* a small brass horn played by blowing into it while operatings its valves with the fingers to produce various tones; the sound produced by this instrument; any similar sound. **Ex.** *The sound of trumpets announced his arrival.* —*v.* blow on a trumpet; make a sound like a trumpet. **Ex.** *Suddenly, the elephant trumpeted.* —**trum'pet·er**, *n.* one who plays the trumpet.

TRUMPET

---

a, far; æ, am; e, get; ey, late; i, in; iy, see; ɔ, all; ow, go; u, put; uw, too; ə, but, ago; ər, fur; aw, out; ay, life; oy, boy; ŋ, ring; θ, think; ŏ, that; ž, measure; š, ship; j, edge; č, child.

trunk (2) [trəŋk'], *n.* 1. the main stem of a tree from the ground up, without the branches and roots. **Ex.** *They sawed the trunk of the tree into boards.* 2. the body of a human being or an animal, except for the head, arms and legs. **Ex.** *They found the trunk of an ancient statue of a man.* 3. the long, tubelike nose of the elephant. **Ex.** *The elephant raised its trunk.* 4. a box larger than a suitcase that will hold many clothes or other articles and is used especially for long journeys. **Ex.** *She packed the trunks for the trip.* 5. space at the rear of a car for storage. **Ex.** *They put the suitcases in the trunk.*

trunks [trəŋks'], *n. pl.* an outer garment covering the body from the waist to above the knees and covering each leg separately, worn by men for swimming and certain other sports. **Ex.** *The boys wore their swimming trunks to the picnic at the beach.*

trust (1) [trəst'], *n.* 1. a sure feeling that another person will do what is needed as far as possible. **Ex.** *We have complete trust in our doctor.* 2. duty; responsibility; care. **Ex.** *The child was put in his trust.* 3. a property arrangement managed by a lawyer, bank, etc. for the benefit of another. **Ex.** *The wealthy man created a trust for his family.* —*v.* 1. have confidence in. **Ex.** *He trusted his brother to handle the money.* 2. believe. **Ex.** *I trust what she says.*

try (1) [tray'], *v.* 1. attempt; seek to do. **Ex.** *She is trying to find him.* 2. test; seek to learn or prove something by testing, using or doing. **Ex.** *We like to try different kinds of food.* 3. conduct the trial of a person or a case in a law court. **Ex.** *The judge is going to try that case tomorrow.* —*n.* attempt; effort; endeavor. **Ex.** *He made a good try.* —**try'ing**, *adj.* difficult; annoying. **Ex.** *She had a trying day.*

tub (4) [təb'], *n.* 1. a wide, round container, usually low and lacking a lid. **Exs.** *The butter was packed in wooden tubs. She washed the clothes in a tub.* 2. a large, usually porcelain-coated metal container in which people bathe that is located in the bathroom. **Ex.** *Please clean the tub after you use it.*

tube (3) [tuwb'], *n.* 1. any long, rounded, hollow piece of glass, rubber, metal, etc. through which fluids or gases can flow; a container like this; a pipe. **Ex.** *He used many glass tubes in his chemistry experiments.* 2. a container of soft metal from which liquids or soft substances are squeezed. **Ex.** *The artist had several tubes of red paint.*

TUBE 1

tuck (4) [tək'], *v.* 1. pull together in folds to make shorter, narrower, etc., or to decorate. **Ex.** *She tucked up her skirt and climbed over the fence.* 2. place the edges of something in or under; cover closely or tightly. **Ex.** *She tucked the child into bed.* —*n.* a sewed fold made in cloth for decoration or for shortening, narrowing, etc. **Ex.** *She put a tuck in the dress to make it smaller.*

Tuesday (1) [tuwz'diy, tyuwz'diy], *n.* the third day of the week.

tuft (5) [təft'], *n.* a small bunch of feathers, hair, etc., loose at one end and close together at the other. **Ex.** *The bird had a tuft of feathers on its head.*

tug (4) [təg], *v.* pull hard at with much effort; haul. **Ex.** *The horse tugged the wagon up the hill.* —*n.* 1. a hard pull. **Ex.** *He gave several tugs before the door opened.* 2. a small boat that pulls or pushes another, usually larger, boat; tugboat. **Ex.** *The tug was pulling a couple of barges of coal.*

tuition [tuwiš'ən], *n.* payment required for instruction at a school, training center, etc. **Ex.** *The cost of tuition has gone up again at my college.*

tulip [tuw'lip], *n.* a flowering plant that grows from a bulb, having a long stem with a cup-shaped blossom at its top. **Ex.** *We enjoy the many different colors of the tulips planted in the park.*

TULIP

tumble (3) [təm'bəl], *v.* 1. fall hard in an uncontrolled way. **Ex.** *She tumbled from the ladder.* 2. roll over and over; roll and toss. **Ex.** *The children tumbled about on the grass.* —*n.* fall. **Ex.** *He had a bad tumble down the steps.*

tumult (5) [tuw'məlt, tyuw'məlt], *n.* 1. a loud confusion of cries, yells and noise created by crowds; any similar condition. **Ex.** *He was greeted by a tumult of angry voices.* 2. a disturbed condition of the mind or emotions. **Ex.** *Her mind was in a tumult.* —**tu·mul'tu·ous,** *adj.*

tuna [tuw'nə], *n.* any of various large ocean fish, some of which are used for food. **Ex.** *We had a salad made from canned tuna.*

tune (3) [tuwn', tyuwn'], *n.* 1. musical tones arranged into a pleasing melody. **Ex.** *He whistled a tune as he walked.* 2. the state of producing a proper musical sound. **Ex.** *All the instruments were in tune with the piano.* 3. agreement. **Ex.** *His* *ideas were in tune with those of the group.* —*v.* fix an instrument so as to produce the proper musical sound. **Ex.** *He tuned the piano.* —**tune in,** set a radio to a particular station or a television to a particular channel in order to receive a desired program. **Ex.** *She tuned in to hear the weather report.* —**tune-up,** *n.* an adjustment of a car engine to put it in good working order. **Ex.** *Your car needs a tune-up.*

tunnel (4) [tən'əl], *n.* 1. a passage dug under the ground. **Ex.** *They drove through a long tunnel under the river.* 2. a hole that looks like this dug by an animal as its home. **Ex.** *The rabbit ran into its tunnel.* —*v.* make or dig a tunnel. **Ex.** *They tunneled under the wall.*

turf (5) [tərf'], *n.* an upper layer of earth at the surface, held together by grass and roots. **Ex.** *His golf club dug into the turf as he tried to hit the ball.*

turkey [tər'kiy], *n.* a large American farm bird with a small bare head and a fan-shaped tail. **Ex.** *Mother roasted a turkey for our holiday dinner.*

turn (1) [tərn'], *v.* 1. change the direction in which one looks, goes, etc. **Ex.** *We saw her turn the corner.* 2. change the position or part in view. **Ex.** *Turn to the next page.* 3. revolve; move or cause to move in a circle; spin slowly. **Ex.** *The mill wheel was being turned by water power.* 4. direct one's attention to. **Ex.** *He turned to her for help.* 5. change color, form, shape, etc. **Ex.** *The leaves turned brown.* —*n.* 1. a regular chance or time to do something. **Ex.** *It was his turn to play.* 2. a change of direction, condition, etc. **Ex.** *The car made a sudden turn.* 3. a revolving; a moving around a center point. **Ex.** *The minute hand of the clock makes a complete turn in an hour.* —**turn down,** refuse. **Ex.** *The boss turned down my request for more money.* —**turn in,** change direction to go into or enter. **Ex.** *He turned in at the last house.* —**turn off,** 1. close; stop the flow, operation, etc. **Ex.** *Turn off the television.* 2. change direction. **Ex.** *Turn off at the next corner.* —**turn on,** open; start the flow, operation, etc. **Ex.** *Turn on the light.* —**turn out,** 1. close; stop. **Ex.** *Turn out the light.* 2. produce. **Ex.** *He turns out a lot of work.* 3. appear; come out. **Ex.** *They turned out to see the President.* 4. force out. **Ex.** *She turned him out of the house.* 5. become. **Ex.** *Everything turned out well.* —**turn up,** 1. appear or arrive. **Ex.** *He turned up at noon.* 2. find. **Ex.** *He turned up the papers for which I was looking.* 3. increase sound, power, etc. **Ex.** *Turn up the radio so I can hear it.*

turnpike [tərn'payk'], *n.* a modern highway on which one is normally able to drive at the maximum legal speed and for the use of which one usually has to pay a toll. **Ex.** *She sped along the turnpike.*

turntable [tərn'tey'bəl], *n.* the revolving part of a phonograph on which one places records.

turtle (4) [tər'təl], *n.* an animal, covered by a hard shell, that can live in water or on land.

TURTLE

tutor (5) [tuw'tər, tyuw'tər], *n.* a teacher who gives private lessons. **Ex.** *His father employed a tutor for him.* —*v.* give private lessons; teach individually. **Ex.** *He tutors during the summer.*

tweed (5) [twiyd'], *n.* a coarse wool cloth, usually made of threads of two or more colors. **Ex.** *The tweed in his jacket was woven by hand.*

twelve (1) [twelv'], *n., adj.* the number between eleven and thirteen; the number *12.* —**twelfth'**, *n., adj.* coming after eleven others.

twenty (1) [twen'tiy], *n., adj.* the number between nineteen and twenty-one; the number *20.* —**twent'ti·eth**, *n., adj.* coming after nineteen others.

twice (2) [tways'], *adv.* two times. **Ex.** *Your friend telephoned you twice while you were gone.*

twig (4) [twig'], *n.* a small branch from a tree or bush. **Ex.** *We used some dry twigs to start the fire.*

twilight (5) [tway'layt'], *n.* 1. the faint light of the sun remaining just before darkness after the sun has set. **Ex.** *It was difficult to see him in the twilight.* 2. the time or period this light lasts. **Ex.** *She came home just at twilight.*

twin (3) [twin'], *n.* 1. one of two persons or animals born to a mother during the same birth. **Ex.** *I cannot tell one twin from the other.* 2. one of two very similar things. **Ex.** *Her dress is a twin to mine.* —*adj.* 1. born at the same birth. **Ex.** *They are twin sisters.* 2. being one of a pair. **Ex.** *She bought twin beds for the guest room.*

---

a, far; æ, am; e, get; ey, late; i, in; iy, see; ɔ, all; ow, go; u, put; uw, too; ə, but, ago; ər, fur; aw, out; ay, life; oy, boy; ŋ, ring; θ, think; ð, that; ž, measure; š, ship; j, edge; č, child.

twine (5) [twayn'], *n.* a cord made of tough threads twisted together. **Ex.** *She used twine to tie the package.* —*v.* twist together; wind around; encircle. **Ex.** *The vine twined around the tree.*

twinkle (4) [twiŋ'kəl], *v.* 1. give off light in small flashes that come and go; sparkle. **Ex.** *The stars twinkled in the sky.* 2. brighten; become sparkling. **Ex.** *Her eyes twinkled when she smiled.* --*n.* 1. a sparkling light. **Ex.** *She could see a twinkle of light in the distance.* 2. a sparkle in the eye. **Ex.** *There was a twinkle of amusement in her eyes.*

twirl (5) [twirl'], *v.* spin rapidly; revolve. **Ex.** *The dancers twisted and twirled.*

twist (3) [twist'], *v.* 1. wind together or around something. **Ex.** *She twisted her hair into a roll.* 2. bend or force something around and out of its usual shape. **Ex.** *He twisted the paper and threw it away.* 3. turn or bend in curves. **Ex.** *The road twisted around the mountain.* 4. purposely give the wrong meaning to. **Ex.** *The reporter twisted my statement.* —*n.* 1. a twisting; something made by twisting. **Ex.** *Put a twist of lemon peel in my drink.* 2. a sudden, sharp pull or turn. **Ex.** *With a twist of the wheel, he avoided the other car.*

twitch (5) [twič'], *v.* pull or move suddenly. **Ex.** *The horse twitched its tail at the flies.* —*n.* a sudden pull or movement, often uncontrollable. **Ex.** *The old man had a twitch in his left cheek.*

two (1) [tuw'], *n., adj.* the number between one and three; the number 2.

two-way [tuw'wey'], *adj.* having movement, communication, etc. in two directions. **Exs.** *This is a two-way street. This taxi has a two-way radio.*

-ty (2) [tiy], *suffix.* 1. quality or condition of. **Exs.** *Cruel, cruelty; safe, safety.* 2. tens; ten times. **Exs.** *Four, forty; eight, eighty.*

type (2) [tayp'], *n.* 1. a group having some characteristics in common; kind. **Ex.** *What type of house do you want?* 2. a person, animal or thing representing a class or group having some characteristics in common. **Ex.** *This is the type of apple I like.* 3. a wooden or metal block bearing a raised letter, figure, etc., an impression of which is transferred, after being inked, to paper; a set of such blocks; the impressions made by them. **Ex.** *This book has clear, easy-to-read type.* —*v.* use a typewriter. **Ex.** *She types rapidly.*

typewriter [tayp'rayt'ər], *n.* a machine with keys for the letters of the alphabet, numbers and other symbols such as a period, question mark, etc. that makes printed letters on paper when the key for the symbol desired is pressed down. **Ex.** *She wrote a letter to her sister on the typewriter.*

typical (3) [tip'ikəl], *adj.* representative of a class, group, person, thing, etc.; characteristic. **Ex.** *This is typical July weather.* —**typ'i·cal·ly,** *adv.*

typist [tayp'ist], *n.* one who writes using a typewriter. **Ex.** *She got a job in the office as a typist.*

tyrant (5) [tay'rənt], *n.* 1. a ruler who has absolute power; such a ruler who uses his power cruelly and unjustly. **Ex.** *Everyone hated the tyrant.* 2. a person in authority who is cruel, unjust, etc. **Ex.** *The clerk complained that the office manager was a tyrant.* —**tyr'an·ny,** *n.* the government or acts of a tyrant. —**ty·ran'ni·cal,** adj. —**tyr'an·nize`,** *v.*

U

U, u [yuw'], *n.* the twenty-first letter of the English alphabet.

ugly (2) [əg'liy], *adj.* not pleasant in appearance. **Ex.** *That is an ugly house.* 2. dangerous; promising unpleasant events. **Ex.** *Ugly clouds filled the sky.*

ulterior (5) [əlti:r'iyər], *adj.* beyond what is stated; purposely concealed. **Ex.** *He was suspected of having ulterior motives for making such a generous offer.*

ultimate (4) [əl'təmit], *adj.* 1. final; last. **Ex.** *What was his ultimate goal?* 2. greatest; farthest; highest. **Ex.** *The plane reached its ultimate speed during the test flight.* —*n.* something that is the best possible. **Ex.** *The car was the ultimate in comfort.* —**ul'ti·mate·ly,** *adv.* —**ul'ti·ma'tum,** *n.* a final statement before threatened action is taken. **Ex.** *The ultimatum* *stated that if the prisoner were not released within two hours, shelling of the village would begin.*

ultra- [əlt'rə], *prefix.* 1. past the limits or reach of; beyond. **Ex.** *Sound, ultrasound.* 2. very; exceeding; extreme. **Ex.** *Nationalism, ultranationalism.*

umbrella (3) [əmbrel'ə], *n.* a round shelter, usually made of cloth, on a folding frame carried over the head to keep one dry in the rain.

umpire [əm'payər], *n.* 1. an official who is in charge of certain games and sports, such as tennis and baseball, and sees that the rules are followed. **Ex.** *The umpire called the game on account of rain.* 2. a person who is chosen or has the power to settle a dispute or some other matter. **Ex.** *Do you know yet who the umpire will be in this dispute? —v.* act as an umpire.

UMBRELLA

un- (1) [ən], *prefix.* 1. not; opposite of. **Exs.** *Able, unable; cut, uncut; sure, unsure.* 2. change the action to the opposite of. **Exs.** *Fold, unfold; tie, untie; lock, unlock.*

unanimous (5) [yuwnæn'əməs], *adj.* completely agreed; with no opposition. **Ex.** *She was elected secretary of the club by a unanimous vote. —***u·nan'i·mous·ly,** *adv.* **u·nan·im'i·ty,** *n.*

uncle (1) [əŋ'kəl], *n.* the brother of one's father or mother; the husband of one's aunt.

under (1) [ən'dər], *prep.* 1. below; below the surface of; beneath. **Ex.** *He carried a book under his arm.* 2. protected, directed or taught by. **Ex.** *We studied under a good teacher.* 3. less than. **Ex.** *The price is under five dollars.* 4. subject to; bound by; limited by. **Ex.** *He is under the doctor's care.* 5. in the group or class of; within. **Ex.** *You will find the word* blue *listed under* B. *—adj.* in a lower place; beneath. **Ex.** *He examined the under part of the car. —adv.* in or to a position below something else. **Ex.** *The drowning man went under for the third time.*

under- (1) [ən'dər], *prefix.* 1. below in position; inside. **Exs.** *Ground, underground; shirt, undershirt.* 2. below in rank. **Ex.** *Secretary, undersecretary.* 3. less in quantity; not enough. **Exs.** *Paid, underpaid; state, understate.*

undercover [ən'dərkəv'ər], *adj.* hidden; secret. **Ex.** *The undercover agent made a surprise arrest.*

underdog [ən'dərdɔ:g'], *n.* one who is likely to lose in a fight or contest. **Ex.** *The lawyer was known as a champion of the underdog.*

undergo (4) [ən'dərgow'], *v.* experience; pass through; suffer. **Ex.** *She must undergo a serious operation.*

undergone [ən'dərgɔ:n'], *v.* past participle of *undergo.* **Ex.** *He has undergone much suffering.*

undergraduate [ən'dərgræj'uwit], *n.* a student at a college or university who is in the first years of study and has not yet received a degree. **Ex.** *This is a course for undergraduates.*

underground [ən'dərgrawnd'], *adj.* 1. down below the surface of the earth. **Ex.** *This city has an underground transit system.* 2. done in secret. **Ex.** *He sent an underground message.* —*n.* a political group forced to hide and act in secret because a government is opposed to it. **Ex.** *During the war the underground had members in many places.*

underhanded [ən'dərhæn'did], *adj.* secretive and unfair. **Ex.** *He used underhanded methods to win the election.*

underline [ən'dərlayn'], *v.* draw a line under; emphasize. **Ex.** *He underlined the important sentences with his pencil.*

undermine [ən'dərmayn'], *v.* 1. dig a tunnel or mine under. **Ex.** *Water had undermined the foundations of the building.* 2. weakened by secret efforts. **Ex.** *His chances for promotion were undermined by a fellow worker's telling lies about him.*

underneath (4) [ən'dərniyθ'], *prep.* below; under. **Ex.** *The ball is underneath the chair.* —*adv.* beneath; on the under surface. **Ex.** *The rock was dry underneath.*

understand (1) [ən'dərstænd'], *v.* 1. know what is meant; grasp the meaning of. **Ex.** *Do you understand the question?* 2. be familiar with; have a knowledge of. **Ex.** *She understands English.* 3. accept as being a fact or settled. **Ex.** *He understands he must come tomorrow.* 4. have sympathy with. **Ex.** *She is a person who understands children.* —**un'der·stand'ing,** *n.* 1. knowing about something. **Ex.** *He has a very good understanding of banking.* 2. the power to understand; intelligence. **Ex.** *She showed a quick understanding of the problem.* 3. agreement. **Ex.** *They have reached an under-*

a, far; æ, am; e, get; ey, late; i, in; iy, see; ɔ, all; ow, go; u, put; uw, too; ə, but, ago; ər, fur; aw, out; ay, life; oy, boy; ŋ, ring; θ, think; ð, that; ž, measure; š, ship; j, edge; č, child.

standing about sharing the costs. —*adj.* having interest in or sympathy with. **Ex.** *She was understanding about the problem.*

understood (1) [ən'dərstud'], *v.* past tense and participle of *understand.* **Exs.** *She understood what he meant. He had never understood what we were trying to do.*

undertake (4) [ən'dərteyk'], *v.* 1. try; attempt. **Ex.** *He always undertakes more than he can do.* 2. agree to do; promise; pledge. **Ex.** *She said she would undertake to write the letter.* —**un'der·tak'ing,** *n.* 1. something undertaken. 2. a promise.

undertaker [ən'dərtey'kər], *n.* a person who prepares a dead person for burial or burning and makes arrangements for the funeral. **Ex.** *The undertaker arranged for cars to take us to the cemetery.*

underworld (5) [ən'dərwərld'], *n.* 1. the criminal class of society. **Ex.** *The two murdered men were members of the underworld.* 2. hell. **Ex.** *The poem described the poet's journey through the underworld.*

unforeseen (5) [ən'fɔrsiyn], *adj.* not seen or known at an earlier time. **Ex.** *Unforeseen difficulties delayed us.*

uni- (3) [yu'nə], *prefix.* characterized by or consisting of one. **Ex.** *Form, uniform.*

uniform (2) [yuw'nəfɔrm], *adj.* not varying; always the same. **Ex.** *The room was kept at a uniform temperature.* 2. each being the same as another. **Ex.** *The price of this book is not uniform in all stores.* —*n.* a special style of dress worn by members of a particular group. **Ex.** *The nurse was proud of her uniform.* —**u'ni·form·ly,** *adv.* —**u·ni·form'i·ty,** *n.*

unify (5) [yuw'nəfay'], *v.* form into one or one group; unite. **Ex.** *Their common beliefs helped to unify the settlers.*

union (3) [yuwn'yən], *n.* 1. the act of uniting two or more things into one. **Ex.** *He urged a union of the two groups opposing the tax.* 2. a number of states or countries joined together in a larger unit for a common purpose. **Ex.** *The United States is a federal union of fifty states.* 3. an organization of workers who have joined together to protect and further their interests. **Ex.** *He is a member of a labor union.* —**un'ion·ize,** *v.* organize into a labor union. **Ex.** *He is trying to unionize the employees of the company.*

unique (4) [yuwniyk'], *adj.* single in kind; lacking anything with which to compare. **Ex.** *This ancient jewel is unique.*

unit (3) [yuw'nit], *n.* 1. one thing or a group of things considered as one part of a larger whole or group. **Exs.** *The family is a unit of society. A word is a unit of speech* 2. a standard of measurement. **Ex.** *An hour is a unit of time.*

unite (2) [yuwnayt'], *v.* 1. combine into one; join together. **Ex.** *The two groups united to form a club.* 2. join together for a purpose. **Ex.** *The nations united for common protection.* —**u'ni·ty**, *n.* a state of being united. **Ex.** *In unity we have strength.*

universal (3) [yuw'nəvə:r'səl], *adj.* present in all; characteristic of all; intended for all. **Ex.** *The need for understanding and love is universal.* —**u·ni·ver'sal·ly**, *adv.* everywhere.

universe (5) [yuw'nəvərs`], *n.* all of space, including the earth, sun, stars, etc. **Ex.** *Space flights have brought us new knowledge of the universe.*

university (2) [yuw'nəvə:r'sətiy], *n.* an institution of higher learning with one or more colleges and usually some professional schools. **Ex.** *That university has a fine school of medicine.*

unless (2) [ənles'], *conj.* except if it happens that. **Ex.** *He will go unless it rains.*

unparalleled [ənpær'əleld`], *adj.* without anything equal or simliar; without parallel. **Ex.** *The movie was an unparalleled success.*

unprecedented (5) [ənpres'əden'tid], *adj.* without a previous example on which to authorize, explain or base. **Ex.** *The judge made an unprecedented decision.*

unrest [ənrest'], *n.* disturbance; unsettled state. **Ex.** *Food shortages caused unrest among the people.*

unseat [ənsiyt'], *v.* 1. remove from a seat. **Ex.** *The rider was unseated when his horse jumped the fence.* 2. cause a person in politics to lose his position by vote. **Ex.** *The senator was unseated in the last election.*

unsightly [ənsayt'liy], *adj.* not pleasing to the sight. **Ex.** *An unsightly old car was rusting in the driveway.*

unsung [ənseŋ'], *adj.* not praised; unknown. **Ex.** *There were many unsung heroes during the war.*

until (1) [əntil'], *conj.* 1. up to the point or time that. **Ex.** *Cook the meat until it is well done.* 2. before. **Ex.** *Do not come until I call you.* —*prep.* 1. up to the time of. **Ex.** *He studied until dinner time.* 2. before. **Ex.** *We cannot leave until tomorrow.*

untold [əntowld'], *adj.* not easily counted, described, expressed, etc. **Ex.** *I have been there untold times.*

up (1) [əp], *adv.* 1. to, in or at a higher position. **Ex.** *The sun came up a little after six o'clock this morning.* 2. to or in an erect position. **Ex.** *Sit up straight.* 3. out of bed. **Ex.** *She is not up yet.* 4. so as to approach, arrive at or equal. **Ex.** *He ran to catch up with his friend.* 5. into discussion; to attention or notice. **Ex.** *Who brought up that question?* 6. to the present time. **Ex.** *This article brings us up to date on the problem.* 7. in or into a complete or collected state. **Ex.** *He added up the figures.* 8. completely. **Ex.** *She used up the sugar.* —*adj.* going or directed up. **Ex.** *The moon is up.* —*prep.* along; in; into; through; to a higher place; toward a point higher or farther along. **Ex.** *He climbed up the stairs.* —**up for,** be a candidate for election. **Ex.** *He is up for reelection.* —**ups and downs,** changes in luck, fortune or condition. **Ex.** *He has had his ups and downs in life.*

upbringing [əp'briŋiŋ], *n.* the training a person receives as a child. **Ex.** *Since his father was dead, his mother was responsible for his upbringing.*

uphold (5) [əphowld'], *v.* support; agree with; aid. **Ex.** *He promised to uphold the laws of the land.*

upkeep [əp'kiyp`], *n.* the act or cost of maintaining. **Ex.** *The upkeep of this big house requires a lot of money.*

upon (1) [əpan'], *prep.* on; up to a position on. **Ex.** *The child climbed upon the bed.*

upper (2) [əp'ər], *adj.* being farther up or above; higher. **Ex.** *He is a member of the upper house of the legislature.* —**up'per hand',** an advantage; a superior position. **Ex.** *Because he knew more about the subject, he had the upper hand in the discussion.*

upright (3) [əp'rayt], *adj.* straight up; erect. **Ex.** *He stood in an upright position.* 2. honest. **Ex.** *He is upright in all his business affairs.*

uproar [əprɔ:r`], *n.* a great disturbance or noise. **Ex.** *There was an uproar when they heard that he was leaving.*

upset (4) [əpset'], *v.* 1. cause to turn over. **Ex.** *The boys upset the table while playing.* 2. disturb; put in a state of disorder. **Ex.** *The rain upset our plans.* —*adj.* 1. overturned. **Ex.** *He was saved from the upset boat.* 2. in a state of disorder; disturbed. **Ex.** *He has an upset stomach.*

upstairs [əp'ste:rz], *adv.* on, to or toward an upper floor; up the stairs. **Exs.** *Is your guest bedroom upstairs? He walked upstairs very slowly.*

up-to-date (3) [əp'tədeyt'], *adj.* current; in fashion. **Ex.** *This is an up-to-date account of the political situation.*

uptown [əp'tawn'], *adv.* in or toward the part away from the business section. **Ex.** *He lives uptown.*

upward (3) [əp'wərd], *adv.* from a lower to a higher place, position, condition, etc. **Ex.** *They climbed upward.* —*adj.* directed to a higher place, position, etc. **Ex.** *He gave an upward glance as I came into the room.*

uranium [yuwrey'niyəm], *n.* a shiny, white, radioactive metallic element, forms of which are used in nuclear energy, nuclear fuels, etc. **Ex.** *It was difficult to separate the uranium because so many other metals were mixed with it in its raw state.*

urban (5) [ər'bən], *adj.* 1. concerning, typical of a city. **Ex.** *Traffic is a major urban problem.* 2. living or located in a city. **Ex.** *American urban populations have greatly increased during the last ten years.*

-ure (1) [ər, yər], *suffix.* act or process; result. **Exs.** *Press, pressure; fail, failure; seize, seizure.*

urge [ərj], *v.* 1. force onward. **Ex.** *The rider urged the horse to greater speed.* 2. beg earnestly; plead. **Ex.** *She urged her children to study.* 3. advise; recommend. **Ex.** *The doctor urged his patient to rest more.* —*n.* a strong desire; an impulse. **Ex.** *He had a sudden urge to speak.*

urgent (5) [ə:r'jənt], *adj.* 1. requiring immediate attention; pressing. **Ex.** *He was called away on urgent business.* 2. insistent; demanding. **Ex.** *The doctor answered an urgent call for help.* —**ur'gent·ly,** *adv.* —**ur'gen·cy,** *n.*

urn (5) [ərn], *n.* 1. a vase with a large flat base or foot. **Ex.** *There was a pair of stone urns beside the gate.* 2. a container with a spout for making and serving tea or coffee. **Ex.** *This urn holds twenty cups of coffee.*

URN 2

us (1) [əs], *pron.* the form of *we* used after a preposition or as an object of a verb. **Exs.** *He said he would write to us. They saw us yesterday.*

a, far; æ, am; e, get; ey, late; i, in; iy, see; ɔ, all; ow, go; u, put; uw, too; ə, but, ago; ər, fur; aw, out; ay, life; oy, boy; ŋ, ring; θ, think; ð, that; ž, measure; š, ship; j, edge; č, child.

usage (5) [yuw'sij], *n.* the manner of using; treatment. **Ex.** *Rough usage had damaged the car.* 2. the customary way of using words, phrases or language in general. **Ex.** *Usage often changes the meaning of a word.*

use (1) [yuwz'], *v.* employ for a purpose; put into action. **Ex.** *He uses the car to drive to work.* 2. spend; exhaust. **Ex.** *She had used all her strength to clean the house.* —**used,** *adj.* that has been used; not new. **Ex.** *He sells used cars.* —**used to,** 1. did at one time in the past but not now. **Ex.** *He used to work in the city.* 2. accustomed. **Ex.** *He became used to seeing her every day.* —**use up,** use until there is no more. **Ex.** *I used up the soap when I took my bath.*

use (1) [yuws'], *n.* 1. the act of using or being used. **Ex.** *The car is in use at present.* 2. a particular purpose, need, etc. **Ex.** *These dishes are for everyday use.* 3. benefit; advantage. **Ex.** *There is no use crying.* 4. ability to use; power. **Ex.** *She has lost the use of her right leg.* —**useful,** *adj.* practical; of help. **Ex.** *These books may be useful to you in preparing your homework.*

usher (4) [əs'ər], *n.* one who leads a person to a seat in a theater, church, etc. **Ex.** *The usher found seats for us.* —*v.* act as an usher; lead to; bring in. **Ex.** *He ushered her into the office.*

usual (1) [yuw'žuwəl], *adj.* such as is most often met, heard, seen, etc.; ordinary; normal. **Ex.** *She took her usual seat at the table.* —**u·su·al·ly,** *adv.* most of the time. —**as usual,** as done most of the time. **Ex.** *As usual, we began work at nine o'clock.*

utensil (5) [yuwten'səl], *n.* container; instrument; etc., especially one used in a kitchen. **Ex.** *She washed the baking utensils.*

utility (4) [yuwtil'ətiy], *n.* 1. usefulness; the ability to be used. **Ex.** *Their furniture was chosen for utility rather than style.* 2. water, gas, electricity, etc. provided to the public; the company that provides any of these. **Ex.** *The landlord paid the cost of all utilities except the telephone.*

utilize (5) [yuw'təlayz`], *v.* use; make use of. **Ex.** *He utilizes all his spare time for study.*

utmost (4) [ət'mowst`], *adj.* of the greatest degree, quantity or number. **Ex.** *I have the utmost respect for her.* —*n.* the most possible. **Ex.** *He tried his utmost to succeed.*

utter (2) [ət'ər], *v.* speak; produce sounds. **Ex.** *He was gone before she could utter a word.* —**ut'ter·ance,** *n.* the act of uttering; that which is said. **Ex.** *I do not remember a word of his utterance.*

utter (2) [ət'ər], *adj.* complete; absolute. **Ex.** *He was in utter despair.* —**ut'ter·ly,** *adv.* completely. **Ex.** *She was utterly happy.*

V

V, v [viy], *n.* the twenty-second letter of the English alphabet.

vacancy (5) [vey'kənsiy], *n.* 1. a job or position that is not filled. **Ex.** *There is a vacancy in our office.* 2. a room, an apartment, etc. that is for rent. **Ex.** *There are still some vacancies in that hotel.*

vacant (4) [vey'kənt], *adj.* 1. unoccupied; empty. **Ex.** *The house on the corner is vacant.* 2. without work to do. **Ex.** *She had a few vacant hours.*

vacation (2) [veykey'šən], *n.* a period of freedom from work or regular activity; a period for rest; a holiday. **Ex.** *The children are on vacation from school.* —*v.* go away for a rest. **Ex.** *They plan to vacation in the mountains.*

vaccinate (3) [væk'səneyt'], *v.* with a needle introduce into the body a weakened germ or virus causing a particular disease in order to protect a person or an animal from that disease; inoculate. **Ex.** *He was vaccinated against several diseases at one time.* —**vac'ci·na'tion,** *n.* the act of vaccinating. 2. the scar left on the body at the place where a person was vaccinated. —**vac·cine',** *n.* a weakened form of a germ or virus causing a particular disease, which is introduced into the body of a person or animal as a protection against that disease. **Ex.** *The nurse said that the vaccine would not be available until next week.*

vacuum (5) [væk'yuwm'], *n.* an enclosed space from which most of the air or gas been removed; a space in which there is no matter. **Ex.** *For that experiment they need a complete vacuum.*

vacuum cleaner [væk'yuwm kliyn'ər], *n.* an electrically operated device for cleaning rugs, floors, etc. by sucking up dust from their surfaces into a bag. **Ex.** *It's your turn to run the vacuum cleaner in the bedrooms today.*

vague (4) [veyg'], *adj.* not certain or definite. **Ex.** *She was vague about the date of her return.* —**vague'ly**, *adv.* —**vague'ness**, *n*

vain (2) [veyn'], *adj.* 1. useless; worthless; without real value. **Ex.** *The boy made vain efforts to reach the shore.* 2. too proud. **Ex.** *She is vain about her appearance.* —**vain'ly**, *adv.*

valiant (5) [væl'yənt], *adj.* brave; courageous; heroic. **Ex.** *They made a valiant effort to rescue the children.* —**val'iant·ly**, *adv.*

valid (5) [væl'id], *adj.* 1. that can be logically or factually supported or defended; sound. **Ex.** *Do you have a valid reason for your absence?* 2. legally sound; legally binding. **Ex.** *They had a valid claim to the property.* —**va·lid'i·ty**, *n.*

valley (1) [væl'iy], *n.* a long, low piece of land between ranges of hills or mountains. **Ex.** *Many of the early families settled in the valley.*

valor (5) [væl'ər], *n.* personal bravery or courage, especially in battle. **Ex.** *The men showed great valor in action.*

value (1) [væl'yuw], *n.* the quality of being useful or desirable; worth; importance. **Ex.** *His work was of great value to the business.* 2. the money a thing will bring if sold. **Ex.** *What is the value of this house?* —*v.* 1. make a careful guess as to the worth of. **Ex.** *Her diamond ring is valued at over eight thousand dollars.* 2. respect greatly; prize. **Ex.** *I value your friendship very much.* —**val'ues**, *n.* the principles, aims, etc. that people consider to be important. **Ex.** *His desire for money has changed his values.* —**val'u·a·ble**, *adj.*

valve (5) [vælv'], *n.* 1. a device by which the flow of a liquid or gas in a pipe can be started or stopped by opening or closing. **Ex.** *He shut the valve before repairing the pipe.* 2. a structure in hollow parts of the body that prevents bodily liquids from flowing backwards. **Ex.** *The doctor performed surgery to repair a valve in the patient's heart.*

VALVE

van [væn], *n.* a large covered truck used for transporting bulky objects; a large heavy-duty car with a high body and removable passenger seats used for transporting passengers or large objects. **Ex.** *They bought a new stove, which they took home in their van.*

vandal (5) [væn'dəl], *n.* one who destroys or damages things of beauty or property in general. **Ex.** *A vandal had slashed the beautiful painting.* —**van'dal·ism,** *n.* the act of a vandal. —**van'dal·ize,** *v.*

vanilla [vənil'ə], *n.* a substance obtained from the bean of a tropical plant used to flavor many different kinds of sweet things, such as cakes, cookies, ice cream, etc. **Ex.** *The recipe for this pudding calls for one teaspoon of vanilla.*

vanish (3) [væn'iš], *v.* 1. disappear; fade quickly. **Ex.** *His speeding car passed and vanished from sight.* 2. cease to exist. **Ex.** *Their fears vanished when the storm ended.*

vanity (4) [væn'ətiy], *n.* too much pride in one's appearance, possessions, etc. **Ex.** *Her vanity caused her to spend more for clothes than she could afford.*

vanquish (5) [væŋ'kwiš], *v.* conquer; overcome. **Ex.** *She finally vanquished her fear of flying.*

vapor (3) [vey'pər], *n.* 1. a visible mist, as fog or steam. **Ex.** *Clouds of smoke and vapor floated behind the train.* 2. anything in a gaseous state which has changed from its usual solid or liquid form. **Ex.** *The vapor from gasoline burns easily.* —**va'por·ize,** *v.* cause to become a vapor.

variable (5) [ve:r'iyəbəl], *adj.* able to vary; changeable. **Ex.** *The weather bureau has announced variable winds for tomorrow.*

variety (2) [vəray'ətiy], *n.* 1. the state of being varied; difference; change. **Ex.** *Lack of variety made him bored with his job.* 2. a number of things different from one another. **Ex.** *That store sells a wide variety of magazines.* 3. a different form or kind. **Ex.** *She has a new variety of rose in her garden.*

various (1) [ve:r'iyəs], *adj.* 1. different; of many kinds. **Ex.** *She tried on various dresses before buying one.* 2. several; many. **Ex.** *Various people at the meeting asked for you.* —**var'i·ous·ly,** *adv.*

---

a, far; æ, am; e, get; ey, late; i, in; iy, see; ɔ, all; ow, go; u, put; uw, too; ə, but, ago; ər, fur; aw, out; ay, life; oy, boy; ŋ, ring; θ, think; ð, that; ž, measure; š, ship; ǰ, edge; č, child.

varnish (5) [var'niš], *n.*, a preparation which is dissolved in oil or alcohol and which, when applied to the surface of wood, metal, etc., dries and leaves a hard, protective and rather shiny finish. **Ex.** *She put a new coat of varnish on the table top.* —*v.* put varnish on. **Ex.** *He varnished the floor.*

vary (2) [ve:r'iy], *v.* 1. change; alter. **Ex.** *Methods of teaching have varied over the years.* 2. make different or free from sameness. **Ex.** *She likes to vary the dishes she cooks.* 3. be different; change. **Ex.** *The prices of certain foods vary from week to week.* —**var'i·a'tion,** *n.*

vase (4) [veys'], *n.* a container usually used to hold flowers. **Ex.** *She filled the vase with water.*

vast (2) [væst'], *adj.* very great in size, extent, degree, etc. **Ex.** *His family has vast wealth.* —**vast'ness,** *n.* —**vast'ly,** *adv.* **Ex.** *His condition is vastly improved today.*

vault (4) [vɔlt'], *n.* 1. an arched ceiling or roof of stone, brick, etc. **Ex.** *The vault of the church is decorated with paintings.* 2. a room covered with a vault, especially one underground. **Ex.** *The wine was stored in a vault.* 3. a room, often built of steel, in which valuable things such as money, jewelry, important papers, etc. are stored. **Ex.** *The vault of the bank cannot be opened until nine o'clock tomorrow morning.*

vault (4) [vɔlt'], *v.* jump over by placing the hands on something for support. **Ex.** *He vaulted over the fence.*

veal [viyl'], *n.* meat from a young calf. **Ex.** *At the restaurant we had thin, tender slices of veal, which had been lightly fried, served with a delicate wine sauce.*

vegetable (2) [veǰ'(ə)təbəl], *n.* a plant grown for food; the edible parts of plants. **Ex.** *His favorite vegetables are beans and potatoes.*

vehicle (4) [viy'əkəl, viy'hikəl], *n.* anything upon or in which a person or thing may travel or be carried, especially anything on wheels, such as an automobile, bus, truck, etc. **Ex.** *The road was crowded with vehicles.* —**ve·hic'u·lar,** *adj.*

veil (3) [veyl'], *n.* a delicate cloth, net, etc. placed to hide or cover something else. **Ex.** *The bride wore a lace veil over her face.* 2. anything which covers or conceals like a veil. **Ex.** *A veil of clouds hid the mountaintop.* —*v.* cover as with a veil. **Ex.** *Fog veiled the city.*

vein (3) [veyn'], *n.* 1. any of the tubelike vessels that carry blood to the heart. **Ex.** *Blood poured from the cut vein.* 2. a body or layer of mineral in rock or in the earth clearly separated from the matter around it. **Ex.** *He discovered a rich vein of gold.* 3. spirit; mood. **Ex.** *There was always a vein of sadness in his writings.*

velvet (3) [vel'vit], *n.* a cloth of silk, nylon, cotton, etc., the threads of which are made to stand up from the base to form a soft surface. **Ex.** *The sofa is covered with velvet.* —*adj.* 1. made of or covered with velvet. 2. smooth or soft like velvet. **Ex.** *She has a velvet skin.*

vengeance (4) [ven'jəns], *n.* the act of harming, troubling, etc. in return for a wrong or an injury. **Ex.** *He vowed vengeance on his father's murderer.* —**with a vengeance**, with great anger or force.

venture (3) [ven'čər], *n.* an activity with risk or danger. **Ex.** *If his business venture succeeds, he will be wealthy.* —*v.* 1. go into a position of danger or risk. **Ex.** *The boys ventured into the cave.* 2. dare to say, do, etc. regardless of the risk of criticism. **Ex.** *He ventured to say that he disagreed.* —**ven'tur·ous**, *adj.* daring.

verb (5) [vərb'], *n.* 1. a word that expresses action. **Ex.** *In the sentence "The children ran to their mother," ran is the verb.* 2. a word that shows existence or state of being. **Ex.** *In the sentence "She looks happy," looks is the verb.* See **A Brief Explanation of English Grammar.** —**ver'bal**, *adj.* spoken, not written. **Ex.** *They made a verbal agreement.* —**ver'bal·ly**, *adv.*

verdict (4) [vər'dikt], *n.* the decision of a jury in a trial. **Ex.** *The verdict of the jury was "not guilty."* 2. any decision. **Ex.** *His father's verdict was that he could not drive the family car to school.*

verge (5) [vərj'], *n.* the edge; the rim; the point where something is about to begin. **Ex.** *She was on the verge of tears.* —*v.* incline toward; approach. **Ex.** *Her reply verged on rudeness.*

verify (5) [ve:r'əfay'], *v.* 1. confirm; prove the truth of. **Ex.** *We verified his story.* 2. check the accuracy of. **Ex.** *Please verify the spelling of these names.*

verse (3) [vərs'], *n.* 1. a poem; poetic writing. **Ex.** *A collection of her verse has just been published.* 2. a section of a poem or song. **Ex.** *This poem has eight verses.*

version (4) [vər'žən], *n.* 1. translation. Ex. *Do you have the English version of this book?* 2. one of several accounts or descriptions. Ex. *Your version of the accident differs from that of the other witness.*

vertical (4) [vər'tikəl], *adj.* exactly upright; straight up and down. Ex. *The sides of this doorway are not vertical.* —**ver'ti·cal·ly**, *adv.*

very (1) [ver'iy], *adv.* 1. extremely; in a high degree. Exs. *He was very late. She walked very slowly.* 2. exactly; really; truly. Ex. *That was the very first time they met.*

vessel (2) [ves'əl], *n.* 1. a ship or boat. Ex. *The vessel sailed at midnight.* 2. anything that is used as a container or a holder. Ex. *Bowls, cups and bottles were among the ancient vessels they found.* 3. a tube in the body in which fluids are contained or move. Ex. *The mark on her skin was caused by broken blood vessels.*

vest (4) [vest'], *n.* a short, tight-fitting, sleeveless garment worn over a blouse or shirt. Ex. *He was wearing a red vest.* —*v.* give some authority or right to a person, organization, etc. Ex. *By the power which was vested in him, the president of the university awarded degrees to the graduates.*

VEST

veteran (4) [vet'(ə)rən], *n.* one who has given a long time to a profession, service, industry, etc., especially to the military service. Ex. *He is a veteran of the stage.* —*adj.* having given long service to some profession, industry, etc. Ex. *He is a veteran politician.*

veto (5) [viy'tow], *n.* 1. the power or right which one branch of a government has to prevent an action or decision of another branch from being carried out. Ex. *The President's veto of the bill stopped Congress from increasing taxes.* 2. the power or right to prevent an action. Ex. *The plan was abandoned because of our veto.* —*v.* refuse to approve; reject. Ex. *He always vetoes my suggestions.*

vex (4) [veks'], *v.* make angry; bother; annoy. Ex. *We were vexed by our neighbor's barking dog.*

via (5) [vay'ə, viy'ə], *prep.* by way of. Ex. *We crossed the river via the new bridge.*

vibrant (5) [vay'brənt], *adj.* 1. moving back and forth rapidly; full of energy. Ex. *The city was vibrant with life.* 2. strong and lively; exciting. **Ex.** *The picture was painted in vibrant colors.*

vibrate (4) [vay'breyt], *v.* 1. move back and forth rapidly; quiver. **Ex.** *The strings of the instrument vibrated when he touched them.* 2. shake; tremble. **Ex.** *The house vibrated as the heavy truck rumbled by.* —**vi·bra'tion,** *n.* a shaking movement up and down or back and forth. **Ex.** *The vibration of the bus made it impossible to read.*

vice (3) [vays'], *n.* 1. a bad habit. **Ex.** *The use of tobacco is his only vice.* 2. evil; wickedness. **Ex.** *He led a life of vice.*

vice- (3) [vays'], *prefix.* one who takes the place of another; one who is next in rank or importance. **Exs.** President, vice president; admiral, vice admiral; consul, vice consul.

vicinity (4) [vəsin'ətiy], *n.* 1. a region near or next to; neighborhood. **Ex.** *We live in the vicinity of the school.* 2. state of being close together; nearness. **Ex.** *Our two favorite shops are in close vicinity.*

vicious (5) [viš'əs], *adj.* 1. bad; wicked; cruel; harmful. **Ex.** *She told vicious lies about him.* 2. savage; dangerous; fierce. **Ex.** *That is a vicious dog.* —**vi'cious·ly,** *adv.* —**vi'cious·ness,** *n.*

victim (3) [vik'tim], *n.* 1. something or someone alive that is injured, killed or made to suffer. **Ex.** *Help was sent to the victims of the flood.* 2. one whose money, property, etc. is taken by a trick. **Ex.** *They were the victims of a dishonest merchant.* —**vic'tim·ize,** *v.*

victor (5) [vik'tər], *n.* the winner. **Ex.** *Our team was the victor.*

victory (2) [vik't(ə)riy], *n.* success in a fight, contest, game, etc. **Ex.** *Victory was ours at last!* —**vic·tor'i·ous,** *adj.*

video [vid'iyow], *adj.* of or having to do with pictures or images as viewed on a television screen. **Ex.** *We made a video recording of the wedding.*

view (1) [vyuw'], *n.* sight; vision. **Ex.** *We watched the ship until it was no longer in view.* 2. that which one sees or a picture of it. **Ex.** *We have a view of the lake from this window.* 3. thought; opinion. **Ex.** *What are your views on this question?* 4. act of looking, seeing, examining or considering. **Ex.** *On closer view, he saw that the driver was a woman.* —*v.* see;

look; examine. **Ex.** *They viewed the results of the storm.*
—**in view of,** in light of; considering. **Ex.** *In view of what
he said, I do not think we shall go.* —**view'point,** *n.* a way
in which or a position from which something is looked at
or considered. **Ex.** *I find it difficult to see things from
your viewpoint.*

vigil (5) [viĵ'əl], *n.* the act of keeping awake to watch or
protect; a period of watching. **Ex.** *She kept an all-night vigil
at the bedside of the sick child.* —**vig'i·lance,** *n.* watchfulness. —**vig'i·lant,** *adj.*

vigor (4) [vig'ər], *n.* strength and force; energy. **Ex.** *He was a
man of great mental vigor.* —**vig'or·ous,** *adj.*

vile (4) [vayl'], *adj.* 1. wicked; sinful. **Ex.** *His vile behavior
made him a hated man.* 2. highly unpleasant; offensive. **Ex.**
They could not eat the vile food.

village (3) [vil'ij], *n.* 1. a very small town. **Ex.** *There are fewer
than fifty houses in the village.* 2. those who live in such a
place. **Ex.** *The village gathered to hear the news.* —**vil'lag·er,**
n. a person living in a village.

villain (5) [vil'ən], *n.* someone who is bad or evil; in fiction
or drama the wicked person who is often in conflict with
the hero and heroine. **Ex.** *The villain slowly revealed his
evil nature.* —**vil'lain·ess,** *n.* a female villain.

vine (3) [vayn'], *n.* 1. any plant with a long slender stem that
extends along the ground or climbs a tree or other support.
Ex. *The garden wall was covered with vines.* 2. a grapevine.
Ex. *They picked the grapes from the vine.* —**vine'yard,** *n.*
an area planted with grapevines. **Ex.** *We could see the vine-
yards from the train.*

vinegar (3) [vin'igər], *n.* a sour liquid formed by chemical
changes in apple juice, wine, etc., used to flavor or preserve
foods. **Ex.** *She mixed oil and vinegar for the salad dressing.*

vinyl [vay'nəl], *n.* any of various plastics which are strong, long
lasting, shiny and easily bendable, used for floor and furniture
coverings, in place of leather, etc. **Ex.** *This suitcase stands up
under hard wear because its covering is made of vinyl.*

violate (4) [vay'əleyt'], *v.* break; fail to obey. **Ex.** *He violated
the rules of the club.* —**vio·la'tion,** *n.* the act of breaking a
law, promise or rule.

violence (3) [vay'ələns], *n.* 1. the great strength or force of
nature. **Ex.** *The violence of the wind tore the roof from the*

house. 2. rough bodily force that causes injury or damage. **Ex.** *The man died by violence.* —**vi'o·lent,** *adj.* —**vi'o·lent·ly,** *adv.*

violet (3) [vay'ələt], *n.* 1. a small, low plant with purple, bluish-purple, white or yellow flowers. **Ex.** *The children were picking violets in the field.* 2. a bluish-purple color. **Ex.** *She found some material for a skirt to match the violet of her sweater.* —*adj.* bluish-purple. **Ex.** *She has violet eyes.*

violin (4) [vay`əlin'], *n.* a musical instrument with four strings, played with a bow. **Ex.** *His sister plays the piano, while he plays the violin.* —**vi·o·lin'ist,** *n.* a violin player.

VIOLIN

virgin (4) [vər'jin], *adj.* untouched; unused; pure. **Ex.** *The land was still covered with virgin forests.* —*n.* a person who has not had sexual relations. —**vir·gin'i·ty,** *n.* state of being a virgin.

virtual (5) [vər'cuwəl], *adj.* in effect, although not in form or actuality. **Ex.** *Their many paintings made their home a virtual art museum.* —**vir'tu·al·ly,** *adv.* almost. **Ex.** *He was virtually penniless.*

virtue (2) [vər'cuw], *n.* 1. moral behavior; moral goodness. **Ex.** *Her truthfulness was a virtue, but sometimes it embarrassed people.* 2. any good quality. **Ex.** *Patience is one of his many virtues.* 3. merit; advantage. **Ex.** *This dress has the virtue of not needing to be ironed.* —**vir'tu·ous,** *adj.*

virus [vay'rəs], *n.* a very tiny living thing that causes diseases in humans, animals and plants and that can grow and reproduce only in living cells. **Ex.** *AIDS is caused by a deadly virus.*

visible (3) [viz'əbəl], *adj.* capable of being seen; in sight. **Ex.** *The house was visible from the road.* —**vis'i·bly,** *adv.* —**vis·i·bil'i·ty,** *n.*

vision (3) [viž'ən], *n.* 1. the sense or power of sight. **Ex.** *Glasses will improve her vision.* 2. something seen in the imagination; a dream, etc. **Ex.** *She had a vision of her son returning home.* 3. the ability to foresee that which does not exist or has not yet been done. **Ex.** *This city was planned by men of vision.* 4. an unusually beautiful person or thing. **Ex.** *The bride was a vision of loveliness.*

visit (1) [viz'it], *v.* 1. go or come to see for friendly, business or professional reasons. **Ex.** *The doctor visited the patient this morning.* 2. stay as a guest. **Ex.** *They visited us for a week.*

—*n.* the act of visiting. **Ex.** *We look forward to your visit.*
—**vis'i·tor**, *n.* one who visits.

visual (5) [viž'uwəl], *adj.* 1. of or having to do with sight. **Ex.**
The contrasting colors created an interesting visual effect. 2.
visible; capable of being seen. **Ex.** *There were still no visual
signs of spring.* —**vis'u·al·ize**, *v.* make visible mentally. **Ex.**
He could not visualize how the new house would look.

vital (4) [vay'təl], *adj.* 1. important to or necessary for life. **Ex.**
The heart is one of the vital organs of the body. 2. very
important or necessary. **Ex.** *The operation of the factory is
vital to the community.* 3. full of life and energy. **Ex.** *He has a
vital personality.* —**vi·tal'i·ty**, *n.* vigor; health and energy.

vitamin [vay'təmin], *n.* 1. any of various substances which are
found in very small amounts in food and are necessary for the
normal functioning and good health of the body. **Ex.** *I've
changed my diet to make sure that I'm eating foods that give
me the vitamins I need.* 2. these substances produced artificially.
Ex. *Because I am just recovering from an illness, I am taking
a dose of vitamins once a day.*

vivid (4) [viv'id], *adj.* 1. brightly or intensely colored; sharp and
clear; strong. **Ex.** *The accident is still vivid in his mind.* 2. full
of life. **Ex.** *He has a vivid style of writing.* —**viv'id·ly**, *adv.*
—**viv'id·ness**, *n.*

vocabulary (2) [vowkæb'yəle:r'iy], *n.* 1. all of the words of a
language used by a group of people, an individual, etc. **Ex.**
That student has an unusually large vocabulary. 2. a list of
words, usually in alphabetical order, with explanations of
their meanings. **Ex.** *There is a vocabulary of scientific terms
included at the back of that book.*

vocal (5) [vow'kəl], *adj.* 1. of, for or having to do with the voice;
made by the voice. **Ex.** *The program will include several
vocal numbers.* 2. expressing one's opinions often and freely.
Ex. *The students have become more vocal in their demands.*
—**vo'cal·ist**, *n.* a singer. —**vo'cal·ly**, *adv.*

vocation (5) [vowkey'šən], *n.* career; a profession for which one
is best suited by talent and interest. **Ex.** *He has not yet
decided upon his vocation.*

voice (1) [voys'], *n.* 1. the sound made by living creatures,
especially by human beings, in speaking, singing, etc. **Ex.** *We
heard voices in the next room.* 2. the quality of such sounds.
Ex. *She has a good voice for public speaking.* 3. the ability or

power to speak. **Ex.** *He lost his voice during his illness.* 4. the right to speak; the act of expressing oneself. **Ex.** *He had no voice in deciding the matter.* —*v.* say; express in sounds; declare. **Ex.** *They voiced their objections to the law.*

void (4) [voyd'], *adj.* 1. empty; containing nothing; vacant. **Ex.** *Their words were void of meaning.* 2. without legal force or effect. **Ex.** *His will is void because he did not sign it.* —*n.* an empty space; a feeling of emptiness. **Ex.** *His death left a void in his political party.* —*v.* 1. cause to be not legally binding. **Ex.** *They voided the will by proving it was not properly witnessed.* 2. empty; discharge. **Ex.** *The medicine caused him to void the poison.*

volcano (4) [valkey'now], *n.* an opening in the earth from which hot melted rock and ash are thrown; a hill or mountain formed around such an opening by these materials. **Ex.** *That volcano has not been active for many years.* —**vol·can'ic**, *adj.*

volume (2) [val'yəm], *n.* 1. a book; one of the books of a set. **Ex.** *The third volume of this set is missing.* 2. a measure of the space something contains. **Ex.** *The volume of the tank was not large enough for their needs.* 3. quantity; amount. **Ex.** *The volume of sales doubled last month.* 4. the loudness or softness of sound. **Ex.** *He turned up the volume of his radio.*

voluntary (5) [val'ənte:r'iy], *adj.* given or done freely and by choice, without being forced or required. **Ex.** *The offer was entirely voluntary.* —**vol'un·tar'i·ly**, *adv.*

volunteer (4) [val'ənti:r'], *n.* one who offers to serve without being forced or required, especially military service. **Ex.** *He is a volunteer in the army.* —*adj.* of or done by volunteers. **Ex.** *The office was staffed by volunteer workers.* —*v.* offer one's services without being asked. **Ex.** *She volunteered to help her friend clean the house.*

vote (2) [vowt'], *n.* 1. a choice or decision expressed by the voice, raised hand, written means, etc.; the means by which one expresses a choice or decision. **Ex.** *The committee counted the votes.* 2. the total number of expressed choices. **Ex.** *A heavy vote is expected.* 3. the right to express such a choice. **Ex.** *Women in the United States did not always have the vote.* 4. the act of choosing by such an expression. **Ex.** *He asked to*

a, far; æ, am; e, get; ey, late; i, in; iy, see; ɔ, all; ow, go; u, put; uw, too;
ə, but, ago; ər, fur; aw, out; ay, life; oy, boy; ŋ, ring; θ, think; ð, that;
ž, measure; š, ship; j, edge; č, child.

have the matter put to a vote. —*v.* 1. express a choice or decision by vote. **Ex.** *They voted for the best-qualified man.* 2. bring about by vote; elect. **Ex.** *They voted him president of the club.* —**vot'er,** *n.* one who votes.

vow (3) [vaw'], *n.* a solemn promise. **Ex.** *He made a vow to return.* —*v.* promise solemnly; bind oneself to do something. **Ex.** *He vowed revenge.*

vowel (5) [vaw'əl], *n.* a speech sound in which the breath is not stopped by the tongue, teeth or lips; the letters *a, e, i, o, u* and sometimes *y* sounded in this way. **Exs.** *In the word* why, *the letter* y *is a vowel. In the word* alphabet, *the letters* a *and* e *are vowels. In the word* boil, *the letters* o *and* i *are vowels. In the word* but, *the letter* u *is a vowel.*

voyage (2) [voy'ij], *n.* a journey across water or through air or space. **Ex.** *She expects to take an ocean voyage this summer.* —*v.* travel across water or through the air or space. **Ex.** *The ship voyaged to distant ports.* —**voy'ag·er,** *n.* one who or that which takes a voyage.

vulgar (4) [vəl'gər], *adj.* bad-mannered; crude; lacking refinement and taste. **Ex.** *He made a vulgar display of his wealth.* —**vul'gar'i·ty,** *n.*

W

W, w [dəb'əlyuw], *n.* the twenty-third letter of the English alphabet.

wade (4) [weyd'], *v.* 1. move on foot through any substance that offers resistance, such as water, snow, etc. **Ex.** *The children were wading in the shallow water.* 2. go through with great effort. **Ex.** *He waded through the uninteresting book.*

waffle [waf'əl], *n.* a somewhat hard but easily broken cake made with a mixture of flour, eggs, milk, sugar and butter and cooked in a special pan which marks the cake with raised squares. **Ex.** *On Sundays we often have waffles for breakfast.*

wag (4) [wæɡ'], *v.* move or swing back and forth rapidly. **Ex.** *The dog wagged its tail.*

wage (2) [weyj'], *v.* engage in; carry on. **Ex.** *He waged a successful political campaign.* **—wage', wag'es,** *n.* that which is paid for services or work; pay. **Ex.** *His wages are paid weekly.* **—wag'er,** *n.* a bet. **Ex.** *I'll make a wager of ten dollars on the first race.* **—v.** bet. **Ex.** *He wagered that she would not win.*

wagon (1) [wæg'ən], *n.* a four-wheeled cart, especially one designed for carrying heavy loads and pulled by a horse or other large animal. **Ex.** *The wagon was filled with stones.*

wail (4) [weyl'], *v.* 1. utter a long, loud cry to show that one is unhappy. **Ex.** *The baby wailed until his mother returned.* 2. make a mournful, crying sound. **Ex.** *The wind wailed through the trees.* **—n.** a mournful, crying sound. **Ex.** *The wails of the children woke us.*

waist (3) [weyst'], *n.* 1. the part of the body just below the ribs; an imaginary line around this part of the body. **Ex.** *She wore a leather belt around her waist.* 2. the narrow part of a woman's dress at this part of the body. **Ex.** *The waist of that dress was too large.*

wait (1) [weyt'], *v.* 1. remain inactive until something expected happens. **Ex.** *I am waiting for him to call.* 2. cause to wait; delay. **Ex.** *We can let the shopping wait until tomorrow.* **—n.** the act of waiting; the time waited. **Ex.** *There will be a short wait before the train starts.* **—wait·ing,** *n.* a time during which one waits. **Ex.** *Waiting for news of him made us nervous.* **—adj.** of a time of waiting. **Ex.** *I had to sit in the doctor's waiting room for an hour.* **—wait on,** act as a servant, a seller in a store, or a waiter or waitress in a restaurant. **Ex.** *The clerk will wait on you next.*

waiter (3) [weyt'ər], *n.* a man who serves food at a table in an eating place. **Ex.** *The waiter brought us our dinner quickly.* **—wait'ress,** *n.* a girl or woman who serves food at a table in an eating place.

wake (2) [weyk'], *v.* stop sleeping; open the eyes from sleep. **Ex.** *I usually wake very early.* **—wake'ful,** *adj.* not able to sleep; alert.

wake (2) [weyk], *n.* the path made behind a ship as it moves in the water; any trail or track left behind. **Ex.** *The flood left destruction in its wake.*

wake (2) [weyk'], *n.* the custom of watching over a dead body before it is buried. **Ex.** *There were many friends at his wake.*

waken (2) [weyk'ən], *v.* 1. stop or cause to stop sleeping. **Ex.** *Please waken me in an hour.* 2. excite; cause to become active. **Ex.** *The book wakened his interest in history.*

walk (1) [wɔːk'], *v.* 1. move along step by step on foot. **Ex.** *He walks to work.* 2. move through or over on foot. **Ex.** *I walk this street every day.* 3. move with on foot; cause to walk. **Ex.** *She walks the dog every evening.* —*n.* 1. the act of going on foot. **Ex.** *We went for a walk.* 2. the distance walked. **Ex.** *The house is a short walk from here.* 3. the manner of walking. **Ex.** *I recognized his walk.* 4. a path intended for walking. **Ex.** *I saw him coming down the walk.* 5. the direction walked; the way one goes, as in life. **Ex.** *People from every walk of life were her friends.* —**walk out,** go away from; quit; refuse to be a part of. **Ex.** *He walked out on a good job because he did not like the company's policies.*

wall (1) [wɔːl'], *n.* 1. stone, wood, etc. made to form one of the sides of a room or building or to enclose a space. **Ex.** *The walls of the room were painted white.* 2. something like a wall. **Ex.** *A wall of fire made them turn back.* —*v.* enclose; separate. **Ex.** *They walled off part of the large room to make two smaller rooms.*

wallet [wal'it], *n.* a small folding container, often of leather, in which to carry bills, identification cards, papers, etc. **Ex.** *How much money do you have in your wallet?*

wallpaper [wɔːl'pey`pər], *n.* paper, usually with a pattern, used to cover walls. **Ex.** *She chose some pretty flowered wallpaper for the bedroom.* —*v.*

Wall Street [wɔːl' striyt'], a street in New York City that is a principal center for American financial affairs; the financially important American businesses collectively.

walnut (5) [wɔlnət'], *n.* 1. a large, almost round nut, the seed of which is edible. **Ex.** *She put walnuts in the cake.* 2. the tree on which this nut grows; the wood of this tree. **Ex.** *The chairs were made of walnut.*

wander (2) [wan'dər], *v.* 1. move about without definite purpose or objective. **Ex.** *The children wandered down the street.* 2.

move from a planned route, course, or path by mistake. **Ex.** *The speaker wandered from the subject of his speech.* —**wand'er·er**, *n.* one who wanders.

want (1) [want'], *v.* 1. have a wish or desire for. **Ex.** *He wants to watch television.* 2. need. **Ex.** *He was hungry and wanted food.* 3. desire that one come, go or do something. **Ex.** *She wants you to come immediately.* 4. look for in order to capture, arrest. etc. **Ex.** *The police want him for questioning.* —*n.* 1. lack; shortage. **Ex.** *He died from want of food.* 2. need. **Ex.** *His wants are few.* 3. a wish or desire for something. **Ex.** *We can supply all your wants.* —**want'ing**, *adj.* lacking; needing. **Ex.** *Is there anything wanting?*

war (1) [wɔ:r'], *n.* 1. a fight with arms against another nation or between parts of a nation; an armed struggle. **Ex.** *They declared war after the enemy attack.* 2. a common effort or struggle. **Ex.** *We are fighting a war against drugs.* —*v.* fight a war. **Ex.** *They are warring with a neighboring country.*

ward (5) [wɔrd'], *n.* 1. a division of a hospital. **Ex.** *The doctor is visiting the children's ward.* 2. a division of a city or town for the purpose of administration. **Ex.** *You have to vote in the ward where you live.* 3. a person who is under legal protection. **Ex.** *After his parents' death, the court made him a ward of his aunt.*

-ward, -wards, (3) [wərd, wərdz], *suffix.* in the direction of. **Exs.** *Up, upward; north, northward; back, backwards.*

warden (5) [wɔr'dən], *n.* 1. an officer who watches over things; a special guard. **Ex.** *The fire warden told us not to light matches in the building.* 2. the chief guard or officer in a prison. **Ex.** *The warden knew most of the prisoners by name.*

wardrobe (5) [wɔrd'rowb'], *n.* 1. clothing in general. **Ex.** *She had a large wardrobe.* 2. a piece of furniture in which clothing is hung or kept in drawers. **Ex.** *Two men carried the wardrobe upstairs.*

ware (4) [we:r'], *n.* articles or manufactured products for sale. **Ex.** *The store displayed some of its wares in the shop window.*

-ware (4) [we:r'], *suffix.* manufactured products made from or of. **Exs.** *silver, silverware; glass, glassware; china, chinaware.*

---

a, far; æ, am; e, get; ey, late; i, in; iy, see; ɔ, all; ow, go; u, put; uw, too; ə, but, ago; ər, fur; aw, out; ay, life; oy, boy; ŋ, ring; θ, think; ð, that; ž, measure; š, ship; j, edge; č, child.

warehouse (5) [we:r'haws'], *n.* a place for storing goods. **Ex.** *We have the item you want in the warehouse.*

warm (1) [wɔrm'], *adj.* 1. having or giving a small, comfortable amount of heat. **Exs.** *Would you like something warm to drink? This room is too warm.* 2. have a feeling of heat. **Ex.** *The back of her neck felt warm.* 3. stopping the loss of, saving or keeping body heat. **Ex.** *The children wore warm clothing.* 4. eager; showing much good feeling; lively. **Ex.** *They received a warm welcome.* —*v.* 1. give heat to; receive warmth from; become warm. **Ex.** *He warmed himself before the fire.* 2. make or become interested or eager; fill with good feelings. **Ex.** *The news warmed my heart.* —**warm'ly,** *adv.* —**warmth',** *n.* state of being warm; heat.

warm-blooded [wɔrm'bləd'id], *adj.* having a body temperature that remains more or less the same, even though the temperature of the air may change. **Ex.** *A snake is not a warm-blooded animal.*

warm-hearted [wɔrm'har'tid], *adj.* kind; loving; friendly. **Ex.** *His mother is a warm-hearted person.*

warn (2) [wɔrn'], *v.* give notice; inform; caution. **Exs.** *I warned her of the danger. The signal warned us of the approaching train.* —**warn'ing,** *n.*

warp (4) [wɔrp'], *v.* 1. turn or twist out of shape. **Ex.** *This piece of wood has warped because it was not properly dried.* 2. turn or twist away from what is normal, natural, etc. **Ex.** *The boy's mind was warped by his cruel father.* —*n.* a bend or twist. **Ex.** *The carpenter immediately saw the warp in the floor.*

warrant (4) [wɔr'ənt], *n.* a written order which gives the right or authorization to do something. **Ex.** *The police have a warrant for his arrest.* —*v.* be a cause for; give the right to. **Ex.** *His work warrants a raise in pay.* —**war'ran·ty,** *n.* a guarantee. **Ex.** *This motor has a five-year warranty.*

warrant officer [wɔr'ənt ɔ:f'əsər], an officer in the military forces of the United States who ranks above enlisted personnel but below a commissioned officer.

warrior (3) [wɔr'iyər], *n.* a person engaged in war or military life; a fighter. **Ex.** *They were brave warriors.*

wary [we:r'iy], *adj.* careful; cautious; watchful and ready. **Ex.** *At night we are wary of walking along poorly lighted streets.* —**war'i·ly,** *adv.*

was (1) [wəz', waz'], *v.* past tense of *be* used with *I, he, she, it* and singular nouns. **Ex.** *She was tired after working in the garden.*

wash (1) [wɔːš', waš'], *v.* 1. clean by dipping, wetting or rubbing, as with water and often soap. **Ex.** *Wash your hands before dinner.* 2. clean clothes by wetting and rubbing with soap and water. **Ex.** *She washes twice a week.* 3. flow against or over. **Ex.** *The waves washed against the boat.* 4. push or carry by means of water or other liquid. **Ex.** *The box was washed ashore.* —*n.* 1. the act of washing. 2. things such as clothes washed or to be washed at one time. **Ex.** *We have a big wash this week.* 3. a flow or rush, as of water; the sound of a flow or rush. **Ex.** *The wash of the waves put me to sleep.* 4. that with which one washes. **Ex.** *He uses a mouthwash each morning.* —**wash'er,** *n.* a machine for washing. —**wash'ing,** *n.* wash. **Ex.** *It will take a good washing to get all this oil off my hands.* —**wash down,** drink liquid to move food to the stomach. **Ex.** *He washed down his cake with some milk.* —**wash one's hands of,** stop being involved with or responsible for. **Ex.** *If he will not do as I ask, I'm going to wash my hands of the problem.* —**wash up,** wash oneself. **Ex.** *Would you like to wash up before dinner?*

washed-out [wɔːšt'awt'] *adj.* faded in color; pale. **Ex.** *Her washed-out looking dress added to her tired appearance.*

wasn't [waz'ənt], short form, contraction of *was not.* **Ex.** *He wasn't at home when I telephoned.*

wasp (5) [wasp'], *n.* a slender flying insect that stings. **Ex.** *The wasps built a nest at the corner of the roof.*

waste (2) [weyst'], *v.* 1. spend uselessly or without need; make poor use of. **Ex.** *He wasted his money.* 2. fail to use as it should have properly been used. **Ex.** *She wasted her chance to go to college.* 3. lose size, weight,

WASP

strength, etc. **Ex.** *The sick man wasted away.* —*n.* 1. a profitless use of money, time, goods, etc. **Ex.** *Going there was a waste of time.* 2. something thrown away or disposed of as worthless. **Ex.** *Many of our rivers have been damaged by waste.* —*adj.* 1. ruined; destroyed; empty. **Ex.** *After the flood, the valley lay waste.* 2. unused; useless. **Ex.** *The basket was filled with waste paper.*

watch (1) [wač'], *v.* 1. look at; observe closely. **Ex.** *We watched the dancers.* 2. look or wait for; expect. **Ex.** *Watch for your* *father to come home.* 3. act as a guard; take care of. **Ex.** *Please watch the baby for me.* 4. be careful. **Ex.** *Watch where you walk.* —*n.* 1. a device that shows time, carried in the pocket or worn on the lower part of the arm. **Ex.** *His watch had stopped.* 2. the act of watching or guarding. **Ex.** *A guard kept watch at the bank.* 3. the period of time during which a guard is on duty. **Ex.** *His watch ended at noon.*

watchman [wač'mən], *n.* a person who acts as a guard of a building, place of business, property, etc., particularly when it is not occupied. **Ex.** *The watchman comes on duty here just before dark.*

water (1) [wɔ:'tər, wat'ər], *n.* the liquid that falls from the sky as rain or that is found in wells, lakes, rivers, etc. **Ex.** *I was warm and asked for a glass of cold water.* —*v.* 1. wet with water; supply with water. **Ex.** *They water the garden every day.* 2. fill with or give off liquid. **Ex.** *The cold made her eyes water.* —**water down,** make weaker by adding water. **Ex.** *This wine tastes as if it has been watered down.* —**wa'ter·y,** *adj.* like or containing water. **Ex.** *This drink is too watery.*

watercolor [wɔ:'tərkəl'ər], *n.* 1. a paint made with coloring matter and water. **Ex.** *She paints with watercolors.* 2. a painting made using watercolors. **Ex.** *I prefer his watercolors to his oil paintings.*

waterfall [wɔ:'tərfɔ:l'], *n.* a steep fall of water from a dam, cliff, etc. **Ex.** *That is a beautiful waterfall.*

waterfront [wɔ:'tərfrənt'], *n.* the land and buildings or the parts of a city, town, etc. which are by a river, lake, etc. **Ex.** *Many large ships were docked at the waterfront unloading goods.*

waterlogged [wɔ:'tərlɔgd'], *adj.* very heavy because of being soaked or filled with water. **Ex.** *The waterlogged boat sank to the bottom of the lake.*

water main [wɔ:'tər meyn'], one of the largest pipes in a system, usually underground, for bringing water to houses, stores, etc. **Ex.** *Until the broken water main is fixed, we will not have water.*

waterproof [wɔ:'terpruwf'], *adj.* covered with a material or chemicals so as to prevent water soaking in. **Ex.** *His waterproof coat kept him dry during the rain.*

waterway [wɔ:'tərwey'], *n.* a river, stream, canal, etc. that is used by boats to carry goods or passengers. **Ex.** *The scenery along the waterway is very interesting.*

waterworks [wɔː'tərwərks`], *n. pl.* a system of pipes, machines, tanks, etc. by which water is furnished to a city, town, area, etc. **Ex.** *The city's extensive waterworks require constant maintenance.*

wave (1) [weyv'], *v.* 1. move or cause to move one way and then the other, as a flag; flutter. **Ex.** *The branches waved in the wind.* 2. signal by moving the hand one way and then the other. **Ex.** *She waved good-by as we left.* 3. seem to flow in curves; be arranged in curves. **Ex.** *Her hair waved softly about her face.* —*n.* 1. a swell which forms in a moving ridge on the surface of the water. **Ex.** *The waves carried him to shore.* 2. something that swells, rises and falls in this manner. **Ex.** *A wave of anger rose in him.* 3. a curved line or group of curved lines. **Ex.** *Is the wave in her hair natural?* 4. the way in which some forms of energy, such as light and sound, move. **Ex.** *They could tell by means of sound waves where the ship was.* —**wav'y,** *adj.*

waver (4) [wey'vər], *v.* sway one way and then the other; quiver; flicker. **Ex.** *The light wavered and went out.* 2. show doubt or indecision; be hesitant. **Ex.** *Once he had decided to go, he never wavered.*

wax (4) [wæks'], *n.* a solid substance made of or containing fats and oils that melts when heated. **Ex.** *Wax from the candles fell on the table.* —*v.* treat, rub or polish with wax. **Ex.** *She waxed the furniture.* —**wax'en,** *adj.* made of or appearing like wax.

way (1) [wey'], *n.* 1. method; manner; style. **Ex.** *That is the wrong way to do it.* 2. direction of travel, motion, etc. **Ex.** *Which way do we go?* 3. a road, passage or opening. **Ex.** *He lives across the way.* 4. distance. **Ex.** *It is a long way from here.* 5. space in which to pass. **Ex.** *It was difficult to make our way through the crowd.* —**by the way,** incidentally; not directly related but of interest. **Ex.** *He brought me your book and, by the way, he had read it.* —**by way of,** through, **Ex.** *He went from Chicago to New York by way of Washington, D.C.* —**give way,** break; yield. **Ex.** *Do you think the crowd will give way to let us pass?* —**make one's way,** move through or ahead. **Ex.** *He is making his way in the business world.* —**out-of-the-way,** *adj.* far from the usual path; remote. **Ex.**

He visited several out-of-the-way places. —**out of the way,** not in a position to hinder or obstruct. **Ex.** *He put the box out of the way.* —**under way,** going forward; moving ahead. **Ex.** *The meeting had been under way for an hour when we arrived.*

waylay [wey'ley'], *v.* wait for and meet; stop and delay, often for the purpose of harming, robbing, etc. **Ex.** *Reporters waylaid the senator after his speech.*

-ways [weyz], *suffix.* manner; direction. **Ex.** *Side; sideways; folk, folkways.*

wayside [wey'sayd'], *n.* the side of a road. **Ex.** *We saw some pretty wildflowers by the wayside.* —*adj.* at or near the side of a road. **Ex.** *We stopped at a wayside fruit and vegetable stand.*

wayward (5) [wey'wərd], *adj.* refusing to recognize authority and insisting on following one's own way. **Ex.** *She is a wayward child.*

we (1) [wiy'], *pron.* plural of *I;* two or more persons, including the speaker or writer. **Ex.** *He and I will go together, and we will also return together.*

weak (1) [wiyk'], *adj.* 1. not strong, bodily or morally. **Ex.** *He has a weak character.* 2. having lost physical strength; yielding to illness. **Ex.** *The sick man is very weak.* 3. lacking skill or mental power; not effective. **Ex.** *Her English is weak.* —**weak'en,** *v.* make or become weak. —**weak'ling,** *n.* one who is weak. —**weak'ly,** *adv.* —**weak'ness,** *n.* state of being weak; lack of strength.

wealth (2) [welθ'], *n.* 1. a large quantity of possessions, money or other desired things; riches. **Ex.** *He was a man of great wealth.* 2. a large quantity. **Ex.** *She found a wealth of information on that subject in the library.* —**wealth'y,** *adj.*

weapon (3) [wep'ən], *n.* 1. anything used for fighting. **Ex.** *The soldiers were cleaning their weapons.* 2. any means by which one seeks to win in opposition to another. **Ex.** *Tears were her favorite weapon.*

wear (1) [we:r'], *v.* 1. use as clothing for the body. **Ex.** *He seldom wears a coat.* 2. change by use; damage gradually by use; make a hole in by rubbing. **Ex.** *You are wearing a hole in the left elbow of your sweater.* 3. remain in good condition through long use. **Ex.** *This heavy material will wear well.* —*n.* 1. the act of wearing; use. **Ex.** *She needed clothes for school wear.* 2. things worn; clothing. **Ex.** *Menswear is sold on the* *second floor*. 3. the gradual lessening in value, beauty, etc., caused by use. **Ex.** *This chair is showing wear*. 4. the quality of remaining in good condition through long use. **Ex.** *There is a lot of wear left in these shoes*. —**wear down,** 1. decrease in size because of use. **Ex.** *He wears down the heels of his shoes very quickly*. 2. decrease opposition by asking, doing, etc., again and again. **Ex.** *He thinks he can wear me down by begging*. —**wear out,** 1. gradually make unusable. **Ex.** *She is wearing out that dress*. 2. gradually become tired. **Ex.** *Teaching all day wears me out*.

weary (3) [wi:r'iy], *adj.* 1. tired; exhausted; lacking strength. **Ex.** *I'm too weary to do any more*. 2. not contented; bored. **Ex.** *She was weary of cooking*. —*v.* become or cause to become tired, unhappy or bored. **Ex.** *He wearies easily*. —**wea'ri·ly,** *adv.* —**wea'ri·ness,** *n.*

weather (1) [weð'ər], *n.* the condition of the air outside with respect to warmth, wetness, wind, etc. **Ex.** *We had good weather for our trip*. —*v.* 1. come safely through. **Ex.** *The ship weathered the storm*. 2. change or cause to be changed by weather conditions. **Ex.** *Sun and rain have weathered the wood so that now it is gray*.

weave (4) [wiyv'], *v.* shape into a material or into some article by passing threads, strips of cloth, etc., over and under each other. **Ex.** *They are weaving baskets*. 2. move in and out, from side to side, etc. **Ex.** *The car was weaving through traffic*. —*n.* a particular manner of weaving. **Ex.** *This wool has a coarse weave*. —**weav'er,** *n.* one who weaves.

web (4) [web'], *n.* the net of threads that a spider makes. 2. anything like a web or that traps like a web. **Ex.** *He was caught in a web of lies*.

we'd [wiyd'] short form, contraction of *we had* and *we would*. **Exs.** *We'd had one letter from him, when he telephoned us long distance. We'd have bought that house if the price had been lower*.

wedding (2) [wed'iŋ], *n.* the act of marrying; the marriage ceremony. **Ex.** *We are going to their wedding*. —**wed',** *v.* —**wedded,** *adj.*

wedge (1) [wej'], *n.* 1. a solid three-cornered piece of metal with one thin edge used to split a log or something similar; anything shaped like this. **Ex.** *She cut him a wedge of cake*. 2. something which gradually divides, splits or prepares the way for change. **Ex.** *The talks held in Washington proved to be the wedge that led to increased trade between the two countries.* —*v.* 1. hold open; hold in place with a wedge. **Ex.** *Wedge the door open, please.* 2. force, crowd or push as if a wedge. **Ex.** *The child's foot was wedged between two rocks.*

Wednesday (1) [wenz'diy], *n.* the fourth day of the week.

weed (3) [wiyd'], *n.* any useless or unwanted plant. **Ex.** *Many weeds were growing among the flowers.* —*v.* 1. remove unwanted plants. **Ex.** *He weeded the garden.* 2. select and remove something or someone not wanted, not useful, etc. **Ex.** *They weeded out the club members who had not paid their dues.*

week (1) [wiyk'], *n.* 1. a period of seven days. **Ex.** *He will be gone a week.* 2. a series of working hours or days within a seven-day period. **Ex.** *She works a forty-hour week.* —**week'ly**, *adj.* happening, appearing or done once a week. **Ex.** *She made weekly visits to them.* —*adv.* once in each week. **Ex.** *I write to her weekly.* —*n.* a newspaper or magazine that appears once a week. **Ex.** *What weeklies do you read?*

weekday [wiyk'dey'], *n.* any day of the week except Sunday.

weekend (3) [wiyk'end'], *n.* the part of the week from Friday night to Monday morning. **Ex.** *We are spending the weekend in the country.* —*v.* spend Saturday and Sunday. **Ex.** *We will weekend in town.*

weep (2) [wiyp'], *v.* 1. cry from grief or any strong emotion. **Ex.** *She was weeping for joy at the news.* 2. mourn. **Ex.** *He was weeping for his dead child.*

weigh (2) [wey'], *v.* 1. be of a certain heaviness. **Ex.** *The meat weighs four pounds.* 2. learn the heaviness of an object or person by means of a measure. **Ex.** *He weighed himself on the bathroom scales.* 3. measure a quantity as on scales. **Ex.** *He weighed out ten pounds of potatoes.* 4. consider carefully. **Ex.** *The judge weighed all the facts before making a decision.* 5. burden or be burdened by something heavy, serious or troublesome. **Ex.** *He was weighed down with problems.*

weight (1) [weyt'], *n.* 1. the heaviness of something or someone. **Ex.** *What is the weight of this box?* 2. the pressure or burden of sorrow, responsibility, etc. **Ex.** *The weight of his worries caused him to lose sleep.* 3. A piece of metal or other heavy material used as a balance in weighing, for holding something in place, etc. **Ex.** *There was a glass paperweight on his desk.*

4. importance; influence. **Ex.** *His recommendation carried a great deal of weight.* 5. a system for expressing heaviness; a unit of such a system. **Ex.** *Sixteen ounces equals one pound in weight.* See **Weights and Measures.** —*v.* burden with something heavy. **Ex.** *She was so weighted down with books that she could hardly walk.* —**weight'y,** *adj.* heavy; important. **Ex.** *They were discussing weighty matters.* —**carry one's own weight,** do one's share. **Ex.** *Everyone must carry his own weight if we are to finish on time.* —**carry weight,** have importance or influence. **Ex.** *His ideas carry weight with me.*

weird (5) [wiyrd'], *adj.* strange; supernatural; mysterious. **Ex.** *We heard a weird cry.*

welcome (1) [wel'kəm], *adj.* 1. received gladly. **Ex.** *He was a welcome guest.* 2. permitted or invited willingly. **Ex.** *You are welcome to use our telephone.* 3. without obligation. **Ex.** *He thanked me and I said, "You're welcome."* —*n.* a friendly greeting. **Ex.** *They extended us a warm welcome.* —*interj.* a greeting given to a person who has just arrived and whom one is glad to see. **Ex.** *Welcome home!* —*v.* greet or accept with pleasure. **Ex.** *He welcomed us upon our arrival.*

welfare (3) [wel'fe:r'], *n.* the condition of being well in regard to health, comfort and happiness. **Ex.** *They did everything for the welfare of their children.*

well (11) [wel'], *n.* 1. a hole dug into the earth to get water, oil, etc. **Ex.** *His oil wells made him rich.* 2. a natural spring of water. **Ex.** *He brought some water from the well.* —*v.* rise; come forth. **Ex.** *Tears welled from her eyes.*

well (1) [wel'], *adv.* 1. in a manner that is good, pleasing, favorable, etc. **Ex.** *He does his work well.* 2. fully; completely; thoroughly. **Ex.** *He knows me well.* 3. greatly; much. **Ex.** *He is well advanced in years.* 4. surely; certainly. **Ex.** *They well know what the trouble is.* —*adj.* 1. in good health; not sick. **Ex.** *She is very well, thank you.* 2. satisfactory. **Ex.** *I hope that all is well with you.* —*interj.* an expression of surprise, agreement, doubt, etc. **Ex.** *Well, I guess I can go.* —**as well,** also. **Ex.** *He wants to go as well.*

we'll [wiyl'], short form, contraction of *we will.* **Ex.** *We'll be glad to drive you home.*

---

a, far; æ, am; e, get; ey, late; i, in; iy, see; ɔ, all; ow, go; u, put; uw, too; ə, but, ago; ər, fur; aw, out; ay, life; oy, boy; ŋ, ring; θ, think; ð, that; ž, measure; š, ship; j, edge; č, child.

well-being [wel'biy'iŋ] *n.* condition of being healthy, happy, etc. **Ex.** *For your own well-being, you should follow the doctor's advice.*

well-founded [wel'fawn'did], *adj.* based on sound thought and information. **Ex.** *He has some well-founded ideas about teaching methods.*

well-known [wel'nown'], *adj.* known to or by many people; famous; generally or widely known. **Ex.** *She is a well-known actress.*

well-off [welɔ:f'], *adj.* fortunate; wealthy. **Ex.** *Our well-off neighbors can afford a vacation abroad.*

well-read [wel'red'] *adj.* having much knowledge because of considerable reading. **Ex.** *His conversation revealed that he was a well-read man.*

well-to-do [wel'təduw'], *adj.* rich. **Ex.** *My mother worked for a well-to-do family.*

went (1) [went'], *v.* past tense of *go.* **Ex.** *He went there yesterday.*

wept (3) [wept'], *v.* past tense and participle of *weep.* **Exs.** *She wept when she read the letter. The children had wept when the dog died.*

were (1) [wə:r'], *v.* past tense of *be* used with *we, you, they* and plural nouns. **Ex.** *Where were you this morning?*

we're [wiyr'], short form, contraction of *we are.* **Ex.** *We're leaving now.*

weren't [wə:r'ənt], short form, contraction of *were not.* **Ex.** *Why weren't you at the meeting last night?*

west (1) [west'], *n.* 1. the direction to the left of one facing north; one of the four points of the compass. **Ex.** *The sun sets in the west.* 2. regions or countries lying to the west; that part of the United States lying west of the Mississippi River. **Ex.** *He comes from a large city in the West.* —*adv.* toward the west. **Ex.** *My bedroom faces west.* —*adj.* 1. toward, in or at the west. **Ex.** *Have you visited the west wing of the White House?* 2. from the West. **Ex.** *A west wind is blowing.* —**western,** *adj.* characteristic of the west; in, of, to or from the west. **Ex.** *He likes western food.* —*n.* a movie or story about the American west. **Ex.** *He likes to see westerns.* —**westerner,** *n.* one who comes from the West.

wet (1) [wet'], *adj.* 1. covered or soaked with water or some other liquid. **Ex.** *She removed her wet clothes.* 2. rainy. **Ex.** *We have just had several days of wet weather.* 3. damp; not yet dry. **Ex.** *The paint on the wall is still wet.* —*n.* water; rain.

Ex. *The children were playing in the wet.* —*v.* cover or soak with liquid. **Ex.** *Wet the cloth and wash your face.*

we've [wiyv'], short form, contraction of *we have.* **Ex.** *We've just returned from our vacation.*

whale [hweyl'], *n.* a very large mammal that looks like a fish and lives in the ocean. **Ex.** *As the huge whale dived, his tail rose high into the air.*

WHALE

wharf (4) [wɔrf', hwɔrf'], *n.* a structure like a platform, sometimes with a roof, extending over the water or along the shore so that vessels may stay beside it to load or unload; a pier. **Ex.** *Passengers were waiting on the wharf to board the ship.*

what (1) [hwət', hwat'], *pron.* 1. the nature of the thing or the particular thing asked about; which particular thing, action, etc. **Exs.** *What is it? What did you say?* 2. that or those which. **Ex.** *Take what you want.* —*adj.* 1. which or which kind. **Ex.** *What ship is that?* 2. as much; as many as. **Ex.** *Take what money you need.* 3. how great; how surprising; etc. **Ex.** *What a sight that was!* —*interj.* an exclamation of surprise, excitement, anger, etc. **Ex.** *What! No bus for another hour!*

whatever [hwətev'ər], **whatsoever** [hwat'sowev'ər], *pron.* 1. anything or any amount that. **Ex.** *Take whatever you want of the cake.* 2. no matter what. **Ex.** *He loves her whatever she does.* —*adj.* 1. no matter what. **Ex.** *I can eat whatever food you have.* 2. any; of any kind or number. **Ex.** *I have no books whatever.*

what's [hwəts', hwats'], short form, contraction of *what is.* **Ex.** *What's the matter?*

wheat (1) [hwiyt'] *n.* a grain that when ground becomes flour and is used in making breads, cakes, etc; the grass bearing this grain. **Ex.** *The fields of wheat were ready to cut.*

wheel (1) [hwiyl'], *n.* 1. a round frame which turns on a central point. **Ex.** *His bicycle has two wheels.* 2. anything like a wheel in shape, purpose or action. **Ex.** *The driver was behind the wheel.* —*v.* 1. pull or move on wheels. **Ex.** *She was wheeling the baby down the street in a carriage.* 2. turn or cause to turn around. **Ex.** *She wheeled around and faced the man*

WHEEL 1

who had been behind her. —**wheel chair,** *n.* a large chair with two wheels attached, used by a person who is not able to walk.

when (1) [hwen'], *adv.* at what time. **Ex.** *When are you planning to leave? —conj.* 1. at what time. **Ex.** *He does not know when he can come.* 2. at any time. **Ex.** *She gets sick when she rides in a car.* 3. after which; and then. **Ex.** *I had just arrived when you called.* 4. during the time; at the time. **Ex.** *We liked that game when we were children.* 5. although. **Ex.** *The boy kept on playing when he knew it was time for bed. —pron.* what certain time. **Ex.** *Since when have you had a car?*

whenever [hwenev'ər], *conj.* at whatever time. **Ex.** *Go whenever you wish.*

where (1) [hwe:r'], *adv.* 1. at or in what place. **Ex.** *Where is my coat?* 2. to what place. **Ex.** *Where did you go last night?* 3. from what source, person or place. **Ex.** *Where did you get that idea? —conj.* 1. at or in what place. **Ex.** *I know where she is.* 2. at or in the place; in or at which. **Ex.** *This is the house where he lives.* 3. to the place to which. **Ex.** *The dog goes where his owner goes. —pron.* 1. what or which place. **Ex.** *Where do you come from?* 2. the place at or in which. **Ex.** *This is where the accident happened.*

whereabouts [hwe:r'əbawts'], *n.* location of a person or thing. **Ex.** *I do not know his whereabouts. —adv.* near what place. **Ex.** *Whereabouts is your school?*

wherever [hwe:rev'ər], *conj.* at, in or to whatever place. **Ex.** *I will go wherever she goes.*

whether (1) [hweð'ər], *conj.* 1. pointing to a choice between two possibilities. **Ex.** *She is calling to find out whether or not you are coming.* 2. pointing to a choice between two possibilities, the choice of which will not affect the result. **Ex.** *Whether you join us or not, we are going.*

which (1) [hwič'], *pron.* 1. what one or ones of a particular group of persons or things. **Exs.** *Which of the students are coming? Which of the books have you read?* 2. that. **Ex.** *The dress which you are wearing is very pretty. —adj.* what one or ones. **Ex.** *Which hat do you want?*

whichever [hwičev'ər], *pron.* any one that. **Ex.** *Buy whichever you like.*

while (1) [hwayl'], *n.* a space of time. **Ex.** *I will see you in a little while. —conj.* 1. at or during the same time that. **Ex.** *The child fell while she was running.* 2. although. **Ex.** *While the work was difficult, it was interesting. —while away,* use time pleasantly. **Ex.** *We whiled away the summer afternoon reading and talking.*

whine (5) [hwayn'], *v.* 1. utter a low cry or sound in complaint, discontent, etc. **Ex.** *The baby whined no matter what we did for him.* 2. utter or beg with a low cry or sound. **Ex.** *The dog whined to be let in the house.* —*n.* a low sound of distress. **Ex.** *We heard the whine of a hungry child.*

whip (2) [hwip'], *n.* 1. an instrument, usually consisting of a stiff handle and a piece of leather or cord at one end, used for striking animals or people. **Ex.** *He urged the horse on with a whip.* 2. a stroke or blow with or as with a whip. **Ex.** *The whip of the wind snapped the sail.* —*v.* 1. strike with or as with a whip. **Ex.** *The boy was whipped for telling a lie.* 2. move, pull, etc. with a sudden motion. **Ex.** *The teacher whipped around when she heard the sound of whispering.* 3. beat eggs, cream, etc. into a light mass with a fork or beater.

whirl (3) [hwərl'], *v.* 1. spin fast; turn around and around quickly. **Ex.** *The dancer whirled on her toes.* 2. move or be carried along rapidly. **Ex.** *He whirled around the corner on his bicycle.* 3. have the sensation of whirling. **Ex.** *My head is whirling.* —*n.* 1. a rapid turning motion. **Ex.** *He gave the steering wheel a whirl.* 2. something that whirls. **Ex.** *He was lost from sight in a whirl of snow.* 3. a mental state of confusion. **Ex.** *My thoughts are in a whirl.*

whiskey (5) [hwis'kiy], *n.* an alcoholic liquor made from various grains. **Ex.** *He liked a drink of rye whiskey before dinner.*

whisper (2) [hwis'pər], *v.* 1. speak softly and low so as to be heard only by the one or ones spoken to. **Ex.** *He whispered that he loved her.* 2. tell privately, as a secret. **Ex.** *People are whispering about their romance.* 3. make a low, hushed sound like a whisper. **Ex.** *The wind whispered through the trees.* —*n.* 1. a soft, low way of speaking. **Ex.** *He spoke in a whisper.* 2. a secret or private utterance. **Ex.** *There were whispers about his past.* 3. a low, hushed sound. **Ex.** *He heard only the whisper of the nearby brook.*

whistle (2) [hwis'əl], *v.* 1. make a high, sharp sound by forcing the breath through the teeth or closed lips. **Ex.** *He whistled for his dog.* 2. make a similar sound by using some mechanical device. **Ex.** *The policeman whistled for traffic to stop.* 3. move with a high, sharp sound. **Ex.** *The winter wind whistled around the house.* —*n.* 1. a sound produced by whistling. **Ex.**

He gave a whistle of surprise. 2. a device for producing a high, sharp sound. **Ex.** *The brass whistle of the locomotive was highly polished.*

white (1) [hwayt'], *adj.* 1. of the color of milk or snow. **Ex.** *She wore a white dress.* 2. relatively light or pale in color. **Ex.** *Her mother's hair is white.* —*n.* a color like that of milk or snow. **Ex.** *They painted the house white.* 2. clothing of this color. **Ex.** *She likes to wear white in the summer.* 3. the colorless part of an egg. **Ex.** *He used three egg whites in the cake.* —**whit'en,** *v.*

whitecap [hwayt' kæp'], *n.* a rough wave with white foam on top.

white flag [hwayt'flæg'], a white cloth raised when one wants to stop fighting or to surrender.

White House [hwayt' haws'], the official home of the President of the United States in Washington, D.C.

white lie [hwayt' lay'], an easily forgiven lie about something unimportant, often told to prevent embarrassment. **Ex.** *She told a white lie to avoid accepting his invitation.*

who (1) [huw'], *pron.* 1. what person or persons. **Ex.** *Who was at the door?* 2. which person or persons. **Ex.** *I do not know who they are.* 3. the person or persons that. **Ex.** *The man who came left a letter.*

who'd [huwd'], short form, contraction of *who had* and *who would.* **Exs.** *He didn't know who'd done it. Who'd believe that he's seventy-seven years old?*

whoever [huwev'ər], *pron.* 1. whatever person or persons. **Ex.** *Whoever comes should be given the money.* 2. no matter who. **Ex.** *Whoever it is, I don't want to see him.*

whole (1) [howl'], *adj.* 1. the complete amount or extent. **Ex.** *Tell me the whole story.* 2. not divided; not cut into pieces. **Ex.** *He served the whole fish.* 3. containing all its parts. **Ex.** *She bought a whole set of dishes.* 4. unbroken; undamaged; etc. **Ex.** *After the storm, not one window was whole.* —*n.* the entire amount or extent; something complete. **Ex.** *The whole of his experience had not prepared him for this trouble.* —**whol'ly,** *adv.* —**on the whole,** usually, generally. **Ex.** *On the whole, I believe his story.*

wholehearted [howl'har'tid], *adj.* completely enthusiastic; sincere; energetic; etc. **Ex.** *He made a wholehearted effort to win.*

wholesale (4) [howl'seyl'], *n.* the selling of goods in large quantities, especially to merchants for resale to the actual users. *Ex. He does business only at wholesale.* —*adj.* 1. of or about the selling of goods in large quantities. *Ex. He bought the medicine at wholesale prices.* 2. extensive; done on a broad scale; general. *Ex. The gang had committed wholesale murder.* —**whole'sal·er**, *n.* one who sells in large quantities, usually not directly to the actual user.

wholesome (4) [howl'səm], *adj.* helpful; of benefit to the mind or body. *Ex. She prepares wholesome meals for her family.*

who'll [huwl'], short form, contraction of *who will. Ex. Who'll be going with you?*

whom (1) [huwm'], *pron.* a form of *who* used as the object of a preposition or verb. *Exs. To whom did you speak? That is the man whom I saw yesterday.*

who's [huwz'], short form, contraction of *who is. Ex. Who's going with you?*

whose (1) [huwz], *pron.* a form of *who* that shows ownership or possession. *Exs. Whose hat is this? We met the man whose son won the race.*

why (1) [hway', way'], *adv.* for what cause, reason, purpose, etc. *Ex. Why did you come?* —*conj.* 1. for which; because of which. *Ex. There is no reason why he cannot go.* 2. the reason for which. *Ex. I do not know why he did it.* —*interj.* an exclamation of surprise, hesitation, etc. *Ex. Why, it's past noon!*

wicked (3) [wik'id], *adj.* sinful; morally wrong; evil. *Ex. The wicked deeds of his youth had made him an outcast.* —**wick'ed·ly**, *adv.* —**wick'ed·ness**, *n.*

wide (1) [wayd'], *adj.* 1. having great extent from one side to the other; broad. *Ex. The travelers crossed a wide plain.* 2. measured from side to side. *Ex. The table is too wide for this room.* 3. not limited; including much; extensive. *Ex. He is a man of wide experience.* 4. opened very much. *Ex. Her eyes were wide with surprise.* —*adv.* 1. over a great extent; to a great distance. *Ex. The news spread far and wide.* 2. fully open. *Ex. Open the door wide.* —**wide'ly**, *adv.* —**wid'en**, *v.* —**width'**, *n.* the extent or distance from side to side. *Ex. What is the width of this material?*

wide-awake [wayd'əweyk'], *adj.* fully awake; alert. *Ex. The wide-awake girl quickly raised her hand to reply.*

widespread [wayd'spred'], *adj.* extending or occurring over a large area or among many people. **Ex.** *The flood damage was widespread.*

widow (2) [wid'ow], *n.* a woman who has not remarried after the death of her husband. **Ex.** *The widow was left with two young children.* —*v.* cause to be a widow. **Ex.** *She was widowed at the age of sixty.* —**wid'ow·er,** *n.* a man who has not remarried after the death of his wife.

wield (5) [wiyld'], *v.* 1. use or handle effectively or skillfully. **Ex.** *His father taught him how to wield an ax.* 2. exercise or use. **Ex.** *In our country, the president wields great power.*

wife (1) [wayf'], *n.* a woman united to a man in marriage. **Ex.** *I have not met his wife.*

wig (5) [wig'], *n.* a covering made of hair or material that looks like hair, worn on the head, usually to conceal the lack of natural hair or to change one's appearance. **Ex.** *He has worn a wig for several years because he is almost bald.*

wild (1) [wayld'], *adj.* 1. living in a natural state; not cultivated. **Ex.** *There are wild animals in these woods.* 2. without inhabitants or cultivation. **Ex.** *The land along the river is wild.* 3. not civilized. **Ex.** *There are still wild people in that jungle.* 4. excited; angry; uncontrolled, etc. **Ex.** *The ship was driven on the rocks by the wild sea.* 5. unreasonable; crazy. **Ex.** *People laughed at his wild ideas.* —*adv.* without control; wildly. **Ex.** *They let their children run wild.* —**wild'ly,** *adv.* —**wild'ness,** *n.*

wilderness (3) [wil'dərnəs], *n.* a region of wild, rough land where few or no people live. **Ex.** *They were lost in the wilderness.*

will (1) [wil'], *n.* 1. desire; wish. **Ex.** *He was forced to sign the paper against his will.* 2. strong intention. **Ex.** *The sick woman has lost her will to live.* 3. the power of making choices and controlling actions. **Ex.** *He has a strong will.* 4. feelings toward another. **Ex.** *There is ill will between them.* 5. a declaration of a person's wishes for disposing of his property after death, usually written. **Ex.** *The dying man changed his will.* —*v.* leave property to someone in a will. **Ex.** *He willed her the house.* —**will'ful,** *adj.* 1. determined to do something or have one's own way. **Ex.** *His willful behavior is difficult to control.* 2. intentional. **Ex.** *It was willful murder.*

will (1) [wil'], *v.* used with other verbs to indicate: 1. future action. **Ex.** *He will probably come tomorrow.* 2. desire;

decision. **Ex.** *Which will you have?* 3. agreement; willingness.
Ex. *Will you help me?* 4. ability. **Ex.** *This box will hold all
your books.* 5. intention. **Ex.** *I will go to see her soon.* 6.
custom or habit. **Ex.** *She will tell you all her troubles if you let
her.*

willing (2) [wil'iŋ], *adj*. 1. consenting; agreeable to doing. **Ex.**
He is willing to come tomorrow. 2. acting, doing, giving, etc.
cheerfully. **Ex.** *They are willing workers* —**will'ing·ly**, *adv*.
—**will'ing·ness**, *n*.

willow (5) [wil'ow], *n*. a tree with long narrow leaves and long
hanging branches which are tough but so easily bent that they
are used for making baskets and woven furniture; the wood
of this tree. **Ex.** *Willows grew beside the stream.* —**wil'ow·y**,
adj. slender and graceful. **Ex.** *She has a willowy figure.*

wilt (5) [wilt'], *v*. 1. droop; lose firmness and freshness. **Ex.**
Water the flowers or they will wilt. 2. become weak; lose
courage. **Ex.** *She seemed to wilt when her request was refused.*

win (1) [win'], *v*. 1. gain, get or arrive at by effort, work, etc.
Ex. *We need to win their help.* 2. gain a victory; defeat others
in a contest. **Ex.** *I'm sure that our team will win.*

wind (1) [wind'], *n*. 1. movement of air. **Ex.** *The wind was
blowing from the south.* 2. a strong, often damaging movement of air. **Ex.** *The wind blew off his hat.* 3. breath. **Ex.** *He
lost his wind during the race.* 4. hint. **Ex.** *He caught wind of
their plans.* —*v*. cause to breathe with difficulty. **Ex.** *The
walk up the hill winded me.* —**wind'y**, *adj*.

wind (1) [waynd'], *v*. 1. wrap or roll something around an object
or itself. **Ex.** *I'll wind this string into a ball.* 2. cover or
surround by turning or twisting; go around. **Ex.** *That vine is
winding its way around the tree.* 3. cause to operate by turning.
Ex. *Remember to wind your watch.* 4. move in or follow in a
curving, turning, twisting way. **Ex.** *The road winds through
our farm.* —**wind up**, finish. **Ex.** *We should be able to wind
up this work today.*

windbreak [win(d)'breyk'], *n*. anything that slows or stops the
force of the wind. **Ex.** *The trees acted as a windbreak for the
house.* —**wind'break'er**, *n*. a jacket that protects one from the
force of the wind.

a, far; æ, am; e, get; ey, late; i, in; iy, see; ɔ, all; ow, go; u, put; uw, too;
ə, but, ago; ər, fur; aw, out; ay, life; oy, boy; ŋ, ring; θ, think; ð, that;
ž, measure; š, ship; j, edge; č, child.

windfall [wind'fɔl'], *n.* an unexpected gain. **Ex.** *The money from his uncle's will was a windfall.*

window (1) [win'dow], *n.* 1. an opening in a wall to admit light and air, usually with a movable frame containing glass. **Ex.** *He opened the window.* 2. a piece of glass in a window opening. **Ex.** *He broke the window.*

window-shop [win'dowšap'], *v.* look at goods for sale through a store window without going into the store to buy anything. **Ex.** *They window-shopped all afternoon.*

windpipe [wind'payp'], *n.* the passage located at the back of the mouth by which air reaches the lungs. **Ex.** *A piece of food lodged in his windpipe.*

windshield [wind'šiyld'], *n.* the window across the front of an automobile. **Ex.** *The windshield was shattered in the accident.*

wine (2) [wayn'], *n.* the juice of grapes or some fruit or plant changed chemically so that it has an alcoholic content. **Ex.** *She served wine with dinner.* —**win'er·y,** *n.* a place where wine is made.

wing (1) [wiŋ'], *n.* 1. one of the paired parts of a bird or other animal that, when spread and moved, carry it into the air. **Exs.** *The bird's wing was broken. The fly spread its wings and flew away.* 2. any part with the appearance of a wing used for flying. **Ex.** *The wing of the plane is being fixed.* 3. any part which extends from the main part. **Ex.** *They are adding a wing to their house.* 4. a section of a larger political group; a political group with rightist or leftist ideas in politics. **Ex.** *The right wing of his party voted for him.* —**under the wing,** under the protection, care, guidance. **Ex.** *He took the new boy under his wing.*

wink (4) [wiŋk], *v.* 1. close and open one of the eyes quickly, usually as a sign. **Ex.** *He winked at the pretty girl.* 2. send out short, rapid sparkles of light. **Ex.** *She saw the lights of the city winking.* —*n.* the act of winking. **Ex.** *She ignored his wink.*

winter (1) [win'tər], *n.* the cold season when few plants grow, in countries north of the equator from December to March. **Ex.** *Yesterday we had the first snow of winter.* —*adj.* characteristic of winter; used in winter. **Ex.** *She bought some winter clothes.* —*v.* pass the winter. **Ex.** *They always winter in the South.* —**win'try,** *adj.* like winter.

wipe (2) [wayp'], *v.* rub with something soft in order to dry, clean or remove. **Exs.** *He wiped the dishes. The mother* *wiped the child's nose.* —**wipe out,** remove completely; get rid of. **Ex.** *He wiped out his debts.*

wire (2) [wayr'], *n.* 1. a piece of metal in a long, threadlike form. **Ex.** *Those men are putting up the telephone wire.* 2. telegram. **Ex.** *She sent me the news by wire.* —*v.* 1. provide with wire; use wire for any purpose. **Ex.** *They are now wiring the building for electricity.* 2. send by wire; telegraph. **Ex.** *Wire me the board's decision at once.* —*adj.* made of wire. **Ex.** *They put a wire fence around their yard.* —**wir'y,** *adj.* thin and physically strong. **Ex.** *He has a wiry build.*

wise (1) [wayz'], *adj.* 1. judging properly what is true or false, good, best to do, etc.; showing sound judgment. **Ex.** *She made a wise choice.* 2. having great learning; knowing much. **Ex.** *His teacher is a wise person.* —**wise'ly,** *adv.* —**wisdom,** *n.*

-wise (1) [wayz'], *suffix.* in the direction or manner of. **Exs.** *Clock, clockwise; like, likewise; edge, edgewise.*

wish (1) [wiš'], *v.* 1. want; long for; express a desire or longing. **Exs.** *She wishes to see the house. We wish the work were finished. I wish him well.* 2. express a greeting. a farewell, etc. **Ex.** *He wished me good morning.* 3. order; request. **Ex.** *He wishes to see you at nine o'clock.* —*n.* 1. a longing to do, get, be, etc., something; a desire that one feels or expresses. **Exs.** *He had no wish to go. She followed her mother's wishes.* 2. that which is desired or hoped for. **Ex** *She got her wish.*

wit (2) [wit'], *n.* 1. the ability to understand and express ideas in a clever and amusing way. **Ex.** *He entertained us with his wit.* 2. a clever and amusing person. **Ex.** *The writer was a well-known wit.* —**wits',** *n. pl.* the power to sense, judge and act. **Ex.** *He kept his wits during the emergency.* —**wit'ty,** *adj.* clever; showing wit. —**at one's wits' end,** no longer able to sense, judge and act; not knowing what to do; completely at a loss. **Ex.** *I have looked everywhere for her, and I am at my wits' end.*

witch (3) [wič'], *n.* a woman believed to practice evil magic. **Ex.** *The villagers thought a witch had caused them their trouble.*

with (1) [wið, wiθ], *prep.* 1. accompanied by; along or by the side of. **Ex.** *His family was with him.* 2. showing a general relationship; because of. **Ex.** *We are pleased with your work.* 3. by means of. **Ex.** *She covered the table with a cloth.* 4. using; showing. **Ex.** *We watched them with interest.* 5. having. **Ex.** *He lived in the house with the red door.* 6. being in

agreement or disagreement. **Ex.** *He was angry with his friend.*
7. as a result of. **Ex.** *She is ill with a cold.* 8. at or about the
same time of. **Ex.** *With these words, she left.* 9. in regard to
sameness or difference. **Ex.** *How do prices here compare with
those outside the city?*

withdraw (4) [wiðdrɔ:'], *v.* 1. take out, away or back; remove.
Ex. *They are withdrawing their son from that school.* 2. go
apart or away from others. **Ex.** *She often withdraws into
silence.* —**with·draw'al,** *n.* the act of going or taking away;
that which one withdraws. **Ex.** *He made a withdrawal from
his savings account.* —**with·drawn',** *adj.*

wither (4) [wið'ər], *v.* 1. become dry and faded. **Ex.** *The grass
withered and died for lack of water.* 2. lose or cause to lose
freshness and strength. **Ex.** *The heat had withered the flowers.*

withhold [wiðhowld'], *v.* hold back; not give; not express. **Ex.**
She is withholding information that we need. —**with·hold'ing
tax',** that part of an employee's wages or salary which an
employer withholds and pays directly to the government as a
portion of the employee's income tax.

within (1) [wiðin'], *prep.* 1. inside a limit of space, time, etc. **Ex.**
We lived within sight of the ocean. 2. inside fixed or required
limits. **Ex.** *He always drives within the speed limit.* —*adv.* in,
into or on the inner side. **Ex.** *He heard noises within.*

without (1) [wiðawt'], *prep.* 1. with no; not having or using; free
from. **Ex.** *He was without fear.* 2. avoiding; not doing, giving,
etc. **Ex.** *He left without saying good-by.* 3. outside. **Ex.** *Everything within and without the house was in order.* —*adv.* 1.
in or into the outer side; outside. **Ex.** *We heard a shout
without.* 2. in need of; lacking. **Ex.** *You can use this or do
without.*

withstand (5) [wiðstænd'], *v.* continue to stand despite some
strong opposing force; endure; resist. **Ex.** *That ship can withstand any storm.*

witness (2) [wit'nes], *n.* 1. one who personally sees or knows
about something that happens or has happened. **Ex.** *He was
a witness to the accident.* 2. one who gives evidence of what
he has seen. **Ex.** *The lawyer asked him to be a witness for the
defense.* —*v.* see personally; observe. **Ex.** *He witnessed the
fight.*

wizard (5) [wiz'ərd], *n.* a person of great, almost magical skill.
Ex. *He is a wizard at mathematics.*

woe (5) [wow'], *n.* 1. grief; great sadness. **Ex.** *Her son's death added to her woe.* 2. misery; suffering. **Ex.** *The flood was a cause of much woe.*

woke (4) [wowk'], *v.* past tense of *wake.* **Ex.** *I woke at ten o'clock this morning.*

wolf (2) [wulf'], *n.* a wild, meat-eating, dog-like animal. **Ex.** *A wolf killed one of our sheep last night.* —*v.* eat rapidly and greedily. **Ex.** *The hungry boy wolfed his lunch.*

WOLF

woman (1) [wum'ən], *n.* 1. an adult female person. **Ex.** *She is a lovely woman.* 2. an adult female human in general. **Ex.** *Some people think that a woman's place is in the kitchen.* 3. a female worker. **Ex.** *We have a cleaning woman once a week.*

women (1) [wum'in], *n.* plural of *woman.* **Ex.** *How many women were there?*

won (1) [wən], *v.* past tense and participle of *win.* **Exs.** *Who won the game? She had won several prizes at school.*

wonder (1) [wən'dər], *v.* 1. feel doubt or curiosity about; ask oneself. **Ex.** *They wondered if it would snow.* 2. feel surprised or astonished. **Ex.** *We wondered at the size of the building.* —*n.* a feeling of surprise or astonishment. **Ex.** *They were filled with wonder at the sight.* 2. something surprising or marvelous. **Ex.** *It is a wonder that she lived so long.* —**won'der·ful,** *adj.* marvelous; remarkable. **Ex.** *He showed wonderful courage.*

won't (1) [wownt'], *v.* shortened form, contraction of *will not.* **Ex.** *He won't go.*

woo (4) [wuw'], *v.* seek the love, affection or support of. **Exs.** *He wooed and won the girl. He wooed the voters with the promise that he would lower taxes.*

wood (1) [wud'], *n.* the hard substance that makes up a tree or bush; this substance prepared for use as building material, firewood, etc. **Ex.** *This kind of wood is often used for making chairs and tables.* —*adj.* made of wood. **Ex.** *That is a heavy wood door.* —**wooden,** *adj.* 1. made of wood. **Ex.** *There was a wooden dish on the table.* 2. without feeling or expression.

Ex. *She stood there with a wooden look on her face.* 3. stiff; without bending. **Ex.** *The wooden way he moved was painful to watch.* **—wooded,** *adj.* covered with trees. **Ex.** *Part of their land was heavily wooded.* **—woods,** a small forest. **Ex.** *I went for a walk in the woods.*

wool (2) [wul'], *n.* 1. the soft, hairy covering of sheep and some other animals. **Ex.** *The wool was shipped to a factory.* 2. thread, cloth or clothing made of the hair of sheep or some other animals. **Ex.** *She bought some wool to make a dress.* **—adj.** made of wool. **Ex.** *He was wearing a wool sweater.* **—wool'en,** *adj.* made of wool. **—wool'ly,** *adj.* of or like wool.

word (1) [wərd'], *n.* 1. a unit of one or more sounds that has meaning; the written form of this unit. **Ex.** *How many English words do you know?* 2. a short talk. **Ex.** *May I have a word with you?* 3. argument. **Ex.** *He was late and we had words.* 4. a promise; a pledge. **Ex.** *She gave me her word that she would write.* 5. a message; news. **Ex.** *Word came that you were ill.* **—v.** express in words. **Ex.** *She worded her request badly.* **—by word of mouth,** by spoken words. **Ex.** *The story spread by word of mouth.* **—word for word,** using the same words exactly. **Ex.** *I told her what you said, word for word.*

wore (1) [wɔ:r'], *v.* past tense of *wear.* **Ex.** *She wore a hat.*

work (1) [wərk'], *n.* 1. effort used to do something; labor. **Ex.** *Gardening is pleasant work.* 2. that which needs effort; a project. **Ex.** *There is much work to be done on this farm.* 3. that which is created by effort, such as a book, painting, opera, etc. **Ex.** *That is a work of art.* 4. the job one does for pay; employment. **Ex.** *He is trying to find work.* **—v.** 1. use mental or physical effort to make or do something; labor. **Ex.** *He works very hard at everything he does.* 2. operate; run; function as it should. **Ex.** *The heating system in this house works very well.* 3. be employed at or by. **Ex.** *He works for the government.* 4. cause to labor. **Ex.** *He works his men too hard.* 5. move slowly and with difficulty. **Ex.** *They worked their way up the mountain.* **—work'er,** *n.* one who works. **—work'ing,** *adj.* 1. concerning work. 2. in operation; functioning. **Ex.** *The number you have dialed is not a working number.* **—works',** *n. pl.* 1. a factory. **Ex.** *This iron is being sent to the steel works.* 2. the parts of a machine that operate or move. **Ex.** *The works of this clock are broken.* **—out of work,** lacking a job; unemployed. **Ex.** *He has been out of work for two months.* **—work out,** 1. end. **Ex.** *Everything* *worked out well.* 2. get out by effort. **Ex.** *He worked his way out of the crowd.* 3. solve. **Ex.** *He worked out the answer to the problem.* 4. engage in physical exercise. **Ex.** *He works out every day for about an hour.* —**work up,** 1. advance; move toward; develop. **Ex.** *He has worked up to office manager.* 2. become excited; awaken strong feelings. **Ex.** *She was worked up about her situation at home.*

workday [wərk'dey'], *n.* 1. a day on which one works. **Ex.** *Sunday is not a workday for me.* 2. the length one works in a day. **Ex.** *He has an eight-hour workday.*

workman [wərk'mən], *n.* a man who works with his hands, often at work requiring skill. **Ex.** *This old clock was made by a clever workman.* —**work'man·like,** *adj.* skillful; well-done. **Ex.** *He did a workmanlike job.*

world (1) [wərld'], *n.* 1. the earth; the globe. **Ex.** *She took a trip around the world.* 2. the people who live on the earth. **Ex.** *The whole world hopes for peace.* 3. the societies and activities of people. **Ex.** *He had to work hard in the world to succeed.* 4. a special group of people, things, etc. **Ex.** *He is studying the animal world.* —**world'ly,** *adj.* wise in matters of the world.

worm (3) [wərm'], *n.* a small, slender, soft-bodied animal without legs. **Ex.** *The bird was looking for worms.* —*v.* move or act in a slow, twisting way. **Exs.** *The boy wormed his way under the fence. She wormed her way into their confidence.* —**worm'y,** *adj.* 1. full of worms. 2. like a worm.

WORM

worn (1) [worn'], *v.* past participle of *wear.* **Ex.** *Have you worn that dress before?* —*adj.* 1. damaged by use. **Ex.** *His clothes looked worn.* 2. tired. **Ex.** *She looked worn at the end of the day.*

worn-out [worn'awt'], *adj.* 1. worn until no longer usable. **Ex.** *His worn-out clothes had had many years of hard use.* 2. exhausted. **Ex.** *The worn-out woman longed for her vacation.*

worry (2) [wə:r'iy], *v.* 1. be anxious; be concerned. **Ex.** *They worry about their son's health.* 2. trouble; bother. **Ex.** *Don't worry me with your problems.* —*n.* 1. anxiety; concern. **Ex.** *Worry is bad for your health.* 2. that which causes anxiety or concern. **Ex.** *They have financial worries.*

worse (2) [wərs'], *adj.* bad, sick, unpleasant, harmful, etc. in a greater degree. **Ex.** *He is feeling worse now than he felt before he drank the medicine.* —*n.* that which is worse. **Ex.**

She was none the worse for her fall. —**wors'en,** *v.* become or make worse. **Ex.** *The storm has worsened.*

worship (3) [wər'šip], *v.* show deep religious respect. **Ex.** *Each worshiped in his own way.* —*n.* the act of showing deep religious respect; a religious service. **Ex.** *They attended morning worship* —**wor'ship·er,** *n.*

worst (2) [wərst'], *adj.* bad, sick, unpleasant, harmful, etc. in the highest degree. **Ex.** *He is the worst boy in the class.* —*n.* that which is most bad, unpleasant, harmful, etc. **Ex.** *We have not yet heard the worst.*

worth (1) [wərθ'], *n.* 1. value measured in money. **Ex.** *The man asked about the worth of his house.* 2. the amount that a sum of money will buy. **Ex.** *Please give me fifty cents' worth of candy.* 3. the quality or qualities that make a thing useful, valuable or desirable; excellence. **Ex.** *Everyone knew the worth of his work.* —*adj.* 1. of value in terms of money. **Ex.** *This car is still worth a lot.* 2. deserving of. **Ex.** *It is not worth my time.* —**wor'thy,** *adj.* deserving; admirable; useful. **Ex.** *The money will be used for a worthy cause.*

worthwhile [wərθhwayl'], *adj.* worth the time or effort. **Ex.** *I find helping children a worthwhile activity.*

would (1) [wud'], *v.* 1. past tense of *will*. **Ex.** *He would often stop there on his way home.* 2. used with another verb to ask a question more politely. **Ex.** *Would you help me clean the kitchen?*

wouldn't [wud'nt], *v.* short form, contraction of *would not*. **Ex.** *He said that he wouldn't be able to come until next week.*

wound (2) [wawnd'], *v.* past tense and participle of *wind*. **Exs.** *He wound his watch. They had wound the alarm clock too tightly and broken a spring.*

wound (2) [wuwnd'], *n.* 1. an injury to the body in which the skin is usually cut or broken. **Ex.** *Blood was pouring from the wound.* 2. an injury or hurt to the feelings, reputation, etc. **Ex.** *The experience caused a wound to her pride.* —*v.* injure; hurt. **Ex.** *He was wounded in the right leg.*

wove (4) [wowv'], *v.* past tense of *weave*. **Ex.** *They wove baskets of grass.*

woven (4) [wowv'n], *v.* past participle of *weave*. **Ex.** *A rug woven from rags lay on the living room floor.*

wrap (2) [ræp'], *v.* 1. fold or wind around so as to cover. **Ex.** *She wrapped a scarf around her shoulders.* 2. cover or enclose in paper and fasten with string or something similar. **Ex.** *She wrapped the package.* —*n.* an outer garment. **Ex.** *Let me help you remove your wrap.* —**wrap'ping,** *n.* covering or paper used to enclose. —**wrapper,** *n.* 1. a covering or paper used to enclose. 2. one who wraps. 3. a woman's robe.

wrath (4) [ræθ], *n.* fierce anger; rage. **Exs.** *He could not face his father's wrath. The wrath of the storm lessened.*

wreath (4) [riyθ'], *n.* a circle made by twisting together flowers, leaves, etc. **Ex.** *The bride wore a wreath of white flowers.* —**wreathe',** *v.* encircle or wind around; decorate with a wreath or something resembling a wreath in shape. **Ex.** *His face was wreathed in smiles.*

wreck (3) [rek'], *v.* 1. damage greatly; ruin. **Ex.** *His hopes were wrecked when he failed the examination.* 2. tear down; demolish. **Ex.** *The building was wrecked because it was unsafe.* —*n.* 1. anything that has been badly damaged, broken or ruined. **Ex.** *The house was a wreck after the fire.* 2. the act of badly damaging, breaking or ruining. **Ex.** *The wreck of the ship was reported yesterday.* —**wreck'age,** *n.* 1. the act of wrecking. 2. pieces of a wreck. **Ex.** *The wreckage of the airplane was scattered for miles.* —**wreck'er,** *n.* 1. that which or one who wrecks. 2. a truck which carries aways wrecks or wreckage. **Ex.** *The wrecker towed the car to a garage.*

wrench (4) [renč'], *n.* 1. a sudden pulling and twisting. **Ex.** *He gave the bottle cap a wrench and off it came.* 2. an injury caused by twisting or pulling. **Ex.** *He has a wrench in his left shoulder.* 3. a sudden grief or emotional pain. **Ex.** *It was a wrench to leave her family.* 4. a tool for twisting nuts onto bolts, turning pipes, etc. —*v.* twist and pull violently. **Ex.** *He wrenched the telephone from the wall.* 2. injure by twisting. **Ex.** *She wrenched her back trying to lift the heavy box.*

WRENCH 4

wrestle (4) [res'əl], *v.* 1. struggle to overcome another and force him to the ground. **Ex.** *The two boys wrestled for several minutes.* 2. try earnestly to overcome or solve a difficulty by thought. **Ex.** *He wrestled with the problem for a long time before he was able to solve it.* —**wres'tler,** *n.* one who wrestles. —**wres'tling,** *n.* a sport or contest in which people wrestle.

wretch (4) [reč'], *n.* 1. a person in great pain or in a very unhappy condition. **Ex.** *The poor wretch asked for food and a place to sleep.* 2. a person despised for his bad character. **Ex.** *She would not speak to the wretch.* —**wretch'ed,** *adj.*

wring (3) [riŋ'], *v.* 1. twist and press with force, as to remove water from wet cloth. **Ex.** *Wring the clothes and then hang them on the line.* 2. obtain by threats of force or actual force. **Ex.** *He tried to wring a confession from the prisoner.* —**wring'er,** *n.* a mechanical device used for forcing water out of clothes when washing them.

wrinkle (4) [riŋ'kəl], *n.* a small fold or ridge on a smooth surface. **Ex.** *There were wrinkles from age on her face.* —*v.* form wrinkles; become wrinkled. **Ex.** *This material wrinkles easily.*

wrist (4) [rist'], *n.* the joint where the hand and the arm meet. **Ex.** *He wore a watch on his left wrist.*

write (1) [rayt'], *v.* 1. form letters, words or numbers on something with a pencil, pen, etc. **Ex.** *My daughter is learning to write.* 2. communicate with or send a message to in writing. **Ex.** *He writes me every week.* 3. be the author of a book, poem, etc.; compose a musical work. **Ex.** *He is writing a short story.* —**writ'er,** *n.* one who writes words, letters, books, etc.; one who does this as his regular work. —**writing,** *n.* the act of one who writes; something written. **Ex.** *I have read all of his writings.* —**write down,** write on paper. **Ex.** *Write down what he says.* —**write up,** write a report of. **Ex.** *Write that news up for tomorrow's paper.*

writhe (5) [rayδ'], *v.* make twisting, bending movements as in pain. **Ex.** *The wounded man writhed in agony.*

written (1) [ritən], *v.* past participle of *write.* **Ex.** *Has he written to you about the matter?* —*adj.* in writing. **Ex.** *They have a written agreement.*

wrong (1) [rɔ:ŋ'], *adj.* 1. not correct; mistaken. **Ex.** *His answers were wrong.* 2. bad; not lawful; not morally right. **Ex.** *It was wrong of her to take his book.* 3. not right for the purpose, occasion, etc. **Ex.** *She wore the wrong dress to the party.* 4. not right in operation or condition. **Ex.** *There is something wrong with the car.* —*adv.* 1. not morally right. **Ex.** *She did* *wrong in taking the money.* 2. not correctly. **Ex.** *She did the work wrong.* —*n.* 1. a morally bad thing. **Ex.** *They are teaching their children to know right from wrong.* 2. an injury or injustice. **Ex.** *She did him a great wrong.* —*v.* do an injustice or injury to. **Ex.** *She wronged him by making a false accusation.*

wrongdoer [rɔŋ'duwər], *n.* one who does wrong. **Ex.** *They will punish the wrongdoers.* —**wrong·do·ing,** *n.* a wrongful act.

wrote (1) [rowt'], *v.* past tense of *write.* **Ex.** *She wrote to him yesterday.*

wrung (3) [rəŋ'], *v.* past tense and participle of *wring.* **Exs.** *She wrung her hands and burst into tears. The machine had wrung the clothes almost dry.*

X

X, x [eks'], *n.* the twenty-fourth letter of the English alphabet.

x-ray (3) [eks'rey'], *n.* 1. a ray similar to light that can pass through solid substances, such as the human body, and affect film the same way as light. **Ex.** *We are going to try treating this condition with x-rays.* 2. a photograph made with such rays. **Ex.** *The doctor studied the x-ray of the broken leg.* —*v.* examine, photograph or treat with such rays. **Ex.** *His teeth were x-rayed.* —*adj.* referring to such rays. **Ex.** *The doctor just bought a new x-ray machine.*

Y

Y, y [way'], *n.* the twenty-fifth letter of the English alphabet.

-y (1) [iy], *suffix.* 1. the act or action of. **Exs.** *Recover, recovery; deliver, delivery; discover, discovery.* 2. full of; characterized by. **Exs.** *Dirt, dirty; rainy, rainy; salt, salty.* 3. the state or quality of being. **Exs.** *Difficult, difficulty; honest, honesty; jealous; jealousy.* 4. having the characteristics of; like. **Exs.** *Bush, bushy; silk, silky; wave, wavy.*

Yankee (4) [yæŋ'kiy], *n.* a familiar name given to English colonists before and during the American Revolution, northerners during the Civil War in the United States, American soldiers in both World Wars and citizens of the United States by people of other countries. **Ex.** *He was surprised to hear himself called a Yankee.*

yard (1) [yard'], *n.* a measure of length; three feet; thirty-six inches. **Ex.** *She bought two yards of material.* See **Weights and Measures.**

yard (1) [yard'], *n.* 1. the ground around a house or building. **Ex.** *They have many flowers in the yard at the side of their house.* 2. an enclosed space that is used for a special purpose. **Ex.** *We bought some boards from the lumberyard.*

yardstick [yard'stik'], *n.* a stick thirty-six inches in length, used for measuring.

yarn (4) [yarn'], *n.* a special thread made from cotton, wool, etc. and used in making knitted and other kinds of material. **Ex.** *She bought some yarn for a sweater.*

yawn (4) [yɔ:n'], *v.* open the mouth wide without wanting to, as when bored or tired. **Ex.** *He yawned several times during the lecture.* —*n.* the act of opening the mouth in this way. **Ex.** *His suggestion was received with a yawn.*

year (1) [yi:r'], *n.* 1. a time period of 12 months or 365 days beginning on January first and ending on December thirty-first; a time period as long as a year, beginning at any mentioned time. **Exs.** *In what year were you married? We are leaving next month and will be gone for a year.* 2. a period within a year having its limits set according to some yearly activity. **Ex.** *The school year begins in September and ends in the following June.* —**year'ly,** *adj.* done, made, happening, etc. once in each year or every year. **Ex.** *The group had a yearly dance.* —*adv.* once in each year. **Ex.** *We see them yearly.* —**years,** *n. pl.* an indefinite time or period. **Ex.** *They met years ago.*

yearn (4) [yərn'], *v.* want very much; desire. **Ex.** *He yearns to go home.*

yeast (5) [yiyst'], *n.* a substance in powder or cake form containing agents which cause chemical change, used in making beer, in lightening dough and sometimes in dieting. **Ex.** *She added yeast to the bread mixture to make it rise.*

yell (3) [yel'], *v.* scream loudly. **Ex.** *The boy yelled with pain.* —*n.* 1. such a cry. **Ex.** *The child's yells of anger could be heard in the next house.* 2. a cry of encouragement. **Ex.** *During the game the students often shouted the school yell.*

yellow (1) [yel'ow], *adj.* of the color of gold, of a ripe lemon, of a banana or of butter. **Ex.** *She is wearing a yellow dress.* —*n.* a color like that of gold, a lemon, etc. **Ex.** *She had the kitchen done in yellow.*

yellow pages [yel'ow peyj'əz], *n.* a section or volume of the telephone directory, printed on yellow paper, arranged alphabetically according to products and services available and giving the names and telephone numbers of the businesses which offer them. **Ex.** *Why don't you look in the yellow pages for the names of dealers selling the kind of car you want to buy?*

yes (1) [yes'], *adv.* used to express: 1. agreement. **Ex.** *Yes, I like this book.* 2. consent. **Ex.** *Yes, I will come here tomorrow.* —*n.* the act of agreeing or consenting. **Ex.** *They replied with a yes.*

yesterday (1) [yes'tərdiy, yes'tərdey'], *adv.* 1. on the day before this present day. **Ex.** *It happened yesterday.* 2. in a past time or period. **Ex.** *Yesterday people only dreamed of flying.* —*n.*

1. the day before this present day. **Ex.** *Since yesterday was the first day of the month, today must be the second.* 2. a past time or period. **Ex.** *We saw some of the oil lamps of yesterday at the museum.*

yet (1) [yet], *adv.* 1. at some time before now; already. **Ex.** *Has he come yet?* 2. now; at this time. **Ex.** *I cannot tell you just yet.* 3. at some future time; regardless of present difficulties. **Ex.** *I will learn how to fix this machine yet.* —*conj.* however; nevertheless. **Ex.** *She tries hard, yet she does her work poorly.*

yield (2) [yiyld'], *v.* 1. produce; bear. **Ex.** *That field yielded a good crop.* 2. surrender; quit; give something to another because of pressure or demand. **Ex.** *The troops yielded to the enemy.* 3. move back or away because of pressure or demand. **Ex.** *The door would not yield when we pushed it.* —*n.* that which is yielded; the amount produced. **Ex.** *The yield of milk from that cow was heavy.*

yogurt [yow'gərt], *n.* a form of milk made thick, soft and slightly sour by the addition of bacteria. **Ex.** *I like to eat plain yogurt with vegetables, but with fruit, such as strawberries, yogurt makes a good dessert.*

yoke (4) [yowk'], *n.* 1. a device in the form of a frame of wood placed on the neck of a pair of animals so that they can pull a plow or load. **Ex.** *He put the yoke on the oxen.* 2. condition of slavery or of submission to the control of another. **Ex.** *They were under the yoke of a foreign power.* —*v.* joins by means of a yoke. **Ex.** *He yoked the oxen together and fastened them to the plow.*

YOKE 1

yolk [yowk'], *n.* the round yellow center of an egg. **Ex.** *This yellow cake requires six egg yolks.*

yonder (5) [yan'dər], *adv.* at or in the place indicated or pointed to; over there. **Ex.** *Go yonder where the two roads cross.* —*adj.* in the place indicated or pointed to; over there. **Ex.** *Yonder fields belong to this farm.*

you (1) [yuw'], *pron.* 1. the person or persons to whom one's words are directed. **Exs.** *You should go now. I saw you yesterday. Did he give all of it to you?* 2. one; any person. **Ex.** *You never know what may happen.*

you'd [yuwd'], short form, contraction of *you had* and *you would.* **Exs.** *You'd better leave now, if you're going to catch the last train. If you'd like me to, I can come tomorrow.*

you'll [yuwl'], short form, contraction of *you will*. **Ex.** *You'll have to wait another week.*

young (1) [yəŋ'], *adj.* 1. not old; in the first years of life. **Ex.** *Our children are young.* 2. fresh and active. **Ex.** *He looks young for his age.* —*n.* young people, as a group. **Ex.** *The young often have little time for the old.* 2. young animals. **Ex.** *The birds fed their young.*

your (1) [yu:r'], *adj.* of or belonging to you. **Ex.** *Is she your sister?*

you're [yu:r'], short form, contraction of *you are*. **Ex.** *You're looking very well.*

yours (2) [yurz'], *pron.* that which belongs to you. **Ex.** *Is this book yours?*

yourself [yərself'], *pron.* 1. your own self. **Ex.** *Do it yourself.* 2. your usual self. **Ex.** *You are not acting like yourself today.*

youth (2) [yuwθ'], *n.* 1. the period of life when one is young; the period of life between childhood and adulthood. **Ex.** *She played the piano in her youth.* 2. a young man. **Ex.** *He was a youth of eighteen.* 3. young people, as a group. **Ex.** *The youth of the community are interested in politics.* 4. the quality or condition of being young, active, etc. **Ex.** *When he was approaching middle age, he still had the strength of youth.*

you've [yuwv'], short form, contraction of *you have*. **Ex.** *You've done a lot of work today.*

Z

Z, z (1) [ziy], *n.* the twenty-sixth letter of the English alphabet.

zeal (4) [ziyl'], *n.* strong, active interest; enthusiasm. **Ex.** *He worked for our cause with great zeal.* —**zeal'ous**, *adj.* —**zeal'ous·ly**, *adv.*

zebra [ziy'brə], *n.* a wild animal found in Africa which is like a horse in appearance but has a striped coat of black or dark brown and white. **Ex.** *We saw herds with hundreds of zebras when we were in East Africa.*

zero (4) [ziːr'ow], *n.* 1. the figure *0*, which symbolizes an absence of quantity; nothing. **Ex.** *Six taken from six equals zero.* 2. a line or point, as on a thermometer, on which a scale measured in degrees is based. **Ex.** *The temperature is going below zero tonight.*

zinc (5) [ziŋk'], *n.* a bluish-white metal used as a protective coat for certain other metals, in mixtures with other metals, etc. **Ex.** *Zinc is combined with copper to make brass.*

zip [zip'], *v.* fasten or close with a zipper. **Ex.** *Don't zip up your jacket all the way while you're inside or you'll be too warm.* —**zip'per,** *n.* a device used to fasten or open clothing, suitcases, etc., consisting of two sets of teeth made of metal or plastic that lock or unlock when a sliding piece is pulled up or down. **Ex.** *Will you please help me pull up the zipper on the back of my dress?*

zip code [zip' kowd'], *n.* a system to speed the delivery of mail using five numbers which are placed after the address to indicate the state or district, the town or city and the post office to which the mail is going. **Ex.** *I had to call the post office to find out the zip code to use on this letter.*

zone (3) [zown'], *n.* 1. an area which can be distinguished from the areas around it by some distinctive feature. **Ex.** *Cars must move slowly in a school zone.* 2. any one of the five areas—the North Frigid Zone, the North Temperate Zone, the South Frigid Zone, the South Temperate Zone and the Torrid Zone—into which imaginary lines running east and west around the earth divide the earth's surface by climate and location. —*v.* divide into zones. **Ex.** *This section of the city is zoned for business.*

zoo (5) [zuw'], *n.* an enclosed area, usually in a park, where animals are kept to preserve them from extinction and to exhibit them to the public. **Ex.** *The children saw the lions at the zoo.*

Appendix I
Marks, Signs and Symbols

I. In Writing

' **apostrophe** [əpas'trəfiy], 1. used at the end of a noun to show ownership or possession by that noun of something mentioned later in the sentence. (The apostrophe is usually but not always followed by an *s* in such a noun.) **Exs.** *John's book; the boy's dog (one boy); the boys' house* (several boys). 2. used to show that a word has been shortened by omitting a letter or letters. Some of the most common forms are: -'*m* =*am* (*I'm* = *I am*); -'*re* = *are* (*you're* = *you are*); -'*s* = *is* (*he's* = *he is*); -'*s* = *has* (*she's* = *she has*); -'*ve* = *have* (*we've* = *we have*); -*n't* = *not* (*isn't* = *is not*); -'*ll* = *will* (*they'll* = *they will*); -'*d* = *would* (*I'd* = *I would*); -'*d* = *had* (*you'd* =*you had*). 3. used to show the plural of letter, signs and figures. **Ex.** *Look in the* A's *and* B's *of that book.*

* **asterisk** [æs'tərisk`], used to show that the word before the asterisk is explained elsewhere, at the place where there is another asterisk, often in a note at the bottom of the page.

: **colon** [kow'lən], 1. used in a sentence before a series of things, a long quotation, examples, etc. **Ex.** *I have the following: two hammers, two saws and plenty of nails.* 2. used at the end of the opening greeting in a business letter. **Ex.** *Dear Sir:*

, **comma** [kam'ə], 1. used to show a pause within a sentence shorter than the pause for a semicolon. **Exs.** *When he called, I was eating dinner. Ethel, my friend, is a teacher.* 2. used between words or numbers in a series, sometimes after the next to the last item, which is separated from the last item by *and* or *or.* **Ex.** *He bought meat, milk, bread and fruit.*

— **dash** [dæš`], used to show a break or interruption in thought. **Ex.** *If we buy it now—and I would like to buy it—we will pay too much.* See **hyphen.**

!   **exclamation point** [eks'kləmey'šən poynt'], used after a word or at the end of a sentence to show surprise, anger, fear or other strong feeling. **Exs.** *You went there alone! Quiet!*

-   **hyphen** [hay'fən], 1. used in a word to show that it is formed from two or more other words or from a prefix and another word. **Exs.** *self-control; ex-smoker.* 2. used to show the syllables of a word, especially when part of a word appears at the end of one line and the rest of the word appears on the next line. **Exs.** *hy-phen; ab-so-lute.*

( )   **parentheses** [pəren'θəsiyz], used around a word or words, figures, etc. which explain or make clearer in some way the other words or the sentence to which the parentheses are added. **Ex.** *The guest speaker (I knew him as a boy) is staying at my home.* **—pa·ren'the·sis,** one of a pair of parentheses.

.   **period** [pi:r'iyəd], 1. used to show a complete stop at the end of a sentence. **Ex.** *He went home.* 2. used to show that a word is in an abbreviated form. **Exs.** *Doctor, Dr.; Senior, Sr.* 3. used to show that words are omitted. **Ex.** *About the book, the magazine writer said, ". . . one of the best."*

?   **question mark** [kwes'čən mark'], used after a word or at the end of a sentence to show that a question has been asked. **Exs.** *Why? Where did you go?*

" "   **quotation marks** [kwotey'šən marks'], 1. used before and after the words of the person speaking. **Ex.** *"When will I see you again?" he asked.* 2. used before and after words that are an exact repetition of something previously written or said. **Ex.** *The song begins with the words, "Tell me, pretty maiden."* 3. used before and after the name of a book, story, movie, etc. **Ex.** *When did you first see "Gone with the Wind"?*

' '   **quotation marks, single** [kwotey'šən marks' siŋ'gəl], used before and after a quotation which is inside another quotation. **Ex.** *"That man is the one who called 'Fire!' the policeman told me."*

;   **semicolon** [sem'iykow'lən], 1. used to show a pause within a sentence between main clauses not joined by *and, but, for, nor, or* or *yet.* **Ex.** *Every day he wrote from nine* *o'clock in the morning until two in the afternoon; then he had his lunch.* 2. used between main clauses when one or more of the clauses contains commas. **Ex.** *It rained on the way to school; and as a result our hats, coats, shoes and socks were soaked.* 3. used between groups of words, some or all of which contain commas. **Ex.** *Three boxes were lost: one containing books, magazines and papers; one containing paintings, drawings and photographs; and one containing silverware, small brass pieces and coins.*

II. In Arithmetic, Measures and Weights

@   **at** [æt'], in the amount or rate of for each. **Ex.** *Six pencils @ $.05 each will cost you $.30.*

¢   **cent(s)** [sent(s)'], a unit of money written after the number; one cent equals 1/100 of a dollar. **Ex.** *These oranges are priced at 25¢ each.*

°   **degree** [dəgriy'], 1. a measure of temperature. **Ex.** *It is only 10° above zero today.* 2. a measure of an angle. **Ex.** *A 90° angle is a right angle.*

÷   **divided by** [dəvay'did bay'']. **Ex.** *8 ÷ 4 = 2.*

$ **dollar(s)** [dəl'ər(z)], a unit of money written before the number; one dollar equals one hundred cents. **Ex.** *The price of this book is $15.00.*

=   **equals** [iy'kwəlz], **Ex.** *2 + 2 = 4.*

'   **foot, feet** [fut', fiyt'], a measure of length equal to twelve inches or one third of a yard. **Ex.** *This window is 3' wide and 6' high.*

"   **inch(ez)** [inč'(əs)], a measure of length equal to one twelfth of a foot. **Ex.** *This material is 54" wide.*

–   **minus** [may'nəs]. **Ex.** *3 – 2 = 1.*

%   **percent** [pərsent'], out of, in or part of 100. **Ex.** *6% of 100 is 6.*

+   **plus** [pləs'], and; added to. **Ex.** *2 + 2 = 4.*

×   **times** [taymz'], multiplied by. **Ex.** *3 × 2 = 6.*

0   **zero** [zi:r'ow], 1. nothing. **Ex.** *1 – 1 = 0.* 2. a point on the thermometer from which other degrees of temperature are measured. **Ex.** *It was 20 degrees below 0 last night.*

&   **and** [ænd'], together with. **Ex.** *I bought this dress at Jones & Sons department store.*

%   **in care of** [in ke:r' ev], used in addresses to show that a person is located at the address of another or can be reached through that other person. **Ex.** *John's address here in town is c/o Henry Smith at 711 Box Street.*

Appendix II
Abbreviations

The following is a partial list of the most frequently used shortened forms in written American English. In many instances, an abbreviation may be written with periods or without them and have the same meaning. (**Ex.** *N.W.*, *NW*). Also, many abbreviations may be written in capital letters or in small letters and have the same meaning. (**Ex.** *P.M.*, *p.m.*) Only when the differing forms have differing meanings are they listed separately. (**Ex.** MA, master of Arts; MA, Massachusetts.)

A

AB	Bachelor of Arts. See **B.A.**
AC	alternating current, one of two common forms of electrical current. Electrical devices marked AC or DC can use only the current indicated.
AD	anno Domini, a Latin phrase; in the year of Our Lord; the stated number of years since the birth of Christ.
adj.	adjective, a part of speech.
adv.	adverb, a part of speech.
AIDS	Acquired Immune Deficiency Syndrome, a fatal disease caused by a virus.
AK	Alaska, a state of the United States.
AL	Alabama, a state of the United States.
A.M., a.m.	ante meridian, a Latin phrase; any hour been midnight and noon.
ans.	answer.
Apr.	April, the fourth month of the year.
AR	Arkansas, a state of the United States.
arr.	arrive, arrival.
art.	article, a part of speech.
Aug.	August, the eighth month of the year.
Ave.	Avenue.
AZ	Arizona, a state of the United States.

B

B.A.	Bachelor of Arts, a first university degree, usually received after four years of study.
BC	before Christ; the stated number of years before the birth of Christ.
BS	Bachelor of Science, a degree in science equivalent to a BA.
bu.	bushel, a unit of dry measure.

C

C	centigrade, referring to a temperature scale.
CA	California, a state of the United States.
COD	Cash on Delivery; payment to be collected when goods are delivered.
CO	Colorado, a state of the United States.
Co.	Company.
conj.	conjunction, a part of speech.
CST	Central Standard Time, official time in the Central time zone of the United States.
CT	Connecticut, a state of the United States.

D

DC	direct current. See AC.
DC, D.C.	District of Columbia, the capital of the United States.
DE	Delaware, a state of the United States.
Dec.	December, the twelfth month of the year.
dep.	depart; departure.
dept.	department.
Dr.	Doctor.
DST	Daylight Savings Time; the time during the period from the first Sunday of April to the last Sunday of October when clocks are

turned ahead one hour in order to have more daylight at the end of the day. **Ex.** *4:30 EST equals 5:30 DST during the months of April through October.*

E

E	East, a direction; eastern.
e.g.	for example; as one example.
esp.	especially.
EST	Eastern Standard Time, official time in the Eastern time zone of the United States.
est.	established.
est.	estimated.
etc.	et cetera, a Latin phrase; and other things of that kind.
ex.	example.

F

F	Fahrenheit; referring to a temperature scale.
Feb.	February, the second month of the year.
fem.	feminine.
FL	Florida, a state of the United States.
ft.	foot or feet, a unit of measure of length.

G

GA	Georgia, a state of the United States.
gal.	gallon, a unit of liquid measure.
govt.	government.

H

HI	Hawaii, a state of the United States.
hp	horsepower, a unit of measure of energy.
hr.	hour, a unit of measure of time.

I

IA	Iowa, a state of the United States.
ID	Idaho, a state of the United States.
i.e.	id est, a Latin phrase; that is.
IL	Illinois, a state of the United States.
IN	Indiana, a state of the United States.
in.	inch, a unit of measure of length.
Inc.	Incorporated; formed into a corporation.
interj.	interjection, a part of speech.
IOU	I owe you; a signed paper promising to pay a debt.
IQ	intelligence quotient; a measure of a person's mental development.

J

Jan.	January, the first month of the year.
Jr.	junior.
Jul.	July, the seventh month of the year.
Jun.	June, the sixth month of the year.

K

KS	Kansas, a state of the United States.
KY	Kentucky, a state of the United States.

L

LA	Louisiana, a state of the United States.
lat.	latitude, a measure of distance.
lb.	pound, a unit of measure of weight.
LLB	Bachelor of Law, a first university degree in the study of law.
long.	longitude, a measure of distance.
lv.	leave.

M

MA	Massachusetts, a state of the United States.
M.A.	Master of Arts, next higher degree after a BA.
Mar.	March, the third month of the year.
masc.	masculine.
math	mathematics.
MD	Doctor of Medicine.
MD	Maryland, a state of the United States.
ME	Maine, a state of the United States.
MI	Michigan, a state of the United States.
mi.	mile, a unit of measure of length.
min.	minute, a unit of measure of time.
MN	Minnesota, a state of the United States.
MO	Missouri, a state of the United States.
mo.	month, a unit of measure of time.
mph	miles per hour, a measure of speed.
Mr.	Mister, a title used before a man's name.
Mrs.	Missiz, a title used before a married woman's name.
ms.	manuscript.
MS	Master of Science, a degree in science equivalent to an MA.
Ms.	Miz, a title used before the last name of a woman who does not wish to use the title of Miss or Mrs.
MS	Mississippi, a state of the United States.
MST	Mountain Standard Time, official time in the Mountain zone of the United States.
MT	Montana, a state of the United States.
Mt.	Mount; mountain.

N

N	North, a direction; Northern.
n.	noun, a part of speech.
NC	North Carolina, a state of the United States.

ND	North Dakota, a state of the United States.
NE	Northeast, a direction; northeastern.
NE	Nebraska, a state of the United States.
NH	New Hampshire, a state of the United States.
NJ	New Jersey, a state of the United States.
NM	New Mexico, a state of the United States.
Nov.	November, the eleventh month of the year.
NV	Nevada, a state of the United States.
NW	Northwest, a direction; northwestern.
NY	New York, a state of the United States.
NYC	New York City, a city in the state of New York.

O

Oct.	October, the tenth month of the year.
OH	Ohio, a state of the United States.
OK	Oklahoma, a state of the United States.
OR	Oregon, a state of the United States.
oz.	ounce, a unit of measure of weight.

P

p., pp.	page, pages.
PA	Pennsylvania, a state of the United States.
pd.	paid.
Ph.D.	Doctor of Philosophy, the highest university degree; the next highest degree after an MA.
pk.	peck, a unit of dry measure.
P.M., p.m.	post meridian, a Latin phrase; any hour from noon until midnight.
PO	Post Office.
POW	Prisoner of war.
pr.	pair.
prep.	preposition, a part of speech.
pron.	pronoun, a part of speech.

P.S.	postscript, words added to a letter after the signature.
PST	Pacific Standard Time, official time in the Pacific time zone of the United States.
pt.	pint, a unit of liquid and dry measure.

Q

qt.	quart, a unit of liquid measure.

R

rd.	1. road. 2. rod, a unit of measure of length.
Rep.	Representative.
Rev.	Reverend, a title before the name of a member of the clergy.
RI	Rhode Island, a state of the United States.
rpm	revolutions per minute, a measure of speed.
RR	railroad.
Ry.	railway.

S

S	South, a direction; southern.
SC	South Carolina, a state of the United States.
SD	South Dakota, a state of the United States.
SE	Southeast, a direction; southeastern.
sec.	second, a unit of measure of time.
Sen.	Senator.
Sept.	September, the ninth month of the year.
Sr.	Senior.
SS	steamship.
St.	1. Saint when used before a name. **Ex.** *St. John.* 2. Street when used after a name. **Ex.** *Main St.*
SW	Southwest, a direction; southwestern.

T

TN	Tennessee, a state of the United States.
TV	television.
TX	Texas, a state of the United States.

U

U.	University.
UN	United Nations.
US	United States.
USA	1. United States of America. 2. United States Army.
USAF	United States Air Force.
USCG	United States Coast Guard.
USMC	United States Marine Corps.
USN	United States Navy.
USS	United States Ship.
UT	Utah, a state of the United States.

V

v.	verb, a part of speech.
VA	Virginia, a state of the United States.
VCR	video cassette recorder.
vol.	volume.
VT	Vermont, a state of the United States.

W

W	West, a direction; western.
WA	Washington, a state of the United States.
WI	Wisconsin, a state of the United States.
wk.	week.
wt.	weight.

| WV | West Virginia, a state of the United States. |
| WY | Wyoming, a state of the United States. |

XYZ

| yd. | yard, a unit of measure of length. |
| yr. | year, a unit of measure of time. |

Appendix III
Weights and Measures

Weight

Unit	Abbreviation	Value in Other U.S. Units	Metric Values
ounce	oz.	1/16 of a pound	28.349 grams
pound	lb.	16 ounces	0.453 kilograms
ton	to	2,000 pounds	0.907 metric ton

Dry Measure

pint	pt.	½ of 1 quart	0.550 liter
quart	qt.	2 pints	1.101 liters
peck	pk.	8 quarts	8.809 liters
bushel	bu.	4 pecks or 32 quarts	35.238 liters

Liquid Measure

pint	pt.	½ of 1 quart	0.473 liter
quart	qt.	2 pints	0.946 liter
gallon	gal.	4 quarts	3.785 liters

Length

inch	in.	1/12 of 1 foot	2.540 centimeters
foot	ft.	12 inches or 1/3 of 1 yard	30.480 centimeters
yard	yd.	3 feet or 36 inches	0.914 meter
rod	rd.	16½ feet	5.029 meters
mile	mi.	5,280 feet	1,609 kilometers

United States Money

Unit	Value	Symbol
1 penny	1 cent	1 ¢
1 nickel	5 cents	5¢
1 dime	10 cents	10¢
1 quarter	25 cents	25¢
1 half dollar	50 cents	50¢
1 dollar	100 cents	$1.00

Heat

Degrees Centigrade	Degrees Fahrenheit	Condition
0°	32°	Freezing Point
100°	212°	Boiling Point

Appendix IV

Place Names

This section provides the American spelling and pronunciation together with identification of the continents, countries of the world and their capitals, states of the United States and their capitals, and some important cities and geographic features of the world. The spelling of these place names is in accord with that given in *The World Factbook,* an annual United States government publication. The *World Factbook* spellings are those approved by the United States Board on Geographic Names. The letters *N, S, E* and *W* refer to direction (North, northern, South, southern, East, eastern, West and western).

Names of natives of countries or areas are usually formed by adding the letter *n* to the names of countries or areas ending in *a, e, i, o* or *u.* (**Exs.** *America, American; Kenya, Kenyan.*) Names ending with other letters are often formed by adding *an* or *ian,* sometimes dropping the final letter before doing so. (**Exs.** *Italy, Italian; Mexico, Mexican.*) These same rules apply in forming the adjective. (**Exs.** *Do you know any African folktales? They have a collection of Korean art.*) Exceptions to these rules are listed. (**Exs.** *Denmark, Danish; Portugal, Portuguese; France, French.*)

A

Abidjan [æ'biyĵan], the administrative center of the Ivory Coast.

Abu Dhabi [a'buw da'biy], the capital of the United Arab Emirates.

Abuja [æbuw'ĵæ], the capital of Nigeria.

Accra [akra'], the capital of Ghana.

Addis Ababa [æd'is a'bəbə], the capital of Ethiopia.

Adelaide [æd'əleyd`], a seaport in S Australia.

Aden [ad'n, eyd'n], 1. Gulf of, a body of water between Yemen and Somalia. 2. the capital of South Yemen when Yemen was divided into North Yemen and South Yemen.

Adriatic Sea [ey`driyæt'ik siy'], an arm of the Mediterranean Sea between Italy and the Balkan Peninsula.

Aegean Sea [iy'jiyan siy'], an arm of the Mediterranean Sea between Greece and Turkey.

Afghanistan [æfgæn'əstæn`], a country in W central Asia between Iran and Pakistan. —**Af'ghan,** *n.* and *adj.*

Africa [æf'rikə], the second largest continent of the earth.

Agana [agan'ya], the capital of Guam.

Ahmadabad [a'mədəbæd], a large city in India.

Alabama [æl`əbæm'ə], a S state of the United States.

Alaska [əlæs'kə], a state of the United States NW of Canada.

Albania [ælbey'niyə], a country in SE Europe between Greece and Serbia and Montenegro.

Albany [ɔ:l'bəniy], the capital of New York.

Albuquerque [æl'bəkə:r'kiy], a large city in New Mexico.

Aleutian Islands [əluw'šən ay'ləndz], a long chain of islands, part of Alaska, stretching westward to the N Pacific Ocean.

Alexandria [æl`igzæn'driyə], a seaport of Egypt on the Mediterranean Sea.

Algeria [ælʝi:r'iyə], a country in NW Africa on the Mediterranean Sea between Morocco and Tunisia.

Algiers [ælʝi:rz'], the capital of Algeria.

Alma-Ata [al'ma ata'], the capital of Kazakhstan.

Alofi [alow'fiy], the capital of Niue.

Alps [ælps'], a mountain range in S central Europe.

Amazon [æm'əzan'], the world's second-longest river, flowing N from Peru through Brazil to the Atlantic Ocean.

America [əme:r'əkə], 1. the United States. 2. North America. 3. South America.

American Samoa [əme:r'ikən səmow'ə], a territory of the United States in the South Pacific Ocean between Hawaii and New Zealand.

Amman [a'man, aman'], the capital of Jordan.

Amsterdam [æm'stərdæm`], the capital of the Netherlands.

Anchorage [æŋ'kəriʝ], the largest city in Alaska.

Andes [æn'diyz], a large mountain system extending the length of W South America.

Andorra [ændɔ:r'ə], a country in W Europe between Spain and France.

Andorra la Bella [ændɔ:r'ə la bel'a], the capital of Andorra.

Angola [æŋgow'lə], a country in SW Africa on the South Atlantic Ocean between Namibia and Zaire.

Anguilla [æŋgwil'ə], an island country in the Caribbean Sea E of Puerto Rico.

Ankara [æŋ'kərə], the capital of Turkey.

Annapolis [ənæp'ələs], the capital of Maryland.

Antananarivo [æntenæn'əriyv'ow], the capital of Madagascar.

Antarctic Ocean [æntark'tik ow'šən], a body of water at the South Pole surrounding Antarctica.

Antarctica [ænark'tikə], a continent at the South Pole.

Antigua and Barbuda [æntiy'gwə ænd barbuy'də], a country made up of two islands in the E Caribbean Sea.

Apia [apiy'a], the capital of Western Samoa.

Appalachian Mountains (æp'əley'čən mawn'tənz], the longest mountain system in the E United States, extending from Canada to Alabama.

Aqaba [a'kaba'], 1. Gulf of, a body of water extending from the Red Sea to Egypt, Israel and Jordan. 2. a seaport of Jordan.

Arabia [ərey'biyə], a peninsula of SW Asia between the Red Sea and the Persian Gulf, including Saudi Arabia, Yemen, Oman, United Arab Emirates, Qatar and Bahrain.

Arabian Sea [ərey'biyən siy'], a part of the Indian Ocean bordered by the S part of the Arabian Peninsula, E Africa and W India.

Arctic Ocean [ark'tik ow'sən], a body of water at the North Pole.

Argentina [a:r'jəntiy'nə], a country in SE South America on the South Atlantic Ocean between Chile and Uruguay. —**Ar·gen·tine**, *n.* and *adj.* —**Ar·gen·tin'e·an**, *n.* and *adj.*

Arizona [e:r'əzow'nə], a SW state of the United States.

Arkansas [ark'ənsɔ:'], 1. a S central state of the United States. 2. a river extending from Colorado through Arkansas, there joining the Mississippi River.

Armenia [armiy'niyə], a country in E Europe between Turkey and Azerbaijan.

Aruba [əruw'bə], an island country in the Caribbean Sea slightly N of Venezuela.

Ashkhabad [æš'kæbad'], the capital of Turkmenistan.

Asia [ey'žə, ey'šə], the largest continent of the world.

Asmara [æzma'rə], the capital of Eritrea.

Asunción [asən'siyown], the capital of Paraguay.

Athens [æθ'ənz], the capital of Greece.

Atlanta [ætlæn'tə], the capital of Georgia.

Atlantic Ocean [ætlæn'tik ow'šən], a body of water between America and W Europe and Africa, extending from the Arctic to the Antarctic.

Augusta [əgəs'tə], the capital of Maine.

Austin [ɔs'tən], the capital of Texas.

Australia [ɔstreyl'yə], a country and continent of the world in the S Pacific Ocean.

Austria [ɔs'triyə], a country in central Europe between Germany and Hungary.

Azerbaijan [a'zərbayǰan'], a country in E Europe on the Caspian Sea, N of Iran and E of Armenia.

Azores [ey'zɔrz], a self-governing group of Portuguese islands in the North Atlantic Ocean W of Portugal.

Azov, Sea of [æz'ɔːf siy' əv], a bay of the Black Sea bordered by Ukraine and Russia.

B

Baghdad [bæg'dæd`], the capital of Iraq.

Bahamas, The [bəha'məz ðiy], a country in the Atlantic Ocean E of the United States and N of Cuba.

Bahrain [bareyn'], a country in the Persian Gulf E of Saudi Arabia.

Baikal, Lake [bay'kɔːl leyk'], a body of water, the deepest lake in the world, in S Russia N of Mongolia.

Baku [bakuw'], the capital of Azerbaijan.

Balkan Peninsula [bɔl'kən pənin'sələ], a part of SE Europe bounded by the Black Sea to the E, the Mediterranean and Aegean seas to the S and the Ionian and Adriatic seas to the W.

Baltimore [bɔl'təmɔr], a seaport of Maryland.

Bamako [bam'əkow`], the capital of Mali.

Bandar Seri Begawan [bən`dər ser`iy bega'wən], the capital of Brunei.

Banghazi [bænga'ziy], a seaport of Libya on the Mediterranean Sea.

Bangkok [bæŋ'kak], the capital of Thailand.

Bangladesh [baŋ`gladesh'], a country in S Asia on the Bay of Bengal, almost entirely surrounded by India but also bordering Burma on the E.

Bangui [bæn'gi], the capital of the Central African Republic.

Banjul [ban'juwl'], the capital of The Gambia.

Barbados [barbey'dows], a country in the Caribbean Sea at its E edge.

Barcelona [bar`səlow'nə], a large city in Spain.

Barents Sea [bær'ənts siy'], a part of the Arctic Ocean, N of Norway and Russia.

Basseterre [bas`teyr'], the capital of Saint Kitts and Nevis.

Basse-Terre [bas'te:r'], the capital of Guadeloupe.

Baton Rouge [bæt'ən ruwž'], the capital of Louisiana.

Beijing [bey'jiŋ], the capital of China.

Beirut [beyruwt'], the capital of Lebanon.

Belarus [belaruws'], a country in E Europe between Poland and Russia.

Belfast [bel'fæst], the capital of Northern Ireland.

Belgium [bel'jəm], a country in W Europe, bordering on the North Sea, N of France and S of the Netherlands.

Belgrade [bel'greyd, bel'græd], the capital of Serbia and Montenegro.

Belize [bəliyz'], a country on the E coast of Central America, bordering the Caribbean Sea, between Guatemala and Mexico.

Belmopan [bel'mowpan'], the capital of Belize.

Belo Horizonte [bey'low hawrəzant'iy], a large city in Brazil.

Bengal, Bay of [ben'gɔl bey'əv], an arm of the Indian Ocean off the E coast of India.

Benin [beniyn'], a country in W Africa on the North Atlantic Ocean between Togo and Nigeria. Formerly Dahomey.

Bering Sea [ber'iŋ siy'], a part of the North Pacific Ocean bounded on the E by Alaska and on the W by Russia.

Berlin [bərlin'], the capital of Germany.

Bermuda [bərmyuw'də], a British dependency made up of a group of more than 350 small islands in the North Atlantic Ocean E of North Carolina.

Bern [bərn'], the capital of Switzerland.

Bhutan [buw'tan], a country in S Asia N of India in the Himalayas.

Birmingham [bər'miŋhæm], a large city in W central England.

Biscay, Bay of [bis'key bey' əv], a part of the Atlantic Ocean bordered by France on the N and E and Spain on the S.

Biskek [biš'kek], the capital of Kyrgyzstan.

Bismarck [biz'mark], the capital of North Dakota.

Bissau [bisaw'], the capital of Guinea-Bissau.

Black Sea [blæk' siy'], a body of water between Turkey and Russia.

Blantyre [blæntayr'], the former capital of Malawi.

Bogotá [bow'gəta], the capital of Colombia.

Boise [boy'ziy, boy'siy], the capital of Idaho.

Bolivia [bəliv'iyə], a country in W central South America bordered by Brazil, Peru, Argentina and Paraguay.

Bombay [bambey'], a seaport of W India.

Bonn [ban'], the capital of former West Germany.

Bosnia and Herzegovina [baz'nia ænd hər'tsəgowviy'na], a country, formerly part of Yugoslavia, in SE Europe between Croatia and Serbia and Montenegro.

Boston [bɔs'tən, bas'tən], the capital of Massachusetts.

Botswana [bat'swa'nə], a country in S Africa between Namibia and Zimbabwe.

Brasília [brəziy'lyə], the capital of Brazil.

Bratislava [bra'tisla'və], the capital of Slovakia.

Brazil [brəzil'], a country in E South America on the Atlantic Ocean.

Brazzaville [braz'əvil], the capital of the Congo.

Bridgetown [briǰ'tawn], the capital of Barbados.

Brisbane [briz'bən], a seaport in E Australia.

Britain [brit'ən], Great Britain. **—Brit'ish,** *adj.* **—the Brit'ish,** *n.*

British Indian Ocean Territory [brit'iš in'diyən ow'šən teːr'ətər'iyz], **BIOT,** islands in the Indian Ocean between Africa and Indonesia.

British Isles [brit'iš aylz'], the islands of Great Britain and Ireland in NW Europe.

British Virgin Islands [brit'iš vər'ǰin ay'ləndz], a group of islands in the Caribbean Sea, E of Puerto Rico.

Brunei [bruwnay'], a country in E Asia on the N coast of Borneo, almost entirely surrounded by Malaysia.

Brussels [brəs'əlz], the capital of Belgium.

Bucharest [buw'kərest], the capital of Romania.

Budapest [buw'dəpest'], the capital of Hungary.

Buenos Aires [bwey'nəs ay'riyz], the capital of Argentina.

Bujumbura [buw'ǰəmbuwr'ə], the capital of Burundi.

Bulgaria [bəlge:r'iyə], a country in SE Europe on the Black Sea between Romania and Greece.

Burkina [bərkiyn'ə], a country in W Africa between Ghana and Mali. Formerly Upper Volta.

Burma [bər'mə], also known as Myanmar, a country in SE Asia on the Bay of Bengal surrounded by India, China, Bangladesh and Thailand. —**Bur`mese'**, *n.* and *adj.*

Burundi [buwruwn'diy], a country in central Africa between Tanzania and Zaire.

Byelorussia [byel'owreš'ə], the former name of Belarus.

C

Cairo [kay'row], the capital of Egypt.

Calcutta [kælkət'ə], a seaport of E India on the Bay of Bengal.

California [kæl`əfɔrn'yə], a W state of the United States.

Cambodia [kæmbow'diyə], a country in SE Asia on the Gulf of Thailand between Thailand and Vietnam.

Cameroon [kæm`əruwn'], a country in W Africa on the North Atlantic Ocean between Nigeria and Equatorial Guinea.

Canada [kæn'ədə], a country in N America, N of the United States.

Canberra [kæn'berə], the capital of Australia.

Canton [kæn'tan, kæntan'], the former name of Guangzhou, a large city in SE China.

Cape Town [keyp'tawn`], the legislative capital of South Africa and a seaport on the S Atlantic Ocean.

Cape Verde [keyp' vərd'], a country in the North Atlantic Ocean made up of a group of islands W of Senegal.

Caracas [kəra'kəs], the capital of Venezuela.

Cardiff [kar'dif[, a port and industrial city in Wales, the United Kingdom.

Caribbean Sea [kæ:r`əbiy'ən siy`, kərib'iyən siy'], a part of the North Atlantic Ocean SE of North America.

Carson City [kar'sən sit'iy], the capital of Nevada.

Casablanca [kæs`əblæŋ'kə], a seaport on the W coast of Morocco.

Caspian Sea [kæs'piyən siy'], a body of water surrounded by Russia, Azerbaijan, Iran, Turkmenistan and Kazakhstan.

Castries [kæstriy', ke:s'triys`], the capital of Saint Lucia.

Cayenne [kayen'], the capital of French Guiana.

Cayman Islands [keymæn' ay'ləndz], islands in the NW Caribbean Sea between Cuba and Honduras, belonging to the United Kingdom.

Central African Republic [sen'trəl æf'rikən ripəb'lik], a country in central Africa between Chad and Zaire.

Central America [sen'trəl əme:r'əkə], the countries and area between Mexico and South America.

Ceylon [silan'], the former name of Sri Lanka.

Chad [čæd'], a country in N central Africa between Libya and the Central African Republic.

Charleston [čarl'stən], 1. the capital of West Virginia. 2. a seaport of South Carolina on the North Atlantic Ocean.

Charlotte Amalie [šar'lət amal'yə], the capital of the Virgin Islands.

Chechnya [češ'niya], a self-governing area in SW Russia. —**Che·chen,** *n.* and *adj.*

Chengdu [čəŋg'duw'], a large city in central China.

Chernobyl [černow'bil], an industrial city in Ukraine, abandoned after an atomic accident in 1986.

Chesapeake Bay [čes'əpiyk` bey'], an inlet of the North Atlantic Ocean between Maryland and Virginia.

Cheyenne [šay'æn], the capital of Wyoming.

Chicago [šəka'gow], a large city in Illinois on Lake Michigan.

Chile [čil'iy], a country in SW South America on the South Atlantic Ocean bordered by Argentina, Bolivia and Peru.

China [čay'nə], a country in Asia between India and Mongolia.

China Sea [čay'nə siy'], a part of the Pacific Ocean extending from S Japan to Malaysia.

Chisinau [kiy`šiyna'ow], the capital of Moldova.

Chongqing [čuŋ'kiŋ'], a large city in central China on the Yangtze River.

Cincinnati [sin`sənæt'iy], a city in SW Ohio.

Cleveland [kliyv'lənd], a large city in Ohio on Lake Erie.

Colombia [kələm'biyə], a country in NW South America between Panama and Venezuela.

Colombo [kələm'bow], the capital of Sri Lanka.

Cologne [kəlown'], a city in Germany on the Rhine River.

Colorado [kal`era'dow], a W state of the United States.

Columbia [kələm'biyə], 1. the capital of South Carolina. 2. a river flowing through the states of Washington and Oregon to the Pacific Ocean.

Columbus [kələm'bəs], the capital of Ohio.

Comoros [kam'ərowz], a country made up of three islands in the Indian Ocean, E of the coast of N Mozambique.

Conakry [kan'əkriy], the capital of Guinea.

Concord [kaŋ'kərd], the capital of New Hampshire.

Congo [kaŋ'gow], 1. a country in W Africa on the South Atlantic Ocean between Gabon and Zaire. 2. a river in central Africa.

Connecticut [kənet'əkət], a NE state of the United States.

Copenhagen [kow'pənhey`gən], the capital of Denmark.

Coral Sea [kɔr'əl siy'], a body of water N and E of Australia and S of New Guinea.

Corsica [kɔ:r'sikə], an island, part of France, in the Mediterranean Sea N of Sardinia.

Costa Rica [kas'tə riy'kə], a country in S Central America between Nicaragua and Panama.

Cotonu [kow'tənuw], the capital of former Dahomey.

Cracow [kra'kaw], a city in S Poland.

Croatia [krowey'šə], a country, formerly part of Yugoslavia, in SE Europe on the Adriatic Sea and having borders with Slovenia and Bosnia and Herzegovina.

Cuba [kyuw'bə], an island country in the Caribbean Sea, E of Florida.

Curaçao [kyuwr`əsaw'], an island in the S Caribbean Sea which is part of the Netherlands Antilles.

Cyprus [say'prəs], a country and island in the E Mediterranean Sea S of Turkey. —**Cyp'ri·ot**, *n.* and *adj.*

Czechoslovakia [ček`əslowva'kiyə], a former country in central Europe, now divided into the Czech Republic and Slovakia.

Czech Republic [ček' ripəb'lik], a country in E Europe between Germany and Slovakia.

D

Dahomey [da'howmey], the former name of Benin.

Dakar [dakar'], the capital of Senegal.

Dallas [dæl'əs], a large city in Texas.

Damascus [dəmæs'kəs], the capital of Syria.

Dane [deyn'], **Danish** [dey'niš], *n.* and *adj.* See **Denmark.**

Dar-es-Salaam [da:r' es səlam'], the capital of Tanzania.

Delaware [del'əwe:r], an E state of the United States.

Denmark [den'mark], a country in NW Europe on the North Sea, bounded on the S by Germany. —**Dane,** *n.* —**Da'nish,** *n.* and *adj.*

Denver [den'vər], the capital of Colorado.

Des Moines [də moyn'], the capital of Iowa.

Detroit [ditroyt'], an industrial city in Michigan.

Dhaka [da'kə], the capital of Bangladesh.

Diego Garcia [diyey'gow gar'siyə], an island which is part of the British Indian Ocean Territory between Africa and India.

District of Columbia [dis'trikt əv kələm'biyə], the area occupied by Washington, the capital of the United States, between Maryland and Virginia.

Djakarta [jəkar'tə], the capital of Indonesia.

Djibhouti [jibuw'tiy], a country and its capital on the E coast of Africa, between Eritrea and Somalia.

Doha [dow'hə], the capital of Qatar.

Dominica [dam'əniy'kə, dəmin'ikə], an island country in the Caribbean Sea between Puerto Rico and Trinidad and Tobago.

Dominican Republic [dəmin'ikən ripəb'lik], a country on a Caribbean island with Haiti, between Cuba and Puerto Rico.

Douglas [dəg'ləs], the capital of the Isle of Man.

Dover [dow'vər], the capital of Delaware.

Dublin [dəb'lən], the capital of Ireland.

Durban [dər'bən], a port city on the E coast of South Africa.

Dushanbe [dušan'ba], the capital of Tajikistan.

Dutch [dəč'], *n.* and *adj.* See **Netherlands.**

E

Ecuador [ek'wədɔr], a country in NW South America at the Equator on the Pacific Ocean between Colombia and Peru.

Edinburgh [ed'inbərʻə], the capital of Scotland.

Egypt [iy'jipt], a country in NE Africa on the Mediterranean and Red seas between Libya and Sudan.

El Salvador [el sæl'vədɔr], a country in Central America on the North Pacific Ocean between Guatemala and Honduras.

England [iŋ'glənd], a part of the United Kingdom off the NW coast of Europe.

English Channel [iŋ'gliš čæn'əl], a body of water between England and France.

Equatorial Guinea [ekˈwətɔr'iyəl gin'iy], a country in W Africa on the North Atlantic Ocean between Cameroon and Gabon.

Erie [i:r'iy], one of the five Great Lakes in central North America. It forms part of the boundary between the United States and Canada.

Eritrea [e:rˈətriy'ə], a country in E Africa on the Red Sea between Djibouti and Sudan and N of Ethiopia.

Essen [es'ən], an industrial city in Germany.

Estonia [estow'niyə], a country in NE Europe on the Baltic Sea between Sweden and Russia.

Ethiopia [iy'θiyow'piyə], a country in E Africa between Somalia and Sudan.

Europe [yu:r'əp], one of the seven continents of the world.

F

Falkland Islands [fɔk'lænd ay'ləndz], a group of islands in the S Atlantic Ocean, SE of Argentina, belonging to the United Kingdom.

Far East [fa:r' iyst'], E Asia.

Faroe Islands [fe:r'ow ay'ləndz], a group of islands in the N Atlantic Ocean between Norway and Iceland which belongs to Denmark.

Far West [fa:r' west'], W United States.

Fiji [fiy'ǰiy], a country made up of a group of islands in the South Pacific Ocean E of Australia and N of New Zealand.

Filipino [fil'əpiy'now], *n.* and *adj.* See **Philippines.**

Finland [fin'lənd], a country in N Europe on the Baltic Sea between Sweden and Russia. —**Finn,** *n.* —**Finn'ish,** *n.* and *adj.*

Florida [flɔ:r'ədə], a SE state of the United States on the North Atlantic Ocean.

Formosa [fɔrmow'sə], the former name of Taiwan.

Fort-de-France [fɔrtˈ də fræns'], the capital of Martinique.

France [fræns'], a country in W Europe on the North Atlantic Ocean between Germany and Spain. —**French'**, *n.* and *adj.*

Frankfort [fræŋk'fərt], the capital of Kentucky.

Freetown [friy'tawn'], the capital of Sierra Leone.

French [frenč'], *n.* and *adj.* See **France.**

French Guiana [frenč' guyæn'ə], an overseas department of France in NE South America on the North Atlantic Ocean between Suriname and Brazil.

French Polynesia [frenč' pal`əniy'žə], a group of islands in the South Pacific Ocean, between Australia and South America, belonging to France.

Frunze [fruwn'zə], an alternate name for Bishkek, the capital of Kyrgyzstan.

Funafuti [fuw`nəfuw'tiy], the capital of Tuvalu.

Funchal [fuwnšal'], the capital of the Madeira Islands.

G

Gabon [gæbɔːn'], a country in W central Africa at the Equator on the Atlantic Ocean between Congo and Equatorial Guinea.

Gabarone [gæb`ərow'nə], the capital of Botswana.

Gambia, The [gæm'biyə θiy], a country in W Africa on the North Atlantic Ocean almost entirely surrounded by Senegal.

Ganges [gæn'ǰiyz], a river in NW India flowing SE through Bangladesh to the Bay of Bengal.

Gaza Strip [ga'zə strip'], an area on the E Mediterranean Sea between Egypt and Israel.

Georgetown [ǰɔrǰ'tawn], the capital of Guyana.

George Town [ǰɔrǰ' tawn'], the capital of Cayman Islands.

Georgia [ǰɔr'ǰə], 1. a SE state of the United States. 2. a country in SE Europe on the Black Sea between Russia and Turkey.

Germany [ǰər'məniy], a country in W Europe on the North and Baltic seas between France and Poland.

Ghana [ga'nə], a country in W Africa on the North Atlantic Ocean between the Ivory Coast and Togo.

Gibralter, Strait of [ǰibrɔl'tər streyt' əv], 1. a body of water in SW Europe joining the Atlantic Ocean and the Mediterranean Sea. 2. a dependency of the United Kingdom on the S coast of Spain.

Glasgow [glæs'gow], a large city in Scotland.

Gobi [gow'biy], a desert area in Mongolia and China.

Godthab [gɔt'hɔp], the capital of Greenland.

Grand Turk [grænd' tərk'] the capital of Turks and Caicos Islands.

Great Britain [greyt' brit'ən], an island off the coast of W Europe made up of England, Scotland and Wales.

Great Lakes [greyt' leyks'], a group of five large lakes—Huron, Ontario, Michigan, Erie and Superior—in central North America.

Greece [griys'], a country in S Europe on the Mediterranean Sea between Bulgaria and Turkey. —**Greek**, *n*. and *adj*. —**Gre'cian**, *adj*.

Greenland [griyn'lənd], an island in the North Atlantic Ocean NE of Canada, a self-governing division of Denmark.

Grenada [grəney'də], an island country in the Caribbean Sea N of South America.

Grozny [grɔːz'niy], a petroleum-producing city in Chechnya.

Guadalejara [gwad`ləhar'ə], a large city in Mexico.

Guadeloupe [gwad'luwp], an overseas department of France made up of a group of islands in the Caribbean Sea SE of Puerto Rico.

Guam [gwam'], an island in the North Pacific Ocean between Hawaii and the Philippines which belongs to the United States.

Guangzhou [kwaŋg'jow], a large city in SE China. Formerly Canton.

Guatemala [gwa`təma'lə], a country and its capital in Central America between Mexico and Honduras.

Guernsey [gərn'ziy], a group of islands in the English Channel belonging to the United Kingdom.

Guinea [gin'iy], a country in W Africa on the North Atlantic Ocean between Guinea Bissau and Sierra Leone.

Guinea Bissau [gin'iy bisaw'], a country in W Africa on the North Atlantic Ocean between Senegal and Guinea.

Guyana [giyæn'ə, giya'nə], a country in N South America on the North Atlantic Ocean between Venezuela and Suriname.

H

Hague, The [heyg' θiy], the seat of government of the Netherlands.

Haiti [hey'tiy], a country on a Caribbean island with the Dominican Republic, between Cuba and Puerto Rico.

Hamilton [hæm'əltən], the capital of Bermuda.

Hanoi [ha`noy'], the capital of Vietnam.

Harare [həra'rey], the capital of Zimbabwe.

Harbin [har'bən], a large city in China.

Harrisburg [hær'isbərg], the capital of Pennsylvania.

Hartford [hart'fərd], the capital of Connecticut.

Havana [həvæn'ə], the capital of Cuba.

Hawaii [həway'iy], a state of the United States in the central part of the North Pacific Ocean. —**Ha·wai'ian Islands,** the group of islands forming the state.

Helena [hel'ənə], the capital of Montana.

Helsinki [hel'siŋkiy], the capital of Finland.

Himalayas [him'əley'əz], a mountain range in S central Asia.

Holland [hal'ənd], the Netherlands.

Ho Chi Minh City [how' čiy' min' sit'iy], a large city in Vietnam. Formerly Saigon.

Honduras [handuw:r'əs, handyuw:r'əs], a country in Central America between Guatemala and Nicaragua.

Hong Kong [hɔ:ŋ' kɔ:ŋ'], a dependency of the United Kingdom on the SE coast of China bordering the South China Sea.

Honiara [how`niyar'ə], the capital of the Solomon Islands.

Honolulu [han'əluw'luw], the capital of Hawaii.

Houston [hyuws'tən], a large city in Texas.

Hudson [həd'sən], 1. a river in the state of New York. 2. a bay in NE Canada.

Hungary [həŋ'gəriy], a country in E Europe between Slovakia and Romania.

Huron [hyu:r'an, hyu:r'ən], one of the five Great Lakes in central North America. It forms part of the boundary between the United States and Canada.

Hyderabad [hay'dərəbæd`, hay'dərəbad`], a large city in India.

I

Iberian Peninsula [aybiyr'iyan pənin'sələ], the area in SW Europe consisting of Spain and Portugal.

Iceland [ays'lənd], a country and island in the N Atlantic

Ocean between Greenland and Norway. —**Ice'land'er,** *n.*
—**Ice·lan'dic,** *n.* and *adj.*

Idaho [ay'dəhow`], a NW state of the United States.

Illinois [il`ənoy', il`ənoyz'], a N central state of the United States.

India [in'diyə], a country in S Asia on the Bay of Bengal and the Arabian Sea between Pakistan and Bangladesh.

Indiana [in`dyæn'ə], a N central state of the United States.

Indianopolis [in`diyənæp'əlis], the capital of Indiana.

Indian Ocean [in'dyen ow'šən], a body of water surrounded by Africa, Asia, Australia and Antarctica.

Indochina [in`dow čay'nə], a peninsula of SE Asia including Vietnam, Cambodia, Laos, Thailand, Burma and Malaysia.

Indonesia [in`dəniy'žə], a country in SE Asia made up of many islands including Java, Sumatra, Celebes, part of Borneo and part of New Guinea.

Indus [in'dəs], a river flowing from Tibet NW to Pakistan, then SW to the Arabian Sea.

Ionian Sea [ayow'niyən siy'], a section of the Mediterranean Sea between S Italy and W Greece.

Iowa [ay'əwə], a N central state of the United States.

Iran [iran', iræn'], a country in the Middle East between the Caspian Sea and the Persian Gulf and Iraq and Afghanistan.

Iraq [iræk', irak'], a country in the Middle East between Iran and Saudi Arabia.

Ireland [ayr'lənd], a country in the North Atlantic Ocean W of Great Britain. —**I'rish,** *n.* and *adj.*

Irish Sea [ay'riš siy'], a part of the North Atlantic Ocean between Ireland and Great Britain.

Islamabad [izlam'əbæd], the capital of Pakistan.

Isle of Man See **Man, Isle of.**

Israel [iz'riyəl], a country in the Middle East on the E Mediterranean Sea between Lebanon and Egypt. **Is·rae'li,** *n.* and *adj.*

Istanbul [is'tanbuwl'], a large city in Turkey.

Italy [it'əliy], a country in S Europe which is a peninsula in the Mediterranean Sea bounded by France, Switzerland, Austria and Slovenia.

Ivory Coast [ay'vəriy kowst'], a country in W Africa on the North Atlantic Ocean between Ghana and Liberia.

J

Jackson [jǎk'sən], the capital of Mississippi.

Jakarta [jəkar'tə], the capital of Indonesia.

Jamaica [jəmey'kə], an island country in the Caribbean Sea S of Cuba.

Jamestown [jaymz'tawn], the capital of Saint Helena.

Japan [jəpæn'], a country in E Asia made up of islands in the North Pacific Ocean lying off the SE coast of Russia and E of the Korean Peninsula. —**Jap`a·nese'**, n. and adj.

Jefferson City [jef'ərsən sit'iy], the capital of Missouri.

Jersey [jər'ziy], an island in the English Channel belonging to the United Kingdom.

Jerusalem [jəruw'sələm], the capital of Israel.

Jidda [jid'ə], the capital of Saudi Arabia.

Johannesburg [jowhæn'isbərg], a large city in South Africa.

Jordan [jor'dən], 1. a country in the Middle East between Israel and Saudi Arabia. 2. a river flowing through Israel and Jordan.

Juneau [juw'now], the capital of Alaska.

K

Kabul [kabuwl'], the capital of Afghanistan.

Kampala [kampa'lə], the capital of Uganda.

Kansas [kæn'zəs], a N central state of the United States.

Karachi [kəra'čiy], a large city in W Pakistan.

Kathmandu [kat'mənduw], the capital of Nepal.

Kazakhstan [kəzak'stan], a country on the Caspian Sea between Russia and Uzbekistan.

Kentucky [kəntək'iy], a N central state of the United States.

Kenya [kiyn'yə, ken'yə], a country in E Africa on the Indian Ocean between Somalia and Tanzania.

Khartoum [kartuwm'], the capital of Sudan.

Kiev [kiyev'], the capital of Ukraine.

Kigali [kiygal'iy], the capital of Rwanda.

Kingston [kingz'tən], the capital of Jamaica.

Kingstown [kingz'tawn], the capital of Saint Vincent and the Grenadines.

Kinshasa [kinša'sə], the capital of Zaire.

Kirghizia [kiːrgiyž'iyə], former name of Kyrgyzstan.

Kiribati [kir'ə`bæs`], a country made up of islands scattered across the equator between Hawaii and Australia in the mid-Pacific Ocean.

Kobe [kow'biy], a seaport of Japan.

Kolonia [kəlow'niya], the capital of the Federated States of Micronesia.

Korea, North [kɔriy'ə nɔrθ'], a country in NE Asia between China and South Korea.

Korea, South [kɔriy'ə sawθ'], a country in NE Asia between North Korea and Japan.

Koror [kow'rar], the capital of Palau.

Kuala Lumpur [kwa'lə lum'puːr], the capital of Malaysia.

Kuwait [kuweyt'], a country in the Middle East and its capital on the Persian Gulf between Iraq and Saudi Arabia. —**Ku·wait·i,** *n.* and *adj.*

Kyoto [kyow'tow, kiyow'tow], a large city in Japan.

Kyrgyzstan [kirgiy'stæn], a country in S Asia between China and Kzakhstan.

Kyzl [kizil'], the capital of Tuva.

L

Lagos [ley'gɔs'], the former capital of Nigeria.

Lahore [ləhɔːr'], a large city in Pakistan.

Lansing [læn'siŋ], the capital of Michigan.

Laos [la'ows, laws', ley'ɔs], a country in SE Asia between Vietnam and Thailand. —**Lao'tian,** *n.* and *adj.*

La Paz [la paz'], the seat of government of Bolivia.

Las Vegas [las vey'gəs], a large city in Nevada.

Latin America [læt'ən ame:r'əkə], South and Central America and Mexico.

Latvia [læt'viyə], a country in E Europe on the Baltic Sea between Estonia and Lithuania.

Lebanon [leb'ənən], a country in the Middle East on the Mediterranean Sea between Syria and Israel. —**Leb'a·nese',** *n.* and *adj.*

Leningrad [len'ingræd`], the former name of St. Petersburg.

Lesotho [ləsow'tow], a country in S Africa completely surrounded by South Africa.

Lhasa [la'sə, las'ə], the capital of Tibet.

Liberia [laybi:r'iyə], a country in W Africa on the North Pacific Ocean between Sierra Leone and the Ivory Coast.

Libreville [liy'brəvil], the capital of Gabon.

Libya [lib'iyə], a country in N Africa on the Mediterranean Sea between Tunisia and Egypt.

Liechtenstein [lik'tənštayn], a country in the Alps in W Europe between Austria and Switzerland.

Lilongwe [liylɔ:ŋ'wey], the capital of Malawi.

Lima [liy'mə], the capital of Peru.

Lincoln [liŋ'kən], the capital of Nebraska.

Lisbon [liz'bən], the capital of Portugal.

Lithuania [liθ'uwey'niyə], a country in E Europe on the Baltic Sea between Latvia and Belarus.

Little Rock [lit'əl rak'], the capital of Arkansas.

Liverpool [liv'ərpuwl], a port city in W England.

Ljubljana [lyuw'blyəna], the capital of Slovenia.

Lomé [low'mey], the capital of Togo.

London [lən'dən], the capital of the United Kingdom.

Long Island [lɔ:ŋ' ay'lənd], an island in the North Atlantic Ocean, part of the state of New York.

Longyearbyen [jɔŋgyi(ə)r'buwe'ən], the capital of Svalbard.

Los Angeles [lɔ:s æn'jələs], a large city in California.

Louisiana [luwiy'ziyæn'ə], a S central state of the United States on the Gulf of Mexico.

Luanda [luwæn'də], the capital of Angola.

Lusaka [luwsa'kə], the capital of Zambia.

Luxembourg [lək'səmbərg'] a country and its capital in W Europe between Belgium and Germany.

M

Macau [məkaw'], a group of three islands in the S China Sea, SW of Hong Kong, belonging to Portugal.

Macedonia [mæs'ədow'niyə], a country in S Europe between Serbia and Greece and Bulgaria and Albania.

Madagascar [mæd'əgæs'kər], an island country in the W Indian Ocean off the coast of Africa E of Mozambique.

Madeira Islands [mədiyr'ə ay'ləndz], a self-governing group of islands in the North Atlantic Ocean, W of Morocco, belonging to Portugal

Madison [mæd'isən], the capital of Wisconsin.

Madras [mədræs', mədras'], a large city in SE India.

Madrid [mədrid'], the capital of Spain.

Maine [meyn'], a NE state of the United States.

Majuro [məˈjuw(ə)r'ow'], the capital of the Marshall Islands.

Malabo [məlab'ow], the capital of Equatorial Guinea.

Malawi [məla'wiy], a country in SE Africa between Zambia and Mozambique.

Malaysia [məley'šə], a country in SE Asia on the South China Sea between Vietnam and Indonesia.

Maldives [mal'dayvz], a country made up of islands in the Indian Ocean SW of India.

Male [ma'ley], the capital of Maldives.

Mali [ma'liy], a country in W Africa between Mauritania and Niger.

Malta [mɔːl'tə], a country made up of three islands in the Mediterranean Sea S of Sicily.

Man, Isle of [mæn' ayl' əv], an island in the Irish Sea belonging to the United Kingdom.

Managua [mana'gwə], the capital of Nicaragua.

Manama [mana'mə], the capital of Bahrein.

Manchester [mæn'česˋtər], a large city in NW England.

Manhattan [mænhæt'ən], an island and part of New York City.

Manila [mənil'ə], the capital of the Philippines.

Maputo [məpuwt'ow], the capital of Mozambique.

Marshall Islands [mar'šəl ay'ləndz], a country consisting of a group of islands in the North Pacific Ocean N of New Zealand and between Hawaii and Papua New Guinea.

Martinique [marˋtiniyk'], an island, which is an overseas department of France, in the Carribean Sea N of Venezuela.

Maryland [meːr'ələnd], an E state of the United States on Chesapeake Bay.

Maseru [mas'əruw], the capital of Lesotho.

Massachusetts [mæsˋəčuw'sits], a NE state of the United States on the Atlantic Ocean.

Mauritania [mɔːr'ətey'niyə], a country in NW Africa on the North Atlantic Ocean between Algeria and Senegal.

Mauritius [mɔriš'əs], an island country in the Indian Ocean E of Madagascar.

Mbabane [əmbaban'], the capital of Swaziland.

Mecca [mek'ə], a holy city in Saudi Arabia.

Medellin [med`liyn'], a large city in Colombia.

Mediterranean Sea [med`ətərey'niyən siy'], a body of water between Africa and Europe.

Melbourne [mel'bərn], a large city in SE Australia.

Mexico [mek'sikow], a country between the United States and Central America.

Mexico City [mek'sikow sit'iy], the capital of Mexico.

Mexico, Gulf of [mek'sikow gəlf' əv], a body of water E of Mexico and S of the United States.

Miami [mayæm'iy], a large city in Florida.

Michigan [miš'əgən], 1. a N central state of the United States. 2. one of the five Great Lakes in central North America.

Micronesia, Federated States of [maykrowniy'žə fed'əreyt'əd steyts əv], a country made up of a group of islands in the mid-Pacific Ocean between Hawaii and Indonesia.

Middle East [mid'əl iyst'], a loosely defined area usually including Egypt, Iran, Iraq, Israel, Jordan, Kuwait, Lebanon, Oman, Saudi Arabia, Syria, United Arab Emirates and Yemen.

Middle West, Midwest [mid'əl west'], the N central states of the United States.

Milan [milæn', milan'], a large city in Italy.

Milwaukee [milwɔ:'kiy], a large city in Wisconsin.

Minneapolis [min`iyæp'ələs], a large city in Minnesota.

Minnesota [min`əsow'tə], a N central state of the United States.

Minsk [minsk'], the capital of Belarus.

Mississippi [mis'əsip'iy], 1. a S state of the United States on the Gulf of Mexico. 2. a river flowing S in the central United States from Minnesota to the Gulf of Mexico.

Missouri [mizuw:r'iy, mizuw:r'ə], 1. a central state of the United States. 2. a river flowing SE from Montana and joining the Mississippi River in the state of Missouri.

Mogadishu [mow'gədiy'šuw], the capital of Somalia.

Moldavia [maldey'viyə], a former name of Moldova.

Moldova [maldow'və], a country in E Europe between Romania and Ukraine.

Monaco [man'əkow`, məna'kow], a country and its capital in Europe, on the Mediterranean Sea, bordering France near its border with Italy.

Mongolia [maŋgow'liyə], a country of E central Asia between Russia and China.

Monrovia [manrow'viyə], the capital of Liberia.

Montana [mantæn'ə], a NW state of the United States.

Monterrey [mantərey'], a large city in Mexico.

Montevideo [man'təvədey'ow], the capital of Uruguay.

Montgomery [mantgəm'əriy], the capital of Alabama.

Montpelier [mantpiyl'yər], the capital of Vermont.

Montreal [man`triyɔ:l'], a large city in Canada.

Montserrat [mant'sərat'], an island in the Caribbean Sea, SE of Puerto Rico, belonging to the United Kingdom.

Morocco [mərak'ow], a country in NW Africa on the North Atlantic Ocean and the Mediterranean Sea, bordering Algeria to the E.

Moroni [mawrown'iy], the capital of Comoros.

Moscow [mas'kaw], the capital of Russia.

Mozambique [mow`zæmbiyk'], a country in SE Africa on the Indian Ocean between Tanzania and South Africa.

Muscat [məs'kæt], the capital of Oman.

Myanmar [myanma'], another name for Burma.

N

Nagoya [nagoy'ə], a seaport of Japan.

Nairobi [nayrow'biy], the capital of Kenya.

Namibia [namib'iyə], a country in SW Africa on the South Atlantic Ocean between Angola and South Africa.

Naples [ney'pəlž], a seaport of Italy.

Nashville [næš'vil], the capital of Tennessee.

Nassau [næs'ɔ:], the capital of The Bahamas.

Nauru [nauw'ruw], an island country in the South Pacific Ocean NNE of Papua New Guinea.

N'Djamena [en`jəmey'nə], the capital of Chad.

Nebraska [nəbræs'kə], a N central state of the United States.

Nepal [nəpɔ:l'], a country in the Himalayas between China and India.

Netherlands [neð'ərləndz], a country in NW Europe on the

North Sea between Germany and Belgium. **—Dutch,** *n*. and *adj.*

Netherlands Antilles [neð'ərləndz æntil'iyz], a group of islands in the S Caribbean Sea belonging to the Netherlands.

Nevada [nəvæd'ə, nəva'də], a SW state of the United States.

Newark [nuw'ərk, nyuw'ərk], a large city in New Jersey.

New Caledonia [nuw' kæl'ədown'yə], a group of islands in the South Pacific Ocean, E of Australia, belonging to France.

New Delhi [nuw' del'iy], the capital of India.

New England [nuw' iŋ'glənd], the NE states of the United States.

New Hampshire [nuw' hæmp'šər], a NE state of the United States.

New Jersey [nuw' ǰər'ziy], an E state of the United States on the Atlantic Ocean.

New Mexico [nuw' mek'sikow`], a SW state of the United States.

New Orleans [nuw' ɔrliynz', nuw' ɔr'lenz], a seaport of Louisiana.

New York [nuw' yɔrk'], an E state of the United States on the Atlantic Ocean.

New York City [nuw' yɔrk sit'iy], a seaport and business center in the state of New York.

New Zealand [nuw' ziy'lənd], an island country in the S Pacific Ocean SE of Australia.

Niamey [niy'amey], the capital of Niger.

Nicaragua [nik`ərə'gwə], a country in Central America between Honduras and Costa Rica.

Nicosia [nik`əsiy'ə], the capital of Cyprus.

Niger [nay'ǰər], a country in W Africa between Algeria and Nigeria.

Nigeria [nayǰi:r'iyə], a country in W Africa on the North Atlantic Ocean between Benin and Cameroon.

Nile [nayl'], the longest river in the world, in Africa, flowing from S to N into the Mediterranean Sea. The White Nile and the Blue Nile join to form the Nile at Khartoum.

Niue [niyuw'ey], a self-governing island in the South Pacific Ocean associated with New Zealand.

Norfolk [nɔr'fək], a seaport in Virginia.

North America [nɔrθ' ame:r'əke], one of the seven continents of the world.

North Carolina [nɔrθ kær`əlay'nə], a SE state of the Un..
States.

North Dakota [nɔrθ dəkow'tə], a N central state of th..
United States.

Northern Ireland [nɔr'ðərn ayr'lənd], a part of the United
Kingdom N of Ireland.

Northern Mariana Islands [nɔr'ðərn mær`iyæn'ə ay'ləndz], a
self-governing group of islands in the North Pacific Ocean,
between Hawaii and the Philippine Islands, associated with
the United States.

North Pole [nɔrθ' powl'], the farthest N point on the earth.

North Sea [nɔrθ' siy'], a part of the North Atlantic Ocean
between Britain and N Europe.

Norway [nɔr'wey], a country in N Europe on the North Atlantic Ocean W of Sweden. —**Nor·we'gian,** *n.* and *adj.*

Nouakchott [nwak`šat'], the capital of Mauritania.

Nouméa [nuwmey'ə], the capital of New Caledonia.

Nuku'alofa [nuw'kuwəlɔ:'fə], the capital of Tonga.

Nuuk [nuwk'], the capital of Greenland.

O

Ohio [owhay'ow], a N central state of the United States.

Oklahoma [ow`kləhow'mə], a S central state of the United
States.

Oklahoma City [ow`kləhow'mə sit'iy], the capital of Okla-
homa.

Olympia [owlim'piyə], the capital of Washington.

Omaha [ow'məha`], a large city in Nebraska.

Oman [owman'], a country in the Middle East on the Arabian
Sea at the SE end of the Arabian Peninsula between the
United Arab Emirates and Yemen.

Ontario [ante:r'iyow], one of the five Great Lakes in central
N America. It forms part of the boundary between the United
States and Canada.

Oporto [owpɔr:'tow], a seaport of Portugal.

Oranjestad [oræn'yəstæt], the capital of Aruba.

Oregon [ɔ:r'əgan`, ɔ:r'əgən], a NW state of the United States.

Orient [ɔ:r'iyənt], E Asia.

Osaka [owsa'kə], a seaport of Japan.

Oslo [as'low, az'low], the capital of Norway.

Ottawa [at'əwə, at'əwaˋ], the capital of Canada.

Ouagadougou [wa'gəduwˋguw], the capital of Burkina.

P

Pacific Ocean [pəsif'ik ow'šən], a body of water between Asia and Australia and the Americas.

Pago Pago [paŋ'gow paŋ'gow], the capital of American Samoa.

Pakistan [pæk'istæn, pakˋistan'], a country in SW Asia on the Arabian Sea between Afghanistan and India.

Palau [palaw'], a country consisting of a group of islands in the North Pacific Ocean SE of the Philippines.

Palestine [pæl'əstaynˋ], an area in the Middle East at the E end of the Mediterranean Sea.

Panama [pæn'əmaˋ], a country in Central America, between Costa Rica and Colombia, and its capital. **—Pan'a·ma Ca·nal'**, a manmade waterway in Panama connecting the Pacific Ocean and the Caribbean Sea.

Papeete [paˋpiyey'tey], the capital of French Polynesia.

Papua New Guinea [pæp'yuwə new' gin'iy], a country in SE Asia occupying the E half of the island of New Guinea in the Pacific Ocean N of Australia.

Paracel Islands [pæra'sel ay'ləndz], a group of islands in the South China Sea.

Paraguay [pæːr'əgweyˋ, pæːr'əgwayˋ], a country in central South America between Brazil and Argentina.

Paramaribo [pærˋəmær'əbowˋ], the capital of Suriname.

Paris [pæːr'is], the capital of France.

Peking [piy'kiŋ'], the former name of Beijing.

Pennsylvania [penˋsəlveyn'yə], an E central state of the United States.

Persia [pər'žə], the former name of Iran.

Persian Gulf [pər'žen gəlf'], a part of the Arabian Sea between Arabia and Iran.

Perth [pərθ'], a large city in Australia.

Peru [pəruw'], a country in W South America on the South Pacific Ocean between Ecuador and Chile. **—Pe·ru'vi·an,** *n.* and *adj.*

Philadelphia [filˋədel'fiyə], a large city in Pennsylvania.

Philippines [fil'əpiynz'], a country in SE Asia made up of islands in the W Pacific Ocean between China and Indonesia. —**Fil'i·pi'no,** *n.* and *adj.*

Phoenix [fiy'niks], the capital of Arizona.

Phnom Penh [pənɔm' pen'], the capital of Cambodia.

Pierre [pi:r'], the capital of South Dakota.

Pittsburgh [pits'bərg], a large city in Pennsylvania.

Plymouth [plim'əθ], the capital of Montserrat.

Poland [pow'lənd], a country in E Europe between Germany and Belarus. —**Pole',** *n.* —**Pol'ish,** *n.* and *adj.*

Polynesia [pal'əniy'žə], a group of islands in the S and N Pacific Ocean stretching from New Zealand to Hawaii.

Ponta Delgada [pan'tə delga'də], the capital of the Azores.

Port-au-Prince [pɔrt'owprins'], the capital of Haiti.

Portland [pɔrt'lənd], 1. a seaport of Oregon. 2. a seaport of Maine.

Port Louis [pɔrt luw'iy], the capital of Mauritius.

Port Moresby [pɔrt mɔ:rz'biy], the capital of Papua New Guinea.

Porto Alegra [pɔ:r'tow aleg're], a large city in Brazil.

Port-of-Spain [pɔrt' ev speyn'], the capital of Trinidad and Tobago.

Porto-Novo [pɔ:rt'ow now'vow], the capital of Benin.

Portugal [pɔr'čəgəl], a country in SW Europe on the North Atlantic Ocean to the W of Spain. —**Por'tu·guese',** *n.* and *adj.*

Port-Vila [pɔrt' viy'lə], the capital of Vanuatu.

Potomac [pətow'mək], a river in Maryland and Virginia that flows into the Chesapeake Bay.

Prague [prag'], the capital of the Czech Republic.

Praia [pray'ə], the capital of Cape Verde.

Pretoria [pritɔ:r'iyə], the administrative capital of South Africa.

Providence [pra'vədəns], the capital of Rhode Island.

Puerto Rico [pwer'tə riy'kow, pɔr'tə riy'kow], a self-governing island in the N Atlantic Ocean between the Dominican Republic and the Virgin Islands, voluntarily associated with the United States.

Pusan [puw'san'], a large city in South Korea.

Pyongyang [pyɔ:ŋ'ya:ŋ'], the capital of North Korea.

Q

Qatar [ka'tar'], a country in the Middle East on the W coast of the Persian Gulf between Saudi Arabia and Iran.

Quebec [kwibek'], a province and its capital in E Canada.

Quito [kiy'tow], the capital of Ecuador.

R

Rabat [rəbat'], the capital of Morocco.

Raleigh [raw'liy], the capital of North Carolina.

Rangoon [ræŋguwn'], the capital of Burma, sometimes translated as Yangon.

Rawalpindi [rɔlpin'diy], the capital of Pakistan.

Red Sea [red' siy'], a body of water between Africa and the Arabian Peninsula.

Réunion [riyyuwn'yən], an island in the W Indian Ocean E of Madagascar, a department of France.

Reykjavik [rayk'yəvik], the capital of Iceland.

Rhine [rayn'], a river in Europe flowing from Switzerland through Germany and the Netherlands to the North Sea.

Rhode Island [rowd' ay'lənd], a NE state of the United States.

Rhodesia [rowdiy'žə], the former name of Zimbabwe.

Richmond [rič'mənd], the capital of Virginia.

Riga [riy'gə], the capital of Latvia.

Rio de Janeiro [riy'ow dey jene:r'ow], a seaport of Brazil.

Rio Grande [riy'ow grænd'], a border river between the United States and Mexico.

Riyadh [riyad'], the capital of Saudi Arabia.

Road Town [rowd' tawn'], the capital of the British Virgin Islands.

Rocky Mountains [rak'iy mawn'tənz], the longest mountain system in North America, extending from Mexico to Alaska.

Romania [ruwmey'niye], a country in E Europe on the Black Sea between Ukraine and Bulgaria.

Rome [rowm'], the capital of Italy.

Roseau [rowzow'], the capital of Dominica.

Russia [rəš'ə], a country in E Europe and N Asia stretching from the Black Sea to the North Pacific Ocean.

Rwanda [ruwan'də], a country in central Africa between Tanzania and Zaire and Uganda and Burundi.

S

Sacramento [sæk`rəmen'tow], the capital of California.

Sahara [səhæːrə, səha'rə], the largest desert in the world, located in N Africa.

Saigon [saygan'], the former name of Ho Chi Minh City.

St. Christopher and Nevis [seynt' kris'təfər ænd niy'vis], the former name of St. Kitts and Nevis.

Saint-Denis [seynt' dəniy'], the capital of Réunion.

Saint George's [seynt' jorj'z], the capital of Grenada.

Saint Helena [seynt' heliy'nə], an island belonging to the United Kingdom in the S Atlantic Ocean between South America and Africa.

Saint Helier [seynt' hel'yər], the capital of Jersey.

Saint John's [seynt' janz'], the capital of Antigua and Barbuda.

Saint Kitts and Nevis [seynt' kitz' ænd niy'vis], a country consisting of islands in the E Caribbean Sea SE of Puerto Rico.

St. Lawrence [seynt' lɔːr'əns], a river in E North America forming part of the boundary between the United States and Canada.

St. Louis [seynt' luw'is], a large city in Missouri.

Saint Lucia [seynt' luwčiy'ə], a country in the E Caribbean Sea.

St. Paul [seynt' pɔːl'], the capital of Minnesota.

Saint Peter Port [seynt' piy'tər pawrt'], the capital of Guernsey.

Saint Petersburg [seynt' piy'tərzbərg], a large city and seaport in Russia.

Saint Pierre and Miquelon [seynt' piyeːr' ænd mik`əlawn'], islands belonging to France in the N Atlantic Ocean off the E coast of Canada.

Saint Vincent and the Grenadines [seynt' vin'sent ænd θiy gren`ədiynz'], a country made up of several islands in the E Caribbean Sea N of Venezuela.

Saipan [saypæn'], the capital of the Northern Mariana Islands.

Salem [sey'ləm], the capital of Oregon.

Salt Lake City [sɔlt' leyk' sit'iy], the capital of Utah.

Samoa See **American Samoa** and **Western Samoa.**

Sanaa [sana'], the capital of Yemen.

San Francisco [sæn' frənsis'kow] a seaport of California.

San Jose [sæn howzey'], the capital of Costa Rica.

San Juan [sæn hwan'], the capital of Puerto Rico.

San Marino [sæn' meriy'now], a country and its capital in S Europe completely surrounded by Italy.

San Salvador [sæn sæl'vedɔr], the capital of El Salvador.

Santa Fe [sæn'tə fey'], the capital of New Mexico.

Santiago [sæntiya'gow], the capital of Chile.

Santo Domingo [sæen'tow dowmiŋ'gow], the capital of the Dominican Republic.

São Paolo [sawn paw'luw], a large city in Brazil.

São Tomé [sawn tuwme'], the capital of São Tomé e Príncipe.

São Tomé e Príncipe [sawn tuwme' e priyn'siypi], an island country in the North Atlantic Ocean off the coast of Africa opposite Gabon.

Sarajevo [sæ'rayeyvow], the capital of Bosnia and Herzegovina.

Sardinia [sardin'iyə], a self-governing region of Italy and the second largest island in the Mediterranean Sea.

Saudi Arabia [sɔː'diy ərey'biyə, saw'diy ərey'biyə], a country in the Middle East between the Red Sea and the Persian Gulf.

Scandinavia [skænˋdəney'viyə], the countries in NW Europe of Denmark, Norway and Sweden.

Scotland [skat'lənd], a part of the United Kingdom occupying the N section of the main British island, N of England. —**Scot,** *n.* —**Scotch,** *n.* and *adj.* —**Scottish,** *adj.*

Seattle [siyæt'əl], a seaport of Washington.

Senegal [sen'əgɔl, sen'əgæl], a country in W Africa on the North Atlantic Ocean between Mauritania and Guinea-Bissau.

Seoul [sowl'], the capital of South Korea.

Serbia and Montenegro [sər'bia ænd mownˋtəniy'grow], a country in SE Europe on the Adriatic Sea between Bosnia and Herzegovina and Bulgaria.

Seychelles [seyšel', seyšhelz'], an island country in the Indian Ocean NE of Madagascar.

Shanghai [šæŋhay'], a seaport on the E coast of China.

Shenyang [šən'yaŋ'], a large city in China.

Siam [sayæm'], the former name of Thailand.

Sicily [sis'əliy], a self-governing region of Italy and the largest island in the Mediterranean Sea.

Sierra Leone [siye:r'ə liyown', siye:r'ə liywon'iy], a country in W Africa on the North Atlantic Ocean between Guinea and Liberia.

Sikkim [siyk'kim], a state in NE India.

Singapore [siŋ'gəpɔ:r'], a country and its capital in SE Asia on the South China Sea between Malaysia and Indonesia.

Skopje [skɔp'ye], the capital of Macedonia.

Slovakia [slowva'kiyə], a country in Europe between Hungary and Poland.

Slovenia [slowviy'niyə], a country in SE Europe on the Adriatic Sea between Austria and Croatia.

Sofia [sow'fiyə, sowfiy'ə], the capital of Bulgaria.

Solomon Islands [sal'əmən ay'ləndz], a country made up of a group of islands in the South Pacific Ocean E of Papua New Guinea.

Somalia [səma'liyə], a country in E Africa on the Indian Ocean E of Ethiopia and Kenya.

South Africa [sawθ' æf'rikə], a country occupying the S end of Africa on the Indian and South Atlantic oceans.

South America [sawθ' əmə:r'əkə], one of the seven continents of the world.

South Carolina [sawθ kæ:r'əlay'nə], a SE state of the United States on the Atlantic Ocean.

South China Sea [sawθ čay'nə siy'], a part of the Pacific Ocean bounded by seven Asian countries including China, Vietnam and the Philippines.

South Dakota [sawθ dəkow'tə], a N central state of the United States.

South Georgia and the South Sandwich Islands [sawθ' jɔr'jə ænd θiy sawθ' sæn(d)'wič ay'ləndz], a group of islands belonging to the United Kingdom in the South Atlantic Ocean SE of Argentina.

South Pole [sawθ' powl], the farthest point S on the earth.

Spain [speyn'], a country in SW Europe on the Mediterranean Sea and the North Atlantic Ocean between France and Portugal. —**Span'ish,** *n.* and *adj.*

Spratly Islands [spræt'liy ay'ləndz], a group of islands in the South China Sea.

Springfield [spriŋ'fiyld], the capital of Illinois.

Stanley [stæn'liy], the capital of the Falkland Islands.

Stockholm [stak'howm], the capital of Sweden.

Sri Lanka [sriylaŋ'kə], an island country in the Indian Ocean off the SE coast of India.

Sucre [suw'krey], the constitutional capital of Bolivia.

Sudan [suwdæn'], a country in NE Africa on the Red Sea between Egypt and Ethiopia. —**Su·da·nese'**, *n.* and *adj.*

Suez Canal [suw'ez, suwez' kənæl'], a man-made waterway in Egypt connecting the Mediterranean Sea and the Red Sea.

Superior [səpi:r'yer], one of the five Great Lakes in central North America. It forms part of the boundary between the United States and Canada.

Surabaya [suwr'əbay'ə], a seaport of Indonesia.

Suriname [sər'ənamə], a country in N South America on the North Atlantic Ocean between Guyana and French Guinea.

Suva [suw'va], the capital of Fiji.

Svalbard [spal'bar], a group of islands in the Arctic Ocean, N of and belonging to Norway.

Swaziland [swa'ziylænd], a country in SE Africa between Mozambique and South Africa.

Sweden [swiyd'ən], a country in N Europe on the Baltic Sea between Norway and Finland. —**Swede'**, *n.* —**Swed'ish**, *n.* and *adj.*

Switzerland [swit'sərlənd], a country in W Europe bordered by Germany, France, Italy and Austria.

Sydney [sid'niy], a seaport of Australia.

Syria [si:r'iyə], a country in the Middle East on the Mediterranean Sea bordered by Turkey, Iraq, Jordan, Israel and Lebanon.

T

Taegu [tayguw'], a large city in South Korea.

Tahiti [ta'hiytiy], an island in the South Pacific Ocean which is part of French Polynesia.

Taipei [tay'pey'], the capital of Taiwan.

Taiwan [tay'wan'], a self-governing island in the China Sea off the SE coast of China between Japan and the Philippines.

Tajikistan [taȷik'istan'], a country in Asia between China and Afghanistan.

Tallahassee [tæl'əhæs'iy], the capital of Florida.

Tallinn [tal'lin], the capital of Estonia.

Tanzania [tæn'zəniy'ə], a country in E Africa on the Indian Ocean between Kenya and Mozambique.

Tarawa [tərɑ'wə], the capital of Kiribati.

Tashkent [taškent'], the capital of Uzbekistan.

T'bilisi [təbil'əsiy], the capital of the Republic of Georgia.

Tegucigalpa [təguw'siygal'pa], the capital of Honduras.

Tehran, Teheran [te'əran'], the capital of Iran.

Tel Aviv [tel' əviyv'], the city in Israel where most countries maintain their embassies.

Tennessee [ten'əsiy'], a SE state of the United States.

Texas [tek'səs], a S central state of the United States.

Thailand [tay'lænd], a country in SE Asia on the South China Sea between Burma and Cambodia. **—Thai,** *n.* and *adj.*

Thames [temz'], a river in S England flowing from N to SE to the North Sea.

Thimphu [θim'puw], the capital of Bhutan.

Tianjin [tiyen'ʝiŋ'], a seaport in NE China.

Tibet [tibet'], a self-governing region in SW China.

Tirana [tirɑ'nə], the capital of Albania.

Togo [tow'gow], a country in W Africa on the North Atlantic Ocean between Ghana and Benin. **—To'go·lese,** *n.* and *adj.*

Tokyo [tow'kiyow'], the capital of Japan.

Tonga [taŋ'gə], a country made up of islands in the South Pacific Ocean NNE of New Zealand.

Topeka [təpiy'kə], the capital of Kansas.

Toronto [təran'tow], a large city in Canada.

Torshavn [tawrshawn'], the capital of the Faroe Islands.

Transjordan [trænsʝɔr'dən], Jordan.

Trenton [trent'ən], the capital of New Jersey.

Trinidad and Tobago [trin'ədæd ænd təbey'gow], an island country in the Caribbean Sea off the NE coast of Venezuela.

Tripoli [trip'əliy], the capital of Libya.

Tulsa [təl'sə], a city in Oklahoma.

Tunis [tuw'nis, tyuw'nis], the capital of Tunisia.

Tunisia [tuwniy'žə], a country in N Africa on the Mediterranean Sea between Algeria and Libya.

Turkey [tər'kiy], a country on the Mediterranean and Black seas between Bulgaria and Iran. **—Turk',** *n.* **—Turk'ish,** *n.* and *adj.*

Turkmenistan [tərk`menistæn'], a country on the Caspian Sea between Uzbekistan and Iran.

Turks and Caicos Islands [tərks' ænd kay'kows ay'ləndz], a group of islands in the W North Atlantic Ocean, SE of The Bahamas, belonging to the United Kingdom.

Tuva [tuw'və], a self-governing republic of Russia N of Mongolia.

Tuvalu [tuwval'uw], a country made up of islands in the SW Pacific Ocean E of Papua New Guinea and N of Fiji.

U

Uganda [yuwgæn'də], a country in E Africa between Kenya and Zaire.

Ukraine [yuwkreyn'], a country in E Europe on the Black Sea between Poland and Russia.

Ulan Bator [uw'lan ba'tawr], the capital of Mongolia.

Union of Soviet Socialist Republics [yuwn'yən əv sow'viyət sow'šəlist ripəb'liks], a former country in E Europe and N Asia. —**Soviet**, *n.* and *adj.*

United Arab Emirates [yuwnay'tid ær'əb emi:r'tis], a country in the Middle East on the S shore of the Persian Gulf between Oman and Saudi Arabia.

United Kingdom [yuwnay'tid kiŋ'dəm], a country in W Europe made up of England, Wales, Scotland and Northern Ireland.

United States of America [yuwnay'tid steyts' əv ame:r'ikə], a country in North America between Canada and Mexico.

Upper Volta [əpp'ər vowl'tə], the former name of Burkina.

Uruguay [yu:r'əgwey`, yu:r'əgway'], a country in South America between Brazil and Argentina.

USSR [yuw' es' es' a:r'], See **Union of Soviet Socialist Republics.**

Utah [yuw'tɔ, yuw'ta], a NW state of the United States.

Uzbekistan [uwzbek'əstæn], a country in central Asia between Kazakhstan and Turkmenistan.

V

Vaduz [faduwts'], the capital of Liechtenstein.

Valletta [vəlet'e], the capital of Malta.

Valley, The [væl'iy ðiy], the capital of Anguilla.

Vancouver [væŋkuw'vər], a seaport of W Canada.

Vanuatu [van`əwa'tuw`], a country made up of a group of islands in the South Pacific Ocean E of Australia and NE of New Caledonia.

Venezuela [ven`əzwey'lə], a country in N South America on the Caribbean Sea between Colombia and Guiana.

Vermont [vərmant'], a NE state of the United States.

Victoria [viktowr'iyə], 1. the capital of the Seychelles. 2. the capital of Hong Kong.

Vienna [viyen'ə], the capital of Austria.

Vientiane [viyen'tiyan], the capital of Laos.

Vietnam, Viet Nam [viyet'nam'], a country in SE Asia on the South China Sea, bordered on the N by China and the W by Laos and Cambodia. —**Viet'nam·ese,** *n.* and *adj.*

Vila [viy'lə], the capital of Vanuatu.

Virgin Islands [vər'jin ay'ləndz], a group of islands in the Caribbean Sea, SE of Puerto Rico, belonging to the United States.

Virginia [verjin'yə], a SE state of the United States.

Volga [vowl'gə], a river flowing from NW Russia S to the Caspian Sea.

W

Wales [weylz'], a part of the United Kingdom occupying a section of the main British Island W of England. —**Welsh',** *n.* and *adj.*

Warsaw [wɔr'sɔ], the capital of Poland.

Washington [waš'iŋtən], a NW state of the United States.

Washington, D.C. [waš'iŋtən diy' siy'], the capital of the United States.

Wellington [wel'iŋtən], the capital of New Zealand.

West Bank [west' bæŋk'], an area between Jordan and Israel.

Western Samoa [wes'tərn səmow'ə], a country in the South Pacific Ocean between Hawaii and New Zealand.

West Virginia [west' vərjin'ye], a SE state of the United States.

Willemstad [vil'əmstat], the capital of the Netherlands Antilles.

Wisconsin [wiskan'sən], a N central state of the United States.

Wuhan [wuwhan'], a large industrial city in China.

Wyoming [wayow'miŋ], a NW state of the United States.

X Y Z

Yangon [yeŋ'gɔːn], another name for Rangoon.

Yangtze [yæŋ'tsiy'], the longest river in Asia, rising in Tibet, flowing SE and then NE into the China Sea.

Yaoundé [yauwn'dey], the capital of Cameroon.

Yaren [yar'ən], the seat of government offices of Nauru.

Yemen [yem'ən], a country on the S end of the Arabian Peninsula bordering the Red Sea and the Gulf of Aden.

Yerevan [iyriyvan'], the capital of Armenia.

Yokohama [yowkəha'mə], a seaport of E Japan.

Yugoslavia [yuw'gowsla'viyə], a former country in SE Europe including Bosnia and Herzegovina, Croatia, Macedonia, and Serbia and Montenegro. —**Yu'go·slav** *n.*

Yukon [yuw'kan], a river rising in Canada and flowing through Alaska into the Bering Sea.

Zagreb [za'greb] the capital of Croatia.

Zaire [za'iːr'], a country in central Africa between Congo and Zambia.

Zambia [zæm'biyə], a country in S central Africa between Zaire and Zimbabwe.

Zimbabwe [zimba'bwey], a country in S Africa between Zambia and South Africa.

Appendix V

Roman Numerals

I	1	XXX	30
II	2	XL	40
III	3	L	50
IV	4	LX	60
V	5	LXX	70
VI	6	LXXX	80
VII	7	XC	90
VIII	8	XCV	95
IX	9	XCVI	96
X	10	XCVII	97
XI	11	XCVIII	98
XII	12	IC	99
XIII	13	C	100
XIV	14	CI	101
XV	15	CII	102
XVI	16	CC	200
XVII	17	D	500
XVIII	18	M	1,000
XIX	19	MCMXC	1990
XX	20		